THE OXFORD HANDBOOK OF

THEOLOGY, SEXUALITY, AND GENDER

THE OXFORD HANDBOOK OF

THEOLOGY, SEXUALITY, AND GENDER

Edited by

ADRIAN THATCHER

OXFORD

UNIVERSITY PRESS

OXFORD
UNIVERSITY PRESS

Great Clarendon Street, Oxford, OX2 6DP,
United Kingdom

Oxford University Press is a department of the University of Oxford.
It furthers the University's objective of excellence in research, scholarship,
and education by publishing worldwide. Oxford is a registered trade mark of
Oxford University Press in the UK and in certain other countries

© Oxford University Press 2015

The moral rights of the authors have been asserted

First Edition published in 2015

Impression: 1

Published in the United States of America by Oxford University Press
198 Madison Avenue, New York, NY 10016, United States of America

British Library Cataloguing in Publication Data

Data available

Library of Congress Control Number: 2014946815

ISBN 978-0-19-966415-3

Printed and bound by
CPI Group (UK) Ltd, Croydon, CR0 4YY

CONTENTS

PART III SEXUALITY AND GENDER IN THE BIBLICAL WORLD

PART IV SEXUALITY AND GENDER IN CHRISTIAN TRADITION

PART V CONTROVERSIES WITHIN THE CHURCHES

PART VI INTER-RELIGIOUS CONVERSATIONS

PART VII CONCEPTS AND ISSUES

PART VIII SEXUAL THEOLOGIES
FOR ALL PEOPLE

List of Contributors

Marilyn McCord Adams, Visiting Professor of Philosophy, Rutgers, and Honorary Professor of Philosophy and Religion at the Australian Catholic University, USA.

Asma Barlas, Professor and Director, Center for the Study of Culture, Race, and Ethnicity at Ithaca College, USA.

Tina Beattie, Director of the Digby Stuart Research Centre for Catholic Studies at Roehampton University, London, UK.

Mandakranta Bose, Professor Emerita at the Centre for India and South Asia Research at the University of British Columbia, Canada.

Brendan Callaghan SJ, The Master at Campion Hall, Oxford, UK.

Patrick S. Cheng, Associate Professor of Historical and Systematic Theology at the Episcopal Divinity School, Cambridge, Massachusetts.

Simon Coleman, Chancellor Jackman Professor in the Department for the Study of Religion at the University of Toronto, Canada.

Colleen M. Conway, Professor of Religious Studies at Seton Hall University, New Jersey, USA.

Pamela Cooper-White, Ben G. and Nancye Clapp Gautier Professor of Pastoral Theology, Care, and Counseling at Columbia Theological Seminary, Canada.

Susannah Cornwall, Advanced Research Fellow in Theology and Religion at the University of Exeter, UK.

Deborah Beth Creamer, Director of Accreditation and Institutional Evaluation, The Association of Theological Schools in the United States and Canada.

Dyan Elliott, Peter B. Ritzma Professor of the Humanities and Professor of History at Northwestern University, Evanston, Illinois, USA.

Andrew Goddard, Associate Director of the Kirby Laing Institute for Christian Ethics (KLICE), Cambridge, UK.

Rita M. Gross is a Buddhist feminist theologian and author. Before retiring, she was Professor of Comparative Studies in Religion at the University of Wisconsin–Eau Claire, USA.

Angelique Harris, Assistant Professor in the Faculty of Social and Cultural Sciences at Marquette University, Milwaukee, USA.

Linda Hogan, Vice-Provost/Chief Academic Officer, Professor of Ecumenics at Trinity College, Dublin, Ireland.

Stephen J. Hunt, Associate Professor in the Sociology of Religion at the University of the West of England, UK.

Mary Jo Iozzio, Professor of Moral Theology at Boston College School of Theology and Ministry, Massachusetts, USA.

Ronit Irshai, Assistant Professor, The Gender Studies program at Bar Ilan University, and Research Fellow at the Shalom Hartman Institute, Jerusalem, Israel.

Lisa Isherwood, Professor of Feminist Liberation Theologies and Director of Theological Partnerships at the University of Winchester, UK.

Theodore W. Jennings Jr., Professor of Biblical and Constructive Theology at Chicago Theological Seminary, USA.

Margaret D. Kamitsuka, Associate Professor of Religion at Oberlin College, Ohio, USA.

Ruth Mazo Karras, Professor and Chair of Department of History, University of Minnesota, USA.

William K. Kay, Professor of Theology at the University of Glyndŵr, Wales.

Thomas Knieps-Port le Roi, INTAMS Chair for the Study of Marriage and Spirituality, Faculty of Theology and Religious Studies, at Katholieke Universiteit Leuven, Belgium.

Mathew Kuefler, Professor in the Department of History at San Diego State University, California, USA.

Michael G. Lawler, Professor Emeritus of Catholic Theology at Creighton University, Nebrasca, USA.

William Loader, Emeritus Professor at Murdoch University, Australia, and Extraordinary Professor, North-West University, South Africa.

Gerard Loughlin, Professor in the Department of Theology and Religion at Durham University, UK.

Neil Messer, Professor of Theology at the University of Winchester, UK.

Cynthia R. Nielsen, Catherine of Siena Fellow at Villanova University, Pennsylvania, USA.

Michael Barnes Norton, Assistant Professor in the Department of Philosophy and Interdisciplinary Studies at the University of Arkansas at Little Rock, AR, USA.

Margaret Robinson, Project Coordinator, Bisexual Mental Health Project, Toronto, Canada.

Eugene F. Rogers, Jr., Professor of Religious Studies and Women's and Gender Studies, at the University of North Carolina at Greensboro, USA.

Todd A. Salzman is Professor of Theology at Creighton University, Nebraska, USA.

Jane Shaw, Dean of Grace Cathedral, San Francisco, USA.

Ola Sigurdson, Professor of Systematic Theology at the Department of Literature, History of Ideas, and Religion at the University of Gothenburg and Director of the Centre for Culture and Health, Sweden.

Anna Stewart, Associate Tutor, School of Global Studies at the University of Sussex, UK.

Ken Stone, Academic Dean & Professor of Hebrew Bible, Culture, and Hermeneutics at the University of Chicago, USA.

Elizabeth Stuart, Deputy Vice-Chancellor at the University of Winchester, UK.

Steve Summers, Principal of the Local Ministry Programme, Guildford, UK.

Adrian Thatcher, Visiting Professor, Department of Theology and Religion at the University of Exeter, UK.

Marta Trzebiatowska, Lecturer in Sociology at the University of Aberdeen, Scotland.

John Witte, Jr., Jonas Robitscher Professor of Law, Alonzo L. McDonald Distinguished Professor and Director of the Center for the Study of Law and Religion at Emory University, USA.

PART I

METHODS

....

CHAPTER 1

INTRODUCTION

....

ADRIAN THATCHER

THIS Introduction describes the academic home of the Handbook, and identifies what is in it, what it does, and how it is done. These are, of course, large questions about its *nature*, *content*, *purpose*, and *method*.

A WORK OF THEOLOGY

....

There are forty-one chapters in the Handbook, including this one, four of them co-authored. Of the forty-four authors, twenty-one are male and twenty-three are female. The attempt at achieving approximate gender balance among the contributors is deliberate.

The Handbook is a work of Christian *theology* within the broader subject or field of religion. The Handbook is not primarily a work of religious studies, except that theology is now often located within that broader genre. As a work of theology it takes for granted that God is, that God is revealed in Jesus Christ, and that God's Spirit is at work in Church and world. Teachers and students of religion do not bring these suppositions to their studies. Teachers and students of theology need not, and increasingly may not, adhere to these suppositions either, but when they study Christianity they will know that they are looking into or speaking out of a tradition which does. Theology and religious studies are different, but related. Both realms of inquiry have their methods and suppositions, and, to avoid confusion, it is better to acknowledge them. In any case, they frequently inform each other. Some of the essays in the Handbook are better situated within religious studies, while those on history and the social sciences can be situated outside both. Some of the essays are clearly locatable within Christian ethics, itself a lively branch of theology.

But what sort of theology? A broad spectrum of theology will be found in the present volume. Authors represent different theologies and traditions. Within a generation sexual theology (Nelson 1979), feminist theology (Fulkerson and Briggs 2012), body theology (Nelson 1992; John Paul II 1997; Isherwood and Stuart 1998), lesbian and gay theology (Stuart 2003), indecent theology (Althaus-Reid 2000), sexual liberation theology (Althaus-Reid 2006), and, more recently, queer theology (Loughlin 2007; Cheng 2011; Cornwall 2011) have appeared, all of them providing novel treatments of the subjects of this Handbook. Some of these theologies have become well established and have generated collections of essays, series of monographs, and—in the case of feminist theology—an Oxford Handbook (Fulkerson and Briggs 2012). Sexuality and gender are not merely contentious and pervasive topics within theology: according to the Norris Hulse Professor of Divinity at the University of Cambridge, they have escalated in importance to the extent that even the very doctrine of the Trinity cannot be contemplated without a prior grappling with each: for

> the problem of the Trinity cannot be solved without addressing the very questions that seem least to do with it, questions which press on the contemporary Christian churches with such devastating and often destructive force; questions of sexual justice, questions of the meaning and stability of gender, questions of the final theological significance of sexual desire.
>
> (Coakley 2013: 2)

THE METHOD OF CORRELATION

The theological plan for this volume was inspired by my studies of the theologian Paul Tillich some forty years ago (Thatcher 1978). Before his exile from Germany in 1933 Tillich advocated what he called 'dialectical' or 'answering' theology. This was to become, in his *Systematic Theology*, volume i (1953: 67–74), the 'method of correlation'. He thought, in dialogue with Karl Barth, that a prior analysis of the situation in which hearers of the Gospel were placed, would enable the proclamation of the Gospel to be nuanced towards particular human needs in particular contexts. Proclaimers required some 'pre-understanding' of the situation of their hearers: hearers required some pre-understanding of the proclamation in order to be able to accept what they heard. Theology, he declared, existed to provide answers to genuine human questions: question and answer were to be brought into correlation. The method has been heavily criticized. Tillich thought that philosophy, and in particular existentialism, could articulate the deepest human or existential questions. Today we look to the natural and social sciences to provide much of this for us. And sometimes theology asked the questions and philosophy provided the answers.

Despite these difficulties, Tillich was right on several counts. He was right to insist that for revelation to occur at all, it must first be received in a human context, and to be received it must be, at least partially, understood. Tillich was right to demand 'answering theology' and the structure of the present Handbook attempts to provide 'answers' to very modern and pressing questions arising from the experience and study of sexuality and gender, within and beyond the Christian faith. Tillich was also right to insist that the answers theology provides are not invented, even by clever theologians, but in some sense already given, since God is already given, and the knowledge of God cannot be reduced to anything else. But different and competing answers to the same questions will be found, and there will be a growing tentativeness to all of them that would have disconcerted the confident Tillich. Each of the eight parts in this volume contributes to a framework which correlates secular and theological studies in a manner which is intended to be mutually beneficial. Theology is brought into correlation with sexuality and gender, and also with the social sciences and history. The method of correlation is the organizing principle of the volume; no more. It is not made into any kind of sophisticated technique, and authors have not been requested to accommodate it in their individual chapters.

SEXUALITY AND GENDER

There are problems with the subjects 'sexuality' and 'gender' greater than the obvious one of defining them. Historians of culture, of medicine, and of ideas are telling us that the idea that there are two sexes belongs to the seventeenth and eighteenth centuries (Schiebinger 1989; Laqueur 1990; Dabhoiwala 2012) and that earlier centuries believed in a single human nature or sex in which women existed as inferior versions of men. 'Sexuality' and the cognate terms associated with it (homo-, hetero-, and bi-) undoubtedly belong to European modernity. The term 'homosexual' first appeared in print in 1869 (see Chapter 36). 'Gender' comes from the Old French *gendre* (now *genre*), which itself derives from the Latin *genus*. It has been used since the fourteenth century as a grammatical term, referring to classes of noun designated as masculine, feminine, or neuter in some languages. 'The sense "the state of being male or female" has also been used since the 14th century, but this did not become common until the mid 20th century' (Oxford Dictionaries Pro 2013). Sexuality is already anchored in a particular discourse, that of medicine (and later the social sciences), which already brings assumptions about what 'it' is, how it is to be studied, how it supposedly supplants earlier discourses, and so on.

When theology provided a 'master discourse' for the discussion of sexual matters, there was in place a framework which related them to God, to God's purpose for humanity, to a good yet marred creation, to marriage as a divinely appointed institution, and to the virtues of love and friendship. The discourse of sexuality consciously eliminates these earlier associations and values. It is invented and closely guarded by the medical and social sciences. 'Gender' becomes a subject of academic study a century later. It too belongs in a context of philosophy and social theory, where there are now two sexes and the relations between each sex are deemed to give rise to 'injustice' and 'inequality', both of which require social action and reaction. Both subjects float, albeit launched from different historical launching sites, on an ebbing tide of secularization of thought and practice.

Language and Change

Theologians need to be aware of two particular problems when handling these topics—those of language and of the pace of the social and behavioural changes accompanying them. First, theology cannot be required merely to operate the chosen discourses of modernity. On the one hand, it may find, from within its own resources for thinking and acting, that these discourses are deficient. They may contain lacunae. They may be reductive, the products of science alone. Terms such as 'homosexual' may confer identities on people which take on an inappropriate fixity and ultimacy. And medical discourse may fail to valorize sufficiently the deep human significance of sexual love. On the other hand, the new discourses enable Christians to learn much about themselves and their relationships, and to locate fault-lines in their own settled and pre-scientific ways of thinking. Correlation is again beneficial: assimilation is not. Theology may be able to warn the churches of some of the dangers of buying into the modern nomenclature of sex. It is ironic that Catholic and evangelical theologians alike are so much at home with this untheological vocabulary. That said, readers will note its presence in the titles and content of many of the essays in this volume. But such nomenclature cannot be ultimate and should not be read back into scripture and tradition as if it had always been there. Theology issues no linguistic veto regarding the use of the modern vocabulary of sex, but it strikes a note of caution about the adequacy of modern discourses and their tendency to supplant older ones.

Second, a study of these twin subjects goes to the heart of immense social, cultural, and behavioural changes in most 'First World' countries. A single generation has known homosexual intimacy to be a criminal offence; then it has seen it partially decriminalized and tolerated; then in some countries the age of consent was reduced to 16; then discrimination against any person on the ground of sexual orientation itself became a crime; then civil partnerships and finally marriage for couples of the same sex has been or is being introduced. Lesbians and gays have entered the cultural mainstream.

Heterosexuality has changed at a similar pace. The liberalization of divorce laws in the 1960s and 1970s caused a threefold rise in the number of divorces within a decade. Abortion became increasingly available and provoked intense social disagreement which still persists. The stigma attached to single parenthood weakened, and in several countries has virtually disappeared. Fewer people married, and those who did increasingly delayed tying the knot. As the average age at first marriage continued to increase, so did the practices of both prenuptial and non-nuptial cohabitation (Thatcher 2002). Patriarchal marriage began to be replaced by egalitarian marriage, in which wives become equal (or less unequal) partners with husbands. The connection between marriage and having children became more tenuous. In some countries children born to unmarried parents are beginning to be a majority. The period has seen an increasing frankness about sex in the media and the wider culture, and of course, on the Internet.

The professions are now open to women (with one obvious, sacerdotal, exception). Accompanying these changes is the advance made by women in social, professional, and domestic life. Women outnumber men in universities (and in British departments of theology and religious studies by a margin of two to one). The impact of the advance of women on family forms and practices has been great. Childcare has become a pressing issue; men are gradually learning to share more of the burden of housekeeping and childminding. The striving for equality between the sexes may already have been overtaken by a concern not just for the recognition of difference between men and women, but more widely for the recognition and negotiation of the differences of race, (dis)ability, class, and wealth.

Faced with changes of this magnitude and pace, it is not surprising that sexuality and gender have risen to the top of contentious and divisive issues within the churches. Yes, God's self-revelation is God's Word, Jesus Christ, but the reception of the Light of life (John 1:4) as it illuminates sexuality and gender, may have been fuzzy and poor. Change generally evokes a degree of resistance; rapid, profound change evokes trepidation and reaction. While Christian doctrine and ethics have always developed, a deep sense of their alleged changelessness remains. The essays will indicate the full brunt of these controversies and the disarray they have caused. As the issues have been argued about, appeals to the alleged authorities that might confirm the truth of one position over another, have caused real people with real needs to disappear in the heat of the accompanying theological struggles. An attempt to address that problem is made in Part VIII.

The Structure of the Handbook

The structure follows the method of correlation. It is influenced also by the (Episcopalian) instinct that the sources of theology are scripture, tradition, and reason, sometimes called 'the three-legged stool', together with the addition (by Methodists and others) of experience. Part I, 'Methods', indicates the priority of questions of method, as this introduction has done. Chapter 2 explores the key methodological approaches evident in recent theologies of sexuality, including those that reject the very notion of sexuality. Chapter 3 traces the academic development of postmodern theology and gender studies, arguing that gender theory restores to theology the forgotten wisdom of its own tradition with regard to language and the interpretation of scripture. Chapter 4 shows how traditional doctrines, such as those of God, Christ, and Trinity, can reinvigorate the theology of sexuality, now dominated by distinctively modern categories.

Reason

Part II, 'What Theologians Need to Know', also follows from the method of correlation, and uncontroversially draws on reason as a distinct source of theology. 'Reason' has several senses (Thatcher 2011: 35), one of which, in contrast to revelation, is the application of critical thinking to the natural and social worlds, in order to discover truths about them not otherwise disclosed to us by God. These worlds are God's creation. The sciences are reasoned and reasonable activities, not contrary to revelation, but potentially a means of illumination of God's creative purposes. Each author in Part II responds to the question 'What do theologians need to know about sexuality and gender as your discipline understands them?' Since sexuality and gender are studied by the sciences, and by philosophy and social theory, these disciplines are vital in 'informing' theological reflection on the same topics.

Chapter 5 introduces evolutionary biology and behavioural genetics (among other topics), and surveys the insights they offer into the evolutionary origins of sex, sexual selection theory and human mating strategies, sexual diversity, sexual dimorphism, and intersex. Chapter 6 surveys some of the insights that have emerged from various theoretical approaches to psychological exploration (including the pervasiveness of sexuality in human experience and the fundamentally relational nature of the sexual drive and motivation), and offers them as a resource for theological reflection. Chapter 7 provides an overview of anthropological research on the ways in which religions both construct and constrain gender and sexuality. It deals with issues of 'discipline', 'reproduction', and 'protest and change' respectively, and reflects on the role of gender in the writing of ethnographic texts.

Chapter 8 hones the social scientific tools for studying religion, gender, and sexuality. Drawing on a range of examples from sociology of religion, it explores the significance of individuals' dispositions on the one hand and opportunities they encounter in their everyday lives on the other. Chapter 9 offers a philosophical analysis of key terms and distinctions such as gender essentialism, gender as a social construction, and gender realism. It assesses the importance of two prominent feminist philosophers, Judith Butler and Linda Martín Alcoff. Chapter 10 provides an overview of what Christian theologians need to know about queer theory, and suggests many ways in which theological reflection on sexuality and gender may benefit from it. The inclusion of queer theory in Part II may occasion some surprise, not least because it is very recent and because queer theorists generally deny their work lies within any academic discipline at all. Queer theory earns its place here as an influential critical methodology for handling sexuality and gender, and as a contributor to queer theology.

Scripture

Part III, 'Sexuality and Gender in the Biblical World', hardly needs explanation. All the churches give priority to the Bible as a source of theology. The danger of the metaphor of the 'three-legged stool' is that if the stool is to support any weight each leg must be exactly equal in length, and Episcopalians do in fact (if not in theory) place more weight on the single leg of scripture than on the other two. The Roman Catholic Church believes there are 'two distinct modes of transmission' of divine revelation, 'Sacred Tradition and Sacred Scripture' (*Catechism of the Catholic Church* 1994: para. 80), and it derives 'certainty' from each. Both 'must be accepted and honoured with equal sentiments of devotion and reverence' (para. 82). Protestants always give priority to the Bible (sometimes to the neglect of tradition and reason). So there are overwhelming grounds for placing the Bible at the forefront of theological inquiry into sexuality and gender (and into anything else). The four essays in this part examine marriage, sexual relations, same-sex relations, and gender in the Bible and in the surrounding biblical world, recognizing continuity and discontinuity between that world and our own.

Contemporary interpreters of the Bible sometimes construct a threefold ordering of their inquiries, into what is 'behind the text', 'in the text', and 'in front of the text' (Turner 2000: 44–70; House of Bishops' Group on Issues in Human Sexuality 2003: 45–47; Green 2010). But if these simple spatial prepositions hint at a simple procedure for arriving at an understanding of the text, the essays in Part III disperse any such suggestion, and enlarge considerably what might be meant by 'behind', 'in', and 'in front of'. Chapter 11 shows that some of the assumptions 'in the text' of the Hebrew Bible about marriage and sexual relations are not merely complex and internally diverse: they actually stand in tension with traditional Jewish and Christian norms for marriage and sexual activity. Chapter 12 delves deep into marriage and sexual relations in the New Testament and the surrounding world as these topics are found within and behind the many relevant texts, finding within them both a positive appreciation of sex and marriage, as well as dire warnings against sexual wrongdoing.

Chapter 13 argues that biblical texts taken to prohibit same-sex love have been misunderstood. These prohibitions turn out not to be 'in the text' at all. Rather, there are multiple forms of same-sex love to be found in the texts of the Hebrew Bible and the New Testament, and this chapter explores them. Chapter 14 describes the application of gender theory in Classical studies. It then concentrates on gender analyses of New Testament writings that demonstrate the differing approaches of masculinity studies, queer theory, and intersectional analysis. All four essays indicate the growing impact of Classical studies on biblical studies. They broaden what is 'behind' the text of the scriptures to what is 'all around the text'. It is a broad circumference.

Tradition

Another problem with the threefold ordering of textual interpretation lies with an over-simplification of what stands 'in front of' the text. Yes, readers stand or sit in front of the text, but outside their direct field of vision (and sometimes conscious awareness) lie nearly two thousand years of tradition. Part IV, 'Sexuality and Gender in Christian Tradition' provides a bridge, albeit a tenuous one, between the biblical world and our own period. Tradition too is a source of theology: indeed the Catechism declares that it 'transmits in its entirety the Word of God which has been entrusted to the apostles by Christ the Lord and the Holy Spirit' (*Catechism of the Catholic Church* 1994: para. 81). The meanings of 'tradition' (like 'reason') are varied, but each has in common that it belongs to the past, and that it belongs to the Church.

These four chapters belong either to the history or to the tradition(s) of the Church. The authors of these chapters embrace historical particularities. Chapter 15 indicates the development of ideas about desire and the body, and about the abandonment of earlier notions of a genderless ideal, in the third to fifth centuries of Christian thought. Chapter 16 is a study of Duns Scotus' estimate of the female gender. Because Mary must be a real mother, he rejects the Aristotelian view that mothers are merely passive causes in reproduction. Chapters 17 and 18 examine ideas about reproduction between 1100 and 1500, including their tension with virginity and celibacy, and the use of fictive parenthood or reproductive metaphors in theology and Church. Chapter 19 analyses the mainline Lutheran, Calvinist, and Anglican models of sex, marriage, and family and their gradual liberalization by Enlightenment liberalism.

These discrete chapters occupy the limited space available in the Handbook for tradition. While each chapter makes an independent contribution to the volume, Part IV as a whole demonstrates (if demonstration were needed) the very different thought-worlds through which the Church of God has passed. There are three further grounds for including a part devoted to tradition. First, there is no direct path from the times of the Bible to our own times. Instead there is tradition, faithful yet flawed, which provides pathways of continuity, some of them parallel with each other. Just as an individual with no memory lacks identity and orientation, so it is with the churches. Second, the pathways of tradition pass through strange territory. Yet this very strangeness, when it is allowed to appear in its barely graspable otherness, can stimulate new insights. The imaginative effort required to understand, say, a patristic quarrel about the superior status of virginity over marriage, or thinking one's way into a pre-scientific understanding of reproduction, or of women's gendered inferiority in the Middle Ages, challenges us to think differently about such matters, to recognize the historical contingency of our present assumptions, and perhaps to be open to new discernments.

Third, and most important of all, the people of God are not merely receivers of tradition: they are tradition *makers*, handing it on, having lived it and changed it in the process. The development of tradition, instead of its mere repetition, is immensely important for the subjects of this Handbook. As Joseph Ratzinger has reminded us,

> Not everything that exists in the Church must for that reason be also a legitimate tradition; in other words, not every tradition that arises in the Church is a true celebration and keeping present of the mystery of Christ. There is a distorting, as well as legitimate, tradition, ... [and] ... consequently tradition must not be considered only affirmatively but also critically.

(1969: 185, cited in Salzman and Lawler 2008: 214)

The Global Religious Context

Parts V and VI embrace the global dimension of both *internal* controversies within the churches, and *external* conversations with some of the non-Christian faiths. Part V, 'Controversies within the Churches' takes readers into some of the contemporary dilemmas which cause pain within the churches and incredulity outside them. There are struggles over male 'headship', female priesthood and episcopacy, gay marriage, and much else. This part describes the processes involved as churches respond to the questions of their members, sometimes proposing, sometimes resisting, refinements to their teachings as they seek the mind of Christ.

Chapter 20 examines the controversies about sex and gender in the Roman Catholic Church within the context of ongoing debates about the nature of the Church, the dynamism of the tradition, and the authority of the Magisterium. It argues that underlying the issues, one can discern fundamentally different theological understandings about the nature of the human body, the relationships between the sexes, and the malleability of sexuality. Chapter 21 examines similar controversies in the churches of the Anglican Communion, leaving open the question whether the acrimony over, for example, openly gay bishops and the blessing and marriage of same-sex couples, will continue at a time when other issues like poverty and environmental degradation take centre stage.

Chapter 22 examines attitudes to homosexuality throughout worldwide Pentecostalism. It uncovers contrasting positions in relation to homosexuality which also generate varying attitudes to what are perceived as the pastoral needs of sexual minorities. Chapter 23 discusses theology and practice in Evangelical churches. Chapter 24 examines the conflicts concerning sexuality and gender within the Black churches of the USA. It discerns a tension between, on the one hand, the tradition of providing for the spiritual needs of Black Americans and fighting for social justice, and, on the other hand, becoming necessarily involved in controversies about gender equality, HIV/AIDS and safer sex education, homosexuality and same-sex marriage.

Part V focuses upon disagreements internal to some of the Christian churches; Part VI turns outward to four of the world's established non-Christian faiths. Four distinguished practitioners of world faiths write about changing attitudes to sexuality and gender from within those faiths. Chapter 25 unravels the 'hitherto unquestioned consensus' in Judaic studies that Judaism embraces a positive attitude towards sexuality. It examines the tension between sexuality in ancient rabbinic thought and issues in modern Halakhah that have just begun to inform scholarly research: the ethos of modesty and the construction of the female body; homosexuality and lesbianism; and reproduction and sexuality. Chapter 26 illustrates that *missing* from Islam's scripture is the imaginary of God as father/male; endorsements of father-rule (the traditional form of patriarchy), and any concept of sexual differentiation that privileges males over females (more modern forms of patriarchy). Hermeneutic principles which do not automatically privilege patriarchal readings are offered.

Chapter 27 shows how Hindu theology weaves sexuality into answers to questions about the origin of existence, about an ultimate spiritual source of phenomena, and about the striving for a relationship between it and human beings. Both on the theogonic plane and the worldly, Hindu thought is shown to associate sexuality with gender, but to treat the latter as a fluid identity rather than a natural and essential one. Chapter 28 shows why Buddhism has multiple evaluations of sexuality. For monastics, it must be avoided because of the entanglements to which it leads, but laypeople can enjoy the pleasures of sexuality without guilt so long as they observe basic sexual ethics. Buddhism has always had male-dominated institutions, but reform is on its way, and the argument that its philosophy or world view is completely gender-neutral and gender-free, is offered.

A dark and constant shadow over all of the religions is the social, cultural, and domestic power of men over women and their use of religious means to retain it. Christian readers will note several similarities between their religion and the ones represented here. Consistent with male hegemony is the continuing influence of a literalist hermeneutic which elevates to ultimacy not merely sacred texts but particular ways of reading them. The agendas of reform and development across the religions, particularly with regard to gender, display many similarities.

Experience

All the chapters in Parts VII and VIII may be located principally within the fourth source of theology: experience. (For the arguments about the inclusion of experience, see Thatcher 2011: 38–40.) They all further the aim of Oxford Handbooks in Religion and Theology to introduce readers to many contemporary debates, and to set the agenda for how those debates might evolve. Essays in Parts VII and VIII count as theological 'answers', within the method of correlation, to some of the questions posed to the churches.

The issues in Part VII, 'Concepts and Issues', arise from sexual and gendered experiences—positive and negative—of people living now, and the engagement of theology with these. Chapter 29 explores the multiple aspects and causes of sexual violence, showing how it is connected to the wider realm of injustice, including social and institutional structures of domination along the lines of gender, race, sexual orientation, class, and other systemic inequalities. It offers an ethic of sexual justice, drawing on a Trinitarian theology that emphasizes relationality and abundant life. Chapter 30 affords some selective historical glimpses into Christianity's long history of anti-sex teachings, and counterposes two dominant themes in contemporary theologies: sexual pleasure as sacred and God-given, and as having liberating and justice-making potential. Sexual pleasure is then surveyed in relation to post-colonialism, disability, ageing, sadomasochism, and transgender and intersex identities.

Chapter 31 suggests that, whereas the problem with the dominant tradition during antiquity and the Middle Ages was that it separated desire *from* a legitimate sexuality, the problem of modern Christianity is that it has reduced desire *to* sexuality. Watchful of the critique of neighbourly love as a form of narcissism, the chapter provides a phenomenologically informed account of the love of the other that avoids narcissism and an 'economy of the same'. Chapter 32 addresses the question how the HIV/AIDS pandemic may be understood in the light of God's extravagance and hope for the future.

Person-Centred Theology

The longest part of the Handbook, Part VIII, 'Sexual Theologies for All People', continues the examination of concepts and issues, but with a difference. This part might well have been arranged under headings such as premarital sex, homosexuality, lesbianism, bisexuality, singleness, and so on. But these headings, while familiar, have several disadvantages. They are impersonal, and abstract discussion of theoretical issues can sometimes conceal the real people who fall under these convenient classifications, together with their loves and longings, their joys and disappointments. 'Sexual theology' (borrowing Nelson's term) is first of all about people, not about categories or practices. It is person-centred more than act-centred or issue-centred. These chapters attempt to avoid categorization and condemnation of sexual minorities. They are conscious attempts to speak Good News to people whose minority status has frequently resulted in persecution, stigmatization, and incomprehension. And the theology that appears in these pages offers good news of acceptance, affirmation, and understanding to them.

The persons considered in Chapter 33 are beginning sexual activity. The chapter develops a theory of virtue and virtue ethics which focuses more on the character of the sexual agent than on the acts the agent does. It sees nuptial cohabitation as a likely first step for many, on a journey that will eventually end in the couple's marriage. The persons considered in Chapter 34 are married. Contemporary sociocultural contexts which render marriage more fragile, are described. The new theological emphasis on conjugal love is highlighted, and it is argued that contemporary theologies of marriage need to catch up with the capacity of committed love among married people to become a locus of divine grace.

The persons considered in Chapter 35 live in families. They are invited to understand family life as it is found in Roman Catholic official teaching and in the Protestant Family, Religion, and Culture project. Many of the issues arising from these understandings are then explored, including the possible stigmatization of 'non-traditional' families, the place of equal-regard love in families, and the place of kin within the Kingdom of God. The persons considered in Chapter 36 are gay. The chapter explores the recent construction of gay identities and considers earlier construals of same-sex affections and the people who had them. It considers gay identity as an affective as well as a political category, and also whether gay identity is superseded by the identity conferred on individuals by being 'in Christ'.

The persons considered in Chapter 37 are lesbian. The question 'Who and what might we be speaking of when we use the term "lesbian"?' is addressed. The chapter neatly reverses the question how lesbians might understand themselves in the light of Christian theology, and asks instead what richness is being offered to theology by 'this rainbow of human experience'. The persons considered in Chapter 38 are bisexual. The chapter describes the diversity and social locations within which concepts of bisexual theory, such as compulsory monosexism, emerge. It demonstrates how Christian theology has unfairly constructed bisexuality as immature, promiscuous, and morally and politically inadequate, and sets directions for further bisexual theological work.

The persons considered in Chapter 39 are intersex and transgender. Both groups of people, while discrete, demonstrate the limitations of existing theologies of sexuality which assume stable and binary models of human maleness and femaleness. Drawing on liberationist theological goods, this chapter points to the necessity for non-pathologizing theological accounts of variant sex and gender. The persons considered in Chapter 40 are disabled. The chapter begins by examining moral assumptions that define people with disabilities as asexual or hypersexual, and offers alternatives to these limiting perspectives. It explores medical understandings of disability, together with the ways in which disability reminds us to attend to embodiment in general more authentically. The people considered in Chapter 41 are friends. The chapter warns that friendship may be losing its legacy as a socially and morally important relationship, and be viewed as a commodity to enhance one's social status or chosen lifestyle. It is argued that by revisiting Jesus' statement to his disciples, 'You are my friends', together with its reception history, the Church has an opportunity to reclaim friendship's legacy, and allow the self-understanding as the 'friends of Christ' to transform its shape and mission.

Perspectives

The broadest possible spectrum of theological contributions has been sought. There have been three kinds of difficulty in achieving this: ecclesiastical, hermeneutical, and geographical. There are churches that are reluctant to admit the troublesome conversations about sexuality and gender within their midst. Some distinguished theologians from within these churches have not wished to contribute to this Handbook, whether or not in any representative capacity, for fear of denominational recrimination. Several inquiries to prospective authors have met with polite refusal for this reason. A mere association with some of the topics given space in the volume has proved an unfortunate deterrent.

The Roman Catholic Church invests authority for maintaining the purity of its teaching to the Magisterium. 'The task of interpreting the Word of God authentically has been entrusted solely to the Magisterium of the Church, that is, to the Pope and to the bishops in communion with him' (*Catechism of the Catholic Church* 1994: para. 100). Official teachers cannot openly question the magisterium without sanction, as many faithful Catholic theologians can painfully attest. An example of Catholic intransigence is the judgement of the United States Conference of Catholic Bishops' Committee on Doctrine, that the book, by two of the authors in this volume, *The Sexual Person: Toward a Renewed Catholic Anthropology* (Salzman and Lawler 2008), reaches conclusions which are 'clearly in contradiction to the authentic teaching of the Church, cannot provide a true norm for moral action and in fact are harmful to one's moral and spiritual life' (USCCB 2010). Not only is doctrinal and moral development harmfully stifled by interventions such as these, adventurous reimagining of Catholic teaching, such as this book provides, together with the enormous pastoral relief it potentially engenders, is effectively discouraged.

There is a growing number of Protestant churches (or sections of churches) which claim to base their teaching on the Bible alone, with little or no regard for tradition and reason. They generally combine the heightened authority ascribed to the Bible with a more or less literal interpretation of it. The theologians of these churches are difficult to engage. There is little new for them to say because the Bible has already 'said' it, and the words of the biblical text are revelation. There is only 'biblical truth' which is to be 'faithfully' expounded. Within these churches there is little commitment either to the additional sources for theological work or to engagement with theological issues other than from what too often appears as a 'biblicist' standpoint. Also, if there are few signs of a theological tradition, people cannot be found *from* it, to speak *about* it, or to contribute anything *to* it.

Third, there is the geographical issue about the location of both authors and readers of the volume, mainly in First World countries. The Christian faith is growing in many other locations where First World theology, especially as it engages with sexuality and gender, is regarded with deep suspicion as too liberal, or still colonial, or secularist, or just plain decadent. I regret it has not yet been possible to do full justice to this growing readership-in-waiting, or to identify the next generation of theological researchers from Developing and Third World countries. Perhaps it is inevitable that the authors are representative of the likely readership of the volume. It is important to keep in mind that the perspectives offered in these pages are not the only ones to be discovered within the worldwide people of God.

Research

Following David Tracy, it is often said that theology has three 'publics'—society, academy, and church (1981: 3–46). All three publics are currently paying much attention to the topics of this Handbook. Because research aims at new understanding, it is the driving force behind the development of traditions of knowledge, including those of theology. Its research emphasis enables it to engage with each public in a timely manner.

Society and academy require more from theology than the mere recapitulation of the Christian tradition: so do substantial sections of church. If replication were all that was required, there would be no need to engage in any research into any of the questions discussed in the forthcoming pages. Handing down what has hitherto been believed would be sufficient. Joseph Monti has rightly claimed that the churches are forgetting how the obligation of fidelity to tradition must be dialectically engaged with the equal obligation of contemporaneity—how Christian life must make sense in its own time, must be truthful and right-making, and promote the good in whatever world we find ourselves (1995: 30). Three arguments in particular reinforce the 'obligation of contemporaneity' especially in relation to sexuality and gender.

First, there is a relativity attaching to all our knowledge. All of the essays provide evidence of this. But there is a subtle inference to be drawn from the facts of epistemological relativity which recognizes the tendency of 'relativists' to relativize all knowledge except their own. The inference is based on the character of the Church itself. Since it sees itself as a 'trans-historical' body, it spans more than one epistemological or 'cosmological world' (Monti 1995: 21), and so it cannot permanently identify itself with *any* historical view, whether ancient or contemporary. The task of interpretation is continual and always provisional.

Second, Christian teaching has always been shaped in part by the contexts in which it has found itself. 'Our own *internal* confessions and self-understandings are always framed by the *external* stories of others—those different from us who challenge our penchant to claim that we have, so to speak, given birth to ourselves' (Monti 1995: 45, emphasis in original). There is a plethora of external stories circulating around theology at the present time, in relation to sexuality and gender. Hearing them discerningly is the prelude to theological conversation and to the development of tradition. It is how the method of correlation works. Third, sexuality and gender both belong to areas of Christian thought and practice where, perhaps more than all other areas, bold development is greatly needed. The same may be true within all the major religions. This Handbook is a series of contributions to that vital task.

References

Althaus-Reid, Marcella (2000). *Indecent Theology*. Abingdon: Routledge.

Althaus-Reid, Marcella (2006) (ed.). *Liberation Theology and Sexuality*. Aldershot and Burlington, VT: Ashgate.

Catechism of the Catholic Church (1994). London: Chapman.

Cheng, Patrick (2011). *Radical Love: An Introduction to Queer Theology*. New York: Seabury.

Coakley, Sarah (2013). *God, Sexuality, and the Self: An Essay 'On the Trinity'*. Cambridge. Cambridge University Press.

Cornwall, Susannah (2011). *Controversies in Queer Theology*. London: SCM.

Dabhoiwala, Faramerz (2012). *The Origins of Sex: A History of the First Sexual Revolution*. London: Penguin Books.

Fulkerson, Mary McClintock, and Sheila Briggs (2012) (eds). *The Oxford Handbook of Feminist Theology*. Oxford: Oxford University Press.

Green, Joel B. (2010) (ed.). *Hearing the New Testament: Strategies for Interpretation*, 2nd edn. Grand Rapids, MI, and Cambridge: Eerdmans.

House of Bishops' Group on Issues in Human Sexuality (2003). *Some Issues in Human Sexuality: A Guide to the Debate*. London: Church House Publishing.

Isherwood, Lisa, and Elizabeth Stuart (1998). *Introducing Body Theology*. Sheffield: Sheffield Academic Press.

John Paul II (1997). *The Theology of the Body*. Pauline Books and Media.

Laqueur, Thomas (1990). *Making Sex: Body and Gender from the Greeks to Freud*. Cambridge, MA, and London: Harvard University Press.

Loughlin, Gerard (2007) (ed.). *Queer Theology: Rethinking the Western Body*. Malden, MA, and Oxford: Blackwell.

Monti, Joseph (1995). *Arguing about Sex: The Rhetoric of Christian Sexual Morality*. Albany, NY: State University of New York Press.

Nelson, James B. (1979). *Embodiment: An Approach to Sexuality and Christian Theology*. Minneapolis: Augsburg.

Nelson, James B. (1992). *Body Theology*. Louisville, KY: Westminster John Knox Press.

Oxford Dictionaries Pro (2013). <http://english.oxforddictionaries.com> (accessed Apr. 2014).

Ratzinger, Joseph (1969). 'The Transmission of Divine Revelation'. In Herbert Vorgrimler (ed.), *Commentary on the Documents of Vatican II*, vol. iii. New York: Herder & Herder, 185.

Salzman, Todd A., and Michael Lawler (2008). *The Sexual Person: Toward a Renewed Catholic Anthropology*. Washington, DC: Georgetown University Press.

Schiebinger, Londa (1989). *The Mind Has No Sex? Women in the Origins of Modern Science*. Cambridge, MA, and London: Harvard University Press.

Stuart, Elizabeth (2003). *Gay and Lesbian Theologies: Repetitions with Critical Difference*. Aldershot and Burlington, VT: Ashgate.

Thatcher, Adrian (1978). *The Ontology of Paul Tillich*. Oxford: Oxford University Press.

Thatcher, Adrian (2002). *Living Together and Christian Ethics*. Cambridge: Cambridge University Press.

Thatcher, Adrian (2011). *God, Sex and Gender: An Introduction*. Chichester: Wiley-Blackwell.

Tillich, Paul (1953). *Systematic Theology*, vol. i. London: Nisbet.

Tracy, David (1981). *The Analogical Imagination: Christian Theology and the Culture of Pluralism*. London: SCM Press.

Turner, Max (2000). 'Historical Criticism and Theological Hermeneutics of the New Testament'. In Joel B. Green and Max Turner (eds), *Between Two Horizons*. Grand Rapids, MI, and Cambridge: Eerdmans, 44–70.

United States Conference of Catholic Bishops' (USCCB) Committee on Doctrine (2010). 'Inadequacies in the Theological Methodology and Conclusions of "The Sexual Person Toward a Renewed Catholic Anthropology" by Todd A. Salzman and Michael G. Lawler'. Sept. 15. <http://www.usccb.org/about/doctrine/publications/upload/Sexual_Person_2010-09-15.pdf> (accessed Apr. 2014).

CHAPTER 2

....

THE THEOLOGICAL STUDY
OF SEXUALITY

....

ELIZABETH STUART

INTRODUCTION

....

FOR the latter quarter of the twentieth century and the first decade of the twenty-first century Western Christianity found itself riven over the issue of homosexuality. As I write I have a sense that Christians of all persuasions and positions are just exhausted with the argument. Meanwhile, across much of the Western world, governments have or are in the process of legalizing same-sex marriage as the culmination of a steady march towards equality which may have been sometimes stalled but never halted by Christian debate. While the Church debates have become predictable and intellectually desiccated, perhaps because the Holy Spirit has been moving elsewhere, theological reflection upon sexuality, largely but not entirely divorced from ecclesiastical spats, has produced a rich seam of theological discourse focused not only on homosexuality, though homosexuality was undoubtedly the catalyst for the emergence of the discourse, but on human sexuality in all its diversity and complexity.

Theologies of sexuality are distinctly modern phenomena. This is because the concept of sexuality is one brought to birth in modernity. In pre-modernity the focus of theological and philosophical discourse regarding matters sexual was on sexual acts and whether they were sinful/immoral or not. There was no sense that a person's sexual behaviour gave an insight into that person's self. It might tell you that person was a sinner when it came to that particular aspect of their life but that was all. Scholars have different views on when precisely the contemporary concept of sexual orientation emerged but agree that it happened between the late eighteenth and late nineteenth century. Different theories as to why it emerged are also evident; some attribute it to the reconstruction of family life under capitalism, others to the development of medical discourse and the modern focus on deviance, others to the development of molly-house culture in London. What scholars tend to agree on is that it was the construction of the homosexual that came first and which led, in turn, to the notion of the heterosexual and bisexual: in other words what began to emerge was the notion that it was possible to classify people according to their sexual desire (as distinct from their sexual activity) and that sexual orientation was a key characteristic of selfhood. Though this classification began as an attempt to order and control perversion, as Foucault (1990) famously pointed out, those so classified were able to use the classification as a form of resistance to construct first an identity, then a community, and finally human rights as a minority group.

Foucault argued that the Roman Catholic Church has played its part in creating the context in which the modern discourse on sexuality could emerge by encouraging the practice of confession and the confession of sexual sins. The Churches, however, had marginal input into the emergence of sexual orientation. That discourse was generated by a new breed of secular scientists—psychiatrists and sexologists—whose claim that sexuality was central to selfhood presented certain theological challenges, particularly to those traditions which had valorized celibacy over marriage. However, the notion that people have a sexual orientation and that the human self is in some sense a sexual self gradually became secular orthodoxy. The homosexual orientation was initially pathologized, but that pathologization began to be challenged by those 'suffering' from the condition. This resistance to the dominant discourse of the homosexual as a sad pervert is symbolized by the Stonewall Riots of 1969 when the patrons of a New York bar popular with all kinds of sexual and other minorities resisted a regular police raid and rioted for four days. The Stonewall Riots are really the creation myths of the gay liberation movement. They symbolize the rejection of the pathologization of homosexuality by those labelled homosexual. Stonewall represents the creation of the lesbian and gay selfhood, the claim of an identity with its own cultural distinctiveness and depth, the claim to belong to a stable minority group, the claim to be able to speak with ultimate authority on their 'condition'. They were able to do this because modernity had displaced external authority with the authority of the self.

In its early days the gay liberation movement adopted a radical approach to sexuality arguing that human sexuality was fundamentally androgynous and polymorphous but that approach gradually gave way to a more reformist agenda based upon a more stable and, indeed, essentialist view of sexuality. It is easier to argue for an equal place in society on the basis of a secure, coherent identity. However, developing in parallel with the gay liberation movement was the lesbian feminist movement. This has retained a more radical attitude to human sexuality with lesbianism understood less as a sexual orientation and more as a defiant choice against patriarchy.

During the 1970s a variety of different identity and sub-identity sexual minority identities emerged, often out of protest against one group (e.g. white lesbian women) claiming to be able to define the experience of all. Often enormous tension existed between these various groups. These debates and discourses coincided with growing tolerance towards sexual minorities in Western secular society. That tolerance was dramatically dissolved with the arrival of AIDS when, once again, sexual minorities found themselves pathologized, stigmatized, and, in many places, subject to increased legal discrimination. However, what AIDs also did was to bring together these diverse and disputatious minorities in solidarity with one another. It also revealed the inadequacy of the contemporary classification of sexual minorities. Sexual behaviour was revealed to have only a tangential relationship to sexual identity. AIDS was also one of the signifiers of the end of modernity with its trust in science, medicine, clearly defined identities, and unstoppable progress. AIDS brought the death of many people and many things including the stable sexual subject but it also gave birth to a new political and philosophy known as 'queer' which subverted all established sexual identities.

It was inevitable that following the example of black and feminist gay and lesbian people, Christians would begin to reflect theologically upon their experience of marginalization and oppression. It was in the mid-1970s that a distinctive branch of theology based upon gay experience began to emerge. The key characteristics of this theology were the existence of a gay self which needs to move into an authentic state and as such is the point of contact with the divine; the existence of particular gay wisdom and spiritual gifts which sometimes incarnate Gospels' values more authentically than heterosexuality; and a belief in the authority of gay experience which exceeds that of scripture and Christian tradition, and reflects cultures which had no concept of a homosexual self.

The 1970s also saw the Churches begin to wrestle with the issue of homosexuality under pressure from gay and lesbian members and contemporary understandings of sexual orientation. Seeking to balance these against readings of scripture and tradition many took the view that, while being gay itself was not sinful, engaging in sexual acts was, or at least fell short of the ideal of heterosexual marriage. With one or two notable exceptions, that debate still goes on at various levels in almost all Christian denominations.

In order to interrogate the dominant methodological approaches used in this discourse I have borrowed some categories from Meister Eckhart (via Matthew Fox's particular interpretation of him—Fox 1991). Eckhart's four paths will provide a theological grid to make some sense of theologies of sexuality. It is artificial, of course; there will be other ways of representing this still quite young theological development, but using Eckhart reminds me at least that what theology, all theology, must be about is the nature of God and our way into union with the divine, and that as we contemplate our confusing, complex, and changing humanity in the dazzling light of the divine we are stumbling our way towards the truth. There is no one royal, direct road but a multitude of paths, some of which may get us further along the road than others but all of which have their obstacles and cul-de-sacs.

VIA POSITIVA

In terms of theological reflection upon sexuality, the *via positiva* is one walked upon by both conservatives and liberal theologians. It is built upon the theological propositions that maleness and femaleness are theological categories and that therefore sexuality is caught up in the drama of salvation. These ideas are thoroughly modern but are claimed to be a legitimate development of scripture and tradition. Both Dietrich Bonhoeffer and Karl Barth proposed that humanity bears the image of God through male–female relationality. Same but also different, men and women find oneness in each other and in that process fulfil their vocation to image God (Grenz 2006: 70–94). Human beings only become truly human when men and women are in relationship to each other. Barth offered some sustained reflection upon this theme. For him marriage between men and women offers the means to participate in and to reflect the divine both in terms of its triune nature and the relationship between Christ and the Church. It is therefore the ful-filment of maleness and femaleness (although Barth did acknowledge that other forms of non-sexual fellowship between men and women also participate in some sense in marriage: Rose 2010: 156–161) that propels heterosexuality to the heart of the Christian project. For him, it is essential for men and women to be in relationship with each other. Obviously, since for Barth humanity is only complete and fulfilled as the *imago dei* in male–female relationships homosexuality is problematic (as is monasticism in this regard). Indeed, in seeking a partner of the same sex, homosexual people commit idola-try, substituting an image of themselves for the other (Barth 1961: 165–166).

For the Roman Catholic theologian Hans Urs von Balthasar (1986) sexual difference was equally theologically important. For him men and women together in their differ-ence constitute the fullness of the Christian life. Balthasar understood the Church to be constituted with two aspects: the Marian and the Petrine. The former refers to subjective holiness, the latter to objective holiness. Together they express the nuptial nature of the Church. The marriage of men and women is therefore the sacrament of the Church. Again sexuality, and more particularly heterosexuality, is at the heart of the theological project.

In a similar vein to Barth, Pope John Paul II (2006) also placed sexuality at the heart of theological anthropology. He developed a theory of the nuptial meaning of the body which suggested that in marriage men and women sacramentally reveal the nature of the divine. For Pope John Paul the nature of the divine is self-giving and generative and therefore reproduction and openness to it is an essential element of the marriage bond. Thus any form of non-marital sex or sex which is closed to procreation is sinful.

The affirmation of the goodness of human (hetero) sexuality and its crucial place in human nature, providing the locus of the *imago dei*, was a radical and innovative asser-tion that signals the moment when Protestant and then Catholic theology embraced the thoroughly modern notions both that people have a 'sexuality' and that their 'sexuality' in some sense tells the truth about who they are and what they are for, more profoundly than any other aspect of their humanity.

Liberal theologians started from the same place but came to different conclusions. If sexuality is the sacred heart of humanity then, liberal theologians such as James Nelson (1992) argue, one must begin theological reflection upon sexuality with the lived expe-rience of it, not with some romanticized ideal. Human experience of sexuality then becomes the starting point of theological reflection. This means speaking the truth about the less than ideal experience of heterosexual marriage for many women living under patriarchy and the love, devotion, and generous self-giving of many of those in non-married, non-reproductive sexual relationships. Apparent biblical prohibitions related to homosexuality can be negotiated on the grounds that the authors knew nothing of the notion of sexual orientation and that there were people for whom same-sex desire might be natural. Thus liberal theologians seek to argue that it is not the gender of those in relationship that matters but whether their sexual relationship manifests the values and virtues of the kingdom of God and one of these is to receive the gift of sex with joy and gratitude. Exactly what these virtues may be are a matter of debate but many liberal theologians would take the view of Jeffrey John (1993) that these virtues include faithful, covenanted commitment. In other words and whether they explicitly acknowledge it or not, liberal theologians, just like their conservative colleagues, accept that marriage is the primordial sacrament or covenant relationship—that which is caught up in, mirrors and mediates, the mysterious relationship between Christ and his Church—but seek to open it to the non-heterosexual. Despite protestations to the contrary, there is little theological space in both conservative and liberal sexual theology for the celibate or single person.

Both conservatives and liberals in reflecting theologically upon human sexuality approach it from a fundamentally essentialist perspective. Sexuality and gender are God-given categories and though their meaning may change through time and across cultures there is nevertheless a transhistorical, transcultural family resemblance between men and women today and men and women of the past, and gay people of today and those who expressed desire for those of the same sex in pre-modernity. What modernity did was to recognize and identify sexual orientations; it did not invent them. These categories are therefore stable enough to invest with theological meaning and build theologies upon. It is this latter assumption that some theologians have sought to challenge.

VIA NEGATIVA

In this methodological approach human beings do not simply manifest the divine when desire draws them into unity with another, rather in the *via negativa* the divine becomes desire; we might even say it *disappears* into desire. The language of *eros* is not alien to Christian theology. Many of the medieval mystics approached the divine through the language and the imagery of the erotic, the soul and body together yearning for God (McGinn 1998). But in the 1980s theologies of sexuality began to emerge which went much further than this. They identified God with the erotic. These theologies are particularly associated with lesbian theologians. Carter Heyward (1989) defined God as erotic power and right relationship, the energy that calls us out of ourselves towards others into relationships based upon mutuality. Heyward acknowledges that not all relationship can be equal, but all relationships can be based upon mutuality, by which she meant that they can be characterized by the desire to call forth the other person into the fullness of their possibilities. In so doing, we are engaging in 'godding', bringing forth God into the midst of our lives.

Her theology does not isolate sexual relating but insists that all relating must be grounded in friendship, from relations with our partner to relations to the earth. Heyward is also reluctant to define how that friendship is best manifest in sexual relating, mutuality being the only defining requirement of right relationship. However, there are certain virtues associated with such mutuality: courage, which requires us to overcome fear to embrace vulnerability; compassion, which recognizes the connectedness of all life; anger, which is a bodily signal when right relationship is not present; forgiveness, by which we release ourselves and others from the past; touch, through which those in right relationship transcend individuality; healing, which is a commitment to live in right relationship with all living creatures; and, finally, faith which involves being determined to live in right relationship in the midst of structures which encourage wrong relating.

Heyward's influence upon theologies of sexuality is hard to overestimate. It is particularly evident in the virtual disappearance of the divine into reflection upon what constitutes right relationship and the implications of living in right relationship. So, for example, Lisa Isherwood (2000), reflecting on the theological implications of body politics, seeks to purge religious constructions of sex and sexuality from patriarchal assumptions. In doing so she postulates the existence of a divine body which it is possible to possess, a body which lives in the world in conscious cognitive dissonance, unconstrained and untethered by power structures and oppressive thinking. This body is a space that is beyond patriarchal control. It is in this space that the possibility of sex becoming a manifestation of erotic power exists. Isherwood refers to this space as a divine body but there is little explicit reflection upon the nature of the 'divine' whose body it is. God, as what Isherwood called a metaphysical concept, is abandoned in such an approach, to be replaced by a trace, a radically immanent presence manifest in the midst of human relating (Isherwood 2000: 20–34).

A similar approach is adopted by some male gay theologians who argue that the tragedy of the AIDS pandemic requires a reconstruction of the concept of God. J. Michael Clark (1989, 1997) argues that AIDS has taught gay theologians to abandon the God of salvation and eschatology. This 'vertical' notion of God has to be replaced by a 'horizontal one', a radically immanent power for justice and right relation. The gay Christian project becomes, in this understanding, living ethically and 'coming out' of heterosexuality and patriarchy. This notion of the gay community as an exodus community (a notion borrowed from liberation theology) became a popular one among gay theologians. Richard Cleaver (1995) argues that scripture reveals the divine to be one who creates new types of peoples, the people of Israel and the Church. Salvation is never just an individual matter, it is about being part of the creation of a community called to be different, to live differently. It would be a tragic mistake, then, for gay and lesbian people to yearn for the same sort of lives as heterosexual people. Marriage and even monogamy cannot just be accepted as the ideal ways of relating. Everything must be open to being rethought from the basis of gay experience. The gay community must resist short cuts to liberation by constructing a mirror image of heterosexuality.

The great value of this approach is that it focuses the theological lens on actual human relationships. It avoids the idealization of particular ways of sexual relating and concentrates instead on the ethics and virtues of relating sexually within the larger context of relationships including non-personal relationships, for example, with the earth. A high concept of relationality requires the consciousness and interrogation of all types of relating. The divine is encountered in the act of relating rightly and in the act of reflecting upon relationality. The focus is not on the self but on what is going on between people and whether the divine is manifest in that or not. Furthermore, the experience of sexual relating (and indeed other types of relating) becomes a source from which to interrogate the tradition. For example, Maaike de Haardt suggests that monotheism undermines relational sexuality by idealizing the one male in whom there is absolute power (de Haardt 2010: 181–194). Or, more positively, many gay theologians find in the relationship between David and Jonathan a covenanted relationship in which God is present in the love between two men.

The dangers of the *via negativa* are that so immersed does God become in the act of right-relating that the erotic can become an idol, engulfing the divine without remainder. There is no transcendent perspective from which to interrogate a relationship or type of relating. This is clear, for example, when Isherwood reflects on the phenomenon of sadomasochism, pointing out that some women reject it on the grounds that violence is always antithetical to right-relating, while other women regard it as an expression of mutuality and trust. She asks who is right and concludes 'ultimately everyone, since I suspect that both claims are true depending on the people and the circumstances ... How we act, in each moment, is charged with divine/political meaning and it is the consciousness of that which shapes reality' (2000: 223). The dangers of the radical privatization of sexuality are evident here—who has the right to question where I find or how I define right relation? This approach to sexuality in fact has all the weaknesses of situation ethics. Theological reflection becomes rather blinkered, focused on the local and even further into personal relationships, which is at once both empowering and seducing. There is nothing in this approach which forces people to lift their sights to a horizon from which to interrogate their relating. Though undoubtedly extremely empowering, the notion of any community as an exodus community constructs it as oppressed and infused with special theological insight. This can lead to a lack of self-reflection and criticism, and a temptation to identify God with a particular experience.

VIA CREATIVA

In the *via positiva*, the divine is manifest through specific types of sexual relations and human beings find their completion in such relationship. Sexuality is therefore an integral part of Christian discipleship. In the *via negativa*, the divine is erotic power, the force of right relationship which cannot be predefined except by the qualities of mutuality. In the *via creativa*, human beings participate with God in the bringing to birth of a new creation, the new creation which Christ inaugurates and into which Christians are baptized. One of the chief characteristics of this new creation, according to St Paul, is that all identity markers are removed including those of gender (Gal. 3:28). It is from this theological proposition that the approach to sexuality known as queer theology begins.

Queer theology is not the preserve of gay people. It is in fact against any notion of sexual identity. It takes its name from queer theory, a post-structuralist approach to gender and sexuality which emerged in the 1990s in the wake of Michel Foucault's work and is particularly associated with the critical theorist Judith Butler. The use of the term 'queer' is a play on the term often applied in a derogatory fashion to gay and lesbian people and also the use of the term to designate oddness. As David Halperin has put it (1997: 82), '"queer" then, demarcates not a positivity but a positionality vis-a-vis the normative'. That positionality involves interrogating and contesting dominant concepts of sexuality and gender. Butler famously argued that gender and desire are not stable categories. Far from being expressive of some inner nature or truth about ourselves, Butler (1992) suggested that gender is in fact a performance, a performance learned from cultural scripts which through repetition are written onto bodies, not least through sexual acts. The performativity is exposed through the art of drag and indeed through lesbian and gay people who perform the dominant scripts of maleness and femaleness badly. However, that performativity is masked by the creation of homosexuality as an essential identity alongside heterosexuality. What many assume was a helpful or, indeed, liberating development has in fact, according to Butler, locked contemporary Western culture into a collective depression as we subconsciously wrestle with desires that are foreclosed to us by the construction of the self in terms of sexual identity and gender.

Critics of Butler have argued that she too quickly erases identities which people have fought and sacrificed much to own and that her theory has no grounding in people's real, everyday (Wolfe and Penelope 1993). How can we live without stable concepts of sexuality or gender? This is where queer theologians come in to argue that there is one community where in fact such living is encouraged and indeed divinely mandated and that is the Church. They argue that the Church should be the place where sexual identity has no ultimate status. Eugene Rogers (1999) notes that, according to St Paul, every Gentile member of the Church is there because God chose to act *para phusin*, contrary to nature (Rom. 11:24) (significantly, a phrase he also uses of people engaged in same-sex activity), in grafting them into the community of salvation. God acts in a queer way, transgressing expectations to include Gentiles, and this reveals that the rhythm of the divine is that of inclusion rather than exclusion.

Kathy Rudy (1997) makes a similar point when she notes that it is baptism, not biology, that incorporates Christians into the people of God, into God's very self, which eclipses all other forms of identity. She maintains that Christians do not need categories of sexual identity or, indeed, of gender. Christianity has never been about biological reproduction; it has always been about conversion. Christianity grows by opening itself to the stranger in hospitable embrace. Rudy maintains that sex has to be understood as part of Christian discipleship and therefore must be judged according to its ability to build up a hospitable Christian community.

Rogers also notes that baptism makes a Christian a citizen of the city of God which requires a different way of being. Rogers argues that the Christian tradition offers two models of being by which believers are moulded into the shape of Christ: marriage and monasticism. Both these ways of life are designed to make the believer hospitable and both swoop up those involved into the life of the Trinity, a community of self-giving love. This community has been represented in the Christian tradition through analogy which makes use of male, female, and neutral imagery. This 'gender-bending' is a vital part of the Christian tradition, according to queer theologians. The original human according to Genesis 1:27 was male and female, non-gendered. The baby Jesus was male but born of no male matter, and chose to transpose himself first into non-gendered bread and wine and then into the omnigendered Church. Scattered throughout history have been saints who have defied and crossed cultural gender roles. Think for example, of St Joan of Arc. Bodies can cross boundaries, and gender and sexuality can be dissolved. Christianity is at its heart what Marcella Althaus-Reid (2000) has termed 'indecent' but it has become 'vanilla' under the reign of patriarchy and heterosexism. It needs to become obscene: instead of dealing with sexuality and gender, the ordered categories by which we are controlled and control, it needs to deal with sex in all its complexity and messiness.

Elizabeth Stuart (2003) explores what it means for the Church to live without categories of sexual identity, believing that notions of sexuality and gender are simply not stable enough to build theologies upon. She argues that this must first mean that no one is excluded from any aspect of Church life on the grounds of sexuality or gender. The celibate life must be valorized as a reminder that desire has its ultimate fulfilment in God, not in human relating. She also argues that the Church is called to parody, to repeat with critical difference, cultural constructions of sexuality and gender whether that be marriage or singleness, the family, the couple, maleness or femaleness, to expose their non-ultimacy.

Many queer theologians claim that there is much in the Christian tradition that can be read as 'queer', and Christian theology often crafts a space full of paradox, fluidity, mystery, and apparent contradiction. Take, for example, the figure of the Virgin Mary, a figure often put to the service of sexual and gender essentialism and yet as often loved by those who suffer under such a system. Tina Beattie (2007) has argued that Mary is a queer space. She is the first to benefit from the new, redeemed humanity wrought by her son, a humanity freed from the cycle of sex, birth, and death, her virginity anticipating the resurrection and death having no hold on her. The significance of the story of the Annunciation is precisely that it is a non-sexual conception, its radical difference from normal conception destabilizing the valorization of sex and, in particular, heterosexuality. The virgin mother catapults the mind beyond the binary opposites with which we constrict our world view to a paradoxical space in which the divine can be encountered. As the 'new Eve' early Church theologians understood Mary as redeeming Eve and all women, not standing in opposition and contrast to her as later theologians have understood Mary.

Beattie argues that the figure of the Virgin Mary invites us into a transgressive space between worlds, a space in which we can learn to become what we are, redeemed selves. This space is a space of paradox and ambiguity in which we can expect to be both delighted and disturbed by the disruption of our identities and constructions. It is a queer space in which identity, gender, and sexuality become playfully fluid. In prayer we too can play with our desire for a God who is both mother and father, lover and brother, husband and wife, and the Virgin Mary plays a key role in that (Beattie 2007: 293–304). Althaus-Reid argued that Mary was the strangest thing in Christianity (Althaus-Reid 2003: 71) and it is not hard to see why: the virgin who gives birth to a son who is also her father and her spouse, and who becomes the mother of us all, she is probably the most obviously queer thing in Christianity.

Another figure often cited by queer theologians is Gregory of Nyssa. This early Church theologian appeals to queer theologians because he suggested that the Christian journey was one towards the resurrection in which the body will be restored to its prelapsarian, non-gendered state, and on its journey to this state the soul moves through male and female roles. So though the soul is propelled towards God by desire and the longing for good, it finds that that desire is fulfilled in a context beyond sexual difference. For Gregory, his sister Macrina in her ascetic state was evidentially moving beyond gender. As Stuart (2003) notes, in his vision of the soul moving through gender categories to a place beyond gender Gregory offers a vision as queer as any contemporary theorist.

If Patrick Cheng is right that sin should be understood as opposition to what God has given humanity in Christ, and Christ has brought in a new creation in which sexual identities are abolished, then, for queer theology, sin is sexual and gender essentialism is the perpetuation of the notion that these categories tell the truth about us and about our relationship with God (Cheng 2011: 71).

Queer theology is not without its weaknesses. It can be accused of being too theoretical and idealistic with no grounding in lived reality, even, and perhaps especially, in the Church which remains in most part hidebound by notions of gender and sexuality. The great danger facing queer theology is that it will atrophy and become another form of fixed identity. It must not itself become normative. Though it can be frustratingly inconclusive, with its tendency to expose and pose rather than answer questions, this is actually its greatest strength because it creates a space for Christians to do some hard thinking. It must always be in the process of contesting and deconstructing as it seeks to map out a space beyond identity. As Susannah Cornwall has put it, the role of queer theology is to pull the rug out from under theology (Cornwall 2011: 252). But in order to have an impact beyond the academy it needs to find a way on to the rug-covered floors of the Churches.

VIA TRANSFORMATIVA

What is the future of theology and sexuality? If the mission of Christianity is to cooperate with the divine in the realization of the kingdom of God upon earth then theologians now need to focus on how the resurrected life, a life beyond gender and sexual identity, can be lived. Such a life must first be piloted and modelled in the Church. However, as previously noted, while the Church has agonized and twisted and turned on these issues, Western society has begun to resolve them. But this should not absolve the Church of its duty to stop talking about sexuality and gender and to focus instead on love, justice, desire, mercy, and equality in relating, including sexual relating. Theologians of sexuality need to turn to issues around the right ordering and channelling of desire towards its end in God.

While both Church and society have been struggling with issues around homosexuality, both the monastic and marriage vocations have been undergoing something of a crisis. Probably the most pressing task for theologians of sexuality at the current moment is therefore reflection upon the demands of faithfulness in sexual relating and its place in the ordering of desire towards the divine. It is interesting that theologians of the *via creativa* have been more open than those on the other paths to the value of the celibate life as pointing to the true end of desire and providing a site of resistance to the notion that sexual identity and relating in some way tells the truth about a person in the way that nothing else does. For, as Sarah Coakley has argued, what Christianity may well be in need of at this current time is a new asceticism, an understanding of the part that desire plays in Christian discipleship that will enable Christians to steer a course between the rampant libertarianism of contemporary culture and a disordered repression of desire. And perhaps, as she suggests, what we also need are living examples of how to live beyond the end of sexuality and gender, how to live according to a proper erotic asceticism (Coakley 2010).

This post-sexuality asceticism will need to wrestle with the extraordinary complexities posed by living in a digital age. Many have claimed that we are becoming cyborgs, creatures in whom the flesh and technology—particularly digital technology—begin to merge. It is possible for us to have a virtual self, indeed many virtual selves, all of whom may engage in cybersex assuming different sexual identities in the process, an activity which engages the fleshy body albeit at a distance from the object of desire. In the process of all this, some claim that we are becoming post-human. If to be human is to be located in a web of relationships, as Elaine Graham has argued, then there is a danger of us moving into a state where at least some relationships are disengaged from our bodily presence and we need to explore whether that does or may undermine the authenticity of the encounter (Graham 2004: 10–32).

Brett Lunceford (2009) has suggested that if the sacred is essentially unmediated experience, then increasingly mediated forms of sexual activity may be luring us further and further from sacred sexuality (2009: 77–96). And if that is the case how is Christian theology to deal with those for whom this is the only possible form of sexual expression? More thought on the relationship between sexuality and social justice needs to be undertaken and the onus there is on those of the *via positiva* who want to suggest that there is a close connection between sexual relating and true humanity.

The *via positiva* approach should be welcomed because it represented a radical change of attitude, particularly in the Roman Catholic Church. No longer was (hetero) sex to be approached with suspicion or fear but celebrated as part of the created order and the human vocation. The *via negativa* goes further in identifying the divine with sexual desire as long as it is ordered towards mutuality. The danger with these two approaches is that they overlook the fact that sex may be violent or exploitative and indeed those who advocate the *via creativa* may move too quickly to the glorious liberty of the resurrection for those who are still pinned to the crucifix of violence and exploitation. In a post-sexuality world, theologians need to find a way of reflecting upon such violence. Sex is not always good. Theologians are naturally wary of a return to a sex-negative discourse but we cannot be afraid of acknowledging the fact that at its worst sex can be a weapon of evil and even in its most loving form it can be, and often is, messy and ambiguous. It may be caught up in the economy of salvation but it itself is not salvation.

There are also groups of people whose lived experience challenge all the *viae* examined in this chapter. Transgendered people challenge the biological essentialism that underpins the theology of the *via creativa* and the dissolution of that essentialism by queer theologians. Asexual people are currently an almost completely silenced group within theology of sexuality. Asexuality is not the same as celibacy, many asexual people are in relationships (Bogaert 2012) and the asexual person should raise uncomfortable questions for all of us who have valorized sex and sexual desire perhaps at the expense of relationship. Have we in the process aided the alienation of our asexual brothers and sisters and placed them outside the economy of salvation? In the Church, intersexed people are beginning to find a voice in theological discourse as are bisexual people and it is vitally important that their voices are heard as theologians begin the project of developing the asceticism needed in a post-sex context. They must become part of the formation of this ascetic.

Conclusion

In 1977 Michel Foucault, the father of queer theology, decried the 'austere monarchy of sex' and suggested that we need to say 'no' to all the systems that valorize sexuality (1990: 159). Ironically, as Foucault was declaring himself bored with sex and issues of sexuality, the theological discourse on these matters was just getting going. It has flourished into a discipline coalesced around a range of methodologies represented in this chapter as four paths or *viae*. These paths have wound around the Christian tradition, the body, heteronormativity, homosexuality, *eros*, the divine and its disappearance, and ended up pretty much where Foucault was in 1977 questioning the fundamental notions of sexuality which dominated the theological discourses of modernity, and regarding them as obstructions on the way to the kingdom. Part of the reason for Foucault's boredom lay in an experience he had in the late 1970s. He was run down by a car and believed he was dying. He described the experience as one of intense pleasure and one of his best memories (Macey 2004: 131). This near-death experience, the joy of death, provided Foucault with a horizon, an ecstatic experience from which to assess other types of pleasure and desire. For him death was an ultimate pleasure and a limitless one, whereas sex is a fleeting, limited pleasure which can only be recalled through repetition. Sex always points beyond itself to a space, to a reality where desire finally finds its consummation. The purpose of theological reflection upon sexuality must be to hasten our journey to that space. Perhaps, then, theologians now need to focus more than they previously have on the dissatisfaction that sex inevitably induces because it is perhaps here in the very limits of sexual satisfaction that God is found. Christian theology cannot just have an affair with sexuality, it has to move beyond the honeymoon period that it has enjoyed with it during modernity and move into the dissatisfaction, disappointment, and boredom because it is these experiences that point us beyond a pleasure anticipated and even experienced in sex, to the joy of death in which we will be making love with God.

REFERENCES

Althaus-Reid, M. (2000). *Indecent Theology: Theological Perversions in Sex, Gender and Politics*. London and New York: Routledge.

Althaus-Reid, M. (2003). *The Queer God*. London and New York: Routledge.

Balthasar, H. Urs van (1986). *The Office of St Peter and the Structure of the Church*. San Francisco: Ignatius Press.

Barth, K. (1961). *Church Dogmatics*, vol. iii, pt. 4. Edinburgh: T&T Clark.

Beattie, T. (2007). 'Queen of Heaven'. In G. Loughlin (ed.), *Queer Theology: Rethinking the Western Body*. Malden, MA, and Oxford: Blackwell Publishing, 293–304.

Bogaert, A. (2012). *Understanding Asexuality*. Lanham, MD: Rowman and Littlefield.

Butler, J. (1992). *Gender Trouble*. New York and London: Routledge.

Cheng, P. S. (2011). *Radical Love: An Introduction to Queer Theology*. New York: Seabury Books.

Clark, J. M. (1989). *A Place to Start: Toward an Unapologetic Gay Liberation Theology*. Dallas: Monument Press.

Clark, J. M. (1997). *Defying the Darkness: Gay Theology in the Shadows*. Cleveland: Pilgrim Press.

Cleaver, R. (1995). *Know My Name: A Liberation Theology*. Louisville, KY: Westminster John Knox Press.

Coakley, S. (2010). 'Best of '10: Rethinking Sex and the Church' [Online]. <http://www.abc.net.au/religion/articles/2010/07/14/2953473.htm> (accessed 10 Sept. 2013).

Cornwall, S. (2011). *Controversies in Queer Theology*. London: SCM.

de Haardt, M. (2010). 'Monotheism as a Threat to Relationality?' In L. Isherwood and E. Bellchambers (eds), *Through Us, With Us, In Us: Relational Theology in the Twenty-First Century*. London: SCM, 181–196.

Foucault, M. (1990). *A History of Sexuality*, i. New York: Vintage Books.

Fox, M. (1991). *Creation Spirituality: Liberating Gifts for the Peoples of the Earth*. San Francisco: Harper.

Graham, E. (2004). 'Post/Human Conditions'. *Theology and Sexuality*, 10(2): 10–32.

Grenz, S. J. (2006). 'The Social God and the Relational Self: Toward a Theology of the *Imago Dei* in the Postmodern Context'. In R. Lints, M. S. Horton, and M. R Talbot (eds), *Personal Identity in Theological Context*. Grand Rapids, MI: Wm. B. Eerdmans, 70–94.

Halperin, D. (1997). *Saint Foucault: Towards a Gay Hagiography*. Oxford: Oxford University Press.

Heyward, C. (1989). *Touching Our Strength: The Erotic as Power and Love of God*. San Francisco: Harper and Row.

Isherwood, L. (2000). 'Sex and Body Politics: Issues for Feminist Theology'. In Isherwood (ed.), *The Good News of the Body: Sexuality and Feminism*. Sheffield: Sheffield Academic Press, 20–34.

Isherwood, L. (2000). 'Safe Sex: A Feminist Theological Reflection'. In Isherwood (ed.), *The Good News of the Body: Sexuality and Feminism*, Sheffield: Sheffield Academic Press, 223–226.

John, J. (1993). *'Permanent, Faithful, Stable': Christian Same-Sex Partnerships*. London: Affirming Catholicism.

Lunceford, B. (2009). 'The Body and the Sacred in the Digital Age: Thoughts on Posthuman Sexuality'. *Theology and Sexuality*, 15(1): 77–96.

Macey, D. (2004). *Michel Foucault*. London: Reaktion.

McGinn, B. (1998). *The Flowering of Mysticism: Men and Women in the New Mysticism 1200–1350*. New York: Crossroad.

Nelson, J. B. (1992). *Body Theology*. Louisville, KY: Westminster/John Knox Press.

Pope John Paul II (2006). *Man and Woman He Created Them: A Theology of the Body*. London: Pauline Books.

Rogers, E. F. Jr. (1999). *Sexuality and the Christian Body: Their Way into the Triune God*. Oxford and Malden, MA: Blackwell.

Rose, M. (2010). *Ethics with Barth: God, Metaphysics and Morals*. Farnham: Ashgate.

Rudy, K. (1997). *Sex and the Church: Gender, Homosexuality and the Transformation of Christian Ethics*. Boston: Beacon Press.

Stuart, E. (2003). *Gay and Lesbian Theologies: Repetitions with Critical Difference*. Farnham: Ashgate.

Wolfe, S. J., and J. Penelope (eds) (1993). *Sexual Practice, Textual Theory: Lesbian Cultural Criticism* (Oxford: Blackwell).

CHAPTER 3

....

THE THEOLOGICAL STUDY OF GENDER[1]

....

TINA BEATTIE

THEOLOGY was the highest of the disciplines—the queen of the sciences—in the medieval universities. In these scholastic institutions, knowledge prayerfully gleaned from scripture and patristic theology was rationally analysed and organized according to the rediscovered texts of ancient Greek philosophy, science, and mathematics, with Aristotle being the most influential source. Gender studies, on the other hand, is one of the most recent disciplines to emerge in the proliferation of intellectual perspectives that is characteristic of postmodernity (Lyotard [1979] 1984), a movement that might eliminate the last traces of Christian Aristotelianism's formative role in the making of Western culture and ideas (D'Costa 2005; MacIntyre 2009; Turner 2013).

In the post-Enlightenment era, theology was displaced from its place of pre-eminence, first by philosophy and then by science. However, while the postmodern fragmentation of knowledge has challenged many academic disciplines and methods, it has left unchallenged the resistance to theology inherent in post-Kantian epistemologies. As Sarah Coakley observes, 'gender studies...is predominantly secular and often actively anti-theological in tone' (Coakley 2009: 2). The converse, however, is not true. Although many theologians are resistant to issues of gender and sexuality, those who take such questions seriously are among the most radical and intellectually rigorous of contemporary theologians (see Loughlin 2007). Coakley goes so far as to argue that '*only* systematic theology (of a particular sort) can adequately and effectively respond to the rightful critiques that gender studies and political and liberation theology have laid at its door. And *only* gender studies, inversely, and its accompanying political insights, can thus properly re-animate systematic theology for the future' (2009: 2, emphasis original). Elaborating upon the theological potential of gender awareness, Coakley (2013) argues that modern theologians misread the emergent Trinitarian theologies of the fourth and

---

[1] The ideas in this essay are elaborated more fully in Beattie (2006, 2013).

fifth centuries, because they fail to recognize how intricately questions of God were bound up with questions of desire, sexuality, and gender.

Sandra Lipsitz Bem refers to 'the lenses of gender' to describe how cultural constructs perpetuate different concepts of gender which she describes as 'gender polarization, androcentrism, and biological essentialism' (1993: p. viii). Bem writes of the need to 'render those lenses visible rather than invisible, to enable us to look *at* the culture's gender lenses rather than *through* them' (1993: 2, emphasis original). Theologians such as Coakley explore the new perspectives that open up when we become aware of how theology has been influenced by the invisible lenses of gender, and when we seek different possibilities for the interpretation of gendered Christian doctrines and their anthropological, sacramental, and ethical applications by making those lenses visible (see also D'Costa 2000).

This means approaching theology in the light of changing interpretations of gender and sexual difference. The work of Thomas Laqueur (1990) is of particular relevance here. Laqueur goes beyond Michel Foucault's influential theories about the social construction of sexuality and its associations with power and knowledge (Foucault [1976] 1998, [1984] 1992, [1984] 1990), to ask wide-ranging questions about pleasure, pain, embodiment, and justice in the context of changing representations of sexual anatomy and physiology in Western history.

Laqueur identifies two overlapping 'masterplots': a one-sex model found in pre-modern texts in which the female body is understood as an inferior anatomical variation on the male body, and a post-Enlightenment two-sex model in which biological differences are interpreted in terms of an essential physiological difference between men and women. Laqueur argues that, in 'pre-Enlightenment texts, and even some later ones, *sex*, or the body, must be understood as the epiphenomenon, while *gender*, what we would take to be a cultural category, was primary or "real"' (1990: 8, emphasis original). Laqueur also argues that 'Anatomy in the context of sexual difference was a representational strategy that illuminated a more stable extracorporeal reality. There existed many genders but only one adaptable sex' (1990: 35). We shall come back to these claims when we look more closely at the theological construction of sexual difference.

Despite the entrenched secularism of Anglo-American feminist theory and gender studies (Beattie 1999), postmodernism constitutes a more hospitable environment for theology than its modern antecedents. The shift away from modern metanarratives about the universality of reason and the progressive nature of scientific knowledge (Kuhn [1962] 2012) towards more contextualized narratives creates a plurality of intellectual spaces within which different cultural and religious ways of knowing can be accommodated, albeit by surrendering their claims to universality. This makes it possible for theology to reclaim its own traditions and methods, beyond the objectifying and rationalizing distortions of post-Enlightenment epistemologies. My approach in this essay belongs within this postmodern perspective, which learns from its secular counterparts but is not afraid to interpret their insights from the perspective of faith.

FEMINISM, GENDER STUDIES, AND THE LINGUISTIC TURN

The paradigmatic shift from modern empirical or rationalist approaches to knowledge towards the more narrative and contextual approaches associated with postmodernism entails an emphasis on the formative influence of language on the construction of knowledge and subjectivity. Linguistic theories displace epistemological claims rooted in the rationalism of the knowing subject, or in empirical descriptions of the material world (Vanhoozer 2003; Ward [2001] 2005; Weeks 2011). This is sometimes referred to as 'the linguistic turn', and it is the context within which gender studies must be situated.

Rejecting any realist claims about the significance of sexuality and gender which appeal to essential sexual characteristics or anatomical differences, this approach draws on resources such as psychoanalysis, Marxist theory, feminism, linguistics, post-structuralism, and post-colonial theory, as well as the evolutionary, social, and behavioural sciences, to explore how questions of gender identity are deeply influenced by dominant cultural norms (see Chopp and Davaney 1997; Tong 2009). Rather than being a divinely given or naturally occurring feature of the biologically sexed body, the linguistic concept of gender is shown to play a formative role in the construction of ideas about subjectivity and personhood, in the formation of ethics, in the attribution of roles and characteristics to different sexes, and in the political organization of social and domestic hierarchies and institutions. That is why gender studies belongs within the broadly defined approach to knowledge known as 'deconstruction'. Gender theorists and feminists argue that culturally constructed heterosexual characteristics and relationships are elevated to a normative status by denying the fluctuating and diverse spectrum of human sexuality, identity, and desire. This results in the hierarchical ordering of the sexes and the exclusion or marginalization of those who fail to conform to the binary heterosexual norms and hierarchies that undergird the social order.

Gender studies emerged from the feminist movements of the late 1960s and 1970s. Like their secular counterparts, feminist theologians were concerned with the religious, political, and social subordination and exclusion of women. They sought to correct this by drawing on women's experiences and perspectives to challenge the androcentrism and patriarchy of Christian theology and ethics, and to draw attention to the neglected presence of women in the Bible and in the making of Christian history and theology. Rosemary Radford Ruether explains this privileging of women's experience in her pioneering book, *Sexism and God-Talk* ([1983] 1992):

> The uniqueness of feminist theology lies not in its use of the criterion of experience but rather in its use of *women's* experience, which has been almost entirely shut out of theological reflection in the past. The use of women's experience in feminist theology, therefore, explodes as a critical force, exposing classical theology, including its codified traditions, as based on *male* experience rather than on universal human

experience. Feminist theology makes the sociology of theological knowledge visible, no longer hidden behind mystifications of objectified divine and universal authority.

([1983] 1992: 13, emphasis original; see also Hogan 1995)

Ruether argues that the 'critical principle' for feminist theology is 'the promotion of the full humanity of women. Whatever denies, diminishes, or distorts the full humanity of women is, therefore, appraised as not redemptive', whereas 'what does promote the full humanity of women is of the Holy' ([1983] 1992: 18–19).

However, this concept of 'woman' soon came under scrutiny. The 'woman' whose full humanity was being affirmed and whose experiences were being validated and given scholarly authority was, in the eyes of many critics, white, liberal, middle class, and heterosexual (Fulkerson 1994; Kamitsuka 2007). A wide range of contextualized feminist voices soon began to speak from positions of otherness in ways which undermined the concept of 'woman' as a singular theoretical category and political subject (King 1994; Pui-lan 2005). This exposed profound and enduring tensions between the feminist quest for justice, which requires some universal or normative claims about women, and recognition of the diversity of women's identities, aspirations, and experiences which defies such universalization. The linguistic turn has prompted ongoing debate as to whether it constitutes the abandonment of the liberative praxis entailed in the feminist theological struggle for justice in favour of more fashionable but less politically engaged theoretical discourses associated with secular academia (Marla et al. 1999).

This process of constructing and then deconstructing 'woman' went hand in hand with the attempt to disentangle the relationship between sex and gender, in order to put a critical distance between the biologically sexed body and the gendered meanings attributed to that body through cultural and linguistic constructs (Ortner 1972). However, dichotomies between sex and gender/nature and culture began to dissolve under the deconstructive gaze, on the basis of the argument that 'sex' and 'nature' are no less linguistic constructs than 'gender' and 'culture' (Butler [1990] 1999). Language maps the biological body with the contours and symbols of socially encoded sexual constructs, and we cannot meaningfully extricate the material givenness of sex—the 'real' body—from language. The linguistic turn leads to the realization that we inhabit a world that is interpreted through and through, and whatever material realities exist beyond that process of interpretation remain incomprehensible to us in and of themselves.

Although it appears in new guise in postmodern theory, this awareness of the aporia between consciousness and materiality and the perplexity to which it gives rise has its origins in much earlier philosophical and theological musings on the nature of the relationship between body and soul, matter and mind. These arguably reach their modern apotheosis in the philosophy of Immanuel Kant, whose refusal to accept the legitimacy of concepts based on metaphysical claims to knowledge has had a formative influence on the making of secular modernity with its rationalist and empiricist underpinnings.

However, while earlier generations sought to overcome the perceived gap between mind and matter through various theological and philosophical appeals to the universality of God or reason in the formation of knowledge and the discovery of truth, postmodernists—including gender theorists—seek to unmask the ideologies of power which they see at work in all attempts to explain the world in terms of any universal truth. From this perspective, language serves not to express truths we discover in an intrinsically meaningful universe, but rather to conform human knowledge and identity to social conventions and laws, maintaining political and sexual hierarchies through the linguistic dynamics of control, exclusion, and negation. Postmodern theorists resist any attempt to fill the ontological void with claims to knowledge or truth based either on rationality and science or on theology and metaphysics. Language itself takes the place of a meaningful cosmos, and the silent abyss takes the place of God.

Postmodern thinkers are concerned with exploring the ways in which the knowing subject is susceptible to unconscious social and psychological influences encrypted within the linguistic structure, which serve both to maintain and disrupt the hierarchies, gendered identities, and claims to knowledge of the established order through the complex interwoven and interdependent dynamics of inclusion and exclusion. Thus, for example, sexual difference would be interpreted not in terms of two equal but different sexes, but in terms of 'woman' as lack and negativity in relation to the positive characteristics of subjectivity and normativity associated with 'man'. Gender theorists seek to dismantle such binary logic in order to bring into play a wider range of gendered meanings and possibilities, by deconstructing the rational masculine 'I' of the modern symbolic order and his excluded, feminized others.

GENDER AND SEXUAL DIFFERENCE

The gender dualism implicit in Western ways of knowing can be traced back to Greek philosophical concepts of paternal form and maternal matter, and their influence on early and medieval theology. From this perspective, material beings exist by way of a copulative encounter between inseminating paternal form and receptive maternal matter. Jacques Lacan argues that these ancient copulative ontologies are perpetuated in post-Christian modernity through the structures of language, so that the symbolic order which constitutes the rationalized linguistic sphere of society's institutions, laws, and values constitutes the paternal form, and the imaginary or unconscious is redolent with the primordial unformed desires and fears associated with maternal matter (Beattie 2013). This constitutes the linguistic perpetuation of the one-sex model described by Laqueur, for when sexual difference is organized around relationships of perfection and lack (associated in Lacanian psychoanalysis with the Phallus as the veiled placeholder once occupied by God in the ordering of knowledge), there is no true difference. This leads to Lacan's controversial assertion that there is no sexual relationship (Lacan 1999), an assertion challenged by Luce Irigaray who argues that sexual difference needs to find linguistic expression in order to allow for the full subjectivity of women as different from men, rather than as 'the other of the same' who serves to define masculine subjectivity by functioning as its negated other (Irigaray 1985a, 1985b, 1993).

Julia Kristeva takes a more nuanced Freudian/Lacanian approach, arguing that rather than seeking the linguistic reformation of culture around the morphology of sexual difference, we need to recognize that sexual difference is a cultural projection of the division of the psyche around the dynamics of love and abjection associated with the Oedipal process. This constitutes the necessary split within the consciousness of a linguistic species (the human) in which separation from the primordial state of union associated with the maternal body is the condition for our entry into culture and language (Kristeva [1980] 1982, [1983] 1987). Kristeva turns to the maternal body rather than the sexual body as a site of possible signification in which the ambiguity of self and otherness, body and language, might be expressed beyond the dualisms and repressions of modern sexual essentialisms ([1983] 1987: 234–263; see also Battersby 1998).

Lacan has had a considerable influence on psychoanalytic theories of gender and sexual difference, particularly in the work of Irigaray and Kristeva and, through them, on postmodern theology. However, the most significant pioneer in the field of gender studies is American cultural theorist and philosopher Judith Butler (Butler 1993 [1990] 1999; Armour and St Ville 2006). Butler's work is dedicated to dismantling the edifice of sexual difference and the identities and political structures that it sustains, by disruptive textual performances of gender that open into multiple gendered identities and subject positions. This parodic mimesis of gendered pluralities exposes the constructed nature of essential heterosexuality, and lays bare its relationship to power within a social order that seeks to divide and rule its subjects/citizens through the control of sexual subjectivities and desires. Summarizing Butler's arguments, theologian Mary McClintock Fulkerson (1999: 193) writes:

> As a dominant ordering of reality, compulsory heterosexuality regulates pleasure and bodies; it cuts up reality into two human identities and defines how they may legitimately experience.... [D]esire is channelled and defined by the sexes it connects; and those sexes are two—male and female. Any thinking about desire and human relations is locked into this grid; any subject which does not conform is disciplined.

However, even this radically deconstructive approach has been called into question by the realization that gender is only one of many characteristics that contribute to the social positioning of the self. Questions of gendered identity have become enmeshed in the tangled intersections of race and ethnicity, class, sexual orientation, ability and disability, post-colonial perspectives, cultural affiliations, etc.—leading to the term 'intersectionality' as a discourse that approaches questions of subjectivity, justice, and politics within these complex and volatile markers of identity and otherness (Yuval-Davis 2011).

Any theologian who seeks to engage with this proliferation of theories must contend with a sometimes blinding array of claims and counter-claims, with complex ethical and political questions of identity politics, human rights (including sexual and reproductive rights), and discourses of alterity and heterogeneity in relation to the dominant cultural discourses of our time. Some might ask why theologians should engage with an often confused and confusing theoretical quest which is so resistant to their insights, and which sometimes tells us more about the narcissism of academics than about the lived realities of ordinary human lives.

I would argue with Coakley that the study of gender draws theology back to its neglected roots, opening up new insights and interpretations. The linguistic turn, involving as it does the rediscovery of the power of language to shape the world, can be interpreted as a call to rediscover the forgotten wisdom of the Christian theological tradition and, even if the invitation is spurned, to hold out to gender theorists the possibility of a dialogue with theology with regard to questions of transcendence, materiality, hope, and meaning. So let me turn to some of the key issues and debates that have arisen through the introduction of gender as a lens for theological and biblical reflection and analysis, beginning with the reaction of the Roman Catholic hierarchy.

Essentializing Sex

The most theologically developed resistance to gender theory has come from the Catholic magisterium and a movement known as 'theology of the body'. This was inspired by a series of reflections on the Book of Genesis given by Pope John Paul II between 1979 and 1980 (1979–1980, 2006; West [2003] 2007), and it has generated an influential following among some North American theologians in particular. A number of Catholic women theologians has welcomed this initiative and has sought to develop it in the form of a 'new feminism' (Schumacher 2004), in response to John Paul II's call to promote 'a "new feminism" which rejects the temptation of imitating models of "male domination", in order to acknowledge and affirm the true genius of women in every aspect of the life of society, and overcome all discrimination, violence and exploitation' (John Paul II 1995b: #99). These 'new feminists' are generally hostile to secular feminism (Beattie 2006) and defend the Church's official teachings on contraception, abortion, homosexuality, and marriage. 'Theology of the body' is almost exclusively concerned with the sexual and reproductive body, and has little to say about how bodies are also affected by economic and political systems.

Janet Martin Soskice points to the striking contrast between what she refers to as the 'sexual "monoculture"' (2007: 45) that informed Catholic theological anthropology up to and including the Vatican II document *Gaudium et Spes*, and the 2004 letter issued by the magisterium and addressed to Catholic bishops, 'On the Collaboration of Men and Women in the Church and the World' (CDF 2004). That letter refers to sexual difference as 'belonging ontologically to creation' (CDF 2004: #12). A similar claim is made in John Paul II's 'Letter to Women' (1995a) when he claims that 'Womanhood and manhood are complementary *not only from the physical and psychological points of view*, but also from the *ontological*' (1995a: #7, emphasis original). While stopping short of claiming that sexual difference is itself ontological, such claims represent a shift in Catholic anthropology—from the predominantly one-sex model described by Laqueur, to a two-sex model shaped by modern biology and romantic sexual stereotypes.

This emphasis on sexual difference can be understood as a reaction against theological campaigns for women's ordination, and political campaigns for women's reproductive rights (Beattie 2009, 2010). The authors of the 2004 CDF letter had some understanding of gender theory, for they associate the struggle for women's equality with a tendency to minimize 'physical difference, termed *sex*,...while the purely cultural element, termed *gender*, is emphasized to the maximum and held to be primary' (CDF 2004: ♮2, emphasis original). The desire to liberate women from 'biological determinism' inspires 'ideologies which...call into question the family, in its natural two-parent structure of mother and father, and make homosexuality and heterosexuality virtually equivalent, in a new model of polymorphous sexuality' (CDF 2004: ♮2). Despite the title of this letter, it says nothing about the contribution of men to either conflict or collaboration between the sexes, but focuses exclusively on the challenges and antagonisms of women and gender politics.

Paradoxically then, the Catholic magisterium has agreed with gender theorists that heterosexual gender roles constitute the bedrock upon which society is constructed, so that to fundamentally change these roles would be to radically undermine the status quo.[2] For conservatives, this poses an apocalyptic threat to modern Western culture. For postmodernists, it offers liberation from oppressive heterosexist norms which sustain cultures of exclusion, inequality, and violence. I want to suggest that neither of these approaches is sufficiently nuanced to offer an adequate theological account of the human body in a graced creation, but first let me turn to questions of gender in the Bible.

GENDER AND THE BIBLE

Whereas Catholic theology appeals to natural law, tradition, and magisterial authority as well as scripture, evangelical theology is more biblically focused. Elaine Storkey points out that 'As both the shaper of a worldview, and as a moral and spiritual guide for personal and communal life, the Bible unites evangelicals and remains the key source of understanding for their faith' (2007: 164). However, she describes the North American debate about gender as being 'polarized between 'complementarians' and 'egalitarians', each claiming biblical justification for their position ('biblical manhood and womanhood' versus 'biblical equality') (2007: 165; see also Storkey 2000). Storkey appeals for the renewal of Trinitarian theology as a way of appreciating the significance of human relatedness for our understanding of gender, and for a recognition of the extent to which the life and teachings of Jesus challenged the patriarchal culture of his time—a claim which is not unproblematic in terms of its representation of first-century Jewish culture (see Kraemer 1998). Storkey offers an alternative to the traditional gender roles supported by more conservative evangelicals (Gallagher 2003; Köstenberger and Jones [2004] 2010).

---

[2] At the time of writing, Pope Francis's papacy might signal a shift in Catholic gender politics, but it is too early to know.

The first three chapters of Genesis are fundamental to the Christian understanding of sex and gender across denominational and historical boundaries, and indeed they remain an indispensable resource for anybody seeking to understand Western attitudes to sexuality and gender. From the beginning of the theological tradition the story of creation has been the lens through which gender has been interpreted, and the story of Adam and Eve in Genesis 2 has been accorded greater significance than that of the creation of male and female in the image of God in Genesis 1 (Børressen [1991] 1995b; Coakley 1997 and 2002).

The account of creation and the fall in Genesis 2 and 3 has been almost universally interpreted to legitimate the subordination of women to men, based on the argument that Eve was created after Adam, she was described as his handmaid, and she was the first to yield to temptation (Kvam, Schearing, and Ziegler 1999). Theologians have also traditionally differentiated between the hierarchical ordering of the sexes which was part of the original goodness of the order of creation, and the marital domination and maternal suffering experienced by women which is a consequence of original sin. This has led to the argument that, while men and women are equal in the order of redemption, the hierarchical relationship between the sexes is part of God's intention for the good ordering of creation and the human relationships and institutions within it (Børressen [1968] 1995a). The oppression of women by men is a consequence of sin and has no place in Christian communities, but the subordination of women to male authority is intended by God (Köstenberger and Jones [2004] 2010).

However, there are different points of view as to the eschatological significance of sexual difference in the body-soul union of the person. The Western tradition has followed Augustine in believing that the creation of sexed humanity in Genesis is an eternal characteristic of the human creature. The resurrected body will retain its sexual characteristics. Both sexes participate in the fall through the actions of Adam and Eve, and in the incarnation and redemption through the participation of Christ and Mary (the New Adam and the New Eve) (Louth 1997; Beattie 2002).

The Orthodox tradition has tended towards a more contingent theology of sexual difference, seeing it as a secondary rather than a primary characteristic of what it means to be human (Ware 1997; Coakley 2002). God created the sexes in anticipation of the fall and death coming into creation, so that reproduction would become necessary to maintain the species in a post-lapsarian world. In this tradition, the risen body will not be sexually differentiated, though feminist theologians point out that there is an orientation towards androcentrism in these ostensibly non-sexed accounts of the resurrected body (Børresen [1991] 1995b).

In her book *God and the Rhetoric of Sexuality* (1978), Phyllis Trible poses one of the most influential challenges to traditional interpretations of Genesis. Through a close reading of the 'liturgy of creation' (Trible 1978: 12) in Genesis 1, she shows that the creation of male and female in 'the image of God' denotes both likeness and difference, and invites the use of male and female metaphors to express this—though this equality is obscured by the fact that 'the Bible overwhelmingly favors male metaphors for deity' (1978: 23). She reads Genesis 2–3 as 'A love story gone awry' (1978: 72), arguing that the Hebrew account does not support the canonical reading of the text which 'proclaims male superiority and female inferiority as the will of God' and 'portrays woman as 'temptress' and troublemaker who is dependent upon and dominated by her husband' (1978: 73). Instead, Trible argues that the emergence of sexual difference is part of the process of creation which begins with the creation of the divinely dependent and 'sexually undifferentiated earth creature' ('ādām) (1978: 80) from the earth (hā-ᵃdāmâ), with sexual difference occurring simultaneously with the creation of the woman, and the introduction of the words female and male ('iššâ and 'îš).

Trible's interpretation has been challenged (Bal 1985; Gellman 2006), but she forms part of a growing scholarly movement, again originating with the questions that feminism posed to biblical studies from the late 1960s and now extending across a range of studies of gender and sexuality in the Bible (Sawyer 2002; Guest et al. 2006). The creation narratives in Genesis continue to provide a focal point for postmodern theologians seeking doctrinally faithful, biblically inspired approaches to such questions. The account of the goodness of creation and of the human male and female made in the image of God requires a delicate balancing act between the affirmation of sexual difference as part of that original goodness, and the recognition that this difference offers itself as a resource for imagining a variety of ways in which gender expresses our capacity for personal maturing and deepening relationality. Soskice (2007: 49) argues that the account of the creation of male and female in the image of God in Genesis 1:27 affirms

> that all human beings are in the divine image, and that sexual difference has something to tell us about God and about ourselves.... The as yet unsung glory of Gen. 1:26–7 is that the fullness of divine life and creativity is reflected by a human race which is male and female, which encompasses if not an ontological then a primal difference.

However, this brings me to a difference between Protestant and Catholic approaches to creation, the Bible, and revelation, which has a subtle but important influence on theologies of gender.

SCRIPTURE, SACRAMENTALITY, AND DESIRE

The linguistic turn has prompted a shift away from historical-critical methods of biblical scholarship towards more narrative approaches, in which the texts are interpreted not in terms of their objective historical meaning but as the unfolding story of faith within Jewish and Christian communities (Frei 1993; Loughlin 1996). This shift is evidence of the extent to which postmodernism restores to Christian scholarship some of its own forgotten insights about reading and interpreting texts. As many theologians point out, the pre-modern approach to the Bible was more linguistically nuanced than its modern counterparts. In patristic and medieval theology, the scriptures opened into ever-deeper meanings and mysteries by way of metaphor and allegory, and literal readings ultimately yielded to more mystical interpretations. Thomas Aquinas explains that scripture is the self-revelation of the mystery of God, so that it constitutes a concealing as well as a revealing. This means, says Thomas, that 'the manner of its speech transcends every science, because in one and the same sentence, while it describes a fact, it reveals a mystery' (*Summa Theologiae* I.1.10, quoted in Beattie 2013: 57–58).

This mystery is, in the Catholic sacramental tradition, a weaving together of nature and grace, reason and revelation, into a single harmonious symphony of creation orchestrated by desire for God and held in being by the active love of God. This 'sacramental imagination' (Hilkert [1997] 2006) has always found expression in Catholic liturgy, art, literature, and music, but it also informs the politicized and historically contextualized perspectives of liberationist and feminist theologies, for the God of scripture is the God of nature and of history. Our capacity to enter more deeply into knowledge of God is understood in terms of the continuity of grace with nature, rather than as a rupture between the two—in the words of Thomas, 'grace perfects nature' (*Summa Theologiae* I.62.5, quoted in Beattie 2013: 40).

Protestant theology tends to have a more radical account of the dis-gracing of nature through the effects of original sin, so that the 'sacramental imagination' of the Catholic tradition is sometimes contrasted with the 'dialectical imagination' exemplified by Reformed theologians such as Karl Barth. In Mary Hilkert's summing-up of Barth's position, 'There can be no continuity between revelation and creation since creation as destroyed by sin reveals only God's "no." The hidden God (*Deus absconditus*) of Christian revelation can never be discovered directly in human history or experience, both of which are deeply scarred by sin' ([1997] 2006: 21; see also Jones 1993). From this perspective, the cross is a scandal which radically interrupts history and stands over and against nature, with no evident continuity between the order of nature and the transformative and redeeming power of grace.

It would be wrong to draw a rigid distinction between these two approaches, for they weave through Catholic and Protestant theologies in different ways. Nevertheless, they shape different theological approaches to questions of gender, as can be seen if we briefly consider Nancy Dallavalle's criticism of Fulkerson's Reformed theology of gender, from the perspective of a Catholic sacramental account of creation.

Fulkerson is one of the most radically deconstructive theologians of gender in her close engagement with Foucault, and her work is a rich resource for understanding the theological potential of gender theory. In her book *Changing the Subject* (1994), she argues that feminist theologians have been insufficiently attentive to the ways in which power operates through the subtle dynamics of inclusion and exclusion which constitute the academic production of knowledge. Fulkerson seeks a new method for feminist theology, in which the story of Jesus becomes a narrative enacted in different communities in a way that destabilizes the subject and entails 'the loss of a fixed notion of human nature' (1994: 393–394). This calls for a 'theological politics of respect for difference' through participation in 'communities that transgress gender hierarchies' (1994: 394). The implications of this are explored in a later essay in which Fulkerson appeals for a theological grammar that is iconoclastic in its refusal 'to require binary gendered identity' as a condition of 'access to the status of child of God' (1999: 199). In its place, she appeals for a

> radical love...displayed in a community whose relations of respect, forgiveness, confession, accountability and agape toward the stranger are made available without conditions...Radical love is invoked in the community to support a reality where there is neither slave nor free, male nor female in Christ Jesus, a reality defined by a grammar of justification by faith alone.
>
> (Fulkerson 1999: 198–199)

Dallavalle compares the ethical emphasis on justice in feminist theologies, with the emphasis on creation in Catholic sacramental theology (1998b). She argues that Fulkerson's critique of feminism is 'shaped by her own Reformed tradition's position of "iconoclasm" with regard to creation', which is, she argues, 'foreign (not "heresy") to both the Catholic tradition of finding biological sexuality to be theologically significant and the Catholic sacramental sensibility' (Dallavalle 1998a: 41). Dallavalle calls for a 'critical essentialism' which 'brings the important insights of gender theory into a deeper and more mutually critical conversation with the profound resonance of biological sexuality in the Catholic theological tradition' (1998a: 24), based on acceptance of the fact that, however much men and women have in common, 'we live our lives not 'embodied' generically, but as male and female' (1998a: 33). The doctrine of creation, interpreted within the unfolding life of the Church, invites us to 'continue to plumb the mystery of biological sexuality as "holy work"', constituting 'an interpretative act by creation on creation' by way of the 'ongoing polyphony of creation and tradition and economy' (1998a: 39).

The idea of 'critical essentialism' has been questioned by those who see it as lending support to more conservative theories of biological determinism and sexual dualism (Abraham 2009), but Dallavalle's critique serves as a reminder that there are limits to deconstruction. Ultimately we cannot escape the particularity of the body with its sexual functions and gendered encryptions. From a sacramental perspective these are not repressive social impositions which violate the freedom of the self, but can be interpreted as a divine invitation to inhabit the freedom and mystery of life in God's graced creation. It is one thing to acknowledge with Fulkerson that 'notions of inner sexual identity and the accompanying matrix that routes and normalizes desire from gendered identity are historically constructed' (1999: 198), but it is another to suggest that we are able to break free of all such historical constructs which confer our identities upon us and weave us into society. The challenge is not to wriggle free of all such constructs, for to do that would be to lapse into some primordial, non-linguistic condition of animality. It is rather to ask how our unique positioning within creation as 'rational animals' (see Beattie 2013: 71) made in the image of the relational, Trinitarian, and Incarnate God enables us to navigate a creative path of limited and fragile freedom between the body's grace and vulnerability, and the spirit's capacity to liberate our bodies into love, or to surrender them to the enslavement of obsessive and destructive desires.

This means attending to the wounded aspects of desire, which Christianity refers to in terms of original sin. There is a fundamental difference between secular anthropology and theological anthropology concerning the nature of desire. In theological terms, desire for God is the origin and end of all desire, and only when we understand this are we free to enjoy the more transient and finite objects of desire that constitute our earthly needs, pleasures, and relationships (Beattie 2013: 71–85). Original sin constitutes a fundamental distortion of the goodness of our desire for God, so that we develop obsessive attachments to and cravings for objects that distract us from the love of God and neighbour.

However, feminist theologians argue that the Christian understanding of sin needs to be analysed in terms of gender. Valerie Saiving's 1960 essay, 'The Human Situation: A Feminine View' introduced a gendered perspective into theological accounts of sin, in a way that anticipates later constructivist theories of gender. Resisting any appeal to essential sexual differences, Saiving argues that women are psychologically conditioned to greater relationality, love, and dependence than men, originating in the maternal relationship. The anxiety that arises as a result of separation from the mother makes men vulnerable to sin understood in terms of 'pride, will-to-power, exploitation, self-assertiveness, and the treatment of others as objects rather than persons' (Saiving 1960: 107). Women, on the other hand, might face the temptation of 'specifically femin-ine forms of sin' (1960: 108), associated with 'underdevelopment or negation of the self' (1960: 109).

Feminist theologians have developed Saiving's insights (Douglas et al. 2012), and have also drawn on the work of psychologists such as Carol Gilligan (1982) to construct a gendered theology of sin. However, the texts of medieval mysticism also provide a rich resource for exploring how gendered concepts of relationality inform the language of sin and grace, desire, and alienation, in the expression of human yearning for God.

GENDER AND MYSTICISM

Grace Jantzen's book, *Power, Gender and Christian Mysticism* (1995) was one of the first to bring feminist analysis to bear on the concept of mysticism. Challenging accounts of mysticism as an intense subjective experience of God, Jantzen engages with Foucault to argue that mysticism is a social construct that must be analysed in terms of gendered power relations which were used to control and exclude women. Other studies have offered a more nuanced and closely contextualized approach, drawing on a range of theoretical perspectives to cast new light on the complex gendering of mystical texts in their historical contexts (Hollywood 2002).

The linguistic style associated with medieval mysticism gains much of its poetic qual-ity from an appreciation of the potency of metaphors of gender to communicate the mysterious and dynamic relationship between creation and God. Barbara Newman observes that 'The permutations of gender in mystical texts, and among mystics them-selves, are endlessly interesting' (2013: 54). However, she cautions that mystical language expresses an intimate personal relationship between the human 'I' and the divine 'Thou', and these direct personal pronouns only become gendered when they are translated into a third-person account:

> As soon as the third person intervenes, the I-Thou relationship becomes a story about He-and-I or I-and-She. It is this necessary, but distorting gap between the experience of relationship and the language of narration that gives gender, fascinating though it is, more prominence than most mystics would say it deserves.
>
> (Newman 2013: 54)

We find clear examples of this if we read the dialogical voices of women mystics in works such as Catherine of Siena's *Dialogue*, in which the author adopts a range of narrative voices to express the relationship between the bodily self, the soul, and God. The soul is the feminized other in relation to the mystical body of Christ and the Church, and the 'I' is the bodily narrator who observes this relationship without ever being able to plumb its depths or say what it means. The soul encounters God in rapture, but the first-person narrator claims to have no understanding of this experience:

> And what shall I say? I will stutter, 'A-a,' because there is nothing else I know how to say. Finite language cannot express the emotion of the soul who longs for you infinitely...I say only, my soul, that you have tasted and seen the abyss of supreme eternal providence.
>
> (Catherine of Siena 1980: 325–326)

Yet this ecstatic union between the soul and God means nothing unless it animates the body to love and serve God in the body of the neighbour, for that is where God is truly to be found. God tells Catherine that 'love of me and love of neighbor are one and the same thing: Since love of neighbor has its source in me, the more the soul loves me, the more she loves her neighbors' (Catherine of Siena 1980: 86). Catherine offers a lavish example of a nuptial theology of erotic delight in the mystical body of Christ, with a passionate and highly politicized commitment to minister to the human body in all its suffering and need, and to cry out for justice in the Church (Beattie 2013: 364–387).

The nuptial language of Christian mysticism is inspired by the Song of Songs, which was interpreted by Origen in the third century in terms of the soul's quest for God. This sowed the seeds for the flowering of the Canticle in Christian mystical writings from the eleventh century (Astell and Cavadini 2013; see also Trible 1978). Although post-Reformation interpreters of the Bible often fought shy of the explicit eroticism of the Canticle, medieval theologians and artists appropriated its lush imagery of erotic love to express the relationship of the soul and/or the Church as bride with Christ the bridegroom, with the Virgin Mary often featuring as a motif of the perfection of this relationship. Images of erotic desire were used interchangeably with images of maternal nurture, so that the mystical body of Christ becomes a polymorphous source of desire, consolation, and joy variously associated with the masculinized eroticism of the bridegroom, the mothering presence of the Church, and the nurturing body of the Eucharist (Bynum 1991).

In that sense, the mystics knew what deconstructionists have rediscovered about how language provides the means for its own liberation from the dualisms and binaries that trap our imaginative possibilities and prevent us from becoming other than we are. However, they repeatedly warn against a solipsistic revelling in contemplative delight for its own sake, because the love that is experienced in contemplation or divine union must always find material expression in love of neighbour and care for the poor.

REDEEMING GENDER

Here we encounter the most significant difference between postmodern theories of gender and the language of classical Christian theology and devotion. The gendered discourses of postmodern theory often have little purchase on the material realities and experiences of ordinary people and show little ethical concern for those who are too young, too old, or simply too caught up in the grinding needs of survival to participate in the gendered parodies of postmodern metrosexuals.

Paradoxically, what theology might bring to this discussion is not the language of eternity and metaphysics, but the language of materiality and incarnation. Finitude, mortality, and creaturely embodiment constitute the human condition, and set limits to what we can achieve in terms of our capacity to transform imaginative possibilities into existential realities. Christian theologians have been repeatedly seduced by various forms of Manichaeism and philosophical dualism in which matter is condemned as meaningless or polluting in relation to the rational and abstract perfection of God. Postmodernism risks becoming another of these Manichaean seductions, for in its privileging of language and its refusal to allow any intrinsic significance to the material world, it constitutes the ultimate triumph of form over matter. The task of theology is not simply to invert this in favour of a romanticized New Age pantheism, but to ask how we can creatively imagine a different world through our playful and prayerful habitation of the in-between, that space which is opened by grace, where Word and flesh encounter one another in the conceptually impossible/impossibly conceived union of the body with God in the womb of the Virgin.

In its engagement with gender theory, theology must ask what is needed to repair the ruptured relationship between language and materiality, and between self and neighbour, without reinscribing bodies within the exhausted sexual essentialisms of modernity. Such questions must also be asked of our relationships with the non-human aspects of creation, for we are becoming aware of how interwoven our lives are with those of the rest of creation, and how dependent we are on the intricate harmonies that create an organic whole out of the myriad forms of being with which we share our threatened planet.

The quest for an incarnational, Trinitarian theology, deeply rooted in the goodness of creation, must attend to the significance of gender if it is to be faithful to the wisdom of its own tradition. Gender theory dissolves the moral certainties and sexual binaries of bourgeois Christian modernity and ushers in a new and as yet unknowable future. It invites renewed reflection on what it means to say with St Paul that 'There is neither Jew nor Gentile, neither slave nor free, nor is there male and female, for you are all one in Christ Jesus' (Gal. 3:28).

Postmodern theologians make visible the lenses of gender in ways that bring strange and sometimes challenging new perspectives into view. In this endeavour, theology is no less constructivist than theory, for the bodies to which it refers are bodies queered by grace (Loughlin 2007). Language clothes the naked human animal with gendered personhood made in the image of God, and theology springing from the graced creativity of contemplation opens our imaginations to the myriad possibilities of gendered loving and being that stream between the two poles of reproductive necessity. Coakley refers to 'gender's mysterious and plastic openness to divine transfiguration' so that 'the 'fixed' fallen differences of worldly gender are transfigured precisely by the interruptive activity of the Holy Spirit, drawing gender into Trinitarian purgation and transformation. Twoness, one might say, is divinely ambushed by threeness' (Coakley 2009: 11).

Theology is called to recognize the extent to which this divine ambushing deconstructs the dualisms which might nevertheless be necessary to orientate us in relation to the knowledge of good and evil from which every other dualism emerges. For as long as history continues, violence and suffering will continue, and the moral reasoning necessary to navigate a complex ethical path through life depends on our ability to do good and avoid evil. But the classical theological tradition tells us that, like all human faculties, our capacity for reasoning does not transcend the time-bound reality of our mortal lives to give us insight into the being of God (Porter 2005). Only by allowing ourselves to be drawn deeply into the mystery of the incarnate and risen God through contemplation and desire, can we experience something of that unknowing which constitutes the undoing of all that we know and enables us to live within the mystery.

Genesis 3 tells us that the first symptom of sin—the first intimation that all is not well in God's very good creation—manifests itself in the space of difference between the man and the woman made in the image of God. Only with the acquisition of the knowledge of good and evil did it become possible for us to banish God from the garden of creation and become like gods, through the dynamics of division, blame, and shame. But Christianity knows that such knowledge is cursed. It is sin's taproot into the human soul, alienating us from God and from creation, and sowing the seeds of conflict within our most intimate relationships.

The theological vocation is to emerge from deep silence into language, to seek to articulate that unsayable mystery experienced by the soul which has 'tasted and seen the abyss of supreme eternal providence'. To allow something of this mystery to seep through, theology needs language that is diaphanous, loosely woven in the 'broken middle' (Rose 1992) between the universal and the particular, the infinity of our imagination and the finite vulnerability and dependence of our bodies. This means that theology must be poetic, but it must also sift and filter its poetry through the fine mesh of wisdom. Wisdom is what remains when the materiality that seeps into our consciousness through the porosity of the senses has been reflected upon, prayed upon, transformed into love, and animated by desire to materialize that love in the world. Only when we know what it means to experience the quiver of desire for God in the sinews and tendons of our flesh and in the deepest yearnings of our souls, only when we can say with the Psalmist, 'I praise you because I am fearfully and wonderfully made' (Ps. 139:14), can theologians begin to ask what place gender and sexuality might have in our being and doing, in our living and loving.

REFERENCES

Abraham, Susan (2009). 'Strategic Essentialism in Nationalist Discourses: Sketching a Feminist Agenda in the Study of Religion'. *Journal of Feminist Studies in Religion*, 25(1): 156–161.

Armour, Ellen T., and Susan M. St Ville (2006) (eds). *Bodily Citations: Religion and Judith Butler*. New York and Chichester: Columbia University Press, 27–40.

Astell, Ann W., and Catherine Rose Cavadini (2013). 'The Song of Songs'. In Julia A. Lamm (ed.), *The Wiley-Blackwell Companion to Christian Mysticism*. Malden, MA, and Oxford: Blackwell Publishing, 27–40.

Bal, Mieke (1985). 'Sexuality, Sin and Sorrow: The Emergence of the Female Character (A Reading of *Genesis* 1–3)'. *Poetics Today*, 6(1–2): 21–42.

Battersby, Christine (1998). *The Phenomenal Woman: Feminist Metaphysics and the Patterns of Identity*. Cambridge: Polity Press.

Beattie, Tina (1999). 'Global Sisterhood or Wicked Stepsisters: Why Aren't Girls with God Mothers Invited to the Ball?' In Deborah Sawyer and Diane Collier (eds), *Is there a Future for Feminist Theology?* Sheffield: Sheffield Academic Press, 115–125.

Beattie, Tina (2002). *God's Mother, Eve's Advocate: A Marian Narrative of Women's Salvation*. London and New York: Continuum.

Beattie, Tina (2006). *New Catholic Feminism: Theology and Theory*. London and New York: Routledge.

Beattie, Tina (2009). 'The End of Woman: Gender, God and Rights Beyond Modernity'. In Patrick Claffey and Joseph Egan (eds), *Movement or Moment? Assessing Liberation Theology Forty Years after Medellín*. Oxford: Peter Lang, 161–181.

Beattie, Tina (2010). 'Catholicism, Choice and Consciousness: A Feminist Theological Perspective on Abortion'. *International Journal of Public Theology*, 4(1): 51–75.

Beattie, Tina (2013). *Theology after Postmodernity: Divining the Void—A Lacanian Feminist Reading of Thomas Aquinas*. Oxford and New York: Oxford University Press.

Bem, Sandra Lipsitz (1993). *The Lenses of Gender: Transforming the Debate on Sexual Inequality*. New Haven: Yale University Press.

Børresen, Kari Elisabeth ([1968] 1995a). *Subordination and Equivalence: Nature and Role of Women in Augustine and Thomas Aquinas*. Rowman & Littlefield.

Børresen, Kari Elisabeth ([1991] 1995b). 'God's Image, Man's Image? Patristic Interpretations of Gen. 1,27 and 1 Cor. 11,7'. In Børresen (ed.), *The Image of God: Gender Models in Judæo-Christian Tradition*. Minneapolis: Fortress Press, 187–209.

Butler, Judith ([1990] 1999). *Gender Trouble: Feminism and the Subversion of Identity*. New York: Routledge.

Butler, Judith (1993). *Bodies that Matter: On the Discursive Limits of 'Sex'*. New York: Routledge.

Bynum, Caroline Walker (1991). *Fragmentation and Redemption: On Gender and the Human Body in Medieval Religion*. New York: Zone Books.

Catherine of Siena (1980). *The Dialogue*, trans. Suzanne Noffke OP. New York and Mahwah, NJ: Paulist Press.

Chopp, Rebecca S., and Sheila Greeve Davaney (1997) (eds). *Horizons in Feminist Theology: Identity, Tradition, and Norms*. Minneapolis: Augsburg Fortress.

Coakley, Sarah (1997) (ed.). *Religion and the Body*. Cambridge: Cambridge University Press.

Coakley, Sarah (2002). 'Creaturehood before God: Male and Female'. In Coakley (ed.), *Powers and Submissions: Spirituality, Gender and Philosophy*. Oxford: Blackwell Publishing, 55–68.

Coakley, Sarah (2009). 'Is there a Future for Gender and Theology? On Gender, Contemplation, and the Systematic Task'. *Criterion*, 47(1): 2–11.

Coakley, Sarah (2013). *God, Sexuality, and the Self: An Essay 'On the Trinity'*. New York and Cambridge: Cambridge University Press.

Congregation for the Doctrine of the Faith (CDF) (2004). 'Letter to the Bishops of the Catholic Church on the Collaboration of Men and Women in the Church and the World'. <http://www.vatican.va/roman_curia/congregations/cfaith/documents/rc_con_cfaith_doc_20040731_collaboration_en.html> (accessed Sept. 2013).

Dallavalle, Nancy A. (1998a). 'Neither Idolatry nor Iconoclasm: A Critical Essentialism for Catholic Feminist Theology'. *Horizons* 25(1): 23–42.

Dallavalle, Nancy A. (1998b). 'Toward a Theology that is Catholic and Feminist: Some Basic Issues'. *Modern Theology*, 14(4) (Oct.), 535–553.

D'Costa, Gavin (2000). *Sexing the Trinity: Gender, Culture and the Divine*. London: SCM Press.

D'Costa, Gavin (2005). *Theology in the Public Square: Church, Academy and Nation*. Malden, MA, and Oxford: Blackwell Publishing.

Douglas, Mark and Elizabeth Hinson-Hasty (2012). 'Roundtable: Fifty Years of Reflection on Valerie Saiving's "The Human Situation: A Feminine View"'. *Journal of Feminist Studies in Religion*, 28(1): 75–133.

Foucault, Michel ([1976] 1998). *The History of Sexuality*, i. *The Will to Knowledge*. Trans. Robert Hurley. London: Penguin.

Foucault, Michel ([1984] 1992). *The History of Sexuality*, ii. *The Use of Pleasure*. Trans. Robert Hurley. London: Penguin.

Foucault, Michel ([1984] 1990). *The History of Sexuality*, iii. *The Care of the Self*. Trans. Robert Hurley. London: Penguin.

Frei, Hans W. (1993). *Theology and Narrative: Selected Essays*. Ed. George Hunsinger and William C. Placher. Oxford: Oxford University Press.

Fulkerson, Mary McClintock (1994). *Changing the Subject—Women's Discourse and Feminist Theology*. Minneapolis: Fortress Press.

Fulkerson, Mary McClintock (1999). 'Gender—Being It or Doing It? The Church, Homosexuality, and the Politics of Identity'. In Gary David Comstock and Susan E. Henking (eds), *Que(e)rying Religion: A Critical Anthology*. New York: Continuum, 188–201.

Gallagher, Sally (2003). *Evangelical Identity & Gendered Family Life*. Piscataway, NJ: Rutgers University Press.

Gellman, Jerome (2006). 'Gender and Sexuality in the Garden of Eden'. *Theology and Sexuality*, 12(3): 319–335.

Gilligan, Carol (1982). *In a Different Voice: Psychological Theory and Women's Development*. Cambridge, MA: Harvard University Press.

Guest, Deryn, Robert E. Goss, and Mona West (2006) (eds). *The Queer Bible Commentary*. London: SCM Press.

Hilkert, Mary Catherine ([1997] 2006). *Naming Grace: Preaching and the Sacramental Imagination*. New York: Continuum.

Hogan, Linda (1995). *From Women's Experience to Feminist Theology*. Sheffield: Sheffield Academic Press.

Hollywood, Amy (2002). *Sensible Ecstasy: Mysticism, Sexual Difference, and the Demands of History*. Chicago: University of Chicago Press.

Irigaray, Luce (1985a). *Speculum of the Other Woman*. Trans. Gillian C. Gill. Ithaca, NY: Cornell University Press.

Irigaray, Luce (1985b). *This Sex Which Is Not One*. Trans. Catherine Porter with Carolyn Burke Porter. Ithaca, NY: Cornell University Press.

Irigaray, Luce (1993). *Sexes and Genealogies*. Trans. Gillian C. Gill. New York: Columbia University Press.

Jantzen, Grace (1995). *Power, Gender and Christian Mysticism*. Cambridge: Cambridge University Press.

John Paul II (1979–1980). *Original Unity of Man and Woman: 'Catechesis on the Book of Genesis'*. <http://www.vatican.va/holy_father/john_paul_ii/audiences/catechesis_genesis/> (accessed Sept 2013).

John Paul II (1995a). 'Letter to Women'. < http://www.vatican.va/holy_father/john_paul_ii/letters/documents/hf_jp-ii_let_29061995_women_en.html> (accessed Sept. 2013).

John Paul II (1995b). *Evangelium Vitae—on the Value and Inviolability of Human Life*. <http://www.vatican.va/holy_father/john_paul_ii/encyclicals/documents/hf_jp-ii_enc_25031995_evangelium-vitae_en.html> (accessed 1 Aug. 2013).

John Paul II (2006). *Man and Woman He Created Them: A Theology of the Body*. Trans. Michael Waldstein. Pauline Books and Media.

Jones, Serene (1993). 'This God Which Is Not One: Irigaray and Barth on the Divine'. In Maggie C. W. Kim, Susan St Ville, and Susan M. Simonaitis (eds), *Transfigurations: Theology and the French Feminisms*. Minneapolis: Fortress Press, 109–142.

Kamitsuka, Margaret K. (2007). *Feminist Theology and the Challenge of Difference*. Oxford and New York: Oxford University Press.

King, Ursula (1994) (ed.). *Feminist Theology from the Third World*. Maryknoll, NY: Orbis Books.

Köstenberger, Andreas, and David W. Jones ([2004] 2010). *God, Marriage, and Family: Rebuilding the Biblical Foundation*. Wheaton, IL: Crossway Books.

Kraemer, Ross Shepard (1998). 'Jewish Women and Christian Origins: Some Caveats'. In Kraemer and Mary Rose D'Angelo (eds), *Women and Christian Origins*. Oxford: Oxford University Press, 35–49.

Kristeva, Julia ([1980] 1982). *Powers of Horror: An Essay on Abjection*. Trans. Leon S. Roudiez. New York: Columbia University Press.

Kristeva, Julia ([1983] 1987). *Tales of Love*. Trans. Leon S. Roudiez. New York: Columbia University Press.

Kuhn, Thomas S. ([1962] 2012). *The Structure of Scientific Revolutions*. Chicago: University of Chicago Press.

Kvam, Kristen E., Linda S. Schearing, and Valarie H. Ziegler (1999) (eds). *Jewish, Christian, and Muslim Readings on Genesis and Gender*. Bloomington: Indiana University Press.

Lacan, Jacques (1999). *On Feminine Sexuality—the Limits of Love and Knowledge: The Seminar of Jacques Lacan, Book XX, Encore, 1972–1973*. Ed. Jacques-Alain Miller, trans. Bruce Fink. New York and London: W. W. Norton & Company.

Laqueur, Thomas (1990). *Making Sex: Body and Gender from the Greeks to Freud*. Cambridge, MA: Harvard University Press.

Loughlin, Gerard (1996). *Telling God's Story: Bible, Church and Narrative Theology*. Cambridge: Cambridge University Press.

Loughlin, Gerard (2007) (ed.). *Queer Theology: Rethinking the Western Body*. Malden, MA, and Oxford: Blackwell Publishing.

Louth, Andrew (1997). 'The Body in Western Catholic Christianity'. In Coakley (1997), 111–130.

Lyotard, Jean-François ([1979] 1984). *The Postmodern Condition: A Report on Knowledge*. Trans. Geoff Bennington and Brian Massumi. Manchester: Manchester University Press.

MacIntyre, Alasdair (2009). *God, Philosophy, Universities: A Selective History of the Catholic Philosophical Tradition*. Lanham, NY, and Plymouth: Rowman & Littlefield.

Marla Brettschneider, Regula Grünenfelder, Jane Naomi Iwamura, Grace Ji-Sun Kim, Patricia Martinez, Emily R. Neill, Debra Washington, and Kirsten White (1999). 'Roundtable Discussion: From Generation to Generation: Horizons in Feminist Theology or Reinventing the Wheel?' *Journal of Feminist Studies in Religion*, 15(1) (Spring): 102–138.

Newman, Barbara (2013). 'Gender'. In Julia A. Lamm (ed.), *The Wiley-Blackwell Companion to Christian Mysticism*. Malden, MA, and Oxford: Blackwell Publishing, 41–55.

Ortner, Sherry B. (1972). 'Is Female to Male as Nature is to Culture?' In M. Z. Rosaldo and L. Lamphere (eds), *Women, Culture, and Society*. Stanford, CA: Stanford University Press, 68–87.

Porter, Jean (2005). *Nature as Reason: A Thomistic Theory of the Natural Law*. Grand Rapids, MI, and Cambridge: Eerdmans.

Pui-lan, Kwok (2005). *Postcolonial Imagination and Feminist Theology*. Louisville, KY: Westminster John Knox Press.

Rose, Gillian (1992). *The Broken Middle: Out of Our Ancient Society*. Oxford and Cambridge, MA: Blackwell.

Ruether, Rosemary Radford ([1983] 1992). *Sexism and God-Talk: Toward a Feminist Theology*. Boston: Beacon Press.

Saiving, Valerie (1960). 'The Human Situation: A Feminine View'. *Journal of Religion*, 40(2): 100–112.

Sawyer, Deborah F. (2002). *God, Gender and the Bible*. London and New York: Routledge.

Schumacher, Michele M. (2004) (ed.). *Women in Christ: Toward a New Feminism*. Grand Rapids, MI, and Cambridge: Eerdmans.

Soskice, Janet Martin (2007). 'Imago Dei'. In Soskice, *The Kindness of God: Metaphor, Gender, and Religious Language*. Oxford: Oxford University Press, 35–51.

Storkey, Elaine (2000). *Men and Women: Created Or Constructed? The Great Gender Debate*. Carlisle: Paternoster Press.

Storkey, Elaine (2007). 'Evangelical Theology and Gender'. In Timothy Larsen and Daniel J. Treier (eds), *The Cambridge Companion to Evangelical Theology*. Cambridge: Cambridge University Press, 161–176.

Tong, Rosemarie (2009). *Feminist Thought: A More Comprehensive Introduction*. Boulder, CO: Westview Press.

Trible, Phyllis (1978). *God and the Rhetoric of Sexuality*. Philadelphia: Fortress Press.

Turner, Denys (2013). *Thomas Aquinas: A Portrait*. New Haven: Yale University Press.

Vanhoozer, Kevin J. (2003) (ed.). *The Cambridge Companion to Postmodern Theology*. Cambridge: Cambridge University Press.

Ward, Graham (1997) (ed.). *The Postmodern God: A Theological Reader*. Oxford: Blackwell.

Ward, Graham ([2001] 2005) (ed.). *The Blackwell Companion to Postmodern Theology*. Oxford and Malden, MA: Blackwell.

Ware, Kallistos (1997) ' "My Helper and My Enemy": The Body in Greek Christianity'. In Coakley (1997), 90–110.

Weeks, Jeffrey (2011). *The Languages of Sexuality*. London and New York: Routledge.

West, Christopher ([2003] 2007). *Theology of the Body Explained: A Commentary on John Paul II's 'Gospel of the Body' (revised)*. Boston: Pauline Books and Media.

Yuval-Davis, Nira (2011). *The Politics of Belonging: Intersectional Contestations*. London: Sage.

CHAPTER 4

···

DOCTRINE AND SEXUALITY

···

EUGENE F. ROGERS, JR.

Iғ you are looking to this chapter for 'strategies' to move the churches on controverted topics in theology and sexuality, your search will misguide you, if you imagine 'strategies' and theology to be at odds. There is no 'strategy' apart from better theology. There is no better theology—and thus no strategy—apart from better exegesis, better Christology, better use of the liturgy, better recovery of patristic and medieval resources, and so on. Precisely when the theology of sexuality *looks*, to its critics, more innovative than it is, it does the Church more good, and receives a better hearing from the critics and the middle. Then it proceeds in a manner recognizably trying to do what the Church as a whole is trying to do.

When theology of sexuality really is doing something innovative, the requirement of doing good for the Church by receiving a hearing is more important still. That is so because what the theologian is doing, among other things, but especially in times of real or apparent change, is suggesting how and what the Church should teach, or proposing doctrine. As in the Christological controversies and the Reformation debates, heresy charges abound. That means that theologians should write in such a way that any anathemas, now hastily proclaimed, can later be more easily removed. Theology of sexuality, like theology in general, should avoid the appearance of special pleading, but seek its own betterment: this is theology's own ascetic practice. This means that much depends, of course, on what one means by 'better'. What counts as better depends, in turn, on the sense of the faithful in the very long term. That means that one should attempt to write theology, or propose doctrine, so that both one's grandparents and one's grandchildren, if God should grant them, can understand it. With appropriate changes, the 'rules' that follow for theology of sexuality go for any theology at all. This means that the present essay belongs at the point where two subgenres of theology overlap: what Karl Barth called 'regular' and 'irregular' dogmatics, or systematic and ad hoc theology. It insists, with Barth, on their unity.

Critics often complain that proposals for articulation of doctrine in the sexuality debates have 'not done the theology'. They mean that the conclusions sound novel or ad hoc and do not obviously follow systematic *loci*. But for so fierce a systematician as Karl Barth, those features are not in themselves disabling. They merely mark 'irregular' dogmatics:

> Dogmatics as free discussion of the problems that arise for Church proclamation from the standpoint of the question of dogma can and must be pursued in the Church outside the theological school and apart from its special task. Such free dogmatics existed before there was the regular dogmatics of the school, and it will always have its own necessity and possibility alongside this. It will differ from it by the fact that it does not cover the whole ground with the same consistency, whether in respect of Church proclamation itself, the decisive biblical witness, the history of dogma, detailed systematics, or strictness or clarity of method. Perhaps for specific historical reasons it will take up a specific theme and focus on it. Perhaps it will be relatively free in relation to the biblical basis or its choice of partners in discussion. Perhaps it will be more of an exposition of results, and will take the form of theses or aphorisms, and will observe only partially or not at all the distinction between dogmatics and proclamation.... In one respect or another, or even in many or all respects, it will be, and will mean to be, a fragment, and it will have to be evaluated as such.
>
> The dogmatic work that has come down to us from the early Church, even from the pens of its most significant and learned representatives, is not for the most part regular dogmatics but irregular dogmatics in the sense described.... On the whole it must be admitted that in spite of its name irregular dogmatics has been the rule, and regular dogmatics the exception, in every age of the Church. It should also be noted that regular dogmatics has always had its origin in irregular dogmatics, and could never have existed without its stimulus and co-operation.... [I]t has also been impossible to deny that the transition from irregular to regular dogmatics—when perhaps the school has ceased to be aware that it had to serve life, i.e., the Church— has often been accompanied by a decline in the seriousness, vitality and joyfulness of Christian insight, by a lameness in the inquiry into dogma, and therefore by a loss of the true scientific character of dogmatics.

(Barth, CD I/1. 277–278)

The 'rules' that follow aim to show how sexual theology may not be regular but must remain rigorous.

RECOVER THE BIBLE

Biblical texts are not going away. *After* the sense of the faithful has changed, they may, like 'slaves obey your masters' (Col. 3:22), go unread. But within a hundred years of controversy we will not have that luxury. As long as texts are controverted, the only strategy is not to ignore them, but to offer a better interpretation. If it's true that the Holy Spirit inspires the reader of Scripture, that's in theory not dangerous. If it's true that the Holy Spirit is not homophobic, then she will cooperate in giving Christians something better than homophobia to do with their texts.

If this sounds like Barth's Second World War cry of 'Exegesis, exegesis, and yet more exegesis!' I do not disagree, but I have different precedents in mind (Barth 1935: 17). One is more traditional. For the great catholic tradition from Augustine to Aquinas and until the Reformation, the enemy of good exegesis was compulsory univocity—the confining of the text to one meaning. The idea that the text has only one meaning is an artefact of the Reformation, reinforced by the fundamentalist attempt to read the Bible as a science book. Earlier interpreters regarded compulsory univocity as a quenching of the Spirit and a misunderstanding of the difference between divine and human authorship. It marks the divine author to intend more than one thing with a text. This conviction got recorded as a rule, which I call the '*non cogere* principle', for the Latin phrase 'do not confine': do not so confine the text to one meaning as to expose the faith to ridicule. You may not confine the text, because any *true* sense that respects the way the words go (*salva litterae circumstancia*) just *is* 'the meaning of the text'.[1] So 'the meaning of the text' is a *collection* of possible readings. Diversity is *required*. To do otherwise is illegitimately to 'confine' the text. Note how deeply unmodern this is. Descartes defines thought as capturing or confining: *Cogito ergo sum*. I think—I get or capture it—therefore I am. But 'cogito' for the medievals is precisely what I *may not do* over against the biblical text. Thinking, yes, by all means, as creatively as possible. 'Capturing', shutting down the variety of readings, no. Yes, there are controls on interpretation, but theory does not determine them—the virtues of the interpreter do. That's another story (Rogers 1996).

The most traditional—unconfining—interpretive procedure is also the most radical. The conservative Catholic anthropologist Mary Douglas would agree with the radical gender theorist Judith Butler that one can think only *with* social forms, and not without them. That goes in spades for the Bible. But (in the clearest passage Butler ever wrote) 'the options for theory [as for biblical hermeneutics] are not exhausted by *presuming* [one side of a binary, such as a traditional interpretation] or *negating* it'. The only option then is to *use* biblical passages—even ones traditionally read homophobically—not ignore them or leave them unchallenged. The only option is to give them something better, more Christian, to mean. The point of using biblical passages, even ones traditionally read homophobically, is then

> not to negate or refuse [difficult passages] ... [but] to continue to use them, to repeat them, to repeat them subversively, and to displace them from contexts in which they have been deployed as instruments of oppressive power. Here it is of course necessary to state quite plainly that the options ... are not exhausted by *presuming* [say, a traditional interpretation] on the one hand, and *negating* it, on the other. It is [the interpreter's] purpose to do precisely neither of these. [This interpretive procedure] does not freeze, banish, render useless, or deplete of meaning the usage of the

---

[1] Thomas Aquinas, *ST* I.1.10 and *De pot.* 4.1–2. The *De potentia* considers precisely the relation of theology to natural science. For an uncontroversial account—because no one cares anymore about the Aristotle's views on the creation of the world—consider how Aquinas and Bonaventure handle the potential conflict between Aristotle and scripture in Marshall (1990). For more along the lines of this paragraph, see Rogers (1996).

[passage]; on the contrary, it provides the conditions to *mobilize* the signifier in the service of an alternative production.[2]

Our models for this are Jesus and Paul, who constantly fill old texts and situations with new meaning. In the most salient example, Jesus anticipates—and we repeat—the breaking of his body to mobilize a violent execution for a new production of the peaceful feast. Paul likewise transcends such scriptural binaries as gender ('in Christ there is no "male and female"', Gal. 3:28 reinterpreting Gen. 1) and Jew and Gentile (when Paul has God, like a giddy gardener, graft Gentiles 'in excess of nature' onto the Jewish olive tree in Rom. 11). The *non cogere* principle of non-confinement operates not only among traditional interpreters like Augustine and Aquinas, and not only among radical gender theorists, but also and most powerfully within the Bible itself, from 'This is my body, given for you' to the letters of Paul.

Romans 1:18–2:1 may not be the most important passage in the sexuality debates, but it is the most important passage to be *reclaimed* in those debates. We ignore it at our peril, because it occupies a prominent, if complex, place in Paul's argument about Jews and Gentiles, and thus about Paul's inclusion of others (Rogers 2011). The traditional reading supposes that Paul's comments about sexuality 'in excess of nature' (*para phusin*, Rom. 1:26) belong to individual morality. But since the 1960s New Testament scholars have taught that Romans is about Jews and Gentiles (1:13–16). Human beings in the text are always about Jews or Gentiles separately or together.[3] When we think to ask to which group Romans 1:26 applies, the answer is immediately obvious: it describes Gentiles. Why would Paul use an ethnic sexual stereotype (Stowers 1994: 108–9) against the Gentiles? After all, Gentiles are his converts. But Paul's Jesus-following Gentiles occupy an ambiguous position. They worship the God of Israel but are not circumcised and do not keep kosher. Are they really Jewish or not? We know from Galatians that rival preachers encourage Gentile Jesus-followers to resolve the ambiguity in favour of more Jewish practice. (Douglas Campbell (2009: 542–547) goes so far as to supply quotation marks where Paul in Romans mimics a rival preacher and remarks that those who can't hear the difference lack a sense of tone.) Some among Paul's congregation in Rome, therefore, are anxious, with the zeal of a convert, to distinguish themselves from the dirty Gentiles they once were. Paul therefore states the anti-Gentile stereotype in the strongest terms, in order to puncture it. Those nodding their heads get stung in verse 2:1. 'Judge not that you be not judged' (Matt. 7:1 KJV).

But that's not the really interesting reversal. The really interesting reversal occurs much later, in 11:24, where God's very *salvation* of the Gentiles takes place 'in excess of nature'. No one to whom the incendiary phrase 'in excess of nature' (traditionally translated 'contrary to nature') has been applied, will soon forget it, even eleven chapters on.

---

[2] Butler (1995: 51–52), paragraphs run together. The original context is not biblical interpretation, but the usage of gendered binary terms such as male and female.

[3] Stowers (1994: 2, 6, 108–9, 256, 269, 284, 306). Remarks about 'all' simply mean both Jews and Gentiles together, while Adam appears as ancestor of both.

God grafts Gentile branches, in excess of typical agricultural practice, as *wild* branches onto the *domestic* olive tree of Israel. 'Normal' would be to graft domestic branches onto wild (more vigorous) rootstock, as we now graft navel oranges onto rough lemon roots. But Paul does not portray God as a prudent agriculturalist. Rather he makes God a giddy plant-fancier sticking wild cuttings into unaccustomed clefts. In a letter abounding with metaphors that stretch the biological realm—adoption, the Spirit teaching Gentiles to call someone else's God 'Father'—this is the most shocking. God takes on a 'dirty Gentile' characteristic—excessive sexuality—in order to save those same Gentiles. Like Judith Butler, Paul reclaims a sexual stereotype: he does not avoid but repeats it, repeats it subversively, and liberates it for an alternative production. You quite miss how shocking God's salvation of the Gentiles is, if you leave out Paul's bold reclamation of the ugly stereotype.

Use the *Non Cogere* Principle

The *non cogere* principle is possible because of course not only Scripture may not be confined to one meaning, but God. Indeed, Scripture may not be confined to one meaning, because God may not be confined to a genus: *Deus non est in genere*, God does not belong in a category, or to translate with a cognate term, God does not belong in a gender. God does not come under a gender, because God stands above gender as its source. So the *non cogere* principle applies first of all to God—God may not be confined—and as a corollary to Scripture as God's word. To capture God within a category is to treat God as a creature—it is idolatry. To confine Scripture to one meaning is therefore also to read the Bible idolatrously. This principle is easy to state, but to see its power, we turn to historical examples, in the next rule.

Recover Historical Examples

Again you must *recover historical examples* to see how the Middle Ages refused to confine God—and therefore also Jesus—to a gender. Already the New Testament interpreted Psalm 110 (111 in the Vulgate) Christologically (Matt. 22:44; Acts 2:34; 1 Cor. 15:25; Eph. 1:20; Heb. 1:3, 13). When interpreters came to the Vulgate's *'ex utero … genui te',* 'out of my womb I bore you' (Ps. 110:2), they heard it already in God's voice. Already, therefore, Augustine had raised the question of God's gender:

> If God hath a Son, hath He also a womb? Like fleshly bodies, He hath not; for He hath not a bosom either; yet it is said, 'He who is in the bosom of the Father *(in sinu Patris),* hath declared Him' [John 1:18]. But that which is the womb, is the bosom also: both bosom and womb are put for a secret place. What meaneth, 'from the

womb'? From what is secret, from what is hidden, from Myself, from My substance; this is the meaning of 'from the womb'... Let us then understand the Father saying unto the Son, 'From my womb before the morning star I have brought Thee forth'.

(Augustine, *In Ps.* 109.10)

You may say, it's easy enough to bend the gender of God in heaven, but Jesus is definitely male. The Middle Ages bent that, too, and did so for Christological reasons. So another rule is:

USE TRADITIONAL CHRISTOLOGY

Christ is fully divine and fully human; and the winning traditional Christology is 'high', that is, God takes on a human nature as God's very own; God does not 'adopt' a pre-existing human being. 'Fully divine', applied to gender, means that Christ, as divine, remains beyond gender, as its source. But what about 'fully human'? Does that mean God is male after all? No, that would confuse the categories, and the Incarnation takes place *inconfuse*, unconfusedly (as Chalcedon has it), with the divine assuming the human for saving purposes. What does it mean that God, who is beyond gender, nevertheless 'takes on' a gender for saving purposes? The short answer is, in order to show men how not to be patriarchal. But the technical answer is more interesting. God becomes human as *anthropos*, human being, not as *aner*, male, although Christ is circumcised. What does this mean for Christ's representatives, priests and laypeople? Do men represent Christ better than women? Or does it mean that priests and laypeople (like God) should suppress their gender, to become sexless? What does it mean that a God beyond gender nevertheless occupies a gender?

Consider first an easier example. God is beyond flesh and suffering, as the Creator. But, the Incarnation shows, God is not 'trapped' beyond those things; God can take them on for God's own purposes: God can take on flesh; God can become human. God can, and does, take on suffering. Similarly, God can take on a gender. Christ need not be sexless. Gender is not, like sin, something Christ must avoid. In the Incarnation, God is neither limited to a gender, nor denied a gender (Rogers 2008: 527–532). This means that priests and laypeople, in representing Christ the incarnate God, are likewise neither limited to a gender, nor denied a gender. They need not be men alone (they are not limited) nor need they be sexless (they are not denied). I consider objections to each half of that statement.

Someone may object that while Christ's body is certainly not denied a gender (he is circumcised) his gender is pretty well limited (he is not female). Not so. The 'body of Christ', because it is the incarnate body of *God*, does escape the limits of the male gender. The 'body of Christ' is not only the body of Jesus: the body of Christ is also the Church, and the Church has traditionally been gendered female. The body of Christ, you might say, undergoes a gender change between Luke and Acts, male in Jesus, female in the Church. Depending on your Eucharistic theology, the body of Christ also appears in an ungendered form, as bread. These are not jokes or puns. These are rigorous theological reflections on deeply embedded ways of talking about the body of Christ, ways that are not going away as long as there are Christians, because the language is too deeply embedded in the way that God's self-offering makes salvation materially available through the body of Christ.

Or someone may object that a gender-suppressed representation of Christ is required after all, since 'in Christ there is no "male and female" ' (Gal. 3:28). There it's very important to note the wording. Paul denies three binaries: in Christ there is no 'Jew or Gentile', no 'slave or free', no 'male *and* female'. The conjunction is different in the last of the three. Paul is carefully retaining the wording of Genesis, whereby God created humanity 'male *and* female'. Paul is not denying that Jesus is male. Paul is denying that Jesus is confined by that gender complementarity. Jesus does not need a wife to be a complete human being. Jesus ushers in a realm in which not procreation but resurrection ensures the continuity of embodied human life. 'No "male and female" ' does not deny Jesus a gender, but compulsory complementarity.

We can turn to traditional Christology, then, to free not only God, but also Christ, from mid-twentieth-century gender binaries. As God, Christ is not limited to a gender; as human, Christ is not denied a gender. Because the body of Christ is the body of *God*, it is not limited to the maleness of Jesus, but becomes female in the Church. Yes, these metaphors are thoroughly gendered: but properly understood they follow Butler's rule: they do not freeze, banish, or render useless the language of gender, but they free it for an alternative production; they burst its limits. 'This is my body,' Jesus says, 'given for you', turning an execution into another invitation to the feast. He mobilizes his death to provide the matter of the Eucharist.

Look to Liturgy

Historical examples become more powerful when embedded in liturgy. What we say in church becomes the most important part of the Bible; before private Bible-reading was widespread, what one said in church just was the Bible. The same practice domesticated Augustine's odd bit of exegesis. Sometime in the sixth century, St Benedict's *Rule* prescribed the Magnificat at Vespers and Psalm 110 for Sundays. So monks throughout western Christendom would have sung the two in close proximity once a week. The Magnificat is Mary's song in Luke about her motherhood, and Psalm 110 became God's song about 'his', God's motherhood. After a century of singing the motherhood of Mary with the motherhood of the Father, the 'womb of the Father' entered official, conciliar theology at the Eleventh Council of Toledo in 675: 'One *must believe* that the Son is begotten *and born* not from nothing, nor from other substance, but *from the womb of the Father [de Patris utero]*, that is, from his substance' (Denzinger and Hünermann 1991: no. 526, emphasis added). 'Begotten and born' gives God both masculine and feminine verbs. And 'one must believe' this. This is a clear example of *lex orandi, lex credendi*: the rule of prayer is the rule of belief. In this traditional phrase, 'prayer' means the public prayer of the Church, not the private prayers of individuals, and is not confined to set prayers beginning with 'Dear God' or ending with 'Amen'. Rather, the phrase means all the set parts of public worship: not only the Lord's Prayer, but the Creeds, the Eucharistic and other liturgies, the collects, the readings from Scripture (which acquire more weight from being publicly read), canticles, psalms, and hymns: everything but sermons, announcements, prayers individual or used once only, or other ad hoc remarks.

Arguments from the liturgy—including favourite hymns—are among the strongest, because they resonate with what churchgoers have been saying, singing, and hearing since they were children. Thus too arguments for same-sex marriage presented to the US Episcopal House of Bishops offered a *lex orandi* case by showing how the marriage rite of the US *Book of Common Prayer* (*BCP*) could already accommodate same-sex couples (Rogers et al. 2011).

In that proposal, the panel argued that the marriage rite in the US Book of Common Prayer centres on the familiar vows: 'to have and to hold from this day forward, for better for worse, for richer for poorer, in sickness and in health, to love and to cherish, until we are parted by death. This is my solemn vow' (*BCP* 1979: 427). This vow makes marriage an ascetic practice. The preface upholds marriage as the best context, '*when it is God's will*, for the procreation of children and their nurture in the knowledge and love of the Lord' (*BCP* 1979: 423, emphasis added), so that procreation is not required. Indeed the vows contain no escape-clause for lack of procreation, as if to say 'for better or worse but not for childlessness'. Nothing in the vows or the preface prevents the rite as it stands from serving for two women or two men, except of course the phrase 'the union of husband and wife', which the authors took as typical rather than exhaustive.

We base our argument, then, not on autonomy, individualism, or personal experience, but on the embodied discipline of marriage by which God may transform longing into charity and dispositions to love into works of virtue. Can we credit what we pray in the marriage rite, that God may 'make their life together a sign of Christ's love to this sinful and broken world, that unity may overcome estrangement, forgiveness heal guilt, and joy conquer despair' (*BCP* 1979: 429)? Our argument arises from the power of prayer, the marriage prayer of the Church. Does it make sense for two women or two men? Do same-sex couples, in spite of all that opposes them, nevertheless fit the marriage prayer?...Does this proposal about marriage fit with our understanding of how God prepares us for life with himself, by binding us to life with another? (Rogers et al. 2011: 52).

USE THE DOCTRINE OF ANALOGY

In the same argument, the panel observed that the Book of Common Prayer did not treat the Genesis passages about male and female alone, but interpreted them by the

New Testament, including a complicated passage about male and female in the fifth chapter of Ephesians. The panel then turned to the doctrine of *analogy* to get a better interpretation of the marriage passage in Ephesians. In theology, 'analogy' does not mean 'A is to B as C is to D'. Rather, it names a procedure for talking about God in which we continue to use human words but insist that in logic the human word applies *properly* to God and only derivatively to human beings—even though in history we learn the word first for human things. (You might say that Butler's insistence that we can transcend our words only by continuing to use them, freeing them from contexts of oppression and mobilizing them for alternative arrangements, constitutes a secular version of theological analogy.) For example, only God is truly good. Human goodness only participates distantly in divine goodness. This procedure frees God from the constraints of human language—God is not in a category—while allowing the words to apply.

As a by-product, the analogical procedure also shows that human values do not necessarily reflect the reality of divine values. In Ephesians 5, we find heavily gendered and hierarchical language applied to God and to married couples. 'The husband is the head of the wife as Christ is the head of the church, his body' (5:23). Conservatives use such passages to reinforce traditional gender roles, less nowadays with regard to hierarchy, but more, recently, with regard to complementarity. Do such passages reinforce the apparent gender complementarity of Genesis by writing it into the New Testament? If progressives ignore the traditional interpretation of such passages, they will leave them uncontested and they will exercise their baleful influence out of conscious sight. But the analogical rule is: we must not use mid-twentieth-century gender roles to tell us what Christ and the Church are like. Rather, we can observe, first of all, that the passage gives biblical evidence for the changing gender of Christ's body, which the author compares to the female-gendered wife. We can observe that the passage overturns late ancient gender roles when it stresses reciprocity: 'be subject to *one another*' (Eph. 5:21). And most important, we can observe that the passage obeys the rule of analogy that it is Christ who sets the meaning of lordship, that is, he *serves*. So much for hierarchy.

But what about gender? Here again the rule of analogy is important. The Pauline author invokes it explicitly. 'This mystery is a profound one, and I am saying it refers to (*lego eis*) Christ and the Church' (Eph. 5:32). That is, Christ and the Church are the primary, heavenly reality that marriage distantly reflects. The mystery is profound because, in the author's opinion, we don't yet really know the profundity of marriage; it points to a heavenly reality beyond our grasp. Logically and analogically, this passage opens up, even explodes rather than reinforces traditional views of marriage. The true roles of spouses, the passage insists, are set by Christ and the Church. Those roles are twofold, symbolic and moral. They raise two questions: (1) May two women or two men symbolize Christ and the Church, or only a cross-sex pair? To my mind, this question of complementarity is *the* question exercising the Church these days, under all the others. It raises the subterranean anthropological question of how societies recruit the (especially binary) categories they perceive as natural—such as day and night, black and white, sun and moon, male and female—to do further socio-conceptual work. The passage also raises another question: (2) What are the *moral* requirements of marriage? I take the second question first.

'Let each one of you love his wife as himself,' the passage concludes, in gendered language. But this 'love the other as oneself' language clearly recalls the second of the Great Commandments, 'love your neighbour as yourself'. In the context of reciprocity and christic lordship-as-service, marriage practises the love of nearest neighbour, the spouse. The *moral* content of marriage is to be a school for neighbour-love. No conservative has ever seriously argued that same-sex couples need practice in neighbour-love any *less* than cross-sex couples (although Stanley Hauerwas (2001) has argued it jocularly).

In these days of egalitarian marriage, the symbolic issue is actually the more serious for same-sex couples. It is the *tableau vivant* of man and wife that sticks in our grandparents' heads. In the passage itself, the woman represents the Church, so apparently that's not a problem. No one would argue that men cannot represent the Church as members, since they have been baptized into the Church from the beginning. One *might* argue that men ought not represent the Church as bishops and priests, since that seems to go against the typology, but of course no one has ever done that. Apparently, then, both women and men can represent the Church half of the typology, since the Church has always been made up of women and men. Similarly, men can clearly represent Christ as priests; and women have always represented Christ as believers. More recently, in some churches at least, they represent Christ also at the altar as priests.

Taken together, the two elements of marriage in Ephesians 5 recall the two Great Commandments: they *represent* the love of God, and they *practise* the love of neighbour. And on examination, the passage offers no reason why two women or two men cannot do both those things. On the contrary, the passage opens marriage up to bear those very meanings, by referring it to one heavenly reality, Christ, who is beyond gender as its source, and another heavenly reality, the Church, composed of women and men. The whole point of typology is to open roles up to be occupied by many players, even those who may not, to others, quite look the part.

Use 'Trinity', But Use It with Care

Students can regard 'Trinity' as a *ménage à trois*, but no one in the tradition has used it that way. Although sexual metaphors are common, they are used in surprising ways. Perhaps the most interesting feature is that procreation metaphors are ruled out. Both Augustine and Richard of St Victor worry about Trinitarian theories that resemble polytheism in turning the Trinity into a fertility cult. Augustine (*De Trin.* xii.6–7, §§8–9) rejects parent–parent–child as an image of the Trinity, and Richard of St Victor (*De Trin.* vi.10) rejects parent–child–grandchild.

Rather, the Trinity consists of one who loves, one who returns love, and one (the Holy Spirit) who witnesses, celebrates, and (in the death and resurrection of Jesus) guarantees the love of two (Rom. 8:11). If God intends human beings to share in the Trinitarian life, and 'if there are such human beings as homosexual persons, then God is committed, in unmerited grace, to take their bodies—somehow—as means rather than impediments to that communion' (Rogers 1999: 45). Same- and cross-sex weddings alike are liturgies that can sweep the spouses up into a lived analogy of the Trinitarian life, for at a wedding feast too there is one who loves, one who returns love, and a whole congregation to witness, celebrate, and (in times of difficulty) guarantee the love of two. For the marriage rite—like the Trinity—consists not of two promises (one from each party), but *three*: the congregation promises also: 'Will all of you witnessing these promises do all in your power to uphold these two persons in their marriage', and the people answer, 'We will' (*BCP* 1979: 425). This sweeps the congregation up into the witnessing and warranting office of the Holy Spirit, and the promising couple up into the love of neighbour that reflects the love of God in Christ. This means that the marriage of any couple, including a same-sex couple, functions not for themselves alone but for the upbuilding of the whole Church. Indeed it furthers the mission that begins in the Trinity when God sends the Word and the Spirit and ends in the Trinity when God receives us into the Trinitarian life (Rogers et al. 2011: 52–56, 76–81). Not just same-sex couples need the Church to bless them, but the Church needs their witness to the Trinitarian love of God.

This may sound very high, ascetic, and asexual, but classic authors have not been so bashful. On the contrary, the erotic poetry of the Song of Songs proved so evocative of God's love for human beings that Gregory Nazianzen could write, with some embarrassment, 'The Father is the Begetter and the Emitter; without passion of course, and without reference to time, and not in a corporeal manner. The Son is the Begotten, and the Holy Ghost the Emission; for I know not how this could be expressed in terms altogether excluding visible things' (Gregory Nazianzen, 'Third Theological Oration', 2).

The Greek word here for 'emission' is *problema*, something thrown out, from *pro* plus *ballein*, as in 'ballistics'. Without the language of fathering and begetting, it might seem colourless; but with them, one sees that Gregory knows very well what he has written before he takes it back, and its translation as 'emission' is justified. Other theological examples appear in Lampe (1961) under *problema*, *problesis*, and *probleus*. Aquinas uses similar language without blushing. About what it means to become 'children of God', Aquinas writes,

> And this is clear from the comparison to physical children, who are begotten by physical semen proceeding from the father. For the spiritual semen proceeding from the Father, is the Holy Spirit. And therefore by this semen some human beings are (re)generated as children of God.—1 John 3:9: 'Everyone who is born of God does no sin, since the semen of God remains in him [*semen Dei manet in eo*]' (*In Rom.* 8:17, para. 636).[4]

---

[4] For more about this passage, see Rogers (2011). The Greek of the quotation from 1 John is *sperma*. The observation that 'semen' also means 'seed' and recalls (say) the parable of the sower, only reinforces the connection evident elsewhere in Romans between sexual and agricultural images. For more on medieval use of sexual metaphors, see Bynum (1982) and Coon (2004). For the suggestion that one of Bynum's passages from Guerric of Igny is homo- rather than heteroerotic, see Rogers (2005: 120).

TREAT OTHER GROUPS WITH CHARITY

Groups at odds with each other frequently fall into comparing the ideal for themselves with the empirical reality (or worse) of those they treat as other. The members of the in-group typically represent redemption, the members of the out-group represent sin. Women, Jews, Gentiles, gay people, and other disfavoured groups have all been used as representatives of sin itself. It is not wrong, therefore, to think of the out-group in ideal terms, but only charitably, as long as one treats *all* groups charitably. Long traditions treat both monasticism and cross-sex marriage as forms of asceticism: vowed relationships for better or worse. Why may not same-sex couples pursue ascetic means ('in sickness and in health', 'for richer for poorer', 'forsaking all others') for the sake of greater goods (faith, hope, and charity)? If marriage is a school for turning *eros* into *agape*, then who is to say that same-sex couples need it any less? (Rogers 1999; Rogers et al. 2011).

KEEP PERSONAL 'EXPERIENCE' IN THE BACKGROUND

At the beginning of any intervention, an appeal to 'experience' can do a lot to gain disfavoured groups an initial hearing. Once a situation becomes polarized, however, the appeal to experience will all too often backfire. If I say 'as a lesbian, I...' then many straight conservatives will stop listening to me. If I say 'as a straight woman married for fifty years, I...' then many members of sexual minorities will stop listening, unless of course I express a solidarity that crosses the identifying experience. Most often, such appeals to experience, once controversy has erupted, simply identify partisans. At the pivot of every article, beginning 'but on the other hand', Thomas Aquinas' *Summa Theologiae* appeals to the Bible, authoritative theologians, or Aristotle: What if instead he had written 'but on the other hand, in my experience...' (Schner 2002: 41 n. 2). What then? Too often, the appeal to personal experience reduces to the exclamation, 'Listen to me!' Better to get the hearer's attention with the subject matter.

Not all appeals to experience, however, are subject to the self-undermining quality of personal experience or special pleading. Confessions of sin and changes of mind tend to enhance the speaker's authority. The example of Peter and Paul in Acts shows Jewish Christians speaking up for members of another group, Gentile Christians (Fowl 1998: 122–127). One's *positive* testimony *on behalf of others* shows a charity that grants a great authority. The word 'testimony' is itself a clue here. 'Experience' is not a biblical word. 'Testimony' is. The implication of 'testimony' is that it is often a witness to someone else rather than oneself. This testimony, should it spread, can become the experience of the Church—the sense of the faithful—rather than of a self-interested individual.

This, when it shows the fruits of the Spirit, can be the work of the Spirit, the advocate, the one who speaks for us through others.

REFERENCES

Aquinas, *see* Thomas Aquinas.

Augustine (1888). *In Ps. = Enarrationes in Psalmos.* Trans. J. E. Tweed. In Paul Schaff (ed.), *Nicene and Post-Nicene Fathers.* Buffalo, NY: Christian Literature Publishing, ser. 1, vol. viii.

Augustine (1964). *De Trin. = De Trinitate. The Trinity in The Fathers of the* Church, xlv. Trans. Stephen McKenna. Washington, DC: Catholic University of America Press.

Barth, Karl (1936–1975). *CD = Church Dogmatics*, 4 vols. in 13 parts, vol. I/1, 2nd edn. Trans. G. W. Bromiley. Edinburgh: T & T Clark.

Barth, Karl (1935). *Das Evangelium in der Gegenwart.* Munich: Christian Kaiser.

BCP (*Book of Common Prayer*) (US) (1979). *Book of Common Prayer.* New York: Church Hymnal Corporation and Seabury Press.

Butler, Judith (1995). 'Contingent Foundations'. In Seyla Benhabib et al. (eds), *Feminist Contentions.* London: Routledge, 35–57.

Bynum, Caroline Walker (1982). 'Jesus as Mother and Abbot as Mother: Some Themes in Twelfth-Century Cistercian Writing'. *Jesus as Mother: Studies in the Spirituality of the High Middle Ages.* Berkeley and Los Angeles: University of California Press, 110–169.

Campbell, Douglas (2009). *The Deliverance of God: An Apocalyptic Reading of Justification in Paul.* Grand Rapids, MI: Eerdmans.

Coon, Lynda (2004). ' "What Is the Word If Not Semen?" Priestly Bodies in Carolingian Exegesis'. In Leslie Brubaker and Julia M. H. Smith (eds), *Gender in the Early Medieval World.* Cambridge: Cambridge University Press, 278–300.

Denzinger, Heinrich, and Hünermann, Peter (1991). *Enchiridion Symbolorum*, 37th edn. Freiburg im Breisgau: Herder. Cited by thesis number.

Fowl, Stephen E. (1998). *Engaging Scripture: A Model for Theological Interpretation.* Oxford: Blackwell.

Gregory Nazianzen (1890). 'Third Theological Oration' = Oration 29. Trans. Philip Schaff, *Nicene and Post-Nicene Fathers.* Buffalo, NY: Christian Literature Publishing.

Hauerwas, Stanley (2001). 'Why Gays (as a Group) Are Morally Superior to Christians (as a Group)'. In John Berkman and Michael Cartwright (eds), *The Hauerwas Reader.* Durham, NC: Duke University Press, 519–521.

Lampe, G. W. H. (1961). *A Patristic Greek Lexicon.* Oxford: Clarendon Press.

Marshall, Bruce (1990). 'Absorbing the World: Christianity and the Universe of Truths'. In Bruce Marshall (ed.), *Theology and Dialogue: Essays in Conversation with George Lindbeck.* Notre Dame, IN: Notre Dame University Press, 69–102.

Richard of St Victor (1979). *De Trin. = De Trinitate.* In Grover A. Zinn (ed. and trans.), *The Twelve Patriarchs, The Mystical Ark, Book Three of the Trinity*, Classics of Western Spirituality. New York: Paulist Press.

Rogers, Eugene F., Jr. (1996). 'How the Virtues of the Interpreter Presuppose and Perfect Hermeneutics'. *Journal of Religion*, 76: 64–81. Reprinted with minor changes in Rogers (2013: 97–118).

Rogers, Eugene F., Jr. (1999). *Sexuality and the Christian Body.* Oxford: Blackwell.

Rogers, Eugene F., Jr. (2005). *After the Spirit.* Grand Rapids, MI: Eerdmans.

Rogers, Eugene F., Jr. (2008). 'Believers and the Beloved: Some Notes on Norris's Christology'. *Anglican Theological Review*, 90: 527–532.

Rogers, Eugene F., Jr. (2011). 'Romans on the Gender of Gentiles'. *Soundings: An Interdisciplinary Journal*, 94: 359–374. Abbreviated in Rogers (2013: 289–297).

Rogers, Eugene F., Jr. (2013). *Aquinas and the Supreme Court: Race, Gender, and the Failure of Natural Law in Thomas's Biblical Commentaries*. Oxford: Wiley-Blackwell.

Rogers, Eugene F., Jr., Deirdre J. Good, Willis J. Jenkins, and Cynthia B. Kittredge (2011). 'A Theology of Marriage including Same-Sex Couples'. *Anglican Theological Review*, 93: 51–87.

Schner, George (2002). 'The Appeal to Experience'. In Eugene F. Rogers, Jr. (ed.), *Theology and Sexuality: Classic and Contemporary Readings*. Oxford: Blackwell, 23–43.

Stowers, Stanley (1994). *A Rereading of Romans: Justice, Jews, and Gentiles*. New Haven: Yale University Press.

Thomas Aquinas (1980). *De pot.* = *Quaestio disputatae de potentia*. In Roberto Busa (ed.), *S. Thomae Aquinatis opera omnia ut sunt in indice thomistico*, 7 vols, vol. iii. Stuttgart-Bad Cannstattt: Friedrich Fommann-Holzboog, 269–352.

Thomas Aquinas (1953). *In Rom.* = *Super epistolam ad Romanos lectura*. In *Super epistolas S. Pauli lectura*, 8th rev. edn, 2 vols, vol. i. Ed. P. Raphael Cai. Turin: Marietti 1–230. Cited by chapter, verse, and paragraph number.

Thomas Aquinas (1952). *ST* = *Summa theologiae*. Ed. Petrus Carmello. Turin: Marietti. Cited by part, question, article, and part of article.

PART II

WHAT THEOLOGIANS NEED TO KNOW

CHAPTER 5

....

CONTRIBUTIONS FROM BIOLOGY

....

NEIL MESSER

INTRODUCTION

....

IN the early 1990s, Dean Hamer and his colleagues at the United States National Institutes of Health published evidence that human male homosexuality was partly influenced by a genetic factor linked to a region on the X chromosome known as Xq28 (Hamer et al. 1993). This result (of which more later) was widely—though inaccurately—reported in the news media as the discovery of a 'gay gene'. It provoked a flurry of interest, excitement, and alarm, with predictably diverse responses. At one end of the scale, some gay activists began wearing T-shirts with the slogan 'Xq28—thanks for the genes, Mom!', while at the other there was concern that there could be demand for prenatal testing and perhaps abortion of male foetuses with the marker. These disparate reactions illustrate both the powerful influence of biological discourses on perceptions of human sex, sexuality, and gender, and the deep ambiguity of that influence.

What light do the biosciences shed on the complex phenomena of sex and sexuality? How much is known or understood about the biology of sex, and how much remains obscure? What kinds of thing can biology tell us about sex, and what kinds of thing can it *not* tell us? If we wish to speak theologically about sex and gender, what do we need to know about biology? My own interest in these questions stems from my research background in molecular biology, followed by a move—also in the early 1990s—into the study of Christian theology and biomedical ethics. What follows in this chapter, therefore, is a survey of some of the things that one biomedically-trained theological ethicist thinks theologians would benefit from knowing about biological understandings of sex and sexuality. The chapter begins with an introduction to two relevant areas of biological science, after which a selection of specific topics in the biology of sex and sexuality will be surveyed: the origins of sex, evolutionary theories of sexual selection and human mating strategies, and evolutionary and genetic studies of same-sex attraction and behaviour. I shall conclude with some brief reflections on what a Christian theologian ought to make of these findings, theories, and debates.

APPROACHES TO THE BIOLOGICAL STUDY OF SEX

Although sex and sexuality can be studied from the perspective of many different bio-scientific disciplines, two fields will be particularly important for the following discussion: evolution and genetics. Some understanding of how these approaches work is necessary in order to appreciate their possibilities and limitations; so in this section, each will be briefly surveyed.

Evolutionary Biology

The theory of evolution by natural selection, independently worked out by Alfred Russel Wallace (1858) and Charles Darwin (1859), is in a sense the working paradigm for more or less all of the modern biological sciences. At heart the theory is very simple: within any population of members of a species, there will be random variations in many physical and behavioural characteristics, and some of these variations will be heritable. Any heritable variant that increases its bearer's chances of surviving and reproducing under the prevailing conditions will, over many generations, become more frequent in the population. Any further change in the same characteristic, if it further enhances the likelihood of survival and reproduction, will likewise become more common. Thus over very long periods, large changes in the characteristics of a species can accumulate as a result of countless tiny incremental steps. Also, different populations descended from a common ancestor can diverge in their characteristics to such an extent that they become distinct species.

One major gap in Darwin's and Wallace's theory was that it lacked a convincing account of the mechanism by which characteristics could be inherited. Unknown to them, at around the same time, the Augustinian friar Gregor Mendel was pioneering the scientific study of inheritance, which later became known as 'genetics'. When Mendel's work was rediscovered at the turn of the twentieth century, it was initially thought to be a rival to Darwinian evolution, but in the 1920s and 1930s a number of biologists showed how Mendel's work supplied exactly the understanding of inheritance that evolutionary theory needed. The resulting theory became known as 'neo-Darwinism' or the 'Modern Synthesis' (see, further, Messer 2007: 7–9). In the subsequent century or so, the theory has of course been developed, extended, and refined in many ways, and various interpretations and applications of it have been hotly debated—as we shall see—but the theory itself remains firmly established and central to the biosciences.

Since the 1960s, one area of increasing interest has been the evolution of non-human and human behaviour. An early example was W. D. Hamilton's theory of 'kin selection' (Hamilton 1964a, 1964b). This was a proposal to explain the evolutionary puzzle of altruistic behaviour—that is, behaviour that increases the recipient's chances of survival and reproduction at the expense of the actor's chances—which is observed in many non-human species. Hamilton's theory was later popularized by Richard Dawkins (1976); in the latter's famous and much misunderstood language, a 'selfish gene' can give rise to unselfish behaviour. In other words, a gene well adapted to ensuring its own survival and spread in the population (the specialized sense in which Dawkins used the adjective 'selfish') might do so by giving rise to forms of altruistic and cooperative—unselfish— behaviour. For example, the workers in a beehive do not reproduce but instead take care of the queen, the only member of the hive to breed. Because the workers are the queen's sisters, they share a high proportion of their genetic inheritance, so many of the workers' genes are successfully passed on to the next generation when the queen breeds.

In the 1970s, these evolutionary studies developed into the field of 'sociobiology', a term introduced to the public by Harvard entomologist Edward O. Wilson (1975, 1978). Wilson held that such evolutionary theorizing would sooner or later offer a complete explanation of human psychology and culture, subsuming the social sciences into biology. This approach not only attracted scientific criticism, but became the focus of fierce political controversy, particularly on the grounds that it lent itself to ideologically motivated use by those with reactionary social agendas in areas such as race and gender (Bateson 2008: 2). However, some sociobiologists, such as the feminist Sarah Blaffer Hrdy (1999), have been highly critical of such ideological distortions but nonetheless sought to use sociobiological methods without incurring such problems.

From the early 1990s, the evolutionary study of human behaviour took a new turn with the growth of evolutionary psychology (EP) (Barkow et al. 1992; Pinker 1997; Buss 2003). EP operates with certain characteristic assumptions, including the following.

- **A modular theory of mind**: human minds are not general-purpose reasoning devices, but complex assemblies of different 'mental modules', each 'designed' by natural selection to perform a specific set of tasks. Our minds are powerful and flexible because we have very many of these modules, which can interact in varied and complex ways. This view is sometimes described as the 'Swiss Army Knife model' of the mind.

- **An adaptationist view of evolution**: any present feature of an organism is assumed to exist because it is a specific adaptation to past evolutionary selection pressures. This allows a 'reverse-engineering' approach to evolutionary explanation, whereby the presence of a characteristic can be explained by asking what problem of survival or reproduction in the evolutionary history of the species it was designed to solve. Critics of this view do not deny the role of adaptation, but emphasize the importance in evolution of other factors such as genetic drift (a chance increase or decrease in the frequency of a gene in the population), 'exaptations' (features that evolved for one purpose but were later co-opted for a quite different function), and 'spandrels' (characteristics that arose as by-products of some other trait that was directly selected for) (Gould 2000).

- **A gene-selectionist answer** to the long-standing debate about the level or levels at which natural selection operates. Do evolutionary selection pressures select for *groups* whose members share a particular characteristic, *individuals* that have that characteristic, or both? The theoretical biology of Hamilton and others, as popularized and developed by Dawkins (1976, 1982), introduced another answer: natural selection is best understood as acting on *genes*, which survive and spread by interacting with countless other genes to build organisms (or as Dawkins called them, 'survival machines') and often by inducing those organisms to cooperate with one another in social groups.
- **An environment of evolutionary adaptedness (EEA):** a high proportion of present-day humans' behavioural as well as physical features arose as adaptations to a postulated ancestral environment during the Pleistocene period (1.8 million to 11,000 years ago), during which humans are thought to have lived as hunter-gatherers in small social groups.

Working with these assumptions, evolutionary psychologists try to identify universal psychological mechanisms (which may give rise to very different behaviours in different contexts) and ask what selection pressures in the EEA these mechanisms would have been 'designed' by natural selection to address. Since the postulated EEA was very different from modern society, the effects of these mental modules now might be very different from those they were originally designed to produce. For example, it has been suggested that motion sickness might be a by-product of a mental module originally 'designed' to cause vomiting to expel poisonous foods whose toxins gave rise to spatial disorientation (Pinker 1997: 264–266).

Though influential, EP has also proved controversial (for examples of the criticisms that follow, see Rose and Rose 2000a). Several of its basic assumptions have been challenged: some evolutionary biologists, including Stephen J. Gould, have questioned its adaptationism, as we have seen; the modular view of mind is critiqued by some developmental psychologists; speculations about the EEA are criticized as vague and untestable. However, Patrick Bateson—by no means an uncritical admirer—remarks that '[e]ven so it has led to some interesting studies' (2008: 3). In addition to these methodological criticisms, though, EP has been described as 'culturally pernicious' (Rose and Rose 2000b: 3), both incorporating and reinforcing prevailing social assumptions about matters such as sex and gender—though the evolutionary psychologist David Buss insists that it has no political agenda, and identifies his personal stance on such questions as progressive rather than reactionary (2003: 18).

Behavioural Genetics

Whereas evolutionary psychologists look for human universals and seek explanations in the shared evolutionary history of our species, behavioural geneticists study differences between individuals and ask how far those differences can be explained by the particular genetic inheritance of each individual. The methods used for such investigations can be divided into what Erik Parens (2004: S6) calls 'classical' and 'molecular'.

An important objective of classical approaches to behavioural genetics is to produce what are known as 'heritability estimates' for particular traits (Parens 2004: S11–12; Schonemann 2006; Wickham and Sham 2006). The heritability of any trait, physical or behavioural, is the fraction of the phenotypic variation in that trait (the variation in the observable characteristics associated with it) that is caused by genetic variation. Thus, a heritability of 0.78 for height in a sample of human adults would mean that 78 per cent of the observed variation in height was due to genetic variation, and the other 22 per cent was due to environmental factors. To estimate the heritability of behavioural traits, geneticists often use *twin* and *adoption studies*. These rely on the fact that identical twins are 100 per cent genetically similar whereas fraternal twins are on average 50 per cent genetically similar. They also rely on assumptions about the environment: twins raised in the same home will have very similar environments, whereas twins with different adoptive parents will have different environments. Therefore if identical twins show a higher *concordance* (likelihood of sharing the same characteristic) than fraternal twins, or if adopted children show higher concordance with their biological relatives than with their adoptive families, some degree of heritability is inferred.

However, these assumptions can be questioned: fraternal twins may have less similar environments than identical twins, and identical twins may be placed for adoption in fairly similar homes (Parens 2004: S11), in which case judgements about heritability become less certain. Also, there are important limitations to what can be concluded from a heritability estimate. First, it will always refer to a population in a particular environment, which means that such estimates cannot supply meaningful comparisons between populations in different environments. For example, even if a trait like IQ is highly heritable *within* a population, it is false to conclude that differences *between* populations have a genetic basis, unless one can be sure that there are no relevant environmental differences (Parens 2004: S14–15, contra Herrnstein and Murray 1994). Second, heritability studies in themselves give no information about the gene or genes responsible for a heritable variation. To identify candidate genes, 'molecular' approaches such as linkage and association studies are needed (Borecki 2005).

Linkage studies make use of the process of 'recombination', which occurs during the generation of each parent's gametes (sperm or egg cells). Most cells in the body are *diploid*: they have two copies of each chromosome, and therefore two copies (alleles) of most of their genes. The two copies can differ—they might for example be different variants of a gene influencing eye colour. When parents generate their gametes, each gamete receives only one copy of each chromosome—they are *haploid*. As a consequence, when the sperm and egg join, the resulting zygote has one copy of each chromosome from each parent. But the chromosome in each gamete has a 'reshuffled' combination of the alleles from the parental cells, so each zygote receives a unique combination of genetic variants from its two parents. Alleles that are closer to one another on a chromosome are less likely to get separated during the recombination (reshuffling) process. So if two traits are seen together more frequently than would be expected by chance, we can infer that the genes influencing them are close together on a chromosome—they are *linked*. Now, suppose we are trying to find a gene that influences a particular phenotype, but we have no idea where it is located. If we can identify another gene whose location we do know, and we frequently find a particular variant of that gene in combination with a particular version of our trait of interest, we can infer that there is a genetic linkage between the two. In other words, there is a gene that influences our phenotype somewhere close to the 'marker' whose location we already know. By identifying a number of different markers all linked to the gene we are seeking, it may be possible to pin down the gene's location more and more precisely.

Association studies test whether some kind of measurable genetic variation (such as a variation in DNA sequence) at a known location in the genome is associated with the phenotypic variation we are interested in. If one variant of the DNA sequence at a particular location is correlated with a particular version of the phenotype more frequently than we would expect by chance, we have identified an association between this genetic variant and our phenotype. Association studies are often used to assess 'candidate' genes: if we suspect that a particular gene might play a part in the phenotype we are studying, carefully designed association studies can help to test that suspicion (Borecki 2005: 4).

A number of cautionary notes must be sounded about these studies (see Parens 2004: S17–24). First, complex behavioural traits are likely to be influenced by a large number of genes, each making only a small contribution to the phenotype. A behavioural trait might have a heritability of 0.4 (40 per cent of the phenotypic variation in that trait is attributable to genetic causes), but the variation at any single genetic locus associated with it might account for as little as 1 per cent of the total phenotypic variation. Contributions that small can be very difficult to identify by linkage analysis. Second, identifying genetic loci associated with phenotypic variation does not necessarily show that the genetic variation *causes* the phenotypic variation. Third, even if this can be demonstrated, that might not tell us much about the mechanism by which the phenotypic variation is caused. It was often assumed in the past that the relationship was simple and direct: 'Genes → behaviour'. It is now generally recognized that this is oversimplified and inaccurate: it would be nearer the mark to say that networks of genes interact with many different environmental factors to influence brain development, which in turn influences behaviour (Hamer 2002). Recent developments in molecular genetics, however, are making it possible to gain an increasing understanding of causal relationships between particular genes and associated phenotypes, by detecting when, where, and to what extent those genes are active.

It is often assumed that if a behavioural trait has a genetic cause it is hard-wired, whereas if it is environmentally caused it will be more amenable to change. However, that is not so. Consider a parallel case: the effects of the metabolic disorder phenylketonuria (PKU), which is 100 per cent heritable, can be entirely prevented by controlling patients' diet—an environmental change. This illustrates an important general point about the biological study of behaviour. Simple dichotomies of 'genes *versus* environment' or 'nature *versus* nurture' are very misleading, because genes interact with one another and their environment in complex, multifarious ways. Not only can environmental factors dramatically alter the effects of genes, as in the PKU example: the expression of genes is very often regulated by environmental influences. It is not a matter of 'nature *versus* nurture' but—as the title of a book by Matt Ridley (2005) puts it—'nature *via* nurture'.

Having surveyed some aspects of evolutionary theory and behavioural genetics, we move on to explore some of the specific questions about sex and reproduction that have been investigated using these and other biological approaches.

THE ORIGINS OF SEX

Perhaps the most basic evolutionary question about sex and reproduction is: Why is there sex at all? How did it come to evolve in the first place, and having evolved, how does it persist and remain so widespread in nature? In this context, 'sexual reproduction' means reproduction that involves recombination, where offspring get half of their genetic material from each of two parents as described earlier. In asexual reproduction, by contrast, the offspring are all essentially identical genetic copies of the parent.

Sexual reproduction presents an evolutionary puzzle because it appears to be more costly than asexual reproduction in various ways (Neiman and Jokela 2010). One is the cost of producing males: since males do not directly produce offspring, a population in which females produce both male and female offspring will grow more slowly than one in which females produce only female offspring, other things being equal. This suggests that if a sexual population finds itself in competition with an asexual one, sooner or later the sexual population should become extinct. Another cost of sexual reproduction is the cost of recombination: because each offspring receives a new combination of genes from its two parents, recombination can break apart favourable combinations of genes.

One possible answer is that sex evolved early in evolutionary history and has persisted because it is difficult to eliminate once it has arisen. However, this does not appear to be the case, because asexual species seem to evolve relatively frequently from sexual ancestors, but asexual lineages also tend to become extinct more quickly than their sexual counterparts (Neiman and Jokela 2010: 2). This suggests that there are not only past, but also present, evolutionary advantages to sexual reproduction for many plant and animal species. One possibility is that recombination functions as a genetic repair mechanism, allows the effects of harmful genetic mutations (changes to the DNA sequence) to be masked. For example, in humans a single mutation in the gene for a protein that transports chloride ions across cell membranes causes the serious disease cystic fibrosis. Yet children only develop the disease if they receive two copies of the faulty version of the gene, one from each parent. Any child who receives only one faulty copy will remain healthy, because the unaffected version inherited from the other parent will mask the effects of the mutation. This masking effect is impossible in asexual reproduction. Since mutations are always occurring, as a result of various environmental causes such as background radiation and ultraviolet light from the sun, asexual populations will gradually accumulate harmful mutations to the point where their ability to survive and reproduce is significantly reduced.

Another possibility is the 'Red Queen' hypothesis, so called after the Red Queen's remark to Alice in Lewis Carroll's *Through the Looking-Glass*: 'Now *here*, you see, it takes all the running *you* can do, to keep in the same place' (Carroll 1871: ch. 2). In this hypothesis, new threats to the members of a species will arise from time to time, for example from parasites or infectious diseases. Sex confers an advantage by continually generating new genotypes (combinations of genetic material), some of which will be better equipped than others to resist the threats. Suppose, for example, a parasite evolves to be highly effective at attacking individuals with a particular genotype. If the host species reproduces asexually, all offspring will have that genotype and will be vulnerable to attack from the parasite. On the other hand, if it reproduces sexually, new genotypes will be generated, some of which will be more resistant to the parasite. However, if these resistant genotypes become more frequent in the population, there will then be an evolutionary selection pressure on the parasite to evolve the ability to attack those genotypes; this in turn will create a selection pressure on the host to generate still more new combinations, and so the 'arms race' continues.

There are theoretical and empirical problems with both these hypotheses, and with others. Because of this, Neiman and Jokela (2010: 7) suggest that the origin and persistence of sex may be best explained by a combination of these mechanisms rather than any one in isolation. Joan Roughgarden, by contrast, is critical of both the 'genetic repair' and 'Red Queen' hypotheses, arguing instead that 'the advantage of sexual reproduction [is] that in every generation all the matings throughout the population rebalance the portfolio of genetic diversity residing in a species' gene pool' (2010: 98).

Sexual Selection and Human Mating Strategies

Sexual selection and related theories are attempts to give evolutionary explanations for various aspects of mating behaviour and reproductive strategy in many species, including humans. Recent applications of these theories to humans have often involved the approaches of sociobiology and evolutionary psychology, and have proved controversial for the kinds of reasons alluded to earlier.

Darwinian Sexual Selection

The theory of sexual selection originates in the work of Charles Darwin (1871) as a way of explaining some apparent problems with his account of evolution by natural selection.

Natural selection suggests that heritable variants which improve their bearers' chances of survival and reproduction will become more common in the population. Darwin was puzzled, however, by some features of male animals which looked like liabilities for survival, such as peacocks' tails and elks' antlers. The peacock's tail would seem to make the bird conspicuous to predators and hinder his escape from them, so how has it persisted in evolution? Darwin's answer was that such features may be liabilities for *survival*, but advantageous for *reproduction*. This can occur, he said, in one of two ways: by competition between males, or by female choice. Antlers are used as weapons in contests between males, in which the winner gets to mate with the females; peacocks' tails confer a reproductive advantage because peahens prefer mates with bright, conspicuous plumage. (This of course raises the question why peahens should have evolved to prefer such mates, which has been the subject of much discussion in more recent evolutionary literature; for a survey, see Cronin 1991: 183–204.)

Darwin's sexual selection theory proved controversial among his contemporaries and was neglected until relatively recently, perhaps partly because it challenged conventional assumptions that females have an essentially passive role in mating (Cronin 1991: 155–164; Hrdy 1999: 36–37; Buss 2003: 2–3; Richards 2010: 2). Even if Darwin was ahead of his contemporaries in this respect, however, critics point out that in other ways his sexual selection theory was still deeply shaped by patriarchal assumptions (Hrdy 1999: 18–23; Roughgarden 2010). Among the general principles of sexual selection, he asserted that '[t]he female . . . with the rarest exception, is less eager than the male . . . she is coy, and may often be seen endeavouring for a long time to escape from the male' (Darwin 1871: i. 273). In relation to humans specifically, he notoriously remarked: 'The chief distinction in the intellectual powers of the two sexes is shewn by man attaining to a higher eminence, in whatever he takes up, than woman can attain—whether requiring deep thought, reason, or imagination, or merely the use of the senses and hands' (1871: ii. 327). As we shall see later, evolutionary biologists who agree in their criticism of Darwin's patriarchal assumptions differ widely in the remedies they propose.

Parental Investment

Although sexual selection was somewhat neglected in the century following Darwin's account, there were exceptions, such as the biologists R. A. Fisher (1930) and A. J. Bateman (1948). Since the 1970s, interest in the theory has grown dramatically, thanks in part to Robert Trivers' influential theory of parental investment (Trivers 1972), which states that the operation of sexual selection is determined by the relative quantity of resources invested by the two parents in their offspring. Differences in parental investment begin with 'anisogamy': male and female sex cells are different sizes. Female gametes (including mammalian egg cells) are fewer, larger, and richer in nutrients, while male gametes (including mammalian sperm) are smaller, contain little nutrient, and are produced in far larger quantities. Since a zygote is the product of one ovum and one sperm, the female investment of resources in each zygote is greater than the male. Differences in parental investment continue through the development of the offspring. In mammals, the minimum investment that will give a male a chance of producing viable offspring is ejaculation, whereas for a female, the minimum investment includes pregnancy and lactation. Different species of mammal vary widely in the relative parental investment of the two sexes: in some species, males invest nothing beyond mating, while in others they play a large role in the care of offspring.

Following Bateman, Trivers theorized that it will be adaptive for the sex which makes the smaller parental investment to mate more frequently, and members of that sex will tend to compete for access to the other. This reasoning is often held to support Darwin's contention that in most species (including humans) males are more eager and indiscriminate in mating, while females are more choosy and coy (Shykoff 2003: 1–2).

Evolutionary psychologists such as David Buss (2003) have elaborated Trivers' theory into extensive accounts of human mating strategies and preferences. Buss has conducted large-scale surveys of sexual preferences among people from many different social, political, cultural, and geographical contexts around the world. He holds that this empirical research reveals many universally human sex differences in mating preferences and behaviour—albeit differently expressed in different contexts—and theorizes these differences in terms of Trivers' parental investment hypothesis and the 'reverse engineering' approach to evolutionary explanation described earlier. For instance, he argues that in the environment of evolutionary adaptedness (EEA), it was adaptive—it tended to maximize reproductive success—for females to be more selective than males in their choice of mates and for males to compete with one another for access to females. Hence men still tend to be more competitive, more indiscriminate in their choice of partners, and more interested in casual sex than women—though with considerable cultural variation in the way these tendencies are worked out. Women tend to seek commitment, social status, and wealth in their mates, because in the EEA it was adaptive for females to have mates who would help rear their offspring and could provide resources such as food and shelter. By contrast, men prefer youth and physical beauty, because in the EEA these would have been signs of a healthy and fertile mate who would have the best chance of bearing and rearing viable offspring.

In Trivers' theory, the sex with the greater parental investment is vulnerable to desertion, while the sex with the lower investment is vulnerable to cuckoldry: a man who helps raise the children could be tricked into raising offspring fathered by another, genetically unrelated man, a waste of his resources in terms of reproductive success. According to Buss this explains a range of sexual differences, from patterns of jealousy (men worry about their partners having sex with someone else, women about their partners leaving them for someone else) to sperm competition (a man who has been away from his partner produces more numerous and active sperm, to maximize his chance of fertilizing her even if she has had sex with someone else in his absence). Moreover, these differences in optimal mating strategies can give rise to sexual conflict, and explain various forms of violence and abuse (Buss 2003: 142–167; for the theory of sexual conflict, see Bondurtansky 2010).

Critiques of Sexual Selection

Buss emphasizes that evolutionary explanations illuminate but do not prescribe or justify the behaviours they explain, nor do they imply that those behaviours are fixed and immutable (2003: 18). By understanding the way our preferred mating strategies have evolved, he maintains, we will be better able to adjust our environments to ameliorate the harmful effects of those evolved preferences: 'Only by examining the complex repertoire of human sexual strategies can we know where we came from. Only by understanding why these strategies evolved can we control where we are going' (2003: 222).

Notwithstanding these avowals, Buss and other evolutionary psychologists have drawn criticism on a number of grounds. Some biologists and social scientists have raised methodological questions about Buss's survey data and criticized the rigour and evidence base of the evolutionary hypotheses by which he explains those data (Fausto-Sterling 2000: 177–182). Various critics have argued that contemporary evolutionary psychologists, like their predecessors from Darwin on, have neglected to pay attention to female agency and sexual strategies—though some do acknowledge that Buss attributes a more active role to female agency than some evolutionary psychologists (Hrdy 1999: 23–24; Fausto-Sterling 2000).

Some of these critics share many of evolutionary psychology's theoretical commitments, but still wish to build on the same theoretical base in their own research, while avoiding the distorting effects of their predecessors' patriarchal bias. For example, Hrdy (1999) has used sexual selection and parental investment theories in her research on mating and parenting in female primates, challenging many of the assertions in older literature about female sexual roles. Topics such as female competition in mating have been more extensively researched recently, and the second edition of Buss's book includes a new chapter on women's 'hidden sexual strategies' (Buss 2003: 223–249; Bro-Jørgensen 2011).

Other critics, however, go further, arguing that these specific weaknesses reflect more basic methodological problems with the EP approach itself (Fausto-Sterling 2000). There are evolutionary biologists—notably Joan Roughgarden (2010)—who, rather than building on sexual selection theory like Hrdy, claim that it should be deconstructed altogether. Roughgarden challenges the empirical evidence for Darwinian sexual selection, argues that it is theoretically self-contradictory, and advocates instead a 'social selection' theory. This takes a broader view of successful reproduction than sexual selection theory, which according to Roughgarden focuses excessively on mating success. She argues that successful mating is only one component of successful reproduction, which also requires systems of social cooperation to ensure that offspring are successfully reared. A good deal of sexual behaviour (including the same-sex matings observed in many different species) can then be explained as building and maintaining social relationships, rather than being directed towards fertilization.

It could be asked how great the distance really is, in principle, between Roughgarden's social selection theory and EP accounts building on sexual selection. Certainly, evolutionary psychologists too emphasize the importance of social relationships and cooperation in maximizing reproductive success, and Roughgarden is not alone in proposing a social bonding function for same-sex intercourse. But there are some clear differences: for example, as we have already seen, she holds a different view of the evolutionary advantage of sex from those favoured by many evolutionary psychologists, and sexual conflict has a less central role in her theory.

SEXUAL DIVERSITY

It is sometimes observed that sexual diversity and particularly homosexuality in non-human animals has been ignored or under-reported (Bagemihl 1999).[1] However, it is by now well established that same-sex sexual behaviour is known among many animal species (Roughgarden 2010: 92–93). In the human species, estimates of the prevalence of same-sex sexual attraction vary, but tend to place the frequency at a few percent of the population, often lower for women than men. In one large Australian study, around 8 per cent of both men and women reported some level of homosexual attraction (Bailey et al. 2000). The patterns of distribution vary, however: most studies find that women are more likely than men to report slight to moderate homosexual attraction and less likely to report mostly or exclusively same-sex attraction.

Evolutionary Theories of Homosexuality

The persistence of homosexual orientation is regarded as a puzzle by many evolutionary biologists, because a behavioural trait that makes its bearers less likely to mate with the opposite sex should reduce reproductive success and therefore be selected against; indeed, empirical evidence confirms that gay men have a lower rate of reproduction than straight men (Buss 2003: 251). Various theories have been proposed to account for the persistence of same-sex orientation in human evolution: homosexual males might have given additional support to their close kin in child-rearing, thereby promoting their own 'inclusive reproductive fitness' by propagating copies of their genes in their nephews and nieces; homoerotic behaviour might have evolved to promote alliance formation and strengthen social relationships; same-sex orientation might be a by-product

---

[1] Although the term 'homosexuality' is often regarded as problematic, and tends to be avoided by members of lesbian, gay, bisexual, and transgender (LGBT) groups and authors in the humanities, it is still the term predominantly used in the biological literature on same-sex sexual attraction and behaviour—including literature by scientists who attribute LGBT identities to themselves.

of 'feminine' traits that were attractive to females and therefore favoured by sexual selection (Buss 2003: 251–254; on alliance formation, see also Roughgarden 2010). However, none of these hypotheses has strong empirical support, and all have conceptual difficulties. So far, evolutionary theorizing about homosexuality seems inconclusive. One possible reason for this is implied by David Buss when he acknowledges that '[h]omosexuality is not a singular phenomenon' (2003: 255, emphasis original). Not only does gay male sexuality differ from lesbian sexuality, but there are also diverse gay and lesbian sexualities, and some of this diversity appears to have morphological and hormonal as well as psychological correlates (Buss 2003: 256).

The Behavioural Genetics of Homosexuality

There have been a number of behavioural genetic studies of homosexuality. Family studies suggest that it clusters in families, but this could be due to genetic or environmental influences or both. Twin and adoption studies usually show higher concordance for identical than fraternal twins. However, the figures vary widely between studies, and there are methodological difficulties with obtaining precise figures (Bailey et al. 2000; Sanders and Dawood 2004: 2). This and other factors make it very difficult to produce reliable heritability estimates, though researchers tend to agree that both male and female homosexuality is at least moderately heritable (Bailey 2005: 1). There must also be environmental causes, because there are well-known environmental correlations. For example, gay men are more likely to be the younger in a sequence of brothers (Bailey 2005: 1).

Among molecular genetic studies, Hamer et al. (1993) found significant linkage of male sexual orientation to genetic markers in a region of the X chromosome labelled Xq28. Hamer's group later published additional data supporting this linkage, together with data from lesbian sisters showing no significant linkage of female sexual orientation to the same markers (Hu et al. 1995). However, other groups have failed to confirm this result, so the evidence overall is inconclusive (Bailey 2005: 2). Some authors argue that this is exactly what one would expect for a complex behavioural trait influenced by many different genes (Sanders and Dawood 2004: 4–5). However, a recent modelling study suggests another possible explanation: that sexual orientation is influenced by epigenetic modifications rather than genetic markers (Rice et al. 2012). Epigenetic modifications are chemical changes to the DNA or to other structural components of the chromosome which play a part in regulating the expression of genes. Rice et al. propose that some sex-specific epigenetic modifications regulate responsiveness to androgens (hormones that influence sexual development) during foetal development. Usually these epigenetic signals are erased between generations, but if they escape erasure, they could have the effect of making female foetuses more sensitive to androgens than usual and male foetuses less sensitive. At present this is only a model based on existing data, but it makes specific predictions which lend themselves to experimental testing.

Sexual Dimorphism and Intersex

'Sexual dimorphism' refers to the physical differences that distinguish males and females, and is obviously relevant to the theories of sexual selection discussed earlier. Some biologists are critical of the notion of sexual dimorphism on the grounds that it promotes a male–female binary which is challenged by the evidence of intersex conditions.

Sexual Dimorphism and Its Critics

As noted in the discussion of sexual selection, it depends on anisogamy—the difference in size between two types of gamete. Biologists hypothesize that anisogamy may have evolved as a trade-off between the dispersability of gametes and the quantity of nutrient they could contain (Grande and Brown 2010: 110–113). Nutrient-rich gametes can support the early development of the offspring, but are not easily dispersed, whereas smaller gametes (such as the pollen of flowering plants) contain little nutrient but can be dispersed much more widely. If smaller gametes were less costly for the organism to produce, it could be adaptive for some individuals to produce such gametes, 'parasitizing' the greater parental investment of others that produced larger gametes with more nutrient. Thus anisogamy and sexual differentiation, rather than the production of undifferentiated gametes, could become an 'evolutionarily stable' reproductive strategy. Joan Roughgarden, however, disputes this account. In the context of her social selection theory, she proposes an alternative model in which anisogamy was selected for as a strategy to optimize the chances of different gametes coming into contact (Iyer and Roughgarden 2008). Standard accounts of sexual dimorphism at the level of the whole organism relate it to sexual selection and parental investment theories, so that large sex differences in size and other characteristics are associated with large differences in the parental investment of the two sexes. As we saw earlier, however, Roughgarden (2010) disputes this conflictual model of the relations between the sexes on both empirical and theoretical grounds.

Sex Determination and Intersex Conditions

Genetically, sex determination is regulated by complex interactions of numerous genes that influence development both before and after birth (Sarafoglou 2005; Ostrer 2006; Simpson 2008). This begins with the sex chromosomes, labelled X and Y. In humans, like other mammals, by far the usual pattern is that a zygote receives one sex chromosome from each parental gamete; normally a zygote with two X chromosomes will develop into a female, while an individual with one X and one Y will be male. Rarely, other karyotypes (numbers of chromosomes) occur: females can have one, three, or (very rarely) four or five X and no Y chromosomes; males might have XXY, XYY, or

XXYY karyotypes. Some of these rare karyotypes give rise to few if any phenotypic differences from the more common karyotype of the same sex, but others can affect fertility, the development of the reproductive organs, or sex differentiation. Some also result in other characteristic physical, cognitive, or behavioural differences.

Early in foetal development, undifferentiated gonads (sex organs) form. In male foetuses, a gene on the Y chromosome known as *SRY* initiates the development of these gonads into testes and regulates the expression of other genes involved in testis formation (Simpson 2008). As the testes develop, they produce two hormones, Müllerian inhibiting hormone (MIH) and testosterone. MIH inhibits the development of the female internal genitalia (oviducts, uterus, cervix, and the upper part of the vagina). Testosterone promotes male secondary sexual characteristics and is converted into dihydrotestosterone (DHT), which is involved in the formation of the penis and prostate. If the genes involved in testis formation are absent or inactive, the gonads will instead develop into ovaries. It is not clear whether the initial formation of ovaries is simply a default pathway in the absence of *SRY* or requires specific genes to occur, but in any event a number of genes on the X and other chromosomes are known to be involved in maintaining the ovaries once they have formed (Simpson 2008: 3–5).

Thus, sexual differentiation depends on complex pathways of interacting genes that regulate the development of reproductive organs and sexual characteristics. Genetic changes affecting any of the steps in these pathways can result in one of a number of diverse intersex conditions (Sarafoglou 2005; Simpson 2008). 'True hermaphrodites' have both ovarian and testicular tissue, and ambiguous or predominantly female external genitalia. 'Female pseudohermaphrodites' have female gonads (ovaries) but ambiguous or virilized external genitalia. 'Male pseudohermaphrodites' have testes, may have ambiguous or predominantly female external genitalia, and may develop breasts and other female secondary sexual characteristics.

Intersex conditions are often referred to in the literature as 'disorders' (e.g. Sarafoglou 2005), though it should be noted that the identification of a condition as a disorder is a complex and contested matter in the philosophy of medicine (for a survey, see Messer 2013: ch. 1). An alternative interpretation is articulated by Grande and Brown (2010: 113): 'Knowledge of biological variation allows us to conceptualize the less frequent middle spaces as natural, though statistically unusual.' A more radical critique of the male–female binary is given by various authors such as Anne Fausto-Sterling (2002) and Joan Roughgarden (2010). The latter argues that at the least, each of the three main intersex groups—true hermaphrodites (whom she calls 'herms'), female pseudohermaphrodites ('ferms'), and male psuedohermaphrodites ('merms') should be considered a sex in its own right.

Concluding Reflections

Surveying this material, I am struck by the contrast between the scientific voices with which this chapter has been concerned and those with which much contemporary writing on sex and gender seems to interact more comfortably, such as critical theorists like Foucault (1978–1986), Butler (1990), and those influenced by them. It is not just that they disagree about specific matters, but that their language, concepts, and basic assumptions seem far apart. Setting up a constructive conversation between these voices is no easy matter (though for one very interesting attempt, see Jung and Vigen 2010). Biologists might be inclined to accuse such critical voices of an 'antinaturalistic fallacy': ignoring the evidence about the way the world and human beings really are (Buss 2003: 17). Their critics in the humanities might be tempted to respond by dismissing evolutionary and genetic claims as discursive exercises of power/knowledge. However, there is a sizeable middle ground in which biologists and social scientists seek to work constructively with evolutionary and genetic insights while remaining critical of some biological theorizing about sex and gender. For some, this means working from a very similar theoretical base, but aiming to free their own research from the biases and distortions they attribute to previous work (e.g. Hrdy 1999). Others advocate larger-scale deconstruction of theoretical frameworks such as sexual selection (Roughgarden 2010) or approaches such as EP (Rose and Rose 2000a), and reconstruction of evolutionary research on different lines.

What, though, is a theologian to make of all this? What light, if any, can these arguments shed on a theological account of what it is to be human? How should scientific perspectives and insights be related to other sources of theological understanding, particularly the Scriptures and Christian traditions of reflecting on them?

Among constructive answers to this question, a wide range of possibilities can be identified (Messer 2007: 49–61). Towards one end of the scale is the late Arthur Peacocke's view that the methods and claims of theology must be brought into line with scientific rationality (e.g. Peacocke 2000). Towards the other is the view I have advocated, under the influence of Karl Barth, in which the agenda must be set by a biblically grounded theology, but that theology can be highly hospitable to critically appropriated insights from many sources, including the biological sciences (Messer 2007: 60–62). Somewhere in between lies the Tillichian approach of critical correlation around which the present volume is organized.

These issues become particularly acute when normative questions come into view. Quite apart from the uncertainty and provisionality evident in much of the biological literature I have surveyed, it is a commonplace that to read normative conclusions off biological accounts is to commit a naturalistic fallacy (e.g. Buss 2003: 16). There is a particular reason why such a move *is* fallacious: since early modern times, the natural sciences have for the most part achieved their extraordinary success precisely by *excluding* questions of purpose and the good from their purview, limiting themselves to matters of description and cause-and-effect explanation (Messer 2009; 2013: 47; *pace* Ruse 2003). If that is correct, then they cannot by themselves suggest answers to normative questions.

This does not mean, however, that insights from biology can safely be ignored by theologians seeking such answers. To a Christian theologian, to ask about the good of a human being is to ask what is good for a physically embodied creature (whether or not one holds that there is any essential or universal human nature). The biosciences have insights to offer about the conditions of such embodied creaturely lives. What theology takes from these insights and the terms on which the conversation is set will no doubt differ in (for example) a natural law ethic (Pope 2007), a Barth-inspired ethics of creation (Messer 2007), and the Tillichian correlational method of this book. But theologians adopting any of these approaches—or others besides—would be ill-advised to leave their bioscientific conversation partners outside the door.

REFERENCES

Bagemihl, B. (1999). *Biological Exuberance: Animal Homosexuality and Natural Diversity*. New York: St Martin's Press.

Bailey, J. M. (2005). 'Sexual Orientation: Genetics'. In *Encyclopedia of Life Sciences (eLS)*, Chichester: Wiley. DOI: 10.1038/npg.els.0005155.

Bailey, J. M., M. P. Dunne, and N. G. Martin (2000). 'Genetic and Environmental Influences on Sexual Orientation and Its Correlates in an Australian Twin Sample'. *Journal of Personality and Social Psychology*, 78(3): 524–536.

Barkow, J. H., L. Cosmides, and J. Tooby (1992) (eds). *The Adapted Mind: Evolutionary Psychology and the Generation of Culture*. New York: Oxford University Press.

Bateman, A. J. (1948). 'Inter-Sexual Selection in Drosophila'. *Heredity*, 2: 349–368.

Bateson, P. (2008). 'Sociobiology, Evolutionary Psychology, and Genetics'. In *eLS*. DOI: 10.1002/9780470015902.a0005855.pub2.

Bonduriansky, R. (2010). 'Sexual Conflict'. In *eLS*. DOI: 10.1002/9780470015902.a0003669.pub2.

Borecki, I. (2005). 'Linkage and Association Studies'. In *eLS*. DOI: 10.1038/npg.els.0005483.

Bro-Jørgensen, J. (2011). 'Sexual Selection and Female Competition'. In *eLS*. DOI: 10.1002/9780470015902.a0023305.

Buss, D. (2003). *The Evolution of Desire: Strategies of Human Mating*, 2nd edn. New York: Basic Books.

Butler, J. P. (1990). *Gender Trouble: Feminism and the Subversion of Identity*. London: Routledge.

Carroll, L. (1871). *Through the Looking-Glass (And What Alice Found There)*. London: Macmillan.

Cronin, H. (1991). *The Ant and the Peacock: Altruism and Sexual Selection from Darwin to Today*. Cambridge: Cambridge University Press.

Darwin, C. (1859). *On the Origin of Species by Means of Natural Selection, Or, the Preservation of Favoured Races in the Struggle for Life*. London: John Murray.

Darwin, C. (1871). *The Descent of Man, and Selection in Relation to Sex*, 2 vols. London: John Murray.

Dawkins, R. (1976). *The Selfish Gene*. Oxford: Oxford University Press.

Dawkins, R. (1982). *The Extended Phenotype: The Long Reach of the Gene*. Oxford: Oxford University Press.

Fausto-Sterling, A. (2000). 'Beyond Difference: Feminism and Evolutionary Psychology'. In Rose and Rose (2000a), 174–189.

Fausto-Sterling, A. (2002). 'The Five Sexes: Why Male and Female Are Not Enough'. In C. L. Williams and A. Stein (eds), *Sexuality and Gender*. Oxford: Blackwell, 468–473.

Fisher, R. A. (1930). *The Genetical Theory of Natural Selection*. Oxford: Clarendon Press.

Foucault, M. (1978–1986). *The History of Sexuality*. Trans. R. Hurley, 3 vols. New York: Random House.

Gould, S. J. (2000). 'More Things in Heaven and Earth'. In Rose and Rose (2000a), 85–105.

Grande, T., and Brown, J., with R. Colburn (2010). 'The Evolution of Sex'. In P. B. Jung and A. M. Vigen (eds), *God, Science, Sex and Gender: An Interdisciplinary Approach to Christian Ethics*. Urbana and Springfield, IL: University of Illinois Press, 105–122.

Hamer, D. H. (2002). 'Rethinking Behavior Genetics'. *Science*, 298(5591): 71–72.

Hamer, D. H., Hu, S., Magnuson, V. L., Hu, N., and Pattatucci, A. M. L. (1993). 'A Linkage between DNA Markers on the X Chromosome and Male Sexual Orientation'. *Science*, 261(5119): 321–327.

Hamilton, W. D. (1964a). 'The Genetical Evolution of Social Behaviour I', *Journal of Theoretical Biology*, 7: 1–16.

Hamilton, W. D. (1964b). 'The Genetical Evolution of Social Behaviour II', *Journal of Theoretical Biology*, 7: 17–32.

Herrnstein, R., and C. Murray (1994). *The Bell Curve: Intelligence and Class Structure in American Life*. New York: The Free Press.

Hrdy, S. B. (1999). *Mother Nature: Natural Selection and the Female of the Species*. London: Chatto and Windus.

Hu, S., Pattatucci, A. M. L., Patterson, C., Li, L., Fulker, David W., Cherny, Stacey S., Leonid Kruglyak, L., and Hamer, D. H. (1995). 'Linkage between Sexual Orientation and Chromosome Xq28 in Males but not in Females'. *Nature Genetics*, 11: 248–256.

Iyer, P., and J. Roughgarden (2008). 'Gametic Conflict versus Contact in the Evolution of Anisogamy'. *Theoretical Population Biology*, 73(4): 461–472.

Jung, P. B., and A. M. Vigen (2010) (eds). *God, Science, Sex and Gender: An Interdisciplinary Approach to Christian Ethics*. Urbana and Springfield, IL: University of Illinois Press.

Messer, N. G. (2007). *Selfish Genes and Christian Ethics: Theological and Ethical Reflections on Evolutionary Biology*. London: SCM.

Messer, N. G. (2009). 'Humans, Animals, Evolution and Ends'. In D. Clough and C. Deane-Drummond (eds), *Creaturely Theology: On God, Humans and Other Animals*, London: SCM, 211–227.

Messer, N. G. (2013). *Flourishing: Health, Disease and Bioethics in Theological Perspective*. Grand Rapids, MI: Eerdmans.

Neiman, M., and J. Jokela (2010). 'Sex: Advantage'. In *eLS*. DOI: 10.1002/9780470015902.a0001716.pub2.

Ostrer, H. (2006). 'Male Sex Detemination: Genetics'. In *eLS*. DOI: 10.1002/9780470015902.a0006235.

Parens, E. (2004). 'Genetic Differences and Human Identities: On Why Talking about Behavioral Genetics Is Important and Difficult'. *Hastings Center Report Special Supplement*, 34(1): S1–S36.

Peacocke, A. (2000). 'Science and the Future of Theology: Critical Issues'. *Zygon*, 35(1): 119–140.

Pinker, S. (1997). *How the Mind Works*. London: Penguin.

Pope, S. J. (2007). *Human Evolution and Christian Ethics*. Cambridge: Cambridge University Press.

Rice, W. R., Friberg, U., and Gavrilets, S. (2012). 'Homosexuality as a Consequence of Epigenetically Canalized Sexual Development'. *Quarterly Review of Biology*, 87(4): 343–368.

Richards, R. A. (2010). 'Sexual Selection: Its Possible Contribution to Recent Human Evolution'. In *eLS*. DOI: 10.1002/9780470015902.a0021788.

Ridley, M. (2005). *Nature via Nurture: Genes, Experience and What Makes Us Human*. London: Fourth Estate.

Rose, H., and S. Rose (2000a) (eds). *Alas Poor Darwin: Arguments against Evolutionary Psychology*. London: Jonathan Cape.

Rose, H., and S. Rose (2000b). 'Introduction'. In Rose and Rose (2002a), 1–13.

Roughgarden, J. (2010). 'Evolutionary Biology and Sexual Diversity'. In Jung and Vigen (2010), 89–104.

Ruse, M. (2003). *Darwin and Design: Does Evolution Have a Purpose?* Cambridge, MA: Harvard University Press.

Sanders, A. R., and K. Dawood (2004). 'Sexual Orientation'. In *eLS*. DOI: 10.1038/npg. els.0001480.

Sarafoglou, K. (2005). 'Intersex Disorders'. In *eLS*. DOI: 10.1038/npg.els.0005508.

Schonemann, P. H. (2006). 'Heritability'. In *eLS*. DOI: 10.1038/npg.els.0005409.

Shykoff, J. A. (2003). 'Sexual Selection'. In *eLS*. DOI: 10.1038/npg.els.0001718.

Simpson, J. L. (2008). 'Mammalian Sex Determination'. In *eLS*. DOI: 10.1002/9780470015902. a0001886.pub2.

Trivers, R. (1972). 'Parental Investment and Sexual Selection'. In B. Campbell (ed.), *Sexual Selection and the Descent of Man*. New York: Aldine de Gruyter.

Wallace, A. R. (1858). 'On the Tendency of Varieties to Depart Indefinitely from the Original Type'. *Journal of the Proceedings of the Linnean Society of London. Zoology*, 3(20 August): 53–62.

Wickham, H., and P. Sham (2006). 'Heritability Wars'. In *eLS*. DOI: 10.1038/npg.els.0005233.

Wilson, E. O. (1975). *Sociobiology: The New Synthesis*. Cambridge, MA: Harvard University Press.

Wilson, E. O. (1978). *On Human Nature*. Cambridge, MA: Harvard University Press.

CHAPTER 6

CONTRIBUTIONS FROM PSYCHOLOGY

BRENDAN CALLAGHAN SJ

INTRODUCTION

EXPLORATIONS of human sexuality by psychologists from varying theoretical traditions have given rise to a range of insights into, and ways of reflecting on, this dimension of our humanity, held by believers to be our humanity-in-the-image-of-God. For
those who share the opinion of William James—that 'psychology' comprises a range
of questions requiring answers along several different lines of approach—this variety
of insights should come as no surprise. It should also be clear, even to a casual reader,
that adherents of these different approaches have not found it easy to discover common
ground. Any survey of the contributions from psychology to what theologians need to
know will necessarily reflect this context.

This chapter sits between discussions of the contributions of biology and those of
anthropology, with a possible measure of overlap in each direction. The focus here
will initially be on what depth psychology and social psychology can offer to theologians, touching en route on the developmental schema and life stages proposed by Erik
Erikson, and the work of John Bowlby which gave rise to attachment theory, as in some
way providing links between the two, and always bearing in mind that each of these
headings itself refers to a range of approaches. A brief introduction to some of these
approaches will be followed by a synthesis of what theologians need to know.

DEPTH PSYCHOLOGIES

Freud

That our experience and behaviours are influenced and shaped by intra-personal processes more or less inaccessible to our awareness is not something that Freud was the

first to notice. But what marks out the end of the nineteenth century is the work of Freud and others, seeking to systematize and to provide some comprehensive understanding of the less-than-conscious.

Christian responses to Freud's work in particular were frequently shaped more by a culturally rooted inability to accept his ideas than by a thought-through critical and theological evaluation of them. Two aspects of his thought relevant to us were problematic to many of his contemporaries: his notion of childhood sexuality, and what was perceived as 'pan-sexualism'. The latter concern betrayed a lack of understanding of what Freud included within the category of 'sexuality'. His recognition of the social and affective elements of our sexuality as inextricably interwoven with the genital and physiological elements was ignored by many of his critics, who then read back into his writings an inappropriate emphasis on the 'biological' aspects of sex as pervading all of our experience. For those looking back from an age when the essential relationality of human experience features in church teachings at all levels, and when the consequences for the church community of widespread denial of the power of the physical and physiological aspects of sexuality are all too clear, there is an obvious irony here.

More troubling to Freud's readers in the early twentieth century was his suggestion that sexuality—in its various dimensions—was not something that emerged with puberty but was present in childhood. It is not necessary to buy into the whole theoretical structure of the Oedipus Complex to accept the essential insight that childhood is a phase of our development as sexual beings: similarly, it is not necessary to accept all Freud's theoretical constructs to recognize the importance of what he describes in terms of the Superego. The first line of an essay by a graduate student at Heythrop memorably expressed why this is the case: 'Sigmund Freud wanted to be a hedgehog' (Murray 2005). In the useful classification of thinkers into hedgehogs—who have 'one big idea', worked out into a complex of mutually interdependent expressions—and foxes—who have many more-or-less-independent ideas (Berlin 1953)—Freud was clearly a fox, who very much wanted to be a hedgehog. The consequence for his readers is that they can be selective in what they choose to accept from his range of insights.

Freud's descriptions of the various stages of psychosexual development, and in particular the names assigned to each, refer to the bodily zones that, in his understanding, provided the most intense experiences at various ages. Whether or not we agree with his interpretations, he points us to the intensely bodily and physical nature of infant and early childhood experience, and the ways in which play and other forms of exploration have a crucial role in development. The small child's discovery of their own body—and those of others—contributes to their development in essential ways. 'I'll show you mine if you'll show me yours' is, in such an understanding, an irreplaceable formative and educational experience. As the child moves through early life, such experiential learning remains an essential component of their psychosexual maturing.

Bringing together these two areas of concern, we can note that Freud sees early childhood as characterized by a shifting focus: the most intense and detailed sense-experience is associated with different bodily zones, giving rise to Freud's labelling of the oral, anal, and genital phases. School-age children are seen by Freud as passing through the 'latency period' in which the intense physicality of earlier years gives way in importance to the establishment and development of friendships and other social relationships. It is with the onset of puberty and adolescence that the genital and physiological elements of our sexuality begin to be integrated with the social and affective elements, with growth in that integration being a lifelong process.

To read back into childhood and early adolescent sexual play a moral code which belongs properly in the costly, risky, and powerful engagements of adult sexuality might seem inappropriate when viewed in this light: to see in this reading-back at least an element of what Freud called 'projection' is to recognize another particular irony.

'Projection' is one example of what Freud speaks of as 'defence mechanisms', less-than-conscious processes which reduce anxiety by distorting perception of external or internal reality. Mary-Anne Coate gives an engaging and perceptive introduction to these in her book *Clergy Stress* (1989), but perhaps the most well-known application of this concept is in the work of Elizabeth Kübler-Ross (1969) on loss, death, and bereavement, in which she pointed to the near-universal operation of denial as a mechanism giving us time to rally our resources. When denial is operating, I have no conscious access to the reality-for-me of what might cause me distress or anxiety: the 'reality-for-me' in question might be an aspect either of external reality (I have not had my pocket picked; the news of this death is not true), or of internal reality (this loss has occurred, but it is not significant for me).

Alongside denial, the most common defence mechanism is probably projection, in which we attribute to others feelings and motives which are in fact our own. Anyone who has noticed the degree of obstructiveness shown by other road users when they themselves are anxious and in a hurry has at least that experience of projection to recognize, but once we move into the realm of sexuality, projection is common, and a fuller range of defence mechanisms frequently comes into play. Rationalization allows me to overlay my real feelings with very reasonable alternative explanations for my experiences (with the sheer reasonableness of the alternative explanations, along with their number, often being a pointer to this mechanism at work); reaction formation allows me access to my own desires by only recognizing them in their 'opposites' (with prominent church leaders seeming particularly vulnerable to public declarations on sexuality which turn out to have been grounded in a mixture of projection and reaction formation); avoidance as a defence mechanism ensures that I never find myself in a situation which might generate sexual anxieties (without ever quite knowing why I am always somewhere else); projection, finally, enables me to see in the other either what I love in myself (or would love to recognize and love in myself), or what I fear to see as an aspect of myself.

Defence mechanisms might helpfully be thought of as sometimes appropriate in the short term—as tactics to allow me to adjust to a changed reality-as-experienced—but as always inappropriate in the long term, as strategies, because they use up energy otherwise available for productive adjustment. They block reality-based development, and more or less inevitably, they eventually break down.

As an area characterized by intense feeling and highly significant value-structures, sexuality is manifestly prone to the operation of defence mechanisms. The experiences of sexual attraction and arousal, of 'falling in love' and obsessions, of who and what characterize my desire: all of these combine powerful experiences with equally powerful questions of value and identity. Add to the mix the social, cultural, and religious restrictions on 'upfront' discussion and self-disclosure in the realm of the sexual, and it is not difficult to see how large swathes of our sexual experience are prone to the influence of defence mechanisms. Conscious decisions are frequently made under the influence of less-than-conscious emotions and desires, while many effective decisions are never made at a conscious level at all. Theologians need to be as sensitive as the great novelists, poets, and playwrights to the ways in which so much of our engagement with each other, in wider social and political settings as well as in the interpersonal and intimate, is in fact shaped and influenced by less-than-conscious elements of experience and desire.

Even at the level of what is accessible to conscious and critical examination, human behaviour turns out, thanks to Freud's insights, to be more complex in its causation than is generally acknowledged: 'Freud was indispensably instrumental in irrefutably showing us how mind is governed by many competing causal forces that operate simultaneously and on stratified levels of dynamic activity and complexity' (Mills 2007: 544).

The character of Mr Spock in *Star Trek* is a gentle caricature of total rationality at work (and frequently somewhat at sea) in the realm of the affective, and may serve as a reassurance that 'rationality is not all' in this dimension of our experience, but some theologizing around sexuality does seem to operate out of a philosophical stance closer to Spock (and his Hellenistic intellectual ancestors) than to the more emotion-rich culture of Christianity's Jewish roots.

A major contribution from Freud to any resource for theologians reflecting on human sexuality is undoubtedly his concept of the Superego. In simple form, the Superego is the mechanism which internalizes the small child's perceptions of what is acceptable and unacceptable to those whose approval and care is essential for the child's survival. As an initially helpless infant, I need you to be happy with me if my more basic needs—for food, for water, for warmth, for being held—are going to be met. Long before I can think my way through what might be right or wrong, I have begun to adapt, not only in my external behaviour but also in my internal patterns of feeling and emotion, according to my perceptions of what pleases and displeases you.

As John W. Glaser (1971) and Richard M. Gula (1996) among others have pointed out, to mistake this primitive, pre-reflective, and fear-driven mechanism for 'conscience' is a serious error: but at an unreflective level, this is an error which we all make on occasion, and many of us make most of the time. In consequence we can be driven by fear-filled perceptions of what will make us acceptable or unacceptable—to others and to God—and these perceptions, and the patterns of response they generate, can limit our capacity to develop adult and autonomous responses to the gospel in our lives. But if this is one risk arising from confusing conscience and Superego, there is also the opposite risk—that of dismissing the workings of conscience as nothing other than the effects of an overactive Superego, to be discounted or totally dismissed. Here, too, there is a need to recognize the influence of the less-than-conscious: my judgements and decisions as to what will form my moral compass are not insulated from neurotic defences.

Manifestly, the dimension of sexuality is one in which Superego mechanisms can exert great influence, the more so because of the various ways in which custom and

culture restrict the measured discussion essential for the formation of a mature conscience and the development of moral decision-making.

Object Relations Approaches

Object relations theory has its origins in the work of Melanie Klein, whose rejection of what she saw as a too-narrow focus on the instinctual by Freud gave rise to a
developing awareness of the more complex ways in which individuals relate to the
objects in their internal and external worlds. Klein's own particular focus on the
mechanisms of introjection and projection has influenced a major school of psychoanalytic thought and therapeutic practice, but in our context it is the essentially
relational nature of human motivation, and the ways in which all our relating (and
indeed all our functioning) are shaped by our patterns of perceiving, that are the
key insights. In the view of object relations theorists, libido, the motive power of
the psyche, is not seeking the discharge of biological tensions, but the building and
maintenance of relationships with good objects, both external and internal: how we
perceive these objects is an active and creative process, a shaping rather than a simple receiving.[1]

This is not the setting for an extended review of the history of Object relations theory,
which was for many years predominantly developed in the work of British psychoanalytical thinkers. But two particular aspects of more contemporary thinking in this area
seem to have considerable relevance in our context, the first being the already-noted
stress on relationality as being at the heart of human motivation, the second being the
more complex but no less important notion of the role of illusion.

For Freud and classical Freudians, illusion was that which was believed (or believed
in) in the absence of reasonable evidence. Maturity should bring with it an abandonment
of such beliefs and the acceptance of truths as supported by scientific method: 'Men
cannot remain children for ever; they must in the end go out into "hostile life"' (Freud
1928: 49). Contemporary psychoanalysts such as Ana-Maria Rizzuto ([1979] 1981, 1991,
1998) and the late William Meissner SJ (1966, 1981, 1984, 1987, 2000) point to an irony
here. What might be judged to be Freud's greatest insight was his recognition of the way
in which all our perceptions are influenced by less-than-conscious factors, but he was
unable to see that his own perceptions of what could lead to truth were themselves so
influenced. As Rizzuto expresses it:

> Freud has shown beyond doubt that man's wishes and needs colour whatever he does
> and whatever he sees. Man is always playing with reality...either to create himself
> through illusory anticipation, to sustain himself through illusory reshaping of what
> does not seem bearable, or simply to fool himself through illusory distortion of what

---

[1] Aquinas got there first: 'whatever is received into something is received according to the condition of
the receiver.' *Quidquid recipitur ad modum recipientis recipitur.* Cf. *Summa Theologiae*, 1a, q. 75, a. 5; 3a, q. 5.

he does not like... Illusory transmutation of reality, however, is the indispensable and unavoidable process all of us *must* go through if we are to grow normally and acquire psychic meaning and substance.... The type of illusion we select—science, religion, or something else—reveals our personal history and the transitional space each of us has created between his objects and himself to find a 'resting place' to live in.

(Rizzuto [1979] 1981: 228, emphasis original)

Object relations theory stresses that we relate to the world as we represent the world to ourselves—that is, we relate to the world via the 'objects' which mediate the world to us, and which are themselves shaped by our own patterns of feeling, our own needs and wishes. The key 'area' for human experience and action is what these theorists refer to in terms of 'transitional space' or intermediate space—that 'outside, inside, at the border, (to use the words of the British psychoanalyst Donald Winnicott in a key article first published in 1953), which is neither purely private nor simply public: neither the 'autistic' totally internal space of my fantasy and imagination, nor the 'objective', measurable, replicable public space of the outside world, but a space which is 'between', the uniquely human zone of functioning which finds its origins in the infant's creation (out of what is available in the world) of some substitute for the never-always-present mother. Culture, religion, art, love: all of these essentially human activities and experiences rely on my capacity to stay at the point of intersection between the outside and the inside, between the autistic and the objective: they depend on my capacity to play, to engage in a healthy manner with illusion.

Rizzuto points to a crucial element of these representations when she notes that these representations of the objects in our internal and external worlds are formed from 'a vast number of complex memories', many of them preconceptual:

To be is to be with others. To be with others is to collect a vast number of complex memories about ourselves, others, and our mutual interactions. The memories belong to all the conceptual levels available: visceral (the milk that 'touches' internally), proprioceptive (pressure and muscle sensations), sensorimotor, eidetic and conceptual. The conceptual modality is the last to emerge in development: the others are present either at birth or very early in life. (1991: 52)

Once again we are reminded that much of what is central in our engagement with one another is preconceptual: not so much 'irrational' as requiring processing in modalities which are not limited to the conscious and rational. It is no surprise, then, that everyday language is stretched to its limits and beyond in the attempt to articulate our experiences of ourselves-intimately-with-others. As we will discuss later, it should not be assumed that psychological theory succeeds where everyday discourse fails (and even poets and playwrights struggle).

Object relations theory contributes to what theologians need to know by stressing the way in which our relating to one another is central to our human functioning and motivation, and by making clear how our relating is shaped by our previous experience, needs, and memories. It enriches classical Freudian theory by pointing beyond the satisfying of biological drives to that which is essentially human in human sexuality, and enables us to see 'play' as a vital and positive element of our sexuality.

Jung

To deal as briefly as is necessary here with the psychology of C. G. Jung is inevitably to misrepresent the complex thought of this subtle (and in the judgement of some critics inconsistent) thinker. Anthony Stevens's book in the 'Very Short Introduction' series (2001) provides an excellent way into this complexity. But two concepts in particular stand out as requiring attention, even at the risk of misrepresentation, because of how they can contribute to a pool of resources for theologians reflecting on sexuality: that of the Shadow, and that of the Anima and Animus. Each of these fits within Jung's psychology of archetypes. As he saw them, these are innate capacities for forming images, and for establishing patterns of feelings associated with these images, which relate to fundamental and universal aspects of our experience. Shadow and Anima/Animus are each encountered—more directly or less directly depending on the individual—in the process of Individuation, Jung's conceptualizing of how we come to discover both who we are and who we are capable of becoming.

Where Freud suggests that our perceptions of what is acceptable and unacceptable give rise to the Superego, Jung suggests that as we form a clearer image of who we wish to be, so there arises a counter-image, comprising all that will not fit with our ideals, which he calls the Shadow. Since it is made up of aspects of ourself, we need to come to terms with it if we are to become whole. Literatures and traditions across the world, and in particular myth and fairy story, provide countless examples of such Shadow images, a fact which Jung saw as indicative of their universal nature. Film-makers provide contemporary renderings of these images, some with more visible roots in folk tale than others: *The Lord of the Rings* and the *Star Wars* sequence both play with archetypal images, with the former reaching back through European myths and the latter attempting to create new mythic figures. (Gollum and Darth Vader, for example, can be seen as Shadow images, and it is in keeping with Jungian thought that each turns out to have a vital contribution to make to the good outcome of their respective stories.)

While misreadings of Jung have suggested that he believed in some sort of shared level of psychic functioning—what might be caricatured as a 'shared file-store in the sky'—Jung's own explanation was based in the commonality of key elements of our experience, and the consequent evolution of key capacities for processing these. Frieda Fordham's description stands the test of time:

> The brain itself has been shaped and influenced by the remote experiences of mankind. But although our inheritance consists in physiological paths, still it was mental processes in our ancestors that created the paths. If these traces come to consciousness again in the individual, they can do so only in the form of mental processes, and if these processes can become conscious only through individual experience and thus appear as individual acquisitions, they are none the less pre-existing traces,

which are merely 'filled-out' by the individual experience. Every 'impressive' experience is such an impression, in an ancient but previously unconscious stream-bed. (1959: 22)

Only when I have come to terms with my Shadow—at least in part—am I then free to encounter my Anima, (or if I am a woman, my Animus), the image of the contrasexual elements within each of us, and so of the feminine within the man and vice versa. Fully to develop as a man, I need to come to terms with these feminine aspects of my sexuality if I am to be able to engage with an other (i.e. another real person) as complementary to me in my sexuality (whether this be an opposite-sex or a same-sex complementarity).

That Jung places the encounter with the Shadow first, that is, prior in time to the encounter with the Animus/Anima, reflects the insight that coming to terms with my sexuality, in the process of encountering my Anima/Animus, can frequently require recognizing aspects of myself that do not at first sight fit in with my Ideal Self. While Jung suggests that the symbolic representations of Shadow and Animus/Anima are distinct, individuals' experience may not always be so neatly classifiable. Individuation works itself out according to a general template in the concrete realities of my experience, rather than according to some absolutely definable flow-chart which is unchanged by particularity. Jung's psychology of archetypes and individuation points to the ways in which our development as individuals—including our psychosexual development—always involves the universal expressed in the particular.

Other

The transpersonal psychologies, such as Assagioli's *Psychosynthesis* (2000), provide additional useful insights, among them the notions of first recognizing the needs and wants of what may be considered subpersonalities, and of then learning to be sufficiently skilful a) to disidentify (from unconscious and unhelpful identifications with these aspects of myself—mistaking the part for the whole), and b) consciously to identify as appropriate (making choices informed by reflective awareness). Understandings of the lived complexities of human sexuality can obviously benefit from this approach, which rejects rigid all-or-nothing dichotomies in favour of a richer description of our conscious and less-than-conscious functioning. A number of the approaches collected under the heading of transpersonal psychology are open to considering an openness to the transcendent as constitutive of human capacity and experience, and this allows them to provide a hospitable base for theologians. Caution needs to be exercised, however, given the wide range of understandings linked to such terms as 'the transcendent' and 'spirituality'.

ERIK ERIKSON

Although Erik Erikson's major works were published in the middle of the twentieth century, mostly between *Childhood and Society* ([1950] 1963) and *The Life Cycle Completed*

(1987), his descriptions of the patterns he observed in psychosocial development remain informative and influential. Richard Stevens provides a helpful introduction to his work (2008). He published a number of books and papers which constitute a rich legacy, only a fragment of which can be touched on here, namely his insights on the stages of adolescence and young adulthood. In Erikson's overall scheme each of these is characterized by an 'existential question', respectively: 'Who Am I and What Can I Be?', and 'Can I Love?'. Adolescence sees the resolution of the 'crisis' between identity and role confusion: I come to discover-and-create who I am in the making and attempted living-out of commitments. In our complex and technological society this process can take many years, depending as it does on our acquiring a measure of mastery of the (increasingly complex) skills of adult living, but the key elements are not directly concerned with external skills as such.

'How can I learn who I am until I see what I can do?' might be another way of articulating the key questions of adolescence, as long as it is recognized that alongside the technological element suggested by 'doing' there is the more fundamental relational aspect: 'What sort of commitments can I make and live by?' As I come to resolve this adolescent crisis, so I acquire the capacity for fidelity—'the ability to sustain loyalties freely pledged in spite of the inevitable contradictions and confusions of value systems' (Erikson 1964). With whatever measure of fidelity I have acquired, I can now embark on enduring commitments to others in relationships which enable intimacy and preserve me from isolation, and so engage with the crisis of young adulthood out of which arises the capacity for love.

In terms of our concerns in this chapter, Erikson points to the way in which our sense of identity and our capacity to engage with others are interwoven. Given what we now know about the varieties of experienced sexual and gender identity (as discussed later), theological reflection around such issues as the capacity and the need for intimacy needs to take account of this complex interplay.

ATTACHMENT THEORY

This more recent development, which serves as something of a bridge between the more 'classical' depth psychologies and the range of approaches which might be summed up as social psychology, has its origins in the work of John Bowlby ([1969] 1999, 1973, 1980). Attachment theory has been fruitful in generating a variety of studies illuminating how early experiences of attachment shape later patterns of relating. Bowlby saw attachment as an emotional-behavioural system which had evolved to maintain proximity between helpless human infants and their caregivers/protectors. To the extent that a secure pattern of attachment is established, the primary caregiver comes to be perceived and experienced as both a haven of safety and a secure base for exploration. This early experience then gives rise to a mental model, or set of expectations, that shapes the individual's engagement and interactions with other people throughout life.

Alongside the secure pattern of attachment there are two further possibilities—labelled 'avoidant' (where proximity to the caregiver has been experienced not as safe and secure, but as threatening), and 'anxious-ambivalent' (which speaks for itself). What is crucial is that these various patterns of early experience result in 'templates' which always have a shaping and sometimes have a determining effect on later patterns of relationship.

Bowlby saw attachment and sexuality as separate but overlapping systems, with different goals. But, as Lawrence Josephs points out in a book review in *Neuropsychoanalysis*: 'Bowlby believed that the relation to attachment figures provided a paradigm of relatedness that forms a scaffold for the developmental unfolding of sexuality…attachment scaffolds psychosexual development, but sexual pleasures and fears may facilitate as well as disrupt attachment relationships' (Josephs 2010: 220).

Attachment theory provides for the theologian concerned with sexuality a further set of insights pointing to the relational complexities of our engagements with each other, expanding the range of reflection beyond any simplistic understanding of biological priorities.

Social Psychology

A recent editorial in the *Archives of Sexual Behavior* (2012) noted sixty-eight peer-reviewed journals concerned with sex and/or gender, the majority of them falling within the area of psychology. Any genuinely comprehensive overview of what concerns social psychologists in the area of sexuality must therefore be sought elsewhere than here, but some key themes can be examined in our quest to uncover what theologians need to know. Distinguishing between the descriptive and the explanatory can sometimes be helpful in this area of psychological research. Just as with the topics emerging from looking at the depth psychologies, so with these themes: it can be helpful to note what psychologists have uncovered and described even if their explanations of what is described may not appear so helpful to theologians or other people of faith.

We have already noted Freud's and Erikson's approaches to psychosexual development. Without being reliant on their particular theoretical formulations, more contemporary accounts of sexual development similarly note a prepubertal phase of sexual awakening when sexual characteristics and differences become matters of intense interest and curiosity (and various versions of 'doctors and nurses' provide the context for that curiosity to be exercised). This is followed by an early school-age stage when psychosexual socialization is key (corresponding to Freud's latency period), before the onset of puberty and the beginnings of the processes leading towards adult psychosexual integration, as social, emotional, physical, and societal pressures all come to bear in new and powerful ways. Explanations of this overall path of development range from those rooted in a biological determinism on the one hand, to social constructivist approaches which see sexual and gender identity as essentially social creations on the other; somewhere between these extremes are various interactionist models which see biology and experience both playing their part.

Staying with the descriptive level, we can note that the study of sexual development by social and other 'empirical' psychologists has made it clear that there is a great range of developmental patterns, and an equivalently large range of outcomes in terms of gender identity and sexual orientation. Any oversimple model of human sexual dimorphism runs into serious questions raised by those who experience themselves as transgendered, while large amounts both of structured research and of personal report have opened up discussion of the area of sexual orientation so as to give rise to richer and more nuanced attempts at understanding. Similarly, studies of sexuality across the increasing lifespan, from early childhood to old age, have revealed a much more complex repertoire of activity and experience than had been previously adverted to, at least in any open manner. Any adequate theology of sexuality has to take account of the sheer diversity of developmental patterns, and their outcomes in terms of diversity of experience and behaviours.

GENERAL COMMENTS

What is intriguing for a psychologist attempting to survey what psychology has to offer to theologians reflecting on sexuality (a slightly different formulation of 'what theologians need to know'), is the degree to which psychological theories have for the most part failed to come up with adequate explanatory accounts of this complex, varied, and rich aspect of human experience and behaviour. In a blog/book review, Danny Wedding (2009) observed:

> Traditionally, issues involving human sexuality have not received a high priority in psychological theory, research, or clinical practice. Perhaps because sexuality is such a complex, value-laden area (particularly in relation to sexual trauma, sexual orientation, abortion, and extramarital involvement), psychology researchers have often left the field of human sexuality to other disciplines. From our perspective, this is a major mistake. The paradox of sexuality is that healthy sexuality contributes a small positive role in individual and relational well-being, but dysfunctional, conflictual sexuality—and particularly sexual avoidance—can play an inordinately powerful negative role in subverting individual and couple satisfaction and stability.

Despite the existence of those sixty-eight peer-reviewed journals noted earlier, Wedding's observation is accurate. So much is this neglect the case that one pair of authors (Jones and Hostler 2005) refer back to psychoanalytic thinking as offering the most holistic and least reductionist theoretical framework within which to understand human sexuality.

This chapter has focused primarily on what might be gleaned from psychology in the academy—that is, from theoretical, clinical, and empirical research and reflection—and it is to this realm of discourse that the earlier comments refer. But alongside this major element of psychology there is a flourishing and highly valuable genre applying psychology in a variety of human settings, and it would be remiss were this not to be noted and recognized, even where some of the writing is already partly theological and as well as psychological. An example of such work is the series of books produced by Evelyn Eaton Whitehead and James D. Whitehead, developmental psychologist and historian of religion respectively. From *A Sense of Sexuality* comes the following observation, which can serve as an appropriate illustration of how a 'pastoral psychology' approach can be illuminating in ways that more formal theorizing cannot:

As a strength of adult maturity, intimacy is the capacity

- to commit ourself to particular people
- in relationships that last over time
- and to meet the accompanying demands for change
- in ways that do not compromise personal integrity.

(Whitehead and Whitehead 1989: 60)

The capacity to account for human sexuality in some adequate manner is a litmus test which points to the differing reductionisms embedded in different psychological theories: the emphasis in classical Freudian thought on fixed patterns of response established in the Oedipal period, paralleled to some degree by the equally 'fixed by past events' approach of evolutionary psychology; the incapacity of classic behaviourism to get beyond simple understandings of 'reward' in terms of physically pleasurable events; the oddly disembodied (or at least 'disincarnate') approach of many of the most influential of the humanistic psychologists on the one hand, and of the social constructivists on the other. Among the former, Abraham Maslow was more responsive to the implications of the human than many of his contemporaries in psychology: 'My whole training...was behaviourist. When my first baby was born, that was the thunderclap that settled things. I looked at this tiny, mysterious thing and felt so stupid. I felt small, weak, and feeble. I'd say that anyone who's had a baby couldn't be a behaviourist' (Maslow, in Hoffman 1992: 73). But this did not prevent him from effectively separating out the physical/physiological and the self-actualizing at the lowest and highest levels of his hierarchy of needs.

Jones and Hostler (2005) single out as the most adequate the Freudian framework, though they suggest that classical Freudianism suffers from biological determinism, and prefer more contemporary relational approaches. While the charge of biological determinism is a debated one among scholars of Freud, it is undoubtedly the case that more recent formulations in psychoanalytic theory, influenced by the Object relations school in particular, have encompassed a much wider range of human experience and activity.

We explored aspects of this earlier. Jones and Hostler (2005: 23) provide an elegant citation that sums up this approach and concludes this brief survey:

> The key claim is that the relevant framework for considering these issues is that sexuality is inside the symbolic order, not purely an expression of instinctual needs. Biological determinants are not wholly cast aside, but the rigidity of their determining role is greatly reduced.... It is now commonplace that sexuality has a history, that is, it is inside the contingency of culture, not merely fixed and innate in a stereotyped way.

What Theologians Need To Know

'Sexuality is inside the symbolic order... it is inside the contingency of culture'. This statement presents itself as a good starting point for approaching the question of what theologians need to know. Despite the surprising paucity of material on sexuality from the discipline of psychology, there are some psychological insights which theologians *do* need to know, and this assertion of the vital importance of the symbolic is the most important of them, if one of the more general in its expression.[2]

From classical psychoanalysis comes the recognition that sexuality is a pervasive dimension of human experience in two senses. Sexuality incorporates the affective and social elements of our lives alongside the genital and physical/physiological: contrary to any oversimplistic reading of Freud, human sexuality is rooted in wider aspects of the human than the release of biological tensions. And sexuality is a dimension of our human experience and behaviour from birth to death, not an attribute which emerges only with the onset of puberty and the coming of adolescence and which somehow retreats or vanishes once the ages of reproductive fertility have passed. Theology needs to take account of both these aspects of the pervasiveness of human sexuality, both to ensure that the richness of adult sexuality is not lost sight of by reducing theological reflection on this dimension of being human to a sterile morality of particular actions, and to avoid imposing on childhood sexuality an understanding which is proper to the powerful and risk-laden place sexuality plays in adult relating. The degree to which the sexual dimension of our being is a field in which defence mechanisms operate is also a crucial contribution to appropriate theologizing around sexuality: the Hellenistic stress on and reliance on the rational does not provide a complete picture of the positive richness and complexity of what it is to be a sexual person.

From the Object relations school come key insights: the essentially relational foundations of human sexuality, making clear that any reading of psychoanalytic theory which reduces sexuality to tension-reduction is an impoverished reading; and the

---

[2] The contributions from anthropology of Mary Douglas complement what psychology has to offer here.

equally essentially creative elements that underpin that relationality, clarifying how our perceiving of and relating to all of reality is coloured by our own needs and desires. The renewed understanding of 'illusion' as an essential element of human experience, and the notion of transitional or intermediate space as the arena in which much of what is most human in our experience takes place: these are key elements in any approach to sexuality which would do justice to the human capacity for symbolization—the same capacity which lies at the heart of a truly sacramental understanding of being a human person before God. The interplay of individual and shared meaning and significance which is at the heart of all truly human engagement, be it intimacy, artistic expression, scientific endeavour, or any other form of creativity and play, takes place in this 'between' space which preverbal and preconceptual experiences have helped to establish. Theologians—themselves engaged in creative 'play' and belonging to a tradition which has made use of the full range of human creativity in its attempts to celebrate the divine–human encounter—can draw on rich resources here, provided they remain alert to the limitations of linear and rational discourse to express the full reality of the human.

Jungian psychology brings in the element of the archetypal—the recognition of those aspects of our individual experience which are universal—and the understanding of the whole of human life as a process of individuation, of becoming the person we are capable of becoming. This is not the place for an extended treatment of how individuation might be understood within a theological framework, but the element of process—of a continuing and continual growing into a fullness of being—provides a foundation for theological reflection on the developmental nature of human sexuality. Richard Sipe, in books ranging from *A Secret World: Sexuality And The Search For Celibacy* (1990) to *Celibacy in Crisis: A Secret World Revisited* (2003), and Aloysius Pieris SJ (1992) have both explored this in more theological terms, opening up the notion of chastity (as distinct from celibacy, which is regarded as one mode of chastity) as growth in a more integrated sexuality lived in the light of the gospel.

In particular, Jung's suggestion that we need to come to terms with the Shadow (all that does not fit in with our notion of our ideal self) in order to be able to engage with the contra-sexual elements of ourselves as symbolized and embodied in the Anima/Animus points to complexities in our experience of our own sexuality of which theologians need to take account.

The transpersonal psychologies, and in particular Assagioli's *Psychosynthesis*, in addition to underpinning a powerful therapeutic system, add two elements in particular to the store of what theologians need to know: the human capacity for identifying with one aspect of our complex selves and thus mistaking the part for the whole, and an understanding of the human from a psychological perspective that recognizes an openness to the transcendent as an essential element of the human. The first points to an element of risk, in for example overidentifying with an element of our sexuality to the point of losing sight of who we are in the totality of ourselves: theological reflection on a proper self-acceptance, as well as on a proper asceticism, can draw on helpful material here. The second offers the possibility of a truly human theological anthropology that could encompass the various elements of our capacity for engagement with God and with each other so as to make clear how our sexuality is involved in our relating to God.

Attachment theory brings into play a further aspect of how our sexuality is shaped by our experience (or perhaps simply another way of looking at how this happens), in its suggestion that early attachment patterns provide templates for later patterns of intimate engagement: 'ideal' patterns of sexual expression and experience have to be tested against what is actually possible in the life of this individual with this early attachment experience. The insights of attachment theory into the ways in which our capacity for positive and healthy emotional engagement can be limited by early experience have something to offer in the realm of theological anthropology and a renewed understanding of 'original sin'.

Erikson's work points us to the inextricable interweaving of identity and intimacy as the capacities for fidelity and love emerge from the crises of adolescence and young adulthood, raising questions for many areas of theological reflection around sexual and gender identity.

From what was drawn together under the general heading of 'social psychology' emerges one key observation—that of the sheer diversity of human sexual behaviour and experience. Even 'gender' appears as a more complex element of being human than much theology has yet got to grips with, while theological debate and discussion around sexual identity and sexual orientation sometimes seem to be conducted in ignorance of even the simply descriptive materials made available by psychological research. It could be suggested that much theological reflection in the area of sexuality has in fact operated on understandings and explanations of the observable facts of human sexual behaviour and experience that are rightly characterized by Richard Sipe (2003) as 'pre-Copernican'.

It has been a deliberately repeated theme of this chapter that theologians do not need to 'buy into' the explanatory levels of the various and varied psychological studies reviewed in order to recognize the real challenges contained in their descriptive elements. That this theme has been repeatedly stressed reflects the way in which some writers from a theological or ecclesiastical background have been unable to see the trees for the wood—that is, they have overidentified the descriptive material made available by various psychologists with the implicit or explicit anthropologies held by the psychologist in question. In rejecting the anthropology, they failed to notice what was there in the descriptions. Thus, the descriptive elements deriving from Freud's willingness to look unflinchingly at the unacceptable were ignored by many Christian writers because of the avowed atheism of this self-described 'Godless Jew', and this despite Freud's own recognition that psychoanalysis could and would be used by religious people. Closer to our theme, a particular Christian anthropology of sexuality has made it impossible for some thinkers to engage with what contemporary sciences (including but not limited to psychology) have brought to light regarding the varieties of sexual development and behaviour.

It has been noted earlier in this chapter that psychological research has neglected sexuality, perhaps because of its combination of being complex and value-laden. A significant element of what has emerged in the course of this chapter is precisely that admixture of complexity and values, or, rather, a mixture of complexity, variety, creativity, play, risk, and the discovery and making of meaning. That sounds like useful and necessary material for theologians to know.

References

Archives of Sexual Behaviour (2012). *Archives of Sexual Behaviour*, 41: 1–4.

Assagioli, Roberto (2000). *Psychosynthesis: A Collection of Basic Writings*. Amherst, MA: Synthesis Center Inc.

Berlin, Isaiah (1953). *The Hedgehog and the Fox: An Essay on Tolstoy's View of History*. London: Weidenfeld & Nicolson.

Bowlby, John [1969] (1999). *Attachment*, 2nd edn. New York: Basic Books.

Bowlby, John (1973). *Separation: Anxiety & Anger*. London: Hogarth Press.

Bowlby, John (1980). *Loss: Sadness & Depression*. London: Hogarth Press.

Coate, Mary-Anne (1989). *Clergy Stress*. London: SPCK.

Erikson, Erik [1950] (1963). *Childhood and Society*, 2nd edn. New York: W. W. Norton.

Erikson, Erik (1964). *Insight and Responsibility*. New York: W. W. Norton.

Erikson, Erik (1987). *The Life Cycle Completed*. New York: W. W. Norton.

Fordham, Frieda (1959). *An Introduction to Jung's Psychology*. Harmondsworth: Penguin Books.

Freud, Sigmund (1928). *The Future of an Illusion*. London: Hogarth Press.

Glaser, John W., SJ (1971). 'Conscience and Super-Ego: A Key Distinction'. *Theological Studies*, 32: 30–47.

Gula, Richard M., SS (1996). *Ethics in Pastoral Ministry*. New York: Paulist Press.

Hoffman, E. (1992) 'The Last Interview of Abraham Maslow'. *Psychology Today*, 25(1): 73.

Jones, S. L., and H. Hostler (2005). 'The Role of Sexuality in Personhood: An Integrative Investigation'. In W. Miller and H. Delaney (eds), *Judeo-Christian Perspectives on Psychology: Human Nature, Motivation, and Change*. Washington, DC: American Psychological Association, 115–132.

Josephs, Lawrence (2010). Review of 'Attachment and Sexuality'. *Neuropsychoanalysis*, 12(2): 220–222.

Kübler-Ross, Elizabeth (1969). *On Death and Dying*. London: Routledge.

Meissner, William W., SJ (1966). *Foundations for a Psychology of Grace*. New York: Paulist Press.

Meissner, William W., SJ (1981). *Internalization in Psychoanalysis*. Psychological Issues, Monograph 50. New York: International Universities Press.

Meissner, William W., SJ (1984). *Psychoanalysis and Religious Experience*. New Haven: Yale University Press.

Meissner, William W., SJ (1987). *Life and Faith: Perspectives on Religious Experience*. Washington, DC: Georgetown University Press.

Meissner, William W., SJ (2000). *Freud and Psychoanalysis*. Notre Dame, IN: University of Notre Dame Press.

Meissner, William W., SJ (2008). 'Psychoanalysis and Catholicism—Dialogues in Transformation'. *Psychoanalytic Enquiry*, 28: 580–589.

Mills, Jon (2007). 'A Response to Grünbaum's Refutation of Psychoanalysis', *Psychoanalytic Psychology*, 24: 539–544.

Murray, Annie (2005). 'Freud & Religion'. MA Psychology of Religion Course Essay. Heythrop College, University of London.

Pieris, Aloysius, SJ (1992). 'The Three Ingredients of Authentic Humanism'. *Vidyajyoti Journal of Theological Reflection*, 56(1): 3–22.

Rizzuto, Ana Maria [1979] (1981). *The Birth of the Living God*. Chicago: University of Chicago Press.

Rizzuto, Ana Maria (1991). 'Religious Development: A Psychoanalytic Point of View'. *New Directions for Child Development*, 52: 47–60.

Rizzuto, Ana Maria (1998). *Why Did Freud Reject God?* New Haven: Yale University Press.

Sipe, Richard (1990). *A Secret World: Sexuality and the Search for Celibacy*. New York: Brunner/Mazel.

Sipe, Richard (2003). *Celibacy in Crisis: A Secret World Revisited*. New York and Hove: Brunner-Routledge.

Stevens, Anthony (2001). *Jung: A Very Short Introduction*. Oxford: Oxford University Press.

Stevens, Richard (2008). *Erik H. Erikson: Explorer of Identity and the Life Cycle*. Basingstoke: Palgrave Macmillan.

Wedding, Danny (March 2009). 'Have Psychologists Ignored Human Sexuality?' PsycCRITIQUES Blog. <http://psycnet.apa.org/> (accessed 28 Aug. 2013).

Whitehead, E. E., and J. D. Whitehead (1989). *A Sense of Sexuality*. New York: Doubleday.

Winnicott, D. W. (1953). 'Transitional Objects and Transitional Phenomena—A Study of the First Not-Me Possession'. *International Journal of Psycho-Analysis*, 34: 89–97.

Young, R. M. (2001). 'Locating and Relocating Psychoanalytic Ideas of Sexuality'. In C. Harding (ed.), *Sexuality: Psychoanalytic Perspectives*. New York: Brunner-Routledge, 18–34.

CHAPTER 7

....

CONTRIBUTIONS FROM ANTHROPOLOGY

....

ANNA STEWART AND SIMON COLEMAN

INTRODUCTION

....

RELIGION, according to one popular anthropological definition, is a realm of experience in which humans confront ultimate categories of meaning. Through religious language, ritual, and ideology human beings come to reside within a 'system of symbols' that colours their experience of and orientation towards the world (Geertz 1973: 90–91). In the years since Geertz's influential definition of religion was proposed, anthropologists have pointed out the importance of looking not only at systems of *meaning* but also at the entanglement of actors in more material and more mundane networks of family, economy, and politics (Asad 1983). Gender (involving cultural expectations about the roles of men and women) and sexuality (involving morality, desire, and physical activity related to sex) have added significant dimensions to the study of religion for they appear to bring together these themes of symbolic meaning and embodied life. Gender and sexuality are also fundamental to our experience of ourselves, each other, and the environment. In *The History of Sexuality* (1976), the French philosopher Michel Foucault argued that people's identities in the West had become increasingly tied to their sexuality from the eighteenth century onwards. However, gender and sexuality are frequently emphasized in religious cultures across the world as a whole (Ramet 1996: 5).

In the following, we divide up our exploration of these themes into three main approaches. Through looking at notions of both 'discipline' and 'reproduction' we examine some of the ways in which gender and sexuality are related to the construction and consolidation of cultural and social order, not least as they reinforce local understandings of religious authority and biological necessity. By looking also at issues of 'protest and change', however, we provide a further dimension to our overview: we show that what is at stake in articulating and controlling gender and sexuality is demonstrated by their ability to challenge, as well as to consolidate, power and authority within a given social group.

Gender, Sexuality, and Discipline

Religions often deal with gender as a kind of essence. Creation myths the world over provide commentaries on the nature of women and men and offer explanations for differences in their religious status. In societies marked by a hierarchical segregation, narratives will contain explanations for this arrangement that are framed not in terms of historical and contemporary politics but rather with reference to the very design and nature of human beings. So it is in the Old Testament story of the Garden of Eden, in which the fate of Eve and all of her female descendants is irreparably damaged by her curiosity, and also for the traditionally matriarchal Seneca people of North America and Canada, who trace their origins to a female progenitor who fell to earth from the sky and conceived children through union with the wind (see Sanday 1981).

Such accounts form part of wider symbolic repertoires of the meaning of male and female. Many religious traditions identify women particularly with the material body, for example, so that where the ensnarements of the physical world are seen to be a barrier to salvation, so too is femininity perceived to be a polluting or restrictive element (Ortner 1974; Humes 1996). At times, however, the specific character of femaleness as opposed to maleness can have a more complex, double-edged, set of associations. In her ethnographic study of Jamaican Pentecostals, Diane Austin-Broos (1997: 140) notes that women's bodies are more readily seen as vessels that can be defiled by fornication—a form of pollution that the Holy Ghost must cleanse. On the other hand (1997: 148–151), it is also said that men find it more difficult to sustain the lived experience of being filled by the Spirit, as women's wombs seem particularly suited to capture spiritual vitality. Indeed, women are able to achieve more intimate, informal relations with Jesus. Such assumptions construct women as more 'open'—with positive as well as negative moral consequences.

Meanwhile, the perception of a general denigration of the traits identified as feminine in Western religious cultures is explicitly criticized in contemporary Wiccan and Goddess faiths, which promote images of a feminine divine, embodied in fertility and emotionality, while often leaving the underlying notion of essential difference and gendered nature undisturbed (Kraemer 2012). Anna Fedele's (2013: 4) account of 'alternative' pilgrimages to Catholic shrines in France shows how many pilgrims who reject conventional Christianity favour visits to shrines linked with Mary Magdalene, whom they associate with the power of the Sacred Feminine. Indeed, Magdalene—the only woman in the canonical gospels who is named without being associated with a man (2013: 7)—provides a role model with both contrasting and complementary identities in relation to those associated with the Virgin Mary: the menstruating and sexual Magdalene is juxtaposed by these pilgrims with the pure, stainless Virgin (2013: 71).

The widespread spiritual significance accorded to masculinity or femininity is demonstrated in the religious status accorded those who are deemed to transgress these categories. People who occupy what anthropologists have termed 'Third' gender categories, recognized socially as neither male nor female but something else, are often found to be possessed of a particular spiritual potency. The Hijra in India are born male though some choose to become eunuchs, and all live in their communities as women. They are often seen as able to bestow blessings or curses upon others in their roles as ritual workers (Nanda 1986). The founder of the millennialist Japanese movement Omoto-kyo was a woman who claimed to have the spirit of a male, and who shared her leadership of the group with a man who supposedly had the spirit of a woman (Hardacre 1990). Outside of such stable non-binary identities cross-dressing frequently features as an important part of religious rituals. Balzer (1996) gives the example of the Siberian bear ceremony, in which men and women don the dress and mannerisms of the other in ribald celebrations. In such ritual 'boundary transcendence' (1996: 174) the distinct essences of male and female are breached and this symbolic accomplishment suggests that the bridges between death and life, gods and humans, may be equally traversable.

Although the (to Western eyes) spectacular gender transgressions embodied in Third gender categories or ritual cross-dressing provide further evidence of the symbolic importance of gender, they also undermine its claims to essence. The collaborative construction of gender can be seen most obviously in coming-of-age rites; for example the various rituals completed by ultra-orthodox Jewish boys through which their commitment to both the text of the Torah and the covenant associated with it is demonstrated (Bilu 2003), or the Kinaalda ceremony during which Navaho girls experience and embody the commitment to family and social cooperation that they will be expected to exhibit as women (Dehyle and Margonis 1995).

The religious habits of the individual are not only constructed within marked ritual practice, however. As anthropologists have become more aware of the construction of gender we see it not only in the drama of ritual but also in more everyday contexts. Roman Catholic men who carry the statue of St Paul during annual festivals to the patron on the Island of Malta are selected on the basis of physical strength, ability to work in groups, and reliability—qualities that are not only embodied in the ritual itself but also in their social lives and family ties (Mitchell 1998). A similar sense of the ritual significance of everyday action is promoted by female mosque movement members in Egypt, who describe their decision to veil not as an expression of an already felt sense of appropriate feminine modesty, but as a way of developing this sense (Mahmood 2001). Through such ongoing religious engagements gender becomes habit, something that is achieved rather than merely expressed.

The anthropological approach of studying religious life in both formal and everyday contexts yields benefits when it comes to understanding the faith of non-elites, particularly women. Since the feminist critiques of the 1970s, anthropologists have become increasingly wary of the tendency for those in positions of religious authority to produce accounts of religious community that focus particularly on male experience, or present the experience of men as universal (see Ardener 1975). Where such models are adopted by anthropologists, religious adherents, particularly women, may become positioned as passive consumers, peripheral to the real stages of religious life. Some work has also revealed the way in which language may draw on metaphors and registers that place female concerns at the margins, even without direct reference to gender distinctions. Thus Susan Harding's (2000: 177) analysis of the American Christian fundamentalist leader Jerry Falwell notes how his voice, his aggressive tone, his military and sports metaphors tend to scan as masculine. Thus for her the forms of fundamentalist public address implicitly privilege men (2000: 176): 'Gender-stratified address among orthodox Protestants, like gender-stratified space in an orthodox Jewish synagogue, which physically situates men inside and women looking in, produces and instils male authority in both men and women.'

Longmann (2002), in a study of Orthodox Jews in Belgium, certainly did find that in the scholarly arenas and public ceremonial life of faith, women appeared as a rather marginal force. The characterization of women as marginal actors within Orthodox Judaism became, however, rather harder to sustain as she grew more aware of the central importance of the home for these believers, and the prominence of women in this setting. The women she spoke to considered the work of wives and mothers to be critically important to the faith of all other members of their family, with one informant describing them as 'priestesses' in their homes (2002: 244). These findings complement Shoshana Feher's (1998: 118–120) observations on attitudes to gender among Orthodox Jews in southern California. Feher notes how private and public domains are demarcated along gender lines, with public ritual life seen as the men's domain. But even as they operate within a patriarchal religious regime, women are bringing men into the home and family and requiring their participation in ways uncommon in some other parts of secular society. Given that this is a religion that gives men a source of identity beyond their work, it offers women the possibility of finding mates who—to some degree—will be supportive in the home. The situation is complicated further by the fact that while Orthodox women tend not to protest against their exclusion from public ritual life, they do not necessarily accept such traditional gender roles in other areas of life. For instance, they would strongly object to the same lack of equality in the workplace.

RITUAL AND REPRODUCTION

Of the various social categories that moderate what it means to be a woman or a man, sexuality presents itself as a special case (Boellstorff 2007). Although sexual practice is not determined and cannot be predicted in any straightforward way by gender, these two realms of classification are often found to be deeply intertwined. Perhaps the most obvious indication of this relationship for our purposes is the very fact that gender and sexuality are twinned as research interests in various academic fields, as indicated by the title of this edited volume. Academics are not alone in making this conceptual pairing. When we look to religious cultures we find a similarly habitual linking of the two.

Sexuality, like gender, appears in a myriad of practices, identities, and social structures across different cultures. Desires and practices that we think of as eminently—perhaps quintessentially—natural are subject to a great deal of cultural mediation.

One area in which we can view the significance of religion in mediating sexual practice is in the many situations in which religious practitioners are convinced to forswear sex altogether. Sexual abstinence is understood by believers in a range of religious movements to confer a parallel spiritual potency (Bell and Sobo 2001: 8) and is often an aspect of religious ritual (see Turner 1964). Filippo and Caroline Osella (2003) describe the temporary renunciation practised by the predominantly male Hindu pilgrims to the top of a mountain in south India, Sabarimala. Participants are honouring the celibate deity Lord Ayyappan, born from two male gods, whose own great powers derive from his celibacy. Pilgrims blend with each other and with the deity through their sacrifice, though it is also notable that sexual desire and potency then become emphasized on the return journeys of the pilgrims, who may for instance round off their period of abstinence by taking pleasure trips to local beach resorts.

For those whose lives are devoted to intense religious observance, celibacy can become a stable part of a sanctified identity, as we see in the case of Catholic priests (Anderson 2007). The less purposeful and more commonplace abstention of those who have not yet become sexually active is also granted religious significance in the category *virgin* (Hastrup 1993). The identities made of sexual abstinence are leant further shades of meaning in their interactions with gender. Female virgins are often regarded as exemplary in their femininity (Hastrup 1993: 40) whereas men who abstain from sex for religious reasons may be understood to be possessed of a masculinity that is in some way uncanny or irregular in comparison to that of their sexually active peers (Almeida 1997: 153; Laven 2012).

The various meanings and methods of sexual abstinence in religious contexts indicate that the manner of interaction between sexual practice and social identity cannot be assumed. Problems of translation remain pertinent throughout anthropology; although we may perceive parallels in the patterns of practice and desire found in geographically distant cultures, it is important to attend to the meaning of sexual engagement in its own context. Rituals of initiation among men in the Sambia culture of Papua New Guinea, for example, include among various observances the ingestion of the semen of older men in acts of fellatio (Herdt 1981). To the outside observer it might seem appropriate to refer to this activity as a kind of ritual homosexuality. The use of such labels, however, may obscure local meanings. For initiates these practices are expected rather as an acquisition of the kind of adult masculinity that is necessary to marry a woman and father children, a stage in the development of a normative heterosexuality. The habit of attaching a specific understanding of selfhood to a given practice may be a result of our own religious legacy. Elliston (2005: 106) suggests that for much of the Christian West a model of 'confessional sexuality' is in operation, in which sexual practice is understood to be the outward expression of an essential inner nature.

A further difficulty in studying sexuality cross-culturally arises from the fact that sexual practice itself is not only typically carried out in private settings (Lyons and Lyons

2005: 2), but also widely considered to be unsuitable for discussion outside of more intimate interpersonal conversation (though see Thomas Gregor's (1980) ethnography of the Mehinaku, an indigenous people in Brazil, for a contrasting case). Despite this somewhat cloistered nature, sexual practices still maintain a significant public presence in many religious communities if only in the form of a pervasive emphasis on hetero-sexual reproduction. It is common for believers to refer to one another in terms express-ing familial relationships, as brothers and sisters, and for religious seniors to be addressed as 'mother' and 'father' (e.g. Toulis 1997; Wedenoja 2001). Reproduction is so central to the spiritual life of American Mormons that the large families that they cultivate on this earth are expected to continue to grow in heaven (Cannell 2005: 336). For the British con-servative Protestants studied by Anna Stewart (2011), marriage and family were regarded not only as desirable but also in some cases a necessary spiritual qualification. Although her informants agreed that it was not necessary for the leader of a church to come from a particular class or background or even to have received any kind of formal training, most insisted that a pastor should be a married man who has ideally fathered children. In these churches male speakers are constantly introduced with reference to the names of their wives and children, and pictures of leaders invariably include their wives smil-ing alongside them. Shoshana Feher's (1998: 119) discussion of Orthodox Jews, referred to earlier, includes the observation that women who do not marry and have children (or who are divorced) may feel alienated and marginalized within the community. She quotes Mark Zborowski and Elisabeth Herzog's (1974: 124) description of life within the eastern European *shtetl*, or small Jewish community, before the Second World War: 'No man is complete without a wife, no woman is complete without a husband. For each individual the idea center of gravity is not in himself, but in the whole of which he is an essential part.'

The elision of religious community and kinship group hints at a possible motivation for religious concerns regarding sexual activities. Dangers to the system of sexual repro-duction, however that system is constituted, represent dangers to the wider social struc-ture. In patriarchal religious cultures the greatest threat to the system is 'sexuality itself' (Abu-Lughod 1986: 119). The linking of political, religious, and sexual life ensures that practices that deviate from the established norm such as infidelity, divorce, masturba-tion, prostitution, or even a marriage marked by too much ardour may be apprehended not only as socially dangerous but also, by the same logic, as spiritually polluting. There are parallels here with the anthropologist Mary Douglas's (1966) influential study of pol-lution, boundaries, and the sacred across cultures. Douglas shows how communities, especially close-knit ones, protect significant social and cultural boundaries by estab-lishing behaviours and attitudes that separate off sacred and profane, while expressing anxieties over practices that appear to cross or contravene such demarcations. She also argues that ideas of boundedness are very frequently expressed through metaphors of the body, whose integrity is to be protected through avoiding activities that may pen-etrate its borders in socially unsanctioned ways such as eating the wrong foods or engag-ing in illicit sexual activity.

For the Brazilian Catholics studied by Parker (2009: 82–83), the association between sex and spiritual pollution was so well established that the words 'sin' and 'sex' were understood to be virtually synonymous. Islamic Bedouin women in Egypt demonstrate a similar understanding of the dangers of sex as they uphold practices of veiling and modesty in order to efface their own sexuality and in so doing minimize the threat that they pose to the social system (Abu-Lughod 1986). Religious concerns regarding the sexual lives of adherents can be seen on a larger scale as Islamic groups ally themselves with the Vatican to oppose moves to enshrine women's reproductive freedom in UN declarations (Petchesky 2003: 229).

A particularly striking example of the interaction between sanctioned religious authority and sexual infraction is provided by the sexual scandals surrounding the supposedly celibate Roman Catholic priesthood in many countries. Kathryn Lofton (2012) has reviewed the documents surrounding such abuses in the United States, and notes how they occurred in the context of hierarchical relationships, both possessive and devotional in relation to younger parishioners, where clergy simultaneously drew on and effectively undermined their ritual authority as representatives of the Church.

As well as activities that are spiritually sanctioned or spiritually taboo, there are sexual practices for which there is no obvious frame of reference at all. An example is provided by the Afro-Brazilian religion Candomblé, which involves forms of possession and animism (investing the natural world with spiritual significance). As a religious culture Candomblé has been noted to be particularly accepting of male homosexuality. Openly gay men preside at many shrines in positions of spiritual leadership, and gay and straight members alike are quick to point out the comparatively liberal attitudes of leaders and laity to sexual matters (Van De Port 2005: 11–16). Gay women have struggled to achieve the same prominence, however—a fact that may have its roots in the theological underpinnings of the faith. Practitioners engage in rituals in which human suppliants are possessed by one of a pantheon of divine beings in a ritual process described as 'mounting'. While penetrative sex between men can be understood within the idioms of mounting, sex between women, though not explicitly advocated or condemned, is rendered literally 'unspeakable' in terms of the wider spiritual grammar (Allen 2012).

This issue of congruence between belief and practice becomes particularly pertinent in an era of increased globalization, where networks of media and migration allow habits and ideas regarding sex to move across cultural and national borders (Boellstorff 2005: 575). Men who have sex with and form romantic relationships with other men in Indonesia, for instance, may adopt the Western label 'gay' to describe their sexual lives and identities; but there is no easy analogy for this term in their own culture, and it is not interpretable within local understandings of Islam (Boellstorff 2005). These men are therefore obliged to perform individual exegeses of love and relationships, forging personal theologies in order to incorporate their sexual lives within a wider Muslim identity (Boellstorff 2005; see also Blackwood 2005).

Similar struggles of incorporation mark the current debates surrounding homosexuality in the Christian Church. The Bible itself is relatively silent on the subject of same-sex sexual practices. The authors of both Testaments seem more concerned with the spiritual significance and regulation of heterosexual marriage, particularly in its reproductive functions, in a manner broadly congruent with the concerns more widely observed within patriarchal societies (see Hunt 2009: 2; Pagels 2011). The growth of lesbian, gay, bisexual, and transgender (LGBT) movements over the last fifty years in many Christian and nominally Christian societies has brought about a more sustained engagement with alternative sexualities and illuminates differences in the various streams of global Christianity. Liberal theologies may highlight the theme of alienation that features in the stories of many gay men and women, drawing this experience into a wider Christian narrative of reconciliation between humanity and God (Lawless 2003: 72). In more conservative streams, however, the incorporation of the concept of homosexuality within official and folk doctrines often denies the inclusion of homosexuals themselves. For many conservative Christians the identities of sexually active gay men and women are considered to be irreconcilable with those of believers to the extent that 'homosexual' has become incorporated into grammars of faith as 'unsaved'. In these movements, non-heterosexuality may be pathologized as evidence of spiritual disorder or even demonic assault from which the adherent requires salvation or healing (see Csordas 1994: 105; Griffifth 1997: 125).

Rather different questions of reproduction in both cultural and physical senses are explored by Louise Ryan and Elena Vacchelli (2013) in their exploration of parenting strategies among mothers of diverse Muslim backgrounds in London. In this case study, mothers are shown to use conservative interpretations of Islamic beliefs and practices to underpin their parenting strategies and to make sense of and give meaning to their experiences and encounters in Britain (2013: 90). Thus religion here both teaches children 'right' and 'wrong' and indicates what are perceived as morally lax attitudes to gender roles and sexuality within the British population at large. In turn, however (2013: 91), gender roles, cultural identities, and religious practices may become sites of intergenerational conflict between migrant Muslim parents and their British-born children.

Power, Protest, and Change

Religious hierarchies associated with gender, sexuality, and sexual reproduction take on political importance in situations of cross-cultural encounter. Those who have found themselves subject to the proselytizing efforts of Christian missionaries and colonialists have often found their existing forms of reproductive organization devalued and even regarded as sinful in the new spiritual context. So it was for the Kaliai people of Papua New Guinea whose preferred system of cross-cousin marriage was termed incest upon the arrival of missionaries and colonial administrators (Lattas 1991: 233), and the traditionally polygamous people of southern Zimbabwe who were informed that the Bible insisted that for a man to have more than one wife was a sin (Engelke 2004a: 78). Relations of domination can themselves be understood in terms of gender. For the Kaliai the God of Christianity was seen as an unequivocally masculine force, in the face of which the locals were endowed in their own imagination with a distinctly feminine passivity. In their origin legends women had been usurped in their prior leadership by men, and they perceived themselves to be similarly alienated within the new order of their world (Lattas 1991).

Such frameworks of subjugation may inspire their own narratives of resistance. The leader of one of the Kaliai cargo-cults that have sprung up in response to the new Christian colonial regime offers 'a powerful deconstructive reading of biblical mythology' as he insists that white people arose from the sexual union of the Virgin Mary with a snake, hidden knowledge that both explains and further reveals the duplicity of these agents of colonialism (Lattas 1991: 240–241). A similar sense of the potential falseness of colonial agents is evidenced in the beliefs of some Zimbabwean Christian converts who discovered upon reading the Bible that polygamy was in fact widely in evidence among the patriarchs of the Old Testament. For members of the Masowe WeChishanu movement the lesson taken was that they could not 'trust the whites or their book' and they rejected the necessity of scripture in their own version of Christianity (Engelke 2004a: 78).

These examples illustrate how religious symbols that are apparently shared among groups can become points of key contention. Hermkens et al. (2009) bring together pieces focusing on the Virgin Mary as catalyst for both conservatism and radicalism in the Roman Catholic Church. Earlier in this piece, we saw the Virgin contrasted with the more dynamic figure of Mary Magdalene. But Hermkens et al. (2009: 5) also argue that from the 1970s onwards, liberation and feminist theologies have presented Mary as an alternative role model for women, as a strong, determined figure who takes action in situations of injustice and resists representations of femininity characterized by purity, modesty, obedience, and sacrificial motherhood.

Even within a more unified religious context the faith of individuals can be a route through which the tensions inherent in the models and practices of gender and sexuality are articulated and sometimes overcome. Phyllis Mack (1992: 9–10) indicates how early Quakers expressed their commitment to radicalism and democracy in part through attributing fluid and interchangeable attributes to men and women, with the result that letters and visionary texts written by the first female prophets were often indistinguishable from those written by men. Women might even assume the personae of biblical prophets (1992: 133–134), in the process denying the relevance of class and status differences by refusing to use verbal or body languages of deference, even as they insisted that they preached as disembodied spirits 'in the light', not as women or men per se.

Possession has typically been approached by anthropologists as a realm in which otherwise proscribed behaviours are awarded temporary licence, and marginal actors are able to partake in a wider range of expression on behalf of the spirit that animates them (Bowie 2006: 278). Female members of the Zar cult in Sudan are plagued by spirit visitors who index and give rise to physical and psychic traumas, particularly the misfortunes of unstable family ties or difficulties bearing healthy male children. Though these visitations are in general regarded as unwelcome, they provide a period during which women are able to act in transgression of local feminine norms of 'dignity and propriety' and burlesque the behaviours of men (Boddy 1989: 131). The logics of possession seem to lend a similar licence to women in Pentecostal churches in America who, filled with the Holy Spirit, may testify for hours in churches where women are not permitted to preach (Lawless 1983).

We must, however, be wary of viewing articulations of difference as innately oppressive, and all expressions of agency as resistance. Though the opposition of masculine and feminine is an important symbolic principle in many faiths, it is important that we do not draw from the prevalence of this opposition an assumption that the relationship between women and men is necessarily adversarial (Strathern 1987: 45). In her study of Catholics in rural north-east Brazil, Mayblin (2011) pursues this point. The men and women she worked with considered the genders as different in crucial ways, but as equally capable of embodying the religious flaw of pride as well as the virtue of sacrifice. The shared responsibilities to eschew the former and embrace the latter were played out in the theatre of marriage, in which husbands and wives were equally susceptible to pride, equally concerned with social position, and equally powerful in their ability to devastate the lives of one another. In some cases, religion may work as a force that actively reduces difference in the preoccupations and aspirations of men and women. Brusco points out that in her study of Catholics in Brazil, religious conversion can become a force for peace in the household. Women whose husbands had entered into evangelical styles of faith found that their converted husbands, able to pursue a new kind of masculinity outside of the traditional fields of drinking and gambling, became more involved fathers and the heads of more peaceful homes (Brusco 1997).

The fact that global Christianities tend to privilege the experience and narrative forms of conversion means that change, at the social and individual level, is perhaps most apparent as a theme in studies of Christians. It may be the case, however, that the Western, Christian background of anthropology as a science (see Cannell 2005) means that we are prevented from clearly seeing change that is meaningful outside of our own cultural framework. Western understandings of individual agency, inherited within much secular social thought and liberal feminism, tend to paint individuation and autonomy as the ultimate aspiration of every human being. Following the removal from power of the Taliban during the 2001 'War on Terror' there was some surprise among Western liberals that Afghan women did not immediately remove their burqas, the all-over garment that they had come to recognize as a symbol of women's oppression under fundamentalist Islam (Abu-Lughod 2002: 285). For those whose subjectivities are formed in different cultural contexts, however, there are different understandings of what it means to lead a good life (Dehyle and Margonis 1995; Abu-Lughod 2002; Robbins 2006). If the burqua is considered by the Afghan women who wear it to be an appropriate means of expressing and experiencing piety, modesty, and closeness to God, why would they discard it upon a change of government (Abu-Lughod 2002: 785–786)? One of the challenges for anthropologists considering gender and sexuality cross-culturally, then, is to come to faithful depictions of the forms of change that are meaningful in a given cultural context, a consideration which lends an ongoing significance to our own disciplinary engagement with religion.

CONCLUSION

Several factors lie behind anthropological understandings of the connections between religion, gender, and sexuality, as well as the shifting and growing interest in the intersections among these themes in recent decades. One important factor is the evolving understanding of gender itself as both a subject for anthropologists to study and a force that has influenced the way scholars themselves have constructed their own discipline. Henrietta Moore (1988) has argued that a significant shift occurred in the early 1970s, as writers began to confront issues of how women were represented in anthropological writing. She quotes (1988: 3) the well-known theory of 'muted groups' proposed by Edwin Ardener (1975), which suggests that dominant groups in society will both generate and control dominant modes of expression, so that if muted groups wish to express themselves they are forced to do so via such modes of expression. We can certainly see how such a perspective might be taken in relation to some of the members of the religious communities we have described in this chapter, but Moore's point is that it might also be applied to anthropology itself, which has tended to order the world 'in a male idiom'.

In thinking about these more reflexive themes, we might consider cases where authorship of jointly produced work has sometimes been attributed more to a male than to a female writer (for a discussion, see Engelke 2004b). We might also think of the writing process itself. In her study of pilgrimage in a Greek island shrine, Jill Dubisch (1995: 3) argues that gender is an important biographical element that has affected her work, and that it is a factor that should not be ignored by seeing the author as gender-neutral in what is observed, analysed, or written. Her work on the pilgrimage site has thus enabled her to explore a number of topics that have multiple significance (1995: 8), including religion, gender, performance, and the nature of Greekness; but also anthropological issues of fieldwork, reflexivity, the nature of anthropological writing, and questions associated with being both a woman and an anthropologist. Dubisch highlights some of the political and epistemological dilemmas of such work, including (1995: 11) the thorny issue of whether female (or male, for that matter) experience can be viewed as sufficiently universal to highlight common issues of oppression or dominance across cultures.

This last dilemma—that of taking cultural, social, often taken-for-granted context into account, while also looking for human universals—is central to the anthropological enterprise at large. One of its strengths in studies of religion is that it has been able to show the difficulty of isolating religion as a lived practice not only from such factors as gender, but also from other features that make up daily social life. We have seen this point illustrated a number of times in this chapter, including Ryan and Vacchelli's explorations of how the migrant experience of parenting both helps to constitute and is constituted by Muslim attitudes to gender and sexuality, as well as Shoshana Feher's explorations of intersections among Orthodox Judaism, gender discriminations, and the world of work in addition to that of the synagogue. A further powerful example of the point, this time related to class, is provided by João Vasconcelos (2007) in an analysis of spirit mediumship at Christian Rationalist Séances in Cape Verde. Vasconcelos remarks on the remarkable congruence between such religious morality and the ethos of middle-class womanhood on the island. Mediums need the time to stay at home and the education to be able to speak well and so tend to be middle-aged as well as middle class. Thus we see how religious practice is often intertwined with other circumstances and social or cultural arrangements in ways that make it very difficult to separate out abstract religious propositions from lived experience and social structures.

This is not to say that anthropology cannot learn from other disciplines including theology, in the study of religion and gender. In a piece on the relationship between theology and anthropology, Joel Robbins (2006: 288) suggests that one discipline can shine where the other falters. While anthropologists have historically sought to show that difference in the world is not only possible but that it exists in abundance, we have at times struggled to convince our audiences and ourselves that the differences we find might have meaning for our own lives. Here, Robbins suggests, theologians have the upper hand, as their discussions of social life have been underpinned by a belief in the possibility of its transformation. Though these disciplines may differ in their understandings of the kinds of changes that are desirable, and how they might be brought about, each argues that there are indeed other ways to live. Theology may therefore present to anthropology the challenge that visions of a better world can not only be described but perhaps more fully realized, even if, as demonstrated in this chapter, the form that this 'better world' would take cannot be assumed (Abu-Lughod 2002). Research on gender and sexuality sheds light on visions of different worlds that are reached towards not only in the exotic rituals of cultural 'others' but also in the everyday circumstances of one's own life. In the symbolic languages of gender, the everyday engagements of the body, the reproduction of the family, and the forms given to desire, religious visions of the relationship between humankind and transcendent forces are formed, affirmed, and contested.

REFERENCES

Abu-Lughod, L. (1986). *Veiled Sentiments: Honour and Poetry in a Bedouin Society*. Berkeley and Los Angeles: University of California Press.

Abu-Lughod, L. (2002). 'Do Muslim Women Really Need Saving? Anthropological Reflections on Cultural Relativism and Its Others'. *American Anthropologist*, 105: 783–790.

Allen, A. (2012). ' "Brides" without Husbands: Lesbians in the Afro-Brazilian Religion Candomble'. *Transforming Anthropology*, 20(1): 17–31.

Almeida, M. (1997). 'Gender, Masculinity and Power in Southern Portugal'. *Social Anthropology*, 5(2): 141–158.

Anderson, J. (2007). 'The Contest of Moralities: Negotiating Compulsory Celibacy and Sexual Intimacy in the Roman Catholic Priesthood'. *Australian Journal of Anthropology*, 18(1): 1–17.

Ardener, E. (1975). 'The "Problem" Revisited'. In S. Ardener (ed.), *Perceiving Women*. London: Malaby, 19–27.

Asad, T. (1983). 'Anthropological Concepts of Religion: Reflections on Geertz'. *Man*, ns 18: 237–259.

Austin-Broos, D. (1997). *Ja'maica Genesis: Religion and the Politics of Moral Orders*. Chicago: University Of Chicago Press.

Balzer, M. (1996). 'Sacred Genders in Siberia: Shamans, Bear Festivals, and Androgyny'. In S. Ramet (ed.), *Gender Reversals and Gender Cultures: Anthropological and Historical Perspectives*. London: Routledge, 164–182.

Bell, S., and E. J. Sobo (2001). 'Celibacy in Cross-Cultural Perspective: An Overview'. In Bell and Sobo (eds), *Celibacy Culture and Society: The Anthropology of Sexual Abstinence*. Madison: University of Wisconsin Press, 3–26.

Bilu, Y. (2003). 'From Milah (Circumcision) to Milah (Word): Male Identity and Rituals of Childhood in the Jewish Ultraorthodox Community'. *Ethos*, 31(2): 172–203.

Blackwood, E. (2005). 'Tombois in West Sumatra: Constructing Masculinity and Erotic Desire'. In J. Robertson (ed.), *Same-Sex Cultures and Sexualities: An Anthropological Reader*. Oxford: Blackwell, 232–260.

Boddy, J. (1989). *Wombs and Alien Spirits: Men and Women in the Zar Cult in North Africa*. Madison: University of Wisconsin Press.

Boellstorff, T. (2005). 'Between Religion and Desire: Being Muslim and Gay in Indonesia'. *American Anthropologist*, 107(4): 575–585.

Boellstorff, T. (2007). 'Queer Studies in the House of Anthropology'. *Annual Review Of Anthropology*, 36: 17–35.

Bowie, F. (2006). *The Anthropology of Religion: An Introduction*. Oxford: Blackwell.

Brusco, E. (1997). 'The Peace That Passes All Understanding: Violence, the Family, and Fundamentalist Knowledge in Columbia'. In J. Brink and J. Mencher (eds), *Mixed Blessings: Gender and Religious Fundamentalism Cross-Culturally*, London: Routledge, 12–24.

Cannell, F. (2005). 'The Christianity of Anthropology'. *Journal of the Royal Anthropological Institute*, 11: 335–356.

Csordas, T. (1994). *The Sacred Self: A Cultural Phenomenology of Charismatic Healing*. Berkeley and Los Angeles: University of California Press.

Dehyle, D., and F. Margonis (1995). 'Navajo Mothers and Daughters: Schools, Jobs, and the Family'. *Anthropology And Education Quarterly*, 26(2): 135–167.

Douglas, M. (1966). *Purity and Danger: An Analysis of Concepts of Pollution and Taboo*. London: Routledge.

Dubisch, J. (1995). *In a Different Place: Pilgrimage, Gender, and Politics at a Greek Island Shrine*. Princeton: Princeton University Press.

Elliston, D. (2005). 'Erotic Anthropology: "Ritualised Homosexuality" in Melanesia and Beyond'. In J. Robertson (ed.), *Same-Sex Cultures And Sexualities: An Anthropological Reader*, Oxford: Blackwell, 91–115.

Engelke, M. (2004a). 'Text and Performance in an African Church'. *American Ethnologist*, 31(1): 76–91.

Engelke, M. (2004b). ' "The Endless Conversation": Fieldwork, Writing, and the Marriage of Victor and Edith Turner'. In R. Handler (ed.), *Significant Others: Interpersonal and Professional Commitments in Anthropology*. Madison: University of Wisconsin Press, 6–50.

Fedele, A. (2013). *Looking for Mary Magdalene: Alternative Pilgrimage and Ritual Creativity at Catholic Shrines in France*. Oxford: Oxford University Press.

Feher, S. (1998). *Passing Over Easter: Constructing the Boundaries of Messianic Judaism*. Walnut Creek, CA: Altamira.

Foucault, Michel [1976] (1998). *The History of Sexuality, i. The Will To Knowledge*. London: Penguin.

Geertz, C. (1973). 'Religion as a Cultural System'. In Geertz (ed.), *The Interpretation of Cultures: Selected Essays*. New York: Basic Books, 87–125.

Gregor, T. (1980). *The Mehinaku: The Drama of Daily Life in A Brazilian Indian Village*. Chicago: University of Chicago Press.

Griffith, R. (1997). *God's Daughters: Evangelical Women and the Power of Submission*. London: University of California Press.

Hardacre, H. (1990). 'Gender and the Millennium in Omotokyo: A Japanese New Religion'. *Senri Ethnological Studies*, 29: 47–62.

Harding, S. (2000). *The Book Of Jerry Falwell: Fundamentalist Language and Politics*. Princeton: Princeton University Press.

Hastrup, K. (1993). 'The Semantics of Biology: Virginity'. In S. Ardener (ed.), *Defining Females: The Nature Of Women In Society*. Oxford: Berg, 34–50.

Herdt, G. (1981). *Guardians of the Flutes*. New York: Mcgraw Hill.

Hermkens, A.-K., W. Jansen, and C. Notermans (2009). 'Introduction: The Power of Marian Pilgrimage'. In Hermkens, Jansen, and Notermans (eds), *Moved by Mary: the Power of Pilgrimage in the Modern World*. Farnham: Ashgate, 1–13.

Humes, C. (1996). 'Becoming Male: Salvation through Gender Modification in Hinduism and Buddhism'. In S. Ramet (ed.), *Gender Reversals and Gender Cultures: Anthropological and Historical Perspectives*. London: Routledge, 123–137.

Hunt, S. (2009). *Contemporary Christianity and LGBT Sexualities*. Farnham: Ashgate.

Kraemer, C. (2012). 'Gender and Sexuality in Contemporary Paganism'. *Religion Compass*, 8(6): 390–401.

Lattas, A. (1991). 'Sexuality and Cargo Cults: The Politics of Gender and Procreation in West New Britain'. *Cultural Anthropology*, 6(2): 230–256.

Laven, M. (2012). 'Jesuits and Eunuchs: Representing Masculinity in Late Ming China'. *History and Anthropology*, 23(2): 199–214.

Lawless, E. (1983). 'Shouting for the Lord: The Power of Women's Speech in the Pentecostal Religious Service'. *Journal Of American Folklore*, 96(382): 434–459.

Lawless, E. (2003). 'Transforming the Master Narrative: How Women Shift the Religious Subject'. *Frontiers: A Journal of Women's Studies*, 24(1): 61–75.

Lofton, K. (2012). 'Sex Abuse and the Study of Religion'. <http://blogs.ssrc.org/tif/2012/07/06/sex-abuse-and-the-study-of-religion/>.

Longman, C. (2002). 'Empowering and Engendering "Religion": A Critical Perspective on Ethnographic Holism'. *Social Anthropology*, 10: 239–248.

Lyons, A., and D. Lyons (2005). *Irregular Connections: A History of Anthropology ond Sexuality*. London: University of Nebraska Press.

Mack, P. (1992). *Visionary Women: Ecstatic Prophecy in Seventeenth-Century England*. Berkeley and Los Angeles: University of California Press.

Mahmood, S. (2001). 'Feminist Theory, Embodiment, and the Docile Agent: Some Reflections on the Egyptian Islamic Revival'. *Cultural Anthropology*, 16(2): 202–236.

Mayblin, M. (2011). 'Death by Marriage: Power, Pride, and Morality in Northeast Brazil'. *Journal of the Royal Anthropological Institute*, 17: 135–153.

Mitchell, J. (1998). 'Performances of Masculinity in a Maltese Festa'. In F. Hughes-Freeland and M. Crain (eds), *Recasting Ritual: Performance, Media, Identity*. London: Routledge, 68–94.

Moore, H. (1988). *Feminism and Anthropology*. Oxford: Polity.

Nanda, S. (1986). 'The Hijras of India'. *Journal of Homosexuality*, 11(3–4): 35–54.

Ortner, S. (1974). 'Is Female to Male as Nature is to Culture?' In M. Rosaldo and L. Lamphere (eds), *Woman, Culture, and Society*. Stanford, CA: Stanford University Press, 68–87.

Osella, C., and F. Osella (2003). ' "Ayyappan Saranam": Masculinity and the Sabarimala Pilgrimage in Kerala'. *Journal of the Royal Anthropological Institute*, 9: 729–754.

Pagels, E. (2011). *Adam, Eve, and the Serpent: Sex and Politics in Early Christianity*. New York: Vintage.

Parker, K. (2009). *Bodies, Pleasures, and Passions: Sexual Culture in Contemporary Brazil*. 2nd edn. Nashville: Vanderbilt University Press.

Petchesky, R. (2003). 'Negotiating Reproductive Rights'. In J. Weeks, J. Holland, and M. Waites (eds), *Sexualities and Society: A Reader*. Cambridge: Polity, 227–240.

Ramet, S. (1996). 'Gender Reversals and Gender Cultures: An Introduction'. In Ramet (ed.), *Gender Reversals and Gender Cultures: Anthropological and Historical Perspectives*. London: Routledge, 1–21.

Robbins, J. (2006). 'Anthropology and Theology: An Awkward Relationship?' *Anthropological Quarterly*, 79(2): 285–294.

Ryan, L., and E. Vacchelli (2013). ' "Mothering Through Islam": Narratives of Religious Identity in London'. *Religion and Gender*, 3(1): 90–107.

Sanday, P. (1981). *Female Power and Male Dominance: On the Origins of Sexual Inequality*. Cambridge: Cambridge University Press.

Strathern, M. (1987). *The Gender of the Gift: Problems with Women and Problems with Society in Melanesia*. London: University of California Press.

Stewart, A. (2011). 'Text and Response in the Relationship between Online and Offline Religion'. *Information, Communication, and Society*, 14(8): 1204–1218.

Toulis, N. (1997). *Believing Identity: Pentecostalism and the Mediation of Jamaican Ethnicity and Gender in England*. Oxford: Berg.

Turner, V. (1964). 'Betwixt and Between: The Liminal Period in Rites de Passage'. *Proceedings of the American Ethnological Society*, 4–20.

Vasconcelos, J. (2007). 'Learning to be a Proper Medium: Middle-Class Womanhood and Spirit Mediumship at Christian Rationalist Séances in Cape Verde'. In D. Berliner and R. Sarró (eds), *Learning Religion: Anthropological Approaches*. Oxford: Berghahn, 121–140.

Van de Port, M. (2005). 'Candomble in Pink, Green, and Black: Re-Scripting the Afro-Brazilian Religious Heritage in the Public Sphere of Salvador, Bahia'. *Social Anthropology*, 13(1): 3–26.

Wedenoja, W. (2001). 'Mothering and the Practice of "Balm" in Jamaica'. In A. Lehmann and J. Myers (eds), *Magic, Witchcraft, and Religion: An Anthropological Study of the Supernatural* (5th edn.), London: Mayfield, 173–180.

Zborowski, M., and E. Herzog (1974). *Life is with People: The Culture of the Shtetl*. Prague: Schocken Books.

CHAPTER 8

....

CONTRIBUTIONS FROM
SOCIOLOGY

....

MARTA TRZEBIATOWSKA

INTRODUCTION

....

SOCIOLOGISTS are concerned with the way human behaviour is patterned. They search for regularities in large bodies of data about patterns of behaviour, ignore the weak patterns that appear occasionally, and attempt to explain why people do what they do in particular situations. What is of interest to sociologists are correlations between two variables, without falling into the trap of selecting from the research data elements that allow them to construct a plausible interpretation of the discerned pattern. Sociologists, then, look for plausible explanations of phenomena that strike them as important due to their objective prevalence in human social life. Depending on the subject under investigation some explanations will be more plausible than others. In other words, good social science is driven primarily by evidence rather than ideological fervour, or partisan passions.

Having said that, sociologists can also perform a valuable public role. They draw attention to inequalities among different groups in society, and endeavour to account for such inequalities by referring to structural rather than purely psychological and individualistic reasons. Pierre Bourdieu, the eminent French sociologist, believed that if everyone possessed a basic understanding of the underlying mechanisms that cause individuals 'to contribute to their own deprivation' the quality of social relations would be greatly improved (1993: 17). Sociology can certainly provide us with a toolbox for making sense of our own position in the world but it is a little more than that: sociology is a martial art because 'you use it to defend yourself, without having the right to use it for unfair attacks' (Bourdieu 2001).

Thus, for example, the absence of women in the higher echelons of the Catholic Church can be plausibly explained by structurally created and maintained barriers, rather than women's personal dispositions or choices. Leadership in the Catholic Church is defined and presented as an exclusively male domain, something only suitable for men; women are kept out of that realm effortlessly and any attempts to alter the situation are met with unanimous objection, if not ridiculed outright as almost utopian in their exoticism.[1] A sociological analysis of women's position in Catholicism would focus on the institutional relations of power and patterns of organization which make it possible, and indeed natural, to exclude them as a group. It would highlight the operation of the religious system as a whole in explaining the reasons behind and the persistence of exclusionary practices. Moreover, sociologists might look at the role women themselves play in perpetuating their own inferior position in the Church. This is in no way to apportion blame to women for the injustice but rather to stress how all social actors contribute to creating the objective conditions they are part of, however beneficial or harmful the conditions are to them personally.

Gender and sexuality are two of the most obvious social divisions and social markers of division. Gender is omnipresent and dictates the rule of identity and engagement in all social situations to a large extent. The difficulty of studying gender lies in its simultaneous rigidity and fluidity, which are both contextual. In the manner of a chemical substance that changes when coming into contact with other substances, gender manifests itself differently depending on the social situation but, unlike many social roles, it never entirely disappears from view, or loses its relevance. Religion is a social structure which both affects and is affected by gender. The relationship is mutually susceptible. This chapter will outline the social scientific tools for studying religion, gender, and sexuality. It will discuss the extent to which we can learn more about a phenomenon by analysing the relative match between individuals' dispositions on the one hand and opportunities they encounter in their everyday lives on the other.

Central to the argument is the notion that in order to study the intersection of religion, gender, and sexuality in a social scientific manner, we must pay attention to the expectations and norms that are internalized and then used to reproduce the symbolic order they were created in. It is not my intention to explore whether such reproduction is a positive or a negative thing, whether it benefits women, or men, or whether it is inevitable. All of these points have been covered evocatively, and in some detail, by others. The primary focus will be on the need for more collaboration between social scientists and theologians, or religious studies scholars. The following section introduces the basic rules of the sociological practice.

The Nature of the Sociological Inquiry and the Power of Unintended Consequences

It is useful to begin with a description of how sociological research works. The British sociologist W. G. Runciman suggests four stages of a social scientific investigation: reportage,

---

[1] This is not to say that no attempts have been made to address the absence of women in the leadership of the Catholic Church. For sociological accounts of such attempts, see Wallace (1992); Byrne (2011).

explanation, description, and evaluation of human behaviour (Runciman 1983). The role of a sociologist consists of these four elements: collecting information in as many ways and places as possible; producing an understanding of the data and, if possible, establishing correlation and causation (with the important caveat that the first does not automatically imply the second); exercising 'sociological imagination' by attempting to see the point of view of those one describes (seeing the world through their eyes, or 'putting oneself in their shoes'); and finally, the most pragmatically-oriented aspect, that is judging the phenomenon under scrutiny with a view to designing social policy, or helping 'those involved to a course of action leading to political transformation' (Runciman 1983: 40). Empiricists are less concerned with description and evaluation. Neither is useful for their purposes, as 'no methodological conclusions can be drawn from this' apart from the fact that researchers get the opportunity to 'subject the objects of their studies to verbal questionnaires' (Runciman 1983: 40). All four elements of social science are of equal importance and relevance in the task of studying the relationship between religion, gender, and sexuality but it is crucial not to conflate them.

The trouble with studying social life is its simultaneous predictability and irrationality. Therefore constant awareness of the power of unintended consequences of social action constitutes a big part of the sociological task. A poem by the Scottish poet Robert Burns contains the famous line that sums up this aspect of the sociological inquiry beautifully: 'the best-laid schemes o' mice an' men gang aft agley'. Individuals, groups, and institutions may set out to achieve a particular goal but they cannot predict the full outcome of their actions. This is largely because we are only semi-conscious, but mostly unaware, of the totality of social influences that have shaped us.

A good example of this would be the case of North American Catholic convents in the aftermath of the Second Vatican Council. The council was an attempt to soften the authoritarian structures of the Catholic Church and to adapt to cultural needs at the time. The document *Adaptation and Renewal of Religious Life: Perfectae Caritatis* (1965) referred specifically to religious orders. In brief, it advocated an adjustment of the community to the changed conditions of the time (Neal 1990: 52; Ebaugh 1993: 20; Wittberg 1994: 215) and the 'elimination of outmoded customs' (Weaver 1995: 102). Nuns were invited to re-evaluate their community's mission statements and restructure their life so that their apostolic activity became more effective. The Second Vatican Council aimed to alter the social perception of nuns as clerics, which in turn was supposed to diminish the gap between the nuns and the laypeople amongst which they carried out their mission. The elements of the traditional religious orders targeted by the renewal were precisely the ones which marked nuns out as sacred and granted them a special status. They included the habit, the cloister, and the organizing of social relationships with laity (Ebaugh 1993: 23). Habit and veil were to be adjusted to look more modern and in some cases exchanged for normal clothing. This was to encourage laypeople to identify with the nuns rather than see them as distant and elevated figures.

Prior to the Second Vatican Council convents were large institutions, closed to non-members, which housed all sisters in the order in one building. In response to *Perfectae Caritatis* (1965) they were split into smaller units and became more open to lay visitors. Consequently, the physical and social isolation of sisters from the outside world disappeared in the case of apostolic orders. A significant number of nuns were sent to universities where they encountered new ideas and alternative lifestyles. Many began to adopt a feminist rhetoric in their mission statements and everyday life choices. The irony of this, largely positive, shift is that traditional religious orders in America face extinction as more nuns decide to leave and the number of new entrants is low (Ebaugh 1993; Wittberg 1994). This does not mean that the demise of Catholic convents in the United States is inevitable but it does show that what began as a renewal resulted in unforeseen changes that are likely to lead to a decline of the religious institution as we know it. This case illustrates the power of unintended consequences on the institutional and individual level, as well as the difficulty of making future predictions on the basis of sociological research.

STUDYING GENDER AND RELIGION SOCIOLOGICALLY

When sociologists set out to explain some naturally-occurring phenomenon, they generally pursue two lines of enquiry simultaneously. First, they search for regularities in large bodies of information about patterns of behaviour. Second, they endeavour to construct a plausible account of why someone in a particular situation, who holds certain beliefs, values, or attitudes, would choose one course of action over another. That is, sociologists search for a correlation between two measures and then try to ensure that they are not making the *post hoc ergo propter hoc* mistake by finding in actors' accounts of what they are doing, the material that would allow us to construct a plausible interpretation of the discerned pattern.

Gender is one of the most obvious social divisions and social markers of division. Once a gender preference pattern is established, it often becomes self-reinforcing. Some social activities, including those related to religiosity or spirituality, gradually become labelled as feminine or masculine, and the feedback loop becomes self-reinforcing: individuals engage in activities they feel most reflect their identities. Therefore, understanding why women, or men (or those who self-identify as 'between-genders') act the way they do can prove challenging because there is a risk of attributing non-existent motives to social actors. Given the frequency with which a social scientific approach to religion is criticized, two simple propositions are worth making. First, the more and more diverse sources of evidence we have the better. Second, it is unwise to make too much of infrequent and unusual patterns. For instance, it may well be the case that a behaviour or belief initially seems commonplace or popular, but it needs to be scrutinized in the wider context against other factors that are present.

Plausible explanations are far harder to produce in sociology than in the natural sciences. There are many features of human behaviour that make it more difficult to study than chemical processes: one obvious difficulty is that our raw material possesses degrees of self-awareness and degrees of freedom that allow it to change. The chemist need not account for the possibility that a substance may learn from, or reflect on, being mixed with another substance and change its reactions as a result. But sociologists have two distinct advantages over natural scientists. First, they can in various ways collect data from their research participants through interviewing them individually and collectively, reading their diaries and letters, initiating informal conversations that allow to subtly probe, as well as observing them as they go about their everyday activities. Second, sociologists share many of the characteristics of their research participants. Max Weber, one of the founding fathers of sociology, famously used the term *Verstehen* to describe a sociological technique for understanding human action whereby our shared humanity allows us to render meaningful a very wide variety of experiences ([1903–1917] 2011). In order to comprehend what others do, sociologists need to recognize the motivations of the actor as intended by them and also acknowledge the context in which the behaviour occurs and makes sense.

THE SIGNIFICANCE OF GENDER IN THE SOCIOLOGY OF RELIGION

Although gender and sexuality have been central to mainstream sociology since the early 1970s, they only appeared on the agenda of the sub-discipline—the sociology of religion—in the mid-1990s. While feminist theologians critiqued patriarchal religions and strove to redefine the religious language and symbols for women, sociologists of religion were preoccupied with the secularization debate (e.g. Berger 1967; Martin 1978; Wilson 1982). In Britain the situation began to change with the publication of a journal article by Tony Walter and Grace Davie (1998) which examined the puzzle of the gender gap in religiosity and symbolically put the question of gender and religiosity on the sociological table. Now the fact that women are more religious than men is considered something of an axiom in the sociology of religion. Both quantitative and qualitative researchers tend to agree that overall women are more likely to describe themselves as religious and/or spiritual, to assent to statements of Christian faith, to believe in life after death, to admit superstitious beliefs and practices, and to engage in New Age spiritualities (Trzebiatowska and Bruce 2012).

The obvious question is, of course, why it took sociologists of religion so long to catch up with reality. Walter and Davie suggest two possible explanations for this (1998). One is the focus of the Protestant churches on the absence of women in leadership roles generally, and female priests and ministers more specifically. Paradoxically, this meant that little attention was paid to the disproportionate numbers of women attending Christian churches in the West. The problem was rectified when the data was finally acknowledged by both sociologists and historians (Davie 2007). The second explanation has to do with the concept of patriarchy and its sociological application to the study of mainstream religious traditions. If religions are irredeemably patriarchal, then women should be leaving oppressive and restrictive religious institutions that act against their interests. At the same time the gender gap in churches widened and men were leaving faster than women. The dominant theoretical framework lagged behind the social changes and, as Grace Davie points out, it was easier to ignore the emerging data than to revise it (2007).

This much-needed revision manifested itself most strongly in Callum Brown's account of the decline of religion in Britain (2001, 2012) and Linda Woodhead's work on 'gendering the secularization theory' (2007). Both authors bring women's behaviour and experiences into the spotlight, albeit they adopt slightly different approaches. In his *Death of Christian Britain* Brown, a social historian, explains the rapid decline of Christianity in Britain in the second half of the twentieth century, as a direct result of 'the simultaneous de-pietisation of femininity and the de-feminisation of piety from the 1960s' (2001: 192). Religion became feminized in the nineteenth century and in the 1960s, as women embraced new secular opportunities in the wake of the sexual revolution, the churches began to empty at an alarming rate because men had already defected.

This argument is updated and developed in Brown's 2012 book *Religion and the Demographic Revolution* where he analyses the role of gender in the secularization processes in Canada, Ireland, UK, and USA since the 1960s. Women still play an important role but they are no longer the solution to the problem of religious decline because they, not men, now leave churches at a faster rate (Brown 2012: 263). More importantly, it has become acceptable for a Western woman to openly declare herself an atheist. The feminine image of Christianity is fading away and being replaced by a more aggressive, militant, and masculine rhetoric in the most successful Christian denominations (Brown 2012: 261).

Woodhead's work echoes Brown to a certain extent but it focuses on the critique of the secularization thesis as a dominant male paradigm which only tells half of the story. Both modernization and secularization are social processes and as such, they are necessarily gendered—experienced differently by men and women—but they have both been considered from the male perspective, taken as the norm. Modernization and secularization go hand in hand. The former creates a world dominated by a rational instrumentalism which is embodied in bureaucracies where people are constrained to interact on the basic of narrow social roles. Modern society is an efficient but soulless place which breaks down communal ties and breeds a sense of alienation in the modern individual.

While men can solve the problem by finding respite from the public realm through family and the home, for women the problem requires a different solution. They are doubly alienated as they already occupy the private sphere and find it unrewarding, hence they need another place to escape to. According to Woodhead (2007), women in post-traditional societies end up doubly deprived as a result of juggling the spheres of work and home simultaneously and becoming dissatisfied with and unfulfilled in both. To illustrate her point Woodhead explains that as women's labour patterns were and still remain different to those of men, their religious behaviour will also differ, depending on their work and lifestyle pattern. She distinguishes between three work patterns in late modern societies: a masculine one based on secular values, a mixture of masculine and feminine, and finally a traditionally feminine option (stay-at-home wives and mothers). The type of religious behaviour will correspond to the lifestyle pattern of particular groups of women. The most traditionally feminine and privatized lifestyle will produce the most traditional and church-based religiosity, while the secular pattern is conducive to irreligiosity. In the middle, there are 'jugglers' who tend to opt for a flexible and individualized form of religiosity—New Age spiritualities (Woodhead 2007).

Both Brown and Woodhead leave no doubt that gender is crucial in the narrative of secularization because it acts as one of the key variables in explaining any social phenomenon sociologically. This brings us to the practical implications of accounting for gender in the social scientific study of religion. Inevitably, sexuality is part and parcel of any such exploration and the topic is discussed in more detail towards the end of this chapter. There are two key debates that have structured this field of study since the 1990s. The first one, concerning the gender imbalance in levels of religious belief, membership, and commitment, is more social scientific in orientation. The second focuses on the position of women in mainstream and minority religions and it is driven by feminist concerns. Predictably, the line between the two becomes rather blurred at times. The remainder of this chapter provides an overview of the debates and offers reflections on possible future directions.[2]

The Universal Gender Gap in Religiosity

Most commentators agree that women are more religious and spiritual than men. Statistical surveys consistently show that the women's involvement in a wide variety of religious practices is disproportionately larger than that of men (see Stark 2002 for an overview). An interesting caveat can be made here. Not only is the gap between genders significantly wider in more secular countries, but it is also greater among those who attend regularly than those who attend rarely. This demonstrates that women are on average more committed and serious about their religious practice than men. If we look at non-Christian worship in Britain, in Islam and Buddhism, men are a majority of regular attenders but when the question is rephrased to read 'do you consider that you are actively practising your religion?' women are more likely than men to describe themselves as observant (Trzebiatowska and Bruce 2012: 5). Although measuring gender differences in religiosity is problematic due to religious and cultural differences between various countries, not to mention the difficulty of translating survey questions, a large body of data shows that the gap is almost universal. This creates an issue for sociologists because, as Rodney Stark remarks (2002), how can we convincingly explain something that is found

---

[2] For a comprehensive account of the impact of secularization on women, see Aune et al. (2008).

universally through references to cultural relativism and social constructionism? Surely, if the difference cuts across cultures and religions, it has to be rooted in biology?

Not necessarily so. Several competing theories have been offered by sociologists as well as psychologists and historians. They can be roughly divided into: gendered socialization (Walter and Davie 1998); risk theory (Miller and Hoffman 1995); degrees of femininity and masculinity (Thompson 1991); power-control theory (Collett and Lizardo 2009); and lagged effects of secularization (Trzebiatowska and Bruce 2012). Though the question about women's greater religiosity can be posed as if it concerned a single unitary social fact, it is actually an amalgam of different social facts, each with their own small explanation, some of which overlap and reinforce each other. That is, the causes of gender differences in religiosity differ with time and place. Insofar as a succinct answer can be produced, it would include several interrelated elements.

First, there is nothing in the biological make-up of men and women that of itself explains the gendered difference in religiosity. Nonetheless, the indisputably different biological role of women and men in reproduction directs women to the social role of carer and thus creates the framework within which complex gendered divisions of labour can be created, sustained, and elaborated. Women's primary responsibility for socialization of children keeps them closer than men to organized religion, makes more attractive belief in the afterlife, and sustains attitudes that find expression in the broader cultural worlds of contemporary spirituality. Second, the role of religion in the control of human sexuality gives men an interest in pressing women to adhere closely to the dominant religious culture. It may also give women who find male sexual demands oppressive a good reason to embrace and promote personal piety. Third, dominant notions of masculine toughness militate against attention to physical and psychological health.[3] This often means that interest in bodily purity — peripheral in more mainstream religion but central to many new religious movements and to holistic spirituality — attracts women more than men.

There is one important point to add to this. The hitherto proposed answers to the question of women's greater religiosity rely on relatively rigid definitions of femininity and masculinity. The inflexible categories of women and men are particularly noticeable in the theories which explain gender differences in religiosity through risk-taking. Risk-preference theorists propose that women are more likely to believe in the supernatural because they are more risk-averse than men, and thus bet the right way in Pascal's wager. In her critical commentary on the nature of the debate on women's greater religiosity, Marie Cornwall (2009) points out that this explanation is premised on a crude and dated definition of both: men and women, and masculinity and femininity. According to Cornwall, contributors to the debate are unreflexive in their use of terminology and concepts that belong more comfortably in the Parsonian sociology of the 1950s. Most mainstream gender scholars would be highly critical of explaining the

---

[3] The persistence of 'masculine toughness' as the norm will differ, depending on social class, education, race, and ethnicity, as well as sexual orientation. Undeniably, dominant definitions of what it means to be a man are shifting but the shift is uneven and its effects tend to be overestimated in the media and popular discourses (O'Brien et al. 2005).

gender gap in religiosity through 'universal' differences between men and women, while ignoring (or dismissing as irrelevant) the social processes that structure masculinities and femininities.

In current sociological thought gender is conceptualized as an institution (hence a macro-phenomenon in itself), which means that it cannot be read as a fixed set of traits and behaviours that span across cultures and nations. Men and women are account-able to the culturally constructed gender order and a lot of gendered behaviour rests on the pressure to act in accordance with a culturally given script (Cornwall 2009: 253). Therefore, for example, quantitative survey respondents may be doing gender when tick-ing boxes or answering open-ended questions. Moreover, the measures used in ques-tionnaires are in themselves social constructs. We know that what is considered devout behaviour for a woman (or a man) will vary, depending on the context. Christianity, Islam, Hinduism, and Judaism make different demands of men and women and com-plex power relations are at play at the level of everyday interactions.

To complicate the matter further, what is required of a 'good Muslim' differs from what would qualify someone as a 'good Christian'. This means that gender processes in themselves are key to any explanation of religiosity because men and women do not act in a vacuum. Their actions are mediated by what they understand themselves to be in a particular social situation and what others expect them to act like. Qualitative research-ers encounter similar bias, depending on the gender of both interviewers and inter-viewees (Williams and Hikes 1993; Sallee and Harris 2011). Although Cornwall aims her criticism at the proponents of the risk explanation specifically, the problem she identi-fies could be extended easily to most work on the gender gap in religiosity produced to date. This reductionism is understandable (and perhaps inevitable) as comparisons require us to define the objects under scrutiny as clearly and efficiently as possible for the sake of methodological rigour. Nonetheless, our constantly developing understand-ing of how gender operates, how it is negotiated, constructed and deconstructed, under-mined and reinforced, manipulated and imposed, means that such simplifications now appear inadequate and redundant. As Cornwall remarks, 'the more interesting ques-tions, when it comes to gender and religiosity, are about the gendering processes that constitute religious expression, experience, and religiosity differently for women and men' (2009: 254).

Perhaps the quest for one definitive answer should be abandoned altogether and the attention shifted to documenting and explaining the changes in religious lives of women and men, while also accounting for other identity components, such as ethnicity, race, class, and sexuality.

Religion and Sexuality

Religion is inextricably associated with the control of sexuality, and the existing themes in the sociology of religion inevitably centre on the extent to which religious individuals are able to exercise their sexual choices and craft identities in light of religious rules and regulations. Because it is often a source of tension and conflict and because parentage often has important implications for inheritance, almost all societies show a strong interest in controlling sexual activity. Who can do what, when, and with whom is the subject of powerful social mores and these are usually legitimated by being given divine justification and underpinning. Although the high theory of most religions places an equal burden on men and women to control their urges, in almost every society women make the sacrifices that are involved in such control. They continue to be the ones responsible for the collective honour of their community and exercising sexual purity on behalf of men.

However, there appears to be a paucity of sociological research that deals specifically with religion and sexuality in the field of sociology. The existing literature could be divided into three categories: the uneasy relationship between religion and homosexuality, religious regulations of women's reproductive lives and family formation, and female sexuality in the context of the New Religious Movements of the 1970s and 1980s.[4] This analytical framework reflects the dualistic approach to the more general question of human existence: to what extent are we, as individuals, free to act otherwise? And how constrained are we by social structures larger than ourselves?

Unsurprisingly, the bulk of sociological research on the intersection of religion and sexuality is concerned with the question of lesbian, gay, bisexual, and transgender (LGBT) individuals and groups in relation to religious institutions and traditions. Granting visibility and voice to powerless or under-represented social groups has long constituted a pivotal part of the sociological agenda. And so, for example, Melissa Wilcox's meticulously researched monograph *Coming Out in Christianity* (2003) is a congregational study of LGBT Christians in the United States. One of the most salient aspects of Wilcox's book seems to be the role of community in the formation of LGBT identities and the conscious element of forging a very particular type of spirituality as a result of being rejected by one's religious organization (2003: 16).

A useful resource for data on the religion/sexuality link is the project entitled *Religion, Youth and Sexuality: A Multi-Faith Exploration* by Andrew Yip, Michael Keenan, and Sarah-Jane Page (2011).[5] The study covers a number of religious traditions and provides a much-needed overview of how young people manage their religious and sexual identities in twenty-first-century Britain. Similar themes are explored by various contributors in the interdisciplinary volumes *Contemporary Christianity and LGBT Sexualities* (2009), edited by Stephen Hunt, and *Religion, Gender and Sexuality in Everyday Life* (2012) edited by Peter Nynas and Andrew Yip. While the former focuses primarily on non-heterosexuals, the latter contains reflections on a wide range of sexualities and

---

[4] For example, a lot of research attention has focused on the sexual behaviour of members in some of the most notorious New Religious Movements, such as the Children of God or the Osho Movement, but the analysis was necessarily locked into the liberation/restriction debate (see, for example, Puttick 1999; Boeri 2002).

[5] Full details of the project can be found at <http://www.nottingham.ac.uk/sociology/research/projects/rys/index.aspx>.

religious contexts. Both collections demonstrate the Janus-faced relationship between religion, gender, and sexuality evidenced most clearly in the constant interplay between oppression and liberation. Relatively absent are studies of sexual behaviour of individuals who consider religion to be a big part of their identity. This could be partly a result of the general secular tendency in mainstream sociology, combined with the automatic association of sexual expression (and thus a potentially rich pool of data) with secular (and sometimes even overtly anti-religious) attitudes. Consequently, researching sexual attitudes and behaviours among individuals who identify as religious has been, yet again, the domain of interdisciplinary researchers.

While the subject matter and questions posed in the publications just discussed are crucial in the sociological task of exposing inequalities in religious institutions, championing diversity and tolerance, as well as exploring the nuances of identity formation in the globalized and mediatized world, very little attention has been given to the sexual experiences of heterosexual religious men and women. In a way, this is not surprising. Minority groups and non-mainstream sexualities constitute important research subjects for sociologists because of their often disadvantaged status and invisibility. Moreover, studying such groups provides a valuable insight into the complexity of human behaviour, which can further illuminate our understanding of the social world as a whole.

Paradoxically, however, a critique of heteronormativity means that sexual identities and experiences that fall into the realm of the socially normative are perceived as unproblematic and thus remain unexplored. Sonya Sharma's work fills this gap to a certain extent. Her elegantly written, and data-rich, book *Good Girls, Good Sex* (2011) explores the constant negotiation between oppression and liberation which young Protestant women engage in on a daily basis. Her study is notable for its focus on (predominantly) heterosexual Christian women and shows the struggle between religious values and personal lives. Sharma's research participants highlighted the power of accountability to their religious tradition, as well as to their fellow Christians, that can provide a comfortable buffer against the oversexualized and secular mainstream society. At the same time this accountability restricts their individual sexual freedom and choices. Perhaps the most striking aspect of this study is the evident difficulty of separating religious and sexual identities—the two are locked together and mutually susceptible against the wider background of the church community.

Religion, Gender, and Value-Neutral Research

Questioning whether religion is bad or good for women (and men), or whether it reinforces male domination, or can be a tool of liberation for women (and men) can be helpful, and such debates do much to further the conversation on the condition and future direction of religious groups and institutions. However, there is another possibility. One constructive way of analysing the relationship between gender and religion would be to adopt a more value-neutral approach. Fact and value should not be confused, and the latter has a very particular place in the social sciences. Obviously, it would be naïve to assume that values should, or can, be eliminated entirely from research, but equally researchers should always inform their audience of their value positions and to keep out value judgement in the process of data collection (Weber [1903–1917] 2011). It follows that we can examine the mechanism behind the creation of the religious conditions in which both women and men find themselves, and thus understand and explain why they do what they do, without necessarily adopting a political agenda at the outset. Instead, data collection should be guided by as little prejudgement as possible and only when objective inequalities are demonstrated in the field of study should value judgements enter the research process.

To give an example, it makes little sense, from the point of view of a rational social actor, to remain voluntarily in a religious tradition that restricts one's freedom of choice as an individual. As Daphne Hampson famously put it: 'for a feminist to be a Christian is indeed for her to swallow a fishbone' (1996: 1). In other words, to be aware of one's prison and remain in it is, to many, incomprehensible. If one were to adhere to this logic (and many do), religious women may be of little interest to a feminist sociologist. She, or he, would assume that to study pious women is futile because their choices can only be put down to false consciousness. And yet qualitative studies of women in conservative religions show that patriarchy in religious settings can be shut out, pushed aside, and comfortably ignored, precisely because of the seemingly restrictive gender segregation on which the groups are based.

Plenty of rich and sophisticated ethnographies demonstrate the complexities of women's membership and involvement in conservative religious institutions. Brenda Brasher's *Godly Women* (1998), R. Marie Griffith's *God's Daughters* (2000), Deborah Kaufman's *Rachel's Daughters* (1991), Lynn Davidman's *Tradition in a Rootless World* (1991), Elizabeth Brusco's *Reformation of Machismo* (1995), Maria Frahm-Arp's *Professional Women in South African Pentecostal Charismatic Churches* (2010), and Christel Manning's *God Gave Us the Right* (1999) all offer a wide range of fascinating examples of how modern women use their religions for the purposes of personal fulfilment and negotiate the contradictions of their respective cultures (see also Ozorak 1996; Mihelich and Storrs 2003; Hartman and Marmon 2004; Yadgar 2006). How do we make sense of this data without falling into the trap of dismissing the women's agency as motivated by false consciousness, or overemphasizing the liberating aspect of the religion while ignoring the structural inequalities?

This is where we can benefit from the sociological toolkit. The guiding theoretical light of this chapter, Pierre Bourdieu, believed that 'the degree to which the world is really determined is not a question of opinion: as a sociologist it is not for me to be "for determinism" or "for freedom", but to discover necessity, if it exists, in the place where it is' (1993: 25). Discovering necessity in the study of religion and gender means uncovering the underlying mechanisms and relations of power that govern particular social fields. This can only be done through relying on empirical evidence and data in forming sociological arguments. Evidence matters because it enables the researcher to unearth structural causes for what appear to be highly personalized and idiosyncratic phenomena.

In the case of religion and gender, emphasis needs to be placed on the amount of work and effort that is invested in presenting the relationship between women and men as natural and ahistorical. Social institutions—the family, religious bodies, the state, the educational system, the media—all contribute to creating the illusion that the gender order is eternal and pre-given, therefore commonsensical and 'just-so'. This commonsensical view of the world, however, is the collection of experiences, beliefs, and norms internalized by individuals throughout their lives, therefore both internal and external to them. This operational toolkit works to match individual expectations to the objective reality, which partly explains why a young woman brought up in a Pakistani village will follow the religious expectations of her community while mistaking them for her own preferences.

The structural and the individual are interconnected and difficult to disentangle. Most individuals do not question the order of gender and there are relatively few transgressions and subversions, which is exactly how the normative order reproduces itself effortlessly. Part of the reason for such lack of subversion is the operation of *symbolic violence* in its reproduction (Bourdieu 1984). Symbolic violence refers to an invisible, subtle coercion exerted over the dominated group. The trouble with challenging masculine domination (in religion, for example) is that even when doing so women are drawing on the 'modes of thought that are the product of domination' (Bourdieu 2001: 5). The ethnographic studies described earlier exhibit this problem to various degrees. Women form female-only groups, or enclaves, convert to a religion that places them in a more advantageous position in the otherwise oppressive system, or skilfully redefine and manipulate religious practices and rituals they find problematic. In this sense, the semi-conscious formative gendering process plays itself out relatively safely because no direct threat is ever levelled against the existing symbolic order, thus ensuring its permanence.

Gender order operates tacitly to the point that neither women nor men fully realize the degree to which they reproduce the relationship of domination through their everyday actions. Even when women draw on the aforementioned strategies to undermine this relationship, they usually end up further reinforcing the androcentric view. This is because their own strategies of resistance are rooted in the very symbols and myths they try to undermine. In a way, unless the tools of emancipation are drawn from outside of the religious traditions they aim to undermine, the potential for subversion, and in effect change, may be slight. This is not to say the relationship between gender and religion remains rigid and unchanged.

It appears that there are several possibilities for the interaction between gender and religion: religions remain overwhelmingly male-dominated, with women leaving at a fast pace; women gain access to positions of power and authority but religious institutions become feminized at all levels; new forms of spirituality are set up by women and for women (for example, the overwhelming majority of women in holistic spiritualities as shown by Heelas and Woodhead 2005). The potential for wide structural change comes from the internal inconsistencies and contradictions in the individuals' own biographies and in the system they inhabit. Mere awareness of gender divisions and inequalities in religion will not suffice to effect transformation, however. Collective efforts, not individual action, lead to gradual transformation of seemingly monolithic structures. The women who engage in subversive practices in private make a difference to their personal lives but their actions only count if they have tangible social consequences.

Conclusion

Interdisciplinary research on the intersection of religion and gender has flourished in the past few decades. Admittedly, in Britain most of this work has been carried out by theologians, religious studies scholars, and religious practitioners, while the contributions from sociologists have been relatively few.[6] In order to advance the sociological study of religion, gender, and sexuality, the continuing importance of religion in the public sphere needs to be acknowledged by mainstream sociologists (and feminist sociologists, in particular). That religious practitioners and scholars who have a personal investment in all things spiritual readily engage with the subject goes without saying, and a wealth of enlightening material is produced as a result.

If the interaction between religion and gender is to be taken seriously, secular scholars need to examine religion as a variable in its own right, not as an element of identity that stands for ethnicity, race, or cultural difference. This is not an easy task, especially since secular feminism and traditional religion have never made easy bedfellows (King 1995). It would be beneficial for both sides to combine the social scientific input from feminist sociologists and the in-depth knowledge and experience of various religious traditions from religious women, in order to conduct truly meaningful and comprehensive studies of what it means to be a religious woman (and man) in the twenty-first century (Llewellyn and Trzebiatowska 2013). In the words of Bourdieu, 'sociology confronts its practitioner with harsh realities; it disenchants' (1993: 10). But a fruitful collaboration with other disciplines could soften the harsh disenchantment and inject hope and potential for a truly socially transformative research. Secular sociologists need to entertain the possibility of change in gender relations within religious contexts, and religious scholars could learn from the sociological method of inquiry to understand better the structurally determined mechanisms which make the symbolic gender order so resistant to change.

---

[6] Feminist philosophers have been far more vocal than sociologists in this regard. See, for example, Braidotti (2008) and Butler (2008).

References

Adaptation and Renewal of Religious Life: Perfectae Caritatis (1965).

Aune, K., S. Sharma, and G. Vincett (2008) (eds). *Women and Religion in the West: Challenging Secularization*. Farnham: Ashgate.

Berger, P. (1967). *The Sacred Canopy: Elements of a Sociological Theory of Religion*. New York: Anchor Books.

Boeri, M. W. (2002). 'Women After the Utopia: The Gendered Lives of Former Cult Members'. *Journal of Contemporary Ethnography*, 31: 323–360.

Bourdieu, P. (1984). *Distinction: A Social Critique of the Judgment of Taste*. London: Routledge.

Bourdieu, P. (1993). *Sociology in Question*. London: Sage.

Bourdieu, P. (2001). *Masculine Domination*. Cambridge: Polity Press.

Braidotti, R. (2008). 'In Spite of the Times: The Postsecular Turn'. *Journal of Theory, Culture and Society*, 25: 1–24.

Brasher, B. E. (1998). *Godly Women: Fundamentalism and Female Power*. New Brunswick, NJ: Rutgers University Press.

Brown, C. (2001). *The Death of Christian Britain: Understanding Secularisation 1800-2000*. London: Routledge.

Brown, C. (2012). *Religion and the Demographic Revolution: Women and Secularisation in Canada, Ireland, UK and USA since the 1960s*. Woodbridge: Boydell Press.

Brusco, E. E. (1995). *The Reformation of Machismo: Evangelical Conversion and Gender in Columbia*. Austin: University of Texas Press.

Butler, J. (2008). 'Sexual Politics, Torture, and Secular Time'. *British Journal of Sociology*, 59: 1–23.

Byrne, L. (2011). *Woman at the Altar: The Ordination of Women in the Catholic Church*. New York: Continuum.

Collett, J., and O. Lizardo (2009). 'A Power-Control Theory of Gender and Religiosity'. *Journal for the Scientific Study of Religion*, 48: 213–231.

Cornwall, M. (2009). 'Reifying Sex Difference is Not the Answer: Gendering Processes, Risk and Religiosity'. *Journal for the Scientific Study of Religion*, 48: 252–255.

Davidman, L. (1991). *Tradition in a Rootless World: Women Turn to Orthodox Judaism*. Berkeley and Los Angeles: University of California Press.

Davie, G. (2007). *Sociology of Religion*. London: Sage.

Ebaugh, H. R. (1993). *Women in the Vanishing Cloister: Organizational Decline in Catholic Religious Orders in the United States*. New Brunswick, NJ: Rutgers University Press.

Frahm-Arp, M. (2010). *Professional Women in South African Pentecostal Charismatic Churches*. Leiden: Brill, 2010.

Griffith, R. M. (2000). *God's Daughters: Evangelical Women and the Power of Submission*. Berkeley and Los Angeles: University of California Press.

Hampson, D. (1996). 'On Autonomy and Heteronomy'. In D. Hampson (ed.), *Swallowing a Fishbone? Feminist Theologians Debate Christianity*. London: SPCK.

Hartman, T., and N. Marmon (2004). 'Lived Regulations, Systemic Attributions: Menstrual Separation and Ritual Immersion in the Experience of Orthodox Jewish Women'. *Gender & Society*, 18: 389–408.

Heelas, P., and Woodhead, L. (2005). *The Spiritual Revolution: Why Religion is Giving Way to Spirituality*. Oxford: Blackwell.

Hunt, S. (2009) (ed.). *Contemporary Christianity and LGBT Sexualities*. Farnham: Ashgate.

Kaufman, D. R. (1991). *Rachel's Daughters: Newly Orthodox Jewish Women*. New Brunswick, NJ: Rutgers University Press.

King, U. (1995). 'Gender and the Study of Religion'. In U. King (ed.) *Religion and Gender*, Oxford: Blackwell, 1–40.

Llewellyn, D., and M. Trzebiatowska (2013). 'Secular and Religious Feminisms: A Future of Disconnection?' *Feminist Theology*, 21: 244–258.

Manning, C. (1999). *God Gave Us the Right: Conservative Catholic, Evangelical Protestant and Orthodox Jewish Women Grapple with Feminism*. New Brunswick, NJ: Rutgers University Press.

Martin, D. (1978). *A General Theory of Secularization*. Aldershot: Gregg Revivals.

Mihelich, J., and D. Storrs (2003). 'Higher Education and the Negotiated Process of Hegemony: Embedded Resistance Among Mormon Women'. *Gender & Society*, 17: 404–422.

Miller, A. S., and John P. Hoffman. (1995). 'Risk and Religion: An Explanation of Gender Differences in Religiosity'. *Journal for the Scientific Study of Religion*, 34: 63–75.

Neal, M. A. (1990). *From Nuns to Sisters: An Expanding Vocation*. Mystic, CT: Twenty-Third Publications.

Nynas, P., and A. Yip (2012) (eds). *Religion, Gender and Sexuality in Everyday Life*. Farnham: Ashgate.

O'Brien, R., K. Hunt, and G. Hart (2005). ' "It's Caveman Stuff, but that is to a Certain Extent How Guys Still Operate": Men's Accounts of Masculinity and Help Seeking'. *Social Science and Medicine*, 61: 503–16.

Ozorak, E. W. (1996). 'The Power But Not the Glory: How Women Empower Themselves Through Religion'. *Journal for the Scientific Study of Religion*, 36: 17–29.

Puttick, E. (1999). 'Women in New Religious Movements'. In B. R. Wilson and J. Cresswell (eds), *New Religious Movements: Challenge and Response*. London: Routledge, 143–160.

Runciman, W. G. (1983). *A Treatise on Social Theory*, vol. i. Cambridge: Cambridge University Press.

Sallee, M. W., and Frank Harris (2011). 'Gender Performance in Qualitative Studies of Masculinities'. *Qualitative Research*, 11: 409–429.

Sharma, S. (2011). *Good Girls, Good Sex: Women Talk about Church and Sexuality*. Winnipeg, MB: Fernwood.

Stark, R. (2002). 'Physiology and Faith: Addressing the "Universal" Gender Difference in Religious Commitment'. *Journal for the Scientific Study of Religion*, 41: 495–507.

Thompson, E. H. (1991). 'Beneath the Status Characteristics: Gender Variations in Religiousness'. *Journal for the Scientific Study of Religion*, 30: 381–394.

Trzebiatowska, M. & Bruce, S. (2012). *Why Are Women More Religious Than Men?* Oxford: Oxford University Press.

Wallace, R. (1992). *They Call Her Pastor: A New Role for Catholic Women*. Albany, NY: SUNY Press.

Walter, T., and G. Davie (1998). 'The Religiosity of Women in the Modern West'. *British Journal of Sociology*, 49: 640–660.

Weaver, M. J. (1995). *New Catholic Women: A Contemporary Challenge to Traditional Religious Authority*. San Francisco: Harper & Row.

Weber, M. [1903–1917] (2011) *The Methodology of the Social Sciences*. New Brunswick, NJ: Transaction Press.

Wilcox, M. (2003). *Coming Out in Christianity: Religion, Identity and Community*. Bloomington, IN: Indiana University Press.

Williams, C. L., and E. J. Heikes (1993). 'The Importance of Researcher's Gender in the In-depth Interview: Evidence from Two Case Studies of Male Nurses'. *Gender & Society*, 7: 280–291.

Wilson, B. (1982). *Religion in Sociological Perspective*. Oxford: Oxford University Press.

Wittberg, P. (1994). *The Rise and Fall of Catholic Religious Orders*. Albany, NY: SUNY Press.

Woodhead, L. (2007). 'Why So Many Women in Holistic Spirituality?' In Kieran Flanagan and Peter Jupp (eds), *A Sociology of Spirituality*, Aldershot: Ashgate, 119–120.

Yadgar, Y. (2006). 'Gender, Religion, and Feminism: The Case of Jewish Israeli Traditionalists'. *Journal for the Scientific Study of Religion*, 45: 353–370.

Yip, A., M. Keenan, and S. J. Page (2011). *Religion, Youth and Sexuality: A Multi-Faith Exploration*. Nottingham: University of Nottingham.

CHAPTER 9

....

CONTRIBUTIONS FROM
PHILOSOPHY

....

CYNTHIA R. NIELSEN AND MICHAEL
BARNES NORTON

INTRODUCTION

....

THE practice of philosophy involves inquiries into the conceptual foundations of being, knowledge, ethics, politics—in short, its questions and analyses touch upon every aspect of human experience. Philosophical questions generally deal with the meaning or nature of concepts that often otherwise go unquestioned, as well as with the uses and effects of concepts within human society. Philosophy also includes the study of the history of these inquiries, with the goal of understanding how this history has influenced contemporary ideas and behaviours. With regard to the study of gender, sex, and sexuality, the most important philosophical contributions have come from the works of feminist and womanist scholars. Feminism, as this chapter will show, is a term that encompasses a broad variety of different and sometimes incompatible perspectives. Notwithstanding their multiple differences and myriad expressions, feminists agree that women exist in situations of oppression (both historically and in the present) and that this oppression should be ended (see, for example, hooks 2000: 26 or Stone 2007: 28). Given this common commitment to end women's oppression, feminist philosophers' theoretical inquiries are always closely tied to practical concerns and sociopolitical goals. Engagement in philosophical inquiry, while motivated by the commitment to end women's oppression, leads feminist philosophers in particular to examine the meanings and effects of concepts like sex and gender—concepts that are operative throughout all social, cultural, and political structures.

Gender, like race, is a controversial and volatile topic. We encounter one another as embodied and thus gendered beings. But what precisely *is* gender? What does it mean be feminine? Conversely, what does it mean to be masculine? Was Jesus a 'masculine man' in the sense that those terms connote in American discourse in the twenty-first century? Does the ability to give birth to a child constitute the essence of womanhood? Questions such as these and many others like them evoke strong emotions, as they affect individuals and collectives in profoundly personal ways. Theologians and ecclesial and religious practitioners—whether clergy, professional educators, or lay ministers—must be prepared to engage questions about gender in ways that demonstrate both a sufficient grasp of the complexity of the topic and compassionate care. Given the history of the oppression of women and gender narratives that adversely affect both men and women, Christian theologians (and all people of goodwill) have an ethical responsibility to devote sustained attention to gender studies and to challenge those views that fall short of Christianity's high ideals of love, liberation, equality, and human flourishing.

Our chapter begins with a discussion of key terms and distinctions. For example, early on, feminists who rejected the claims and implications of biological determinism and gender essentialism saw the need to distinguish between biological sex and socially shaped gender. Here biological sex is understood as fixed and is presented in binary terms: one is (in most, but importantly not all, cases) either male or female and biology has the final, definitive word on the matter.[1] Gender, however, is dynamic and influenced by history, culture, and other sociopolitical forces. In other words, gender is socially constructed. The notion of gender as socially shaped shall be discussed both analytically and through specific examples (see also Haslanger 1995).

As feminist theorists continue to reflect upon gender, questions and challenges arise regarding the viability of the sex/gender distinction. Consequently, debates emerge between various expressions of gender realists and gender nominalists. Roughly and simplistically speaking (and, as we shall see, the story is significantly more complex), gender realism in its essentialist variant claims that there is some common, essential feature or core constitutive of 'womanness', whereas gender nominalists deny that individual women possess shared, essential features that constitute what it is to be a woman. In the context of this debate, we examine feminist and womanist theorists critical of gender realism because of its failure to address class, race, ethnic, and other sociopolitical factors that significantly affect women's lived experience. Although gender realism of the essentialist sort has been severely criticized and abandoned by many contemporary feminist theorists, we shall mention some of the leading voices who continue to argue for a sophisticated and historically attuned version of gender realism. Lastly, we discuss briefly Alison Stone's critical analysis of the sex/gender distinction, in particular her claim that (biological) sex must be understood not as a fixed, binary distinction but as a continuum.

The next sections are devoted to two prominent feminist philosophers, Judith Butler and Linda Martín Alcoff. In these sections, our goal is to present the key aspects of Butler's and Alcoff's views of gender as clearly as possible; we do not attempt to bring

---

[1] For the sake of clarity, the terms 'female' and 'male', following established feminist conventions, denote biological sex. Unless noted otherwise and thus made clear by the context, the terms 'woman' and 'man' and 'feminine' and 'masculine' denote gender.

their views into critical or complementary dialogue with one another. Butler's notion of performing gender has been both highly influential and appropriated across disciplinary boundaries. According to Butler, gender is an unstable concept and to define terms such as 'woman' or 'feminine' is in effect to engage in an exclusionary and oppressive act. That is, gender identity categories are never purely descriptive; rather, they are normative and thus give rise to categories such as 'deviants' and those deemed 'abnormal'. For Butler, gender comes into being through repeated, habitual acts; that is, gender *becomes* when performed. However, on Butler's account, sex is also socially shaped. If this is the case, then 'hard' binaries such as nature/culture, sex/gender, feminine/masculine, and so forth become fuzzy, fluid, and spectral. In short, Butler argues that feminists should give up the attempt to define the term 'woman' and likewise abandon identity politics. Instead of pursuing these endeavours, feminists would do well to appropriate and develop for their own purposes Foucault's insights regarding power relations, normativity, and genealogy.

Alcoff, on the other hand, argues that some definition of woman must be retained in order to address social justice issues such as gender equality, discrimination, and violence against women. Having developed a view of identity as an open, dynamic, multi-layered 'horizon of agency'—always and ever socially and relationally shaped—Alcoff is poised to offer a compelling case for a historically and materially sensitive gender realism and to further elaborate her view of gender as positionality. While in no way affirming gender essentialism, biological determinism, or a rigid, absolute distinction between sex and gender, Alcoff acknowledges (contra Butler) that certain aspects of biological sex are not constructed. As she explains, 'the objective basis of sex categories is in the differential relationship to reproductive capacity between men and women' (Alcoff 2006: 154).

In short, our hope is that by raising awareness of the complexity of gender (and sex), a new openness to interdisciplinary dialogue will awaken—an openness that will allow historically marginalized voices to be heard and better understood. Such a dialogue will no doubt challenge but likewise strengthen and reinvigorate religious traditions and ecclesial communities called to minister to a diverse and ever-changing social body.

WHY DISTINGUISH BETWEEN (BIOLOGICAL) SEX AND (SOCIALLY CONSTRUCTED) GENDER?

The usefulness for feminism of the distinction between sex as a biological fact and gender as a social construct was, initially, largely to do with countering claims of biological determinism—i.e., the idea that not only the psychological and behavioural traits of male and female individuals but also the social positions of men and women as groups are natural expressions of their biological differences. To the extent that feminists for at least two centuries have been arguing that psychological, behavioural, or social traits that many women share (and especially those that put them at a disadvantage to men) are the result not of their biology but of social pressures, writers from Mary Wollstonecraft to Simone de Beauvoir can be said to have implied or at least anticipated the sex/gender distinction (Stone 2007: 11).

However, prior to the late 1960s, the word 'gender' referred only to a linguistic distinction (e.g., *le/la* in French; *der/die/das* in German). It was first applied to persons by Robert Stoller (1968) in the context of psychological research into transsexuality; if 'sex' applied only to biological characteristics and 'gender' to psychological ones, it became easier to describe how an individual could feel that her sex was not appropriate to her. Taking up this distinction, feminists were able to argue that the elements that constitute gender, while historically understood as necessarily coupled with biological traits of which they were simply the expression, come together in ways that are socially constructed and thus malleable. At the same time, they could take sex to be a biological fact that divides humans into (at least) two separate groups and that not only accounts for physiological differences but may also account for some pervasive differences at the psychological and social levels (Fausto-Sterling 2003: 123).

On the one hand, distinguishing between sex and gender does not necessarily result in a complete dissociation of one from the other. It is still possible to argue that gender, while it is a social construct, is an expression of sex. Thus, within a given society it would be seen as appropriate for members of one sex to take on one set of gender-related traits while members of the other sex took on a different set. Female bodies may be expected to express themselves by taking on feminine characteristics, and the same for male bodies *mutatis mutandis*. On the other hand, once this distinction has been made it seems reasonable to make the argument that there is no natural connection between a person's sex and her gender. The phenomenon of transsexuality that gave rise to the distinction, along with the fact that different cultures sometimes have very different ideas of which traits are feminine and which are masculine, seems to lend support to the idea taken up in a variety of ways by many feminist and womanist writers that sex and gender are entirely separable.

If gender is socially constructed and bears no necessary relationship to a person's biological sex, then of what exactly does gender consist? According to early definitions from the 1960s and 1970s, genders are sets of social expectations about the appropriate behaviours for females and males, upheld by the beliefs and practices of social institutions as well as individuals. To have a gender is to occupy a certain role (or set of roles) with a given society, to conform to a set of expectations about one's actions and attitudes, and to identify oneself as a belonging to one's gender (Stone 2007: 56). This fairly broad understanding of gender allows for a variety of more detailed interpretations. It can accommodate the perspectives of both gender realists and gender nominalists, insofar as they agree that femininity is not a result of (and thus does not entirely depend on) having a female body but is rather a matter of occupying a certain social role and taking up a certain set of traits and activities. Since feminine traits and activities have historically been undervalued compared to those understood as masculine, the distinction between socially constructed gender and biologically determined sex supports ethical and political arguments that women's subordination can be done away with if the social conditions that uphold it are altered or discarded. More recently, though, many feminist theorists have criticized this distinction, arguing for example that the concept of sex should also be seen as (at least partly) socially constructed. We will examine some of these arguments in upcoming sections, after a deeper exploration of the social construction of gender.

MORE ON THE NOTION OF GENDER AS A SOCIAL CONSTRUCTION

Having explained the notion of gender as a social construction, we turn now to further elucidate the dynamism and historical character of gender via a more sustained focus on particular examples. As noted in the previous section, many contemporary feminist theorists (especially womanists and post-structuralists) argue that gender is socially conditioned rather than a 'natural' or fixed essence. That is, our notion of what it is to be a man or a woman, feminine or masculine, changes over time and varies according to the particularities of each historical context. There are no universal traits, qualities, practices, or dispositions that constitute what it is to be a woman and apply to all women transculturally and transhistorically. For example, Aristotle considered women morally inferior to men and believed that wives ought to be 'ruled' by their husbands owing to the husband's 'natural' superiority (see, for example, *Nic. Ethics* 7.1158b13–28; see also, Cooper 1980: esp. 307). St Augustine also held that in the marital relation, the wife's 'natural' role was one of subordination and subservience (see, for example, Augustine, *Conf.* 9.9.19; 224–225 (Boulding trans.); see also Hunter 2003). In fact, he often described the marital relation as analogous to a master/slave relation, wherein the husband was identified as master, the wife as dutiful slave (again see, for example, Augustine *Conf.* 9.9.19; 224–225 (Boulding trans.); see also, Patricia Clark 2001).

In addition to claims of moral inferiority, women have often been considered intellectually inferior to men. This assumed intellectual deficiency was the basis of many nineteenth-century arguments against women's suffrage. For example, Frederick Douglass, the well-known abolitionist and advocate for women's suffrage, opposed such views in his third autobiography, *Life and Times*. As Douglass explains, he had been convinced (by arguments such as Elizabeth Cady Stanton's) that women possess rational capacities equal to men and thus must be granted equal opportunities to develop and exercise their capacities. Douglass unabashedly admits that his former attempts to counter Stanton's arguments were based on 'the shallow plea of "custom," "natural division of duties," "indelicacy of woman's taking part in politics," the common talk of "women's sphere," and the like' (1994: 907).

These examples (and they could be multiplied) highlight how gender, gender-coded roles, and what qualifies as feminine or masculine are highly contingent, dynamic, and historically conditioned. As Douglass observes in the quote, stereotypes, customs, and biases play a significant role in the social construction of gender. Once a stereotype or particular view becomes dominant and is reflected and reinforced via institutional structures as well as social, religious, political, and legal discourses and sociocultural practices, it then functions as a norm and is often perceived as 'natural' or as a necessary, universal, or essential characteristic of womanhood. For example, stereotypes and socially accepted beliefs that women are more emotional, nurturing, pure, and less logical (than men) have been employed to argue that a woman's 'natural' place is in the domestic sphere. As many feminist and womanist theorists have pointed out, these highly contested beliefs and conclusions have been used to oppress women through denying them equal (political, civic, and legal) rights, educational and employment opportunities, and the ability to reach their fullest potential (see, for example, Hoff 1991 and de Beauvoir 2011; on the dual effects of racism and sexism, see hooks 1981).

Gender stereotypes of course also harm men. To be masculine, for example, is often connected with physically aggressive behaviour, and men who exhibit such behaviour (e.g., via team sports or hunting) are considered more 'manly' than those who prefer less aggressive activities (e.g., fashion design or ballet). Moreover, particular gender-coded behaviours are learned behaviours that are taught by parents, teachers, clergy, and so forth and are reinforced through films, television, video games, and other social narratives and practices. Young boys are frequently encouraged to be tough and to play violent make-believe games (such as games involving plastic assault weapons), as these are ways to show themselves as males and to 'be boys'. In addition, from an early age males are encouraged to initiate romantic and sexual relations with females (and thus to show themselves as active 'leaders' rather than passive recipients—as passivity is an assumed 'natural' female trait); those who fail to do so are often teased by family members and even bullied by friends for not living up to an assumed norm of what it is to be a 'man' (see, for example, Kimmel and Mahler 2003).

Similarly, from a very early age young girls are socially conditioned to be physically attractive so that they can 'win' a male's attention and affection. Females (and males) are constantly bombarded with media images depicting women as objects to satisfy (heterosexual) male sexual desire. Such gender-coded social structures, practices, and narratives assume that women are not complete subjects by themselves; rather, their femininity (or womanhood) is essentially tied to fulfilling male desire (see, for example, the introduction to de Beauvoir 2011: esp. 10). Thus, females come to believe that what it is to be a woman or to be *feminine* is fundamentally related to particular clothing styles, body types, and so forth, and that in order to succeed as a woman, they must attract a man. (Especially in religious circles, whether in the form of direct instruction or understood as an assumed social requirement confirming or validating one's feminine 'nature', females are frequently either straightforwardly taught or strongly encouraged to get married and bear children.) Females who have no desire to marry, who cannot or choose not to bear children, or who either do not fit the socially conditioned norms for what it is to be 'sexy' (i.e. here, sexy = feminine) or choose not to conform to such standards often struggle to achieve a positive self-image—some even harm their bodies through unhealthy diets and drugs.

Having further explicated and illustrated how gender is socially constructed, we now turn to analyse whether the legitimacy of the sex/gender distinction is valid.

DOES THE SEX/GENDER DISTINCTION HOLD?

As we have seen, even if the sex/gender distinction is taken as given, gender itself may be understood as possessing a determinate essence that is shared by every member of that gender. As briefly explained earlier, this position—called gender realism—holds that there is some characteristic trait, condition, or experience that all women share, by virtue of which they are women. For example, Nancy Chodorow holds that women and men are distinguished in large part on the basis of whether or not they see themselves as (potentially) acting as a mother—and importantly, this remains a social and psychological issue, not one of biological ability (Chodorow 1978). Others argue that what all women share is their social and political subordination to men (see, for example, Haslanger 2003).

Some feminist and womanist theorists reject gender realism because it ignores factors such as class, race, ethnicity, nationality, and religion. While it may be true that all women experience some form of subordination, it is also obviously the case that not all women experience the same form of subordination. Consider the contrast between the experiences of black female house slaves and white plantation owners' wives in the antebellum American South. Both were subordinate to white males and subject to treatment as sexual objects by them. However, the divergences between the two groups' racial and socio-economic status produced drastically different experiences of their subordination to white men. Elizabeth Spelman criticizes Chodorow's account for not acknowledging the degree to which different experiences of womanhood are inseparable from experiences of race or class discrimination (Spelman 1988). Spelman insists that there cannot be one universal category of womanhood to which all women belong, but rather only 'particular kinds of women' (Spelman 1988: 113).

Importantly, it is nearly always middle-class white Western women whose experiences have been taken to coincide with those of all women (Spelman 1988: 3). For this reason as well as others, some women have been reluctant to align themselves with the theoretical and political positions of feminists—or at least to adopt the term 'feminism' (hooks 2000: 24). These feminists, their critics argue, have failed to attend to their own social, political, racial, and class conditions, especially those which afford them some kind of privilege over others, and thus have taken their own particular experience of their gender as a universal norm for womanhood. Ways in which, for example, particularly lower-income women, women of colour, or non-Western women are oppressed have been downplayed or ignored. An exemplary target of this criticism is Betty Friedan's famous argument that the central problem of modern women was their relegation to the role of the housewife—an argument made at a time when over one-third of women were already in the workforce (hooks 2000: 2). Without a unified concept of womanhood, on the other hand, it can become difficult to see how the feminine gender can be meaningfully distinguished from the female sex.

Some gender theorists argue that the distinction between gender and sex is invalid not because there are multiple particular experiences of what we ordinarily call a single gender but rather because 'sex' is also a social concept. Fausto-Sterling argues that even biological factors are not necessarily immutable and thus may be affected by social conditions (2003: 125). Even if this were not the case, one may argue that there is no biological feature or group of features that necessarily marks a body as belonging to a particular sex without socially constructed concepts coming into play. This can be seen most starkly in the case of intersexed individuals, who are born with some characteristically female features and some that are characteristically male (or features that fall somewhere in between), and who are often surgically altered to conform to one sex only (Stone 2007: 39).

However, for any particular biological trait that may mark a body with a particular sex there may be instances where such a definition would be problematic. If being a female consists, for instance, in having ovaries, XX chromosomes, or the ability to bear children, then some women who are born intersexed, transsexual women, and women who are infertile or post-menopausal would not count as female. Stone suggests instead that sex be understood as a 'cluster concept' that is defined by a group of traits that often (but not always) occur together (2007: 45). She also argues that sex is a continuum, stretching between female and male but also incorporating intermediate positions, rather than a simple dichotomy (Stone 2007: 44). An individual's place on this continuum would be determined not only by biological factors but also by the way in which they are interpreted socially and psychologically.

Judith Butler's account of gender as performance also offers strong criticisms of the sex/gender distinction. We will consider this account in the next section.

Judith Butler on Gender
as Performance

In her influential work *Gender Trouble*, Butler begins by pointing towards criticisms of the notion that sex is biologically determined, thereby questioning the tenability of the sex/gender distinction. She suggests that, if sex is culturally constructed in much the same way as gender, then perhaps sex simply is gender (Butler 1999: 11). However, the core of Butler's argument is that gender is an unstable and necessarily incomplete concept that is experienced in multiple ways that depend on race, class, and other social factors (1999: 21). Not only is womanhood not a feature or experience common to all women; the construction of even particular instances of womanhood is an ongoing process, one which can be accepted or contested but never fully accomplished. Since gender is always already culturally, discursively, and linguistically mediated, she argues, ' "being" a sex or a gender is fundamentally impossible' (1999: 25). Instead, gender is something that individuals in particular social contexts *do*—it is performance.

Butler rejects both the idea that there are particular traits or experiences that naturally belong to particular genders and the idea that individuals possess core gender identities. She argues, rather, that gender is a product of the power relations that are manifest in multiple social structures. Drawing on the work of Michel Foucault and Monique Wittig among others, she emphasizes the ways in which heterosexuality is normative throughout society, producing masculine and feminine subjects of desire within a purely dimorphic gender structure. In this 'heterosexual matrix', only (heterosexual) men and women are recognized, while those with desires or gender traits that do not conform are considered dangerous or unnatural deviants (Butler 1999: 42). Furthermore, this power structure works to conceal its own operation, so that the gender categories it produces—along with their respective traits, experiences, and desires—are seen as natural rather than socially constructed. It is here that the notion of a fixed sex as the underlying foundation of gender emerges, and Butler sees in this distinction a complicity with the gender hierarchy: nature is to be dominated by culture, just as women are to be subordinate to men (1999: 48).

Butler's rejection of the sex/gender distinction and her critique of normative gender structures go hand in hand, insofar as they both point towards her conclusion that gender must be understood as an act, or rather as a series of acts. After detailed analyses of the ways in which taboos against both incest and homosexuality ground the traditional gender dichotomy, she argues that individual bodies produce their gender through repeated acts, gestures, and behaviours. By taking up the acts that are already socially associated with a particular type of body, bodies produce internal gender identities for themselves as effects of their external habits—that is, a body *performs* its gender (Butler 1999: 173). The internalization of gender, though, leads an individual to experience her gender such that her performance of it is understood as an expression of a fixed essence that exerts a normative influence. Butler challenges the idea of a fixed gender essence precisely in order to highlight possibilities for subverting this influence (1999: 180).

It is important to recognize two basic points about Butler's notion of gender as performance. First, for the most part the performance of gender does not happen as a conscious choice on the part of an individual. Second, the performance of gender never consists of only one discrete act, or even a small group of acts, performed at a particular time. The performance of gender always involves a repetition across time, and it is always already a repetition of socially significant acts. The repetitive performance that produces gender is 'at once a reenactment and reexperiencing of a set of meanings already socially established' (Butler 1999: 178). Insofar as gender is an effect of discursive power structures, operative in multiple ways throughout society, bodies are always already under the influence of gender norms. Yet, since the ways in which gender is constructed and performed are not naturally determined but contingent, there remain performative possibilities for reconfiguring gender in ways that challenge dominant social norms. Butler looks to drag performance both as a way to reveal the performative structure of gender as such and as an example of a particular performative strategy that exposes the possibility of generating gender identities that do not conform to the standard dimorphic model (1999: 175). The explicit realization, which drag displays, that gender (and identity more broadly) is a fabricated effect can, according to Butler, give rise to new possibilities for conceptualizing political agency outside traditional hierarchies (1999: 187).

Since Butler rejects the sex/gender distinction one may wonder why, according to her account, certain kinds of bodies perform one gender identity while other kinds of bodies perform another. In other words, if sex is no more a biological reality than gender, then why do the large majority of bodies with female sex characteristics identify as women? Part of the answer to this question is that the features that constitute sex are, as much as gender traits, socially constructed as such. Following Fausto-Sterling, Butler points out that even understandings of how sexes are biologically determined rest on discursive assumptions about the respective natures of the sexes—assumptions that are grounded in gender norms (Butler 1999: 139). This is not to deny that our bodies exist as material entities and that there are important differences between different kinds of bodies that play significant roles in gender performance. It is only to say that the significances of biological sex characteristics are no more naturally determined than the behavioural traits associated with gender; their meaning is similarly established through the operation of multiple social discourses.

While in *Gender Trouble* Butler seems to argue that there is no aspect of the body that is not subject to discourse, in her more recent work she allows that there is an extent to which the materiality of bodies escapes the reach of discursive structures (see Meijer and Prins 1998: 278). In *Bodies that Matter*, Butler acknowledges a certain irreducibility of basic bodily experiences while maintaining that the intelligibility of such experiences depends on contingent discursive frameworks (Butler 1993: p. xi). 'For there is an "outside" to what is constructed by discourse,' she writes, 'but this is not an absolute "outside" ' (1993: 8). The materiality of the body, on which the social construction of gender works and through which bodies perform gender, is not exhausted by this process. Exploring the ways in which matter eludes determination by discursive structures even as it is always already enmeshed in them can open up possibilities for resistance to gender oppression.

Butler advocates the multiplication of identities as a political strategy, suggesting that feminists cease trying to define 'woman' but rather to utilize it tactically while at the same time submitting it to thoroughgoing critique (Butler 1993: 29). Appropriating insights from Foucauldian genealogy and Derridean deconstruction, she champions exposing the ways in which unstable concepts of sex and gender present themselves as natural and universal—and thus normative. Recognizing the extent to which these concepts are fluid and contingent makes possible the more radical goal of leaving them behind.

Linda Alcoff on Gender as Positionality: An Account of Fluid Identity and Embodied Difference

Having provided a summary of the key aspects of Butler's notion of gender as performance, we now turn to Alcoff's position. Alcoff develops an account of subjectivity as positionality as a way to stress how gender acquires its meaning(s) from particular social and historical contexts (Alcoff 2006: 151). Her attention to gender's social and historical location motivates her criticism of both cultural feminism and feminist post-structural theory. On the one hand, Alcoff finds the cultural feminist (essentialist, realist) position that emphasizes select 'feminine' characteristics (e.g. nurture, intuition, etc.) problematic both for its essentialist tendencies and its failure to explain under what conditions such characteristics come about. In other words, the cultural feminists present a dehistoricized and decontextualized account of alleged 'feminine' attributes (2006: 151).

On the other hand, while eschewing essentialism and embracing nominalism, feminist post-structuralists engage in an 'ahistorical approach to resistance' (Alcoff 2006: 151). That is, feminist post-structuralists often fail to give sufficient attention to the material particularities of our bodies. However, as race theorists have shown, phenotypic differences such as skin colour do matter when it comes to one's lived experience (see, for example, Nielsen 2011b and 2013). The same is true of gendered bodily differences such as having breasts or the appearance of having breasts. Moreover, feminist post-structuralism's variant of feminism is limited 'to the negative tactics of reaction and deconstruction', as meanings, definitions, and descriptions of 'woman' are variously taken as inherently prescriptive and normative, and thus as oppressive (on 'negative feminism', see Alcoff 2006: 141).

Alcoff's critical remarks are not meant as a complete dismissal of either cultural feminism or post-structural feminism. In fact, Alcoff incorporates what she sees as the best insights of both views into her own account. For example, like the feminist post-structuralists, Alcoff is attentive to the myriad ways that power relations and discourses shape and produce gender. However, Alcoff takes issue with a feminist post-structuralist tendency to claim that we are constructed 'all the way down'. That is, Alcoff rejects the conclusion that because gender is socially constructed, we must embrace 'a total erasure of individual agency within a social discourse or set of institutions, that is, the totalization of history's imprint' (Alcoff 2006: 140). For Alcoff, an individual is able to resist dominant and constraining gender (and racialized) discourses and practices and can renarrate her subjectivity. An individual agent's intentional strategies and acts of resistance do not take place 'outside' particular social and historical contexts; yet such actions occur regularly and often result in significant social and political advances as well as new collective identities. (Consider, for example, Frederick Douglass's acts of resistance against the dominant racist narratives of his day; see Nielsen 2011a.) While collective identities, for Alcoff, are socially constructed, they are nonetheless real and gain their unity through social location, common experiences, and so forth.

Even so, Alcoff's notion of identity is fluid and multiple rather than fixed and homogeneous. Here she draws upon the philosophical hermeneutical tradition, utilizing and advancing Gadamer's notion of an agent's hermeneutical horizon (itself consisting of multiple, mutable perspectives) as an interpretive grid for understanding and being-in-the-world (see, for example, Gadamer 2004: esp. 302–307). Thus, one's horizon may include one's experience *as* a Latina, which is different from one's experience *as* a lesbian, which is also different from one's experience *as* an upper-class female in a male-dominated profession. Each of these aspects or multiple identities (of oneself) involves a different set of social practices, discourses, expectations, and recognitions. Some identities within one's horizon can be more easily compartmentalized than others; however, one's gender and race, given their visibility and typical identification via select physical markers, must be navigated daily and cannot be relegated to a private (i.e. non-public and non-sociopolitical) realm. Even though one's horizon and one's various identities can congeal and become determinate and describable, they are not fixed; instead horizons and identities (political or otherwise) can be altered and expanded via new experiences, gains in understanding, and changes in sociopolitical structures, discourses, and practices.

Moreover, on Alcoff's (2006: 100) account an interpretative horizon is not analogous to a magnifying glass; rather, a horizon constitutes the self and thus is productive or co-creative of one's world (lived experience). One sees and experiences the world *as* an Asian woman or *as* a black man. Here not only does one's embodied difference matter, but one's socio-economic location and political standing (i.e. one's positionality) are also significant, as they impact how an individual is (or is not) recognized socially and legally and what opportunities she can pursue. Alcoff's emphasis on our embodiment and social location constitutes a needed corrective to certain universalizing tendencies of the hermeneutical tradition. On the point of embodiment, Alcoff finds company with many cultural feminists who also highlight how women's bodily and gender-coded difference must be recognized (whether we are speaking against the objectification of women in pornography or advocating for maternity leave so that a female's body may heal). However, as noted earlier, Alcoff's position does not necessitate an embrace of essentialism, as gender qua social construction is a *social* (not a natural) reality. To affirm gender as a social reality does not require one to make universal claims about alleged transhistorical feminine characteristics, activities, or roles or about women's 'nature' per se. In addition, on Alcoff's view (contra Butler) our discourse about gender is not in itself oppressive and constraining; it also enables us to describe real issues and concerns affecting women and to create more liberating narratives.

In agreement with Sally Haslanger's realist position, Alcoff affirms that sexed identity is an objective type, that is, it describes a 'unity without an underlying essence', and the basis for this unity is neither random nor arbitrary (Alcoff 2006: 168; cf. Haslanger 2000a). Here a type's objectivity means that 'the unifying factor is independent of us' (Alcoff 2006: 168). Alcoff's argument for an objective basis for sexed identity does *not* entail affirming that sexed identity (or gender) is unmediated linguistically, untouched by human practices, or that the narratives about sexed identity are never used to oppress women. Rather, one can (as Alcoff does) embrace gender as a social construction and simultaneously argue that sexed identity is based on objective differences that are not mere products of discourse. For Alcoff, this objective basis is our differential labour divisions in biological reproduction. Specifically, Alcoff formulates her position as follows: 'women and men are differentiated by virtue of their different relationship of possibility to biological reproduction, with biological reproduction referring to conceiving, giving birth, and breast-feeding, involving one's own body' (2006: 172).[2]

Here the idea is that certain activities involving one's body are expected of *females only* such as the ability (whether actual, potential, or assumed) to give birth to children and to lactate (Alcoff 2006: 172). By articulating her position in terms of possibility or concrete potentiality, Alcoff's view can account for infertile, prepubescent, and post-menopausal females as well as females who have no desire to bear children. Such is the case because all who fall under the category 'women' (including those just mentioned) 'will have a different set of practices, expectations, and feelings in regard to reproduction, no matter how actual their relationship to possibility is for it' (2006: 172). Of course, the degree, particular sociopolitical consequences, and so forth of a female's reproductive potential will differ from society to society; yet this variation in no way negates the objective embodied aspects that Alcoff specifies.

Lastly, Alcoff argues that her account of sexed identity as an objective type 'does not prescribe compulsory heterosexuality in the sense of mandating heterosexual coupling as the necessary means for the reproduction of children' (Alcoff 2006: 173). While conception does require uniting male and female biological material, human reproduction in the broad sense demands significantly more than a mere biological union. Human reproduction involves caring for the child and bringing it to full maturity—a process that can be accomplished by stable, loving adults and is not limited to heterosexual couples only. 'Putting biological reproduction as the basis of sexual difference is not the same as putting heterosexuality at the basis or linking heterosexuality with reproduction in the broad sense' (2006: 173).

Alcoff mentions several examples of how compulsory heterosexuality can have harmful effects on both the children and the mothers. For example, women who are forced through religious or cultural traditions or socio-economic structures to marry or remain

---

[2] For more on Alcoff's non-absolute account of nature and culture, see Alcoff (2006: 175).

in an unhealthy marriage are often subject to domestic violence and their children are likewise subject to child abuse. In addition, many children have been lovingly cared for and have thrived in single-parent households and adoptive (both non-biological heterosexual and same-sex) families. In short, reproduction in this broad sense—from the support a pregnant women needs to the long-term nurture necessary to successfully bring a child into adulthood—is not the exclusive domain of heterosexual couplings. One can recognize an objective type based on a biological division of reproductive roles, reject the claim that such a recognition logically entails sustained heterosexual relationships, and argue for a dialectical relation between 'nature' and 'culture' where both are amenable to change via human practices (for example, various medical and other technologies; see Alcoff 2006: 175).

CONCLUSION

Having explained some of the important terms and concepts in gender studies and presented overviews of some of the leading feminist theorists, our hope is that our readers have come to understand and appreciate both the complexity involved in a philosophical analysis of gender and the sociopolitical significance and influence of gender narratives on society as a whole. Given the impact on the lives of countless men, women, and children of false, overly simplistic, and unjustified gender narratives—many of which can and do cause psychological, spiritual, and relational injury—it is crucial that theologians and ecclesial and religious practitioners take time to study the topic of gender (and sex) and to familiarize themselves with the insights of feminist theorists and philosophers. For such theological and religious leaders to fail to take gender and gender narratives seriously is not only a failure in the realm of ethics and social justice but also a failure in love. If Christian leaders and all people of goodwill (religious or otherwise) hope to make an impact not only on the present generation but also on the generations to come, then they must be willing to engage in genuine dialogue with feminist thinkers, and when necessary and applicable, to revise some of their most cherished—but perhaps unwarranted and un-*natural*—assumptions and beliefs.

REFERENCES

Alcoff, Linda (2006). *Visible Identities: Race, Gender, and the Self*. Oxford: Oxford University Press.

Augustine (2004). *Confessions*. Trans. Maria Boulding. New York: New City Press.

Augustine of Hippo (1998). *City of God Against the Pagans*. Ed. and trans. R. W. Dyson. Cambridge: Cambridge University Press.

Aristotle (2002). *Nicomachean Ethics*. Trans. Joe Sachs. Newburyport, MA: Focus Publishing.

de Beauvoir, Simone (2011). *The Second Sex*, complete and unabridged. Trans. Constance Borde and Sheila Malovany-Chevallier. New York: Vintage.

Butler, Judith (1993). *Bodies that Matter*. New York: Routledge.

Butler, Judith (1997). *The Psychic Life of Power*. Stanford, CA: Stanford University Press.

Butler, Judith (1999). *Gender Trouble*, 2nd edn. New York: Routledge.

Chodorow, Nancy (1978). *The Reproduction of Mothering*. Berkeley and Los Angeles: University of California Press.

Clark, Patricia (2001). 'Women, Slaves, and the Hierarchies of Domestic Violence: The Family of St. Augustine'. In Sandra R. Joshel and Sheila Murnaghan (eds), *Women and Slaves in Greco-Roman Culture*. New York: Routledge, 109–129.

Cooper, John (1980). 'Aristotle on Friendship'. In Amélie Oksenberg Rorty (ed.), *Essays on Aristotle's Ethics*. Berkeley and Los Angeles: University of California Press, 301–340.

Douglass, Frederick (1994). *Life and Times of Frederick Douglass*. In Henry Louis Gates Jr. (ed.), *Douglass Autobiographies: Narrative of the Life of Frederick Douglass, an American Slave, My Bondage and My Freedom, Life and Times of Frederick Douglass*. New York: Library of America, 453–1045.

Fausto-Sterling, Anne (2003). 'The Problem with Sex/Gender and Nature/Nurture'. In Simon J. Williams, Lynda Birke, and Gillian A. Bendelow (eds), *Debating Biology: Sociological Reflections on Health, Medicine and Society*. New York: Routledge, 123–132.

Gadamer, Hans-Georg (2004). *Truth and Method*, 2nd edn. Ed. and trans. Joel Weinsheimer and Donald G. Marshall. New York: Continuum.

Haslanger, Sally (1995). 'Ontology and Social Construction'. *Philosophical Topics*, 23: 95–125.

Haslanger, Sally (2000a). 'Feminism in Metaphysics: Negotiating the Natural'. In Miranda Fricker and Jennifer Hornsby (eds), *The Cambridge Companion to Feminism in Philosophy*. Cambridge: Cambridge University Press, 109–126.

Haslanger, Sally (2000b). 'Gender and Race: (What) are They? (What) Do We Want Them to Be?' *Noûs*, 34: 31–55.

Haslanger, Sally (2003). 'Future Genders? Future Races?' *Philosophic Exchange*, 34: 4–27.

Haslanger, Sally (2005). 'What Are We Talking About? The Semantics and Politics of Social Kinds'. *Hypatia*, 20: 10–26.

Hoff, Joan (1991). *Law, Gender, and Injustice: A Legal History of U.S. Women*. New York: New York University Press.

hooks, bell (1981). *Ain't I a Woman? Black Women and Feminism*. Boston: South End Press.

hooks, bell (2000). *Feminist Theory: From Margin to Center*, 2nd edn. Cambridge, MA: South End Press.

Hunter, David G. (2003). 'Augustine and the Making of Marriage in Roman North Africa'. *Journal of Early Christian Studies*, 11: 63–85.

Kimmel, Michael S., and Matthew Mahler (2003). 'Adolescent Masculinity, Homophobia, and Violence: Random School Shooting 1982–2001'. *American Behavioral Scientist*, 46: 1439–1458.

Meijer, Irene Costera, and Baukje Prins (1998). 'How Bodies Come to Matter: An Interview with Judith Butler'. *Signs* 23(2): 275–286.

Nielsen, Cynthia R. (2011a). 'Resistance is Not Futile: Frederick Douglass on Panoptic Plantations and the Un-Making of Docile Bodies and Enslaved Souls'. *Philosophy and Literature*, 35(2): 251–268.

Nielsen, Cynthia R. (2011b). 'Resistance Through Re-Narration: Fanon on De-constructing Racialized Subjectivities'. *African Identities: Journal of Economics, Culture, and Society*, 9(4): 363–385.

Nielsen, Cynthia R. (2013). *Foucault, Douglass, Fanon, and Scotus in Dialogue: On Social Construction and Freedom*. New York: Palgrave Macmillan.

Spelman, Elizabeth (1988). *Inessential Woman*. Boston: Beacon Press.

Stoller, Robert J. (1968). *Sex and Gender: On the Development of Masculinity and Femininity*. New York: Science House.

Stone, Alison (2007). *An Introduction to Feminist Philosophy*. Cambridge: Polity Press.

CHAPTER 10

CONTRIBUTIONS FROM QUEER THEORY

PATRICK S. CHENG

INTRODUCTION

QUEER theory is a critical approach to sexuality and gender that challenges what is 'normal' or 'natural'. Specifically, queer theory contends that identities—including identities relating to sexuality and gender—are socially constructed across different times and places, and thus are fluid and not fixed. Furthermore, queer theory recognizes that such identities are constructed through the deployment of social power, including the power of discourse and naming. Since the term 'queer theory' was first coined by Teresa de Lauretis in the journal *Differences* (1991), it has deeply influenced scholarship in the realm of literary, historical, and cultural studies.

Religious studies scholars and theologians—especially those who identify as lesbian, gay, bisexual, transgender, and intersex (LGBTI)—have also used queer theory in their work since at least 1993 (Shore-Goss 2010: 188). Several articles have been published in recent years that provide a helpful overview of the intersections of queer theory and religious studies (Schippert 2011; Jenzen and Munt 2012; Wilcox 2012; Brintnall 2013) as well as the intersections of queer theory and theology (Lowe 2009; Schneider and Roncolato 2012).

There is some irony, of course, in the fact that an anti-identitarian discourse like queer theory has taken on an identity of its own. It is for this reason that at least one religious studies scholar has wished that he could wave his fairy wand and 'erase the words *queer* and *queer theory* from our lexicon' (Brintnall 2013: 55, emphasis original). Similarly, Teresa de Lauretis herself disavowed the use of the term 'queer theory' as a 'conceptually vacuous creature of the publishing industry', just three years after she coined the term (de Lauretis 1994: 297).

Notwithstanding its contested use, queer theory has become an important part of the field of sexuality studies. Accordingly, this chapter will provide an introduction to what theologians should know about queer theory. Recalling the work of the late Eve Kosofsky Sedgwick on 'minoritizing' and 'universalizing' views of homosexuality (Sedgwick 2008: 82–86), this chapter will argue that queer theory is not just a narrow, or minoritizing, topic of interest to LGBTI-identified theologians alone. Rather, queer theory is also a 'universalizing' topic of interest to *all* theologians, particularly to the extent that Christian theology has always challenged and questioned issues of identity, whether relating to God or humanity. For this reason, Gerard Loughlin has argued that theology 'is' and 'has always been' a 'queer thing' (Loughlin 2007a: 7).

This chapter is organized into four sections. This introduction will be followed by a section examining the word 'queer' and outlining four marks, or characteristics, of queerness: (1) identity without essence; (2) transgression; (3) resisting binaries; and (4) social construction. A section providing an overview of queer theology—that is, 'queer talk about God'—and discussing four strands of queer theology that correspond to each of the four marks of queerness will then follow. Finally, some future directions for queer theology will be proposed; in particular, six ways in which queer theory might inform the future work of queer theologians.

FOUR MARKS OF QUEERNESS

Queer theory is a notoriously difficult concept to define. Because queer theory is a critical methodology that challenges the stability of identities—including sexual and gender identities—it resists attempts to reduce itself to an 'essence' or a core definition. Indeed, Lauren Berlant and Michael Warner have suggested that the term 'queer commentary' might be a better way of describing queer theory. In their view, it is 'not useful' to treat queer theory as a 'thing' or an 'academic object' because it cannot be 'assimilated into a single discourse' (1995: 343).

Similarly, Lee Edelman has criticized attempts by scholars to describe the state of queer theory as a 'fantasy'. For Edelman, queer theory resists any effort to create a 'communal site', a 'safe harbor', or an 'image of home'. Rather, queer theory must resist 'every totalization' that would describe it as a 'unified field of vision' (1995: 343, 348). Edelman's warning should be taken seriously by anyone—including this author—who tries to capture or boil down the essence of queer theory.

Keeping in mind the reservations of Berlant, Warner, and Edelman, this chapter does attempt to address the practical need of introducing queer theory to those who are unfamiliar with its slippery contours. In addition to this chapter, there are a number of helpful book-length introductions to queer theory (Jagose 1996; Turner 2000; Hall 2003; Sullivan 2003), as well as shorter articles (Schneider 2000; Murfin and Ray 2009: 420–423), that provide a useful overview of queer theory for pedagogical purposes.

A key task of queer theory is to observe and document the deployment and effects of the word 'queer'. According to the *Oxford English Dictionary*, 'queer' can be traced back to at least the fourteenth century, when it originally meant 'to question' or 'to

inquire'. In the sixteenth century, the word took on the meaning of 'strange, odd, pecu-
liar, eccentric', and, in the early nineteenth century, the word became a synonym for
transgression—that is, 'to put out of order' or 'to spoil'. At the end of the nineteenth
century, 'queer' had become a derogatory term for a male homosexual (*OED Online*
2013).

In the late 1980s, gay and lesbian activists, including those involved with organizations such as Queer Nation, sought to reclaim the term 'queer' in a positive way. For
example, one of the slogans of Queer Nation was 'We're here, we're queer, get used to
it!' By doing so, however, the word 'queer' became a shorthand term for describing people who self-identified as sexual and gender minorities. To this day, 'queer' is still often
used as an umbrella term to refer to a variety of sexual and gender minorities, including LGBTI people. This can be particularly useful in the context of an ever-expanding
alphabet soup of identities, including lesbian, gay, bisexual, transgender, intersex, queer,
questioning, allied, asexual, pansexual, and two-spirit identities.

This chapter, however, will focus less on the shorthand or umbrella definition of
'queer'—which is grounded primarily in sexuality and gender identity categories—and
more on understanding queerness as strangeness or transgressivity. In particular, this
chapter will propose four marks, or characteristics, of queerness: (1) identity without
essence; (2) transgression; (3) resisting binaries; and (4) social construction. These four
marks are not intended to be an essentialist definition of queerness, but they are simply one way of documenting the various strands of what queer theorists have observed
about queerness since the early 1990s. Like the classical four marks of the Church, which
describe a 'body' that is remarkably queer (Ward 1999: 176–177; Thatcher 2011: 135–154),
these four marks of queerness describe a fluid body of ideas that is constantly in the process of becoming.

Identity Without Essence

The first mark of queerness is *identity without essence*. A key characteristic of the word
'queer' is its resistance to stable identity categories. Accordingly, it is not surprising that
'queer' lacks a stable definition itself. As David M. Halperin has famously noted in his
book *Saint Foucault: Towards a Gay Hagiography*, queerness is an 'identity without an
essence'. That is, '*There is nothing in particular to which it necessarily refers*' (emphasis original). Queerness is less a 'positivity' than a 'positionality vis-à-vis the normal'
(1995: 62).

As noted earlier, the word 'queer' is commonly used as a shorthand or umbrella term
for LGBTI persons and other sexual and gender minorities. However, the notion of
queerness as 'identity without essence' is actually at odds with these sexual and gender
identity categories. Rather than reaffirming such categories, queerness challenges the
stability and naturalness of such categories. Notwithstanding the pop artist Lady Gaga
and her LGBTI-affirming anthem of 'Born This Way'—in which she asserts that 'I'm
beautiful in my way | 'Cause God makes no mistakes | I'm on the right track, baby | I was

born this way' (2011)—queerness is about questioning and challenging identities, and not reaffirming them.

Queer theory differs from gay and lesbian studies to the extent that the latter discipline treats the identity of 'gay' and 'lesbian' as a given and becomes the focal point for reflections about marginalized or non-normative sexualities. Gay and lesbian studies reflect the traditional ethnic studies model of thinking about race, and the contemporary LGBTI-rights movement has adopted such a model in arguing for LGBTI civil rights based upon immutable characteristics. Queerness, by contrast, resists and challenges this essentialist way of thinking about sexual and gender identities.

According to Annamarie Jagose, the 'definitional indeterminacy' and 'elasticity' of queerness is one of its 'constituent characteristics' (1996: 1). Not surprisingly, queer theory has moved far beyond its original focus on sexuality and gender issues, and into the realms of race, post-colonialism, temporality, and neo-liberalism (Eng with Halberstam and Muñoz 2005). Some of these topics will be covered in the final section of this chapter about possible future directions in queer theology.

Transgression

The second mark of queerness is *transgression*. Queerness, as David Halperin describes it, is 'whatever is at odds with the normal, the legitimate, the dominant' (1995: 62). In other words, queerness can be understood more by what it *opposes* than what it is. To that end, it may be helpful to think about the word 'queer' as a verb instead of a noun. To queer something—for example, the Bible or Christian theology—is to subvert, deconstruct, and challenge it, as opposed to merely reaffirming it.

The connection between transgression and queerness arose in the 1980s and 1990s, when activist groups such as AIDS Coalition to Unlease Power (ACT UP) and Queer Nation engaged in 'confrontational and controversial' direct actions in order to protest governmental and ecclesial apathy with respect to the HIV/AIDS pandemic as well as institutional homophobia. For example, in 1989, ACT UP engaged in a 'Stop the Church' action at St Patrick's Roman Catholic Cathedral in New York City that involved the disruption of Sunday Mass. It was around this time that activists began using the term 'queer' to describe their 'unwillingness to conform' to social norms of silence with respect to their sexualities (Gibson, Alexander, and Meem 2013: 76–77).

Michael Warner has written about the important connections between queerness and transgression in his book *The Trouble With Normal: Sex, Politics, and the Ethics of Queer Life*. In constructing an ethics of queer life, Warner argues that the fight by LGBTI activists for marriage equality is actually 'a mistake' and a 'loss of vision', particularly in light of queer culture's historical affirmation of sexual autonomy. For Warner, queerness must resist the 'norms of straight culture' as the standard by which 'queer life should be measured' (1999: 1, 88).

Similarly, Lee Edelman has strongly rejected the 'compulsory narrative of reproductive futurism' in his book *No Future: Queer Theory and the Death Drive*. For Edelman, it

is time to stop kneeling at the 'shrine of the sacred Child' that 'marks the fetishistic fixa-
tion of heteronormativity'. That is, our society is often more interested in protecting the
needs of the fictional 'fantasmatic Child'—for example, saving children from the 'threat'
of LGBT people—than protecting the 'actuality of freedom itself' (2004: 11, 21). It should
be noted that Edelman's critique of reproductive futurism and the 'Child' is not a critique
of actual children or the raising of children. Rather, it is a critique of a 'Save Our Children'
ideology that curtails the freedoms and civil liberties of actual people in the name of a fic-
titious 'innocence' that is 'continuously under siege' (2004: 21–22). For both Edelman and
Warner, transgression is a queer value that must be embraced instead of being rejected.

Resisting Binaries

The third mark of queerness is *resisting binaries*. Queerness challenges the gender binary
system in which there are only two options—male and female—with respect to biological sex, gender identity, and sexual orientation. Under this system, a person who is classified as a 'man' with respect to biological sex is automatically assumed to have a male
gender identity as well as have a heterosexual orientation (that is, be sexually attracted
to only women). Similarly, a person who is classified as a 'woman' with respect to biological sex is automatically assumed to have a female gender identity and to be sexually
attracted only to men.

Queerness challenges this binary view of the world. First, not all people can be classified as either 'men' or 'women' with respect to biological sex. Approximately 1.7 per cent
of all births involve intersex conditions in which a baby is born with ambiguous sexual
organs or with genitalia that do not match the baby's chromosomal make-up (Thatcher
2011: 12–13). Second, one's biological sex does not necessarily determine one's gender
identity. A person who is classified as a man in terms of biological sex may have a female
gender identity. Third, not all people have a heterosexual orientation (that is, are sexually attracted primarily to persons of the other biological sex). A person who is classified as a woman in terms of biological sex can be sexually attracted primarily to other
women, or to both women and men.

Queerness also challenges the heterosexual/homosexual binary. As Eve Kosofsky
Sedgwick notes in her book *Epistemology of the Closet*, this binary is highly problematic.
First, Sedgwick observes that the concept of 'heterosexuality' is actually meaningless
without the concept of 'homosexuality' to define itself against. That is, heterosexuality is
not so much set apart from homosexuality, but it is actually *dependent upon* homosexuality for its meaning. As a result, the heterosexual/homosexual binary is 'irresolvably
unstable' (2008: 9–10).

Second, Sedgwick noted that there are actually a myriad of factors relating to sexual identity for any given person—for example, one's preferred sexual acts, one's most
eroticized sexual organs, one's sexual fantasies, one's main locus of emotional bonds,
and one's enjoyment of power in sexual relations—that do not necessarily depend on
the biological sex of one's partner (1993: 7). Why then, Sedgwick asked, is the biological

sex of one's partner the single classification that is lifted up above all others? Again, Sedgwick challenged the 'naturalness' of the heterosexual/homosexual binary in terms of how sexual identity is classified.

Similarly, Gayle S. Rubin has challenged binary thinking with respect to sexuality. In her influential essay 'Thinking Sex: Notes for a Radical Theory of the Politics of Sexuality', Rubin lists twelve pairs of binaries that distinguish 'good' sexual acts from 'bad' ones. These binary pairs include heterosexual/homosexual; married/unmarried; monogamous/promiscuous; and procreative/non-procreative sex (2011: 152). By exposing the stark differences between the 'charmed circle' (that is, the first element in each pair) and the 'outer limits' (the second element in each pair), Rubin reveals the importance of resisting binary thinking with respect to sexuality.

Social Construction

The fourth mark of queerness is *social construction*. Queer theory, as noted earlier, subscribes to a social constructionist view of sexuality and gender. That is, queer theorists have argued that there is nothing natural, universal, or fixed about contemporary categories of sexuality and gender, including the categories of 'gay' and 'lesbian'. Rather, these categories are fluid and are constructed by the societies and cultures in which they exist. Furthermore, these categories result from the deployment of social power, including the power of discourse and naming (Thatcher 2011: 24–28).

To be sure, people have engaged in same-sex acts throughout history. However, the contemporary identity categories of 'homosexuality' and 'heterosexuality' have not always existed throughout history. In ancient Greece and Rome, for example, men defined their sexualities in terms of being active (that is, the one who penetrates others) or passive (that is, the one who is penetrated), but *not* in terms of the biological sex of their sex partners (Halperin 2002: 113–117).

The late Michel Foucault argued in the first volume of *The History of Sexuality* that our contemporary understanding of homosexuality as an identity—that is, as a distinct 'personage', 'life form', and 'species' of humanity—only came into existence in the nineteenth century as a result of the classifying work of sexologists and the discourses of 'psychiatry, jurisprudence, and literature'. Before then, people who engaged in sodomy were viewed merely as a 'temporary aberration'; they did not have an identity based upon their acts. Foucault also argued that, ironically, as a result of the medicalization of homosexuality in the nineteenth century, homosexuals were subsequently able to organize around such an identity and demand the recognition of their 'legitimacy' or 'naturality' (1990: 43, 101).

Similarly, Judith Butler has argued that gender is not a matter of nature, but rather of performativity. Drawing upon the notion of performative acts—in which certain linguistic statements not only describe reality but change it (for example, 'I pronounce you man and wife')—Butler argued in her book *Gender Trouble: Feminism and the Subversion of Identity* that gender is not determined by biology, but is rather a 'repeated stylization of the body' that 'congeal[s] over time' to produce the '*appearance* of substance' (1990: 45, emphasis added). For example, drag is a powerful reminder of the constructed nature of gender because it disrupts the norms of gender performativity. Butler has acknowledged, however, that gender is not something that can be merely turned on or off at will. Rather, gender is a 'ritualized production' that is ultimately a 'constrained repetition of norms' that is 'regularized' and enforced over time through taboo, ostracism, and even death (1993: 60).

In sum, queer theory challenges the notion that sexuality and gender is fixed and unchanging throughout different times and places. As the work of Michel Foucault and Judith Butler has demonstrated, sexual and gender identities are socially constructed, as opposed to being 'timeless' and 'transhistorical' categories that are 'innate and unchanging' (Bristow 2011: 225).

FOUR STRANDS OF QUEER THEOLOGY

Shifting from queer theory to queer theology, this section will examine how contemporary Christian theologians have used queer theory in their work. In particular, it will focus on the academic discipline of queer theology and how queer theologians have incorporated the four marks of queerness discussed in the previous section—(1) identity without essence; (2) transgression; (3) resisting binaries; and (4) social construction—in their scholarship.

Queer theology, broadly speaking, is 'queer talk about God' (Cheng 2011: 2). Like the word 'queer', however, queer theology has several definitions. One definition views queer theology as theological reflection by, for, and about LGBTI people. This identity-based definition stems from the umbrella definition of 'queer' that includes a wide spectrum of sexual and gender minorities, including LGBTI persons.

Under this first definition, queer theology has existed since at least 1955, when the Anglican priest Derrick Sherwin Bailey published *Homosexuality and the Western Christian Tradition*, one of the first books to argue that the anti-homosexual tradition in Western Christianity was actually 'erroneous' and 'defective' (1955: 172–173). Since the early 2000s, several books (Goss 2002: 239–258; Stuart 2003; Cheng 2011: 26–42; Cornwall 2011: 43–71) and anthology chapters (Spencer 2004; Shore-Goss 2010) have been published that provide a helpful overview of theologies that have been written by, for, and about LGBTI persons.

A second (and narrower) definition of queer theology relates to how theologians have intentionally used queer theory in their work. It can be argued that, to the extent that Christianity is a very strange thing from the perspective of the secular world, theology has exhibited the four marks of queerness from its very beginnings. Despite the argument that theology 'is' and 'has always been' queer (Loughlin 2007a: 7), it has only been since 1993 that queer theologians have engaged explicitly with queer theory in their writings (Shore-Goss 2010: 188). (This is not surprising, of course, as the term 'queer theory' was not coined until 1991.) To this end, this section will now explore the four strands of queer theology that correspond with each of the four marks of queer theory.

Identity Without Essence

The first strand of queer theology relates to *identity without essence*. This strand of queer theology recalls apophaticism, which was an important theme in early Christianity. Apophaticism, which means 'turning away from speech' (McGuckin 2004: 23), can be traced back to the early Church theologians Clement of Alexandria (*c*.150–215) and Origen (*c*.186–255), and was more fully developed by Pseudo-Dionysius in the early sixth century.

According to apophatic theology—also known as negative theology—God can only be known by what God is *not*. That is, God transcends all speech and thought, and is ultimately 'above all essence'. Indeed, theologians have consistently recognized the 'profoundly limited capacity' of human language and of thought to 'capture the deity' (McGuckin 2004: 23). Thus, to the extent that both God and queerness are 'identities without essence', it can be said that God is queer.

Gerard Loughlin makes an explicit connection between God and queerness in his introductory essay to the anthology *Queer Theology: Rethinking the Western Body*. According to Loughlin, 'queer' can in fact be 'offered as a name for God'. Citing traditional theological sources, including the scholastic theology of Thomas Aquinas, Loughlin argues that we cannot know what God is, but only what God is not. In other words, 'God in Godself is an identity without an essence.' At most we can only say that 'God *is*', in the same way that we can only say that '*queer is*' (emphasis original). God is queer precisely because God is 'radically unknowable' (2007a: 10).

Virginia Burrus also makes a strong connection between theology and queerness. In her essay 'Queer Father: Gregory of Nyssa and the Subversion of Identity', Burrus explores the asceticism of the early Church Fathers. She equates asceticism with queerness because both are practices that 'center on *resistance* to normative discourses of sex and sexuality' (emphasis original). Citing David Halperin's definition of queerness as 'identity without essence', Burrus argues that Christian asceticism is not so much a 'positivity' but rather a 'positionality vis-à-vis the normative' (Burrus 2007: 147).

As both Loughlin and Burrus have demonstrated, Christian theology is queer because it understands God—as well as certain practices such as asceticism—as identities without essence. Furthermore, as Burrus notes, queer readings of traditional theological texts can be 'therapeutic' to the extent that they take 'theological hate speech' about queerness and reproduce it as 'counterspeech' within such texts (2007: 147–148).

Transgression

The second strand of queer theology relates to *transgression*. Transgression is a key theme in Christian theology to the extent that it is relates to the destruction of 'traditional boundaries' or the undermining of 'established paradigms' (Goss 2002: 229). From the perspective of the secular world, Christianity is a highly transgressive belief system. That is, the incarnation, crucifixion, resurrection, and inbreaking of God's reign are all highly transgressive events with respect to the powers and principalities of the world. As Paul writes, God chose what is foolish, weak, low, and despised to shame those who are wise, strong, and powerful (1 Cor. 1:27–28).

Indeed, Jesus Christ can be understood as the 'Transgressive Christ' because he was tortured and put to death by the religious and political authorities of his day for daring to queer, or to challenge, the status quo. In fact, he is accused by the assembly of elders of 'perverting' their nation (Luke 23:2). To the extent that grace can be understood in Christological terms (that is, by imitating Christ), grace in light of the Transgressive Christ can be seen as *deviance*. Similarly, to the extent that sin can be understood in Christological terms (that is, by opposing Jesus Christ), sin can be seen as unthinking *conformity* with the status quo. For example, bystanders who silently acquiesce to horrific acts of bullying or scapegoating of LGBTI people—whether by students or by church leaders—can be understood as exhibiting the sin of conformity (Cheng 2012: 101–110).

Robert E. Shore-Goss has argued that transgression is a central metaphor for queer theologies. For Shore-Goss, transgression is at the heart of queer theology because queer theology 'turns upside down, inside out, and defies heteronormative and homonormative theologies' (Goss 2002: 225). In his book *Jesus Acted Up: A Gay and Lesbian Manifesto* (Goss 1993), Shore-Goss argues that Jesus Christ is the 'model for transgressive practice'. Like activist groups such as ACT UP that disrupted church services to call attention to the Roman Catholic Church's complicity in the HIV/AIDS pandemic, Jesus Christ held his own 'action in the Temple' by overturning the money changers' tables and challenging the established religious system of his day (Goss 1993: 147–149).

For Shore-Goss, queer transgression is not limited to religious and political activism. Transgression also includes 'gender-bending and nonconventional sexualities' (Goss 2002: 225). To that end, Goss writes about the spiritual dimensions of a variety of queer sexual practices including erotic massage, full-body orgasm, polyamory, and barebacking in his book *Queering Christ: Beyond Jesus Acted Up*. These practices are described in a number of provocative chapters, including 'Finding God in the Heart-Genital Connection' and 'Is There Sex in Heaven?' (2002: 56–87).

Similarly, the late Marcella Althaus-Reid also used transgression to construct her 'indecent' theologies. In her groundbreaking book *Indecent Theology: Theological Perversions in Sex, Gender and Politics*, Althaus-Reid uses a transgressive methodology of indecent theology to critique the absence of sexual discourse in traditional Latin American liberation theologies. By juxtaposing explicitly sexual topics with theological reflection (for example, 'Oral sex: sexual *hi/storias* in oral theology' (emphasis original) and 'Black leather: doing theology in corsetlaced boots'), Althaus-Reid demonstrates how liberation theologies fail to discuss the connections between economic and sexual oppression and thus erase the sexual lives of the poor (2000: 134, 148).

The theologies of Shore-Goss and Althaus-Reid demonstrate that Christian theology is fundamentally queer to the extent that it transgresses and challenges the world's religious, political, and sexual norms. Queer theologies of transgression are important to the extent that they remind us of the scandal of a Messiah who was born in the midst of an excrement-filled manger and who was crucified as a common criminal on the cross.

Resisting Binaries

The third strand of queer theology relates to *resisting binaries*. Notwithstanding the current obsession of the religious Right with male/female complementarity, the Christian theological tradition has long resisted binary, either-or thinking. For example, the ancient ecumenical councils concluded that Jesus Christ is both fully human *and* fully divine, refusing to choose one nature over the other. Similarly, the Trinitarian Godhead consists of three co-equal persons, which deconstructs binary thinking as well as pair-bonded relationships. Finally, theological doctrines such as the Roman Catholic doctrine of Purgatory create middle or third spaces in which binary structures such as heaven and hell are deconstructed.

The erasure of binaries—and, indeed, of boundaries generally—is an important theme for Patrick S. Cheng. In his book *Radical Love: An Introduction to Queer Theology*, Cheng argues that both queerness and Christian theology can be understood in terms of 'radical love', which is defined as 'a love so extreme that it dissolves our existing boundaries' (2011: p. x). In the same way that queerness deconstructs the binaries of male/female and of heterosexual/homosexual, Christian theology deconstructs the binary of divine/human. According to Cheng, Jesus Christ can be understood as the 'boundary-crosser extraordinaire', whether this relates to 'divine, social, sexual, or gender boundaries'. That is, the theological doctrine of Christology can be understood as 'showing how the boundaries between the divine and the human are forever dissolved in the person of Jesus Christ' (2011: 79).

Laurel C. Schneider also resists binary thinking in her queer theological work. In her book *Beyond Monotheism: A Theology of Multiplicity*, Schneider proposes a 'logic of multiplicity' that moves beyond binary thinking. According to Schneider, monotheism and the 'logic of the One' is actually 'dualistic' in that it demands a separation of 'truth from falsehood' and that 'God be clearly and absolutely distinguished from not-God'. By contrast, the logic of multiplicity results in 'fluidity, porosity, a-centered relation, nomadic generativity, promiscuous love, and impossible exchange' (2008: 74, 152). Schneider's logic of multiplicity is a creative example of how contemporary theologians have used queer theory to resist binary thinking.

Finally, queer theology resists binaries to the extent that it is not limited only to the perspectives of gay men and lesbians. Bisexual, transgender, and intersex voices inherently resist the binaries of heterosexual v. homosexual (sexual orientation), male v. female (gender identity), and man v. woman (biological sex). Although several books have been published on bisexual (Kolodny 2000; Robinson 2010; Hutchins and Williams 2012), transgender (Mollenkott 2001; Tanis 2003), and intersex (Cornwall 2010) theologies in recent years, more work needs to be done in this area.

Social Construction

The fourth strand of queer theology relates to the theme of *social construction*. The Christian theological tradition has long held that earthly identities—whether secular or religious—are actually *not* of ultimate significance, particularly from an eschatological perspective. The one identity that matters is one's incorporation into the Body of Christ through the sacrament of Baptism. In this way, theology is strangely consistent with the social constructionist view of queer theory that challenges the 'naturalness' of one's sexual and gender identities.

As already noted, the work of Michel Foucault and Judith Butler has been central to queer theory, and in particular with respect to the notion that categories of sexuality and gender are contingent upon historical and other factors such as social power, as opposed to being 'natural' and 'universal'. Indeed, several important works have been published since the late 1990s that explore the contributions of Foucault (Foucault 1999; Carrette 2000; Bernauer and Carrette 2004) as well as Butler (Armour and St Ville 2006) to religious studies and theology.

Along these lines, Elizabeth Stuart has written extensively about queer theory and social construction in her theological work. In particular, she has critiqued gay and lesbian liberation theologies—that is, the precursor to queer theologies—for replicating traditional identity categories as opposed to transcending them. In her book *Gay and Lesbian Theologies: Repetitions with Critical Difference* (2003), Stuart argues that Christianity, akin to queerness, deconstructs sexual and gender identities through one's 'baptismal incorporation to the body of Christ'.

For Stuart, queer theology is 'not really "about" sexuality in the way that gay and lesbian is about sexuality'. That is, queer theology recognizes the inherent instability of sexual and gender categories and, as such, it must interrogate sexuality (as opposed to sexuality interrogating theology). For Stuart, sexuality and gender categories ultimately lack any ultimate or 'eschatological significance' (2003: 102–103, 114–115). Theology is queer only to the extent that it recognizes this truth.

Mark Jordan has also written extensively about queer theory and how sexual identities—including the 'Sodomite'—have been shaped by Christianity throughout history. In his book *The Invention of Sodomy in Christian Theology* (1997), Jordan challenges Michel Foucault's distinction between pre-nineteenth-century homosexual acts on the one hand (that is, the ancient 'practice' of sodomy), and post-nineteenth-century homosexual identities on the other (that is, the 'personage' of the homosexual). Jordan explores the personage of the 'Sodomite', which dates back to at least Peter Damian and the eleventh century, and suggests that the 'rapid acceptance' of homosexuality as an identity in the twentieth century might actually not have happened without 'medieval theology's preoccupation' with the Sodomite (1997: 163).

Jordan continues his exploration of church-influenced scripts about sexual identities in *Recruiting Young Love: How Christians Talk About Homosexuality* (2011). According to Jordan, this book is 'a sort of sequel' to *The Invention of Sodomy in Christian Theology* because it documents the 'invention or improvisation of new characters'—such as 'inverts, homophiles, and gays'—who can only 'speak in the space of the sodomite's retreat' in twentieth-century American churches (2011: p. xx). Jordan, like Stuart, demonstrates how these sexual identities are neither 'natural' nor 'universal', but rather are socially constructed by the Christian tradition.

FUTURE DIRECTIONS FOR QUEER THEOLOGY

This final section will explore some possible future directions for queer theology. As noted earlier, queer theory has moved far beyond issues of sexuality and gender in its current iterations. Queer theology, however, has yet to 'catch up' with respect to many of the areas addressed by contemporary queer theory. Accordingly, this section will propose six issues for future queer theological reflection: (1) queer of colour critique; (2) queer post-colonial theory; (3) queer psychoanalytical discourse; (4) queer temporality; (5) queer disability studies; and (6) queer interfaith dialogue.

One issue for future queer theological reflection is *queer of colour critique*. Queer of colour critique emerged in the late 1990s as a response to the 'normativity of whiteness in mainstream North American gay culture' (Muñoz 1999: 9). A key principle of queer of colour critique is that sexuality is 'constitutive of race and gender' (Hong and Ferguson 2011: 2). That is, issues of race and gender cannot be separated from issues of sexuality. Queer of colour critique recognizes its roots in women of colour feminism and has proposed an alternative genealogy for queer theory that is grounded in the work of writers such as James Baldwin, Audre Lorde, and Gloria Anzaldúa (Hames-García 2011: 26–28). One work that addresses queer of colour critique from a theological perspective is *Rainbow Theology: Bridging Race, Sexuality, and Spirituality* (2013) by Patrick Cheng. Although there are an increasing number of theologians who are addressing these issues in their scholarship (for example, there is a 2011 special issue of *Theology and Sexuality* on queer Asian theologies), queer of colour critique remains a promising area for future theological reflection.

A second issue for future queer theological reflection is *queer post-colonial theory*. Queer post-colonial theory emerged in the late 1990s as a challenge to the binary notion of the 'deeply ingrained homophobia' of post-colonial discourse on the one hand and the perception of gay and lesbian studies as 'white' and 'elitist' on the other (Hawley 2001a: 1). Although several books have been published in this area (Hawley 2001b, 2001c), few scholars have addressed queer post-colonial issues from a theological perspective. One scholar who has done so is Jeremy Punt. In his essay 'Queer Theory, Postcolonial Theory, and Biblical Interpretation: A Preliminary Exploration of Some Intersections', Punt proposes a queer post-colonial biblical hermeneutic that focuses on how 'sexual, racial, colonial, and class domination' identities are 'constructed and disestablished', and how the 'suppressed voices of the subalterns' might emerge in biblical texts (Punt 2011: 337).

A third issue for future queer theological reflection is *queer psychoanalytical discourse*. Psychoanalytic discourse has been an important resource for queer theory from its very beginnings. Queer theorists such as Leo Bersani, Judith Butler, Teresa de Lauretis, Tim Dean, Lee Edelman, and Eve Kosofsky Sedgwick have all engaged with psychoanalytic theory in their work (Brintnall 2013: 54), and a key resource in this area is *Homosexuality and Psychoanalysis* (Dean and Lane 2001). As Kent L. Brintnall has noted, however, it is surprising that this strain of queer theory 'is virtually absent from religious studies and theology'. According to Brintnall—who has addressed these intersections in his own work (2011: 65–99)—queer psychoanalytical discourse should be of particular interest to religious studies scholars and theologians who are interested in discourses about mysticism, apophaticism, and the sacred (2013: 54–55). It remains to be seen whether and how queer theologians rise to Brintnall's challenge.

A fourth issue for future queer theological reflection is *queer temporality*. Time has been an important theme for contemporary queer theorists, as illustrated by the recent anthology *Queer Times, Queer Becomings* (McCallum and Tuhkanen 2011). As J. Jack Halberstam has observed, queer time is not only about the 'compression and annihilation' resulting from the HIV/AIDS pandemic, but it is also about the ways in which LGBTI people often live their lives outside the logic of heteronormative time—that is, how queer lives are 'unscripted by the conventions of family, inheritance, and child rearing' (2005: 2). Whether this relates to queer folk who come out later in life and experience a second adolescence, or queer folk who remain immersed in youthful club culture well into their thirties and forties, queer time is about challenging linear notions of temporality. As with the case of queer psychoanalytical discourse, there is a surprising lack of queer theological work on queer temporality, particularly given the importance of time with respect to liturgy and theological doctrines such as eschatology.

A fifth issue for future queer theological reflection is *queer disability studies*. Since the mid-2000s, a number of significant works have been published in queer disability studies, including *Crip Theory: Cultural Signs of Queerness and Disability* (2006), and *Sex and Disability* (2012). As Robert McRuer has noted, there is a strong connection between able-bodiedness and heterosexuality. Able-bodiedness, like heterosexuality, still 'largely masquerades as a nonidentity, as the natural order of things' (2006: 1). Similarly, Anna Mollow has critiqued the societal bias towards a disability-free future. Citing Lee Edelman's critique of reproductive futurism, Mollow notes that some disability-related fund-raising events, with their 'ritual displays of pity' that 'regularly demean disabled people', operate under a logic of 'rehabilitative futurism' that is threatened by the future presence of disability (2012: 288). Unfortunately, most queer theorists—not to mention queer theologians—have yet to make the connections between queerness and disability in their work.

A sixth issue for future queer theological reflection is *queer interfaith dialogue*. Several works have addressed queer theory from the perspective of non-Christian faith traditions. One such work is the anthology *Balancing on the Mechitza: Transgender in Jewish Community* (2010b). This work engages with queer theory by challenging the gender binaries that are present in many traditional Jewish practices. For example, Noach

Dzmura draws upon Talmudic texts in his essay 'An Ancient Strategy for Managing Gender Ambiguity' to find an 'ambiguous or indeterminate third space' within the context of a 'binary norm' (2010a: 170–171; see also Michaelson 2009 on non-dual Judaism). Another such work, from a Buddhist perspective, is 'Towards a Queer Dharmology of Sex' (2004). This essay, by the late Roger Corless, argues that Buddhism itself can be considered queer to the extent that queer consciousness can be understood in terms of Buddhist principles of non-duality. It is critical for queer theologians to be in dialogue with such works—and to be engaged in a constant decentring of their Christian identities—if they are to take queerness seriously.

In conclusion, it is important to note that the foregoing list is merely one possible roadmap for future work in queer theology. As Eve Kosofsky Sedgwick has noted, 'People are different from each other' (2008: 22). Accordingly, other people may be interested in issues that were not mentioned in this section, such as queer affect theory, queer ecofeminism, and queer animal studies. It does seem appropriate, however, to close this chapter with non-closure, since 'queer theory curves endlessly toward a realization that its realization remains impossible' (Edelman 1995: 348). To paraphrase Reinhold Niebuhr, queer theology is an 'impossible possibility'. As such, theologians are called, in the words of Lee Edelman, to the following: 'Reinvent it. Resist it. Refuse it. Pursue it. Get over it. Just do it' (1995: 348).

References

Althaus-Reid, M. (2000). *Indecent Theology: Theological Perversions in Sex, Gender and Politics*. London: Routledge.

Armour, E. T., and S. M. St Ville (2006). *Bodily Citations: Religion and Judith Butler*. New York: Columbia University Press.

Bailey, D. S. (1955). *Homosexuality and the Western Christian Tradition*. London: Longmans.

Berlant, L., and M. Warner (1995). 'What Does Queer Theory Teach Us About *X*?' *Proceedings of the Modern Language Association*, 110(3): 343–349.

Bernauer, J., and J. Carrette (2004) (eds). *Michel Foucault and Theology: The Politics of Religious Experience*. Aldershot: Ashgate.

Brintnall, Kent L. (2011). *Ecce Homo: The Male-Body-in-Pain as Redemptive Figure*. Chicago: University of Chicago Press.

Brintnall, K. L. (2013). 'Queer Studies and Religion'. *Critical Research on Religion*, 1(1): 51–61.

Bristow, J. (2011). *Sexuality*, 2nd edn. Abingdon: Routledge.

Burrus, V. (2007). '*Queer Father: Gregory of Nyssa and the Subversion of Identity*'. In Loughlin (2007b), 1–34.

Butler, J. (1990). *Gender Trouble: Feminism and the Subversion of Identity*. New York: Routledge.

Butler, J. (1993). *Bodies That Matter: On the Discursive Limits of 'Sex'*. Abingdon: Routledge.

Carrette, J. R. (2000). *Foucault and Religion: Spiritual Corporality and Political Spirituality*. Abingdon: Routledge.

Cheng, P. S. (2011). *Radical Love: An Introduction to Queer Theology*. New York: Seabury Books.

Cheng, P. S. (2012). *From Sin to Amazing Grace: Discovering the Queer Christ*. New York: Seabury Books.

Cheng, P. S. (2013). *Rainbow Theology: Bridging Race, Sexuality, and Spirit*. New York: Seabury Books.

Corless, R. (2004). 'Towards a Queer Dharmology of Sex'. *Culture and Religion*, 5(2): 229–243.

Cornwall, S. (2010). *Sex and Uncertainty in the Body of Christ: Intersex Conditions and Christian Theology*. London: Equinox Press.

Cornwall, S. (2011). *Controversies in Queer Theology*. London: SCM Press.

de Lauretis, T. (1991). 'Queer Theory: Lesbian and Gay Sexualities—An Introduction'. *Differences: A Journal of Feminist Cultural Studies*, 3(2): pp. iii–xviii.

de Lauretis, T. (1994). 'Habit Changes'. *Differences: A Journal of Feminist Cultural Studies*, 6(2–3): 296–313.

Dean, T., and C. Lane (2001) (eds). *Homosexuality and Psychoanalysis*. Chicago: University of Chicago Press.

Dzmura, N. (2010a). 'An Ancient Strategy for Managing Gender Ambiguity'. In Dzmura (2010b), 170–181.

Dzmura, N. (2010b) (ed.). *Balancing on the Mechitza: Transgender in Jewish Community*. Berkeley: North Atlantic Books.

Edelman, L. (1995). 'Queer Theory: Unstating Desire'. *GLQ: A Journal of Lesbian and Gay Studies*, 2: 343–346.

Edelman, L. (2004). *No Future: Queer Theory and the Death Drive*. Durham, NC: Duke University Press.

Eng, D. L., with Halberstam, J., and Muñoz, J. E. (2005). 'Introduction: What's Queer About Queer Studies Now?' *Social Text*, 84–85, 23(3–4): 1–17.

Foucault, M. (1990). *The History of Sexuality*, i. *An Introduction*. New York: Random House.

Foucault, M. (1999). *Religion and Culture*. Selected and ed. J. Carrette. New York: Routledge.

Gibson, M. A., J. Alexander, and D. T. Meem (2013). *Finding Out: An Introduction to LGBT Studies*, 2nd edn. Thousand Oaks, CA: SAGE Publications.

Goss, R. (1993). *Jesus Acted Up: A Gay and Lesbian Manifesto*. New York: HarperCollins.

Goss, R. E. (2002). *Queering Christ: Beyond Jesus Acted Up*. Cleveland: Pilgrim Press.

Halberstam, J. (2005). *In a Queer Time and Place: Transgender Bodies, Subcultural Lives*. New York: New York University Press.

Hall, D. E. (2003). *Queer Theories*. New York: Palgrave Macmillan.

Halperin, D. M. (1995). *Saint Foucault: Towards a Gay Hagiography*. New York: Oxford University Press.

Halperin, D. M. (2002). *How to Do the History of Homosexuality*. Chicago: University of Chicago Press.

Hames-García, M. (2011). 'Queer Theory Revisited'. In M. Hames-García and E. J. Martínez (eds), *Gay Latino Studies: A Critical Reader*. Durham, NC: Duke University Press, 19–45.

Hawley, J. C. (2001a). 'Introduction'. In Hawley (2001c), 1–18.

Hawley, J. C. (2001b) (ed.). *Postcolonial and Queer Theories: Intersections and Essays*. Westport, CT: Greenwood Press.

Hawley, J. C. (2001c) (ed.). *Postcolonial, Queer: Theoretical Intersections*. Albany, NY: State University of New York Press.

Hong, G. K., and R. A. Ferguson (2011). 'Introduction'. In Hong and Ferguson (eds), *Strange Affinities: The Gender and Sexual Politics of Comparative Racialization*. Durham, NC: Duke University Press, 1–22.

Hutchins, L., and H. S. Williams (2012). *Sexuality, Religion and the Sacred: Bisexual, Pansexual and Polysexual Perspectives*. Abingdon: Routledge.

Jagose, A. (1996). *Queer Theory: An Introduction*. New York: New York University Press.

Jenzen, O., and S. R. Munt (2012). 'Queer Theory, Sexuality and Religion'. In Stephen J. Hunt and A. K. Yip (eds), *The Ashgate Research Companion to Contemporary Religion and Sexuality*. Farnham: Ashgate, 45–58.

Jordan, M. D. (1997). *The Invention of Sodomy in Christian Theology*. Chicago: University of Chicago Press.

Jordan, M. D. (2011). *Recruiting Young Love: How Christians Talk About Homosexuality*. Chicago: University of Chicago Press.

Kolodny, D. R. (2000) (ed.). *Blessed Bi Spirit: Bisexual People of Faith*. New York: Continuum.

Lady Gaga (2011). 'Born This Way'. *Born This Way*. New York: Interscope Records.

Loughlin, G. (2007a). 'Introduction: The End of Sex', in Loughlin (2007b), 1–34.

Loughlin, G. (2007b) (ed.). *Queer Theology: Rethinking the Western Body*. Malden, MA: Blackwell.

Lowe, M. E. (2009). 'Gay, Lesbian, and Queer Theologies: Origins, Contributions, and Challenges'. *Dialog: A Journal of Theology*, 48(1): 49–61.

McCallum, E. L., and M. Tuhkanen (2011) (eds). *Queer Times, Queer Becomings*. Albany, NY: State University of New York Press.

McGuckin, J. A. (2004). *The Westminster Handbook to Patristic Theology*. Louisville, KY: Westminster John Knox Press.

McRuer, R. (2006). *Crip Theory: Cultural Signs of Queerness and Disability*. New York: New York University Press.

McRuer, R., and A. Mollow (2012). *Sex and Disability*. Durham, NC: Duke University Press.

Michaelson, J. (2009). *Everything Is God: The Radical Path of Nondual Judaism*. Boston: Trumpeter Books.

Mollenkott, V. R. (2001). *Omnigender: A Trans-Religious Approach*. Cleveland: Pilgrim Press.

Mollow, A. (2012). 'Is Sex Disability? Queer Theory and the Disability Drive'. In McRuer and Mollow (2012), 285–312.

Muñoz, J. E. (1999). *Disidentifications: Queers of Color and the Performance of Politics*. Minneapolis: University of Minnesota Press.

Murfin, R., and S. M. Ray (2009). *The Bedford Glossary of Critical and Literary Terms*. Boston: Bedford/St Martin's.

OED Online (2013). Oxford: Oxford University Press.

Punt, J. (2011). 'Queer Theory, Postcolonial Theory, and Biblical Interpretation: A Preliminary Exploration of Some Intersections'. In T. J. Hornsby and K. Stone (eds), *Bible Trouble: Queer Reading at the Boundaries of Biblical Scholarship*. Atlanta: Society of Biblical Literature, 321–341.

Robinson, M. (2010). 'Reading Althaus-Reid: As a Bi Feminist Theo/Methodological Resource'. *Journal of Bisexuality*, 10: 108–120.

Rubin, G. S. (2011). 'Thinking Sex: Notes for a Radical Theory of the Politics of Sexuality'. In Rubin (ed.), *Deviations: A Gayle Rubin Reader*. Durham, NC: Duke University Press, 137–181.

Schippert, C. (2011). 'Implications of Queer Theory for the Study of Religion and Gender: Entering the Third Decade'. *Religion and Gender*, 1(1): 66–84.

Schneider, L. C. (2000). 'Queer Theory'. in A. K. M. Adam (ed.), *Handbook of Postmodern Biblical Interpretation*. St Louis: Chalice Press, 206–212.

Schneider, L. C. (2008). *Beyond Monotheism: A Theology of Multiplicity*. Abingdon: Routledge.

Schneider, L. C., and C. Roncolato (2012). 'Queer Theologies'. *Religion Compass*, 6(1): 1–13.

Sedgwick, E. K. (1993). *Tendencies*. Durham, NC: Duke University Press.

Sedgwick, E. K. (2008). *Epistemology of the Closet*, updated edn. Berkeley and Los Angeles: University of California Press.

Shore-Goss, R. E. (2010). 'Gay and Lesbian Theologies'. In S. M. Floyd-Thomas and A. B. Pinn (eds), *Liberation Theologies in the United States: An Introduction*. New York: New York University Press, 181–208.

Spencer, D. T. (2004). 'Lesbian and Gay Theologies'. In M. A. De La Torre (ed.), *Handbook of U.S. Theologies of Liberation*. St Louis: Chalice Press, 264–273.

Stuart, E. (2003). *Gay and Lesbian Theologies: Repetitions with Critical Difference*. Aldershot: Ashgate.

Sullivan, N. (2003). *A Critical Introduction to Queer Theory*. New York: New York University Press.

Tanis, J. (2003). *Trans-Gendered: Theology, Ministry, and Communities of Faith*. Cleveland: Pilgrim Press.

Thatcher, A. (2011). *God, Sex, and Gender: An Introduction*. Malden, MA: Wiley-Blackwell.

Turner, W. B. (2000). *A Genealogy of Queer Theory*. Philadelphia: Temple University Press.

Ward, G. (1999). 'The Displaced Body of Jesus Christ'. In J. Milbank, C. Pickstock, and Ward (eds), *Radical Orthodoxy*. Abingdon: Routledge, 163–181.

Warner, M. (1999). *The Trouble With Normal: Sex, Politics, and the Ethics of Queer Life*. Cambridge, MA: Harvard University Press.

Wilcox, M. M. (2012). 'Queer Theory and the Study of Religion'. In D. L. Boisvert and J. E. Johnson (eds), *Queer Religion: LGBT Movements and Queering Religion*, vol. ii. Santa Barbara, CA: Praeger, 227–251.

PART III

SEXUALITY AND GENDER IN THE BIBLICAL WORLD

CHAPTER 11

MARRIAGE AND SEXUAL RELATIONS IN THE WORLD OF THE HEBREW BIBLE

KEN STONE

THE Hebrew Bible is sometimes understood as one of the sources of what is assumed to be a 'traditional', 'Judaeo-Christian' model of marriage and sexual relations. Descriptions of such a model usually emphasize heterosexual reproductive monogamy and companionate marriage as the foundation of society and the context for all appropriate sexual activities. Readers who attempt to ground this model in the Hebrew Bible often highlight the opening chapters of Genesis, especially 1:26–28 and 2:22–25, as sources or prescriptions for traditional marriage. These verses are, themselves, then interpreted in light of the very assumptions about marriage, gender, and sexual practice that are said to be derived from the Bible (see, e.g., Davidson 2007).

Yet a closer look reveals a more complicated picture. The opening chapters of Genesis and many other texts do recognize the importance of reproductive heterosexuality for ancient Israelite society. When the entirety of the Hebrew Bible is taken into account, however, there appears to be less continuity than is often assumed between the so-called traditional view of marriage and the actual assumptions about family, kinship, and sexual practice that are articulated in, or presupposed by, biblical literature. Indeed, as scholars increasingly note (e.g., Pressler 2006; Knust 2011), the Hebrew Bible contains a wider range of perspectives on sex, gender, and kinship than references to any single 'biblical view' should allow.

Methodologically, it is important to note that the Hebrew Bible can be a flawed source of information about marriage and sexual relations as they actually existed in the historical and social world of ancient Israel. Most of the texts found in the Hebrew Bible are separated by long periods of time, often hundreds of years, from the time periods they claim to recount. Moreover, biblical literature in the form that we have it was largely produced by, and has been shaped by the perspectives of, an elite, literate, urban, and male set of authors who probably represent only a small minority of the population of ancient

Israel in their own time (Meyers 2013). Thus one must be cautious about the conclusions one draws from the Hebrew Bible about actual circumstances in ancient Israel, especially in earlier periods of its history or away from urban areas.

Nevertheless, a number of important observations can be made about marriage and sexual relations in the Hebrew Bible. In the pages that follow, I will attempt to describe some of the attitudes that we find in biblical literature about such relations. In distinction from the more common approach just referred to, this description will underscore both the diversity of biblical perspectives and the gaps that exist between the literature of the Hebrew Bible and more contemporary attitudes that are often associated with the 'traditional' view.

LANGUAGE, 'MARRIAGE', AND PATRIARCHAL ECONOMY

One way to begin to explore biblical perspectives on marriage is to examine the language used to describe marriage relations in the texts. In fact, there does not exist any single word in the Hebrew Bible that corresponds in a straightforward way to the English word 'marriage'. When the word 'marriage' appears in English translations, as it occasionally does, translators have used the word in an attempt to refer idiomatically to a relationship that the Hebrew text describes in other ways.

Most English translations do make frequent use of the English words 'wife' and 'husband.' Already in the much-cited passage in Genesis 2:24, we read in the New Revised Standard Version (hereafter NRSV) that 'a man leaves his father and his mother and clings to his wife'; in 3:6 we find that the woman, after eating fruit, 'also gave some to her husband'. The words 'wife', 'wives', and to a lesser extent 'husband' then occur multiple times in the remainder of Genesis and throughout the English Bible. In Hebrew, however, the words translated here and in many other passages as 'husband' and 'wife' are actually the same words used more generally, including elsewhere in these same verses of Genesis, to refer to a 'man' and a 'woman': *ish* and *ishshah*. English translators decide whether to translate *ishshah* as 'woman' or 'wife' and *ish* as 'man' or 'husband' based solely on considerations of context.

This translation practice is so common that very few scholars raise questions about it. Yet the appearance in English Bibles of words that readers associate with contemporary marriages may give the impression that biblical concepts of marriage are more similar to modern concepts than they actually are. As Jon Berquist (2002: 60–62) notes, the decision to make frequent use of English words that do not have precise Hebrew counterparts ('wife' instead of simply 'woman', 'husband' instead of simply 'man'), while perhaps pragmatically justifiable, obscures the fact that ancient marriage conventions were sometimes different from our own. In addition, such decisions can lead translators to supply spouses for biblical characters who may not have them, as arguably happens when Deborah is routinely understood in Judges 4:4 as 'wife of Lappidot' rather than the alternative possibility 'woman of torches' or 'fiery woman' (see Schneider 2000: 63–69).

If the Hebrew Bible doesn't contain a term for 'marriage', and if the terms most often translated as 'husband' and 'wife' are in fact simply common Hebrew words for 'man' and 'woman' used in contexts that translators associate with marriage, what language does the Hebrew Bible actually use to indicate that something like a marriage has taken place? One of the most common phrases occurs already in Genesis 4:19, where we read that 'Lamech took for himself two women. The name of the one was Adah and the name of the second was Zillah.' Comparable descriptions of men 'taking', 'giving', and 'bringing' women appear frequently throughout the Bible. To cite only a few examples: Abram and his brother Nahor 'took' Sarai and Milcah respectively (Gen. 11:29). Isaac 'took' Rebekah and she becomes his 'woman', usually translated here and in comparable passages as 'wife' (Gen. 24:67). Esau 'took' Mahalath, the daughter of Ishmael, alongside other women that he already had (Gen. 28:9). Later Esau also 'took' women from the Canaanites (Gen. 36:2). The Israelites 'took' daughters from their neighbours and 'gave' daughters to the sons of their neighbours (Judg. 3:6). As the latter verse indicates, fathers can also be the subjects of these verbs of taking and giving. Thus Abraham tells his servant that he should not 'take' a Canaanite woman for Isaac, but rather 'take' a woman from Abraham's relatives (Gen. 24:3–4). Rebekah's father Bethuel and her brother Laban later tell the same servant to 'take' Rebekah and 'she will be a woman to the son of your master' (Gen. 24:51). Laban also 'took' his daughter Leah and 'brought' her in to Jacob (Gen. 29:23). Subsequently Laban 'gave to him his daughter Rachel' as well (Gen. 29:28). Reuel 'gave' his daughter Zipporah to Moses (Exod. 2:21). In the latter case as in some comparable instances, NRSV adds 'in marriage' without explicit linguistic justification but rather as a means to bridge the cultural gap between the language about marriage found in the Hebrew Bible and the conventions of marriage assumed by English readers.

Gendered Hierarchy

The connotations of acquisition associated with these and other examples of men 'taking' and 'giving' women throughout the Bible need to be recognized. Although it is too simple to say that marriage is understood in the Hebrew Bible as an outright property relation, women do fall under the authority of the men who are primarily the actors in the arrangement of marriages. Women do not 'take' or 'give' men. Rather, in numerous texts, marriage appears to be primarily a transaction between men, especially the father of a young woman and the man who wishes to take her. To be sure, mothers can be involved in the arrangement of marriages as well, as we find with Hagar (Gen. 21:21). Hagar, however, has no husband. A more conventional role for the mother in the arrangement of marriages may be reflected in Samson's request to both his father and his mother to 'get' (literally the same word as 'take') for him the Philistine woman he has seen (Judg. 14:2). Moreover, the story of Rebekah indicates that a young woman's own wishes were, at least on occasion, taken into account by her family before a marriage was made final (Gen. 24:8, 58). In most cases, however, men are the subjects, and women are the objects, of the transactions that constitute marriage in the Hebrew Bible.

The gendered hierarchy that structured this understanding of marriage becomes clear not only from the language of 'taking' and 'giving', but in other ways as well. For example, there are two Hebrew words in addition to *ish* that are sometimes translated into English as 'husband': *baal* and *adon*. Both of these words literally mean 'master' or 'lord'. They are used to refer not only to the relation between a husband and wife but also relations between masters and slaves and, in some cases, relations between deities and their worshippers. Indeed, both *baal* and *adon* are used as names or titles of deities, whether Israel's god Yahweh or his chief rival, Baal. The fact that the same terms can be used to describe the male participants in marriage relationships underscores the hierarchical nature of those relationships: husbands are 'lords' over their wives in the language used for biblical marriages.

Yet the terms *baal* and *adon*, even more than *ish* and *ishshah*, are usually obscured in English translations when they appear in marriage contexts. For example, when Sarah, according to NRSV, observes in Genesis 18:12 that 'my husband is old', the Hebrew term translated as 'husband' is actually *adon*, 'master' or 'lord'. Where NRSV refers in Exodus 21:3 to a slave who 'comes in married, then his wife shall go out with him', the Hebrew text actually says that 'if he is master (*baal*) of a woman (*ishshah*), his woman (*ishshah*) will go out with him'. In Deuteronomy 24:4, where NRSV refers to a woman's 'first husband', the Hebrew text actually refers to 'her first master (*baal*)'. The verbal root of *baal* is also used several times to describe the acquisition of a woman that constitutes marriage. Thus in Deuteronomy 24:1, where NRSV begins 'Suppose a man enters into marriage with a woman', the Hebrew actually reads more literally: 'If a man takes a woman and he becomes her lord'. In Isaiah 62:5, where English translators tell us a man 'marries' a young woman, the Hebrew text actually uses the verbal form of *baal* to indicate that he has become lord or master over her.

In these and other passages, translators have introduced the terms 'marriage' and 'husband' into the English text, while the language of male lordship has been suppressed. A feminine passive participial form of the verb can also refer to a married woman, literally, as 'the one [feminine] lorded over', though English translations inevitably obscure this language, too, by referring to the woman simply as 'married' (e.g., Isa. 54:1; 62:4). The use of this type of vocabulary across the Hebrew Bible to refer to marriage is consistent with the implications of lordship found already in Genesis 3:16, where God says explicitly to the woman (using a different verb) that her man 'will rule over you'.

The connotations of gendered mastery in biblical references to marriage are even apparent from the Ten Commandments. Thus Exodus 20:17 uses masculine linguistic forms to warn a male audience that 'You will not covet the house of your neighbour. You will not covet the woman of your neighbour, or his male slave, or his female slave, or his ox, or his donkey, or anything that belongs to your neighbour' (see also Deut. 5:21). This prohibition lists things belonging to one male Israelite that another male Israelite might desire, including women, slaves, and animals. Indeed, the language of 'taking', 'giving', and 'lordship' that we have already seen in contexts associated with marriage is also used to refer to the acquisition of slaves and animals in the Hebrew Bible. The owner of an ox (Exod. 21:28–29) or a donkey (Isa. 1:3) is also the animal's *baal*. Such texts help us understand the extent to which a married woman was positioned under the authority of her husband in ancient Israel, even as an unmarried woman living in the house of her father was under the authority of her father or brothers prior to marriage.

Thus, while it may go too far to say that women were routinely reduced to the status of property or chattel in ancient Israel, from an anthropological perspective marriage in the Hebrew Bible does appear to be conceptualized as the 'exchange' or 'traffic in women' that generates relations of kinship between groups of men in many traditional, male-dominated societies (Stone 1996; cf. Rubin 1975). As Genesis 34:13–24 indicates, the exchange of daughters alongside animals and other property serves to establish alliances and obligations between kinship groups. The economic dimensions of these exchanges become explicit through such associated biblical practices as bride-price and dowry (e.g., Gen. 34:12; Exod. 22:16–17; 1 Kgs 9:16; cf. Gen. 24:53, 29:15–30; Deut. 22:28–29; Judg. 1:12–15; 1 Sam. 18:25). Women are taken and given in the Bible in hostile situations as well, as with the kidnapping of women as wives (Judg. 21) and the use of women among defeated enemy populations as wives (Deut. 21:10–14).

It is of course true that husbands or wives could love their spouses, as the love of Isaac for Rebekah (Gen. 24:67), the love of Jacob for Rachel (Gen. 29:18), or the love of Michal for David (1 Sam. 18:20) indicate. Yet Jacob has to work fourteen years to acquire Rachel and her sister Leah from their father Laban, just as he has to work an additional six years to acquire flocks of sheep and goats from Laban (Gen. 31:41). David has to deliver a hundred Philistine foreskins to Saul as bride-price for Michal (1 Sam. 18:25). Thus even love for a spouse cannot separate marriage from the economic and hierarchical assumptions that structure it. Such marriages are properly referred to as 'patriarchal', since they assume a father's authority over his daughter prior to her marriage and a husband's authority over his wife after marriage. Indeed, the most common Hebrew term for a family or household is, literally, 'house of the father'.

POLYGYNY, CONCUBINAGE, AND STATUS

If marriage in the Hebrew Bible is frequently conceptualized as an economic transaction in which one man acquires a woman from another man, there is no reason in principle why a man of means might not use his resources to acquire more than one woman. This is exactly what we find in numerous biblical texts. We have already seen that Lamech and Jacob each have two wives, while Esau appears to have several. Other male characters who acquire multiple women include Noah's grandson Ashur, Abraham, Gideon, Elkanah, Saul, David, Solomon, a number of other kings, and possibly Moses. This structure of marriage is appropriately referred to as 'polygyny' or 'many women', rather than 'polygamy' or 'many spouses', since there is no indication in the Hebrew Bible that women could have multiple husbands.

The Hebrew Bible nowhere forbids polygyny. Indeed, the law on primogeniture in Deuteronomy 21:15–17 acknowledges that polygyny is permitted in a matter-of-fact way when it confirms the priority of the firstborn son even in cases where one wife is loved and a second wife, though disliked, gives birth to the first son. Exodus 21:10 also specifies that a man must continue to take care of his first woman after he takes a second one. Although the rejection of Solomon by God in 1 Kings 11 is sometimes misunderstood as a condemnation of polygyny, God's anger is not provoked by the number of Solomon's women but rather by the fact that Solomon's foreign wives lead him to worship other gods. The story is characterized not by a suspicion of polygyny but rather by a suspicion that foreign women may lead Israelite men astray, a theme I return to later.

Pilegesh

A man's multiple women may not all share the same status, however. Some of the women acquired by men in the Hebrew Bible are referred to with the obscure Hebrew term *pilegesh*. This term has most often been translated into English as 'concubine', a word derived from Latin that was used to refer to individuals in a Roman system of non-marital but recognized sexual relationships (both opposite-sex and same-sex) other than, or in addition to, the relationship of husband and wife. Because the Hebrew Bible precedes the Roman institution, however, it is unwise to assume that an Israelite *pilegesh* exactly parallels a Roman concubine. A closer linguistic relationship may exist between *pilegesh* and the Greek *pallake*, which referred to a woman other than a wife in a permanent sexual relationship with a man; but the social contexts are, again, rather different. Any attempt to understand and translate *pilegesh* is complicated by the fact that the women who are referred to as *pilegesh* in the Hebrew Bible do not always appear to function in identical ways.

Susan Ackerman has argued that most of the women who are referred to as *pilegesh* actually fall into one of two categories. In some cases, a *pilegesh* appears to be 'a wife of secondary rank' (Ackerman 1998: 236). This may be true, for example, of the Levite's *pilegesh* in Judges 19; for the Levite is referred as both the woman's *ish* in 19:3 and her *adon* in 19:26–27. The woman's father is also referred to as the father-in-law of the Levite three times (19:4, 7, 9). On the other hand, a *pilegesh* may be in some cases 'a woman who is a part of a man's harem but is not one of his actual wives' (Ackerman 1998: 236). This category could cover those instances in which such kings as Saul, David, and Solomon as well as the judge Gideon are specified as having both wives and concubines (Judg. 8:30–31; 2 Sam. 5:13, 15:16, 16:21–22, [cf. 3:2–5], 19:5; [Heb. 19:6], 21:11; [cf. 1 Sam. 14:50]; 1 Kgs 11:3); and it might also include the concubines Abraham has, in addition to his two wives (Gen. 25:6).

Ackerman's categorization provides a useful way to approach the heterogeneity of the texts that refer to a *pilegesh*. Our understanding of the norms and conventions that shaped the life of a *pilegesh* in ancient Israel remains obscure, however; and some scholars suggest that it is better to leave the term untranslated (e.g., Schneider

2000: 128–130). What is clear is that the term reflects a system of marriage and sexual relations in which a man could legitimately have more than one woman as ongoing or permanent sexual partners, and that these women did not always fill the same role or hold the same status. Both wives and concubines could bear a man's children, though Genesis 25:6 may indicate that the children of a *pilegesh* were less likely to inherit a man's property after his death. The well-known stories of Abraham, Sarah, and Hagar and of Jacob, Leah, and Rachel indicate as well that a woman could give her own slave or maid to her husband in order that the slave woman might bear children for the man in place of the wife (a custom also known from other ancient Near Eastern texts). One of these women, Bilhah, is also referred to once as a *pilegesh* (Gen. 35:22). Similarly, in the book of Judges the mother of Abimelech is referred to once as the *pilegesh* of Abimelech's father (Judg. 8:31) and once as the slave woman of Abimelech's father (Judg. 9:18).

While it is acceptable for a man to have multiple women in the Hebrew Bible, in practice the resources required to do so probably meant that most Israelite men had only one wife. The ability of a man to collect multiple women appears to be an indication of his wealth, status, or power. This is made clear in 2 Samuel 3:1–5, where David's ability to grow stronger as the house of Saul grows weaker is illustrated by David's acquisition of multiple women and his siring of multiple sons. The growth in David's strength, women, and sons demonstrates the potency of the future potentate. On the other hand, David's subsequent inability to have sexual relations with Abishag, the young woman who shares his bed and keeps him warm in his final days, communicates to readers that David is now becoming impotent in both senses of the word (1 Kgs 1:1–4).

This function of women as indications of a man's power also makes them vulnerable to becoming objects in struggles between men for power and prestige (Stone 1996; 2005: 68–89). Thus, when Absalom attempts to replace his father David on Israel's throne, he demonstrates his power and shames his father by raping David's ten concubines on the palace roof, 'before the eyes of all Israel' (2 Sam. 16:22). Saul's son, Ishbaal, appears to fear that his father's cousin Abner may be making a comparable bid for the throne when he asks Abner why Abner has had sexual relations with Saul's *pilegesh*, Rizpah (2 Sam. 3:7). Solomon is similarly suspicious when his half-brother and rival for the throne, Adonijah, attempts to acquire Abishag, the young woman who had shared their father's bed (1 Kgs 2:13–25). The rape of a Levite's *pilegesh* in Judges 19 appears to function in part as a way for Gibeahite men to dishonour the Levite.

It is sometimes suggested that, while biblical literature acknowledges the existence in Israel of polygyny, concubinage, and the use of women in male struggles for power, the stories describing such phenomena are narrated in such a way as to underscore their negative consequences, indicating thereby that monogamy is the form for marriage mandated by the Hebrew Bible (e.g., Davidson 2007). It is therefore important to recall that Israel's God is also sometimes characterized as participating in these male contests over wives and concubines. When Nathan delivers an oracle to David condemning his adultery with Bathsheba and killing of Uriah, Nathan reports that God had previously given David 'your master's house and the women of your master' as part of the process by which God gave David the throne of Israel (2 Sam. 12:7–8). The women referred to here may be Ahinoam, since that name is given to both a wife of Saul and a wife of David (1 Sam. 14:50, 25:43; 2 Sam. 3:2); Abigail, who was the wife of David's enemy Nabal before becoming David's wife (1 Sam. 25:2–42; 2 Sam. 3:3); or other unnamed wives and concubines of Saul or other enemies of David. In any event, Nathan's oracle makes clear that God gave multiple women to David. Moreover, it goes on to state that God will give David's women to another rival of David who will 'lie with your women before the eyes of this sun' (2 Sam. 12:11), a turn of phrase that surely anticipates Absalom's subsequent public rape of David's concubines 'before the eyes of all Israel' (2 Sam. 16:22). God is therefore not represented here as a passive observer of these male contests over wives, concubines, and status, but rather as an active subject in them. Thus, polygyny, concubinage, and status cannot be cordoned off from biblical theology. They are rather a part of it, since Israel's discourse on God—its *logos* on *theos*—characterizes God in terms of them.

ADULTERY AND WHORING

Adultery is a very serious offence in the Hebrew Bible. In Genesis 20:9, Abimelech refers to it as a 'great sin' or 'great guilt'. According to the law codes, both the woman and the man who participated in adultery could be put to death (Lev. 20:10; Deut. 22:22). Like the notion of marriage, however, the notion of adultery in the Hebrew Bible is premised on the assumption that a married woman falls under the authority of her husband, who has exclusive rights to sexual intercourse with her. Adultery appears to be defined solely on the basis of the female partner's status (Brenner 1997: 134; Knight and Levine 2011: 318–320). If a man has sexual relations with a woman who is betrothed or married to another man, he and the woman have both committed adultery whether or not the male partner is married. The offence of the adulterous man is not against his own wife, but rather against the man who is supposed to have authority over the offending woman's sexuality.

This understanding may even be reflected in the language used to prohibit adultery. In Leviticus 20:10, the male partner in the adulterous couple is the subject of the verb 'to have adultery' at the beginning of the verse. No mention is made of the male partner's marital status, however, while the marital status of his female partner, the object of his adulterous activity, is described explicitly as 'the woman [or 'wife'] of his neighbour'. The right to the woman's sexuality belongs to the adulterous man's neighbour, hence both she and her male partner have committed adultery in violation of her husband's rights. The male adulterous partner's own marital status is immaterial: he cannot commit adultery against his wife, if he has one. If a married man has sexual relations with an unmarried prostitute, there is no indication in the Hebrew Bible that he has committed adultery even though he is, himself, married. Since his female partner is not married, and so does not fall under the authority of another man, adultery is not possible. Adultery violates a man's right to have exclusive sexual access to his woman, but it does not violate a woman's right to have exclusive sexual access to her husband. As far as we can tell, no such right existed.

Purity and Promiscuity

Just as marriage in the Hebrew Bible appears to come close at times to being a gendered property relationship, it is tempting to understand adultery as something like a property offence. Things are not quite so simple, however. Since the female partner in adultery is also put to death, responsibility or agency on her part is assumed: she is not simply the passive object of a theft. Moreover, the punishment for the offence is more serious than the punishment for theft. Indeed, sexually promiscuous women are viewed very negatively in much of the Hebrew Bible.

A lengthy and troubling passage in Numbers 5 describes a procedure that could be followed when a man suspected his wife of adultery even though she has not been caught in the act and he may simply be jealous. Several times in the description, the language of uncleanness is used (5:13, 14, 20, 27, 28, 29). Thus, it appears that a woman who participated in adultery was understood to have defiled herself or made herself impure in some way. The text also specifies that the woman is 'under' her husband, in other words, under his authority (5:19, 20, 29); and it exempts the husband from being punished for subjecting her to the ordeal described (5:31). It is not known whether, or how often, this type of procedure was actually followed.

The biblical regulation of women's sexuality does not begin with betrothal and marriage, however. A number of texts also evince a concern about the sexual purity of a young woman before marriage. Thus, Deuteronomy 22 describes a scenario in which a man accuses his wife of having been sexually active prior to their marriage. If her parents are able to produce the bloody cloth from her wedding night, the man who accused his wife has to pay a fine to her father and cannot divorce her. On the other hand, if his charge turns out to be true, the young woman is stoned to death at 'the entrance of the house of her father' (22:21). Her actions are described quite negatively as 'disgraceful', 'whoring the house of her father', and 'evil'. No comparable restrictions are given for premarital sexual activity of a young man.

Because female sexual promiscuity is viewed so negatively, several biblical writers use sexual rhetoric metaphorically to talk about perceived religious and political misconduct on the part of the Israelites, especially the worship of other deities instead of or alongside Yahweh. Within the terms of this metaphorical language, Yahweh is usually represented as a husband who has been wronged by Israel, his sexually promiscuous or adulterous wife. The rhetoric assumes that Israelite men will be able to relate to the anger and dishonour that a husband would feel if his wife were sexually unfaithful (Weems 1995). In some instances, it also represents God's punishment of Israel symbolically as the violent response of a wronged husband, suggesting that such violence might be an appropriate response to female sexual misconduct. A particularly troubling example of such rhetoric appears in Ezekiel 23, where the northern and southern kingdoms, and especially their capital cities Samaria and Jerusalem, are represented as two 'whoring' sisters who receive a violent punishment they deserve. A brief note at the end of this passage (23:48) seems to serve as a warning to human women: If God can treat 'his' promiscuous wives, Israel and Judah, this way, human women should take care not to act lewdly.

Although biblical rhetoric harshly condemns adultery and singles out women's promiscuity in particular when using sexual promiscuity as a theological trope, some scholars suggest that actual prosecution of cases of adultery may not have been as common as such rhetoric implies. The Bible does not actually describe any such cases, though it does narrate in detail one story, that of David and Bathsheba, in which the offspring of the adulterous union dies while both of the sexual partners are permitted to live (in contradiction to the laws on adultery). Knight and Levine point out that Deuteronomy 17:6 and 19:15 put a high burden of proof on capital cases, requiring two or three witnesses rather than a single witness. Thus, 'the law code's requirements for conviction of a capital crime would make the prosecution of adultery difficult at best, unless the couple were remarkably careless' (Knight and Levine 2011: 320).

Prostitution

In spite of the negative attitude taken towards adultery and the sexual activity of daughters who are still living in their fathers' houses, the Hebrew Bible does not prohibit prostitution as such. Prostitution may have been considered a shameful or stigmatized occupation for women, and Deuteronomy 23:18 prohibits the use of a prostitute's fee as payment for a vow in the temple. Jephthah's reputation also appears to suffer in Judges 11 because his mother is a prostitute. Nevertheless, prostitution was tolerated in ancient Israel as in other ancient Near Eastern societies; and it plays a role in several biblical narratives, including those involving Tamar, Rahab, Samson (who visits a prostitute in Gaza), and the prostitutes who come before Solomon after one of their children dies (Bird 1997). Women who had no father, husband, or other male relative to take care of them in the patriarchal societies of the ancient Near East may have had few other options for survival.

At one time, biblical scholars claimed that some women, and possibly some men as well, also served as temple, sacred, or cultic prostitutes. It is now increasingly recognized, however, that no such institution as sacred prostitution is likely to have existed in Israel or elsewhere in the ancient Near East (Budin 2008). The *qedeshim* and *qedeshot*, non-Yahwistic cultic functionaries who are viewed negatively in the Hebrew Bible, likely came to be associated with prostitution as a consequence of biblical rhetoric that uses the language of 'whoring' to disparage the worship of other gods.

Prohibited Unions

Not all marital unions between women and men are permissible in the Hebrew Bible. Leviticus 18:6–18, 20; 20:11–14, 17, 19–21; and Deuteronomy 27:20, 22–23, prohibit or curse a number of specific types of sexual union between various categories of kin. It is possible that the child of an illicit union who is not to be admitted to the 'assembly of Yahweh' in Deuteronomy 23:2 (23:3 in Hebrew) is the product of such an incestuous union, though some translators prefer 'bastard' in the latter case. The prohibitions against incest stand alongside prohibitions and curses against bestiality (Lev. 18:23, 20:15–16; Deut. 27:21; see also Exod. 22:19), perhaps because both types of violations were considered improper confusing of boundaries or categories that ought to remain separate and clear. Similarly, condemnation of male same-sex intercourse in some of these same chapters (Lev. 18:22, 20:13) appears to be grounded in a concern about confusing or mixing of boundaries between male and female (Stone 1996: 75–79; Knust 2011: 147–150). A prohibition against sexual intercourse during a woman's menstrual period (Lev. 18:19, 20:18) indicates that purity concerns also play a role in these lists of proscribed sexual activities.

The Bible is not entirely consistent in its attitude towards some of these types of prohibited unions, however. For example, the marriage between Abraham and Sarah appears to be viewed positively in the book of Genesis. Yet according to Genesis 20:12, Abraham and Sarah have the same father. This type of union is ruled out explicitly in Leviticus 18:9 and 20:17. Similarly, Leviticus 18:18 prohibits sexual contact between a man and two women who are sisters. Yet just this type of union is the origin of the twelve tribes of Israel, as Jacob marries and has children by the two sisters Leah and Rachel. David's daughter Tamar also indicates that David would allow her half-brother Amnon to marry her (2 Sam. 13:13), although it is unclear whether Tamar's statement is an indication of permitted practice, an example of exceptional practice among royalty, or a desperate ruse to prevent her own rape.

Intermarriage

A number of biblical texts also take a negative attitude towards intermarriage between Israelite men and non-Israelite women. Thus, Deuteronomy 23:3 (23:4 in Hebrew), immediately after indicating that those who are born from an illicit union are not to be admitted to the assembly, also rules out the admission of Ammonites and Moabites. In Nehemiah 13, this passage appears to be quoted (13:1–2) as justification for separating the Israelites from foreigners with whom they have intermarried. Later in the same chapter, Nehemiah explicitly disapproves of Judahites who are living with women of Ashdod, Ammon, and Moab; and he cites the negative example of Solomon as a king who was led astray by foreign women. Ezra goes even further, actively breaking up marriages between Israelite men and non-Israelite women (including Ammonites and Moabites; cf. 9:1) and sending the foreign women and their offspring away. This negative polemic against Ammonites and Moabites may also shape the narrative in Genesis 19, where we are told that the Ammonites and Moabites originated from incestuous unions between Lot and his daughters, who made of their father a passive sexual object. In Numbers 25, sexual relations with Moabite and Midianite women provoke divine disapproval and a plague, as such women are thought to be responsible for leading Israelite men astray. The *ishshah zarah*, or 'strange woman', who provokes anxiety in the book of Proverbs may also be a foreign woman, though this is less certain.

Yet on the matter of mixed marriages, too, biblical literature takes an inconsistent approach. Moses has both a Midianite woman (Exod. 2:16–22) and a Cushite (probably Ethiopian) woman (Num. 12:1); and his sister Miriam is punished by God when she and Aaron speak out against Moses on account of his Cushite wife (Num. 12:1–15). Although Samson's parents oppose his desire for a Philistine woman, the narrator indicates that God is responsible for it (Judg. 14:4). More significantly, Ruth is a Moabite woman who not only seduces and marries an Israelite man but, according to the genealogy that serves as the 'punchline' for the book of Ruth, is the great-grandmother of David (Ruth 4:18–22) and hence ancestress of the chosen Judahite dynasty. It is therefore possible to read the book of Ruth as having been shaped by intentional opposition to the approach taken to intermarriage in the books of Ezra and Nehemiah. André LaCocque, for example, refers to the book of Ruth as a 'politically subversive pamphlet' written to critique those alternative biblical views (LaCocque 1990: 100, *passim*; cf. Havrelock 2011: 40–63). Similarly, both Tamar, who is cited positively in Ruth 4:13 for seducing her father-in-law Judah in order to continue the Judahite line, and her mother-in-law appear to be Canaanite women in Genesis 38, though Canaanites are also explicitly ruled out as appropriate marriage partners in Deuteronomy 7:1–4 and Ezra 9:1–4 (cf. Stone 2005: 46–67). It is therefore hard to disagree with Jacques Berlinerblau when, in the course of discussing the topic of biblical interpretation and inter-ethnic marriage, he refers to the Hebrew Bible as 'a document that we want to nominate for the award of Worst Proof Text Ever' (2005: 88). The Bible simply does not contain a single or consistent view on marriages between Israelite men and non-Israelite women, sometimes condemning such marriages and sometimes accepting them (cf. Brett 2000).

If Tamar and Ruth are lifted up positively in spite of taking sexual actions that might be considered controversial, this is partly because, like Leah and Rachel, they 'built up the house of Israel' (Ruth 4:11). This text and numerous others place a high value on the generation of offspring in Israel. Indeed, the biblical concern about women's sexual purity as well as the fierce condemnation of adultery with a woman who is betrothed or married to another man are likely to be grounded at least in part in a concern about proper paternity. Descent in Israel is predominantly patrilineal, that is, traced through the male line; and fathers were probably concerned to ensure that the child or children who inherited their name and property were truly their own.

SEXUAL PLEASURE

The picture I have drawn so far of the approach taken to marriage and sexual relations in the Hebrew Bible may appear to be somewhat negative. It is therefore important to stress that, in general, the Hebrew Bible does not stigmatize sexual desire or pleasure. It does attempt to set limits on such activity, particularly (but not exclusively) for women. However, the negative consequences of these limits for women have more to do with the patriarchal nature of Israelite society (or at least of the views found in the Hebrew Bible) than with a negative valuation of sexual pleasure, as such.

More positively, Deuteronomy 24:5 states that a man who has taken a new woman will not go out with the army for a year. He is rather to stay home and enjoy the woman he has taken. Ecclesiastes 9:9 and Proverbs 5:18–19 also commend a man's enjoyment of his wife, though in Proverbs this advice is coupled with suspicion of 'strange' and 'foreign' women (5:20). Ruth makes a sexual overture to Boaz in Ruth 3 that is nowhere stigmatized, though the language used to describe her seduction is somewhat euphemistic. Women's sexual pleasure is referred to in a positive way by Sarah in Genesis 18:12, though it appears that she believes both she and Abraham are too old for her to experience such pleasure any longer.

The most positive representation of sexual pleasure in general, and of women's sexual desire and pleasure in particular, is found in the Song of Songs. Although the book has often been read as an allegory of the love between God and Israel, or Christ and the Church, it clearly was written as a poem or series of poems about sex and desire. Indeed, many of its characteristics are shared with a genre of ancient Near Eastern love poetry known especially from Egyptian literature. Although many of the passages found in the Song of Songs are very provocative, its most remarkable feature is perhaps the fact that it attributes sexual desire and pleasure to a female speaker without stigmatizing women's sexuality in any way. Indeed, some scholars of the Song (e.g., Walsh 2000) have noted that some of the metaphors and symbols used in it—particularly the metaphors of fruit—are more easily associated with women's bodies and pleasure than are the agricultural metaphors of seed more often associated with phallic sexuality in the ancient world. More significantly still, in spite of a tendency on the part of some readers to turn the Song of Songs into a celebration of marriage, there is no indication in the book that the lovers are married. To the contrary, they appear to want to be together sexually even though some members of their society are trying to keep them apart.

Yet the Song also indicates that women's sexual agency and pleasure could be viewed with suspicion by others, particularly men. The female speaker's brothers appear to be concerned about guarding her sexual purity (1:6, 8:8–9). Thus, they are characterized in terms of a male vigilance about a sister's sexual honour that can be found elsewhere in the Hebrew Bible (Gen. 34:14; 2 Sam. 13:20–22) and beyond (cf. Stone 1996: 44, 107).

Similarly, the woman's search for her lover in the streets at night provokes a harsh reaction from city guards, who at one point beat her up (S. of S. 5:7; cf. 3:2–3). The woman's insistence on seeking her lover and maintaining control of her own sexuality (8:12) are therefore even more remarkable, since she appears to be actively resisting norms and suspicions prevalent within the patriarchal society that gave us the text. Some scholars go so far as to suggest that a woman may even have written the Song to contest the negative images of women's sexual pleasure and agency that we find in certain biblical prophets (e.g., LaCocque 1998).

A less positive evaluation of the consequences of women's sexual desires may be found in Genesis 3. There, as part of a series of 'etiologies of life's hardships' (Bird 1997: 190) put into God's mouth at the conclusion of the Garden of Eden story, God says to the woman, 'I will greatly increase your pain and your pregnancies. In pain you will bear children, yet towards your man will be your desire, and he will rule over you' (Gen. 3:16). This verse recognizes that, when it was written, and as we have already seen, men often exercised some sort of dominion over their women. It also underscores the difficulty of childbirth for women, whose chances of dying while giving birth were much greater in the ancient world than today (cf. Meyers 2013). Other difficulties of life are noted as well, such as the fact that food was normally secured through arduous agricultural labour involving a struggle against thorns, thistles, and recalcitrant soil in the dry highlands of Canaan (Gen. 3:17–19). Although the labour required for agriculture is assigned to men in Genesis 3, women played important roles in the ongoing survival of a family as well (cf. Meyers 2013). Indeed, the picture of the 'excellent' or 'capable' woman in Proverbs 31 shows her to be engaged in a large number of activities, from morning to night. Precisely because of the need for more labour for the intensive subsistence agriculture practised in ancient Israel, however, women may have felt the pressure to produce more children for their husbands, as we see in such stories as that of Leah and Rachel. The tension produced between this desire for more children, on the one hand, and the dangers of childbirth, on the other, may well account for the fact that women's sexual desire is seen in Genesis 3 as a punishment. The woman's desire for the man is referred to with other difficulties because, in the specific context of ancient Israel, that desire encourages her to participate in an activity—heterosexual intercourse with a man who rules over her—that she might, on the basis of self-interest and chances of survival, prefer to avoid.

This is only one side to childbirth, however, even in ancient Israel. As the conclusion to the book of Ruth indicates, the birth of a child could be a source of great joy among women, not only within a single family but in a larger women's network. Moreover, in spite of the patriarchal structure of marriage and family, women participated actively in raising their children, who are therefore told in Exodus 20:12 and Deuteronomy 5:16 to 'honour your father and your mother'. Even an adult son such as Isaac could remain close to his mother, and desire comfort after her death (Gen. 24:67).

CONCLUSION

It should be apparent even from this summary picture that the attitudes taken towards marriage and sexual relations in the Hebrew Bible are less unified than is often assumed. Moreover, such attitudes do not supply twenty-first-century readers with a timeless mandate for family structures or sexual behaviour. To the contrary, biblical attitudes are shaped by the specific ancient contexts in which the literature was written. This is particularly true where attitudes towards women and women's sexuality are concerned. Thus, before attempts are made to 'apply' biblical texts to contemporary debates about marriage or sexual practice, one should take care to recognize the extent to which those texts incorporate assumptions we no longer wish to reproduce.

Nevertheless, the careful study of biblical literature may have surprisingly positive consequences for contemporary debates as well. When we recognize from the ancient disagreements over, for example, marriages between Israelite men and Moabite women that there has never been a single view about appropriate and inappropriate marriages, or when we are inspired by the Song of Songs to make greater room for women's sexual pleasure and desire, we carry on the legacy of custom, dissent from custom, and change to custom, that have always shaped marriage and sexual relations in Judaism and Christianity.

REFERENCES

Ackerman, Susan (1998). *Warrior, Dancer, Seductress, Queen: Women in Judges and Biblical Israel*. New York: Doubleday.

Berlinerblau, Jacques (2005). *The Secular Bible: Why Nonbelievers Must Take Religion Seriously*. New York and Cambridge: Cambridge University Press.

Berquist, Jon L. (2002). *Controlling Corporeality: The Body and the Household in Ancient Israel*. New Brunswick, NJ: Rutgers University Press.

Bird, Phyllis A. (1997). *Missing Persons and Mistaken Identities: Women and Gender in Ancient Israel*. Minneapolis: Fortress Press.

Brenner, Athalya (1997). *The Intercourse of Knowledge: On Gendering Desire and 'Sexuality' in the Hebrew Bible*. Leiden: Brill.

Brett, Mark G. (2000). *Genesis: Procreation and the Politics of Identity*. New York: Routledge.

Budin, Stephanie Lynn (2008). *The Myth of Sacred Prostitution in Antiquity*. Cambridge and New York: Cambridge University Press.

Davidson, Richard M. (2007). *Flame of Yahweh: Sexuality in the Old Testament*. Peabody, MA: Hendrickson Publishers.

Havrelock, Rachel (2011). *River Jordan: The Mythology of a Dividing Line*. Chicago: University of Chicago Press.

Knight, Douglas A., and Amy-Jill Levine (2011). *The Meaning of the Bible: What the Jewish Scriptures and Christian Old Testament Can Teach Us*. New York: HarperCollins.

Knust, Jennifer Wright (2011). *Unprotected Texts: The Bible's Surprising Contradictions about Sex and Desire*. New York: HarperCollins.

LaCocque, André (1990). *The Feminine Unconventional: Four Subversive Figures in Israel's Tradition*. Minneapolis: Fortress Press.

LaCocque, André (1998). *Romance She Wrote: A Hermeneutical Essay on Song of Songs*. Harrisburg, PA: Trinity Press International.

Meyers, Carol (2013). *Rediscovering Eve: Ancient Israelite Women in Context*. Oxford and New York: Oxford University Press.

Pressler, Carolyn (2006). 'The "Biblical View" of Marriage'. In Linda Day and Carolyn Pressler (eds), *Engaging the Bible in a Gendered World: An Introduction to Feminist Biblical Interpretation in Honour of Katharine Doob Sakenfeld*. Louisville, KY: Westminster/John Knox Press, 200–211.

Rubin, Gayle (1975). 'The Traffic in Women: Notes on the "Political Economy" of Sex'. In Rayna Reiter (ed.), *Toward an Anthropology of Women*. New York: Monthly Review Press, 157–210.

Schneider, Tammi J. (2000). *Judges*. Collegeville, MN: Liturgical Press.

Stone, Ken (1996). *Sex, Honour and Power in the Deuteronomistic History*. Sheffield: Sheffield Academic Press.

Stone, Ken (2005). *Practicing Safer Texts: Food, Sex and Bible in Queer Perspective*. New York and London: T&T Clark.

Walsh, Carey Ellen (2000). *Exquisite Desire: Religion, the Erotic, and the Song of Songs*. Minneapolis: Fortress Press.

Weems, Renita (1995). *Battered Love: Marriage, Sex, and Violence in the Hebrew Prophets*. Minneapolis: Fortress Press.

....

CHAPTER 12

MARRIAGE AND SEXUAL RELATIONS IN THE NEW TESTAMENT WORLD

....

WILLIAM LOADER

UNDERSTANDING what New Testament writers thought or said about marriage and sexual relations is at least as much about what they are likely to have assumed as it is about what they wrote. In their world, as in some societies today, marriages were mostly arranged between families. Wise heads might have noted an existing attraction between a couple, but the priority was family economy and welfare. With negligible help from elsewhere, families had to make ends meet. Extended families mattered as did producing new generations, for they were essential for caring for the older ones. A family's survival rested mainly on its own undertakings, whether craft or agriculture. Such household priorities and practices were by and large similar across Jewish, Greek, and Roman cultures (Satlow 2001: 20).

Threats to families would include famine, illness, and natural disaster, but also childlessness, unwanted pregnancy, especially where adultery made paternity uncertain, and divorce. Inadequate contraception and so fear of unwanted pregnancy drove strict controls, especially of women. Thus fathers married off their daughters as early as possible, also on the widespread assumption that women lacked emotional control. Their husbands, often twice their age, were usually far more experienced, including sexually, sometimes using prostitutes, allegedly spurned by Jews according to Philo, and a capital offence.[1] A virginal wife gave some hope of continuing chastity. In age, experience, authority, physical strength, education and most other categories, she was his inferior, explaining the plausible conclusion that women were in any case inferior (with exceptions proving the rule). Wealthy households might have slaves, who were at the master's disposal, including sexually, though not the males in Jewish households.

---

[1] *Ios.* 42; *Spec.* 3.51; *Hypoth.*7.1.

THE IMPACT OF THE GENESIS CREATION STORIES

Both bare necessity and community values informed norms and expectations. In Jewish society the Genesis creation stories were foundational. Their retelling in the book of *Jubilees* (*c*.160 BCE) has angels show Adam on successive days the animals which God created and Adam observe their coupling and want something similar for himself (*Jub.* 3:1–7) (Loader 2007: 236–285). The account has God agree and so create woman from Adam's rib, bring Adam to her, making fulfilment possible: 'he knew her', a designation for sexual intercourse. Thus it celebrates sexual union in companionship as God's intent, which happens before they enter the garden of Eden, where they abstain, and without focus on procreation, something only of interest after they leave that holy place (*Jub.* 4:1). Companionship and procreation typify the book's high view of marital intimacy. Josephus appears also to know *Jubilees'* story (*Antiquitates judaicae* [A.J.] 1.35), all the more impressive because of his heavy emphasis elsewhere on procreation (Loader 2011b: 265–270).

Philo similarly emphasizes procreation, but, despite his frequent and often extreme warnings against passion, affirms sexual desire and its pleasure in the service of procreation in his retelling of how the first man and woman became one flesh (*De opificio mundi* [*Opif.*]. 161; Gen. 2:24) (Loader 2011b: 21–31, 56–76). Even when procreation ceases to be possible, he defends marital intercourse as something positive (*De specialibus legibus* [*Spec.*] 3.35). Positive pleasure in intimacy marks the difference between the purely functional sex between Abraham and Hagar and that between Abraham and Sarah (*Quaestiones et solutions in Genesin* [QG] 3.21; *De Abrahamo* [*Abr.*] 253). Sexual union even serves as a favourite metaphor to depict the union between the soul and God or Wisdom, and between the mind and the senses (Loader 2011b: 136–141).

The Book of Wisdom has Solomon declare that his conception was the fruit of sexual pleasure as his parents slept together (Wis. 7:1–2) (Loader 2011a: 414–415). Similarly in *Genesis Apocryphon*, when confronted by her husband's fear that their wondrous child, Noah, might be the fruit of her flirting with angels, Bitenosh recalls the heightened pleasure of their last intercourse, reflecting the still plausible view that heightened orgasm enhances conception (2.1, 9–10) (Loader 2009: 285–291).

In *Instruction*, whose fragments survive among the Qumran Scrolls, an exposition of the Genesis accounts affirms marriage, including women's subordination within it, but also sexual union as positive (4QInstr[b]/4Q416 2 iii.15b–iv.13) (Loader 2009: 300–12). Another scroll, the *Vision of Amram*, cites Amram's love for Jochabed, as the reason why during a long absence he refrained from the usual option in polygamous marriages of taking a second wife (Loader 2009: 324–326).[2] In its opposition to polygamy (strictly

---

[2] 4Q543 4 2–4 = 4Q544 1 7–9 = 4Q547 1–2 iii.6–9a.

'polygyny' = having many wives) the *Damascus Document*, recovered from the Cairo Genizah and preserved among Qumran fragments, appeals to God's creating male and female and by implication to the two (only two) becoming one (Gen. 2:24) (CD 4.20–5.2) (Loader 2009: 108–119). Tobit has Tobias' prayer on the wedding night allude to Genesis 2:24, beside 1:27a and 2:7 (Tob. 6:18) (Loader 2011a: 176–177). In the *Tale of the Three Youths* (1 Esdras 3–4), one of them twice cites Genesis 2:24 to argue the power of marital love (4:20–21, 25) (Loader 2011a: 142–147). Imagery from Genesis 2–3 and Canticles colours the romantic tale of *Joseph and Aseneth*, which celebrates both love and the legitimacy of Joseph's marrying a foreigner (Loader 2011a: 300–334). Pseudo-Phocylides cites Homer's depiction of life-long marital bliss (Ps.-Phoc. 195–197). Not surprisingly Jewish inscriptions often refer to marital love (Chapman 2003: 211).

Arranged marriages could become loving ones. Occasionally we find reference to pre-marital attraction as in *Joseph and Aseneth*, but normally all liaisons between young women and men were strictly controlled for the family's sake. Modern patterns of dating and extensive pre-marital experience had no equivalent. As in the famed biblical encounters of Rebecca and Isaac, Rachel and Jacob, and Zipporah and Moses at wells, negotiations were short. Tobias meets Sarah first on the day of the wedding.

Ben Sira, for all his concerns with unruly daughters and the dangers posed by women, affirms the sexual attractiveness of a wife (Sir. 26:1–4, 13–18), claiming that the pleasure it elicits exceeds all else (36:22–24), even comparing a wife's beauty to sacred objects in the temple (26:16–18) (Balla 2011: 54–80). *Genesis Apocryphon* hails Sarah's sexual attractiveness (20.2–6) and the book of Judith, hers, which lured Holofernes to his death (10:3).

Such positive views of sexuality also inspired images of the age to come as characterized by fertility and abundance,[3] even where people would live for a thousand generations in a state of radiance.[4] *Sefer ha-Milhamah* has the presence of God and his angels guarantee fulfilment of the promise in Exodus 23:26 of no miscarriages.[5] Philo uses the same text to declare: 'No man shall be childless and no woman barren' (*De praemiis et poenis* [*Praem.*]107; 98–105). Wisdom promises that sterile woman will bear fruit (3:13); 2 *Baruch*, that childbirth will be without pain (73:7). The future would be as the present, only working as it should, and so sex have its rightful place and be off limits only in holy precincts. The *Temple Scroll* extended holy precincts to encompass Jerusalem, and *Jubilees*, followed by the *Damascus Document*, expanded the ban to the sabbath.[6] Otherwise sex in the right time and place was seen as normal and good (Loader 2009: 376–390).

Only rarely do we find the future portrayed as entirely sacred, ruling out sex. *Jubilees* depicted Eden as a temple, hence the first couple's abstinence there (3:12, 4:26, 8:19), perhaps envisaging a future return to paradise similarly (cf. 23:28) (Loader 2007: 275–285). *Liber Antiquitatum (Pseudo-Philo) (L.A.B.)* may imply this when it describes the future

---

[3] 1QS/1S28 4.6b-8; 4Q257/4QSᶜ 5.4-5; CD 2.11b–12a; 4QInstrᵍ/4Q423 3 1–5 / 1QInstr/1Q26 2 2–4; 11QTᵃ/11Q19 59.12.

[4] 4QpPsᵃ/4Q171 1–10 iii.1–2a; *1 Enoch* 10:17–18.

[5] 11Q14 1 ii.14b; 4Q285 8 10–11.

[6] *Jub.* 50.8; cf. also CD 11.5; 4QDᶠ/4Q271 5 i.1–2; possibly CD 12.4; 4QDᵉ/4Q270 2 i.18–19; 4QHalakhah A/4Q251.

abode of the righteous as a 'place of sanctification' (19:12–13; cf. also 26:13, 33:5) (Loader 2012: 70–74). Those imagining the future as an eternal sabbath, inspired by Isaiah 60:19–20,[7] and who shared *Jubilees'* sabbath ban on sex, would have ruled it out. Yet neither *L.A.B.* nor *Jubilees* disparages sex in itself when retelling biblical stories.

Negative attitudes to sex are rare. *Sibylline Oracles (Sib. Or.)* 1–2 (early second century CE) reduces Adam and Eve's intercourse to pleasant conversation (1:22–37) and sees no place in the world to come for marriage (2:238) (Loader 2011a: 68–78). The *Apocalypse of Moses* describes sexual desire as poison which the snake sprinkled on Eve's fruit, trapping her into the 'sin' of forever wanting sex with her husband (19:3; cf. also 2:4, 7:2, 28:4) (Loader 2011a: 68–78, 336–341). These are atypical of Jewish literature of the period, which affirms sex and not least the command to multiply (Gen. 1:28).[8]

SEX BEFORE MARRIAGE

Controls on sex confined sex to marriage. Thus, while rarely addressed, pre-marital chastity was standard. While Tobias and Sarah, meeting first on the wedding day, had no other option, the report of the deaths of her previous would-be husbands and her virginity assumes it (Tob. 3:8). Mary and Joseph's story (Matt. 1:18–19) makes sense only if we assume pre-marital chastity. Suggestions that this was so only in Galilee, not Judea (Satlow 2001: 167) rest on misunderstanding (Katzoff 2005: 140).

The various reinterpretations of Deuteronomy 22: 13–21 about accusations of brides' not being virgins assume it,[9] as does Jacob's assurance to Rebecca that in 63 years of his life he had never touched a woman (*Jub.* 25:4). In *Joseph and Aseneth* Joseph insists that they not have sex before the wedding night (21:1). Similarly Paul's advice to those with strong sexual desire that they marry assumes it (1 Cor. 7:8–9).

Even before matches were made and partners promised, chastity, especially of young women, was a paramount responsibility of fathers. Ben Sira deems it irksome (Balla 2011: 33–56). Daughters cannot be trusted. Like quivers they parade around looking for arrows (26:12, 42:9–14), and should be kept indoors and away from married and so sexually experienced women (42:11–13). Keeping daughters indoors away from public gaze was a common theme.[10] The *Damascus Document* concerns itself with daughters' behaviour and also with how to find them suitable partners.[11] Agents sometimes acted for fathers, as Zebul for Kenaz's daughters (*L.A.B.* 29:2). Paul acts in that role metaphorically in indicating that

---

[7]   *1 Enoch* 58:3, 5–6; *2 Enoch* 65:7–11; *4 Ezra* 7:39–42; *L.A.B.* 19:10, 26:13; cf. also Rev. 21:22–25, 22:5.

[8]   So *1 Enoch* 67:13; 65:12; *2 Enoch* 42:11; 71:37; *Sib. Or.* 1:65; Ps.-Phoc. 176; 4 Macc. 16:10, 18:9; *L.A.B.* 13:10.

[9]   11QT^a/11Q19 65.7–15; 4QD^f/4Q271 3 13b–15a; 4QOrd^a/4Q159; Philo *Spec.* 3.79–82; Josephus *A.J.* 4.246–248.

[10]   Ps.-Phoc. 215–217; 2 Macc. 3:19–20; 3 Macc. 1:18; 4 Macc. 18:7; Philo *Spec.* 3.169; *Jos. Asen.* 2:1–6.

[11]   4QD^e/4Q270 2 i.16–17a; 4QD^f/4Q271 3 8–16; similarly 4QInstr^a/4Q415 11; 4QInstr^d/4Q418 167b).

he wants to present the Corinthians as a chaste virgin to Christ to whom they are promised and not let them be seduced like Eve (2 Cor. 11:2–3; cf. also 1 Cor. 7:36–38).

Weddings were no private affair, but occasions for serious negotiation (about dowries and so-called bride prices) and celebration (Collins 1997: 107–115; Satlow 2001: 163–717, 213–217; Loader 2012: 45–51). Arranging marriages entailed prior promises, amounting to betrothal or engagement, though not necessarily formalized (Satlow 2001: 69–76; Loader 2012: 43–44). Paul accedes that fathers having made such promises of their daughters should feel free to fulfil them (1 Cor. 7:36–38) (Loader 2012: 214–219). Weddings belonged to those rare occasions where one could indulge in rich food. They served as images of hope (4Q434 2 6; Matt. 22:1–4; Luke 14:7, 15–24; Matt. 25:1–13; cf. Isa. 62:5), the joy of bride and bridegroom, an image of bliss (Bar. 2:23; 2 *Bar.* 10:13–16; 1 Macc. 1:27).

INCEST

The cultures of those times commonly rejected incestuous marriages. Jewish rules banned sexual relations and therefore also marriage with one's mother, stepmother, sister, granddaughter, stepsister, aunt, daughter-in-law, sister-in-law, wife's mother or wife's grandchildren, or living wife's sister (Lev. 18:6–18, 20:11–12), to which Pseudo-Phocylides added one's father's concubine (179–183). John the Baptist, apparently with Jesus' support, applied the ban to one's stepbrother's divorced wife, accusing Antipas accordingly, who, seduced by his step-daughter's dancing, acceded to his execution (Mark 6:17–18)[12] (Loader 2012: 143–146). Paul censured a Corinthian for sleeping with his deceased father's wife, his stepmother (1 Cor. 5:1). Both instances would be acceptable in most modern legislatures.

Debate raged over whether one could marry a niece, a position later championed by the Pharisees against the Sadducees according to tradition preserved in the Jewish Mishnah (*m. Git* 9.10; *b. Git* 90a). Essenes argued that banning marriage to aunts implies banning marriage to nieces.[13] (Loader 2009: 121–124, 354–356). Thus *Jubilees* prefers to depict Sarah not as Abraham's niece but as his sister[14] (Loader 2007: 249–250). By contrast, *Aramaic Levi Document*, the *Testament of Qahat*, and the *Visions of Amram*, have no hesitation in affirming not only marriages to nieces, but also Amram's marriage to his aunt (Exod. 6:20; Numb. 26:59; similarly *L.A.B.* 9:9, 12).

Concern with incest apart from the issue of marriage was widespread.[15] Expositions typically focus on Reuben and Bilhah (Gen. 35:22, 49:5; 1 Chr. 5:1)[16] and Judah and Tamar

---

[12]   See also Josephus *A.J.* 17.341, 349–363; *B.J.* 2.114–116.

[13]   11QT^a/11Q19 66.15–16, as uncontested; but clearly contested in CD 5.7b–11a. Cf. also 4QD^e/4Q270 2 ii.16; *4QHalakha A*/4Q251 17 2, 4–5.

[14]   *Jub.* 12:9; cf. Gen. 11:29; Josephus *A.J.* 1.151.

[15]   CD 7.1; 8.5b–6a; 4Q477 2 ii.8; 4QApocJer C^b/4Q387 fr.; and probably 4QInstr^d/4Q418 101 ii. 5; 4QApocrJer A/4Q383 fr. A; *Pss. Sol.* 8:9–11.

[16]   *Jub.* 33:2–20; 4QcommGen A/4Q252; *4QNarrative A*/4Q458; *T. Reub.* 1:6–10.

(Gen. 38:1–30; *Jub.* 41:1–26). Philo alleges that Persians allow incest (similarly *Sib. Or.* 7:42–45) and among the Greeks, deplores Solon's permitting marriage to half-sisters and Spartans' to full-sisters (*Spec.* 3.12–28).

INTERMARRIAGE

The general rule for choosing marriage partners was that they should be Jews and preferably from one's own extended family (endogamy), also a Roman preference, rather than from beyond it (exogamy), a Greek preference. In Tobit the concern is family inheritance,[17] but frequently it is to avoid Gentile religious and moral contamination. The prohibitions of Exodus 34:11–16 and Deuteronomy 7:1–6, and more acutely, those of Ezra 9:1–2 and Nehemiah 10:28–30; alongside Phinehas' execution of those who defied the ban (Num. 25), inspired a hard line on the issue.[18] *Jubilees* uses Dinah's abduction to condemn all marriage to foreigners, even if circumcised, and, like *Aramaic Levi Document*, hails Levi and Simeon as heroes (30:1–26) (Loader 2007: 87–105, 155–195; Frevel 2011). Similarly *4QHalakhic Letter (4QMMT)* B 39–49 uses Deuteronomy 23:2–4 to exclude not only Ammonites and Moabites, but all non-Jews from entering God's people by marriage. Prohibitions on mixing fibre and seed (Lev. 19:19 and Deut. 22:9–11) serve the same end in B 75–82; and in C 4–32, where the concern may be captive wives. The argument is made with allusion to Solomon (cf. Sir. 47:19–21) and Phinehas (Loader 2009: 53–90; Harrington 2011: 259–265).

Captive wives, as foreigners, resulting from the Hasmonean conquests, would have become a problem. Deuteronomy 21:10–14 allowed men to force sexual relations onto female prisoners with only the provisos that this should not happen straightaway allowing them time to grieve and that they be released if it does not work out. The new source of additional wives or concubines may well have reignited the issue of intermarriage. Polygynous marriage allowed for such additions, but may well have come under fire as a result.

Qumran writings reflect concern about intermarriage in relation to both priests[19] and people[20] (Loader 2009: 356–359). The Additions to Esther turn the tale on its head by having Esther deplore marrying not only any uncircumcised man but also any foreigner (C 26–28 / 14:15–17) (Loader 2011a: 236–243). *L.A.B.* has Amram advocate Tamar as a model in choosing incest for procreation as a lesser evil than intermarriage, in order to counter those who advocated withdrawing from sex altogether (9:5). It also crudely tones down outrage at the concubine's rape at Nob by suggesting she partly deserved it for having previously slept with foreigners (45:3, 47:8; cf. Judg. 19:1–30). Rejecting

---

[17] 4:13b, 6:12; cf. 8:21, 10:10, 14:13; similarly Jdt 8:1; *L.A.B.* 9:9; Esther C 26/14:15.
[18] E.g. Philo *Spec.* 1.56; cf. also *Mos.* 1.147; 2.193; *Migr.* 144–145.
[19] 4QOrd^b/4Q513; 4QApocrJer C^e/4Q390 2 i.10; 4QTestament of Qahat and 4QVisions of Amram.
[20] 4QHalakhah A/4Q251 17; and possibly 4QMiscellaneous Rules/4Q265; 4QCatena^a/4Q177 1–4.

intermarriage was a common theme.[21] It may well be targeted in 1 Maccabees 1:11–15, given the allusion to Numbers 25:3 and Phinehas in 2:53–54, and to changing the Law in 1:49[22] (Loader 2011a: 490–492). Josephus rejects it, despite toning it down in his comment that Isaac had 'no desire to form ties of affinity with the indigenous population' (*A.J.* 1.265) (Loader 2011b: 345–348). The Babatha archive contains reference to a woman now free 'to marry any Jewish man' (*Papyrus Murabba'at* 19). Similarly Paul assures widows that they are free to remarry 'in the Lord' (1 Cor. 7:39). Concern with believers' marrying non-believers may also underlie 2 Corinthians 6:14–7:1 (Loader 2012: 222–226).

The stories of Hagar, Tamar, Aseneth, Rahab, Ruth and Esther inspired alternative views. Defiantly, the legend in *Joseph and Aseneth* not only affirms marriage to a foreigner turned proselyte, but has Levi of all people champion her cause (22:11–13) (Loader 2011a: 300–334). Philo portrays Hagar and Tamar as converts (*Abr.* 250–251; *De Virtutibus* 220–221), as probably does Josephus on Ruth (*A.J.* 5.318–340). Plutarch's advice that women should submit to their husband's religion coheres with such a stance (*Moralia* 140D).

POLYGYNY

An influx of captive women may have made polygyny a phenomenon not only of the rich. Polygyny is certainly assumed in pre-Hasmonean times. Ben Sira addresses the problems of polygynous marriages, such as rivalry among wives,[23] a phenomenon already attested in Genesis of Jacob's marriage (29:31–30:24) and developed further in its various retellings.[24] *L.A.B.* recounts the rivalry between Manoah and Eluma (42:1–10) and Elkanah and Hannah (50:1–5), similarly about fertility. The Babatha archive reports similar tensions. The *Temple Scroll* assumes polygyny in discussing both captive women, including among priests (63.10–15), and levirate marriage (4QT[b]/4Q524), though it interprets Deuteronomy 17:17 as prohibiting it for the king. The *Damascus Document* then extends the prohibition to all (4.20–5.2) on the basis of linking Genesis 1:27 implicitly with 2:24; citing the entry of animals into the ark in pairs (Gen. 6:9), and perhaps by taking the prohibition of marrying two sisters (Lev. 18:18) as referring to two fellow Israelites (Loader 2009: 37–48, 97–125; Harrington 2011: 265–271). When it cites the regulation about captive wives (4QD[e]/4Q270 4.19), we must assume that it considered this as acceptable only for single men. Both Philo and Josephus assume polygyny, the latter explaining it as 'an ancestral custom of ours to have several wives at the same time' (*A.J.* 17.14). Jesus' encounter with the

---

[21] *2 Baruch* 42:4–5; 48:22–24; 60:1–2; *T. Job.* 45:3; Theodotus 4 18–21; *Aristeas* 139, 142; *Pss. Sol.* 17:28; *Sib. Or.* 5:264.

[22] Cf. also 2 Macc. 14:37–38; 14:3.

[23] Sir 26:5–6; 28:15; 37:11a.

[24] *Jub.* 28:11–24; Josephus *A.J.* 1.307–308; *LAB* 61:6; *T. Iss.* 1:2–2:5.

Sadducees about the woman widowed seven times also assumes it, though without addressing it (Mark 12:18–27).

Polygyny provided a way of dealing with marital dissatisfaction without requiring divorce. There were, indeed, stories of wives falling out of, and then back into favour. *Jubilees* has Leah eventually become Jacob's darling (36:23–24; similarly *Testament of Issachar* 1:2–2:5) (Loader 2007: 270–274). While its use as a cover for importing foreign captive wives made it controversial, polygyny also faced rejection from Greek and Roman culture (Baugh 2003: 116; Treggiari 2003: 169). Where it became less acceptable, a new problem would have arisen. Men would choose to divorce their wives, rather than supplement them. But that would raise the question: what justified such radical dismissal with its harsh consequences for women?

DIVORCE

Such will be the context for the debates of which rabbinic tradition contained in the Jewish Mishnah preserves fragile memory (*m. Git* 9.10; *b. Git* 90a) (Jackson 2008: 194, 205–207; Meier 2009: 94–95, 121, 126) and which must still have been an issue in Jesus' time. In the incidental reference to divorce in Deuteronomy 24:1, which informed the debate, the issue was the meaning of *'rwth dvr* (*lit.* 'shame of a matter'; *aschēmon pragma* 'a shameful matter'). The position attributed to Hillel and Akiba is very liberal and probably reflects what had been the common understanding, so that anything from bad cooking to insubordination would do (Meier 2009: 77–95). By contrast Shammai, it is alleged, argued for a narrow view, namely a sexual misdemeanour of some kind (apart from adultery) (Sigal 2007: 111–112). Josephus notes that there could be a range of grounds (*A.J.* 4.253), as does Philo, but in his exposition of Deuteronomy 24:1–4 he presumes that the woman has committed adultery, thus bringing the biblical law into harmony with Augustan law (*Spec.* 3.30–31), and disapproves of men who look for any pretext for divorce simply because their wives have fallen out of favour (*Spec.* 3.80) (Loader 2011b: 199–201). The lax practice of divorce may underlie Pseudo-Phocylides' criticism of those who multiply marriages (205–206).[25]

Debate about divorce appears to have influenced the transmission of Malachi 2:14–16, whose unamended text *sn' shlkh* may originally have referred critically to a man who 'hates' and 'divorces' his wife, as the LXX reads it (*alla ean misēsas exaposteilēs* 'but if in hating her you divorce her'), and so not be about hating divorce as such. A Hebrew text found at Qumran appears to have reversed the focus when it reads: *ky 'm snth shlkh* 'for if you hate her, send her away' (*4QMinor Prophets*[a]/4Q76). The original critique seems not to be of divorce but of its loose application and to include allusion to Genesis 2:24, about becoming one, and to Genesis 1:28, about bearing fruit (Collins 1997: 126–127).

[25] Similarly *Sib. Or.* 3:357–358 of Cleopatra; Josephus *A.J.* 17.349–353; *B.J.* 2.114–116 of Glaphyra.

It is further early evidence of disquiet in some circles about the way divorce was being exercised, especially its flippant use.

Divorce was simply assumed to be part of everyday life, so that references to it are often incidental. Thus it appears in reworkings of laws about seduction, binding the man to forgo any future option of divorce,[26] and of laws about vows.[27] Fragments of the *Damascus Document*, once read as opposing divorce in 4.20–21, now show on the contrary that divorce was a facet of community, and that the document provides for oversight for widows, divorcees, and their children as community members.[28] Its rule that men not marry divorcees probably has in mind women divorced for adultery (4QD[f]/4Q271 3) (Loader 2009: 114–115). Ben Sira commends divorcing a recalcitrant wife (25:26) and appears to reflect the use of 'hated' as a semi-technical term for a divorced woman,[29] present also among the Elephantine papyri and in the Judean desert archive.

Josephus insists that only men had the right to divorce, disapproving of Herod's sister Salome's divorcing of her husband Costabarus (*A.J.* 15.259–260) and of divorces by later women of the Herodian family. They probably acted under Roman law which allowed divorce from either side (Jackson 2005: 365–367; Loader 2011b: 318–320). Salome, however, seems to be using Jewish law, since she followed the distinctly Jewish practice of providing a certificate of release, which, as Josephus explains (*A.J.* 4.253), guarantees the termination of sexual relations and frees the partner to remarry (Jackson 2005: 355), the same being assumed in non-Jewish contexts but without the certificate.

ADULTERY AND DIVORCE

Early debates about divorce appear unrelated to adultery, for which the penalty was not divorce but execution, at least in biblical law (Lev. 20:10; Deut. 22:22; Prov. 2:16–19, 7:25–27) and both Philo and Josephus proudly acclaim the fact to underline the superiority of Jewish religion.[30] Prohibition of adultery (Exod. 20:14; Deut. 5:18; cf. also Lev. 20:10; Deut. 22:22), never in question, is widely attested.[31] The link with the prohibition of coveting another man's wife, alongside 'his field, male or female slave, or ox, or donkey' (Deut. 5:21) was also recognized.[32] Adultery was serious; it was stealing another man's property (Countryman 2007: 152–155; Loader 2012: 4–5). The Septuagint translation has it head the list on the second table of the ten commandments (Loader 2004: 5–25), leading Philo to declare adultery 'the greatest of crimes' (*De Iosepho* 42–44), and, like

---

[26] 11QT[a]/11Q19 66.8–11; 4Q159/4QOrd[a] 2–4+8 8–10; Philo *Spec.* 3.70; cf. Deut 22:28–29.

[27] 11QT[a]/11Q19 54.4; cf. Num. 30:10 MT.

[28] 4QD[a]/4Q266 9 iii.5; CD 13.16–17.

[29] 7:26; 42:9; cf. also Mal 2:16; 4QInstr[a]/4Q415 2 ii.4–5.

[30] Philo *Spec.* 3.11; *Hypoth.* 7:1; Josephus *A.J.* 3.274–275; 7.130–131; *Ap.* 2.215; cf. also Sir 9:9; Sus 22.

[31] Sir 23:23; *L.A.B.* 11:12; 25:10; 44:6–7, 10; 4 Macc 2:4–6; Ps.-Phoc. 3, 177; *Sib. Or.* 3:594–595, 764; Philo *Hypoth.* 7.1; Josephus *A.J.* 3.92; *Ap.* 2.201.

[32] *L.A.B.* 44:6–7, 10; 4 Macc. 2:4–6; and *Pseudo-Philemon*.

many others, to use it as an umbrella under which to gather all sexual wrongdoing (*De Decalogo*[*Decal.*] 122–131; *Spec.* 3.12–82; cf. also Ps.-Phoc. 3; Mark 7:21–23; Matt. 15:19; 1 Cor. 6:9–10) (Loader 2011b: 188–229).

Present-day concerns about adultery include hurt to a partner, hinted at in Ben Sira, who writes of 'wounds of the heart' (Sir 25:13) and of committing offence against one's own bed (23:18; cf. 26:19–21). He deplores its secrecy (23:18–26; cf. also *Psalms of Solomon* [*Pss. Sol.*] 4 and Susanna) and insists that men should keep themselves exclusively for their wives (36:24–27; cf. also 25:1; similarly Josephus *Ap.* 2.201.). His main concern was on dishonouring another male (Sir 23:23) and destroying his household (*Pss. Sol.* 4:9–10, 20, 15:11), amongst other things by creating offspring of doubtful paternity[33] (Loader 2011a: 503–504; Loader 2011b: 349–350). Philo expands this to include harm done not only to the wronged man's family, but also to the perpetrator's and to his friends (*Decal.* 126–131). Joseph features frequently as the hero who resisted adultery.[34]

Under Roman rule Jews lost the right of capital punishment. The story now preserved in John 7:53–8:11, about Jesus being presented with a woman charged with adultery, plays on the conflict between Jewish law and Roman law, which Jesus avoids by turning the charge back on the accusers (Loader 2012: 135–138). Until 70 CE the rite of Bitter Waters (Num. 5:11–31) apparently applied in disputed cases, supposedly causing any guilty woman to die (Instone-Brewer 2002: 94–97). In undisputed cases the alternative to execution was divorce. This then filled the reason given for divorce in Deuteronomy 24:1 with new meaning. Now 'a matter of shame' included adultery, indeed became its primary reference. Understood this way Deuteronomy 24:1–4 illustrates its own logic: the woman became unclean for the husband, doubly so. Philo accordingly runs the two aspects together: she is divorced for the adultery which initiates the new marriage (*Spec.* 3.31). Adultery was not just the ground for divorce but required it.

In this way Jewish law came to share what was the rule in both Greek and Roman law and which the Augustan *Lex Iulia* reforms (18 BCE) reinforced, namely that adultery mandated divorce. About this there was no choice (Baugh 2003: 116; Treggiari 2003: 165–168). The *Lex Julia* demanded that men refusing to divorce their wives for adultery were to be prosecuted. The assumption that adultery mandated divorce and, therefore, that a man must never again sleep with his adulterous wife, is widely attested. Thus when Joseph suspects Mary of the equivalent of adultery during betrothal, he had to divorce her one way or another and as a 'righteous man' chose the less shaming alternative (Matt. 1:18). Nir, husband of the pregnant Sopanim, reached the same conclusion (2 *Enoch* 71:6J; similarly 6A). Similarly Jacob never slept again with Bilhah after Reuben defiled her.[35] Retellings of Abraham's troubles with Pharaoh over Sarah's abduction (Gen. 12:10–20) take pains to show that no intercourse took place, since otherwise her return to Abraham would have been impossible.[36] Absalom's sleeping with David's concubines similarly cut the latter's access to them (2 Sam. 20:3).

---

[33] Sir 23:23; Wis 3:12, 16–18; 4:3–6; Josephus *A.J.* 3.274.

[34] Wis. 10:13; 4 Macc. 2:2–3; Philo *Ios.* 40–44; Josephus *A.J.* 2.41–60; *Jos. Asen.* 7:3.

[35] *Jub.* 33:9; *T. Reub.* 3:15; cf. Gen. 35:22.

[36] *Jub.* 13:11–15; Josephus *A.J.* 1.161–165; *B.J.* 5.380–381; 1QapGen/1Q20 20.15–15; *Pseudo-Eupolemus* 6–7 and Philo *Abr.* 98; *QG* 4.63, 66–67; cf. Gen. 12:10–20.

PASSION AND ORDER

Roman and Greek societies were more tolerant of men engaging in sexual relations with slaves and prostitutes, male or female, before marriage and to some degree during marriage. While banquets in Jewish life and those known to attend them, like Jesus, often attracted disapproval, Jewish authors like Philo railed especially against pagan banquets as typified by drunken and indiscriminate promiscuous behaviour.[37] Critique of such excess also came from within Hellenistic culture, especially from philosophers, whose views many Jews welcomed. When Stoics promoted order as the fundamental principle of life, Jews like Philo could easily identify that with God's created order and the Law. While some philosophers advocated extinguishing sexual passion, allowing only passionless sexual intercourse for procreation (Ocellus; Seneca; Musonius Rufus), Jewish writers were reluctant to call God's creation into question, preferring the more common view which urged rational control of the passions and avoiding excess (Loader 2012: 93–94; Deming 2004: 47–104; Ellis 2007: 96–146). Even Philo, who sometimes makes extremely negative statements about passions and pleasure[38] (Loader 2011b: 84–91), cannot bring himself to bedevil them. Emerging from such influence is a strong emphasis on sexual intercourse for procreation and on attitudes and states of mind rather than simply acts.

JESUS AND DIVORCE

In the New Testament one of the best known issues related to sexuality is Jesus' reported prohibition of divorce, in response to the ongoing issue of its abuse, preserved in five sayings, three of which are independent of one another (Matt. 5:32; 19:9; Mark 10:11–12; Luke 16:18; 1 Cor. 7:10–11) and one dialogue (Mark 10:2–9; revised in Matt. 19:3–9) (Loader 2012: 240–292).

In Mark the saying (10:11–12) follows the tradition about the conversation (10:2–9), but in a separate scene involving only the disciples. The conversation begins with some Pharisees asking, 'Is it lawful for a man to divorce his wife?' (10:2), reflecting presumably the ongoing concern. Jesus has them recall the Mosaic Law central to such discussions (Deuteronomy 24:1–4), then declares: 'Because of your hardness of heart he wrote this commandment for you' (10:5). This is not an attack on Moses' Law, but an assertion that this was a compromise to address human failure. Like others of his time Jesus appeals to the Genesis creation stories to identify God's original intent. He cites 1:27 ('God made them male and female') and 2:24 ('For this reason a man shall leave his father and

---

[37] *Contempl.* 53–56; *Abr.* 134–135; *Somn.* 1.122–125; *Ebr.* 21; *Spec.* 2.50; *Legat.* 14.
[38] *Leg.* 3.129–132; *Spec.* 1.9.

mother and be joined to his wife, and the two shall become one flesh') (Mark 10:7–8), adding to the latter: 'So they are no longer two, but one flesh' (10:8).

The conclusion follows, pithily formulated in two parts, one introduced by the word, God, the other, by the word for human being. Literally translated it reads: 'What God therefore has yoked together, let a human being not separate'* (10:9).[39] 'Yoke' was common imagery for marriage; 'separate', standard terminology for divorce. Divorce is thus rejected as an affront against God, by a human being unjoining what God has joined. Perhaps it once stood on its own as Jesus' only response, but it stands now with Genesis as its rationale.

The assumption is that such joining, through sexual intercourse, creates a permanent bond. The Hebrew words for 'man' and 'woman', *ish* and *ishshah*, underline their common substance. Greek could not reproduce the wordplay, but achieved something similar by adding the words 'the two' into the text, focusing on the two becoming one rather than on their returning to common substance (Loader 2004: 39–42). The notion of permanence is central to the argument.

Matthew reframes the original question to include whether one can divorce 'for any cause' (19:3) and then reverses the elements of Jesus' response. He first has him cite Genesis in confrontational style ('Have you not read...' 19:4), then continues right through to the statement about not unjoining what God had joined (19:6). Only then does he refer to Mosaic Law and then as part of their question. As in 5:32, he has Jesus set his own response in contrast to Deuteronomy 24:1–4 and their understanding of it, beginning 'but I tell you' and going on to cite his version of the divorce saying which Mark locates in a separate scene (Mark 10:10–12). In that scene Matthew has Jesus say something else (19:10–12).

His main change is to modify Mark's version of the saying. To understand its significance we turn to a discussion of all five prohibition sayings. They read as follows:

> Whoever divorces his wife and marries another commits adultery against her; and if she divorces her husband and marries another, she commits adultery.
>
> (Mark 10:11–12)

> And I say to you, whoever divorces his wife, except for sexual wrongdoing, and marries another commits adultery.*
>
> (Matt. 19:9)

> It was also said, 'Whoever divorces his wife, let him give her a certificate of divorce.' But I tell you that anyone who divorces his wife except regarding a matter of sexual wrongdoing makes her commit adultery, and whoever marries a divorced woman commits adultery* (Matt 5:31–32).
>
> Everyone divorcing his wife and marrying another commits adultery, and the one marrying a woman divorced from her husband commits adultery.*
>
> (Luke 16:18)

---

[39] The English translation used throughout this chapter is the New Revised Standard Version, with asterisks indicating the author's modified translation.

> To those who are married I give this command, though not I but the Lord, that a woman not divorce (*lit.* separate) from her husband—but even if she divorce (*lit.* separate), let her remain unmarried or be reconciled to her husband again—and that a husband not divorce (*lit.* dismiss) his wife.*
>
> (1 Cor. 7:10–11)

Unlike the absolute prohibition of divorce in the dialogue ('What God therefore has yoked together, let a human being not separate'—Mark 10:9; Matt. 19:6), all go beyond it to address remarriage. While some argue that, unlike Mark 10:9, the sayings address divorce only if followed by remarriage (Hays 1996: 352), the charge of adultery in all but Paul's version assumes that the original marriage remains intact and so by implication also condemns any attempt to dissolve it. The charge in itself is unusual because adultery was normally understood as committed against another man, but is committed here against the perpetrator's marriage, in effect, as Mark makes explicit, against his wife. Mark alone refers unambiguously to a woman divorcing (possibly implied in Matt. 5:32; Luke 16:18). This matches Roman practice, but could also reflect ancient Jewish practice.

Luke places the saying directly after the assertion that the Law in all its detail remains intact (16:17), to prove that comprehensiveness. He also sets it within the context of an attack on greed, perhaps targeting divorce and remarriage for sake of monetary gain, an issue also addressed in Jewish literature. Paul clearly assumes that the original marriage remains intact, so he rules out remarriage, though he does not use the charge of adultery in this context. The divorced person should at least remain single, which implies the same. Paul's practical bent has him qualify the prohibition where unbelievers demand divorce (1 Cor. 7:12–16). Peaceableness outweighs sticking to the prohibition (1 Cor. 7:15). It justifies believers' acceding to divorce and then no longer feeling 'enslaved'*, best read as implying, as divorce normally meant, that they were free to marry another (Instone-Brewer 2002: 201–202; cf. Fee 1987: 303). His hermeneutic of letting what he sees as loving and healthy have priority echoes the stance of Jesus for whom the biblical mandate of caring for human need overrode lesser commands such as sabbath or purity law.

Unlike the others, Matthew's two sayings have Jesus identify an exception to the prohibition of divorce, namely 'sexual immorality' (*porneia*), best understood as referring to adultery (Loader 2012: 246–249; Davies and Allison 1997: 16). Fitzmyer suggests incestuous marriage (1998: 88–89), and reads Acts 15:20, 29; 21:25 similarly, but incestuous marriage needed no divorce since it was invalid in the first place. The broad term *porneia* frequently referred to adultery (e.g. Jer 3:8–9 LXX; Sir 23:23; Sus 64). The exception in Matthew's two sayings does probably derive from a narrow reading of 'shame of a matter' in Deuteronomy 24:1, but in both instances is presented as standing in contrast to the way that both Matthew's and Jesus' dialogue partners understood Deuteronomy 24:1. Otherwise the contrast between what people heard that passage saying and what Matthew's Jesus said in 5:32 and 19:9 would not make sense (Loader 2012: 284).

One could see Matthew as somewhat uncharacteristically softening a prohibition of Jesus to bring it into line with Deuteronomy 24:1 (Gundry 1994: 90), or, more likely, as expressing what all prohibition sayings would have assumed from the beginning, namely that adultery mandated divorce, but that divorce for any other reasons was out-lawed (Loader 2012: 286). There is a coherence between belief that sexual intercourse both creates a permanent union and can sever a previous union. Paul assumes this in 1 Corinthians 6:12–20, where he cites Genesis 2:24 about becoming one flesh, to declare that sex with an immoral woman creates a permanent union, severing the previous one, here referring metaphorically to the believers' union with Christ. When barely a few verses later he cited Jesus' prohibition of divorce, he surely understood it in the light of this assumption. It went without saying that adultery required divorce because it broke the previous union. Unlike with adultery there is insufficient evidence to judge whether other exceptions could have counted, such as violent abuse or severe neglect, as Instone-Brewer suggests (2002: 184–187).

Options for divorced women were limited: returning to one's family, making a living on one's own, in desperation by prostitution, or remarrying, the preferred option which the sayings ruled out. Matthew 5:32 presumes remarriage would follow, so speaks of divorce causing one's wife to commit adultery. Problems remain. What probably began as Jesus' reaction against irresponsible use of the divorce mechanism by men could become in itself an oppressive injunction if deemed infallible and absolute, especially in abusive marriages. Today people recognize that much else can go wrong and be wronging beside adultery, so most opt for the flexibility which characterized Jesus by seeking the most loving and healthy response to what is going on.

AFFIRMING SEXUALITY

Jesus' appeal, like many of his time, to the creation stories, also reflects a positive affirmation of sexual intimacy in the context of marriage. People valued weddings and marriages and used them as a rich source of positive imagery. Thus Jesus could be described as like a bridegroom;[40] future hope, as like a wedding feast (Matt. 22:1–14; John 2:1–12); the new Jerusalem, as like a bride (Rev. 21:1–14); the church, as Christ's bride (Eph. 5:25–33); and the Corinthians, as Paul's virgin daughter whom he seeks to present to Christ chaste and pure (2 Cor. 11:1–3). Jesus emphasized sexual union and permanence independently of concern with procreation. The same is true of Paul. Echoing Stoic models, but informed also by his belief in creation, Paul affirms marriage in 1 Corinthians 7:1–7. This is all the more significant because it is not his personal preference. He sees it both negatively as a means to control sexual deviance (7:2), and positively as partners giving themselves to each other sexually and belonging to each other. The belonging does not imply obligatory sex, a precursor to marital rape, but mutual respect, the opposite of one partner claiming rights over the other. Hence his insistence that couples reach mutual agreement about when to have or not have sex (1 Cor. 7:5). Paul assumes that marriage entails mutual love between man and wife, even though he considers it a distraction (1 Cor. 7:33–34).

---

[40]   Mark 2:19–20; Matt. 25:1–13; John 3:29; cf. also 4:1–42.

Against some with much more negative attitudes to sex, Paul makes a special effort to refute suggestions that following one's desire for sexual union with a loved one by marrying is sin. He emphasizes this in relation to the unmarried and widowed (1 Cor. 7:8–9, 39–40), the divorced (7:15), virgins male or female (7:25–26), and fathers giving away daughters, already promised in marriage or not (7:36–38) (Loader 2012: 214–218), or, as some understand it, men and their potential spouses (Fitzmyer 2008: 322–327). Like Philo, Paul could never bring himself to declare sexual desire, which God created, sin. When Paul contrasted 'flesh' and 'Spirit', the target was not sexual desire but lifestyle and behaviour. Thus the 'works of the flesh' in Galatians 5:19–21 include many sins which are matters more of mind and attitude than body: 'idolatry, sorcery, enmities, strife, jealousy, anger, quarrels, dissensions, factions, envy'.

Paul's concern is misdirected passion, as in his view of same-sex relations (Rom. 1:24, 26–28) and in 1 Thessalonians 4:4–6, where he tells men to control their bodies, perhaps literally, their penises (Fee 2009: 149), though some argue, their wives (Collins 2000: 104), and so not to be carried away into wronging one another through adultery like people in the world around them (Loader 2012: 152–160, 293–338). He links their depravity to their idolatry, as in Romans 1:18–32.[41] Misdirected passion also includes cavorting with immoral women, probably prostitutes (1 Cor. 6:12–20), and incest (1 Cor. 5:1).

In lists of evils sexual immorality often comes first, as it did in the second table of the Septuagint decalogue (Mark 7:22; 1 Cor. 5:10, 11; 6:9–10; Gal. 5:19–21; Col. 3:5, 8; Eph. 5:3, 5; 1 Tim. 1:10; Rev. 9:21; 21:8; 22:15). Frequently such lists associate sexual wrongdoing with drunkenness and debauchery at banquets, the common context for such behaviour in that world. Thus 1 Peter warns against 'doing what the Gentiles like to do, living in licentiousness, passions, drunkenness, revels, carousing, and lawless idolatry') (4:3; cf. also 1 John 2:15; 2 Pet. 2:10, 13–14; Jude 11–12).

ADULTERY AND ATTITUDE

The prohibition of adultery is frequently alluded to (e.g. Jas. 2:11; Heb. 13:4) and serves metaphorically as in Old Testament tradition to depict idolatry.[42] When Matthew portrays Jesus as pitting his own interpretation of biblical law against the way it was heard in his time, he begins by shifting the focus from murder to hate and harboured anger (5:21–26), and then moves to adultery: 'But I tell you, that everyone who looks at a woman with a view to lusting after her has committed adultery with her already in his heart,'* (5:27–28) (Loader 2012: 109–119). 'Woman' here means 'married woman'. Adultery is with married women. 'With a view to lusting after', could be translated: 'with the result that he lusts after', but Matthew's Greek usage elsewhere (6:1, 23:5) indicates that the focus is intent, not effect. Read as effect it would amount to a condemnation of

---

[41] Cf. also 1 Cor. 10:7–8; and Wis 14:12, 22–27; *Sib. Or.* 3.29–45.

[42] Jas. 4:4; Rev. 2:22; cf. also Matt. 12:39; 16:4; Mark 8:38.

males finding a woman sexually attractive, and so condemn all sexual feeling as adulterous. That could (and did) lead to the conclusion that women and women's sexuality are dangerous, who must therefore be controlled (and could frequently be blamed) (See Luz 2007: 389–390 on its impact). The focus on intent does the opposite, addressing the danger posed not by women but by men who look with lustful intent at married women, declaring it adulterous attitude, adultery in the heart/mind. What is condemned is not sexual feelings but what one does with them, for which men must take responsibility (and not blame women). Effectively it expresses what is already implied in the decalogue, 'Neither shall you covet your neighbour's wife' (Deut. 5:21). Where women were not, as was sometimes assumed, regarded as dangerous because of their sexuality, community with men and women became possible even though lingering prejudice about their inferiority remained. The focus on attitude and not just behaviour also finds expression in Mark 7:21–23 (also Matt. 15:18–20), which targets what comes out of the mind and heart as what truly defiles.

Matthew has Jesus reinforce his warning against adulterous attitudes by challenging men in hyperbole to be prepared to excise their right hand or pluck out their right eye, if that is what it takes (5:29–30). Mark used similar sayings in the context of child abuse (Mark 9:42–48; Matt. 18:6–9) listing hands, eyes, and feet, though without sexual reference (Loader 2012: 119–135). Some like Origen read 'foot' and 'hand' as euphemisms for penis and castrated themselves (Davies and Allison 1988: 524), surely not the intent and difficult when thinking of *right* hand or foot, while others suggest 'hand' might refer to masturbation as in the Mishnah (*m. Nid.* 2.1), but attaching special meanings to eye, hand, and foot seems over-interpretation.

The attitudes to marriage and sexuality of New Testament writers belong to the world of their time with occasional intrusions of strictness, as is typical also of their approach to wider issues like same-sex relations and family. Sex was positive as God's creation, but exposed to dangers.

References

Balla, Ibolya (2011). *Ben Sira on Family, Gender, and Sexuality*. Berlin: de Gruyter.

Baugh, S. M. (2003). 'Marriage and Family in Ancient Greek Society'. In Ken M. Campbell (ed.), *Marriage and Family in the Biblical World*. Downers Grove: IVP, 103–131.

Chapman, David W. (2003). 'Marriage and Family in Second Temple Judaism'. In Ken M. Campbell (ed.), *Marriage and Family in the Biblical World*. Downers Grove: IVP, 183–239.

Collins, John J. (1997). 'Marriage, divorce, and family in Second Temple Judaism'. In Leo G. Perdue, Joseph Blenkinsopp, John J. Collins, and Carol Meyers (eds), *Families in Ancient Israel*. Louisville: Westminster John Knox, 104–162.

Collins, Raymond F. (2000). *Sexual Ethics and the New Testament*. New York: Crossroad.

Countryman, L. William (2007). *Dirt, Greed, and Sex*, 2nd edn. Minneapolis: Fortress.

Davies, William D. and Dale C. Allison (1988/1991/1997). *Matthew*, 3 vols. Edinburgh: T&T Clark.

Deming, Will (2004). *Paul on Marriage and Celibacy*, 2nd edn. Grand Rapids: Eerdmans.

Ellis, J. Edward (2007). *Paul and Ancient Views of Sexual Desire*. London: T&T Clark.

Fee, Gordon D. (1987). *The First Epistle to the Corinthians*. Grand Rapids: Eerdmans.

Fee, Gordon D. (2009). *The First and Second Letter to the Thessalonians*. Grand Rapids: Eerdmans.

Fitzmyer, Joseph A. (1998). 'The Matthean Divorce Texts and Some New Palestinian Evidence'. In Joseph A. Fitzmyer, *To Advance the Gospel*, 2nd edn. Grand Rapids: Eerdmans, 79–111.

Fitzmyer, Joseph A. (2008). *First Corinthians*. New Haven: Yale University Press.

Frevel, Christian (2011). ' "Separate yourselves from the Gentiles" (Jubilees 22:16): Intermarriage in the Book of Jubilees'. In Christian Frevel (ed.), *Mixed Marriages*. London: T&T Clark, 220–250.

Gundry, Robert H. (1994). *Matthew*, 2nd edn. Grand Rapids: Eerdmans.

Harrington, Hannah (2011). 'Intermarriage in Qumran Texts: The Legacy of Ezra–Nehemiah'. In Christian Frevel (ed.), *Mixed Marriages*. London: T&T Clark, 251–279.

Hays, Richard B. (1996). *The Moral Vision of the New Testament*. Edinburgh: T&T. Clark.

Instone-Brewer, David (2002). *Divorce and Remarriage in the Bible*. Grand Rapids: Eerdmans.

Jackson, Bernard S. (2005). 'The Divorces of the Herodian Princesses: Jewish law, Roman law, or Palace law?' In Joseph Sievers and Gaia Lembi (eds), *Josephus and Jewish History in Flavian Rome and Beyond*. Leiden: Brill, 343–68.

Jackson, Bernard S. (2008). ' "Holier than thou"? Marriage and divorce in the Scrolls, the New Testament and early Rabbinic Sources'. In Bernard S. Jackson (ed.), *Essays on Halakhah in the New Testament*. Leiden: Brill, 167–225.

Katzoff, Ranon (2005). 'On P.Yadin 37 = P.Hever 65'. In Ranon Katzoff and David Schaps (eds), *Law in the Documents of the Judaean Desert*. Leiden: Brill, 133–144.

Loader, William (2004). *The Septuagint, Sexuality, and the New Testament*. Grand Rapids: Eerdmans.

Loader, William (2007). *Enoch, Levi, and Jubilees on Sexuality*. Grand Rapids: Eerdmans.

Loader, William (2009). *The Dead Sea Scrolls on Sexuality*. Grand Rapids: Eerdmans.

Loader, William (2011a). *The Pseudepigrapha on Sexuality*. Grand Rapids: Eerdmans.

Loader, William (2011b). *Philo, Josephus, and the Testaments on Sexuality*. Grand Rapids: Eerdmans.

Loader, William (2012). *The New Testament on Sexuality*. Grand Rapids: Eerdmans.

Luz, Ulrich (2007). *Matthew 1–7*. Hermeneia. Minneapolis: Fortress.

Meier, John P. (2009). *A Marginal Jew: vol. 4. Law and Love*. New Haven: Yale University Press.

Satlow, Michael L. (2001). *Jewish Marriage in Antiquity*. Princeton: Princeton University Press.

Sigal, Phillip (2007). *The Halakhah of Jesus of Nazareth according to the Gospel of Matthew*. Atlanta: Society for Biblical Literature.

Treggiari, Susan (2003). 'Marriage and Family in Roman Society'. In Ken M. Campbell (ed.), *Marriage and Family in the Biblical World*. Downers Grove: IVP, 132–182.

CHAPTER 13

....

SAME-SEX RELATIONS IN THE BIBLICAL WORLD

....

THEODORE W. JENNINGS, JR.

HOMOPHOBIC HERMENEUTICS

....

FOR much of Christian history it has been regarded as self-evident that biblical literature is characterized by a blanket prohibition of same-sex love. Increasingly, however it
is becoming apparent that there is far more to biblical literature than meets the 'homophobic' eye. The homophobic hermeneutics of scripture was a long time in the construction. Homophobic hermeneutics has less to do with personal loathing of same-sex
love, than with cultural and philosophical constructs that become regulative for the
interpretation of texts, and for the selection of those texts that are determinative for
assessing the scriptural archive with respect to same-sex love. Thus even those who
are by no means personally homophobic find themselves faced with what may appear
to be a uniform biblical rejection of same-sex sexuality and love (Jennings 2009).
More recent advances in biblical interpretation have rendered this monolithic edifice
questionable.

In order to see how this is so it will first be useful to consider some of the texts that
have been interpreted as rejecting same-sex love, asking whether these texts have in fact
the 'self-evident' meaning so often attributed to them. For this assembly of a handful of
verses has prevented readers of biblical literature from recognizing that there may be
multiple perspectives in this literature that often take same-sex love for granted, or even
celebrate certain forms of same-sex love. Thus after consideration of some of the ways a
socially or culturally homophobic selection and interpretation of rather isolated texts
in the Bible have been taken to represent the whole of biblical literature on this subject,
it will be important to attend to the multiple ways in which biblical literature deals with
forms of same-sex sexuality and love.

The approach to be taken here will be thematic, drawing on materials from Hebrew
Scriptures as well as the early Christian documents collected in the New Testament.

The (Alleged) Rejection of
Same-Sex Love

We begin with the story of Sodom that for many centuries lent its name to the acts that give expression to same-sex love (Jordan 1997). The messengers of God are first welcomed with lavish hospitality by the sojourner Abraham (Gen. 18:1–8). They inform Abraham that their purpose is to bring retributive punishment upon the wealthy urban centres of Sodom and Gomorrah for their manifest injustice (18:20–21). Abraham pleads that the cities be saved for the sake of a few just persons living there (18:22–33). The bargaining over the requisite number of just persons being concluded, the messengers go to Sodom to attempt to find at least ten just persons. They are welcomed by Abraham's kinsman Lot, likewise a sojourner (19:1–3). The people of Sodom, however, resolve to do violence to the vulnerable strangers. This is said to be the agreement and intent of all the people, young and old of the city (thereby confirming the absence of even ten just persons in the entire city). In order to assuage their thirst for violence Lot offers his own daughters as a sacrifice to the blood lust of the city. When this offer is refused, the messengers lead Lot's household out of the city which then is destroyed by fire, thereby fulfilling the original intent of the divine messengers (there being no just persons whether men, women or children, left in the city).

This story was recalled in biblical and intertestamental literature as emphasizing the punishment inflicted by God on the injustice of prosperous and arrogant cultures, an injustice that is narratively summarized as the determination of the whole city to violate and do violence to vulnerable strangers. We may recall here the repeated injunctions of biblical literature to show hospitality to the vulnerable, especially sojourners, strangers, immigrant labourers (Ex. 22:21; Lev. 19:34; Heb. 13:2) together with repeated warnings that social injustice will be met with divinely ordained destruction of the societies and empires that exhibit injustice.

It is now generally recognized that this story has nothing whatever to do with same-sex love. The prophet Ezekiel speaks for a nearly universal Jewish and early Christian interpretation of this tale when he attributes the sin of Sodom to arrogance, avarice, and violence (Ezek. 16:49; cf. Isa. 1:10–17; Zeph. 2:9). However both Philo of Alexandria and Josephus use this story to assimilate Jewish tradition to a tradition associated with the later Plato of the repudiation of same-sex love. Breaking with emergent Judaism (Loader 1990) the tale is re-interpreted to agree with Platonic homophobia. While Jewish exegesis seems not to have been influenced by Philo, some early Christian exegetes came under the influence of this Platonizing project. As late as the fifth century CE theologians like Augustine and Jerome could still read the story as having to do with crimes against hospitality and so against justice (Jennings 2009: 190–198). However, it became increasingly common to adopt Philo's example and read the text in conjunction with homophobic presuppositions, something discernible in the imperial edicts of

Justinian and Theodosius. Thus a text that warns against the injustice of the wealthy and powerful—injustice especially directed against the vulnerable—comes to license injustice toward the vulnerable on the part of the powerful.

LEVITICUS

While the story of Sodom was regularly deployed by Christian writers to characterize same-sex love from the sixth century onward, it took several more centuries before Christian moralists appropriated the proscriptions found in Leviticus 18:22 and 20:13 to criminalize (and, in the early modern period, even provide the death penalty for) same-sex love. The lateness of the homophobic appropriation of this text by Christian writers may be due to the function of Leviticus to establish or at least recall a specifically Jewish identity, as well as the recollection of Paul's critical approach to the Mosaic Law.

Late modern exegesis has again begun to cast doubt upon the appropriateness of the use of Leviticus to promote a homophobic agenda. There is, of course, an emergent revulsion against the imposition of the death penalty for same-sex love, a penalty applied by early Protestantism and early modern Catholicism and reaching its feverish height in the Nazi policies of extermination camps. In spite of the significance of Leviticus for articulating Jewish identity, Judaism itself has never been known to have taken these texts literally in such a way as to enact capital punishment for these alleged crimes (Bamberger 1979).

To this we may add the fact that the text of Leviticus imposes a great many requirements upon its readers that Christians have never been willing to apply to themselves. Whether these have to do with dietary restrictions, the mixing of fabrics, or the development of techniques for hybridization, the arbitrary selection of a particular prohibition as the law of God, while ignoring virtually all the rest, places those who would appropriate these two verses in an embarrassing position.

In addition there is considerable discussion about what exactly these texts prohibit. Some exegetes have focused attention upon the cultic language of abomination in order to suggest that what is prohibited is some set of cultic sexual practices associated with fertility cults (Boswell 1980: 100–102). Others have suggested rape as the prohibited behaviour although there is the difficulty that both parties are subjected to the penalty of death. This hardly seems just. The text itself seems to suggest that what is prohibited is taking on the role of a woman in sexual intercourse; that is, lying with a man in a woman-like way is a likely interpretation (Olyan 1994). But if the prohibition here is the desire to be penetrated, this might comport with the ethos of a holiness code that seeks to defend emergent Judaism from cultural and social penetration by alien cultures. If the holiness code is the latest of the codes of law, and if it must be dated at the earliest to the Persian period and the latest to the early Hellenistic period, then such an interpretation would make sense. This would be all the more true, if the desire to be penetrated by the more powerful male figure of the deity is characteristic of the cultural unconscious of a religious tradition that emphasizes the maleness both of the deity and of the ideal worshipper (Eilberg-Schwartz 1994).

However the legal texts are to be understood, it is noteworthy that it is only in the very latest stratum of legal codes that we have a text that in any way takes same-sex sexual practices into account. The use of this late and isolated text to characterize the attitude of the whole of the Hebrew Bible is itself remarkable. It may owe more to a Christian desire to associate Judaism with the Law and to understand law as a set of commandments (ignoring the narratives of much of the Torah) than to a fair reading of the texts. In any case the result has been to use these two verses to blind readers to the wealth of homoerotic narrative of the bible.

MALACHOI AND *ARSENOKOITAI*

For a homophobic project it has been an inconvenient truth that nowhere in the New Testament is it recorded that Jesus had anything negative to say about same-sex love. Into the breach, however, have been wrested a few verses from Paul. In two texts attributed to Paul are terms that in modern Christian exegesis (and translation) have come to be understood as references to same-sex practices. They are *malachoi* and *arsenokoitai* (1 Cor. 6:9–10; 1 Tim. 1:9–10). The term *malachoi* is used both in the New Testament and in Hellenistic literature to designate the softness of those who live in luxury. It thus suggests the self-indulgence of the idle rich. Jesus uses the term in this way to refer to the court of Herod (Matt. 11:8; Lk. 7:25). Hellenistic writers like Musonius Rufus likewise use the term to refer to those who pamper themselves with idleness and luxury instead of becoming accustomed to manual labour (Jennings 2003: 115–116). As late as the middle of the twentieth century this term was used in Catholic moral teaching to refer to that form of self-indulgence termed masturbation. Contemporary translation of the term to imply a reference to 'effeminate' partners in male–male sexual practices seems tendentious at best.

Arsenokoitai is a term not known otherwise in literature contemporary with Paul. It is sometimes later quoted from Paul but when it is actually given a context that would suggest its meaning it is associated with one of the most famous rapes in history, Zeus' rape of Ganymede (Jennings 2009: 124). It therefore would have to do with the male-type sex that has rightly given to Roman male culture the title of rape culture (Williams 1999: 125–159). This impression is heightened in the use of this term in 1 Timothy 1:9–10 where it is associated with other references to extreme violence: not disobeying parents but killing them, not stealing objects but other persons and so on. Once again a text that indicts the violence of the powerful comes to license violence against the vulnerable, as Christianity came to solicit the favourable attentions of the prosperous and powerful in order to become an established religion of the Empire.

Something similar seems to have happened with Paul's references in Romans 1:26–27 to what may be sexual practices against nature (by women) and to men burning with desire for other men. The first having to do with women seems to be interpreted in a sexual sense primarily in the late modern period (Brooten 1996). A look at the accounts of the practices of imperial women in the time of Paul gives ample testimony to unnatural practices: murders of husbands and sons, offering one self, and requiring other imperial women to offer themselves, as prostitutes to the highest bidder, and so on (Elliott 1994: 194–5).

Similarly the reference in Romans 1:27 to males burning in desire for one another may be best understood as depicting the sexual crimes of the ruling class, especially those alleged to characterize emperors like Tiberius, Caligula, and Nero of raping not only women but also men. Caligula was stabbed (penetrated) to death by members of his own bodyguard who had either been raped by the emperor or whose women had been raped by him. Thus Caligula received in his own body a punishment befitting his crimes. This interpretation of the references in Romans is strengthened when the context of Paul's argument is taken into account: his critique of the Roman Empire and its 'legal' order, the empire that had legally executed the one Paul regarded as Messiah and divine Son (Jennings 2009: 129–155).

One of the features common to the homophobic appropriation of these few texts of the Bible is that they have so often been turned on their heads by a violent exegesis. Texts that condemn the viciousness of wealthy and powerful patrons have been appropriated in order not only to deflect criticism away from these patrons but to inculpate as scapegoats vulnerable members of society. But focusing attention on these texts also serves as a kind of screen to prevent readers from recognizing the wide array of diverse depictions of same-sex love in the Bible. It is to this that we now turn. We should bear in mind that the stories we are going to consider will not give us information about what specific sexual practices, if any, give expression to the variety of same-sex loves that appear in biblical texts.

LESBIAN ROMANCE

If one reads the Hebrew Bible in its canonical order the first extended depiction of same-sex love, and one of the most beautiful and impressive, is the love of Ruth the Moabite for her Judean mother-in-law Naomi. So moving is this love story of two women that it is not uncommon for Ruth's words to Naomi (1:16–17) to be the centre-piece of marriage ceremonies, even when those to be married are of 'opposite' sexes.

These passionate words of commitment of one person to another are preceded by the notice that Ruth 'cleaved' to Naomi (1:14), a word that echoes the words of Genesis 2:24 to designate the passionate embrace of male and female in creation (Pardes 1992). The subsequent narration develops this love in a number of ways. The women must find a way to shelter their love within the patriarchal confines of Judean society. This will entail Ruth's seduction of the elderly Boaz with the considerable assistance and direction of Naomi so as to assure their survival within that society (Linafelt and Beal 1999). Essentially Boaz is embarrassed into marrying Ruth. But when a child is born the village women are not misled: instead of rejoicing at a son being born to Boaz they celebrate that a son has been given to Naomi (4:15)! Like lesbian couples in our own day they have found a 'sperm donor', a surrogate father, to give them a child to raise. And not just any child, for this will be the ancestor of David and, as Matthew will recall, the ancestor of Jesus the messiah. It does not seem that Matthew is oblivious to the socially irregular character of this relationship for in Matthew's genealogy of Jesus (1:2–17) we have a group of somewhat 'disreputable' women: Tamar the cultic prostitute, Rahab the prostitute of Jericho, the adulterous wife of Uriah (Bathsheba), not to mention Mary whom Joseph sought to protect from the ignominy of public shaming and execution for the crime of becoming pregnant by someone other than her intended spouse (Matt. 1:19). Matthew's inclusion of Ruth in this company suggests that the Gospel writer was not unaware of the potentially shocking character of the relationship.

There are other stories that have been found to be suggestive of what we now term lesbian relationships. In the Hebrew Bible, material that comes under consideration includes Vashti remaining with the women of the harem rather than being at the service of her emperor husband's whim (Esth. 1:12) as well as the story of Jephthah's daughter that includes the notice that the young women of Israel had the custom of going into the wilderness together in memory of her (Judg. 11:39–40). In the New Testament we may mention the odd household of Mary and Martha (Lk. 10:38–42; Jn. 11:1–44, 12:1–11), with or without Lazarus. Nevertheless this story of Ruth must surely rank as not only the earliest but also one of the most beautiful depictions of female same-sex love.

WARRIOR LOVE

The son of Ruth and Naomi becomes the ancestor of David who is the protagonist of the most extended story of same-sex love to be found in the Bible. The convoluted story of David and his male lovers is set within a context in which warriors are often accompanied in their exploits by younger male companions who share in the adventures and the dangers of their 'lovers' (See Judg. 9:54 and 1 Sam. 9 for Saul and his companion. See 1 Samuel 14 for Jonathan and his companion). The idea of love between older and younger warriors is familiar not only from the later stories of classical Greece but also from stories of 'flower' warriors in Korea, and Samurai love in Japan (Leupp 1995). But the earliest extended account of this sort of love after the Babylonian Enuma Elish is the story of David (Halperin 1990: 73–87).

What is remarkable about this story is that David is always the beloved of more powerful males. In Greek terms his is the tale of an *eromenos* (beloved) rather than an *erastes* (lover). This is the very sort of tale that may have evoked the horror of the much later priestly writers of Leviticus, as well as the discomfort of even those Greek authors who celebrated the conventions of pederasty. David's first human lover appears to have been King Saul who chose David to be his armour bearer and to attend him in private with his soothing music. David seems to earn this position by his beauty (1 Sam. 16:12, 17:42), his bravery (17.33) and his gentleness as a musician (16:15–18, 23). But almost before the beginning of such a potentially idyllic love story, things are complicated by Saul's warrior son Jonathan who also desires David: 'The soul of Jonathan was knit to the soul of David' (18:1). Jonathan chooses David as his own armour bearer (18:4). Saul's jealous rage then becomes the motor for the story's unfolding (18:10–30:31). It is Jonathan who seeks to protect David from his father's murderous passion. When they meet in secret Jonathan expresses his own undying love for David (20: 13–17; see also 18:1, 19:1, 20:41–42). Saul in fury accuses Jonathan of having uncovered the nakedness of his father (20:30–34), a metaphor otherwise used to refer to someone having sexual relations with another person who has intimate relations with a third party whose nakedness is thereby uncovered (Lev. 18:7–8). The metaphor may also remind the reader of Ham's violation of Noah's nakedness in Genesis 9:22–23.

There follow a number of campaigns in which Saul seeks the death of his formerly beloved David. During these campaigns David seeks out opportunities both to find Saul at his most vulnerable, and to demonstrate his own loyalty to his former lover (chs 24 and 26). Eventually David is taken in as companion by Achish, the military leader of the Philistines (chs 27–30). But he begs off from joining in the final attack upon Saul and Jonathan who perish in the battle. Then we have David's mourning for his former lovers (2 Sam. 1:11–27) and his words about Jonathan: 'Your love to me was wonderful, passing the love of women' (2 Sam. 1:26). Subsequently David demonstrates his love for Jonathan by taking in Jonathan's orphaned son Mephibosheth (2 Sam. 9:7) who thereby has two fathers.

These powerful warriors are not David's only lovers however. The ultimate warrior king of Israel, YHWH, is also David's warrior lover, his first and last lover. David is chosen to be the warrior companion of YHWH on account, in part, of his surpassing beauty (1 Sam. 16:12), a trait that had previously been mentioned as the reason for the selection of Saul (1 Sam. 9:2). David's love for YHWH is expressed in his naked dance that leads the ark (the body) of YHWH into Jerusalem (2 Sam. 6:14–16) thereby earning the scorn (and jealousy?) of his wife Michal. But David had not been blinded to the faults of his powerful lover. When the Ark arbitrarily slays one who touched it David let it stay out in the countryside until it became more stable (2 Sam. 6:6). Perhaps from Saul David had learned the danger of unstable lovers.

The account of David's entering into the tent where the ark stands; his offering to build YHWH a house, together with the reply of YHWH—'I don't want a house but I will love you forever'—bears some resemblance to a sort of marriage (2 Sam. 7; see Jennings 2005: 50–62). While the remainder of the story has many twists and turns and the love of David and YHWH sometimes turns cold and quarrelsome, the upshot is that YHWH never goes back on his promise of steadfast love for David. Indeed Psalms will recall that it is precisely YHWH's steadfast love for David that ensures YHWH's steadfast love for Israel itself (Ps. 89). Just as David's music had drawn the attentions of Saul, so also David will be recalled as the composer of songs for YHWH. Thus does homoerotic narrative open upon the theme of the divine love to which we shall return later.

THE CENTURION'S LAD

A story from the Gospels seems to pick up this trope of warrior love from the Hebrew Bible as well as the theme of extraordinary loyalty that runs through it. In Matthew (8:5–13) a centurion comes to Jesus to ask for aid for his beloved lad. In this Gospel the term used by the centurion to designate the object of his care is *pais*, a term regularly used in Hellenistic literature to designate the *eromenos* of an *erastes*, the younger beloved of same-sex love (Jennings 2003: 131–144). The audacity of the centurion's coming to Jesus in this manner is underscored in a variety of ways. The centurion is begging for the help of a lowly member of the society he is supposed to rule, control, and dominate. Moreover when the centurion rejects Jesus' offer to come to his house he makes clear that he supposes that Jesus is a commander of demonic forces (8:8–9), precisely what many of Jesus's opponents also claim about him (Matt. 12:24). When Jesus exclaims 'in all Israel I have not seen such faithfulness' (8:10) he is not commenting on the centurion's Christology (or rather demonology). He is remarking upon a love for a beloved that will take any risk of humiliation and danger to restore the beloved to wholeness. When this story is read against the background of the warrior love of the David saga, the warrior love of Greek and even Roman literature, as well as that which is related of centurions who could not marry women during their terms of service (Jennings and Liew 2004), the endorsement of at least certain forms of same-sex love on the part of Jesus becomes evident: love that includes unswerving loyalty and the care of lovers for their beloveds.

EUNUCHS

Some contemporary writers have seized upon the biblical figure of the eunuch as emblematic of the place of gay people in our society, since both are regarded with contempt within patriarchal and heterosexist structures (Wilson 1995). The eunuch, normally castrated by the cutting off of testicles may be regarded as incapable of fulfilling the proper functions of manhood, and so as effeminized in ways that may be analogous to the situation of at least some gay males.

However much this figure of the eunuch may be the object of disdain in much ancient literature (Greenberg 1988: 101–109) and was the subject of condemnation in one of Israel's law codes (Deut. 23:1), there is no question but that the eunuch is also the subject of considerable affirmation as well in biblical literature. We may recall the role of the eunuch in rescuing Jeremiah from the death to which the authorities had consigned him (Jer. 38:7–13); or the promise to eunuchs made in the oracle of Isaiah (Isa. 56:3–5); or the place of the Ethiopian eunuch as among the first to be baptized (by Philip) as a follower of the way of the Messiah (Acts 8:26–39).

Perhaps the most extended story of one who has the function of the eunuch is the saga of Joseph. In this story Joseph, as Jacob's favourite, youngest and most beautiful son, is garbed in the robe of a princess (Jennings 2005: 177–198). The favouritism, as well as perhaps the offending garb, arouse the ire of the other brothers who bully him, beat him, and initially leave him for dead. He is rescued only to be sold to slave-traders who bring him to Egypt where his beauty attracts the attention of the eunuch Potiphar as well as his wife. Even when he finds himself in prison he gains the affection of his jailers. Eventually he rises in the service of the Pharaoh assuming the traditional place of the eunuch administrator of the kingdom. Eunuchs often seem to have this role since they do not beget progeny and so do not become competitive with the royal lineage (Greenberg 1988: 122). After Joseph has used his position to confront his brothers and to provide his family with refuge in Egypt he apparently has two sons by a woman provided by Pharaoh. He in turn presents her to Jacob as if he were Jacob's wife Rachel who had died in child birth. Jacob then assumes paternity of the sons Ephraim and Manesseh who round out the number of the sons of Jacob/Israel and, indeed, lend their names to the later kingdom of Israel.

It is a decidedly odd story, rich with often unnoticed tropes of same-sex roles and romance. Joseph's 'cross-dressing', his being the object of bullying, his finding favour with powerful men on account of his talent, temperament, and notable beauty, rising to a position from which he can control the destinies of those who had tormented him in his youth, all prefigure recognizable motifs of modern gay romance.

In the Gospel of Matthew Jesus affirms the place of the eunuch: those who are born that way (that is, without the capacity or desire for heterosexual procreative acts), or who are made that way by others (*castrati*), or who make themselves to be like eunuchs (perhaps ascetics) for the sake of the reign of God (Matt. 19:10–12; see Jennings 2003: 146–154). As we have seen in the case of Matthew's genealogy and the account of the centurion's beloved *pais*, the First Gospel appears to be quite open to unconventional sexualities.

TRANSGENDERED AFFAIRS

The fear of feminization has long been associated with antipathy towards same-sex love. Similarly, on those rare occasions when any attention at all was directed to female same-sex love, the derision addressed to the supposedly 'mannish' lesbian has been a staple of literature since the days of ancient Greece and Rome (Brooten 1996: 29–56).

In spite of the presumably masculinist views of the Hebrew Bible there is much space given to the deployment of transgendering, especially in ways to figure the relationship between the divine being and a treacherous but ultimately faithful Israel. In order to

see how important the role of the transgender person is in this literature, it is necessary to keep clearly in mind that Israel (as well as Ephraim and Judah) is the name of a
putatively male character. Moreover in these texts the divine being is also cast as a male
character, who will be the lover or husband (irate or merciful) of Israel.

Beginning with Amos (5:2) and Hosea (1–3, 5:1, 6:10, 9:1) and continuing through
Jeremiah (chs 2, 13) and Ezekiel (chs 16, 23) the prophets give an account of the relation
between YHWH and YHWH's people by feminizing (transgendering) Israel (Jennings
2005: 131–176). This will enable the prophets to deploy the trope of the adulterous or
unfaithful wife in order to clarify this relationship.

This transgendering enables depictions of YHWH falling in love with the lovely and
vulnerable Israel figured as a maiden in the desert (Amos 5:2; Ezek. 16:7–8); of the gifts
bestowed upon this lovely beloved by which YHWH actively collaborates in transvest-
ing Israel (Jer. 2:32; Ezek. 16:9–14); of Israel's search for better and more astonishingly
endowed lovers—Egyptians with very large penises (Ezek. 23:19–20); dashing Assyrian
cavalrymen (Ezek. 23:5–6, 12:23), or Chaldeans adorned with sumptuous garments
(Ezek. 23:14–17). Thus the prophets render intelligible the rage of YHWH as a jealous
and betrayed husband in order to account for the horrifying punishments inflicted
upon Israel for his/her unjust infidelities (Jer. 13:22, 26). Finally the prophets are able to
use this allegory to bring to expression YHWH's repentance of his jealous rage and his
taking Israel back into his loving embrace (Jer. 31:4; Isa. 54:6–7). Legal codes that may
come from a later period would make this reconciliation with an unfaithful 'wife' a capital offence (Deut. 24:4; Jer. 3:1)!

The problem as seen by the prophets who elaborate this rather daring analogy is not
that Israel acts the part of a woman. The problem is only that of unfaithfulness, of seeking better lovers to embrace than the one who first loved Israel. Thus, as with same-
sex love, the problem is not with the love itself, however unconventional. The problem
instead is a lack of justice and faithfulness. Accordingly these same prophets may also
transgender the divine being as well likening YHWH to a mother who protects her
young (Hos. 13:8. See Mollenkott 1985).

This transgendering also finds echoes in the New Testament. We find it in certain
depictions of Jesus who like a hen wills to gather Jerusalem under her protective wings
(Matt. 23:37; Lk. 23:37), or the depiction of Jesus as the lady Sophia (Lk. 7:33). But the
most dramatic example of such transgendering comes in the dramatic story of Jesus
washing the feet of his companions (Jn. 13:1–15). While there is much that may be
remarked upon in this story, one feature is that elsewhere in biblical literature washing
the feet of others is always the work of a woman (Jennings 2003: 162–166).

Paul also transgenders himself in writing to his congregations presenting himself
both as mother, giving birth to believers (Phile. 1:10; Gal. 4:19), and as nurse-maid giving
of his own body to nourish his communities (1 Thess. 2:7; see Gaventa 2007). Perhaps
relying upon the earlier prophetic tradition, Paul will also speak of presenting his congregations as virgin brides (2 Cor. 11:2). The later church, identified as an all-male hierarchy, will nonetheless think and speak of itself as a bride enamoured of its 'groom', thereby
appropriating the prophetic tradition of transgendering Israel.

STRANGE LOVES

In addition to the more readily recognizable examples of lesbian, gay, and transgender forms of same-sex love, there are a number of biblical narratives with allusions to somewhat less familiar forms of same-sex relationships and practices. These also fall into obscurity if the basic hermeneutical approach is that of finding cognates to those sexually mediated relationships for which the reader seeks to gain societal and ecclesial approval. Such an approach may unduly restrict the forms of same-sex eroticism to be discerned in biblical literature.

One example of an eroticism associated with the cult of YHWH comes from the accounts of the 'sons of the prophets' first associated with Samuel and then subsequently with Elijah and Elisha. We first encounter them as the frenzied dancers who accompany Samuel and initiate Saul (1 Sam. 10:5–11). Later in the story Saul will seek them out in order to reassure himself of YHWH's favour. In this case he is found unconscious and naked—a state which occasions the repeated exclamation 'Is Saul also among the prophets?' (1 Sam. 19:19–24). The role of a company of male prophets is continued in the stories of Elijah and Elisha in 1 Kings 17 through 2 Kings 13. That naked men represent YHWH is also found in the comportment of at least two of the 'writing prophets' (Mic. 1:18; Isa. 20:25) although in these cases what may be expressed is not erotic ecstasy but impending woe.

Another example may be perceptible in the reference to male cultic sex workers, the *quedasim* who, like the sons of the prophets, are encountered in the narrative cycle concerning Elijah and Elisha in 1 and 2 Kings. While earlier biblical interpretation sought to explain this phenomenon by claiming the importation of fertility practices from Canaanites, the evidence for such practices among the Canaanites has been hard to come by (Greenberg 1988: 92, 99). However one possible interpretation of the evidence is to suppose that these male cult functionaries were indigenous to the worship of the male deity YHWH (Jennings 2005: 115–130). In that case they may have engaged in the sexual penetration (perhaps anally) of worshippers (male and female) who were thereby possessed by the deity and 'his' potency. Certainly this would comport with the very strong evidence that Israel's male deity was regularly represented in terms of male erotic potency.

Somewhat more startling may be references that can be interpreted as the sexual awakening of quite young males, reminiscent of certain practices associated with Papua New Guinea. In the narratives concerning Elijah and Elisha (1 Kgs 17:17–24; 2 Kgs 4:32–35), each of these early prophets is summoned to cure a stricken lad. In each case the prophet enters into the private chamber of the lad, stretches out upon him and shouts and shudders. The result is the transmission of vital energy into the lad who is thereby restored to life (Jennings 2005: 99–106). We may note that in the Acts of the Apostles a somewhat similar story (although shorn of many of the specifically erotic details of the earlier sagas) is told of the Apostle Paul who restores to life a lad who had fallen asleep during Paul's discourse and fallen from the window ledge into the street (Acts 20:9–12). If we focus upon the erotic features of the awakening of youth we may also recall the call of Samuel who is accosted in his bedchamber by the (phallus-like?) representation of YHWH, by which he is commissioned to serve as YHWH's delegate in Israel (1 Sam. 3; see Jennings 2005: 106–112).

Even more disturbing are ways in which the divine sexual potency may be represented as a forcible sexual assault upon others. We have seen in the case of the story of Sodom that rape could be understood as one of the ways of establishing domination over others. We have all too many examples of this in modern war zones. A story in which YHWH is depicted as a sort of rapist of his enemies is found in the account of the seizure of the ark by the Philistines. The ark is placed alongside the representation of the victorious god Dagon, but the next day Dagon is found smashed and face down as though raped by YHWH (1 Sam. 5:2–4). Subsequently the Philistines themselves are afflicted with haemorrhoids (1 Sam. 5:6–12), a possible sign of anal rape, and are led to beg the Israelites to take back the embodiment of their deity.

Even more alarming are the stories that seem to implicate God as a rapist even of those who are divine favourites. The story of the assault upon Jacob by night either by a messenger of YHWH (Gen. 3:22–32) or by YHWH himself (Hos. 12:2–4) is one such story, an assault that leaves Jacob with a permanent limp. Another such tale concerns YHWH's apparently unprovoked assault upon Moses which is warded off by Moses' wife by means of the blood of circumcision (Ex. 4:24–26). Indeed the prophet Jeremiah could extend this metaphor to describe himself as having been effectively raped by YHWH (Jer. 20:7).

These odd tales from the literature of ancient Israel suggest the wild variety of ways in which eroticism, especially male–male eroticism is represented as suggestive of the relationships among Israelites, and between them and their deity.

DIVINE LOVE

One of the most astonishing features of the imaging of same-sex eroticism in biblical literature is the role this plays in identifying the divine character. That is to say it is not only between human persons of the same sex that biblical narratives depict same-sex erotic practices but also between the divine and the human, thereby implicating the divine being in same-sex eroticism as well.

As we have seen, this includes episodes in which the eroticism is characterized more by violence and violation than by what we have come to know as love. These tales of homoerotic terror are not isolated, for the divine may wreak havoc upon friends and enemies alike in many strands of biblical literature. But at various points we can also detect a sort of transformation of this divine being into one whose love is steadfast rather than arbitrary, tender rather than violent. We notice this already in the accounts of YHWH's sexual assault upon those who are or become his favourites. Thus Jacob will be recalled as the recipient of YHWH's steadfast love (Jer. 31:2–3) as will Moses (Ex. 34:6–7). While one might not regard these relationships as morally exemplary, involving as they do aspects of violent assault, they may be suggestive of aspects of BDSM romantic fantasy.

One of the principal ways by which the emergence of steadfast love, as an ingredient of same-sex love, is brought to narrative life, is in the Davidic narratives in which David's faithfulness to YHWH comes to be reciprocated by YHWH's steadfast love, not only for David but, on account of David, for David's people as a whole. Similarly the transgendered affair between Israel and YHWH recounted by Hosea, Jeremiah, Ezekiel, and Isaiah, seems to pass through the elemental rage of jealous love toward the vow of unending tenderness.

THE BELOVED DISCIPLE

In the Gospel of John the depiction of the (male) divine being as the lover of another man may influence the characterization of Jesus who in this narrative is sometimes so identified with, and as, the divine, that it becomes the proof text for later Christological developments in the Church. It is also the narrative text in which the idea of divine love is most highly developed. Given the material which we have considered in this survey of biblical literature it should come as no surprise that the divine-human can be depicted as a protagonist in same-sex love. The suggestion is found in allusions, toward the end of the Gospel, to 'the (male) disciple Jesus loved' (Jennings 2003: 13–102).

This figure first appears in the final banquet scene in which the question of love is thematized in various ways (Jn. 13–17). Thus the scene has been compared to that of Plato's famous Symposium (Steiner 1996: 404). The man Jesus loved is introduced as the disciple who enjoys the greatest physical proximity to and intimacy with Jesus (13:21–26). This way of characterizing the love that unites Jesus and this man will be recalled in subsequent episodes (21:20).

A further episode finds this disciple among the group of women who are witnesses to the death of Jesus (19:25–27). In that episode Jesus commends the disciple to the care of his mother Mary and charges Mary to treat his beloved as if he were her son. The account may be read as having the effect of declaring the disciple to be Mary's son-in-law.

A later episode has the beloved and Peter together after the death of Jesus and hurrying to the tomb when they are told that the body is no longer there (20:1–10). One of the features of three of the four episodes in which the beloved appears is his relationship to Peter. In this case the speed of the beloved is often taken as evidence of his relative youth, while his reluctance to enter the tomb may owe to the trauma of having witnessed his lover's execution.

The final episode is in the last chapter of the Gospel which some have seen as a sort of appendix. This chapter concludes with Jesus charging Peter with the care of Jesus's sheep (21:15–20) while reserving for himself alone the care of his beloved (21:20–24).

Taken together these brief episodes involving the one called 'the disciple Jesus loved' (known to tradition as the youthful Apostle John) may serve to make concrete the theme of divine love while avoiding the circumscription of human love within the strictures of traditional marriage and family values. The divine love becomes human love in all its possibilities (including erotic ones) without thereby enforcing conventions, institutions, and frameworks that limit love.

While the theological and exegetical literature has regularly ignored the homoerotic aspects of these allusive episodes, these possibilities in the texts have not gone unnoticed in wider literary and artistic circles (Jennings 2011). They may also be viewed as carrying forward into early Christian literature traces of the homoerotic tendencies found in the literature of ancient Israel.

Conclusion

In this chapter I have surveyed some of the most important material in biblical literature that may be relevant for a consideration of same-sex love in the Bible. In recent decades the literature exploring this theme has grown exponentially. The number of texts that have been found fruitful for consideration of same-sex love (Guest et al. 2006) in these documents has also grown. These are important not only for understanding better the 'Abrahamic' faiths of Judaism, Christianity, and Islam but also for the cultural worlds impacted by these traditions. Indeed it may be that as these texts become loosened from the dogmatic and moralizing confinements of aspects of these traditions, they may offer up more possibilities for attentive and rewarding readings.

In this chapter I have indicated how a queer-positive or gay-friendly interpretive strategy may deal fruitfully with some of these texts. I by no means suppose that such a strategy exhausts the possible meanings of such texts either in the cultural world(s) in which they originated or in our own time and circumstance. We are increasingly aware that the interpretation of ancient texts will always be multiple owing both to the ineradicable uncertainty of our knowledge about the worlds from which they come and to the diverse questions and interests that shape contemporary readers. It may be that in our time the reading of these texts is coming to be less dominated by the sedimented homophobia of tradition, thereby permitting aspects of these texts to become readable in ways that would be quite surprising for some of our forebears.

An early stage of this process was the attempt to pry the texts loose from the attempts to stabilize social homophobia by reference to the authority of the Bible (Bailey 1955). A further stage was to seek exemplars within the texts that would offer sanction for burgeoning forms of same-sex love in the modern world. Thus, stories of David and Jonathan, or Ruth and Naomi, or even the disciple Jesus loved, have been read in this way. However, as we become more aware of the sheer diversity of the forms in which erotic attraction may express itself, additional material becomes readable, not in order to license practices of which we approve but in order to take into account the sheer diversity of human erotic practices and arrangements reflected in biblical literature. It has long been recognized that the narrative materials of the bible are replete with erotic adventure. But in the past this recognition has been restricted to heterosexual relationships and practices. A closer look, however, suggests a much wider variety of same-sex sexual relationships and practices than is found even in the literature of Ancient Greece. This also means that it would be most misleading to characterize the agents in these ancient narratives as lesbian or gay or homosexual in the ways that are familiar to us in modern culture. As is true also for other categories like marriage or even gender, there is a vast gulf between our own time and conceptuality, and the conceptualities of the diverse times and cultures given expression in biblical literature.

But perhaps beneath the categories we may discern familiar patterns of desire and delight, of jealousy and betrayal, of violence and tenderness, of commitment and loyalty, that enable sympathetic identification and perhaps even a growing hope for love wherever it may be encountered.

REFERENCES

Bailey, Derrick Sherwin (1955). *Homosexuality and the Western Christian Tradition*. London: Longmans.

Bamberger, Bernard J. (1979). *Leviticus*: vol. 3. of *The Torah: A Modern Commentary*. New York: Union of American Hebrew Congregations.

Boswell, John (1980). *Christianity, Social Tolerance, and Homosexuality: Gay People in Western Europe from the Beginning of the Christian Era to the Fourteenth Century*. Chicago: University of Chicago Press.

Brooten, Bernadette J. (1996). *Love Between Women: Early Christian Responses to Female Eroticism*. Chicago: University of Chicago Press.

Eilberg-Schwartz, Howard (1994). *God's Phallus and Other Problems for Men and Monotheism*. Boston: Beacon Press.

Elliott, Neil (1994). *Liberating Paul: The Justice of God and the Politics of the Apostle*. Maryknoll: Orbis Press.

Gaventa, Beverly (2007). *Our Mother Saint Paul*. Louisville: Westminster John Knox Press.

Greenberg, David F. (1988). *The Construction of Homosexuality*. Chicago: University of Chicago Press.

Guest, Deryn et al. (2006) (eds). *The Queer Bible Commentary*. London: SCM Press.

Halperin, David M. (1990). *One Hundred Years of Homosexuality*. New York: Routledge.

Jennings, Jr., Theodore W. (2003). *The Man Jesus Loved: Homoerotic Narratives from the New Testament*. Cleveland: Pilgrim Press.

Jennings, Jr., Theodore W. (2005). *Jacob's Wound: Homoerotic Narrative in the Literature of Ancient Israel*. New York: Continuum.

Jennings, Jr., Theodore W. (2009). *Plato or Paul: The Origins of Western Homophobia*. Cleveland: Pilgrim Press.

Jennings, Jr., Theodore W. (2011). 'The "Gay" Jesus.' In Delbert Burkett (ed.), *The Blackwell Companion to Jesus*. Oxford: Wiley-Blackwell, 443–457.

Jennings Jr., Theodore W. and Benny Tat-Siong Liew (2004). 'Mistaken Identities but Model Faith: Reading the Centurion, the Chap and the Christ in Matthew 8:5–13.' *Journal of Biblical Literature*, 123(2): 467–494.

Jordan, Mark (1997). *The Invention of Sodomy in Christian Theology*. Chicago: University of Chicago Press.

Leupp, Gary (1995). *Male Colors: The Construction of Homosexuality in Tokugawa Japan*. Berkeley: University of California Press.

Linafelt, Tod, and T. K. Beal (1999). *Ruth and Esther*. Ed. Berit Olam. Collegeville MN: Liturgical Press.

Loader, J. A. A. (1990). *A Tale of Two Cities: Sodom and Gomorrah in the Old Testament, Early Jewish and Early Christian Traditions*. Kampen: J.H. Kok.

Mollenkott, Virginia Ramey (1985). *The Divine Feminine: The Biblical Imagery of God as Feminine*. New York: Crossroad.

Olyan, Saul M. (1994). 'And with a Male You Shall not Lie the Lying Down of a Woman: On the Meaning and Significance of Leviticus 18:22 and 20:13.' *Journal of the History of Homosexuality*, 5(2): 179–206.

Pardes, Ilana (1992). 'The Book of Ruth: Idyllic Revisionism'. In Ilana Pardes (ed.), *Countertraditions in the Bible: A Feminist Approach*. Cambridge, MA: Harvard University Press, 98–117.

Steiner, George (1996). *No Passion Spent: Essays, 1978–1995*. New Haven: Yale University Press.

Williams, Craig A. (1999). *Roman Homosexuality: Ideologies of Masculinity in Classical Antiquity*. New York: Oxford University Press.

Wilson, Nancy (1995). *Our Tribe: Queer Folks, God, Jesus and the Bible*. New York: HarperCollins.

CHAPTER 14

....

THE CONSTRUCTION OF GENDER IN THE NEW TESTAMENT

....

THEORETICAL BACKGROUND

....

THE term 'construction' in the title of this chapter indicates a theoretical approach to gender identity that emerged with the linguistic turn in the humanities, especially under the influence of Michel Foucault. Foucault, along with scholars such as Judith Butler (1990, 1993, 2004) and Joan Scott (1986) played a crucial role in destabilizing the definitions of 'men' and 'women,' exposing them as cultural categories open to deconstruction. While these theorists provided the theoretical foundation for the study of gender, it was the application of this theory to classical texts that illustrated what these new ideas had to offer to the study of sex and gender in the ancient world.

For instance, Thomas Laqueur's (1990) *Making Sex: Body and Gender from the Greeks to Freud* detailed the very different way that ancient Greeks and Romans conceived of human bodies and sexual difference. According to Laqueur, ancient writers such as Aristotle and Galen operated on the basis of a one-sex model (male versus less than male) rather than a two sex one (male versus female). Or, to put it another way, rather than a horizontal axis with male and female as polar opposites, they operated on the basis of a vertical hierarchy with elite free males at the top, and less perfect versions of the male sex populating the space below (freed men, women, slaves, barbarians). Because it showed the fundamentally different way that ancient thinkers 'constructed' the male and female bodies, Laqueur's work highlighted the dangers of importing contemporary ideas of sexual difference onto these ancient texts, including the New Testament.

Masculinity Studies and the Ancient World

Laqueur's *Making Sex* is only one contribution to a significant body of work on gender and sex in the ancient Mediterranean that has informed New Testament scholars. While Laqueur focused primarily on constructions of the body and biological sex differences, gender theory also generated an interest in studying cultural constructions of masculinity in the ancient world. Feminist criticism had rightly called into question the association of men and masculinity with the universal so that giving focused attention to the mechanisms for the cultural construction of masculinity became a natural next step in gender studies. The study of masculinity in the Greco-Roman world by scholars such as Maud Gleason (1995), Jonathan Walters (1997), Lin Foxhall and J. B. Salmon (1998a, 1998b), Craig Williams (1999), and Carlin Barton (2001) helped New Testament scholars undertake a more nuanced, culturally contextualized study of gender construction in the New Testament.

Together this work in classical studies provided New Testament scholars with abundant evidence for how an ideal man looked, sounded, and especially acted, from the perspective of ancient Greco-Roman writers. While much could be said about these protocols, Fredrick Ivarsson (2006: 165–166) helpfully summarizes the 'ground rules of Greco-Roman masculinity' as follows:

> 1) Mastery is the basic criterion of masculinity. Being fully gendered as a man, as opposed to merely having the physical features held to signify a male, means being on top in relation to non-men (women, slaves, children, barbarians) and being able to control one's own passions and desires. 2) Manliness is an achievement and has to be constantly proven in competition with other men. Masculinity is always under construction. 3) Manliness is a moral quality.... Being manly is always a positive value, even when applied to a woman. By contrast, being effeminate or soft is morally reprehensible.

In sociological studies, the sort of dominant masculinity described by these elite authors has been designated *hegemonic masculinity*. R. W. Connell (Connell and Messerschmidt 2005: 832), reflecting on the origin on the concept, explains:

> Hegemonic masculinity was not assumed to be normal in the statistical sense; only a minority of men might enact it. But it was certainly normative. It embodied the currently most honoured way of being a man, it required all other men to position themselves in relation to it, and it ideologically legitimated the global subordination of women to men.

Although this concept emerged from contemporary studies of gender, evidence from Greek and Roman writers makes clear that hegemonic masculinity was a factor in cultural negotiations in the imperial Roman world of the New Testament writers. Even if ideas regarding proper masculine deportment are available only by way of elite texts, and even if this masculinity was enacted by only a select minority in the first century CE, this gender ideology affected and must have been supported by many more people lower down the hierarchy. Such observations have led to a proliferation of studies of masculinity in the New Testament and early Christianity, for example, Moore (1996), Burrus (2000), Kuefler (2001), Moore and Anderson (2003), Penner and Vander Stichele (2007a), Conway (2008), and Cobb (2008).

Outside biblical studies, the emergence of gender criticism, including masculinity studies, has drawn significant criticism. Although Joan Scott asserted that adding gender to historical studies would advance feminist politics, others argued that gender criticism effectively moved women to the margins and men to the centre of study once again (Hoff 1994; see Meyerowitz 2008: 1347–1348). Similar objections are found in biblical scholarship (see Guest 2012: esp. 23–41). Others have noted that in New Testament studies, the study of gender construction in the ancient world has been largely descriptive and absent the political critique inherent to feminist analysis (see, for example, Myles 2010: 70). Studies of masculinity tend to show how New Testament writers are complicit in advancing the cultural values of imperial masculinity without offering explicit critique of this complicity. On the one hand, one could argue there is an *implicit* critique in this work insofar as it points to places where the New Testament writings subvert or trouble hegemonic masculinity. On the other hand, what ultimately emerges is often a rather grim picture of the overriding power of hegemonic discourses (a critique also raised about Foucault and Butler's work, see Hornsby 2006).

Queer Theory, Intersectionality, and the New Testament

The recent addition of queer theory to the study of gender construction in the New Testament might be seen as a response, at least in part, to these objections. Here again, the work of Foucault and Butler, along with that of Eve Kosofsky Sedgwick (1985, 1990), and Teresa de Lauretis (1991) helped to shape the contours of queer theory. If studies of ancient masculinity tend to be primarily descriptive, queer approaches to the Bible take a decidedly political approach, looking to expose aspects of the biblical text that disrupt the 'normal'. To the degree that queer interpretation of the New Testament discomfits readers' views of normative sex/gender identities and creates space for a variety of expressions of human sexuality, it is doing the work it sets out to do. In advocating queer interpretation of the Bible, Robert Myles maintains, '... we have the ethical responsibility to ask questions of power and control when it comes to biblical interpretation, no matter how transgressive it might seem. Normalcy, as an ideological means of control, obscures our perception of reality' (2010: 79).

Biblical scholarship has seen the publication of several collections of essays devoted to queering biblical texts (Moore 2001; Stone 2001; Hornsby and Stone 2011), along with a growing number of articles that find queer spaces in the New Testament (e.g. Townsley 2006; Punt 2007; Myles 2010). Meanwhile, feminist scholarship has recently taken another turn by adopting an 'intersectional' approach that analyses the 'interactive complexity of the social and discursive relations of inequality within and across analytical categories' including race, gender, class, sexuality, and imperialism (Schüssler Fiorenza 2009: 109). Analytical work on the New Testament using this approach has only begun, but promises to continue the political and liberationist direction of feminist biblical interpretation (see, for example, Bailey et al. 2009; Nasrallah and Schüssler Fiorenza 2009; Kartzow 2012).

The remainder of this chapter will discuss gender construction in the New Testament in relation to these various approaches—examining constructions of masculinity, highlighting queer aspects of gender construction, and exploring the intersectional aspects of identity markers. The most extended discussion will be on constructions of masculinity because much of the recent work on gender construction in the New Testament has concentrated on masculine ideologies. This is true not only because masculinity was and still is a category sorely in need of deconstruction, but also because in the ancient Mediterranean context the basic Christian story about a crucified saviour would have been heard by many as a story about failed masculinity. Potential followers of this saviour would need to make sense of this 'gender failure', both with respect to their understanding of Jesus, and perhaps even more critically, with respect to the implications for their own gendered identity should they become adherents. Consideration of the ways that construction of gender in the New Testament writings takes such factors into account is the critical starting place for gender analysis of the New Testament that seeks to be historically and contextually grounded.

Gender Construction in the Letters of Paul

The undisputed letters of Paul offer a rare opportunity in the New Testament to analyse the construction of gender by way of rhetorical self-presentation. Maud Gleason's (1995) work on the rhetorical 'self-fashioning' of the Sophists encouraged an analysis of Paul's own gendered self-fashioning as well as how he used gender-coded rhetoric to encourage new believers and to attack his opponents. At points, Paul appears to resist normative concepts of masculinity, as in when he boasts of his weakness (e.g. 2 Cor. 11:30). At the same time, he regularly assumes positions of dominance and authority over his followers and attacks his opponents with language that is very much in keeping with the rhetoric of hegemonic masculinity in the Greco-Roman world. Similarly, while Paul famously proclaims that in Christ there is no 'male and female' (Gal. 3:28), he also draws clear distinctions between what he considers appropriate conduct for men and women in the community (1 Cor. 11:2–16).

To begin, the sections of moral exhortation in Paul's letters are infused with metaphoric language that is culturally cued as masculine. Paul suggests that like warriors, believers are to don armour, such as helmets and breastplates (Rom. 13:12; 1 Thess. 5:1).

Paul speaks of wielding weapons of warfare (2 Cor. 6:7, 10:4) and envisions himself as an athlete in training, a runner, a boxer, and one who beats his body into submission. Believers, too, are runners who should compete to win and, like athletes, must exercise self-control in all things (1 Cor. 9:24–27). While we might consider self-control to be a non-gender specific trait, as noted earlier, this was not the case in Paul's world. One who lacked self-mastery was prone to excess, whether in food, drink, or sexual desire (even for one's own wife), and was deemed effeminate (for a more detailed overview, see Conway 2008: 21–29).

It may not be surprising to see Paul conforming to Greco-Roman standards of masculinity in the area of moral exhortation. But his interest in masculine comportment is not limited to exhortation. For instance, when Paul refers to self-control as a fruit of the spirit (Gal. 5:23), he implies that the benefits gained from belief in Christ include a rise in status on the gender hierarchy. Even more, as Stanley Stowers (1994) has convincingly argued, the entire letter to the Romans can be read through the theme of self-mastery, where Paul presents this coveted virtue as a goal that his gentile audience can attain through salvation in Christ. According to Stowers, the story of sin and salvation in Romans is a story of the loss and recovery of self-control. And it is Christ who 'becomes an enabler of the restored and disciplined self' (1994: 78). For Paul's ancient audience this restored and disciplined self is a masculine self, so that, as Stephen Moore reinforces, 'righteousness in Romans is essentially a masculine trait; it is, in fact, the very mark of masculinity' (2001: 163, emphasis original). Similarly, in his work on the Corinthian correspondence, Fredrick Ivarsson argues that Paul constructs Christian identity as true masculinity. Belief in Christ offers the Corinthians the benefit of being morally superior (hence, more masculine!) compared to the non-believers around them. Paul suggests this status is possible even for those who are weak and marginalized, including women and slaves. Nevertheless, in so doing, he confirms the value and ultimate status of masculinity (Ivarsson 2008: 171).

If masculinity is a benefit gained through Christ, then Paul himself must provide an example of true masculinity. It is in this context that we should view Paul's self-description as a paternal authority figure in relation to the communities he founded. Not only does he refer to himself as their father who has begotten them (1 Thess. 2:11; 1 Cor. 4:15, see also Philem. 1:10), but he uses this paternal authority to discipline them. He threatens to 'come with a stick' to the Corinthians and warns that if he must come again, he will not spare them (1 Cor. 4:21; 2 Cor. 13:2). And like a father, Paul imagines himself betrothing the Corinthians to Christ as a chaste virgin (2 Cor. 11:2). When his authority is challenged, Paul responds with attempts to effeminize his opponents (thereby elevating his own masculine status). The most blatant such attack is seen in his wish that his opponents in Galatia would castrate themselves (Gal. 5:12). More subtly, as Ivarsson has shown, the vice lists in 1 Corinthians 5:10–11 and 6:9–10 are 'descriptions of deviant masculinity', that Paul deploys to chastise the arrogant young men in Corinth who would challenge his authority (2007: 164). Similarly, Paul points out the effeminate conduct of Corinthians who are swayed by the so-called super-apostles: 'For you put up with it when someone makes slaves of you, or preys upon you, or takes advantage of you, or puts on airs, or gives you a slap in the face' (2 Cor 11:20, NRSV). All of this evinces Paul's basic acceptance and rhetorical use of the culturally dominant view of masculinity.

Paul's Weakness as Subversive Masculinity?

Alongside these claims of manly authority, however, are Paul's calls of attention to his own weakness, a quality *not* associated with manliness in the ancient world (1 Cor. 2:1; 2 Cor. 11:30, 12:10). Does this mean that Paul subverts cultural valuations of masculinity by presenting an alternative, marginal masculinity? If so, it is only when he is forced to do so. Moreover, if he presents an alternative, it is only an alternative *means* of achieving the elevated status of masculinity. It was not a fundamental challenge to the association of superiority with masculinity.

First, one should note that it is only in the Corinthian correspondence that Paul embraces weakness as part of his identity. Elsewhere, he typically uses the word to refer to those who are weaker in faith that he is (Rom. 14:1–2, 15:1). It is no coincidence that Paul's most concentrated discourse on weakness comes in 2 Corinthians 10–12 where he addresses accusations that have been made against him by the 'super-apostles' (2 Cor. 11:5, 12:11). According to Paul, these opponents accuse him of writing bold and weighty letters, but appearing weak and submissive in person (2 Cor. 10:1, 10). Moreover, they label his speaking abilities as 'contemptible' and 'untrained' (2 Cor. 10:10, 11:6). Gleason's (1995) work has shown how one's public presence and rhetorical prowess were key determiner of manliness, so such attacks challenged Paul's masculinity.

Both J. Albert Harrill (2001, 2006) and Jennifer Larson (2004) elaborate this point in their respective work on 2 Corinthians. Harrill situates the invective against Paul in the context of Greco-Roman practice known as physiognomics that relied on physical appearance (eyelids, eyebrows, neck, limbs, gait, voices) to determine virtue/manliness or lack thereof (see Barton 1994; Gleason 1995). In this context, Harrill argues, accusing Paul of a weak bodily presence effectively likened him to a slave, thus deeming him unmanly. Larson points to other possible attacks on Paul's manliness—that he was inconsistent (becoming all things to all people, 1 Cor. 9:22), a flatterer, and engaged in manual labour. These were all practices that signalled a loss of autonomy because they were signs of self-abasement, or putting oneself under the whims of another.

While one might be tempted to read Paul's emphasis on weakness as a subversion of masculine gender ideology, this does not appear to be Paul's objective. Larson (2004: 94) admits as much when she notes both that Paul rejects 'certain traditional standards of masculinity' but also that this rejection is not complete, nor is Paul consistent in this effort. Indeed, not only does Paul designate weakness as one of the traits he merely takes on in order to relate to others who are weak (1 Cor. 9:22), his sarcastic reference to his own weakness in 2 Corinthians 11:21 suggests that he does not consider himself weak compared to the Corinthians themselves. Harrill may be on target when he situates Paul's admission of weakness in the context of a debate between the sophists and the Socratic-Cynic philosophers regarding the use of physiognomics to persuade. If this is the case, Paul is not primarily valorizing weakness, as much as refuting the argument of his opponents which mistakenly relies on physical appearance (Harrill 2001, 2006).

Clearly when Paul embraces the charges of weakness, he does so in a way that ultimately exerts his own power and authority. To be sure, his famous saying, 'Whenever I am weak, then I am strong' (2 Cor. 2:10) suggests a reversal of traditional masculine qualities. The claim comes in the context of addressing the mysterious 'thorn' in his flesh, where he contends also that through it he gains power in Christ. We might read this claim alongside Paul's defence of the 'God's weakness' manifest in the crucifixion, which is above any human strength (1 Cor. 1:25). Achieving power and strength remains the goal, but both are gained by means of an alternative route—through the apparent weakness of the crucifixion. The question for interpreters is whether this amounts to a positing of an alternative masculinity. How one answers this question may depend, in part, on one's hermeneutical aim. If the goal is to disrupt dominant gender norms and to use scripture to do so, emphasizing Paul's alternative expressions of masculinity may open up possibilities for alternatives in the contemporary world. We might see these as moments of disruption of hegemonic masculinity, even while recognizing that elsewhere Paul is firmly embedded and seemingly formed by the normative gender constructs of his time. And it is true that Paul does not limit himself exclusively to masculine metaphors in his self-descriptions. He can, at times, draw on birth imagery (Gal. 4:19), or speak of himself as a 'nurse tenderly caring for her children' (1 Thess. 2:7, NRSV). While this type of imagery is rare compared to the multiple ways that Paul asserts manly authority of his communities, some have argued that it should be seen as a de-centering of maleness, especially when viewed in the light of Paul's most famous gender statement, 'in Christ there is no male and female' (as for example Kahl 2000).

Gender Egalitarianism in Galatians 3.28?

In Galatians 3.28 Paul appears to sweep away race, class, and gender binaries with a single verse causing almost endless debate as to his meaning. Indeed, as Dale Martin points out, in the late twentieth century the verse became the *locus classicus* for debate on gender equality (for an insightful history of interpretation, see Martin 2006: 77–90). Most historical critics remain convinced by Wayne Meeks' (1974) influential article, in which he argues that Galatians 3:28 reflects the philosophical ideal of the unification of opposites that was widespread in the ancient world, especially as this ideal was expressed in the myth of the primal androgyne. By the first century, the two Genesis creation stories were frequently interpreted through the lens of this myth, where Genesis 1:27 detailed the creation of an original androgynous progenitor of the human race, and Genesis 2:22 expressed the tragic bifurcation of that being into two distinct sexes. According to Meeks, when Paul claims that in Christ there is 'no male and female', he is quoting an early Christian baptismal formula which imagined the reunification of the divided male and female. As Meeks put it, the formula 'suggests that somehow the act of Christian initiation reverses the fateful division of Genesis 2:21–22' (1974: 185).

For Meeks, this reunification also implied that Paul advocated equality between male and female in his churches, but this particular aspect of his interpretation has been disputed. Others building on his work have shown that in the ancient world androgyny did not mean equality, as if this primal being was understood to be equal parts male and female. Such ontological perfection was typically understood as incorporeal and as masculine (Boyarin 1994; MacDonald 2000; Martin 2006). Philo clearly expresses the association of spiritual perfection with masculinity when he states, 'For progress is indeed nothing else than giving up the female genus by changing into the male, since the female gender is material, passive, corporeal and sense-perceptible while the male is active, rational, incorporeal and more akin to mind and thought (*Questions and Answers on Exodus 1:8*). This idea is evident in a saying from the Gospel of Thomas (114) in which Jesus tells the disciples that he will transform Mary into a male and a living spirit like the other male disciples so that she will be able to enter the kingdom of God. In short, while Paul describes some type of unified existence 'in Christ' (and it is unclear what that meant exactly), he was not likely envisioning men and women as equals in a socially transformative way.

For those looking for a liberating or just word in the New Testament about gender categories, this is where the gender ideology of the ancient world is particularly unyielding. But, according to Martin, all hope need not be lost. With him, I would argue that there is no theological reason that interpretations of the biblical text need be constrained by the 'hegemony of historical criticism' (2006: 88). Here queer theory may do better work, both recognizing the reality of the New Testament's historical context and then reading deliberately against it. So, with Martin, one could tweak Paul's phrase, 'there is no male and female' to mean that this binary is false. There is more to human gender construction than these two options, so in saying no to them, we dispense with the idea that one must be either male or female. As Martin notes, 'We admit the queer observation that gender is multiplex not duplex' (2006: 89). This may be a more fruitful approach in the long term than hoping to discover any sustained programme of cultural resistance on the part of these ancient authors.

Men and Women in 1 Corinthians 11:2–16

If Galatians 3:28 teases the contemporary reader with possibilities of gender equality, 1 Corinthians 11 confuses with Paul's seeming vacillation between assertions of female difference and subordination, and claims to sexual mutuality. And until recently, the majority of interpreters have assumed that the passage is about women's behaviour, in spite of the fact that Paul refers to the men nearly as much as he refers to the women, and he expressly mentions the inappropriateness of men's long hair (see Murphy O'Connor 1980; Brooten 2000: 294; Townsley 2006: 17.2). Many link Galatians 3:28 and 1 Corinthians 11, seeing Paul's declaration of 'no male and female in Christ' being taken in directions that he did not intend by the Corinthians (as in, women subverting customary dress by wearing their hair loose, or unveiled). Many have connected this behaviour to the prominence of the Dionysius cult in Corinth, suggesting that the behaviour of the women and/or Paul's protest was related to this cult. But what happens when the passage is read as Paul's displeasure with both men and women's behaviour?

Drawing on Butler's theory of gender performance, Gillian Townsley offers one way of 'que(e)rying' the text along these lines. Building on the work of Meeks and MacDonald, she suggests that perhaps the Corinthians were acting out the myth of androgyny that Paul heralded in Galatians 3:28 (Townsley 2006: 17.8–17.9). She posits that 'Based on their understanding of Paul's teaching behind Galatians 3:28, the Corinthians—both the men and the women—may have decided to symbolically dramatise their belief in a re-unified humanity through their appearances' (2006: 17.6). If such gender blurring is the case, she argues, Paul is seeking to re-establish clear gender boundaries. She further suggests that there is precedent for this type of cross-dressing in the Dionysus rituals which were practised in Corinth. Meeks himself had already noted that transvestism in ritual initiation was not unusual in the ancient world, although he denied any 'hint' of evidence for it in Christianity (Meeks 1974: 184; on cross dressing in the ancient world, see also Brooten 2000: 295–296). Townsley's reading suggests otherwise—that is, there may at least be a hint of evidence for just this type of ritual cross dressing. To be sure, as Townsley notes, this would still not amount to creating a state of gender equality, but it shows that one may find places in the New Testament that destabilize the normalized heterosexual gender binary. Whether one is fully convinced by this reading, Townsley's work is a good example of analysis influenced by gender and queer theory.

GENDER CONSTRUCTION IN THE CANONICAL GOSPELS

Given their narrative genre, gender-critical work on the gospels has largely focused on characterization, especially the gender construction of the main character, Jesus, and to a lesser degree the minor characters with whom he interacts. Most recently, this work has also been influenced by postcolonial theories, so that the gendered presentation of Jesus is considered in the context of Roman imperial occupation and colonization. What has become clear from these investigations is an inherent ambiguity in the gendered portrayal of Jesus. On the one hand, the gospel writers have an interest in highlighting the ways that Jesus measures up to the standards of hegemonic (and imperial) masculinity. As we will see below, the gospel writers find ways to make clear that Jesus' power and authority surpasses that of the emperor. On the other hand, all of the gospels relate the story of Jesus' passion which, in the context of the first century is a story of humiliation and emasculation. It is not surprising, then, that gender analyses have produced interpretations of Jesus as a figure who assimilates Roman imperial masculine ideology as well as one who represents alternative, marginal expressions of masculinities. The following examples of studies of the Markan Jesus will illustrate the point.

The Markan Jesus

Eric Thurman's reading of the gender construction of the Markan Jesus is guided by postcolonial theory and by his reading of first- and second-century Greek romances. Thurman suggests that the construction of male subjects across these ancient narratives (both the Gospel and the romances) expose similar strategies of resistance and ambivalence toward the colonial social order. He notes, for example, that the protagonist of *An Ephesian Tale* by Xenophon of Ephesus, and the Markan Jesus are both subjected to 'servile punishments and... reduced to a state of unmanly humiliation' (Thurman 2007: 223). Thurman sees the Markan Jesus as one who displays increasingly emasculated conduct beginning with his loss of manly self-control in the Garden of Gethsemane, and continuing to greater degrees of passivity in the passion narrative. In this way, he argues, the hero of Mark's Gospel (like the hero of *An Ephesian Tale*) destabilizes the hegemonic masculinity of the empire. Still, both men are also transformed by the end of their respective narratives so that their humiliated stated is 'converted into a triumphant spectacle of reclaimed manly honour' (Thurman 2007: 223; see also Thurman, 2003). Thurman's aim is to show how these stories share a 'simultaneous desire for and suspicion of Roman dominion' (2007: 228). In this way, they reveal the ambivalent position of many non-Roman men in the empire who find their status undercut by imperial power structures.

My own reading of the Markan Jesus focuses on the way the Gospel presents him as a 'strong man,' who pre-emptively defines his death as a manly death on behalf of others, rather than an emasculating crucifixion (Conway 2008: 90–100). He teaches his disciples to live a life of service, but this is so that they can be like the ideal kings as defined in Greek and Roman traditions, that is, humane in their leadership, rather than tyrannical like the 'great ones' currently in charge (Mark 10:42–46). In other words, there is much about the Gospel's presentation of Jesus that aims to shore up his masculine status, even while he makes his way to the emasculating cross. He urges his audience, indeed threatens them, in advance not to be ashamed of him, anticipating the shameful death he is about to undergo, while simultaneously offering an alternative image of divine power and glory on the other side of this death (Mark 8:38).

Nevertheless, like Thurman, I suggest there remains an inescapable ambivalence in the gender construction of Jesus. In spite of claims that he must die as a ransom for many, the Markan Jesus nevertheless asks to avoid the painful death altogether (Mark 14:36). Even more telling, the Markan crucifixion scene exposes the gruelling and deadly demand of hegemonic masculinity in Jesus' anguished cry from the cross (Mark 14:37), that is, the expendability of the male body, or as Carlin Barton (2001: 277) puts it, 'the willingness, on behalf of the collectivity to lose everything, to become nothing'.

The Johannine Jesus

The Johannine Jesus is often placed in contrast to the Markan Jesus, and in terms of gender, one might argue that he is arguably the manliest of the New Testament presentations of Jesus (Conway 2003, 2008). This Jesus appears to be in absolute control of events throughout the narrative, even of his own death (10:17–18, 19:26–30). Others have no authority over him, with the exception of his divine father who surpasses him in authority. Nevertheless, the Johannine Jesus must still undergo death on the cross. Peter-Ben Smit has seen in this an undercutting of the 'macho-Christology' in John. In his view, 'the hypermasculine Jesus constructed in the course of John is de(con)structed at the cross'. In this way, 'the paradoxical glorification of Jesus becomes the sign which destabilises … much to the benefit of those who are looking for new and creative ways of (re)defining human gender and sexuality (Smit 2006: 31.9). I suggest that such a reading is true only if we read *against* the narrative which takes pains to circumvent a reading of this death as emasculation, never referring to it as crucifixion, but always as a glorification, or 'lifting up' (3:14, 8:28, 12:32). Having Jesus lay down his own life, 'for his friends' (15:13) suggests that we should see his death as a voluntary death for others. To the extent that this attempt at preserving the masculine image of Jesus does not convince (though much of Christian history suggests otherwise), we might view it as a failed effort that leaves the instability of the Johannine Jesus' gender identity exposed.

Still, the fact that the Johannine Jesus is presented as divine Wisdom incarnate, a figure that is often personified as a woman in the Hebrew scriptures, also raises questions about gender. Whether the Johannine Jesus completely subsumes this feminine aspect in a dominant masculine characterization is a point of debate. Positions range from Martin Scott's, who argues 'Jesus Sophia is not mere man, but rather, the incarnation of both the male and female expression of the divine, albeit within the limitations of human flesh' (Scott 1992: 172) to that of Wayne Meeks, who claims 'in the Fourth Gospel there is no trace of the usual feminine Sophia; she has become entirely the masculine Logos, the Son of Man' (Meeks 1972: 722; see Conway 2008: 152–156).

Faced with these extremes, Tat-siong Benny Liew has offered a queer reading of the Johannine Jesus, observing that, in most cases, interpreters' own restricted views of gender have precluded interpretations beyond the male/female binary. He offers a transgressive reading of the Johannine Jesus as neither male nor female, but more as transvestite. Liew teases out a reading of the Johannine Jesus that is intended to 'displace the male and/or female structure' and encourage the reader to look at Jesus' 'cross-dressing body' (2009: 260). Liew's reading is also intersectional as it analyses the desire of John's *Ioudaioi* (typically translated as 'the Jews' but left untranslated by Liew) to keep 'the racial-ethnic, class, gender, and sexual hierarchies intact in their nation-building project' (2009: 276). Liew's reading is creative and provocative, if not always convincing in its historically based arguments. But, again, productive readings of the biblical text need not always be historical readings.

These two examples of the Markan and Johannine Jesus give a sense of the varying ways that interpreters have viewed the gender construction of the canonical Jesus. One could find similar variation in accounts of Matthean Jesus and the Lukan Jesus, but here those gospels will be discussed in relation to other aspects of gender construction in the New Testament in the final section.

Symbolic and Metaphorical Gender Construction in the New Testament

Beyond Pauline rhetoric, or gospel characterization, gender construction also takes place symbolically throughout the New Testament, and often intersects with other prominent ideologies in the ancient world. For example, householder, or *oikos* ideology, in which the father/householder has ruling authority over the women, children, and slaves of the household, plays an important role across the New Testament. The Gospel of Matthew regularly depicts God and Jesus as 'master of the house' (*oikodespotēs*) and conveys parables with the master as a central character. At the same time, the Gospel frequently undercuts biological kinship ties, thereby threatening the erosion of the traditional household structure. In this way, as Anderson and Moore have shown, the Gospel 'embodies multiple, contradictory assumptions regarding masculinity' (2003:71). Myles's queer reading of the Gospel of Mark makes a similar point about Jesus' call to the male disciples to leave their homes and occupations to follow him. He notes, 'The very act of moving away from secure familial attachments meant surrendering to widespread imperial discourses asserting the importance of male headship and the relative impotence of falling outside these conventional institutions' (Myles 2010: 72).

Perhaps the most puzzling teaching of Jesus, lying well outside of householder ideology, and unique to Matthew's gospel, is his saying about eunuchs 'who have made themselves eunuchs for the sake of the kingdom of heaven', with the accompanying admonition 'Let anyone accept this who can' (Matt. 19:12 NRSV). In essence, Jesus here lifts up an alternative masculinity as a model of discipleship. This model is not grounded in traditional concepts of marriage and reproduction (which are reinforced in Matt. 19:3–9), but in the culturally threatening, gender-blurred figure of the eunuch. Matthew Kuefler (2001) argues that options such as this one for alternative expressions of manliness were critically important to the later spread of Christianity (see also Moxnes and Kartzow 2010).

Householder/*oikos* ideology is also evident in the Pastoral Epistles, as Jennifer Glancy (1994) and Mary Rose D'Angelo (2003) have shown. D'Angelo focuses on how this gendered ideology structures power in relation to others. As she notes, an answer to the question posed in 1 Timothy 3:5, ('if someone does not know how to manage his own household, how can he take care of God's church?') requires the display of a household, women, children, and slaves over which the dominant man (and church leader) exhibits control (D'Angelo 2003). Similarly Rebecca Anna Solevag argues that *oikos* ideology 'saturates' the Pastorals, providing a governing principle (2012: 7). She details the way the ideal man is constructed as the householder, while the ideal woman is constructed using the language of domesticity and subordination. Focusing especially on the (in) famous teaching on women's salvation through childbearing (1 Tim. 2:15), Solevag makes the case that the author, on the basis of his reading of Genesis, believed that

Eve's transgression (sexual seduction) created an ontological difference between men and women. Because of their unique condition that they inherited from Eve, women demand a special means of redemption, namely childbearing coupled with the proper set of female virtues. Not only does childbearing fit within the householder ideology of the Greco-Roman culture, it also echoes the punishment in Genesis, becoming also part of women's redemption.

Gender and imperial ideology are closely related in Luke–Acts which builds a portrait of Jesus and the disciples/apostles in relation to imperial claims to power and authority. More than any other gospel, it uses imperial rhetoric to describe Jesus, including a twice told apotheosis scene recalling the deification of Roman emperors (Luke 24:51; Acts 1:1–9). D'Angelo (2003) has detailed the elite masculine construct offered by the prologue, which elevates the author (as patron of the 'most excellent Theophilus') into the ranks of other elite males of the empire, a point reinforced by the successive appearance of various men of rank through the narrative. The point seems to be an appeal to those who were versed with this imperial ideology and an attempt to show Jesus as surpassing the emperor's ability to bring peace to the nations.

Todd Penner and Caroline Vander Stichele's work on Acts is a good example of how gender intersects with other social power dynamics, in this case, religion, imperial expansion, and the deployment of the 'past' to support the particular ideological agendas. They show how the author of Acts, like other ancient Greek authors, links the male authority figures of his narrative to the great men of the Jewish past (Moses, Abraham, and David) and to the geographical advancement of early Christianity. They place the author of Luke–Acts alongside other elite Greek authors of the east who write about the 'past' in ways that assert their control and authority in the present. In so doing, they resist Roman authority, even while living ever more in submission to it (Penner and Vander Stichele 2007b).

In terms of gender symbolism, it is appropriate to end this discussion with an all too brief mention of the final book in the Christian canon, Revelation. Gender construction takes place here through symbolic figures—the Son of Man, the Lamb, the whore of Babylon, the woman clothed with the sun, the 144,000 male virgins, and the new Jerusalem adorned as a bride for her husband (to name a few). Scholarship on these images is extensive, much of it focused on the perverse scene in chapters 17–18, in which the reader is asked to gaze on the destruction of Rome/Babylon personified as a woman/whore. Tina Pippin has argued that this picture is thoroughly misogynistic, with all female figures, including the whore, constructed with respect to male fantasies. Twenty years later, after the emergence of postcolonial studies and queer theory, Lynn Huber (2011) writes of the tension involved in identifying with the whore, even as she supports the destruction of imperial power she represents. Engaging the image of the whore in its first-century context, Glancy and Moore (2011) have investigated whether her figure would be recognizable to a first-century reader as a prostitute. They read Revelation in the context of first-century political discourse which commonly featured sexual invective against the imperial family. They conclude that the whore of Babylon, with her self-identification as empress (Rev. 18:7), more closely resembles the *whore-empresses* along the lines of Messalina as she was negatively portrayed in political invective and the population imagination (Glancy and Moore 2011; see also Moore 2009). Beyond these studies, other gender critical work has been done on the figure of the Lamb. For example, Chris Frilingos (2004) sees the Lamb as an unstable figure, shifting from feminine to masculine. Meanwhile, Huber (2008) has read the 144,000 male virgins as metaphors of resistance against Roman imperial discourses on the family and masculinity.

Future 'Construction' Projects

Although much work on gender construction in the New Testament has proliferated rapidly over the past two decades, more remains to be done. A better understanding of the interactions between elite and non-elite forms of gender performance in the ancient the world may illumine gender constructions in early Christian writings, as will the work on intersecting identity markers of race, class, and ethnicity. Similarly, while a great deal of work has been done on the rhetorical construction of gender in ancient texts, this work could benefit from interaction with materially focused studies, along the lines of Bernadette Brooten's (1982) classic study on women leaders in the synagogues. Meanwhile, there remains an important place for both historically grounded examinations of gender in the ancient world and more creative readings aimed at cultural resistance and transformation. Historical investigations offer important correctives for potential misreadings and misuses of readings that claim the authority of the past. They also make us more acutely aware of our own culturally embedded assumptions about gender. What they cannot consistently do is offer transformative readings for the present. Queer readings can and do offer creative challenges to embedded gender assumptions, both in the New Testament and in our own context. At a theoretical level, more explicit work should be undertaken as to how these differing approaches can mutually benefit and learn from each other.

REFERENCES

Anderson, J. C. and S. D. Moore (2011). 'How Typical a Roman Prostitute is Revelation's "Great Whore"?' *Journal of Biblical Literature*, 130: 551–569.

Bailey, R. C., T.-S. B. Liew, and F. F. Segovia (2009). *They Were All Together in One Place: Toward Minority Biblical Criticism*. Leiden & Boston: Brill.

Barton, C. A. (2001). *Roman Honor: The Fire in the Bones*. Berkeley: University of California Press.

Barton, T. (1994). *Power and Knowledge: Astrology, Physiognomics, and Medicine Under the Roman Empire*. Ann Arbor: University of Michigan Press.

Boyarin, D. (1994). *A Radical Jew: Paul and the Politics of Identity*. Berkeley: University of California Press.

Brooten, B. (1982). *Women Leaders in the Ancient Synagogue: Inscriptional Evidence and Background Issues*. Chico, CA: Scholars Press.

Brooten, B. (2000). 'Response to Corinthian Veils and Androgynes', in *Images of the Feminine in Gnosticism*. Harrisburg, PA: Trinity Press International, 293–296.

Burrus, V. (2000). *Begotten, Not Made: Conceiving Manhood in Late Antiquity*. Stanford, CA: Stanford University Press.

Butler, J. (1990). *Gender Trouble: Feminism and the Subversion of Identity*. New York: Routledge.

Butler, J. (1993). *Bodies That Matter: On the Discursive Limits of 'Sex'*. New York: Routledge.

Butler, J. (2004). *Undoing Gender*. New York & London: Routledge.

Cobb, L. S. (2008). *Dying to be Men: Gender and Language in Early Christian Martyr Texts*. New York: Columbia University Press.

Connell, R. W. and James W. Messerschmidt (2005). 'Hegemonic Masculinity: Rethinking the Concept'. *Gender & Society*, 19: 829–859.

Conway, C. M. (2003). '"Behold the Man!" Masculine Christologies and the Fourth Gospel' Masculine Christology and the Fourth Gospel'. In S. D. Moore and J. C. Anderson (eds), *New Testament Masculinities*. Atlanta: Society of Biblical Literature, 163–180.

Conway, C. M. (2008). *Behold the Man: Jesus and Greco-Roman Masculinity*. Oxford & New York: Oxford University Press.

D'Angelo, M. R. (2003). '"Knowing How to Preside Over his Own Household": Imperial Masculinity and Christian Asceticism in the Pastorals, *Hermas*, and Luke-Acts'. In S. D. Moore and J. C. Anderson (eds), *New Testament Masculinities*, Atlanta: Society of Biblical Literature, 265–295.

de Lauretis, T. ed. (1991). 'Queer Theory: Lesbian and Gay Sexualities.' Special issue of Differences: *A Journal of Feminist Cultural Studies*, 3.

Foxhall, L. and J. B. Salmon (1998a). *Thinking Men: Masculinity and its Self-representation in the Classical Tradition*. London and New York: Routledge.

Foxhall, L. and J. B. Salmon (1998b). *When Men were Men: Masculinity, Power, and Identity in Classical Antiquity*. London and New York: Routledge.

Frilingos, C. A. (2004). *Spectacles of Empire: Monsters, Martyrs, and the Book of Revelation*. Philadelphia: University of Pennsylvania Press.

Glancy, J. (1994). 'Unveiling Masculinity: The Construction of Gender in Mark 6:17–29'. *Biblical Interpretation*, 2: 34–50.

Glancy, J. and S. D. Moore (2011). 'How Typical a Roman Prostitute is Revelation's Whore?' *Journal of Biblical Literature*, 130: 551–569.

Gleason, M. W. (1995). *Making Men: Sophists and Self-presentation in Ancient Rome*. Princeton, NJ: Princeton University Press.

Guest, D. (2012). *Beyond Feminist Biblical Studies*. Sheffield: Phoenix Press.

Harrill, J. A. (2001). 'Invective Against Paul (2 Cor. 10:10): The Physiognomics of the Ancient Slave Body, and the Greco-Roman Rhetoric of Manhood'. In A. Y. Collins and M. M. Mitchell (eds), *Antiquity and Humanity: Essays on Ancient Religion and Philosophy*. Tubingen: Mohr Siebeck, 189–213.

Harrill, J. A. (2006). *Slaves in the New Testament: Literary, Social, and Moral Dimensions*. Minneapolis: Fortress Press.

Hoff, J. (1994). 'Gender as a Postmodern Category of Paralysis'. *Women's History Review*, 3: 149–169.

Hornsby, T. J. (2006). 'The Annoying Woman: Biblical Scholarship after Judith Butler'. In E. T. Armour and S. M. S. Ville (eds), *Bodily Citations*. New York: Columbia University Press, 71–89.

Hornsby, T. J. and K. Stone ed. (2011). *Bible Trouble: Queer Reading at the Boundaries of Biblical Scholarship*. Leiden and Boston: Brill.

Huber, L. R. (2008). 'Sexually Explicit? Re-reading Revelation's 144,000 Virgins as a Response to Roman Discourses'. *Journal of Men, Masculinities and Spirituality*, 2: 3–28.

Huber, L. R. (2011). 'Gazing at the Whore: Reading Revelation Queerly'. In T.J. Hornsby and K. Stone (eds), *Bible Trouble: Queer Reading at the Boundaries of Biblical Scholarship*. Leiden and Boston: Brill, 301–320.

Ivarsson, F. (2006). 'Vice Lists and Deviant Masculinity: The Rhetorical Function of 1 Corinthians 5:10–11 and 6:9–10', in T. Penner and C. Vander Stichele (eds), *Mapping Gender in Ancient Religious Discourses*. Leiden and Boston: Brill, 163–184.

Ivarsson, Fredrick (2008). 'Christian Identity as True Masculinity'. In Bengt Holmberg (ed.), *Exploring Early Christian Identity*, WUNT 1.226. Tubingen: Mohr Siebeck, 159–171.

Kahl, Brigitte. (2000). 'No Longer Male? Masculinity Struggles behind Galatians 3.28', *Journal for the Study of the New Testament*, 79: 37–49.

Kartzow, M. B. (2012). *Destabilizing the Margins: An Intersectional Approach to Early Christian Memory*. Eugene, OR: Pickwick Publications.

Kuefler, M. (2001). *The Manly Eunuch: Masculinity, Gender Ambiguity and Christian Ideology in Late Antiquity*. Chicago: University of Chicago Press.

Laqueur, T. W. (1990). *Making Sex: Body and Gender from the Greeks to Freud*. Cambridge, MA: Harvard University Press.

Larson, J. (2004). 'Paul's Masculinity'. *Journal of Biblical Literature*, 123: 85–97.

Liew, T.-S. B. (2009). 'Queering Closets and Perverting Desires: Cross-Examining John's Engendering and Transgendering Word Across Different Worlds'. In R. C. Bailey, T.-S. B. Liew, and F. F. Segovia (eds), *They Were All Together in One Place? Toward Minority Biblical Criticism*. Leiden and Boston: Brill, 251–288.

MacDonald, D. R. (2000). 'Corinthian Veils and Gnostic Androgynes', in K. L. King (ed.), *Images of the Feminine in Gnosticism*. Harrisburg, PA: Trinity Press International, 276–292.

Martin, D. (2006). *Sex and the Single Savior: Gender and Sexuality in Biblical Interpretation*. Louisville, KY: Westminster John Knox.

Meeks, W. A. (1972). 'The Man from Heaven in Johannine Sectarianism'. *Journal of Biblical Literature*, 91: 44–72.

Meeks, W. A. (1974). 'The Image of the Androgyne: Some Uses of a Symbol in Earliest Christianity'. *History of Religions*, 13: 165–208.

Meyerowitz, J. (2008). 'A History of "Gender"'. *American Historical Review*, 113: 1346–1356.

Moore, S. D. (1996). *God's Gym: Divine Male Bodies of the Bible*. New York: Routledge.

Moore, S. D. (2001). *God's Beauty Parlor: And Other Queer Spaces in and around the Bible*. Stanford, CA: Stanford University Press.

Moore, S. D. (2009). 'Metonymies of Empire: Sexual Humiliation and Gender Masquerade in the Book of Revelation'. In T.-S. B. Liew (ed.), *Postcolonial Interventions*. Sheffield: Sheffield Phoenix Press, 71–97.

Moore, S. D. and J. C. Anderson eds.(2003). *New Testament Masculinities*. Atlanta, GA: Society of Biblical Literature.

Moxnes, H. and M. B. Kartzow (2010). 'Complex Identities: Ethnicity, Gender and Religion in the Story of the Ethiopian Eunuch (Acts 8:26–40)'. *Religion and Theology*, 17: 184–204.

Murphy O'Connor, J. (1980). 'Sex and Logic in 1 Corinthians 11:2–16'. *Catholic Biblical Quarterly*, 42: 482–500.

Myles, R. J. (2010). 'Dandy Discipleship: A Queering of Mark's Male Disciples'. *Journal of Men, Masculinities and Spirituality* [Online], 4. <www.jmmsweb.org> (accessed 24 June 2013).

Nasrallah, L. S. and E. Schüssler Fiorenza eds. (2009). *Prejudice and Christian Beginnings: Investigating Race, Gender and Ethnicity in Early Christian Studies*. Minneapolis, MN: Fortress Press.

Penner, T. and C. Vander Stichele eds. (2007a). *Mapping Gender in Ancient Religious Discourses*. Leiden and Boston: Brill.

Penner, T. and Vander Stichele, C. (2007b). 'Script(ur)ing Gender in Acts: The Past and Present Power of *Imperium*'. In T. Penner and C. Vander Stichele (eds), *Mapping Gender in Ancient Religious Discourses*. Leiden and Boston: Brill, 231–266.

Philo of Alexandria. (1953). *Philo: Questions and Answers on Exodus*. Trans R. Marcus. Loeb Classical Library. Cambridge, MA: Harvard University Press.

Punt, J. (2007). 'Sex and Gender, and Liminality in Biblical Texts: Venturing into Postcolonial Queer Biblical Interpretation'. *Neotestamentica*, 41: 382–398.

Satlow, M. L. (1996). '"Try to Be a Man": The Rabbinic Construction of Masculinity'. *Harvard Theological Review*, 89: 19–40.

Schuössler Fiorenza, E. (2009). *Democratizing Biblical Studies: Toward an Emancipatory Educational Space*. Louisville, KY: Westminster John Knox Press.

Scott, J. W. (1986). 'Gender: A Useful Category of Historical Analysis'. *American Historical Review*, 91: 1053–1075.

Scott, M. (1992). *Sophia and the Johannine Jesus*. Sheffield: Sheffield Academic Press.

Sedgwick, E. K. (1985). *Between Men: English Literature and Male Homosocial Desire*. New York: Columbia University Press.

Sedgwick, E. K. (1990). *Epistemology of the Closet*. Berkeley: University of California Press.

Smit, P.-B. (2006). Jesus and the Ladies: Constructing and Deconstructing Macho-Christology. *The Bible and Critical Theory* [Online], 2. <http://bibleandcriticaltheory.org/index.php/bct> (accessed 24 June 2013).

Solevag, A. R. (2012). 'Salvation, Gender and the Figure of Eve in 1 Timothy 2:9–15. *lectio difficilior*' [Online], 2. <http://www.lectio.unibe.ch/12_2/solevag_anna_rebecca_salvation_gender_eve.html> (accessed 24 June 2013).

Stone, K. ed. (2001). *Queer Commentary and the Hebrew Bible*. Cleveland, OH: Pilgrim Press.

Stowers, S. K. (1994). *A Rereading of Romans: Justice, Jews, and Gentiles*. New Haven, CT: Yale University Press.

Thurman, E. (2003). 'Looking for a Few Good Men: Mark and Masculinity'. In S. D. Moore and J. C. Anderson (eds), *New Testament Masculinities*. Atlanta: Society of Biblical Literature, 137–161

Thurman, E. (2007). 'Novel Men: Masculinity and Empire in Mark's Gospel and Xenophon's *An Ephesian's Tale*'. In T. Penner and C. Vander Stichele (ed.), *Mapping Gender in Ancient Religious Discourses*. Leiden and Boston: Brill, 185–229.

Townsley, G. (2006). 'Gender Trouble in Corinth: Que(e)rying Constructs of Gender in 1 Corinthians 11:2–16'. *Bible and Critical Theory* [Online], 2. <http://bibleandcriticaltheory.org/index.php/bct/index> (accessed 24 June 2013).

Walters, J. (1997). 'Invading the Roman Body: Manliness and Impenetrability in Roman Thought'. In J. P. Hallett and M. B. Skinner (eds), *Roman Sexualities*. Princeton: Princeton University Press, 29–43.

Williams, C. A. (1999). *Roman Homosexuality: Ideologies of Masculinity in Classical Antiquity*. Oxford and New York: Oxford University Press.

PART IV

....

SEXUALITY AND GENDER IN CHRISTIAN TRADITION

....

CHAPTER 15

DESIRE AND THE BODY IN THE PATRISTIC PERIOD

MATHEW KUEFLER

INTRODUCTION

FEW historical periods have influenced the shaping of Christian theology on gender and sexuality as the patristic period, the third through the fifth centuries CE, also called late antiquity. These centuries witnessed a number of significant developments in the nature of Christianity itself. Among them were the establishment of clearer mechanisms for defining doctrines, more formal hierarchies of authority to promulgate these doctrines, and a Roman government that turned from persecuting to supporting Christians. The flip side to such changes is obvious, and there was less tolerance for diversity of belief and state-sponsored suppression of alternative religious ideas and practices. The term 'patristic' derives, of course, from the bishops and theologians who directed the churches, the so-called Church Fathers, a name first used at the end of this period and one that reinforces the sense of paternalism and patriarchy within late ancient Christianity.

The Church Fathers dominate the historical record for Christianity in this period, and most of what we know about it comes from them. They were mostly men of the upper classes of Roman society, privileged, used to being heard, well educated, and they wrote in cultured Latin or Greek. In earlier centuries they would probably have become civic or military leaders; in the fourth and especially the fifth centuries they led in ecclesiastical fashion, and many of them were bishops. There were other Christian voices speaking—those of less well educated Syriac- or Coptic-speaking monks, for example; those of dissenters labelled heretics; or those of women—but almost invariably we hear them only through the intermediacy of these Fathers. Scholars long assumed that these men represented a 'mainstream' of belief that was shared by the silent mass of late ancient Christians. To be sure, the theological standing of these men reflects the overall historical impact of their ideas. Yet we must not be too quick to see theirs as the sole or even the majority opinions in their day. As Peter Brown described it in his inimitable prose, 'The day-to-day life of Christians is a darkened landscape, intermittently lit up for us by the flashes of polemical fireworks that crackled far overhead' (Brown 1988: 142).

Scholars are nowadays trying to supplement the historical record left by the Church Fathers—largely in the form of theological treatises, sermons, and letters—with other writings from the period, especially hagiography, including apocryphal acts of the saints, the stories of Egyptian monks and nuns known as 'Sayings of the Fathers' (*Apophthegmata patrum*), and even literary romances, most of which afford a greater role to women than that found in patristic writings, and perhaps reveal a broader glimpse into the Christian society of late antiquity (see, e.g., Cooper 1996; Coon 1997; Alwis 2011; Harper 2013). Finally, there is also a long tradition of smoothing over the roughness in the differences between the ideas held by individual Church Fathers, to see them as all reflecting the same orthodoxy through time, though scholars are now more willing to admit to variations in emphasis or even to outright contradictions among the patristic writers. In what follows, these caveats must be kept in mind. Even so, the broad outlines of a patristic theology on gender and sexuality and on desire and the body can be sketched out, and the importance of that theology for later Christians even to the present day readily admitted.

BODY

All theological reflection on gender and sexuality began with thinking about the body. The Church Fathers may have taken what they knew about it from ancient medical writers, though it is not easy to know how widely read those medical writers were. Lactantius, for example, the fourth-century bishop who was also tutor to the sons of the emperor Constantine, passed along the notion that the sex of a child was determined by the flow of the man's seed in the uterus, either to the right for a male or to the left for a female—and to the middle in the case of a male child born with some female characteristics or a female child with some male characteristics (*De opificio Dei* 12). This is what medical writers were saying, too, and individuals like Lactantius may have absorbed such ideas from their reading and then passed them along to others. When attempting to understand the reproductive body, medical writers differed on whether men alone provided the seed that became a child and that was simply nurtured within the woman, or whether women also provided seed that mingled with a man's. The same medical writers also agreed that the generalized or 'default' body was a male one, unless some accident in gestation turned it into a female one (Laqueur 1990: ch. 2). Christian writers echoed these opinions in their own discussions about whether males alone or females along with them were created in the image of God (see, e.g., Augustine, *De trinitate* 12.7.10; also

Power 1995). Augustine of Hippo mentioned intersex individuals briefly, also suggesting that they were usually considered as male (*De civitate Dei* 16.8).

Christians also had the Bible to help them in understanding the nature of the body, and they read it with their traditional preconceptions. The legend of Adam and Eve, for example, was often understood as reinforcing the male primacy and superiority that was so much a part of ancient Mediterranean culture (Pagels 1988). Paul's disquiet about sin and the distorted will (Rom. 7) reminded patristic writers about the need to subordinate the body to the mind in ways much like those already taught by Plato and the Stoics. And Jesus' teaching that both men and women would live like the angels in heaven (Matt. 22:30) seemed to support the idea of a disembodied, even genderless afterlife that fit easily with neo-Platonic notions of the ascent of the soul out of materiality.

Some of these understandings were hard to reconcile with other Christian teachings equally derived from the Bible. How could the inferiority of the body be set alongside a belief in its future glorification? (Bynum 1995: chs 1–2). Origen of Alexandria had argued for a radical human transcendence in paradise out of the body and, with it, beyond gendered difference, but his ideas were condemned at the end of the fourth century for their apparent incompatibility with Christian teachings on the resurrection of the flesh. Docetist Christians could not believe in a bodily Jesus, that is, a perfect God taking form in imperfect matter, and their ideas were repeatedly condemned. Yet the assertion of the perpetual virginity of Mary also required patristic writers to explain how an embodied Jesus could be born from Mary while leaving her bodily virginity intact (see, e.g., Jerome, *Adversus Helvidium* 20; see also Otten 1997 on Tertullian).

DESIRE

Sexual desire was arguably the most problematic characteristic of the body. Again, there were longstanding cultural traditions that made this claim: for Stoics, the passions of lust and anger were the elements that most disturbed the human mind, and for many medical writers, sexual excess dangerously weakened the body. The Bible seemed to encourage these notions. Perhaps Adam and Eve would not have had sex if they had not sinned, as some Church Fathers believed, but would have brought children into the world by other means. Even if God had always intended Adam and Eve to have sex, though, it would have been an efficient and dispassionate activity if they had not sinned (see, e.g., Augustine's changing opinion on this question, from *De bono coniugalis* 1 to *De nuptiis et concupiscentia* 1.5; also Dunning 2011). Lust was at the heart of this problem. It was, for Augustine, that punishment that God intended to fit the crime, since our human rebellion against God's command in the Garden of Eden was infinitely repeated in our bodies' unruly refusal to obey our minds in uncontrolled sexual desire (*De nuptiis et concupiscentia* 1.6).

The fact that lust remained even after baptism also meant for Augustine that it served as the chief reminder of original sin (*De nuptiis et concupiscentia* 1.25; for more on Augustine's views about sex, see Brown 1988: ch. 19). Several patristic writers even wondered about the sinfulness of sexual dreams, and of the physical arousal that might accompany them: was it sinful to dream about sex or to have an erection or seminal emission, if such things happened during sleep and without the individual's consent? (Brakke 1995). The connections between sexual desire and sin were forcefully laid out: indeed, Augustine's views on lust only confirmed for him our inability to be sinless and thus our utter dependence on God's grace for salvation.

Augustine went further than most in his theological reflections on lust and sin, but most of the Church Fathers elaborated all too gladly on Jesus' and Paul's brief injunctions against sex and marriage (Matt. 19; 1 Cor. 7). The encouragement of virginity, chastity, and celibacy predates the patristic period, since already in the first Christian centuries some individuals and groups were rejecting sex and marriage—as, too, were some non-Christians, like the Jewish Essenes in Judaea or Therapeutae in Egypt. The Christian groups, present throughout the third, fourth, and fifth centuries, are often called Encratites (from the Greek *enkrateia*, meaning 'self-control'), and some rejected all sex and marriage as sinful for Christians, though by the end of the fourth century it was declared heretical to consider marriage or sex within marriage as sinful (on the ascetic tradition within early Christianity see Brown 1988). Nonetheless, almost all of the Church Fathers deemed sex and marriage inferior to virginity, chastity, and celibacy. It was like the difference between not doing evil and actually doing good, according to Jerome (*Adversus Jovinianum* 1.13).

Sexual Renunciation

Almost all of the Church Fathers who wrote about sex wrote to encourage sexual renunciation. Unmarried persons were urged in letters and sermons to remain so. Even married persons were invited to vow to each other and before God no longer to have sex in what were called spiritual marriages; the individuals joined in such unions were called *syneisaktoi* in Greek and *subintroducti* in Latin. They may have begun as means for Christians to live sexless lives in an earlier era when unmarried persons risked financial penalties under Roman law; after Constantine removed these penalties (*Codex Theodosianus* 8.16.1; also Kuefler 2007), married Christians who wished to renounce sex were more often encouraged to separate. Spiritual marriages were particularly insisted upon for married men of the clergy by the late fourth century, at least in the western parts of the empire (see, e.g., Jerome, *Adversus Jovinianum* 34, or canons 27 and 33 of the early fourth-century Council of Elvira; see also eastern support in Cyril of Jerusalem, *Catechesis* 12.25). Clerical marriage was defended in *Codex Theodosianus* 16.2.44 (on spiritual marriages see Elliott 1993; Alwis 2011).

Monasticism

Perhaps the most obvious consequence of the impulse toward chastity in the patristic period is seen in the rise of monasticism. The origins of the movement are complex and varied, involving both men and women in either urban or rural settings, temporarily or permanently, alone or in formal or informal groups. Some individuals fled into the wilderness of desert, forest, or mountain, while others simply remained in their family's homes, and while we hear more about men doing the former and women the latter, we have only anecdotal evidence for both. What the early participants in monasticism shared was a desire to escape the obligations and preoccupations of normal life in favour of lives devoted to prayer and asceticism (Brown 1988; Elm 1994; Coon 1997: chs 4–5). The abandonment of marriage and family life formed a common element within the early movement: some of the earliest monks, according to stories in the Egyptian writings about them, left wives and children behind when they took up the monastic lifestyle. The importance of restraining one's sexual impulses, through harsh regimes of bodily punishments, also frequently appeared in early monastic writings. Fasting was also encouraged as key to monastic asceticism, and patristic writers noted the parallels between the desire for food and sexual desire (Shaw 1998). Modern scientific studies suggest that the limited diets of these early practitioners of monasticism may have often resulted in amenorrhoea in women and chronic impotence in men, both of which were likely welcomed (see Rousselle 1988: ch. 10).

Castration

Still, the drive to sexual renunciation among Christians in late antiquity can be seen in myriad ways. Self-castration was one technique men used to achieve it. Eunuchs existed in large numbers in Roman society in the third, fourth, and fifth centuries CE, serving as domestic slaves guarding wealthy women in their homes or escorting them out-of-doors, and even achieving high government offices, so while self-castration may seem an extraordinary act of mutilation to us today, it probably did not seem so to those who lived in this period. A variety of castration methods existed from tying up the scrotum to sever the vas deferens to amputation of the penis; eunuchs who had undergone the former, less risky method of castration might still be able to achieve erections, so it did not necessarily preclude even penetrative sexual relations, let alone other kinds.

Whether eunuchs felt sexual desire was debated among ancient writers: Basil the Great said in a discussion of castration that a dehorned bull will still try to butt with its head (*De virginitate* 63; on castration, see Kuefler 2001: 31–36, 96–102; and, into later periods, also Ringrose 2003; Tougher 2008). Again, if compared to modern studies, men who had been castrated before puberty were far likelier not to develop sexual interests that those castrated in adulthood. Castration served religious ends, too: pagan priests of the Phrygian goddess Cybele often castrated themselves as a sacrifice of their fertility, and in the first centuries CE the cult had spread across the Mediterranean (see, e.g., Firmicus Maternus, *De errore profanarum religionum* 4.1–3; also Roller 1999). So it should not seem too surprising that some Christian men castrated themselves, especially given Jesus' instructions that his followers do so for the sake of the kingdom of heaven (Matt. 19:12). Whenever the Church Fathers mentioned this passage they reminded their readers not to take it literally, which suggests that some men were.

Perhaps the most famous individual to have himself castrated was the theologian Origen of Alexandria (see Eusebius, *Historia ecclesiastica* 6.8), but the first decree of the Council of Nicaea condemned self-castration in Christian clerics, so it was obviously a more general practice than most scholars have acknowledged. Ambrose of Milan decried it still in the late fourth century, arguing that Christian men should restrain their sexual impulses with the force of their wills rather than resorting to self-castration (*De viduis* 13.75–77). John Chrysostom went further, stating that eunuchs gained no merit from their virginity because they could not do otherwise (*De virginitate* 8.5). And John Cassian praised the Egyptian monk Serenus for waiting for God to send an angel to castrate him in a dream rather than doing it himself (*Conlationes* 7.2; on eunuchs in early Christianity generally, see Kuefler 2001: ch. 8).

Brides of Christ

Many of the Church Fathers regularly resorted to metaphorical language to strengthen the appeal of sexual renunciation among Christians. They often quoted from the Song of Songs, which permitted them to imagine the celibate individual as married to Christ and the virginal individual as enjoying His embraces. Both men and women might be called 'brides of Christ' in patristic writings, urged to forgo the temporary pleasures of carnal passion for the eternal pleasures of celestial bliss, but also to prefer the perfect divine spouse to any inferior earthly version (see, e.g., Jerome's letter 22 to the young woman Eustochium to encourage her not to remarry after the death of her husband; also Cooper 1996; Kuefler 2001: ch. 5). The peculiarities of so sublimated an understanding of sexuality in late antiquity have intrigued many scholars (see, e.g., Burrus 2004; Burrus et al. 2010).

Opposition to Sexual Renunciation

Not all Christians celebrated the joys of sexual renunciation. The fourth-century theologian Jovinian, whose ideas we know only from his opponents, criticized the emphasis on asceticism in late ancient Christianity. Those who insisted that Christians abandon sex and marriage and live lives of asceticism, he countered, erred in not recognizing baptism as sufficient to salvation (Hunter 2007). Julian of Eclanum responded to Augustine's ideas about lust and original sin by saying that since sexual desire remained after baptism it could not be sinful, since baptism removed all sin. (It must be kept in mind that most Christians were baptized in adulthood in the patristic period; on Julian, see Brown

1988: 408–419.) We cannot know how many Christians held opinions like these rather than like those of the Church Fathers.

MARRIAGE

Virtually all patristic writings about marriage were intended to discourage it (see, e.g., Tertullian, *De exhortatione castitatis*; Gregory of Nyssa, *De virginitate*; or John Chrysostom, *De virginitate*; see also generally Brown 1988). Augustine stands alone in having written two treatises on marriage that described its benefits (*De bono coniugalis* and *De nuptiis et concupiscentia*). He maintained that there were three 'good things' about it (*bona*, which he also called its fruits, *fructus*, and its bonds, *vinculi; De nuptiis et concupiscentia* 1.10). First was the begetting of children, what he called *proles*. Second was its encouragement of faithfulness, *fides*. Third was its symbolic recreation of the sacred relationship between Christ and the Church, a model derived from Paul or someone writing as Paul, its *sacramentum* (*De nuptiis et concupiscentia* 1.17; from Eph. 5:32).

Each of these three elements reflects important things believed about marriage in the patristic period, which can be seen even in those authors who did not devote whole treatises to the subject of marriage. First, procreation provided the only moral justification for sexual activity among the Church Fathers. Already at the start of the third century, Clement of Alexandria insisted that sex within marriage was fully permissible but only if it were potentially procreative (*Paedagogus* 2.10.83; also Brown 1988: ch. 6; Hunter 1992).

Second, the faithfulness expected in marriage required its indissolubility in a way not in keeping with Roman or Biblical traditions, both of which permitted divorce and remarriage. Cyril of Jerusalem maintained that marriage united two individuals for life (*Cathesesis* 5.3). Augustine said much the same, and recognized that he differed from both Mosaic and secular law in opposing all divorce (*De nuptiis et concupiscentia* 1.10). Christian women who devoted themselves to widowhood after their husband's death were highly praised by the Church Fathers (see, e.g., Ambrose, *De viduis*). Little was said to widowers about not remarrying, but given the differences in ages of marriage in late antiquity, when a woman might well marry someone twenty years her senior (Shaw 1987), the absence of such discussion may not indicate any particular moral stance. Augustine, in *De bono viduitatis*, permitted remarriage if a widow felt she could not live in chastity. In contrast, Tertullian, in *De monogamia*, thought that remarriage should be prohibited to all Christians (Kuefler 2014b).

Third, the comparison of husband and wife to Christ and the Church provided an opportunity to describe the male domination and female subordination within marriage that reflected Roman standards. In his letter to the married woman Celantia, the theologian Pelagius suggested that a Christian woman should honour and obey her husband even more than a pagan would, since he represented Christ to her (*Ad matronam Celantiam* 26; on Christian marriage and family life generally, see Reynolds 1994; Nathan 2000; Cooper 2007).

Sexual Sins

Augustine's enumeration of the three good things found in marriage also provides us with guidelines for thinking about sexual sins as imagined by the Church Fathers.

Within Marriage

The breach of the first, *proles*, might take place when sexual acts happened, even within marriage, without procreative potential, that is, through oral or anal sex, or use of contraceptives or abortifacients, or any of these things—and always alluded to euphemistically (see, e.g., Augustine, *De bono coniugalis* 9, who mentioned only 'the use of nature [*naturalis usus*]' in sex contrasted with 'that which is against nature [*iste, qui est contra naturam*]'; on contraception and abortion in late antiquity, see Riddle 1992). A rupture of the first might also occur through immoderate sexual activity between married persons, which was repeatedly discouraged by the Church Fathers.

The breach of the second, *fides*, might be found in divorce or remarriage but also in adultery. Roman and Greek Christians in late antiquity disagreed with their ancestors in considering husbands bound by the same requirement of sexual faithfulness as wives. Traditionally while any wife could be found guilty of adultery if she had sex outside of her marriage, a husband could be charged with it only if he had had sex with a married woman. In other words, it was the marital status of the woman that mattered, and the man's was irrelevant. The fact that many patristic writers had to spell out the equal obligations of husbands probably means it was still open to question among Christians in late antiquity (see, e.g., John Chrysostom, *Propter fornicationes* 1.4–5; or Lactantius, *Divinae institutiones* 6.23; also Kuefler 2001: 164–165).

Divorce and remarriage were considered breaches of the third, *sacramentum*. Perhaps motivated by Christian sentiment, the emperor Constantine forbade divorce except in limited circumstances, in 331 CE (*Codex Theodosianus* 3.16.1). While the language of the law is not entirely clear, it seems that a man was prevented from divorcing his wife unless she had committed adultery or was involved in prostitution or had procured an abortion (or maybe, in this last case, she had dealt in poisons); a woman was forbidden from divorcing her husband unless he was a murderer, a tomb robber, or an abortionist (or maybe again, in this last case, a poisoner instead). The law remained in effect through the rest of the period, though it was briefly abrogated between 439 and 452 (*Novella Theodosiani* 12.1 and *Novella Valentiniani* 35.1; see also Kuefler 2007). The law could not prevent a couple from separating, but it did greatly restrict their ability to remarry.

Long before the enactment of this law, Christian theologians regularly condemned remarriage, even when marriages ended by the death of one partner, some more vociferously than others (see, e.g., John Chrysostom, *De virginitate* 37.1; Jerome, *Adversus Jovinianum* X, or the Council of Elvira, canon 64). In other words, the faithfulness expected in Christian marriage was a singular and lifelong obligation; the ancients called it monogamy, though it differs from our modern definition of the term.

Outside of Marriage

While the Church Fathers condemned all sex outside of marriage, they railed most frequently against what we would call male homosexuality. This may indicate a greater hostility toward it than towards other forms of non-marital sex, or it may mean simply that unmarried Roman women, at least those of the upper classes, were too closely supervised to become entangled in casual sexual relations. Homoeroticism was part and parcel of ancient Greek and Roman society, though it had rules different from those of today. Sex happened mostly in age-differentiated relationships between adult men and adolescent boys that the ancients called pederasty, though relations between young men of roughly similar age were not unknown. In these relations, the younger or socially inferior partner was supposed to be the one penetrated, putting himself at the sexual service of the older or socially superior partner. Accordingly, the penetrated partner was usually regarded as having been feminized, with considerable resulting social censure, though more excused in the young or in slaves.

Patristic writers tried to attach similar opprobrium to the penetrating partner in same-sex relations, arguing that it was just as shameful and equally feminizing (see, e.g., Salvian of Marseilles, *De gubernatione Dei* 7.20). In their lumping together of both partners as equivalent in sin, though, the Church Fathers might be considered as having helped to establish a new type of homosexual identity. They also worried occasionally about the possibilities for sexual relationships among the men brought together in monasticism (Masterson 2006; Krueger 2011). Less often they spoke out against female homoeroticism but when they did it was with equal animosity and with parallel concerns about the masculinization of women who participated in it (Brooten 1996: ch. 11).

A few of the Church Fathers denounced prostitution, though it was legal within the Roman Empire, regulated, and even taxed (McGinn 1997). And some criticized Christian men who had sex with their own slaves, which was probably a longstanding social custom (see, e.g., Augustine, *De bono coniugalis* 5; see also Council of Elvira, canon 31, which excluded men who had engaged in illicit sexual activities from communion; on Christian sexual morality in late antiquity generally; Kuefler 2001: 161–170; Harper 2013).

GENDER

The dangerous slippage between male and female that the Church Fathers warned against in homoeroticism points to the centrality of gender to their views about the human condition. Like others living in their day, the patristic writers believed strongly in the necessity of gendered divisions, separating those with public roles from those with private ones. At the same time, some of the traditions of earliest Christianity—'in Christ there is no more male or female' (Gal. 3:28)—challenged that conventional perspective with what has been called the genderless ideal. The emphasis on sexual renunciation in patristic Christianity itself offered the possibility of redefining or even eliminating gender roles, since without sex, marriage, or family life, little remained to mark the distinction between the social roles of men and women (Brown 1988: esp. ch. 7).

The Renunciation of Gender

Some Christians in the third, fourth, and fifth centuries CE remained intrigued by the genderless ideal. The dozens of accounts of women who disguised themselves as men, like Thecla, to become a wandering preacher, or like Eugenia, to become the abbot of a male monastery, reveal that interest clearly, even if the women may not actually have existed (Castelli 1991; also Salisbury 1992: esp. ch. 7). Many ascetic women were praised for the 'manliness' of their self-control, though some were criticized for acting 'too much' like men, unveiling themselves in public or wearing the *pallium* associated with philosophers and monks (see Kuefler 2014a; on ascetic women, also Clark 1986; on the symbolic importance of clothing in late ancient Christianity, also Coon 1997: ch. 3).

Scholars have sometimes wondered whether the elimination of gender meant more of an erasure of the feminine (see, e.g., Burrus 2000; but also Dunning 2011). There is some truth to this assertion, yet the abandonment of masculine identities also held some appeal. The Christian men who castrated themselves or who thought of themselves as brides of Christ, as noted above, provide some evidence for this perspective, as do the monks Augustine criticized for wearing their hair long and saying they were no longer men (*De opere monachorum* 32). A few stories also circulated about men who dressed as women: the soldiers Sergius and Bacchus, for example, who after their conversion to Christianity were forced to dress as women so as to humiliate them before being martyred, or the unnamed soldier who exchanged his clothing with a Christian virgin condemned to a brothel so that she could escape (the latter tale was told several times, including by Ambrose, *De virginibus* 2.4, and by Palladius, *Historia lausiaca* 148–149; also Kuefler 2001: 238–244; Harper 2013: 206–218; on Sergius and Bacchus, see Woods 1997).

The Affirmation of Gender Difference

Nonetheless, the patristic period witnessed a general movement away from the genderless ideal and toward a greater conformity to gender norms. That much can be seen in the exclusion of women from leadership roles in the churches. The extent to which women exercised sacerdotal functions in the early churches is debated, but they were certainly deaconesses, though they were increasingly excluded from this role, too

(Torjesen 1993; Macy 2007). Women remained as important patrons of religious work—the wealthy Roman noblewoman Paula financed Jerome's translation of the Bible into Latin, and Pulcheria, the sister of the emperor Theodosius II, helped to steer the course of the Council of Ephesus in 431—but public roles were denied to most of them (on women's lives in late antiquity, see Clark 1986; Salisbury 1992; Clark 1993; Cloke 1995; Cooper 1996). Indeed, too great a role for women in any church was regarded in itself as a sign of heresy by some of the Church Fathers.

Instead, women were encouraged to remain secluded, whether in monasteries or at home, and the biblical metaphor of the 'locked garden' from the Song of Songs (4:12), often directed at Christian women, reinforced this message politely but insistently. Even while being discouraged from entering marriage and family life, then, Christian women could be encouraged to take up domestic roles. Men's self-perceptions were also reinforced in traditional ways, by defining sexual renunciation and asceticism as heroic and using gladiatorial and military metaphors for Christian men, such as 'soldiers of Christ,' a term used only for men in the patristic era (see Kuefler 2001: ch. 4, for military metaphors, and 2001: 170–178 for sporting metaphors; see also Burrus 2000). The importance of gender difference was affirmed in multiple ways. The Church Fathers repeatedly condemned the gender fluidity of Roman stage performances, within which men sometimes played women's roles, as well as their sexual immodesty, which might include nudity and live sex acts (see, e.g., Tertullian, *De spectaculis* 17 and 23). At the end of the fourth century a debate about whether the glorified resurrected body would be genderless was resolved firmly in favour of the opinion that gender difference would remain in the afterlife (Clark 1992).

The importance of the patristic period to the Christian tradition on gender and sexuality cannot be overstated. If the Bible provided the foundations for theological reflection, and the earliest Christian centuries the occasion for experimentation with the possibilities permitted from those foundations, it was the patristic period that crafted a systematic—and hegemonic—theology. Once established, there was little variation in that rough consensus for a thousand years, and some elements of it have only recently been questioned.

ACKNOWLEDGEMENTS

I am very grateful to Adrian Thatcher for inviting me to participate in this handbook; I dedicate this essay to Elizabeth A. Clark, who has long been an inspiration and mentor to me on matters related to Christianity, late antiquity, gender, and sexuality.

REFERENCES

This bibliography contains only recent scholarly works in English. Each will direct the reader to the far larger bibliography of works published on these subjects. Those interested in reading the writings of the Church Fathers themselves can find modern editions of many of the texts mentioned in this chapter in the series published by Brepols, en titled *Corpus christianorum, series latina* and *series graeca*. The rest may be found in the older *Patrologiae cursus completus, series latina* or *series graeca*. English translations of many may be found in the series *Classics of Western Spirituality*, published by the Paulist Press, or in the *Fathers of the Church: A New Translation*, published by the Catholic University of America, or the older and sometimes inaccurate *Ante-Nicene Fathers*, 10 vols, and *Nicene and Post-Nicene Fathers*, series 1, 14 vols, and series 2, 14 vols, published by T. and T. Clark, Edinburgh.

Alwis, A. (2011). *Celibate Marriages in Late Antique and Byzantine Hagiography: The Lives of Saints Julian and Basilissa, Andronikos and Athanasia, and Galaktion and Episteme*. London: Continuum.

Brakke, D. (1995). 'The Problematization of Nocturnal Emissions in Early Christian Syria, Egypt, and Gaul'. *Journal of Early Christian Studies* 3: 419–460.

Brooten, B. (1996). *Love between Women: Early Christian Responses to Female Homoeroticism*. Chicago: University of Chicago Press.

Brown, P. (1988). *The Body and Society: Men, Women, and Sexual Renunciation in Early Christianity*. New York: Columbia University Press.

Burrus, V. (2000). *'Begotten, not Made': Conceiving Manhood in Late Antiquity*. Stanford, CA: Stanford University Press.

Burrus, V. (2004). *The Sex Lives of Saints: An Erotics of Ancient Hagiography*. Philadelphia: University of Pennsylvania Press.

Burrus, V., M. Jordan, and K. MacKendrick (2010). *Seducing Augustine: Bodies, Desires, Confessions*. New York: Fordham University Press.

Bynum, C. (1995). *The Resurrection of the Body in Western Christianity, 200–1336*. New York: Columbia University Press.

Castelli, E. (1991). '"I will Make Mary Male": Pieties of the Body and Gender Transformation of Christian Women in Late Antiquity'. In J. Epstein and K. Straub (eds), *Body Guards: The Cultural Politics of Gender Ambiguity*. New York: Routledge, 29–49.

Clark, E. (1986). *Ascetic Piety and Women's Faith: Essays on Late Ancient Christianity*. Lewiston, NY: Edwin Mellen.

Clark, E. (1992). *The Origenist Controversy: The Cultural Construction of an Early Christian Debate*. Princeton, NJ: Princeton University Press.

Clark, G. (1993). *Women in Late Antiquity: Pagan and Christian Life-Styles*. Oxford: Oxford University Press.

Cloke, G. (1995). *This Female Man of God: Women and Spiritual Power in the Patristic Age, 350–450*. London: Routledge.

Coon, L. (1997). *Sacred Fictions: Holy Women and Hagiography in Late Antiquity*. Philadelphia: University of Pennsylvania Press.

Cooper, K. (1996). *The Virgin and the Bride: Idealized Womanhood in Late Antiquity*. Cambridge, MA: Harvard University Press.

Cooper, K. (2007). *The Fall of the Roman Household*. Cambridge: Cambridge University Press.

Dunning, B. (2011). *Specters of Paul: Sexual Difference in Early Christian Thought*. Philadelphia: Pennsylvania University Press.

Elliott, D. (1993). *Spiritual Marriage: Sexual Abstinence in Medieval Wedlock*. Princeton, NJ: Princeton University Press.

Elm, S. (1994). *Virgins of God: the Making of Asceticism in Late Antiquity*. Oxford: Oxford University Press.

Harper, K. (2013). *From Shame to Sin: the Christian Transformation of Sexual Morality in Late Antiquity*. Cambridge, MA: Harvard University Press.

Hunter, D. (1992). 'The Language of Desire: Clement of Alexandria's Transformation of Ascetic Discourse'. *Semeia*, 57: 95–111.

Hunter, D. (2007). *Marriage, Celibacy, and Heresy in Ancient Christianity: The Jovinianist Controversy*. Oxford: Oxford University Press.

Krueger, D. (2011). 'Between Monks: Tales of Monastic Companionship in Early Byzantium'. *Journal of the History of Sexuality*, 20: 28–61.

Kuefler, M. (2001). *The Manly Eunuch: Masculinity, Gender Ambiguity, and Christian Ideology in Late Antiquity*. Chicago: University of Chicago Press.

Kuefler, M. (2007). 'The Marriage Revolution in Late Antiquity: the Theodosian Code and later Roman Marriage Law'. *Journal of Family History*, 32: 343–370.

Kuefler, M. (2014a). 'Clothes (Un)make the (Wo)man: Dress and Gender Crossings in Late Antiquity'. In *Atti del VI Congresso della Società Italiana Delle Storiche*. Forthcoming.

Kuefler, M. (2014b). 'The Merry Widows of Late Antiquity: the Evidence of the Theodosian Code'. In T. Pierre (ed.), *On the Shoulders of Giants: Essays in Honor of Glenn Olsen*. Toronto: Pontifical Institute for Medieval Studies, forthcoming.

Laqueur, T. (1990). *Making Sex: Body and Gender from the Greeks to Freud*. Cambridge, MA: Harvard University Press.

McGinn, T. (1997). 'The Legal Definition of Prostitute in Late Antiquity'. *Memoirs of the American Academy in Rome*, 42: 73–116.

Macy, G. (2007). *The Hidden History of Women's Ordination: Female Clergy in the Medieval West*. New York: Oxford University Press.

Masterson, M. (2006). 'Impossible Translation: Antony and Paul the Simple in the Historia Monachorum'. In M. Kuefler (ed.), *The Boswell Thesis: Essays on Christianity, Social Tolerance and Homosexuality*. Chicago: University of Chicago Press, 215–235.

Nathan, G. (2000). *The Family in Late Antiquity: The Rise of Christianity and the Endurance of Tradition*. New York: Routledge.

Otten, W. (1997). 'Christ's Birth of a Virgin who became a Wife: Flesh and Speech in Tertullian's *De carne Christi*'. *Vigiliae Christianae*, 51: 247–260.

Pagels, E. (1988). *Adam, Eve, and the Serpent*. New York: Vintage.

Power, K. (1995). *Veiled Desire: Augustine on Women*. New York: Continuum.

Reynolds, P. (1994). *Marriage in the Western Church: The Christianization of Marriage during the Patristic and Early Medieval Periods*. Leiden: Brill.

Riddle, J. (1992). *Contraception and Abortion from the Ancient World to the Renaissance*. Cambridge, MA: Harvard University Press.

Ringrose, K. (2003). *The Perfect Servant: Eunuchs and the Social Construction of Gender in Byzantium*. Chicago: University of Chicago Press.

Roller, L. (1999). *In Search of God the Mother: The Cult of Anatolian Cybele*. Berkeley: University of California Press.

Rousselle, A. (1988). *Porneia: On Desire and the Body in Antiquity*. Trans. F. Pheasant. Oxford: Blackwell.

Salisbury, J. (1992). *Church Fathers, Independent Virgins*. New York: Verso.

Shaw, B. (1987). 'The Age of Roman Girls at Marriage: Some Reconsiderations'. *Journal of Roman Studies*, 77: 30–46.

Shaw, T. (1998). *The Burden of the Flesh: Fasting and Sexuality in Early Christianity*. Minneapolis: University of Minnesota Press.

Torjesen, K. (1993). *When Women were Priests: Women's Leadership in the Early Church and the Scandal of their Subordination in the Rise of Christianity*. San Francisco: Harper.

Tougher, S. (2008). *The Eunuch in Byzantine Society and History*. London: Routledge.

Woods, D. (1997). 'The Emperor Julian and the Passion of Sergius and Bacchus'. *Journal of Early Christian Studies*, 5: 335–367.

CHAPTER 16

DUNS SCOTUS ON THE FEMALE GENDER

MARILYN MCCORD ADAMS

CERTAINLY, it would be not only anachronistic but positively misleading to represent John Duns Scotus (1265–1308) as a radical feminist. What he well and truly was, was 'the Marian Doctor', a champion of 'Marian privilege', of the conviction that the Blessed Virgin Mary is pre-eminent among merely human saints. Scotus makes it a methodological rule 'to praise her too much rather than too little'. Scotus' devotion to Mary colours his views about the female gender in what were (for the late thirteenth and early fourteenth century) striking ways.

MARY AND OTHER MOTHERS

The council of Ephesus (431) declared Mary to be the 'mother of God'. Scotus took this claim to mean two things: first, that Mary was a real mother; and second, that the individual whose mother she was, is the Divine Word who assumed the human nature formed in her womb.[1]

---

[1] The works of Duns Scotus have been published in two editions, a seventeenth-century edition due to Lucas Wadding, and the not yet complete modern critical edition known as the Vatican edition. The references are to Scotus' commentaries on Peter Lombard's *Sentences*. The Wadding edition (hereafter Wad) includes the Oxford commentary or *Opus Oxoniense* (hereafter *Op.Ox.*) and the Paris commentary or *Reportata Parisiensia* (hereafter *Rep.Par.*). So far the Vatican edition (hereafter Vat) includes the earlier *Lectura* (hereafter *Lect.*) and refers to its edition of the later Oxford commentary as the *Ordinatio* (herafter *Ord.*). The present reference is to *Ordinatio*, Book III, distinction 4, the single question, paragraph numbers 12–13 in Vatican volume X, pages 199–200. References hereafter will be abbreviated in the following format: *Ord.* III, d.4, q.u, nn.12–13; Vat X.199–200.

Challenging Aristotelian Biology

Probing what it takes to be a real mother forces Scotus' attention onto theories of reproductive biology. Everyone agreed on the basics: normally and naturally, mother and father are partners in the production of the organic body of their offspring. The father plants a seed, while the mother furnishes most of the matter out of which the foetal body is formed. Then-contemporary Aristotelian science charted a process: first the matter is relocated to a suitable place in the mother's womb; then the matter is condensed and altered so that it will be differentially disposed to receive the form(s) of organic body.[2] The last instant of this process is eventful. A substantial change occurs in which the matter receives not only the form(s) of organic body but the animating principle or soul as well. At the same instant of time, God the Son becomes Incarnate: the human nature in Mary's womb is assumed by the Divine Word.[3] For Scotus, it is important that all of these things occur simultaneously, because—strictly speaking—if an agent X ceases to act before Y comes to be, X is not the generative cause of Y. If the organic body to which the parents have contributed were finished for some time before animation occurred, it wouldn't be true that the parents were mother and father of the animal. They would be producers only of its body. Likewise, if animation occurred before Incarnation, then the completed human nature would exist for a time without belonging to Christ, and Mary would not be mother of God![4]

What was controversial and consequential for ancient and medieval views of the female gender, was the question whether the mother is an active, or only a passive cause in reproduction. Albert the Great, Thomas Aquinas, and Giles of Rome, among others, followed Aristotle in insisting that the father alone is active. The mother furnishes most of the matter, but the active formative power is in the father's seed.[5] Scotus is emphatic in rejecting this position. So far as appeals to authority are concerned, Galen thinks that the mother is an active cause, and Galen trumps Aristotle for medical expertise![6] Reproductive powers are essential to animal species. But male and female are of the same species. Even where animals engage in bisexual reproduction, the differentiation of male and female powers cannot be so great that the former are active while the latter are merely passive.[7] Moreover, there is the empirical fact that, not infrequently, offspring resemble the mother more than the father. Scotus dismisses Aristotle's explanation that some obstacle in the matter keeps 'father-likeness' from 'taking'. On the contrary, a positive likeness requires an active cause to explain it.[8] Scotus mocks: Aristotle's

---

[2] *Ord.* III, d.2, q.3, nn.102 & 117; Vat IX.162 & 168.
[3] *Ord.* III, d.2, q.3, nn.115–116; Vat IX.167–168; *Ord.* III, d.4, q.7, n.38; Vat IX.210–211.
[4] *Ord.* III, d.2, q.3, nn.107, 111–112; Vat IX.163, 165–166.
[5] *Ord.* III, d.4, q.7, nn.16–17; Vat IX.201–202.
[6] *Ord.* III, d.4, q.7, n.69; Vat IX.224.
[7] *Ord.* III, d.4, q.u, n.19; Vat IX.202–203.
[8] *Ord.* III, d.4, q.u, nn.21-23; Vat IX.203–204.

picture reduces mothers to containers of stuff out of which life is formed. Should we call rubbish bins or compost heaps 'mothers' because maggots are (according to medieval biology) spontaneously generated there under the influence of an external active cause (namely, the sun)? Do not think that this suggestion be blocked because rubbish bins and compost heaps are not of the same species as maggots. Think of the mothers of mules.[9]

Normally and naturally, Scotus insists, mother and father are both active causes that are essentially ordered to one another in reproduction. To be sure, Scotus still identifies the father as the principal and the mother as the secondary active cause.[10] His reason is that normally and naturally, when an Aristotelian agent is sufficiently proximate to a well-disposed patient, action takes place: put the fire under the kettle for a while, and the water heats up to a boil. Normally and naturally, if the principal cause is close to the patient, then—even if the secondary cause is lacking—the principal cause will try to produce the effect all by itself. But the stuff out of which babies are made is always inside the mother. If she were the principal cause, she would be perpetually pregnant—which is contrary to experience. Scotus concludes that, normally and naturally, the mother is a secondary cause whose active powers of foetal-formation are triggered by the introduction of the father's seed.[11]

Scotus' seeming depreciation of the mother's active power is balanced by his further reflection on the father's causal contribution. Back to reproductive biology. Mammals reproduce their own kind 'mediately', by producing seeds that are things of a different kind (substances of a different species) and endowing them with active powers to transform matter.[12] The father expels his seed into the mother's womb, and the active power of the seed cooperates with the mother's active power to move the material stuff to the womb, to condense and to alter it into something ready for the substantial change into the organic body. Some accounts imply that the matter of the father's seed gets mixed in with the matter that is instantaneously converted and animated. Even if the father's seed were not so incorporated and still existed at the moment of substantial change, its active powers to move and dispose matter are too low-grade to be partial causes of substantial forms. The father's own action is over when the seed is expelled. In the interval between copulation and foetal animation, the father could drop dead and be causally active no more. By contrast, the mother is present to exercise her active powers at the moment of that substantial change of the stuff into an animated organic body. Genuine causes are simultaneous with the production of their effects. Scotus concludes that, normally and naturally, the father is a per se cause in reproduction, since without his contribution the process of foetal formation would not get started. But, normally and naturally, the father is not an essentially ordered cause in the production of the animal, because his action

[9] *Ord.* III, d.4, q.7, n.24; Vat IX.204–205.
[10] *Ord.* III, d.4, q.u, n.43; Vat IX.213.
[11] *Ord.* III, d.4, q.u, n.50; Vat IX.217.
[12] *Lect.* II, d.18, q.2, nn.18–23; Vat XIX.158–159.

is over by the time that happens.[13] It is the mother who is an essentially ordered active cause in producing the offspring.[14]

Motherhood, Natural and Miraculous

Mary was a fertile female, when the angel Gabriel appeared. Scotus concludes that she must have had the same active reproductive powers as other mothers.[15] But to be a real mother, it is not enough to *have* such powers. She would have actually to *exercise* them. Theological consensus had it that the Holy Spirit acted to produce baby Jesus in her womb at the very instant at which she finished pronouncing the sentence: 'Be it unto me, according to your word!' The relocation and configuration of the matter to receive the substantial forms was instantaneous. Surely the powers Mary shared with other mothers were powers to produce changes over an interval of time—powers whose exercise would have been prevented by the precipitous and instantaneous action of the Holy Spirit to do the whole thing all by Itself.[16]

Nor—Scotus thinks—would it do any good to suppose that a supernatural power was conferred on Mary, so that she would be able to cooperate with the Holy Spirit's instantaneous action. Normally and naturally, real mothers act to form the bodies of their offspring by active powers consequent upon their own natures. Such supernatural power would not belong to Mary normally and naturally; action through it would not make her a mother by nature but only accidentally.[17] Anyway, if what allegedly keeps powers from producing shaped-up foetal matter instantaneously is the fact that they are created, the supernaturally infused power would suffer from the same limitation.[18] Even if the power were supernatural because God alone could cause it, it would still be a quality *created* by God. Moreover, the cause must be at least as excellent as its effect, but accidents are less noble than substance. Even if supernatural because God alone could cause it, the proposed power would be *an accident*, all the same.[19]

Scotus' own view is that whether or not Mary got to exercise her powers to relocate and condense the matter, she was still able to act instantaneously (as usual) for the production of the substantial form(s) of the organic body. Normally and naturally, that action is instantaneous, even when location and shaping of the matter in the womb takes time.[20] Normally and naturally, mothers perform many actions in foetal formation. But what happens before a given action is not essential to *that* action. The power and disposition of the agent and patient at the time of the action are what count, however they got

[13] *Lect.* II, d.18, q.2, nn.31–36; Vat XIX.162–163.
[14] *Ord.* III, d.4, q.u, nn.52–55; Vat IX.218–219.
[15] *Ord.* III, d.4, q.u, n.43; Vat IX.213.
[16] *Ord.* III, d.4, q.u, nn.26–28; Vat IX.205–207.
[17] *Ord.* III, d.4, q.u, n.31; Vat IX.208–209.
[18] *Ord.* III, d.4, q.u, n.33; Vat IX.209.
[19] *Ord.* III, d.4, q.u, nn.34–35; Vat IX.209.
[20] *Ord.* III, d.4, q.7,nn.41–44; Vat IX.213–214.

that way. So the fact that Mary does not act to move or condense the matter, does not keep her from being in a position to perform her other action: of cooperating in the substantial change that turns the stuff into an organic body.[21] Exercising this natural power was enough to make her a real and natural mother. Because she did not cooperate with a merely human father in the production of Christ's human nature, and because the Holy Spirit collapsed the 'preparation' of the matter into the instant of substantial change, her motherhood was also miraculous.[22] Of course, Mary had no active power to bring it about that the human nature she actively cooperated in producing was assumed by God the Son. Just as that human nature was in obediential potency to being assumed, so she was in obediential potency to being the mother of God.[23]

IMMACULATE CONCEPTIONS?

The motherhood of Mary makes the saving work of Christ possible, but it also seemed to put obstacles in its way. In medieval theology, Christ is supposed to save the human race from the consequences of Adam's fall. Recall how Adam allegedly began with a highly functional agency that was easily able to obey all of God's commands. But Adam disobeyed, and the consequences of his sin—death, physical vulnerability, psycho-physical disarray—redound to all of his descendants (allegedly, the whole human race). On the one hand, such inheritance was explained in *juridical or quasi-legal* terms of inherited guilt and liability to punishment. Defenders of inherited guilt distinguished between the guilt or sin one has by virtue of one's origin (original guilt or original sin) from that the individual incurs because of his/her own acts (actual guilt/sin). On the other hand, Augustine advanced the theory of seminal transmission, as a *causal* explanation of how such penalties get passed on from generation to generation. After the fall, sexual intercourse is always accompanied by lust or concupiscence. Uncleanness is 'catching': lustful intercourse engenders contaminated flesh, and contaminated flesh infects the offspring's soul. Christ can accomplish his saving work, only if God takes a sinless human nature from Adam's race. But how can this happen when the Blessed Virgin Mary was a post-fall product of bisexual reproduction?

Anselmian Anticipations

Anselm offered two answers to this question. In *Cur Deus Homo* II, he argues from Christ's excellence as Saviour: Christ's obedience unto death was so pleasing to God that it was efficacious, not only for then-present and future members of Adam's race.

---

[21] *Ord.* III, d.4, q.u, nn.45–48, 53; Vat IX.214–216, 218.
[22] *Ord.* III, d.4, q.u, nn.60–61; Vat IX.219–220.
[23] *Ord.* III, d.4, q.u, n.51; Vat IX.217.

It reached backward to cleanse the elect among Christ's forebears already during their *ante-mortem* careers. Anselm does not elaborate as to exactly when or from precisely what they are cleansed, but presumably the Blessed Virgin Mary was freed from whatever Christ needed not to 'catch' in his biological derivation.[24]

In his later work *De conceptu virginali et originali peccato*, Anselm delved deeper. Stressing that merely material stuff cannot be, but rather the soul alone is, the subject of sin, he rejects Augustine's seminal transmission theory. Biologists held with 'mediate animation'—the view that what is seminally produced in the mother is not immediately animated (infused with a soul) but only after the material is shaped into an organic body (40–46 days after conception for males, 80 days for females). It follows that original sin cannot begin with conception, but only at animation. Because, normally and naturally, the parents produce only the flesh and not the soul, original sin cannot be seminally transmitted in the process of conception itself.[25] Rather, inheritance of original sin must be understood juridically or quasi-legally.

Anselm distinguishes between those of Adam's race whose propagation lies, broadly speaking, within natural human powers and the parents' will to exercise them, from those whose propagation lies outside the scope of such powers. All human beings reproduced by bisexual reproduction fall in the first category, while Eve formed from Adam's rib is an example of the second. (Anselm counts births from over-aged parents in the first category, because any miracles involved with Abraham and Sarah, Zechariah and Elizabeth were directed towards restoring their natural reproductive powers.) Anselm's theological hypothesis is that God decreed that if Adam's descendants refrained from sin, natural offspring would be reproduced in the condition in which Adam was created; but if Adam or his descendants sinned, their offspring would be born in the condition into which Adam fell. These do not apply to miraculously produced offspring and so Christ can be animated without original sin.[26] Such Divine decrees neither require nor leave any loopholes for the immaculate animation or later cleansing of Mary. Anselm covers her case with a separate argument from propriety: 'it was fitting that the Virgin be beautified with a purity than which a greater cannot be conceived except for God's'.[27]

Liturgical Controversies

Philosophical theologians were not alone in magnifying Mary. Popular Marian devotion found its focus in certain feasts. The liturgical rule of thumb was that saints should be celebrated only for those occasions when they were already sanctified. Anselm's theology readily underwrites the feast of the Annunciation: surely she was cleansed when

---

[24] Anselm, *Cur Deus Homo* II, c.16; Schmitt II.116, 16–24.

[25] Anselm, *De conceptu virginali et de originali peccato*, cc.1–4; Schmitt II.140–145; c.7; Schmitt II.147–149.

[26] Anselm, *De conceptu virginali et de originali peccato*, cc.10–13; Schmitt II.151–155.

[27] Anselm, *De conceptu virginali et originali peccato*, cc.18–19; Schmitt II.159–160.

Christ's immaculate conception/animation occurred. Patristic authority insisted that God maintained her in a state of freedom from any and all sin forever after. Hence, the feast of the Assumption was easily accepted. But Bernard of Clairvaux—himself an ardent promoter of Marian privilege—was scandalized by the custom (spreading from England and Gaul) of celebrating her Conception. Surely, her bisexual reproduction by Joachim and Anna meant that Mary's was *not* an immaculate conception. To suppose otherwise would undermine Mary's own pre-eminence. If Mary were immaculately conceived, Mary would not be the only mother to conceive a child without original sin. More importantly, immaculate conception for Mary would detract from Christ's excellence as universal Saviour. If Mary were born without original sin, she would not need to be saved by Christ.[28]

Convinced by arguments like Bernard's, many looked for a *via media* that would locate Mary lower than Christ but higher than everyone else on the great chain of sanctification. Suppose Mary contracts original sin at animation, but is cleansed before birth. Perhaps purification occurs in two stages: at animation, cleansing from original sin and suppression of concupiscence; at the annunciation, extinction of concupiscence. Alternatively, perhaps her time as an *in utero* sinner could be shrunk to an instant.[29]

Franciscan Refocusing

Although Bonaventure follows theological consensus against both immaculate conception and immaculate animation for Mary, he pauses to rehearse a case for the opposite conclusion that includes an observation of considerable importance. Bernard's argument—that immaculate conception/animation for Mary would mean that she did not need a Saviour—fails to distinguish between *always* having a trait and having a trait *independently*. The immaculate conception/animation of the Blessed Virgin Mary would depend on Christ just as much as the graces given to other sinners do. While others were freed from original sin by Christ *after* they fell, Mary was sustained by Christ *lest* she fall.[30] Immaculate animation for Mary is not incompatible with Christ's excellence as universal Saviour after all.

Scotus joins William of Ware and Peter Aureol in taking this argument a step further: not only is Christ's excellence as a Saviour *compatible* with immaculate animation for some naturally begotten member of Adam's race; Christ's standing as the maximally perfect mediator *positively requires* it. Scotus defends his major premiss—that the maximally perfect mediator has a maximally perfect act of mediating for some person whose mediator he is—from three angles. First, to be *maximally well-pleasing to God*,

---

[28] Bernard of Clairvaux, *Epistola 174: Ad canonicos Lugdunenses de Conceptione S. Mariae*, PL 182, cols.332–336.

[29] For a more extensive discussion of such authors, see Lottin (1941: 26–64); Wolter (1954: 26–69); and Adams (2010: 133–159).

[30] Bonaventure, *Sent.* III, d.3, p.1, a.1, q.1; Quaracchi III.63–68.

the mediator's deed would have not simply to remove offence, but to prevent God from being offended in the first place. Second, to be *maximally efficacious in shielding the beneficiary from evil*, the mediator's deed would have to take away the greater evil as well as the lesser—original sin which is worse than actual sin. Third, to be *maximally obliged to the mediator*, the beneficiary would need to receive from him the maximal good that can be had from him—innocence or preservation from guilt and not just guilt-removal. Once maximally perfect mediation is in the offing, Marian pre-eminence takes over to identify her as the winner of the prize.[31]

Like many maximizing principles, Scotus' premiss threatens to prove too much. Mary could have received more: tradition has it that she tasted many of the consequences of Adam's fall—hunger and thirst, fatigue and pain, and eventually death. Scotus replies that Mary's humanity was subjected only to those defects that were useful for earning merit.[32] Universalism also invites: wouldn't the maximally perfect mediator confer maximum benefits on all souls? Scotus himself envisions spreading advantages, when he asks rhetorically why many souls should be indebted to Christ for grace and glory and none for innocence? Why should there be many innocent angels in heaven and no innocent souls but the soul of Christ?[33] But he does not engage the question of universal salvation in this connection. Relative to some of his successors, Scotus' conclusion is quite cautious: whether or not Mary was subject to immaculate animation, God only knows. 'But if it is not incompatible with the authority of the Church or the authority of Scripture, it seems defensible that what is more excellent should be attributed to Mary.'[34]

Real Marriage and Other Vows

For medieval Christian thinkers, sexual intercourse was an activity that needed to be contained, and heterosexual marriage was the institution provided to house it. The ascetical tradition (inherited from the church fathers and nurtured by monasticism) fostered the following argument voiced by Richard of St Victor: reason is what distinguishes humans from beasts; therefore whatever interferes with the use of reason is *prima facie* evil; therefore, because sexual intercourse interferes with the use of reason, it cannot be right either to engage in it or to contract to engage in it without there being some compensating good. Put otherwise, people who engage in such behaviour need to have a good excuse.[35] Aristotelians objected: surely this position is too extreme. Many conditions—sleep, for instance—interfere with the use of reason, but are not for that reason *prima facie* evil. Richard distinguishes those conditions (such as sleep) that actually strengthen soul and body for vigorous intellectual functioning, from those (such as

---

[31] *Ord.* III, d.3, q.1, nn.17–25; Vat IX.175–178.
[32] *Ord.* III, d.3, q.1, n.27; Vat IX.179.
[33] *Op.Ox.* III, d.3, q.1, n.7; Wad VII.1.93.
[34] *Op.Ox.* III, d.3, q.1, n.9; Wad VII.1.95.
[35] *Op.Ox.* IV, d.31, q.u, nn.2–3; Wad IX.668–669.

sexual intercourse) that drain energy and make it more difficult to intellectualize after-wards.[36] Scotus retains the traditional language of excuse, while insisting that good reasons are to be found in the ends and fruits of marriage.

Repeatedly, Scotus maintains that marriage is a mutual and indissoluble obligation that arises when a man and a woman give themselves to each other so far as power over their bodies is concerned. Like all tribes and nations, the medieval church assumes the primary purpose of reproduction to be securing group survival by swelling the population. Because in the beginning devotees of God were few, the primary purpose of marriage was to procreate offspring and rear them up to worship God and so to fill out the company of the faithful.[37] After the fall, marriage serves a second and secondary purpose as a way of dealing with carnal lust. Before the fall, procreation—obeying God's command to be fruitful and multiply—was paramount. After the fall, when the human psyche became disordered and the rule of right reason proved insecure, spousal power over each other's bodies loomed large in preserving conjugal chastity.[38] The primary purpose of marriage 'excuses' by putting sexual intercourse in service of a great enough good, while the secondary end 'excuses' because sex acts within marriage can avoid a worse evil.

Expanding on the common opinion that marriage partners contract to exchange power over each other's bodies, Scotus introduces the Franciscan distinction between dominion and use. What partners transfer in the marriage contract is dominion over their bodies. The husband's dominion over his wife's body, and the wife's dominion over her husband's body, gives rise to what Scotus calls 'conditional' obligations: affirmatively, to concede to the spouse use should the spouse ask, and negatively, not to concede use to someone other than the spouse should they ask.[39] Just as dominion and use can break apart in the case of real estate—for example, the Holy See holds dominion over buildings that are used exclusively by Franciscans—so Scotus envisions cases of genuinely contracted marriage in which there is mutual dominion without use.[40]

Ideally, marriage is one-to-one and indissoluble: once vows are taken, the bond between husband and wife is meant to be lifelong.[41] Nevertheless, Scotus acknowledges, marriage regulations are not natural law in the strict sense. That is, the claims that marriage is one-to-one and indissoluble are neither self-evident principles (propositions that are true by definition) nor obvious entailments therefrom. For the exchange between the two spouses to have 'complete justice' and obligatory force requires the act of a higher lord consenting to, or at least not dissenting from the contract. God is the lord of all bodies, and God is the primary legislator who lays down the statutes as to

[36] *Op.Ox.* IV, d.31, q.u, n.3; Wad IX.669.
[37] *Op.Ox.* IV, d.26, nn.8, 16; Wad IX.582, 597; IV, d.31, q.u, n.4; Wad IX.670–671; *Rep.Par.* IV, d.28, q.7, nn.11, 14, 19–20; Wad XI.2.788–790.
[38] *Op.Ox.* IV, d.32, q.u, n.2; Wad IX.688; *Rep.Par.* IV, d.33, q.1, nn.3,5; Wad XI.2.810–811.
[39] *Op.Ox.* IV, d.31, q.u, n.5; Wad IX.671.
[40] *Op.Ox.* IV, d.30, q.2, n.6; Wad IX.655.
[41] *Op.Ox.* IV, d.31, q.u, n.6; Wad IX.671.

how the bodies of spouses are to be justly exchanged relative to each end.[42] Scotus goes so far as to say that the statutes of the higher lord are the *principal* cause and the wills of the contracting partners the *instrumental* cause of their obligations to one another.[43] Thus, even if one-to-one life-long indissolubility is the ideal that God enjoins at creation and that Christ reinstitutes in the Gospels, God can revoke the marriage statutes and/or dispense individuals from them.[44] The bible and canon law expose a variety of cases in which God has done just that.

Polygamy

Marriage is ideally one-to-one and indissoluble, but polygamy is tolerated under Mosaic law. Scotus worries about how this comports with spousal justice in marriage. Strict commutative justice would require equality of value in things exchanged. But value is relative to the end, and there are two ends in the marriage, with respect to which the calculations come out different.

What is exchanged is dominion over bodies. Relative to the principal end of procreation, Scotus maintains, the male body is more valuable than the female body, because the male could impregnate many females at once, while—even considering twins and triplets—the female can have only one pregnancy at a time. Scotus infers that so far as the end of procreation is concerned, a man could exchange his single body for the bodies of many women, and that this would not be contrary to the natural law, even in the state of innocence (although there would have been no need for polygamy in the state of innocence because there were then equal numbers of women and men).[45]

Relative to the secondary purpose of marriage—to serve as a remedy against fornication and adultery—Scotus reckons that male and female bodies are of equal value: the woman's body is able to preserve the chastity of the man, and vice versa. According to strict justice, relative to this purpose, the marriage exchange should be one-to-one. For one spouse to have two or more partners would be contrary to natural law and to strict justice.[46]

Scotus speculates that in the patriarchal period there was good reason for God to dispense from the ideal of monogamy: viz., that the number of the faithful was small and the number of infidels was large. It was expedient for God to prioritize procreation, the principal end of marriage, over the secondary end of preserving conjugal chastity, and to allow the men to take many wives.

---

[42] *Op.Ox.* IV, d.26, q.u, nn.9–10; Wad IX.583, 599. See also *Op.Ox.* IV, d.33, q.1, nn.3,7; Wad IX.703, 706; *Op.Ox.* IV, d.33, q.3, n.5; Wad IX.719–720; and *Rep.Par.* IV, d.33, q.1, n.4; Wad XI.2.810.

[43] *Op.Ox.* IV, d.33, q.3, n.9; Wad IX.721–722.

[44] *Op.Ox.* IV, d.26, q.u, n.18; Wad IX.599; *Op.Ox.* IV, d.33, q.1, n.4; Wad IX.705; *Rep.Par.* IV, d.33, q.1, n.6; Wad XI.2.811.

[45] *Op.Ox.* IV, d.33, q.1, n.2; Wad IX.703; *Rep.Par.* IV, d.33, q.1, n.3; Wad XI.2.810.

[46] *Op.Ox.* IV, d.33, q.1, n.3; Wad IX.703; *Rep.Par.* IV, d.33, q.1, n.3; Wad XI.2.810.

Scotus explains that God can dispense with the one-to-one requirement 'without injury and injustice to the woman', because the woman can appreciate God's reason—the need to accelerate the growth of the company of the faithful—and renounce her right to have sole dominion over the body of 'her man'. She can choose to settle for partial dominion, according to right reason.[47] Scotus does not discuss whether Divine permission of polygamy would be unjust to women who do not consent. Rather Scotus seems to assume that the women would number themselves among the wise and follow right reason.[48]

Nevertheless, Scotus insists, right reason sees departures from monogamy as an emergency measure. The population had increased enough by the time of Christ that he revoked the dispensation, so that polygamy is no longer licit.[49] Scotus is equally confident that God would never dispense from monogamy in favour of polyandry, because there could never be a comparably good reason for it. True, many husbands would satisfy the wife's libido and be a good way to contain her sexual activity within the bonds of marriage. But it would rarely if ever increase the reproductive yield.[50]

Divorce

Ideally, marriage is ''til Death do us part' indissoluble. But Mosaic provision for divorce and Jesus' controversy with the Pharisees about it (Matt. 19) are matters of biblical record. Scotus re-emphasizes, indissolubility is not a matter of strict-sense natural law. Spouses could contract to give their bodies to each other for a certain time, or for one or two uses, if that were instituted by a higher lord for a greater good.[51] Just as God instituted the law of marriage as an indissoluble chain, so God can temper, revoke, or modify it. Just as he willed monogamy except where a greater good would follow, so God willed marriage as a life-long obligation except where a greater evil would ensue. Scotus follows his predecessors in identifying this greater evil as uxoricide: an inclination of men to kill their wives when they got tired of them and wanted to marry someone else. Not only would this be bad for the wife. It could lead to public strife if the wife's family sought revenge and killed the husband. Likewise, if the man received a death penalty under the law, the family would be destroyed and the upbringing of the orphaned children jeopardized.[52] According to Scotus, God's response was to revoke the prior law of indissolubility and to permit divorce as licit because of male cruelty.[53]

---

[47] *Rep.Par.* IV, d.33, q.1, nn.6–7; Wad XI.2.811.
[48] *Op.Ox.* IV, d.33, q.1, n.6; Wad IX.706; *Rep.Par.* IV, d.33, q.1, n.1; Wad XI.2.811.
[49] *Op.Ox.* IV, d.33, q.1, n.6; Wad IX.706; *Rep.Par.* IV, d.33, q.1, n.7; Wad XI.2.811.
[50] *Op.Ox.* IV, d.33, q.1, n.8; Wad IX.706; *Rep.Par.* IV, d.33, q.1, n.9; Wad XI.2.812.
[51] *Rep.Par.* IV, d.33, q.3, nn.5, 7; XI.2.815–816.
[52] *Op.Ox.* IV, d.33, q.2, n.5; Wad IX.719–720.
[53] *Rep.Par.* IV, d.33, q.3, nn.9–10; Wad XI.2.817.

Nevertheless, although spouses have equal dominion over each other's bodies, there was no corresponding dispensation for a wife to divorce her husband. Scotus' explanations—that no matter how much women might hate their men, they would never dare to kill them; that women are more restrained than men in taking revenge—may reflect mistaken judgements about strength and courage, cruelty and vindictiveness in 'the weaker sex'. On whichever basis, Scotus concludes that there is no worse evil to be avoided that would justify allowing women to divorce.[54]

Vows of Chastity

Because he is so clear that Christ restored the original institution of marriage as life-long monogamy,[55] Scotus finds it particularly problematic that medieval canon law allowed, and counsels of perfection encouraged married couples to take vows of chastity. Richard of St Victor and Bonaventure explained that this practice was consistent, because marriage is dissolved by death, and the one who enters religious life dies to the world. Scotus counters: it is physical, not spiritual death that ends a marriage.[56] Henry of Ghent maintained that the marriage contract is not dissolved, but it is spiritualized. If the husband enters the monastery, he is no longer obliged to grant use-rights because he has dedicated his body to a sacred use. But if the wife remains in the world, she may re-marry, whereupon she will be spiritually married to one and carnally married to the other.[57] Scotus objects that the negative obligation—to deny another bodily use if asked—is life-long. The wife could re-marry (thereby granting use-rights to another) only if the first marriage were dissolved.

For Scotus, the only condition besides physical death that could dissolve a new-law marriage, would be an act of the legislator who instituted marriage as indissoluble in the first place. If the Church allows married people to enter religious life while their spouse is still alive, Christ himself must have revoked or relaxed the requirement for the sake of the greater good of chastity.[58] If marriage vows confer bodily dominion on the partner, medieval canon law allowed that for the first two months spouses could refuse each other while each and both deliberated whether to enter religious life after all.[59] The clearest case is when the contract has been ratified but the marriage has not been consummated, and both parties vow chastity and enter the religious life. Here the marriage is dissolved. If the husband enters the monastery and vows chastity, and the wife publicly gives him leave before the proper authorities, and she either vows chastity or is old enough to be beyond suspicion, she thereby renounces her right of asking in perpetuity.

---

[54] *Op.Ox.* IV, d.33, q.3; Wad IX.721; *Rep.Par.* IV, d.33, q.3, n.8; Wad XI.2.816.

[55] *Op.Ox.* IV, d.33, q.3, nn.6, 8; Wad IX.720–721; *Rep.Par.* IV, d.33, q.3, nn.9–10; Wad XI.817.

[56] *Op.Ox.* IV, d.31, q.u, n.6; Wad IX.671; *Rep.Par.* IV, d.31, q.u, n.13; Wad XI.2.805.

[57] *Op.Ox.* IV, d.31, q.u, n.6; Wad IX.671; *Rep.Par.* IV, d.31, q.u, nn.15–16; Wad XI.2.805.

[58] *Op.Ox.* IV, d.31, q.u, nn.7–8; Wad IX.671–672.

[59] *Op.Ox.* IV, d.32, q.2, nn.2–3; Wad IX.688.

If, however, the woman remains in the world and is unable or unwilling to remain continent, or if she renounces her right but not before the relevant officials, the man should be recalled from the monastery. Because of his vow of chastity, he is obliged not to ask. Because of his marriage vow, he is obliged to pay the conjugal debt when his wife asks. He does not commit mortal sin, because he vowed chastity in good faith in the mistaken belief that he was free to do so. He renounced sexual intercourse so far as it was within his power. But he could not renounce someone else's right. As things turned out, his wife had not sufficiently renounced it either.[60]

Mary and Joseph

Where canon law is at pains to say when vows of chastity dissolve the marriage bond, the marriage of Mary and Joseph presents the problem in reverse. Theological consensus had it that before the angel Gabriel appeared, Mary had vowed perpetual virginity. Scotus insists that her vow of chastity was absolute,[61] binding her not to concede use no matter what. How, then, could she be free to marry, when marriage would transfer bodily dominion to her spouse?

Scotus replies that the dominion carries only a conditional obligation to concede use if asked. To be sure, a use-request from Joseph would put Mary in a bind: she would be both obliged not to concede use by her vow of chastity, and obliged to concede use by her marriage bond. Happily, Mary was assured by revelation that Joseph would never ask. Scotus suggests that just as the angel told Joseph not to be afraid to take Mary as his wife, so an angel told Mary not to be afraid to take Joseph as spouse. She was given to understand—whether by the Holy Spirit or by Joseph himself—that Joseph had taken a matching vow of chastity, that he would guard her virginity and preserve her from the stigma of being an unwed mother.[62] For good measure, Scotus adds the alternative reassurance that God would absolve Mary from fulfilling her marriage obligation, should Joseph ever ask.[63] Unlike the couple who enter the religious life, Mary and Joseph are really married, because each holds dominion over the other's body. But both have renounced their right to use, and never using, both remain chaste.

The Ordination of Women

Scotus' promotion of Marian privilege and his sensitivity to gender-justice factor into his conclusions about the ordination of women in a surprising way.

---

[60] *Op.Ox.* IV, d.32, q.2, nn.3–4; Wad IX.688–689.
[61] *Op.Ox.* IV, d.33, q.2, nn.4–6; Wad IX.654, 655; *Rep.Par.* IV, d.30, q.2, nn.1, 5; Wad XI.2.800–801.
[62] *Op.Ox.* IV, d.30, q.2; Wad IX.654.
[63] *Rep.Par.* IV, d.30, q.2, nn.6, 9; Wad XI.2.801–802.

Scotus defines holy orders as an eminent rank in the ecclesiastical hierarchy, a rank that confers a character or disposition empowering the recipient to execute an excellent act in the Church.[64] Scotus clarifies: the rank itself is not a spiritual power, but it disposes a person to have both the authority and an indelible spiritual power to execute such an act.[65] Thus, bishops receive an indelible power to ordain, to confirm, and to consecrate the oils for confirmation and extreme unction; priests, an indelible power for eucharistic consecration and for absolving penitents.[66] Such indelible power is not only power to do such acts rightly and well; it is the *sine qua non* of doing such acts at all. Canon law and church courts can cut persons off from performing such noble acts *de jure*, but, no matter what, bishops and priests *de facto* retain their indelible power. Thus, ecclesiastical penalties can make their acts illegal, but not invalid.[67]

Like all eminent ranks, holy orders are not for everyone! Obstacles to ordination may arise from propriety or from necessity. Scotus contrasts necessity arising from precepts that limit what is legal, and necessity arising from fact that bears on the validity of the orders allegedly conferred. Urgent on the late thirteenth-century agenda was the question whether under-aged boys and women could and/or should be ordained?

Propriety is an obstacle to ordaining extremely young boys who lack the capacity to receive the sacrament with suitable reverence. Moreover, it is against the canons, which stipulate that candidates must have reached the age of discretion to be competent to take the vow of chastity that ordination involves.[68] The latter laws make ordaining under-aged boys illegal, but apparently not invalid. Ordination is an unrepeatable sacrament. If hands are laid on boys below the canonically required age, ordination is not repeated when they grow old enough. It 'took' the first time; even if illegal, it was valid all the same.[69]

By contrast, Scotus voices the common conclusion that female gender 'absolutely obstructs' the reception of this order, with respect both to propriety and to necessity, both to the necessity of precept and to the necessity of fact. Scotus shows no sympathy with an ancient rationale that ordination is only for those who bear the image of God, and only males are made in God's image.[70] By contrast with Bonaventure and Aquinas, Scotus does not rest his case with 'signification' arguments: that priests and bishops signify Christ the Mediator and only males can naturally represent a male Christ;[71] or that priests and bishops essentially signify excellence of rank, which women cannot signify because they are in a state of subjection to males.[72] Scotus is in no position to insist that women are unfit for leadership because incurably weak-minded and emotionally

---

[64] *Rep.Par.* IV, d.24, q.u, n.12; Wad XI.2.778.
[65] *Rep.Par.* IV, d.24, q.u, nn.5–7; Wad XI.2.776.
[66] *Rep.Par.* IV, d.24, q.u, n.8; Wad XI.2.776–777.
[67] *Rep.Par.* IV, d.25, q.1, n.18; Wad XI.2.782.
[68] *Rep.Par.* IV, d.25, q.2, n.3; Wad XI.2.784.
[69] *Rep.Par.* IV, d.25, q.u, n.4; Wad XI.2.784.
[70] Cited without sympathy by Bonaventure, *Sent.* IV, d.25, a.2, q.1; Quaracchi IV.649.
[71] Bonaventure, *Sent.* IV, d.25, a.2, q.1; Quaracchi IV.650.
[72] Aquinas, *Summa theologica, Suppl.* q.39, a.1, c.

unstable. Marian privilege means that Mary is pre-eminent among all merely human saints, that she is full of grace to a degree that exceeds all of Christ's male apostles and prelates. Scotus recognizes Pauline prohibitions against women speaking in the church (I Tim. 2:11–15) or praying with uncovered—much less tonsured—heads (I Cor. 11:13), but insists that gender-justice keeps these from being the heart of the matter. Scotus insists that it would be *unjust* for the Apostles and the Church to take away from any one person—much less the whole gender—any rank that would be useful for her salvation and the spiritual good of those around her, unless Christ the head of the Church had commanded it in the first place. The fact that Christ did not confer priesthood on the Blessed Virgin Mary is evidence that Christ commanded that the priesthood be restricted to males.[73]

Scotus does consider a range of putative counter examples. Talk of *presbytera* refers to widows or to the wives of Greek priests; of 'deaconesses', to the custom of allowing an abbess to read a homily at matins. The office of abbess is not ordained. Women are allowed leadership in female communities, because of the dangers to chastity of men and women living in the same house.[74] More challenging is the case of Mary Magdalene, who was traditionally considered to be an Apostle, a preacher, and the leader of all women penitents. Scotus' startling reply is that Christ treated her as a singular exception and assigned her to these offices as a personal privilege, where personal privilege dies with the person, is not passed on to heirs, carries no empowerment to ordain successors, and sets no precedents.[75]

The prohibition against women's ordination is a function of divine positive law. It is free and contingent divine policy that subjects women to male domination after the fall.[76] It is Christ's command that—with the possible exception of Mary Magdalene—only males can be ordained. Because God is the ultimate legislator of sacraments, however, the upshot is that the ordination of women is not only illegal, but invalid. A bishop attempting to confer orders on a woman, 'not only does badly', because it is contrary to the precept of Christ; he 'does nothing'. She is not 'fit matter for the sacrament', not because of any natural properties—after all, male and female are naturally of the same species—but because Christ has freely and contingently instituted that ordination can be conferred only on human males.[77] The soaring declaration of Galatians 3:28—that in Christ there is neither Jew nor Greek, neither male nor female, neither slave nor free—is not concerned with ecclesiastical rank, but points to what is for Scotus the most important fact about the female gender: women as much as men are candidates for salvation and eternal life![78]

---

[73] *Rep.Par.* IV, d.25, q.2, nn.5–6; Wad XI.2.784.
[74] *Rep.Par.* IV, d.25, q.2, n.9; Wad XI.2.785.
[75] *Rep.Par.* IV, d.25, q.2, n.6; Wad XI.2.784.
[76] *Rep.Par.* IV, d.25, q.2, n.8; Wad XI.2.785.
[77] *Rep.Par.* IV, d.25, q.2, n.8; Wad XI.2.785.
[78] *Rep.Par.* IV, d.25, q.2, n.9; Wad XI.2.785.

CONCLUSION

For Scotus, the most important thing about the female gender, philosophically, is that the female is of the same species as the male. Not only are women and men alike active causes in reproduction, women as much as men are rational animals capable of governing their choices and behaviour by the dictates of right reason and so competent to forfeit and/or not press rights to which they have legitimately contracted, when this is clearly for the sake of a great enough good.

For Scotus, the most important thing about the female gender, theologically, is that women as much as men are candidates for grace and glory. In the Incarnation, God the Son assumes a male human nature, so that it is a male human nature that not only belongs to a divine person, but also is fitted out with as much grace and supernatural upgrades as it can hold and still be capable of suffering and dying on a cross. Yet, it is a female human being who is pre-eminent among the merely human saints and so receives more grace and supernatural upgrades in her *ante-mortem* career than any of the others do. Scotus does take over the traditional idea that women are subject to men as a consequence of the fall. But he does not understand this to mean that female capacities for moral agency are more diminished. Nor does such subjection figure in Scotus' analysis of the nature of marriage either with respect to its ideal nature or with respect to Divine dispensations for polygamy and divorce.

REFERENCES

Adams, Marilyn McCord (2010). 'The Immaculate Conception of the Blessed Virgin Mary: A Thought-Experiment in Medieval Philosophical Theology'. *Harvard Theological Review*, 103(2): 133–159.

Anselm (1946–61). *Opera Omnia*. Ed. F. S. Schmitt. Edinburgh: T. Nelson.

Aquinas, Thomas (1952–56). *Summa Theologiae*. Ed. Petrus Caramello. Turin and Rome: Marietti.

Bernard of Clairvaux (1854). *Ad canonicus Lugdenenses de Conceptione S. Mariae. Patrologia Latina, Cursus Completus*. Ed. J. P. Migne. Paris: apud Garnier, vol. 182.

Bonaventure (1882–1902). *Opera Omnia*. Ad Claras Aquas Quaracchi: Collegium S. Bonaventurae.

Lottin, D. O. (1941). 'Le traité du péché originel chez les primiers maitres fanciscaines de Paris'. *Ephemerides Theologicae Lovainienses*, XVIII: 26–64.

Scotus, John Duns (1950–2008). *Opera Omnia*. Ed. Carl Balic et al. Civitas Vaticana: Typis Polyglottis Vaticanis.

Scotus, John Duns (1639). *Opera Omnia*. Ed. L. Wadding. Lyon [Reprint: Hildesheim 1968–69].

Wolter, Allan B. (1954). 'Doctrine of the Immaculate Conception in the Early Franciscan School'. *Studia Mariana cura commissionis Marialis Franciscanae edita*, IX: 26–69.

CHAPTER 17

REPRODUCING MEDIEVAL CHRISTIANITY

RUTH MAZO KARRAS

RECENT scholarship on medieval women has focused on virginity and its meanings. It opened up independence for women, and was a way of asserting control over their own bodies and lives, but at the same time it put all other women, who did not wish to choose virginity or were prevented from doing so by family pressures, in the position of being held up to an unattainable standard of virtue. Virginity was also an ideal for medieval men, at least so the church argued, and was certainly one strand in a web of competing masculinities.

But the importance of virginity should not blind us to the centrality that reproduction held in medieval Christianity, not only as a second best for those who could not achieve virginity, or as a transgressive activity. Reproduction was a central site for Christian thinking in many ways, from the miraculous conception of Christ to precepts for everyday believers. In the western European Middle Ages, in particular, reproduction provides a crucial link among theology, sexuality, and gender. The discussion here focuses on the period from 1100 to 1500, but inevitably includes the ongoing traditions in which medieval Christians participated, and also discusses how Jews interpreted some of the same traditions quite differently.

Medieval Christianity had a complex relationship with reproduction. The church held that celibacy was a higher state than marriage. Churchmen preached constantly (although not always with the same degree of emphasis) about the sinfulness of sexual activity that did not tend toward reproduction, and some even spoke of the sinfulness of that which did. But the audience of many of the surviving texts, it must be remembered, was celibate clergy, monks, and nuns. Although the church's teachings could well have made non-celibate lay people feel second-rate—and in some cases may well have been intended that way—it is hard to argue that something practised by 95 per cent of the population was transgressive. Reproducing was not, perhaps, the most spiritually valuable act a medieval Christian could perform, but it was neverthe-less an expected and important part of life for most medieval Christians, as well as non-Christians.

REPRODUCTION AND SEXUALITY

Medieval people connected sexuality closely with reproduction. This, of course, is not unique to medieval Europe; the connection between sex and fertility was only disrupted by the widespread availability of contraceptive technology in the twentieth century. But medieval understandings were particularly conditioned by Christian interpretations of the Bible, particularly that of St Augustine (354–430), who held in his later (although not his earlier) commentary on Genesis that reproductive intercourse became sinful because of Adam and Eve's disobedience (Brown 1988: 400–406; Cohen 1989: 245–259). Had it not been for the Fall, the first couple, and their descendants, would have reproduced sex-ually but without concupiscence or carnal longing. 'I do not see what could prevent them from having honorable marriage and an immaculate bed . . . so that they could beget off-spring of their seed without any disturbing burning of lust, without any labor or pain of childbirth' (Augustine 1894: 9:3, 272–273). Just as people may eat to maintain their bodies, but when they desire food may fall into gluttony, people could have had inter-course in order to establish or maintain the human race, but when they desire each other may fall into lust. Medieval Christians did not suggest that reproduction ever could have taken place without genital activity (except in the case of Mary), but the sin of Adam and Eve meant that what could have been done by movement of body parts controlled by will rather than desire was henceforth inevitably accompanied by the sin of concupiscence.

In a society with no effective contraception, causality went both ways. Reproduction inevitably required sexual activity (and therefore implied sin), but penile–vaginal inter-course also almost inevitably implied reproduction.[1] Symbols of opposite-sex love were symbols of fertility, for example the rabbit, the name of which in Old French (con) also made a sexual pun (Camille 1998: 96). Today the connection between penile–vaginal intercourse and reproduction is much more tenuous, in the sense that it is possible to have the first without the second, and even the second without the first. The way peo-ple today talk about reproductive or contraceptive technologies, and react against them, indicates the extent to which the modern era has inherited from the Middle Ages an idea that reproductive sex is natural, and sex without reproduction or reproduction without sex are somehow not.

---

[1] Herbs with a contraceptive or abortifacient effect were known, as well as coitus interruptus and possibly barrier methods, but while these may have had some effect on the overall fertility of the population, they were not reliable enough to be able to detach heterosexual intercourse from reproduction. There is remarkably little discussion in medieval sources of heterosexual oral or anal sex, or manual stimulation except as foreplay.

Building on Augustine

Medieval thinking about the liceity of sexual activity extended the writings of St Augustine. In several treatises on marriage and virginity, he praised the latter but shied away from criticizing the former too harshly. St Jerome had written to Eustochium in 384: 'I praise weddings, I praise marriage, but because they generate virgins' (Jerome 1949: letter 22:20, 1:130), but for Augustine marriage was not to be considered a lesser evil: rather, it was a good, although virginity was a greater one. Augustine articulated three goods of marriage, of which reproduction was only one. (The others were the promotion of fidelity and the creation of a sacrament.) A marriage could be faithful and sacramental without carnal activity, and indeed as Dyan Elliott (1993) has shown, a wide range of people throughout the Middle Ages entered into such chaste but sacramental marriages. For many Christian writers, then, there were other reasons for marriage, but reproduction was the only thing that justified sexual activity within it. While it might be considered a spouse's duty to have intercourse in order to prevent his or her partner from straying, Augustine did not think that was always the case. There were certain acts— non-reproductive ones—that were so sinful that a wife should refuse them to her husband, even if it means his visiting a prostitute: if she engages in them the blame is hers.

The fact is that intercourse necessary for begetting children carries no blame, and it alone is proper to marriage. But the intercourse which goes beyond this necessity is no longer subject to reason, but to lust.... if both partners are slaves to such lustfulness, their behaviour is clearly alien to marriage.... Whereas the natural exercise of sex in its stealthy progression beyond the marriage-compact, that is, beyond the requirement to bear children, is pardonable in a wife but mortally sinful in a prostitute, the unnatural use of it is abominable in a prostitute, but more abominable still in a wife... when a man seeks to exploit a woman's sexual parts beyond what is granted in this way, a wife behaves more basely if she allows herself rather than another to be used in this way (Augustine 2001: 24–27).

Presumably the man's sin would also be less if he committed these acts with a prostitute, since she was already a committed sinner and he would not be causing his wife to sin; but Augustine frames it in terms of the culpability of the wife.

Most medieval texts participated to a greater or lesser extent in the Augustinian tradition, placing reproduction as the main justification for sexual intercourse. Other forms of sexual behaviour, including inappropriate positions used by married couples as well as fornication, same-sex relations, and incest, were penalized in early medieval penitentials, and later fulminated against by canonists and preachers (Payer 1984; Brundage 1987: 396). Although if a husband and wife were prompted by concupiscence to have sexual relations, they were still committing a sin, medieval authors generally held that as long as they were at the same time attempting to reproduce, or at least not doing anything to prevent reproduction, their marriage was still a valid one (Biller 2000: 158–177). As the twelfth-century canonist Gratian wrote, 'what happens beyond the intention of generation is not an evil of marriages, but venial' (Biller 2000: 159). Thus couples who were beyond the age of likely conception could continue to have sex, as long as they remained open to and desiring of offspring (Brundage 1987: 280; Payer 1993: 87). Medieval authors did not make the full-fledged argument made by Christian theologians today, that sex as an expression of (marital) love is a gift of God in and of itself, but they left the door open to it.

The Rise of Nature

By the central and later Middle Ages this idea of reproduction as the only acceptable justification for sexual intercourse, and even that reproductive sex outside of marriage was less sinful than non-reproductive sex within it, was expressed in terms of 'nature'. The 'sin against nature' came largely, though not exclusively, to mean same-sex activity. Alain of Lille, the twelfth-century writer whose dialogue *Complaint of Nature* used a variety of metaphors to emphasize the sterility of same-sex intercourse, clearly made the connection between fertility and the natural, but was not so clear that only same-sex coupling violated nature (Jordan 1997: 80–87). 'The human race, derogate from its high birth, commits monstrous acts in its union of genders, and perverts the rules of love by a practice of extreme and abnormal irregularity', said Alain, but it does so 'under the lyre of frenzied Orpheus', whose story certainly involved love of the opposite sex. The examples include Helen (for her harlotry), Pasiphae (for her bestiality), Myrrha (for her incest), and Narcissus (for his self-love) (Alain of Lille 1972: 36–37).

A great many treatises on morality, focused on various ways of categorizing sins, both in Latin and in the vernacular, appeared from the later thirteenth through fifteenth centuries, and many of them followed the views of William Peraldus on the seven deadly sins. Peraldus's work was extraordinarily popular, used as the basis for treatises in many European vernaculars as well as scholarly discussions, and may have influenced Aquinas. It treated the 'sin against nature' as the most serious of the branches of the sin of Lust (Peraldus 1588: 2:9–10), which included using the wrong part of a woman, the crime of Onan, the destruction of Sodom and Gommorah, and the Levitical prohibition against lying with a man as with a woman. The *Fasciculus Morum*, a fourteenth-century English text based on Peraldus, specifically refers to 'the diabolical sin against nature called sodomy', and also uses the trope of its unmentionability: 'I pass over it in horror and leave it to others to describe it' (Wenzel 1989: 686–687), although it then goes on to give several paragraphs of discussion which describe its punishment (Karras 2005).

The most influential author on the relation of nature to reproduction, however, was the Dominican Thomas of Aquino (1225–1274). Whereas the twelfth-century canon lawyer Gratian had distinguished five kinds of illicit coitus, without mentioning nature, Aquinas gave six types of lust (*luxuria*): simple fornication, adultery, incest, deflowering a (female) virgin, abduction, and the vice against nature. The latter was subdivided to include pollution without *concubitus* (literally lying together, or coitus),[2] which refers

---

[2] Although Jordan (1997: 144 n. 20), says that *concubitus* is not a synonym for *coitus* because Aquinas uses the latter only for penile–vaginal intercourse.

to masturbation either on one's own or with an object, intercourse with a member of another species, intercourse with someone not of the proper sex, and intercourse in other than the 'natural' way, either by using an 'improper instrument' (which could mean a body part as well as an object) or 'monstrous and bestial manners' (Jordan 1997: 145). The latter certainly included anal intercourse between a man and a woman, and probably the use of contraceptives, as well as other acts, although the term 'sodomitic' was applied only to intercourse between two men or two women. 'Monstrous and bestial', the harshest words Aquinas used, were used only of behaviour between two people who might otherwise have reproduced, although he did say that sex with an animal is actually the worst form of *luxuria* (Jordan 1997: 145).

The idea that reproductive sex was closely connected to nature continued to be widespread for the rest of the Middle Ages, even being used to justify prostitution (Rossiaud 1988: 86–103). The use of contraception, even by married people, came to be considered unacceptable, for the same reason as well as others (Noonan 1986: 231–257). Even to prevent adultery or protect the life of a wife, any human action that prevented reproduction was wrong (although human inaction, i.e. chastity, was laudable). As Müller (2012: 3–4) points out, however, the sinfulness of contraception does not mean that it was criminal, and it was treated quite differently from abortion.

Put another way: reproduction was the natural consequence of sex. In church teaching—and probably in the lives of most married couples in the Middle Ages—it was a desirable consequence, rather than a punishment for the sin of lust. Even when it was undesirable—the pregnancy of an unmarried woman—theologians considered it preferable to unnatural behaviour.

The corollary of this evaluation of sex acts as reproductive or not is that medieval people did not think about sexual orientation or even about acts in the same way as modern ones. Although I use 'heterosexual intercourse' here as shorthand for 'sex between a woman and a man', the gender of the partners was not what made the difference between natural and unnatural in medieval discourse. Rather, it was whether or not the act was reproductive. A (potentially) reproductive act, penile–vaginal intercourse between two unmarried people, or even between two people each married to someone else, was not as sinful as a non-reproductive spilling of seed by a married couple. Thus, Karma Lochrie (2005: xi–xxvii) is quite right that 'heteronormative' is an anachronistic concept for the Middle Ages, but not because there were no such things as norms. Rather, it makes sense to speak of reproduction being the norm, and all non-reproductive acts, regardless of who the partners were, as deviant, in terms of medieval thought.

Jewish Traditions on Fertility

Although it drew on many of the same Biblical traditions—Adam and Eve, and the commandment to 'be fruitful and multiply' come from the Hebrew Bible—Jewish tradition was on the whole somewhat less condemnatory of non-reproductive sex. The Talmud allowed married couples to practise withdrawal if the woman were nursing a child (Cohen 1989: 138).

Lists of prohibited sex acts include bestiality and homosexual intercourse, but they focus mainly on incest and on a man taking a woman who belongs to someone else. Certainly the Jewish practice of menstrual separation, with intercourse to follow the woman's ritual bath after the end of her period and 'white days', functioned in part, and probably intentionally so, to encourage intercourse during a woman's fertile period. The woman's right to sexual intercourse from her husband (but not the other way around, probably because he could divorce her if she was 'rebellious' and refused sex) also promoted reproduction.

Rabbinic literature shows several conflicting traditions on the legitimacy of marital sex: as witnessed in the Babylonian Talmud, some rabbis seem to have thought that it should be carefully controlled and not engaged in for pleasure, others that 'Anything a man wishes to do with his wife, he may do.' As Boyarin (1993: 110) notes, although the Talmud presents this from an androcentric perspective, as indeed it does much else, it elsewhere stresses the importance of the woman's consent and even desire. The 'evil inclination' was always to be avoided, and at times this was the case even between husband and wife (Biale 1992: 43–46), but it was also good because necessary for reproduction (Boyarin 1993: 63)—a dialectical rather than dualist position.

Certain religious movements within medieval Judaism urged the avoidance of sexual intercourse where at all possible, for example various Kabbalistic groups (Biale 1992: 109–113). Ascetic tendencies may have been influenced by the majority Christian culture. Mainstream medieval Judaism, however, both in Ashkenazic and Sephardic Europe, considered reproductive sex a commandment, and also allowed marital sex for the purpose of pleasure (Biale 1992: 78–82). Some rabbis permitted women to use contraceptive devices, such as sponges, especially after the family already had children and when further childbearing would endanger her life or the family's economic well-being (Karras 2012a: 93–94). This must be understood within an overall context that very much promoted childbearing and did not seek to liberate women from it; the rabbis who commented on the permissibility of contraception seem to have assumed that the couples considering it already had children.

The overall tenor of Jewish teaching was in many ways similar to Christian. Sexual organs and desires existed for the purpose of creating children, which was an important social goal; as Boyarin puts it for the Talmud, 'Procreation, then, is not the 'purpose' or the justification or excuse for sexuality but its very essence in rabbinic thought' (Boyarin 1993: 75), and the same might be said, though a bit wishfully, about Christian thought. Sexual pleasure was not to be sought as an end in itself, though it was permissible within marriage both to prevent illicit sex elsewhere and to make the partners happier with each other. However, the two sets of beliefs and practices took this basic teaching in different directions, which had in large part to do with the way they understood marriage.

REPRODUCTION AND MARRIAGE

Much of the legacy of marriage that the Middle Ages has left the modern world is one of sacramentality (in the Christian case) or religious sanction (in others). Even though not all Christian denominations make marriage a sacrament, they all make it a religious event, something done in accordance with divine commandment. The number of couples who choose to have a religious ceremony is on the decline in most Western countries, but the history of marriage as religious still haunts it, whether in the form of words used or in the claim of religious authorities to determine whom the state should allow to marry.[3]

Marriage as Sacrament

Participating in a sacrament of the church was probably not what prompted most medieval Christians to marry. The idea of the sacrament was certainly there. Augustine had described the sacramental bond as permanent: it remained even if the marriage were dissolved by divorce (with the consequence, as Christian marriage developed, that divorce meant only a separation and not the opportunity to remarry; see Reynolds 1994: 281, 297–99).

The idea of marriage as a sacrament persisted throughout the early Middle Ages. It was developed in discussions among canon lawyers and theologians during the twelfth century. Hugh of St Victor (1096–1141) discussed it extensively, including the idea that the sacrament was created by the consent of the parties, but that idea came to dominate due to the work of Peter Lombard (1100–1160), the Paris theologian whose *Sentences* became the most widely used textbook of medieval theology. Peter laid out the sacramental permanence of marriage, and the importance of the consent of the two parties, rather than that of the parents or anyone else, in creating it, as well as the importance of sexual union: marriage is made 'according to the consent of souls and according to the union of bodies' and that consent, the efficient cause of marriage, must be given 'not in just any manner, but in express words, and not in the future tense but in the present' (Colish 1994: 2: 628–698, quotes at 651, 652). This became the basis of the church's established theology and canon law of marriage; the position of the canon lawyer Gratian, who did not think consent sufficient to create a permanent and complete marriage, lost out. Marcia Colish sees as key the Lombard's acknowledgement that marriage was about more than just procreation, that sex in marriage was not merely a concession to prevent greater sin but something sacramental itself.

---

[3] For example, in England and Wales the number of couples choosing civil rather than religious ceremonies first broke 50 per cent in 1992 and now stands at 68 per cent. Office for National Statistics, Statistical Bulletin, 29 February 2012, *Marriages in England and Wales 2010*, 5. In Australia, 31 per cent were religious ceremonies in 2010, down from 58 per cent in 1990. Australian Bureau of Statistics, Bulletin 4102.0—*Australian Social Trends*, March Quarter 2012, 12. Numbers are lower for much of the rest of Europe. For the USA and Canada, these statistics are compiled on a state or provincial basis and therefore not so readily available, but the USA, while it still has a higher percentage of religious ceremonies, shows a similar trend.

But just because sacramental marriage became the teaching of the church does not mean that this was the reason why people chose to marry. Indeed, the reiteration of the sacramental nature of marriage in medieval sources intended for the laity suggests that the latter understood marriage in a different way. David D'Avray's (2005) monumental study of marriage sermons, which were extremely widespread, argues that marriage symbolism was used to discuss Christ's relation to the church in order to make it easier to give lay people an understanding of the complex theology of that relation. But it might also have had a different purpose and effect: to use marriage as a metaphor for the divine union in order to persuade people that it was in fact a sacrament, that there was something special and spiritual about the bond.

We must not forget that everyone who wrote about the sacramental nature of marriage in the Middle Ages was unmarried. In fact the bulk of surviving texts on many topics were written by priests or male or female religious. But in the case of marriage it is important to remember that we do not have the views of people who chose to enter into it, and if we wish to know them we must infer them from behaviour.

Social Reproduction

It is clear throughout the Middle Ages, as in most societies, that there are a variety of motivations for marriage. Some are in fact motivations for the formation of stable couples—a means of support, a gendered division of household labour—that become reasons for marriage when marriage is the only sanctioned type of couple. People who were too poor to marry were so not because the marriage process itself cost a lot. One was supposed to pay a priest for the ceremony, and it was customary to hold some kind of celebratory meal afterwards, but in fact a clandestine but valid marriage could be created by a private exchange of vows. What people could not afford was the setting up of a household (unmarried workers frequently lived in the homes of their employers) and supporting a family.

Other purposes more directly required formal marriage. For example, the transmission of property to the next generation, under Roman law, had required legitimate birth (or adoption), and Christian societies accepted this as they did so many other provisions of that law. Thus marriage was, as one Roman jurist put it, for the purpose of engendering legitimate heirs (Treggiari 1991: 379). This might matter considerably more at levels of society in which there was property to transmit, and indeed, because most of the documentation of medieval marriage that survives—or was ever created—was about property, we know remarkably little about the marriages of poorer and lower-status people. Nevertheless poor people might also wish to have legitimate heirs: they could help work the land on which the family were tenants, and even unfree tenancies generally passed to sons (or sometimes daughters). Thus, although marriage was not actually required for biological reproduction, it was required for social reproduction, in the sense that legitimate heirs were needed.

It was also required for social reproduction in the sense that while one could create a household as an unmarried couple, there could still be considerable social pressure to be formally married. Late medieval court records are full of cases of couples who lived together without being married—it certainly happened. But it also found its way into court records because these people were informed upon by their neighbours. Even if we acknowledge that for a number of medieval couples—particularly those who moved from place to place—contemporaries never knew whether there was a formal marriage or not, it was a distinct social advantage to be reputed as married. Single women who did not take up a religious life or live with relatives were often sexually suspect (Karras 1999; Beattie 2007: 48–49 disagrees). But so were men; late medieval sources are very concerned with the depredations caused by young unmarried men, especially in groups (Rossiaud 1988: 11–26; Muchembled 2012: 45–81). Marriage and the formation of a household brought respectability, or at least a striving for respectability, and was thought to calm people down.

Thus the opportunity for biological and social reproduction was an important factor in medieval marriage, which was not just a matter of a spiritual bond. And from Augustine's time (and earlier) the theology of marriage reflected this. Even when talking about the way marriage allowed people to participate in the union of Christ and the church, thinkers constantly mentioned the practical features, that is, a gender division of labour to support the family. And in these discussions 'marriage' substituted for 'coupling': although it might theoretically be possible to get the benefits of household formation and offspring without marrying, this was not considered. It was not other forms of domestic partnership, but rather virginity, with which marriage was most often compared.

Marriage versus Virginity

Medieval writers generally followed Augustine in considering marriage a lesser good than virginity, with some variation. Some writers valued virginity exceptionally highly, especially as a critique of clerical marriage. Virginity, especially for women, could be encouraged by stressing the pains of childbirth and the troubles of childrearing. The late twelfth- or early thirteenth-century letter on virginity, *Holy Maidenhood*, for example, described them thus:

> In conceiving it, her flesh is at once defiled with that indecency... in carrying it there is heaviness and constant discomfort; in giving birth to it, the cruelest of all pains, and sometimes death; in bringing it up, many weary hours.... Your rosy face will grow thin, and turn green as grass; your eyes will grow dull, and shadowed underneath, and because of your dizziness your head will ache cruelly... discomfort in your bowels and stitches in your side, and often painful backache; heaviness in every limb; the dragging weight of your two breasts, and the streams of milk that run from them. Your beauty is all destroyed by pallor; there is a bitter taste in your mouth, and everything that you eat makes you feel sick; and whatever food your stomach disdainfully receives... it throws it up again. Then when it comes to it, that cruel

distressing anguish, that fierce and stabbing pain, that incessant misery, that torment upon torment, that wailing outcry...we do not blame women for their labor pains, which all our mothers suffered for ourselves; but we describe them as a warning to virgins, so that they should be the less inclined towards such things.

(Millett and Wogan-Browne 1990: 33)

Since the twelfth century, in response to heretical beliefs (whether real or imagined) about the absolute evil of the body and of reproduction, notably among the Cathars in southern France, orthodox opinion was careful not to deny the value of marriage and children (Noonan 1986: 171–199). Even *Holy Maidenhood* had to stop periodically to note that 'the indecent heat of the flesh, that burning itch of physical desire before that disgusting act, that animal union, that shameless coupling, that stinking and wanton deed, full of filthiness' that is sex, 'is, nevertheless, to be tolerated to some extent within marriage' (Millett and Wogan-Browne 1990: 9). And even when a constant stream of material in praise of virginity, for both women and men, issued from the pens of churchmen, both in Latin and in the vernacular, marriage and reproduction was the expected norm for most medieval people. That does not mean that they all married. At least 10 per cent of the population in northwestern Europe—far more than those in religion—never married and probably never formed a long-term domestic partnership (Kowaleski 2013).

The tension between virginity, or lacking that, celibacy, and marriage with its sexual and reproductive implications, was thus a constant one for medieval society. It could create tensions for the individual who preferred a life of virginity but was pushed into marriage by familial and social expectations. Christina of Markyate (*c*.1100–*c*.1155), for example, managed to persuade her husband not to consummate their marriage, despite her family's urging him to force her (Fanous and Leyser 2004). Maria Sturion of Venice (*c*.1379–1399), whose husband left her when he went off to war and who 'deserted' him by returning from her father-in-law's home to her parents', also clearly would have preferred a virginal life (Stuard 2008; for more examples see Elliott 1993).

The tension between virginity and marriage could also create tensions within the society at large. It could be argued that virginity was the hegemonic ideal, that the privilege of the celibate class was such that its vision of proper sexuality dominated society even though the group was numerically small, and that those who married (or otherwise coupled) were in some way 'othered' or 'queer'. This would be going too far. The praise of virginity has the tone of a losing battle, or of protesting too much. The Protestant reformers would note that very few people were actually called to chastity, but this was in fact widely recognized in the fifteenth century, and not always deplored; there were suggestions at fifteenth-century church councils that clerical marriage should be allowed (Karras 2012b: 122–125). Churchmen had tried to draw a line between the married and the chaste in order to bolster their own prestige (Karras 2012b: 121–122), but by the later Middle Ages it was widely understood that many churchmen were crossing that line and the prestige of the clerical order as a whole was not such as to make its ideal dominant.

The example of Judaism is once again instructive as a comparison. There virginity was not valued as in medieval Christianity. Women were expected to remain virgins until they were married, as in Roman society and many others, but this was a matter of life stage rather than a matter of a state of the soul. Although of course not all Jews married, they were urged, even commanded, to do so by Rabbinic texts. Marriage could be postponed due to economic circumstances, especially for a man, but it remained an important goal. Despite the presence of misogynist literature in this culture as in Christianity, there was also a great deal that praised wives—not women in general, but wives in support of their husbands—and rabbinic stories of famous sages often spoke of their wives as virtuous. The best-known example of an admired wife from medieval western Europe is Dolce of Worms, the wife of the pietist Rabbi Eliezer ben Judah ha-Rokeah, who was murdered in 1196, whose husband wrote poetry in her memory (Baskin 2001). Marriage and reproduction were as connected in Jewish culture as they were in Christian, but there was less of the ambivalence about them that haunted medieval Christian society.

FICTIVE REPRODUCTION

Christian ambivalence about reproduction was nowhere as clear as in the status of the clergy. As of 1139 the marriages of priests were declared invalid, and even before that they were not supposed to marry (McLaughlin 2010: 31–36). They did, of course, reproduce, even though they were not supposed to. We have more records of priests and monks who had children than nuns, likely reflecting that they had more opportunity. Still, stories like that told by Aelred of Rievaulx about the nun of Watton (Salih 2001: 152–165), indicate that monastic women did become pregnant, and that it could be extremely disruptive to their houses, whose chastity was collective. In a similar legend found in various places in Europe, an abbess's illegitimate child, miraculously delivered by the Virgin Mary, redeems the story by growing up and becoming a bishop (Karras 1988).

Priests and Fatherhood

In a real world where it was customary for sons to follow their fathers' profession, however, the illegitimate sons of priests who wished to become priests themselves were perceived as a real problem (Wertheimer 2006). A man of illegitimate birth could not become a priest, or a man or woman head a monastery, without a dispensation from the pope. The records of the papal penitentiary from 1449 to 1533 indicate that 56 per cent of those seeking such dispensations were the children of men in higher religious orders, seeking to follow their fathers; in some cases they may even have wished to take over their father's parish (Schmugge 1995: 33, 183). But such behaviour was still frowned upon, as the term 'illegitimate' indicates.

The clergy were deprived of legitimate biological fatherhood, but they were metaphorical fathers in several ways. One way was linguistic. The words 'pope' (*papa* in Latin) and 'abbot' (*abbas* in Latin, from the Aramaic for 'father') carried a paternal sense that at least in the case of the pope people would have been aware of. And an abbess, too, was the mother of her house. But the metaphor extended much farther than titles alone. From the early Middle Ages abbots and abbesses are called the father and mother of their monks or nuns (who were brothers or sisters to each other). Metaphors of fatherhood were used, and indeed taken quite seriously by and for bishops, up to and including the Bishop of Rome (McLaughlin 2010: 187–218). Pope Innocent III used both paternal and maternal metaphors of himself and of other bishops, associating the three qualities of 'authority, reproduction, and nurture ... in the contexts of divine, biological, spiritual and surrogate fatherhood' (Rousseau 1999: 27). He took biological fatherhood in terms of reproduction as negative, and he limited the ability of the clergy to provide for their biological children. Authority, and spiritual nurture, remained important.

Where a priest or abbot was called a father, he played that role in that he was responsible not for engendering but for providing for his flock—spiritually, and in the case of abbots materially as well—educating them, and disciplining them where necessary. Similarly, when abbots were referred to as maternal, as Caroline Bynum has shown was not unusual in twelfth-century Cistercian discourse, this was not in the sense that they had metaphorically given birth. Rather, they nurtured and protected their monks (Bynum 1984). The maternal metaphor in the same sense was used for Jesus, by these twelfth-century writers and by Julian of Norwich (1342–1416). Jesus fed people with his blood as a mother fed them with her milk (Bynum 1984). Describing abbots in this way, then, was a powerful religious message as well as gender-bending.

On the local level, the paternal metaphor was less obvious. Priests, especially parish priests, were supposed to lead, teach, and admonish their flock on a daily basis, all activities which we might see as fatherly. But 'Dominus' or 'Sir,' rather than 'father', was the typical title given them. Nor was fatherhood very common as a metaphor for priests' relation to their flocks. A fine collection of recent scholarship on clerical identities and masculinities in the Middle Ages has no index entry for 'fatherhood' nor do any of the chapters focus on fatherhood as an aspect of clerics' masculinity (Thibodeaux 2010). Although it is hard to prove a negative, well-known handbooks for priests from the later Middle Ages do not use it (Myrc 1902; Guido 2011). On the pastoral level, the relationship between a penitent and the priest who was his or her confessor was more often likened to a marital or romantic love relationship, as was the case with holy women like Eve of Wilton who engaged in what Dyan Elliott calls an 'alternative intimacy' with her confessor Goscelin (Elliott 2012: 150–171 for this and other examples). It was less often expressed as one of spiritual fatherhood.

Technically a priest who had sexual relations with a woman of his flock was guilty of spiritual incest, since he was her spiritual father, but actual accusations of this were rare (Karras 1992: 3). Sexual abuse by clerics could be considered analogous to incest in that it represents a violation of trust on the part of someone in a position of presumably benevolent authority. However, for medieval people it was not an analogy; a spiritual kinship relation was real. Similarly, godparenthood also created a kin relationship to which the forbidden degrees within which one could not marry also applied; while it created an impediment to marriage in canon law, however, it was not treated nearly as seriously as nuclear family incest (Archibald 2001: 26–41).

Metaphorical versus Biological Parenthood

An analysis of what paternal metaphors meant to medieval people, even to the average parish priest, must be largely speculative. It is clear, however, that medieval Christianity considered having children a good thing, and also considered being chaste a good thing. The only person who had managed to achieve literal reproduction without sexual activity was the Virgin Mary, who was not only 'alone of all her sex' but alone of all her species; Jesus, of course, was also without sin, but he did not have biological children. Mary was the most honoured saint in the medieval world, and it was the unique combination of her parenthood of God and her unsullied purity that made her so. There were some particularly feminine devotions to the Virgin Mary; because of her miraculous motherhood she was believed to help women in childbirth, for example (Smith 2005: 762–763). Overall, however, devotion to the Virgin was extremely popular among both men and women, and most of the writings we have that are devoted to her are by men (Rubin 2009). She was held up to women as a model to emulate, but to men also, just as people of both sexes would at the end of the Middle Ages be asked to imitate Jesus. Augustine had written that all virgins (he meant female virgins) 'in company of Mary are mothers of Christ, as long as they do the will of the Father' (Augustine 2001: 70), and many later Christian authors picked up on this theme. But for men, too, what better way to imitate the saint who had become a parent while remaining a virgin than by making oneself a parent while remaining chaste?

In part, the clergy were reluctant to relinquish an area of superiority to the laity. The reformers of the eleventh and twelfth centuries stressed that the clergy were purer and therefore superior to the laity. The laity may have been able to get some comfort out of the fact that they, unlike the clergy, were able to establish dynasties (Moore 2000: 65–111). But the clerical hierarchy were reluctant to allow the laity even this restricted area of exclusivity. They too claimed parenthood—and in fact a higher form. Indeed, although Bynum reads the metaphor of abbot as mother as a sign of gender fluidity, this could also have a darker connotation: it was a gender fluidity that allowed males to appropriate the positive characteristics of females, claiming not only to be holier and more rational than women but also better mothers.

But it would be wrong to see the fictive parenthood accorded to bishops and abbots as due to the denial of literal parenthood to them. A comparison with medieval European Jewry is helpful because there it was possible, indeed desired and expected, for the religious leaders of the community to father legitimate children. Even Judah ben Samuel the Pious of Regensburg (1140–1217) and Eleazar ben Judah of Worms (1176–1238), leaders of the Rhineland Pietist movement which expressed perhaps more qualms about sexual temptation than mainstream Ashkenazic Judaism, married and had children. Rabbinic dynasties, indeed, were quite common, for example Joseph Qimhi (1105–1170) of Provence and his sons Moses and David, Biblical commentators, or Rashi (Shlomo benYitzhak) of Troyes (1040–1105), perhaps the best-known medieval Ashkenazic rabbi, who had no sons, but whose daughters married other major Talmudic scholars and whose grandsons, notably Samuel ben Meir (Rashbam 1085–1158) and Yaakov ben Meir (Rabbeinu Tam 1100–1171) were influential halakhic authorities. In addition to relationships by what Christians would have called consanguinity or affinity, intellectual dynasties could also be traced from teacher to student, as in Christian culture, without the need for biological relationship. The language of fatherhood was not prominent on the level of an individual teacher and his students, although it could occasionally be said that a religious leader was like a father to his followers, in a way not that different from Christianity.

Of course, within both Christian and Jewish culture, metaphors of parenthood were very common on a broader level than the individual. The Latin word for a homeland was *patria*, 'fatherland'. The most common Hebrew phrase for 'Jews' was *bnei Yisrael*, 'children [or sons] of Israel'. God, of course, was the father in both traditions. It cannot simply be that biological or social, as opposed to metaphorical, parenthood was precisely what was lacking to the Christian leaders. Rather, the patriarchal notion of the father as the one who shapes and teaches, as well as protects, his children was so central in Judeo-Christian culture (and perhaps in Western culture; this does not only grow out of the Hebrew Bible) that God had to be discussed in such a way. Religious leaders, who helped their students or penitents get closer to God, and in the case of Christianity actively mediated between them, were parents in the image of God. Where biological reproduction was problematized, spiritual reproduction could replace it, and where biological reproduction was welcomed, spiritual kinship took a place alongside it.

REFERENCES

Alain of Lille (1972). *The Complaint of Nature*. Trans. Douglas M. Moffat. Yale Studies in English, 36. Hamden, CT: Archon Press.

Archibald, Elizabeth (2001). *Incest and the Medieval Imagination*. Oxford: Oxford University Press.

Augustine (1894). 'De Genesi ad litteram'. In J. Zycha (ed.), *Corpus scriptorum ecclesiasticorum latinorum* 28:1. Vienna: F. Tempsky.

Augustine (2001). *De bono coniugali, De santa virginitate*. Ed. and trans. P. G. Walsh. Oxford: Clarendon Press.

Baskin, Judith (2001). 'Dolce of Worms: The Lives and Deaths of an Exemplary Medieval Jewish Woman and her Daughters.' In Lawrence Fine (ed.), *Judaism in Practice: From the Middle Ages through the Early Modern Period*. Princeton: Princeton University Press, 429–437.

Beattie, Cordelia (2007). *Medieval Single Women: The Politics of Social Classification in Late Medieval England*. Oxford: Oxford University Press.

Biale, David (1992). *Eros and the Jews: From Biblical Israel to Contemporary America*. New York: Basic Books.

Biller, Peter (2000). *The Measure of Multitude: Population in Medieval Thought*. Oxford: Oxford University Press.

Boyarin, Daniel (1993). *Carnal Israel: Reading Sex in Talmudic Culture*. Berkeley: University of California Press.

Brown, Peter (1988). *The Body and Society: Men, Women, and Sexual Renunciation in Early Christianity*. New York: Columbia University Press.

Brundage, James A. (1987). *Law, Sex, and Christian Society in Medieval Europe*. Chicago: University of Chicago Press.

Bynum, Caroline (1984). 'Jesus as Mother and Abbot as Mother: Some Themes in Twelfth-Century Cistercian Writing.' In *Jesus as Mother: Studies in the Spirituality of the High Middle Ages*. Berkeley: University of California Press, 110–169.

Camille, Michael (1998). *The Medieval Art of Love: Objects and Subjects of Desire*. New York: Harry N. Abrams, Inc.

Cohen, Jeremy (1989). *'Be Fertile and Increase, Fill the Earth and Master It': The Ancient and Medieval Career of a Biblical Text*. Ithaca: Cornell University Press.

Colish, Marcia (1984). *Peter Lombard*, 2 vols. Leiden: E.J. Brill, 1994.

D'Avray, David (2005). *Medieval Marriage: Symbolism and Society*. Oxford: Oxford University Press.

Elliott, Dyan (1993). *Spiritual Marriage: Sexual Abstinence in Medieval Wedlock*. Princeton: Princeton University Press.

Elliott, Dyan (2012). *The Bride of Christ Goes to Hell: Metaphor and Embodiment in the Lives of Pious Women, 200–1500*. Philadelphia: University of Pennsylvania Press.

Fanous, Samuel, and Henrietta Leyser (2004) (eds). *Christina of Markyate*. London: Routledge.

Guido of Monte Rochen (2011). *Handbook for Curates: A Late Medieval Manual on Pastoral Ministry*. Trans. Ann T. Thayer. Washington: Catholic University of America Press.

Jerome (1949). *Lettres*. Ed. Jérôme Labart. Paris: Les belles lettres.

Jordan, Mark (1997). *The Invention of Sodomy in Christian Theology*. Chicago: University of Chicago Press.

Karras, Ruth Mazo (1988). 'The Virgin and the Pregnant Abbess: Miracles and Gender in the Middle Ages.' *Medieval Perspectives*, 3: 112–132.

Karras, Ruth Mazo (1992). 'The Latin Vocabulary of Illicit Sex in English Ecclesiastical Court Records.' *Journal of Medieval Lati*, 2: 1–17.

Karras, Ruth Mazo (1999). 'Sex and the Singlewoman.' In Judith M. Bennett and Amy M. Froide (eds), *Singlewomen in the European Past 1250–1800*. Philadelphia: University of Pennsylvania Press, 127–145.

Karras, Ruth Mazo (2005). 'The Lechery That Dare Not Speak Its Name: Sodomy and the Vices in Medieval England.' In Richard Newhauser (ed.), *In the Garden of Evil: The Vices and Culture in the Middle Ages*. Toronto: PIMS, 193–205.

Karras, Ruth Mazo (2012a). *Sexuality in Medieval Europe: Doing Unto Others*, 2nd edn. London: Routledge.

Karras, Ruth Mazo (2012b). *Unmarriages: Women, Men, and Sexual Unions in the Middle Ages*. Philadelphia: University of Pennsylvania Press.

Kowaleski, Maryanne (2013). 'Gendering Demographic Change in the Middle Ages.' In Judith M. Bennett and Ruth Mazo Karras (eds), *Oxford Handbook of Women and Gender in Medieval Europe*. Oxford: Oxford University Press, 181–196.

Lochrie, Karma (2005). *Heterosyncrasies: Female Sexuality When Normal Wasn't*. Minneapolis: University of Minnesota Press.

McLaughlin, Megan (2010). *Sex, Gender, and Episcopal Authority in an Age of Reform, 1000–1122*. Cambridge: Cambridge University Press.

Millett, Bella, and Jocelyn Wogan-Browne (1990) (eds). *Medieval English Prose for Women: Selections from the Katherine Group and Ancrene Wisse*. Oxford: Clarendon Press.

Moore, R. I. (2000). *The First European Revolution c. 970–1215*. Oxford: Blackwell.

Muchembled, Robert (2012). *A History of Violence: From the End of the Middle Ages to the Present*. Cambridge: Polity.

Müller, Wolfgang P. (2012). *The Criminalization of Abortion in the West: Its Origins in Medieval Law*. Ithaca: Cornell University Press.

Myrc, John (1902). *Instructions for Parish Priests*. Ed. Edward Peacock. London: Kegan Paul Trench, Trübner & Co.

Noonan, John T., Jr. (1986). *Contraception: A History of Its Treatment by the Catholic Theologians and Canonists*, 2nd edn. Cambridge, MA: Harvard University Press.

Payer, Pierre (1993). *The Bridling of Desire: Views of Sex in the Later Middle Ages*. Toronto: University of Toronto Press.

Payer, Pierre (1984). *Sex and the Penitentials*. Toronto: University of Toronto Press.

Peraldus, Guillielmus (1588). *Summae Virtutem et Vitiorum*. Antwerp: Marinus Nutius.

Reynolds, Philip Lyndon (1994). *Marriage in the Western Church: The Christianization of Marriage During the Patristic and Early Medieval Periods*. Leiden: E.J. Brill.

Rossiaud, Jacques (1988). *Medieval Prostitution*. Trans. Lydia G. Cochrane. Oxford: Basil Blackwell.

Rousseau, Constance (1999). 'Pater Urbis et orbis': Innocent III and his Perspectives on Fatherhood', *Archivum Historiae Pontificae*, 37: 25–37.

Rubin, Miri (2009). *Mother of God: A History of the Virgin Mary*. London: Allen Lane.

Salih, Sarah (2001). *Versions of Virginity in Late Medieval England*. Cambridge: D.S. Brewer.

Schmugge, Ludwig (1995). *Kinder, Kirche, Karrieren: Päpstliche Dispense von der unehelichen Geburt im Spätmittelalter*. Zurich: Artemis & Winkler.

Smith, Katherine Allen (2005). 'Mary or Michael? Saint-Switching, Gender, and Sanctity in a Medieval Miracle of Childbirth', *Church History*, 74: 758–783.

Stuard, Susan Mosher (2008). 'Satisfying the Laws: The Legenda of Maria of Venice'. In Ruth Mazo Karras, Joel B. Kaye, and E. Ann Matter (eds), *Law and the Illicit in Medieval Europe*. Philadelphia: University of Pennsylvania Press, 197–210.

Thibodeaux, Jennifer D., ed. (2010). *Negotiating Clerical Identities: Priests, Monks, and Masculinity in the Middle Ages*. Basingstoke: Palgrave.

Treggiari, Susan (1991). *Roman Marriage: Iusti Coniuges from the Time of Cicero to the Time of Ulpian*. Oxford: Clarendon Press.

Wenzel, Siegfried (1989) (ed. and trans). *Fasciculus Morum: A Fourteenth-Century Preacher's Handbook*. University Park: Pennsylvania State University Press.

Wertheimer, Laura (2006). 'Children of Disorder: Clerical Parentage, Illegitimacy, and reform in the Middle Ages'. *Journal of the History of Sexuality*, 15: 382–407.

....

CHAPTER 18

CHASTE BODIES, SALACIOUS THOUGHTS

The Sexual Trials of the Medieval Clergy

....

DYAN ELLIOTT

INTRODUCTION: THE HIGH COST OF CHASTITY

....

IN theory, the medieval cleric was set apart from laypeople by virtue of his chastity. Although this was a portentous, and often onerous, commitment, it was nevertheless a condition that offered substantial rewards. Chastity brought with it extra merit in heaven—an opportunity to join the 144,000 unsullied virgins who followed the Lamb (Rev. 14:3–4). But the high premium placed on the undefiled body meant that a vow of chastity was not only irrevocable, but could not be parsed or converted into anything else because there was nothing else of equal value. Yet while a cleric may be chaste by vocation, and perhaps even inclination, his exposure to sexual matters of both a theoretical and practical nature was not only something of an occupational hazard, but one that would increase as the Middle Ages progressed. What follows is a survey of the many licit, and even obligatory, ways that sex impinged on the cleric's life both discursively and experientially.

THE TEMPTATIONS OF LITERACY

....

Because the Bible was perceived as the unfolding of God's plan for humanity, medieval society revered literacy and learning to a degree that has no parallel in contemporary society. The clergy was necessarily literate in order to interpret scripture, so part of this reverence was projected onto them. Yet a heightened adulation of learning was concomitant with the awareness that literacy could work to both positive and negative ends: Augustine was converted by a passage of a bible he opened at random; but Dante's Paolo and Francesca fell into adultery while reading about the adulterous love of Lancelot and Guinevere.[1] The tendency was, of course, to regard scripture itself as a source of edification, even though there was considerable sexual content that did not easily conform with this expectation. In such instances, medieval intellectuals looked for the allegorical meaning. Medieval readings of the Song of Songs exemplify this tendency. On the most literal level, it is a very sensual, often sexually explicit, love poem regarding an expectant bride's longing for her groom. Even the most learned exegete would be bound to acknowledge this. Traditionally, however, the poem was read allegorically with the groom as Christ and the bride either as the soul, the Virgin Mary, or the Church. The many monastic commentaries on the Song of Songs are invariably allegorized (Turner 1995). This interpretative strategy may strip it of explicit sexual innuendo, but the sensuality still remains.

Besides the Song of Songs, there were any number of sexually explicit passages in the Bible that might not seem to lend themselves so easily to allegory. Consider, for example, the instance of Lot offering his virginal daughters to the people of Sodom and Gomorrah to forestall their sexual abuse of the messengers of God (Gen. 19:4–9). Yet, medieval exegesis demonstrates that it was possible to allegorize just about anything. According to the moralization of Nicholas of Lyra (d.1340), for example, the two daughters represented temporal pride and a life devoted to the body, which explains why the girls deserved to be sacrificed.[2] But the literal meaning was still considered edifying if it were used to proscribe certain sexual practices deemed unacceptable. Hence, Nicholas advances that Lot was prepared to prostitute his daughters in order to avoid a worse crime.[3]

Solitary Thoughts

The earliest monks were solitaries who lived in the deserts of modern-day Syria and Egypt. Tales concerning their valiant efforts at taming their bodies were destined to become one of the staples of clerical reading. One such ascetic, Abba Poemen, is credited with saying that fornication was one of two thoughts (the other was slander) that 'should never be talked about or pondered in the heart, it does no good' (Ward 1975: 158). But since the purpose of ascetical discourse was primarily to discuss questions of temptation, topics such as fornication were constantly 'talked about' and 'pondered'. Moreover, such discussions are often accompanied by provocative images. When a certain monk announced that he had overcome the spirit of fornication, Abba Abraham tested this claim by asking '"If you were to find a woman lying on your mat when you entered your cell would you think that it is not a woman?"' (Ward 1975: 29).

---

[1] Augustine, *Confessions*, 8.12.29; Dante, *Divine Comedy, Inferno*, 5.1308–1321.
[2] Nicholas of Lyra 1603: i. 243 (Gen. 19, *Moraliter* ad v. *Habeo duas filias*).
[3] Nicholas of Lyra 1603: i. 243 (Gen. 19, Nicolaus de Lyre, ad v. *Habeo duas filias*).

An elder suffering from a grave illness goes to Egypt to seek a cure, maintaining all the while that he is virtually dead to the world. But he recovers sufficiently to rape the faithful virgin attending him.[4] A holy man is afflicted by demons transformed into beautiful women who for forty days try to tempt him into 'filthy intercourse'.[5] A harlot makes a bet with some ribald youths that she can seduce a holy man, turning up at his cell at night in order to make good her claim.[6] Even tales associated with allaying sexual temptation can evoke images of the female body. For instance, a brother asks an elder for help with his sordid thoughts in the following terms: 'When a woman wishes to wean her son, she rubs something bitter on her breasts and when he comes to suck as usual, he senses the bitterness and flees. Therefore send me some bitterness in my thoughts.'[7]

Such 'sayings' tend to be short and anecdotal, but this is not invariably the case. The *Conferences* of John Cassian (d. *c.*435) consist of twenty-three extended conversations between different holy men intended to provide a coherent discussion of the trials confronting an ascetic. The penultimate book is devoted to a discussion of nocturnal emissions, beginning with why they occur: 'Our forebears have taught that there are three causes for this onslaught, which occurs at irregular and inopportune moments. It is either stored up due to a surfeit of food, or it flows forth due to a careless mind, or it is provoked by the snares of the mocking enemy' (John Cassian 1997: 763–764 (22.3.1). After analysing the three causes in depth, Cassian engages moral questions like the ramifications of such emissions for cultic purity, or the degree of culpability during sleep. Although written for remedial purposes, the discussion was sufficiently frank that the venerable series of translations contained in the *Library of Nicene and Post-Nicene Fathers of the Church* saw fit to omit it altogether, presumably to forestall the prurient reader.[8]

Hagiography also had its sexual moments. A discussion of a given saint's conversion to a more holy life frequently entailed extensive treatment of a salacious past. Mary of Egypt, one of the few desert mothers, was a courtesan so filled with lust that she often refused money for her favours. She went to the Holy Land in search of new clients and paid for her passage with her body—a journey which she describes as follows:

> Whose tongue can tell, whose ears can take in all that took place on the boat during that voyage! And to all this I frequently forced those miserable youths even against their own will. There is no mentionable or unmentionable depravity of which I was not their teacher. I am amazed, Abba, how the sea stood our licentiousness, how the earth did not open its jaws, and how it was that hell did not swallow me alive, when I had entangled in my net so many souls.
>
> (Andrew of Crete 1967: 88)

---

[4] *Verba seniorum*, 5.35, in *PL* lxxiii. 833.
[5] *Verba seniorum*, 5.36, in *PL* lxxiii. 883.
[6] *Verba seniorum*, 5.37, in *PL* lxxiii. 844.
[7] *Verba seniorum*, 5.30, in *PL* lxxiii. 881.
[8] <http://www.newadvent.org/fathers/3508.htm>. Bk. 22 is now translated by Ramsey in John Cassian (1997: 761–82).

In matters of the imagination, however, less is often more. Thus in the *Life of Saint Antony*, when Athanasius (d.373) recounts how the devil, appearing as a woman, 'imitated all her acts simply to beguile Antony', the reader is tacitly invited to fill in the blanks created by this euphemistic treatment (Athanasius 1994: iv. 197 (c. 5)). Such tales of ascetical heroics also share in the medieval tendency to teach by negative example. Hence when discussing the insidious snares of the spirit of fornication, there are instances in which monks fall not only to women, but even to donkeys (John Climacus 1982: 174–175 (c. 17); Salisbury 1991: 175–176).

The Temptations of Texts

Theology could provide considerable food for sexual thought, the influence of the Church Father Augustine of Hippo (d.430) being paramount in this regard. Many theologians prior to Augustine had tended to see the sexed body, sexual activity, and in some cases even embodiment, as punitive repercussions of the sin of Adam and Eve. These authors understood God's injunction to be fruitful and multiply in purely spiritual terms. Although Augustine was initially sympathetic to this view, he vehemently denounced it in his later works, maintaining not only that Adam and Eve had been created in sexed bodies, but also that they were intended to have sex in Eden (Brown 1987: 399–401). Unfortunately, the fall forced the first couple to relocate before they had a chance to engage sexually, so the first sex act was, in fact, post-lapsarian. This did not stop Augustine from speculating what sex would have been like had Adam and Eve not fallen, positing that the body would have been entirely subjected to reason and that the penis would be moved voluntarily like any other member. By the same token, a woman's hymen would somehow remain intact after sex. Augustine's authoritative views made their way into *The Sentences* of Peter Lombard (d.1164)—a work upon which every aspiring master of theology would be required to write a commentary well into the early modern period (Peter Lombard 2007–2010: ii. 86–87 (2.20.1.3)). The potential salaciousness of Augustine's treatment is again recognized by the editors of *The Library of Nicene and Post-Nicene Fathers of the Church*: in their translation of *The City of God*, the offending passages are left in the original Latin.[9]

The rise of scholasticism in the high Middle Ages was animated by a rediscovery of Aristotle and the philosopher's incumbent emphasis on nature. This, in turn, inspired an ardent interest in all of God's creation, including demons. Scholastic purview even extended to their fiendish erotics. Biblical warrant for discussion of demonic sexuality could be found in the episode in which the sons of God, often understood as angels, begot children of the daughters of men, giving rise to a race of giants (Gen. 6:2). Out of deference to angels, later patristic authorities were inclined to allegorize the sons of God as holy men or members of the clergy (Elliott 2012: 55–56). Yet in the thirteenth

---

[9] Augustine, *City of God*, 14.26; <http://www.newadvent.org/fathers/120114.htm>.

century, when it was determined that angels and demons were entirely immaterial, theologians nevertheless had not abandoned the belief that there were incubi who had sex, and even offspring, with mortals—giving rise to some bizarre explanations. According to Thomas Aquinas (d.1274), angels, both good and bad, would assume bodies that they had contrived in order to appear to men, and even have sexual relations:

> Still if some [children] are occasionally begotten from demons, it is not from the seed of such demons, nor from their assumed bodies, but from the seed of men taken for the purpose; as when the demon assumes first the form of a woman, and afterwards of a man; just as they take the seed of other things for other generating purposes, as Augustine says (De Trin. ii.), so that the person born is not the child of a demon, but of a man.[10]

Popular writers, such as the Cistercian Caesarius of Heisterbach (d.1240), were well informed about the overtures that sexually predatory demons made to religious personnel—particularly nuns (Caesarius of Heisterbach 1929: i. 130, 140–141, 377–382 (3.6, 3.13, 5.44–7); Elliott 2012: 239–241).

All of the texts just discussed were unmistakable products of a clerical ambience. But medieval clerics were also exposed to a series of profane texts in the course of attaining their mandatory literacy. Certain classical authors, like Ovid, became staples of the medieval classroom, regaling students with both excellent rhetorical models and spicy stories involving sex (Coulson 2011; Pairet 2011). Eventually works like the *Ovid moralisé* arose in an attempt to find edifying analogies for these pagan tales. The rise of schools in the twelfth century also coincided with a renewed interest in the classical art of memory, which cultivated imaginative techniques as mnemonic devices. For instance, students were encouraged to associate material they wished to commit to memory with striking, even shocking, images. To this end, Peter of Ravenna devised an alphabet of human figures featuring alluring women: 'these greatly stimulate my memory' (Carruthers 1990: 109).

An influx of medical writings from the Arab world provided the clerical intelligentsia with an unprecedented opportunity to make the body and sexuality the actual focus of study. Among the earliest of such texts was *On Coitus*—translated from the Arabic by Constantine the African (d.1078). The influential *Canon of Medicine*, whose author was the Persian physician and polymath Avicenna (d.1037), was translated from the Arabic in the twelfth century.[11] There was also a corpus of literature on the female reproductive system, and its diseases, circulating under the name of *Trotula* (Green 2001). These texts provide very frank discussions of human sexuality. Their impact will, in turn, be reflected by the authors who imbibed these materials. Albert the Great (d.1280), who

---

[10] Thomas Aquinas, *Summa Theologica*, 1a a. 51 art. 3, resp. ad 6, <http://www.newadvent.org/summa/1051.htm>.

[11] Constantine the African 2010: 511–23; Avicenna 1574: fols. 279^r–293^v (bk. 3, fen. 20–21). See Jacquart and Thomasset (1988); Cadden (1993).

was technically a theologian, nevertheless wrote voluminously on nature and the animal kingdom, including the human animal. His book *On Animals* provides a frank and non-judgemental discussion of sexual desire in a young pubescent girl, describing how the changes in her body provoke sexual fantasies that result in masturbation (Albert the Great 1890–9: xi. 497 (26.9.1.1); Elliott 1999: 45–46).

Albert the Great's student, Thomas of Cantimpré (d.1272), wrote *On the Nature of Things*, which discusses the sexual organs, generative seed, and conception. Thomas seems more sensitive to the volatility of his subject matter than his teacher, however, beginning his treatment of the genitalia with the disclaimer that 'Many things that ought to be written about the penis and the womb we are dismissing on account of the modesty of those who do not care to read or hear about such things' (Thomas of Cantimpré 1973: 65 (1.60)). The subsequent discussions tend to focus on diseases of the genitalia, while the treatment of generation privileges seed and temperature over the sex act itself. But medical discourse also contributed to, and doubtless stimulated, the ever-present anti-feminism of the Middle Ages. This is epitomized in a work entitled *Women's Secrets*—a thirteenth-century treatise falsely attributed to Albert that circulated in theological circles. The commentaries that circulated with the text are especially virulent, alleging, for example, that there were women who implant iron in their vaginas specifically to damage the penis (Lemay 1992: 87, 88). Such scare tactics may have been crude efforts to counterbalance the effects of any salacious thoughts inspired by the subject matter.

THE STRUGGLE FOR CHASTITY

Thus far I have been treating clerical chastity as if that discipline were omnipresent or uncontested, neither of which is true. Even though the ascetical tradition privileging chastity was present from the earliest days of the Church, the first concerted efforts to impose chastity on the priesthood only begin in the fourth century and make little headway for centuries. In fact when the papal reform was initiated in the mid-eleventh century, many, if not most, members of the clergy were married. Although the reformers would eventually succeed in making clerical marriage illegal, it proved impossible to eradicate clerical concubinage (Karras 2012: ch. 3).

This ongoing struggle for chastity gave rise to a burgeoning discourse stigmatizing sexually errant priests—often appearing in stray, anecdotal indictments across many different genres. For instance, the historian Flodoard relates how Genebaud (d. *c*.555), bishop of Laon, had separated from his wife when he became bishop but still continued to visit her for 'religious instruction'. The children that resulted from these conjugal visits were assigned punitive names like Latro (thief) or Vulpecula (little fox) (Flodoard 1881: xiii. 425 (1.4)). Fornicating priests who continued to say Mass were perceived as risking their souls by drinking unworthily to their own damnation (1 Cor. 11:29). A biography of Charlemagne recounts how the emperor, having heard a rumour about a fornicating bishop, sent two court officials to investigate by insisting on a Mass without warning:

> Fearing men more than he feared God, he bathed his sweaty limbs in ice-cold spring-water and then went forward to offer the awe-inspiring sacraments…He was brought to his death by a frightful attack of fever and compelled to submit his soul to the decree of the strict and eternal Judge.
>
> (Notker 1969: 121–122 (1.25))

In the high Middle Ages, such disparate accounts are supplemented by a number of spiritual miscellanies which highlight clerical misdemeanours by way of dramatic deterrents. Caesarius of Heisterbach claims (without any justification) that the priest Oza died when he stretched out his hand to steady the Ark of the Covenant because he had had sex with his wife the night before (2 Kings 6:7). The moral is: 'If a priest going to raise the figurative ark is punished with death for this cause, what punishment do you think the priests deserve if being adulterers and fornicators they touch the true body of Christ with defiled hands?' (Caesarius of Heisterbach 1929: ii. 157–158 (9.53)). Sometimes divine intervention forestalls such defilement. Caesarius recounts how a fornicating priest is spared the fate of the Carolingian bishop by a dove, which miraculously drinks the wine in the chalice and carries off the Host. This happens repeatedly until the priest confesses. But often the clerical offenders end up dying tragically. When an apostate monk fell grievously ill, he deliriously began shouting out the names of his past lovers in despair (Caesarius of Heisterbach 1929: i. 70–72, 21–22 (2.5, 1.14)).

The Sin Against Nature

While the discourse condemning the clergy's heterosexual infractions will remain a constant throughout the period, it is only in the high Middle Ages that a discourse stigmatizing same-sex relations begins to emerge. An early instance occurs during the eleventh century, when most reforming zeal was focused on the suppression of clerical wives. The monk and cardinal Peter Damian (d.1072) luridly describes clerical wives as concubines of the devil bent on raping a vulnerable priesthood (Peter Damian 1989–2005: v. 276–277 (Ep. 122, c. 34–5); Elliott 1999: 100–106). Yet Peter Damian was rather exceptional in his vision of a clergy that was not just free from sexual contact with women, but entirely chaste. The result was a treatise entitled *The Book of Gomorrah* which denounced the same-sex relations that he claimed were endemic among the clergy. In the course of determining which type of offence merits greater penance, he provides a very detailed description of the vice he sought to suppress:

> [T]here appear to be four varieties of this criminal vice. There are some who pollute themselves; there are others who befoul one another by mutually handling their genitals; others still who fornicate between the thighs and others who do so from the rear. Certainly a greater penance must be imposed on those who sin with others than on those who masturbate alone; and more severe judgment is to be passed on those

who corrupt others through anal intercourse than on those who couple between the thighs.

(Peter Damian 1989–2005: ii. 6–7 (Ep. 31, c. 8); Jordan 1997: 45–66)

Peter Damian's treatise received a cool reception from Leo IX, to whom it was dedicated (Boswell 1972: 210–213). But at the end of the twelfth century, Alan of Lille's *Plaint of Nature* would again attack same-sex relations. Taking the form of a rather ironical allegory, *The Plaint* casts sexual transgression as a contravention of grammatical rules:

He is subject and predicate: one and the same term is given a double application. Man here extends too far the laws of grammar. Becoming a barbarian grammar, he disclaims the manhood given him by nature…That man, in whose case a simple conversion in the Art causes Nature's laws to come to naught, is pushing logic too far. He hammers on an anvil which issues no seeds. The very hammer itself shudders in horror of its anvil.

(Alan of Lille 1980: 68–69 (meter 1); Boswell 1972: 310–311; Jordan 1997: 67–92)

By the thirteenth century, same-sex relations (progressively known as sodomy) will start to be stigmatized in various spiritual miscellanies as a sin against nature. According to Thomas of Cantimpré, offenders rarely repent—remaining as mute as the people from Sodom. The few who do confess tend to backslide. This is in spite of the fact that clerics guilty of the crime literally die screaming with horror. Thomas tells of a classmate—'especially good, chaste, and dear'—who was seduced by one of his masters. At the behest of his family and friends, he attempted to give up the vice many times, but always returned to it. He died in despair, telling his friends to warn his seducer to repent, but recognizing it was too late for himself. He could already see the demons ready to drag him off to hell. According to Thomas, sodomy was considered sufficiently heinous to postpone the incarnation. When Christ, the epitome of purity, finally did arrive, all sodomites perished. The 'unnaturalness' of sodomy is even reflected by the response of the natural world: the very ground that a sodomite walks or sits upon was said to dry up (Thomas of Cantimpré 1627: 323–326 (2.30.8–13); Elliott 1999: 151–152).

More Sins Against Nature

While presenting sodomy as an exclusively male vice, Thomas of Cantimpré followed his teacher, Albert the Great, in the conviction that women, especially nuns, were more prone to masturbation—also classified as a sin against nature. On the authority of Albert, Thomas argues that such an individual 'polluted by the delight of the flux of concupiscence' is no longer a virgin—even with her hymen intact (Thomas of Cantimpré 1627: 315 (2.29.35)). There are also posthumous consequences: a wicked old woman, pretending sanctity while indulging in this vice, was buried in the cloister. But the next day a black sow and her piglets dug up her body and spread her entrails throughout the cloister. The nuns could not see the pigs but could hear their demonic grunting very clearly. Fortunately, most of the women depicted seem to confess this sin and do sufficient penance (or, if they die prematurely, time in Purgatory) and not suffer relapses (Thomas of Cantimpré 1627: 320–322 (2.30. 3–5)).

As in Cassian's time, nocturnal emissions continue to be flagged as an area of concern in such works. Although not technically considered sinful (unless the person in question somehow solicited the experience or consented to the inherent pleasure after the fact), such emissions were often regarded as the result of a previous sin, such as gluttony, and evidence of a less-than-perfect nature.[12] The general consensus was that it was safest to confess such experiences just in case—a point frequently made in extremely vivid ways. Peter Damian relates how a resistant demon taunted his exorcist as follows: "'Have you forgotten what I did to you last night?... [A]fter I disguised myself as a wild boar in the forest, you pursued me as the hunter...But...I suddenly took the form of a beautiful woman, and running up to give you a kiss so that you would pollute yourself, was gloriously successful.'" If the devil is so triumphant over someone because of 'vivid dreams', just imagine his joy over adultery and incest, Peter Damian reasons. He takes this opportunity to segue into the tale of Robert the Pious, who was punished for an incestuous marriage by the birth of a goose-headed son (Peter Damian 1998: v. 135–136 (Ep. 102, c. 21–22)). Thomas of Cantimpré also has a tale about a monk who was humiliated when a demoniac said: "'Wasn't that a beautiful woman I brought you in your dreams last night?'"—a painful reminder that the monk had failed to confess his nocturnal emission (Thomas of Cantimpré 1627: 541 (2.57)).

With dramatic exempla such as these, it is not surprising that the nocturnal emission's degree of sinfulness remained an area of confusion. James of Vitry (d.1240) holds up for ridicule a priest who, allegedly thinking that nocturnal emissions were worse than fornication, told his various penitents that they should visit a prostitute rather than endure such pollution (James of Vitry 1914: 110–111 (24)). Indeed, John Gerson (d.1429) will eventually see fit to write treatises on both nocturnal emissions, specifically addressed to the clergy, and diurnal emissions in response to the confusion of clergy and laity of both sexes (Gerson, *De praeparatione ad missam*, 1973b: ix. 35–49; *De cognitione castitatis*, 1973a: ix. 64).

THE DANGERS OF CLERICAL DUTIES

But much of the clergy's exposure to sexual matters occurred in the line of duty, arbitrating questions of sexual morality. In his *Pastoral Rule*, Gregory the Great speaks very explicitly about the way such responsibilities could take their toll on the clerical psyche.

[12] See Thomas Aquinas on whether nocturnal emissions are mortal sins. *Summa Theologica*, 2a 2ae q.154, art. 5, <http://www.newadvent.org/summa/3154.htm>.

Now, it happens that, while the ruler's mind in his condescension learns of the trials of others, he also is assailed by the temptations that he gives ear to; for in the case of the laver, too, that was mentioned as serving the cleansing of the multitude, it is certainly defiled. In receiving the filth of those who wash in it, it loses its limpid clearness. But the pastor need not fear these things at all, for when God weighs all things exactly, the pastor is the more easily delivered from temptation, as he is the more compassionately afflicted by the temptations.

(Gregory the Great 1978: 59 (2.5))

A celebrated case in the Carolingian era suggests the extent to which a prelate might be required to condescend to the trials of others. In 858, Emperor Lothar II attempted to repudiate his sterile wife, Theutberga, in order to marry his mistress, Waldreda. When the empress refused to go quietly, Lothar and his agents developed a number of trumped-up charges indicting Theutberga, claiming that she had conceived as a result of incest with her brother and subsequently procured an abortion. Since she was allegedly impregnated in the course of anal sex, however, she remained an intact virgin when she married Lothar (Hincmar of Reims 1992: 114 (interr. 1)). Hincmar, archbishop of Reims, dedicated an entire treatise to refuting these charges. Not surprisingly, the treatise was prefaced with a carefully worded disclaimer: '[N]o one ought to shun us as unchaste [because of our attention to] the unchaste things of this kind, whose modest ears flee, blushing.' To his mind: 'Nobody ought even to be provoked hearing the filthy things of illnesses, which the venomous cunning of diabolical malignity inflicts on human fragility.' In the event that contact with such provocative material does have a deleterious effect, Hincmar cites the passage from Gregory the Great's *Pastoral Care* by way of reassurance (Hincmar of Reims 1992: 113 (preface); Heidecker 2010; Bishop 1985).

As the Middle Ages progressed, the Church developed a hegemony over marriage, which would be consolidated at the end of the twelfth century with its inclusion in the definitive list of seven sacraments. Marital problems were now unequivocally the domain of the Church, inviting the clergy into the private life of the laity in an unprecedented manner (Brundage 1987: chs. 6–9). The clergy were also responsible for policing the sexual relations of husband and wife, referred to as the conjugal debt. This term was inherited from Paul (1 Cor. 7:3), who had described husband and wife as sexual debtors to one another, incapable of refusing sex lest the other fall into fornication (Makowski 1977). That church officials took Paul at his word is evident by the range of problems they were prepared to address. First there was the concern that both parties were both capable of rendering the debt in the first place. In the event that the husband seemed impotent, a procedure arose in which the courts assigned matrons to examine and sometimes attempt to arouse the male to see if the impediment were permanent (Murray 1990). Canon lawyers discussed what to do in the event that a woman's hymen was too thick to be penetrated or the man's organ was too large. Then there were the difficult conditions under which you would still be compelled to render the debt if asked. In one of his rulings, Alexander III required a wife to pay the debt to a leprous husband. Theologians debated whether the debt could be exacted during holy days; in church; during a wife's pregnancy; her period—usually resolving these questions in favour of the debt (Brundage 1987: 283, 335, 339, 451–452; Elliott 1993: 146–162; Elliott 1996: 168–200; Elliott 1999: 61–80).

Ecclesiastical courts treated cases in which the marriage contract had been breached—whether through adultery, desertion, bigamy, or consanguinity (Helmholz 1974). They also meted out punishment for the sexual misdemeanours of the unmarried. The following entry from 1347, appearing in the court register for the dean and chapter of Lincoln, is representative:

> William Wythlack is noted for fornication with Alicia de Torkeseye...The woman appeared and confessed the sin and was assigned a pilgrimage to Lincoln barefoot to offer a bound of wax at the altar of Blessed Mary. She abjured her sin with the penalty of 18 d.
>
> (Poos 2001: 217)

The succinct nature of such accounts should not eclipse the fact that the clergy, in the course of these cases, would necessarily become intimately involved in the personal lives of their spiritual charges. And sometimes this would mean they became privy to some rather strange scenarios. The case brought before the deanery of Wisbech in 1460 is suggestive in this context:

> Johannes [Freman] appeared dressed in women's clothing around the middle of the night the last Sunday before Advent and at the same time, his wife entered the bedroom of the said John Digby with others, illicitly breaking the law and [acting] against her honesty. And what she was looking for and did there or for what reason is not known.
>
> (Poos 2001: 316)

One can only imagine what (sexual) bodies are buried in this inflected account.

Of course, the higher clergy were also responsible for policing the lower clergy. Bishops were required to make the rounds of their dioceses, correcting the clergy's sexual misconduct which, in some cases, may have been a full-time job. The following entry in the register of Bishop Eudes of Rouen is not unusual.

> [24 January 1252] Walter, priest at Herecourt, has for many years been ill famed of incontinence, and is still so, albeit he has been warned many times about this. However, after the said warnings he promised us that he would resign his aforesaid church at our command, if it should happen that he should be again defamed of this crime and the ill fame should be substantiated, and he could not purge himself of this vice. Today he appeared before us and confessed that after all the warnings and the promises he had made he had scandalously suffered a relapse, and he resigned his church.
>
> (Eudes of Rouen 1964: 170)

Penitence and Penitents

But undoubtedly the priest's most intimate look into the sexual lives of his parishioners occurred in the course of hearing of confession. In the early Middle Ages, special handbooks known as penitentials were developed to assist the priest with this task. Private auricular confession began in, and was probably largely confined to, clerical circles in the early period. These works still included special sections devoted to offences to which a layperson might be prone, however. Hence we find terse sanctions against a husband's intercourse with his wife 'from behind' or 'in the anus'—characterizations which could be construed as provocative by themselves—even if there was no penitent involved (McNeill and Gamer [1938] 1990: 62; Payer 1984).

In the twelfth century, confession became more widespread among the laity, culminating in the mandate by the Fourth Lateran Council (1215) that every person confess a minimum of once a year. The penitentials had consisted primarily of crude lists of tariffs that often seemed arbitrary in assigning penance. Sacerdotal aids became much were sophisticated both anticipating and in the wake of Lateran IV, deploying casuistry as a means of understanding how both external and internal circumstances might affect a priest's assessment of a sin (Payer 2009). Robert of Flamborough's *Liber poenitentialis* (1208 × 1213) shows an awareness of the seductiveness of discourse itself, warning that sins against nature should only be extorted with great caution but the manner of extortion should not be written down (Robert of Flamborough, 4.224, 1971: 197). Others were sensitive to the interactive nature of confession and the way it might scandalize the priest. Peter the Chanter (d.1197) raises the question of a layperson who 'has a simple priest who would be corrupted easily if he were to make new discoveries in sin, in the 1000 ways of having sex... should confess to him his sins with the circumstances'. He ultimately answers the question in the negative (Peter the Chanter 1957: pt. 2, 310 (c. 134)).

Female penitents were construed as a particular challenge when it came to confession because of the temptation they afforded. Thomas of Cantimpré admits freely that his experience with female penitents was excruciating—at least until of St Lutgard of Aywières intervened with her prayers (Murray 1998: 72–3; Elliott 2003: 31–51; Thomas of Cantimpré 2008: 65–66). Some authorities will devise strategies for reducing temptation: Raymond of Peñafort (d.1275) advises priests to sit across from women and avoid looking into their faces; Humbert of Romans (d.1277) insists that confessions be made in public where both parties can actually be seen by others.

Antoninus of Florence (d.1459) urges confessors to be stern and speak harshly (Raymond of Peñafort 1603: 464–465 (3.34.30); Humbert of Romans 1888: ii. 368 (46.11); Antoninus of Florence 1507?: fo. 28^r (3.11)). Even so, the relationship between confessor and penitent was often extremely close. This was especially true when a woman was attempting to live a holy life in the world, in which case her confessor generally becomes the de facto spiritual director. Matthew of Cracow (d.1410) is extremely suspicious of the kind of spiritual intimacy that ensues from such relationships—urging confessors to distance themselves, but cynically observing that the women will probably just change confessors. This is also at the root of Humbert of Romans' apprehension of Beguines, warning confessors to guard against their desire for frequent confession and conversation. But John of Freiburg (d.1314) acknowledges that, however cautious the confessor might be, a certain amount of temptation is inevitable when it comes to carnal sins—especially when he is learning about certain acts for the first time. He is philosophical about it, however, citing Gregory the Great's rationale, and arguing that the temptation would be that much more bearable if occasioned in the line of duty (Matthew of Cracow, before 1501: c. 20 [no pagination]; Humbert of Romans 1888: ii. 368 (46.11); John of Freiburg, 1518: fo. 192^r).

Of course, the confession of a priest to another priest could be just as provocative as any lay penitent—perhaps more so. The seventh-century Penitential of Theodore censures the *Various Failings of the Servants of God* as follows:

1. If a priest is polluted in touching or in kissing a woman he shall do penance for forty days....
6. A monk or a holy virgin who commits fornication shall do penance for seven years....
7. He who pollutes himself through the violence of his imagination shall do penance for twenty days....
8. He who when asleep in a church pollutes himself shall do penance for three days....
9. For masturbation, the first time he shall do penance for twenty days, on repetition, forty days.
10. If 'in femoribus' [he ejaculates between another's thighs], one year... (McNeill and Gamer [1938] 1990: 191–192)

In the high Middle Ages, moreover, a hypothetical confession was inserted in Robert of Flamborough's (1971: app. B, 297–299) text that reads like a high comedy routine.

PRIEST: Did you approach a menstruating woman, a pregnant woman or a woman not yet purified?
PENITENT: Often ...
PRIEST: Have you sinned with a man?
PENITENT: With many.
PRIEST: Did you introduce any innocent party to this?
PENITENT: Three scholars and one subdeacon.
PRIEST: Tell how many you abused and how often and your rank and their ranking ...
PENITENT: I am a subdeacon and [I did it with] three subdeacons for half a year; and a married man once ...
PRIEST: Have you had nocturnal pollutions?
PENITENT: Frequently.

The degree to which an individual cleric would be affected by matters sexual was bound to be highly idiosyncratic, as would the strategies advanced for addressing the problem. For some, the most banal experience could be sexually provocative. Gregory the Great tells how the devil appeared before Benedict in the form of a little blackbird, which somehow brought to mind 'a woman he had once seen, and before he realized it his emotions were carrying him away'. The saint threw himself into a convenient thorn bush to combat the feeling of pleasure. Others became impervious to temptation over time. Gregory maintains that Abbot Equitius' sexual temptation was vanquished by an angelic castration while still a young man (Gregory the Great 1959: 58–59, 16 (2.2, 1.4)). For those who are not this fortunate, Gregory prescribes a regimen of hard work, confident that time will eventually come to the rescue: 'It is a well-known fact … that temptations of the flesh are violent during youth, whereas after the age of fifty concupiscence dies down … God's chosen servants must therefore obey and serve and tire themselves out with strenuous work as long as they are still subject to temptations' (Gregory the Great 1959: 60 (2.2)).

For the priest who is impervious to every strategy, even the passage of time, there is always the advice that Abelard gave to his son: if you can't be chaste, be careful (Dronke 1970: 149).

REFERENCES

Primary Sources

Alan of Lille (1980). *The Plaint of Nature.* Trans. James J. Sheridan. Toronto: Pontifical Institute of Mediaeval Studies.

Albert the Great (1890–1899). *Animalium libri XXVI.* In *Opera Omnia*, vols. xi–xii. Ed. A. Borgnet. Paris: Vivès.

Andrew of Crete (1967). *The Great Canon.* Compiled by the Holy Trinity Monastery. Jordanville, NY: Printshop of St Job of Pochaev.

Antoninus of Florence (1507). *Confessionale Anthonini.* Paris: Jehan Petit.

Athanasius ([1892] 1994), *Life of Antony. In A Select Library of Nicene and Post-Nicene Fathers*, 2nd ser., iv. 188–221. Ed. Philip Schaff and Henry Wace. Repr. Peabody, MA: Hendrickson.

Avicenna (1574). *Liber canonis medicine.* Venice: Andrea Bellunensis.

Caesarius of Heisterbach (1929). *The Dialogue on Miracles*, 2 vols. Trans. H. Von E. Scott and C. C. Swinton Bland. London: Routledge.

Constantine the African (2010). *De coitu.* In Faith Wallis (ed.), *Medieval Medicine: A Reader.* Toronto: University of Toronto Press, 511–523.

Eudes of Rouen (1964). *The Register of Eudes of Rouen.* Trans. Sydney M. Brown. New York: Columbia University Press.

Flodoard (1881). *Historia Remensis ecclesiae.* In J. Heller and G. Waitz (eds), *Monumenta Germaniae Historica, Scriptores*, xiii. 405–599. Hanover: Impensis Bibliopolii Hahniani.

Gerson, John (1973a). *De cognitione castitatis.* In *Œuvres complètes*, 10 vols. in 11. Ed. Palémon Glorieux. Paris: Desclée, ix. 50–64.

Gerson, John (1973b). *De praeparatione ad missam. In Œuvres complètes,* 10 vols. in 11. Ed. Palémon Glorieux. Paris: Desclée, ix. 35–49.

Green, Monica (2001) (ed. and trans.). *Trotula: A Medieval Compendium of Women's Medicine.* Philadelphia: University of Pennsylvania Press.

Gregory the Great (1959). *Dialogues.* Trans. Odo John Zimmerman. *Fathers of the Church,* vol. xxxix. New York: Fathers of the Church.

Gregory the Great (1978). *Pastoral Care.* Trans. Henry Davis. *Ancient Christian Writers,* vol. xi. New York: Newman Press.

Hincmar of Reims (1992). *De divortio Lotharii Regis et Theutbergae Reginae.* Ed. Letha Böhringer, *Monumenta Germaniae Historica: Concilia,* iv, suppl. 1. Hanover: Hansche.

Humbert of Romans (1888). *Opera de vita regulari,* 2 vols. Ed. Joachim Joseph Berthier. Rome: A. Befani.

James of Vitry (1914). *Die Exempla des Jacob von Vitry.* Ed. Goswin Frenken. Munich: C. H. Becksche.

John Cassian (1997). *Conferences.* Trans. Boniface Ramsey. New York: Paulist Press.

John Climacus (1982). *The Ladder.* Trans. Colm Luibheid and Norman Russell. New York: Paulist Press.

John of Freiburg (1518). *Summa confessorum.* Rome: n.pub.

Lemay, Helen Rodnite (1992) (trans.). *Women's Secrets: A Translation of the Pseudo-Albertus Magnus's 'De secretis mulierum' with Commentaries.* Albany, NY: State University of New York Press.

McNeill, J. T., and Helena M. Gamer ([1938] 1990) (eds. and trans.). *Medieval Handbooks of Penance.* New York: Columbia University Press.

Matthew of Cracow (before 1501). *De modo confitendi et de puritate conscientiae.* Paris: n.pub.

Nicholas of Lyra (1603). *Postilla. In Bibliorum Sacrorum cum Glossa: Ordinaria,* 6 vols. Venice: n. pub.

Notker the Stammerer (1969). *Charlemagne: In Two Lives of Charlemagne.* Trans. Lewis Thorpe. Harmondsworth: Penguin, 93–172.

Peter Damian (1989–2005). *Letters of Peter Damian,* 7 vols. Trans. Owen J. Blum and Irven M. Resnick. *Fathers of the Church, Mediaeval Continuation.* Washington, DC: Catholic University of America Press.

Peter Lombard (2007–2010). *The Sentences,* 4 vols. Trans. Giulio Silano. Toronto: Pontifical Institute of Mediaeval Studies.

Peter the Chanter (1954–1967). *Summa de sacramentis et animae consiliis,* 3 pts. in 5 vols. Ed. Jean-Albert Dugauquier. Analecta Mediaevalia Namurcensia, vols iv, vii, xi, xvi, xxi. Louvain: Nauwelaerts; Lille: Librairie Giard.

Poos, Lawrence Raymond (2001). *Lower Ecclesiastical Jurisdiction in Late-Medieval England: The Courts of the Dean and Chapter of Lincoln, 1336–1349, and the Deanery of Wisbech, 1458–1484.* Records of Social and Economic History, ns 32. Oxford: Oxford University Press.

Raymond of Peñafort (1603). *Summa de poenitentia et matrimonio.* Rome: Joannes Tallini.

Robert of Flamborough (1971). *Liber poenitentiales.* Ed. J. J. Firth. Toronto: Pontifical Institute of Mediaeval Studies.

Thomas Aquinas. *Summa theologica.* <http://www.newadvent.org/summa/3154.htm>.

Thomas of Cantimpré (1627). *Bonum universal de apibus.* Douai: B. Belleri.

Thomas of Cantimpré (1973). *Liber de natura rerum.* Ed. H. Boese. Berlin: Walter de Gruyter.

Thomas of Cantimpré (2008). *Life of Lutgard of Aywières. In Thomas of Cantimpré: The Collected Saints Lives.* Trans. Margot King and Barbara Newman. Turnhout: Brepols, 211–296.

Verba seniorum. In Patrologiae cursus completus...series Latina (1846), ed. J.-P. Migne, 221 vols. Paris: Garnier Fratres and J.-P. Migne, lxxiii. 739–809.
Ward, Benedicta (1975) (trans.). *The Sayings of the Desert Fathers: The Alphabetical Collection.* London: Mowbrays.

Secondary Sources

Bishop, Jane (1985). 'Bishops as Marital Advisors in the Ninth Century'. In Julius Kirshner and Suzanne F. Wemple (eds), *Women of the Medieval World*. Oxford: Basil Blackwell, 54–84.
Boswell, John (1972). *Christianity, Social Tolerance, and Homosexuality: Gay People in Western Europe from the Beginning of the Christian Era to the Fourteenth Century*. Chicago: University of Chicago Press.
Brown, Peter (1987). *The Body and Society: Men, Women, and Sexual Renunciation in Early Christianity*. New York: Columbia University Press.
Brundage, James. A. (1987). *Law, Sex, and Christian Society in Medieval Europe*. Chicago: University of Chicago Press.
Cadden, Joan (1993). *Meanings of Sex Difference in the Middle Ages: Medicine, Science, and Culture*. Cambridge: Cambridge University Press.
Carruthers, Mary (1990). *The Book of Memory: A Study of Memory in Medieval Culture*. Cambridge: Cambridge University Press.
Coulson, Frank T. (2011). 'Ovid's *Metamorphoses* in the School Tradition of France, 1180–1400: Texts, Manuscript Traditions, Manuscript Settings'. In James G. Clark et al. (eds), *Ovid in the Middle Ages*. Cambridge: Cambridge University Press, 49–82.
Dronke, Peter (1970). *Poetic Individuality in the Middle Age*. Oxford: Clarendon Press.
Elliott, Dyan (1993). *Spiritual Marriage: Sexual Abstinence in Medieval Wedlock*. Princeton: Princeton University Press.
Elliott, Dyan (1996). 'Bernardino of Siena versus the Marriage Debt'. In Jacqueline Murray and Konrad Eisenbichler (eds), *Desire and Discipline: Sex and Sexuality in Premodern Europe*. Toronto: University of Toronto Press, 168–200.
Elliott, Dyan (1999). *Fallen Bodies: Pollution, Sexuality, and Demonology in the Middle Ages*. Philadelphia: University of Pennsylvania Press.
Elliott, Dyan (2003). 'Women and Confession: From Empowerment to Pathology'. In Mary Erler and Maryanne Kowaleski (eds), *Gendering the Master Narrative: Women and Power in the Middle Ages*. Ithaca, NY: Cornell University Press, 31–51.
Elliott, Dyan (2012). *The Bride of Christ Goes to Hell: Metaphor and Embodiment in the Wives of Pious Women, 200–1500*. Philadelphia: University of Pennsylvania Press.
Jordan, Mark D. (1997). *The Invention of Sodomy in Christian Theology*. Chicago: University of Chicago Press.
Helmholz, R. H. (1974). *Marriage Litigation in Medieval England*. Cambridge: Cambridge University Press.
Heidecker, Karl (2010). *The Divorce of Lothar II: Christian Marriage and Political Power in the Carolingian World*. Trans. Tanis M. Guest. Ithaca, NY: Cornell University Press.
Jacquart, Danielle, and Claude Thomasset (1988). *Sexuality and Medicine in the Middle Ages*. Trans. Matthew Adamson. Princeton: Princeton University Press.
Karras, Ruth Mazo (2012). *Unmarriages: Women, Men, and Sexual Unions in the Middle Ages*. Philadelphia: University of Pennsylvania Press.

Makowski, Elizabeth M. (1977). 'The Conjugal Debt and Medieval Canon Law'. *Journal of Medieval History*, 3: 99–114.

Murray, Alexander (1998). 'Counseling in Medieval Confession.' In Peter Biller and Alastair Minnis (eds), *Handling Sin: Confession in the Middle Ages*. University of York: York Medieval Press in association with Boydell and Brewer, 63–77.

Murray, Jacqueline (1990). 'On the Origins and Role of "Wise Women" in Causes for Annulment on the Grounds of Male Impotence'. *Journal of Medieval History*, 16: 235–249.

Pairet, Anna (2011). 'Recasting *Metamorphoses* in Fourteenth-Century France: The Challenges of the *Ovide moralisé*'. In James G. Clark et al. (eds), *Ovid in the Middle Ages*. Cambridge: Cambridge University Press, 83–107.

Payer, Pierre J. (1984). *Sex and the Penitentials*. Toronto: University of Toronto Press.

Payer, Pierre J. (2009). *Sex and the New Medieval Literature of Confession: 1150–1300*. Toronto: Pontifical Institute of Mediaeval Studies.

Salisbury, Joyce (1991). 'Bestiality in the Middle Ages'. In J. Salisbury (ed.), *Sex in the Middle Ages: A Book of Essays*. New York: Garland, 173–186.

Turner, Denys (1995). *Eros and Allegory: Medieval Exegesis of the Song of Songs*. Kalamazoo, MI: Cistercian Publications.

CHAPTER 19

....

SEX AND MARRIAGE IN THE PROTESTANT TRADITION, 1500–1900

....

JOHN WITTE, JR.

SEX, marriage, and family life were hotly contested issues during the sixteenth-century Protestant Reformation and were some of the first institutions to be reformed.[1] The leading Protestant theologians of the sixteenth century all prepared lengthy tracts on the subject, and scores of leading Protestant jurists worked together to develop a new family law for Protestant lands. Virtually every city and territory on the Continent that converted to the Protestant cause in the first half of the sixteenth century had new marriage laws on the books within a decade after accepting the Reformation. And it was King Henry VIII's 'great marriage affair' with Catherine of Aragon that prompted the English break with Rome.

The Protestant reformers' early preoccupation with marriage was partly driven by their critique of the Roman Catholic sacramental theology and canon law of marriage that had dominated the West for the prior half millennium. The medieval Church's expansive jurisdiction over marriage was, for Protestants, a usurpation of the state's authority. The sacramental concept of marriage on which the Church predicated its jurisdiction was for the reformers a self-serving theological fiction. The canonical prohibition on the marriage of clergy and monastics ignored the Bible's warnings against sexual sin as the reformers understood them. The church's intricate rules governing sexual desire and expression, even within marriage, were seen as a gratuitous insult to God's gift of marital love. The canon law's many impediments to engagement and marriage and its prohibitions against complete divorce and remarriage stood in considerable tension with the Protestant understanding of the natural and biblical right and duty of each fit adult to marry.

---

[1] For detailed sources covered in this summary chapter, see my volumes in the bibliography: (2002: 177–256; 2012: chs 3–8); and Witte and Kingdon (2005).

Many Protestant theological leaders acted on these new teachings about sexuality and marriage in the first decades of the Reformation. The first Protestant clergy were mostly ex-priests or ex-monastics who had forsaken their orders and vows, and married shortly thereafter. New Protestant converts followed their examples by marrying, divorcing, and remarrying in open contempt of canon law rules. A few early Anabaptists even experimented with polygamy.[2] As Catholic Church courts and their secular counterparts firmly punished these flagrant sex crimes, Protestant theologians and jurists rose to the defence of their coreligionists, producing a new Protestant gospel of marital and sexual freedom.

Political leaders rapidly translated this new Protestant gospel into new civil laws in place of the Catholic Church's canon laws. Viewed together, these new state laws (1) shifted marital jurisdiction from the church to the state; (2) abolished monasteries and convents; (3) commended, if not commanded, the marriage of clergy; (4) rejected the sacramentality of marriage and the religious tests traditionally required for valid unions; (5) banned secret marriages and required the participation of parents, peers, priests, and political officials in marriage formation; (6) sharply curtailed the number of impediments used to annul engagements and marriages; and (7) introduced fault-based complete divorce with a subsequent right for divorcees to remarry. The Western legal tradition would not see such sweeping reforms of its marital laws again until the liberal, cultural, and constitutional reforms of the last half century.

MAINLINE PROTESTANT MODELS OF SEX AND MARRIAGE

Mainline Protestants—Lutherans, Calvinists, and Anglicans—all started their marital teachings with the Bible. For them, Genesis 1 and 2 were axiomatic statements of the created order and natural law of marriage. God had created marriage as a 'two-in-one-flesh union' between a man and a woman designed for them to 'be fruitful and multiply' and to be protected from sexual sin. Also axiomatic was the Decalogue that commanded children to 'honour' their parents, and spouses to avoid adultery or even 'coveting' their neighbour's wife or maidservants. Instructive, too, were the intricate Mosaic laws on sex, marriage, and family life, which the Hebrew Prophets wove into a robust ethic of enduring and exclusive monogamous marriage modelled on Yahweh's covenantal love for his elect people.

From Matthew 19 and Romans 7, Protestants drew the lessons that a lawful Christian marriage should not be 'rent asunder' too easily and that a second marriage should not be entered too quickly. 1 Corinthians 7 stipulated the 'conjugal rights' that husbands

---

[2] I am largely omitting herein Anabaptist reforms of marriage, which soon settled into a conventional Protestant marriage ethic without polygamy. See Williams 1992: 756–798.

and wives alike could enjoy in each other's bodies rather than 'burning' with lust, and allowed parties to separate in the event of desertion by one spouse. The household codes of Colossians 3, 1 Peter 2–3, and Ephesians 5–6 governed the interactions of husbands and wives, parents and children, masters and servants. These codes, together with sundry New Testament injunctions against sexual immorality, informed a rich Protestant tradition of confessional, catechetical, and casuistic teachings on sex, marriage, and family life that lasted into the twentieth century.

While a few early Protestant groups used the Bible alone, most Protestants also drew heavily on the Western tradition—the marital wisdom of Aristotle, the Stoics, and the Church Fathers, the domestic norms of pre- and post-Christianized Roman law, and, before long, even some of the marital theology and law of the medieval Church. Protestants accepted the traditional teaching that marriage was both a natural institution created by God and a contractual unit formed in its essence by the mutual consent of the parties. The marital contract prescribed for couples a life-long relation of love, service, and devotion to each other, and proscribed any unwarranted breach or relaxation of their connubial and parental duties. Protestants also recognized traditional sex crimes like adultery, concubinage, prostitution, incest, polygamy, sodomy, abortion, infanticide, and child abuse as violations of natural and biblical morality.

Unlike medieval Catholics, however, Protestants rejected the medieval Church's subordination of marriage to celibacy and its celebration of marriage as a sacrament. According to common Protestant lore, the person was too tempted by sinful passion to forgo God's soothing remedy of marriage, and the celibate life had no superior virtue and was no prerequisite for ecclesiastical service. Moreover, Protestants did not believe marriage to be a sacrament. The marital household was, in their view, a social order ordained by God and equal in dignity to the church, state, and other estates. From this common foundation, Lutherans, Calvinists, and Anglicans each constructed their own models of sex, marriage, and family life.

Lutheranism

The Lutheran tradition that dominated Germany and Scandinavia from the sixteenth to the nineteenth centuries, developed a social model of marriage, grounded in the two kingdoms theory of Martin Luther (1483–1546) (Dieterich 1970; Ozment 2001). Marriage, Luther and his colleagues taught, was a social estate of the earthly kingdom of creation, not a sacred estate of the heavenly kingdom of redemption. Though divinely ordained and biblically governed, marriage was directed to human ends and social 'uses'. Marriage revealed to persons their sin and their need for God's marital gift: this was its theological use. Marriage restricted prostitution, promiscuity, and other public sexual sins: this was its civil use. Marriage taught love, restraint, and other public virtues: this was its pedagogical use.

All fit men and women were free and encouraged to marry or remarry, clerical and lay alike, unless they had the rare gift of continence. We are all sinful creatures, Lutherans argued; lust has pervaded the conscience of everyone. Marriage is thus not just an option but a necessity. For without it, a person's distorted sexuality becomes a force capable of overthrowing the most devout conscience. A person is enticed by nature to concubinage, prostitution, masturbation, voyeurism, and other sexual sins. 'To spurn marriage is to act against God's calling... and against nature's urging,' Luther wrote. The calling of marriage should be declined only by those who have received God's special gift of continence. 'Such persons are rare, not one in a thousand, for they are a special miracle of God' (Luther [LW] 1955: vol. 28: 912, 927–931; vol. 45: 18–22).

This understanding of marriage as a protection against sin undergirded Lutheran and other Protestants' bitter attacks on the Catholic tradition of mandatory clerical celibacy. To require celibacy of clerics, monks, and nuns, the reformers believed, was ultimately a source of great sin. Celibacy was a gift for God to give, not a duty for the church to impose. It was for each individual, not for the church, to decide whether he or she had received this gift. By demanding monastic vows of chastity and clerical vows of celibacy, the church was seen to be intruding on Christian freedom and contradicting Scripture, nature, and common sense. By institutionalizing and encouraging celibacy the church preyed on the immature and the uncertain. By holding out food, shelter, security, and economic opportunity, the monasteries enticed poor and needy parents to oblate their minor children to a life of celibacy, regardless of whether it suited their natures. Mandatory celibacy was not a prerequisite to true clerical service of God. Instead, wrote Luther, a former monk, it led to 'great whoredom and all manner of fleshly impurity and... hearts filled with thoughts of women day and night.' It was far safer that all clergy be married. And, indeed, marriage would enhance a pastor's ministry to couples and families, and his marital parsonage could provide a model for proper Christian domestic living.

Marriage not only protected humanity against sexual sin, Lutherans insisted, but also offered them the sublime divine gift of marital love. Luther extolled the 'love' of husband and wife to be 'over and above' all other loves,' indeed a 'foretaste of the love of heaven' (Luther [WA] 1883–1987: vol. 2: 167; see also 13: 11, 17/2: 350ff). He did not deny the traditional leadership of the *paterfamilias* within the marital household, but he also did not betray these warm sentiments to the point of becoming the grim prophet of patriarchy, paternalism, and procreation *über alles* that some modern critics make him out to be. For Luther, love was a necessary and sufficient good of marriage. He supported marriages between loving couples, even those between young men and older women beyond child-bearing years or between couples who could not have children. He stressed repeatedly that husband and wife were spiritual, intellectual, and emotional 'partners,' each to have regard and respect for the strengths of the other. He called his own wife Katharine respectfully 'Mr Kathy' and said of her: 'I am an inferior lord, she the superior; I am Aaron, she is my Moses' (in Ozment 2001: 36–37). He repeatedly told husbands and wives alike to tend to each other's spiritual, emotional, and sexual needs and to share household duties (LW 45: 39ff).

Marriage sometimes brought the divine gift of children as well. Luther treated procreation as an act of co-creation and co-redemption with God. He wished for all marital couples the joy of having children, not only for their own sakes but for the sake of God as well. Childrearing, he wrote, 'is the noblest and most precious work, because to God there can be nothing dearer than the salvation of souls....Most certainly, father and mother are apostles, bishops, [and] priests to their children, for it is they who make them acquainted with the Gospel' (LW 45: 46). Only on this sure foundation of parental love, nurture, and education, could the church do its proper catechesis and the state its public education of children.

This Lutheran model of sex, marriage, and family life remained at the core of German and Scandinavian culture and law until the nineteenth century. One of the richest distillations of Lutheran teachings on love and marriage came from Danish philosopher, Søren Kierkegaard (1813–55), whose views on love were later elaborated by Anders Nygren. One of the best early legal syntheses of Lutheran laws on marriage and divorce came from Prussian jurist Justus Henning Böhmer (1674–1749), whose work remains at the heart of a burgeoning German and Scandinavian scholarship on Lutheran marriage law today.

Calvinism

The Calvinist tradition, first established in Geneva, set out a covenantal model of marriage. (Köhler 1942; Seeger 1989; Kingdon 1995) Marriage, John Calvin (1509–1564) and his followers taught, was a public covenant modelled on the ancient covenant between Yahweh and Israel. A variety of parties participated in the formation of this marital covenant. The marital parties themselves swore their betrothals and espousals before each other and God—rendering all marriages tripartite agreements, with God as third party witness, participant, and judge. The couple's parents, as God's 'bishops' for children, gave their consent to the union. Two witnesses, as God's priests to their peers, served as witnesses to the marriage. The minister, holding God's spiritual power of the Word, blessed and instructed the couple in a mandatory church wedding. The magistrate, holding God's temporal power of the sword, registered the couple and protected them in their person and marital property. Each of these parties—parents, peers, ministers, and magistrates—was considered essential to the legitimacy of the marriage, for they each represented a different dimension of God's involvement in the covenant. To omit any such party was, in effect, to omit God from the marriage covenant.

The covenant of marriage, said Calvin, was grounded in the order of creation and governed by the moral law of God set out in Scripture, reason, and conscience. God's law set out two tracks of marital norms, Calvin taught: civil norms, which are common to all persons, and spiritual norms, which are distinctly Christian. This moral law, in turn, gave rise to two tracks of marital morality: a simple morality of duty demanded of all persons regardless of their faith, and a higher morality of aspiration demanded of believers in order to reflect their faith. The moral law not only coerces them against violence and violation, but also cultivates in them charity and love. It not only punishes harmful acts of adultery and fornication, but also prohibits evil thoughts of passion and lust. It not only punishes wife abuse or child neglect, but also counsels a sacrificial love, tenderness, patience, and kindness towards a spouse and children that goes beyond that given to anyone or anything else.

It was the church's responsibility to teach aspirational spiritual norms for marriage and family life. It was the state's responsibility to enforce mandatory civil norms. This division of responsibility was reflected in sixteenth-century Geneva and later Calvinist polities in the procedural divisions between the church consistory and the city council. In family cases, the consistory was the court of first instance, and would call parties to their higher spiritual duties, backing their recommendations with instruction, admonition, confession, Eucharist bans, and in extreme cases, excommunication. If such spiritual discipline failed, the parties were referred to the city council to compel them, using civil and criminal sanctions, to honour at least their basic civil duties for marriage.

This Calvinist covenantal model mediated both contractual and sacramental understandings of marriage. On the one hand, it confirmed the traditional contractual qualities of marriage—without subjecting it to the personal preferences of the parties. Marriage depended for its validity and utility on the voluntary consent of the parties. But marriage was more than a mere contract, for God was a third party to every marriage covenant, and set its basic terms in the order and law of creation. Freedom of contract in marriage was thus effectively limited to choosing maturely which party to marry—with no real choice about the form, forum, or function of marriage once a fit and willing spouse was chosen.

On the other hand, this covenant model confirmed the sacred qualities of marriage—without ascribing to it sacramental functions. Marriage, Calvin argued, was a holy and loving fellowship, a compelling image of the bond between Yahweh and his elect, Christ and his church. But marriage was no sacrament. Yes, Ephesians 5:32 analogized the loving and sacrificial union of a Christian husband and wife to the 'great *mysterion*' of Christ's union with the church, but the Bible was not thereby making marriage a sacrament. It was just using a striking image to drive home a moral lesson. The Bible did this all the time, said Calvin. 'Faith is like a mustard seed': it grows even if tiny. 'The kingdom of heaven is like yeast': it leavens even if you cannot see it. Or 'the Son of man will come like a thief in the night'. So be ready at all times for his return. The marriage analogy is similar: 'Marital love is like the union of Christ and the church.' So be faithful and sacrificial to your spouse, as Christ is to his church. (See Calvin 1960: 4.19.34; see also LW 36: 97ff.)

Denying the sacramental quality of marriage had dramatic implications for how a marriage should be formed and dissolved in Calvinist and other Protestant lands. First, there were no formal religious or baptismal tests for marriage. To be sure, parties would certainly do well to marry within the faith for the sake of themselves and their children. But interreligious marriage was permissible, as Calvin himself showed in marrying an Anabaptist widow. Second, divorce and remarriage were licit, sometimes necessary. To be sure, marriages should be stable and presumptively indissoluble. But this presumption could be overcome if one of the essential marital goods was chronically betrayed by adultery, desertion, cruelty, or felony. If the parties could not be reconciled, either the husband or wife had the right to divorce and remarry another.

This covenantal model of marriage came to dominate numerous Calvinist communities in Switzerland, Germany, Hungary, France, the Netherlands, Scotland, England, and later North America. Until well into the nineteenth century, both church and state authorities in Calvinist lands governed in copious detail marital formation, maintenance, and dissolution, child care, custody, and control, spousal rights, responsibilities, and remedies and more. They also set stern codes of sexual ethics for Calvinist communities designed to curb fornication, adultery, sodomy, pornography, prostitution, dancing, and other sexual expression. These firm moral codes formed the backbone of Puritan sexual ethics in early America and also animated the chastity and modesty ethics of nineteenth-century Victorians. And, in the twentieth century, great theologians like Karl Barth, Emil Brunner, and Helmut Thielieke worked out an intricate covenant theology of sex, marriage, and family life rooted in various strands of the Calvinist tradition.

Anglicanism

The Anglican tradition brought forth a commonwealth model of marriage (Powell 1917; Ingram 1987; Carlson 1994). This model embraced the social and covenantal models of marriage taught by Lutherans and Calvinists, but also went beyond them. Marriage, Anglican writers argued, was at once a gracious symbol of the divine, a social unit of the earthly kingdom, and a solemn covenant with one's spouse. But the most essential cause, condition, and calling of the family was that it served and symbolized the common good of the couple, the children, the church, and the state all at once. For Anglican divines like William Gouge (1578–1653), marriage was appointed by God as 'a little commonwealth' to foster the mutual love, service, and security of husband and wife, parent and child. It was also designed as a 'seedbed and seminary' of the broader commonwealth of church and state to teach essential Christian and political norms and habits (Gouge 1622).

Like the political and ecclesiastical commonwealths, Anglican divines argued, the domestic commonwealth was created as a hierarchical structure. God had created Eve as 'a help meet' for Adam. He had called Adam and Eve to mutual society among themselves and to the mutual procreation of children (Gen. 1:28, 2:18). After the Fall, He had commanded that Adam 'shall rule over' Eve (Gen. 3:16). As heir of Adam, the modern husband was thus the head of his wife. As heir of Eve, the modern wife was his subject, his 'help meet'. Together husband and wife were the heads of their children and the rest of the household. Each of these offices in the family hierarchy was bound by a series of duties, rooted in the Bible and natural law, which dozens of thick household manuals and catechisms of the day elaborated. Faithful maintenance of domestic duties and offices, Anglican divines believed, was the best guarantee of individual flourishing and social order within the broader commonwealths of church and state. Robert Filmer's' *Patriarcha* (c. 1642), gave this conservative, patriarchal rendering of the commonwealth model of marriage its classic formulation—and his work helped to distil and anchor both political theories of absolute monarchy and theological theories of absolute male headship within the marital household.

Until 1640, the commonwealth model served to rationalize the traditional hierarchies of husband over wife, parent over child, church over household, state over church. To call the marital household 'a little commonwealth' was to signal its subordinate place within the new hierarchy of social institutions that comprised 'the great church and commonwealth' of England. It was also to call the household to an internal hierarchy of offices that matched the royal and episcopal offices of the great commonwealth— with the *paterfamilias'* role of ruler within each family serving as a miniature model of the king as the supreme head of the church and commonwealth of England. The commonwealth model was thus used to integrate a whole network of parallel domestic and political duties rooted in the Bible and English tradition. Anglican divines and moralists expounded at great length the reciprocal duties of husband and wife, parent and child, master and servant that would produce a well-ordered little commonwealth. And, in keeping with the tradition of stability of the great political commonwealth of England, these same Anglican writers prohibited the dissolution of this little domestic commonwealth of the family by divorce.

As the political concept of the English commonwealth was revolutionized and democratized in the seventeenth century, however, so was the English commonwealth model of marriage. Particularly during the English Commonwealth period of 1642–60, when a coalition of Protestant revolutionaries overthrew the church and state establishment, these traditional domestic hierarchies were challenged with a revolutionary new principle of equality. The biblical duties of husband and wife and of parent and child were recast as the natural rights of each household member against the other. The traditional idea of a created natural order met with a new idea of marriage, society, and state formed voluntarily by contracts by individuals in the state of nature. Just as the English commonwealth could be rent asunder by force of arms when it abused the people's natural rights, so the family commonwealth could be put asunder by suits at law when one spouse abused the other's marital rights. Just as the King could be beheaded for abuses in the Commonwealth, so the paterfamilias could be removed from the head of the little commonwealth for abuses in the household.

Locke, Blackstone, and the Common Law Tradition

The most famous exposition of this new democratic reading of the commonwealth model of marriage came from English philosopher, John Locke (1632–1704), who straddled the Anglican, Puritan, and early Enlightenment worlds. Especially in his famous *Two Treatises on Government*, Locke sought to refute Robert Filmer's *Patriarcha* (1949). God did not create Adam and Eve as ruler and subject, but as husband and wife, said Locke. Adam and Eve were created equal before God. Each had natural rights to use the bounties of Paradise. Each had natural duties to each other and to God. After the fall

312 JOHN WITTE, JR.

into sin, God expelled Adam and Eve from the Garden. He increased man's labour in his use of creation. He increased woman's labour in the bearing of children. But God, said Locke, did not abrogate the natural equality, rights, and duties with which God created Adam and Eve, and all persons after them. Nor did God render all wives to be eternally subject to their husbands. Men and women are born free and equal in the state of nature.

As humans moved from the state of nature, 'the first Society' to be formed 'was between Man and Wife, which gave beginning to that of Parents and Children'. This 'conjugal society', like every other society, 'is made by a voluntary Compact between Man and Woman'. The marriage of a man and woman is 'necessary not only to unite their care and affection, but also necessary to their common offspring, who have a right to be nourished and maintained by them, till they are able to provide for themselves'. For Locke, men and women have a natural and equal right to enter into a marital contract. But their children also have a natural right to survival, support, protection, and education. This imposed on their parents the natural duty to remain in their marriage once contracted, at least until their children were emancipated (Locke 1960: II.2, II.77–86).

Locke's arguments—and their elaboration by other philosophers like Baron Montesquieu (1689–1755), Jean-Jacques Rousseau (1712–88), and Mary Wollstonecraft (1759–97), all childhood Protestants—were critical to the development of the rights of men and women, parents and children within the Western legal tradition. William Blackstone (1723–80), the leading English common lawyer of the eighteenth century, for example argued:

> The duty of parents to provide for the maintenance of their children is a principle of natural law....The main end and design of marriage [is] to ascertain and fix upon some certain person, to whom the care, the protection, the maintenance, and the education of the children should belong.
>
> (Blackstone 1765: 1.16.1)

Blackstone set out in detail the reciprocal rights and duties that the natural law imposes upon parents and children, and which the common law must enforce. It requires parents to maintain, protect, and educate their children, and in turn protects their rights to discharge these parental duties against undue interference by others. These 'natural duties' of parents are the correlatives of the 'natural rights' of their children to be nurtured, protected, and educated. And, in turn, once they become adults, children acquire reciprocal natural duties toward their parents as they enter into their second childhood, and need the support, care, and protection of their children and other kin (Blackstone 1765: I.15.1; 1.16.1–3).

The common law was gradually reformed in line with these new teachings on marital equality and intra-familial rights. In England, Parliament passed the famous Matrimonial Causes Act of 1857 that authorized innocent husbands and wives alike to sue for absolute divorce on proof of cause with a right to remarry, and empowered courts to place minor children in the custody of that parent who was best suited to care for their maintenance, nurture, and education. This and later new legislation on elementary education, bastardy protection, and prevention of cruelty to children, slowly bent the law toward the presumption that custody of a child, particularly a minor, be granted to the mother, and that the father be charged with support payments but entitled to visitation rights until the child reach the age of majority.

Furthermore, a series of Married Women's Property Acts after 1870 slowly released married women from the traditional bonds of coverture that legally subsumed a woman's person, property, and identity into that of her husband. Married women slowly gained stronger title and control over the property they brought into the marriage, or acquired after the wedding. They also gained increasing capacities to enter contracts of sale, lease, and mortgage of their properties, and the capacity to execute wills, trusts, and other dispositions. These early reforms of marital property law eventually strengthened the pursuit of gender equality outside the marital home as well. After their rights to property were enhanced, women were able to gain broader rights and access to higher education, learned societies, trade and commercial guilds and unions, and a variety of professions, occupations, and societies historically closed to them. On the strength of these achievements, women ultimately gained the right to vote and to hold public office in 1918 (Shanley 1987; Staves 1990). Comparable reforms in favour of women's rights and children's rights emerged in other common law lands, notably in Canada, the United States, and Australia which all had comparable sweeping new marital and family reforms in the later nineteenth and early twentieth centuries.

FROM PROTESTANT CONFESSIONALISM TO ENLIGHTENMENT LIBERALISM

Protestants, on both sides of the Atlantic, continued to expound their rich theologies of marriage until the twentieth century. They continued to mine the Bible for further insights into the fundamentals of sex, marriage, and family life. While these Protestant theologies of marriage did change in accent and application over time and across denominational lines, the main Protestant teachings on marriage introduced in the sixteenth and seventeenth centuries did not change much before the twentieth century.

Lutherans, Calvinists, Anglicans, Anabaptists, and the hundreds of denominations eventually derived from these mainline groups, all generally expounded the same basic teaching. God had created marriage for the mutual comfort of men and women, their mutual procreation of children, and their mutual protection from sin and temptation. All fit and able adults should marry, unless uniquely called to a single life. Monogamous marriage between unrelated parties was the sole legitimate form and forum for sex and procreation. Incest, polygamy, adultery, fornication, concubinage, prostitution, sodomy, and bestiality were all strictly forbidden. Marriages should proceed first with an engagement, then with public banns, and finally with a church wedding. Valid marriages required parental consent, peer witnesses, and civil registration with the state to complement the pastor's consecration in the church. Marital parties should support and care for each other throughout their lives, and provide for each other and for their children in their last wills and testaments. Both fathers and mothers must share in the care, education, and protection of their children. Divorce is allowed on proven grounds of adultery, malicious desertion, or other serious fault, with remarriage allowed at least to the innocent party and ongoing household support required of the guilty party.

Natural Law Theory

The more innovative changes in Protestant teachings theory in the eighteenth and nineteenth centuries came at the philosophical level. Selected Protestants in Europe and America allied with Enlightenment liberals to develop a fuller natural law theory that defended the equal rights of women and children, but also defended the traditional norms of enduring and exclusive monogamous marriages and no extramarital sex. Rather than simply adducing the Bible and Christian tradition, however, these later Protestant writers sought to build a natural account of these main features of marriage and sexual morality—using rational, empirical, and utilitarian arguments designed to be cogent even to those with different religious convictions (See Waters 2007; Yenor 2011).

These Protestant natural law theorists used various methods to make their case. Some drew increasingly sophisticated inferences from bonding patterns and reproductive strategies among animals, building on Aristotelian-Thomistic insights and anticipating the findings of modern evolutionary biologists (see Browning 2003). Some uncovered the common forms and norms of marriage that were shared by Greeks, Romans, Jews, Catholics, Protestants, and others—all of which they took as evidence of a common natural law at work. Orthodox Protestant theologians often decried these efforts, especially as some philosophers moved toward the more anti-clerical, if not anti-Christian formulations of the later French Enlightenment. But most Protestant natural law theorists on marriage saw their efforts as a complement to, even a confirmation of, the work of the Christian tradition.

The writings of Henry Home, known as Lord Kames of Scotland (1696–1782), are a good illustration. A leading man of letters and a leading justice of the highest Scottish court, Home was a friend of Frances Hutcheson, David Hume, Adam Smith, and other Scottish Enlightenment luminaries. He was best known for his brilliant defence of natural law, principally on empirical and rational grounds which were designed to give it more universal and enduring cogency. A devout and life-long Protestant, Home believed in the truth of Scripture and the will of God. But he wanted to win over even sceptics and atheists to his legal and moral arguments and to give enduring 'authority to the promises and covenants' that helped create society and its institutions. (Home 2005: 1.2).

Among many other institutions and 'covenants', Home defended monogamous marriage as a 'necessity of nature', and he denounced polygamy and non-marital sex as 'a vice against human nature'. He recognized that polygamy had been practised in early

Western history and was still known in some Islamic and Asiatic cultures in his day. But, Home insisted, polygamy exists only 'where women are treated as inferior beings', and where 'men of wealth' buy their wives like slaves and adopt the 'savage manners' of animals. Among horses, cattle, and other grazing animals, he argued, polygamy is natural. One superior male breeds with all females, and the mothers take care of their own young who grow quickly independent. For these animals, monogamous 'pairing would be of no use: the female feeds herself and her young at the same instant; and nothing is left for the male to do'. But other animals, such as nesting birds, 'whose young require the nursing care of both parents, are directed by nature to pair' and to remain paired till their young 'are sufficiently vigorous to provide for themselves' (Home 2007: Book 1, Sketches VI–VI; Book III, Sketch III).

Humans are the latter sort of creature, said Home, for whom pairing and parenting are indispensable. Humans are thus inclined by nature toward enduring monogamous pairing of parents—indeed, more so than any other creature given the long fragility and helplessness of human offspring:

> Man is an animal of long life, and is proportionally slow in growing to maturity: he is a helpless being before the age of fifteen or sixteen; and there may be in a family ten or twelve children of different births, before the eldest can shift for itself. Now in the original state of hunting and fishing, which are laborious occupations, and not always successful, a woman, suckling her infant, is not able to provide food even for herself, far less for ten or twelve voracious children.... [P]airing is so necessary to the human race, that it must be natural and instinctive.... Brute animals, which do not pair, have grass and other food in plenty, enabling the female to feed her young without needing any assistance from the male. But where the young require the nursing care of both parents, pairing is a law of nature.
>
> (Home 2007: Book 1, Sketch 6)

Not only is the pairing of male and female a law of nature, Home continued. 'Matrimony is instituted by nature' to overcome humans' greatest natural handicap to effective procreation and preservation as a species—their perpetual desire for sex, especially among the young, at exactly the time when they are most fertile. Unlike most animals, whose sexual appetites are confined to short rutting seasons, Home wrote, humans have a constant sexual appetite which, by nature, 'demands gratification, after short intervals'. If men and women just had random sex with anyone—'like the hart in rutting time'—the human race would devolve into a 'savage state of nature' and soon die out. Men would make perennial and 'promiscuous use of women' and not commit themselves to the care of these women or their children. 'Women would in effect be common prostitutes.' Few women would have the ability on their own 'to provide food for a family of children', and most would avoid having children or would abandon them if they did (Home 2007: Book 1, Sketches VI–VI).

Monogamous marriage is nature's safeguard against such proclivities, said Home, and 'frequent enjoyment' of marital sex and intimacy 'endears a pair to each other', making them want only each other all the more. 'Sweet is the society of a pair fitted for each other, in whom are collected the affections of husband, wife, lover, friend, the tenderest affections of human nature.'

> The God of nature has [thus] enforced conjugal society, not only by making it agreeable, but by the principle of chastity inherent in our nature.... Chastity is essential even to the continuation of the human race. As the carnal appetite is always alive, the sexes would wallow in pleasure, and be soon rendered unfit for procreation, were it not for the restraint of chastity.
>
> (Home 2007: Book 1, Sketch VI)

Hume and Paley

Similarly, the famous Scottish philosopher, David Hume (1711–1776), for all his scepticism about traditional morality and Christianity, thought traditional legal and moral norms of sex, marriage, and family life to be both natural and useful. Hume summarized the natural configuration of human marriage crisply: 'The long and helpless infancy requires the combination of parents for the subsistence of their young; and that combination requires the virtue of chastity and fidelity to the marriage bed' (Hume 1963: 206–207). Like Home, Hume denounced polygamy. This 'odious institution' denied the natural equality of the sexes. It fostered 'the bad education of children'. It led to 'jealousy and competition among wives', and more. Moreover, said Hume, polygamy forced a man, distracted by his other wives and children, to confine his other wives to the home—by physically threatening, binding, or even laming them, by isolating them from society, or by keeping them so poor and weak they could not leave. All this is a form of 'barbarism', with 'frightful effects' that defy all nature and reason (Hume 1987: 182–187).

Hume offered similar arguments against 'voluntary divorce'—no-fault, unilateral divorce, as we now call it. Many in Hume's day argued for divorce as a natural expression of the freedom of contract and a natural compensation for having no recourse to polygamy despite a man's natural drive to multiple partners. Hume would have none of this. To be sure, he recognized that divorce was sometimes the better of two evils—especially where one party was guilty of adultery, severe cruelty, or malicious desertion, and especially when no children were involved. But, outside of such narrow circumstances, he said, 'nature has made divorce' without real cause the 'doom of all mortals'. First, with voluntary divorce, the children suffer and become 'miserable'. Shuffled from home to home, consigned to the care of strangers and step-parents 'instead of the fond attention and concern of a parent', the inconveniences and encumbrances of their lives just multiply as the divorces of their parents and step-parents multiply. Second, when voluntary divorce is foreclosed, couples by nature become disinclined to wander, and instead form 'a calm and sedate affection, conducted by reason and cemented by habit; springing from long acquaintance and mutual obligations, without jealousies or fears'.

'We need not, therefore, be afraid of drawing the marriage-knot, which chiefly subsists by friendship, the closest possible.' Third, 'nothing is more dangerous than to unite two persons so closely in all their interests and concerns, as man and wife, without rendering the union entire and total. The least possibility of a separate interest must be the source of endless quarrels and suspicions.' Nature, justice and prudence alike require their 'continued consortium' (Hume 1987: 187–190).

William Paley (1743–1805), a Cambridge philosopher and Anglican cleric, added a utilitarian argument against fornication—'sex or cohabitation without marriage'. Even though some humans by nature are inclined to wander, Paley argued, society must forbid fornication because it 'discourages marriage' and 'diminishes the private and public goods' that marriage offers. The male part of the species, Paley wrote, will not undertake the encumbrance, expense, and restraint of married life, if they can gratify their passions at a cheaper price; and they will undertake anything rather than not gratify them' (Paley 2002: 3.3.2). Paley recognized that he was appealing to general utility, but he thought an absolute ban on fornication was the only way to avoid the slippery slope to utter sexual libertinism:

> The libertine may not be conscious that these irregularities hinder his own marriage…much less does he perceive how *his* indulgences can hinder other men from marrying; but what will he say would be the consequence, if the same licentiousness were universal? or what should hinder its becoming universal, if it be innocent or allowable in him?
>
> (Paley 2002: 3.3.2)

Fornication furthermore leads to prostitution, Paley went on, with its accompanying degradation of women, erosion of morals, transmission of disease, production of unwanted and uncared for children, and further irregularities and pathos. Fornication also leads naturally to a tradition of concubinage—'the kept mistress', who can be dismissed at the man's pleasure, or retained 'in a state of humiliation and dependence inconsistent with the rights which marriage would confer upon her' and her children. No small wonder that the Bible condemned fornication, prostitution, concubinage, and other such 'cohabitation without marriage' in no uncertain terms, said Paley. But, again, in these injunctions the Bible is simply reflecting the natural order and common moral sense.

Adultery is even worse than fornication, said Paley, because it not only insults the goods of marriage in the abstract. It injures an actual good marriage, leaving the innocent spouse as well as their children as victims. For the betrayed spouse, adultery is 'a wound in his [or her] sensibility and affections, the most painful and incurable that human nature knows'. For the children it brings shame and unhappiness as the vice is inevitably detected and discussed. For the adulterer or adulteress, it is a form of 'perjury' that violates their marital vow and covenant. For all parties in the household, adultery will often provoke retaliation and imitation—another slippery slope to the erosion of marriage and the unleashing of sexual libertinism and seduction. Both nature and Scripture thus rain down anathemas against it (Paley 2002: 3.3.2). Paley's utilitarian arguments in favour of traditional understandings of sex, marriage, and family life would find enduring provenance among many utilitarians into the nineteenth century, including the most famous of them, Jeremy Bentham (1748–1832).

Locke, Home, Hume, and Paley were only a few of the scores of Western writers from the seventeenth to the nineteenth centuries who defended traditional Western norms of sex, marriage, and family using this surfeit of arguments from nature, reason, fairness, prudence, utility, pragmatism, and common sense. Some of these writers were inspired, no doubt, by their personal Protestant faith, others by a conservative desire to maintain the status quo. But most of these writers pressed their principal arguments on non-biblical grounds. And they were sometimes sharply critical of the Bible—denouncing St Paul's preferences for celibacy, the Mosaic provisions on unilateral male divorce, and the many tales of polygamy, concubinage, and prostitution among the ancient biblical patriarchs and kings. Moreover, most of these writers jettisoned many other features of the Western tradition that, in their judgement, defied reason, fairness, and utility—including, notably, the establishment of Christianity by law and the political privileging of the church. Their natural law theory of the family was not just a rationalist apologia for traditional Christian family values or a naturalist smokescreen for personal religious beliefs. They defended traditional family norms not out of confessional faith but out of rational proof, not just because they uncritically believed in them but because they worked.

Later Enlightenment Reforms

The key move made by the early (often Protestant) Enlightenment philosophers was to remove the necessary religious dimension of sex and marriage. This liberalized the marital household somewhat, and gave parties the choice whether to involve the church or to obey the Bible in their sex, marriage, and family lives. But the early Enlightenment philosophers left in place the idea that marriage was at once a natural, social, and contractual association, with a number of its basic terms pre-set by nature and society in order to protect the natural rights and duties of husbands and wives, parents and children. They also left in place traditional prohibitions on no-fault divorce, extramarital sex, and other sex crimes in order to protect the rights of women and children.

The key move made by liberal philosophers in the twentieth and early twenty-first century was to gradually remove the necessary natural and social dimensions of marriage as well. This liberalized the institution of marriage even more, reducing it to a private contract between a man and a woman who had reached the age of consent. These parties were now free to enter, exercise, and exit their marriage contract without interference from church, state, or society. They were free to renegotiate the terms of their marital contract. And they were free to live in various intimate relationships without any contracts at all. This posed dramatic new challenges to contemporary Protestants. Western Protestants have thus joined Catholics and others in a new modern marriage movement designed to protect and privilege the marital household, even while protecting personal liberty (Thatcher 1999).

REFERENCES

Blackstone, William (1765). *Commentaries on the Laws of England*, 4 vols. Oxford: Oxford University Press.

Browning, Don S. (2003). *Marriage and Modernization*. Grand Rapids, MI: Eerdmans.

Calvin, John (1960) [1559]. *Institutes of the Christian Religion*. Trans. F. L. Battles, ed. John T. McNeill. Philadelphia: Westminster Press.

Carlson, Eric Josef (1994). *Marriage and the English Reformation*. Oxford: Blackwell.

Dieterich, Hartwig (1970). *Das protestantische Eherecht in Deutschland bis zur Mitte des 17. Jahrhunderts*. Munich: Claudius Verlag.

Filmer, Robert (1949) [1642]. *Patriarcha and other Political Works*. Ed. Peter Laslett. Oxford: Oxford University Press.

Gouge, William (1622). *Of Domesticall Duties: Eight Treatises*. London: John Haviland.

Home, Henry (2005) [1779]. *Essays on the Principles of Morality and Natural Religion*, 3rd edn. Ed. Mary Catherine Moran. Indianapolis: Liberty Fund.

Home, Henry (2007). *Sketches of the History of Man, Considerably Enlarged by the Latest Additions and Corrections of the Author*. Ed. James A. Harris, 3 vols. Indianapolis: Liberty Fund.

Hume, David (1963) [1777]. *Enquiries Concerning the Human Understanding and Concerning the Principles of Morals*. 2nd edn. Ed. L. A. Selby-Bigge. Oxford: Clarendon Press, 1902, 2nd impr., 1963.

Hume, David (1987). *Essays Moral, Political, and Literary*, rev. edn. Ed. Eugene F. Miller. Indianapolis: Liberty Fund.

Ingram, Martin (1987). *Church Courts, Sex, and Marriage in England, 1570–1640*. Cambridge: Cambridge University Press.

Kingdon Robert M. (1995). *Adultery and Divorce in Calvin's Geneva*. Cambridge, MA, and London: 1995.

Köhler, Walter (1942). *Zürcher Ehegericht und Genfer Konsistorium*, 2 vols. Leipzig: Verlag von M. Heinsius Nachfolger.

Locke, John (1960) [1689]. *Two Treatises on Government*. Ed. Peter Laslett. Cambridge: Cambridge University Press.

Luther, Martin [WA] (1883–1987). *D. Martin Luthers Werke: Kritische Gesamtausgabe*, repr. edn, 78 vols. Weimar: H. Böhlaus Nachfolger.

Luther, Martin [LW] (1955). *Luther's Works*. Trans. and ed. Jaroslav Pelikan et al., 55 vols. Philadelphia: Westminster Press.

Ozment, Steven (2001). *Ancestors: The Loving Family in Old Europe*. Cambridge, MA: Harvard University Press.

Paley, William (2002) [1785]. *Principles of Moral and Political Philosophy*. Ed. D. L. LeMahieu. Indianapolis: Liberty Fund.

Powell, Chilton L. (1917). *English Domestic Relations 1487–1653: A Study of Matrimony and Family Life in Theory and Practice as Revealed by the Literature, Law, and History of the Period*. New York: Columbia University Press.

Seeger, Cornelia (1989). *Nullité de mariage divorce et séparation de corps a Genève, au temps de Calvin. Fondements doctrinaux, loi et jurisprudence*. Lausanne: Méta-Editions.

Shanley, Mary Lyndon (1987). *Feminism, Marriage, and the Law in Victorian England, 1850–1890*. Princeton, NJ: Princeton University Press.

Staves, Susan (1990). *Married Women's Separate Property in England, 1660–1833*. Cambridge, MA: Harvard University Press.

Thatcher, Arian (1999). *Marriage After Modernity: Christian Marriage in Post-Modern Times*. New York: New York University Press.

Waters, Brent (2007). *The Family in Social and Political Thought*. Oxford: Oxford University Press.

Williams, George H. (1992). *The Radical Reformation*, 3rd edn. Kirksville, MO: 16th Century Essays & Studies.

Witte, John, Jr. (2002). *Law and Protestantism: The Legal Teachings of the Lutheran Reformation*. Cambridge: Cambridge University Press.

Witte, John, Jr., and Robert M. Kingdon (2005, 2014). *Sex, Marriage and Family in John Calvin's Geneva*, 2 vols. Grand Rapids, MI: Eerdmans.

Witte, John, Jr. (2007). *The Reformation of Rights: Law, Religion, and Human Rights in Early Modern Calvinism*. Cambridge: Cambridge University Press.

Witte, John, Jr. (2012). *From Sacrament to Contract: Marriage, Religion, and Law in the Western Tradition*, 2nd enl. edn. Louisville, KY: Westminster John Knox Press.

Yenor, Scott (2011). *The Idea of Marriage in Political Thought*. Waco, TX: Baylor University Press.

PART V

CONTROVERSIES
WITHIN THE
CHURCHES

....

CHAPTER 20

CONFLICTS WITHIN THE ROMAN CATHOLIC CHURCH

....

LINDA HOGAN

INTRODUCTION

....

FOR over five decades the Roman Catholic Church has been embroiled in a series of theological controversies about sex and gender. The debates have revolved primarily around the meaning and significance of embodiment—and particularly of gendered embodiment—and have drawn the Church into a series of debates about the extent to which the tradition has been shaped by misogynistic and patriarchal views of women. Moreover, these controversies about sex and gender have occurred within the context of ongoing debates about the nature of the Church, the dynamism of the tradition, the primacy of conscience, and the authority of the magisterium. Thus these controversies about sex and gender have also tended to catalyse and intensify the more ecclesiologically focused debates, particularly those that have centred on the meaning of Vatican II and its legacy.

Both within the Church, and in society more generally, the late twentieth century was a period of great change, a time both of innovation and of turmoil. New moral questions were being raised as a result of technological and social change, and the traditional perspectives on morality were beginning to be challenged. The renewed ecclesiology of Vatican II also changed the ways in which Roman Catholics related to the tradition's teaching on morality and created an expectation that the laity would have a stronger voice in the articulation of the Church's position on these new and emerging issues. This intersection of the internal debates about the nature of the Church with the more broadly-based societal controversies about sex and gender has, therefore, led to a highly contested and fraught situation within Roman Catholicism.

Underlying many of the most contentious disagreements, especially disagreements about reproductive rights and same-sex relationships, one can discern fundamentally different theological understandings of the nature of the human body, the relationships between the sexes, and the malleability of sexuality. The chapter begins, therefore, with a discussion about the diversity of perspectives on embodiment, particularly female embodiment, and on the ethical significance of sexual difference. In addition to these questions which are centred on the meaning of the gendered body, this chapter will consider a parallel, and no less significant, set of discussions within Roman Catholicism, about the nature of moral truth and the capacity of human beings to apprehend that truth. These debates about natural law and the primacy of conscience have had a major impact on the credence given to the teachings of the magisterium on issues of sexuality and gender and on the extent to which they have been accepted. Having examined these underlying theological controversies, this chapter will go on to consider the contours of the contemporary debates about reproductive rights and same-sex relationships. Nor is there any sign of these controversies abating. Rather, the positions are becoming more polarized and the divisions more intractable.

INTERPRETING THE BODY

The publication, in 1968, of Mary Daly's *The Church and the Second Sex* marked a sea change in how the theological discussion about the female body was conducted. Prior to Daly's searing critique of Catholicism on account of its endemic misogyny, little attention was given to the ongoing impact of this patriarchal heritage. Subsequent to Daly's initial intervention, feminist theologians began to analyse the scale and depth of the misogyny inherent in the traditions and practices of Christianity and, as a result, today we are more clear-sighted about the nature and extent of the problem. Throughout the 1960s and 1970s, feminist scholars excavated the biblical and theological canon, unearthing the ideologies of subordination that were embedded in the tradition. Early seminal works, such as Kari Borresen's *Subordination and Equivalence: The Nature and Role of Women in Augustine and Aquinas* ([1968] 1995) and Rosemary Radford Ruether's *Religion and Sexism* (1973), highlighted how thoroughly and energetically ideologies of subordination were adopted, developed, and promoted within the Christian tradition more generally, and Roman Catholicism in particular. Later, the historical works of feminist philosophers and theologians like Margaret Miles (1989) and Caroline Walker Bynum (2001) explained how deeply embedded in Western theological and philosophical thinking this misogyny has been.

In particular, this work has revealed that, running through all of the different historical periods of Western theo-politics, there has been a deep-seated ambivalence, not only towards the body, but especially towards the female body. As the carrier of new life or as mother, she is to be revered and respected, but as carnal woman, as a sexual being, she evokes anxiety and dread. Within the theological traditions of Western Christianity, and especially within Roman Catholicism, these tensions are highly visible. On the one hand, there is the 'fear and loathing' of bodies, particularly of women's bodies. Moreover, the fear and loathing is exaggerated because of the tradition's tendency to view the meaning and significance of bodiliness exclusively, or at least primarily, through the lens of sexuality. Indeed, many of the more infamous misogynistic theological statements about women's nature exemplify this and regard women's bodies, paradoxically, as both the cause and consequence of their inferior status.

Yet this anti-body strain of the tradition exists alongside another, potentially contradictory theological narrative, expressed through the tradition's incarnational theology. This incarnational theology, underdeveloped and hesitant though it has been, offers a different way of conceptualizing and relating to the body. In this theological framework, the body is an intrinsic part of God's good creation and the vehicle of God's redemptive presence in the world. It has a consistent presence in theological analysis throughout the centuries although, for the most part, it has been overshadowed by the more negative and sceptical approach to the body. In the context of this incarnational strand, however, James Keenan argues that the view that Christianity has an unambiguously negative theology of the body does not stand up to scrutiny (1994: 330–346). Nonetheless, even with this important corrective, the negativity towards the female body continues to surface. Indeed, the Vatican's 1976 *Declaration on the Admission of Women to the Ministerial Priesthood* exemplifies this inability to conceptualize the female except through her body. As a result, in this text, as throughout that tradition, despite the broadly incarnational framework, women's bodies remain the stumbling block.

INTERPRETING THE GENDERED BODY

Critiques of the misogyny of the tradition quickly gave way to an interrogation of the nature and significance of sexual difference. A central preoccupation of second-wave feminism, this question about the ethical significance of the biological differences between men and women immediately became a lightning rod within Roman Catholicism. Feminism, especially in its earliest phases, was essentially a protest against the idea that biology is destiny. Taking its cue from Simone de Beauvoir's insistence in *The Second Sex* that 'one is not born, rather one becomes a woman', much of the early feminist theological analyses were premised on the insistence that each person can shape the meaning of her embodiment, even against the dominant cultural interpretations. This early definitive claim has been the catalyst for a highly contested and still unfinished debate about what it means to be in a sexually differentiated body and about the extent to which governing ideologies of gender and gender relations affect the ways in which the body is conceptualized.

Within Roman Catholicism, the ideology that has traditionally governed gender relations has been that of complementarity. This doctrine of complementarity is based on the claim that the differences between male and female are ontological, not social, part of our essential anthropological make-up. Indeed this claim that the categories of masculinity and femininity represent an ontological distinction in the nature of human beings is a fundamental premise on which much Roman Catholic moral theology has historically been based. Up until very recently, the tradition interpreted this ontological distinction hierarchically. Thus, the embedded misogyny combined with the idea of gender complementarity led to the construction of a theological anthropology which reinforced the inferiority of women. Indeed, threaded throughout the tradition, one can see evidence of this hierarchical interpretation of gender complementarity.

The personalist theology of the twentieth century attempted to reinvigorate the concept of gender complementarity, while resisting the hierarchical interpretations with which it had traditionally been associated. In the early decades of the twentieth century, the phenomenological approaches of Dietrich von Hildebrand ([1966] 1992) and Edith Stein (2002) led to a renewed interest in this idea of ontological complementarity. However, it was only when the Polish theologian Karol Wojtyla took this up in earnest—first in his 1960s study, published as *Love and Responsibility* (1981)—that the contemporary Roman Catholic theology of complementarity began to gain traction. Moroever, as Pope John Paul II, Wojtyla developed this anthropology further and promoted it through his teaching, most notably through his apostolic letter on women, *Mulieris dignitatem* (1988) and his apostolic exhortation on marriage, *Familiaris consortio* (1981). John Paul II did acknowledge that the concept of gender complementarity has, in the past, been interpreted in a hierarchical manner. However, through his exegesis of the Genesis text, he insists that Adam and Eve, the original man and woman, are images of God as a 'unity of two' and that their masculinity and femininity allow them to make the sincere mutual gift of self to one another (John Paul II 1988: 7). This complementarity, he argued, is one that is premised on a fundamental equality, so that although men and women play distinct roles in Church and society, they are nonetheless to be regarded as different but equal. Moreover, he insisted that this differentiation is seen in the biological structure of the male and female, so that the woman fulfils her femininity in motherhood and the man in fatherhood (1988: 8). Indeed, for the mother the 'unique contact with the new human being developing within her gives rise to an attitude towards human beings—not only towards her own child, but every human being—which profoundly marks the woman's personality' (1988: 18).

There is no doubt that John Paul II's promotion of this distinctive reading of complementarity has made a significant impact on the politics of sex and gender both within and outside the Church. For example, the growth of what is called 'new Catholic feminism', which draws its inspiration from the theology of John Paul II and of Hans Urs von Balthasar ([1976] 1990), has ensured that the idea of gender complementarity continues to have a popular as well as an academic voice within the Church (see Schumacher 2004, Bachiochi 2010; and the contributions of Sr. Prudence Allen and of Pia de Solenni in the popular press). This strongly essentialist reading of gender continues to be a contested position, however, not least amongst many feminists who refute the notion that there is an ontological difference between the sexes.

This concept of gender complementarity assumes a convergence between certain biological facts and the social interpretation of those facts. Liberal, socialist, and radical feminists, in contrast, do not accept such an analysis, but rather argue that there is a clear and unambiguous distinction between biology and culture, between the body and its cultural elaboration. The body is therefore regarded as the material upon which society inscribes particular meanings, albeit meanings that can be oppressive. Moreover, although oppressive, these are meanings that can be refused, reinterpreted, or transcended. Postmodern feminism has developed an even more anti-essentialist position, questioning the assumption that there is any definitive distinction between biological 'givens' and the cultural elaborations of these biological givens. Judith Butler has led the field in this context, suggesting that feminism, too, has wrongly accepted the established patriarchal construction of the natural world in which gender is assumed to be dichotomous. (It is interesting to note that even classics like Elizabeth Spelman's *Inessential Woman* (1988), although focused on the differences among women, do not question the binary nature of gender.) Butler argues that we believe the world to be divided into two genders because this is what we expect. Moreover, not only do we construct two genders because we look for them, we also construct an account of the two distinct sexes because that too is what we expect to find.

Butler's *Gender Trouble* ([1990] 2007), as well as her subsequent work, especially *Undoing Gender* (2004), has challenged in a radical way the assumption that gender is binary and that sexual difference falls naturally and biologically along dualistic lines. The presence of transsexual and intersex individuals, for example, confirms that the existing categorizations are too narrowly defined and that biological identity is often blurred or indeterminate. However, such is the force of this ideology that those whose morphologies are different tend to be remade and corrected, and ultimately are shaped according to the normative conceptualization of sex and gender as binary.[1] Nonetheless, what this analysis reveals is that the biology that is taken to underlie gender identity and on which the assumption of gender dichotomy is based, is far more complex and multifarious than most societies or religions are willing to acknowledge. Moreover, not only is the gender essentialism that underlies the ideology of complementarity challenged, but so too is the heteronormativity that flows from this.

Thus, it can be concluded that Roman Catholic tradition has, for the most part, essentialized sexual difference and sacralized complementarity. Alternative ways of narrating sexual identity have tended to be ignored, criminalized, or pathologized. However, in contemporary society, especially in Western society, these long-dominant assumptions are currently undergoing interrogation. Moreover, theologies of complementarity are especially under the spotlight, and are the subject of ongoing contestation. As shall be discussed later, one can see these debates being played out, not only in the ongoing disagreements about reproductive rights, but also in the disputes about same-sex relationships.

---

[1] Judith Butler discusses the complex and tragic story of David Reimer in 'Doing Justice to Someone: Sex Reassignment and Allegories of Transsexuality', in Butler (2004: 57–74).

INTERPRETING THE NATURE OF
MORAL TRUTH

Alongside the turmoil in the Roman Catholic Church on issues pertaining to gender and sexuality, an equally turbulent, although less well-known, set of debates about the nature of moral truth and the capacity of individuals to discern that truth was also under way. The immediate background to these debates was the development of what is now called the revisionist strand of moral theology that began in the 1940s and 1950s by Odon Lottin, Fritz Tillmann, and Klaus Demmer (see Keenan 2010: chs. 3 and 4). The later work of Bernard Häring, Charles Curran, and Margaret Farley, amongst others, added impetus to this revisionism, recasting in fundamental ways how Catholic moral theology thought about the nature of the human person, about our capacity to discern the truth, about the nature of the truth we seek, and about the extent to which human knowledge and reason can apprehend the good.

Although these fundamental epistemological concerns have been rehearsed in different guises over the past five decades, the publication of *Veritatis splendor* in 1993 provided the occasion for a comprehensive but deeply divisive debate on these issues. In *Veritatis splendor*, Pope John Paul II developed a response to what he claimed was the crisis of truth that engulfs the world today. With his characteristic anti-relativistic stance, John Paul II reaffirmed the universality and immutability of the moral commandments (1993: 173), arguing that the Church's magisterium 'teaches the faithful specific particular precepts and requires that they consider them in conscience as morally binding' (1993: 164). The implications of such a position for the putative primacy of conscience will be discussed later. As crucial, however, is the debate about the role that historical and cultural contexts have in determining how human beings come to know the moral truth.

Debates on this matter have dominated moral theology for decades and have revolved around a number of critical and related issues including the legitimacy of the concept of intrinsic evil, the normative significance of the direct–indirect distinction (Schüller 1979), and the absoluteness of moral norms (Fuchs 1983). Within the broad spectrum of theologians who are classed as revisionists, there is a strong commitment to a more dynamic understanding of the way in which human beings come to know and understand the truth, namely, one that can reckon with the historicity of human experience and the context-dependent nature of moral norms. Much of the disagreement has revolved around Aquinas' discussion of the 'secondary' precepts of the moral law (in qu. 94, a. 4 of the *Prima Secundae*, the details of which need not detain us here). The core of the issue, however, is that, for the classicists like John Paul II, William May, Robert George, and Germain Grisez, 'some moral norms are absolute, with no exceptions whatsoever, and that among such norms are those prohibiting always and everywhere acts such as the intentional killing of the innocent, adultery, fornication, contraception'

(May 2005: 2). By contrast, for the revisionists, including Richard McCormick, Franz Scholz, Daniel Maguire, Louis Janssens, and Charles Curran, when we deal with complex moral problems 'one must examine in great detail all aspects of the complex human reality before coming to an answer to a complex moral question about what should be done in a particular situation' (Curran 2005: 33).

INTERPRETING THE ROLE OF CONSCIENCE

There is a parallel and intersecting point of debate about the nature and authority of the moral conscience, much of it associated with the ambiguities that flow from the presence of conflicting characterizations both of the moral conscience itself and of the differing conceptualizations of the ecclesial context present in the texts of Vatican II. One of the classic articulations of the role of conscience is found in *Gaudium et Spes*, para. 16 (Flannery 1996: 916) which states that

> Deep within their consciences men and women discover a law which they have not laid upon themselves and which they must obey. Its voice ever calling them to love and to do what is good and to avoid evil, tells them inwardly at the right moment: do this, shun that. For they have in their hearts a law inscribed by God. Their dignity rests on observing this law, and by it they will be judged. Their conscience is people's most secret core, and their sanctuary. There they are alone with God, whose voice echoes in their depths... Through loyalty to conscience, Christians are joined to others in the search for truth and for the right solution to so many moral problems

In the early part of the passage, conscience is situated within the paradigm of law. Its function is articulated in terms of obedience to the objective moral law. Its task: to obey. Further on, the idiom changes substantially, with the paradigm of law ceding to that of person. Now conscience is 'the voice of God echoing in one's depths'. In his commentary on this text, Pope Benedict XVI, then Cardinal Ratzinger, argues that this text indicates that the authority of the conscience derives from its transcendent character. Thus, he concludes, 'Over the pope as the expression of the binding claim of ecclesiastical authority there still stands one's own conscience, which must be obeyed before all else; if necessary even against the requirement of ecclesiastical authority' (Ratzinger 1969: 134). However, although Cardinal Ratzinger's commentary reinforces this idea that conscience is the supreme and ultimate tribunal, the last resort which is beyond the claim of external social groups, even of the official Church, he is, nonetheless, critical of the text because he claims that it fails to explain 'how conscience can err if God's call is directly to be heard in it'.

Thus, *Gaudium et spes* instantiates the broader theological struggle between legalist and personalist readings of the tradition, and between differing models of the Church. Moreover, in *Veritatis splendor*, a comparable tension is also in evidence. In the sections on conscience, *Veritatis splendor* follows the tradition in insisting that the judgement of the individual conscience has an imperative character and that the maturity and responsibility of its judgements are measured by 'an insistent search for truth and by allowing oneself to be guided by that truth in one's actions' (John Paul II 1993: para. 61). Alongside this narrative, however, there is an insistence that 'the magisterium does not bring to the Christian conscience truths which are extraneous to it; rather it brings to light the truths which it ought already to possess'. In fact it contends that 'the Church puts herself always and only at the *service of conscience* ... helping it ... to attain the truth with certainty and to abide in it' (1993: para. 64.2, emphasis original). Precisely how these two contrary impulses will ultimately be reconciled is unclear. In the meantime, however, they continue to fuel the debate about the authority of conscience in the context of a tradition of magisterial teaching.

The last fifty years has seen a transformation of the discipline of moral theology. As has been widely acknowledged, there has been a move away from the act-centred, legalistic, minimalistic, and casuistic enterprise of the manuals, to the more biblically-based, historically-conscious, and context-sensitive theologies of today. However this transformation has not been uncontested. In fact, it has occasioned a series of debates about the nature of moral truth, the absoluteness of moral norms, the primacy of conscience, and the authority of the magisterium on matters of morals. Moreover, not only have these issues been hotly contested in their own right, but, in addition, their impact is discernible in the deeply divisive debates on the ethics of sex and gender, to which we now turn.

REPRODUCTIVE RIGHTS

Although the debates about reproductive rights have already been raging for at least five decades, they still show no signs of abating. There are many contentious issues, which range from contraception, abortion, and IVF, to extramarital sex and same-sex relationships. Over the decades these different issues have been to the fore in terms of being the ground on which the battles over sexual ethics have been fought. However, in each case, the central theological preoccupation of the magisterium had been to insist on maintaining what it regards as the fundamental link between the unitive and procreative dimensions of sexuality. For much of its history, the Church's teaching on sexuality has been focused on procreation, and particularly on procreation as one of the primary ends of the marital relationship. Particularly in the twentieth century, however, the language and emphasis of this traditional framework began to change, much of it driven by the early personalist theologies of Doms and Haaring, and also of Karol Wojtyla, later Pope John Paul II. Thus, by the 1960s, the Church had moved away from the traditional language of the primary and secondary ends of sex (procreation, mutual help, and the alleviation of concupiscence) and instead had begun to adopt the language of the equal ends of love and procreation. For example, Pope John Paul II speaks about the 'inseparable connection, established by God, which man on his own initiative may not break, between the unitive significance and the procreative significance which are both inherent in the marriage act' (John Paul II 1997: 421). However, he does so in the context of his strong understanding that the marriage act shows 'the value of total self-giving', which is 'the inner truth of conjugal love' (John Paul II 1981: 32). The rather mechanistic and reductive language of the primary and secondary ends of marriage is thus replaced by the language of mutual self-giving. Notwithstanding the change in idiom, however, the theological position on the inseparability of these two dimensions of the sexual relationship remained unchanged. Moreover, with the issuing of *Humanae vitae* in 1968, this fundamental premise of Catholic sexual ethics was further reinforced.

Even though the Papal Commission in 1963 recommended a change in the Church's approach to the question of the permissibility of the use of artificial contraception, *Humanae vitae* reiterated the ban on contraceptive methods that interrupted or altered biological processes with the purpose of preventing conception. The global reaction to the encyclical is well known, with *Humanae vitae* becoming synonymous with the increasing alienation of many Roman Catholics from their Church. The reaction was immediate and extensive. Dr Leo Alting von Geusau, for the interdenominational Centre for International Documentation on the Contemporary Church (Johannes [1969] 1970), monitored the reaction and reported that by May 1969 the centre had received over 4,000 communications from different geographical regions and different fields of expertise, including demography, medicine, economics, and theology. This material confirms what is commonly understood to be the case, namely that the initial reaction was almost entirely negative. The politics of the reception of *Humanae vitae* are too complex to detail here. However, it is clear that over the decades it has become the fault-line along which the Roman Catholic Church's sexual ethics has fractured. For the most part during the remainder of the papacy of Paul VI, *Humanae vitae* was ignored and very little effort was spent trying to influence the family planning policies of governments worldwide, or attempting to silence the ever-growing dissent. By contrast, however, during the papacy of John Paul II, a vigorous defence and promotion of *Humanae vitae* was begun. Moreover, this was pursued, not only by attempting to shape the personal choices of individual Catholics through an extensive catechetical programme, but also by promoting its public policy agenda, particularly in the run-up to the 1994 Cairo World Conference on Population and Development, during which a campaign to influence world leaders—including leaders of other religious traditions—was pursued.

For the most part, the Church's ban on artificial contraception has been ignored, particularly in countries where access to these products and services is not a problem. However, the HIV/AIDS pandemic reignited the debate about the Church's ban, specifically on the use of condoms. The debate has focused around a number of major issues, although for the most part it has not occasioned a change in the Church's ban on artificial contraception but rather on how, and to what extent, the case for use of prophylactics can be made within the context of the Church's moral teaching. Theologian James Keenan and medic Jon Fuller have been to the fore in this, arguing that the traditional principle of toleration could be invoked to allow for the use of condoms, and that this can be seen in terms of a method that protects the common good rather than one that cooperates in an illicit sexual union (see especially Keenan 1989: 205–220; 2000: 163–174).

Indeed, the Administrative Board of the US Bishops revealed that it, too, was open to such an approach, when, in its 1987 document *The Many Faces of AIDS*, it suggested that if it is obvious that a person (with HIV) will not act without bringing harm to others, 'a health professional could reasonably advise, on a personal level, that the person use condoms to minimize the harm' (Administrative Board of the US Bishops 1987). Moreover, it also suggested that, if grounded in a broader moral vision, church programmes could include accurate information about prophylactic devices (see Fisher 2009: 329–359).

Theologians, leaders of Catholic NGOs, and laity have been vocal in their opposition to the Church's refusal to use these mechanisms within the tradition to facilitate the use of condoms in the fight of AIDS.[2] Moreover, the stakes were raised further in 2006 when Bishop Kevin Dowling of the diocese of Rustenburg, South Africa called for the Church to lift its ban on the use of condoms. Dowling has been extensively involved in social justice work in South Africa and has seen at first hand the immiseration and violence with which hundreds of thousands of people live daily, and which creates the vulnerability that allows the pandemic to thrive. His argument is that, in the context of the AIDS pandemic, condoms should be accepted as a tool for protecting millions of vulnerable lives, especially the lives of the women and children forced into prostitution because of poverty. He insists that the Church's teaching is premised on the sanctity of life and that this should allow the Church to focus on condoms, not as a contraceptive device, but rather as a life-protecting intervention in the fight against AIDS (see Boustany 2006). However, notwithstanding the evidence that public health initiatives which use an ABC approach (Abstain, Be consistent, use Contraception) are successful, the Church continues to insist on an abstinence-only approach (see Benedict XVI 2005, 2006, 2007, 2009).

INFERTILITY

The technological advances of the late twentieth century also transformed the experience of infertility and provided new opportunities for those who, for a range of reasons, could not conceive naturally. Here again, the Church's response to these opportunities was entirely determined by the concern to maintain an unbreakable link between the unitive and procreative dimensions of sex. The first shot in this debate was issued as early as 1897 when, in answer to a question about whether artificial insemination was licit or not, the Congregation deemed that it was not (*Acta Sanctae Sedis* 1896–1897: (29): 704). Moreover, even as the various technological advances created more innovative solutions to the diverse physiological, medical, and psychological causes of infertility, the position of the Church was unchanged. Thus, the unambiguous condemnation of all

---

[2] The works of James Keenan, Tina Beattie, Kevin Kelly, and Enda McDonagh are of interest in this regard.

interventions remains premised essentially on the argument that the unitive and pro-creative dimensions of the sexual act are inseparable and must remain thus.

Notwithstanding the Church's fundamental objection to these technologies, however, it seems that Roman Catholics choose these options when they are medically appropriate. Some may opt for processes that only fertilize and implant one ovum so as to ensure that no supernumerary embryos are created, although there is no evidence to allow one to assess the extent to which this limitation is something that Roman Catholics choose more than other citizens. For the most part it seems that Catholics are not concerned about the moral legitimacy of the technical process that separates the unitive and pro-creative dimensions of sexual intercourse. However, if they decide to pursue fertility treatments that only implant one fertilized ovum it is usually because they believe that the pre-emplanted embryo should be regarded as having an equivalent status to a person and therefore they refuse procedures that create supernumerary embryos.

This issue of the status of the embryo also arises in the context of abortion. Indeed, within the realm of reproductive rights there is probably no issue more contentious or politicized than abortion. Moreover, the Roman Catholic Church's position has hardened considerably in the last century when the focus has been on the inviolability of human life from the moment of conception' (Congregation for the Doctrine of the Faith 1987). This is in contrast to the earlier theological discussion that, although it was framed in the context of the sanctity of life, tended to have a more gradualist approach to the status of the embryo and distinguish between early and late abortion (see Noonan 1970; Dombrowski and Deltete 2000). Pope John Paul II's 1995 encyclical *Evangelium vitae* articulated an absolutist position in terms of the condemnation of abortion, arguing that it is symptomatic of what he calls 'the culture of death'. His framing of the issue persisted into the papacy of Benedict XVI. Debates about the persuasiveness of this position revolve around the question of when personhood can be attributed to the fertilized ovum, with significant criticism focused on this idea of 'the moment of conception' and analogous concepts. Feminist theologians have argued that the tradition has consistently failed to acknowledge women's autonomy in decision-making and has allowed its latent misogyny to shape its approach to this fundamental issue. Although both sides of this debate acknowledge that the issue is a complex one, nonetheless the positions continue to harden and the politics of abortion continues to become more antagonistic.

SAME-SEX UNIONS

Many of the same fundamental issues are perceived to be at stake when the issue of same-sex relationships is discussed. In particular, the motif of the inseparability of the unitive and procreative elements of each and every sexual encounter also runs through the tradition's approach to the ethics of same-sex relationships. The contemporary debate about the ethics of homosexuality was essentially begun with the 1975 *Declaration on Certain Questions Concerning Sexual Ethics*, commonly referred to as *Persona humana*. It maintained this fundamental theological premise although it also introduced an important distinction between 'the homosexual condition or tendency and individual homosexual actions' which it believed has facilitated a more pastoral approach to homosexual persons. Not wanting this distinction between persons and acts to lead to a misunderstanding of the Church's position, the Congregation for the Doctrine of the Faith issued a further communication in 1986 which insisted that although 'the particular inclination of the homosexual person is not a sin, it is a more or less strong tendency ordered toward an intrinsic moral evil; and thus the inclination itself must be seen as an objective disorder' (Congregation for the Doctrine of the Faith 1986: para. 3). Thus, although it maintained this new position on not condemning the person on account of his or her sexual orientation, one is in no doubt that, although not culpable for the fact of the orientation, nonetheless the orientation itself is to be regarded as disordered. Moreover, in a further reinforcement of the original negative approach, the Congregation for the Doctrine of the Faith reiterated its unambiguous condemnation of homosexual activity so that when homosexual persons 'engage in sexual activity they confirm within themselves a disordered inclination which is essentially self-indulgent' (1986: para. 5).

COMPLEMENTARITY

The case for this position is made with arguments from natural law. Fundamental is the claim that there is a natural complementarity of the sexes, an ontological complementarity that is written into the structure of our natures. It is simply something from which we cannot deviate. Moreover, the tradition holds that the nature of marriage is premised on this natural gender complementarity and that the only reproductive sexual acts that can be regarded as morally acceptable are those between a married man and woman. These arguments from natural law tend to be supplemented by arguments from scripture, based on particular interpretations of key texts, as well as by arguments from tradition, based on the claim that there has been an unchanging and constant tradition of condemnation. However, it is the natural law argument that is regarded as decisive.

The feminist challenge to this concept of gender complementarity has been discussed earlier. In addition to the feminist critiques, however, there has also been an important and fiercely contested debate about the precise meaning of complementarity in the context of the discussion about the ethics of same-sex relationships. Todd Salzman and Michael Lawler have led the way, challenging the tradition's interpretation of this complementarity and arguing that it mistakenly conflated the host of different ways in which couples can be said to share a complementarity in the context of a sexual relationship. Within that context they suggest that the Church fails to appreciate the range of ways in which there may be a sexual complementarity between couples, and suggest that one must distinguish between biological complementarity and personal complementarity, and, within biological complementarity, one must distinguish between heterogenital complementarity and reproductive complementarity. According to Salzman and Lawler, the tradition conflates all of these different ways in which there may be a complementarity between couples. Moreover, they argue that the tradition refuses to accept the possibility that within a sexual relationship, personal complementarity can be achieved without heterogenital complementarity. In proposing a development of the tradition based on a more nuanced reading of the body, Salzmann and Lawler argue that in both same-sex and heterosexual relationships, the partners, as sexual human beings,

> give their bodies to one another and are theologically communicative that is, they are witnesses to the community of God's constancy and steadfast fidelity. In their witness, homosexual couples have iconic significance in their sexuality through embodied interpersonal union, just as heterosexual couples, both fertile and infertile have iconic significance in their sexuality in their embodied interpersonal union. Heterogenital complementarity is not a determining factor. Rather, two genitally embodied persons, heterosexual or homosexual, in permanent interpersonal union, who reflect God's constant love and steadfast fidelity, represent the determining factor.
>
> (Salzman and Lawler 2006: 635)

Others, including James Alison, Gareth Moore, and Margaret Farley, also question the way in which complementarity functions within the arguments about the ethics of same-sex relationships, although they do not pursue the argument in quite the same way as do Salzman and Lawler. For example, Margaret Farley's *Just Love: A Framework for Christian Sexual Ethics* (2006) suggests an alternative approach to sexual ethics that dislodges the question of sexual orientation from the central place it has traditionally occupied and replaces it with a question about the relationship between sexuality and justice in all forms of sexual expression. When one thinks this through in terms of same-sex relationships one can see that it is no longer characterized as an incomplete or less perfect expression of human sexuality. Rather, a person's sexuality can be recognized as being part of one's embodied identity. The moral questions are thus raised in terms of the quality of the relationships within which sexual desire is expressed. As one might expect, opposition to these positions has been strong and vocal. Robert George and Patrick Lee have been to the fore in challenging the reinterpretation of complementarity. Their particular argument is that 'only sexual acts between a man and a woman who have consented to the kind of union that would be fulfilled by the conceiving, bearing and raising children together (that is marriage) can consummate or actualise marital communion' (George and Lee 2008: 641). Other criticisms of these revisions have focused on the interpretation of natural law, on the status attributed to magisterial teaching, and on the extent to which the Church's moral tradition can change.

Same-sex unions are now formally recognized in approximately forty countries around the world. However, the Church's formal response to any proposal to recognize same-sex unions has been shaped by its condemnation of homosexual sex. An important text in this regard is 'Responding to Legislative Proposals on Discrimination Against Homosexual Persons' (Congregation for the Doctrine of the Faith 1992). For the most part there has been a reluctance to advocate for any form of social protection for same-sex unions, on the basis that, to quote Mario Conti, Archbishop of Glasgow, it will wound the body politic and trivialize the respect due to marriage.

However, there is some degree of variation in the responses of the different episcopal conferences. So, while all the episcopal conferences share a conviction that marriage, in both its sacramental and legal forms, should be reserved for heterosexual couples, nonetheless some of the episcopal conferences accept that there should be some protection for same-sex unions, with the caveat that they would only accept a form of protection that did not imply equivalence with heterosexual marriage. For example, the Irish Episcopal Conference in its submission to the All-Party Oireachtas Committee on the Constitution says:

> it may, in certain circumstances, be in the public interest to provide legal protection to the social, fiscal and inheritance entitlements of persons who support caring relationships which generate dependency, provided always that these relationships are recognised as being qualitatively different from marriage and that their acceptance does not dilute the uniqueness of marriage.
>
> (Irish Episcopal Conference and the Office for Public Affairs of the Archdiocese of Dublin 2005: 7–9)

The debate is further complicated by the question of whether same-sex couples should be permitted to adopt children and, moreover, where the law permits this, whether Roman Catholic bodies such as adoption agencies should facilitate it.

Conclusion

There is a large and growing chasm between the Roman Catholic Church's approach to sex and gender and the views and practices of a significant number of Catholics worldwide. The traditional views on women and gendered bodies have been completely repudiated and there is a suspicion among many that a residue of misogyny persists despite the relatively new rhetoric of egalitarianism. In terms of the Church's teachings on sexual morality, the experience of the last five decades suggests that these too are rejected or ignored by countless millions worldwide. The systematic sexual abuse of children by Catholic clergy has also highlighted, in the most shocking way possible, how a malignant nexus of sexuality and power could undermine a tradition so completely. On matters of sex and gender, therefore, the Church is facing a host of major challenges. However, it will only be able to begin to deal with them if it can find a way to deal with the internal divisions while attempting to forge a degree of consensus on these important ethical issues. The Church ought to be capable of creating a space wherein new insights are approached in an open and generous manner and wherein a shared sense of purpose will ameliorate the damage that disagreement on serious moral issues brings. Although, thus far, the Church has not managed to do this, its future credibility depends on this happening.

References

Acta Apostolicae Sedis (1896–1897). 'Dubium quod artificialem foecundationem'. *Acta Apostolicae Sedis*, 29: 704.

Administrative Board of the US Bishops (1987). *The Many Faces of AIDS*. Washington, DC: Office of Publishing and Promoting Services, US Catholic Conference. usscb.org/sswp/international/mfa87.html.

Alison, James (2001). *Faith Beyond Resentment: Fragments Catholic and Gay*. New York: Crossroad.

Bachiochi, Erika (2010) (ed.). *Women, Sex and the Church: The Case for Catholic Teaching*. Boston: Pauline Books & Media.

Beauvoir, Simone de ([1949] 1984). *Le Deuxième Sexe*. Paris: Gallimard. Trans. as *The Second Sex*. Harmondsworth: Penguin.

Benedict XVI (2005). 'Address to the Bishops of South Africa, Botswana, Swaziland, Namibia and Lesotho', 10 June. <www.vatican.va/holy_father/benedictxvi/spe_20050610_ad-limina-south-african_en.html>.

Benedict XVI (2006). 'Interview on the Way to Bavaria', 5 Aug. <www.vatican.va/holy_father/benedictxvi/spe_20060805_intervista_en.html>.

Benedict XVI (2007). 'Address to the Ambassador of Namibia to the Holy See', 13 Dec. <www.vatican.va/holy_father/benedictxvi/spe_20071213_namibia_en.html>.

Benedict XVI (2009). 'Address to Journalists enroute to Cameroon', 17 Mar. <www.vatican.va/holy_father/benedictxvi/spe_20090317_africa-interview_en.html>.

Borresen, Kari ([1968] 1995). *Subordination and Equivalence: The Nature and Role of Women in Augustine and Aquinas*. Kampen: Kok Pharos.

Boustany, Nora (2006). 'AIDS Crisis Shapes Bishop's Stance'. *Washington Post*, 26 Apr.

Butler, Judith (2004). *Undoing Gender*. New York and London: Routledge.

Butler, Judith ([1990] 2007). *Gender Trouble: Feminism and the Subversion of Identity*. New York and London: Routledge.

Bynum, Caroline Walker (2001). *Metamorphosis and Identity*. New York: Zone Books.

Congregation for the Doctrine of the Faith (1975). *Declaration on Certain Questions Concerning Sexual Ethics*. <http://www.vatican.va/roman_curia/congregations/cfaith/documents/rc_con_cfaith_doc_19751229_persona-humana_en.html>.

Congregation for the Doctrine of the Faith (1986). 'Letter to the Bishops on the Pastoral Care of Homosexual Persons', 1 Oct. *Origins*, 16 (13 Nov.).

Congregation for the Doctrine of the Faith (1987). *Instruction on Respect for Human Life*. <http://www.vatican.va/roman_curia/congregations/cfaith/documents/rc_con_cfaith_doc_19870222_respect-for-human-life_en.htm>.

Congregation for the Doctrine of the Faith (1992). 'Responding to Legislative Proposals on Discrimination Against Homosexual Persons'. *Origins*, 22 (6 Aug.).

Curran, Charles E. (1987). *Faithful Dissent*. London: Sheed & Ward.

Curran, Charles E. (1999). *The Catholic Moral Tradition Today: A Synthesis*. Washington, DC: Georgetown University Press.

Curran, Charles E. (2005). *Moral Theology of John Paul II*. London: T&T Clark.

Daly, Mary (1968). *The Church and the Second Sex*. New York: Harper & Row.

Dombrowski, Daniel A., and Robert Deltete (2000). *A Brief, Liberal Catholic Defense of Abortion*. Urbana and Chicago: University of Illinois Press.

Doms, Herbert (1939). *The Meaning of Marriage*. New York: Sheed & Ward.

Farley, Margaret (1990). *Personal Commitments: Beginning, Changing, Keeping.* New York: Harper & Row.

Farley, Margaret (2006). *Just Love: A Framework for Christian Sexual Ethics.* New York: Continuum.

Fisher, Anthony (2009). 'HIV and Condoms within Marriage'. *Communio: International Catholic Review*, 36: 329–359.

Flannery, Austin, OP (1996). *The Basic Sixteen Documents Vatican Council II Constitutions, Decrees, Declarations: A Completely Revised Translation in Inclusive Language.* Dublin: Dominican Publications.

Fuchs, Josef, SJ (1983). *Personal Responsibility and Christian Morality.* Washington, DC: Georgetown University Press / Gill and MacMillan.

George, Robert, and Patrick Lee (2008). 'Questio Disputata—'What Male–Female Complementarity Makes Possible: Marriage as a Two-in-One-Flesh Union'. *Theological Studies*, 69(3) (Sept.): 641–662.

Häring, Bernard (1978, 1979, 1981). *Free and Faithful in Christ: Moral Theology for Priests and Laity*, vols. i–iii. Slough: St Paul's Publications.

Irish Episcopal Conference and the Office for Public Affairs of the Archdiocese of Dublin (2005). *Joint Submission of the Committee on the Family.*

Johannes, F. V. ([1969] 1970). *Humanae Vitae: Dossier Delle Reazioni.* Milan: Mondadori. Published in English as *The Bitter Pill: Worldwide Reaction to the Encyclical Humanae Vitae.* Philadelphia: Pilgrim Press.

John Paul II (1981). *Apostolic Exhortation, Familiaris Consortio, to the Clergy and all the Faithful of the Whole Catholic Church, on the Role of the Christian Family in the Modern World.* <http://www.vatican.va/holy_father/john_paul_ii/apost_exhortations/documents/hf_jp-ii_exh_19811122_familiaris-consortio_en.html>.

John Paul II (1988). *Apostolic Letter, Mulieris Dignitatem, of the Supreme Pontiff, on the Dignity and Vocation of Women on the Occasion of the Marian Year.*

John Paul II (1993). *Veritatis splendor.* London: Catholic Truth Society.

John Paul II (1997). *The Theology of the Body: Human Love in the Divine Plan.* Boston: Pauline Books.

Keenan, James (1989). 'Prophylactics, Toleration and Cooperation: Contemporary Problems and Traditional Principles'. *International Philosophical Quarterly*, 29(2) (June): 205–220.

Keenan, James (1994). 'Christian Perspectives on the Human Body'. *Theological Studies*, 55: 330–346.

Keenan, James (2000). 'Collaboration and Cooperation in Catholic Healthcare'. *Australasian Catholic Record*, 77 (Apr.): 163–174.

Keenan, James F. (2010). *A History of Catholic Moral Theology in the Twentieth Century: From Confessing Sins to Liberating Consciences.* London and New York: Continuum.

May, William (2005) "Charles Curran's Grossly Inaccurate Attack on the Moral Theology of John Paul II", <http://www.christendom-awake.org/pages/may/curran.htm>.

Miles, Margaret R. (1989). *Carnal Knowing: Female Nakedness and Religious Meaning in the Christian West.* Kent: Burns & Oates.

Moore, Gareth (2005). *The Body in Context: Sex and Catholicism.* London: Bloomsbury.

Noonan, John (1970) (ed.). *The Morality of Abortion: Legal and Historical Perspectives.* Cambridge, MA: Harvard University Press.

Papal Birth Control Commission (1995). 'Responsible Parenthood Majority Report of the Papal Birth Control Commission' (Appendix 1). In Robert McClory, *Turning Point: The Inside*

Story of the Papal Birth Control Commission and How Humanae Vitae Changed the Life of Patty Crowley and the Future of the Church. New York: Crossroad.

Paul VI (1969). *Humanae Vitae.* London: Catholic Truth Society.

Ratzinger, Joseph (1969). *Gaudium et Spes.* In Herbert Vorgrimler (ed.), *Commentary on the Documents of Vatican II*, vol. v. New York: Herder and Herder, 115–163.

Radford Ruether, Rosemary (1973). *Religion and Sexism.* New York: Simon & Schuster.

Salzman, Todd A., and Michael G. Lawler (2006). 'Catholic Sexual Ethics: Complementarity and the Truly Human'. *Theological Studies*, 67: 625–652.

Salzman, Todd A., and Michael G. Lawler (2008). *The Sexual Person: Towards a Renewed Catholic Anthropology.* Washington DC: Georgetown University Press.

Schüller, Bruno (1979). 'Direct/Indirect Killing' In Charles E. Curran and Richard A. McCormick (eds), *Moral Norms and Catholic Tradition: Readings in Moral Theology.* New York: Paulist Press, 138–157.

Schumacher, Michele (2004) (ed.). *Women in Christ: Toward a New Feminism.* Grand Rapids, MI: Eerdmans.

Spelman, Elizabeth (1988). *Inessential Woman.* Boston: Beacon Press.

Stein, Edith (2002). *Finite and Eternal Being.* Washington, DC: ICS Publications.

von Balthasar, Hans Urs ([1976] 1990). *Theo-Drama: Theological Dramatic Theory, ii. Dramatis Personae: Man in God.* Trans. G. Harrison. San Franscico: Ignatius.

von Hildebrand, Dietrich ([1966] 1992). *Man and Woman: Love and the Meaning of Intimacy.* Manchester NH: Sophia Press.

Wojtyla, Karol (1981). *Love and Responsibility.* London: Collins.

CHAPTER 21

CONFLICTS WITHIN THE ANGLICAN COMMUNION

JANE SHAW

GENDER

IN the late 1960s and early 1970s, debate about the ordination of women in the Anglican churches was reignited, against the backdrop of the civil rights movement and the women's movement. The admission of women to the three 'orders'—deacon, priest, and bishop—became the subject through which the churches of the Anglican Communion argued about gender into the twenty-first century.

Historical Background to the Ordination of Women

This was not a new debate. In the late nineteenth century the deaconess order had been revived, and the early decades of the twentieth century saw disagreement about whether deaconesses were in holy orders or not. The Lambeth Conference—that once-a-decade gathering of bishops from all around the Anglican Communion—flip-flopped on the issue. In 1920, the Lambeth Conference declared that deaconesses were ordained; in 1930, it declared they were not. Nevertheless, the work of deaconesses in parishes and made people think about women in ministry.

As women were given the vote, went to university, and increasingly entered the professions, people began to ask why they could not also be ordained to the priesthood. In England, Maude Royden, an Oxford graduate, became the leading campaigner on the subject, and a renowned preacher. Denied a pulpit in the Church of England, Royden remained a devout Anglican but started to hold 'fellowship services' at The Guildhouse, a converted chapel near Victoria Station in London. She preached all over the world in the 1920s—the USA, Australia, New Zealand, Japan—and on her return founded, in 1930, the Anglican Group for the Ordination of Women (AGOW). The Church of England responded by producing reports.

In the middle of the Second World War, and for expedient reasons, the first woman was ordained as a priest in the Anglican Communion. Florence Li Tim-Oi was working in an isolated region of China, where she was pastor to an Anglican church of about a hundred, and Bishop Ronald Hall of Hong Kong and South China thought it more regular to ordain a woman than to allow a layman to exercise a sacramental ministry, including the celebration of communion. Geoffrey Fisher, who took up the post of Archbishop of Canterbury a few months after this ordination, did not look kindly on it, and put pressure on Florence Li Tim-Oi to resign. She agreed to stop functioning as a priest, but did not resign her orders. The Church in South China declared that it was spiritually wounded and grieved in heart by the Western Church's discrimination against women.

The Ordination of Women as Deacons, Priests, and Bishops

So in the 1960s, when Jim Pike, the radical bishop of California and supporter of the civil rights movement, pressed the question of the status of deaconesses in the Church, it was not new. But his declaration that he was going to recognize a deaconess in his diocese, Phyllis Edwards, as a deacon, provoked consternation and disagreement. At the liturgy in Grace Cathedral in San Francisco, Bishop Pike gave Phyllis Edwards the traditional deacon's stole and a copy of the Gospels. He also listed her as a full member of the clergy in diocesan directories. The issues at stake were not so much about gender but about authority and power, as the historian Pamela Darling comments: 'The Edwards recognition service...clearly linked the issue of women's ordination with questions of authority and collegiality, a connection that would reappear again and again' (Darling 1994: 111).

Pike's action pressed the issue for the whole Anglican Church. In 1968, the Lambeth Conference recommended, in Resolution 32, that those made deaconesses by the laying-on of hands with appropriate prayers be declared to be within the diaconate (that is, deacons). Decisions made at the Lambeth Conference are not, however, binding on the provinces and churches of the Communion, and never have been. They merely represent the 'mind' of the gathered Anglican bishops at that moment. It was now up to individual provinces of the Anglican Communion to decide whether or not they would follow Lambeth's recommendation. The churches of Canada, Hong Kong, Kenya and Korea quickly did so, as did the American Episcopal Church. Given that ordination to the diaconate was, in most cases, transitional, leading to ordination to the priesthood, the larger question of women's entry into the priesthood was necessarily opened up by this change.

The 1968 Lambeth Conference, while endorsing the ordination of female deacons, declared in Resolution 34 the evidence for or against women as priests to be inconclusive.

In Resolution 35, it sent that question out for debate in the provinces. Three further resolutions, 36–38, attempted both to encourage discussion and yet retain control. It was the Anglicans in Hong Kong who once again led the way in the Communion as a whole. In 1971, Jane Hwang and Joyce Bennett were ordained priest there by Bishop Gilbert Baker, and Florence Li Tim-Oi's priesthood was again recognized. This ordination took place hot on the heels of the very first meeting of the Anglican Consultative Council (ACC), a pan-Anglican committee recently set up to consider the controversial issues that faced the whole Communion. That meeting, in Kenya in early 1971, had called upon all churches in the Communion to report their views on female priests to the next meeting of the ACC in 1973. But Bishop Baker of Hong Kong reported back much earlier: his diocesan synod had already passed a motion in favour of the ordination of the women as priests, and he wanted to get on with it. The ACC gave him their blessing, by twenty-four votes to twenty-two, also stating that it would use its influence to encourage all provinces to stay in communion with the dioceses and provinces, which took the step of ordaining women as priests. The Synod of the Church of Burma followed in 1972, voting for women as priests. The Church of England, on the other hand, continued its tradition of producing reports and having debates.

Meanwhile, in the Episcopal Church in the USA, some women who felt called to the priesthood, and their male and female supporters including bishops, were getting frustrated and restive. To their great disappointment, the Church's General Convention in 1973 had voted against ordaining women. In 1974 the recently retired bishop of Philadelphia, Robert DeWitt, agreed to ordain eleven women, despite General Convention's vote of the previous year. His decision followed calls from a number of prominent churchmen for the bishops to ordain women equally alongside men. The presiding bishop of the Episcopal Church, John Allin (who was opposed to the ordination of women) telegrammed each of the women, asking them to reconsider this move, but to no avail. On 29 July, the Feast of Mary and Martha, eleven women were ordained priest at the church of the Advocate in Philadelphia. They became known, ever after, as the Philadelphia Eleven. Four bishops were involved, and a congregation of 2,000 witnessed the historic event. The event was distressing to many because these women and their supporters had declined to wait for the Church's permission. Pamela Darling interprets their actions as following 'the model of the civil rights movement, appealing to the "higher" authority of conscience informed by the Holy Spirit, accountable to a community which valued the full humanity of women above the claims of ecclesiastical tradition' (Darling 1994: 129).

Opinion was divided and many were shocked because the Episcopal Church prided itself on being democratic, with authority held in General Convention, the three-yearly decision-making meeting of bishops, priests, and clergy. The House of Bishops met quickly after the Philadelphia ordination; they condemned the ordinations as invalid (while many others saw them as irregular but still valid) and rounded on their four brother bishops who had been involved, for breaking the ranks of collegiality. But they were powerless to do much—for the power of the House of Bishops only exists when they meet in the context of General Convention—and this was made clear when a second 'illegal' or irregular ordination took place a year later, in Washington DC, this time of four women. It was only when General Convention met in 1976 that the issue could be resolved, and they voted to make women eligible for ordination to the priest-hood and the episcopate.

Back in the Church of England, in 1975 the General Synod debated the topic, though, as historian Sean Gill wryly notes, they did so 'with all the enthusiasm of men and women asked to cross a minefield wearing magnetic boots—and perhaps, in the view of all sides—with the same results' (Gill 1994: 251). A resolution stating that there were no fundamental theological objections to the ordination of women to the priesthood was passed in all three houses (bishops, clergy, and laity), but motions to remove the legal barriers to the ordination of women failed. Courtesy, restraint, and patience were all urged. The shadow of how women had been ordained in the Episcopal Church made some people nervous, while others were impatient, knowing that the churches in Canada and New Zealand had voted to ordain women as priests (and indeed bishops) in 1975 and 1976 respectively.

When General Synod once again rejected a motion to ordain women in 1978, disap-pointment was high. In 1979, the Movement for the Ordination of Women (MOW)—a national movement whose activism was rooted in diocesan branches—was begun. England finally got female deacons in 1987, a year after Australia's first female deacons had been ordained in Melbourne. The English General Synod voted for women to be priests in 1992, the year that the first women were ordained as priests in Perth, Australia (Lindsay and Scarfe 2012). Women were finally ordained as priests in the Church of England in 1994, nineteen years after General Synod had declared 'that there are no fundamental theological objections to the ordination of women to the priesthood'. By then other parts of the Anglican Communion already had female bishops, the first being Barbara Harris, consecrated as a suffragan (assistant) bishop in the Diocese of Boston in 1989. Florence Li Tim-Oi was a concelebrant at the Eucharist following the ordination and consecration. The following year saw the first female diocesan bishop in the Communion: Penny Jamieson in Dunedin, New Zealand. In 1993, Victoria Matthews was elected a suffragan bishop in the Diocese of Toronto, Canada, and consecrated early in 1994. In 2007, Nerva Cot Aguilera was ordained a bishop in the Episcopal Church of Cuba and in 2008 Kay Goldsworthy was ordained as an assistant bishop for the Diocese of Perth. In 2013, the Church of Wales voted for female bishops, and the Church in Ireland appointed their first female bishop, Pat Storey. The Church of England, which had rejected women bishops in November 2012 by just six votes in the House of Laity, was looking like it was out in the cold, and was suffering a crisis about its credibility.

A comparison between the Episcopal Church in the USA and the Church of England, and how each church went about the ordination of women, may be instructive here. The General Convention of the Episcopal Church was forced to respond to the irregular ordinations in Philadelphia and Washington, DC, at its meeting in 1976, just as it had been forced to consider the question of female deacons after Bishop Jim Pike's actions at Grace Cathedral ten years earlier. But when it came to debate the matter, it did so proactively, and voted for women to be ordained to the priesthood and episcopate. There was opposition, but there was no capitulation, with the consequence that now, some thirty years on, women have been ordained in all 110 dioceses of the Episcopal Church; seventeen women have been elected and consecrated as bishops in the United States; and in 2006, Katherine Jefferts Schori was elected to a nine-year term as the presiding bishop (the head of the Episcopal Church).

The Church of England has gone about things very differently. Those who worked for the ordination of women did so methodically, acting through the mechanisms and procedures of General Synod to achieve their result. This was a laborious process, and took until 1992, and even then Synod only voted for women to be ordained to the priesthood. The question of women in the episcopate is still, in 2013, being debated. The attempt to hold things together has often meant not facing the question squarely, or deferring it. As Margaret Webster writes,

> Since 1984 the House of Bishops had supported the ordination of women as priests. Even in 1978, influenced by the Lambeth Conference, the majority had voted in favour. But they wanted that support to be consistent with a quiet life, and for many of them the policy had been to sidestep the questions at the heart of the matter.
>
> (Webster 1994: 192)

As a consequence, the Church of England, especially perhaps the bishops, capitulated to opposition. While all other churches in the Anglican Communion that have female priests (and in some cases female bishops) have dealt pastorally but informally with those opposed to the ordination of women, the Church of England decided it needed to cater for that opposition by creating 'flying bishops' or Provincial Episcopal Visitors (PEVs). This phenomenon came about *after* General Synod had voted for the ordination of women as priests, but before the legislation went to Parliament, and was an attempt by bishops to keep opponents in the Church when some were vociferously threatening to leave (and when the Church of England had promised a £30,000 payout to each leaver). This synodical (not parliamentary) legislation, enabled individual priests and parishes opposed to the ordination of women to choose the oversight of a PEV rather than a diocesan bishop. It has been much criticized for institutionalizing the opposition to female priests and setting a problematic precedent for the whole Anglican Communion by suggesting that oversight is no longer territorial but can, rather, be *issue*-based. It paved the way for all kinds of groups to think that they can choose their own bishop; in the recent controversies about gay bishops, some churches have opted for oversight from bishops of other provinces, in a form of 'border-crossing' which has been frowned upon but not disciplined (Furlong 1998). Secondly, a precedent has been set in how the Church of England has gone about considering the ordination and consecration of women as bishops: it has started with the question 'what do we do about the opponents?' as opposed to the more rational and obvious starting point, 'how do we have women bishops?' The Church of England will have female bishops, probably sooner rather than later, but on what terms? Will it be on the same terms as male bishops or not? (Shaw 2008).

Theology and Gendered Roles

There are more issues in relation to gender and the Church than the ordination of women as deacons, priests, and bishops, but the Anglican Communion has discussed gender—and the related questions of power, authority, and the broader organization of society—largely through debates on this topic. Conservatives on the evangelical end of the Church have voiced their opposition to the ordination of women with the use of certain biblical texts, especially those that seem to advocate 'male headship' such as Ephesians 5:21–33. Such arguments relate to larger questions of social order. A theology of divinely ordered gendered hierarchy, appealing to such biblical texts and also to the idea that the Son is subordinated to the Father in the Trinity, has been especially developed and promulgated in the ultra-conservative Diocese of Sydney in Australia where women cannot be ordained priests (Porter 2006).

Theological anthropology is also at the heart of these debates about ordination. Opponents of the ordination of women at the 'high' end of the Anglican Church appealed to Jesus' maleness and a particular understanding of a priest as an 'icon of Christ', to say that women could not represent Christ at the altar. This strikes at the very heart of orthodox Christian anthropology, which says that women and men are made equally in the image and likeness of God. High Church opponents have also appealed to the notion that all Jesus' twelve apostles were male and their successors, bishops, were all male (Baker 2004). Feminist historians, employing more sophisticated tools of analysis, have pointed to the archaeological evidence for female *episcope* (Eisen 2000), and have also pointed to the problems inherent in a notion of a seamless chain of bishops, given the diversity and geographical diffusion of the early churches (Lyman 2004).

Powerful cultural norms about the role of women and men are challenged when we admit women to the priesthood and episcopate, and these vary across the different cultures represented in the Anglican Communion. In English society, for example, we might point to the 'clubbable' homosocial nature of the House of Bishops, embedded in the Established Church, which acts subtly against the admission of women. The Kenyan Anglican theologian Esther Mombo, outlining the sociocultural factors that prevent women becoming bishops in Africa, notes that the Church there is strongly patriarchal, but also powerfully tribal. This causes great wrangles in episcopal elections, as the dominant tribe tries to get their own man in. As she notes,

> This [emphasis on the tribe] affects women because women are generally viewed as outsiders in the tribe in which they are born and strangers in the tribe into which they are married. In this case the social and ethnic expectations of episcopacy make it hard for a woman to be nominated to the post.

> (Mombo 2004: 165)

Such cultural norms about gender, especially around sexual difference and the problems and presumptions of gender complementarity, also affect the discussions on sexuality. But before discussing those norms and presumptions, let us look at the history of these debates in the Anglican Communion over the last few decades.

SEXUALITY

The Lambeth Conference has been debating sex and sexuality since its third meeting in 1888. It was at that meeting that it first addressed the question of polygamy amongst converts, an issue that would return for discussion exactly a hundred years later in 1988. Homosexuality was first discussed in 1978, and has been discussed at every Lambeth Conference since. The recurring nature of debates at Lambeth Conference about sex and sexuality over more than a hundred years indicates how pressing and puzzling the Church has found this topic; the conference's resolutions reveal when the Church has made new decisions as well as reversals of thought about these questions, changing the tradition or moving it in new directions.

The recurring nature of these debates is not surprising. Marriage has been vigorously defended by the Church in the modern era precisely because of its rather chequered history in the Christian tradition, particularly in the long period between the fourth and sixteenth centuries when celibacy was regarded as the greater good (Shaw 2005). The nature of 'family' is always going to be debated because what family is, and what it means, varies so widely amongst the 77 million Anglicans across the world. The question of reproduction will always be an issue because it touches on the status of women and relates to demographical questions. Homosexuality has become the touchstone for all these issues, and many more—not least post-colonialism—in the last two decades, leading to fierce debates across the Anglican Communion that have yet to be resolved.

Homosexuality

The Anglican churches are not alone in making homosexuality the vehicle by which conversations about sex can occur amongst Christians. Society, anxious about sex at a time of rapidly changing values and practices, has found homosexuality to be a convenient path into a discussion of broader issues about sex, and, for some, a way of avoiding real conversation about heterosexuality (Herzog 2008). Similarly, as civil rights for gays and lesbians have increased and been largely accepted by democracies in the West, religion is a way for the larger society to have a debate about the role of gay and lesbian peoples, and the Church provides a location for the expression of continued unease in some quarters about that granting of civil rights.

The Anglican churches, including the bishops in conference at Lambeth, debated many aspects of sex and sexuality long before they began to talk about homosexuality, but it was the ferocity of recent debates, ostensibly at least about the ordination of openly gay men and lesbians as priests—and, in particular, as bishops—and the blessing of same-sex unions and gay marriage, that led many to declare the Communion to be in crisis (Hassett 2007). Mary-Jane Rubenstein expressed in 2008 (the year of a Lambeth Conference) what many people thought: that 'the current quality of internecine rancour might ultimately prove too much for the Communion to bear' (Rubenstein 2008: 134). Nevertheless, the proposed Anglican Covenant, designed to hold the Communion together by encouraging provinces to covenant together while at the same time making some churches 'second rank' if they strayed too far from a general consensus on issues such as homosexuality, was rejected by a range of Anglican provinces, including the Church of England. Despite threats from some parties, the Anglican Communion has not split, though some splinter groups have left.

At the Lambeth Conference in 1978 a resolution was passed asking for wider discussion of homosexuality in the Church. It was the first of many calls for learning and listening. The 1988 Lambeth Conference reaffirmed this 1978 resolution and its call for 'dispassionate study of the question of homosexuality', and also asked each province to 'reassess, in the light of such study and because of our concern for human rights, its care for and attitude towards persons of homosexual orientation'.

By the time the 1998 Lambeth Conference met, some provinces in the Communion, most notably the Episcopal Church of the USA, the Anglican Church in Canada, and the Church of England, had been studying the subject of homosexuality, as urged by the 1978 and 1988 meetings. The Episcopal Church had gone beyond study and had begun to ordain openly gay men and lesbians as priests. In 1977, Bishop Paul Moore of New York ordained Ellen Barrett, the first openly lesbian priest. In 1994, the Episcopal Church's General Convention had passed a resolution stating: 'No one shall be denied access to the selection process for ordination in this Church because of race, color, ethnic origin, age, national origin, marital status, sexual orientation, disabilities or age, except as otherwise specified by these Canons.' Nevertheless, it clarified, 'No right to ordination is hereby established,' and Episcopalians continued to disagree about the issue.

In Britain, the Lesbian and Gay Christian Movement (LGCM) had been founded in 1976. Official reports had assessed the subject, such as the 1979 document *Homosexual Relationships: A Contribution to Discussion*. This was considered too liberal, so in 1986, a standing committee of the Church of England House of Bishops asked the Board for Social Responsibility to form a working party that would advise the House of Bishops on homosexuality and lesbianism. The Revd June Osborne chaired the working party, and the result was the Osborne Report of 1989, which drew on the direct testimony of gay and lesbian Christians. The working party did precisely what the Lambeth resolutions had asked national churches to do: it set out to report the 'experiential facts' as well as the choices that gay Christians made about their lives, so that any discussion faced up to 'what actually happens'. As a result, the working party suggested the Church of England should be more welcoming to gays and lesbians, and should actually listen to them. 'Homosexuality is about homosexual people. We should never lose sight of the painful and stressful journey many homosexual people

have to make in the church and in society—with little understanding from either'
(Osborne 1989: 34).

The Osborne Report was also considered too liberal and was never published. Over
twenty years later, in 2012, as the Church of England was responding to the British
Government's proposals for gay marriage, the *Church Times* decided to publish it on its
website, indicating its enduring importance for discussion (*Church Times*, 20 January
2012). One reason that the Osborne Report had not been published was the eruption of
a fierce debate in the Church of England General Synod in 1987, a year after the Osborne
Report was commissioned, and two years before it was completed. The conservative
resolution that emerged from that bitter debate led the bishops to publish their own
document in 1991, *Issues in Human Sexuality*, which also called for further dialogue and
discussion. As George Carey, then Archbishop of Canterbury, put it, 'we do not pretend
[this] to be the last word on the subject' (Carey 1991: p. vii). Crucially, this report drew
a distinction between ordained and lay, saying that gay priests needed to remain celibate, while considering it permissible (though not ideal) for gay and lesbian laypeople to
enter into same-sex monogamous relationships.

Meanwhile, official reports and debates aside, in both the Church of England and the
Episcopal Church, the blessing of such same-sex unions had been happening unoffi-
cially for some time. The LGCM in Britain had a confidential list of forty clergy willing to officiate at such services and, by the late 1990s, was getting about 500 enquiries a
year. In 1997, the year before the Lambeth Conference was to meet again, the House of
Deputies at the Episcopal Church's General Convention debated a resolution to prepare
liturgical materials for blessing same-sex partnerships, and that failed by just one vote.
For some people, as Stephen Bates puts it, 'The gays seemed to be winning the argument.
And then came the 1998 Lambeth Conference' (Bates 2004: 124).

The 1998 Lambeth Conference was a turning point. The tenor of the event is caught in
one single image: Bishop Emmanual Chuckwuma of Enugu, Nigeria—outside the conference halls—attempting to exorcize the homosexual demons out of Richard Kirker,
the coordinator of the LGCM, after telling him that Leviticus demanded the death penalty for homosexuality (Bates 2004: 125–141). The 1998 Lambeth Conference did not
set the tone or provide the environment for a respectful discussion across the divides.
The bishops failed to meet formally (or, in most cases, informally) with gay and lesbian
Christians to hear their experiences, despite requests for them to do so. It was as if all
the calls for careful listening and greater education over the past three decades had
been for naught. Resolution 1.10 on homosexuality was far more conservative than the
1978 and 1988 resolutions. It called for further education and dialogue as those previous resolutions had, and yet at the same time undermined that call by rejecting 'homosexual practice as incompatible with Scripture' and declaring that it could 'not *advise*
the legitimizing or blessing of same sex unions nor ordaining those involved in same
gender unions [emphasis added]'. The word 'advise' is significant: despite the fact that
Lambeth resolutions are not, and never have been, binding on individual provinces,
many conservatives would go on to evoke Resolution 1.10 as if it were 'holy writ' (Bates

2004: 140) in the years following, as openly gay, partnered bishops were proposed in the USA and England, the first by election, the second by appointment.

Gene Robinson, an openly gay, partnered man, was elected as diocesan bishop of New Hampshire in June 2003, and ratified as bishop at the Episcopal Church's 2003 General Convention. It was a matter of some contention in the Church, and the 2003 meeting of General Convention also passed a moratorium on gay bishops and same-sex blessings by way of a compromise (Robinson 2008). Robinson entered office as bishop of New Hampshire in 2004. The Archbishop of Canterbury, Rowan Williams, did not invite him to the 2008 Lambeth Conference. That conference steered clear of any votes, sticking to its remit of conversation. A group of about 200 conservative bishops chose not to go, and had an alternative conference (in a group known as GAFCON). In 2009, the General Convention of the Episcopal Church lifted the moratorium on gay bishops; Mary Glasspool, an openly lesbian priest with a partner, was elected suffragan bishop of Los Angeles later that year, and consecrated in the spring of 2010. That convention also mandated its liturgy group to draw up a draft of a same-sex blessing covenant.

While the USA forged ahead, the Church of England—or at least Dr Rowan Williams, the Archbishop of Canterbury—backed down. When Richard Harries, Bishop of Oxford, appointed Jeffrey John as his suffragan bishop of Reading in 2003, he cleared it first with the archbishop, because Dr John was an openly gay man with a partner, though he affirmed that they had a celibate relationship, in accordance with the *Issues in Human Sexuality*. But that document had itself become 'holy writ' rather than the discussion document it was intended to be, and when it looked as if Dr John might be consecrated a bishop, the conservatives swung into action, using as a weapon an article that he had written in favour of same-sex relationships. The opposition became bitter; the Archbishop of Canterbury backed down and put pressure on Dr John to resign and, unlike the Episcopal Church, England was not to have an openly gay, partnered bishop after all.

Meanwhile, as the Church of England and the Episcopal Church in the USA were discussing gay bishops, parts of the Anglican Church in Canada were attracting attention over the issue of blessing same-sex unions. In May 2003 the Bishop of New Westminster, Michael Ingham, announced that he had given permission to priests in his diocese to bless same-sex unions, and issued a rite for that. The General Synod of the Church in Canada did not give its full approval, however, even as individual dioceses voted in favour of such blessings over that decade.

As these events played out, it became clear that battle lines had been drawn up during the 1998 Lambeth Conference, and the conservatives, having triumphed then, swung into action as soon as Gene Robinson was elected bishop of New Hampshire, Jeffrey John was appointed bishop of Reading in England, and Michael Ingham allowed same-sex blessings in church in western Canada. In the USA, a group of nineteen US bishops, led by Robert Duncan of Pittsburgh, made a statement warning the Church of a possible schism between the Episcopal Church and the Anglican Communion; five years later, Duncan himself left the Episcopal Church to head up a small splinter church

(Anglican Church in North America, known by its acronym ACNA), taking some parishes from the Diocese of Pittsburgh with him.

The differences of opinion about homosexuality are often rather crudely drawn in the press as being between conservatives and liberals, the Global South and the West. But none of these groups spoke with one voice. Once Gene Robinson's election was announced, conservatives in the West, especially North America, harnessed the conservative voices of the Global South, especially in Africa, in their opposition to Robinson. One of the earliest conservative, and most controversial, groups to create transnational ties of this sort was Anglican Mission in America; it had formed even before the election of Gene Robinson as bishop. It was the earliest to put itself under the authority of foreign primates, and in 2000 had two American priests consecrated as bishops in Singapore by foreign primates. These moves were widely regarded as an attack on Anglican unity and orthodoxy, and Rowan Williams, the Archbishop of Canterbury, publicly questioned the legitimacy of the consecrations.

Nevertheless, the Global South was not, and still is not, united in its views on homosexuality. The Anglican Church in Nigeria has been a leading voice against homosexuality, especially under the lead of Archbishop Peter Akinola (who retired in 2010). By contrast, the Church in South Africa resolutely stood in favour of a more liberal view, with Archbishop Desmond Tutu taking the lead on that. In 2013, he declared that he would rather choose hell than worship a homophobic God. And even when the (usually male) bishops of a particular country have spoken out against homosexuality, individual theologians have voiced the diversity of views actually held: in Kenya, theologian Esther Mombo has been such an alternative public voice.

The often bitter arguments, ostensibly about homosexuality, tapped into many issues in the Communion as a whole, not least central control v. provincial autonomy and the interpretation of scripture, but in many ways they were about who would ultimately 'own' the 'Anglican franchise'. This ongoing set of controversies about homosexuality was shot through with questions about identity, colonialism and post-colonialism, and gender, just as other debates about sexuality have been.

In the debates about homosexuality, conservatives set up a false dichotomy between 'traditionalists' and 'revisionists', regarding scripture and tradition as having spoken with a unitary, unchanging, and timeless voice on that subject. This problematic hermeneutic has been employed to try and impose Communion-wide uniformity, despite the long history of provincial autonomy. However, even a cursory look at the Anglican Church's thinking and decisions shows reversals about various aspects of sexuality over the twentieth century, indicating that tradition is dynamic, not static, and scripture is always necessarily interpreted in relationship to the context in which it is read. In the cases of polygamy and divorce, it is clear that in the modern period the principle of provincial autonomy was firmly held until very recently.

Take polygamy, for example. The 1988 Lambeth Conference not only addressed the issue of polygamy; it reversed its previous resolution, passed in 1888, on the subject. Nineteenth-century missionaries encountered polygamy in many of the societies they travelled to, and faced the problem of what to do about this practice, so clearly rejected by Christian tradition, despite its prevalence in the Hebrew scriptures. It proved a particularly tough issue in parts of Africa. Incentives to give up polygamous house-holds—such as hut taxes—were introduced by the colonial administration, but the issue remained, especially in parts of Southern Africa. By the 1860s, missionaries were writing back to the Church of England for advice on what to do, as polygamy seemed an impos-sible problem. How could someone remain in a pre-existing polygamous relationship and convert to Christianity? Some missionaries baptized polygamous men; others did not (Jones 2011).

Some churchmen working in Africa argued for a more lenient approach, especially Bishop John Colenso of Natal, who believed that a polygamous man could be admitted to the Church, but his more open view did not prevail. Thus the Lambeth Conference of 1888 stated in Resolution 5 that polygamous men could not be baptized, though they could be admitted as candidates for baptism 'until such time as they shall be in a posi-tion to accept the law of Christ'. The accompanying report made it clear that polygamy was 'inconsistent with the law of Christ'. The wives of polygamists were, in some cases, to be admitted to baptism on the grounds that they were faithful to one husband, and usu-ally had 'no personal freedom to contract or dissolve a matrimonial alliance' (Davidson 1929: 120, 134). Polygamy was discussed at several twentieth-century Lambeth confer-ences (1920, 1958, 1968) but the bishops' position remained consistent until 1988. For example, Resolution 23 on 'Marriage Discipline' passed in 1968, was very clearly opposed to making any concessions to those in polygamous marriages.

The cultural conflict inherent in these deliberations, and with which nineteenth-century missionaries struggled, remains. In African countries with large Muslim populations, the question repeatedly occurs when a Muslim man is con-verted to Christianity: if he is polygamous, should he give up all but one of his wives when baptized? If he does, he knows that those women will be rejected by his tribe (into which they have married) and by their tribe of birth, and therefore will have few means of financially supporting themselves, the most obvious being prostitution. So it can be argued that as a matter of compassion the polygamous man should retain all his wives after he has been baptized as a Christian, even though polygamy has been clearly rejected by Christianity. It also takes into account the woman's perspective and experi-ence, which is rare in most Christian conversations about sexuality.

In 1972, the Anglican archbishops in Africa asked the Roman Catholic priest and aca-demic historian Adrian Hastings to research Christian marriage in Africa and produce a report. Hastings was an outspoken critic of colonialism and, while holding monogamy as the ideal of Christian marriage, he recommended: 'while Christians should not feel free to take on a second wife, people within a polygamous marriage should, if other-wise suitably disposed, be received to baptism and communion' (Hastings, quoted in Jones 2011: 406). Hastings' report came out at just the moment that some African writ-ers, such as Felix Ekechi, were arguing for the full acceptance of polygamy as a legiti-mate form of Christian marriage. Ekechi wrote: 'the espousal of monogamy as the only ideal Christian family life is now being interpreted as merely reflecting European values, which invariably, conform with the Western nuclear family structure as opposed to the African extended family system' (quoted in Jones 2011: 406).

The Anglican Consultative Council (one of the four 'instruments' of Communion) commended Hastings' report in 1973, and in 1984 asked the African provinces to prepare a proposal to bring to the next Lambeth Conference in 1988, which a Kenyan bishop did, stating that the matter of polygamy was a local African matter, and the African bishops should be given the discretion to address it in their own way. The Western bishops at the 1988 conference, while disagreeing with polygamy and regarding it as unchristian, understood this argument, and decided to see it as a local African issue, trusting their colleagues to deal with it in a sensitive way. Resolution 26 upheld 'monogamy as God's plan' and yet said that a polygamous man may be baptized and confirmed providing:

> (1) that the polygamist shall promise not to marry again as long as any of his wives at the time of his conversion are alive; (2) that the receiving of such a polygamist has the consent of the local Anglican community; (3) that such a polygamist shall not be compelled to put away any of his wives, on account of the social deprivation they would suffer.

The decision of 1888 had, just a hundred years later, been reversed.

As Timothy Willem Jones points out, the nineteenth-century debates about polygamy were entwined with discussions about divorce. Civil divorce was only established in England in 1857. The Matrimonial Causes Act, which made divorce possible, automatically permitted remarriage; this caused controversy in the Church, which was, largely, vehemently opposed to remarriage because of Jesus' teaching that anyone who divorced and remarried committed adultery against their spouse. Jesus' words in Matthew 5:32 and 19:9 allow divorce and remarriage on the grounds of adultery; this 'Matthean exception' as Jones points out, was, at the end of the nineteenth century, interpreted primarily to mean that the Church would accept divorce only for adultery but would not permit remarriage during the lifetime of the other spouse. Those who remarried could face excommunication, depending on their bishop's attitude. This was essentially the position of the 1888 Lambeth Conference as it discussed polygamy.

Throughout the twentieth century, the bishops at Lambeth reasserted lifelong monogamy as the ideal Christian model for marriage, but as divorce rates increased, there was pressure for the Christian churches to rethink this position. Within Anglicanism, this was done piecemeal, reflecting provincial autonomy. As early as 1920, the Lambeth Conference had produced Resolution 67 allowing provinces to act as they believed fit on this matter (Davidson 1929: 44). Knowing that it could not infringe the autonomy of the national churches, the Lambeth Conference of 1930 followed up its 1920 resolution with a cautiously worded statement (Resolution 11) against the remarriage of divorced persons while a former spouse was alive (Lambeth Conference 1930: 42).

In many places, change happened on the ground and the Canons of the Church caught up with the reality later. In the Episcopal Church for example, different dioceses had their own canons, and the remarriage of divorcees was allowed in certain circumstances even before the Second World War; in 1973 the Episcopal Church's General Convention passed a canon that allowed the remarriage of those divorced in circumstances other than those traditionally allowed by scripture. In the Anglican Church in Australia, a canon of 1981 reaffirmed that the remarriage of divorcees in church could only occur in accordance with scripture and with the permission of the diocesan bishop; in 2007, these conditions were modified. In 2002 the Church of England agreed that divorced people could remarry in church in certain circumstances, according to the discretion of the priest. Individual provinces of the Anglican Communion dealt with divorce in their own time and governance structures, while the Lambeth Conference resolutions continued to affirm the monogamous, lifelong nature of Christian marriage.

Marriage as a lifelong, monogamous relationship between two people of the opposite sex, primarily intended for reproduction, has been challenged in various ways in the modern Anglican Church, as these examples illustrate. The history of Anglican deliberations and Lambeth Conference resolutions on sex, marriage, polygamy, and homosexuality highlights that a so-called 'traditional' position on sexuality and marriage has been far more diverse and contested than is usually admitted.

Debates about gender and sexuality across the Anglican Communion have therefore raised the question of uniformity, unity, and provincial autonomy, precisely because certain issues and arguments have a geographical and historical specificity. So for example, the particular context in which North American, and to some extent British, churches wished to be able to include gay and lesbian people in the ordained ministry, and provide blessings for same-sex unions, was not taken seriously by other Anglicans, in the ways that the particular context that gave rise to a new decision on polygamy was in 1988. At Lambeth 1988, polygamy was treated as a local issue, and the Anglican provinces for which this was a live issue were given the autonomy to address it as they saw fit. It may have been something of a shock to other bishops, especially many North Americans, expecting the same courtesy from fellow bishops with regard to their own live issue, namely homosexuality, that it was debated with such acrimony and bitterness ten years later in 1998. But by then, the long-standing ideal of local autonomy was being largely jettisoned.

The Windsor Report (Anglican Consultative Council 2004) and the proposed Anglican Covenant that emerged from the Windsor process, set up by Archbishop Williams after Gene Robinson was consecrated a bishop in November 2003, sought to address the debates and arguments about homosexuality by imposing uniformity. There was a new desire to impose like-mindedness. There were also many new alignments across national and provincial boundaries, which were largely confessional, and in opposition to a wider sense of communion. *The Windsor Report* and the proposed covenant seemed to interpret Communion as being of one (or common) mind. Mary-Jane Rubenstein reminds us that genuine community consists of constant, mutual interruption. She goes so far as to call that *contamination* 'when bodies exist in community with one another, the integrity of each is constantly undermined and contaminated by otherness'. She suggests that the choice is between a communal model of relationship which operates 'on the principle of subsuming differences under one essence' or a community model of relationship which embraces differences and finds ways of living with those differences—as in the Eucharist for example (Rubenstein 2008: 152, 159–160). Winnie

Varghese's description of communion 'across borders we might not otherwise cross' and the narrative of her meeting with the Bishop of Madras of the Church of South India one day in New York, including the conversations they had across their differences about sexuality, is such an example of the community model. She argues that if the Anglican Communion is to have a covenant, then it should be one that encourages the unrealized potential in transformative encounters of that sort. 'It would be quite something,' she writes, 'if we generated a document that strengthened or organized some of that potential, but I don't think we've seen that document yet' (Varghese 2011: 54).

SEXUAL DIFFERENCE

Finally, these debates about sexuality and gender have raised the crucial question of how we understand sexual difference and the related modern phenomenon of gender complementarity. The French feminist philosopher Luce Irigaray has described sexual difference as *the* philosophical issue of our time (Irigaray 1993). This has certainly been borne out in religious arguments against both the ordination of women and gay marriage. For example, as countries such as England, Australia, and New Zealand and different states in the USA have considered the possibility of legislation in favour of gay marriage in the second decade of the twenty-first century, opponents have argued against it from the assumption that both sexual difference and gender complementarity are universal and timeless concepts. And yet, historians of medicine have convincingly shown that both are modern concepts, emerging in particular political and social circumstances in the West in the eighteenth and nineteenth centuries. Only then did the idea develop that women and men have distinctly different qualities (and that these are rooted in biology) and this suits them for different (but 'complementary') roles in life (Laqueur 1990).

These ideas of 'natural' gender roles and complementarity did not go uncontested, as the shifts in gender relations, women's rights, and gay rights over the twentieth century indicate (Webster 1995), but they continued to have an impact on theology and have been repeatedly used in the Christian debate about gay marriage as, for example, in a report on marriage produced by the Faith and Order Commission of the Church of England in 2013, *Men and Women in Marriage*. Published just as legislation for gay marriage was going through the British Parliament, the report claimed to outline the long meaning of marriage but it created controversy and was dismissed precisely because it did not discuss the history of marriage adequately, instead appealing to ahistorical concepts of sexual difference and gender complementarity.

As governments in the West have taken on the idea of gay marriage with surprising speed in the twenty-first century, the Anglican churches have responded in a variety of ways. In Britain, for example, the Church of England bishops dropped their vociferous opposition to the bill when it became clear that it had overwhelming support in the House of Lords, but nevertheless the legislation exempts the Church of England from performing gay marriages in church. In the USA, as different states passed legislation for gay marriage, episcopal dioceses responded individually, some clearing the way for gay marriages to be celebrated in church alongside heterosexual marriages—as in California and Washington, DC, for example—but using the special rite for same-sex couples sanctioned at the 2012 General Convention rather than the Book of Common Prayer marriage rite.

The twentieth century saw debates about many issues of gender and sexuality in the Anglican churches, from the ordination of women to polygamy to divorce to homosexuality. In the first decade of the twenty-first century, these debates crystallized into heated controversy. They were focused through the issue of homosexuality, and resounded throughout the Anglican Communion. By the second decade, the heat was going out of some of the arguments, especially in the West, as society began to shift its attitudes and a younger generation developed more liberal ideas about sexuality. In some contexts, the disconnect between the Church and society made the Church less credible; this was apparent in England when the Church of England once again voted against women bishops in November 2012. Meanwhile, global issues of poverty, economics, and the environment began to take centre stage, and it remains to be seen whether the arguments about gender and sexuality will, with hindsight, look simply like quaint domestic squabbles, or whether they will continue to generate the same kind of acrimony in the future.

REFERENCES

Anglican Church in Australia (1981). 'Marriage of Divorced Persons Canon 1981'. <http://www.anglican.org.au/docs/canons/Canon%201985-07%20Divorced%20persons.pdf>.

Anglican Consultative Council (2004). *The Windsor Report*. London: The Anglican Communion Office.

Baker, J. (2004). *Consecrated Women? A Catholic and Evangelical Response*. Norwich: Canterbury Press.

Bates, S. (2004). *A Church at War: Anglicans and Homosexuality*. London: I. B. Tauris.

Board for Social Responsibility of the Church of England (1979). *Homosexual Relationships: A Contribution to Discussion*. London: CIO.

Carey, G. (1991). 'Introduction'. In House of Bishops, *Issues in Human Sexuality*. London: Church House Publishing, p. vii.

Darling, P. (1994). *New Wine: The Story of Transforming Leadership in the Episcopal Church*. Cambridge, MA: Cowley Press.

Davidson, R. (1929). *The Six Lambeth Conferences 1867–1920*. London: SPCK.

Eisen, U. (2000). *Women Officeholders in Early Christianity: Epigraphical and Literary Studies*. Trans. L. Mahoney. Collegeville, MN: Liturgical Press.

Faith and Order Commission (2013). *Men and Women in Marriage*. London: Church House Publishing.

Furlong, M. (1998). *Act of Synod—Act of Folly?* London: SCM Press.

Gill, S. (1994). *Women and the Church of England, from the Eighteenth Century to the Present*. London: SPCK.

Harris H., and J. Shaw (2004) (eds). *The Call for Women Bishops*. London: SPCK.

Hassett, M. (2007). *Anglican Communion in Crisis: How Episcopal Dissidents and Their African Allies are Reshaping Anglicanism*. Princeton: Princeton University Press.

Herzog, D. (2008). *Sex in Crisis*. New York: Basic Books.

House of Bishops' Group on Issues in Human Sexuality (2003). *Some Issues in Human Sexuality: A Guide to the Debate*. London: Church House Publishing.

Irigaray, L. (1993). *An Ethics of Sexual Difference*. Trans. C. Burke and G. Gill. Ithaca, NY: Cornell University Press.

Jones, T. W. (2011). 'The Missionaries' Position: Polygamy and Divorce in the Anglican Communion, 1888–1988'. *Journal of Religious History*, 35(3): 393–408.

Lambeth Conference (1888). *Lambeth Conference Resolutions*. <http://www.lambethconference.org/resolutions/1888/1888-5.cfm>.

Lambeth Conference (1930). *Lambeth Conference 1930: Encyclical Letter from the Bishops with the Resolutions and Reports*. London: SPCK.

Lambeth Conference (1968). *Lambeth Conference Resolutions*. <http://www.lambethconference.org/resolutions/1968/>.

Lambeth Conference (1988). *Lambeth Conference Resolutions*. <http://www.lambethconference.org/resolutions/1988/1988-34.cfm>.

Lambeth Conference (1998). *Lambeth Conference Resolutions*. <http://www.lambethconference.org/resolutions/1998/1998-1-10.cfm>.

Laqueur, T. (1990). *Making Sex: Body and Gender from the Greeks to Freud*. Cambridge, MA: Harvard University Press.

Lindsay E., and J. Scarfe (2012). *Preachers, Prophets & Heretics: Anglican Women's Ministry*. Sydney: University of New South Wales Press.

Lyman, R. (2004). 'Women Bishops in Antiquity: Apostolicity and Ministry'. In Harris and Shaw (2004), 37–50.

Mombo, E. (2004). 'Why Women Bishops are Still on the Waiting List in Africa'. In Harris and Shaw (2004), 163–167.

Osborne, J. (1989). 'The Osborne Report'. Unpublished Manuscript. <http://thinkinganglicans.org.uk/uploads/osborne_report.pdf>.

Porter, M. (2006). *The New Puritans: the Rise of Fundamentalism in the Anglican Church*. Carlton, Vic.: Melbourne University Press.

Robinson, G. (2008). *In the Eye of the Storm: Swept to the Center by God*. New York: Seabury.

Rubenstein, M.-J. (2008). 'Anglicans in the Postcolony: On Sex and the Limits of Communion'. *Telos*, 143 (Summer), 133–160.

Shaw, J. (2005). 'Marriage, Sexuality and the Christian Tradition'. In N. Coulton (ed.), *The Bible, the Church and Homosexuality*. London: Darton, Longman and Todd, 49–79.

Shaw, J. (2008). 'The Calling of Women as Bishops'. In J. Tigney (ed.), *Women as Bishops*. London: Mowbray, 3–12.

Varghese, W. (2011). 'The Covenant we have been offered is not the Covenant we need'. In Jim Naughton (ed.), *The Genius of Anglicanism: Perspectives on the Proposed Anglican Covenant*. Chicago: Chicago Consultation, 53–58.

Webster, A. (1995). *Found Wanting: Women, Christianity and Sexuality*. London: Cassell.

Webster, M. (1994). *A New Strength, A New Song: The Journey to Women's Priesthood*. London: Mowbray.

CHAPTER 22

PENTECOSTAL CHURCHES AND HOMOSEXUALITY

WILLIAM K. KAY AND STEPHEN J. HUNT

CULTURAL AND COUNTER-CULTURAL TENDENCIES

COLLECTIVELY, 'classical' Pentecostalism, emerging in the first decade of the twentieth century, and its charismatic variant (neo-Pentecostalism) from the middle of that century, became a Christian renewal movement, a series of free-standing denominations, and a miscellaneous collection of networks. Within a relatively short time—during the first half of the twentieth century—its churches and agencies spread across the globe. It is now credibly claimed, in all its variant forms, to comprise between 300 million and 520 million people (Kay 2011). Its relationship with the modern world is ambiguous. Andrew Walker, on the one hand, has stressed how Pentecostalism has been open to cultural changes such as the utilization of contemporary media to advocate its distinct gospel message. More recently, in parts of the world where it has grown rapidly, perhaps most notably South America, it has carried a strong work ethic concomitant with a rapidly expanding capitalist economy (Walker 1998). On the other hand, across its various 'streams' Pentecostalism has largely remained counter-cultural in respect of preserving conventional moral positions, especially those related to sexuality. Given that Pentecostalism's distinct theology emphasizes the presence and power of the Holy Spirit, it is inevitable that its expectations of personal morality, including sexual morality, are demanding. It proclaims the reality of reformed and empowered lives assisted by the Spirit and it cannot deny this message without self-contradiction. Its understanding of how personal morality should be defined is based upon a wide range of biblical texts which have long been read by Christians (and Jews) as condemning certain behaviours. Thus, Pentecostalism has long taken a stand against adultery, sex before marriage, divorce (except on the grounds of adultery), and homosexuality.

Given the traditional stance taken towards the subject, at least until relatively recently, homosexuality has not been a topic that has lent itself to much deliberation in Pentecostal circles. The subject historically has largely remained 'closed', not needing discussion, and has usually only been dealt with as a matter of pastoral discipline. The requirement to reflect on the subject of homosexuality, if not other minority sexual orientations, became more urgent with the emergence of the gay rights movement, the legalization of homosexuality and accompanying civil rights, and issues such as same-sex marriage in the Western world. Pentecostalism is however a global phenomenon and engages with diverse cultures. This has led to radically contrasting, or at least nuanced, positions in relation to homosexuality which also generate varying attitudes to what are perceived as the pastoral needs of sexual minorities.

North American and British Traditions

Pentecostalism has until relatively recently not felt it necessary to issue public condemnations of homosexuality since, even between consenting adults, homosexual acts were illegal in the United Kingdom till 1967. The situation in the USA was somewhat different because of the judicial variation between states. By the mid-1980s, however, the Supreme Court was starting to move in a direction of liberalization. Occasional preachers might apocalyptically condemn homosexuality but the major Pentecostal denominations were more measured in their public pronouncements and only issued statements against what they took to be general immorality. More strident views can be found in the developing world and these will be discussed later.

In Britain denominations such as the Assemblies of God and the Elim churches have forged their own statements but have tended to leave detailed discussions to umbrella organizations to which they belong (such as the Evangelical Alliance, the organization to which two-thirds of Pentecostal and charismatic churches belong (Evangelical Alliance 2012a, 2012b)) to express more coherent and detailed views. By contrast, in the USA the prevailing religious culture permits Pentecostal/fundamentalist outlooks greater social legitimacy. In addition North American Pentecostals have until the 1990s been better educated than European Pentecostals and therefore been capable of turning to scholars within their ranks for succinctly worded public statements or more discursive 'position papers'.

Conventional Statements

A number of negative statements on homosexuality (but generally not other minority sexual orientations) were made by the major Pentecostal denominations in the late 1970s at a time when homosexuality was becoming more socially acceptable in Western democracies and lesbian, gay, bisexual, transgendered, and intersex (LGBTI) groups more mobilized and vocal.[1] Official statements of the Assemblies of God and the United Pentecostal Church International (UPCI) nonetheless exemplified what amounted to a reiteration of traditional views on homosexuality (and only homosexuality).

The Assemblies of God's General Presbytery adopted a report on homosexuality in 1979 (Assemblies of God USA [1979] 2001). It began with the declaration that

> Increasingly political and religious advocacy for homosexuality has prompted us to restate our position on this critical issue…This reaffirmation of the truth has become all the more urgent because writers sympathetic to the homosexual community have advanced revisionist interpretations of the relevant biblical texts that are based on biased exegesis and mistranslation.

The reinterpretation of biblical texts alarmed Pentecostals because their main beliefs were anchored in what they took to be the plain meaning of Scripture. The report continued with reference to a general moral decline associated with the 'permissive society' of the post-1960s, and in this respect it eschewed possible accusations of homophobia:

> A nation's tolerance or intolerance of homosexuality is one indication of the nation's spiritual condition…Since the Bible speaks to the issue of homosexuality, it must be considered the authoritative rule by which a position is established…Scripture considers it a sin against God and man. The church's concern about this problem is not a matter of discrimination against a minority group. This is a moral issue…Homosexuality is a sin (1) because it is contrary to the principles of sexuality which God established in the beginning…(2) because the Bible refers to it as evil…[and] (3) [because] it comes under divine judgment.

The report was revised in 2001 and there was no significant shift in views (although there was a more than a hint that sexual *orientation* was being differentiated from *behaviour* and that abstinence was ideal for those with such tendencies):

> It should be noted at the outset that there is absolutely no affirmation of homosexual behavior found anywhere in Scripture. Rather, the consistent sexual ideal is chastity for those outside a monogamous heterosexual marriage and fidelity for those inside such a marriage. There is also abundant evidence that homosexual behavior, along with illicit heterosexual behavior, is immoral and comes under the judgment of God.
>
> (Assemblies of God USA [1979] 2001)

The UPCI (otherwise known as 'Oneness' or non-Trinitarian Pentecostalism)[2] belongs to the 'holiness' Apostolic tradition and traces its roots back to 1916. Among

---

[1] The subject increasingly surfaced in Pentecostal publications, for example, 'Homosexuality', International Pentecostal Church of Christ.

[2] Subscribing to the non-Trinitarian dogma of God conceived as a singular spirit who is manifested in diverse ways: the Father, Son, and Holy Spirit.

Pentecostals its style (e.g. on dress codes) has been seen as more 'old-fashioned' than that of the larger more mainline (i.e. Trinitarian) denominations. In 1977 its General Conference adopted a succinct Position Paper on Homosexuality (UPCI 1977). The document made reference to Romans 1 as declaring that homosexuality is 'vile, unnatural, unseemly and an abomination in the sight of God,' and an expression of 'moral decadence and sin'. There was also strong disapproval of liberal groups within Christianity who were accepting 'the so-called "gay-right" [sic] movement as a legitimate lifestyle'. The paper implies that any UPCI pastor involved in homosexual activity would be expelled and never reinstated.

Two decades later the felt need to restate the conventional biblical stand on homosexual practice (but not necessarily *orientation*) became even more urgent. The Foursquare Church, in 2000, claimed a worldwide membership of over 8 million, with almost 60,000 churches in 144 countries (National Council of Churches 2008). Its position was affirmed in 1993 through a denominational statement that placed human sexuality within the context of heterosexual marriage. It reads:

> The Biblical record shows that sexual union was established exclusively within the context of male-female relationship and formalized in the ordinance of marriage... The Scriptures identify the practice of homosexuality as a sin that, if persisted in, brings grave consequences in this life and excludes one from the Kingdom of God.
>
> (International Church of the Foursquare Gospel 1993)

Similarly, the Pentecostal Assemblies of Canada (PAOC), with a membership of nearly a quarter of a million, adopted a resolution by its General Conference in 1994 that emphasized that for two millennia Christian churches had held a strong anti-divorce stance, and it then went out of its way to categorize homosexuality activity, like heterosexual adultery, as giving a legitimate ground for divorce. The PAOC declared that it 'stands firmly in the mainstream of historical Christianity. It takes the Bible as its all-sufficient source of faith and practice, and subscribes to the historic creeds of the universal church... Marriage can only be broken by *porneia* which is understood as marital unfaithfulness involving adultery, homosexuality, or incest'.

The International Pentecostal Holiness Church (IPHC), with a reported worldwide membership in 2007 of over 1 million—a number rising to over 3 million when its affiliates are added—included in its *Vision and Mission* (2013) a reiteration of its stance against homosexuality but also a reference to lesbianism, suggesting that the significance of other sexual minorities was at last being noticed: 'We have maintained a strong position against premarital, extramarital, and deviant sex, including homosexual and lesbian relationships, refusing to accept the loose moral standards of our society. We commit ourselves to maintaining this disciplined lifestyle with regard to our bodies.'

After a series of legal changes stemming from the extension of human rights, many Western nations had by the end of the twentieth century recognized same-sex unions as 'civil partnerships'. Before the second decade of the twenty-first century same-sex marriages on equal terms with the marriages of heterosexual couples had been passed into law in many countries. This development was met with strong condemnation by many Christian churches, with Pentecostal denominations stressing their own long-held position. For example, the Church of God in Christ (COGIC), a Pentecostal 'holiness' denomination with a predominantly African-American membership and some 5 million members and 12,000 congregations in the United States, joined with the Assemblies of God USA and other Christian bodies to criticize President Barack Obama's endorsement of same-sex marriage:

> The president's position regarding 'same-sex marriage' has set off a 'firestorm', unlike any other debate in our civil society, perhaps, since the civil rights unrest of the mid-20th century... The advocacy for same-sex marriage, while in conflict with our nation's long-standing moral posture, has indeed created opportunity for the church to communicate our unequivocal position about God's design and foundation for humanity, the biblical mandate for heterosexuality through the bonds of matrimony and the centuries-old understanding of the only acceptable means of procreation, habitation and the establishment of the family.
>
> ('Black Pastors Fight Gay Marriage' 2004)

The IPHC (resolution 1, passed 1990), mainly situated in North America, adopted a resolution in its 2013 General Conference, stating,

> Inasmuch as modern society has eroded the biblical ideal of the family and its practical existence, and inasmuch as homosexual couples, unmarried heterosexual couples, and even groups of persons simply maintaining a common household are seeking to gain legal and social status as families, with all due rights and privileges given to families, including but not limited to social benefits or rights such as child rearing and custody, spousal or dependent insurance, inheritance rights, and tax exemptions, and inasmuch as a growing number of states, with the support of certain national leaders, have attempted to change the legal definition of marriage to include same-sex couples... Be it resolved that the United Pentecostal Church International (UPCI) uphold the biblical ideal of the basic family as one man and one woman... married by law in accordance with all biblical injunctions; and all offspring of such a couple, biological or adopted...; with the extended family being comprised of the various relatives of blood and marriage resulting from the lawful union of a man and woman.

Here the extension of the concept of marriage, with all its social, legal, and economic privileges, and the formation of families generated by this extended concept, was opposed by IPHC. The opposition is not merely to homosexuality as a private practice but to what was seen as a fundamental shift in the future composition of the family and society as a whole.

Also of concern to Pentecostals has been the teaching and advance of gay rights in American schools. An article in the *Pentecostal Evangel* (Assemblies of God General Council's official weekly magazine) strongly objected to the teaching of 'diversity' and 'tolerance' courses to stop 'homophobia'; stocking library shelves with pro-homosexual literature; inviting speakers from homosexual activist groups to address students; forming homosexual clubs for students; and sponsoring special 'diversity' and 'pride' days

(Kennedy 2004). Again, the objection to homosexual practice was broadened to include criticism of what was seen as a quantum shift in educational and social norms.

GLOBAL VARIATIONS

Major movements of Pentecostalism and charismatic revival have been evident in specific regions of the world—a revival frequently attributed to socio-economic and political challenges wrought by the complex processes of modernization. This would particularly appear to be the case in sub-Saharan Africa and Central and South America (Cox 1995; Martin 2002; Anderson 2004; Kay 2009), but not exclusively so, given the revivals which have also appeared in South East Asia, notably South Korea. The subject of sexual minorities, and in particular sexual rights which are observably a product of liberalizing agendas, has proved to be troublesome for Pentecostals and charismatics across these global regions, obliging them to connect with political and public spheres as champions of religious conservatism.

In Africa the condemnation of homosexuality by Pentecostal/charismatic churches also resonates with robust political forces forged by post-colonial nationalism, regional religious movement discourses, and the condemnation of homosexuality by elements of the American Christian Right. More often than not, Pentecostals/charismatics hold in common the conventional Christian view that homosexuality constitutes a threat to national interests and a challenge to the decrees of God (with HIV and AIDs often seen as divine judgement accompanied by the claim that homosexuals could be 'healed'). This is made clear via a brief survey of Pentecostal/charismatic constituencies in Nigeria and Ghana in West Africa and Uganda in the East in their broad condemnation of homosexuality.

Pentecostalism is not new to Nigeria and there have been various 'waves' of Pentecostal revival since the 1920s. Many of these 'waves' held strong associations with Western churches (Anderson 2001: 86–87) and, as elsewhere in the world (Coleman 2000), have frequently come to advocate a health and wealth gospel of personal material advancement under the influence of North American Pentecostal ministries. Unlike earlier revivals, those which emerged in the 1970s embraced a political activism originating with the founding of the Christian Students' Social Movement of Nigeria in 1977. A defining aspect of this early activism was an accent on the dogma that spiritual forces governed the political sphere and conservative reform could be instigated through prayer (Freston 2001: 185–186). 'Spiritual' world views of this kind are compatible with traditional African culture (which never passed through the rationalistic critique of the Enlightenment) and have affinity with Pentecostalism.

In the 1980s, Pentecostals became active in the interdenominational Christian Association of Nigeria via the Pentecostal Fellowship of Nigeria (PFN, the principal Pentecostal umbrella organization in the country) and the Organization of African Instituted Churches (Freston 2001: 184). In 2011, the PFN announced its unwavering support of the nation's Senate for having the 'moral courage' to pass a bill making same-sex marriage in Nigeria a crime that carried a fourteen-year jail term and banning gatherings of sexual minorities within nightclubs. The organization also chastised some Western countries for threatening Nigeria with sanctions should the bill be passed into law. The chairman of the Kaduna state chapter of the PFN, Bishop David Bakare, stated:

> It is time we begun to have such great Nigerians who could look at any so called donor nation in the face and tell them to go to hell with their donations if they don't like the laws of Nigeria.... This is one of the best things that ever happened to Nigeria through the Senate. This Act by the National Assembly has brought hope, courage, and pride to the Nigerian people that we are once again the giant of Africa indeed.

(Vendornaija World Press 2011)

Thus, according to this reading of events, international pressure to liberalize laws pro-scribing homosexuality is just another piece of post-colonial meddling and one, more-over, connected with the implicit threat of a withdrawal of financial aid. This said, an accurate understanding of Nigerian history is complex since contradictory assertions are made about the acceptability of homosexuality in traditional African society.

Similarly, among Pentecostals in Ghana, there is open opposition to same-sex mar-riages, a widespread denial of church membership to homosexuals, and strong emphasis on deliverance in accordance with what Onyinah (n.d.) refers to as 'witchdemonology [sic]' concerning the 'demonization' of the African traditional practices which 'they [Pentecostals] believe are threats to their successful living'. In viewing homosexuality as immoral, Ghanaian Pentecostals are at one with mainline conservative denominations. The document *The Position of Christian Church in Ghana on Homosexuality* (signatures to the document include two from the Ghana Pentecostal and Charismatic Council (Christian Council of Ghana)) refers to 'homosexuals [having] adopted an open life-style describing their otherwise shameful practice in a more positive term "gay"'. The document speaks of the significant threat emanating from Western lifestyles, com-mends the government for preventing a global conference on homosexuality, and calls on 'traditional rulers' and 'decent-loving Ghanaians' to campaign against homosexual-ity, 'fearing the wrath of God' should homosexual rights be advanced in the country. This harsher attitude by which Ghanaian Pentecostal churches approach the subject is nonetheless supplemented by a more conciliatory tone. For instance, Dr Fred Deegbe, chairman of the Ghana Pentecostal Council, assured those struggling with homosexu-ality that the Church was there to help them, not punish them: 'We do not by our con-demnation of the practice asking [sic] communities to either stone or kill those who are found to be homosexuals... But, we want to accept them and provide the necessary help they may require to heal them' (Christian Council of Ghana, 19 July 2011).

Uganda has proved to be the test case in respect of the major gay rights issues. Same-sex relationships have long been illegal in Uganda and punishable by incarcera-tion for up to fourteen years. The law is a remnant of British colonialism designed to pun-ish what colonial authorities deemed 'unnatural sex' among native Ugandans. However, attitudes in the country have become more draconian. In 2009 the Anti-Homosexuality Bill (a private member's bill) was submitted by a Member of Parliament, David Bahati, proposing the broadening of the criminalization of same-sex relations domestically, and further including provisions for Ugandans who engage in same-sex relations outside Uganda, asserting that they may be extradited for punishment back to Uganda.[3]

The bill received international condemnation including criticisms from Christian organizations.[4] However, the proposed legislation in Uganda was thought by several news agencies to be inspired by American evangelical Christians who were accused of taking advantage of social and economic circumstances in Uganda to export the North American 'culture war' to Africa.[5] Pentecostal clerics have certainly made their objection to gay culture one of their core messages. According to the controversial Pentecostal pastor Martin Ssempa, spokesman for the Interfaith Rainbow Coalition Against Homosexuality in 2007, homosexuality 'breaks the laws of God, the laws of nature and the laws of Uganda'. It was Ssempa who organized several anti-gay rallies in Kampala, claiming that homosexuals (including the pressure group Sexual Minorities Uganda) were using the summit to intimidate Uganda into changing the country's laws. Nevertheless, given that Pentecostals only constitute 4.6 per cent of the total population, it would be unrealistic to see them as the major cause of Ugandan anti-homosexual prejudice (CIA 2013).

In a globalized world, Pentecostal churches have been 'planted' by some of the larger African international ministries in countries beyond their original national contexts. Many carry their cultural and religious views into Western countries where homosexuality is more acceptable and the rights of sexual minorities are advanced. In such environments social boundary maintenance against what is often perceived as a morally corrupt 'host' culture becomes imperative. For example, the view that homosexuality is a specifically Western import is impressed on a younger generation of Nigerian Pentecostals. Among those with a high-impact international outreach is the Redeemed Christian Church of God. The Church's Sunday School Teachers' Manual includes a 'Prayer Point' instructing young people to 'Pray that God will deliver the nations of the world from the sin of homosexuality and lesbianism', understood to have originated as a liberation movement in the West. In outlining what constitutes homosexuality and lesbianism these sexual orientations are seen as being on par with paedophilia and bestiality, and Leviticus 18 is the authority for this. Homosexuals and lesbians are said to 'use their money, intellect, power and position to fight God's word and invariably to fight God Himself' (enforced by a reference to Romans 1:18) (Redeemed Christian Church of God 2011).

---

[3] The proposed bill, supported by many Pentecostal leaders, included penalties for individuals, companies, media organizations, or NGOs that know of gay people or support their rights.

[4] The Roman Catholic Archbishop of Kampala Cyprian Lwanga stated in December 2009 that the bill was unnecessary and 'at odds with the core values' of Christianity, expressing particular concerns at the death penalty provisions.

[5] This includes California pastor Rick Warren who became influential in the shaping of public policy in Uganda, Nigeria, and, to a lesser extent, Kenya and Uganda. Kaoma, Kapya (Winter 09/Spring 10). *The U.S. Christian Right and the Attack on Gays in Africa*. <PublicEye.org> (accessed 4 March 2013).

In South Korea the views of Pentecostals towards sexual minorities are set against a very different cultural backdrop from that of Africa, but nevertheless traditional Asian culture regards homosexuality as repulsive and it is not publicly acknowledged. However, male and female same-sex sexual activity is legal in South Korea even if same-sex couples and households headed by same-sex couples are not entitled to the same legal protections as those granted to heterosexuals. Pentecostals have become increasingly politically active in the context of this more liberal legal framework, and from a position of strength. According to the Pew Forum's 2006 Pentecostal survey, Pentecostals and charismatics account for some 10 per cent of South Korea's urban population, while approximately four in ten Korean Protestants are either Pentecostal or charismatic (Pew Forum Survey on Religious and Public Life 2006).

In 2000, 107 of the 273 members of the national Congress were Protestants, including five who attend the David Yonggi Cho's Full Gospel Church (affiliated with the Assemblies of God and generally accepted as the largest church congregation in the world) (Lee 2009: 338). For the 2004 National Assembly elections, Yonggi Cho supported the creation of the conservative Korean Christian Party, although it failed to attract enough support to field its twenty-three candidates (Freston 2004: 68). Leading up to the 2012 general and presidential elections conservative Christian leaders including David Yonggi Cho and Kumnan Methodist Church pastor Kim Hong-do established a forum to discuss what was perceived as the moral collapse of South Korean society. The forum gathered together pastors from 3,000 churches featuring discussions on a number of topics including the possibility of creating a Christian political party, the propagation of Islam in South Korea, human rights issues in North Korea, and, surprisingly, the possibility of repealing laws regarding homosexual rights. In this way, the contrast between African and Korean Pentecostalism is manifested by their separate diagnoses of moral liberalization within their cultures. According to Hyung-Jin Kim,

> Anti-gay sentiments run deep through South Korean society amid a complex mix of several elements that include a large, vocal conservative Christian community; a deep-rooted Confucian heritage that has long put strains on open talks on sex-related topics; and rapid economic developments under past military-backed dictatorships that ignored the voices of minority groups.
>
> (Zonkel 2013)

As in South Korea, South and Central America Pentecostals, while numbered among the *evangélicos*, represent the most rapidly growing sector of Protestantism. For example, in Brazil, which has by far the region's largest Protestant population, the national census shows that Pentecostals constituted 68 per cent of Protestants in 2000. As Pentecostals have approached from a quarter to a third of the population in some Latin American countries, they have sought a greater share of public influence and political representation. In Brazil an evangelical congressional caucus consists largely of Pentecostals and includes about 10 per cent of the country's parliamentarians. In Chile the Pentecostals host an annual Independence Day celebration attended by the president, while in Nicaragua Pentecostals founded a political party that has fielded presidential candidates and won seats in Congress. In many such countries governments historically provided special benefits to the Catholic Church, including direct subsidies, control over religious education in government schools, and a monopoly on hospital and military chaplaincies. Pentecostals have entered politics partly to share the benefits previously afforded exclusively to the Catholic Church and to insist that they be made available to the region's growing Protestant communities as well. In doing so, Pentecostals have rivalled the Catholic Church in providing a distinct religio-moral leadership (Serbin 1999).

In Latin America moral issues such as abortion and homosexuality have not kindled the kind of 'culture wars' witnessed in the US partly because much of the region remains fairly conservative on such issues. However, left-of-centre groups in some countries have advanced and occasionally successfully initiated proposals to liberalize government policies on abortion, divorce, and homosexuality. In the case of Brazil, homosexuality had been legal since 1830, after the passing of a penal code which eliminated sodomy laws that had been in force during Portuguese rule.[6] In 2005 São Paulo hosted the world's largest gay pride event with an estimated 2 million marchers. These developments helped spur Pentecostal political mobilization. For example, it was partly in order to obstruct the further proposed liberalization of constitutional provisions concerning abortion and homosexuality that Pentecostals in Brazil increased their political participation after the country's post-junta political 'opening' (*abertura*) in 1986 (the effort to block liberalization succeeded on homosexuality but failed on abortion). Such successful opposition, however, proved short-lived. President Lula da Silva's administration was in favour of sexual minority rights and in 2011 the Supreme Federal Court voted in support of permitting same-sex couples the same legal rights as married couples.

There have been a number of campaigns by Brazilian evangelicals to reach out to sexual-minority men and women. *Movimento pela Sexualidade Sadia* (Social Movement for a Healthy Sexuality), an evangelical group headed by an ex-homosexual, spearheads attempts to evangelize in gay parades and deliver leaflets featuring the testimonials of ex-gays and ex-lesbians. State representative Edino Fonseca, an Assemblies of God government minister, introduced a bill in the Rio de Janeiro state legislature (in 2008) to establish social services to support men and women wanting to change their sexual orientation (he also introduced a bill to protect evangelical groups offering assistance to such men and women from discrimination and harassment). However, this more yielding approach has been accompanied by harsh condemnation of homosexuality. Lula de Silva's variety of socialism came to be viewed as 'demonic' by Pentecostals,[7] while Silas Malafaia (former pastor of Brazil's largest Pentecostal megachurch and associated

---

[6] There may be a religious factor in Brazilian homosexuality. A minority of the Brazilian population adheres to Candomblé and other Afro-Brazilian religions (similar to Santería) which tolerate homosexuality.

[7] Da Silva had initially gained some support among Pentecostals during his successful presidential campaign in 2002 (Hunt 2011: 168–169).

with Assemblies of God) became known for his verbal attacks on a broad array of foes, including the leaders of Brazil's movement for gay rights, and led to self-described 'crusades' in Fortaleza, a city in the north-east of the country, where he headed an event mixing scripture and hymns for a gathering of about 200,000 people. He has stated that 'Homosexuals are parasites of the State' (Daily Kos 2012). In 2013, Brazil's House of Representatives elected Marco Feliciano, a right-wing Pentecostal pastor from the country's Social Christian Party (PSC), as president of the lower chamber's Human Rights and Minorities' Commission and this may well have future implications for sexual minority rights.

The cases of United States, Korea, and Brazil indicate the complexity of politico-cultural interactions with Pentecostalism in different countries. In general terms, it would appear that in Western societies which have long been shaped by Christian values and ideals, there is, or has been until recently, a basic agreement between Pentecostalism's social conservatism and the default tradition of conventional morality. In South Korea, which has long been shaped by Asian religions, Christianity arrived as a progressive force and Pentecostalism has intensified the drive towards modernity. In Brazil the situation is different again because of the prevalence of multi-faceted Roman Catholicism. Here Pentecostalism may sometimes define itself against its religious competitors as well as against secularism.

LGBTI-Affirming Groups

Pentecostals attempting to reconcile their faith with homosexuality have been few and far between. One exception was James S. Tinney, a leading authority on Black Pentecostalism (with a chair at Howard University, USA). When he identified himself publicly as a gay man in 1979 (in an address to the Third World Lesbian and Gay Conference in Washington, DC) and subsequently founded a church for black lesbians and gays, he was excommunicated from his denomination, the Temple Church of God in Christ. In 1980, he founded the Pentecostal Coalition for Human Rights as part of his mission to help lesbians and gay men to reconcile their Pentecostalism with their homosexuality. In 1982, he organized a three-day revival for gays and lesbians and several conferences to help build bridges between fundamentalist churches and the LGBTI community.[8]

While Tinney was one early voice, in recent years LGBTI caucuses have increasingly emerged representing adherents from Pentecostal backgrounds. The tendency for such Pentecostal groupings to form somewhat later than those in the more mainstream denominations, and largely in the context of the Western world, is arguably a reflection of biblically-based theological conservatism. Some have retained allegiance with their home church, for example, the Assemblies of God Gay Pentecostals (while

---

[8] Tinney died age 46 in 1988, from complications related to AIDS.

the AOG USA is the largest set of Pentecostal churches, it has only a small number of gay outreaches). Alternatively, some caucuses have evolved into a growing number of independent LGBTI-affirming Pentecostal churches. Although many such organizations adhere to distinctive core Pentecostal doctrines, and in some instances those of particular Pentecostal denominations, they differ in forging a stance based on a revised theological reading of Old and New Testament texts that finds no wholesale condemnation of homosexuality and other sexual minority behaviours.

LGBTI Pentecostal groupings are particularly well represented in the Apostolic tradition. This tradition, unlike Assemblies of God for instance, vests authority in individuals who are recognized as carrying apostolic gifting and authority. In Assemblies of God in the USA governance is through committees, conferences, and voting by ballot. Consequently, Apostolic churches may alter their theological or social stance more nimbly than is the case in denominations where a majority of ministerial voters has to be persuaded to accept new policies and positions.

The Gay Apostolic Pentecostals (GAP) constituted the first LGBTI-affirming Apostolic cadre to organize separately from mainline Apostolic churches, having formed in Schenectady, New York, in 1980. The founders of the movement imagined an international network of affirming Apostolic churches endorsing an otherwise conventional apostolic theology identified with such denominations (while affirming LGBTI people, it refrained from advancing itself as an LGBTI organization). This was realized in the establishment of the National Gay Pentecostal Alliance (NGPA) with the opening of its first church in Omaha, Nebraska. The NGPA was organized in 1980 as a Pentecostal group open to persons of all sexual orientations. Co-founder Revd William H. Carey wrote in 1993: 'Given the intense homophobic nature of most Pentecostal denominations, setting up any type of organization within any of those bodies, or even comprised of members of any of those bodies, was not possible. Open homosexuals are not tolerated in Pentecostal churches. Some are excommunicated' (Religious Tolerance. org 2012).

Although the NGPA is an Apostolic Pentecostal organization, due to the lack of affirming Trinitarian Pentecostal churches, it initially encouraged all its members to remain in their churches. Early in the twenty-first century, NGPA merged with a smaller organization, the Apostolic Intercessory Ministries (AIM), under the new name Apostolic Restoration Mission (ARM). In 2010, the organization claimed fifty ministers in nineteen states across the USA and with representation in five other countries. Its growth at this time was partly a result of incorporating the Global Alliance of Affirming Apostolic Pentecostals (GAAAP) centred in Thonotosassa, Florida. It was in 2010 that GAAAP amended its constitution to become a denomination and began to affiliate churches (some twenty).

In recent years, further LBGT-affirming Apostolic Pentecostal organizations have come into existence. These include the Affirming Pentecostal Church International (APCI, which is currently the largest such group, operating churches around the world), Reconciling Pentecostals International and Covenant Network. The APCI was founded in 2010 in Indianapolis, Indiana (the city of its headquarters). The APCI, which also has strong roots in the Pentecostal Apostolic tradition,[9] has established congregations in the USA (some fifteen), as well as in countries as far flung as Albania, Brazil, Portugal, Mexico, and the UK. It has attempted to establish churches in Peru, Trinidad, and the Ukraine, but found it difficult to do so in African countries where, as noted earlier, cultural disapproval of sexual minorities is well ingrained, although the APCI has extensive ministries in Nigeria, through their Chicago church, High Praises International Ministries.

As with other LGBTI-affirming Christian organizations, Pentecostal or otherwise, the APCI is a fully affirming church open to all persons and complements this conviction with a stress on diversity rights and a strong anti-discrimination policy including numerous social categories, such as race, sexual orientation, and gender identity. Its Apostolic Institute of Ministry exists for the purpose of providing APCI ministers and student ministers with a quality education, offering classes in theology, history, eschatology, and church administration. In addition, the school offers teaching seminars at APCI churches as required. The statutes of the organization assert that such churches provide 'a social climate that encourages and supports monogamous relationships and solid family units... (and a) "city of refuge" for the healing of those who have been abused and hurt in other churches' (Affirming Pentecostal Church International 2012: 1).

In May 1998, independent of the developments discussed so far, several Apostolic ministers assembled in Little Rock, Arkansas, for the purpose of examining the possibility of formation of a new Pentecostal fellowship. All of these ministers came from a 'Oneness' (= non-Trinitarian) background and had been subject to rejection by the various affirming Pentecostal organizations that existed at that time. The vision was to form a Pentecostal fellowship for ministers, churches, and ministries that would provide a home for Apostolic people leaving their traditional churches and organizations, and to create a single affirming fellowship that would unite both Oneness and Trinitarian believers who shared the Pentecostal message and forms of worship. The Rock of Christ Church of Little Rock advances itself as 'A Progressive Pentecostal Church with an Outreach to the Gay and Lesbian Community. Teaching an Acts 2:38 Message for Whosoever!'.

It was not until 2000 that the Fellowship of Reconciling Pentecostals International (FRPI) was founded and functioned for over two years under the auspices of the Potter's House Fellowship in Tampa, Florida. In doing so, the requirement of baptism in the name of Jesus only for full licence or ordination was abandoned. The Fellowship of Reconciling Pentecostals International was legally and independently incorporated in Scottsdale, Arizona in June 2003. The spirit of the FRPI is exemplified by the Chief Presiding Presbyter who writes: 'Since its inception in 2000, the FRPI strives to be a home for all disenfranchised Pentecostals for whatever reason and wherever you find yourself at this present time. Our goal is to assist those who are struggling or confused in understanding where they really stand with God' (Duncan 2013).

---

[9] In matters of doctrine, APCI beliefs are similar to those of most Apostolic Pentecostal churches: the oneness of God; water baptism by full immersion in the name of Jesus for forgiveness of sins; the baptism of the Holy Ghost with the initial evidence of speaking in other tongues; and holiness. The APCI remains firmly wedded to these teachings, and does not give ministerial credentials to those holding other beliefs.

While all of these groupings were established in the USA, LGBTI caucuses have emerged independently elsewhere. For example, the umbrella organization Freedom 2 Be in Australia which holds monthly meetings in Sydney, Melbourne, Brisbane, and Perth, organizes regular gatherings and hosts an online community offering support for LGBTI people (in its websites 'I' denoting 'Inter-sex' is added) from Pentecostal and charismatic traditions. Its website states that,

> At some stage, most have believed that homosexuality is against God's order and must change in order to fulfill God's purpose. In other words, there are only two options: 1. Be heterosexual and a Christian or 2. Be gay or lesbian and go to hell... This creates a psychological dissonance between faith and sexuality.
>
> (Freedom 2 Be 2013)

There are several groups of people that Freedom 2 Be claims to assist: LGBTI people who have left their churches; those in churches but who are not 'out'; those who are 'out'; those exploring 'other' spiritual paths; and heterosexual friends, family, and supporters.

These LGBTQI groupings have come into existence outside denominational structures and would be classified as being neo-Pentecostal in the sense that their governance is non-hierarchical and their linkages are made through networking. Their growth has undoubtedly been assisted by Internet communication. A further example of developments can briefly be mentioned in the Brazil cultural context. *Igreja Contemporanea* (Contemporary Church) and *Cidade de Refúgio* (City of Refuge) are among the freshly established Brazilian LGBTQI-inclusive Christian movements tending to be of a broad evangelical persuasion that encourages young members to find permanent partners and refrain from promiscuity.

Pre-dating these organizations the movement to create gay-affirming churches had begun in Brazil with the formation of a Metropolitan Community Church (MMC) around 2010.[10] There are now eight such churches in the country, with roughly 3,000 members. While the MMC is a liberal Protestant denomination it has come to embrace something of a Pentecostal culture in Brazil popular throughout the country with recent waves of revival in worship and the baptism of the Holy Spirit and the spiritual gifts derived from it, which has been described as 'Presbycostal', while simultaneously non-judgemental regarding sexual activity before marriage and alcohol consumption (Global Post 2013).

SHIFTING GROUND?

In some quarters it might appear that Pentecostalism in Western societies is starting to shift its ground in respect of views of homosexuality. One space in which conventional attitudes

---

[10] Founded by Troy Perry, a former pastor of the Church of God of Prophecy, a holiness Pentecostal denomination in the US.

have been challenged is within Pentecostal academic circles. Controversy was generated during the Society for Pentecostal Studies in 2013, the largest and most prominent academic society within the Pentecostal tradition, when President Paul Alexander of Palmer Seminary (a licensed Assemblies of God minister) in his address argued for the opening up of discussions of homosexual, transgender, and intersex 'realities' as faithful representations of Pentecostal and charismatic Christianity (Institute on Religion & Democracy, n.d.). Alexander's address was suffused with liberation theology and cited inspiration by feminist theologians (a reading of the Exodus narrative that portrayed both oppressive biblical Egypt and later freed Israelites inhabiting the Promised Land as 'the construct of Whiteness'). These were theological themes which he utilized to denounce 'white racing' and 'male sexing' and urged gathered Pentecostal academics to accept 'LGBTQI [lesbian, gay, bisexual, transgender, queer, and intersex realities' in their churches and seminaries.

Individual pastors have also advanced revisionist views in recent times. For example, Jonathan Stone, the pastor of discipleship and evangelism at Westmore church of God in Cleveland, Tennessee, stated at a meeting of Pentecostal pastors: 'I have come to realize that we as Pentecostals are not just ignoring the issue of homosexuality, but sexuality in general. Our unwillingness to talk about these issues has created several blind spots for us. For example, the greatest sexual societal issue facing the church is not homosexuality, but pornography' (see also Behrens 2006).

The debate seems to have been enhanced by a website blog post by Rob Buckingham in 2009, a pastor of a large Pentecostal megachurch called 'Bayside' in Melbourne, Australia, and a high-profile pastor in the movement. His blog post was entitled, 'Is Jesus Anti-Gay?' and made the case for 'acceptance' being the true Christian attitude towards homosexuals.[11] He stated: 'As a Christian, and pastor of a church, I sometimes find the attitudes of fellow Christians embarrassing. We have a number of gay men and women in our church and they are accepted just the way they are—just like everyone else is.'

Paul Bailey, raised in the strict Pentecostal denomination Bibleway Church of Our Lord Jesus Christ and co-pastor of the Regeneration Project based in south London, became the first black Pentecostal church leader in Britain to state publicly his support for same-sex relationships. He is reported as saying in 2013 that

It is important to note that in the Bible marriage was fluid and amorphous. There are many kinds of marriage in Scripture. It is only in Jesus that we move towards a concrete definition...Marriage is a legally binding covenant of love and commitment. Gay people are uniquely created by God to reflect the beauty and diversity of His creation, just as [sic] heterosexual people. They should enjoy the same rights. Our failure to interpret and apply Scripture accurately has resulted in murder, persecution and oppression for the way gay people have been created, i.e., their sexual orientation.

(BCCNI-UK 2013)

---

[11] Strom, Andrew (nd), 'PENTECOSTALS ACCEPT GAYS—It Begins'. The fellowship is part of the 'C3' (Christian City Church) denomination—one of the largest mainstream Pentecostal groups in Australia.

Bailey explained that he arrived at his views on same-sex relationships after providing pastoral care to gay people for a number of years. According to Bailey, the Bible encourages Christians to support people excluded from society, including same-sex couples:

> The statements in Leviticus, Deuteronomy, Romans, 1 Corinthians and 1Timothy refer to a range of homosexual acts, but not to the issue of same-sex orientation or to loving relationships between people of the same gender. Scripture should be applied in the light of God's welcome of excluded peoples. If the Scriptures do not prohibit same-sex love then who are we to exclude those who God has included? Some may say we are stretching [*sic*]—we are. We are trying to reach out to our lost and excluded brothers and sisters.

Pastoral and Counselling Issues

Fundamentally, the principal Western Pentecostal bodies see homosexual behaviour as sinful but they do so because of their belief that sexual activity properly belongs within heterosexual marriage. This belief was widely, if not universally, held by churches right up until the late twentieth century and Pentecostals, who saw themselves as restoring the condition of the early Church, accepted it without question. It follows that redemption is achieved by repentance and a change of lifestyle and sexual activity. Typically the Assemblies of God USA report of 1979 on homosexuality declared, 'The homosexual who wants to be delivered from the penalty and power of sin must come to God in the same way other sinners come to God...through repentance and faith in Jesus as Lord and Saviour' (Assemblies of God USA [1979] 2001). What is notable here is that homosexual activity was regarded as no more or less reprehensible than any other sexual sin; on this evidence one should not regard Assemblies of God USA as homophobic.

Statements about dealing with homosexuality may be brief and to the point. The UPCI simply calls for members to 'encourage prayer for the deliverance of those enslaved by that satanic snare' (UPCI 1977). However, there has been a softening of harsh condemnation in some quarters. The following affirmations summarize the position of the Evangelical Alliance in the UK in its 2012 Report 'Biblical and Pastoral Responses to Homosexuality':

> We encourage evangelical congregations to be communities of grace in which those who experience same-sex attraction and seek to live faithfully in accordance with biblical teaching are welcomed and affirmed. Such Christians need churches which are safe spaces where they are able to share and explore their stories with fellow believers for mutual encouragement and support as we help each other grow together into maturity in Christ.
>
> (Evangelical Alliance 2012b)

According to the 1979 Assemblies of God USA position paper 'Homosexuality', homosexual orientation is taken to mean sexual attraction to other members of the same sex. Homosexual *behaviour* is understood to denote participation in same-sex genital acts, and it is stated that orientation may pose temptations to lustful thinking and behaviour, like heterosexual temptations, which a person may not necessarily act on and may resist and overcome in the power of the Holy Spirit. Here, only homosexual lust and homosexual behaviours are therefore sinful.

In an article in the *Enrichment Journal* produced by Assemblies of God USA reference is made to counselling the sexually immoral (adulterers, prostitutes, homosexuals). This is differentiated from mental health issues which are said to be ideally dealt with by a Christian mental health professional. Since Assemblies of God USA believe that sexual activity should be confined within marriage, and since same-sex marriage was not on the horizon twenty years ago, homosexual acts, like heterosexual acts outside marriage, are categorized as being sinful. However, the purpose of counselling is to 'to set people free, forgive them of their sins, and restore their lives' and the counsellor should treat the counselee [as] a person of worth, made in the image of God' (Goodall n.d.).

CONCLUSION

Pentecostal beliefs about the love of God expressed through Christ are inclusive of all peoples and sexual orientations even if the traditional position of Pentecostals has sharply distinguished between the act and the person: 'God loves the sinner but hates the sin.' The dispute is now a hermeneutical one between the traditionalists who define sin to include LGBTI sexual behaviour and the newer voices who define sin more narrowly or, at any rate, differently. Consequently, it is possible that the debate over LGBTI issues within Pentecostalism may follow a similar trajectory to the debate on divorce. In other words, Pentecostalism may dispute progressive opinion but eventually and slowly adjust its interpretations of Scripture so as to accept a more liberal position, though with various doctrinal or other reservations.

Pentecostals have historically held a strong position on holiness (as defined by abstinence from drugs, alcohol, gambling and sexual activity outside traditionally defined marriage) and this position has been reinforced by a belief in the indwelling Holy Spirit as a source of individualized religious experience. Any changes to Pentecostal beliefs will only occur in a piecemeal fashion as separate denominations, each with their own form of governance, accept new understandings of what constitutes holiness. In general, those denominations that function democratically through voting are likely to change more slowly than those led by gifted individuals since in the latter case the process of change is simpler. Fragmentation of Pentecostalism over the years has led to diversity and growth and it is reasonable to expect further fragmentation, as well as possibly further growth, on LBGT issues.

References

Affirming Pentecostal Church International (2012). 'Constitution and Bylaws'. <http://rpifellowship.com/uploads/Constitution___Bylaws_March2012.pdf> (accessed 23 Apr. 2013).

Anderson, A. (2001). *African Reformation: African Initiated Christianity in the 20th Century.* Trenton, NJ: Africa World Press.

Anderson, A. (2004). *An Introduction to Pentecostalism: Global Charismatic Christianity.* Cambridge: Cambridge University Press.

Assemblies of God USA ([1979] 2001). 'Homosexuality: Statement of the General Presbytery of the Assemblies of God USA', 14 August 1979 and revised 6 August 2001. <http://ag.org/top/Beliefs/Position_Papers/pp_downloads/pp_4181_homosexuality.pdf> (accessed 20 Apr. 2013).

BCCNI-UK (2013). 'Bailey Becomes First Black UK Pentecostal Church Leader to Support Homosexual Marriage'. <http://www.blackchristiannews.com/uk/2013/04/bailey-becomes-first-black-uk-pentecostal-church-leader-to-support-homosexual-marriage.html> (accessed 18 Oct. 2013).

Behrens, Samuel D. (2006). *Anti-Gay Equals Anti-God: A Minister of the Assemblies of God Explains How the Evangelical Church Has Things Wrong.* Tajique, NM: Alama Square Press.

Bonner, William L. (1976). *The Apostolic Dilemma: The Apostolic Church Against Homosexuality.* New York: Crossroad.

'Black Pastors Fight Gay Marriage' (2004). *Charisma* (November). No named author.

Christian Council of Ghana, 'Christian Council joins calls to condemn homosexuality in Ghana'. <http://www.ghananewsagency.org/social/christian-council-joins-calls-to-condemn-homosexuality-in-ghana-31187> (accessed 7 June 2014).

Central Intelligence Agency (CIA) (2013). <https://www.cia.gov/library/publications/the-world-factbook/fields/2122.html> (accessed 26 Aug. 2013).

Coleman, S. (2000). *The Globalisation of Charismatic Christianity: Spreading the Gospel of Prosperity.* Cambridge: Cambridge University Press.

Cox, H. (1995). *Fire From Heaven: The Rise of Pentecostal Spirituality and the Reshaping of Religion in the 21st Century.* Cambridge, MA: Da Capo Press.

Daily Kos (2012). 'Meet Brazil's Religious Right Star: Silas Malafaia'. <http://www.dailykos.com/story/2012/04/17/1084003/-Meet-Brazil-s-Religious-Right-Star-Silas-Malafaia> (accessed 23 Apr. 2013).

Duncan, Randy (2013). 'A Message from Our Chief Presiding Presbyter', Reconciling Pentecostals International. <http://rpifellowship.com/Welcome_Message.html> (accessed 3 Mar. 2013).

Epprecht, Marc (2009). *Heterosexual Africa?: The History of an Idea from the Age of Exploration to the Age of AIDS.* Athens, OH: Ohio University Press.

Evangelical Alliance (2012a). 'Resources for Church Leaders—Biblical and Pastoral Responses to Homosexuality'. <http://www.eauk.org/church/resources/theological-articles/resources-for-church-leaders-biblical-and-pastoral-responses-to-homosexuality.cfm>.

Evangelical Alliance (2012b). '2012 Report: Biblical and Pastoral Responses to Homosexuality'. Update of Evangelical Alliance, *Faith, Hope and Homosexuality* (1998).

Freedom 2 Be (2013). 'About Us'. <http://www.freedom2b.org/about/> (accessed 2 Apr. 2013).

Freston, P. (2001). *Evangelicals and Politics in Asia, Africa and Latin America.* Cambridge: Cambridge University Press.

Freston, P. (2004). *Protestant Political Parties: A Global Survey.* Aldershot: Ashgate.

Global Post (2013). 'LGBT-Inclusive Pentecostal Churches Growing in Brazil'. <http://www.globalpost.com/dispatches/globalpost-blogs/belief/lgbt-inclusive-pentecostal-churches-growing-brazil> (accessed 4 Apr. 2013).

Goodall, Wayde, I. (n.d.). 'Pastoral Counseling: 10 Key Principles'. *Enrichment Journal.* <http://enrichmentjournal.ag.org/199803/096_key_principles.cfm> (accessed 10 May 2013).

Hoad, Neville (2007). *African Intimacies: Race, Homosexuality, and Globalization.* Minneapolis: University of Minnesota Press.

Hunt, Stephen (2011). 'Evaluating Prophetic Radicalism'. In C. Smith (ed.), *Pentecostal Power: Expressions, Impact and Faith of Latin American Pentecostals.* Leiden: Brill.

Institute on Religion & Democracy (n.d.). Report by Juicy Ecumenism. <http://juicyecumenism.com/> (accessed 18 Apr. 2013).

International Church of the Foursquare Gospel (1993). 'Resolution'. Quoted in 'Gay Christian Movement Watch, Official Denominational Positions on Homosexuality', 21 June 2010. <http://www.gcmwatch.com/4911/official-denominational-positions-on-homosexuality> (accessed 21 Oct. 2013).

International Pentecostal Church of Christ. 'Homosexuality'. <http://www.ipcc.cc/position%20statements.htm#HOMOSEXUALITY_> (accessed 7 June 2014).

IPHC (International Pentecostal Holiness Church) (1990), Resolution 1. <http://blogs.christianpost.com/student-of-the-word/upc-resolution-strengthens-stance-on-marriage-11258/> (accessed 8 June 2014).

IPHC (International Pentecostal Holiness Church) (2013). *Vision and Mission.* <https://www.iphc.org/men/vision-mission> (access 7 June 2014).

UPCI (United Pentecostal Church International) (1977) Position paper. <http://www.upci.org/resources/instructional-devotional-leadership/75-homosexuality> (accessed 8 June 2014).

Kaoma, Kapya, *The U.S. Christian Right and the Attack on Gays in Africa* (Winter 09/Spring 10). <PublicEye.org> (accessed 4 Mar. 2013).

Kay, W. K. (2009). *Pentecostalism: Core Text.* London: SCM.

Kay, W. K. (2011). *Pentecostalism: A Very Short Introduction.* Oxford: Oxford University Press.

Kennedy, John W. (2004). 'Homosexual Rights Activists Gain Influence in Public Schools'. *Pentecostal Evangel.* <http://www.tpe.ag.org/Articles2004/4719_kennedy_news.cfm>. (accessed 27 Apr. 2013).

Lee, Y. (2009). *The Holy Spirit Movement in Korea: Its Historical and Theological Development.* Oxford: Regnum.

Martin, D. (2002). *Pentecostalism: The World Their Parish.* Oxford: Blackwell.

Menzie, Nicola (2011), 'Ghana Fears Acceptance of Homosexuality Will Bring God's Wrath'. <http://www.christianpost.com/news/ghana-fears-acceptance-of-homosexuality-will-bring-gods-wrath-52514/#yo53VFrJ6bMuxhVs.99>. (accessed 8 June, 2014)

National Council of Churches (2008). *Yearbook of American & Canadian Churches.* <http://www.ncccusa.org/news/080215yearbook1.html> (accessed 19 Mar. 2013).

Onyinah, O. (n.d). 'Deliverance as a Way of Confronting Witchcraft in Modern Africa: Ghana as a Case History'. *Cyberjournal for Pentecostal-Charismatic Research.* <http://www.pctii.org/cyberj/cyberj10/onyinah.html#_ftn85> (accessed 21 Mar. 2013).

Pew Forum Survey on Religious and Public Life (2006). 'Spirit and Power'—A 10 Country Survey of Pentecostals'. <http://www.pewforum.org/Christian/Evangelical-Protestant-Churches/Spirit-and-Power.aspx> (accessed 18 Mar. 2013).

Redeemed Christian Church of God (2011). 'Christianity and Homosexuality (One—Two)' (Sunday School Teacher's Manual). <http://ss.rccgnet.org/teacher/christianity%20and%20homosexuality1_2.html> (accessed 2 Apr. 2013).

ReligiousTolerance.org (2012). 'Homosexuality and the Pentecostal Movement'. <http://www.religioustolerance.org/hom_upci.htm> (accessed 19 October 2013).

Serbin, K. (1999). 'Brazil: Religious Tolerance: Church–State Relations, and the Challenge of Pluralism'. In P. E. Sigmund (ed.), *Religious Freedom and Evangelization in Latin America: The Challenge of Religious Pluralism*. New York: Orbis Books, 204–219.

Strom, Andrew (nd). 'PENTECOSTALS ACCEPT GAYS—It Begins'. <http://www.revivalschool.com/pentecostals-accept-gays-it-begins-andrew-strom/> (accessed 7 June 2014).

United Pentecostal Church International (1977). 'Homosexuality', quoted by Religious Tolerance.org (2012). <http://www.religioustolerance.org/hom_upci.htm> (accessed 21 Oct. 2013).

United Pentecostal Church International (2011). 'Homosexuality'. <http://www.upci.org/resources/instructional-devotional-leadership/75-homosexuality> (accessed 12 Sept. 2013).

van Klinken, Adriaan (2011). 'The Homosexual as the Antithesis of "Biblical Manhood"? Heteronormativity and Masculinity Politics in Zambian Pentecostal Sermons'. *Journal of Gender and Religion in Africa*, 17(2): 129–142.

van Klinken, Adriaan (2013). 'Gay Rights, the Devil and the End Times: Public Religion and the Enchantment of the Homosexuality Debate in Zambia'. *Religion*, 43(4): 519–540. <http://www.tandfonline.com/doi/full/10.1080/0048721X.2013.765631>.

Vendornaija World Press (2011). 'Ban on Same Sex: PRN Back's Senate'. <http://vendornaija.wordpress.com/2011/12/03/ban-on-same-sex-pfn-backs-senate/> (accessed 2 Apr. 2013).

Walker, Andrew (1998). *Restoring the Kingdom* (4th edn). Guildford: Eagle.

Zonkel, Phillip (2013). 'South Korean Gay Film Maker in News Over Wedding Plans'. *Presstelegram*. <http://blogs.presstelegram.com/outinthe562/2013/07/24/south-korean-gay-film-maker-in-news-over-wedding-plans/> (accessed 13 Aug. 2013).

CHAPTER 23

THEOLOGY AND PRACTICE IN EVANGELICAL CHURCHES

ANDREW GODDARD

EVANGELICAL churches and evangelicals within mainstream churches are often identified as at the heart of current struggles over issues of sexuality and gender, portrayed as taking a conservative stance, resisting changes in wider society, and opposing attempts to revise church teaching and practice. Although there is much truth in this characterization, the reality is more complex than evangelicals or their critics acknowledge. This chapter sets two currently contentious issues—premarital sex and homosexuality—within an examination of evangelical responses to earlier controversies over contraception, divorce, and remarriage, and the role of men and women in church. These highlight different patterns of evangelical response as new and challenging questions were raised. First, however, it is necessary to define 'evangelical' churches and approaches.

EVANGELICALISM

Although some churches identify themselves as 'evangelical', evangelicalism has always been more of a global, interdenominational movement and tradition, present to varying degrees within a large number of different Protestant churches, and lacking any ecclesial authority structures. One challenge in surveying evangelical attitudes, particularly on contentious subjects, is therefore that the definition of 'evangelical' itself is highly contested. Debates about sexuality and gender have sometimes been drawn into such definitional controversies with arguments as to whether someone holding a particular view is still recognizably an evangelical and David Bebbington claiming that 'by the twenty-first century the issues that divided Evangelicals most sharply surrounded issues of gender relations' (Bebbington 2009: 104). There is also the important but sometimes hard-to-define distinction between evangelicalism and fundamentalism, and differences between evangelicalism in different countries.

In sketching the hallmarks of evangelicalism, Bebbington's four distinguishing marks of conversionism, activism, biblicism, and crucicentrism (Bebbington 1989) have been highly influential.

First, faced with major social changes, evangelicals' emphasis on personal *conversion* has, at times, led some to focus on 'saving souls' with individuals being 'born again' out of a corrupt world and personally transformed by the Spirit (in relation to UK evangelicalism see James 2011). This more pietistic strand can lead to a failure to understand or address social and cultural shifts and produce blindness as to how changes either force evangelicals into a strongly counter-cultural, perhaps reactionary, pattern of life or gradually lead them to adapt (Bebbington 1989 shows evangelicalism has been more shaped by cultural context than many acknowledge).

Second, in contrast, evangelical *activism* has led to social engagement seeking cultural conversion. This has often been in a socially conservative form as shown by groups such as CARE in the United Kingdom and Focus on the Family in the United States but evangelical activism can be shaped as much by a high level of pragmatism as any carefully thought-through theology.

Third, evangelicals are marked by their avowal of the supremacy of *Scripture*, often articulated prominently in the statements of faith for evangelical churches and networks (the UK's Evangelical Alliance affirms the 'supreme authority of the Old and New Testament Scriptures, which are the written Word of God' and the Bible as 'fully trustworthy for faith and conduct'). Evangelical conflicts and differing responses over sexuality often get focused on this issue, being largely shaped by whether, and how clearly, Scripture is understood to address directly the specific issue under discussion rather than by a wider theology of humanity or sexuality, the Christian tradition, or human experience within the contemporary context. Conservatives can view others as sitting loose to Scripture's authority and not authentically evangelical.

Fourth, the evangelical emphasis on the *cross* has less obvious impact in the area of sexuality and gender. However, the desire to gain a hearing for the gospel of justification by faith can lead to discussions of ethics, including sexual ethics, being seen as secondary and a pragmatic toleration of what may be described as a 'lesser evil' in order not to alienate potential converts.

CONTRACEPTION

The first major challenge to traditional Christian sexual ethics in recent times was the increasing availability and acceptability of contraception. Despite a strong long-standing Christian tradition opposed to the prevention of conception, by the 1960s, with the widespread availability of simple oral contraception, evangelicals, like most Protestant Christians, were supportive of contraception for married couples (Poulson 2006). In August 1968, the Christian Medical Society and *Christianity Today* (the leading American evangelical publication) held a 'Protestant Symposium on the Control of Human Reproduction' involving evangelical theologians, medics, sociologists, and lawyers. Its published papers (Spitzer and Saylor 1969) supported the symposium's affirmation that 'procreation need not be the immediate intent of husband and wife in the sex act. Coitus may be simply the expression of love and a mutual fulfilment of normal desires' (p. xxiv) and that 'the prevention of conception is not in itself forbidden or sinful providing the reasons for it are in harmony with the total revelation of God for married life' (p. xxv).

Leading Southern Baptist Al Mohler (1998: 24) summed up the evangelical response clearly:

> Most evangelical Protestants greeted the advent of modern birth control technologies with applause and relief. Lacking any substantial theology of marriage, sex, or the family, evangelicals welcomed the development of 'The Pill' much as the world celebrated the discovery of penicillin—as one more milestone in the inevitable march of human progress and the conquest of nature.

The subject has, until recently, received limited attention in evangelical discussions of sex and marriage, as most evangelicals do not even consider it an important issue. A number of factors contributed to this consensus. The primary reason is evangelicals' emphasis on biblical authority and the lack of direct biblical teaching but other elements included widespread evangelical concern about the problems caused by overpopulation, a pragmatic recognition that rejecting contraception would lead to unwanted pregnancies and abortion, and perhaps remnants of evangelicalism's historic anti-Catholicism. The reality is that 'in contrast to Catholic writers, evangelicals have addressed this issue pragmatically rather than theologically. Protestant critics have tended to condemn Catholic opposition as legalistic' (James 2011: 110). The lack of a direct, clear biblical prohibition of contraception is the fundamental basis for evangelical disinterest. The only specific text which could be argued to address contraception directly is Onan's condemnation for preventing fulfilment of his duties within Levirate marriage when he 'spilled his semen on the ground' (Gen. 38:9). The 1968 affirmation decisively stated that 'The Bible does not expressly prohibit contraception'—if the Bible did prohibit it, evangelicals would have been much more cautious and probably openly hostile to its development.

Evangelicals responding to the Vatican's arguments against contraception have argued that the fundamental flaw was to insist on upholding the need for the relational and procreative goods of sexual union and marriage to be expressed equally in every act of sexual intercourse (O'Donovan 1984: 77). In contrast, evangelicals tend to emphasize marriage and sexual intercourse within marriage having multiple goods and purposes taken as a whole. All of these should be embraced but 'contraceptive intercourse may sometimes be a fitting means by which husband and wife aim to nourish simultaneously the procreative and unitive purposes of their marriage' and there is no 'coherent rationale by which to reject contraceptive intercourse within marriage as long as procreation is not excluded *in principle* from the overarching good of the one flesh union' (Meilaender and Turner 1998, emphasis original).

Few evangelical Christians, however, thought through these questions until recent years when some who have done so have rejected contraception. This has been prompted by a number of developments including the cultural impact of the separation of sexual intercourse and procreation, the development by Pope John Paul II of a much more biblically rooted and rich theology of the body, and the recognition that many contraceptives are effectively abortive if one believes life begins at conception. A young evangelical couple described their rethinking in *Open Embrace* (Torode and Torode 2002) and a much more thorough, systematic, and polemical case has recently been made in *The Christian Case Against Contraception* (Hodge 2009). This not only highlights the anti-contraceptive stance of theologians respected in the evangelical tradition (Luther, Calvin, Wesley) but argues that the common assumption the Bible has nothing to say is false and that, in accepting contraception, modern evangelicalism 'denies the trajectory taken by the New Testament and the historical Christian Church to establish sexual ethics', and instead has accepted 'the methodology of argumentation of the larger culture' thus weakening its stance on other issues, notably homosexuality.

Anti-contraception arguments have little purchase on either the thinking or behaviour of most evangelicals but some, looking back at the Vatican's *Humanae Vitae* (1968), now acknowledge 'the prophetic character of the encyclical's warning about the inevitable result of the contraceptive mentality.... Once the sex act was severed from the likelihood of childbearing, the traditional structure of sexual morality collapsed' (Mohler 1998: 24) and regret that 'evangelicals have been unwilling to acknowledge the profound implications of the acceptance of the contraceptive culture, and have been slow to realise that it led directly to the collapse of traditional morality and family life' (James 2011: 114).

Divorce and Remarriage

In contrast to decisions about contraception, decisions about divorce and further marriage after divorce are public, addressed explicitly by Scripture, and often require church policies. Here evangelicals have expressed a range of views.

Most evangelicals have a non-sacramental understanding of marriage and thus reject a Roman Catholic doctrine of indissolubility. Perhaps the predominant model for understanding marriage among evangelicals is in terms of a covenant, called to reflect God's covenant with his people (Atkinson 1979). In line with wider Protestantism, they would hold that sin can destroy a marriage covenant and so divorce (though a product of sin) is possible and most would then accept remarriage, under certain conditions.

The disagreements among evangelicals focus primarily on the interpretation of Scripture where there are different voices even within the Gospels. This polyphony presents a challenge for a tradition looking to the Bible as its supreme authority. It is clear that divorce and further marriage were permissible in Old Testament Israel both from Deuteronomy 24 and widespread evidence of Jewish practice. Jesus, according to the Gospels, took a strongly critical and negative stance. In Mark 10 and Luke 16 this appears to be an absolutist prohibition on remarriage after divorce, equating it with adultery, whereas in Matthew 5 and 19, there is the famous 'Matthean exception' in relation to *porneia*. Paul had to face new questions relating to marriages between Christian

believers and non-believers and he addresses these in 1 Corinthians 7, seemingly permitting divorce where an unbeliever leaves (the 'Pauline Privilege') and, in the view of most
scholars, allowing remarriage.

These different canonical voices have resulted in a number of evangelical approaches
to the question, helpfully captured in two multi-authored volumes which also illustrate the developments within evangelicalism. The fact that the earlier volume (House
1990) contains four views whereas the later volume only three (Wenham, Heth, and
Keener 2006), omitting the most conservative view of 'no divorce and no remarriage',
is itself telling. By 2006 the most conservative view thought to be worth including was
'no remarriage after divorce'. This was represented in 1990 by Old Testament scholar
William Heth who had earlier articulated it with fellow Old Testament scholar Gordon
Wenham (Heth and Wenham, 1984) who defends it in the 2006 volume. From this perspective the teaching of the New Testament, confirmed by its interpretation by the overwhelming majority of Church Fathers, permits separation on the grounds of *porneia*
(Matt. 19) and Christian consent to divorce by an unbelieving spouse who seeks it (1 Cor.
7). In both situations, however, neither party is free to remarry. They remain bound for
life to their original spouse and divorce cannot destroy this reality.

This view is most fully expounded and pastorally applied in the work of Anglican evangelical Andrew Cornes, who roots marriage's indissolubility in the creation order where
marriage is, according to Genesis, a 'one flesh union' ('They have become, at the most fundamental level of their being, a unity. It is a more important fact about them that they are
now one person than that they continue to be two individuals' (Cornes [1993] 2002: 130)).
This view places a strong commendable emphasis on the need to work for reconciliation
after marriage breakdown but is clear any further marriage during the lifetime of the former spouse is sinful. Remarriages are thus not to be celebrated in church; those entering them need to repent; and some evangelical churches holding this view would enact
church discipline against unrepentant members. Cornes, however, denies that the logic
of his position is that such marriages are ongoing adultery, arguing that 'God views your
new married relationship primarily as a marriage; as a marriage which should not have
been entered into, as a mistake, but nevertheless a true marriage' (Cornes 1998: 114–115).

The 'no remarriage' position remains a minority evangelical view. Most evangelicals
permit remarriage when divorce has been on the grounds of adultery or desertion by
an unbeliever as this is held to be biblically sanctioned. Significantly, Heth now holds
such a view and articulates it in the 2006 volume. This view, stated by Calvin and the
Westminster Confession, reads the Matthean exception and the Pauline privilege as
extending to remarriage after divorce in these two contexts. In such cases churches lift
the blanket prohibition but may still be strong in relation to church discipline for 'unbiblical' remarriages where there is no repentance (as seen in Bethlehem Baptist Church led
by leading conservative evangelical John Piper which also states, appealing to 1 Timothy
3, that those remarried after divorce must forgo being elders or deacons in the Church).

Finally, an increasing number of evangelicals extend these two explicit biblical per-
missions to argue that there are other circumstances where remarriage is permitted.
This is still claimed to be evangelical and faithful to Scripture which is read as showing

marriages can be ended with freedom to marry another. Some argue that Jesus' strict sayings are hyperbole and not to be read literally. It is also claimed that the Church today must, like Paul in Corinth, discern new situations not explicitly addressed in Scripture. In the words of Keener, who advocates this view, it involves 'extrapolating Scripture's principles to resolve questions not explicitly addressed in the biblical text' (Wenham, Heth, and Keener 2006: 93). An alternative defence has been extensively argued by evangelical biblical scholar David Instone-Brewer who, drawing on ancient Jewish and other documents and Exodus 21:10–11, argues that neglect of food, clothing, and conjugal love are all also biblical grounds for legitimate divorce and subsequent legitimate remarriage and that Jesus' message, set in its cultural context, was simply to reject the lax view that divorce could be granted for 'any cause' (Instone-Brewer 2002).

In this area, therefore, evangelicals, while insisting on being biblical, have come to quite different (and increasingly more permissive) understandings of Scripture's teaching. Three further features of evangelical practice are noteworthy.

First, divorce and remarriage are not uncommon among evangelical Christians, including public leaders, who take strongly conservative views in other areas. A controversial 1999 US study by the evangelical Barna Research Group even suggested evangelicals' divorce rates were higher than average. The tendency for evangelicals to move to less rigorist ethical approaches is likely connected to this experience and in 2010 the Southern Baptist Convention passed a resolution entitled 'The Scandal of Southern Baptist Divorce' which acknowledged 'the complicity of many among us for too often failing to show the world the meaning of the gospel through marital fidelity'.

Second, despite the increase in divorce and its impact on family life, evangelicals in the UK took some time to engage with the issue in relation to legal changes and it has never been particularly prominent in their social involvement. This situation is even more stark in the USA, with political scientist Mark Smith highlighting it as a surprising missing 'culture war': 'instead of following a fixed and enduring moral compass on divorce, religious groups in America—including those that view the Bible as the inerrant Word of God—gradually accommodated a cultural trend that gained widespread acceptance' (Smith 2010: 59).

Third, the issue of divorce and remarriage has neither produced tensions between evangelicals and others within mainstream churches nor led to competing movements within evangelicalism advocating their view and attacking other evangelicals. This is very different from evangelical views on gender and the proper roles and relationship of men and women.

Gender: Men and Women in Church Leadership

Historically, evangelicalism has a strong tradition, particularly in the 'holiness' and revivalist strands, of encouraging women's gifts and ministries, sometimes resulting in prominent women preachers and leaders, especially in mission. In each century from the eighteenth-century evangelical revival onwards, women such as Sarah Osborn, Phoebe Palmer, the Countess of Huntingdon, Mary Fletcher, and Hannah More were influential evangelicals. In recent decades, however, responding to wider social changes and the rise of feminism, evangelicals have often been bitterly divided in their teaching and practice (see Storkey in Larsen and Treier 2007: 161–176).

Evangelicals, like most in Christian tradition, believed men had authority over women, especially in marriage and the Church. This was based on an understanding of biblical, particularly Pauline (e.g. 1 Cor. 11; 1 Tim. 2; Eph. 5), teaching placing limits on women's exercise of authority in church and teaching the wife's submission to her husband as 'head'. From the 1970s onwards, this interpretation came under increasing challenge and, in response, was defended more vociferously and often in novel ways.

Within the revival of evangelical concern for social action, and influenced by growing evangelical interest in biblical hermeneutics and resistance to certain doctrines of Scripture's 'inerrancy', a movement arose of evangelical or biblical feminism (Cochran 2005 is the best historical survey; see also Creegan and Pohl 2005). An early influential articulation was a work by two women theologians entitled *All We're Meant to Be: A Biblical Approach to Women's Liberation* (Scanzoni and Hardesty 1974) and the Evangelical Women's Caucus (EWC) was formed. That book and Paul Jewett's study (1975) argued Scripture was truly liberating and egalitarian and was being misinterpreted and misused to restrict women unjustly. It also raised questions within evangelicalism about the cultural conditioning of biblical texts and the possibility that apostolic teaching in some areas may be limited and no longer directly applicable or even, more radically, flawed. This deepened conservative suspicions and reactions and played into developing differences among evangelical feminists over homosexuality, inclusive language, and other issues. Divisions ultimately led to a split and the formation in 1986 of Christians for Biblical Equality (CBE) which became the main evangelical group supporting an egalitarian reading of Scripture. Following this split, the EWC became the Evangelical and Ecumenical Women's Caucus (EEWC), adopted a less conservative statement of faith in relation to Scripture's authority, and became less identified as evangelical.

Debates took longer to develop among British evangelicals. The 1977 National Evangelical Anglican Congress (NEAC) had no women speakers and passed a resolution showing an awareness of a problem but maintaining a traditional distinction: 'We repent of our failure to give women their rightful place as partners in mission with men. Leadership in the Church should be plural and mixed, ultimate responsibility normally singular and male.' British evangelicals gradually began to engage with the issue more seriously from the perspective upheld by CBE and 1985 saw the formation of the Men, Women and God network by leaders such as Elaine Storkey (1985) with support from John Stott (who never fully embraced an egalitarian theology).

The biblical theology for equality was rooted in Christ's example, reading the biblical narrative as a whole with men and women being made and restored in God's image, exemplary women leaders in both Testaments (e.g. Deborah in Judges 4–5 and Junia, the female apostle mentioned in Romans 16), and a reinterpretation of the restrictive texts. It has become the dominant evangelical view in theory—an Evangelical Alliance survey in 2013 found that 73 per cent thought women should hold senior positions in the Church and 80 per cent believed women should preach or teach—if not in practice (only 16 per cent of those surveyed attended churches with women as senior leaders). It has, however, engendered a strong conservative reaction defending and providing theological arguments for the previous standard evangelical practice.

The focus of this has been the Council for Biblical Manhood and Womanhood (CBMW). It offers what it calls a 'complementarian' view of gender and sees itself resisting 'unbiblical teaching'. Its 1987 Danvers Statement on Biblical Manhood and Womanhood speaks of equality but also 'distinctions in masculine and feminine roles' which 'are ordained by God as part of the created order' and thus of male headship in marriage and a conviction that 'some governing and teaching roles within the church are restricted to men'. For many conservatives, rejecting this vision starts a slippery slope away from evangelicalism. CBW's 1991 book, *Recovering Biblical Manhood and Womanhood: A Response to Evangelical Feminism* (Piper and Grudem 1991) spread this theological and social vision. It empowered some American evangelical denominations to apply clear restrictions on women's ministry and found supporters in other contexts (the evangelical group Reform in the Church of England requires its council members to sign the Danvers Statement). Most controversially, the argument has gone beyond appealing to biblical texts to argue (from 1 Cor. 11) for a subordination within the Trinitarian Father–Son relationship as the ultimate basis for ordering male–female relationships in terms of 'male headship' (for an evangelical critique of this see Giles 2002).

These differences have created divisions within evangelical denominations such as the Southern Baptists and differentiation amongst evangelicals in more mainstream denominations such as that between 'open' and 'conservative' evangelicals in the Church of England over women priests and bishops (Goddard and Hendry 2010 offers the views of two Anglican evangelical women discussing their different interpretations of Scripture).

The theological differences in part reflect different views on biblical inspiration but relate more to biblical interpretation. Egalitarians (Pierce and Groothuis 2005 is the best compendium) emphasize the broad and progressive sweep of biblical teaching and locate the Pauline restrictions within that, and within their particular original context. Conservatives, in contrast, maintain that the restrictions are universally binding and rooted in creation order. They have developed a much more systematic and programmatic approach, rebutting egalitarian readings (Grudem 2005) and claiming biblical and theological justification for restrictions that in the past evangelicals applied (mirroring wider social norms) but, at times, pragmatically ignored.

Evangelical responses are clearly also shaped by issues of personality, experience, and responses to wider social change. A recent volume of testimonies from those abandoning a conservative position (Johnson 2010) also demonstrates that, although evangelicals continue to appeal to Scripture as their authority, the positive experience of leading as a woman or the example of women's good leadership has been a major factor in causing people to re-examine the biblical witness.

Such moves away from a conservative position are less evident among evangelicals on perhaps the two most contentious issues on sexuality today—premarital sexual relationships and homosexual relationships.

SEX, SINGLENESS, AND MARRIAGE— PREMARITAL SEX AND COHABITATION

In evangelical culture, the basic sexual ethic is, in principle, clear and not distinctively evangelical but the historic Christian consensus summed up by C. S. Lewis as 'Either marriage, with complete faithfulness to your partner, or else total abstinence' (Lewis 1955: 86). Whilst this ethic was widely accepted in the Church, and much of society, it required little serious defence. Evangelicals focused more on encouraging people to live it out and resist sexual temptation than defending it biblically and theologically. Recent decades, however, have witnessed a sea change in social mores and practice and the need to face new challenges (evangelical responses include Winner 2005; Brandon 2009; Kuehne 2009). Among the key changes are that people are marrying much later; cohabitation prior to marriage has now become the norm; there has been a rapid rise in the number of children born outside marriage; and the proportion of the population who are unmarried and indeed never-married has significantly increased.

As a result of such changes, the traditional ethic is now clearly counter-cultural and questions are asked as to its truth, rationale, and viability. Among evangelical Christians, the question is raised whether, while there are clear biblical condemnations of adultery, any specific text of Scripture explicitly condemns all sexual intercourse prior to marriage. There is, however, a clear and consistent condemnation of 'sexual immorality' in both Old and New Testaments. Although a strong case can be made that this includes all non-marital sexual intercourse, evangelicals have, nevertheless, acknowledged the need for more than simply a biblicist, rule-based approach and articulated a theology of sex, marriage, and singleness (discussed later) which, though perhaps more self-consciously seeking to root itself in Scripture, is not distinctively evangelical but rather expresses the traditional Christian consensus.

Appealing to the opening chapters of Genesis, as Christ himself does, evangelicals give a central place in thinking about sexuality to the doctrine of creation. Marriage as a created institution for human flourishing (see Ash 2003) and the created good of being made male and female (the focus of the opening section of Grenz [1990] 1997) are at the heart of evangelical thought in this area. In describing the purpose of marriage, Grenz writes of it as the context for sexual expression (citing 1 Cor. 7), directed towards procreation and child-rearing, the focus of companionship, and a spiritual metaphor of the divine will to community. Sexual intercourse, which Scripture describes in terms of 'becoming one flesh' and Grenz describes in terms of expressing both mutual submission and openness to others through openness to the gift of new life, is therefore good in the context of marriage. At times popular evangelicalism has promoted supposedly biblically-based celebrations of sexual pleasure within marriage amounting to evangelical sex manuals (Wheat 1977; Driscoll and Driscoll 2012).

In evangelical theology, all these created goods are also, to varying degrees and in multiple ways, damaged and distorted in our experience due to human sin. Evangelicals are therefore generally cautious about giving a significant place to our experience of sexuality in developing a theology (Scanzoni 1984 and Bell 2007 are among the exceptions). God's redemptive work seeks to restore his purposes in creation and so Christians are called to live in accordance with these, fleeing sexual immorality, and honouring their bodies and others' bodies as temples of God's Holy Spirit (1 Cor. 6).

In practice much of evangelical culture is so focused on marriage and the family that it is weak in theology and practice in relation to singleness. While singleness receives little attention in the Old Testament, Jesus' teaching and example reveal that 'marriage is not fundamental in the building of God's people in the new covenant as it was in the old covenant' and 'singleness anticipates the age to come in which marriage itself will be obsolete. Singleness visibly heralds the coming of the new age' (Danylak 2010: 172). This vision is elaborated further by Paul, notably in 1 Corinthians 7 where singleness is understood as a spiritual gift. Evangelicals have, however, generally failed to recognize, honour, and support this calling and gifting within their churches in the positive ways that other Christian traditions have done, often narrowing the focus to the need for sexual abstinence when unmarried.

Guided by this theological vision, evangelicals have generally resisted and often actively opposed trends in contemporary society regarding sex outside marriage. Within the USA, this has found expression in clear codes of sexual conduct in evangelical colleges and popular campaigns among young people such as True Love Waits which, since 1992, has encouraged young people to 'make a commitment to God, myself, my family, my friends, my future mate, and my future children to a lifetime of purity including sexual abstinence from this day until the day I enter a biblical marriage relationship'.

In response to cohabitation, evangelicals have advanced pragmatic arguments for preferring marriage such as its unambiguous nature concerning the couple's mutual consent and commitment due to public promises, the wider familial and public involvement compared to living together, and the stronger protection for the vulnerable given by legal recognition (Ash 2003: ch. 11). Most evangelicals continue to understand cohabitation in terms of 'premarital sex' and hence immorality, some encouraging cohabiting couples to separate or at least refrain from sex until they marry or disciplining sexually active unmarried church members.

Although no evangelical authors have developed a positive alternative interpretation of cohabitation, a number have signalled a more accommodating and nuanced stance, often highlighting the difference between marriage and a wedding. Lewis Smedes noted that 'it is perverse to identify real marriage with weddings. A marriage without a wedding is not per se an immoral arrangement'. Nevertheless, he concluded that 'a cogent case can be made that getting married is more responsible than living together without bothering with the institution' (Smedes 1979: 138). Grenz, discussing 'pre-ceremonial sex', notes that 'a biblical case could be made for greater laxity in sexual matters among engaged couples. The Old Testament, for example, stipulated that unmarried persons who engaged in sexual relations ought simply to be married, whereas persons who committed adultery were to be stoned. On that basis it could be argued that preceremonial sexual relations are not sinful' (Grenz [1990] 1997: 213). He still concludes, however, that 'the sex act is best reserved for marriage. Couples ... demonstrate great wisdom when they refuse to allow the pressures of the present to move them from a commitment to abstinence prior to marriage' ([1990] 1997: 214). At a more popular level, Rob Bell has recently drawn attention to the close connection biblically between sex and marriage and written, 'sometimes when a couple is living together, one of their friends tells them they should make things right in God's eyes by making their relationship a legal marriage. But maybe it's already a marriage in God's eyes' (Bell 2007: 137).

It is clear that evangelicals upholding the traditional view face major challenges in pastoral care and mission. Their biblical vision of marriage and sex within marriage is now alien to most people outside the Church. Many, particularly younger, evangelicals therefore experience growing cultural dissonance and face a stark choice: support a minority counter-cultural witness and reappropriate the evangelical tradition of mission as cultural conversion or rethink teaching to become more positive and accommodating of these cultural changes while still being faithful to Scripture. Similar choices arise in the final area of same-sex relationships.

SAME-SEX RELATIONSHIPS

The evangelical position in relation to homosexuality is also the historic teaching of the Church, arising in part as a logical consequence of the sexual ethic discussed earlier. As summed up in one of the most significant evangelical statements on the subject, the 1995 *St Andrew's Day Statement*, issued by the Church of England Evangelical Council: the Church, in bearing good news,

> assists all its members to a life of faithful witness in chastity and holiness, recognising two forms or vocations in which that life can be lived: marriage and singleness (Gen. 2. 24; Matt. 19. 4–6; 1 Cor. 7 passim). There is no place for the church to confer legitimacy upon alternatives to these.
>
>   (*Statement* and responses to it in Bradshaw 1997 [rev. edn. 2003])

Alongside the emphasis on sex being for marriage between a man and a woman, evangelicals also emphasize the complementarity and fundamental created otherness of male and female, a theme still important even amongst those who are 'egalitarians' in relation to church leadership.

The evangelical view is also based on specific biblical texts which refer to sexual conduct between people of the same sex. Although small in number, these are found in both Old (Gen. 19; Lev. 18:22 and 20:13) and New (1 Cor. 6:9–10; 1 Tim. 1:9–10; Rom. 1:26–27) Testaments. Crucially, they are (in contrast to texts relating to some of the issues discussed earlier) of one voice: consistently, often strongly, negative. They have been understood by both Jews and Christians down the centuries as expressing divine disapproval of all homosexual behaviour and a strong scholarly case can still be made for this reading (Gagnon 2001 is the most detailed study, more briefly on each text see Bird and Preece 2012). This issue of uniform biblical teaching, authoritative for evangelicals, explains why most evangelicals strongly maintain a traditional stance, sharing the assessment but not the ultimate conclusion of Professor Diarmaid MacCulloch: 'This is an issue of biblical authority. Despite much well-intentioned theological fancy footwork to the contrary, it is difficult to see the Bible as expressing anything else but disapproval of homosexual activity, let alone having any conception of a homosexual identity' (MacCulloch 2004: 705).

The main evangelical response to gay and lesbian people has, in recent years, been summed up in the title of one of the most influential evangelical studies: 'welcoming, but not affirming' (Grenz 1998). This acknowledges and repents of the hostile, rejecting attitude which evangelicals have often shown in the past to those with homosexual attraction and seeks to welcome them in evangelical churches, but it refuses to affirm same-sex sexual relationships or, in many cases, a gay identity. In the United Kingdom, the Evangelical Alliance report *Faith, Hope and Homosexuality* (Evangelical Alliance 1998) articulated this vision, recently reiterated in ten affirmations alongside more detailed pastoral reflections to evangelical church leaders on its outworking (Goddard and Horrocks 2012). Socially, evangelicals have also taken a non-affirming stance, often being prominent in opposition to gay rights, greater legal recognition for gay and lesbian couples, reduction of the age of consent, and, most recently, same-sex marriage.

A central element in contemporary evangelical approaches is the distinction between orientation (although some evangelicals prefer to avoid this term, with its potential implications for ontology and identity, and speak simply of 'same-sex attraction'—the best evangelical discussion of sexual identity is Paris 2011) and practice. Although some evangelicals remain unwelcoming and rejecting of people simply because of their orientation, most now focus on behaviour, stressing the need to refrain from same-sex sexual activity and for the Church to offer guidance and support in this discipline. New Testament scholar Wesley Hill offers a powerful theological reflection on this calling from his own experience (2010) and evangelical psychologist Mark Yarhouse has addressed a range of questions often raised by family members and church leaders (2011). Various groups, such as True Freedom Trust (TfT) in the UK, support those seeking to live according to traditional teaching.

Some, particularly from charismatic and Pentecostal evangelicalism, have offered ministries of healing in various forms including prayer, counselling, and more formal reparative therapy. This has led to people identifying as 'ex-gays' who testify to some level of change in their sexual attractions or orientation (Bergner 1995). There has been much criticism of these groups, some warranted, and some have abandoned the approach (most dramatically, in summer 2013, the closing of the main global network Exodus by Alan Chambers). Some have become more affirming of gay partnerships while remaining broadly evangelical (Marks 2008 recounts the best-known British example of Courage). An important study of 'ex-gay' ministries by two evangelical scholars has, however, rejected the common hypotheses of their opponents that 'change of sexual orientation is impossible' and 'the attempt to change is harmful' (Jones and Yarhouse 2007: 365; see also Goddard and Harrison 2011).

The evangelical consensus opposed to same-sex relationships has not gone unchallenged. One of the earliest more sympathetic Christian discussions was by evangelical theologian Helmut Thielicke who warned that an evangelical approach to Scripture required not merely citing texts but 'interpreting the quotations in accord with the kerygmatic purpose' (Thielicke 1964: 277). Although insisting that theologically 'homosexuality is in every case *not* in accord with the order of creation' (1964: 282) and so 'questionable', Thielicke sought to articulate a view of ethically responsible living. In this 'the homosexual has to realise his optimal ethical potentialities *on the basis* of his irreversible situation', and so 'one must seriously ask whether in this situation ... the same norms must not apply as in the normal relationship of the sexes' when considering 'how the homosexual in his actual situation can achieve the optimal ethical potential of sexual self-realisation' (1964: 285, emphasis original). In relation to homosexual acts, he wrote of 'that freedom which is given to us by the insight that even the New Testament does not provide us with an evident, normative dictum with regard to this question' (1964: 284). A similar stance was taken by American evangelical Lewis Smedes who, discussing homosexuality as a form of distorted sexuality, argued for the need 'to recognise that the optimum moral life within a deplorable situation is preferable to a life of sexual chaos' (Smedes 1979: 68).

More recently, some evangelicals have become even more affirming. Rereading the texts traditionally cited as condemning all homosexual behaviour they have understood them to be much narrower in scope, concluding with Presbyterian evangelical Jack Rogers that 'none of them, properly interpreted, refers to contemporary Christian people who are homosexual' (Rogers 2006: 89; see also Vasey 1995 and, most thoroughly, Brownson 2013). Exhibiting traditional evangelical activism, those reaching such conclusions have formed groups to advocate their new understanding (Evangelicals Concerned led by Ralph Blair in the USA and Accepting Evangelicals led by Benny Hazelhurst in the UK). Justin Lee, founder of the Gay Christian Network, has recently defended such a viewpoint in the context of telling his personal journey as a young gay evangelical (Lee 2012) and, in response to debates about gay marriage, a number of often already controversial evangelical leaders such as Rob Bell, Brian McLaren, and Steve Chalke have begun publicly challenging the dominant traditional viewpoint.

Evangelical concerns for mission and evangelism have also led to questioning of traditional understandings and approaches as unnecessarily alienating gay and lesbian people from the gospel at the heart of evangelicalism. Some, such as Tom Hanks's Other

Sheep ministry, have combined a traditional evangelistic message with a fully affirming stance to sexual minorities. Andrew Marin, without embracing a fully affirmative stance, has gained a high and influential profile for his commitment to building understanding and relationships between Christians and the lesbian, gay, bisexual, and transgendered (LGBT) community (Marin 2009).

As this issue is dividing various mainstream Protestant denominations, evangelicals remain overwhelmingly traditionalist, with those who are conservative on the roles of men and women being particularly committed, due to their biblical understanding of differences between men and women. There is however a recognition by some evangelicals that there needs to be a fresh engagement with the issue (O'Donovan 2009) and some have been rethinking their stance. It is possible that evangelicalism will to some extent fracture or follow earlier trajectories and divide into polarized camps (as over gender and the role of women) or settle down into more peacefully tolerating a certain diversity of approaches (as over divorce and remarriage). The issue, however, differs from all those discussed previously in that there is nothing positive within Scripture about same-sex sexual relationship and a number of clearly negative texts. There is also a wider biblically-based framework for thinking about sex and marriage which would need revision for evangelicals to become not just more accommodating but genuinely affirmative. The signs therefore are that this issue—unlike others—is seen by many as a case of *Scriptura sacra locuta, res decisa est* (Sacred Scripture has spoken, the matter is decided), and that most evangelicals would agree with Wolfhart Pannenberg that

> Here lies the boundary of a Christian church that knows itself to be bound by the authority of Scripture. Those who urge the church to change the norm of its teaching on this matter must know that they are promoting schism. If a church were to let itself be pushed to the point where it ceased to treat homosexual activity as a departure from the biblical norm, and recognized homosexual unions as a personal partnership of love equivalent to marriage, such a church would stand no longer on biblical ground but against the unequivocal witness of Scripture. A church that took this step would cease to be the one, holy, catholic, and apostolic church.
>
> (Pannenberg 1996)

Conclusion

Despite their reputation for conservatism and, even more unfairly, for unthinking conservatism, evangelical contributions to these five different debates relating to sexuality and gender demonstrate there is extensive serious evangelical thinking with its own conflicts and different paths. From the 1960s to the end of the century, evangelicals were quickly and almost universally accepting of contraception, then increasingly accommodating to a range of acceptable evangelical views over divorce and remarriage. The move to a more egalitarian view of gender has been much more contentious with a strong 'headship' tradition leading to polarization and division but most now viewing this as a 'second-order' issue where evangelicals can disagree. On premarital and homosexual sexual behaviour evangelicals do remain more conservative, more consistently upholding the Christian tradition, but with varying degrees of pastoral accommodation to those disregarding its norms and signs of a possibly growing minority more positive about same-sex relationships. Across this diversity, a key question is whether a significant number of evangelicals can recognize a particular view (even if they do not share it) as seeking to be faithful to Scripture. This is therefore the main challenge facing those evangelicals seeking to change attitudes to any sex outside heterosexual marriage.

If evangelicals continue to view all sex outside heterosexual marriage as falling short of God's purposes (see Rom. 3:23) and sinful, thus requiring repentance, they face a number of challenges which can be related to each of Bebbington's four characteristics. In relation to *biblicism*, which has proved so central, evangelicals must move beyond interpretation of specific texts to view all five of these issues (and others not discussed here) holistically, relating them to each other within a deeper biblical and theological vision of sexuality and gender. The seemingly irreversible change in the understanding and practice of Western societies will then also require evangelical *activism* to be more theologically thoughtful and expressing a commitment not just to individual conversion and transformation but cultural *conversion* through offering an alternative vision, in word and deed, of human flourishing in relation to sexuality. This, in turn, may lead to evangelicals rediscovering a *cruci-centrism* which is not simply doctrinal but practical, as witnessing to traditional Christian teaching on sexuality is increasingly counter-cultural and requires a cruciform way of life for individuals and the evangelical church as a whole.

REFERENCES

Ash, C. (2003) *Marriage: Sex in the Service of God.* Leicester: Inter-Varsity Press.

Ash, C. (2007). *Married for God: Making your Marriage the Best It Can Be.* Nottingham: Inter-Varsity.

Atkinson, D. J. (1979). *To Have and To Hold: The Marriage Covenant and the Discipline of Divorce.* London: Collins.

Bebbington, D. W. (1989). *Evangelicalism in Modern Britain: A History from the 1730s to the 1980s.* London: Unwin Hyman.

Bebbington, D. W. (2009). 'Evangelical Trends 1959–2009'. *Anvil*, 26: 93–106.

Bell, R. (2007). *Sex God: Exploring the Endless Connections between Sexuality and Spirituality.* Grand Rapids, MI: Zondervan.

Bergner, M. (1995). *Setting Love in Order: Hope and Healing for the Homosexual.* Grand Rapids, MI: Baker Books.

Bird, M., and G. Preece (2012) (eds). *Sexegesis: An Evangelical Response to Five Uneasy Pieces on Homosexuality.* Sydney: Anglican Press Australia.

Bradshaw, T. (1997 [rev. edn. 2003]). *The Way Forward? Christian Voices on Homosexuality and the Church*. London: Hodder & Stoughton.

Brandon, G. (2009). *Just Sex: Is It Ever Just Sex?* Nottingham: Inter-Varsity Press.

Brownson, J. V. (2013). *Bible, Gender, Sexuality: Reframing the Church's Debate on Same-Sex Relationships*. Grand Rapids, MI: W. B. Eerdmans.

Cochran, P. (2005). *Evangelical Feminism: A History*. New York and London: New York University Press.

Cornes, A. (1998). *Questions about Divorce and Remarriage*. London: Monarch.

Cornes, A. ([1993] 2002). *Divorce and Remarriage: Biblical Principle and Pastoral Practice*. Fearn: Mentor.

Creegan, N. H., and C. Pohl (2005). *Living on the Boundaries: Evangelical Women, Feminism, and the Theological Academy*. Downers Grove, IL: InterVarsity Press.

Danylak, B. (2010). *Redeeming Singleness: How the Storyline of Scripture Affirms the Single Life*. Wheaton, IL: Crossway.

Driscoll, M., and G. Driscoll (2012). *Real Marriage: The Truth about Sex, Friendship & Life Together*. Nashville: Thomas Nelson.

Evangelical Alliance (1998). *Faith, Hope & Homosexuality: A Report*. London: ACUTE.

Gagnon, R. A. J. (2001). *The Bible and Homosexual Practice: Texts And Hermeneutics*. Nashville: Abingdon.

Giles, K. (2002). *The Trinity & Subordinationism: The Doctrine of God and the Contemporary Gender Debate*. Downers Grove, IL: InterVarsity Press.

Goddard, A., and G. Harrison (2011). *Unwanted Same-Sex Attraction: Issues of Pastoral and Counselling Support*. London: Christian Medical Fellowship.

Goddard, A., and D. Horrocks (2012) (eds). *Resources for Church Leaders: Biblical and Pastoral Responses to Homosexuality*. London: Evangelical Alliance.

Goddard, L., and C. Hendry (2010). *The Gender Agenda: Discovering God's Plan for Church Leadership*. Nottingham: Inter-Varsity Press.

Grenz, S. J. ([1990] 1997). *Sexual Ethics: A Biblical Perspective*. Louisville, KY: Westminster John Knox Press.

Grenz, S. J. (1998). *Welcoming But Not Affirming: An Evangelical Response to Homosexuality*. Louisville, KY: Westminster John Knox Press.

Grudem, W. (2005). *Evangelical Feminism & Biblical Truth: An Analysis of 118 Disputed Questions*. Leicester: Inter-Varsity Press.

Heth, W. A., and G. J. Wenham (1984 [rev. edn. 2002]). *Jesus and Divorce: Towards an Evangelical Understanding of New Testament Teaching*. London: Hodder and Stoughton.

Hill, W. (2010). *Washed and Waiting: Reflections on Christian Faithfulness and Homosexuality*. Grand Rapids, MI: Zondervan.

Hodge, B. C. (2009). *The Christian Case Against Contraception: Making the Case from Historical, Biblical, Systematic, and Practical Theology & Ethics*. Eugene, OR: Wipf & Stock.

House, H. W. (1990) (ed.). *Divorce and Remarriage: Four Christian Views*. Downers Grove, IL: InterVarsity Press.

Instone-Brewer, D. (2002). *Divorce and Remarriage in the Bible*. Grand Rapids, MI: Eerdmans.

James, S. (2011). 'Evangelical Response to the Reconfiguration of Family in England 1960–2010'. Unpublished PhD, London, Spurgeon's College.

Jewett, P. K. (1975). *Man as Male and Female: A Study in Sexual Relationships from a Theological Point of View*. Grand Rapids, MI: Eerdmans.

Johnson, A. F. (2010) (ed.). *How I Changed My Mind About Women in Leadership: Compelling Stories from Prominent Evangelicals*. Grand Rapids, MI: Zondervan.

Jones, S. L., and M. A. Yarhouse (2007) *Ex-Gays? A Longitudinal Study of Religiously Mediated Change in Sexual Orientation.* Downers Grove, IL: IVP Academic.

Kuehne, D. S. (2009). *Sex and the iWorld: Rethinking Relationship beyond an Age of Individualism.* Grand Rapids, MI: Baker Academic.

Larsen, T., and D. J. Treier (2007). *The Cambridge Companion to Evangelical Theology.* Cambridge: Cambridge University Press.

Lee, J. (2012). *Torn: Rescuing the Gospel from the Gays-vs.-Christians Debate.* New York: Jericho Books.

Lewis, C. S. (1955). *Mere Christianity.* Glasgow: Fontana.

MacCulloch, D. (2004). *Reformation: Europe's House Divided, 1490–1700.* London: Penguin.

Marin, A. P. (2009). *Love is an Orientation: Elevating the Conversation with the Gay Community.* Downers Grove, IL: IVP Books.

Marks, J. (2008). *Exchanging the Truth of God for a Lie: One Man's Spiritual Journey to Find the Truth About Homosexuality and Same-Sex Partnerships.* Walton-on-Thames: Courage UK.

Meilaender, G., and P. Turner (1998). 'Contraception: A Symposium'. *First Things*, 88: 22–23.

Mohler, A. (1998). 'Contraception: A Symposium'. *First Things*, 88: 24.

O'Donovan, O. (1984). *Begotten or Made?* Oxford: Clarendon Press.

O'Donovan, O. (2009). *A Conversation Waiting to Begin: the Churches and the Gay Controversy.* London: SCM Press.

Pannenberg, W. (1996). 'Revelation and Homosexual Experience'. Trans. M. Bockmuehl. *Christianity Today*, 11 November: 35, 37.

Paris, J. W. (2011). *The End of Sexual Identity: Why Sex Is Too Important to Define Who We Are.* Downers Grove, IL: IVP Books.

Pierce, R. W., and R. M. Groothuis (2005) (eds). *Discovering Biblical Equality: Complementarity without Hierarchy.* Leicester: InterVarsity Press.

Piper, J., and W. Grudem (1991). *Recovering Biblical Manhood and Womanhood.* Wheaton, IL: Crossway.

Poulson, A. L. (2006). 'An Examination of the Ethics of Contraception with Reference to Recent Protestant and Roman Catholic Thought'. Unpublished PhD, King's College London.

Rogers, J. B. (2006). *Jesus, the Bible, and Homosexuality: Explode the Myths, Heal the Church.* Louisville, KY: Westminster John Knox.

Scanzoni, L. (1984). *Sexuality.* Philadelphia: Westminster Press.

Scanzoni, L., and N. Hardesty (1974). *All We're Meant To Be: A Biblical Approach to Women's Liberation.* Waco, TX: Word Books.

Smedes, L. (1979). *Sex in the Real World.* Tring: Lion.

Smith, M. (2010). 'Religion, Divorce and the Missing Culture War in America'. *Political Science Quarterly*, 125: 57–85.

Southern Baptist Convention (2010). 'The Scandal of Southern Baptist Divorce' (a resolution). <http://www.sbc.net/resolutions/amResolution.asp?ID=1205>.

Spitzer, W. O., and C. L. Saylor (1969). *Birth Control and the Christian.* Wheaton, IL: Tyndale House.

Storkey, E. (1985) *What's Right with Feminism.* London: SPCK.

Thielicke, H. (1964). *The Ethics of Sex.* London: James Clarke.

Torode, S., and B. Torode (2002). *Open Embrace: A Protestant Couple Rethinks Contraception.* Grand Rapids, MI: Eerdmans.

Vasey, M. (1995). *Strangers and Friends: A New Exploration of Homosexuality and the Bible.* London: Hodder & Stoughton.

Wenham, G. J., W. A. Heth, and C. S. Keener (2006) (eds). *Remarriage after Divorce in Today's Church:* vol. 3. *Views.* Grand Rapids, MI: Zondervan.

Wheat, E. (1977). *Intended for Pleasure: Sex Technique and Sexual Fulfilment in Christian Marriage.* London: Scripture Union.

Winner, L. F. (2005). *Real Sex: The Naked Truth about Chastity.* Grand Rapids, MI: Brazos Press.

Yarhouse, M. A. (2010). *Homosexuality and the Christian: A Guide for Parents, Pastors, and Friends.* Grand Rapids, MI: Baker.

CHAPTER 24

....

CONFLICTS WITHIN THE
BLACK CHURCHES

....

ANGELIQUE HARRIS

INTRODUCTION

....

THIS essay examines conflicts concerning sex, sexuality, and gender within Black churches. Black churches are Protestant churches in America with a predominantly Black leadership and congregation. Black churches are based on Protestant Christian beliefs and are often rooted in the history of slavery and colonialism that Blacks from across the African diaspora have historically endured. Serving their often poor and underprivileged congregants and community members, these Black churches have a history of fighting for equality, against racial/ethnic discrimination, and for the rights of the oppressed. Within recent years, however, further controversies have arisen within these religious institutions. These controversies include gender equality, HIV/AIDS and safer sex education, and, perhaps the most controversial, the increased societal acceptance of homosexuality and same-sex marriage. This essay explores how Black churches have responded to these issues and how HIV/AIDS has influenced these responses. Additionally, it will provide examples of the role of women and sexual minorities in Black church denominations and congregations.

THE BLACK CHURCH DEFINED

....

Although 'Black churches' exist throughout the world, the 'Black Church', as an institution, is uniquely American. Black churches are made up of different Protestant religious centres and houses of worship that are often grouped together into denominations that primarily consist of, and are led by, Black Americans (Lincoln and Mamiya 2003; A. Harris 2010). These Black churches make up the institution of the Black Church, which is the most influential social and cultural institution within Black American communities (Lincoln and Mamiya 2003).

Black churches are typically characterized by their jubilant services that often encourage worship through music, song, and dance (Lincoln and Mamiya 2003). Black churches are also known for promoting liberation theology—an interpretation of Christian beliefs that emphasizes freedom and acceptance (Cone 1996). Theologian James Cone explains, 'Black theology is a theology of liberation because it is a theology which arises from an identification with the oppressed Blacks of America, seeking to interpret the gospel of Jesus in light of the Black condition. It believes that the liberation of the Black community is God's liberation' (Cone 1996: 11). Liberation theology is a social movement that uses aspects of Christian doctrine to address social problems and injustices. Often, the concern for justice and freedom is infused in worship services, songs, and sermons. To illustrate this, religious scholars C. Eric Lincoln and Lawrence H. Mamiya (2003: 4) quote a famous Black spiritual:

> Before I'll be a slave
> I'll be buried in my grave
> And go home to my Father
> And be free...

The vast majority of Black Christian Americans are members of the original seven Black church denominations that have their origins in the struggles most Blacks endured as a result of slavery and emancipation. These denominations are the African Methodist Episcopal Church; the Christian Methodist Episcopal Church; the African Methodist Episcopal Zion Church; the National Baptist Convention, USA, Incorporated; the National Baptist Convention of America, Unincorporated; the Progressive National Baptist Convention; and the Church of God in Christ (Lincoln and Mamiya 2003). Additional Black churches include African Union First Colored Methodist Protestant Church; Fire Baptized Holiness Church of God of the Americas; Mount Sinai Holy Church of America; Spiritual Israel Church and Its Army; and the United Pentecostal Council of the Assemblies of God, Inc. Religious scholars Lincoln and Mamiya explain, 'Today, the seven major Black denominations with a scattering of smaller communions make up the body of the Black Church and it is estimated that more than 80 per cent of all Black Christians are in these seven denominations, with smaller communions accounting for an additional 6 per cent' (Lincoln and Mamiya 2003: 1). Although new Christian denominations with Black leadership continue to emerge, they often are modelled on the traditions of the seven original Black church denominations.

Highlighted in the early writings of sociologists W. E. B. DuBois (1903) and later, E. Franklin Frazier (1969), scholars have noted the significant role of the Black Church in the lives of Black Americans. Black churches served as both a safe haven and second family for Black Americans, helping to shield them from some of the trails and hardships of slavery, Emancipation, Reconstruction, and then the Great Migration from southern to northern states (Wimberly 1979). During slavery in the Americas, slave masters often used religion to encourage docility and obedience among the already extremely spiritual enslaved African population. Instead, Christian beliefs were reappropriated and then used as a form of resistance by emphasizing aspects of Christianity that focused on liberation and spiritual salvation (Genovese 1972). Consequently, a culture developed among Black Americans whereby religion and spirituality were used as the impetus for the fight for social justice and equality. This was further exacerbated by the fact that many Blacks, both freed and enslaved, were denied entry into public spaces and were prevented from congregating without the 'supervision' of Whites. The only exception to this was during worship services. Therefore, many plans for freedom and the abolition of slavery took place in early Black churches.

After slavery, Black churches continued to provide for the social and economic needs of Black Americans and served as the primary location for community action (Pattillo-McCoy 1998). As Blacks were still often barred from civic institutions and public spaces, the Black Church went on to serve as 'a school, a bank, a benevolent society, a political organization, a party hall, and a spiritual base' (Pattillo-McCoy 1998: 769) for many Blacks. Black churches provided an early home for political and social activists during the civil rights movement of the 1950s and early 1960s, where many Black community leaders actively fought against discrimination and Jim Crow era segregation. The history books are filled with stories of how charismatic civil rights leaders such as Martin Luther King, Jr., Joseph Lowery, Jesse Jackson, and Wyatt T. Walker used the oratory and organizing skills they learned as leaders within Black churches to organize Black community members and congregants in the struggle for civil rights.

Today, Black churches are an important space for providing and even encouraging racial and cultural pride and solidarity among Black Americans. Many churches often host neighbourhood block parties as well as social and cultural community events. Furthermore, Black churches are known for providing emotional and social support for their congregants and communities by providing soup kitchens, food pantries, health ministries, counselling, and other forms of community outreach (Ellison and Sherkat 1995).

The centrality of the Black Church in the lives of Blacks in Americans varies by gender, age, sexual orientation, marital status, education, and geography. Among Blacks in the rural South, for example, researchers Christopher G. Ellison and Darren E. Sherkat (1995) claim that the Black Church serves as a 'semi-involuntary institution' where southern Blacks are *expected* to join a church. Similarly, because of the Black Church's role during slavery, the effect of Jim Crow's segregation and discrimination, and the prohibition on secular gatherings in public and private spaces for Blacks, the Black Church took on a significant role in the lives of many Blacks, particularly in the South. Conversely, in major metropolitan areas, primarily in the northern states where Blacks had increased freedom, Blacks had much more of a 'voluntary' involvement with the church (Ellison and Sherkat 1995: 1416). 'The availability of (1) a wider range of secular lifestyles and (2) secular sources of benefits usually provided by the church in rural southern communities may make urban religious institutions less central' (Ellison and Sherkat 1995: 1416).

Irrespective of geographic location, however, Black Americans are highly religious. A National Survey of Black Americans (Billingsley and Caldwell 1991: 428) found that

- 84 per cent of African American adults considered themselves to be religious
- 80 per cent considered it very important to send their children to church
- 78 per cent indicated that they pray often
- 76 per cent said that the church was a very important institution in their early childhood socialization
- 77 per cent reported that the church was still very important
- 71 per cent attended church at least once a month
- nearly 70 per cent were members of a church.

In fact, Black women are the most religious racial/ethnic group in the United States. A 2013 study conducted by the *Washington Post* and Kaiser Family Foundation found the following:

- 74 per cent of Black women and 70 per cent of Black men believe 'that living a religious life' is 'very important' as compared to 57 per cent of White women and 43 per cent of White men.
- 87 per cent of Black women and 79 per cent of Black men believe that 'religion or faith in God' plays a very important role 'in helping [respondents] get through tough times' as compared to 66 per cent of White women and 51 per cent of White men (*Washington Post* 2013).

Interestingly, this survey also found that Black women had the highest rates of life satisfaction with 51 per cent reported being very satisfied with their lives, compared to 46 per cent among Black men, 50 per cent among White women, and 48 per cent among White men. These findings are not surprising as research has often noted the major influence that religion and spirituality have in providing a more positive outlook and overall physical well-being (Wilson 2000). For instance, one study indicates that Black Americans who attend church regularly, as defined by two to three times a month, are healthier than Blacks who do not attend church regularly (Wilson 2000). The mediation and optimism offered through prayer and the social support provided by worshipping in a communion with others and also by participating in social and community activism elevates the role of religion and of the Black Church in the lives of many Black Americans and communities. As such, many Black churches have routinely provided their parishioners and communities with everything from food pantries, to parish nurses who check vital signs for high blood pressure, to community health fairs. Black church pastors, religious leaders, and congregants are often even expected to visit sick and bedridden church and community members. This responsibility of caring for community members and for the sick was greatly challenged during the early years of the HIV/AIDS epidemic in Black American communities. In particular, the challenge for Black churches centred around providing care, support, and HIV education while also adhering to their traditional beliefs and concerns. Most of this tension centred on the Black Church's perception of sexuality.

HISTORY AND SEXUALITY

Like most other religious institutions, the Black Church, overall, tends to take a particularly conservative stance towards issues of sex and sexuality. Black churches often promoted abstinence from sex until marriage. This belief was not only fuelled by scripture but also by the desire of the church and the middle class, primarily women, to discourage any form of sexual expression or accusations of depravity. These church folk believed that one way to increase positive perceptions of Black Americans among Whites was to promote a culture of respectability among Blacks—working class and poor Blacks in particular (Higginbotham 1993). With the exception of promoting abstinence until marriage, Black church leaders often silenced discussions of sex and sexuality in the church, with this silence reverberating into larger Black communities. Kelly Brown Douglas (2003) argues that disapproval of liberal sexual expression by Black church leaders, in large part, originated with the dehumanization of Blacks during slavery in the Americas.

Although the Black Church is not exceptional in its avoidance of explicit discussions of sex and sexuality, the reasons for such avoidance are unique. During slavery Blacks were depicted as little more than hypersexual beasts without intellect, morals, or decency who were worthy of ownership, thus justifying their enslavement to Whites (West 2001; Douglas 2003). Whites strengthened their power over Blacks by degrading both Black sexuality and the Black body (Douglas 2003; Collins 2004). To distance themselves from this negative portrayal of Black sexuality, the Black Church and Black communities took a very conservative stance towards all perceived forms of sexual deviance—such as premarital sex, out-of-wedlock births, extramarital affairs, and homosexuality (Douglas 2003). In the early twentieth century, Black reformers claimed that sexual depravity caused societal ills, such as poverty and illness (Gaines 1996). The Black Church worked to 'clean up' 'the image of Black sexuality in Black communities' (Cohen 1999: 72), by policing the Black body. In fact, a number of Black churches denounced all forms of perceived deviant behaviour, such as illicit drug use, alcohol consumption, and even dancing (Higginbotham 1993). These community leaders believed that '[r]espectability was part of a larger interracial pedagogy on earning civil rights and gaining self-respect through proper conduct' (Mitchell 2004: 85).

Therefore, this silencing of sexuality has allowed for Black communities to avoid explicit discussions of sex and sexuality. It has harboured a culture of sexual conservatism that created what Cathy Cohen (1999) referred to as a 'boundary of Blackness', whereby those groups who were perceived as being sexually deviant—such as prostitutes and homosexuals—were openly shunned within not only Black churches but also Black communities. This has had a particularly major impact on the creation of homophobia and heterosexism in Black churches and communities.

HOMOSEXUALITY

Within many Black communities homosexuality is seen as a sexual perversion that is rooted in White society (Somerville 2000; McBride 2005; Griffin 2006). At the core of this heterosexism and homophobia is the belief among many Blacks that homosexuality did not exist in Africa prior to European contact. Many scholars have implied that homosexuality was a Western European and Arab import that colonized Africans either adopted or were forced to adopt (Johnson 2001). A number of early twentieth-century White scholars assumed that, being 'closer to nature', Blacks only practised purely heterosexual acts, mainly for the purposes of procreation, and did not practise homosexuality, which they believed was something invented by more advanced societies (Murray and Roscoe 1998). Conversely, the belief arose among some Blacks that homosexuality does not exist in African societies because African societies are more civilized and moral, and as such, too advanced for homosexual sex (Ajen 1998; Murray and Roscoe 1998).

There are countless instances of same-sex behaviour and the bending of traditional gender roles and norms in Africa. For instance, male transvestites were referred to as *makhanith* or *mahanisi* in Zanzibar and *mashoga* in Mombasa, and *magai* is the Swahili word for homosexual women and men (Amory 1998: 68). Nonetheless, each culture understood and responded to these behaviours differently and ascribed different meanings and values to them. Some cultures found them to be acceptable while others found them to be deviant (Murray and Roscoe 1998).

In his account of the history of homosexuality, David Greenberg (1990) notes that the construct of homosexuality began with the association of sex and sin. As women were not thought of as having a sexuality independent of men, female same-sex attractions have been notoriously under-examined within historical writings and accounts. Consequently, the bulk of Greenberg's work focuses on male homosexual sex and he argues that it was frowned upon as being a 'wasteful loss of semen...no different from throwing away money' (Greenberg 1990: 362). Believing in a limited supply of semen, religious leaders considered it a sin to 'spill' semen during same-sex behaviours and masturbation. Birth control was also a sin. Religious doctrine encouraged that 'intercourse between spouses should not take place too frequently' (1990: 362), and when it did occur, it should only take place for the explicit purposes of procreation. Religious leaders attempted to regulate society through their control of sex, sexuality, and procreation (Foucault 1990). Michel Foucault maintained that religious leaders believed deviant forms of sexual expression should be 'driven out, denied, and reduced to silence' (1990: 4).

Historically, in the United States, homosexuality was criminalized, perceived as a sickness, and eventually became an identity (Conrad and Schneider 1992), but among a majority of Black Americans, homosexuality became a deviant identity (Constantine-Simms 2001). Although Black church leaders routinely ignored homosexuality, there were instances whereby these leaders preached against homosexual behaviour. For example, beginning in the late 1920s Adam Clayton Powell Sr., then pastor of Harlem's influential Abyssinian Baptist Church, and father of Congressman Adam Clayton Powell Jr., began his well-known campaign against homosexuality by actively preaching against it and the influence he felt it was having on Black churches and communities (A. Harris 2010). Much of Powell's contention surrounding homosexuality and other forms of alleged depravity stems from what he witnessed during the Harlem Renaissance, a social and cultural movement that took place during the 1920s that was heavily influenced by the works of lesbian, gay, and bisexual artists, such as Gladys Bentley, Zora Neale Hurston, and Langston Hughes.

Pastors such as Powell often turned to passages found in the King James Version of the Bible to promote heterosexism as well as an acceptance of an open hostility towards homosexuals. As with mainstream, Western reactions to Black sexuality, where Black sexuality is treated with fascination and repulsion (West 2001), homosexuality within Black churches has received similar treatment. Many Black church leaders and congregants consider the phrase 'love the sinner, hate the sin' in their 'perceived acceptance' of homosexuality within congregations. For although they may accept 'out' lesbian and gay individuals, they may not accept the behaviour (A. Harris 2010). As premarital sex is generally frowned upon within these churches, this helps to provide justification for accepting homosexual individuals but not the behaviour (A. Harris 2010). Consequently, although today homosexuality is generally prohibited in Black churches, homosexual men in particular are, according to Fullilove and Fullilove, 'accorded a special status in many churches... [as] gay men provide creative energy necessary for the transcendent religious experience' (1997: 2). They write, 'gays in the church are responsible for creating the music and other emotional moments that bring worshippers closer to God' (1997: 2). However, they argue that these lesbian and gay church members often have to remain closeted.

Research on homosexuality in Black communities is increasingly focusing on the influential role that Black churches have in shaping the values and opinions of Black Americans towards homosexuality and other forms of sexual expression and of the impact this has on the lives of Black lesbians and gays (West 1997; Johnson 2001; A. C. Harris 2009). In the end, researchers agree that homosexuality and same-sex attractions are frowned upon among Blacks because gay men are perceived to have freely given up their male privilege—often the only privilege that Black men have (Riggs 2001)—and lesbians to have given up their femininity by not procreating with Black men (hooks 2001). Research on the Black Church and sexuality increased substantially in the early 1990s, due, in large part, to the impact of the AIDS epidemic on Black communities in the United States and abroad.

AIDS AND THE BLACK CHURCH

Prior to the AIDS epidemic, Black churches and communities avoided open and frank discussions of sex, sexuality, and homosexuality. However, AIDS made it clear that acknowledging homosexuality was a matter of life and death for Blacks. Worldwide, HIV/AIDS has had a disproportionate effect on Blacks, with the greatest impact being in sub-Saharan Africa where, in countries such as Swaziland and Botswana, one out of four adults is infected with HIV (Trinitapoli and Weinreb 2012). In the United States, Black women and men make up almost half of all those with HIV/AIDS (CDC 2013). Additionally, Blacks are also significantly more likely to die from the opportunistic infections and ailments that arise as a result of AIDS (CDC 2013).

The intricacies of HIV and modes of transmission vary around the world (Trinitapoli and Weinreb 2012). For example, in sub-Saharan Africa, HIV/AIDS is a disease primarily found among heterosexuals; in the United States, although HIV is found among all populations, it is heavily concentrated among men who have sex with men—some of these men are homosexual, while others are bisexual and some identify as heterosexual (Ford et al. 2007). Most research on AIDS in Black American communities maintains that homophobia within Black communities, and especially within the Black Church, has had great implications for the perceived susceptibility of HIV infection among Blacks, particularly during the early years of the epidemic (Dalton 1989; Fullilove and Fullilove 1997; Cohen 1999; A. Harris 2010).

In the early 1980s, as AIDS killed thousands in the United States and abroad, attention was placed on the four groups identified by researchers who were associated with HIV transmission—gay men, haemophiliacs, Haitians, and intravenous drug users (Shilts 1987). As AIDS in the United States was first identified among otherwise healthy gay men, gay and bisexual men were stereotyped as being the vectors of HIV, transmitting it to heterosexuals (Shilts 1987). The little information known about it concerned its almost certain mortality rates and its association with stigmatized populations. This ambiguous threat led to the further stigmatization of infected individuals. Medical personnel refused to treat those believed to be infected; HIV-positive students were turned away from schools; funeral homes even refused to bury those who died from AIDS (Cohen 1999). Although Blacks always had the highest rates of HIV/AIDS in the United States, within Black American communities AIDS was seen as a White gay disease (Cohen 1999). Consequently, believing they could not be infected, many Blacks ignored warnings from health officials allowing for rates of HIV/AIDS to increase substantially among Black Americans (Dalton 1989; Cohen 1999).

In response to these increasing rates of HIV within Black American communities, a number of Black churches have begun to openly discuss issues of sex and sexuality in an effort to provide AIDS education to their communities. Nonetheless, many churches are still reluctant to address HIV/AIDS as they fear that even mentioning HIV would draw attention to 'deviant' elements in Black communities. Additionally, many Black church leaders and congregants feared that by providing safer sex education they would suggest to congregants that they condoned such behaviours (Shelp and Sunderland 1992; Weatherford and Weatherford 1999; Douglas 2003). This response of Black church leaders to the threat of AIDS was akin to the responses of a majority of religious and social institutions in the United States and abroad during the early years of AIDS (Shilts 1987). The Black Church's reluctance to discuss AIDS was particularly hurtful for those living with HIV, as Black church leaders are expected to come to the aid of those who are sick and oppressed (Williams 1987; Cone 1996; Gaines 1996; Wilmore 2004). Instead, a majority of these churches not only condemned and shunned those with HIV; they actively worked to discriminate against groups associated with the virus (Cohen 1999).

Importantly, not all Black churches discriminated against those with AIDS. Some did provide support and guidance, as they recognized early on the toll that AIDS was taking on Black communities (Cohen 1999; A. Harris 2010). These churches were often in urban areas that were the hardest hit by AIDS—such as in Harlem, Brooklyn, Chicago, and Philadelphia.

Research has shown that reaching out to Black churches plays a vital role in curbing the high rates of AIDS in Black communities as it increases AIDS education and awareness and reduces stigma (Shelp and Sunderland 1992; Weatherford and Weatherford 1999; Newman 2002; Douglas 2003). AIDS education provided through Black churches has a particularly important impact on Black women, who make up a majority of Black church congregations and of HIV/AIDS cases among women in the United States (CDC 2013).

WOMEN

Although Black women make up a large majority of the congregants within Black churches, they are significantly less likely to hold leadership positions within these churches than their male counterparts (Gilkes 2001). Many of the reasons for this stem from both interpretations of the role of women found within religious texts and from social and cultural customs (Douglas 2003). Researchers have often noted the role that spirituality plays in the lives of Black women (Gilkes 2001; Douglas 2003; Frederick 2003). As a group who has historically endured racism, class oppression, and gender discrimination, Black women experience a unique oppression resulting in increased levels of spirituality and religiosity (Gilkes 2001). For many women in Black churches, spirituality and religion are distinct. The ethnography of Marla F. Frederick (2003), a scholar who examines religion and spirituality in the lives of Black women, found that although the women attended church regularly, prayed frequently, and believed that the church played a major role in their lives, they were sceptical of the church as well as its leadership.

As noted earlier, 74 per cent of Black women and 70 per cent of Black men believe 'that living a religious life' is 'very important' as compared to 57 per cent of White women and 43 per cent of White men (*Washington Post* 2013). The influence of religion and spirituality spreads to their participation within Black churches. Within Black churches women are often noted as being actively engaged in church, attending services regularly, as well as helping to lead various church ministries and outreach programmes. However, research also notes that within most Black churches women are discouraged from taking on leadership positions, such as that of a pastor (Gilkes 2001; Frederick 2003). Within most Black churches, ministers are allowed to teach and speak the word of the gospel to followers and congregants. Pastors, on the other hand, lead congregants and churches. Within individual Black churches pastors and to a lesser extent the church board control decisions concerning church affairs and even beliefs. Although the largest Black church denomination, the Church of God in Christ (COGIC), allows for women to function as ministers, they are barred from ordination as pastors except in extreme cases such as when the widow of the pastor is allowed to take over pastoral duties for the church in the event of her husband's death (Pitt 2012).

Other Black churches give women different routes to ordination than men (Gilkes 2001). For example, in some Black church denominations, such as the Church of the Living God (Christian Workers for Fellowship), women are required to serve as missionaries before ordination whereas men are able to be ordained without missionary duties (Gilkes 2001). The justification for not ordaining women is often rooted in the argument that since Jesus is male, only men can lead followers to God. There have been divisions within some Black church denominations concerning the role of women in these churches. For instance, angered that women could help elect bishops but not serve as bishops in the United Holy Church, many church members broke away and formed the Mount Sinai Holy Church of America (Gilkes 2001). The lack of leadership roles for women is not unique to Black churches; many of the world's largest churches such as the Roman Catholic Church and the Latter Day Saints also do not ordain women.

Black church scholar Marla Frederick (2003) describes the complex relationship that Black American women have with Black churches and explains how Black churches foster a culture of resistance as well as a culture of self-help. This tradition of resistance and self-help provides support and motivation for dealing with injustice. Frederick (2003: 7) explains that '[t]here are everyday forms of resistance that people use that do not necessarily require organizing for direct protest; nevertheless, they demonstrate opposition to the status quo or to practices with which they disagree'. Even though within many Black church denominations women cannot serve as pastors, they can still be ordained as ministers and often take on ministerial responsibilities and church governance positions.

Additionally, Black women make up a vast majority of the congregants within these churches, and as such, in reality, have access to power within these institutions (Gilkes 2001; Frederick 2003). Frederick states, 'women who work in these places do not resist politically or with confrontation; instead, in the midst of struggle, they create lives and sustain communities and develop opportunities for success (2003: 7). Even though Black churches do not often provide women with the opportunity to lead congregations, they do often encourage them to be involved in their communities (Gilkes 2001). In her discussion of the 'powerful and respected older women' in Black communities who she describes as 'community mothers' or what Patricia Hill Collins (2000) refers to as 'other mothers', Cheryl Townsand Gilkes (2001: 61) states:

> In secular settings, such mothers are often the heads of Black women's organizations and hold positions of power and authority in more broadly based

community and civil rights organizations. In sacred places...they are occasionally pastors, sometimes evangelists, more often pastors' wives and widows, but most often leaders of organized church women (missionaries, deaconesses, mothers' boards, etc.)

Thus, interestingly, Black churches, although often oppressive to women, have helped to cultivate a culture of activism among Black Americans, women in particular (Gilkes 2001). This culture of activism is evident in various activities, from addressing education and voting rights, to reproductive rights and HIV/AIDS education among Blacks (Giddens 1984; Gilkes 2001).

THE BLACK CHURCH MOVING FORWARD

As with all religious institutions, how the Black Church responds to issues of gender, sex, and sexuality is heavily determined not only by religious doctrine but also by the unique history and culture of followers and congregants. Concerns such as women in leadership positions, same-sex marriage, and HIV/AIDS have forced some Black churches to take even more stringent stances against these issues, while allowing for other, more inclusive churches that actively welcome the emergence of women leaders as well as those with HIV/AIDS, and homosexuals. In fact, it appears as if the largest challenge to Black church traditions and norms has been the increasing presence and recognition of homosexuality. These denominations grew, in large part, because many Black lesbian, gay, bisexual, and transgender (LGBT) church and community members were forced out of their churches by unaccepting congregants and church leaders. Consequently, a number of Black churches with predominantly LGBT congregants have increased in number; the largest of these LGBT Black Church denominations is the Unity Fellowship Church of Christ.

Unity is unique in that it was founded not just as a Black church denomination, but as a social movement with the expressed purpose of responding to the impact that AIDS was having on both the physical and spiritual well-being of Blacks, and in particular, Black members of the LGBT community. As an out gay Black man who did not feel welcomed in his church, in 1982, Unity's founder, Carl Bean, a former gospel singer and Motown recording artist, began to host worship meetings in his home. Unity filled a spiritual void for many Black LGBT people who were ostracized from their churches and communities. From its inception, the work of the church was intertwined with the work of serving those affected by AIDS and HIV. Formed at a time when many churches were hostile and condemnatory towards gay men and people with HIV/AIDS, in some cases stating that their illness was God's judgement against their sexual orientation, Bean saw Unity as a vehicle to demonstrate unconditional love to those affected. This message contrasted with the hostile messages of other religious leaders and placed Unity's theology and actions firmly within the realm of liberation theology. It focuses on serving those who have been oppressed. Unity's core philosophies are described as follows:

> Not a male dominated hierarchy; Not oppressive to women; Not just European in scope; Must relate to People of Color and their various cultures around the world; Not oppressive to Lesbian, Gay, Bi-sexual and Transgender people; Allows us to think and discern through human reason and experience; Not oppressive to Native Americans or their spirituality nor any other oppressive use of scripture; We believe in the teachings of Jesus but we DO NOT dismiss all other faiths and beliefs as wrong or second to our way of believing.
>
> (Unity Fellowship Church Movement 2013)

Today, Unity has sixteen churches located throughout the United States. For a relatively new Black church denomination that caters to such a small demographic, the spread of Unity has been quite remarkable. In addition to Unity, other, more traditional Black churches have taken the steps to confront HIV/AIDS within Black communities and believe that the first step is to openly accept LGBT community members. Throughout the years, organizations such as 'The Balm in Gilead' worked to address this concern, helping to use Black churches as a conduit to provide AIDS education and intervention services to Black communities while also working to address homophobia in these institutions (A. Harris 2010). The Black Church Week of Prayer for the Healing of AIDS takes place during the first week of March and encourages Black churches throughout the United States to take part in AIDS education events, programmes, and sermons.

Importantly, HIV has forced many churches to openly discuss sex and sexuality. Yet, a vast majority of these churches promotes abstinence and provides abstinence-only education to its youth, even though research suggests this form of intervention is ineffective at reducing rates of HIV and other sexually transmitted infections, and also unplanned pregnancy (Hernandez and Smith 1990). Nonetheless, AIDS activists argue that at least getting these churches to talk about AIDS is the first step and is better than ignoring the HIV infection rates in Black communities (Cohen 1999; A. Harris 2010). In addition to the challenges of HIV/AIDS, Black churches have also been confronted with how they will respond to equal rights for same-sex couples.

As same-sex marriage becomes a reality in states across the United States, and the federal government's recent recognition of the rights of married same-sex couples in states that recognize these unions, many Black churches are actively rallying against these unions. Often compared to the fight for racial equality and the civil rights movement, advocates for same-sex marriage argue that not allowing legal recognition of same-sex marriage is a form of discrimination that is not only immoral but also violates constitutional law. Many Black leaders, with most stemming from Black churches, on the other hand, take offence at this comparison and argue that homosexuality is a sin, and such behaviour should not be condoned and their unions not legalized. Additionally, they fear that their religious institutions would have to acknowledge and perform such marriages.

The distain of Black church leaders for same-sex marriage was so great that, in 2004, Black church leaders were credited with helping to secure then President George W. Bush's re-election, based on his promise to back an amendment to the United States Constitution defining marriage as union between a man and a woman (Hutchinson 2005). Also, in California during the 2008 election season, Blacks went to the polls in record numbers to vote for Barack Obama. During the same time legislation was on the ballots reversing the legalization of same-sex marriage that had taken place several months earlier in the state. By a close margin, same-sex marriage was briefly prohibited in this state once more and many political pundits blamed Black church leaders for encouraging members to vote against same-sex marriage (DiMassa and Garrison 2008). Even as recently as 2013, Black political leaders in Illinois were hesitant to support a law legalizing same-sex marriage in the state as they feared losing the support of Black religious leaders (Stone 2013). Nonetheless, just as there have been a number of Black churches that have actively condemned same-sex marriage, there are also Black churches which have supported these unions. For example, there are some Black churches in Massachusetts and New York (states which legally recognize same-sex marriage) that do perform same-sex marriages. Furthermore, a number of Black church leaders, such as the prominent pastor of the West Point Missionary Baptist Church in Chicago, Revd Bernard Jakes, have come out in support of same-sex marriage.

Conclusion

For almost 150 years Black churches have fulfilled a great need among Black Americans. Black churches have worked tirelessly to improve the living conditions of parishioners and the members of their communities by addressing social justice concerns and providing spiritual and social support. Nonetheless, concerns that Black churches have historically grappled with, such as issues of respectability, women in leadership positions, homosexuality, and sexual promiscuity—continue to challenge church leadership. Although these issues were always addressed periodically within individual Black churches, they were not addressed in a more systematic manner until HIV/AIDS began to devastate Black communities. The direct association of AIDS with promiscuity, homosexuality, and illicit drug use barred Black church leaders from addressing AIDS. Nevertheless, a number of Black churches discovered that the devastating effect of AIDS on their congregations and larger Black communities required that they look past sex, homosexuality, and drug use to tackle the disease. This has allowed for larger Black communities to also openly address these issues. However, issues of sex, sexuality, and the role of women in these churches have always been contested and will likely continue to do so into the distant future. Only time will tell how Black churches will respond to these challenges and if they will provide women and members of the LGBT community with the same sense of justice and spiritual fulfilment they were founded to achieve.

REFERENCES

Ajen, N. (1998). 'West African Homoeroticism: West African Men Who Have Sex with Men'. In Murray and Roscoe (1998), 129–140.

Amory, D. P. (1998). '*Mashoga, Mabasha,* and *Magai*: "Homosexuality" on the East African Coast'. In Murray and Roscoe (1998), 67–90.

Billingsley, A., and Caldwell, C. H. (1991). 'The Church, the Family, and the School in the African American Community'. *Journal of Negro Education,* 60(3): 427–440.

CDC (Centers for Disease Control and Prevention) (2013). *Health Disparities in HIV/ AIDS, Viral Hepatitis, STDs, and TB.* <http://www.cdc.gov/nchhstp/healthdisparities/ AfricanAmericans.html> (accessed 19 June 2013).

Cohen, C. J. (1999). *The Boundaries of Blackness: AIDS and the Breakdown of Black Politics.* Chicago: University of Chicago Press.

Collins, P. H. (2000). *Black Feminist Thought: Knowledge, Consciousness, and the Politics of Empowerment,* 2nd edn. New York: Routledge.

Collins, P. H. (2004). *Black Sexual Politics: African Americans, Gender, and the New Racism.* New York: Routledge.

Cone, J. H. (1996). *A Black Theology of Liberation.* Maryknoll, NY: Orbis Books.

Conrad, P., and Schneider, J. W. (1992). *Deviance and Medicalization: From Badness to Sickness.* Philadelphia: Temple University Press.

Constantine-Simms, D. (2001). 'Is Homosexuality the Greatest Taboo?' In D. Constance-Simms (ed.), *The Greatest Taboo: Homosexuality in Black Communities.* Los Angeles: Alyson Books, 76–87.

Dalton, H. L. (1989). 'AIDS in Blackface'. *Daedalus* 118(3): 205–227.

DiMassa, C. M., and Garrison, J. (2008). 'Why Gays, Blacks are Divided on Prop. 8: For Many African Americans, It's Not a Civil Rights Issue'. *Los Angeles Times,* 8 November. <http:// articles.latimes.com/2008/nov/08/local/me-gayblack8> (accessed 19 June 2013).

Douglas, K. B. (2003). *Sexuality and the Black Church: A Womanist Perspective.* Maryknoll, NY: Orbis Books.

DuBois, W. E. B. (1903). *The Souls of Black Folk.* Mineola, NY: Dover Publications, Inc.

Ellison, C. G., and Sherkat, D. E. (1995). 'The "Semi-Involuntary Institution"—Revisited: Regional Variations in Church Participation among Black Americans'. *Social Forces,* 73(4): 1415–1437.

Frazier, E. F. (1969). *The Negro Church in America.* New York: Schocken Books.

Frederick, M. F. 2003. *Between Sundays: Women and Everyday Struggles of Faith.* Berkeley and Los Angeles: University of California Press.

Ford, C. L., Whetten, K. D., Hall, S. A., Kaufman, J. S., and Thrasher, A. D. (2007). 'Black Sexuality, Social Construction and Research Targeting "the Down Low"'. *Annals of Epidemiology,* 17(3): 209–216.

Foucault, M. (1990). *The History of Sexuality: An Introduction,* vol. i. New York: Vintage Books.

Fullilove, M. T., and Fullilove, R. E., III. (1997). 'Homosexuality and the African American Church: The Paradox of the "Open Closet"'. In The Balm in Gilead (ed.), *Though I Stand at the Door and Knock: Discussions on the Black Church Struggle with Homosexuality and AIDS.* New York: The Balm in Gilead, 1–14.

Gaines, K. K. (1996). *Uplifting the Race: Black Leadership, Politics, and Culture in the Twentieth Century.* Chapel Hill: University of North Carolina Press.

Genovese, E. D. (1972). *Roll, Jordan, Roll: The World the Slaves Made.* New York: Vintage Books.

Giddens, P. (1984). *When and Where I Enter: The Impact of Black Women on Race and Sex in America.* New York: Perennial.

Gilkes, C. T. (2001). *If It Wasn't for the Women*. Maryknoll, NY: Orbis Books.

Greenberg, D. F. (1990). *The Construction of Homosexuality*. Chicago: University of Chicago Press.

Griffin, H. (2006). *Their Own Received Them Not: African American Lesbian and Gays in Black Churches*. Cleveland, OH: Pilgrim Press.

Harris, A. (2010). *AIDS, Sexuality, and the Black Church: Making the Wounded Whole*. New York: Peter Lang Publishers.

Harris, A. C. (2009). 'Marginalization by the Marginalized: The Problem of the 21st Century'. *Journal of Gay and Lesbian Social Services*, 21(4): 430–448.

Hernandez, J. T., and Smith, F. J. (1990). 'Abstinence, Protection, and Decision-Making: Experimental Trials on Prototypic AIDS Programs'. *Health Education Research*, 5(2): 309–320.

Higginbotham, E. B. (1993). *Righteous Discontent: The Women's Movement in the Black Baptist Church, 1880–1920*. Cambridge, MA: Harvard University Press.

hooks, b. (2001). 'Homophobia in Black Communities'. In D. Constance-Simms (ed.), *The Greatest Taboo: Homosexuality in Black Communities*. Los Angeles: Alyson Books, 67–75.

Hutchinson, E. O. (2005). 'Black Evangelicals: Bush's New Trump Card'. *AlterNet*, 26 January. <http://www.alternet.org/story/21096/black_evangelicals%3A_bush's_new_trump_card> (accessed 19 June 2013).

Johnson, E. P. (2001). 'Feeling the Spirit in the Dark: Expanding Notions of the Sacred in the African American Gay Community'. In D. Constance-Simms (ed.), *The Greatest Taboo: Homosexuality in Black Communities*. Los Angeles: Alyson Books, 88–109.

Lincoln, C. E., and Mamiya, L. H. (2003). *The Black Church in the African American Experience*. Durham, NC: Duke University Press.

McBride, D. (2005). *Why I Hate Abercrombie and Fitch*. New York: New York University Press.

Mitchell, M. (2004). *Righteous Propagation: African Americans and the Politics of Racial Destiny after Reconstruction*. Chapel Hill: University of North Carolina Press.

Murray, S. O., and Roscoe, W. (1998) (eds). *Boy-Wives and Female Husbands: Studies of African Homosexualities*. New York: St Martin's Press.

Newman, S. (2002). *Oh God!: A Black Woman's Guide to Sex and Spirituality*. New York, NY: The Ballantine Publishing Group.

Pattillo-McCoy, M. (1998). 'Church Culture as a Strategy of Action in the Black Community'. *American Sociological Review*, 63: 767–784.

Pitt, R. N. (2012). *Divine Callings: Understanding the Call to Ministry in Black Pentecostalism*. New York: New York University Press.

Riggs, M. (2001). 'Black Macho Revisited: Reflections of a SNAP! Queen'. In R. P. Byrd and B. Guy-Sheftall (eds), *Traps: African American Men on Gender and Sexuality*, Bloomington, IN: Indiana University Press, 292–296.

Shelp, E. E., and Sunderland, R. H. (1992). *AIDS and the Church: The Second Decade*. Louisville, KY: Westminster/John Knox Press.

Shilts, R. (1987). *And the Band Played On*. New York: Penguin Group.

Somerville, S. B. (2000). *Queering the Color Line: Race and the Invention of Homosexuality in American Culture*. Durham, NC: Duke University Press.

Stone, G. R. (2013). 'Same-Sex Marriage in Illinois: The Role of the Black Church'. *Huffington Post*, 1 June. <http://www.huffingtonpost.com/geoffrey-r-stone/same-sex-marriage-in-illi_b_3372938.html> (accessed 2 Jan. 2014).

Trinitapoli, J., and Weinreb, A. (2012). *Religion and AIDS in Africa*. New York: Oxford University Press.

Unity Fellowship Church Movement (2013). *What We Believe.* <http://www.unityfellowship-church.org/mainsite/?page_id=7> (accessed 19 June 2013).

Washington Post (2013). 'Washington Post—Kaiser Family Foundation poll of Black women in America. *Washington Post,* 19 June. <http://www.washingtonpost.com/wp-srv/special/nation/black-women-in-america> (accessed 19 June 2013).

Weatherford, R. J., and Weatherford, C. B. (1999). *Somebody's Knocking at Your Door: AIDS and the African-American Church.* New York: Haworth Pastoral Press.

West, C. (2001). "Black Sexuality: The Taboo Subject." In R. P. Byrd and B. Guy-Sheftall (eds), *Traps: African American Men on Gender and Sexuality.* Bloomington, IN: Indiana University Press, 301–307.

West, C. (1997). 'The Black Church Beyond Homophobia'. In The Balm in Gilead (ed.), *Though I Stand at the Door and Knock: Discussions on the Black Church Struggle with Homosexuality and AIDS.* New York: The Balm in Gilead, 15–22.

Williams, J. (1987). *Eyes on the Prize: American's Civil Rights Years 1954–1965.* New York: Penguin Books.

Wilmore, G. S. (2004). *Black Religion and Black Radicalism: An Interpretation of the Religious History of African Americans.* Maryknoll, NY: Orbis Books.

Wilson, L. C. (2000). 'Implementation and Evaluation of Church-Based Health Fairs'. *Journal of Community Health Nursing,* 17 (1): 39–48.

Wimberly, E. P. (1979). *Pastoral Care in the Black Church.* Nashville: Abingdon.

PART VI

....

INTER-RELIGIOUS CONVERSATIONS

....

CHAPTER 25

JUDAISM

RONIT IRSHAI

INTRODUCTION

A leading premise in the field of Judaic studies asserts that Judaism embraces an affirmative attitude towards sexuality (Biale 1992; Boyarin 1993; Feldman 1995). It attributes to Judaism a life-sanctifying theological stance, which, as distinct from Christianity, does not set abstinence from the physical life as the spiritual ideal. This theological stance is well represented in the legal (Halakhic) sphere, which for example makes it a husband's obligation to have regular sexual relations (termed *onah*) with his wife in the marital context (Maimonides 1972: 14:1–7), separate from, and in addition to, the biblical obligation to 'be fruitful and multiply' (1972: 15:1). These conjugal rights are perceived as essential to the marital bond.

Biale (1992) was in the forefront of the development of a more nuanced picture of sexuality in Judaism. In his study he portrays opposing conceptions of the Jewish attitude towards sexuality: on the one hand, because Judaism did not accept the principle of abstinence, Jews were perceived as having a more positive attitude towards *eros* than Christians (even to the extent that some anti-Semites see Judaism's positive attitude towards sexuality as a 'barbaric affront to civility' (Biale 1992: 1)). Contrastively, others view Judaism's biblical God, who zealously erased all traces of the eroticism of the pagan deities, as the source of the patriarchal oppression which arrests and suppresses sexuality and romantic feelings.

Biale further argues that the nineteenth-century *Wissenschaft des Judentums* scholars, who inaugurated the historical study of Judaism, framed it as a monolithic system, expunging irrational ideas, such as mysticism, or social movements that countered what they wished to delineate as 'the essence of Judaism'. Although sexuality is an inseparable part of Jewish mystical theology, sectors of rabbinic literature and medieval Jewish philosophy relegated it to the secular world. Accordingly, the place of the body in Jewish intellectual culture was, until recently, 'assumed to be a factor to be ignored or even entirely nullified, because it opposed culture' (Biale 1994: 13). Biale offers alternatives to the *Wissenschaftlich* imagination which separated a homogeneous Judaism from the actual lives of Jews and studied intellectual elites as its sole representatives (Biale 1992: 6–8). Instead of a false monolithic view of an asexual Judaism, he suggests a different, more nuanced study:

> The contradictions in Freud's view of Jewish sexuality capture the central argument of this book: the Jewish tradition cannot be characterized as either simply affirming or simply repressing the erotic. Our story is about the *dilemmas* of desire, the struggle between contradictory attractions, rather than the history of a monolithic dogma. As such, it is the story of a profoundly ambivalent culture [emphasis original].
>
> (Biale 1992: 5)

Together with Biale's *Eros and the Jews* (1992, 1994), Daniel Boyarin's *Carnal Israel* (1993) also marked a shift to renewed interest in topics related to the body and sexuality in Judaic studies and a multifaceted, polyvalent approach. Boyarin focuses on what is denoted rabbinic Judaism, which flourished in the first centuries CE, and comprised the foundation for the future development of Judaism. He outlines the central thesis of his book as follows:

> Rabbinic Judaism—the cultural formation of most of the Hebrew—and Aramaic-speaking Jews of Palestine and Babylonia—was substantially differentiated in its representations and discourses of the body and sexuality from Greek-speaking Jewish formations, including much of Christianity. My fundamental notion ... is that rabbinic Judaism invested significance in the body which in the other formations was invested in the soul.
>
> (Boyarin 1993: 5)

Boyarin maintains that, for the rabbis, the essence of the person was a body with a soul, whereas for Christianity, it was a soul in a body. The importance of this distinction cannot be underestimated: the notion that physical existence is but a 'shadow' of the true essence (the soul or the spirit) facilitates the reduction, and even the denial, of the value of sexuality and procreation. In contrast, an emphasis on the body as the definitive site of human significance and essence does not foster reduction of the value of sexuality, procreation, or consanguinity. Nonetheless, Boyarin's book is no apologetic interpretation of rabbinic Judaism. Indeed, as Boyarin observes, the ascription to rabbinic Judaism of a positive attitude towards the body, sexuality, or sexual pleasure is not unproblematic, and the insistence on physicality and sexuality as a fundamental component of the human essence almost inevitably creates gender segregation and divisions:

> Some Christians (whether Jewish or Gentile) could declare that there is no Greek or Jew, no male or female. No rabbinic Jew could do so, because people are bodies, not spirits, and precisely bodies are marked as male or female, and also marked, through bodily practices and techniques such as circumcision and food taboos, as Jew or Greek as well.
>
> (Boyarin 1993: 10)

Some denote the shift represented by these studies the 'corporeal turn' in Jewish studies (Kirshenblatt-Gimblett 2005). As feminist theories, cultural studies, and postmodern thinking have penetrated Judaic studies, this has impacted on the hitherto unquestioned consensus that Judaism affirms sexuality. The new scholarship challenges the ostensibly 'neutral', gender-free treatment of theology and formal Halakhah in the classic scholarship of Judaic studies, turning attention to the practical implications of theological and halakhic viewpoints for the lives of *actual* women and men. Contemporary scholars, both male and female, have begun to question the underlying gender principles within Jewish thought, theology, and law that shape couplehood and the family as a patriarchal institution, and also the meaning of sexuality itself and its functions in Jewish tradition: the relationship between the husband's Halakhic obligation to have sex with his wife (*onah*), sexual enjoyment (of both partners), and procreation; the male sexual drive as opposed to the female one; and 'solitary' sexuality (masturbation) by men and women. The emergence of queer theory has seen intensive consideration of the question of the Jewish attitude towards heteronormative sexual identities.

The new theoretical frameworks, gender and cultural studies in particular, have sparked a number of questions not addressed by traditional Judaic studies' research. Thus, feminist researchers have begun to ask how the religious laws (Halakhot) concerning women's bodies (modesty, menstrual impurity (*niddah*), procreation), especially their theological and sociological ramifications, affect women's lives today. In this context, harsh feminist criticism is levelled at the construction of the female body in Jewish law as a problematic sexual site which must be distanced from the public arena and loci of holiness and religious activity (Adler 1983; Plaskow 1991).

This chapter singles out four focal issues: (1) sexuality in ancient rabbinic thought, to which the most scholarly attention has been directed; and issues in modern Halakhah that have just begun to inform scholarly research: (2) the ethos of modesty and the construction of the female body; (3) homosexuality and lesbianism; and (4) reproduction and sexuality. All four reflect the tension between the new scholarly trends of gender analysis and feminist critique, and between the conceptual-theological stratum of Judaism and its reflection in the practical-legal sphere of the Halakhah.

SEXUALITY, BODY, AND GENDER IN ANCIENT RABBINIC THOUGHT

An intriguing shift in the study of gender and sexuality in ancient rabbinic literature has been documented by Rosen-Zvi (2012). What can be termed 'liberal feminism' was the initial orientation of study, with scholars addressing such questions as the attitude towards women in this literature, some underscoring its patriarchal and misogynist aspects (Greenberg 1981; Ozick 1983; Wegner 1988; Plaskow 1991; Adler 1998, 2001;

Baskin 2002), and others citing the legislation that favours women and typical rabbinic attempts at enhancing their status (Aiken 1992; Hauptman 1998). We can chart a shift, however, from this framework to the use of gender as an analytic category, including the consideration of gender relations and the formation of gender identities (Satlow 1995; Fonrobert 2000, 2007; Baker 2002; Rosen-Zvi 2012).

These 'second wave' studies have broadened the discussion to encompass the relationship between the sexes and the gender image that emerges from rabbinic literature. Focusing on topics such as sexuality and marriage, the female and male bodies, and adultery and seduction, among others, they widened and challenged the existing viewpoints in Judaic studies. Thus, for example, Satlow questions the premise that the rabbinic commandment of obligatory conjugal rights comprehended sexual enjoyment, arguing that the rabbis defined sex 'as the penetration of the penis into a woman's vagina or anus', and this did not need to result in orgasm. 'This seemingly trivial fact points toward a far more reaching assumption. Sex was about penetration. An active male penetrates a passive female' (Satlow 1995: 316).

Fonrobert's study of the laws of menstrual impurity (*niddah*) represents movement from a discussion of sexuality to a focus on the body. Fonrobert explores the gynaecological-psychological knowledge inherent in the laws of *niddah* as a gateway to understanding Talmudic gender doctrines (2000: 112–115). For the rabbis, the female body, and its secretions, became a new object of complex knowledge and sophisticated mapping. Their application of house-related metaphors to a woman's organs sheds light on the rabbinic formation of female gender identity.

Rosen-Zvi's study (2012) of the *sotah* ceremony (for a woman suspected of adultery; see Num. 5:11–31) as constructed in the Mishnah places at its centre rabbinic concern with the female body. He identifies the Mishnaic shaping of the biblical ceremony (which he adduces was not carried out) as another manifestation of the rabbinic treatment of, and attempt to address, the threat of female sexuality. His analysis of this ceremony and its unusual features reveals a rabbinic effort to achieve total mastery over women, which is limited neither by the ethos of modesty and refraining from the exposure of women's bodies, nor by the sanctity of the body and the prohibition against physical injury.

Other studies by Rosen-Zvi challenge the prevailing trend in current Talmudic research that places the evil inclination (*yetser ha-ra*) primarily in sexual contexts. This trend adduces an almost inescapable conclusion: that the evil inclination functions according to the known rabbinic gender definition which constructs women as attractive and seductive and men as either prone to seduction or forced to battle their inclination. In such a context, there is almost no room to speak of women's sexual drive. Rosen-Zvi's complex portrayal of male *yetser* raises new questions regarding its gendered characterization (2000, 2009).

Pursuing the research direction initiated by Rosen-Zvi, Fisher (2009) explores the ambivalence displayed by rabbinic sources towards female sexuality and desire, which ranges from passivity to unbridled, seductive libido that threatens to erupt momentarily. Her analysis shows that the shared view that female sexuality comes to serve (or ensnare) male sexuality, makes male sexuality, and its needs, the referent for both poles.

The rabbinic stances that attribute sexual passion to women grasp it as an uncontrollable biological 'given', which the surrounding 'culture' is expected to restrain. This in turn explains the paucity of attention to, or limitations on, female observation of men in sexual terms: the demands made of women in the sphere of 'modesty' (such as keeping their bodies covered) are aimed at assisting men to restrain their inclination. Women, however, are not required to take active steps to rein in their passion, either because this passion does not exist (or is weakened) or because it is uncontrollable. Both possibilities are consistent with Wegner's (1988) analysis of the status of women in the Mishnah. She assigns the sources to two broad categories: personhood as opposed to chattel. The defining characteristics are as follows: 'Personhood means the legal status defined by the complex of an individual's powers, rights, and duties in society. An entity possessing no powers, rights or duties is no person at all but merely an object or chattel' (Wegner 1988: 10). The ability to control one's inclination and passion is a central feature of personhood.

Indeed, we can state that the more that the scholarship has studied the means and sites of gender-identity formation in ancient rabbinic literature, the further it is from exhausting the topics of sexuality and passion in that context. Moving to the present, one cogent question is whether the construction of female and male sexuality, passion, and *yetser* in rabbinic literature influences current Halakhic and theological discourse. Three examples from contemporary Orthodox Halakhic discourse are treated in the following sections; note, however, that study of current trends in modern Halakhic literature from a gender perspective, in the context of sexuality in particular, is still in its infancy.

MODESTY AND THE WOMAN'S BODY

'Modesty' is another province that calls the premise of an overridingly positive Jewish attitude towards sexuality into question. This concept encompasses many broad spheres, including norms related to the relationship between the sexes before and after marriage (physical contact before marriage, laws of marital relations), and rules governing the covering of the body. Alternatively, it can address lifestyle and ethical mores: such as the value of making do with little, and education for humility, among others. Feminist scholars note the different treatment of male and female modesty, especially as concerns exposure of the body (Hartman 2007; Fisher 2009).

In this context, the Halakhic restrictions that apply to the female body, limitations that may be directly related to the status of women as subjects in the theological realm, constitute a major issue. As opposed to men, to whom some restrictions apply but who are primarily required to cover themselves only in the presence of God, women must cover themselves in the presence of men and also accept a degree of responsibility for the prospect that they may make men sin by provoking sexual arousal. The major stipulations of the laws of modesty require that married women cover their heads; forbid women to sing in the presence of men; and mandate the wearing of non-revealing clothing. The degree of exposure of different parts of the body depends on Halakhic exegesis, but most Orthodox branches forbid women to wear pants because they outline the body; skirts have to be below the knee and sleeves elbow-length or longer; and blouses must have high necklines. Stricter approaches forbid women to wear strong colours, red especially.

A statement by Rabbi Ovadia Yosef, one of the leading Orthodox Halakhists in the Jewish world today, exemplifies this stringent approach:

> It is obvious that women who go outdoors dressed provocatively transgress the prohibition against placing 'a stumbling block before the blind' (Leviticus 19:14), for they make men look at them and think lascivious thoughts that are even worse than sin...And Rabbenu Jonah wrote that the sin of looking at women transgresses a pentateuchal prohibition.
>
> (Yosef 1977–1980: *Yehaveh da'at*, 3:67)

Female Sexuality and the 'Problem' of Men

Feminist writings train the spotlight on the fact that it is women who are charged with taking responsibility for the ostensible 'problem' of men (Hartman 2007; Ross 2011) and, furthermore, that Halakhic standards are usually set according to male needs. However, because masculinity is the prevailing, but 'transparent', norm in Halakhic rulings, it is not recognized as a problematic bias on the rabbis' part (Irshai forthcoming). Borrowing Laura Mulvey's coinage 'to-be-looked-at-ness', Fisher (2009) notes that Talmudic Halakhic discourse on women asserts that they 'are *not* supposed to-be-looked-at' (emphasis original). But, like the Hollywood film on which Mulvey focuses, here too the norms of how to avoid such observation are dictated by male inclinations and needs.

A definitive example of this issue in everyday life is the polemic in Israel surrounding the Talmudic prohibition that equates a woman's voice with nudity (*qol ba-isha ervah*, lit. 'a woman's voice is nakedness'), especially in the context of women singing in the army, where men and women, both religious and secular, serve. Some rabbis have prohibited religious male soldiers from participating in ceremonies where women sing. Tamar Ross underscores the male bias inherent in this prohibition:

> Women today ask why all the anxiety about the purity of men's thoughts is not accompanied by any concern about women's experiences. Has any halakhist made the effort to weigh the spiritual loss suffered by women through the silencing of their voices against the supposed benefit to men? If modesty is a problem for men, why must women pay the price? Moreover, are women's voices in fact as seductive as they are said to be? A negative answer to that question brings us back to the conclusion that the *halakhah* imposes inappropriate responsibility on women, for the traditional bounds of modesty are always formulated exclusively in terms of women's seductiveness to men.
>
> (Ross 2011: 47)

Fisher (2009) notes another problematic, conflicting message that is conveyed regarding female sexual identity. The premise that women must cover themselves primarily to prevent men from having 'impure thoughts', without its counterpart, in which men cover themselves for the same reason, imparts a sense that men alone have active sexual desires/needs, whereas women possess a restrained, passive sexual drive. The total absence of Halakhot requiring men to cover their bodies in order to prevent women from having impure thoughts can be interpreted as lack of recognition of women as sexual beings with sexual needs. Hartman (2007) distils this point. In her view, the extreme messages of liberal culture regarding exposure of women's bodies, and of religious society that demands their maximum concealment, in actuality reflect the same notion of the woman and femininity—as a sexual object for men.

One of the harshest critiques of the Halakhic requirement that married women cover their hair was voiced in a study by Weiss (2009). According to Weiss, modern Halakhah-observing women attribute various meanings to the requirement that they cover their hair: for some it denotes marriage, or identification with the tribe; for others it is a symbol of piety and humility, an act of deference to the Divine Will, or signals sexual modesty. Weiss challenges these unquestioned associations, arguing that as *myths* which have taken on discernible form they obscure the underlying power relations signified by head-covering. She maintains that, like the Jewish marriage ceremony and laws of divorce, head-covering demarcates a Jewish husband's exclusive and unilateral property rights in his wife's sexuality.

These insights, which amply demonstrate how modesty laws can actually heighten the perception of a woman as a sexual object, are applied by Irshai (2010) to the interface between the generation of female gender and the theological sphere:

> Uncovering the moral paradigm underlying the exclusion of women from religious rituals is even more obvious. The primary basis for that exclusion is the image of woman as a 'ticking sexual time-bomb'. The idea of holiness is profoundly tied to this—the more a woman is hidden, the holier the atmosphere. In other words, woman is equated with the unholy or even the 'anti-holy'; at the same time, man is seen as a 'sex-obsessed hormone dump'. Halakhic genealogy can uncover this paradigm, present it to Modern Orthodox men and women, and ask whether they are prepared to look in the mirror and then buy into this image.
>
> (Irshai 2010: 70)

The Premarital/Marital Divide

In that vein, we must note that there is an ostensibly unbridgeable gap between the laws of modesty before and after marriage. If the message conveyed to a woman while single is that her body must be concealed, that any sign of sexuality is unfitting and violates sanctity, this is seemingly reversed the moment she enters the marital realm. In a sharp volte-face, she is asked to expose her body and reveal her sexual nature. This is even seen as a religious obligation. Despite the fact that they were just previously deeply contradictory, holiness and sexuality are now seen as inseparable.

It is sociological and psychological research that captures the dialectical nature of the relationship between sexuality, the body, fertility, and sanctity among Jews who adhere to Halakhic demands (Ribner and Rosenbaum 2005; Labinsky et al. 2009). Sociological studies that give rein to the voices of observant women who face this gap effectively demonstrate the real difficulties they face and point to the cognitive dissonance created by the sharp transition from life as a single woman, ruled by modesty and concealment, to married life in which the body and sexuality play an important role (Debow 2009; Prins 2011).

All in all, here feminist critique and gender analysis function harmoniously and both expose the links between the laws of modesty and theology. Women's challenge to the religious system from personal experience, their refusal to silence their voices, heightens the awareness of underlying theological assumptions regarding to what extent women are considered religious subjects and who is speaking in the name of God.

'Queer Jews': Homosexuality and Lesbianism

As noted, only in recent decades have scholars of Judaic studies begun to focus on questions of sexual/gender identities. If, as shown earlier, the discussion of gender formation in the female context has flourished, the discussion of maleness from a Jewish perspective is just beginning. Daniel Boyarin's *Unheroic Conduct: The Rise of Heterosexuality and the Invention of Jewish Men* (1997) marks the turning point. It treats, for the first time, the topic of Jewish maleness, particularly as exemplified in rabbinic literature:

> This book is intended as one small chapter...on rabbinic Jewish maleness...of the possibility of an embodied male who fully within the order of sexuality and even paternity, is nevertheless not 'masculine' or 'manly' in the terms of the dominant fiction and thus inscribes the possibility of male subjects who refuse to be men.
>
> (Boyarin 1997: 11)

The new perspective on 'maleness' and 'femaleness' as an anti-essentialist identity formed through cultural activities, and the emergence of queer theories in the 1990s, sparked intense consideration of the question of gender identities within Jewish communities as well as in Jewish studies. For generations addressed only sporadically by Halakhists in the *responsa* literature activities (authoritative replies to queries on matters of Jewish law), this topic did not assume a central place on the agenda of the Jewish world for several reasons: homosexual (but not lesbian) intercourse is considered a biblical prohibition that carries the death penalty; persons with such tendencies, if they existed (such was the claim), were a small minority; and the violation of the religious *nomos* by individuals did not challenge the religious narrative. Until the mid-1980s the question of 'non-heteronormative' sexual identities was barely touched on in the various branches of Jewish literature; including Halakhic literature.

Nonetheless, as the Western social attitude towards individuals with homosexual preferences and identities changed, the painful stories of religious homosexuals and lesbians began to be heard, at first privately and then publicly. In effect, this is an instructive example of how a shift in the Western narrative regarding sexuality in general, and sexual difference in particular, also influenced liberal Western legislation and the Jewish world respectively, both in terms of the attitude towards those with different sexual identities in the various religious branches and in scholarly writing. Thus, for example, the Reform movement was the first which saw the ripening of a respectful, legitimate attitude towards different sexual identities.[1] The more liberal Jewish movements began to ordain rabbis with different sexual identities and even to permit same-sex marriage, providing varied religious rationales for their divergence from the traditional Jewish norm. Even in the Orthodox movement, where the prohibition against homosexuality is still in force, we find shifts in the rhetoric, as surveyed in what follows.

Landmark Publications

Several landmarks can be noted in the public divulgence of Jews with sexual identities that diverge from heteronormativity. Between 1982 and 2002 three seminal books appeared: *Nice Jewish Girls: A Lesbian Anthology* (1982), edited by Evelyn Torton Beck; *Twice Blessed* (1989), an anthology edited by Christie Balka and Andy Rose; and *Queer Jews* (2002), edited by David Shneer and Aviv Caryn. All three books shared the burning need 'to write our life into visibility' (Shneer and Caryn 2002: 16) Shortly thereafter, a first book in Hebrew on this topic was published in Israel: Irit Koren's *Altering the Closet* (2003), which stimulated religious homosexuals and lesbians to tell their stories, and which, beyond garnering empathy for, and identification with, their suffering, also identified the first cracks in Orthodox Halakhic discourse that might create an attitudinal shift towards such individuals.

Rebecca Alpert's *Like Bread on the Seder Plate: Jewish Lesbians and the Transformation of Tradition* (1997), published several years earlier, already marks a quasi-turning point because it does not simply content itself with raising consciousness. She seeks something more—*the inclusion of the lesbian voice in Jewish tradition*. She suggests three steps essential to this process: new exegeses of traditional texts (for example, reading the book of Ruth as mirroring female love); the dissemination of contemporary texts that reflect lesbian experience; and the creation of new Jewish texts that manifest this identity. Alpert is convinced that Jewish tradition has the ability to incorporate her

---

[1] <http://urj.org/cong/membership/diversity/glbtq/>.

identity. Rabbi Steven Greenberg's *Wrestling with God and Men* (2004) continues this trend by challenging Orthodoxy's uncompromising attitude towards sexual identities that diverge from heteronormativity, at the same time as it addresses the thorny problem of how to mediate between absolute commitment to Halakhah, which negates legitimation of same-sex love, and a homosexual identity. He asks whether it is possible to believe, based on new views of reality, that Halakhic decisions on homosexual relations are wrong and still remain faithful to the Halakhic system.

Shifting Halakhic Attitudes

Indeed, in her article, Ross (forthcoming) surveys Halakhic developments in the different branches of Judaism, noting that, whereas in the past, Orthodox Halakhists considered homosexuality as twisted carnality that required correction (Feinstein: 'those who transgress in this regard are considered evil and vulgar' (1973–2011: *Yoreh De'ah* 3:115)), a growing number of rabbis in the Orthodox wing also now feel a need to provide emotional support to homosexuals, which does not necessarily encompass an attempt to change their sexual orientation. One Halakhic-legal strategy distinguishes between *orientation* and *act*. As opposed to what Rabbi Feinstein's ruling implies, the fact that a person has a homosexual orientation does not make him a criminal; his divergent orientation is not inherently incriminating. This stance is in harmony with Boyarin's (1997) study, which makes a distinction between homosexuality and the prohibition against homosexual intercourse. Boyarin argues that the strong negative reactions currently aroused by homosexuality, especially within the religious establishment, are missing from rabbinic literature, and that the attitude towards those who commit undesirable deeds never included their perception as 'others'. Thus, biblical law mandates the death penalty for Sabbath desecrators, but the cultural attitude towards them is far removed from the emotional negativity displayed towards homosexuals. Boyarin is convinced that the biblical prohibition is grounded in the confusion of the categories of male and female; therefore, the real topic is gender and not the 'homosexual' identity. In fact, with the exception of anal intercourse, Jewish law does not prohibit other types of homo-erotic relations.

Returning to the distinction between orientation and act, some rabbis and Halakhic scholars who endorse this stance continue to treat homosexuality as a disease and not as an irreversible condition. They propose that, instead of condemnation, sufferers from this disease should be directed to pharmaceutical treatment intended to return them to normative life (Lamm 1974; Spero 1979). If their orientation cannot be altered, it is then perhaps worthwhile convincing them to 'lower their expectations' and aspire to the creation of a heterosexual family with a spouse who accedes after full disclosure (Rothstein 2010). Another viewpoint supports marriage between a homosexual and a lesbian, so that, together, they can build a Jewish family. Some apply to them the legal category of 'duress' (Hebrew: *ones*), arguing, namely, that they deserve sympathetic treatment because they are impelled to their orientation by sexual desire (Lamm 1974: Matt 1987;

Leibowitz 1999). Others maintain that this topic should not be aired in the public arena, neither by the religious gay community nor in public statements by rabbis. Silence is considered the best policy in order not to grant homosexuality legitimation (Lamm 1974).

With the greater public exposure of homosexuals and lesbians and of their personal stories—in the context of their families and communities, as well as in the media and other public forums—came their refusal to relinquish their religious worlds in spite of their total exclusion by the rabbinic establishment. The tone of some modern Orthodox Halakhists also shifted dramatically (Lubitz 1996; Ettinger 2010). First of all, Halakhists began to address this matter. Second, even if this did not harbinger significant change for religious-Orthodox homosexuals and lesbians, there were now calls for respect towards them, a separation of acceptance of the individual as a person and a believer from Halakhic, but not social, opposition to their sexual behaviour. In practical terms, this means a call not to exclude them from the community or religious educational frameworks, nor to encourage heterosexual marriage 'at any cost', or to automatically direct every person struggling with his sexual identity to 'conversion' therapy. This despite the fact that the religious (mainly the Orthodox) sector still retains strong principled and emotional objections to events such as the Gay Parade. The emerging questions touch on the level of the *nomos*—on the possibility of incorporating religious-Orthodox homosexuals and lesbians, and their families, including marital and parental agreements, in religious communities, and on the widening of the scope of discussion to include issues relating to religious transgenders (Irshai and Tzion-Waldoks forthcoming).

FERTILITY AND SEXUALITY

Of the divine commandments in Jewish tradition, childbearing is regarded as one of the most important. Rooted in the blessing bestowed on Adam and Eve jointly just after their creation: 'God blessed them and God said to them, "Be fertile and increase, fill the earth and master it..." ' (Gen. 1:28), by the Tannaitic period (late first to early third century CE), however, procreation had become an obligation imposed only on men (as distinct from a blessing applicable to both men and women). The profound importance of the commandment to reproduce is evidenced by the long list of Talmudic and post-Talmudic rabbinic discourses and statements on this point as well as its Halakhic implementation (Daube 1977; Gafni 1989; Boyarin 1993; Satlow 2001).

Nonetheless, a clash between the requirement to reproduce and a positive perception of sexuality is not inevitable. Indeed, one of the usual proofs tendered for the existence of a positive attitude towards sexuality in Judaism is the (Halakhic) distinction between the requirement to have conjugal relations in the marital context and the obligation to bear children (Biale 1992: 53–54).

As Feldman (1995) suggests, in order to understand Jewish attitudes towards fertility and family planning one must first consider the importance of marriage and marital sex. Although the main purpose of marriage is to fulfil the commandment of bringing children into the world, marriage does possess autonomous value and, as noted earlier, a husband is required to have regular sexual relations with his wife (the *onah* commandment).

To this we must add the Halakhic licence to have sexual relations during pregnancy and with infertile women, as well as the permission granted to women to use birth control in certain contexts. As long as these methods do not involve the forbidden destruction of semen, they are in principle permissible, on condition that the man has fulfilled the commandment of procreation (at least one son and one daughter) (Irshai 2012). Indeed, Biale (1992: 54) notes that it is possible that rabbinic thought did not distinguish between sexual pleasure and reproduction. Boyarin expands on and explains this statement. The usual Western dichotomy sees sexuality and reproduction as a 'contamination or a devaluing of sexuality, as if it were a purely instrumental approach to the body', or 'as repressive vis-à-vis Eros itself' (Boyarin 1993: 71). Modern culture has a strong tendency to separate sexuality for pleasure from sexuality for reproduction; in effect constructing two distinct bodies for them. Boyarin argues, however, 'it is that the split we make between desire and procreation is the continuance of the split between flesh and spirit for which Christianity was the vehicle of achieving hegemony in the West' (1993: 71). In contrast, rabbinic culture did not in his opinion separate sexuality and procreation, so that the essence of sexuality is the continued existence of the body, in conjunction with the understanding that this does not displace other values and purposes from the sexual act.

In this sense, the rabbinic interpretation is in harmony neither with medieval Christian theological conceptions regarding the sinfulness of the flesh, nor with modern discourse which responds to this duality by viewing the distinction between sex and procreation as sexual liberation, which, in effect maintains the distinction between the high value of sexual pleasure and opposes it to the utilitarian purpose of procreation. When pleasure becomes an essentially spiritual matter, then flesh and spirit remain divorced from each other. In this context Satlow (1995: 290–293) maintains that in the Babylonian Talmud women's pleasure is a valid rationale for marital relations within marriage, whereas the Palestinian Talmud justifies sexual relations using the rhetoric of procreation.

Even if we understand the primary Jewish obligation to procreate as not intrinsically neutralizing sexuality, its enhancement can lead to reduction of the independent valence of sexuality. But did the Halakhah, throughout its history, really maintain that understanding of the obligation to procreate? I suggest (Irshai 2012) that a careful reading of the Halakhic sources reflects a more balanced picture, a viewpoint that does not insist on the supremacy of procreation. Numerous Halakhic analyses aim to circumscribe rather than to broaden the scope of the commandment: some give weight to other values seen as no less important; others recognize different interests or needs that may arise during the course of a person's life. One nineteenth-century

Halakhic authority, Rabbi Yehiel Michel Epstein, suggests that the rabbinic commandment to procreate cannot trump all economic considerations; on the contrary, the ability to support additional children is clearly relevant to any decision to enlarge one's family and the welfare of the children who may be born must be considered. Finally, Epstein's ruling implies that the decision to have more children is a personal one—not only in the sense that it must be reached in light of an individual's concrete circumstances but also in the sense that there is no 'objective' test for assessing those circumstances (1992: *Even ha-ezer* 1:8).

In my opinion, however, an examination of recent Orthodox Halakhic decisions on fertility and procreation reveals the following picture: concerning abortion and birth control, the prevailing tendency is to rule strictly and to impose significant limitations on both. With respect, however, to artificial insemination, *in vitro* fertilization, and surrogacy, the prevailing tendency is towards marked leniency, to the point of disregarding some weighty ethical questions. This attitudinal contrast suggests an underlying ideology at work: if the rabbis tend to stringency in prohibiting 'sex without procreation' but to leniency in permitting 'procreation without sex', we can infer that they are ideologically committed to pronatalism, to promoting fertility and childbearing at almost any price. This tendency within hegemonic Halakhic trends has clear gender implications, especially its narrow view of a woman's role: to give birth and raise children, and not as full subjects (Irshai 2012).

Improper Emission of Seed and Male/Female Sexuality

The Jewish attitude towards male masturbation, especially in the context of fertility treatments that require production of semen other than through normal sexual relations, is an intriguing checkpoint for how the relationship between sexuality and procreation has been viewed in the past generation. A discussion of this relationship raises the question of the permissibility, according to Jewish law, of 'solitary' sex outside the marital context. If Judaism embraces a positive attitude towards sexuality, and procreation remains high on the scale of religious values, there is then no reason to assume that masturbation would be forbidden. This, however, is not the case.

Women's Sexuality

With respect to how women's sexuality and their ability to reach independent sexual satisfaction were constructed in rabbinic and later Halakhic literature, the scholarship is in its infancy. As a definitively male corpus, the Talmud does not provide substantive insight on this matter; nor does later Halakhic literature address much attention to the question of female masturbation. Meachem (2013) maintains that, given the almost total absence of women's voices in the Talmudic text, the rabbinic reliance on the male understanding of their bodies as the basis for understanding the female body led to the blurring of the sexual differences between them. The confusion between the female orgasm and the process of ovulation—of which the ancient rabbis were unaware—lies in their equation of male orgasm, which is equivalent to ejaculation, and female orgasm, also seen as involving emission of seed. Despite the fact that the Babylonian Talmud (Nid. 13a) states that women are not sexually aroused by the required post-menstruation vaginal checks for bleeding, some early authorities were concerned with the possibility that these internal examinations could result in sexual release. Nonetheless, because the female emission of seed is internal, it does not constitute the prohibited 'destruction of seed'; therefore, as seen in this light, there should be no obstacles to female masturbation.

At the same time, a recently published study (Englander and Sagi 2013) clearly demonstrates the problematic attitude of certain current branches of Orthodoxy towards the sexual female body. Although aware that from a formal Halakhic perspective female masturbation is not forbidden, these Orthodox rabbis view it as 'unnatural' because a woman's essence should be directed to the male other and not to the self. Their view of female sexuality is in relation to her partner and her inherent sexual satisfaction comes from pleasuring him. In line with this thinking, female masturbation is an invented modern sexuality and should therefore be opposed (Englander and Sagi 2013: 107).

Male Sexuality and Masturbation

This is not the case for men. For them, the prohibition against destruction of seed connected to autarkic sexuality is perceived as especially harsh. This can be understood, in my opinion, in a number of ways:

1. The reproductive approach. In this case, the law applies to the seed itself, making every non-procreative emission of semen wasted and therefore prohibited. It in turn allows for two possibilities:
   a. A strong reproductive approach, which places great emphasis on the value of the semen itself, forbidding any non-procreative sexual activity. In such instances, ejaculation will be seen as 'wasted seed' in the literal sense of the word, because it does not realize its unique purpose, which is to impregnate. Such an approach is difficult to identify in Jewish sources, although various historical analyses attest the existence of trends that, in response to sexual licentiousness, verged on such stringent attitudes (Yahalom 2011; Ta-Shma 1995).
   b. A weak reproductive approach, which stresses the value of the semen itself but weighs it against other values. According to this viewpoint, in the absence of reproductive ability the semen is not necessarily wasted even if it does not realize its procreative potential. Thus, if the sexual relations are

permitted and even desirable, ejaculation will be permissible in such a case. Alternatively, we can argue that if there is no systematic abstention from fulfilling the reproductive imperative, it may from time to time be permissible to ejaculate for non-procreative purposes.

2. The sexual approach views the law as applying to the proper sexual praxis, linking the prohibition against wasting seed to normative sexuality. The semen itself can at times be wasted, namely, not impregnate (even if there is reproductive potential), but it is the man's obligation to make certain that the ejaculation occurs only via 'correct' or 'desirable' practices and it is these that define the essence of the prohibition. In other words, proper sexual praxis may not be considered wasting of semen even if it does not lead to procreation. On the other hand, an incorrect practice may be considered wasting semen even if in practical terms it leads to reproduction (such as masturbating into a test tube for fertility treatments).

We can of course posit a link between these two distinctions. Perhaps some who place the emphasis on sexual praxis do so out of concern for reproduction. Thus, whereas masturbation and coitus interruptus may not be perceived as intrinsically problematic and even as permissible in some circumstances, their prohibition stems from their association with systematic abstention from procreation. That is, perhaps the control of sexuality is grounded in the desire to control procreation. If correct, this implies that the higher the value of the reproductive imperative on the ladder of priorities of the religious public and the greater its identification with this value, the less need will there be to control 'problematic' sexual activities (such as masturbation).

On the other hand, even where reproduction is a firm value, if there is intense concern with permissible sexual practices then the wasting of seed indeed belongs more to the category of forbidden sexuality than to that of abstention from reproduction. In this context Englander and Sagi (2013) show that, even though procreation ranks high on their ladder of religious values, the sexual discourse in certain sectors of contemporary Orthodox society in Israel (especially National Religious circles) seeks to control sexuality and grasps masturbation as an especially severe prohibition. They identify a dramatic shift in the nature of National Religious discourse, namely, a new preponderance of pastoral discourse on sexuality-related Halakhot, whereas confession or personal salvation are not part of the classic role of Halakhah. As they put it: 'Pastoral discourse invites creation, empowerment, and policing of the sexual subject itself. Because this discourse grants it legitimation through the conversation, it heightens sexuality' (Englander and Sagi 2013: 47–48). The strategies employed range from reduction of guilt feelings to criticism of modern values which place the 'I' and the body at the centre (2013: 56).

Returning to the Talmudic context, Satlow (1994) maintains that the prohibition against non-procreative ejaculation is later than the Talmudic stratum; Rosen-Zvi (1999) disagrees. In any event, the prohibition on wasted ejaculation of semen became, especially under the influence of mystical Jewish literature (Pachter 2006), one of the harshest prohibitions, leaving its imprint on the legal corpus as well. There is a Halakhic debate regarding the severity of the prohibition: some see it as a less stringent rabbinic provision only; others as harsher Pentateuchal law. This impacts both the question of permissible forms of contraception and modern fertility treatments (Irshai 2012).

With respect to fertility treatments, recent medical enhancements and the current possibility of detaching sexuality from procreation have thrown the question of the prohibition against wasting seed into sharper relief. As opposed to the lack of clarity in previous generations, the advent of more sophisticated contraceptive means obviates the need to equate contraception with the wasting of semen; also the development of fertilization technologies, *in vitro* fertilization in particular, invalidates the premise that the emission of semen outside a woman's body necessarily leads to abstention from procreation.

In this context, although some Halakhic approaches do not find use of masturbation in order to extract semen for the purpose of medical examination problematic, the more accepted approach—that of Rabbi Moshe Feinstein—permits extraction of semen for examination or test-tube insemination, but not through masturbation. Feinstein views the prohibition against masturbation as autonomous, separate from the prohibition against the destruction of seed, and equates it with adultery (1973–2011: *Even ha-Ezer* 3:14). There is however no doubt that, despite the profound Halakhic disputes regarding the severity of the prohibition against non-procreative ejaculation, some current Halakhic trends perceive the crude, threatening modern manifestations of sexuality as a harsh danger; therefore, without reference to reproduction, they attempt to channel sexuality to established paths within the institution of heterosexual marriage.

Conclusion

This chapter has traced the emergence of new foci—sex, body, and gender—and new approaches—feminist critique and gender study—in the field of Judaic studies, starting in the 1990s. These new perspectives have engendered fresh bodies of knowledge and insights, with respect to rabbinic thought in particular. Regarding sexuality and gender in modern Halakhic literature and modern Jewish theological trends, the scholarship is still in its early stages. I have attempted to exemplify how the Halakhic discourses within the different streams of Judaism, which embody theological approaches that respond to new trends in sexuality and gender, will inform future research. These still await systematic analysis, both in relation to rabbinic thought and to each other with regard to their legal and practical-ethical implications. Overall, a closer examination of the Jewish attitudes towards sexuality, in light of the new scholarship, leads to the conclusion that despite the fact that Judaism indeed affirms sexuality, this should not be grasped in a simple, superficial, or monolithic fashion. As Biale and Boyarin have shown, the Jewish attitude towards sexuality and gender, and its theological ramifications, is more complicated, nuanced, and dialectical than its representations within the older scholarship.

References

Adler, R. (1983). 'The Jew Who Wasn't There: Halakha and the Jewish Woman'. In S. Heschel (ed.), *On Being a Jewish Feminist: A Reader*, New York: Schocken, 12–18.

Adler, R. (1998). *Engendering Judaism: An Inclusive Theology and Ethics*. Jerusalem and Philadelphia: Jewish Publication Society.

Adler, R. (2001). 'Innovation and Authority: A Feminist Reading of the Women's Minyan "Responsum"'. In W. Jacob and M. Zemer (eds), *Gender Issues in Jewish Law*, New York: Berghahn, 3–32.

Aiken, L. (1992). *To Be a Jewish Woman*. Northvale, NJ: J. Aronson.

Alpert, R. (1997). *Like Bread on the Seder Plate: Jewish Lesbians and the Transformation of Tradition*. New York: Columbia University Press.

Baker, C. M. (2002). *Rebuilding the House of Israel: Architectures of Gender in Jewish Antiquity*. Stanford, CA: Stanford University Press.

Balka, C., and Rose, A. (1989) (eds). *Twice Blessed: On Being Lesbian, Gay, and Jewish*. Boston: Beacon.

Baskin, J. R. (2002). *Midrashic Women: Formations of the Feminine in Rabbinic Literature*. Hanover, NH: University Press of New England for Brandeis University Press.

Beck, E. T. (ed.) (1982). *Nice Jewish Girls: A Lesbian Anthology*. Watertown, MA: Persephone.

Biale, D. (1992). *Eros and the Jews: From Biblical Israel to Contemporary America*. New York: Basic Books.

Biale, D. (1994). *Eros and the Jews*. Trans. Carmit Guy. Tel Aviv: Am Oved (in Hebrew).

Boyarin, D. (1993). *Carnal Israel: Reading Sex in Talmudic Culture*. Berkeley and Los Angeles: University of California Press.

Boyarin, D. (1997). *Unheroic Conduct: The Rise of Heterosexuality and the Invention of the Jewish Man*. Berkeley and Los Angeles: University of California Press.

Daube, D. (1977). *The Duty of Procreation*. Edinburgh: Edinburgh University Press.

Debow, Y. (2009). 'Sexuality among Modern Orthodox Teenage Girls in Israel: A Study of the Effects of an Educational Intervention'. PhD thesis (Bar-Ilan University, Ramat Gan).

Englander, Y., and Sagi, A. (2013). *The New Religious-Zionist Discourse on Body and Sexuality*. Jerusalem: Shalom Hartman Institute (in Hebrew).

Epstein, Y. M. (1992). *Arukh ha-shulhan*, 8 vols. Jerusalem: Hamosad leidud limud hatorah (in Hebrew).

Ettinger, Y. (2010). 'Dozens of Orthodox Rabbis Penned a Manifesto Calling for Recognition of Homosexuals and Lesbians'. *Ha-aretz*, 29 July. <http://www.haaretz.co.il/news/education/1.121433> (accessed 10 July 2013) (in Hebrew).

Feinstein, M. (1973–2011). *Igrot Moshe*, 9 vols. New York: privately printed (in Hebrew).

Feldman, D. M. (1995). *Birth Control in Jewish Law: Marital Relations, Contraception, and Abortion as Set Forth in the Classic Texts of Jewish Law*, 3rd edn. New York: New York University Press.

Fisher, E. (2009). 'The Ethos of "Female Modesty" in Rabbinic Literature: Between the Woman's Obligation to Conceal Her Body and the Male Prohibition against Looking'. Master's thesis (Bar-Ilan University, Ramat Gan) (in Hebrew).

Fonrobert, C. E. (2000). *Menstrual Purity: Rabbinic and Christian Reconstructions of Biblical Gender*. Stanford, C: Stanford University Press.

Fonrobert, C. E. (2007). 'Regulating the Human Body: Rabbinic Legal Discourse and the Making of Jewish Gender'. In Fonrobert (ed.), *The Cambridge Companion to the Talmud and Rabbinic Literature*. Cambridge: Cambridge University Press, 270–294.

Gafni, I. M. (1989). 'The Institution of Marriage in Rabbinic Times'. In D. C. Kraemer (ed.), *The Jewish Family: Metaphor and Memory*. New York: Oxford University Press, 13–30.

Greenberg, B. (1981). *On Women and Judaism*. Philadelphia: Jewish Publication Society.

Greenberg, S. (2004). *Wrestling with God and Men: Homosexuality in the Jewish Tradition*. Madison: University of Wisconsin Press.

Hartman, T. (2007). 'Modesty and the Religious Male Gaze'. In T. Hartman, *Feminism Encounters Traditional Judaism: Resistance and Accommodation*. Waltham, MA: Brandeis University Press, 45–61.

Hauptman, J. (1998). *Rereading the Rabbis: A Woman's Voice*. Boulder, CO: Westview.

Irshai, R. (2010). 'Towards a Gender-Critical Approach to the Philosophy of Jewish Law (Halakhah)'. *Journal of Feminist Studies in Religion*, 26(2): 55–77.

Irshai, R. (2012). *Fertility and Jewish Law: Feminist Perspectives on Orthodox Responsa Literature*. Waltham, MA: Brandeis University Press.

Irshai, R. (forthcoming). 'Halakhic Discretion and Gender Bias: A Conceptual Analysis'. *Democratic Culture* (in English and in Hebrew).

Irshai, R., and Tzion-Waldoks, T. (forthcoming). 'Modern Orthodox Feminism in Israel: Between Nomos and Narrative'. In *Law and Governance* (in Hebrew).

Kirshenblatt-Gimblett, B. (2005). 'The Corporeal Turn'. *Jewish Quarterly Review*, 95: 447–461.

Koren, I. (2003). *Altering the Closet*. Tel-Aviv: Yediot Aharonot (in Hebrew).

Labinsky, E. et al. (2009). 'Observant Married Jewish Women and Sexual Life: An Empirical Study'. *Conversations*, 5. <http://www.jewishideas.org/articles/observant-married-jewish-w omen-and-sexual-life-empi> (accessed 2 July 2013).

Lamm, N. (1974). 'Judaism and the Modern Attitude to Homosexuality'. In L. I. Rabinowitz (ed.), *Encyclopedia Judaica Year Book*. Jerusalem: Keter, 194–205.

Leibowitz, Y. (1999). *I Wanted to Ask You, Prof. Leibowitz: Letters to and from Yeshayahu Leibowitz*. Jerusalem: Keter, 178–179 (in Hebrew).

Lubitz, R. (1996). 'The Jewish Stance on Homosexual Relations and Guidelines for Its Didactic Realization'. *Mayim mi-delayav*, 233–251 (in Hebrew).

Maimonides. (1972). *The Code of Maimonides: Book Four. The Book of Women*. New Haven and London: Yale University Press.

Matt, H. J. (1987). 'Homosexual Rabbis?' *Conservative Judaism*, 39(3): 29–33.

Meachem, T. (2013). '"Women Are Not Sensitive": On Sexual Stimulus in Halakhic Writings'. In T. Cohen (ed.), *To Be A Jewish Woman—Contemporary Feminist-Religious Discourse*. Jerusalem: Kolech and Reuven Mas Publishing, 153–171 (in Hebrew).

Ozick, C. (1983). 'Notes toward Finding the Right Question'. In S. Heschel (ed.), *On Being a Jewish Feminist: A Reader*. New York: Schocken, 120–151.

Pachter, S. (2006). 'Shmirat Habrit: The History of the Prohibition of Wasting Seed'. PhD thesis (Hebrew University, Jerusalem) (in Hebrew).

Plaskow, J. (1991). *Standing Again at Sinai*. 2nd edn. New York: Harper.

Prins, M. (2011). 'The Coping of Orthodox Women with Body and Sexuality after Marriage'. MA thesis (Bar-Ilan University, Ramat Gan) (in Hebrew).

Ribner, D. S., and Rosenbaum, T. Y. (2005). 'Evaluation and Treatment of Unconsummated Marriage among Orthodox Jewish Couples'. *Journal of Sex and Marital Therapy*, 31: 341–353.

Rosen-Zvi, I. (1999). 'The Evil Inclination, Sexuality, and Prohibitions against Men and Women Being Alone (Yihud): A Chapter in Talmudic Anthropology'. *Theory and Criticism*, 14: 55–84 (in Hebrew).

Rosen-Zvi, I. (2000). 'Do Women Possess Yetzer? Anthropology, Ethics, and Gender in Rabbinic Literature'. In H. Kreisel, B. Huss, and U. Ehrlich (eds), *Spiritual Authority: Struggles over Cultural Power in Jewish Thought*. Beer Sheva: Ben Gurion University, 21–33 (in Hebrew).

Rosen-Zvi, I. (2009). 'Sexualising the Evil Inclination: Rabbinic "Yetzer" and Modern Scholarship'. *Journal of Jewish Studies*, 60(2): 264–281.

Rosen-Zvi, I. (2012). *The Mishnaic Sotah Ritual: Temple, Gender and Midrash*. Leiden: Brill.

Ross, T. (2011). 'The Feminist Contribution to Halakhic Considerations: Qol be-ishah ervah as a Test Case'. In A. Rosenak (ed.), *Philosphy of Halakhah: Halakhah, Meta-Halakhah and Philosophy: A Multi Disciplinary Perspective*. Jerusalem: Magnes, 35–64 (in Hebrew).

Ross, T. (forthcoming). 'The Current Halakhic Status of Homosexuals: A Test Case'. In A. Rosenak (ed.), *Proceedings of the Conference on 'Halakhah as an Event: New Trends in the Study of the Philosophy of Halakhah'*, Van Leer Institute (in Hebrew).

Rothstein, G. (2010). 'Should Orthodox Homosexuals Be Encouraged to Marry?' *Hirhurim—Musings*, 22 August. <http://torahmusings.com/2010/08/homosexuality-and-marriage> (accessed 3 July 2013).

Satlow, M. L. (1994). '"Wasted Seed": The History of a Rabbinic Idea'. *Hebrew Union College Annual*, 65: 137–175.

Satlow, M. L. (1995). *Tasting the Dish: Rabbinic Rhetorics of Sexuality*. Atlanta, GA: Scholars Press.

Satlow, M. L. (2001). *Jewish Marriage in Antiquity*. Princeton: Princeton University Press.

Shneer, D., and Aviv, C. (2002) (eds), *Queer Jews*. New York: Routledge.

Spero, M. H. (1979). 'Homosexuality: Clinical and Ethical Challenges'. *Tradition*, 17(4): 53–73.

Ta-Shma, I. M. (1995). *Ha-Nigle She-Banistar: The Halachic Residue in the Zohar*. Tel Aviv: Hakibbutz Hameuchad, 35 (in Hebrew).

Wegner, J. R. (1988). *Chattel or Person? The Status of Women in the Mishnah*. New York: Oxford University Press.

Weiss, S. (2009). 'Under Cover: Demystification of Women's Head Covering in Jewish Law'. *Nashim*, 17: 89–115.

Yahalom, S. (2011). 'Moch: Family Planning in the Jewish Communities of France and Catalonia in the Middle Ages', *Pe'amim*, 128: 99–162 (in Hebrew).

Yosef, O. (1977–1980). *Responsa: Yehaveh Da'at*, 6 vols. Jerusalem: Alefbet Press.

CHAPTER 26

···

ISLAM

···

ASMA BARLAS

FOR believers, sacred knowledge has the power to shape both their perceptions of God and of themselves, which is why 'a culture's idea of divinity is central not only to that culture's religious life but also to its social, political, familial institutions and relationships' (Bennett 1989: 7). For instance, by sexualizing and engendering God, religions can also authorize male privilege, and even the oppression of women, since 'the source of ultimate value is often described in anthropomorphic images as Father or King' (Bynum 1986: 1). In light of this, I will begin my chapter on Islamic and, specifically Qur'anic, perspectives on theology, sexuality, and gender with an overview of its depictions of God.

GOD BEYOND SEX AND GENDER

···

Knowing something of God's self-disclosure in the Qur'an is also necessary for understanding my own hermeneutical approach to the text, which I read as being anti-patriarchal. I define patriarchy as a continuum at one end of which is the historical tradition of father-rule that draws on the imaginary of God-the-Father in some of its religious iterances. At the other end, is a politics of sexual differentiation that transforms 'biological sex into politicized gender, which prioritizes the male while making the woman different (unequal),[1] less than, or the "Other"' (Eisenstein 1990: 90). The Qur'an, I will argue, does not support either form of patriarchy and I will start by examining its repudiation of a 'patriarchalized' God as well as of father-rule.

God, says the Qur'an, is one, uncreated, and incomparable. Of the many verses to this effect, the main one, which comprises a *surah*, or chapter, by itself, proclaims:

> Say: [God] is God
> The One and Only;

[1] In some of her later work, Eisenstein concedes that difference does not mean inequality.

God, the Eternal, Absolute;
He begetteth not,
Nor is He begotten;
And there is none
Like unto Him.

(112: in Ali 1988: 1806)

In spite of its own references to God as 'He' and 'Him', the Qur'an prohibits using similitude for God, suggesting that its masculinizations of God are a function of the Arabic language rather than statements about God's being. However, even though the principle of divine incomparability attests that God is unlike anything created, thus also beyond sex or gender, Muslims continue to map some sort of gender symbolism onto God. For instance, classical theology (*kalam*) refers to God in masculinist terms as lord and king whereas Sufism tends to highlight God's 'feminine' attributes. These contrasting depictions originate in the ninety-nine divine names in the Qur'an (the just, the loving, the compeller, the subtle, and so on) as do the four 'Creator models'—the Qur'anic, the mystical, the allegorical, and the neo-Platonic—that Muslims have used historically to depict 'their one God' (Netton 1989: 2). The Qur'an itself, however, does not classify any divine (or human) attribute as being masculine or feminine.

Significantly, masculinizations of God never shade into representations of God as father since the Qur'an strictly forbids Muslims to call God that, in both a literal and a metaphorical sense. Thus, while it refers to the virgin birth of Jesus, it also says Jesus was an apostle who forbade both his own deification and also any sacralization of God as father. Those who allege otherwise, it states, are 'In blasphemy indeed' (5.19: in Ali 1988: 246–247). Another verse rejects the doctrine of Trinitarianism since 'God is One God: Glory be to [God] (Far Exalted is [God]) above Having a son' (4.171: in Ali 1988: 234). How 'can [God] have a son When [God] hath no consort?' asks the Qur'an (6.100–101: in Ali 1988: 319). Along the same lines, it says that those Jews who call the prophet Uzair God's son are 'deluded Away from the Truth'(9.30: in Ali 1988: 448).

Not only is God not a literal father, but God is not a symbolic father also. In response to those Jews and Christians who call themselves 'sons of God, and His beloved', the Qur'an instructs the Prophet Muhammad to ask, 'Why then doth [God] Punish you for your sins? Nay, ye are but men,—Of the men [God] hath created" (5.20: in Ali 1988: 247). As for the polytheists, says the Qur'an, they 'falsely, Having no knowledge, Attribute to [God] Sons and daughters. Praise and glory be To [God Who] is above What they attribute to [God]!' (6.100–101: in Ali 1988: 319). When another verse condemns them for saying God has only daughters, it is not because girls are less worthy than sons, but because God rejects the trope of fatherhood altogether. And, as the Qur'an points out, the polytheists assign to God 'What they hate (for themselves)' (16.62: in Ali 1988: 672).

OPPOSITION TO 'FATHER-RULE'

These categorical rejections of the patriarchal imaginary of God-the-Father make it impossible to ascribe readings of Islam as a patriarchy to its idea of the divine. For, if God is not a patriarch then there is no *theological* model on which father-rule can draw in Islam. To make a more radical claim, if God is not a patriarch, then God's speech (the Qur'an) may not be patriarchal either since there is a coherence between divine ontology and discourse; that is, between who (we believe) God *is* and what (we believe) God *says*. It is partly on this basis that I describe the Qur'an's *episteme* as anti-patriarchal (Barlas 2002). Partly, however, my characterization stems from its pointed attacks on following 'the ways of the fathers', which reads like an unmistakable reference to traditional patriarchy.

Several instances in the Qur'an illustrate this conflict between adhering to one's father's beliefs and heeding God's messages. For example, when Moses calls on Pharaoh to turn to God, his subjects mockingly ask if he has 'Come to us to turn us Away from the ways We found our fathers following?' (10.78: in Ali 1988: 504). In the Qur'anic—as in the Biblical—account, it is their rejection of God's call that leads God to drown Pharaoh and his people in the end. In a similar vein, God rebukes those Arabs of the Prophet's times (the Qur'an was revealed to him in the seventh century), who turn a deaf ear to him:

> When it is said to them:
> 'Come to what God
> Hath revealed; come
> To the Apostle:'
> They say: 'Enough for us
> Are the ways we found
> Our fathers following.'
> What! even though their fathers
> Were void of knowledge
> And guidance?
>
> (5.107: in Ali 1988: 275)

Although the Qur'an tells the Prophet that his task is only to convey God's message, not to oblige compliance to it, this verse disparages people who cling unquestioningly to patriarchal custom. However, the most explicit expression of the Qur'an's opposition to father-rule is to be found in the story of Abraham's life, which is in two parts. The first involves Abraham's confrontation with his father, a confrontation he himself instigates by calling his father's beliefs into question:

> Behold! he said
> To his father and his people
> 'What are these images,
> To which ye are
> (So assiduously) devoted?'

> They said: 'We found
> Our fathers worshipping them.'
> He said, 'Indeed ye
> Have been in manifest
> Error—ye and your fathers'.

(21.51–56: in Ali 1988: 834)

Their quarrel escalates after Abraham breaks most of the idols his father worships, which, he says, 'heareth not And seeth not, and can Profit thee nothing,' and then urges him,

> O my father! to me
> Hath come knowledge which
> Hath not reached thee:
> *So follow me: I will guide*
> *Thee* to a Way that
> Is even and straight.

(19.43: in Ali 1988: 776,
emphasis added)

This sequence of events attests that it is Abraham's faith in God that not only leads him to destroy his father's deities but also to break with his father's authority. In fact, in a stark reversal of patriarchal traditions, Abraham then presses his father to follow *his* lead in turning to God. For his transgressions, his father has him thrown into a fire from which God rescues him, much as God rescues Abraham's son from *him* years later.

The story about Abraham's near sacrifice of his son is very different, of course, but it also reveals the Qur'an's resistance to father-rule, even if the father in question is a prophet. Thus, although it is read as confirming Abraham's status as a patriarch, the scriptural account of the sacrifice lends itself to exactly the opposite reading:

> He said, 'I am going to my Lord; He will guide me. My Lord, give me one of the right-eous.' Then We gave him the good tidings of a prudent boy; and when he had reached the age of running with him, he said, 'My son, I see in a dream that I shall sacrifice thee; *consider, what thinkest thou?*' He said, 'My father, do as thou art bidden; thou shalt find me, God willing, one of the steadfast.' When they had surrendered, and he flung him upon his brow, We called unto him, 'Abraham, thou has confirmed the vision; even so We recompense the good-doers. This is indeed the manifest trial.'

(37: 99–105: in Arberry 1955: 153–154, emphasis added)

This tantalizingly minimalist narrative attests that, unlike the Biblical Abraham (and his own father), Abraham does not exercise absolute authority over his son. Not only does he not set out to kill an unsuspecting or unwilling son, but he *asks* him what he makes of Abraham's own dream. It is only when the son also interprets it literally and agrees to his sacrifice that both father and son embark on it only to have God call them off. Abraham's authority as a father is thus subject both to his son's moral choices and to God's will and it is this subordination of the father's rights to God's will (Islamic monotheism) that I believe poses an 'insoluble... contradiction' in the Qur'an (Derrida[2] in Barlas 2011: 58).

Numerous other verses emphasize that accountability to God—God's rights over believers—takes precedence over one's parents' rights. For instance: 'Be ever steadfast in upholding equity, bearing witness to the truth for the sake of God, even though it be against your own selves or your parents and kinfolk' (4.135: in Asad 1980: 130). An even more direct command is

> 'Show gratitude
> To Me and to thy parents:
> To Me is (thy final) Goal.'
> But if they strive
> To make thee join
> In worship with Me
> Things of which thou hast
> No knowledge, then *obey them not*;
> Yet bear them company
> In this life with justice
> (And consideration), and follow
> The way of those who
> Turn to Me (in love):
> In the End the return
> Of you all is to Me.'
>
> (31.14–15: in Ali 1988: 1083,
> emphasis added)

This is the context in which the Qur'an warns Muslims to 'fear (The coming of) a Day When no father can avail Aught for his son, nor A son avail aught For his father' (31.33: in Ali 1988: 1089). In the end, each individual can only bear their own burdens and only be their own witnesses. It is this approach to ethical/moral individuality that I will now consider, along with the Qur'an's teachings about human creation, ontology, and sexuality, as a way to explore its attitude towards the second form of patriarchy.

SEX/GENDER, CREATION, AND MORAL INDIVIDUALITY

Some feminists criticize 'patriarchal religions' for treating biological differences between men and women as explaining the 'psycho-social distinctions' between them,

---

[2] Derrida is referring to the Biblical Abraham in a very different context. See Barlas (2011).

and for regarding these as evidence of their inequality (Millett 1970: 26). In fact, not just religious, but also secular, patriarchies confuse sex (biology) with gender (the social meanings ascribed to sex and sexual difference), claiming that women's biology renders them deficient in reasoning and morality and therefore hostile to civilization (Hewitt 1995: 64). Such views then lead to treating the man as a 'constituting Cartesian subject' and the woman as his 'other' (Hekman 1990: 79). It is these tendencies that I define cumulatively as the second mode of patriarchy and which, I will argue, the Qur'an does not support, since it does not espouse a view of sexual differentiation that privileges males.

ONTOLOGICAL EQUALITY

The most significant Qur'anic teaching which demonstrates that sexual equality in Islam is ontological is that God created women and men from a single self:

> Reverence
> Your [Creator], Who created you
> From a single *Nafs*[3]
> Created, of like nature,
> (its) *zawaj* [mate] and from them twain
> Scattered (like seeds)
> Countless men and women;—
> Reverence God, through Whom
> Ye demand your mutual (rights).

(4.1: in Ali 1988: 178)

Several other verses allude to the ontological identity of men and women, for instance, 'It is [God] Who hath Produced you From a single person' (6.98: in Ali 1988: 317); 'And among [God's] Signs Is this, that [God] created for You mates from among Yourselves, that ye may Dwell in tranquillity *[sukun]* with them' (30:21: in Ali 1988: 1056); and, most notably,

> O [human!] We created
> You from a single (pair)
> Of a male and a female,
> And made you into
> Nations and tribes, that
> Ye may know each other
> (Not that ye may despise
> Each other). Verily
> The most honoured of you

[3] *Nafs* is feminine plural.

> In the sight of God
> Is ([the one] who is) the most
> Virtuous of you.

> (49.13: in Ali 1988: 1407)

In other words, the Qur'an does not sexualize, or pathologize, differences. Nor do gender distinctions play much of a role in its creation narrative. Thus, more often than not, it uses generic terms to refer to creation, like 'an-nas', 'al-insan', and 'bashar', and where it refers to Adam, it does so in twenty-one out of twenty-five cases to designate not a male but humanity. As Riffat Hassan (1999: 345) notes, the word 'Adam' derives from the Hebrew 'Adamah', which simply means 'of the soil'. More importantly, she says, none of these verses can be 'interpreted as asserting or suggesting that man was created prior to woman or that woman was created from man. In fact there are some passages which could—from a purely grammatical/linguistic point of view—be interpreted as stating that the first creation (*nafs in wahidatin*) was feminine, not masculine!' (Hassan 1999: 345)

In brief, then, the Qur'an does not share the view ascribed by some Christian feminists to the Old Testament that 'man is not out of woman but rather woman out of man. Because also man was not created for the sake of the woman, but rather woman for the sake of the man' (in Ali 1991: 206). According to feminists, it is Eve's derivative status and her role in the Fall that explains the 'otherising' of women in some Christian traditions. There is, however, no 'hierarchy of being'[4] in the Qur'an since it does not say that the woman was created from the man or that she is inferior to him; nor that priority of creation establishes superiority since Satan was created before humans and is not, for that reason, better than them! Also, with 'one exception, the Qur'an always uses the Arabic dual form to tell how Satan tempted both Adam and [his spouse] and how they both disobeyed [God]; this much is clear: woman is never singled out as the initiator or temptress of evil' (Wadud 1999: 25).

MORAL INDIVIDUALITY

The Qur'an's depiction of moral individuality/personality also does not suggest that men, whether in their biological capacities as males or in their social roles as fathers or husbands, are better equipped than women to cultivate it. To the contrary, it holds them to the same standards of behaviour, judges them by the same criteria, and often addresses them in the same terms as well:

> For believing men and women,
> For devout men and women,

---

[4] This is how Margaret Hodgen (1964) refers to the Bible's account of creation.

For men and women who are
Patient and constant, for men
And women who humble themselves,
For men and women who give
In charity, for men and women
Who fast (and deny themselves).
For men and women who
Guard their chastity, and
For men and women who
Engage much in God's praise,
For them has God prepared
Forgiveness and great reward.

(33.35: in Ali 1988: 1116–1117)

In other words, the Qur'an does not associate 'moral voice with gender'[5] which is also clear from the fact that it calls men and women God's vice-regents (*khilafa*) on earth and one another's *awliya*, who have parallel and mutual obligations:

The Believers, men
And women, are [*awliya*],
One of another: they enjoin
What is just, and forbid
What is evil: they observe
Regular prayers, practice
Regular charity, and obey
God and [God's] Apostle.
On them will God pour
[God's] mercy: for God
Is exalted in power, Wise.

(9171–72: in Ali 1988: 461)

Awliya, often translated as 'protectors', has a deeper meaning, which is that women and men are 'guides or in charge of one another', a mutuality they can express in 'actions that cover the whole spectrum of existence' (Davies 1988: 84). Indeed, this mutual care and guardianship is essential for nurturing a moral personality. But guardianship also has a negative side for the Qur'an additionally refers to the hypocrites as 'the men and the women, [who] (Have an understanding) with each other: They enjoin evil, and forbid What is just, and are close With their hands' (9.67: in Ali 1988: 459–60).

---

[5] I borrow this phrase from Carol Gilligan (1988: ii).

In the Qur'an, then, the basic distinction is between "'the believers" and the "unbelievers." In all the perspectives of Islamic life and thought people are separated into groups according to the degree to which they fulfil the purpose of life' (Murata 1992: 44). There is no scriptural narrative to the effect that the two sexes are unequal, incompatible, or incommensurable, or that women are inferior to men. In fact, there is 'no *concept* of woman' or of 'gendered man' in the Qur'an (Wadud 1999: xxi, emphasis original). This is because it does not locate gender dimorphisms in sex. That is, while it recognizes the biological differences between men and women (and thus their sexual specificity), the Qur'an does not ascribe any symbolism to sex itself.

The Qur'an and Sex/Uality

Sex, argues Jeffrey Weeks (1985: 16), is 'a transmission belt for wider social anxieties, and a focus of struggles over power, one of the prime sites in truth where domination and subordination are defined and expressed.' Ancient societies, for instance, associated women with sex because of their allegedly 'carnivorous' sexuality which, they feared, could 'threaten male order, male life and sanity' (Padel 1993: 3–4). Women were thus not only forced to veil and seclude themselves but were also subjected to heinous forms of violence (Ahmed 1992). The view that sex is 'an overpowering force which the social/moral/medical [*sic*] has to control' (Weeks 1985: 8) has endured over time and is also evident in how patriarchal religions treat it. Some feminists, for instance, claim that Christianity also considers sex 'unclean, sinful, and debilitating' and tends to 'lump the female and sex together as if the whole burden of the onus and stigma [attached] to sex were the fault of the female alone' (Millett 1970: 51). Although most Muslims also hold such views, the Qur'an does not make pejorative claims about sex or associate it with women. And, while it seeks to regulate sex, it approaches the sexual needs, desires, and actions of men and women without always differentiating between them.

Desire, Chastity, and Sex

The Qur'an often addresses sex and desire indirectly as, for instance, when it says God 'created for you helpmeets from yourselves that ye might find *sukun* in them, and [God] ordained between you love and mercy' (30.21: in Pickthall, n.d.: 291). Some translators interpret *sukun* as love, but others argue that it evokes the sense of mental peace that ensues from a sense of sexual fulfilment (Mir 1987). Whatever its exact meaning, the Qur'an signals that mutual love and satisfaction should be the basis of a marriage, a rather revolutionary idea in the seventh century. So, too, is its view that women and men are not all that different in their sexual needs or conduct. A number of passages convey this sentiment, including those that deal with the all-important issue of sexual purity and impurity:

> Women impure are for men impure
> And men impure for women impure.
> And women of purity
> Are for men of purity,
> And men of purity
> Are for women of purity.

(24.26: in Ali 1991: 902)

Although there is an equivalence between women and men (the pure are for the pure and the impure for the impure), (im)purity does not have to do with a person's sex, but with their conduct. And the conduct the Qur'an considers pure or chaste depends on the context. In some cases, it involves sexual abstinence: in others, it means not engaging in extra-marital sex (fornication); and in yet others, it means avoiding lustful and lewd actions in a marriage. Thus, for instance, the Qur'an declares that 'lawful' to men

> Are (not only) chaste women
> Who are believers, but
> Chaste women among
> The People of the Book [Jews and Christians]—
> Revealed before your time,—
> When ye give them
> Their due dowers, and desire
> Chastity, not lewdness
> Nor secret intrigues.

(5.6 in Ali 1991: 241–242)

Notably, not just Muslim, but, also Jewish and Christian women can be chaste and men, too, must behave chastely. This is a critical directive since another verse (2.223) appears to give them a licence to treat their wives as they want because their wives are their sexual 'property':

> They question thee (O Muhammad) concerning menstruation. Say: it is an *adan* so let women alone at such times and go not in unto them till they are cleansed. And when they have purified themselves, then go in unto them *as Allah hath enjoined upon you*. Truly Allah loveth those who turn unto [Allah] and loveth those who have a care for cleanness. Your women are a *harth* for you (to cultivate)[6] so go to your *harth* as ye will, and send (good deeds) before you for your souls, and fear Allah, and know that ye will (one day) meet [Allah].

(2.222–23: in Pickthall, n.d. 53, emphasis added)

[6] This is Pickthall's (n.d.) interpolation since it is not in the Arabic text. I use different translations of the Qur'an depending on how closely they are thought to approximate to its meanings in Arabic.

The root meanings of *adan*, the word used to define menstruation, are 'damage, harm, injury, trouble, annoyance, and grievance' (Cowan 1976: 12). Significantly, *adan* does not mean pollution and nor does the Qur'an call menstruating *women* polluting. Its reference to cleanliness is also not atypical since all believers are required to cleanse after calls of nature and sexual intercourse. As for '*harth*,' which is translated as tilth (also, as tillage and harvest), it cannot mean property for a number of reasons. First, the Qur'an does not designate any human being as another person's property, even when dealing with the vexed issue of slavery; there is, therefore, no reason to think it would consider wives as property. Indeed, this would go against the grain not only of the marriage contract—which is a contract between legal equals—but also the entirety of the Qur'an's teachings on marriage summarized thus far. Second, there was no concept of landed property in the seventh century and the Qur'an would not have used *harth* to refer to it since it would have meant nothing to its first audience. In fact, it is questionable that *harth* even means land in a literal sense if we look at how the Qur'an uses the term in other contexts. For instance,

> To any that desires
> The *harth* of the Hereafter,
> We give increase
> In his *harth*; and to any
> That desires the *harth*
> Of this world, We grant
> Somewhat thereof, but he
> Has no share or lot
> In the Hereafter.

> (42.20: in Ali 1991: 1311)

Since neither this world nor the next are in the nature of land or property, *harth* is merely a metaphor for something else, both in this verse and in 2:223. (In fact, most classical exegetes took it as an allusion to sowing, that is, to vaginal sex.) Lastly, the reference to 'what Allah hath enjoined,' can be read narrowly as having sex *after* menstruation, since that is what the preceding sentence recommends. Or, it can be read more broadly as adhering to other Qur'anic teachings about spousal relationships that emphasize love and *sukun* and prohibit coarse and vulgar behaviour. If one keeps all these principles in mind, then the permission to husbands to go into their wives is not as open-ended as it seems.

POLYGYNY

Paradoxically, it is the Qur'an's conception of polygyny which reveals that it does not view marriage as catering just to men's sexual needs. While the practice of marrying many wives predates Islam (among the Hebrews, for instance, some were also polygynous), the Qur'an restricted it in specific ways. There are, incidentally, only two verses on the subject and both are directed to the guardians of female orphans:

Give the orphans their property, and do not exchange the corrupt for the good [i.e., your worthless things for their good ones]; and devour not their property with your property; surely that is a great crime. If you fear that you will not act justly towards the orphans, marry such women as seem good to you, two, three, four; but if you fear you will not be equitable, then only one, *[aw]* what your right hands own;[7] so it is likelier you will not be partial.

(4.1: in Arberry 1955: 100)

In other words, polygyny is not the inalienable right of all Muslim men but only *those* who are charged with the care of female orphans. Then, too, not all of these have the right to marry multiple wives but only *those* who fear they will not be able to treat their wards justly outside of the marriage tie. This implies that polygyny is restricted *to* the orphans, a reading the second verse also bears out. God's will, it says, 'is being conveyed unto you through this divine writ about orphan women [in your charge], to whom—*because you yourselves may be desirous of marrying them*—you do not give that which has been ordained for them' (4.127: in Asad 1980: 129, emphasis added).

Both verses, then, are warning guardians not to short-change their wards and both mention polygyny only in relation to *orphans*, thus restricting it further. Finally, the Qur'an says that since a man is unlikely to treat all his wives equally, he should marry just one. (Monogamy, it should be noted, was not the dominant form of marriage in seventh-century Arabia.) Polygyny, as the Qur'an conceives of it, therefore, is not meant to accommodate men's sexual needs or their desire to produce male heirs; it is simply a way to secure the interests of female orphans. The gap between this egalitarian scriptural vision and the lurid history of Muslim harems is too obvious to belabour.

FEMALE BODIES AND VEILING

So far, nothing has been said about the Qur'an's attitude towards the female body, specifically, whether it considers it to be pudendal and corrupting, and orders it to be veiled in order to protect men's sexual piety. Tellingly, there are only two sets of verses on the 'veil', both of which address the Prophet:

> O Prophet! Tell
> Thy wives and daughters,
> And the believing women,
> That they should cast
> Their *[jilbab]* over

---

[7] A reference to war captives and slaves who were part of the structure of Arabia in the seventh century and for whose emancipation and equitable treatment the Qur'an made provisions.

Their persons (when abroad)
That is most convenient,
That they should be known
[as free women, not slaves] and not molested
[by the] Hypocrites,
And those in whose hearts
Is a disease, and those who
Stir up sedition in the City [al-Madina].

(33.59–60:, in Ali 1988: 1126–27)

These are rather straightforward verses: if Muslim women don an outer garment (*jilbab*), *non-Muslim* men will recognize them as such and not harass them. In early slave-owning societies, like Arabia, the 'law of the veil' set apart free women from slaves and therefore women who were off-limits from those who 'were fair game' (Lerner in Ahmed 1992: 15). This was the society in which the first Muslim community took shape and it seems to have been under siege at the time. It should be noted that the verses do not mention women's bodies or call into question either their virtue or that of Muslim men. The second verse, on the other hand, deals squarely with how Muslim men and women should dress and behave in public, and it asks the Prophet to instruct the

believers, that they cast down their eyes and guard their private parts; that is purer for them. God is aware of the things they work. And say to the believing women, that they cast down their eyes and guard their private parts, and reveal not their adornment save such as is outward; and let them cast their *[khumur]* over their bosoms, and not reveal their adornment save to …'.[8]

(24.30: in Arberry 1955: 49–50)

This verse is not as clear-cut as the first two but it is open to a better reading than the traditional one which is that the gaze is an invitation to fornication and that women's bodies are pudendal and polluting. However, the verse can be read as moderating *mutual* sexual desire by prescribing modest behaviour for both men and women. And, while it has more to say about women's dress and adornment than it does about men's, it merely limits the *public display* of women's sexual appeal. After all, they do not need to observe the same dress etiquette in front of men whom they cannot marry. Unlike the conservative aspects of Muslim tradition which holds that women's faces, hair, hands, and feet are pudendal and need to be hidden, this verse does not mandate covering the entire body. I should also note that the Qur'an does not use the word 'hijab' for women's clothing or call for their segregation.

---

[8] Here follows a list of men who are not in a marriageable category.

The Qur'an's emphasis on dress and demeanour and, more importantly, on sexual purity, shows that it seeks to manage the expression of sexual desire but it does not describe the desire itself, or sex, as unclean or associate it with women. Nor does it depict women's bodies as uniquely corrupt, corrupting, or corruptible. However, it does speak about women to men and often in a manner that affirms male authority. It is this fact, together with the so-called 'anti-women' verses, that generate readings of Islam as a patriarchy and so it is important to consider them as well.

'ANTI-WOMEN' VERSES AND PATRIARCHY

Among the injunctions, words, and verses Muslims read as being inimical to women is the word *darajah*, which is taken to mean that men are ontologically superior to women even if only by a single degree. However, the context in which the word is used—just once in the entire text—has absolutely nothing to do with ontology:

> Women who are divorced shall wait, keeping themselves apart, three (monthly) courses. And it is not lawful for them that they should conceal that which Allah hath created in their wombs if they are believers in Allah and the Last Day. And their husbands would do better to take them back in that case if they desire a reconciliation. And they (women) have rights similar to those (of men) over them *in kindness [ma'ruf]*, and men are a degree *[darajah]* above them. Allah is Mighty, Wise.

> (2.228: in Pickthall n.d.: 53, emphasis added)

The verse is about three interrelated subjects: how long a wife must wait before a divorce is finalized; the possibility of a reconciliation with her husband during that time, and the need for mutual kindness. It is only in the context of kindness that the Qur'an mentions the degree men have above their wives and it does so after it talks of a reconciliation. This suggests that the husband has the advantage of being able to *rescind* a divorce he has pronounced (Asad 1980: 50, footnote 216) since that is the only way the couple can reconcile. Even if one disagrees with this reading, however, the degree is plainly not referring to the nature of men's being or to their rights in general; rather, it is an explicit and narrow reference to what is allowed to a husband during a divorce.

There are two other stipulations in the Qur'an that are interpreted as favouring men. One is about inheritance and it gives a son twice the share of a daughter and a brother twice that of a sister, from a deceased parent's and sibling's properties respectively. The other concerns evidence-giving and says that if two men are not available to witness a debt transaction, one man and two women can be called as witnesses so that, if one forgets something, the other can remind her. These provisions have led Muslim law to regard two women as equalling one man across the board even though there are *clear* counter examples in the Qur'an with respect to both inheritance and testimony. Thus, mothers and fathers get equal shares from a deceased child's estate and, in the very crucial matter of adultery, a wife's testimony outweighs that of her husband. If he accuses her of adultery on his own recognizance, she has the right to refute his charge on her own behalf and, if she pleads her innocence, he has no legal recourse against her. In effect, there are a range of examples in the Qur'an that challenge the 'two-for-one' formula (Wadud 1999) which Muslim jurists have devised, to women's detriment.

The last verse I will consider, the so-called 'beating verse', is taken to be the most irrefutable proof of male superiority in the Qur'an:

> [men are] *qawwamuna 'ala* [of] women with the bounties which God has bestowed [more on some of them than on the others] and with what they may spend out of their possessions. And the righteous women are the truly devout ones, who guard the intimacy which God has [ordained to be] guarded. And, as for those women whose *[nushuz]* you have reason to fear, admonish them [first]; then leave them alone in bed: then *[idribuhunne]* them; and if thereupon they pay you heed, do not seek to harm them.
>
> (4.34: in Asad 1980: 109–10)

Although Muslims consider the meanings of this verse (and of the entire Qur'an) to be fixed and transparent, in actuality, these depend on who reads it, how, and in what contexts. For instance, *qawwamun* does not just mean 'guardians', as most Muslims hold; it also means 'financial maintainers' and 'bread-winners' (al-Hibri 1982). If men were indeed women's guardians, then the Qur'an would not say that men and women are in charge of one another and each other's guides (*awliya*). Similarly, *nushuz* is construed as a wife's disobedience to or rebellion against her husband, but the Qur'an also speaks of a husband's *nushuz*. Unless one accepts that (dis)obedience applies to both husband and wife—a proposition at which most Muslims would baulk—*nushuz* is probably better understood as referring to a state of 'marital discord' (Wadud 1999).

There remains the most contentious word of all: *idribuhunne*, from the root *d-r-b*, on which Muslims have hung an entire ontology of abuse by translating it as 'beat/strike'. This is, of course, one of its meanings but it has several more, some of which the Qur'an also uses, for instance, 'ignore', 'leave/go/travel' (e.g., 3:156; 4:101); 'set an example' (14:24; 45; 16:75–76), 'take away' (43:5), and so on. Like all words, therefore, *d-r-b* is also polysemic and there is no obligation to interpret it only as 'beat'. Even if that is what one insists on doing, there is a difference between what the Qur'an permits and what it says is obligatory. It does not say husbands *must* strike wives: nor does it oblige wives to live with abusive husbands. Significantly, there are two more instances of marital discord in the Qur'an both of which counsel temperate behaviour towards wives. One tells men that some of their wives are 'enemies unto you', but asks them to 'forbear and forgive' such women so as to receive God's forgiveness in turn (64.14: in Asad 1980: 871). The other says men should consort with their wives 'in kindness, for if ye hate them it may happen that ye hate a thing wherein Allah hath placed much good' (4.19: in Pickthall n.d.: 81). If husbands must treat even such wives with restraint, there is no cause for them to beat a wife over a dispute, as most Muslims believe. In fact, the Prophet, whose life serves as an exemplar of the Qur'an's teachings, forbade men to hit their wives. (To say, as some apologists do, that he was opposed to God's will on this issue makes for a truly bad theology since it very questionably pits God and God's Prophet against one another.)

AN 'OPEN' HERMENEUTIC

Lastly, the Qur'an praises 'Those who listen to the Word and follow the best (meaning) in it' (38.18: in Ali 1988: 1241), confirming both that it can be read in different ways and that not all readings may be equally good. Rather, it is for Muslims to pick the best, a concept whose meaning is open to continual redefinition, making an interpretive closure of the Qur'an hermeneutically impossible and ethically indefensible. As such, if drawing on other meanings of *d-r-b* yields better readings of verse 4:34, there is no reason to stick to the most punitive. This is not just a concession to the Qur'an since 'plurivocity is typical of the text considered as a whole', as Paul Ricoeur (1981: 109) says of texts in general. This is why a 'key hypothesis of hermeneutical philosophy is that interpretation is an open process which no single vision can conclude' (1981: 212). Tying the meanings of the Qur'an irrevocably to the imaginations of Muslims who lived a millennium ago not only forecloses its own liberatory promise but also ignores basic hermeneutic principles.

Of course, reinterpreting the Qur'an does not address a more fundamental issue, which is that it speaks to men *as if* they have power over women, thus confirming their superiority in the eyes of most Muslims. Yet, the reality is that men *were* the locus of power and authority in the seventh-century tribal Arab patriarchy to which the Qur'an first spoke. That it took this reality seriously does not mean that God has some special affinity with men or that the Qur'an upholds Arab patriarchy as a timeless norm; there is simply nothing to this effect in the entire text. What it does show, however, is that the Qur'an was not 'immune from history'. The very nature of its revelation to the Prophet, over the span of twenty-three years, means that its verses 'impinge upon a succession of temporal events', which is why ignoring history also risks making the Qur'an's 'own history irrelevant' (Cragg 1994: 114–115). This idea, argues Kenneth Cragg (1994: 121–122) 'emerges indisputably from the Qur'anic text itself. There are several important passages which underline the necessarily periodic and contextual nature of its contents.' It is, he contends, the refusal 'to reckon with moving time' that transforms the '"incidentalism" of the days of the Qur'an [into] the "fundamentalism" of the centuries'.

A historicizing approach to the Qur'an that reckons 'with moving time' would consider the tribal Arab patriarchy to which it first spoke one of the 'incidentalisms' of history, since it has long since vanished. As such, this approach would see no point in freezing the Qur'an in time by making its meanings hostage to that patriarchy. As the source of universal truths, sacred texts cannot be tied to any society, or its history, or its interpretive choices. Besides, what makes the Qur'an a living scripture are not just its decrees but the moral and ethical principles they embody. These, Fazlur Rahman (1982) argues, are evident even in verses one might regard as once addressed to the exigencies of seventh-century Arabia; indeed, the Qur'an itself 'provides, either explicitly or implicitly, the rationales behind [its] solutions and rulings, from which one *can deduce general principles*' (Rahman 1982: 20, emphasis original).

In contrast, the kind of historicism that generates the fundamentalism of which Cragg speaks periodizes the Qur'an by treating only those interpretations of it as real and authentic that date from over a millennium ago. (This is what makes the religious knowledge produced in the first few centuries of Islam canonical.) Ironically, this fundamentalism is a feature not just of conservative thought but of progressive and feminist thought as well. For conservatives, clinging to ancient readings of the Qur'an is a way to secure traditional patriarchal structures against erosion. For many progressives and feminists, on the other hand, patriarchal interpretations demonstrate the need to secularize not just Muslim societies but Islam itself. Both sides are therefore equally invested in treating the Qur'an as being closed to new readings (Barlas 2012).

In the meanwhile, however, growing numbers of Muslims, especially women, are beginning to read it as the liberatory speech of a just and non-patriarchal God, and their readings are opening up space to rethink its message. As for the secular project of desacralizing the Qur'an, it seems unlikely to succeed since, for observant Muslims, it is not just a religious text but the speech of an eternally existing God. To the extent that Muslims can only know their God through God's word, the Qur'an will endure as the most sacred symbol of Islam.

As this chapter demonstrates, I am one of those Muslims who read the Qur'an as a liberating text and what drew me to do so is the disturbing fact that there is a 'striking difference between what can be safely inferred from the Qur'an itself and what has frequently been read into it' (Robinson 1996: 29). It is this disjuncture that led me not only to reread the Qur'an but also to explore why Muslims have interpreted it as a patriarchal text for the last fourteen hundred years. The reasons have to do with history and hermeneutics and, most importantly, with configurations of political, sexual, and religious power in Muslim societies (Barlas 2002).

In my own work, I have tried not only to challenge patriarchal readings of the Qur'an but also to propose a method for interpreting it that can lead to better ones. For instance, I read the Qur'an by the Qur'an, which is an old method in Islamic theology. For me, however, this means not only reading one verse in light of another but seeking the hermeneutic keys for interpreting the text in the text itself. For instance, the Qur'an warns against dividing 'Scripture into arbitrary parts', and making it 'Into shreds' (15.89–93: in Ali 1991: 653), and focusing only on some aspects of revelation while concealing 'much (Of its contents)' (6.91: in Ali 1991: 314). It also criticizes changing the 'words From their (right) places' (5.14: in Ali 1991: 245). I take these references to mean that one should read the Qur'an as a unity rather than in a decontextualized or piecemeal way. I also look for the best meanings in a verse, keeping in mind the historical circumstances to which it might have been addressed. Last and most importantly, I read the Qur'an in light of a theological understanding of God that does not violate God's self-disclosure in the Qur'an. The results of this method are for readers to judge and for Muslims who are interested in doing so, to employ in defence of arguments about the need for sexual equality based in a regime of mutual care between women and men.

REFERENCES

Ahmed, L. (1992). *Women and Gender in Islam*. New Haven, CT: Yale University Press.

Al-Hibri, A. (1982). 'A Study of Islamic Herstory'. *Women's Studies International Forum, Special Issue: Women and Islam*, 5(2): 212–215.

Ali, A. Y. (1988). *The Holy Quran*. New York: Tehrike Tarsile.

Ali, C. A. (1991). 'The Equality of Women'. In R. S. Sugirtharajah (ed.), *Voices from the Margin*. New York: Orbis Books.

Arberry, A. J. (1955). *The Koran Interpreted*. New York: Allen and Unwin.

Asad, M. (1980). *The Message of the Quran*. Gibraltar: Dar al-Andalus.

Barlas, A. (2002). *'Believing Women' in Islam*. Austin: University of Texas Press.

Barlas, A. (2011). 'Abraham's Sacrifice in the Qur'an'. In T. Ahlback (ed.), *Religion and the Body*. Åbo, Finland: Donner Institute, 55–71.

Barlas, A. (2012). 'Uncrossed Bridges: Islam, Feminism, and Secular Democracy'. *Philosophy and Social Criticism*, 39(4–5): 417–425.

Bennett, A. (1989). *From Woman-Pain to Woman-Vision*. Minneapolis: Augsburg Fortress.

Bynum, C. W. (1986). '…And Woman his Humanity'. In C. Bynum, S. Harrell, and P. Richman (eds), *Gender and Religion*. Boston: Beacon Press, 257–288.

Cowan, J. M. (1976). *Arabic-English Dictionary*. Ithaca, NY: Spoken Language Services.

Cragg, K. (1994). *The Event of the Quran*. Oxford: Oneworld.

Davies, M. W. (1988). *Knowing One Another*. London: Mansell Publishing.

Eisenstein, Z. (1990). *The Female Body and the Law*. California: University of California Press.

Gilligan, C. (1988). 'Remaking the Moral Domain'. In C. Gilligan, J. V. Ward, and J. M. Taylor (eds), *Mapping the Moral Domain*. Cambridge, MA: Harvard University Press.

Hassan, R. (1999). 'An Islamic Perspective'. In K Lebacqz (ed.), *Sexuality: A Reader*. Cleveland: Pilgrim Press.

Hekman, S. (1990). *Gender and Knowledge*. Boston: Northeastern University Press.

Hewitt, M. A. (1995). *Critical Theory of Religion—A Feminist Analysis* Minneapolis: Fortress Press.

Hodgen, M. T. (1964). *Early Anthropology in the Sixteenth and Seventeenth Centuries*. Philadelphia: University of Pennsylvania Press.

Millett, K. (1970). *Sexual Politics*. New York: Doubleday.

Mir, M. (1987). *Dictionary of Quranic Terms and Concepts*. New York: Garland Publishing.

Murata, S. (1992). *The Tao of Islam*. Albany, NY: State University of New York Press.

Netton, I. (1989). *Allah Transcendent*. New York: Routledge.

Padel, R. (1993). 'Women: Models for Possession by Greek Daemons,' in A. Cameron and A. Kuhrt (eds), *Images of Women in Antiquity* (rev. edn.). London: Routledge, 3–19.

Pickthall, M. M. (n.d.). *The Meaning of the Glorious Koran*. New York: Mentor Books.

Rahman, F. (1982). *Islam and Modernity*. Chicago: University of Chicago Press.

Ricoeur, P. (1981). *Hermeneutics and the Human Sciences*. Trans. J. Thompson. Cambridge: Cambridge University Press.

Robinson, N. (1996). *Discovering the Qur'an*. London: SCM Press.

Wadud, A. (1999). *Quran and Woman*. Oxford: Oxford University Press.

Weeks, J. (1985). *Sexuality and its Discontents*. London: Routledge & Kegan Paul.

CHAPTER 27

....

HINDUISM

....

MANDAKRANTA BOSE

INTRODUCTION

THINKING about divinity, about the human body's urges and about its social identity are tasks, in themselves challenging enough, that may seem to be pulling in different directions. But reflections on the Hindu cogitative tradition show how necessary and possible it is to weave them into a unified system. The challenges begin with theological ideas.

The theology of the Hindus is so vast and varied, stretching back so many millennia and stemming from such varying spiritual visions, with no single source of acknowledged authority, that all observations on Hindu theology must be hedged with disclaimers. The narratives that comprise its cosmic history give obscure, competing, or conflicting accounts of key events, such as the origin of existence, the appearance of matter, life-forms, gods and goddesses, with little if any chronological coherence. To extract from them the ideas central to Hinduism, caution is needed to avoid confusing mythology with theology, intertwined as they often are. Besides, Hinduism consists as much in philosophical speculation and theorizing as in worship regimens derived from a wide variety of theological concepts, while its ideas and practices have evolved and changed over time. Still, it is possible to pick out from this vast expanse common threads that run through the vast tapestry that is Hinduism.

The present study will follow these threads to see how one part of that tapestry is woven, that which delineates the interrelationship of divinity, sexuality, and gender in the Hindu way of thinking. Put simply, the Hindu belief-system places the sexual impulse at the core of creation and procreation, and identifies it as an essential condition of existence. Understanding Hinduism, then, cannot be done without understanding how it reads sexuality and extends it into the social category of gender.

Essentials

Through the rich mass of theology and social ideas oriented to it, the one idea that has continued as the core of Hinduism is that of the existence of a Supreme Being, an Absolute. This singularity is sometimes obscured by the fact that Hinduism is founded neither on a single scriptural text that asserts a specific creed, nor on a single founder to set down the truth of its cardinal doctrines or moral values. However, it is precisely the plurality of philosophical ideas and arguments that has allowed Hindu thinkers to develop theology as a many-sided but systematic study of spirituality and religion, and of their influence on worldly life.

In addition to the unalterable belief in a single Supreme Being, a continuing theme is the affirmation of sexual energy as a fundamental creative principle. Correlated with it is the gender division of roles in the play of life from its creation to its social expressions. As Jeffrey S. Lidke puts it, in Hinduism the sexual impulse 'is regarded as a powerful inner fire whose ultimate source is the very same creative fire that gives rise to the universe itself' (2003: 128).

Grounded in theological speculation, the idea of sexuality as a basic impulse of existence occupies a central place in Hindu thought balanced by a degree of unease about sexual desire as a frequently uncontrollable force. Against the deep reverence in which Hindus hold sexuality as the key to the propagation of life, runs a distrust of its power to subvert moral laws, leading even gods and holy ascetics into transgressions of natural and social codes, as O'Flaherty has demonstrated (1981a: 173–175, 296–302). The theme of sexuality as an indispensable yet potentially disorderly impulse sounds continually through a wide range of literature from early times, illustrated by narratives of extreme lapses, including incest (Bhattacharji 1970: 93–94, Bhattacharyya 1999: 131–133;), ravishment, and deception.

THE INVISIBLE CENTRE

Accommodating such lapses into the cosmic design is only one mark of the complexity of Hindu theology, both in philosophical exposition and in worship practices, a complexity reflected in the vast changes to it over millennia and multivalent doctrinal positions accommodated within Hinduism. Yet there is an elemental consistency in the variety of belief that underlies even rote-learned rituals, for all these proceed from an axiomatic acknowledgement of a supreme power as the source of all existence, reality, and knowledge, and the impossibility of acquiring verifiable knowledge of that power. The seminal texts of Hinduism, the Vedas, along with exegetic works such as the Brāhmaáṇas and Āraáṇyakas, and the meditative Upaniṣads that comprise the philosophy of Vedānta (i.e. the end or goal of the Vedas), assert the existence of a Supreme Being, termed Brahman or Ātman, even as they insist on the impossibility of limiting the identity and nature of that being to particulars or of capturing its lineaments. That is what the sage Yājnavalkya explains to King Janaka in the *Bṛhadāraáṇyaka Upaniṣad* (4.1.1–7).[1]

The same view is taken by another early theologian, Uddālaka Āruṇi, when he tells his son Śvetaketu to keep splitting up a fruit and its seeds into the smallest particles to show graphically that just as one cannot grasp the essence of the fruit's life force by regression, so may one *not* work one's way back through phenomena to find Brahman, who remains

---

[1] All references to the Upaniṣads are to Radhakrishnan (1953).

beyond perception, transcendent, and materially unknowable (*Chāndogya Upaniṣad*, 6.12.1–3). This fundamental assertion has not lost its power or its currency through later developments of theological exposition and practical worship in the various schools of thought in India, including those that arose in the Buddhist and Jain systems.

BEGINNINGS

Like most other theologies, Hindu theology begins with reflections on the fountainhead of existence and its origin. First voiced in the *Ṛg Veda*, these reflections acknowledge an abstract Supreme Being who is self-originating and the source of all phenomena. But speculations on the origin of reality are not all that the text contains; much of it takes for granted a world of personified manifestations of divinity in the form of gods and goddesses who exist in time and space in matrices of social order and do so in relation to humankind and other forms of earthly life (Bhattacharji 1970; Danielou c1991).

Set against the links of need and supplication that the poet-seers of the hymns seek to establish with deities, stands the consistent affirmation of a key Hindu concept, that 'Existence, in the earliest age of Gods, from Non-existence sprang' (*RV* 10.72.3).[2] But reflections on beginnings lead equally to an acknowledgement of an insoluble mystery that can be formulated only as a paradox, as we find in the opening line of the famous *Nāsadīya* hymn of the *Ṛg Veda*: 'there was neither existence nor non-existence then' (*RV* 10.129.1).[3] It is a theme that sounds insistently in the Hindu intellectual tradition.

A later work, the *Chāndogya Upaniṣad*, contains a dialogue swaying between doubt and affirmation:

> 1. In the beginning, my dear, this was Being alone, one only without a second. Some people say 'in the beginning this was non-being alone, one only; without a second. From that non-being, being was produced.' 2. But how, indeed, my dear, could it be thus? said he, how could being be produced from non-being? On the contrary, my dear, in the beginning this was being alone, one only, without a second.'
>
> (*Chāndogya Upaniṣad* 6.2. 1–2)

This 'being alone' remains undefined. Posited thus beyond space and time, beyond the reach of definition, and beyond the limits of description as one who is at once without attributes and the sum of all attributes, the Supreme Being can be thought of simultaneously as formless yet expressible in all forms.

Max Müller describes this entity as

> an unlimited and absolute power, as the primary cause of all created things. No name that expressed ideas connected with the male or female sex...was considered as fit

---

[2] The text of the *Ṛg Veda* cited here is the translation by O'Flaherty (1981b).
[3] The word 'nāsadīya' is derived from 'na' and 'asat,' meaning 'that which is not non-existent'.

for such a being, and thus we see that as early as the Vedic hymns it was spoken of as Tad Ekam, that One, as neither male nor female'.

(Müller 1919: 48)

The poet-seers of the *Ṛg Veda* are so careful in stopping short of ascribing personhood to this abstraction that they begin by eschewing personal pronouns as referents. Speaking of the original One in the *Nāsadīya* hymn, the *Ṛg Veda* uses the impersonal, gender-free pronouns 'that one' and 'it' in what seems to be a deliberate refusal to impute person-hood and thus gender. The verse runs: 'That one breathed, windless, by its own impulse' (*RV* 10.129.2).

But this impersonality in language seems to be hard to sustain and the hymn seg-ues into the third-person personal pronoun when it admits the limits of knowl-edge: 'Whence this creation has arisen—perhaps it formed itself, or perhaps it did not—the one who looks down on it, in the highest heaven, only he knows—or perhaps he does not know' (*RV* 10.129.7). The progress from the gender-neutral 'that one' and 'it' to the masculine referent 'he' is decisive, and the speculative thrill of the 'perhaps . . . per-haps not' paradox must not blind the reader to the insertion of 'he', which is a tacit attri-bution at once of personhood and gender. But the denial of personhood, indeed of an embodied original being is compromised in even earlier verses of this hymn when it states, 'That one breathed, windless, by its own impulse' (*RV* 10.129.2), attributing at least one bodily function, that of breathing, to the nameless one.

Personhood

Leaving this Supreme Being nameless, the seers of the *Ṛg Veda* level their gaze at a deity of a lower degree of abstraction as the first creator god, who can be named because he is conceived in human terms. The *Hiraṇyagarbha* hymn of the *Ṛg Veda* (*RV* 10.121) asks in every verse, who is this creator spirit? To whom should we offer oblations? More con-cretely described than he who is imagined in the *Nāsadīya* hymn, this being is named the Hiraṇyagarbha, or the Golden Germ, which is imagined at once as floating on the primal waters of creation (*RV* 10.121.7) and as producing those waters (*RV* 10.121.9). The pronoun used is the unambiguous 'he' who is the 'one lord of creation' (*RV* 10.121.1), and the hymn concludes by naming him 'Prajāpati, lord of progeny'.

In the post-Vedic era Prajāpati came to be identified with and eventually superseded by the god Brahmā, who became increasingly better known as the creator member of the Hindu Trinity with Viṣṇu and Śiva. Later on Prajāpati became the collective title of a group of ruling deities, the word functioning more as a title than a personal name, but in the *Ṛg Veda* Prajāpati is the primary creator god, the lord and beget-ter of all creatures. However, he is not the Supreme Being. He is a person to whom prayers can be addressed and who is, as the masculine pronoun indicates, a male fig-ure. Here as elsewhere in the myths the biological process of earthly life as inscribed in the sexual relationship between male and female beings is a constant element of the creation myth.

From the Metaphysical to the Physical

The question of origins thus becomes a puzzling issue, muddied further by early myths of world-making that adduce the idea of creator spirits endowed with personhood and the one original person dividing itself into two, or being dismembered into many, thereby initiating the creation of the world. Yet these speculations about the origin of phenomena, metaphysical as they are, do draw upon observations of biological processes. The idea of the one becoming two or more is a neat solution to the problem of answering how propagation may take place without partners, a solution that sidesteps the model of propagation by the union of two partners. But it is still not independent of biology, considering that it invokes the phenomenon of asexual reproduction.[4]

The theme of unitary reproduction has resounded in myths of origins, which are never entirely untouched by biological experience. Although Hindu theology does not specify the physical character of the creative process, it seems to draw upon a biological analogy, for it rests on the assumption that creation at the minimum requires two partners, whether produced by the self-splitting of the original one, and that after the original act there must be two for propagation to continue. Further, the key to propagation is tacitly acknowledged to be sexual reproduction, as we see in the myths of union between male and female persons. Sexuality as a creative energy is unambiguously affirmed in the explicit description of the original male's act of impregnating his daughter (*RV* 10.61.5–7).

From these early, generally cryptic conceptions of creation to the detailed and often convoluted accounts of sexual acts in the *purāṇas* and *kāvyas* that constitute the later sourcebooks of Hindu theology, sexuality continues to be taken as an essential factor of both material existence and its spiritual drive. In brief, Hindu theology holds that existence was jumpstarted by asexual reproduction through the self-splitting of the original One and was followed by the union of the two parts producing offspring, signifying an act of sexual reproduction.

Biology

The fundamental role of biology is never in question even in the more abstract speculation about origins that we have noted above. We see how forcefully sexuality and gender are invoked in the statement, 'There were seed-placers; there were powers. There was impulse beneath; there was giving-forth above' (*RV* 10.129.5). The paired imagery of the givers and receivers of the seeds of life strongly suggests male and female partners,

---

[4] It is an intriguing question whether the idea of one organism reproducing itself was derived at this very early age from observations of asexual reproduction in nature, for instance, fungi, some flatworms, and bacteria.

as understood by O'Flaherty in her note to this verse in her translation of the *Ṛg Veda* (1981b: 26, n.6). Not only does this ascription thereby tacitly recognize the impossibility of escaping anthropomorphism, but it also shows an acknowledgement of the formulas of social relations. As in most other systems of human thought, then, in Hindu theology the idea of sexuality and its implication of gender seem fundamentally entrenched.

Perpetuation

These questions of origin carry over into the related question of continuation. If the origin of life is a mystery, its propagation seems no less of a riddle. How does one become many? Much of Indian philosophy, not only in the Hindu intellectual tradition but also the Buddhist, has been occupied with this problem and has put forward many answers.

An early answer comes again from the *Ṛg Veda*. The hymn known as the *Puruṣa Sukta* (*ṚV* 10.90) or Hymn to Man—'man' here meaning the primordial cosmic Person or Puruṣa—speaks of a gigantic being possessing 'a thousand heads, a thousand eyes, a thousand feet' who pervades all earth and splits himself into four parts, one part then forming into all creatures and three parts remaining in heaven. The crucial two-step event that follows is the birth of a second being from Puruṣa who is called Virāj and from whom in turn 'the Man' is born. This 'Man' is sacrificed by the gods and from his dismembered body appear the sky, the earth, birds, animals, sacred verses, chants and spells, while particular parts of his body produce the different classes of humankind in the social order as well as the gods Indra, Agni, and Vāyu (*ṚV* 10.90.1–16).

Two aspects of this theory are to be noted: first, both stages of procreation, that is, Man dividing into two and then Virāj giving birth to Man, follow the biological model, mysterious as the biological process may be. Secondly, the division of Man results in the appearance of a male and a female, that is to say, in sexual differentiation and the advent of gender. The force of the metaphysical imagination at work in this myth should not, however, distract us from a similar anthropomorphic account in an earlier section of the tenth book of the *Ṛg Veda*, which maintains that 'existence was born from non-existence' (10.72.2–3) and immediately proceeds to proclaim that 'the quarters of the sky were born from her who crouched with legs spread ... the earth was born from her who crouched with legs spread' (*ṚV* 10.72.3–4). Identifying this 'she' as Aditi, the story reverses the generative order of the *Puruṣa Sukta* by giving precedence to female agency in the procreative process. The sentence goes on to repeat that order: 'From Aditi, Dakṣa was born, and from Dakṣa Aditi was born' (*ṚV* 10.72.4).

However, although it is the female who is the first progenitor contrary to the sequence in the *Puruṣa Sukta*, what remains unaltered is the process of the same pair of male and female being born from one another. That the process implies an apparent paradox suggests that early Hindu thought may have conceptualized, at least by implication, the first vital entity as an androgynous one consisting of both male and female elements. Androgyny as an explanation of the beginning of life, biological in its implication, and its perpetuation through the partnership of differentiated sexes is not of course unique to Hindu thought but occurs in many mythologies around the world. The idea of an androgynous godhead was a powerful one and took concrete form later, around the first century CE, in the potent icon of *ardhanārīśvara*, a composite of Lord Śiva and his consort Pārvatī.

Gender Distinction

The assumption of creative roles differentiated by gender became a crucial part of Hindu thought early on, through the assertion that all phenomena result from the interaction of the complementary ontological principles known as *puruṣa* and *prakṛti*. At least partly traceable to the *Puruṣa Sukta* of the *Ṛg Veda* and inherent in Upaniṣadic philosophy, from the early common era onwards, this became a key concept of the Vedic philosophical school known as *sāá¹fkhya*, which traces existence not to a creator but to the interaction of two principles *puruṣa* and *prkṛti*. To simplify an exceedingly abstruse theory, *puruṣa* is pure consciousness, the 'male' principle of existence, and *prakṛti* is inert, unmanifest matter, the corresponding 'female' principle upon which *puruṣa* acts to produce all objects.[5]

Since a principle is by definition abstract, calling a principle male or female reflects the (as yet) incorrigible human habit of thinking and speaking in terms of gender, rather than any sexual property inherent in *puruṣa* and *prakṛti*. Given how commonly human discourse is socially constructed, it is not accidental that *puruṣa* and *prakṛti* should have passed into the nomenclature of gender or that the explanation of creation, of being and becoming, should have been sexualized in Hindu theology.

Necessary Transgressions

One aspect of the problem of one becoming many is that after the initial separation, the first couple must be parent and child or siblings, rendering the continuation of propagation incestuous. Thus we find that incest is an insistent theme in early accounts of procreation. Incest is indeed plainly recognized in Vedic thought. The *Ṛg Veda* describes an explicit sex act between 'the manly one' and 'his daughter' that leads to the creation of the world (*ṚV* 10.61.5–7). The myth of Puruṣa (the 'Man') is followed up in the *Bṛhadāraṇyaka Upaniṣad* where Puruṣa recognizes himself as an amalgam of man and woman. After splitting himself into two he unites with the female he has generated, and 'from this mankind was born', whereupon she 'reflected, "How can he unite with me after engendering me from himself?"' (O'Flaherty 1975: 34). The *Aitareya Brāhmaṇa*

---

[5] Note, though, that an opposite position is taken in some tāntric views. Lorillai Biernacki cites the *Bṛhanīlatantra* to argue that 'the *feminine* principle is not matter, but spirit', and that against the pervasive view that 'the feminine is matter and the masculine is spirit,' this tāntric text holds that 'the masculine principle is coded as matter, the insentient "dead" body' (Biernacki 2007: 62).

(O'Flaherty 1975: 29) relates how the creator god Prajāpati desires his daughter, variously identified as the sky or dawn, to the outrage of the gods.

The idea of incest as a necessary mode of initiating the procreative chain runs persistently through Hindu mythology. Moving ahead from the Vedic texts to the Purāṇas, we find the *Matsyapurāṇa* relating how Brahmā commits incest with his daughter Sarasvatī (3.30–43). A sense of discomfort is, however, evident in its specious defence that judging gods is no business of humans and since no corporeal body is involved, the act is not actually incestuous (4.1–6).[6] The subtext is of course that procreation must go on.

Theorizing Sexuality

Striking though they are, early explanations of procreation as consequences of self-splitting or androgyny or sexual union hardly represent a systematic philosophical approach. Rather, they take the division of the one into two and the resultant gender difference as part of existence without scrutinizing or expanding upon its place within material life.

Nevertheless, these accounts show how theorizing sexuality as a fundamental principle of creation gained weight in Hindu theology early on. It became especially important to the tradition of discourse and regimen known as tantra. The abstract and impersonal nature of the Absolute does place a hurdle in the way of biologically deriving from that abstraction the creation of phenomena, for bodily processes cannot be imputed to one who transcends personhood. On the other hand, they can indeed be so imputed if the Supreme Being is conceived as one who comprises all attributes. It follows then that conceptualizing a creative act as a biological one is by no means untenable.

This conceptualization further supports the identification of sexual energy as the animating force of the universe. It also insinuates gender into the discourse. Since Brahman is beyond description, free of attributes and yet acknowledged as a sum of all imaginable attributes, Brahman may be conceived as at once gendered and gender-free, as both male and female. Here then is a self-contained, self-sufficient, and self-empowered locus of existence from which all reality might be derived, admittedly with perennial uncertainty as to its precise operation.

Relating to the Divine

It is evident then that theologically the most profound parts of the Vedic texts are questions of the nature and processes of existence, of being and becoming. But the speculative corpus soon began to acquire a different body of enquiry that came to invest Hindu

---

[6] Brahmā's act brings down upon him Sarasvatī's curse, which denies him worship in the world. Harsher still is another story: in his anger Lord Śiva assumes his terrible Bhairava form and tears out the fifth head Brahmā had added to his usual four in order to gaze lustfully upon Sarasvatī.

theology with not only intellectual but also emotional intensity. This is the issue of the enquirer's—in general of humankind's—relationship with the divine spirit.

As we have seen, affirmations of belief in a transcendent Absolute co-existed comfortably with the idea of multiple gods and goddesses from the beginning, preoccupied (as the bulk of the *Ṛg Veda* is) with hymns to Indra, Varuna, Agni, and others, who are worshipped and offered sacrifices in the expectation of worldly benefits. The idea of relationships between human worshippers and manifest forms of divinity is thus as ancient as the concept of an abstract Supreme One. It is also fairly straightforward, based as it is on the idea of revering and serving higher powers for gain.

In time, however, this early understanding of relationship evolved into infinitely more varied, finely nuanced and problematic fields of intuition, speculation, and argument. One of the boldest and perennially renewed perceptions is that of the essential unity of the human self with the universal soul; as the sage Uddālaka Āruṇi says to Śvetaketu, the highest realization is 'tat tvam asi' ('you are that', *Chāndogya Upaniṣad*, 6.8.7), even though 'that' may not be open to sense perceptions. The discourse spills out of specifically sacred texts into literary, historical, and ethical texts, including the large body of myths known as the Purāṇas and the two hugely influential epics of India, the *Rāmāyaṇa* (100 CE) and the *Mahābhārata* (400 BCE–300 CE), of which the section known as the *Bhagavad Gītā* is the most influential sacred text for the majority of Hindus.

FROM THE ABSTRACT TO THE MANIFEST

In the post-Veda era, then, religious belief was moving from the contemplation of an abstract Supreme Being to that of a humanized divinity. But the idea of human relationships, even when it is metaphorical, presumes personhood, the body, and by extension gender. Nor is that presumption alien to the concept of the godhead in Hinduism. As we have seen, the earliest Hindu reflections on divinity include the metaphysical abstraction of the nameless One as well as the manifest Many, the gods and goddesses with whom the human seeker establishes a relationship as suppliant in the Vedic hymns.

However, the sacred and philosophical literature of the Hindus, as indeed that of many other spiritual systems, leaves no doubt that such a relationship is not confined to worldly benefits but is equally invested with joy, wonder, and excitement at closeness to the source of all existence. Getting to know that source then becomes as important a need for the thinker as—ultimately—personal union with it. Such a union and the desire for it are understood by some to constitute a sexual state because of its intensity of yearning and the expectation of total assimilation.

The *Bṛhadāraṇyaka Upaniṣad* expresses that aspiration by an erotic analogy: 'As a man when in the embrace of his beloved wife knows nothing without or within, so the person when in the embrace of the intelligent self knows nothing without or within'

(*BrUp* 4.3.21).[7] The idea of so intimate a relationship with the godhead gains particular force when divine beings are endowed with bodily identities, including sexual desire, incorporeal though such bodies might be. Upon such speculations came to rest two of the most influential strands of Hindu religiosity, tantra and bhakti, both formidably complex in their theory and practice.

Tantra

The word tantra, literally 'loom', is properly applied to a set of texts, collectively called Tantras,[8] that has built up over time one of the most complex systems of reflecting on and attaining to the godhead through meditation and esoteric worship rituals. The word itself dates back to the *Ṛg Veda* (*RV* 10.71.9), but the numerous Tantras that constitute the philosophical bases of tantra and its hugely varied worship regimen began to emerge from about the sixth century, taking root mainly in Assam, Bengal, and notably in Kashmir, though not without adherents elsewhere, for instance, Kerala. In time tantra permeated other philosophical systems as well, including Buddhism.

In broad terms, tantra holds that the universe we experience is nothing other than the concrete manifestation of the divine energy of the godhead that creates and preserves that universe. André Padoux speaks of the 'Tantric vision' as 'the cosmos as permeated by power (or powers), a vision wherein energy (*śakti*) is both cosmic and human and where microcosm and macrocosm correspond and interact' (2002: 19). Through rituals that correlate the divine macrocosm with the human microcosm, tantra seeks to seize that cosmic energy and channel it within the human body and mind to liberate the individual soul from the trappings of the world and unite it with the universal Absolute. As Gavin Flood puts it, 'the cosmos is mapped on to the body' (2006: 100).

Tantra takes the human body as the site where humankind's spiritual journey begins, and sexual energy as the key that unlocks the sacred power latent within the human body. It therefore enjoins upon its adherents the most rigorous and elaborate cultivation of the senses, including sexual desire, all of which is formalized as rituals leading to union with the godhead. In the extreme form of the branch of tantra known as the left hand path, these rituals comprise a secret regimen of energizing the body through transgressive action, especially sexual congress, for it is by violations of the norm that the seeker shrugs off the chains of common existence. All worldly codes, be they of diet

---

[7] It is worth quoting Radhakrishnan's gloss on this verse: 'We get on Earth to the Kingdom of heaven. In sex intercourse when it is rightly conceived, we have an act of pure delight which is not mere physical satisfaction but a psycho-spiritual communion. The rich deep fulfilment of love between a man and a woman is a condition of earthly beatitude so simple, so natural and so real, that it is the happiest of all earthly conditions and many mystics employ this as the symbol of divine communion' (Radhakrishnan 1953: 262).

[8] This chapter capitalizes the word 'Tantra' to indicate the set of texts of the belief system 'tantra', put here in lower case and without diacritical marks. So are the words 'tantric' (a practitioner of tantra) and 'tantrism' (the way of tantra), except as the initial word of a sentence.

or habitation or sex, are broken by the tantric seeker who inhabits cremation grounds, eats meat, drinks and smokes intoxicants, and has sex outside marriage.

Because tantra treats sex as the key that unlocks and channels the spiritual energy considered to be inherent in the body, sex has become the defining insignia of tantra for many and its public face. The internet, for instance, is packed with offers of 'tantric' manuals and workshops for enhancing the sex lives of men and women. By extension of tantra's reputation for untrammelled sex, the idea of Hinduism at large has often been coloured by reports of degenerate sexual practices, especially during early Western encounters with India, a telling literary evocation of which occurs—albeit with ironic reservations—in E. M. Forster's *A Passage to India* (1924). Hugh B. Urban has illustrated the Western fascination with the 'sex magic' attributed to tantrism in a study of the nineteenth century occultist Aleister Crowley (Urban 2003).

This sensationalism has been countered by modern scholars such as Narendra Nath Bhattacharyya (1999), Gavin Flood (2006), Loriliai Biernacki (2007), and Hugh B. Urban (2010), who have been at considerable pains to demonstrate from tantric texts that tantrism is not a subterfuge for orgiastic sex and black magic. They do not deny that tantrism is preoccupied with theologically validating sexual acts outside conventional social practices, and that there have been decadent formulations of tantra to serve opportunistic male exploitations of the female body, and also that much of the construction of tantra is part of the Western lubricious imaginary of a decadent Orient. But the recovery and analysis of the tantric tradition on solid grounds of textual evidence (Gupta 1972; Flood 2006) and observed practice (White 2000) have consistently highlighted the spiritual instrumentality of the sexual deployment of the human body, male and female.

Sex and Power

Divested of sensationalism, tantra can be seen to elevate sexuality to a transcendental level by holding the human male–female relationship as one mirroring the union of Śiva and Pārvatī. Considering their lovemaking as the original act of creation, tantric theology transposes their procreative energy from the metaphysical to the physical to provide the basis of the material universe, and it is their union that forms the basis of the esoteric rites of tantra. It is that thread of sexual union that the tantric follows but in reverse. The functionality of sex also foregrounds women as indispensable to tantric rites, but whether as equal agents with male partners or as mere vessels of their purposes remains a perennially debated issue, as noted by Urban (2010: 125–145).

Tantra proclaims the veneration of women and views women as earthly forms of *śakti*, the ultimate locus of energy manifest in many forms of Devī, the essential feminine power at the core of existence. In the theology of *śakti*, which forms the Śākta tradition, all female deities are forms of the Great Goddess, or Devī, and therefore deserving of worship, especially Śiva's consort Pārvatī in her many forms. But in tantra a form of *śakti* particularly venerated is Kālī, the dark and fierce manifestation of Devī, that is, Pārvatī in a different form, and Kālī's other, still more fearsome aspects.

The adoration of Kālī is not limited to tantra, much of Śākta theology being a philosophy of love that aims to realize her benign aspect as the universal Mother. Tantra, however, emphasizes the overwhelming power of *śakti* that underwrites the transgressive roles of the divine feminine by which she sets the devotee free from the illusions of worldly vision to facilitate union with the godhead. Not surprisingly, the adoration of female divinity has led some feminists to see in tantra the restoration of gender balance by the valorization of women (Biernacki 2007: 5–6).

The importance of sexuality in tantra makes the question of gender particularly challenging in the shifting light of the sexual consumption of women on the one hand and the paramountcy of *śakti* on the other, especially as in tantric rites women are theoretically transformed into embodiments of *śakti* and because tantra recognizes spiritually advanced women as *gurus*. Digging deeper into tantra's basis, one may find a constant discrepancy between Śiva's supremacy as instructor and Pārvatī's dependency as disciple, and the equally constant assertion of Devī as the source of power in the universe. Although some scholars have viewed tantra as a theology that elevates women (Gupta 1972: xvi–xvii), promotes gender equivalence (Khanna 2000), and empowers women, the actual world of tantra remains male-dominated in its secret, sex-driven rituals and everyday preceptor–disciple relationships. The socially determined entity that Gavin Flood (2006: 36) calls the tantric body struggles towards the deity under gender constraints.

Sacred Desire

Sex and gender are even more intriguing in the ideology of bhakti, perhaps the most influential belief system within Hinduism in its extent and currency. While the quest for union with the godhead adopts a neuro-physical strategy in tantra, it takes a different direction in bhakti. In both tantra and bhakti the yearning for union with the godhead is intense. But while tantra expects sexual energy to empower the devotee to rise towards union with the universal soul, bhakti theology provides for and indeed often expects an erotic attachment to the deity to achieve such a union.

This erotic stance is not the only position taken in bhakti, its complex soteriological doctrine being based rather upon seeking the deity's compassion through *prapatti* or total dependency and surrender in a state of spiritual elation. But because the deity is ascribed personhood, surrender to the deity evokes a sense of nearness and in its heightened state may take on an erotic coloration. The trope of the individual self's immersion into the universal Self is in itself an erotic vision.

The idea of the unity of the individual with the supreme spirit of the universe, with Brahman, with Ātman, and with 'That' of the *Ṛg Veda*, is of course one that took shape in Upaniṣadic thought, as in the dictum 'you are that' (*Chāndogya Upaniṣad*, 6.8.7). A later work, the *Śvetāśvatara Upaniṣad*, views the distinction between the Lord and the individual soul being progressively erased through rebirth until the union of the two by the grace of the Lord. This is the earliest text to use the term bhakti, and although it occurs in a verse of debatable authenticity, the seeds of bhakti theology certainly seem to lie here (Flood 1996: 153). But at that point the idea of the supreme spirit is still abstract and impersonal.

Bhakti on the other hand is committed to the personhood of the deity who is directly and personally accessible, be it as friend, child, parent, or lover, even as it accommodates belief in god as an abstraction. The fifteenth-century poet Kabir scoffs at the idea of a corporeal god and yet addresses his god as a person. *Śakti* theology also personalizes the deity but without the intimate dependency of bhakti bordering on erotic feelings. Personal and highly charged emotional attachment marked the culture of bhakti from its beginnings around the first century CE and its flowering in South India from about the third century CE among the Vaiṣṇava Ālvārs and the Śaivaite Nāyanmārs.

This division marked the development of bhakti theology and practice along two main branches, the Vaiṣṇava and the Śaiva, but in the southern tradition as well as in the later wave of bhakti initiated by the eleventh-century theologian Rāmānuja that swept across northern India from the twelfth century, the pulse of spirituality was the same, namely, an all-consuming love for the godhead conceived as a person. In whatever form that personal god was imagined, whether as Viṣṇu or Śiva, the devotee claimed for him 'identity with Brahman, which is the All' (Gonda 1970: 34) and yearned to unite with him, the 'iṣṭa-devatā' (the chosen deity) as with an actual person.

It is also possible for the same devotee to pray to both Viṣṇu and Śiva, as the fifteenth-century Maithili poet Vidyāpati, a Śaivaite, did when he celebrated the love of Rādhā and Kṛṣṇa. Tulsīdās, the vastly influential sixteenth-century author of the *Rāmcaritmānas* and a celebrated Vaiṣṇava, includes 'Śiva, great giver' in his poetry of adoration (Hawley and Juergensmeyer 1988: 166). But the goal is union with a personally realized divinity. In the *Bhagavad Gītā* Kṛṣṇa is the warrior Prince Arjuna's closest friend and he assures the prince that one who treads the path of devotion reaches salvation and attains Brahman through his loving grace. In a famous passage Kṛṣṇa promises, 'Abandoning all creeds, seek shelter only with me. I shall deliver you from all wrongdoings. Do not despair' (18.66, author's translation).

The grace promised in bhakti is not reserved for the learned or well-born alone, nor only for male devotees but is accessible to low caste people and women. It also enables the individual to set aside social conventions, to the extent where the twelfth-century Vīraśaiva poet Mahādevyākkā could wander about naked because she would allow nothing to veil her from her beloved Śiva.

One might even say that bhakti particularly privileges women. A. K. Ramanujan calls attention to 'the extent to which bhakti itself appears as "feminine" in nature', its 'chief mood' being the 'erotic (*śrá[1]...gāra*) seen almost entirely from an Indian woman's point of view whether in its phase of separation or of union' (1999: 270). Female subjectivity is so dominant that a male devotee may assume a female persona, sometimes even in his social transactions, for the surest approach to one's god would be as a lover.

When the Kṛṣṇaite scholar Jīva Gosvāmī refused to meet the legendary Rajput devotee Mīrābāī because he refused to be distracted by a woman, she declared that the only male in the universe being her beloved Kṛṣṇa, there could be no gender distinction between her and Jīva. As Ramanujan observes, 'Before God all men are women' (1999: 277). Mīrā knew herself as Kṛṣṇa's bride, asserting that

> in dream he grasped my hand;
> in dream he led me around the wedding fire
> and I became unshakably his bride.

> (Hawley and Juergensmeyer
> 1988: 137)

But it was not only a woman poet who took on the bride persona, and we see a more overtly erotic relationship in Mīrā's predecessor Kabir's poetry:

> They all say I am Your wife
> but I have my doubts—
> If we don't sleep together on one couch
> what kind of love is that?

> (Vaudeville 1993: 270)

The tradition of explicitly sexual confessions was established well before Kabir and Mīrā. The ninth-century Vaiṣṇava woman Āṇṭāl wrote:

> Bless me,
> So that Trivikrama,
> Who spanned the world three times,
> May caress with his sacred hands
> My breasts and my waist
> With love,
> Granting me fame on earth and glory eternal!

> (Sundaram 1987: 104)

This sexually charged spirituality found a ready literary vehicle in India's tradition of love poetry from Sanskrit to regional languages. Spilling out of its devotional context, the idiom of bhakti has supplied the code of Indian romanticism in the widest cultural fields across centuries. From the delicate celebration of the love of Rādhā and Kṛṣṇa in Jayadeva's twelfth-century *Gīta Govinda* and the fourteenth-century poet Vidyāpati's courtly and erotic adoration of a royal couple as a transparent allegory of Viṣṇu and Lakṣmī's union, the imaginary of bhakti has travelled to the modern era in Rabindranath Tagore's poetry of love, nature, and devotion, which melds the secular with the spiritual, and even to the romantic escapism of Bollywood films.

Because it is so emotionally charged, bhakti spread beyond formal theological discourse from very early times to be enunciated in the idiom of common folk. As we have seen, its accessibility has also challenged established forms of social and political power to a degree, though without actually revolutionizing social relations. Inverting gender authority in the human part of the human–divine relationship certainly sets bhakti apart from most other theologies. Bhakti does not dispense with the idea of gender, nor of the superiority of the male, but only redraws the boundary of gender identity, for the only person worshipped must also be the only locus of authority and that person is a male.

In truth, bhakti turns gender into a fluid selfhood determined as much by the will as by the body, never a natural and essential necessity. This idea of gender fluidity is inherent in Hindu thought as evidenced by the myths of androgyny and sex change, which affect the bodies of both mortals and gods. Viṣṇu turning himself into the alluring female Mohinī is only one of many tales. A modern exemplar of de-gendering (as well as de-sectarianism) was the charismatic Ramakrishna Paramahamsa, a Kālī devotee who often dressed up as a *gopī*, one of the women who loved Kṛṣṇa. Desire for god pre-empts bisexual desire within the community of bhakti worshippers but remains no less potent between the human worshipper and her iṣṭa-devatā.

Again, bhakti does not expunge sex. Rather, it constructs a deferred sexuality for all and an intoxicating state altogether different from other modes of yearning for the Supreme Being. In tantra, for instance, sexual congress among devotees is an immediate, concrete act of mystical mimesis whereby the godhead may be realized but one constrained by the limitations of the body whereby the quest becomes a fragmented process. By contrast, desire in bhakti creates a seamlessly uninterrupted intimacy.

Given the diversity of philosophical choices in Hindu theology from the Vedic to modern times, it is not surprising that multiple religious traditions should remain vigorously followed to this day, from ritualistic, elaborate, and often socially constraining regimens to free and simple confessions of faith. Upaniṣadic thought in particular has greatly influenced modern Hinduism, especially in colonial times when it became urgent to reclaim national self-esteem, wilting under attack from Western liberalism and Christian missionary morality. Modern sects such as the Brahmo Samaj in Bengal and the Arya Samaj in northern India set about divesting the Hindu religion of its burden of ritual and custom, in the process turning away from what they saw as the debased ritualism of tantra and the effeminacy of bhakti. Influenced by the Protestant ethic, they adopted a puritanical resistance to sexuality, preferring the intellectualism of Upaniṣadic spirituality.

But the bleaching of mystery and emotion has not worked well, nor the exile of sexuality, although in present-day practices of both bhakti and tantra it is incipient rather than overt. Historically speaking, it is in tantra and bhakti that we see the heaviest impress of sexuality and gender on theological discourse and social practice. In addition, the transition from contemplating an abstract Supreme to searching for a realizable deity has not only been a theological upheaval but also a social revolution in that the ascription of personhood to divinity has created models of conduct valorised by their association with the sacred. It is through this transformative theology that spirit and body meet in the Hindu way of faith and life.

Sexuality as a seminal explanation of existence and the gendering of divinity associated with it are then at the core of Hindu theology. At the same time, since theology

fosters not only theory but also practice, the religious life of Hindus and the social attitudes derived from it have been deeply imbued with spiritually derived positions on
sexuality and gender. Shorn of sectarian delusions, Hindu theology is less a matter of
doctrinaire assertion than of systematic enquiry and analytical speculation. At once
spiritual and worldly, Hinduism holds that the human body, both physical and social, is
a correlative of an eternal entity with which all human action seeks connections.

Hindu theology accepts that the search is at once intellectual, emotional, physical and
social, shaped as it is by the properties of the physical body, especially of sexuality as a
unifying urge, and by the institution of gender as a property of the social body. Through
its competing philosophies spread over millennia, Hinduism continues to affirm the
possibility—perhaps the certainty—of the unity of humanity and divinity.

References

Bhagavad Gītā (c1984). Trans. Winthrop Sargeant. Albany: State University of New York Press.

Bhattacharji, Sukumari (1970). *The Indian Theogony*. Cambridge: Cambridge University Press.

Bhattacharyya, Narendra Nath (1999). *History of the Tantric Religion*, 2nd edn. New Delhi: Manohar.

Biernacki, Loriliai (2007). *Renowned Goddess of Desire: Women, Sex, and Speech in Tantra*. Oxford and New York: Oxford University Press.

Danielou, Alain (c1991). *Myths and Gods of India*. Rochester, VT: Inner Traditions International.

Flood, Gavin (1996). *An Introduction to Hinduism*. Cambridge: Cambridge University Press.

Flood, Gavin (2006). *The Tantric Body: The Secret Tradition of Hindu Religion*. London and New York: I.B. Tauris.

Gonda. J. (1970). *Viṣṇuism and Śivaism*. London: The Athlone Press for the University of London.

Gupta, Sanjukta (1972). *Lakṣmī Tantra: A Pāncarātra Text*. Leiden: Brill.

Hawley, John Stratton, and Mark Juergensmeyer (1988). *Songs of the Saints of India*. New York and Oxford: Oxford University Press.

Khanna, Madhu (2000). 'The Goddess-Woman Equation in *Śākta* Tantras'. In Mandakranta Bose (ed.), *Faces of the Feminine in Ancient, Medieval and Modern India*. New York: Oxford University Press, 109–123.

Lidke, Jeffrey S. (2003). 'A Union of Fire and Water: Sexuality and Spirituality in Hinduism'. In David W. Machacek and Melissa M. Wilcox (eds), *Sexuality and the World's Religions*. Santa Barbara, CA: ABC-CLIO, 103–132.

Matsyapurāṇa (1892). Ed. Pandit Gokulchandra, Pandit Kalicharan, and Pandit Vastirama. Lucknow: Munshi Navalkishore.

Müller, Max (1919). *The Six Systems of Indian Philosophy*. London: Longmans, Green.

O'Flaherty, Wendy Doniger (1975). *Hindu Myths*. Harmondsworth: Penguin.

O'Flaherty, Wendy Doniger (1981a). *Śiva the Erotic Ascetic*. Oxford: Oxford University Press.

O'Flaherty, Wendy Doniger, trans. (1981b). *The Rig Veda*. London: Penguin Books.

Padoux, André (2002). 'What do we mean by Tantrism?' In Katherine A. Harper and Robert L. Brown (eds), *Roots of Tantra*. Albany: State University of New York Press, 17–24.

Radhakrishnan, S. (1953). *The Principal Upaniṣads*. London: George Allen & Unwin.

Ramanujan, A. K. (1999). 'Men, Women and Saints.' In *The Collected Essays of A. K. Ramanujan*. Ed. Vinay Dharwarker. New Delhi: Oxford University Press, 279–294.

Sundaram, P. S. (1987). *The Poems of Andal: Tiruppavai and Nacciyar Tirumozhi*. Bombay: Ananthacharya Indological Research Institute.

Urban, Hugh (2003). 'Unleashing the Beast: Aleister Crowley, Tantra and Sex Magic in Late Victorian England'. *Esoterica*, **5**: 138–192.

Urban, Hugh B. (2010). *The Power of Tantra: Religion, Sexuality and the Politics of South Asian Studies*. London and New York: I. B. Tauris.

Vaudeville, Charlotte (1993). *A Weaver Named Kabir: Selected Verses*. Delhi: Oxford University Press.

White, David Gordon (ed.) (2000). *Tantra in Practice*. Princeton, NJ: Princeton University Press.

CHAPTER 28

....

BUDDHISM

....

RITA M. GROSS

BUDDHISM is older than Christianity by about four hundred years. Like Christianity, it has spread far beyond its land of origin, in which, like Christianity, it is no longer practised to any great extent. At one time, Buddhism was perhaps the most widespread religion in Asia, though its borders shrank with the success of Islam in Western Asia and the triumph of communism in parts of East Asia. Like Christianity, it has spread around the world in the modern period and is now quite widespread in Western countries, but it is probably more culturally diverse than Christianity because the various forms of Buddhism lost contact with each other in Asia long before the modern period. They then developed independently for centuries in East Asia (Korea, Japan, and China), in Tibet, and in South East Asia (Sri Lanka, Thailand, Burma, Laos, Cambodia, and Vietnam), though all forms of Buddhism have always relied on texts and practices that originally came from India. All varieties of Buddhism are now practised in the geographic West by both immigrants from Asia and Western converts.

Asian Buddhists were subjected to European colonialism and introduced to modernity in diverse ways. Some countries, such as Sri Lanka, were colonized and subjected to Western influences very early, beginning in the sixteenth century, while others, such as Tibet, encountered Western and modern influences very late, only in the mid-twentieth century and only in the form of Chinese communist domination. Between these extremes, places such as Japan modernized and Westernized very rapidly in the nineteenth century, while others, such as most of South East Asia, both accommodated and resisted modernity and Westernization.

Today, Asian Buddhists have largely modernized in terms of accepting and utilizing technology and industrialization. However, theologically, except for some Japanese philosophical schools, there has been little sustained, systematic effort on the part of Asian Buddhist religious leaders to think through the implications of modernity for traditional Buddhism. Topics such as how valuing human rights and equality would impact traditional understandings of karma or the implications of accurate history for traditional Buddhist narratives are largely unexplored. Western convert Buddhists imbibed modernity while growing up and during their education, but few of them have done critical and constructive Buddhist theology. This lag is understandable because understanding Buddhist thought and practice accurately is a lengthy process and we are still in the first generation during which large numbers of Westerners have taken on that project. Therefore, the enterprise of modern critical and constructive Buddhist thought is just beginning.

Buddhist 'Theology'

Because, technically speaking, Buddhism is a non-theistic religion, the discipline of theology exists only by analogy in Buddhist contexts. Nevertheless, Buddhism has a highly developed, diverse philosophical tradition with complex concepts of ultimate reality. What Buddhists generally mean by 'non-theism' is the lack of any notion of a creator god, which they contrast with parallel Hindu concepts of deities who create the world. To Buddhists, the question of an ultimate origin of the universe is unanswerable and illogical, leading only to an infinite regress of beginnings. Furthermore, the question of how the presently existing world came into being is irrelevant to solving the more pressing problem of how to live well within that world. A more central meaning of non-theism for Buddhists is that there can be no vicarious enlightenment, by contrast to the vicarious atonement that is so prominent in Christian theories of how humans cope with their lot. For Buddhists, each being must eventually clarify its own confusion about reality. No one can perform that task for anyone else and everyone is capable of eventually cutting through their own confusion.

Nevertheless, in its Mahayana, but not its Theravada, forms—which may be closer to original Buddhism—Buddhism has developed a large repertoire of non-empirical beings who play an important role in the spiritual lives of Buddhists. These beings are extremely numerous and quite varied in how they are depicted, though usually they are recognizably humanoid in form despite, in some cases, having multiple heads, arms, and legs. They appear in virtually all the colours of the rainbow, though white, black, green, red, blue, and yellow predominate. They appear routinely in both male and female form. Thus, a central problem of Western theological imagery, the maleness of its deity, is non-existent in Buddhism. To Buddhists, it has always been clear that if their religion is to include anthropomorphic, 'mythical' beings, these beings would, like their human devotees, appear in both genders. In Vajrayana forms of Buddhism, but not in other forms of Buddhism, these beings are frequently depicted in sexual union.

What role do these beings play in the spiritual lives of Buddhists to whom they are important? To call upon the key Buddhist concept of emptiness (Garfield 1995) that is still not well understood in the West, they are empty of inherent, independent existence. They do not exist eternally, independent of references to them. Nevertheless, they have considerable 'reality' for some Buddhist practitioners, in that they model more completely the ideal Buddhist mind-state than do most ordinary human beings. Especially noteworthy are those beings, both female and male, who model and represent the ideal Buddhist virtues of wisdom and compassion. Some forms of Buddhist meditation consist primarily of visualizing these beings and eventually identifying completely with them. When the identification is complete, one has overcome the mistaken identity that is the most common Buddhist diagnosis of human malaise. We humans persistently and consistently make the mistakes of both self-limitation and self-cherishing. But, according to Buddhism, we also have all the tools we need to overcome our case of mistaken identity. One of those tools is to visualize ourselves as beings who are supremely wise and compassionate while cultivating those virtues in every possible way.

This 'theology' is vastly different from anything found in the West and not well understood by most Westerners. However, it accords well with some forms of Western psychology that stress the relevance of symbols and imagination to human well-being. Because these beings were never thought to be creator, saviour gods having independent, eternal existence, they are immune to modern atheistic deconstructions. The intersection of modernity and Buddhist 'theology' will concern other questions, such as those already mentioned: the impact of historical consciousness on much conventional Buddhist thinking and how notions of human rights and this-worldly justice will affect traditional interpretations of karma. Both of those questions also deeply implicate traditional Buddhist understandings of and practices surrounding gender.

Buddhist Evaluations of Sexuality

Because Buddhism has a very long tradition of celibate monasticism, many observers have mistakenly concluded that Buddhism is anti-sexual or regards sexuality as inherently negative or problematic. But this conclusion, deriving from some Western and Christian evaluations of sexuality, is highly inaccurate. To put it bluntly, it is not sexuality itself, but the results of sexuality—children and domestic responsibilities—that are problematic. They are problematic because they are so demanding and time-consuming, leaving little time and energy for the spiritual disciplines leading to self-transformation and transcendence. They are also problematic because family relationships and domestic responsibilities tend to foster attachment and emotional entanglement. Buddhism regards such states of mind as unhealthy because they inevitably lead to suffering. Instead, it recommends a lifestyle promoting detachment leading to equanimity. Monasticism is often regarded as the lifestyle most conducive to those states of mind, though Buddhism has also developed ethics for detachment in householder lifestyles.

In its early years in India of the fifth and sixth centuries BCE, Buddhism participated in a developing world view characterized by consistent interest in introspection and exploration of the inner world. This new intellectual and spiritual milieu was also increasingly sceptical about the ability of conventional 'worldly' pursuits involving economic activity and physiological reproduction to lead to a deeply satisfying life or to plumb the depths of reality. For that, a quieter, less busy, more secluded lifestyle involving more contemplation, introspection, and reflection was required. These values have remained central to Buddhism, whatever social forms it may take on. But because, until very recently, heterosexual sexual activity almost inevitably led to children, which led to time-demanding childcare and economic activities, as well as lack of solitude and silence, it seemed to most early spiritual seekers in India that conventional householder life and deep spiritual insight were incompatible. Either choice of lifestyle was valorized, but they could not both be practised as the same time, as early Buddhists saw it. That is why monastic celibacy is so highly valued by Buddhists, not because sexuality, per se, is defiling or negative.

Monasticism has remained important throughout Buddhist history, though it has become much less dominant in some Buddhist cultures in more recent times. For example, most Japanese religious leaders and teachers are married, a practice that was introduced some centuries ago and has prevailed since then, though initially Japanese Buddhism did emphasize monastic celibacy. To date, the Western Buddhist movement is almost entirely a lay movement, in part because a system of economic support for monastics simply does not exist in the West. If these conditions persist, Western Buddhism as a form of Buddhism initiated and led almost entirely by lay Buddhists will be an important experiment in Buddhist institutional forms.

Buddhists also have always recognized that a celibate lifestyle is not appropriate for everyone, that there is no one-size-fits-all religion or lifestyle. Thus, for those who choose the more conventional and common lifestyle of production and reproduction, sexual pleasure is entirely appropriate, not in any way to be shunned or avoided. In universal Buddhist ethics, the fourth precept is to avoid sexual misconduct. For monastics, the rules are very carefully laid out. Any kind of sexual contact whatsoever must be avoided and breaking that rule could result in permanent expulsion from the monastic community. But for non-monastics, the rules are much looser and generally follow the norms of the culture in which Buddhists live. Thus, Buddhists have practised and still do practise monogamous, polygynous, and polyandrous forms of marriage, depending on the culture. Concubinage and prostitution have also been widely tolerated for laypeople, though there is disapproval of sexual activity with a woman who is pledged to another man. Emerging Western Buddhism is developing its own lay Buddhist sexual ethic, which will be discussed more fully later.

Within a few years of its founding, Buddhism developed forms of monasticism for women, an option that was unusual for that time and place, although the ancient Jain religion also had monastic orders for women. While today celibate monasticism is a hard sell to most women, especially younger women, in an era in which sexual activity almost inevitably meant endless pregnancies and little opportunity for education or spiritual discipline, it is obvious why celibate monasticism would be attractive to women. It gives women real options and an alternative to domestic drudgery and the subservience of patriarchal marriage. Though female monasticism met with varying fates in different Buddhist cultures throughout the long history of Buddhism, it has never died out completely, even in countries in which full ordination for women has been lost. It is thriving today in many parts of the Buddhist world, especially in East Asia. An important contemporary gender issue for Buddhists is reviving women's monastic institutions in some parts of the Buddhist world and improving nuns' education in others.

'Tantric Sex'

Finally, Buddhist evaluations of sexuality must include some discussion of the wildly misunderstood topic of 'Tantric sex'. As is well known, in Tantric or Vajrayana Buddhism, sexual symbolism abounds and images of couples in sexual union are omnipresent. In fact, one could say that the 'yab-yum' or 'father-mother' image, as it is called, is the dominant religious symbol in Vajrayana Buddhism. However, to claim that this image is primarily a glorification of mundane human sex is about as accurate as to claim that the crucifix is about valorizing torture and extreme violence. It is well known that in Asian contexts, an image of a crucifix can elicit horror rather than reverence or awe. In the same way, the yab-yum image often elicits prurient titillation in Westerners, who are more used to seeing sexual imagery in pornography than in sacred settings.

The image is primarily a symbol rather than a portrayal of social reality and should not be taken as an endorsement of mundane copulation aimed solely at producing momentary egoistic pleasure and gratification. The information one gains when one googles 'Tantric sex' should be taken with a large grain of salt. Ritual physiological sexual practices may have been part of Vajrayana Buddhism in some contexts, and may still be used in some highly esoteric settings, but it is very difficult to gain accurate information about such practices. Anything one can learn on the Web or in publicly available published sources should not be trusted.

As a symbol, the 'yab-yum' image is about the non-duality and inseparability of wisdom and compassion, the two primary Buddhist virtues. Compassion is represented by the masculine element and wisdom by the feminine. Though obvious in the 'yab-yum' icon, this symbolism recurs on many levels in Vajrayana Buddhist practice. One's ritual implements, the bell and sceptre, also reproduce the feminine and masculine principles, as do one's hands, especially when crossed in a specific ritual gesture. Even the vowels and consonants of words repeat this symbolism as do the primary colours of red and white. In this dense symbolic universe, people, individual practitioners, whether women or men, seek to embody both the feminine and the masculine, both wisdom and compassion. It would be a serious misunderstanding of the symbolism to presume that women are more representative of the symbols labelled as feminine or that men have more affinity with symbols labelled as masculine. An accomplished practitioner should embody both wisdom and compassion. Sexual symbolism is especially effective in portraying non-duality, a state in which opposites are neither obliterated nor in conflict with each other.

Buddhism, Feminism, and Gender

Despite the lack of modern theological reconstructions concerning many issues in Buddhism, regarding questions of gender, considerable investigation, much of it done by Western Buddhists, has already occurred (Paul 1979; Horner 1989; Cabezon 1992; Gross 1993, 2013; Boucher 1993; Klein 1995; Simmer-Brown 2001). The main gender question pertains to the roles and status of women within Buddhism, a tradition that is as patriarchal, misogynist, and male-dominated as any other major religion. Upon closer investigation, the issue of gender turns out to be more complicated and multi-faceted than simply being about women and patriarchy. Sexual orientation is a closely related issue, as is sexual exploitation by Buddhist teachers. Discussion of women's serious participation in Buddhist practice throws into question traditional understandings of work and family roles, including child-rearing practices. Thus, simply questioning the appropriateness of women's limited roles in traditional Asian Buddhism eventually brings up a whole host of related issues.

Though there is a worldwide Buddhist feminist movement today, much of the impetus for it does stem from Western Buddhists, who, beginning in the early 1980s, began to seriously question what they saw as the patriarchy and male dominance of Asian Buddhism. The fact that all the notable Asian teachers who came to teach in the West were men did not alleviate their impressions about traditional Buddhist male dominance. In those early days of a large Western Buddhist movement, which began in the early 1970s, many women were attracted to Buddhist teachers and Buddhist practice. In keeping with emerging trends in Western secular and religious women's movements, these women did not take a back seat to their boyfriends or other men in their Buddhist communities. They practised Buddhist meditation as equals and expected to be treated as equals, including taking on whatever leadership roles their Asian teachers would let them assume. By the 1990s, their participation as equals in Buddhist study and practice led to a situation in which about half the Western Buddhist teachers were women, a situation unprecedented in Buddhist history. Thus, I have often argued (Gross 1993) that there was an 'auspicious coincidence'[1] involving the feminist movement and the arrival of Asian Buddhist teachers in the West that greatly spurred the development of a much more egalitarian form of Buddhism. By contrast, imagine what would have happened if those Asian Buddhist teachers had arrived in the West in large numbers in the 1950s, one of the darkest periods in history regarding women's equal participation in society at large. As I have often put it, instead of meditating and studying side by side with their men, the women would have done all the childcare so that men could be free to study and practise and they would also

---

[1] 'Auspicious coincidence' is a term used in some Buddhist contexts to name the intersection of two seemingly independent lines of cause and effect that results in very positive developments. It is often used to describe the meeting of teacher and student when the student is ready to take on serious dharma practice.

have taken on responsibility for holding bake sales to finance building a more adequate meditation centre in which the men could engage in Buddhist practice!

However, despite their immersion in Buddhist study and practice, many who led the way to a more egalitarian Buddhism rejected the label 'feminism' completely. In the early 1980s, I was repeatedly told by other Buddhists that, as a Buddhist, I should not be involved in 'causes' and eventually would see the light and stop talking about Buddhism and feminism. Much of this animosity to 'feminism' was due to the ideological hard edge of much secular feminism. Their opposition, however, led me to define what I meant by feminism—freedom from the prison of gender roles—a definition that applies equally to women and men, to straights and gays, and to any other position on the gender rainbow. Nevertheless, many Buddhists remain reluctant to talk openly about gender equality and equity, even though they participate in more egalitarian forms of Buddhism. They also overlook an undercurrent of people who are initially interested in Buddhism but eventually turn away from Buddhism because no one will admit to or talk about Buddhism's heritage of sexism and patriarchy. Instead, many throw out superficial slogans such as 'enlightened mind is beyond gender', as if such a truism, by itself, was sufficient to undo a centuries-long history of male dominance, the ordinary, everyday, ongoing gender stereotyping that is routinely applied to all genders in much Buddhist discourse, or the expectations that such stereotypes are accurate and reliable.

An Indigenous Feminist Voice

Nevertheless, a significant body of research on Buddhism and gender, as already noted, has been produced. While it is difficult to summarize such a large body of research, several generalizations hold up. First of all, such research definitively demonstrates that, historically, Buddhist *institutions* have been thoroughly male-dominated and have consistently favoured men over women. Women's monasticism has always been far less well supported economically than men's and was allowed to die out in some parts of the Buddhist world. Nuns had far less prestige than monks and women teachers were few and far between. Most problematic of all, being a woman was evaluated as far less fortunate than being a man, mainly because so much that Buddhism values was not available to women, and women were confined to taking care of men and children as their lifework. The solution to the misfortunes of female rebirth proposed by traditional Buddhism was eventual rebirth as a man, rather than by changing society and Buddhist institutions. It must be conceded that, though such a solution seems completely inadequate to many modern people, in circumstances in which fertility control was virtually impossible, it may well have seemed easier to turn women into men than to change society to be more egalitarian. These facts are unknown to and unacknowledged by many Western Buddhists who are familiar only with their relatively egalitarian contemporary sanghas (Buddhist communities). Because they know so little about Buddhist history or about traditional Asian Buddhist societies, many simply refuse to acknowledge these facts and ridicule those who point them out.

But, secondly and more important, male dominance has always been contested by both male and female Buddhists (Gutschow 2004; Schaeffer 2004). In other words, if by 'feminism' we mean promoting egalitarian institutions and values over male-dominant ones and resisting rigid gender roles, Buddhism has always included an 'indigenous feminist' voice. It is not the invention of the twentieth-century Western feminist movement at all, contrary to the claims of many, both Asians and Westerners, who are uninformed about or unsympathetic to the goals of 'feminism'.

For example, some Asian novice nuns who favour restoring nuns' full ordination try to curry favour with their male counterparts, who would have to approve of this change by proclaiming that they are not feminists (Mohr and Tsoedren 2010). Quasi-nuns in Buddhist societies that lack even novice ordination sometimes oppose introducing nuns' ordination because they associate such a project with 'Western feminism' which they regard as egotistical and self-centred. Especially problematic are the conclusions of some non-Buddhist Western social scientists who claim that those who lead movements to restore nuns' ordination in Theravada and Tibetan forms of Buddhism are mainly motivated by 'Western feminism'. It is true that such movements are sometimes led by fully ordained nuns who happen to be Westerners, but it is inaccurate to claim that their motivation to support nuns' ordination movements is due solely to their Western ethnicity. Such claims totally ignore their intense dedication to Buddhism and *Buddhist* grounds for their activities, which are far more important to them than 'feminism', with which most of them do not identify.

What might be called 'indigenous Buddhist feminism', as defined earlier, is found in texts and other evidence from every period of Buddhist history. Even if one resists the label 'feminism', such information is important and accurate for any discussion of Buddhism and gender. Everyone needs to know that the male dominance that is so apparent within a superficial knowledge of Buddhism is not the whole story about Buddhism. One could write a substantial book detailing a history of notable Buddhist women and explicit refutations of Buddhist male dominance. Most of this material is just becoming known to Western scholars and Western Buddhist practitioners. Furthermore, it is very easy to demonstrate that in its most important teachings, such as teachings on egolessness, emptiness, and Buddha-nature, Buddhism is completely gender-neutral and gender-free. These teachings simply cannot be made to support gender hierarchy, male dominance, or misogyny, even though such phenomena are widespread in Buddhist institutions. In fact, thorough understanding of key Buddhist teachings can only result in realizing that gender has no inherent reality but is merely a conventional label. Therefore, I have long contended (Gross 1993) that the single most important statement regarding Buddhism and gender is that, as a whole, Buddhism is characterized by an intolerable contradiction between its gender-neutral, gender-free view and its institutional male dominance. This internal contradiction must be resolved in favour of its world view or central teachings.

However, because Western scholars are often so androcentric themselves, they have overlooked much of the less male-dominant material and emphasized the more male-dominant materials in many of their earlier presentations of Buddhism. As more and more materials come to be known to Western scholars, it is becoming clearer and clearer that Buddhists themselves have always been uncomfortable with their own misogyny and male dominance. Such discomfort does not depend on 'Western feminism' but is built into the very fabric of Buddhism and has always been present in Buddhist discourse, often hidden in plain sight in narratives that have mainly been used to shore up male-dominant interpretations of Buddhism.

For example, in a famous and controversial narrative that is often used against women's interests and needs by both Asians and Westerners, the Buddha's foster-mother Mahaprajapati successfully negotiates with the Buddha to initiate the nuns' order (Oldenberg 2007: 521–524). In this narrative, the Buddha initially rejects her request that women also lead the renunciant, homeless life. For many reasons, contemporary scholarship regards this story as a later interpolation into an older text, but because it has been taken as authentic for so long in Buddhist sources, it is interesting to analyse the story, whether or not it accurately reports opinions and actions of the historical Buddha. Though traditional interpretations of the story emphasize the Buddha's reluctance to allow the nuns' order and often use that interpretation as an excuse to oppose reinstating nuns' ordination, it could just as easily be interpreted as the first instance of indigenous Buddhist feminism. Mahaprajapti refuses to take 'no' for an answer but instead cuts her hair, puts on yellow robes, and with her attendants, follows the Buddha to his next stopping point, where he finally gives in to her request. This is one of the few records, if not the only record, of the Buddha changing his mind about a decision he has previously made.

That point goes unnoted in traditional interpretations, but, in orally retelling the story I have often added the point that the Buddha becomes a great role model for patriarchal authority figures in Buddhism. If even the Buddha could change his mind about the roles and status of women when presented with good arguments opposing his previous position, surely any contemporary male authority can do the same! Yet the reaction I have sometimes received to this interpretation of the narrative is shock and hostility, even a denial that the Buddha had changed his mind at all. Such are the politics of interpretation and scholarship. Unfortunately, women socialized in male-dominant cultures often want to please men more than anything else and lack both the education and the confidence to suggest alternative interpretations of familiar stories that have been used against women. When people are educated enough and confident enough, much different interpretations of traditional stories, which are at least as cogent as the male-dominant interpretations, are easily forthcoming.

SAKYADHITA AND MAJOR CONTEMPORARY ISSUES REGARDING BUDDHISM AND GENDER

Contemporary worldwide interest in the well-being and flourishing of Buddhist women has led to the founding and success of Sakyadhita (2012). Its name translates as 'Daughters of Buddha' and it describes itself as an international organization of women (and men) dedicated to improving conditions for women in Buddhist societies. It was founded in 1987 at the conclusion of the first international Buddhist women's conference held in Bodhgaya, India (Tsomo 1988). The organization met again in Bangkok, Thailand in 1991 and has held major international conferences about every two years thereafter, always in an Asian country because, as its founder, Karma Lekshe Tsomo, says, 'most Buddhist women live in Asia'. Furthermore, Western women can more easily attend conferences in Asia than Asian women can attend conferences in a Western country where costs are generally much higher. These conferences are leisurely, well-organized events and are much less competitive than the standard academic conference. They include not only papers and panel discussions but cultural events, chanting, and meditation practice. They usually conclude with a pilgrimage to local Buddhist temples and other sacred sites. Sakyadhita also has chapters in many countries around the world which sometimes hold more local events.

Some of the themes that recur at conferences sponsored by Sakyadhita indicate well some of the major gender issues in contemporary Buddhism. None recurs more frequently or insistently than the question of nuns and contemporary Buddhism, which has often been referred to already. In brief, Buddhism has classically said that its community (*sangha*) consists of four 'orders'—monks, nuns, laymen, and laywomen. That fourfold community was initiated during the lifetime of the historical Buddha. It persisted for about 1,500 years in all forms of Buddhism and to the present day in Chinese, Korean, and some Vietnamese forms of Buddhism. But the nuns' sangha died out in Sri Lanka in about 1100 CE and was probably never transmitted to the rest of the Theravada Buddhist world in South East Asia. Probably only the novice ordination was transmitted to Tibet. Thus, today, two of the three major forms of Asian Buddhism—Theravada and Tibetan Vajrayana Buddhism—lack full ordination for nuns. In Tibet, novice ordination is available and nuns wear robes in the monastic colours—maroon in the Tibetan case. But in Theravada Buddhist countries, even novice ordination is lacking, leaving women only with an informal 'ordination' that is not recognized as monastic ordination by the male sanghas. These women take eight precepts and wear robes that cannot be in the monastic colour preferred in that country. They are neither truly monastics nor truly laypeople. Often they lack both monastic privileges, such as free transportation or medical care and lay privileges, such as voting and participating in political activities. For example, in Thailand, it can be dangerous for women to wear robes the same colour as those worn by men and it is illegal for monks to participate in women's ordination ceremonies in any way.

In the cases of both Tibet and South East Asia, many women and men, including Tibet's Fourteenth Dalai Lama, support restoring monastic ordination for women. But many obstacles can be found by those who oppose this development and thus far, the men who have the most authority in Buddhist sanghas lack the resolve to act decisively to restore nuns' ordination. Basically, the issue is that ordination must be conferred by those who already hold the vows in question and since no Tibetan or Theravada women currently hold the vows, those who oppose nuns' full ordination claim it cannot be restored 'until the next Buddha comes'. Given that many Chinese, Korean, and Vietnamese nuns hold these vows, one wonders why they cannot give them to Tibetan or Theravadin women, but there are several sets of monastic rules. Even though the basic rules are identical in the different monastic codes, those opposed to nuns' ordination insist that nuns belonging to a different monastic lineage from that practised by the local monks cannot properly give monastic vows to local women (Mohr and Tsedroen 2010). The whole issue is exceedingly technical and complex, often trying the patience of those with less legalistic values.

However, a start has been made in restoring nuns' full ordination. Women of means and determination can travel to a place in which full ordination is still given and receive the vows there. This solution is utilized by many Westerners. In the Tibetan case, they do so with the Dalai Lama's approval and wear Tibetan-style monastic robes rather than the robes characteristic of the country in which they were ordained. But Tibetan and Himalayan women, as opposed to Western women, often cannot or do not wish to take this step and want to receive ordination in their local communities. That is impossible at present, though many say the situation will soon change. In the Theravada world, some monastic authorities are quite sympathetic to women who want full ordination and ways have been found for them to receive it and be recognized, at least informally, as fully ordained monastics. Currently, there are individuals and communities of fully ordained women in both Sri Lanka and Thailand, though not in Burma or Cambodia. From all reports, they are generally well received by the local lay communities, which means they are economically supported. Theravada male monastics are divided on the issue.

In Taiwan, Korea, and other places which never lost nuns' full ordination, recent developments have greatly favoured nuns. Because of East Asian economic prosperity and a well-established ethic of generosity to religious institutions, monastic institutions are very well supported. But because secular economic opportunities are much greater for men than for women and because many women want to avoid patriarchal marriages and get an education, currently, there are many more nuns than monks in East Asian Buddhist countries. This combination of abundant economic support for monastics and many fewer male monastics means that the lack of economic support, which has often doomed women's monastic institutions, is not an issue. Nuns now receive excellent educations, both in meditation and in scholastic subjects. Many of them receive Western PhDs in addition. At Sakyadhita conferences and other places, the Taiwanese and Korean nuns are impressive indeed—disciplined, dignified, and highly confident.

Sakyadhita is careful to include laywomen almost as equals in its activities, despite its heavy emphasis on monastic women and their needs. However, as lay Buddhists become much better educated as Buddhists and become Buddhist teachers and leaders, not only in the West, but increasingly in Asia, it seems inevitable that the traditional hierarchy between monastics and laypeople will be questioned. Well-educated senior Buddhist leaders and teachers who are laywomen are unlikely to be willing to be ranked lower than child nuns indefinitely, even though such ranking prevails at more formal Sakyadhita events and other Buddhist events in Asia. Most such female leaders and teachers are more likely to evaluate monasticism and lay life as different but equal life-style choices appropriate for different people, perhaps at different stages of their lives. But they are unlikely to tolerate indefinitely an evaluation that sees every nun, no matter how young and inexperienced, as superior to every laywoman, no matter how venerable she is or the enormity of her contributions to the Buddhist community. Such a hierarchy is uncomfortably imitative of the traditional hierarchy between monks and nuns, which has been so disadvantageous to nuns and which nuns rightfully resent. However, discussion of this issue has not even begun in any serious fashion.

THE ULTIMATE BUDDHIST GENDER ISSUE—WOMEN TEACHERS

Because Buddhism is a non-theistic religion that does not promise vicarious atonement or divine intervention in one's life, no role is more important than that of the dharma teacher. Ultimately, each individual is responsible for their own enlightenment and the only external aid in that quest comes from one's spiritual mentor who is more experienced with Buddhist spiritual disciplines. It is always said that one's guru or spiritual teacher is more important than one's visualized meditation deity, if one practises a form of Buddhism that relies on such practices. But it is also said that the guru is also more important than the Buddha. This judgement is made because only through a spiritual mentor is one introduced to the Buddha and his teachings. The amount of prestige accorded to spiritual teachers varies in different forms of Buddhism, but all agree that without a teacher, one would have little chance for success in one's spiritual quest.

But throughout Buddhist history, because women have not been educated in Buddhist philosophy and spiritual disciplines, women teachers, though not completely absent, have been few. Nothing more completely expresses the contradiction between Buddhism's male-dominant institutional practices and its gender-free and gender-neutral teachings than the male near-monopoly on the role of guru or spiritual teacher. Nothing is more disempowering or discouraging to serious women students of the dharma (Buddhist teachings). No wonder Western Buddhists are proud of the fact that within a generation, the situation has changed from an almost total lack of women teachers to about half the dharma teachers being women, a situation unprecedented in Buddhist history. Furthermore, some of these women teachers are highly respected and very popular. Such information demonstrates definitely that widespread and popular Buddhist stereotypes about women's inability to meditate successfully, to become enlightened, or to be competent dharma teachers are simply false. Women who tried to learn Buddhist meditation in Asia in the 1950s and 1960s and were told that women could not meditate successfully no longer need to put up with such prejudice.

However, while congratulations are in order, there are still problems. Many of the women dharma teachers mainly teach in local centres while most of the nationally and internationally known teachers who travel extensively and teach at major meditation centres are men. A close look at advertisements for retreats in nationally circulated Buddhist magazines quickly confirms this generalization. Thus, it is still appropriate to watch and wait for the day when Buddhists finally overcome the contradiction between their male-dominant institutions and their egalitarian views because, at all levels, about half their gurus and dharma teachers are women.

CONTEMPORARY GENDER ISSUES

In the past fifty years, some issues not discussed in traditional Buddhist contexts to any great extent have come to the fore among Western Buddhists and, to a lesser extent, among Asian Buddhists. One of these issues is sexual misconduct on the part of (male) teachers. (Very few, if any, women teachers have been charged with sexual misconduct.)

Sexual Misconduct

American Buddhists are particularly vociferous on this topic and many sexual 'scandals' have occurred in American Buddhism (Edelstein 2011). Sexual misconduct is an old, well-established category in Buddhist ethics and avoiding sexual misconduct is a basic ethical responsibility for all Buddhists, whether lay or monastic. If teachers are monastics, any sexual contact between them and their students would be prohibited by rules of monastic discipline. But many of the most prominent teachers of Buddhism in the West have not been monastics and charges of sexual misconduct against them have been frequent.

It is very difficult to sort out to what extent these charges are valid. Most cases of alleged sexual misconduct involve sex between adults of consenting age. Charges of sex with children or minors on the part of Buddhist teachers are very rare. Nevertheless, sex between a teacher and a student is usually discouraged because of perceived power differentials between the teacher and student.

Some of these scandals involved secret adultery between a teacher and a community member, something very problematic for a community in which transparency is valued. In other cases, the teacher has made no attempt to keep his affairs secret. Nor has he forced students in any way to become his partners. The affair is genuinely consensual. Nevertheless, many object to such liaisons because of the power differential between students and teachers. Especially in the case of a young, inexperienced, but very attractive female student, it is often claimed that the relationship could not be genuinely consensual because of power differences between men and women and the even more obvious differences of power and prestige between the teacher and the student. It is difficult to sort out how much discomfort with such conduct is due to a puritanical strand in American culture. Generally, European Buddhists seem to be much less judgemental about these affairs. Additionally, it is difficult to sort out cultural difference between Asian and Western cultures, especially in the cases involving Asian teachers. Asian men often overestimate the sexual availability of Western women, as any Western female traveller to some Asian countries knows very well. Some of the Asian teachers most notorious for their sexual affairs with Western students may well have expected sexual favours from their Western students that they would never expect from Asian women, due to cultural differences and intercultural misunderstandings. Nevertheless, the female students did consent, or did not consent, as the case may be. In cases of consent, they cannot be completely absolved from their own responsibility for consensual relationships.

Homosexual Relationships

Because of extremely rapid changes in many Western societies regarding homosexual relationships, Buddhist communities are also caught up in this issue (Layton 1998). However, Western Buddhists, usually being well-educated liberals, are well ahead of the curve on this issue. Both gays and lesbians and their relationships have been more or less accepted in most Western Buddhist sanghas since their beginnings. Most, but not all, Buddhist teachers who teach in the West, whether Asian or Western, are also accepting of such relationships. In many cases, lesbian or gay couples openly live together at meditation centres.

For many people, the question of homosexual relationships is not a separate question at all, but a question of general sexual ethics. The same sexual ethic is applied to all sexual relationships, whether heterosexual or homosexual and that overall guideline for Buddhist sexual ethics derives from its most basic overall ethic—as much as possible do no harm. Therefore, teachers usually emphasize fidelity between partners as their basic teaching about sexual ethics. Many now discourage promiscuity in all cases, both heterosexual and gay/lesbian, though many Buddhist communities did participate enthusiastically in the 'sexual revolution' during its height in the 1970s. To be faithful to the basic guideline regarding sexual ethics, one should always evaluate whether pursuing a specific sexual relationship could cause harm to anyone, one's self, one's partner, or anyone else. That is why promiscuity and affairs outside of a committed relationship are discouraged by so many Buddhist teachers today. This guideline would also apply to the question of sexual misconduct on the part of teachers. Their affairs may be consensual but they could still involve harming others.

However, in traditional Buddhist literature, the topic of homosexuality is seldom discussed, though there is some literature on Japanese monastic male homosexual practices (Cabezon 1992). Traditional literature prohibiting or discouraging sexual activity involving use of forbidden orifices—the mouth and the anus—which would also apply to heterosexuals, has, for obvious reasons, been very difficult for some gay Buddhists to accept. It is difficult to ascertain how seriously these prohibitions were taken in traditional Buddhist societies, either by lay heterosexuals or by gays and lesbians. Among monastics, because all sexual contact is forbidden, the topics of orifices and partners should be irrelevant, though often they were not.

Abortion

Regarding another contentious modern gender issue, abortion, the Buddhist position, both Asian and Western, is that abortion should be avoided if at all possible. Nevertheless, again, the most basic Buddhist ethical position is, as much as possible, to avoid harming any being. Some Buddhist teachers recognize that sometimes carrying through a pregnancy can be very harmful to a woman and even to society at large. Thus Traleg Kyabgon, an important contemporary Buddhist teacher, has said 'abortion may not be a good thing, but in certain circumstances it may be more beneficial to have an abortion than not to have one' (Kyabgon 2001: 19–21). Much can also be learned from contemporary Japanese Buddhist practices of providing religious services that recognize both their spiritual needs and the sadness of the situation to women and men who suffer needing abortions (LaFleur 1992).

Childcare

Finally, as Buddhism becomes more a lay movement, not only in the West but also in Asia, and as women become more serious dharma practitioners in their own right, the topic of childcare and child-rearing as dharma practice must come to the fore. Historically, Asian Buddhism has a very ambivalent relationship with mothering and child-rearing. This too is not surprising for a tradition that so values monasticism because monastics do not have to deal directly with children and are absolved from direct responsibility for raising the next generation. However, it must also be recognized that in Asia, monasteries and nunneries do often function as orphanages or run schools.

On the one hand, Buddhist literature is full of encomiums to 'mother sentient beings'. The obligation to be compassionate to all sentient beings is based on a claim that every sentient being has, at some point in the endless cycle of samsaric existence, been one's mother. Recognizing how dependent one is on one's mother in this life and recognizing that all beings have been one's mother in some lifetime or another, one should repay one's debt to 'mother sentient beings' through compassionate activity on their behalf. But, as is so often the case in male-dominated religions, theoretical praise of and respect for mothers in the abstract does not necessarily result in high status or social respect and dignity for the actual women who are mothers, even though individual sons often have a great deal of affection for their individual mothers. Women are not only praised for being endlessly self-sacrificing mothers but also are expected to be so, and have few other options. Despite all this praise, women's self-sacrificing motherhood has not brought them any real power, prestige, or equality in traditional Buddhism. Women are praised as mothers, but discriminated against and limited as human beings—a combination that is very common in male-dominated societies. One of the insights of modern feminism has been to point out the hypocrisy involved in praising self-sacrificing *mothers* while, at the same time, *women* have low status, little freedom of choice, and few opportunities. Instead, women have been told that they need to be reborn as men before they can attain enlightenment; have not been fully educated in Buddhist disciplines; and have not become teachers of compassionate activity, despite being lauded as examples of compassion in popular Buddhist literature. In the early days of Western feminism, Asian men often had great difficulty understanding these points.

In traditional societies, including Buddhist societies, such lack of consonance between theory and practice is due mainly to the fact that men absolved themselves from responsibility for the everyday aspects of child-rearing, assigning them to women, who were then praised for being self-sacrificing mothers. In modern Buddhist practice, especially in its Western manifestations, such pious but self-contradictory ways of dealing with child-rearing simply are not acceptable. Men, who often want children as much as women do, must be expected to take on some responsibility for the less glamorous and far more boring aspects of raising the next generation. Men need to take on some responsibility especially for those aspects of raising the next generation that may curtail their free time to study and practise the dharma formally, so that women have more of an equal opportunity situation. Regarding this issue, the modern Buddhist situation parallels the secular situation, in which one of women's most common frustrations is the way in which they are subjected to the 'double shift' in which they help provide livelihood but are still expected to do most of the domestic work, and especially the childcare.

In addition, as their members became parents, many Western Buddhist institutions have become far more sensitive to the need for organized childcare, enabling both parents, not just the fathers, to participate in ongoing education and practice. It is now a common feature of many, though not all, meditation centres, whether urban or residential land centres located in rural areas. Such practices also work on the problem of rearing Buddhist children in a largely non-Buddhist culture.

Furthermore, the fundamentally low evaluation of childcare as something that could be foisted off by men onto women and disvalued, except for pious rhetoric, must change. Many lay Buddhists, but also some monastics, long for much more discussion of child-rearing as a spiritual practice, not merely a mundane activity (Miller 2006). Buddhists will always value non-reproductive, celibate lifestyles, but even celibate practitioners have parents and depend upon them. It has also been pointed out that monastics actually perform many of the same duties as domestic householders, including cooking and other kitchen work. Anyone who has ever lived at a meditation centre is more than familiar with food preparation being regarded as an integral part of their training and spiritual discipline. As lay Buddhist life becomes more normative as *Buddhist* practice, not merely the economic basis on which monastic practice depends, we can expect more recognition that the state of mind with which an activity is done is more important than whether it is done in a monastery or a domestic home. But part of the challenge to contemporary Buddhists who want to demonstrate the cogency and appropriateness of serious lay practice is to equalize the opportunities and responsibilities of women and men as parents, so that men take on more responsibility for maintaining the domestic realm and raising children while women are more free to develop their full human potential rather than being limited to domestic roles. Freedom from the prison of gender roles demands nothing less.

REFERENCES

Boucher, Sandy (1993). *Turning the Wheel: American Women Creating the New Buddhism*. Boston: Beacon Press.

Cabezon, Jose Ignacio (1992) (ed.). *Buddhism, Sexuality, and Gender*. Albany, NY: State University of New York Press.

Edelstein, Scott (2011). *Sex and the Spiritual Teacher: Why It Happens, When It's a Problem, and What to Do about It*. Boston: Wisdom Publications.

Garfield, Jay L. (1995). *The Fundamental Wisdom of the Middle Way: Nagarjuna's Mulamadhyamikakarika*. New York: Oxford University Press.

Gross, Rita M. (1993). *Buddhism after Patriarchy: A Feminist History, Analysis, and Reconstruction of Buddhism*. Albany, NY: State University of New York Press.

Gross, Rita M. (2013). 'Buddhism and Gender'. *Oxford Bibliographies Online: Buddhism*. Editor-in-chief Richard Payne. New York: Oxford University Press.

Gutschow, Kim (2004). *Being a Buddhist Nun: The Struggle for Enlightenment in the Himalayas*. Cambridge, MA: Harvard University Press.

Horner, I. B. (1989). *Women under Primitive Buddhism: Laywomen and Almswomen*. Delhi, India: Motilal Banarsidass Publishers.

Klein, Carolyn Ann (1995). *Meeting the Great Bliss Queen: Buddhists, Feminists and the Art of the Self*. Boston: Beacon.

Kyabgon, Traleg (2001). *The Essence of Buddhism: An Introduction to Its Philosophy and Practice*. Boston and London: Shambhala.

LaFleur, William R. (1992). *Liquid Life: Abortion and Buddhism in Japan*. Princeton: Princeton University Press.

Layton, Winston (1998) (ed.). *Queer Dharma: Voices of Gay Buddhists*. San Francisco: Gay Sunshine Press.

Miller, Karen Maezen (2006). *Momma Zen: Walking the Crooked Path of Motherhood*. Boston: Shambhala.

Mohr, Thea, and Jampa Tsedroen (2010) (eds). *Dignity and Discipline: Reviving Full Ordination for Buddhist Nuns*. Boston: Wisdom Publications.

Oldenberg, Hermann (2007 [1881]). *Vinaya Texts*, vols i, ii, iii. Forgotten Books.

Paul, Diana Y. (1979). *Women in Buddhism: Images of the Feminine in the Mahayanà*... *Tradition*. Berkeley: Asian Humanities Press.

Sakyadhita (2012). <http://www.sakyadhita.org/> (accessed Aug. 2013).

Schaeffer, Kurtis R. (2004). *Himalayan Hermitess: The Life of a Tibetan Buddhist Nun*. New York: Oxford University Press.

Simmer-Brown, Judith (2001). *Dakini's Warm Breath: The Feminine Principle in Tibetan Buddhism*. Boston: Shambhala Publications.

Tsomo, Karma Lekshe (1988) (ed.). *Sakyadhita: Daughters of the Buddha*. Ithaca, NY: Snow Lion. <http://www.sakyadhita.org/>.

PART VII

CONCEPTS AND ISSUES

CHAPTER 29

···

VIOLENCE AND JUSTICE

···

PAMELA COOPER-WHITE

INTRODUCTION

··

In Tahrir Square, Cairo, Egypt, July 2013, a group of young boys chase women through crowds of political protestors, taunting them with sexual epithets. An Independent Television News correspondent recently reported, 'While trying to participate in recent protests and the shaping of their country's future, nearly 100 Egyptian women have been sexually assaulted in Tahrir Square by attackers who may be systematically planning their crimes' (Hilsum 2013).

> Such sweet boys full of energy and fun. They have just been chasing a young woman up the street. The interviewer asks them why. 'If a lady is respectable, no one will harass her,' says a kid in red. The others pile in. 'Why do they wear short skirts or tight trousers?' 'Some young women, when we flirt with them, they smile.' That's how it starts. This is how it ends. A mob attacks a young woman on the corner of Tahrir Square....This is one of more than a hundred assaults in Tahrir Square during last week's demonstrations. This is the very place. Women still come to the square, but it's dangerous. This corner of Tahrir Square has become notorious for attacks on women...
>
> And the most horrific thing I have heard is that these attacks are planned, and, sometimes, women think that the men coming for them are trying to save them from being assaulted, but in fact they take them away and attack them again.
>
> (Hilsum 2013)

In seemingly peaceful fields across the United States, migrant women workers are repeatedly sexually assaulted and harassed by employers exploiting their poverty, some-times illegal status, and fears of deportation, loss of work, or further violence to them-selves and their families:

> In Molalla, Ore., a worker at a tree farm accused her supervisor of repeatedly raping her over the course of several months in 2006 and 2007, often holding gardening

shears to her throat. If she complained to anyone, he allegedly told her, he would fire her and kill her entire family.

(Yeung and Rubenstein 2013)

In a news investigation based on thousands of documents and interviews from California to Florida to the Pacific northwest, University of California journalists documented that

> Hundreds of female agricultural workers have complained to the federal government about being raped and assaulted, verbally and physically harassed on the job, while law enforcement has done almost nothing to prosecute potential crimes. In virtually all of the cases reviewed, the alleged perpetrators held positions of power over the women. Despite the accusations, these supervisors have remained on the job for years without fear of arrest.

(Yeung and Rubenstein 2013)

Thousands more individuals, mostly women, experience sexual violence every day, including rape, assault, stalking, and sexual harassment. The World Health Organisation, extrapolating from research in thirty-five countries, estimates that between 10 and 30 per cent of women worldwide are sexually assaulted, and from 10–52 per cent of women are victims of intimate partner violence (WHO 2005: 1). Literally millions of women and young girls are kidnapped and held captive as sex slaves in a vast underground network of sex trafficking (e.g. UN Population Fund 2000: ch. 3) In the USA alone, not just in dark alleys and in parks at night but on dates, at work, and in the sanctity of their own homes and bedrooms, close to one in every five women experience attempted or completed rape in their lifetimes, as well as three in every hundred men (Tjaden and Thoennes 2000: iii, 13).[1] In spite of recent improvements in US law enforcement, resulting in significant decreases in reported rapes, approximately 350,000 rapes and sexual assaults are still reported to police annually (US FBI 2009a, 2009b) with many more left unreported (Cooper-White 2012: 265n9), and over 200,000 women are raped each year by a husband or intimate partner (Tjaden and Thoennes 2000: 9–10).

Sexual assaults, especially by acquaintances, is still estimated by rape crisis experts to be under-reported by as much as 90 per cent, for reasons ranging from fear of revictimization by the judicial process, fear of reprisal by the offender, or shame and humiliation compounded by a culture that still too often blames victims and makes excuses for the perpetrators. In US society, experts estimate that only a quarter of rape suspects are arrested, only slightly over half are convicted (US Bureau of Justice Statistics 1998; National Center for Policy Analysis 1999), and when factoring in under-reporting, 'only 3% of rapists will ever serve a day in prison' (Jameson 2013). In spite of slowly improving arrest rates, there are still more deterrents to victims to report sexual assaults than to offenders to commit them.

---

[1] For more statistics and information on prevalence studies, see Cooper-White (2012: 2, 107).

Sexuality is a domain of experience that has been variously described as embodied, deeply personal, intimate, ecstatic, and even sacred. Yet precisely because of some of these qualities and the emotions associated with them, it is also a domain that entails not only pleasure but also the possibility of intrusion, coercion, harassment, violation, assault, pain, and even terror. It is a ground on which wars are fought (including intra-psychic, familial, social, political, and even military) over issues of desire and fulfilment, personal morality and boundaries, social mores and taboos, groundrules for procreation and child-rearing, commodification and exploitation, politics of privacy, and civil and criminal safeguards. Because social constructions of 'sex' and 'gender' are so closely identified, sexuality is also intertwined with definitions of gender—including psychological identifications, performativity, social norms and transgressions, and access to privilege and power. By extension, these categories further implicate race, age, ability/disability, and virtually all arenas of embodied experience. Therefore, sexuality, and in particular sexual violence, constitute a domain that calls for ethical reflection regarding multi-dimensional and multi-textured issues of sexual justice, and in particular, the use and abuse of power.

Sex and Power

In the anti-rape movement in the 1970s, a pithy slogan signalled the gist of the feminist political analysis of sexual assault: 'Rape is about power, not sex'. This saying contradicted the (still common) myth that men cannot control their sexual impulses once aroused. It rightly shifted the definition of rape from uncontrollable lust to inexcusable violence, in which sexual body parts are used to dominate and subjugate victims, but the primary motivation is physical force, not sexual desire. As an object lesson, we taught that any body part could be used or targeted for tenderness or violence: a hand can gently caress or bring healing, or it can be made into a fist to pummel another person; a penis can be an instrument of mutual desire and love, or a weapon. Sexual assault is an extreme form of violence precisely *because* erogenous zones of the body are experienced as the most intimate and vulnerable; however, the primary *purpose* of sexual assault is not to discharge sexual tension, but to conquer, humiliate, and violate. The victim of sexual assault is not an 'object of desire', but a literal object of domination and dehumanization.

At the same time, the statement that 'rape is about power, *not* sex', perhaps deserves further clarification and examination. As a slogan, it conveys an important message sharply and memorably. However, there are complexities involving both power and sex that invite further analysis. More nuanced substitutes might lose the pithy utility of a slogan, but might be helpful in understanding the ways in which sex, power, aggression, and violence can overlap and intertwine. Simple slogans, further, tend toward simplistic solutions. The saying 'rape is about power, not sex', helpfully combats myths about sexual assault, but the solution it implies is narrowly focused: to stop perpetrators from abusing power. While this is, indeed, a core insight of prevention and education pro-grammes, perpetrators rarely stop abusing power simply because they are taught or told to do so. Neither re-education/therapy nor containment—mainly through incarcera-tion (where further sexual violence often occurs)—have a strong track record in ending sexual assault.

What, then, would a more nuanced statement be? The following are three pos-sible alternatives that are not meant to undo the important insights of the anti-rape movement, nor to offer an all-encompassing substitution, but to bring greater com-plexity to bear on the causes and dynamics of sexual injustice: 'Rape is about power, *and* sex'; 'Rape is about power, *using* sex'; and 'Rape is about power, gender, and race'.

Rape is about Power, *and* Sex

The main objection to the original slogan is that one cannot escape the fact that sexual assault involves sexual acts. 'Of course rape is sexual', some argue, 'after all, it's *sexual assault*'. If rape is about power, *not* sex, how do we account for the sexual arousal of the offender?

Physiologically, there is a link between sex and aggression—intuited by Freud as the two primary instincts or 'drives' of human nature (Freud 1955: 3–66). Freud viewed sex (libido) and aggression as having their origins, respectively, in the instincts for procreation and for self-defence or self-preservation. Viewed more broadly, if sex is the drive for pleasure, which (at least some of the time) is connected with the potential to propagate the species, aggression is the drive to have an impact, to make a difference in one's environment, to move forward, and to live for oneself. Pastoral theologian Kathleen Greider has pointed out that especially in Christian theology aggression has been branded as negative and sinful, a sign of human bro-kenness. However, she argues:

> The brokenness in our aggression is perhaps most easily identified in its two extremes: violence and passivity, or lack of vitality. At one extreme, aggression explodes into incalculable incidents of hatred and violence. When violent, we are not adequately in charge of our aggression and overuse it, which results in injury and sometimes death....At the other extreme, aggression implodes, a major source of our passion and power drains away, and we are left with too little vitality and vulnerable to passivity. When passive, we are not adequately in charge of our aggression, and underuse it, resulting in ineffectualness.

> (Greider 1997: 13–14)

Sexual activity requires a certain degree of aggression—well modulated between the extremes of violence and passivity—in order for anything to happen. Initiative is required to move sexual relating from the realm of fantasy to mutual activity. Healthy sexual activity requires energy and agency—that is, healthy aggression. Libido, as life force or energy for life, therefore encompasses both sex and aggression, and is necessary to all forms of creativity.

There is an important difference, of course, between healthy aggression and violence. Without aggression, we would have no motivation to get up and do anything at all. Violence, on the other hand, as the word implies, involves violation. Rape and sexual assault are by definition violent, not merely aggressive, because the offender forces unwanted sexual touching or penetration on the other—who becomes a victim. Here physiological explanations for sexual violence become troubling with regard to human nature, and perhaps especially masculinity. There is some emerging scientific research that identifies sex and aggression as involving the same neuronal networks in the brain (Calloway 2011). This view converges with earlier psychoanalytic theories suggesting that sexual fantasies and behaviours labelled as 'perversions' exist on a spectrum with 'normal' sexuality, rather than belonging to entirely separate domains of pathology versus health. Robert Stoller, in particular, whose writings focused on gender identity and the dynamics of erotic life, even proposed that aggression in the form of *hostility* (i.e. aggression directed toward another person) was a necessary ingredient in healthy sexual excitement—albeit in minute proportions, comingled with love and intimacy:

> as one proceeds along the continuum toward less use of hostile mechanisms, one is proceeding from the bizarre (psychotic) through the character disorders we diagnose as perversions and on into the range of the normative, where the mechanisms propelling the excitement are energized by hostility but where affection and capacity for closeness also thrive. At the far end of the spectrum is a small group of contented people who enjoy (even in fantasy) loving, unhostile relationships with others and who are not so frightened by intimacy that they must fetishize the other person. For them the other is a person; they do not have to dehumanize. If hostility is present in their excitement, it is microscopic....Is it, nonetheless, essential?...Perhaps this dynamic [of tension and climax] holds for all excitements, rites of passage, myths, and miracles. What we call 'sublimation' may be a state that has been non-hostilely depleted of hostility.
>
> (Stoller 2012: 31–32)

Stoller is quick to observe, however, that the amount of hostility present in fantasy and modulated in healthy sexuality is not equivalent to violence: 'we should not equate the small amount of hostility that powers a daydream with the much greater degree of hostility needed for hostile acts in the real world' (Stoller 2012: 31).

If healthy sexuality, then, contains at least a minute component of aggression, does the converse also hold, that violence contains an element of sexual arousal? The answer from both social and biological sciences would seem to be a qualified 'Yes'. This is in no way to undermine the essential insight of the anti-rape movement that rape is primarily about power—since rape and sexual assault, and other forms of sexual abuse and exploitation are defined by the use of coercion, unequal power and authority, and/or physical force. Yet the phenomenon of physiological arousal to violence exists, and if there is a tincture of hostility in loving sex, there is more than a tincture of sexual excitement in violence—perhaps especially male violence. While neither a single biological expla-nation (e.g. it's all about testosterone), nor a simplistic social analysis that *all* men are socialized to use violence,[2] are sufficient to explain the connection between sex and vio-lence, history attests to a long record of sexual excitement in violent settings that are not primarily intended as erotic, particularly in war. Numerous ancient frescoes and vases depict scenes of men with full erections competing in athetic races (e.g. Panathenaic Amphora, *c*.530 BCE, Metropolitan Museum of Art 2013) chasing after women, and rap-ing or murdering women in enemy tribes. (e.g. 'Tydeus and Ismene' Amphora, *c*.560 BCE, Musée du Louvre 2013) In ancient Rome, gladiators were imbued with sexual mag-netism even after death—new brides sought to have their hair parted by a spear, pref-erably dipped in the blood of a slain gladiator—and the word for sword, *gladius*, was common slang for penis (Hopkins 1983: 12).[3] Rape, military conquest, and colonization were intertwined in both rhetoric and image in the ancient world, and rape was a tool of domination by both men and gods (Dougherty 1993; Foxhall and Salmon 1999).

Women were regularly regarded worldwide as part of the 'property' belonging to the enemy, and therefore were part of the 'spoils of war' that went to the victor in the form of rape and sexual slavery. Only in the eighteenth century were efforts to respect the sanc-tity of the family and the rights of civilians, or non-combatants, commonly written into legal codes for the conduct of war in the west, although some attempts were made in the middle ages in Europe as well (Askin 1997). Only as recently as 2008 the United Nations classified rape as a 'war tactic' (UN Security Council 2008). However, rape as a form of terrorizing the enemy and a crude and brutal form of reward for conquest reach back to the dawn of human history and persist in wars throughout the world today (Askin 1997). This long history of rape in war has fed a military culture of hyper-masculinity that, in turn, is all too prone in spite of a rhetoric of honour to turn a blind eye to sexual assault within the ranks of the military (an estimated 26,000 victims, both women and men, in 2012 alone—Steinhauer 2013) and leads to sadistic acts of torture and sexualized degradation against enemies objectified as the 'other', as in the prison at Abu Ghraib (*New York Times* 2013).

Sexual arousal to violence is more common than is often supposed or admitted. (Malamuth et al. 1977) It should be noted, in this regard, that male erections occur not only as arousal to pleasure, but to fear and more mundane urges such as the need to uri-nate (SMSNA 2013). At the same time, sexual excitement can be produced in direct con-nection with exposure to violence. That the connection between penises and swords, sex and war, is not relegated only to ancient times is attested by the very existence of the contemporary slang term 'war boner' defined in the *Urban Dictionary* as

> the process of an erection due to being aroused by machine gun fire, explosions, jet engines and large amounts of blood and gore'—as in 'As I was massacring my

---

[2] For a more nuanced multi-variate model, see Harway and O'Neill (1999).
[3] The word *vagina*, which means 'sheath' or 'scabbard' in Latin was not used in the anatomical sense in ancient times, but the sword-and-covering etymology pertains to its first use in English, late seventeenth century. Harper (2013).

opponents in COD I earned a chopper gunner and the sound of the chain and the propeller meshing together fueled my raging war boner!'

(Valley's Own 2011)

To complicate the categories of sex, aggression, power, and violence, then, it must be acknowledged that there is often an element of sexual arousal in violence, as well as a well sublimated and modulated element of aggression, if not hostility, in healthy sexuality.

All too often, moreover, there is a dangerous fusion of sex and violence, not only in a hyper-masculinized psychology of war, but also in pornography, and in mainstream cultural media.[4] This is where biology may entail a link between sexuality and aggression, but socialization can strongly enhance or incite a more dangerous merger of the two. Pornography is not obscene because it is too sexual, *per se*, but because it is dehumanizing. If *eros* is love that includes physical passion but also includes the whole person, body, and soul together, then the *erotic* is that life force that reaches out toward the other for intimacy, mutual creativity, and exchange. The erotic is, in the words of Audre Lorde, 'a measure between the beginnings of our sense of self, and the chaos of our strongest feelings' (Lorde 1980: 296; Griffin 1981; Brock 1988; Heyward 1989). In contrast, pornography 'is a direct denial of the power of the erotic, for it represents the suppression of true feeling. Pornography emphasizes sensation without feeling' (Lorde 1980: 296). The erotic is relational, empathic, whole, spirited, and imaginative; pornography is episodic, performance-oriented, fragmented, standardized, and addictive (Giddens 1992: 119–20; Eberstadt and Layden 2010). The root word *porne* has nothing to do with love—in classic Greek a *porne* was a sexual slave held captive in a low-cost brothel (Hays 2012). Pornography is obscene precisely because its aim is to deny and even murder the soul of those portrayed in it—by *de*eroticizing them, robbing them of their deepest life-giving and life-seeking energy (Griffin 1981). These observations lead to the second alternative statement about rape, power and sex: that rape is about power *using* sex.

Rape is about Power, *using* Sex

In an often cited typology of sex offenders developed in the late 1970s (Groth 1979), the 'angry-hostile offender' was understood to be the type of rapist who used sexual assault to act out his anger and hostility toward women, while the power rapist used rape primarily to enforce dominance. The aim of the third type, the sadistic rapist, was explicitly to inflict pain and torture. However, all these typologies implicate power, and all forms of rape, sexual assault and abuse, stalking and harassment, are abuses of power using sexual language and/or contact as their medium—whether that power is physical force (including the use of weapons), psychological coercion, professional authority, or the use of other means such as alcohol, drugs, or threats to overcome a victim's resistance.

---

[4] For further analysis, see Cooper-White (2012: 64–82). This paragraph draws especially from pp. 80–81.

Sexual violence is sexualized violence—dominating power exercised through sexual words and deeds. Sexualized violence exists on a spectrum from seemingly 'milder' forms of sexual harassment and exploitation (as in professionals crossing sexual boundaries with those over whom they have authority, for example, to hire and fire, teach, preach, or counsel), to stalking and threats, to sexual abuse and molestation, sexual assault, trafficking and sexual enslavement, and rape. The psychological impact of these behaviours, however, is not a simple series of gradations. All can cause trauma. The younger or more vulnerable the victim, and/or the more overpowering, overwhelming, and/or painful the act, the greater the victim's terrorization and often, as well, the greater her subsequent second-guessing, guilt, and self-blame. It does not really help to compare victimizations, since experiences of dehumanization, humiliation, confusion, terror, and pain—emotional, mental, and physical—all fall within a place in the psyche that survives at times by multiple self-numbing mechanisms of rationalization, fragmentation, rage, depression, and self-destructiveness. All such acts of violence are violations of the fundamental personhood of the victim, and are at their core an abuse of power in relation to another human being—which is a theological problem (Poling 1991).

No single aetiology/theory of causation for sexual violence fully accounts for its prevalence, or for its dehumanizing acts. 'Single factor theories' that focused narrowly on particular biological, behavioural, or social causes have been found wanting by social scientists and law enforcement professionals (West 2013). Sexual violence is caused by a confluence of factors that lead a perpetrator to violating another person's humanity. These can include biological, developmental, environmental, cultural, and situational factors in combination with an offender's personal character formation, impairments, and vulnerabilities (Marshall and Barbaree 1990: 257–275). Abnormally high testosterone, relational deficits in early parenting (including but not limited to sexual abuse), violence and aggression learned from parents and/or others in the childhood environment, and a culture saturated in film and media images of sexualized violence may all contribute to damaging a child's developing sense of identity, self-esteem, self-control, capacity for empathy, and relationally directed sexual intimacy—although it should be cautioned that many adults experience some or all of these factors and do not become violent. Both internal and external factors are also considered important in the acting out of sexual domination: there must be an internal motivation involving fantasies of violation, but these must be further facilitated by opportunity (either discovered or premeditated). Often some disinhibition precedes the offender's final step of taking action—either by rationalizing the violence through objectification of the victim, and/or by using drugs, alcohol, pornography, or other means to desensitize himself from the meaning and impact of his desired violent behaviour (Malamuth et al. 1993: 63–97).

Further, individuals who engage in sexual assault, rape, exploitation, and harassment share a common trait of narcissism which, either situationally or permanently, impairs their ability to feel empathy for their victims, or to fully comprehend the meaning and impact of their actions (Cooper-White 2004: 110–116, 172–180). The sociopathic individual, defined by a complete lack of a social sense and conscience, is only the extreme version of the more garden variety narcissist who exploits and uses other persons because his own needs and wishes are the only ones he can see and feel. As the early British psychoanalyst and pediatrician D. W. Winnicott observed, the 'antisocial' or sociopathic personality type is one who inwardly feels 'the world owes me', often because of a very early childhood sense of some perceived goodness that was withheld or taken away (Winnicott 1975: 306–315). While this does not fully explain individuals who for some hormonal or other physiological reason cannot control their sexual and aggressive impulses (e.g. due to traumatic head injury—Gannon and Ward 2008: 356–383), Winnicott's observation implicates not only individual parents and families, but entire communities and the wider society in our failure to provide the reasonable supports necessary to help households become places of safety and nurture, and, moreover, to become 'crucibles of justice' (Anderson and Johnson 1994), fostering in children a sense of openness and generosity toward others in the wider world.

Rape is about Power, Gender, and Race

The injustice of sexual abuse and assault is, therefore, also connected to the wider realm of injustice, including social and institutional structures of domination along the lines of gender, race, sexual orientation, class, and other systemic inequalities. Although a generous humanistic analysis would want us to equalize such demographic factors, and say that women are as prone to violence as men—'they just express it differently'—or that violence is colour-blind, statistical research and studies of the specific dynamics of sexual violence (as well as all violent crime) consistently show that sexual and intimate partner violence are overwhelmingly perpetrated by men against women. And contrary to the myth of the black rapist, statistics show that white men are three times more likely to be the perpetrators of sexual assaults (extrapolating from US Bureau of Justice Statistics 2008).

Sexual violence, then, is unavoidably an issue not only of sexual words and acts, but of gender—in the vast majority of instances, a crime of men against women. Reinforced and exacerbated by patriarchal myths about women as property, possessions, and conquests, sexual violence actually fits the definition of a hate crime, although in the USA it is not prosecuted as such. The distinguishing feature of a hate crime is that it is motivated by bias against an entire category of persons (ODIHR 2009: 16). The US Congress, however, still declines to include 'women' in its list of protected categories: 'race, religion, disability, ethnic origin and sexual orientation' (US FBI 2013). Nevertheless, given the vast preponderance of sexual violence directed by men against women, it is difficult to see how rape, sexual assault, and other forms of sexual violence do not constitute a gender-based hate crime. Gender is considered a protected characteristic in the legal codes of a number of European and other countries, including, for example, Canada and France (ODIHR 2009: 16). Sexual violence, then, is fundamentally a violation of human rights, and needs to be addressed not only in relation to individual victims, but as a systemic and societal injustice.

Toward an Ethic and Theology of Sexual Justice

No one of the alternative sayings described at the start of this chapter entirely captures the motivation of perpetrators, nor the suffering of victims. Nor do the three alternative statements exhaust the possible understandings of sexual violation. What the alternatives do, perhaps, is point toward the need for both an ethic of sexual behaviour *and* an ethics of power. Further, as theologians, we need a theology that emphasizes the relationality of both God and humanity—to provide an adequate and appropriate foundation for an ethic of sexual justice.

Sexual Ethics

Too often, sexual ethics have been reduced to traditional moral teaching about specific *acts* that are considered inherently taboo. These are presented in numerous cultures and religions, including the Judaeo-Christian biblical tradition, as deontological—'natural' laws and purity codes deriving from the very essence of life and goodness, even commanded by God. Yet in other ancient cultures, such as Rome, both homosexual and bisexual relationships were permitted as equal to heterosexual relationships for both gods and men, in part because they were thought to reinforce virtues of brotherly love, and to provide the social glue of a civil society (Boswell 1980). Ancient 'natural laws' prohibiting homosexuality and bisexuality often disguised a teleological intent, however—to maximize procreation for the purposes of increasing a tribe, a religion, and a people. Certain other sexual acts, such as masturbation, were not necessarily considered harmful in and of themselves, but were described as sinful in certain contexts because they did not lead to the increase of the tribe, as when Judah's Onan 'spilled his semen on the ground whenever he went in to his brother's wife, so that he would not give offspring to his brother' (Gen. 38:10). The mystification of the teleological foundation—procreation—has resulted in the unmooring of sexual laws and taboos from their original purpose, thereby holding the (false) status of unquestionable divine law. While the idea of sin is a constant in Christian moral teaching, much of what is considered to be sinful behaviour is socially constructed, and changes according to cultural norms (Portman 2007)—often using biblical interpretation to support contextual *mores*.

Whenever sexual morality has been justified deontologically on the grounds of acceptable versus unacceptable acts, rather than by a transparent teleological foundation, many issues of gender injustice, the treatment of certain persons as property—notably women, children, and servants—and larger issues of sexual ethics based on justice, equality, and freedom have been obscured in moral discourse. For example, Christian moral teachings have traditionally defined marriage as a sacred sexual preserve of one man and one woman largely for the purpose of procreation, and have prohibited sexual activity outside an officially sanctioned marital bond. But this narrow definition of appropriate sexuality has had unintended consequences of turning a blind eye toward rape in marriage (reframing it as the husband's right to sexual congress), sexual abuse of children, and historically the rape of one's slaves or servants (as *droigt du seigneur*—a man's right to treat his property as he wishes). It has demanded celibacy and chastity of loving and committed gay and lesbian persons, and viewed sexual harassment and exploitation in both church and workplace only as moral lapses or 'affairs' rather than abuses of professional power and authority. The emphasis on procreation has further narrowed the definition of what constitutes sexual activity to sexual intercourse *per se*, rendering invisible or unimportant those forms of sexual assault and harassment that do not involve penetration.

What is needed in sexual ethics is not a new set of deontological rules—simple 'do's and don't's'—but a transparent teleological foundation that is informed by modern scientific and psychological understandings of sexuality, as well as by modern problems facing humanity and the planet. Many myths and superstitions about sexual behaviour have long been scientifically unfounded—such as notions that certain acts would lead to insanity, blindness, or hairy palms (!). The ancient drive toward propagation of the human species no longer makes good sense in a world plagued by overpopulation, pollution, and endangered food supplies. For modern Jews and Christians, the Bible still offers sacred truths as a foundation for ethics, but not by proof-texting individual verses anachronistically and out of context. Rather, the Bible offers an over-arching ethical norm of love and justice, expressed by the ten commandments, the prophetic witness of care for the poor and the vulnerable, the injunction to 'do justice, love kindness, and walk humbly with your God' (Mic. 6:8), and the centrality in both the Hebrew Bible and the New Testament of loving one's neighbour as oneself (Lev. 19:18; Mark 12:31, Rom. 13:9; etc.)— even loving one's enemies (Matt. 5:43).

With this biblical foundation, individual sexual activities are re-evaluated in light of their ultimate aim and consequences. Actions are ethical when they promote love and justice, protect the vulnerable, and hold the other in mutual regard and respect. They preserve life in its abundance (John 10:10). Some acts, under this teleological view, will remain forever taboo because by their very nature they violate another person: physical violence, sexual assault or rape, and sexual abuse of children or other persons who are unable to give authentic consent by their relative lack of power, authority, or physical or mental capacity. Other sexual behaviours, however, can be evaluated situationally, taking into consideration such issues as context, intent, and the personal and social meaning of the act in a given place and time. A whole array of formerly taboo activities may or may not be ethical depending upon complex—and at times, competing—factors.

To use the example already given above, masturbation may be healthy or unhealthy depending on its purpose. If a person masturbates compulsively to the detriment of forming loving intimate relationships and even as a form of addiction that diminishes his or her overall thriving, then we might well view this activity as a problem (although, along the lines of other addictions, it might not be considered sinful *per se* unless it causes harm to others (as in frotteurism and exhibitionism). Researchers have also documented harm associated with 'offence-specific fantasies', or masturbating to pornographic material that fuses sex with violence (Gee et al. 2004: 315–331). On the other hand, a person who masturbates to explore what is pleasurable, to learn about one's own body, to ease loneliness, or to enhance a loving and mutual sexual relationship, can be both healthy and ethical.

The line between what is morally sinful versus what is scientifically pathological or 'deviant' is complex, since scientific norms are socially constructed, and shift across continents and centuries (Foucault 1978, 1985; Cushman 1995) Some 'deviant' behaviours may be considered harmless unless they are distressing to the person or others in his or her environment, while sexualized violence nearly always requires both clinical treatment and incarceration or inpatient containment for the sake of safety.

Following this reasoning, a number of formerly taboo behaviours can be re-examined in light of modern understandings of sexuality. Sexual fidelity in marriage and committed partnerships remains an ethical norm, not any more to protect a man's assurance that his children are 'really his', but because deception, secrecy, and the violation of solemn vows inherently cause pain and suffering. At the same time, the impulse to cheat on a partner can be an important signal of deeper trouble within the relationship, and require honest mutual dialogue in order to address what needs to change—including, in some cases, the need to separate. New biomedical issues present further ethical dilemmas regarding extramarital sex—for example, should a spouse with dementia be prohibited from extramarital sexual activity when there is no longer comprehension of the marital vows? Should a non-impaired spouse likewise be prohibited from all extramarital intimacy when this is no longer possible with his or her legal spouse? (Portman 2013).

Even the issue of informed consent, which is key to most ethical decision making, is fraught with complexity. In an 'open marriage', where partners have agreed to have other sexual relationships outside their own relationship, do both partners truly consent to sexual relationships outside their primary bond, or is unequal consent or subtle coercion present? In the practice of sado-masochism, does one person ever truly consent to acts of sexual violence in a relationship, or are other psychological dynamics of power and control subtly or not-so-subtly involved? How do unconscious dynamics come into play in sexual relationships where there is a potential for physical or emotional harm, or in relationships where there has been overt violence? When is consent freely given, and when is engaging in certain activities a reenactment of previous experiences of abuse? Some theorists would further question the entire social construction of gender as binary, with its stereotypical norms of masculinity and femininity, as both a reflection of culture and a reinforcer of male, heterosexist domination. They advocate for a queering, or interrogation, of gender dichotomy through the performance of multiple, alternative, and expanded gender identities (e.g. Butler 2004).

These questions, and more, complicate any attempt to lay down universal rules for behaviour in the grey areas beyond outright sexual violence and abuse.[5] Often, when intentions are hard to determine, and outcomes difficult to predict, the grounds for

---

[5] For thoughtful essays dealing further with these questions, see, e.g., Nelson (1994); Ellison and Douglas (2010); Thatcher (2011).

discerning ethical versus unethical behaviour do circle back to the statement 'rape is about power', because sexual ethics often depend finally upon an examination of the dynamics of power in relationships.

An Ethic of Power

Power, finally, is inseparable from an over-arching ethic of love and justice. The concept of justice itself depends upon a framework of the rights of individuals and groups to exercise power with responsibility, mutual accountability, and care. This is not to argue for an absolute levelling of all power, which, given the multiplicity of forms of power, and the interconnectedness of all living beings, is unlikely within the web of competing human interests and desires—at least this side of the Eschaton. Nevertheless, every form of power has both strengths and limitations, and beyond every well-intended act of power lies the potential for unintended consequences. Furthermore, power cannot be self-regulated as if it were only a phenomenon of conscious intent. The unconscious of each individual has multiple wishes, anxieties, aims, and powers of its own. Families, groups, and nations are, then, an almost impossibly rich amalgam of such contending and contesting motivations.

An ethic of power, therefore, in my view, requires a corresponding ethic of *community*. Hannah Arendt located power finally not in any one individual or group, but in the *polis*, the collective (Arendt 1958: 201). Tyranny succeeds, in Arendt's view, more effectively through the isolation of people from one another than through brute force. Relationship is required for the peaceful negotiation of power, and solidarity through knowledge of the other is made possible. In truth, every theory of power implies a corresponding theory of community. An ethic of constructive, communally shared, and mutually authorized power—what I have termed '*power-in-community*' (Cooper-White 2012: 52–63), is a vision not unlike Isaiah's vision of the peaceable kingdom (Isa. 11: 6, 9): 'The wolf shall live with the lamb, the leopard shall lie down with the kid, the calf and the lion and the fatling together, and a little child shall lead them....They will not hurt or destroy on all my holy mountain; for the earth will be full of the knowledge of the LORD as the waters cover the sea'. This last phrase further suggests that as humans we do not achieve this on our own, but we require a theology, a 'knowledge of the Lord', to support and inspire such cooperation and justice.

A Trinitarian Theology of Relationality

Within Christianity, we have the deep symbol of the Trinity to support an ethic of power-in-community. Following Catholic theologian Elizabeth Johnson:

> At its most basic the symbol of the Trinity evokes a livingness in God, a dynamic coming and going with the world that points to an inner divine, circling around in unimaginable relation....God's relatedness to the world in creating, redeeming, and renewing activity suggests...that God's own being is somehow similarly

differentiated. Not an isolated, static, ruling monarch—but a relational, dynamic, tripersonal mystery of love. Who would not opt for the latter?

(Johnson 1994: 192)

The Trinity is itself an image of power-in-community, the dynamic power (*dunamis*) of mutually empowering and empowered love and care. While it would be unwise to ascribe human character traits to the 'persons' of the Trinity, the image of *perichoresis* with its inherent relationality reveals the ultimate floundering emptiness of narcissism and unempathic self-preservation. The Trinity is a symbol of life that is eternally mutual in its sustenance—enlivened by relationship, the love of the Divine spills over into the creation, and animates us as creatures to reach out similarly in trust and love.

This is by no means a naive exhortation to victims to suppress their righteous outrage and to offer instant forgiveness to individual perpetrators (Cooper-White 2012: 251–261). This line of thinking tends to revictimize survivors, and to aid bystanders in retreating from the reality of violence into a mist of sentimental pseudo-Christian niceness. Jesus stood for justice, and for a love that is deeper and stronger than mere sentimentality. In keeping with the communal ethic of power advocated above, the relationality of the Trinity calls us to a relational form of restoration of justice—not to be carried out on the backs of individual victims—who are revictimized by communities' insistence that they forgive—but to be carried out on the shoulders of all of us together, in community, as we see, hear, and tell the truth of the horrors of violence, and hold up an alternative Trinitarian vision of life lived most fully in mutual communion and kenotic, self-giving joy.

Is this possible, given the human condition? I honestly do not know. As Freud famously said, 'Man is wolf to man' (Freud 1961: 58)—and to woman. It is inherent in human nature to project human nature onto God and in our depictions and doctrines—even our sacred texts—and make God over in our own image (Rizzuto 1979; Cooper-White 2007: 36–38). So our theologies from ancient times and multiple cultures all too often reflect a God-*imago* of patriarchal lordship that serves to reinforce structures of domination and violence. Yet a central symbol of Christian theology is the Incarnation. In spite of many Christian doctrines that perpetuate images of divine domination, the God revealed in Christ is not a dominating lord and master, but a refugee baby in a borrowed feed-stall, a poor itinerant prophet, and a broken body dangling lynched on an instrument of imperial torture. The Jesus of the Gospels and the doctrine of his Resurrection anticipated the coming of God's Realm of peace and justice on earth, and an apocalyptic overturning of the world's structures of oppressive power. We are not yet given a present time that is so full of the knowledge of God that we and the earth are healed of all violence. But through scripture, tradition, and our own reason and experience, we have a vision of the peaceable Realm of God—an erotics of justice that points, however haltingly, toward to God's gift of abundant life.

References

Anderson, Herbert and Susan Johnson (1994). *Regarding Children: A New Respect for Childhood and Families*. Louisville: Westminster John Knox.

Arendt, Hannah (1958). *The Human Condition*. Chicago: University of Chicago Press.

Askin, Kelly Dawn (1997). *War Crimes against Women: Prosecution in International War Crimes Tribunals*. Leiden, Netherlands: Martinus Nijhoff.

Boswell, John (1980). *Christianity, Social Tolerance, and Homosexuality: Gay People in Western Europe from the Beginning of the Christian Era to the Fourteenth Century*. Chicago: University of Chicago Press.

Brock, Rita Nakashima (1988). *Journey by Heart: A Christology of Erotic Power*. New York: Crossroad.

Butler, Judith (2004). *Undoing Gender*. New York: Routledge.

Calloway, Ewen (2011). 'Sex and Violence Linked in the Brain'. *Nature: International Weekly Journal of Science*, 9 Febuary. <http://www.nature.com/news/2011/110209/full/news.2011.82.html> (accessed 23 July 2013).

Cooper-White, Pamela (2004). *Shared Wisdom: Use of the Self in Pastoral Care and Counseling*. Minneapolis: Fortress.

Cooper-White, Pamela (2007). *Many Voices: Pastoral Psychotherapy in Relational and Theological Perspective*. Minneapolis: Fortress.

Cooper-White, Pamela (2012). *The Cry of Tamar: Violence against Women and the Church's Response*, 2nd edn. Minneapolis: Fortress.

Cushman, Philip (1995). *Constructing the Self, Constructing America: A Cultural History of Psychotherapy*. New York: Perseus.

Dougherty, Carol (1993). *The Poetics of Colonization: From City to Text in Ancient Greece*. Oxford: Oxford University Press.

Eberstadt, Mary and Mary Anne Layden (2010) (eds). *The Social Costs of Pornography*. Princeton, NJ: Witherspoon Institute.

Ellison, Marvin and Kelly Brown Douglas (2010). *Sexuality and the Sacred: Sources for Theological Reflection*, 2nd edn. Louisville: Westminster John Knox.

Foucault, Michel (1978). *The History of Sexuality, Vol. 1: An Introduction*, trans. Robert Hurley. New York: Random House/Pantheon.

Foucault, Michel (1985). *The History of Sexuality: Vol. 2. The Use of Pleasure*. Trans. Robert Hurley. New York: Random House/Pantheon.

Foxhall, Lin and John Salmon (eds) (1999). *When Men Were Men: Masculinity, Power, and Identity in Classical Antiquity*. London: Routledge.

Freud, Sigmund (1955). Beyond the Pleasure Principle. In James Strachey (ed.), *The Standard Edition of the Complete Psychological Works of Sigmund Freud*, vol. 18. London: Hogarth, 3–66.

Freud, Sigmund (1961). *Civilization and Its Discontents*. In Strachey J. (ed.), *The Standard Edition of the Complete Psychological Works of Sigmund Freud*, vol. 21. London: Hogarth, 59–148.

Gannon, Theresa A. and Tony Ward (2008) 'Rape: Psychopathology and Theory'. In D. Richard Laws and William T. O'Donohue (eds), *Sexual Deviance: Theory, Assessment, and Treatment*, 2nd edn. New York: Guilford, 356–383.

Gee, Dion, Grant Devilly, and Tony Ward (2004). 'The Content of Sexual Fantasies for Sexual Offenders'. *Sexual Abuse: A Journal of Research and Treatment*, 16(4): 315–331.

Giddens, Anthony (1992). *The Transformation of Intimacy: Sexuality, Love and Eroticism in Modern Societies*. Stanford, CA: Stanford University Press.

Greider, Kathleen (1997). *Reckoning with Aggression: Theology, Violence, and Vitality*. Louisville: Westminster John Knox.

Griffin, Susan (1981). *Pornography and Silence: Culture's Revenge against Nature*. New York: Harper & Row.

Groth, Nicholas (1979). *Men Who Rape: The Psychology of the Offender*. New York: Perseus.

Harper, Douglas (2013). 'Vagina'. *Online Etymology Dictionary*. <http://dictionary.reference.com/browse/vagina> (accessed 23 July 2013).

Harway, Michele and James M. O'Neill (1999). *What Causes Male Violence against Women?* Thousand Oaks, CA: Sage.

Hays, Maggie (2012). 'Pornography: A Definition'. <https://www.againstpornography.org/definition.html> (accessed 23 July 2013).

Heyward, Carter (1989). 'The Erotic as the Power of God'. In Carter Heyward (ed.), *Touching Our Strength*. San Francisco: HarperSanFrancisco.

Hilsum, Lindsey (2013). 'In Tahrir Square, Recent Protests Have Been Scene of Rampant Sexual Assault'. PBS News Hour, 11 July. <http://www.pbs.org/newshour/bb/world/july-dec13/egypt_07-11.html> (accessed 23 July 2013).

Hopkins, Keith (1983). *Death and Renewal: Sociological Studies in Roman History*, vol. 2. Cambridge: Cambridge University Press.

Jameson, Harriet (2013). *'Reporting Rates'*. Washington, DC: Rape, Abuse & Incest National Network (RAINN), 2 May. <http://www.rainn.org/print/288> (accessed 23 July 2013).

Johnson, Elizabeth (1994). *She Who Is: The Mystery of God in Feminist Theological Discourse*. New York: Crossroad.

Lorde, Audre (1980). 'Uses of the Erotic: The Erotic as Power'. In Laura Lederer (ed.), *Take Back the Night*. New York: Harper Perennial.

Malamuth, Neil, Seymour Feshbach, and Yoram Jaffe (1977). 'Sexual Arousal and Aggression: Recent Experiments and Theoretical Issues'. *Journal of Social Issues* 33(2): 110–33. <http://www.sscnet.ucla.edu/comm/malamuth/pdf/77jsi33.pdf> (accessed 23 July 2013).

Malamuth, Neil, Christopher Heavey, and Daniel Linz (1993). 'Predicting Men's Antisocial Behavior against Women: The Interaction Model of Sexual Aggression'. In Gordon C. Nagayama Hall et al. (eds), *Sexual Aggression: Issues in Etiology, Assessment, and Treatment*. Washington, DC: Taylor & Francis, 63–97.

Marshall, William L. and Howard E. Barbaree (1990). 'An Integrated Theory of the Etiology of Sexual Offending'. In William Marshall, D. Richard Laws, and Howard E. Barbaree (eds), *Handbook of Sexual Assault*. New York: Plenum, 257–275.

Metropolitan Museum of Art (2013). Panathenaic Amphora, c.530 BCE. New York. <http://www.metmuseum.org/toah/works-of-art/14.130.12> (accessed 23 July 2013).

Musée du Louvre (2013). 'Tydeus and Ismene' Amphora, c.560 BCE. Paris. <http:// www.hellenicaworld.com/Greece/Mythology/en/TydeusIsmeneLouvreE640.html> (accessed 23 July 2013).

National Center for Policy Analysis (1999). *Crime and Punishment in America, 1999*. Washington, DC: NCPA.

Nelson, James (ed.) (1994). *Sexuality and the Sacred: Sources for Theological Reflection*. Louisville: Westminster John Knox.

New York Times (2013). Online digest of articles on Abu Ghraib. <http://topics.nytimes.com/top/news/international/countriesandterritories/iraq/abu_ghraib/index.html> (accessed 23 July 2013).

Office for Democratic Institutions and Human Rights (2009). *Hate Crime Laws: A Practical Guide*. Warsaw, Poland: ODIHR. <http://www.osce.org/odihr/36426?download=true> (accessed 23 July 2013).

Poling, James (1991). *The Abuse of Power: A Theological Problem*. Nashville: Abingdon.

Portman, John (2007). *A History of Sin: How Evil Changes, but Never Goes Away*. New York: Rowman and Littlefield.

Portman, John (2013). *The Ethics of Sex and Alzheimer's*. New York: Routledge.

Rizzuto, Ana-Maria (1979). *The Birth of the Living God: A Psychoanalytic Study*. Chicago: University of Chicago Press.

Sexual Medicine Society of North America, Inc. (SMSNA) (2013). 'Male Erection Frequency', *Sex Health Matters*. <http://www.sexhealthmatters.org/did-you-know/male-erection-frequency> (accessed 23 July 2013).

Steinhauer, Jennifer (2013). 'Sexual Assaults in Military Raise Alarm in Washington', *New York Times*, 7 May. <http://www.nytimes.com/2013/05/08/us/politics/pentagon-study-sees-sharp-rise-in-sexual-assaults.html?pagewanted=all> (accessed 23 July 2013).

Stoller, Robert (2012). *Sexual Excitement: Dynamics of Erotic Life*. London: Karnac. (Originally published 1979.)

Thatcher, Adrian (2011). *God, Sex, and Gender: An Introduction*. Oxford: Wiley Blackwell.

Tjaden, Patricia and Nancy Thoennes (2000). *Full Report of the Prevalence, Incidence, and Consequences of Violence Against Women: Findings from the National Violence Against Women Survey*, NCJ 183781, National Institute of Justice and Centers for Disease Control and Prevention, November. <http://www.ncjrs.gov/pdffiles1/nij/183781.pdf> (accessed 23 July 2013).

United Nations Population Fund (2000). 'Ending Violence against Women and Girls', ch. 3 in *State of the World Population 2000*. New York: United Nations. <http://www.unfpa.org/swp/2000/english/ch03.html> (accessed 23 July 2013).

United Nations Security Council (2008). Resolution 1820. <http://www.un.org/News/Press/docs/2008/sc9364.doc.htm> (accessed 23 July 2013).

US Bureau of Justice Statistics (1998). 'Crime and Justice in the United States and in England and Wales, 1981–1996'. <http://bjs.ojp.usdoj.gov/content/pub/html/cjusew96/cpp.cfm> (accessed 23 July 2013).

U.S. Bureau of Justice Statistics (2008). Table 40, 'Personal Crimes of Violence, 1996–2008'. <http://www.bjs.gov/content/pub/pdf/cvus/current/cv0840.pdf> (accessed 12 July 2013).

US Bureau of Justice Statistics (2011). 'Personal Crimes of Violence, 2008'. <http://bjs.ojp.usdoj.gov/content/pub/pdf/cvus/current/cv0840.pdf> (accessed 23 July 2013).

US Federal Bureau of Investigation (2009a). '2008 Crime in the United States', Table 1. <http://www2.fbi.gov/ucr/cius2008/data/table_01.html> (accessed 23 July 2013).

US Federal Bureau of Investigation (2009b). '2008 Crime in the United States', Table 1a. <http://www2.fbi.gov/ucr/cius2008/data/table_01a.html> (accessed 23 July 2013).

US Federal Bureau of Investigation (2013). 'Hate Crime—Overview'. <http://www.fbi.gov/about-us/investigate/civilrights/hate_crimes/overview> (accessed 23 July 2013). Hate crime based on sexual orientation was added in 2009 (the Matthew Shepard and James Byrd, Jr., Hate Crimes Prevention Act).

Valley's Own (pseudonym) (2011). 'War Boner', *Urban Dictionary*, 5 April.

West, Rachel (2013). 'The Etiology of Sexual Offending Behavior and Sex Offender Typology: An Overview', Center for Sex Offender Management (CSOM), US Dept. of Justice, <www.csom.org/train/etiology> (accessed 23 July 2013).

Winnicott, D. W. (1975). 'The Antisocial Tendency'. *Through Paediatrics to Psycho-Analysis: Collected Papers*. New York: Basic Books, 306–315.

World Health Organization (2005). *WHO Multi-Country Study on Women's Health and Domestic Violence against Women: Summary Report*. Geneva: WHO. <http://www.who.int/gender/violence/who_multicountry_study/summary_report/summary_report_English2.pdf> (accessed 23 July 2013).

Yeung, Yeung and Grace Rubenstein (2013). 'Female Workers Face Rape, Harassment in U.S. Agriculture Industry', 25 June. Center for Investigative Reporting, University of California at Berkeley. <http://www.pbs.org/wgbh/pages/frontline/social-issues/rape-in-the-fields/female-workers-face-rape-harassment-in-u-s-agriculture-industry/> (accessed 23 July 2013).

CHAPTER 30

SEXUAL PLEASURE

MARGARET D. KAMITSUKA

MOST people living in the Christianized West associate the church with the notion: 'the less pleasure, the more spiritual goodness' (Obach 2009: 55) an apt if simplified notion associated with the late sixth-century pope Gregory the Great. Such associations are not groundless, since they re-emerge with regularity in contemporary popular Christianity, as found in a sermon by renowned Baptist minister John Piper, who warned his congregation 'If you turn from the Lord as your treasure and your all-satisfying pleasure, and make a master out of sex, sooner or later you will meet the wrath of God' (Piper 2002). How should Christians think about sexual pleasure? Is it possible to break out of the binary of sexual temptation versus spiritual fulfilment? Are there other binaries lurking in Christian discourses that set acceptable sexual pleasures against unacceptable ones—and what are the ramifications of this either/or approach?

In recent decades, many progressive theologians are attempting to formulate broadly life-affirming understandings of sexual pleasure for more than just a specific category of individuals—namely, monogamously heterosexual married couples with primarily reproductively oriented coupling practices. This is no easy task given Christianity's long history of anti-sex teachings surrounding a kernel of cautious procreationist mandates. After some selective historical glimpses into that history in Roman Catholicism and Protestantism, this chapter focuses on the affirmation of sexual pleasure in contemporary feminist, womanist, and queer theological writings where two themes emerge: sexual pleasure as God-given; and the justice-making capacities of sexual pleasure. These themes are not mutually exclusive but will be discussed separately in order to show more clearly how they address the binaries mentioned above and to allow for specific critical questions to be raised.

In order to evaluate critically how contemporary theologies construe pleasure, this chapter takes as its critical staring point, Kathleen Sands' caveat that sexual theologies may be asking too much of sex (Sands 1992). Specifically, 'asking too much' regarding the first theme (the God-givenness of sexual pleasure) stems from inadequacies in the mode of theorizing about sexual identity. Regarding the theme of how sexual pleasure contributes to justice-making, 'asking too much' stems from inadequate theorizing about resistance to oppressive power—in this case, heteronormativity. After surveying some new theological investigations regarding sexual pleasure, this essay makes a modest proposal for how an eschatological perspective on pleasure can promote non-binary ways of thinking about sexuality outside this-worldly patriarchal heteronormativity and human finitude.

HISTORICAL OVERVIEW

That Christian thinkers over the centuries have spilled much ink excoriating the pursuit of sexual pleasure is well known. The New Testament is marked by a dim view of *eros*: 'And those who belong to Christ Jesus have crucified the flesh with its passions and desires' (Gal. 5:24). Historians, however, do not lay the blame for the anti-sex rhetoric exclusively at the feet of early Christian writers, noting that their condemnation of pleasure draws in part from Greco-Roman medical views about the regulation of sexual activity in relation to healthy and unhealthy bodily humours. Second-century Roman physician and philosopher Claudius Galen, for example, counselled a moderate diet in order to prevent the unhealthy accumulation in men and women of 'warm semen' that could most appropriately be expelled by intercourse (Shaw 1998: 58). Immoderation in diet was thought to cause immoderation in sexuality, which Galen and his peers frowned upon as distracting one from higher pursuits of virtue and cultivation of the soul.

Greco-Roman teachings on moderation, however, gave way to Christian polemics that pitted pleasure against ascetical purity. A two-tiered worldview emerged that ranked virginity as a higher spiritual vocation than marriage. Christian leaders struggled to keep factions of the church from slipping into gnostic anti-procreationism. For Clement of Alexandria in the late second century, this meant promulgating a stringent view of sexual pleasure even in marriage. Clement envisioned the possibility of marital sexuality whereby Christians might procreate continently. That is, with the grace of Christ, Christians could fulfil God's biblical mandate to be fruitful and multiply 'without loss of self-control', meaning they could 'produce children by a reverent, disciplined act of will' (Clement 1991: 288, 292). As one scholar puts it, Clement painted a picture of saintly married Christians who 'neither want nor feel sexual pleasure when they have genital contact with procreationist resolve' (Gaca 2003: 264).

Augustine and Aquinas

Augustine of Hippo also took a procreationist stance—an even more pessimistic one than Clement. Navigating between a Manichean rejection of sexual bodies and a Pelagian acceptance of conjugal pleasure, Augustine maintained that bodies, originally part of God's good creation, were tainted after the Fall. Procreation, ordained by God, could no longer be accomplished without the sin of concupiscence. Augustine was not against all sensual pleasures; he appreciated many, from art to music, always being careful not to let enjoyment of them draw his attention too far from God, as he discusses in Book 10 of his *Confessions*. In his early fifth-century anti-Pelagian treatise *On Marriage and Concupiscence* (II.14), he condemned sexual pleasure because it caused a particularly pernicious loss of rationality that produced shame: 'For why is the especial work of parents withdrawn and hidden even from the eyes of their children, except that it is impossible for them to be occupied in laudable procreation without shameful lust?' (Augustine 1902: 288). Shame was the existential proof for Augustine's somewhat tortured conscience that sexual pleasure—even within the bounds of marriage—was in fact sinful.

Thomas Aquinas in the twelfth century somewhat rehabilitated concupiscence. In his *Summa Theologiae* (II-II, q. 153), he used Aristotelian philosophy to categorize sexual pleasure as a natural (not inherently sinful) appetite that could be rightly employed by the married person who acts on that appetite for moral and rational reasons. Aquinas affirmed, contrary to Clement, that the amount of pleasure experienced in the conjugal act is not what determines concupiscence. Aquinas diverged from Augustine who saw the interruption of reason by passion to be proof of its sinfulness. Aquinas argued that 'the abundance of pleasure' in sexual intercourse is not necessarily sinful, and the 'fact that the reason's free attention to spiritual things cannot be simultaneous with the pleasure' is not an indication of loss of virtue. Indeed, if suspension of reason meant the automatic loss of virtue, 'it would be against virtue to go to sleep' (Aquinas 1968: 193–194). Sin enters in when sex is pursued for the sake of pleasure alone. Hence, even if Aquinas was able to break free from the pessimism of the Augustinian notion of the transfer of original sin in the concupiscence of intercourse, he nevertheless helped to entrench the notion that married sexual pleasure was meant properly for procreation alone. Although Aquinas was able to pronounce 'licit the suspension of consciousness in orgasm', he rejected the pursuit of sexual pleasure for any other intention than that of procreation (Kochuthara 2007: 220).

Protestant and Catholic Approaches to Pleasure

Some considerably more lenient views on sex in marriage developed in Counter Reformation marriage manuals of the sixteenth century. Jesuit Thomas Sanchez held that married couples could engage in a pleasurable touching in order to foster affection in their marriage, and not just for the objective of procreation. 'Laxist' views such as these opened the door in Roman Catholic teachings in the modern period for an affirmation of sexual pleasure apart from directly procreative intents and purposes (Kochuthara 2007: 237). Peter Gardella comments on the surprisingly open discussion of female orgasm in Bishop Francis Patrick Kenrick's mid-nineteenth-century *Theologiae Moralis*, which says (discreetly in Latin): 'a married woman had the right to bring herself to orgasm "by touches" after intercourse, if she had experienced no climax during lovemaking' (Kenrick quoted in Gardella 1985: 9). We can also see the theme of godly marital sexuality in Pope Benedict XVI's encyclical that calls for a unity of *eros* and *agape* in the intimacy of the conjugal act (Benedict XVI 2005). For the Vatican, the pleasure of sex not just for the purpose of reproduction is licit as long as the couple remains always open to the possibility of procreation and does nothing to impede it.

While Protestant and Catholic theologies may differ greatly, the history of Protestant teachings on sexual pleasure follows a pattern similar to that of Roman Catholicism. Despite their rejection of celibacy, the Reformers took a dim view of sex. Martin Luther, in his *Lectures on Genesis*, for example, displays a thoroughly Augustinian view of sex, stating that 'if Adam had persisted in the state of innocence ... [t]he very work of procreation ... would have been most sacred'. Luther colourfully describes how, as a result of the Fall, sex became 'so hideous and frightful a pleasure that physicians compare it with epilepsy' (Luther 1958: 117, 119). Later Puritan writers, while admonishing the faithful to maintain 'modesty and decency' and avoid the excesses of brutish passion, nevertheless, counselled that husband and wife should give 'due benevolence' sexually to one another (Doriani 1991: 132, 133). They rejected the idea that sex was tainted with sin and did not reduce marital union exclusively to its benefit of procreation. Also, since Puritans did not have fixed fast days, there were few calendar days where marital intercourse was forbidden.

Many of the well-known American Protestant theologians of the nineteenth century preached parsimony regarding all forms of pleasure. Congregational minister Horace Bushnell spoke of sexual intercourse as the 'coarsest sensuality' (Bushnell 1876: 284). Presbyterian minister Sylvester Graham inveighed against sexual excess in marriage as part of his larger philosophy of hygiene and health that advocated moderation and a high fibre diet. He was convinced that the 'convulsive paroxysms attending venereal indulgence' were so debilitating to the whole digestive and nervous system that they should be avoided as much as possible. He believed that the more semen is retained, the more a man will acquire 'sprightliness, vivacity, muscular strength, and general vigor' (Graham 1849: 49, 51).

By the twentieth century, mainline Protestant thinkers moderated their criticisms of sexual pleasure by bringing it under the umbrella of biblical covenantal theology. Karl Barth promoted the view of marriage as ordained by the Genesis 2:24 call to become one flesh—a communion whose deeper significance should be seen as separate from the children it may produce. Under God's providential care, husband and wife have the possibility of experiencing the kind of *eros* without shame exemplified in the Song of Songs—a book that Barth called, the 'second Magna Carta of humanity' (Barth 2004: 293) after the first Magna Carta—the story of God giving the woman to the man in Genesis 2 (291).

Conservative evangelicals in the contemporary period have attempted to surmount the early church's disdain of sexual pleasure. For example, marriage manuals with explicit instructions about how to foster mutual sexual satisfaction abound in popular evangelical publishing.[1] The evangelical promotion of marital pleasure comes under the umbrella of conservative teachings about biblically based male and female gender roles

---

[1] Some titles include: *Intended for Pleasure: Sex Techniques and Sexual Pleasure* (Wheat & Wheat,

where the husband is the head and the wife is subject to him (Piper 2006). The embrace of marital pleasure by some conservative Christians has meant the explicit exclusion of the erotic 'other' (gays, bisexuals, transgender persons). This exclusion has taken various forms. Begun in the United States, a parachurch organization called 'Exodus', promotes therapy programmes to help homosexuals refrain from homosexual behaviours and, if possible, redirect same-sex desires toward heterosexuality.[2]

Whether in the Catholic or Protestant traditions, there is an overwhelming history of official teachings emphasizing the repression, at worst, and the moderation, at best, of sexual pleasure. Even when sexual pleasure is affirmed, that affirmation comes at a cost: for Roman Catholics, the requirement that sexual intimacy—to be licit—be directed to an act that ultimately could result in procreation; for conservative Protestants, that sexual intimacy in marriage reflect specific gender roles and family hierarchy. Many contemporary Catholics and Protestants find these teachings unsatisfactory or impractical for various reasons. Progressive theologians, moreover, who find the underlying assumptions in the church's teachings about sexual pleasure, gendered desire, and sexed identity to be problematic, are both affirming pleasure and rethinking the spiritual and societal importance of sexual relating.

GOD-GIVEN PLEASURE IN FEMINIST AND QUEER THEOLOGIES

Feminist and queer scholars are expanding the definition of sexual pleasure beyond married, male–female coupling that is more or less reproductively oriented. This change is in part a factor of theological advocacy on behalf of sexual identities outside of normative heterosexuality. One group of writings about pleasure approaches this issue by making the case that sexual pleasure is a God-given aspect of human embodiment and hence the suppression of pleasure is, in effect, a rejection of God's gift to humankind.

Episcopal priest Carter Heyward is one of many theologians emphasizing the category of *eros* as integral to the human person as a creature of God and a social being. She states that 'celebration of the erotic and of our desire to express it sexually' is integral to one's relation to God and to others (Heyward 1989: 27). She and fellow lesbian feminist theologian Mary Hunt challenged other feminists to take more seriously the theological, epistemological, and political contribution of 'sexual love between women' within patriarchal, heterosexist culture (Heyward and Hunt 1986: 96). While affirming Adrianne Rich's broad

---

1997); *The Act of Marriage: The Beauty of Sexual Love* (LaHaye & LaHaye, 1998); *Real Questions, Real Answers about Sex: The Complete Guide to Intimacy as God Intended* (McBurney, L. & M. 2005).

[2] See their website at <http://exodusinternational.org/>. On 19 June 2013 Exodus International leaders publicly apologized to the LGBT community and announced they would close their thirty-year ministry (see: <http://wespeaklove.org/exodus/>; accessed 15 November 2013).

definition of lesbianism to include all 'woman-identified women', Heyward and Hunt insist on the *sui generis* 'sexual groundedness of lesbianism' (Heyward and Hunt 1986: 99).

Working with notions from the *Catechism of the Catholic Church*, Jane Grovijahn also emphasizes the groundedness of sexual identity, which she refers to as 'deep authenticity' given in God's 'work of creation' (Grovijahn 2008: 129n28, 122). All human beings, Grovijahn claims, are created with some mode of sexual relating infused with God's grace and are called by God to reach beyond themselves and connect to others—including and perhaps especially by means of sexual intimacy. The experience of sexual pleasure—a mode of 'fleshly flourishing'—reflects God's own relational and covenanting *eros* with the created world (Grovijahn 2008: 125). Queer believers proclaim that in coming out into the experience of sexual intimacy, they find spiritual wholeness and the sacramentality of 'an unapologetic pleasuring of the flesh that is "*capax Dei*"' (Grovijahn 2008: 141).

Heyward's writings exhibit an identity politics view of lesbian sexuality and Grovijahn's exhibit her self-proclaimed queer perspective,[3] but both make theological claims for sexuality as an authentic manifestation of the God-given life force of *eros*. One concern arises regarding the possible essentialism entailed in their appeals to embodied sexual authenticity. There exists a long theological tradition of appealing to a prethematic core of the human person oriented to the divine. Some theologians have called into question this 'experiential-expressive' orientation to religious experience (Lindbeck 1984), preferring to take a more historicized or poststructuralist approach (Davaney 1987; Fulkerson 1994).

A poststructuralist approach, when applied theologically to sexual experience, does not appeal to the divine givenness of an essential human *eros*; rather, poststructuralist theologians employ notions like Judith Butler's 'performativity' in order to display the ways in which identities, including sexualities, are constituted and performed in complex processes of negotiating with and possibly resisting cultural rules and conventions (Kamitsuka 2007). A performative approach to sexuality presumably allows the theologian to affirm its goodness while also recognizing how it is variously mobilized in material contexts of both pleasure and disciplinary constraint. This approach avoids essentializing claims—so difficult to sustain philosophically—about a core human identity. Moreover, a performative approach contests the imposition of gender and sex binaries (masculine/feminine; male/female) which feminist theorists have long associated with what Adrienne Rich has called 'compulsory heterosexuality'—namely, that patriarchy imposes an ideology of innate heterosexuality in order to maintain male dominance and suppress women-oriented women (Rich 1980). Instead of subverting male/female binaries, essentialist approaches to sexuality have few recourses other than to attempt to step outside of the binary, as seen in Monique Wittig's slogan 'lesbians are not women' (Wittig 1992: 32).

That said, there are also important political reasons to continue to invoke, at times, the authenticity of lesbian, gay, bisexual, transgender, or other sexual identities.

---

[3] Heyward has mostly described her 'coming out' as that of a lesbian (Heyward 1995: 112–113), an identity that she has only recently associated more closely with the notion of queer (Heyward 2011). Grovijahn describes herself as 'Catholic and queer to the core' (Evans and Healy 2008: 345).

Individuals in daily life have to engage institutions—including ecclesial ones. In denominations working out their polity regarding the ordination of homosexuals or support for already ordained pastors who have 'come out of the closet', the public assertion of authentic sexual identity has been a practical necessity—along with being a personal and moral necessity for some. These assertions can be seen as 'here I stand; I can do no other' moments for queer clergy in relation to their governing denominational entities.

Not surprisingly, it has not been enough for queer Protestant pastors that their denominations refrain from condemning their sexual 'inclination'; these pastors are demanding the right to express their sexual desire and therefore not to have to take a vow of celibacy in order to keep their church job. In mainline Protestant churches, the movement by ordained ministers for the right to love whom they will has provoked a splintering within many denominations. The worldwide Anglican Church teeters on the edge of a major schism as more conservative Anglican churches, particularly of the 'Global South', reject the Church of England's decision allowing celibate gay bishops, not to mention the decisions in the US Episcopal Church (under the leadership of a female presiding bishop) to bless same-sex marriages and ordain openly gay bishops (Malnick 2013). It seems as though conflicts over the God-givenness of some sexual pleasures will lie at the heart of intra-denominational debates in coming years.

Pleasure as a Mode of Justice-making

Another set of theological writings focuses on sexual pleasure as having the ethical potential to foster more just and healing ways of being in the world. Roman Catholic feminist Patricia Beattie Jung calls for recognizing women's sexual delight as a moral good that awakens self-worth and awareness of the worth of others. Jung argues that female sexual dysfunction is more widespread than commonly thought and that it constitutes a moral problem to the extent that it is 'culturally grounded and sustained' (Jung 2000: 32). Jung charges that the patriarchal church has historically affirmed the reproductive contribution of male orgasm while ignoring female pleasure, which is arguably incidental to human reproduction. A male partner's lack of concern for a woman's pleasure in heterosexual coitus can lead to discomfort and pain and can be a form of violence. If this were not ethical reason enough for giving more serious attention to women's sexual pleasure, Jung further claims that fostering women's sexual pleasure brings vital additional goods: it enables female self-worth and concern for others. If 'self-love and neighbour-love are ultimately congruent', then it is a moral and religious imperative that women achieve sexual self-love (Jung 2000: 45).

Feminists who see the moral potential in fostering women's sexual pleasure also caution that it is important not to lose sight of diversity in women's sexual experience (Pellauer 1994). Womanist theologians have argued that the need for African American women to foster sexual health and well-being emerges out of the historical context of systemic violence against black women's bodies from the slave period up to the present.[4] Hence, the moral affirmation of women's sexual pleasure in African American circles may need to happen in what Karen Baker-Fletcher calls the 'hush harbor'— a term with origins in the ante-bellum South meaning a place where slaves could be away from their masters. Baker-Fletcher uses 'hush harbor' to mean safe and sacred spaces where black women can talk among themselves and with God about sexuality (Baker-Fletcher 2004). Alternatively, some womanist writers argue that the tradition of 'blues-singing women' has been an avenue for liberating black women's sexual pleasure from black church constraints because 'the blues rescues sexuality from its sinful place' (Douglas 2011: 120). Hence, whether in the 'hush harbor' or the nightclub, affirming sexual pleasure, womanist theologians insist, is of moral importance.

Presbyterian minister and social ethicist Marvin Ellison, argues for an ethics that rejects the erotophobic, patriarchal 'shame-based' views of sexuality that pervade Christianity. These views have long marginalized women, gays, lesbians, and other sexual minorities and have channelled men into paths of abuse and violence. Moral discourse must attend to the voices and experiences of those who have been disenfranchised from the 'right to love and be loved'. Honouring sexual self-acceptance and 'eroticism as a spiritual resource' will transform the church's social ethics, giving Christians new resources for subverting systems of domination and promoting 'respectful touching', compassion, justice, and moral responsibility (Ellison 1996: 116, 92).

Argentinian theologian Marcella Althaus-Reid, known for her critique of how Latin American liberation theologies 'desexualise the communities of the poor' (Althaus-Reid 2003: 115), argues for the justice-making aspect of the sexual pleasures of society's poor and marginalized. She insists that the queer lust of present-day 'sexual and political dissidents' must be integrated into liberation theological discourse if it is ever to free itself from its own neo-colonialist trappings (Althaus-Reid 2003: 165). Althaus-Reid argues that queer people play a 'pedagogic role' for theology and politics today (Althaus-Reid 2003: 169). Their experiences and their stories can disrupt the patriarchal–capitalist–heteronormative structures and ideologies that oppress sexually marginalized people: 'Binary thought can only be challenged in theology and capitalism alike by people whose bodies are living parables of transgression … [from whom] we may be able to learn something about difference' (Althaus-Reid 2000: 179–180). The alternative to learning about sexual differences is to forget that the Christianized conquest of Latin America depended on the binary of the masculine colonizer subjugating feminized indigenous peoples.

Critical Reflections on Pleasure and Justice

The feminist and womanist call for the moral imperative to foster women's sexual pleasure, Ellison's claim that non-patriarchal *eros* has the potential to rechannel male violence, and Althaus-Reid's vision for a queer liberation theology—all these theologies

---

[4] For a discussion of the effects on black men's sexuality of the history of slavery and subsequent Jim Crow and other racist structures in the United States, see Hopkins (2006).

suggest that sexual pleasure is more than just enjoyment; it can be ethically productive and socially transformative. Showing the ethical contributions of sexual pleasure is important, but some critical reflection is also needed. This view of pleasure echoes a certain strand of Michel Foucault's writings in which he explored how 'bodies and pleasures' could be a site of resistance to oppressive sexual and gender norms (Foucault 1978: 157). Judith Butler calls into question this utopian vision of bodily pleasures freed from disciplinary mechanisms; moreover, Butler indicates that Foucault himself moved away from the notion of 'bodies and pleasures' and instead focused his final research projects on the issue of how the individual's subjectivity is discursively constituted.

Butler joins with the later Foucault to insist that pleasure, poststructurally understood, is not an avenue of freedom from oppression but is constructed in relation to 'control and constraint ... where constraint is also productive, crafting sexuality and desire' (Butler 1999: 20). From this perspective, the theological appeal to the justice-making potential of sexual pleasure may ask too much of sex by investing it with the moral power to transcend the binary of hegemonic systems of control versus libertarian sexual pleasures. Sexual ecstasy may be marked by moments of transcendent—almost mystical—experience for some, but practices of pleasure never take place outside of what Foucauldians call disciplinary power. The modes of resistance that, for example, sexual minorities mount in opposition to the constraints of heteronormativity are in part the productive 'excessive' and 'confounding' effects that arise precisely in relation to those constraints—so argues Butler (Butler 1999: 20).

How can theologians promote the moral power of sexual pleasure without asking too much of sex? Foucault, who championed pleasure, also advocated *askesis*, technologies of the 'care for oneself', via self-knowledge, as a basis for ethics (Foucault 1988: 43). He was particularly interested in ancient Greco-Roman ethics, which did not pit pleasure against purity but emphasized self-cultivation so that pleasure would have its proper place in a life well lived. Sexual pleasure, in other words, is one of many discursive mechanisms that the individual negotiates in order to achieve, not freedom, but self-knowledge and wisdom. This approach avoids the binaries of corrupting sex versus purifying continence or licit versus illicit desire; the practices of pleasure are regulated not because some are intrinsically evil but because virtue comes from 'mindfulness' in all things. (Foucault 1988: 168). This approach neither overinflates the justice-making potential of pleasure nor labels pleasure as intrinsically corrupting.

OTHER PLEASURES; OTHER BODIES

Affirming the pleasures of sexual touch is a helpful corrective to Christianity's anti-sex and anti-body history. Nevertheless privileging sexual pleasure—especially orgasmic pleasure—may be a too narrow focus for theologians hoping to promote human bodily flourishing. Focusing too narrowly on orgasmic pleasure may marginalize other pleasures and other bodies—namely, those that are not highly libidinous and virile; temporarily celibate or consecrated celibate bodies; bodies recovering from sexual trauma; bodies with physical challenges that impede genital expression; or just plain tired and overworked bodies. Once we open the door into forms of sexual pleasure that are not exclusively or even predominantly genitally orgasmic, a number of sexualities, sexual bodies, and sexual practices become topics of inquiry. We have just a glimpse of what is to come in some recent theological proposals. All of these share a similar methodological starting point—namely, sexual pleasure as experienced by particular groups of people.

Broadening the Focus of Pleasure

Postcolonial theologians have been active in reinterpreting classic Christian texts and addressing ethical issues from a decolonizing perspective, including issues of sexuality. Episcopal theologian Kwok Pui Lan, who experienced British colonial rule in Hong Kong, reflects on how Asian Christians might develop a decolonizing interpretation of *eros* that taps indigenous cultural histories while also exploring new hybrid postcolonial sexualities and pleasures (Kwok 2010). Indian American Roman Catholic theologian Susan Abraham seeks to mobilize 'space and resources' to allow the subaltern subject (who, as Gayatri Chakravorty Spivak has famously and controversially said, is mostly 'silent') to speak (Abraham 2007: 205, 40). Feminist and queer thinkers in the West will need to resist the urge to impose on the subaltern body their own neo-colonizing sexual agendas—whether it be the celebration of 'clitoral pleasure' (Abraham 2007: 114) or the white Western feminist fascination with a narrowly auto-erotic interpretation of *jouissance*, a term coined by French-speaking European feminists (Kwok 2010: 41).

Theologies of disability note that while feminist and queer theologians have given considerable attention to embodiment, they have been largely silent on non-able-bodied experience (Creamer 2009). Disabilities scholars challenge their theological colleagues not to overlook the experience of chronic bodily pain which, though never welcome, can sometimes function as a 'moral compass' (Betcher 2010: 113). Wendy Farley reflects on pleasure and pain from a Buddhist-Christian dialogical perspective. Farley suggests how Buddhist and Christian classic teachings about the superficiality of bodily pleasures can bring about a 'transformation of desire from concupiscence to compassion' that productively reorients privileged religious practitioners in a world where most people live in conditions of physical deprivation and suffering (Farley 1999: 301). Linda Holler similarly believes that through Buddhist meditation practices of 'mindfulness, our daily acts can open up and extend our sensory lives in ways that allow us to feel … [and to be] capable of change and empathy, in short, empowered … by erotic intimacy' (Holler 2002: 168). Through mindfulness about pleasure as well as bodily pain and physical limitations, one is able to look upon and respond to suffering with compassion rather than to look away and isolate oneself from it.

Pleasure and ageing will no doubt continue to be an important topic, given that demographics point to an ageing global population. Ever since Mary Daly's retrieval of the category of 'Hag' and 'Crone' in the late 1970s (Daly 1978), feminists have criticized patriarchal ageism that relegates older women to the dustbin of history while idolizing the stereotypical sexually available ingénue. While many people are living longer and maintaining healthy and sexually active lives into older age, other elderly people experience debilitating illnesses and physical restrictions. This reality calls for a reassessment of the acclamation of pleasure in light of the stark bodily finitude and the inevitability of growing old (Saiving 1988).

A growing circle of theologians is giving attention to masochism, sado-masochism, and various domination/submission and bondage practices that explore nongenitally focused sexual acts. These theologians argue that serious examination of these practices fruitfully prompts reflection on: pleasure outside of procreativity; the ongoing effects of the history of Christian ascetic pain rituals and of hierarchical church authority; and whether the pleasure–pain intensity in BDSM practices can illumine theological questions of God–human relations and vice versa (MacKendrick 1999; Carrette 2005).

Another fast-growing area for theological research is transgender, intersex, and other variant sex/gender identities. The reality of intersex people—those with atypical genitalia who were not surgically altered at birth to resemble most other male or female persons—presents a challenge to assumptions about what is physiologically required to achieve gratifying sexual intimacy. The cultural, ecclesial, and medical imposition of either a male or female sex identity, and rigid definitions of sexual intercourse, argues Susannah Cornwall, devalue 'the sexual and erotic quality of non-genital human relationships' that many intersex (and other) couples have (Cornwall 2010: 84). The church, in particular, should revisit its singular definition of what constitutes the conjugal act—a definition that weighs heavily on the psyche of Christian and non-Christian people.[5]

A significant voice that has emerged to promote equality within the church for transgender people is that of Virginia Mollenkott. Known for her work in the 1970s in the area of evangelical feminism, she came out as a lesbian and considers herself a transgender 'masculine woman' (Mollenkott and Sheridan 2003: 38)—a realization of which she did not become fully conscious until she was sixty-four years old. Having been raised as a conservative Christian, Mollenkott speaks poignantly of the strict sexual and gender codes that were imposed on her (she recalls being required to wear nylon stockings at Bob Jones University, even while playing tennis). As she struggled with her lesbianism, the advice she was given was that if she 'married heterosexually and pretended to be a heterosexual, eventually [she] would become heterosexual' (Mollenkott 2001: 43). After a long and painful journey that echoes the stories of so many other gay and transgender people, Mollenkott now writes about the integration of sexuality and spirituality. Mollenkott and other transgender Christians who maintain an involvement in evangelicalism are in a unique position to mediate between what seemed in the past to be two irreconcilable worlds: evangelical Christianity and transgenderedness.[6]

---

[5] Adrian Thatcher argues that the church's overemphasis on the post-nuptial genital consummation of marriage is detrimental to heterosexual couples as well (Thatcher 1999).

[6] Mollenkott is active in the Evangelical & Ecumenical Women's Caucus; see <http://www.eewc.com/>.

Christology and Ambiguous Bodies

Scholars are also integrating transgender issues into their theology, opening up a wide range of constructive theological possibilities. Susannah Cornwall explores how the 'uncertainty, liminality and even paradox' of transgender experience resonates with the apophatic tradition's view of God's unknowingness (Cornwall 2009: 16). The way in which apophatic theology navigates between God's knowability and ineffability provides resources for speaking about how the human body can be known in its materiality and yet also be elusive and not reducible to culturally dominant gender and sex categories. Moreover, the apophatic approach allows transgender people of all persuasions to see themselves as created richly in the image of God who is multiple and mysterious.

Tricia Sheffield explores the transgressive nature of Chalcedonian Christology, seeing there a theological metaphor for the 'complicated bordercrossing' that is often the case in transgender experience (Sheffield 2008: 239). Even with the church's creedal canonizations of a binary God–Man nature, Jesus' body has remained a 'place of cultural ambiguity' (Sheffield 2008: 241). For Sheffield (2008: 237), this is a good thing because it creates theological room for other ambiguous bodies:

> Jason is a genetic male who is married to a genetic female named Helen. Jason has made the decision to live as an androgynous person full time and now goes by the name Betty. Betty chooses not to undergo hormone therapy treatment or sexual reassignment surgery because it makes it easier for her and Helen to be together. She and Helen live together in what they describe as a married queer relationship.

It is precisely transgender narratives of love like this one that enables us to see anew the queerness of the doctrine of Christ's two natures. The Chalcedic body, Sheffield affirms, is 'a body full of trouble and a body that matters' (Sheffield 2008: 242)—a word play on Judith Butler's book titles (Butler 1990, 1993). Analogously, the bodies and pleasures of transgender people today should trouble the dominant sex/gender assumptions of our culture and matter deeply to those who profess membership in the body of Christ.

A MODEST THEOLOGICAL PROPOSAL: PLEASURE AND THE AFTERLIFE

How can theologians think fruitfully about sexual pleasure? As we have seen in the second and third sections of this chapter, theologians arguing for the God-givenness or the justice-making potential of pleasure take an experiential methodological starting point—namely, the experience of pleasure (and of its repressions). When that methodology is combined with theological assumptions about the goodness of the created order or God's liberating spirit of *eros* in the world, then conclusions may be drawn that affirm a wider range of sexual expressions than has been traditionally named by the church as licit sexual pleasure. The emerging theological discourses about marginalized sexual practices and sexual identities, discussed in the previous section, also take as their starting point human experience.

There are advantages and disadvantages to an experience-based approach. An advantage is that it highlights the lived realities of overlooked groups and attends to subaltern voices. A disadvantage is that despite these theological affirmations of the goodness of sex, in actuality, sexual relationality is often—if not ubiquitously—weakened or even corrupted by the foibles and failings of human nature. Whether one has an Augustinian view of sexual pleasure as concupiscence linked to original sin, or a queer Foucauldian view of pleasure as a mode of resistance to disciplinary heteronormativity, no one would deny that human sexual intimacy can be a site of great pleasure and also of anxiety, betrayal, heartbreak, exploitation, and many other painful experiences. In part, for this reason perhaps, theologians have historically seen the afterlife as a release from all bodily desires. The bulk of classical theological writings on the bodily resurrection denies that there will be any bodily gratification in the afterlife, because the saints in heaven are completely taken up with the soul's beatific vision of God—a vision, which 'once bestowed, spilled out from impassible souls into a gift of impassibility for body'.[7]

Eschatological *Eros*

There are a number of contemporary theologians attempting to envision the proper and perfect end (to use Thomistic language) of human sexuality who argue, as we will see in the following discussion, that sexual expression should not be precluded from the notion of resurrected bodies. If one entertains this possibility a number of questions arise: If we only see dimly in this life, what would sexuality mean for resurrected bodies in the next? Should we expect perfect erotic pleasure in heaven, and, if so, what would it entail?

These questions about eschatological *eros* are speculative but not, for that reason, insignificant. It may very well be that in order to break out of the repressive and heteronormative views of sexual pleasure discussed above, the last bastion of anti-sexual theological anthropology (i.e. humans in heaven) needs to be transformed as well. Doing so, I suggest, could reveal much about how we view sexual pleasure and treat bodies in this life. Discussions of eschatological pleasure, hence, are relevant and heuristically illuminating because they are not just about the end times but are also very much about the here and now. Some sexual theologies may be asking too much of sex, but we also need to ask enough of sex.

Ronald Long argues from a gay theological perspective in favour of the notion of sexual pleasure in heaven. Long affirms that 'desire for other men is something that is

---

[7] See Caroline Bynum's discussion of the medieval debates over whether the body is even needed for the soul to experience the beatific vision (1995: 289).

sacred' and he considers heavenly sex to be a kind of eschatological vindication of gay men's desires, which have been and continue to be so denigrated in the church (Long 2005: 36). Elizabeth Stuart affirms the value of a 'dissident' eschatological feminism that can envision sexual relationships beyond heteronormative structures of monogamous marriage (Stuart 1997: 195).

I have explored elsewhere an approach to the notion of eschatological sexuality, based on the work of Julia Kristeva (Kamitsuka 2010). In this approach, the sexual pleasure of resurrected bodies is viewed through a feminist psychoanalytic lens. If resurrected believers carry their individual embodied identities—including memories—into heaven, then the category of memory, when inflected psychoanalytically, brings into play theories of pre-Oedipal desires and pre-Oedipal wounds. For Freudian-based feminist thinkers like Kristeva, the experience of *jouissance*—which I interpret as female pleasure that may or may not involve genital sexual expressions—has its origins in the deeply rooted maternal pre-Oedipal experience. It is an experience lost to memory because of the violence of birth and the subsequent entry into the symbolic, phallic organization of the libido at the Oedipal stage of development. Abjection is the term Kristeva uses in her effort to emphasize the impact of the infant's violent split from the maternal body at birth and subsequent gradual separation from the mother's body, which is the original source of nurture, bonding, nourishment, pleasure, and nascent desire. There remains, according to Freudian theories of the unconscious, 'a deep well of memory' of that early quasi-borderless pleasure of the mother's body, a maternal *jouissance* (Kristeva 1982: 6); however, at the level of consciousness, abjection predominates once the child enters the phallic, symbolic world. The situation is more acute for the female child who, in abjecting the mother's body, in some way abjects her own. Nevertheless, abjection and its attendant expression of melancholy is apparently a psychic reality for all to some degree.

If psychoanalysts like Kristeva are right, the path to healing psychic scars, deeply embedded in the unconscious, has to do with the *jouissance* of bringing one's repressed losses to speech in the presence of a caring other. Heavenly *eros* could thus be envisioned as encompassing a range of sexual pleasures including, and perhaps necessarily presupposing, the experience of a perfect, healing, interpersonal *jouissance*.

Pleasures beyond Binarisms

Being able to imagine even dimly what heavenly *eros* would look (beatifically) like seems to open up a range of ways to think theologically about pleasure beyond binarisms of body versus spirit or licit versus illicit sex. If bodies are to be thought of in God's presence in heaven, the desires of those bodies would presumable be holy—including sexual desires. Thinking about sexual pleasure as sacred is an open door, some would say, to anything goes. Certainly some who are already prone to self-justification without introspection will think this way. However, I suggest that imagining the sexual pleasures to which one is drawn as unfolding before the angels—so to speak—is a good way to test how sacred and liberating one really wants to insist that sexual practice is. If a sexual practice withstands this eschatological litmus test, it may well prove to be a pleasure that contributes to more compassionate, healing, playful, and liberating experiences of *jouissance* for many types of bodies, ages, and desires. Theologians reflecting on pleasure beyond old binaries would not want to exclude such experiences of *jouissance* from a new theological imaginary about sexual pleasure *coram Deo* within the constraints of disciplinary discourses in this world.

REFERENCES

Abraham, S. (2007). *Identity, Ethics, and Nonviolence in Postcolonial Theory: A Rahnerian Theological Assessment*. New York: Palgrave Macmillan.

Althaus-Reid, M. (2000). *Indecent Theology: Theological Perversions in Sex, Gender and Politics*. London: Routledge.

Althaus-Reid, M. (2003). *The Queer God*. London: Routledge.

Aquinas, St Thomas. (1968). *Summa Theologiae*, vol. 43. Trans. T. Gilby O.P. London: Blackfriars.

Augustine, St (1902). *On Marriage and Concupiscence*, in P. Schaff (ed.), *Nicene and Post-Nicene Fathers of the Christian Church*, vol. 5. *Anti-Pelagian Writings*. Edinburgh: T & T Clark, 263–308.

Baker-Fletcher, K. (2004). 'The Erotic in Contemporary Black Women's Writings', in D. N. Hopkins and A. B. Pinn (eds), *Loving the Body: Black Religious Studies and the Erotic*. New York: Palgrave Macmillan, 199–213.

Barth, K. (2004). *Church Dogmatics, III/2, Doctrine of Creation*. Ed. G. W. Bromiley and T. F. Torrance, trans. G. W. Bromily. London and New York: T. & T. Clark.

Benedict XVI, Pope (2005). *Deus Caritas Est*. Vatican City: Libreria Editrice Vaticana.

Betcher, S. (2010). 'Becoming Flesh of My Flesh: Feminist and Disability Theologies on the Edge of Posthumanist Discourse'. *Journal of Feminist Studies in Religion*, 26(2): 107–118.

Bushnell, H. (1876). *Christian Nurture*. New York: Scribner, Armstrong.

Butler, J. (1990). *Gender Trouble: Feminism and the Subversion of Identity*. New York: Routledge.

Butler, J. (1993). *Bodies That Matter: On the Discursive Limits of 'Sex'*. New York: Routledge.

Butler, J. (1999). 'Revisiting Bodies and Pleasures'. *Theory, Culture & Society*, 16(2): 11–22.

Bynum, C. (1995). *The Resurrection of the Body in Western Christianity, 200–1336*. New York: Columbia University Press.

Carrette, J. (2005). 'Intense Exchange: Sadomasochism, Theology and the Politics of Late Capitalism'. *Theology & Sexuality*, 11(2): 11–30.

Clement of Alexandria (1991). *Stromateis*, Books I–III. Trans. J. Ferguson. Washington, DC: Catholic University of America Press.

Cornwall, S. (2009). 'Apophasis and Ambiguity: The "Unknowingness" of Transgender'. In L. Isherwood and M. Althaus-Reid (eds), *Trans/formations*. London: SCM, 13–40.

Cornwall, S. (2010). 'Ratum et Consummatum: Refiguring Non-penetrative Sexual Activity Theologically, in Light of Intersex Conditions'. *Theology & Sexuality*, 16(1): 77–93.

Creamer, D. B. (2009). *Disability and Christian Theology*. Oxford and New York: Oxford University Press.

Daly, M. (1978). *Gyn/Ecology: The Metaethics of Radical Feminism*. Boston: Beacon Press.

Davaney, S. G. (1987). 'The Limits of the Appeal to Women's Experience'. In C. W. Atkinson, C. H. Buchanan, and M. R. Miles (eds), *Shaping New Vision: Gender and Values in American Culture*. Ann Arbor, MI: UMI Research, 31–49.

Doriani, D. M. (1991). 'The Puritans, Sex, and Pleasure'. *Westminster Theological Journal*, 53(1): 125–143.

Douglas, K. Brown (2011). 'It's All About the Blues: The Black Female Body and Womanist God-talk'. In L. M. Alcoff and J. D. Caputo (eds), *Feminism, Sexuality, and the Return of Religion*. Bloomington: Indiana University Press, 103–123.

Ellison, M. M. (1996). *Erotic Justice: A Liberating Ethic of Sexuality*. Louisville, KY: Westminster John Knox.

Evans, A. M. and T. Healey (2008) (eds). *Queer and Catholic*. New York: Routledge.

Farley, W. (1999). '"The Pain-Dispelling Draft": Compassion as a Practical Theodicy'. *Perspectives in Religious Studies*, 26(3): 291–302.

Foucault, M. (1978). *The History of Sexuality*: vol. 1. *Introduction*. Trans. R. Hurley. New York: Vintage.

Foucault, M. (1988). *The History of Sexuality*: vol. 1. *The Care of the Self*. Trans. R. Hurley. New York: Vintage.

Fulkerson, M. M. (1994). *Changing the Subject: Women's Discourses and Feminist Theology*. Minneapolis: Augsburg Fortress.

Gaca, K. (2003). *The Making of Fornication: Eros, Ethics, and Political Reform in Greek Philosophy and Early Christianity*. Berkeley: University of California Press.

Gardella, P. (1985). *Innocent Ecstasy: How Christianity Gave America an Ethic of Sexual Pleasure*. New York: Oxford University Press.

Graham, S. (1849). *A Lecture to Young Men on Chastity; Intended Also for the Serious Consideration of Parents and Guardians*. Boston: George W. Light.

Grovijahn, J. (2008). 'Godly Sex: A Queer Quest of Holiness'. *Theology & Sexuality*, 14(2): 121–141.

Heyward, C. (1989). *Touching Our Strength: The Erotic as Power and the Love of God*. San Francisco: Harper & Row.

Heyward, C. (1995). *Staying Power: Reflections on Gender, Justice, and Compassion*. Cleveland: Pilgrim.

Heyward, C. (2011). *Keep Your Courage: A Radical Christian Feminist Speaks*. New York: Seabury.

Heyward, C. and M. Hunt (1986). 'Roundtable Discussion: Lesbianism and Feminist Theology'. *Journal of Feminist Studies in Religion*, 2(2): 95–106.

Holler, L. (2002). *Erotic Morality: The Role of Touch in Moral Agency*. New Brunswick, NJ: Rutgers University Press.

Hopkins, D. N. (2006). 'The Construction of the Black Male Body: Eroticism and Religion'. In A. B. Pinn and D. N. Hopkins (eds), *Loving the Body: Black Religious Studies and the Erotic*. New York: Palgrave Macmillan, 179–197.

Jung, P. B. (2000). 'Sexual Pleasure: A Roman Catholic Perspective on Women's Delight'. *Theology & Sexuality*, 6(12): 26–47.

Kamitsuka, M. (2007). *Feminist Theology and The Challenge of Difference*. Oxford and New York: Oxford University Press.

Kamisuka, M. (2010). 'Sex in Heaven? Eschatological Eros and the Resurrection of the Body'. In M. Kamitsuka (ed.), *The Embrace of Eros: Bodies, Desires, and Sexuality in Christianity*. Minneapolis: Fortress, 261–276.

Kristeva, J. (1982). *Powers of Horror: An Essay on Abjection.* Trans. L. S. Roudiez. New York: Columbia University Press.

Kochuthara, S. G. (2007). *The Concept of Sexual Pleasure in the Catholic Moral Tradition.* Rome: Gregorian University Press.

Kwok, P. L. (2010). 'Body and Pleasure in Postcoloniality'. In L. Isherwood and M. D. Jordan (eds), *Dancing Theology in Fetish Boots: Essays in Honour of Marcella Althaus-Reid.* London: SCM, 31–43.

LaHaye, T. and B. LaHaye (1998). *The Act of Marriage: The Beauty of Sexual Love.* Grand Rapids, MI: Zondervan.

Lindbeck, G. (1984). *The Nature of Doctrine: Religion and Theology in a Postliberal Age.* Philadelphia: Westminster.

Long, R. (2005). 'Heavenly Sex: The Moral Authority of an Impossible Dream'. *Theology & Sexuality,* 11(3): 31–46.

Luther, M. (1958). *Lectures on Genesis 1–5.* In J. Pelikan (ed.), *Luther Works,* vol. 1. Saint Louis: Concordia.

McBurney, L. and M. McBurney (2005). *Real Questions, Real Answers about Sex: The Complete Guide to Intimacy as God Intended.* Grand Rapids, MI: Zondervan.

MacKendrick, K. (1999). *Counterpleasures.* Albany: State University of New York Press.

Malnick, E. (2013). 'New Archbishop of Canterbury Facing Showdown with Senior Bishops', *The Telegraph,* 26 May. <http://www.telegraph.co.uk/news/religion/9859632/New-Archbishop-of-Canterbury-facing-showdown-with-senior-bishops.html> (accessed 26 May 2013).

Mollenkott, V. R. (2001). *Omnigender: A Trans-religious Approach.* Cleveland: Pilgrim.

Mollenkott, V. R. and V. Sheridan (2003). *Transgender Journeys.* Cleveland: Pilgrim.

Obach, R. E. (2009). *The Catholic Church and Marital Intercourse: From St. Paul to Pope John Paul II.* Lanham, MD: Lexington.

Pellauer, M. (1994). 'The Moral Significance of Female Orgasm: Toward Sexual Ethics that Celebrates Women's Sexuality'. In J. B. Nelson and S. P. Longfellow (eds), *Sexuality and the Sacred.* Louisville, KY: Westminster/John Knox, 149–168.

Piper, J. (2002). 'This Is the Will of God for You: That You Abstain from Sexual Immorality'. In *Desiring God: God-centered Resources from the Ministry of John Piper* (13 October 2002); <http://www.desiringgod.org/resource-library/sermons/this-is-the-will-of-god-for-you-that-you-abstain-from-sexual-immorality> (accessed 1 March 2012).

Piper, J. (2006). 'A Vision of Biblical Complementarity: Manhood and Womanhood Defined According the Bible'. In J. Piper and W. A. Grudem (eds), *Recovering Biblical Manhood and Womanhood: A Response to Evangelical Feminism,* Wheaton, IL: Crossway, 31–59.

Rich, A. (1980). 'Compulsory Heterosexuality and Lesbian Existence'. *Signs: Journal of Women in Culture & Society,* 5(4): 631–660.

Saiving, V. (1988). 'Our Bodies/Our Selves: Reflections on Sickness, Aging, and Death'. *Journal of Feminist Studies in Religion,* 4(2): 117–125.

Sands, K. (1992). 'Uses of the Thea(o)logian: Sex and Theodicy in Religious Feminism'. *Journal of Feminist Studies in Religion,* 8(1):7–33.

Shaw, T. M. (1998). *The Burden of the Flesh: Fasting and Sexuality in Early Christianity.* Minneapolis: Fortress.

Sheffield, T. (2008). 'Performing Jesus: A Queer Counternarrative of Embodied Transgression'. *Theology & Sexuality,* 14(3): 233–258.

Stuart, E. (1997). 'Sex in Heaven: The Queering of Theological Discourse on Sexuality'. In G. Loughlin and J. Davies (eds), *Sex These Days: Essays on Theology, Sexuality and Society*. Sheffield: Sheffield Academic Press, 184–204.

Thatcher, A. (1999). *Marriage after Modernity*. Sheffield: Sheffield Academic Press.

Wheat, E. and G. Wheat (1997). *Intended for Pleasure: Sex Techniques and Sexual Pleasure*, 3rd edn. Grand Rapids, MI: Fleming H. Revell.

Wittig, M. (1992). *The Straight Mind and Other Essays*. Boston: Beacon.

CHAPTER 31

......

DESIRE AND LOVE

......

OLA SIGURDSON

INTRODUCTION

'OUR heart is restless until it rests in you.' 'Everybody's got a hungry heart.' Augustine of Hippo, one of the most important theologians in the history of Western Christianity, is the source of the first quote. The second is by Bruce Springsteen, one of the most successful singer-songwriters in American popular music. Between them, there is a time difference of 1,600 years or so. Nevertheless, they share some of the same themes: the heart as the centre of the person and its ubiquitous longing. It seems safe to say, as the quotes exemplify, that desire and love run through the history of humankind, as central in ancient Christian theology as in contemporary popular culture.

Desire and love might be ever-present in ancient culture and in contemporary times, but there is still the question whether we might mean the same thing by love today as earlier in history. And what do we mean when we talk about love? Is it an emotion, an attitude, or a relation? Is love the same thing as desire, or should one, on the contrary, understand desire and love as opposed to each other? Who or what is the proper object of love? Oneself? A person of the other sex or the same? Money and power? God? Further, perhaps because of the ever-presence of desire and love throughout history and different cultures, is there not a need for a critique of desire and love, as emotions, attitudes, or relations need not be good just because they are omnipresent? This chapter will explore these questions from the perspective of systematic theology, and present an outline of a relevant and responsible theology of desire and love for today.

It is important for an inquiry into desire and love to establish from the beginning that the meaning of neither of the terms is self-evident. As Werner G. Jeanrond puts it in one of the recent works on the theology of love: 'The single English term love has contributed to the widespread illusion that we here are dealing with a well-defined phenomenon and its unambiguous expression' (Jeanrond 2010: 31). But it is not so, and this means, among other things, that we will have to expect ambiguity in our attempt to understand desire and love, whether as concepts or as human phenomena. Rather, desire and love are multifaceted, with the result that any account of desire and love in theology or elsewhere, needs to be vigilant with regard to the cultural and historical context of a specific use of these expressions. This is in a way the same thing as saying that love and desire as phenomena always already are embodied, gendered, and social—i.e. incarnated. There is perhaps no Christian desire and love as such, but only different historical configurations of desire and love. At the same time, given among other things the permanence of the phenomena in human history, such an ambiguity must not mean that desire and love are completely equivocal concepts. What I will do in the following is to render a critical theology of desire and love through significant contributions with an eye on history, highlighting how different eschatological horizons have given rise to differing conceptualities that we might deem more or less adequate to the phenomena they are supposed to express.

THE ESCHATOLOGICAL HORIZON

When Friedrich Nietzsche in his *Beyond Good and Evil* writes that 'Christianity gave Eros poison to drink:—he did not die from it, but degenerated into a vice' (Nietzsche 2002: §168), one might well want to ask whether this is true. Should ancient Christianity really be the cause of Eros' sickening? To suggest that the Christian Church has had an ambivalent attitude towards sexuality throughout history might not be an exaggeration. But *eros* has been a central and omnipresent theme, and even if one has doubts about how well it has been managed, as Nietzsche has, it would be foolish to deny its presence and importance. It is only in the last two or three centuries that a theological erotics has fallen into disrepute. This might, at least in part, be a consequence of the modern association of *eros* with sexuality, but such an association is not typical for the ancient Christian tradition: to Augustine or Gregory of Nyssa, *eros* or its Latin equivalent *amor* stood for the love of God (on Augustine, see Arendt 1996). A theological erotics was, in other words, high on the theological agenda even for those theologians who had little to spare for human sexuality.

In contrast to those pre-modern theologians we can compare the quite negative attitude on the part of modern—especially Protestant—theology towards *eros*. The Swedish theologian Anders Nygren, to whom I will return later, tried to establish a radical disjunction between *agape* and *eros*, while his Swiss colleague Karl Barth, despite some attempts to integrate *eros* into his theology, commented that 'sexual *eros*' is a 'dangerous demon' (Barth 1958: 314). A contributing reason for modern Protestant theology's problematic relationship to *eros* is that the concept has come to be associated with human sexuality in a new way. Between Augustine and Barth a decisive historical change of how *eros* is understood to relate to human sexuality takes place. Its eschatological horizon, i.e., the purpose and meaning of love for human existence (including its cosmology and/or ontology), is transformed in a way that also had consequences for theology. Let me give a very short account of this development.

It is through the emergence of what Michel Foucault calls *scientia sexualis* from the seventeenth century and beyond, the progress of the modern medical sciences as well as the more general sexualization of Western society during the twentieth century, that *eros* and sexuality have more or less came to be identified with each other (Foucault 1978: 53–73). According to the sexologist Volkmar Sigusch, 1789 is a symbolic year for the birth of sexuality as form and concept (Sigusch 1989: 11; and see Ammicht Quinn 1999). This is the year when the Christian view of the world symbolically gave way to capitalism. As both Foucault and Sigusch describe, sexuality came to be secularized in the modern period in the sense that human intercourse was disengaged from religion; the norm that upheld the relation between intercourse and religion—not only Christianity—was dissolved. This did not mean, however, that human sexuality no longer was under moral scrutiny; on the contrary, medical science was as interested as Christianity ever was to implement good conduct with regard to sexual acts. Nor did moral theology cease to proscribe certain human sexual acts, but the discourse about them became a medical one. In short: sexuality was established as a distinct field of specialized medical knowledge, and moral theology always had to utilize this discourse whenever it wanted to say anything about sexuality.

What was lost in the process, to cut a long story short, was for theology an understanding of human sexual acts against the eschatological horizon of the erotic love of a transcendent God. To a pre-modern lover, it was more or less self-evident that the *telos* of desire could not be found in any human being, but only in God. But through the emergence of sexuality, *eros* came to be reduced to the immanent eschatology of human reproduction. And human reproduction was to take place in the family. As Elizabeth Stuart puts it: 'The loss of an eschatological imagination, not just in gay and lesbian theology, but across much of western Christian theology, has impoverished Christian discourse on sexuality and allowed the collapse of desire into heterosexuality and discipleship into marriage and modern constructions of the family' (Stuart 2003: 110).

To be sure, human reproduction was considered by theology to be a family affair even before *scientia sexualis*. Recall, for instance, Augustine's reflections in 'The Good of Marriage', where offspring, fidelity, and sacrament are the purpose of the institution, but where love curiously enough (at least for us living now) is not mentioned at all (Augustine 2002: 71–86). Nevertheless, what changed through modernity was the shortening of the eschatological horizon of desire as such, as it came to be identified as sexuality—especially reproduction—and sexuality was understood biologically. To put it very briefly, if the problem with the dominant tradition during antiquity and the Middle Ages was that it separated *eros* from a legitimate sexuality, the problem of modern Christianity is that it has reduced desire to sexuality. There are two things that I want to emphasize here: that love and desire always are understood against an eschatological horizon that explains their purpose and meaning, but also that the historical shift had consequences for the understanding of desire as well as, per implication, love. Both these traits of a modern understanding of desire and love come to expression in an exemplary fashion in Nygren's disjunction between *agape* and *eros*.

AGAPE AND EROS

The two parts of Anders Nygren's *Agape and Eros* were originally published in Swedish as *Den kristna kärlekstanken genom tiderna* in 1930 and 1936 and were promptly translated into several other languages. The first English editions were published in 1932 and 1938/9. Although a theological work on love by a professor in systematic theology and subsequently a bishop in the Church of Sweden, Nygren's treatise on love had a profound influence on the intellectual discourse on love during the twentieth century, far outside academic theological circles; the psychoanalyst Jacques Lacan, for instance, was guided by Nygren's work in his account of love in several of his seminars (Lacan 1999: 75–76). It may have had a more profound influence among more popular media, however: sermons, essays, literature, and so on.

One may suspect that part of the popularity of Nygren's thesis has to do with its simplicity: according to Nygren, history exhibits several different 'fundamental motifs' of love, sometimes in relative purity but more often in a mixed state. These fundamental motifs are not just relatively innocent terminological differences, however. They exemplify 'different general attitudes to life' (Nygren 1982: 34)—something akin to what I earlier called 'eschatological horizons'. Nygren's task in *Agape and Eros* is to show what has characterized such different general attitudes to life throughout history, i.e. how they have manifested themselves in different authors, epochs, and religions, especially with regard to the relationship between God and human beings. His emphasis is on the uniqueness of the Christian motif of *agape* in contrast to the Jewish association of love with law (or *nomos*) and the Greek conception of an erotic love. Although all these three motifs only occasionally exist in a pure state, this does not diminish the fundamental differences between them.

Nygren's claim, in *Agape and Eros*, is that his inquiry is purely historical without any commitment, as a historian, to a particular motif or to any value judgement. This is typical for the state of academic research at Nygren's time; for a later observer, it is not beyond suspicion that Nygren's preference for *agape* as a bishop informs his belief, as a historian, in the possibility of such a neat typology. If such a clear-cut distinction between different motifs is possible, at least on a fundamental level if not in actual history, this may explain some of its popularity at the time. Nygren belonged to a theological era where many theologians were reacting against the previous (liberal) theology and the contemporary alleged confusion of Christianity and culture (*die deutsche Christen*), and it is in the same spirit that Nygren insists on not confusing *eros* and *agape* with each other. Finally, *Agape and Eros* should also be understood as an interjection in a confessional polemics, as will be clear in what follows.

So what, then, is the difference between these three motifs as general attitudes? The Jewish *nomos* motif, which is the one that Nygren devotes the least space to elaborate, conceives of the human relationship towards God in legal terms: 'From the point of view of Jewish legal piety, it is self-evident that God loves the righteous and the godly, and that He does not love the unrighteousness and the sinner' (Nygren 1982: 200). Love, in this motif, is conditioned by law, but such a conception, despite the continuity between Judaism and Christianity, is completely shattered by the *agape* motif: 'Agape is the opposite of "Nomos", and therefore a denial of the foundation on which the entire Jewish scale of values rested' (1982: 201). Despite the fact that the apostle Paul had been reciting the *Shema Israel* (Deut. 6:4–5) throughout his entire life, where the love of God with one's entire heart is commanded, Paul's silence in his letters on the human love of God (in contrast to the love of neighbour) is taken by Nygren as evidence of a fundamental reorientation of the apostle's understanding of love (1982: 124–125). For Nygren, pure agapeic love is spontaneous and could never be commanded, and neither could human beings achieve spontaneity in relation to God.

Most of Nygren's intellectual effort in his book is devoted to the radical distinction between *eros* and *agape*, however. The fundamental difference here is the distinction between the 'egocentric attitude' and the 'theocentric attitude'. *Eros* stands for an 'egocentric attitude' (in a non-ethical meaning of the word) since *eros* basically is the human being's own desire for God, whereas *agape* is 'theocentric' since it stands for a spontaneous and unmotivated kind of love. This difference results in two separate ways of bringing about a fellowship with God, by human ascension to the divine or by divine condescension to the human. According to Nygren, 'Agape comes to us as a quite new creation of Christianity' (1982: 48) whereas *eros* characterizes almost 'all religious life outside of Christianity' (1982: 49). Note also who is the subject of love in these different fundamental motifs: in Christianity, it is God who is loving and even *is* love in an agapeic way: 'The subject of Christian love is not man, but God Himself, yet in such a way that the Divine love employs man as its instrument and organ' (1982: 733–734). *Agape* is associated with the New Testament's emphasis on faith as the appropriate response to God's loving presence in Christ—a distinction that to Nygren as a Lutheran is similar to the distinction between works and faith. Whereas for the Greeks, 'it is self-evident that the gods do *not love*' (1982: 201, emphasis original), so it is we as human beings who do the loving and God who is the object of love. Nygren associates *eros* with a tradition of human desire mainly stemming from Plato's *Symposium* (Plato 1999). With regard to *agape*, it is God who is the active agent and human beings who are passive, but with regard to *eros*, it is the other way around. Nygren stresses, then, the utter incommensurability of *eros* and *agape* as 'different general attitudes to life'.

Nevertheless, Nygren is very well aware that the tension between *agape* and *eros* has slackened in their historical instantiations. Interestingly, not even the entire New Testament exhibits the pure *agape* motif. Nygren is, for instance, slightly suspicious of the Johannine literature's emphasis on human love for God at the same time that he endorses his idea that God *is* agapeic love: 'while John says the last word as to its form, Paul has a deeper insight into its essential meaning and content' (Nygren 1982: 149–150). Hypothetically, at least, there might be a Hellenistic influence on the Johannine conception of love that explains why it might be the culmination of the *agape* motif at the same time as its weakening through the influence of a more Greek *eros* motif. It was further weakened of course, in the outright synthesis of Augustine's understanding of love as *caritas* (Nygren 1982: 449–562). His concept of *caritas* is a new and unique contribution in the history of love, as *eros* and *agape* here for the first time form a spiritual unity. God's love for human beings is a kind of pedagogy mediated through the revelation in Christ for the right ordering of human love. Through this pedagogy of love, the love of the world, *cupiditas*, is turned into the love of God, *caritas*. What *eros* asks for but cannot give, only *agape* achieves through the incarnation of Christ. *Agape* cures human beings of their *superbia*, which prevents us from reaching our heavenly goal, through *humilitas*. Augustine's conception of love thus is, according to Nygren, in continuity both with the (Neo)Platonic tradition and the Pauline tradition, and it is a witness to Augustine's great originality that *eros* becomes the means by which Augustine discovers, in relation to his predecessors, a more profound understanding of *agape*. But even though Nygren regarded Augustine as having achieved a historically important synthesis, Nygren also thought that Augustine never fully understood the unavoidable difference between the two motifs and ultimately he employed *agape* in the service of *eros*. Augustine came to set the tone for the Middle Ages through his synthesis, but he never truly understood the radicality of the unmotivated agapeic love.

What Augustine joined together in *caritas*, Luther tore asunder through his doctrine of justification through faith alone (Nygren 1982: 560). Luther's understanding of love is the climax of *Agape and Eros*, because in Luther, according to Nygren, the *agape* motif was restored in its purity in a way that had not been the case since the apostle Paul. In a way, the *eros* motif was restored too at the same time, through Renaissance philosophers and humanists such as Marcilio Ficino, where philosophy becomes a way of salvation. Luther, however, 'insists, in opposition to all egocentric forms of religion, upon a purely theocentric relation to God' (Nygren 1982: 681). Nygren presents Luther's understanding of love in congruity with his doctrine of justification; in fact, there is not much of a direct exegesis of what Luther has to say about love in *Agape and Eros*, but instead Nygren draws out the implication of love from his understanding of the doctrine of justification. Instead of the ascension to God by human beings through *caritas*, as was proposed by Augustine and all the traditions of the Middle Ages, it is God who descends, in his love, and is received by us in faith. There is indeed a form of Christian love, but this is only a love towards the neighbour, and in principle, this is no human love but God's own love towards human being, channelled through the Christian: 'Christian love is through and through a Divine work' (Nygren 1982: 734). As such, it is utterly and completely removed from any form of erotic love of God, neighbour, or self.

With Luther, it is as if we have come to the end of the history of love: Nygren concludes *Agape and Eros* with just a few pages reiterating the distinction between *agape* and *caritas*, now as the fundamental distinction between Luther and Catholicism—and despite the historical scope of the book, we may assume that such a confessional polemics was still a live question for Nygren. Despite the different versions of historical intermingling between the different motifs, Nygren regards them as transhistorical phenomena, always at hand to be reactualized in form or the other. Through Luther, the purity of the *agape* motif had been restored.

THE BODY'S LOVE

There are several reasons why I have dwelled upon Nygren's book: its importance for the general discourse on desire and love in general during the twentieth century; its specific theological impact; and, not least, the very uncompromising way in which Nygren represents his comprehensive hypothesis. Even theologians sympathetic to the viability of a distinction between *agape* and *eros*, as for instance Karl Barth, tended to be more moderate in its execution. Others, for example, Paul Tillich, Hans Urs von Balthasar, and Karl Rahner, doubted, explicitly or implicitly, that a distinction between differing conceptions of love could be so neatly drawn (Tillich 1954; Rahner 1966; Balthasar 2004; Jeanrond 2010: 135–152). Whatever one wishes to say about Nygren's *Agape and Eros*, however, it exemplifies what I referred to as the eschatological horizon of love through its exposition of the different motifs. Love, whatever we mean by it, is more than just a feeling as it, in fact, concerns how we perceive of our 'attitude' or relation towards God, our fellow human beings, and ourselves. At the same time, *Agape and Eros* also exemplifies, for the most part implicitly, a modern 'secularization' of desire in the form of sexuality. To Nygren, sexual love is not something wicked, it just falls out of the horizon of his discussion of love altogether and becomes theologically indifferent—it loses its theological horizon.

   With his emphasis on the passivity of human beings in matters of love, it is not very surprising that sexual expression is not on the agenda for Nygren. But the complete lack of phenomenological descriptions of human love in any of its forms should make us question the adequacy of Nygren's account of love (Stock 2000: 83; for a phenomenology of erotic love, see Marion 2006). If human beings cannot even be the subjects of love, but just the organs or instruments of divine love, is agapeic love experienced by us at all, or is it so utterly other that it quietly sails past us, like a ship in the night? And what about the phenomena that we usually call love—are they in no way of any theological significance? I would suggest that *agape* in the theology of Nygren becomes strangely disembodied, as a consequence of his unilateral understanding of its manifestations; love seems to be on the way down or up in Nygren, and not much happens in between (on embodiment from a theological perspective, see Sigurdson 2006). Embodiment requires situatedness and intersubjectivity, but in *Agape and Eros* it is hardly clear whether agapeic love can actually be experienced in the body.

   One way to counter Nygren's conception would be to dispute the adequacy of his method for interpreting love in the biblical literature as well as in the history of theology. Through his methodologically motivated search for a 'religious a priori' where he categorically distinguishes between different 'basic motifs', it might be that the expressions of love in the biblical literature are inscribed from the outset within an uncongenial horizon. It is true, of course, that *agape* is used by the New Testament as a term for love. But does this necessarily mean that love is understood by the New Testament authors as a specific concept of love? In the Gospel of Matthew, the noun *epithumia*, which we can translate with desire, is used in a negative sense in 5:28, where the looking at a woman with *epithumia* is condemned, but at the same time, in 13:17, *epithumia* is used in a positive sense, where prophets and righteous people long for the sight of the kingdom with a longing that is characterized as *epithumia*. In other words, there is a legitimate longing, desire, or yearning for the kingdom, at least in Matthew, raising our suspicion whether such clear-cut distinctions between different concepts of love really apply here and if the meaning of *agape* is as univocal as implied (on themes of desire and love in the biblical texts, see Boyarin 1993; Martin 1995; Watson 2000; Countryman 2001).

A more disturbing, though implicit, critique against the strict separation of *agape* and *eros* is produced by Rowan Williams, also taking into consideration the role of embodiment for love. For Williams, to be significant for an other or even wanted is a part of what it means to be loved, even with the love that is divine in origin. Williams provides a Trinitarian account of love in his article 'The Body's Grace', which is also phenomenologically sensitive to how love is experienced by both lover and beloved (Williams 2002: 309–321). Human beings are created in such a way that we may be caught up in the loving relationships that characterize the divine Trinity, and this means not only being the object of a unilateral *agape* for which the loveliness or love-worthiness of the object is irrelevant, but also actually being desired, as well as being able, in some way, to return the love. To love and hope for the return of love, according to Williams, is always a risk, since it exposes us to the vulnerability of not being loved or having our intentions misunderstood. Such a love is, as Williams points out, an embodied experience: 'To desire my joy is to desire the joy of the one I desire: my search for enjoyment through the bodily presence of another is a longing to be enjoyed in my body' (2002: 313). There is much here that Nygren would have found disagreeable, at least from a theological point of view: not only desire, but also enjoyment. To him, this would mean not only a compromising of the unilateral character of agapeic love but also a dangerous mix of *agape* with eudaimonistic motifs. But to Williams, this bodily experience of love is also an experience of grace in a theological sense.

Another aspect of Williams's implicit critique of the sharp distinction between *agape* and *eros* is that a unilateral conception of agapeic love actually seems to want to escape from the inescapable vulnerability of human existence. From an anthropological perspective, if a true agapeic love is a love that is strictly unilateral—meaning that the possible love-worthiness of the object of love is irrelevant to my loving—I become, in a sense, indifferent to the response of the other and thus invulnerable. As Williams points out in a further implicit critique of much of the Christian tradition, the flight from vulnerability is a strong reason why sexual desire so seldom is seen as a matter of grace. Speaking anthropologically, what do we think about a person who is always and only giving, but never able to receive anything, always loving but never wanting to be loved? Is this not a neurotic attempt to protect and control one's own limits, never daring to risk these limits in one's relation to the other? Of course, things might look different if we speak of love in a theological context where God is supposed to be the sole creator of everything that exists, but even here we might want to ask why God, if so, created human beings in such a way that no creaturely response was allowed for or even wanted. According to

Williams, however, God wants to be God even to what is not God, and this means that God *wants* human beings. If erotic love is a love where the lover does not want to be who he or she is without the beloved, then God's love for human beings is a kind of erotic love; as is God's wish to be God for human beings, as actually wanted as Godself, which is expressed in the incarnation.

Indeed, there is a theologically (as well as anthropologically) important aspect of love and grace according to which we might be loved even when we do not deserve it. But love does not have to do with economic desert; loveliness does not equate with merit in the sense that I can demand love or count on love from someone; in love, I cannot calculate my own worth, but have to trust the generosity of the other's love instead of trying to control it. That love is, in some way, a relationship that goes to and fro does not destroy its character as gift or grace, but on the contrary makes it possible to experience as such. The context of a theology of both creation and redemption makes it possible, according to an argument such as Williams's, to trust in love, even in the face of our own embodied vulnerability, because we are, from the beginning, wanted. To such an account, *agape* and *eros*—or love and desire—are not two distinct forms of love that can or should be joined together; rather, it is a different account that tries to do justice to the fact that love is a multidimensional phenomenon where activity and passivity, or the 'egocentric' and the 'theocentric', are not mutually exclusive, but are integrated and interrelated moments of this complexity. Through his phenomenological account of the complexities of human love, Williams challenges both the bifurcation of *agape* and *eros* in Nygren's account, and the eschatological horizon of modernity that tends to reduce sexuality to reproduction.

THE PSYCHOANALYTIC CRITIQUE OF NEIGHBOURLY LOVE

Is the kind of distinction between *agape* and *eros* that Nygren advocates to be counted merely as a surpassed moment in the history of theological conceptions of love? It is true that recently there has been increasing attention to the historical and the constructive role that desire has played and still plays in Christian theology in a way that seems to belie Nygren or any conception similar to his (see, for example, Ward 2000; Loughlin 2003; Farley 2005; Shults and Henriksen 2011). However, attempts to put the distinction between *agape* and *eros* to critical and constructive use are far from over. A conception of love similar to Nygren's has recently been advocated by the philosopher and psychoanalyst Slavoj Žižek. Given Lacan's already-mentioned interest in Nygren, maybe this is not as surprising as it sounds. It is in this tradition that Žižek, who advocates a radical political philosophy, suggests that only agapeic love, not desire, can live up to a truly radical practice. He also presents a critique of love of the kind I presented earlier, which is why we need to take note of it here.

This is not the place to deal with all the intricacies of what psychoanalysis has to say about desire, but let me just give a short overview before I get to what Žižek has to say about desire and neighbourly love. Desire, to a psychoanalytic account, is socially produced; according to Lacan, 'Man's desire is the other's desire' (Lacan 1998: 235). This means that what I desire is not something that spontaneously arises within me, but instead I learn to desire what I desire through the desire of the other. What I want is secondary to what others want from me. But how do I know what others want from me? The truth is that I don't, so I have to fantasize about what they want from me. It is through fantasy that the object of my desire is given. But, and here comes the turning point, the arbitrariness of this object cannot appear to me as such but must seem to be given or necessary. One obvious example, often repeated by Žižek, is the function of the king: the king is believed to be king and respected as king because of some inherent property but in reality the king is king because his subjects treat him like one (Žižek 1992: 33). If the king is not believed to be king because of some inherent 'kingness', his status dissolves into thin air. Why is this so? Why must the arbitrariness of the object-cause of desire be hidden from our view? The reason is that the illusion of the necessity of the object-cause hides from our view the nothingness of our desire; what I desire is really nothing. Whatever I take to be the object of my desire can never really fulfil my wishes, which becomes clear if I happen to attain the goal of my desire; if I desire a new home I will discover when I move into it that this new home really was not *it*, and my desire is relocated onto another object of my desire. The aim of psychoanalysis, however, is to dissolve the fantasy.

What happens when the fantasy is dissolved? What remains is the sheer nothingness of my desire, or what in psychoanalysis is called the drive. The drive is a psychoanalytical concept that has its origin in Sigmund Freud's notion of the death drive in *Beyond the Pleasure Principle* from 1920 (Freud 1989). Unlike desire, drive is not entangled in a social or symbolic network of wishes or desires, and so has no ground in any conscious wish or desire. Instead, it is described as a certain mechanical persistence that goes beyond anything that has to do with the happiness or welfare of the individual; it is also senseless, having no motive outside itself, and could thus be described as an empty gesture. Through assuming the drive as my own, I gain a freedom from being caught up in the endless trickery of ever-substitutable objects of desire. But the drive is not the final consummation of our inmost being, but an eternal wandering or an 'undead' urge.

This returns us to the psychoanalytic critique of a malign version of neighbourly love, in Žižek's version (Žižek 2005: 134–190, 2010: 98–119). The trouble with neighbourly love (or most of what goes for it) is that it remains within desire, which means that it is narcissistic, a form of paternalism, where I desire someone who is like me or who is the bearer of the same human rights in me. In an account of desire such as Williams's discussed earlier, there is a symmetrical or intersubjective relationship presupposed that assures me that I share a certain reciprocality with the person I love; I expect to get love in return. I share a common world in an amorous relationship. But this is actually, according to Žižek, a 'gentrification' of the radical nature of agapeic love. Žižek goes to some rhetorical lengths to show the difference between (ordinary) neighbourly love and agapeic love: the true neighbour is not someone that I can enter into a relationship with, and so is no 'person' but rather a 'thing'; the true neighbour is a 'monster', an 'abyss' or 'inhuman'. Desire hides this radical non-reciprocality of true love through empathy, whereas true love is violent and intolerant and does not affirm the other's expectations but instead tries to unplug the beloved from the network of desire. Thus, true love appears (to the lover caught in the desirous but illusory network) under its opposite, as that kind of hatred and cruelty that unplugs a person from such a network; this is, according to Žižek, 'a direct expression of what St. Paul, in 1 Corinthians 13, described as agape, the key intermediary between faith and hope' (Žižek 2010: 106). True love is above all not a benevolent feeling but a violent act. In much the same way as Nygren's *agape*, Žižek's version of agapeic love appears as thoroughly unilateral. It is a matter of drive rather than desire, and as such, it is a critique of the narcissism that is the result of not distinguishing properly between *agape* and *eros* or love and desire.

Žižek is not addressing erotic love as such in this context, but it is easy to see how an erotic love which is a yearning for another, supposedly corresponding to some lack in the lover, could be turned into a kind of complementarity or mirror image. It is also a fact that Žižek, although endorsing Christianity as an experience necessary for a dialectical materialist, brings forth a theology without God. The ultimate subject of agapeic love is, consequently, not God but human subjectivity as drive, and although this is taking Nygren to the extreme, there is a certain consistency in thus radicalizing a love that would regard any mutuality or response as a betrayal. At the same time, Žižek is as convinced as Nygren that *agape* stands for a 'different general attitude to life' than *eros*, and the ultimate reason is the eudaimonistic and perhaps also reciprocal nature of erotic love. Again, like Nygren, Žižek is not opposed to erotic love (in the sense of sexuality), but sees it as at most a by-product of the revolutionary love that is expressed by *agape*.

THE LOVE OF THE OTHER

Žižek together with psychoanalysis points out a persistent problem with love. There is always the possibility that love turns into some form of narcissism or a form of *do ut des*, an economical exchange rather than the giving of gifts without calculation. His critique is therefore helpful for any theology of love. To a theology of erotic love, there is indeed the necessity of a critical vigilance especially with regard to the temptation of projecting one's needs or desires on the other, turning the other into the same. Žižek goes to some rhetorical length in addressing the question 'who is the true neighbour?'. Nevertheless, what is gained thereby in the clarity of the alternatives is perhaps lost in the description of the nuances of loving relationships. Said otherwise, I would presume that there is a certain richness in the phenomenality of love to which such a stark alternative does not do justice. To be sure, reciprocality in the loving relationship leads our thoughts to an economic transaction, but that does not rule out all forms of giving and taking in love, as not all such relations take place in an economic register. The challenge, then, is to try to understand if and how the love of the other—both as the desire for the other and the other's desire—can take place beyond such an economy.

This is not a new question for theology; a critique of desire and love such as Žižek's is not unheard of in theology. For example, Augustine had already warned against the narcissistic curving in of human beings on ourselves. Against quite another eschatological horizon than Žižek's, Augustine's *Confessions* could be interpreted as a discourse on the fantasy through which human beings hide a certain immeasurability in the midst of self—in more traditional theological language: sin—in the illusion of having a transparent access to the objects of one's desire. The sinful self takes itself to be a simple, clear, and stable identity, but this complacency is shattered by a traumatic encounter with God. This encounter gives rise to an instability of self, a certain sickness: 'In your eyes I have become a problem to myself, and that is my sickness' (Augustine 2008: X. xxxiii. 50). (For a fuller account of Augustine and a comparison with Žižek, see Sigurdson 2013.) Through it, one is liberated from narcissism; God stops the circling around self that is its main characteristic, opening up the self to new possibilities. Central to these possibilities is to love, and as any reader of *Confessions* is aware, this is a love that is full of longing and yearning and restlessness, and even if there is a sense in which this erotic love is sated by its further history with God, there is also a sense in which desire is infinite since there is always more to love. In sum, *Confessions* could be read as a critique of an idolatrous love that confines God as well as the self within a limited horizon set up by the human gaze. But despite this critique, Augustine does not give up on desire.

The question then becomes whether a non-narcissistic and non-reciprocal love is possible. My wager is that this is the case. The complexity of a loving relationship is not exhausted by the alternatives of either possessing the other in erotic love or in freely giving without receiving in agapeic love. To reduce erotic love to an economic transaction would mean that the other in the loving relationship is just a projection of the self and thus not other in any genuine sense. Neither can I consume the other out of love, as this would mean the incorporation of the other into myself and consequently the loss of the other's alterity. If the question of the lover to the beloved is 'Will you love me?'—or, more generally, 'Does anyone love me?'—any answer from an other reduced to the same can never be sufficient, because it is in fact not an answer but only an echo of myself. As Jean-Luc Marion puts it:

> For the question 'Does anyone love me?' will in effect only be able to receive a response (if it ever could) by coming upon me from elsewhere than myself; it thus assigns me an irreversible dependency upon that which I can neither master, nor provoke, nor even envisage—an other than myself, eventually someone other for me (*alter ego*), in any case a foreign instance, coming from I know not where—in any case, not from me.
>
> (Marion 2006: 41)

The vulnerability mentioned hitherto gives rise to the question of the other's love, and even if the lover can hope for a loving response from the beloved, if this response is not in some sense freely given but bought, forced, or presumed, it is not a genuine response after all but void of erotic meaning. The to-and-fro of erotic play is in its free giving of gifts; an expression of a goodness going beyond reciprocality that only gives so that you might give. What the other will give me, in love, I can only hope for but neither prescribe nor demand. That said, I think it would be a mistake to turn the difference between an economy of love and the excess of love into an absolute contrast; if promises and legal structures (given that they are just and fair) can confer stability on the loving relationship without prescribing its limits, this can liberate the relationship from a certain neurotic anxiety. To be 'wounded by love' and thus vulnerable is, however, a condition of the possibility of love, never to be exhausted by contract. In love, we give ourselves even before any assurance of a return.

Such an understanding of love could also possibly shed some light on the matter of so-called same-sex relationships in the Christian tradition. In the Christian tradition, especially in its early phase but continuing at least up until modernity, biology, family, and kinship were not the primary characteristic of significant relationships, but rather the community (*koinonia*) established by the Church (*ekklesia*). Reproduction of Christianity took place not through biology but through conversion and baptism (Brown 1989). Relations between Christians should, then, have their basis in conceptions of a more radical difference than just genital differences. What matters most is not whether a couple can have children but their relationship to the other. Any biological idea of sexual difference—especially, perhaps, in modernity, with its reduction of desire to reproductive sexuality—falls too short, theologically speaking, of the ideal of a non-reductive heterosociality or relation to the other. If 'heterosexual' love means a sexual love of the other (the Greek prefix *heteros* meaning 'other'), then not all heterosexual love is truly a love of the other. And, vice versa, the same is true of 'homosexual' love, i.e. 'sexual love of the same', as a love between persons of the same genital configuration does not in itself run the risk of a love that is just a reduction of the other to my mirror image any more than does a love between persons of different genital configurations. To be homosexual means just that one finds the other and discovers oneself in relation to a person of the same sex. The real worry within the Christian tradition should not be homosexuality, then, but homosociality, of which, for a long time, heterosexuality has been the prime expression. If a genuine human relationship to God is a relation to a transcendent other that is not just a mirror image of ourselves, the same must be true, *mutatis mutandis*, of our interpersonal relations. But, nevertheless, parts of the Christian tradition have insisted in remaining in either a utilitarian or a narcissistic understanding of sexual relations.

Turning, finally, to the question of the human love of God, it has been a continuing emphasis in most of the Christian tradition that we both shall and can love God. The worry of a modern theologian such as Nygren has been that such theology will become eudaimonistic, and consequently reduce God to someone or something that could fill the longings of the hungry heart; if that were the case, we would all be the consumers of divinity. God becomes the prisoner not only of reciprocality but of human utility. However, I have suggested that such a mirror image of ourselves never will be sufficient for love; human longing is eschatological in the sense that no thing or object could ever satisfy it. One might on the contrary venture to ask whether the absence of a legitimate theological erotics or erotic theology in parts of the Christian tradition has to do with a domestication of the transcendence of God or, in other words, reducing the alterity of God to a conception of God as the rival of human beings. If God is my rival, then the struggle for sovereignty could only end as one of us engorges the other. But if God is not a rival but other, then human love need not be understood as a bleak image of God's own love; but liberated to become a proper human love. Instead of endlessly falling short of a divine love, we are free to experience and explore the richness of human love in its many forms. As the Benedictine theologian Sebastian Moore suggests, theology from a Christian perspective should not result in the repression of desire but the liberation of desire—the liberation *of* desire, not *from* desire (Moore 2002: 157–169). The restlessness or hunger of the human heart is a divine gift, and if difference is the motor, beyond all calculation, in the love that moves us towards the other, then an uncancellable difference only corresponds to an eternal desire. A hungry heart indeed.

REFERENCES

Ammicht Quinn, R. (1999). *Körper—Religion—Sexualität: Theologische Reflexionen zur Ethik der Geschlechter*. Mainz: Grünewald.

Arendt, H. (1996). *Love and Saint Augustine*. Ed. Joanna Vecchiarelli Scott and Judith Chelius Stark. Chicago: University of Chicago Press.

Augustine (2002). 'The Good of Marriage'. In Rogers (2002), 71–86.

Augustine (2008). *Confessions*. Trans. Henry Chadwick. Oxford: Oxford University Press.

von Balthasar, Hans Urs (2004). *Love Alone is Credible*. Trans. D. C. Schindler. San Francisco: Ignatius Press.

Barth, K. (1958). *Church Dogmatics, iii. The Doctrine of Creation, Part One*. Ed. G. W. Bromiley and T. F. Torrance, trans. J. W. Edwards et al. Edinburgh: T&T Clark.

Boyarin, D. (1993). *Carnal Israel: Reading Sex in Talmudic Culture*. Berkeley and Los Angeles: University of California Press.

Brown, P. (1989). *The Body and Society: Men, Women and Sexual Renunciation in Early Christianity*. London: Faber and Faber.

Countryman, L. W. (2001). *Dirt, Greed and Sex: Sexual Ethics in the New Testament and Their Implications for Today*. London: SCM Press.

Farley, W. (2005). *The Wounding and Healing of Desire: Weaving Heaven and Earth*. Louisville, KY: Westminster John Knox Press.

Foucault, M. (1978). *The History of Sexuality*: vol. i. *An Introduction*. Trans. Robert Hurley. New York: Pantheon Books.

Freud, S. (1989). *Beyond the Pleasure Principle*, Standard Edition. Trans. and ed. James Strachey. New York and London: Norton.

Jeanrond, W. G. (2010). *A Theology of Love*. London and New York: T&T Clark.

Lacan, J. (1998). *The Four Fundamental Concepts of Psychoanalysis*. The Seminar of Jacques Lacan, Book XI, 2nd edn. Ed. Jacques-Alain Miller, trans. Alan Sheridan. New York: Norton.

Lacan, J. (1999). *On Feminine Sexuality: The Limits of Love and Knowledge: 1972–1973 (Encore)*. The Seminar of Jacques Lacan, Book XX. Ed. Jacques-Alain Miller, trans. Bruce Fink. New York: Norton.

Loughlin, G. (2003). *Alien Sex: The Body and Desire in Cinema and Theology*. Oxford: Wiley-Blackwell.

Marion, J.-L. (2006). *The Erotic Phenomenon*. Trans. Stephen E. Lewis. Chicago: University of Chicago Press.

Martin, D. (1995). *The Corinthian Body*. New Haven and London: Yale University Press.

Moore, S. (2002). 'The Crisis of an Ethic without Desire'. In Rogers (2002), 157–69.

Nietzsche, F. (2002). *Beyond Good and Evil: Prelude to a Philosophy of the Future*. Ed. Rolf-Peter Hortmann and Judith Norman, trans. Judith Norman. Cambridge: Cambridge University Press.

Nygren, A. (1982). *Agape and Eros: The Christian Idea of Love*. Trans. Philip S. Watson. Chicago: University of Chicago Press.

Plato (1999). *The Symposium*. Trans. C. Gill. London: Penguin.

Rahner, K. (1966). 'The "Commandment" of Love in Relation to the Other Commandments'. In *Theological Investigations*, vol. v. Trans. Karl-H. Kruger. London: Darton, Longman and Todd, 439–59.

Rogers, E. F., Jr. (2002) (ed.). *Theology and Sexuality: Classic and Contemporary Readings*. Oxford: Blackwell.

Shults, F. L., and Henriksen, J.-O. (2011) (eds). *Saving Desire: The Seduction of Christian Theology*. Grand Rapids, MI: Eerdmans.

Sigurdson, O. (2006). *Himmelska kroppar: Inkarnation, blick, kroppslighet*. Logos/Pathos 6. Göteborg: Glänta.

Sigurdson, O. (2013). 'The Trauma of a Hungry Heart: Augustine, Žižek, and (Pre)Modern Desire'. In Anders Cullhed, Carin Franzén, Anders Hallengren, and Mats Malm (eds), *Pangs of Love and Longing: Configurations of Desire in Premodern Literature*. Newcastle upon Tyne: Cambridge Scholars Press, 41–59.

Sigusch, V. (1989). *Kritik der disziplinierten Sexualität: Aufsätze 1986–1989*. Frankfurt and New York: Campus.

Stock, K. (2000). *Gottes wahre Liebe: Theologische Phänomenologie der Liebe*. Tübingen: Mohr Siebeck.

Stuart, E. (2003). *Gay and Lesbian Theologies: Repetitions with Critical Difference*. Aldershot: Ashgate.

Tillich, P. (1954). *Love, Power, and Justice: Ontological Analyses and Ethical Applications*. Oxford: Oxford University Press.

Ward, G. (2000). *Cities of God*. London: Routledge.

Watson, F. (2000). *Agape, Eros, Gender: Towards a Pauline Sexual Ethics*. Cambridge: Cambridge University Press.

Williams, R. (2002). 'The Body's Grace'. In Rogers (2002), 309–21.

Žižek, S. (1992). *Looking Awry: An Introduction to Lacan through Popular Culture*. Cambridge, MA, and London: MIT Press.

Žižek, S. (2005). 'Neighbors and Other Monsters: A Plea for Ethical Violence'. In Žižek, Eric L. Santner, and Kenneth Reinhard (eds), *The Neighbor: Three Inquiries in Political Theology*. Chicago and London: University of Chicago Press, 134–90.

Žižek S. (2010). *Living in the End Times*. London and New York: Verso.

CHAPTER 32

HIV/AIDS

MARY JO IOZZIO

INTRODUCTION

THIRTY years into the HIV/AIDS pandemic and still people of faith wonder what can be done to reduce mortality and bring transmission of HIV to zero. Religious leaders and theologians have responded, in practical ways with succour to those who are infected with and affected by the virus, and in philosophical ways with argumentation for more effective relief than is presently offered. However, faith-based initiatives can do only so much, especially in the contexts of developing nations; even more, public policy to support those who are vulnerable is as necessary as the support available from these initiatives and other non-governmental organizations.

Now widely known, HIV is transmitted through the same routes of all blood-borne infections (oral, vaginal, and anal sexual intimacy, needle-sharing, and mother-to-foetus *in utero* and during parturition). Despite these multiple infection routes, most religious traditions focus on infection through sexual intimacy. Not since Augustine, expanding on Paul's First Letter to the Corinthians (1 Cor. 7), proposed marriage as an antidote to sexual promiscuity and/or lust have faith communities so baldly faced discussions and determinations on licit sex and what to do when sexual intimacy includes the risk of an infection that to date has no cure (Augustine 1887; see also Fullam 2012). Unfortunately, many of those discussions––particularly those emphasizing married heteronormative sexual intimacy—and their determinations have been counter-productive regarding education for awareness and prevention of HIV and AIDS.

Some traditions suggest that HIV and its unhappy descent into AIDS is God's punishment for one's own (or another's) wrongdoing. Other traditions reject this conclusion and continue to work through a theology that will inform their teaching in ways to support the sexual expressions of their faithful, while challenging unjust practices that contribute to the vulnerability many have to infection. Unjust personal action and unjust social structures contribute to vulnerability. Chief among these structures are gender (with women bearing disproportionately the burdens of infection), illiteracy, migration, poverty, and war (see Bachelet et al. 2012). These more enlightened traditions remain dedicated to providing care, resources, and mercy to those in need. Regrettably, while banal banter and provocative propositions are commonplace, thoughtful sex talk remains difficult to engage and all too rare to find. But thoughtful sex talk is absolutely necessary when the stakes of silence are premature death, single parenthood, and orphaned children. In an age of HIV/AIDS the difficulty to speak openly must be overcome and venues for discussion multiplied.

Bob Vitillo of Caritas Internationalis thinks similarly. He writes:

> I am convinced that the pandemic of HIV/AIDS will force theologians to grapple more seriously with the fundamental theological premises related to human nature, and, more specifically, related to human sexuality. Notice that I have placed the need for theological reflection related to sexuality within the fundamental rather than the moral order. It seems to me that theologians have not yet faced the daunting task of elaborating a substantive theology of human sexuality as a creation of God who willed this to be such a strong, dominant, and constitutive element of human nature. Nor have we sufficiently considered how God's grace has elevated the totality of the human person (including his/her sexuality) to a level which is different from the rest of animal or plant life.
>
> (Vitillo 1994)

In this essay I offer one way to overcome the difficulty of thoughtful talk about HIV/AIDS with a consideration that sex is one of the gifts that human beings receive at the hands of a God of extravagance: a God of infinite possibility, liberal generosity, and unparalleled solidarity. Arguing that creation is a manifestation of a fecund imagination and God's own joy writ large enough to witness sexual diversity—from asexual to heterosexual, lesbian, gay, bisexual, transgender, queer, and intersex—among all living beings, I propose that sex and one's identity as a sexual being is a gift that includes the purposes and promises of the extravagance that is sexual diversity. I ask: What insights can theology bring to the purposes of sex as creativity/generativity and intimacy-building communion/pleasure? What intuitions can be brought to the promises of sex as transcendent experience and hope for the future? How is the pandemic to be understood in the light of God's extravagance? How can we talk openly—without fear of impropriety, coquettish giggles, or sneers, and trivialization of the meanings attached to conjoined embodiment—about sex?

SEX AND SEXUAL DIVERSITY: AN EXTRAVAGANT GIFT FROM AN EXTRAVAGANT GOD

The God that Christians worship is a God who initiated the material universe and who continues to create the manifold world of which we are all a part. Without denying the scientific evidence of the Big Bang as the signal start of this iteration of the cosmos,

Christians have long recognized the origin of creation in the God who spoke 'in the beginning' and made it so. I have long thought that God's speech must have been very loud indeed (like a big bang) in the void that pre-dated those first words. Moreover, and regardless of creation out of a void or from something primordial, Christians believe in a God who fashioned a world that became the material of the universe we know today. And, judging by the diversity evident in this world—from dust and rocks, plants and animals, seas and sea creatures, birds on the wing, and humankind—an extravagant, eccentric (see Kelsey 2009), and exuberant imagination animates God's creativity even as it challenges human perceptions and our inadequate constructs about God. I consider next the relationship that the Christian Trinity has to an evolving cosmos inclusive of the diversity present in creation and in humankind. Following the insights of evolutionary cosmology and biology, few doubt the evidence that the world was in the beginning, is now, and will continue to be a work in progress. And, following the insights of evolutionary theology, God continues to be involved in the progress of creative diversity (McFague 1993; Haught 2004; Peacocke 2007).

Often consideration of God's involvement in time is linked with questions of theodicy/God's judgement in occasions of natural or moral cataclysms and human suffering, including the suffering that accompanies HIV/AIDS, an infection unfortunately blamed on variations of the human-fabricated norm of heterosexism. The Holocaust perpetrated by Nazism signalled a decisive shift in thinking of an omniscient, omnipotent, omnibenevolent God (see Perkins 2009). Yet, the assignment of blame to God for the tragedies of suffering from HIV/AIDS or cancers or the after-effects of hurricanes, earthquakes, and the like is ill-placed—however correct it is to question God in the midst of tragedy. The assignment of praise to God for what is more palatably perceived as good would be similarly ill-placed, though it would be as correct to question God in the midst of joy. Rather, a paradigm of relationality and distinctions, found, for example, in the Trinitarian theology of Catherine Mowry LaCugna, explains satisfactorily where God is in the happy days of human weal and in the catastrophes of woe (LaCugna 1991). If God is for us then God is for us before, during, and after our joys as well as before, during, and after the storms of nature and those of our own making. LaCugna builds on an Aristotelian-Thomist understanding of relations that I take to be definitive for understanding the *imago Dei* that is humankind in relational dependence. Thus, as Christians know the Trinity by the relations distinguishing the three persons (Father, Son, and Spirit), so relationality is expressed also in human persons, though on a radically different level of distinction. (See Iozzio 2005 and forthcoming.)

EVOLUTION'S DIVERSITY

The relationship that God established with the universe reveals a constant exercise of divine creativity as solidarity 'in, with, and under the very processes of the natural world from the "hot, big, bang" to humanity' (Peacocke 1986: 95–96). God remains with all that God has breathed into being through God's own creative/productive/fecund fashioning, particularly since diversity throughout what was created and in creation's residual effects—change, upheaval, adaptation, joy, and suffering—was no afterthought but an *ad extra* kind of bonus, surprising, perhaps, even for God the Creator. Evolutionary processes include positive and negative effects: geologic upheavals from tectonic shifts cause earthquakes and stimulate volcanoes which, in doing so, produce and scatter terrain, and its flora and fauna then take hold of or adapt to a new land or flora and/or fauna fail and give rise to evolutionarily-related new species, including human beings. Given what we can see with our own eyes, hear with our own ears, sense with our own feelings and tactile experiences, if any of us can divine God's purposes, surely a near riotous diversity ranks highly among them. Perhaps more than any other purpose, diversity demonstrates God's own splendour and glory: the composite manifestation of God's own creative being in the physical material of primordial cosmic stuff.

God was, is, and will be in relation to the cosmos as it evolves, perhaps even because it evolves. When God chooses outward relationality (evident in God's having created the world), that choice is exercised with what becomes the relational dependence of the cosmos upon evolutionary creative activity. Following LaCugna's thought, this creative activity results from an explosion of tri-personal love, which eccentric love will not be forestalled if God is for us. This God permeates the cosmos, suffers with evolution's processes, as well as revels in its twists and turns through diversity towards God's purposes, however divined. This tri-personal love explodes in such force that the genesis of humankind follows the billions of years that began with a word: 'Be!'

The world thus begun evolves from fragments to sentient life revealing a diversity of form and function that supports fecundity throughout the known world. Believing that God creates the world grounds this diversity as an inherent expression of the relation between God and those things God has created. Further, believing that God is tri-personal relationality grounds this diversity as the way in which fecund creation relates to God, to the individual expressions among similar species, and to others. When the symbol of God thus functions as the ground of reality then both diversity and relationality can be recognized as normative for the *imago Dei* writ across the cosmos. The implications of this norm—the both/and of diversity and relationship—extend readily to earth or eco-theologies and to the context-diverse liberation theologies of the feminist, Black, Hispanic/Latina(o), Queer, and disability movements.

Relational Fecundity

Fecundity and relationality then serve as a paradigm for a diversity that can deconstruct the myths of the dominant story told primarily in a heterosexist patriarchal voice. That story and its presuppositions have often limited the scope of the *imago Dei* to the observable good belonging to an ideal man. This distortion has resulted in and witnesses still to widespread oppression and marginalization of those who do not fit into what must now be recognized as a quite narrow norm (Johnson 1996): white, male, and independent, heterosexual, non-disabled, youthful, and robust. Context-based studies have convinced most that, indeed, the Western philosophical and theological traditions—from ancient thought to today—focus their attention on things proper to what is (only) an implied norm. The paradigm of relationality challenges the implications of implied norms to which each instance of humankind is to conform and from which determinations of value are assigned. Such conceptions fail to recognize the gift that is diversity —when diversity is God's own revelation of God's way of being in the world— as much as they fail to recognize the *imago Dei* therein.

Here is an image of God that broadens the ways in which God can be imagined by considering the creation for which Christians believe God is responsible. Theological traditions contend that God can be known, at least in part, by God's effects, the most evident and concrete of which is what God has created (e.g., Aquinas 1947: I.2.2c). Counted among this creation is the material that sprang from the primordial stuff of God's word. Over time and under the processes of evolutionary change, that matter assumed forms recognizable today in the diversity of and within species. Thus, if any conclusions can be made definitively about creation and God's effects (and, by extension, at least in part, about God) it is surely that creation is as extravagant, eccentric, and exuberant as God's imagination.

To turn then to sex as gift, I add 'flagrant', 'vast', and 'diverse' to the observations that can be made by observing God's creation and ongoing creative (sexual?) presence in the world. Nothing escapes the believers' reality that this or that thing or being is here because it has participated in, been shaped by, and then loved into being by an extravagantly creative God. That extravagance includes participation in the creative activities of making/fashioning and procreation, the pleasure and delight that accompany what becomes manifest from those creative acts (God delights in God's creation: Psalm 104), and an active kind of complacence that bespeaks the language of consummate love. I suggest with Frederick Crowe, that complacence can be a moment when the moral agent recognizes the possibilities that await fulfilment. The moment is able to move the agent towards making the possible real (the descent into particulars and diversity). Complacence is identified here with the fulfilment—even afterglow—of consummate love (see Crowe 1959).

Once love is engaged as a means of expressing the nature of God, the argument for sexual intimacy as one of the gifts that attends the *imago Dei* reveals a Godlike relational quality to the activity as it is expressed in human terms in the 'conjoined embodiment' of sexual intimacy. Conjoined embodiment signifies the physical experience of sexual intimacy as well as its transcendent counterpart: the sharing of an ecstatic pleasure that is at one and the same time other-directed. The distinctiveness of one body from another is implicated in such experiences (see Copeland 2009). To the extent that such intimacy is extravagant in generosity, exuberant in playfulness, and eccentric in its thoroughgoing other-directedness on the paths it follows to consummation, it will be Godlike. Here too is one way to begin to think about how the natural law tradition functions in light of God's eccentric existence and human/species diversity. The tradition of the natural law 1) holds that all beings are to seek that which is good and to avoid evil and 2) offers a guide in determining the good, which determination reflects those activities that support the being on the path towards consummation and flourishing (see Aquinas 1947: I.II. 94.2). For human beings, the natural law proposes creative activities that express our ways of participating in God's providence: to flourish as individuals, as intimates, in light of truth, and as members of community (Aquinas 1947: I.II. 94.4). Moving beyond a singular focus on procreative productivity in much of natural law thinking, sexual intimacy is a gift that includes diverse procreative fruits: trust, companionship, mutual support, hospitality, and sometimes even children. Further and as part of the creative love that is *imago Dei*, sexual identity is the subject gift that comes with diversity and the power to distinguish oneself—from others—in creation.

I raise the discussion on sexual identity in connection with diversity in creation both to illuminate the difficulties that those whose identities differ from the heterosexist norm experience, and to expose the unhappy identification of HIV/AIDS with homosexuality and other heterosexist-labelled deviant behaviours. Narrow norms have harmed those who failed the rule established in these norms by the dominant purveyors of power. Here, Michel Foucault is instructive for a critique of knowledge that informed these determinations, and of the use and abuse of power on the basis of values assigned particularly to this or that person or people (Foucault [1970] 1994, 1972). Additionally, power abuse defies the God of creative extravagance and insults the God of love whose effects clearly include diversity in sexual identity, however much it may be denied by this or that dominant and dominating voice. If God is extravagant, exuberant, and eccentric and if God shares God's own refulgence with creation, then among that refulgence will be those identities that manifest diversity inclusive of sexual diversity, not deviance.

LET'S TALK ABOUT SEX: DEFINING THE SUBJECT'S ACT

Before proceeding with my considerations of the possibilities of something different (I limit my remarks to the Roman Catholic Church, which has been, at best, ambiguous in its comfort level on matters of sex), let's be clear about what the Church teaches. The Church is steadfast in holding its teaching on sexual intimacy under the sacramental covenant of matrimony. From this starting position, any sexual intimacy outside the marital relationship is wrong; such offences include adultery, polygamy, incest, premarital sex, and—to the extent that homosexual persons do not enjoy the sacramental forum— homosexual acts (*Catechism of the Catholic Church* 1994: #s1601–1666, 2351–2359, 2380– 2391). Further, these offences qualify as sins against the sixth commandment: 'Thou shall not commit adultery.' Thus, the Church teaches that heterosexuality is normative. A primarily physicalist/procreative interpretation of the natural law guides determinations of how sexual intimacy is regulated (through permanency, fidelity, and openness to fertility), and sacramental marriage crowns the good of the couple with grace to perfect their love and make them holy. For anyone standing outside these conventions, the Church offers a spirituality of suffering through sexual abstinence for the Kingdom of God (see Congregation for the Doctrine of the Faith 1986; Crowley 2004).

Alternately and unambiguously, the hip-hop music group Salt-N-Pepa took a bold move in the early 1990s with their hit song 'Let's Talk About Sex', adapted and later rerecorded for release as a charity single to raise awareness and break the silence as 'Let's Talk About AIDS'.[1] The lyrics in both versions challenge the naïvety or innocence of some when it comes to thinking of sex as an expression of romantic love; they challenge the callousness of others when sex is brokered in an economic exchange, a display of power/prowess, or revenge; and they challenge those caught off guard (in the heat-of-the-moment kind of way) only to find themselves unprepared emotionally, materially, and/or spiritually for a sexual encounter. Abstinence programmes in particular can render those who are sexually naïve unaware and unprepared (see Fraser 2005). They sing: 'Let's talk about sex, baby; let's talk about you and me; let's talk about all the good things and the bad things that may be. Let's talk about sex' (Azor 1990). What is fresh about the song, including its rhythm and cadence, is Salt-N-Pepa's challenge to ubiquitous banality and a no-nonsense approach at the core of an intimacy left dangerously unspoken. While HIV/AIDS can be and is contracted by other means, the principal mode of transmission is sexual intercourse. To the extent that sex remains the primary route of infection, the failure of parents, teachers, clergy and faith communities, health-care professionals, and others to talk openly, frequently, and thoughtfully about sex exposes both the negligence of our duties to inform our children, teenagers, and young adults (and older folks) of 'all the good things' and a failure to extend our concern for the parameters of this or that individual's health and well-being to the common good—'the bad things that may be'.

Consider the statement 'The Body of Christ has AIDS,' popularized in Catholic networks, uniting the metaphorical and eschatological dimensions of the ecclesial community. In this corporate type of thinking, when one member of the Church has AIDS, the Church in its entirety is infected and bears the burdens of suffering, grief, and premature and preventable death that accompanies the virus in the community (see Cimperman 2005; van Klinken 2010).

Breaking the Silence

Silence about the power of sex contributes to ignorance and, in the case of HIV/AIDS, leads to a steady or, more than likely, an increasing rate of infection among those who are vulnerable. So, let's talk about sex in order to inform and protect:

> Yo, let's talk about AIDS (go on) to the unconcerned and uninformed. You think you can't get it. Well, you're wrong.... Now if you go about it right you just might save

---

[1] 'Let's Talk About Sex', written by hip-hop music producer Hurby 'Love Bug' Azor, was released with Salt-N-Pepa's third album, *Blacks' Magic* (1990), London Records; alternate version release (1992), Next Plateau Records.

your life. Don't be uptight, come join the fight. We're gonna tell you how you can get it and how you won't; all of the do's and all of the don't's. I got some news for you so listen, please. It's not a black, white, or gay disease.

(Azor 1992)

If sex is an extravagant gift of an extravagant God, and extravagance reveals a God who shares with creation an eccentricity of being, then thinking in a key of extravagance offers the potential to move talk about sex out of the shadows and into the light, while it raises whispers to direct conversation on what's good about sex and strategies for prevention on what can harm. If the global community present in the United Nations can mobilize its member states to acknowledge the continuing threat that is HIV/AIDS and commit their activist efforts to zero new infections, zero discrimination, and zero AIDS-related deaths, surely our faith communities can join UNAIDS and its partners in championing prevention as the cornerstone of the global response to the pandemic (see UNAIDS 2013a, 2013b; UN General Assembly, 65th Session 2011)? Let's talk about sex!

What insights does theology bring to the extravagant potential of the purposes of sex as creativity/generativity and intimacy-building communion/pleasure—'how it could be' of Salt-N-Pepa's song—and to the extravagant promises of sex as transcendent experience and hope for the future—'how it should be'—in spite of HIV/AIDS? Perhaps not since before Augustine and his teaching on the purposes of marriage has the question of sex been so separate from its social function. For Augustine, the purposes of marriage included sexual relief as well as mutual support between spouses and the promise of children, three among other effects of the sacrament that contribute to the social common good (see Clark 1996). It seems appropriate today to reintroduce some of the less patriarchal dimensions of his teaching on companionship as the key to a theological appreciation of the gift of sex as an extravagant ecstatic encounter between friends who are lovers—the conjoined embodiment of a sexual intimacy that is loving and just.

While the commodification of sex is broadcast widely and globalization of the sex trade thrives and increases inequalities between women and men, between those who are poor and the better-off, and between gender minorities and heterosexuals, serious and sustained talk of sex has been increasingly isolated from its social function and towards a (selectively) privatized personal preference (Altman 2004). The often-virulent public campaigns against non-heterosexual civil unions and/or marriage indicate the selectivity of these preferences. Further, whereas in previous generations and much of history, sex and sexual intimacy held a place in the social structures of cultural and ethnic communities, the contemporary world lacks the (implicit) social cohesion of the past (on the social construction of sexual norms, see Tipton and Witte 2005). Granted, sexual intimacy remains the standard method of contributing to the survival of the species—one of the common goods—and has been institutionalized in marriage and other forms of civil unions so as to ensure the socialization and protection of offspring. However, that very institutionalization has been subject also to the corruptions present in the dominant narratives of the system's power brokers and, paradoxically, often to the neglect of those the institution presumably protects (Traina 2003; Germond 2004).

Moreover, and given a feminist or liberationist hermeneutics of suspicion, even the presumption of social cohesion may have never really existed (the seeming worldwide inescapability of Western culture successfully occludes recognition of the difference and diversity present then and now).

As an antidote to this tendency, Margaret Farley offers a context-rich consideration of lived experiences to recognize the 'plasticity of human sexuality, its susceptibility to different meanings and expressive forms' (Farley 2006: 104). She notes that if we are to understand best what it is to be fully human, to experience the achievement of our potentials and flourishing as individuals and as members of communities, as embodied spirits and inspirited bodies, as unified and self-transcendent 'on the way, and in the end, this [anthropology] is the framework in which human sexuality must somehow also be understood' (Farley 2006: 132). Farley then admits both diversity and extravagance as she outlines the requirements for sexual intimacy that is just in its loving.

The Church does not necessarily disagree with Farley's conclusions. However, it takes exception when Farley argues that same-sex and opposite-sex relational intimacy can both be justified by the same sexual ethics held as sacrosanct by the Church (Farley 2006: 288): fidelity and fecundity (*Catechism of the Catholic Church* 1994: #2362, #2366). (On the Vatican position on Farley's book see Congregation for the Doctrine of the Faith 2012.) In their rejection of Farley's reach outwards to sexual minorities and her recognition of sexual diversity, the official magisterium stands unable to accept the illogic of its position that on the one hand it condemns homosexual acts while on the other hand it calls the heterosexist Church to 'accept' persons having homosexual tendencies and to 'treat' them with respect, compassion, and sensitivity. The illogic is exposed in the long-held teaching of the Church and its philosophical traditions that action follows being (Aquinas 1947: I.75.2c; I.105.5c.) Further, as Josef Fuchs asserts,

> It should be repeated that ethics is not concerned with deducing the 'ought' from the 'is' but invariably with coming to a correct understanding of the adage *agere sequitur esse* ... There is a normative aspect to such ethical reflection, since it investigates not only the understanding of one's athematic-transcendental ethical experience ... but [it investigates] also the understanding of categorical experience or of concrete problems.
>
> (Fuchs 1983: 93)

If homosexual persons are to be accepted and treated with respect, acceptance of a homosexual identity indicates logically a pre-recognition of the concrete reality of being homosexual. Thus, the conclusion of the maxim when applied to sexual diversity must be that non-heterosexual intimacy (action) will follow, rightly, from non-hetero persons (being).

A Guide: Because 'Not Just Anything Goes'

Here then is the crux of my advocacy to guide the welcome of sexual diversity: that the virtues and norms governing sexual intimacy follow the theological and anthropological insights found in the perichoretic/circumincession relations of the Trinitarian God for us. God *in se* and *ad extra*, giving and receiving through creative intimacy, loves eccentrically and rests at last enveloped complacently therein. The guide begins with a norm for moral agency of mutuality and maturity: 1) that the moral agents have certain equality or mutuality and have reached physical, emotional, social, moral, and spiritual maturity. Such determinations of mutuality and maturity will vary from culture to culture. Variations aside, certain limits would be held at 16 years of age minimum, an independent personality, the exercise of an ability to contribute to the common good, self-determination and responsibility for action, and a willingness to seek truth beyond the confines of personal experience and towards the transcendent. If any of these conditions of mutuality or maturity are missing, sexual intimacy ought not to be engaged. For example, however disguised as consent, sexually intimate violence belies the moral agency of women and men worldwide, as victims of rape, revenge, hate, paedophilia, and exploitation will testify. Sexual violence reveals the vulnerability of thwarted-agency in the unbalanced exercise of power.

The guide continues with virtues: 2) *chaste fidelity*—that they are thereby able to commit without fear or coercion to an intimate relationship and to remain faithful and chaste in loving. 3) *Creativity/imagination*—that they be ready and willing to serve the common good in their openness to co-creative fecundity. 4) *Courageous humility*—that they protect one another from the vulnerabilities attendant to sexual intimacy, namely, physical abuse or rape, emotional battering or blackmail, social subjugation or stigmatization, moral neglect or abandonment, and/or spiritual disregard or contempt. 5) *Generous conjoined self-care*—that they answer the call to eccentricity as loving mutuality in their experiences of conjoined embodiment from its ecstasy to its embers in the sexually intimate embrace.

Even if scientific conclusions on human sexual diversity remain unconvincing to some, can the Church continue to deny the possibility that sexual diversity reflects another manifestation of God's eccentric extravagance in creation? Can it continue to deny that that possibility would have consequences expressed in concrete actions, including sexual intimacy of a non-heterosexual sort? Among other considerations, perhaps the magisterium has not yet envisioned fully a non-biologically pregnant fecundity that accompanies sexual intimacy as found, for example, in the fruitfulness of friendship and mutual support as well as service to others—as part of the village it takes to raise our children—in many childless marriages. If fecundity is a hallmark of marital sexual intimacy, what besides 'acceptance' does the Church make of childless couples? Are their lives fruitless? The Church's failure to see beyond the narrow norms inherited from a tradition guilty of failure in its determinations of truth and falsehood on many social ills harms the faithful as well as those who look to the Church for clarity in an otherwise confused and confusing world. While surely the Church has met with success in its praise and condemnation of good and evil in the world, it has admitted only a few mistakes, if only in recent memory, mistakes still in need of attention and repair: the Crusades, the treatment of Galileo, the Inquisition, the Holocaust, slavery, racism, and its treatment of women (International Theological Commission 1999). Heterosexism ought now to be included on the list, culpability acknowledged, and repairs made.

Sadly, the official magisterium remains steadfast in its unwillingness to expand its talk about sex. Centuries of a celibate (or continent) clergy has stifled the ability, if not the willingness, to engage seriously the multiple occasions of sex among, and its immanent affects upon, God's people. It has clouded the more recent exposure of the paedophile scandal and other sexual abuse by clergy upon the vulnerable. Moreover, the Church seems averse to genuine dialogue inclusive of the people who stand at the margins on account of their sexual identity and/or those whose experience is at odds with a tradition hiding behind patriarchal heterosexism. In an age of HIV/AIDS the Church must emerge from its closet to engage its fears and apprehensions about sex which manifest in diverse expressions, among diverse peoples, with diverse gifts. It's time to talk about sex.

SEX TRANSCENDING TIME AND SPACE: A KAIROS DEFINING MOMENT

HIV/AIDS is a global phenomenon, presenting a pandemic of epic proportions immortalized in memories of personal and communal loss, in the performing and material arts, and in medical, social, economic, political, and religious literature.[2] Insofar as the popular imagination, via religious and secular spheres, locates HIV/AIDS in sexual activity and to the extent that such activity includes a potent ecstatic quality, all just and loving sex can be understood through the going out of oneself towards another as a transcendent event. In the same way that God transcends time and space in presence to the *imago Dei* throughout the world, so too does the *imago Dei* transcend the limits of physical and temporal existence in the letting go of the strengths and weaknesses that can interfere with consummate love. HIV/AIDS has provided an opportunity to think differently about sexual intimacy, differently from an emphasis on biological fecundity, and differently from the relief of lust. Sex in an age of HIV/AIDS requires forethought, which thought might profitably lead to an ever more fully human determination that this or that act of sexual intimacy is just. Since HIV infection is preventable through fastidious care of blood exchanges between non-infected persons and people with HIV/AIDS, anti-retroviral therapies for women who are HIV+ during pregnancy, and sexual abstinence or, when abstinence is not an option, consistent use of condom prophylaxis, thinking well and being well prepared before an occasion of sex can lead to ever more just expressions and experiences of sexual intimacy along the lines of the norms and virtues outlined earlier.

The Church has been hesitant to encourage the legitimacy of procreative sexual intimacy that is closed to pregnancy. That hesitancy has prevented the Church from advocating prophylactic-preventative condom use among sero-discordant spouses. It has also prevented acceptance of non-heterosexual intimacy and preventative condom use

---

[2] Among others, see Kimmelman (1989); Amedeo Medical Literature Guide (1997–2014); Dickinson (2006); NAMES Project Foundation (2009); Orban (2009); HARC (2013).

between partners. However, Kevin Kelly suggests that this time of HIV/AIDS is a time of grace, an opportunity that 'presents us with a "creation" moment, an invitation to set in motion another "big bang"' (Kelly 1998: 207). Not to be apocalyptic but eschatological, HIV/AIDS may very well be the occasion of conversion from one among many forms of oppression and marginalization to liberation and the freedom to claim ever more worthily that we—all of us, whether hetero, gay, lesbian, bi, transgendered, queer, or intersex—are the children of a loving and just God, whose care for us extends to work that will undo the social vulnerabilities that the pandemic has exposed. HIV/AIDS has mobilized the social consciences and consciousness of people across the globe—a sign of increasing comfort with diversity of many kinds, as well as solidarity between developed nations and the developing world, across religious, cultural, and ethnic divides, and among those with power for those who are oppressed and otherwise marginalized—kairos indeed!

A Practical Theology

On his 2009 visit to Africa, Benedict XVI weighed in on the question of condom use in reference to HIV. In spite of previous intimations of flexibility on the matter, including a study by the Pontifical Council for Health Care (see Suaudeau 2000; Tlhagale 2000; Fuller and Keenan 2000), the Vatican's official position remains unchanged with an unqualified 'No' to their use (Butt 2009; Shinkongo 2009). The persistence of this position is troubling in face of the tremendous devastation and loss that accompanies HIV/AIDS wherever it is present—35.3 to 38.8 million people living with HIV/AIDS worldwide—and particularly in Africa, where 28 million people are living with HIV/AIDS. Since 1981 more than 36 million people have died of AIDS (UNAIDS 2013a). The evidence confirming condom/prophylactic use as one among other effective HIV prevention methods is compelling (see AVERT 2009). The Church must find a way to move beyond its thinking on condom use as contraceptive or as contributive to sexual licentiousness to make their use licit for preventive purposes and to provide easy access for sero-discordant couples, those single who are already infected, and others who are vulnerable to infection on account of age, gender, and/or socio-economic status.

The life-critical gravitas of a more effective response than 'sorry, no' to thwart transmission of HIV demands a return to the subtle nuances that previous methodologies of casuistry, theological reflection, and Catholic social teaching commend. Benedict XVI, employing casuistry, seemed at one time to loosen the condom prohibition, suggesting their use may reduce HIV infection (see Seewald and Pope Benedict XVI 2010: 119). Further, the teachings regarding the preferential option for, and solidarity with, those who are poor and otherwise vulnerable require an unapologetic life-affirming response to those most at risk to and affected by HIV/AIDS. Thus, contrary to the spirit of the law, insistence on the letter of the law results in a compromise of safety, flourishing, and the common good (e.g., Mark 2:23–3:6 and John 5:1–18). However, Jesus demonstrates God's mercy and power to make things right even on the Sabbath (see Brown 1997: 344–345).

Similarly, James Keenan draws attention to the tension between law and a humanitarian spirit: 'Catholics ...try at once both to admit the importance of the law and to uphold the spirit that animates the law. They want, for instance, to affirm their teachings about sex and marriage, but they also want to entertain cases that highlight the humanity underlying these laws' (Keenan 1999: 497). The kairos moment requires that the Church hold firm to people over law, not the other way around. As Kelly concludes, 'Theologically, our world is faced with a redemptive moment. If that is not a challenge to Christians and Christian Churches, what is?' (Kelly 1998: 213).

What is known for certain is that the Church has responded positively and forcefully to the global challenge of HIV/AIDS even as it has been slow to consider sexual diversity. A consideration of this might lead to a revision of its teaching on sex to reflect more accurately contemporary understandings from empirical studies and the experiences of the faithful in matters of sexuality. (For a global Catholic theological reflection on the pandemic, see Keenan et al. 2002; Iozzio et al. 2009.) On the ground and in some of the hardest and most remote sites where the pandemic ravages God's people, the Church has clinics, support, and outreach ministries for those infected with and affected by HIV/AIDS (see e.g. Caritas Internationalis 2012). There and elsewhere, as Agbonkhianmeghe Orobator suggests, 'the church ought to discover in the crisis engendered by the epidemic a radical understanding of its identity and commitment to its mission to renew humanity as well as facilitate the advent of a new community of faith' (Orobator 2005: 123). Such an understanding emerges in the Church as it listens to its people becoming a learning Church while retaining its role as teacher. 'Mutual listening and learning from the context and among the various sectors of the church, and a respect for the principle of subsidiarity, enhance the credibility of the church as a caring and responsive community of faith in the time of AIDS' (Orobator 2005: 127). Kairos, then, inspires more than just a clinical response, particularly to the vulnerability of God's people exposed in the pandemic.

CODA

If the Church is to learn from its members, from the pandemic, and from those who wait for a sign of welcome, it will need to exercise its learning-listening and teaching-advising roles boldly. If the response to HIV/AIDS reveals God's tri-personal relationality extending care for the diverse expressions of creation, then our exercise of relational fecundity in this kairos moment should witness an unfettered care for all God's people. And if the sexual diversity accompanying HIV/AIDS—as God divines—supports the purposes and promises of conjoined embodiment in eccentric other-directedness, then the imposition of stagnant norms that prevent the expression of physical and transcendent intimacy must be replaced with Godlike mercy, solidarity, and love.[3]

---

[3] Pope Francis, whose motto is *Miserando atque Eligendo*, names 'this time is a kairos of mercy'.

REFERENCES

Altman, Dennis (2004). 'Sexuality and Globalisation'. *Agenda: Empowering Women for Gender Equity*, 18(62): special issue *Sexuality in Africa*, 22–28.

Amedeo Medical Literature Guide (1997–2014). 'HIV Infection', FlyingPublisher Free Medical Information. <http://www.amedeo.com/medicine/hiv.htm>.

Aquinas, Thomas (1947). *Summa Theologiae*. Trans. Fathers of the English Dominican Province. New York: Benziger Bros.

Augustine (1887). 'On the Good of Marriage'. Trans. Revd Charles Lewis Cornish. *Nicene and Post-Nicene Fathers*, vol. iii. London: T&T Clark; and Grand Rapids, MI: Christian Classics Ethereal Library. <http://www.ccel.org/ccel/schaff/npnf103.v.ii.html>.

AVERT (2009). 'Condoms: Effectiveness, History and Availability'. <http://www.avert.org/condoms.htm>.

Azor, Hurby (1990). 'Let's Talk About Sex'. Salt-N-Pepa recording, *Blacks' Magic*. London: London Records.

Azor, Hurby (1992). '*Let's Talk About AIDS*'. *Salt-N-Pepa, charity single remix*. New York: Next Plateau Records Incarnation. Video: 1993 The Island Def Jam Music Group (uploaded 23 Nov. 2009). <http://www.youtube.com/watch?v=5aco4hUr4WM>.

Bachelet, Michelle, Jennifer Gatsi-Mallet, and Michel Sidibe (2012). *Women Out Loud: How Women Living with HIV Will Help the World End AIDS*. New York: UNAIDS. <http://www.unaids.org/en/media/unaids/contentassets/documents/unaidspublication/2012/20121211_Women_Out_Loud_en.pdf>.

Brown, Raymond E. (1997). *An Introduction to the New Testament*. New York: Doubleday.

Butt, Riazat (2009). 'Pope Claims that Condoms Could Make Africa's AIDS Crisis Worse'. *The Guardian* (17 Mar.). <http://www.guardian.co.uk/world/2009/mar/17/pope-africa-condoms-aids>.

Caritas Internationalis (2012). 'How Caritas Works: HIV and AIDS'. <http://www.caritas.org/activities/hiv_aids/sinethemba_a_caritas_response_to_aids.html>.

Catechism of the Catholic Church (1994). Vatican City: Libreria Editrice Vaticana.

Cimperman, Maria (2005). *When God's People Have HIV/AIDS: An Approach to Ethics*. Maryknoll, NY: Orbis Books.

Clark, Elizabeth A. (1996) (ed.). *St. Augustine on Marriage and Sexuality*. Washington, DC: Catholic University of America Press.

Congregation for the Doctrine of the Faith (1986). *Letter to the Bishops of the Catholic Church on the Pastoral Care of Homosexual Persons*. <http://www.vatican.va/roman_curia/congregations/cfaith/documents/rc_con_cfaith_doc_19861001_homosexual-persons_en.html>.

Congregation for the Doctrine of the Faith (2012). 'Notification on the Book *Just Love: A Framework for Christian Sexual Ethics* by Sr. Margaret A. Farley, RSM' (30 Mar.). <http://www.vatican.va/roman_curia/congregations/cfaith/documents/rc_con_cfaith_doc_20120330_nota-farley_en.html>.

Copeland, M. Shawn (2009). *Enfleshing Freedom: Body, Race, and Being*. Minneapolis: Fortress Press.

Crowe, Frederick (1959). 'Complacence and Concern in the Thought of St. Thomas'. *Theological Studies*, 20: 1–39, 198–230, 343–395.

Crowley, Paul G., SJ (2004). 'Homosexuality and the Counsel of the Cross'. *Theological Studies*, 65(3): 500–529.

Dickinson, Clare (2006). 'The Politics of National HIV/AIDS Responses: A Synthesis of Literature'. London: HLSP Institute (Mar.). <http://www.hlsp.org/LinkClick.aspx?fileticket =dovYhXrLRnU%3D&tabid>.

Farley, Margaret A. (2006). *Just Love: A Framework for Christian Sexual Ethics*. New York: Continuum International.

Foucault, Michel (1972). *The Archaeology of Knowledge and the Discourse on Language*. New York: Pantheon Books.

Foucault, Michel ([1970] 1994). *The Order of Things: An Archaeology of the Human Sciences*. New York: Vintage Books.

Francis, Pope (2013). Apostolic Journey to Rio de Janeiro. Press Conference during the Return Flight (28 July). <http://www.vatican.va/holy_father/francesco/speeches/2013/july/documents/ papa-francesco_20130728_gmg-conferenza-stampa_en.html>.

Fraser, Jane (2005). 'Teenage Pregnancy: Are the Churches to Blame?' In Julian Filochowski and Peter Sanford (eds), *Opening Up: Speaking Out in the Church*. London: Darton, Longman, & Todd, 81–94.

Fuchs, Josef (1983). *Personal Responsibility and Christian Morality*. Washington, DC: Georgetown University Press.

Fullam, Lisa (2012). 'Toward a Virtue Ethics of Marriage: Augustine and Aquinas on Friendship in Marriage'. *Theological Studies*, 73(4): 663–692.

Fuller, Jon D., and James F. Keenan (2000). 'Tolerant Signals: The Vatican's New Insights on Condoms for H.I.V. Prevention'. *America*, 183(8) (23 Sept.). <http://www.americamagazine. org/content/article.cfm?article_id=2281>.

Germond, Paul (2004). 'Sex in a Globalizing World'. *Journal of Theology for Southern Africa*, 119 (July): 46–68.

HARC (The HIV, AIDS and Religion Collaborative) (2013). Homepage. <http://www. harc-network.org>.

Haught, John F. (2004). *Purpose, Evolution, and the Meaning of Life*. Kitchener, ON: Pandora Press.

International Theological Commission (1999). *Memory and Reconciliation: The Church and the Faults of the Past* (Dec.). <http://www.vatican.va/roman_curia/congregations/cfaith/ cti_documents/rc_con_cfaith_doc_20000307_memory-reconc-itc_en.html>.

Iozzio, Mary Jo (2005). 'The Writing on the Wall … Alzheimer Disease: A Daughter's Look at Mom's Faithful Care of Dad'. *Journal of Religion, Disability & Health*, 9: 49–74.

Iozzio, Mary Jo, with Mary M. Doyle Roche and Elsie M. Miranda (2009) (ed.). *Calling for Justice Throughout the World: Catholic Women Theologians on the HIV/AIDS Pandemic*. New York: Continuum International.

Iozzio, Mary Jo (forthcoming). *Radical Dependence: A Theo-anthropological Ethics in the Key of Disability*. South Bend, IN: University of Notre Dame Press.

Johnson, Elizabeth (1996). *She Who Is: The Mystery of God in Feminist Theological Discourse*. New York: Crossroad Publishing.

Keenan, James F., SJ (1999). 'Applying the Seventeenth Century Casuistry of Accommodation to HIV Prevention', *Theological Studies*, 60: 492–512.

Keenan, James F., with Jon Fuller, Lisa Sowle Cahill, and Kevin Kelly (2002) (ed.). *Catholic Ethicists on HIV/AIDS Prevention*. New York: Continuum International.

Kelly, Kevin T. (1998). *New Directions in Sexual Ethics: Moral Theology and the Challenge of AIDS*. London: Geoffrey Chapman.

Kelsey, David H. (2009). *Eccentric Existence: A Theological Anthropology* (Louisville, KY: Westminster John Knox Press.

Kimmelman, Michael (1989). 'Bitter Harvest: AIDS and the Arts'. *New York Times* (19 Mar.). <http://www.nytimes.com/1989/03/19/arts/bitter-harvest-aids-and-the-arts.html?pagewanted=all&src=pm>.

LaCugna, Catherine Mowry (1991). *God for Us: The Trinity and Christian Life*. San Francisco: HarperCollins.

McFague, Sallie (1993). *The Body of God: An Ecological Theology*. Minneapolis: Augsburg Fortress.

NAMES Project Foundation (2009). 'The AIDS Memorial Quilt'. <http://www.aidsquilt.org>.

Orban, Clara (2009). 'AIDS Literature: A Cross Cultural Perspective'. *Hektoen International: A Journal of Medical Humanities*, 1(2). <http://www.hektoeninternational.org/Journal_AIDS_Literature.html>.

Orobator, Agbonkhianmeghe E. (2005). *From Crisis to Kairos: The Mission of the Church in the Time of HIV/AIDS*. Nairobi: Paulines Publications Africa.

Peacocke, Arthur C. (1986). *God and the New Biology*. London: JM Dent and Sons, 95–96.

Peacocke, Arthur (2007). *All That Is: A Naturalistic Faith for the Twenty-First Century*. Minneapolis: Augsburg Fortress Press.

Perkins, Anna Kasafi (2009). 'God (Not) Gwine Sin Yuh: HIV/AIDS in the Caribbean'. In Iozzio (2009), 84–93.

Seewald, Peter, and Pope Benedict XVI (2010). *Light of the World: The Pope, the Church, and the Signs of the Times*. San Francisco: Ignatius Press.

Shinkongo, Joseph Shipandeni, OMI (2009). 'Intervention #00275-02.02'. *Synodus Episcoporum Bulletin* 23, II Ordinary Special Assembly for Africa of the Synod of Bishops (4–15 Oct.). <http://www.vatican.va/news_services/press/sinodo/documents/bollettino_23_ii_speciale-africa-2009/02_inglese/b22_02.html>.

Suaudeau, Jacques (2000). 'Prophylactics or Family Values? Stopping the Spread of HIV/AIDS'. *L'osservatore romano* (9 Apr.). <http://www.ewtn.com/library/CURIA/PCFHIV.HTM>.

Tipton, Steven, and John Witte, Jr. (2005) (eds). *Family Transformed: Religion, Values, and Society in American Life*. Washington, DC: Georgetown University Press.

Tlhagale, Buti (2000). 'The Killer Disease: A South African Bishop Looks at AIDS in His Country'. *America*, 182(15) (29 Apr.). <http://www.americamagazine.org/content/article.cfm?article_id=682>.

Traina, Cristina (2003). 'Sex in the City of God'. *Currents in Theology and Mission*, 30: 5–19.

UN General Assembly, 65th Session (2011). 'Political Declaration on HIV and AIDS: Intensifying Our Efforts to Eliminate HIV and AIDS'. Resolution 65/277 (10 June 2011). <http://www.unaids.org/en/media/unaids/contentassets/documents/document/2011/06/20110610_UN_A-RES-65-277_en.pdf>.

UNAIDS (2013a). '2013 Fact Sheet' (Report on the Global AIDS Epidemic). <http://www.unaids.org/en/resources/campaigns/globalreport2013/factsheet/>.

UNAIDS (2013b). Homepage. <http://www.unaids.org/en/>.

van Klinken, Adriaan S. (2010). 'When the Body of Christ Has AIDS: A Theological Metaphor for Global Solidarity in Light of HIV and AIDS'. *International Journal of Public Theology*, 4: 446–465.

Vitillo, Robert J. (1994). *Theological Challenges Posed by the Global Pandemic of HIV/AIDS*. Boston College (23 Mar.). <http://natcath.org/NCR_Online/documents/VitilloHIVreport.htm>.

PART VIII

....

SEXUAL THEOLOGIES FOR ALL PEOPLE

....

....

CHAPTER 33

PEOPLE BEGINNING SEXUAL EXPERIENCE

....

MICHAEL G. LAWLER AND TODD A. SALZMAN

FIRST SEX AND
VIRTUE: NECESSARY COMPANIONS

....

THIS chapter reflects on two issues related to first sexual experience. The first issue is a set of questions about human sexuality. What specifically is human (not animal) sexuality? What is its relation to gender? What is its place in human relationships? When and under what conditions ought human relationships to become sexual relationships? Embedded in this issue is a subset of questions about the virtues that ought to be at work when humans are in relationship and specifically in sexual relationship: We suggest three virtues: justice, love, and chastity. The second issue is a set of questions about marriage, the most crucial of which is whether heterosexual marriage is still the exclusive norm for stable sexual relationships and the education of children or whether there are other stable sexual relationships that function as well as heterosexual marriage. The two main contemporary alternatives to heterosexual marriage are cohabitation and same-sex unions. Since same-sex unions are treated specifically elsewhere in this section we focus on the widespread phenomenon of cohabitation, asking questions about its relationship to marriage and marital commitment.

The above questions are complicated by the fact that, for many, their first sexual activity happens early in life, long before they have reached the personal and social maturity that enables them to understand the full implications of sexual intercourse; long before, as Aristotle and Aquinas would say, reason is capable of educating passion. This same lack of maturity may block those who engage in their first sex early in life from fully grasping the ethical arguments we offer in this chapter. Fully human sexual activity, however, needs ethics and we offer what follows as an adult approach to sexual ethics that will need to be learned, if not before the first sex, at least as soon as possible in the on-going journey of an interpersonal, sexual life.

In the Western world, the traditional approach to sexual ethics is in crisis. Marriage rates are down and age at first marriage is up. Better nutritional habits have seen an earlier onset of puberty for both girls (about 13) and boys (about 14). There is, therefore, a 13–15 year gap between puberty and marriage. That is a long time for the immature to resist the powerful urges of the pleasurable sexual drive and to abstain from sex, and research data show that the vast majority of emerging adults neither abstain nor think that their sexual activity before marriage is at all wrong. This situation, and the tragedies that regularly accompany it, cry out for some kind of relationship and sexuality education. We deliberately use the term 'sexuality education' rather than the more common 'sex education' ' to insinuate that the education that is needed is not merely physiological but, more importantly, personal, interpersonal, and relational; not so much the 'how to' of sex as the 'why', the 'with whom', and the 'in what context'? What we offer about virtue in what follows, we believe, is an integral part of that sexuality education. So too is its necessary community location.

The futures of both societies and church, in John Paul II's felicitous phrase, 'pass through the family' (John Paul II 1982: n.75). For that reason he urged the Catholic Church to promote better programmes of *marriage preparation* to eliminate as far as possible the difficulties many *married couples* find themselves in, and even more to favour the establishing of maturing and successful *marriages*' (John Paul II 1982: n.66, emphasis added). The simple substitution of the italicized terms by 'sexuality education', 'sexually-related couples', and 'sexual relationships', respectively, captures the essence of what we believe to be necessary. Sexuality education is best offered by the churches which have in place already, in their catechumenate programmes, an exemplary form of what we believe to be necessary (Lawler: 2007). The influence of the churches on sexual matters, however, is on the wane in the Western world and therefore, failing the churches, the obligation of sexuality education also falls on the larger society which has its own stake in flourishing sexual relationships and families. Whether offered by churches or societies, with the onset of puberty and the 'birth' of possible 'first-sexers', sexuality education is required for the human flourishing of individuals, dare we say especially women, couples, families, churches, and societies. We note here what we will develop when speaking of virtue, namely, that sexuality education is more about respected and valued role models than about words or arguments. Persons who are 'role figures' (Stratman 1997: 15) first exemplify what it means to be sexually virtuous and then, by personal repetition of sexually virtuous actions, individuals establish those virtues as their own.

SEXUALITY AND SEXUAL PRACTICE

We make distinctions between the meanings of the words sexuality, sex, and gender. *Sexuality* refers to a fundamental component of human persons through which they both experience themselves as heterosexual, homosexual, bisexual, or transgendered beings and express themselves sexually in relation to other sexual beings. *Sex* refers to both the biological aspects of being a sexual being and the physical expression of sexuality. *Gender* refers to the way a person expresses his or her sex within a culture. Sex determines sexual being and is itself determined biologically. Gender determines masculinity and femininity and is itself determined culturally. By sex male and female humans are the same in every culture; by gender men and women differ across cultures.

Sex has three distinct meanings: it is pleasurable, it is relational, and on occasion it is procreative. It is the pleasure that accompanies sexual activity that has always raised moral concerns for the Christian churches and has led to their traditional sexual ethic. Sexual pleasure has always been morally suspect in the Christian traditions, even though it is accepted by them as a good created by God. It can be used, of course, for either good or evil, and the abuses of sexual pleasure and a hedonistic morality based *exclusively* on pleasure are fully evident in the historical past and present. Such abuses, however, ought not and do not diminish the essential and valuable place of sexual pleasure as an intrinsic component of sex and sexual ethics.

Suspicion of the pleasure associated with sexual activity has a long history in the Christian traditions. Plato and Aristotle held that sexual activity belonged to the lower powers of human nature and were deeply suspicious of it. Their suspicion was shared by the Stoics who restricted moral sexual acts to acts within marriage open to procreation, and these Stoic views were incorporated into early Christian views on sexuality and sexual ethics. Stoic teaching and the Christian teaching shaped by it did two crucial things: it restricted moral sexual activity to marriage and specifically to acts within marriage open to procreation.

Augustine affirmed that sexual activity in marriage is good because it was created good by the good God, but he also affirmed that its goodness is always threatened by the powerful pleasure associated with it and by the unbridled concupiscence engendered by original sin. He writes that sexual activity in marriage is good when it is for the purpose of procreation and venially sinful when, 'even with one's spouse, [it is] to satisfy concupiscence' (Augustine 1844: 6.6). The suspicion of sexual pleasure reached a high point toward the end of the sixth century when Pope Gregory the Great banned from access to church anyone who had just had *pleasurable* intercourse. James Brundage's 's judgement of the effect of this history is accurate: 'The Christian horror of sex has for centuries placed enormous strain on individual consciences and self-esteem in the Western world' (Brundage 1987: 9). This enormous strain continues to be evident.

The Christian suspicion of and negative attitude to pleasurable sexual activity created a negative sexual ethics. From the earliest Christian days, moral sexual intercourse was restricted to marriage, and in marriage was further restricted to intercourse open to the possibility of the procreation of new life. By the beginning of the third century, Christian Fathers taught that it was better not to engage in sexual activity at all, and virginity was judged a better state in life than marriage. The Fathers in general were not opposed to marriage; they just expressed a preference for virginity. Commenting on Paul's 's 'It is better to marry than to burn with passion' (1 Cor. 7:9), Tertullian argues that it is better neither to marry nor to burn with passion. Virgins, he teaches, have full holiness because 'continence is more glorious than marriage' (1844: 1). Chrysostom agrees: 'I believe that virginity is a long way better than marriage, not because marriage is evil, for to those who would use it correctly [for procreation] it is the doorway to continence' (1912: 9). A twentieth-century Father, Pope John Paul II, also agrees. 'The Church throughout her history has always defended the superiority of this charism [virginity] to that of marriage' (1982: n.14). Starting in the fourth century, the theological judgement of the superiority of virginity to marriage yielded a new ascetic practice which still continues in various Christian churches, namely, the practice of celibacy as a more perfect way to live a Christ-like life. The suspicion of, and negative approach to, sexual pleasure continues to be prominent in the teachings of the churches, but not without challenge from the body of believers.

VIRTUE THEORY

In contemporary ethics, there are three normative approaches to answering the question about the morality of any action. There is the utilitarian approach: the moral sexual act is the one that maximizes the utility of the couple. There is the deontological approach: the moral sexual act is the one that adheres to the rules governing sexual activity. There is the virtue ethical approach that emphasizes the personal character and virtues of sexual agents: the moral sexual act is the one that advances the moral character and human flourishing of the couple. We share with Alasdair MacIntyre the judgement that neither utilitarianism nor deontology offers an adequately comprehensive moral philosophy: indeed that, because of them, 'We have—very largely if not entirely—lost our comprehension, both theoretical and practical, of morality' (MacIntyre 1981: 2). We, therefore, join the many contemporary thinkers who advance virtue ethics as a normative ethics more promising to moral life than utilitarianism or deontology. We give here a brief account of virtue ethics as it relates to sexuality in general and to first sex in particular. That requires, first, a virtue *theory* and, then, based on that theory, a virtue *ethics*.

We need to be clear from the outset what we mean by *virtue*. We may begin, as we may frequently begin in the Western tradition, with Aristotle. He defines virtue as 'a state of character concerned with choice...determined by reason by that principle by which the man of practical wisdom would determine it' (2009: II. 6, 1106b). Aquinas rephrases Aristotle's definition. A virtue, he argues, is a habit or a disposition ordered to an act (1962: I–II, 49, 1 and 3). As a character state or habit, virtue not only explains why a person acts this way on this occasion but also why the person can be relied on to act this way always or, at least, given human sinfulness, most of the time. Immediately, then, we can isolate two dimensions of a virtue: it is a character-state, habit, or disposition and it involves rational judgement and choice of action. Virtues involve getting things right, 'for each involves practical wisdom, which is the ability to reason correctly about practical matters' (Hursthouse 1999: 12). Without practical wisdom, no virtue is possible, which is a problem for those engaging in their first sex at a young age for, Aristotle points out, practical wisdom comes only with lived experience and early first-sexers do not yet have sufficient lived experience.

The choice of one action rather than others is made of the action that is judged appropriate and proportionate for this particular person, on this particular occasion, and for this particular right reason. Aristotle's 's virtue ethics and ours have a final goal, namely, human happiness or flourishing. Virtuous actions are means to that end, and deliberation and choice are about those means and their contribution to the end. It is, of course, because humans are rational that they can know they can choose this action or that action, this virtuous action or this vicious action. Virtue is a thoroughly rational activity and to fully understand it a theory of rationality and knowledge is required. To that we now turn.

KNOWLEDGE

To act rightly is first to know rightly. To understand rightly the process of human knowing, we espouse the theory of critical realism instantiated by Bernard Lonergan in his magisterial *Insight* (1957), because we believe that theory fully elucidates not only the process of coming to know but also the process of coming to virtue. Aristotle teaches that human beings desire to know by nature. Lonergan agrees, arguing that human knowing begins in what he calls the 'pure, detached, disinterested desire simply to know' (Lonergan 1957: 74). Human knowing is endlessly discursive, that is, it cycles and recycles through various levels of cognitive activity until knowledge and truth are reached in the judgement, deliberated on, and a choice is made for action according to the truth of the situation. It begins with attention, cycles on through perception and understanding, and culminates in the judgement of truth (Lonergan 1957: 273–4). It is in the judgement of truth and only in the judgement of truth that genuine human knowledge and truth are achieved. The achievement of knowledge and truth may be followed by choice and action and it is only at the moment of choice and action that morality enters in. Every activity prior to choice and action is inescapably pre-moral.

Perception is a critical activity in the process of coming to know. It is a person's active patterning of external objects. External objects do not simply impress themselves fully formed upon rational animals, as they impress themselves upon non-rational animals, nor do rational persons simply construct or project them. Rather, the appearances of the external world are shaped by persons' attention and in general the character lens through which they view the external object. The outside world persons encounter and attend to is not a world of naked sense data that is neutrally 'out, there, now, real' (Lonergan 1957: 251), but a world already shaped by their interpretations called perceptions. What I 'see' is a function of who I am. My character is a set of enduring states or habits that affect how I see, perceive, judge, choose, and act. It shapes my being and my action. It shapes not only all my relationships, including my sexual relationships, but shapes also the morality of those relationships. Moral character or the lack thereof is at stake in every sexual relationship, including the first sexual relationship. Again, that is a problem for early first-sexers, for character and especially virtuous character take time to develop.

VIRTUE AND CHARACTER

Words and expositions will never make anyone virtuous, for virtues are habits or stable character-states learned only by repeated performance. It is via habitual performance, endlessly and critically questioned and re-questioned in the cycle of attention, perception, understanding, judgement, and choice, that we come to learn and value the goodness of just, loving, and chaste actions. The perception of ethical relevance is the product of both the experience and the habituation of virtue. Not only are virtues learned but they are learned within particular communities; they can be *sustained* only in communities; they get their *content* from communities; and they get their *worth* only from and in communities. Persons who are role-figures first exemplify what it means to be just, loving, and chaste, and then by personal repetition of just, loving, and chaste acts, individuals establish those virtues as their own.

Virtuous role models became virtuous and morally excellent in their own way, and so too must all moral agents become virtuous and morally excellent in their own way. They must become virtuously and morally themselves, not simply clones of their role models. Yet we do learn from those whom we judge to be virtuous and moral. The virtuous role models from whom we learn virtue by imitation offer a respected account of human flourishing and a demonstration that the virtues are both means toward and constituents of that flourishing. Having learned from role models, however, we must then submit them and their character to critical attention, perception, understanding, and the judgement that these role models are indeed virtuous persons and their virtues are means to their flourishing and will be to ours *in our own ways*. Children's virtues are never really *their* virtues but the virtues of those who are their role models, which places a serious moral obligation on parents and other adults who are to introduce children to sexuality and its moral use. To be successful in this task, these adults must, first, become comfortable with their own sexuality and exercise it morally so that, second, they can openly discuss it with children and offer a model of just, loving, and chaste living that children can imitate. To be deemed virtuous and moral, however, children must develop into *their* virtue and *their* adulthood. There is a problem here again with early first-sexers, for the development of their own virtue and character takes time which they have not yet had.

It is common to assert that virtue ethics focuses on the *being* of a personal subject and that the ethics of duty or consequences focuses on the subject's *doing* or actions. That assertion is true enough but, if it is understood to mean that virtue ethics ignores *doing*, it is untrue, for we expect the virtuous person to *do* or *act* virtuously. We expect the person and character with the virtue of justice to *do* just actions; we expect the person with the virtue of chastity to *do* chaste actions; and so on for all the other virtues. Contrary, therefore, to critics who suggest that virtue ethics does not offer ethical rules or norms, it surely does offer norms. It offers prescriptive norms: do justly when justice is called for, do lovingly when love is called for, do chastely when chastity is called for, and do just, loving, and chaste actions in the right circumstances, towards the right people, and for the right reasons. It offers also prohibitive norms: do not do what is unjust or unloving or unchaste. Moral action is action that is according to some virtue, vicious action is action that is contrary to some virtue. Virtue ethics is, indeed, an ethics of being, but action always follows being. It is, in fact, as we argued above, the repeated doing of acts of justice, chastity, and so on that first instils and then reinforces habits that are virtues and the actions to which they are ordered. This repeated doing of virtuous acts takes time, and time is precisely what early first-sexers have not yet had to fashion their own character and their own virtue.

VIRTUE ETHICS FOR SEXUAL RELATIONSHIP

The search for ethical judgement in sexual activity today frequently ends with the claim that sexual activity is ethical when it is loving. We agree with Margaret Farley: 'love is the problem in ethics, not the solution' (Farley 1983: 100), and it is the problem precisely because it is devoid of content. Here we give it content. We begin with an ancient definition: 'to love is to will the good [well-being] of another' (Aquinas 1962: I–II, 28, 1). Love is essentially a personal activity, a decision to will and to seek the well-being of another person, even over my own well-being. True love, as every lover knows, is ecstatic; persons in love go out of themselves to other selves who are absolute and unique. That there are two absolutely unique and yet like selves in any loving relationship links love to the virtue of justice, 'according to which, with constant and perpetual will, someone renders to someone else his due rights' (Aquinas 1962: II–II, 58, 1). When asked what does justice, rendering to others their due rights, have to do with sex, we respond that, since sex is between two, equal persons, justice has everything to do with it.

One modern characteristic of persons is their equality with every other person. That is true in every sexual situation, including first sex. A sexual act that is just and loving wills the good of equality for, and renders all the rights flowing from equality to, both partners. Any sexual act that involves inequities, of power, status, maturity, for example, will be *ipso facto* not just and not virtuous. Flowing from the personal character of equality is the related personal character of freedom. A sexual act that is just and loving renders the rights associated with freedom to the other partner, and wills the good of freedom for both partners. That means that a loving and just sexual act will require the free consent of both partners and that any sexual act that subverts free consent is *ipso facto* not just and not virtuous. The use of power or violence against an unwilling partner will, therefore, never be just. With the modern 'discovery' that women are as free as men, free consent may be seriously interfered with, or even precluded entirely, by any sex that is marked by male domination or female subordination. The same reasoning applies to anyone of diminished capacity, the immature, the dependent, the drugged, the drunk, for example, for diminished capacity will automatically mean diminished consent—something for real men and women to consider before engaging in their first sex.

A consistently recognized goal of sex is the expression and enhancement of relationship and love; sex is a way to 'make love'. To express and enhance the relationship, however, sex must be *mutual*; it must be wanted by and freely participated in by both partners. Both Aristotle and Aquinas teach that love happens, not when I love another, but only when my love is reciprocated by the other. True love, truly willing the well-being of another, is never one-sided; there is no true love until love is mutual. That leads us to a further specification of the mutuality between lovers, namely, mutual, long-term commitment or, in common parlance, fidelity. Long-term commitment is required to give a just and loving relationship time to mature for the well-being of both the couple and their community. Lack of maturity, as in early first sex, always runs the risk of damaging a relationship and preventing growth in virtue.

James Keenan suggests that we think of virtues 'as rightly realizing the ways that we are related' (Keenan 2002: 122). We suggest we each have three sets of relationships: to ourselves, to others in general, and to some others in particular. These three sets of relationship demand and give rise to virtues for relationship. Each of us, first and necessarily, is in a relationship to our own self that may be described as 'selfish' or 'self-loving'. That selfishness, however, is not to be understood as exclusively self-centred and inward-looking but as self-attention, self-perception, self-understanding, and self-judgement leading to self-correction and greater outward-looking to the well-being of others, particularly of that particular other with whom I may be in a serious, perhaps sexual, relationship. Psychological studies suggest that one of the greatest threats to healthy human development, including sexual development, is poor self-esteem. The Western tradition, Christianized by Jesus' commandment to 'love your neighbour as yourself' (Mk. 12:28–34), has not always done an adequate job of emphasizing healthy self-esteem, because it has not always noticed that Jesus' commandment is actually *two* commandments: love the neighbour *and* love the self.

Typically, the Christian tradition has interpreted neighbour love as other-centred and self-sacrificing and self-love as self-centred and selfish. That certainly *can* be the case, and cultures that emphasize radical individualism encourage self-centred love, but self-centred love is neither the healthy self-love demanded by the gospel nor the healthy self-love that nurtures a relationship. Healthy self-love first affirms oneself as a good self, valuable and lovable, and then, in other-centred love, turns towards the other and gives this good, valuable, and lovable self to the other. Sexual love affirms the goodness and uniqueness not only of the other but also of the self, and thus creates a community of love. This is why it is so important that, to make love in sexual intercourse, the partner never be objectified, as is the case in both promiscuous and overly-early sexual encounters. Many people, unsure of themselves, seek affirmation of who they are, seek to prove their manhood or womanhood and to build self-esteem through early and casual sex but, since casual sex is not really a giving of self to the other, the search is constantly frustrated and neither self-identity nor self-esteem is ever truly established or affirmed.

CHASTITY AND STATES OF LIFE

In addition to the virtues of justice and love there is another virtue intimately associated with sexual activity, namely, the virtue of chastity. The *Catechism of the Catholic Church* provides an accepted definition. Chastity, it teaches, is

> the successful integration of sexuality within the person and thus the inner unity of man in his bodily and spiritual being. Sexuality, in which man's belonging to the bodily and biological world is expressed, becomes personal and truly human when it is integrated into the relationship of one person to another.
>
> (*Catechism of the Catholic Church* 1994: 2337)

In this description, chastity, like every other virtue, is about person and character, before it is about acts. It is about personal integrity, the integrity first of the individual sexual person and then of the self-gift of that person to another in a committed sexual relationship. In addition to acting justly, lovingly, and faithfully as already described, chaste persons, precisely because they are chaste persons, act chastely toward themselves and towards those with whom they are in particular, sexual relationships. Embedded in chastity is another virtue, a by-product of justice, namely, respect for both oneself and one's partner. In any genuine human and sexual relationship that respect needs to be mutual.

The *Catechism* goes on to state that 'People should cultivate [chastity] in a way that is suited to their *state of life....* Married people are called to live conjugal chastity; others practice chastity in continence' (*Catechism of the Catholic Church* 1994: 2349, emphasis added). Two things are notable about this statement. First, there is the linking of chastity to states of life; not all are called to practise chastity in the same way. Second, only two states of life are envisioned, the married state and the unmarried or single state; the married are to practise 'conjugal chastity' the single are to remain 'continent'. The engaged are specifically singled out and instructed to 'live chastity in continence'. The envisioning of only two states of life is true to official Western teaching from the mid-eighteenth to early twentieth centuries. It is untrue of the earlier and actual Christian and Western traditions, and manifestly untrue in the twenty-first century in which there are, at least, three states of life: the single state, the married state, and a state in between these two called cohabitation. That third state needs clarification.

MARRIAGE AND COHABITATION

Marriage has always been the societally-approved institution for a legitimate and moral, stable sexual relationship. It may have been structured polygynously or monogynously but it has always been the institution for child-rearing and caring for related others in health, sickness, and old age. It also was, and continues to be, important to both civil and religious societies as the institution for producing new members. Marriage was, therefore, and continues to be, despite individualistic aspirations to the contrary, always a public, not a private institution. Its context is inevitably a particular community in which it is located and from which the partners learn how to live their lives as spouses and parents. That is why couples must always have a licence to marry from the community, and risk community penalties if they fail either as spouses or as parents.

In its beginning in Western civilization, marriage was undertaken for the economic, political, and social benefit of family groups, but in the seventeenth and eighteenth centuries a major shift away from that community-dominated arrangement to a choice on the basis of interpersonal love took place. That choice appeared to uproot marriage from its traditional public context in community and to place it in the private context created by the couple, though a licence to marry from the community was and is still required and community penalties for failure are still in place. That apparent privatization of marriage and family has led in the twenty-first century to what many are calling a 'crisis' in both. We cannot, however, endorse this talk of crisis in marriage and family or the nostalgia for the so-called traditional family that frequently accompanies it, and this for two reasons. First, we are persuaded by family historians that the so-called crisis is nothing new: 'For thousands of years people have been proclaiming a crisis in marriage [and family] and pointing backwards to better days' (Coontz 1992: 1). Second, the so-called traditional family is not as traditional as the historically uninformed like to think (Coontz 1992).

Closely allied to early sex in the contemporary world is the phenomenon of cohabitation, the state of a man and a woman who, though not legally husband and wife, live together as husband and wife, and enjoy intimate sexual relations. The sharp increase in cohabitation is one of the most fundamental social changes in Western countries today. Over half of all first marriages in Britain are preceded by cohabitation, and studies find a similar trend in Europe, the United States, Canada, and Australia (Lawler 2002: 166–168). Not all cohabitors, however, are equal, a thesis endorsed by the most recent researchers (Teachman and Polanko 1990; Schoen 1992; Waite 2000). Those who are particularly at risk from premarital cohabitation are those who have not already decided prior to cohabitation that this is the person they want to marry. Linda Waite sums up this thesis: cohabitors 'on their way to the altar look and act like already-married couples in most ways, and those with no plans to marry look and act very different. For engaged cohabiting couples, living together is a step on the path to marriage, not a different road altogether' (Waite 2000: 18). We call those cohabitors who are already committed to marry one another, who are perhaps even engaged, *nuptial* cohabitors, and those cohabitors who are not committed to marry one another *non-nuptial* cohabitors. What we propose in what follows is proposed only for nuptial cohabitors, that is, those cohabitors who have already committed to marry one another.

Empirical research clearly shows that commitment to both the relationship and the partner is a distinctive determinant in relationship stability, whether that relationship is nuptial cohabitation or marriage. Couples with a double commitment to both the relationship and the partner do not think about possible alternatives to their partner; they are more satisfied with their life in general and their sexual life in particular; and they have no need to consider infidelity (Stanley 2005: 93–95). Recent social scientific research, as already noted, suggests that the once-common generalization that cohabitation, without distinction, is linked to subsequent marital instability is too un-nuanced to be accepted uncritically. Non-nuptial cohabitation alone is linked to an increased likelihood of divorce after marriage. We align with those researchers who demonstrate recently that not all cohabitors are alike and, to contribute to the stability of nuptial cohabitation, we suggest the restoration of a societally-approved betrothal ritual grounded in the historical practice of the Christian tradition.

BETROTHAL

The modern phenomenon of cohabitation is easily assumed to be new, but it is not. Early Christian and Western debates on the nature of marriage agreed on the bedrock: marriage is a union and a communion between a man and a woman embracing the whole of life. But how is marriage effected in these two traditions which, up to the Reformation, were identical? As early as the sixth century, Justinian's 's *Digesta* (1997: 35, 1, 15) decreed the Roman tradition: the mutual consent of both parties makes marriage. The northern European custom was different; there vaginal penetration and intra-vaginal ejaculation makes marriage. This different approach to what makes valid marriage provoked a widespread legal debate in medieval Europe that was ended in the mid-twelfth century by Gratian, Master of the University of Bologna, who proposed a compromise solution. Consent, he argued, *initiates* a marriage and subsequent sexual intercourse *consummates* it. Gratian's compromise ended the debate over what makes marriage and it continues to be enshrined in Western law codes.

Consent, however, could be given in either the future tense ('I will thee wed') or the present tense ('I thee wed'). When it was given in the future tense, the outcome was called betrothal, and the process from cause (consent) to effect (betrothal) was known as *sponsalia* or spousals; that is, the couple became spouses. When consent was given in the present tense, the result was called marriage, and the process from cause (consent) to effect (marriage) was known as *nuptialia* or nuptials; that is, the couple became wedded. The first sexual intercourse between the spouses usually followed the betrothal, and this is a fact of both the Christian and Western traditions that has been obscured by the modern sequence of wedding, marriage, sexual intercourse, and possible fertility.

This 'marital' situation has been well documented. Jean Rémy describes the situation in France: 'In the sixteenth century the engagement or betrothal carried great weight. If the Church frowned on the unblessed marriage she did not forbid it. Very often, above all in the country, the Church marriage took place when the woman was pregnant, sometimes towards the end of her pregnancy' (Rémy 1979: 9). Lawrence

Stone describes the situation in England: 'The formal betrothal ceremony seems to have been at least as important, if not more so, than the wedding. To many, the couple were from that moment man and wife before God' (Stone 1979: 626). Alan Macfarlane emphasizes that 'the engaged lovers before the nuptials were held to be legally husband and wife. It was common for them to begin living together immediately after the betrothal ceremony' (Macfarlane 1987: 291). The betrothal, he adds, 'was in effect the legally binding act; it was, combined with consummation, the marriage (Macfarlane 1987: 309). Later, a celebration of the marriage, an occasion for relatives and friends to bring gifts and to feast (hence the wedding cake), was held but, up to the sixteenth-century the Council of Trent in the Catholic tradition and up to the mid-eighteenth-century the Hardwicke Act in England, the central event of the *sponsalia* or betrothal was held separately from the ceremonial event of the *nuptialia* or wedding. After the betrothal, the couple were considered husband and wife and, therefore, their sexual intercourse was held to be moral and virtuous. This meant, of course, that there was little of what we call pre-marital sex. 'Most of the acts seen as such by Church and State were interpreted by the village [again the community] as activities within marriage—a marriage begun with the promise and irreversibly confirmed by pregnancy' (Quaife 1979: 61).

The parallel between the pre-Tridentine, pre-modern, and modern practices is striking. Pre-modern betrothal led to full sexual relations and pregnancy which, in turn, led to indissoluble marriage; modern nuptial cohabitation leads to full sexual relations and, in turn, to indissoluble marriage, with or without pregnancy. 'The full sexual experience practiced by betrothed couples [in pre-Tridentine and pre-modern times] was...*emphatically premised by the intention to marry*' (Thatcher 1999: 119, emphasis original); so too is contemporary nuptial cohabitation. It is this commitment to marry one's cohabiting partner that establishes nuptial cohabitation as a third state of life between the single and the married states and as a modern analogue to the medieval betrothed state. As a clearly-defined state of life, it calls for the practice of chastity appropriate to it, the same chastity as that required of married couples which, through betrothal, nuptial cohabitors have inchoately become.

A Proposal

We offer here a straightforward proposal; a return to the marital sequence of community-sanctioned-and-guaranteed betrothal, sexual intercourse, possible fertility, ceremonial wedding to acknowledge and to mark the consummation of valid marriage. This period of betrothal would include a community-based sexuality, relationship, and ethical education as proposed throughout this chapter. What we propose is an adaptation of marriage to a diverse cultural situation. It is time, we suggest, to abandon the received model of becoming married as synonymous with becoming wedded, of marriage taking place at a moment in time, the moment of mutually given public consent, and to replace it with a developmental model, in which marriage takes place in stages, in *petits pas* as Jean-Claude Kaufman (1993: 44) describes it. The received Western model of marriage is now being shown to be incapable of responding for all to the developmental nature of sexuality, love, and marriage in new, post-modern cultural conditions. A real, if inchoate, marriage, we suggest, exists from the moment of the private or public commitment to marry, and a consummated and indissoluble marriage exists when the couple have fully expressed in their marital life the marital virtues and values of their culture. Above all, and we repeat this again to avoid any misunderstanding, we judge as moral first and every sexual intercourse between unmarried couples only between couples who have seriously committed themselves, privately or publicly, to marry one another; that is, to those couples who are in what we have called nuptial cohabitation.

A stumbling block to granting moral legitimacy to this suggestion in the Western, Christian tradition is the exclusive connection this tradition has established between marriage, sexual intercourse, and procreation. That tradition is well expressed by the Vatican's Congregation for the Doctrine of the Faith: 'every genital act must be within the framework of marriage' (1975: n.7). That teaching certainly appears to be a major stumbling block to our claim that *some* 'pre-marital' sexual activity is morally legitimate. There can be no way forward until the traditional and exclusive connection between sexual activity and marriage, which is, in fact, the exclusive connection between sexual activity and procreation, is severed. To get really honest about sexuality and sexual activity in the modern world, the exclusive connection between sexual intercourse and procreation has to be abandoned (Gudorf 1994: 29–50).

Reason based on inductive experience shows that all that is expected and desired from a just, loving, chaste, and mutually faithful relationship is best delivered in a stable relationship. Sexual intercourse so radically involves all the potentials of a person that it is best expressed and safeguarded in a stable, faithful relationship between two people. What has happened in the modern age is that, for nuptial cohabitors, that stable relationship is initiated by their mutual consent, articulated not in a wedding ceremony but in their genuine commitment to one another. Though they may not yet have articulated that commitment in public, communal, and legal ritual, they have expressed it to one another in their decision to marry when the psychological and, especially today, the economic restrictions modern society puts upon their right to marry, are removed. Their nuptial, perhaps their engaged or betrothed, cohabitation is their first 'little step' in their journey toward marriage (Bressoud 1998). In the legal words of the received tradition, their consent to marry *initiates* their marriage; their first sexual intercourse *consummates* their marriage; and their subsequent ceremonial wedding *ratifies* their marriage and makes it indissoluble. Since their betrothal however expressed—and we prefer that it be expressed in a public ritual (Lawler: 2007)—initiates their marriage, their cohabitation is not premarital. Their cohabitation and intercourse are certainly pre-ceremonial (though that could be easily remedied by the introduction of a public betrothal ceremony) but they are far from pre-marital.

A major change in the approach of modern ethicists to sexual actions parallels the change in the approach to marriage we propose. The majority of ethicists have agreed for years that decisions about virtue or vice, morality or immorality, in sexual ethics should be based on *interpersonal relationship* and not simply on *physical sexual acts* (Curran 1993: 411–414; Gudorf 1993: 411–414, 1994: 14–18). Lisa Sowle Cahill states that approach succinctly: 'A truly humane interpretation of procreation, pleasure and intimacy will set their moral implications in the context of enduring personal relationships, not merely individual sexual acts' (Cahill 1996: 112). Serious vice or immorality, what the religions call serious sin, is not decided on the basis of individual sexual acts but on the basis of human goods and human relationship built upon them. Cahill suggests such human goods as 'equality, intimacy, and fulfillment as moral criteria'. We add the virtues of love, justice, and chastity to make more fully explicit what she clearly intends. Immoral sexual behaviour is defined not by any sexual act but by anything less than a just, loving, chaste, and mutually fulfilling act.

In the case of nuptial cohabitors, whose pre-wedding but nuptial sexual intercourse takes place in a context of commitment to their relationship, to one another, and to a future marriage, the moral theological argument proceeds along these lines. A man and a woman have a fundamental freedom to marry. Modern society has established socio-economic conditions for marriage which the couple is presently unable to fulfil. That their intercourse under these conditions is not a moral evil would appear to be true especially, Philip Keane argues, 'when the committed couple whose rights are unreasonably prejudiced by society do not experience themselves as genuinely free to take the more ideal route of abstaining from that intercourse that cannot be publicly proclaimed as part of a marriage' (Keane 1977: 107). We accept the probative value of this argument with one addition. In the proposal we present, the mutually committed nuptial cohabiting couple are already, if inchoately, married, and their intercourse, therefore, is not premarital but inchoately marital. Our proposal envisages a marriage that happens not in an instant at a wedding ceremony but in a step-by-step process that is initiated by mutual commitment and consent, is lived in mutual love, justice, chastity, and fulfilment in a nuptial cohabitation progressing to a wedding (see Ntakarutimana 1996; Legrain 1996, 2009). In such a marital process, we believe, sexual intercourse meets the legitimate moral requirement that any sexual activity, including a first, ought to take place within a stable marital relationship.

References

Aquinas, Thomas (1962). *Summa Theologiae Sanctae Thomae de Aquino*. Roma: Editiones Paulinae.
Aristotle (2009). *Nicomachean Ethics*. Trans. David Ross. Oxford: Oxford University Press.
Augustine (1844). *De Bono Coniugali*. In J. P. Migne (ed.), *Patrologiae Cursus Completus: Series Latina*, vol. 40. Ann Arbor, MI: University of Michigan Press
Bressoud, Pierre-Olivier (1998). *Église et couple à petits pas. Vers une réévaluation théologique des formes de cohabitation contemporaine*. Fribourg: Editions Universitaires.

Brundage, James A. (1987). *Law, Sex, and Christian Society in Medieval Europe*. Chicago: University of Chicago Press.

Cahill, Lisa Sowle (1996). *Sex, Gender and Christian Ethics*. New York: Cambridge University Press.

Catechism of the Catholic Church (1994). Mahwah, NJ: Paulist Press.

Chrysostom, John (1912). *De Virginitate*. In J. P. Migne (ed.), *Patrologiae Cursus Completus: Series Graeca* 48. Ann Arbor, MI: University of Michigan Press.

Congregation for the Doctrine of the Faith (1975). *Persona Humana. Acta Apostolicae Sedis* 68: 77–96. Roma: Typis Polyglottis Vaticanis.

Coontz, Stephanie (1992). *The Way We Never Were: American Families and the Nostalgia Trap*. New York: Basic Books.

Curran, Charles E. (1993). 'Sexuality and Sin: A Current Appraisal'. In Charles E. Curran and Richard A. McCormick (eds), *Moral Theology No. 8: Dialogue about Catholic Sexual Teaching*. New York: Paulist Press.

Farley, Margaret (1983). 'An Ethic for Same-Sex Relations'. In Robert Nugent (ed.), *A Challenge to Love: Gay and Lesbian Catholics in the Church*. New York: Crossroad.

Gudorf, Christine E. (1994). *Body, Sex, and Pleasure: Reconstructing Christian Sexual Ethics*. Cleveland: Pilgrim Press.

Hursthouse, Rosalind (1999). *On Virtue Ethics*. Oxford: Oxford University Press.

John Paul II (1982). *Familiaris Consortio. Acta Apostolicae Sedis* 74: 81–191. Roma: Typis Polyglottis Vaticanis.

Justinian Augustus (1997). *Digesta*, ed. Alan Watson. College Park, PA: University of Pennsylvania Press.

Kaufmann, Jean-Claude (1993). *Sociologie du couple*. Paris: Presses Universitaires de France.

Keane, Philip (1977). *Sexual Morality: A Catholic Perspective*. New York: Paulist Press.

Keenan, James, F. (2002). 'Justice and Social Justice'. In Daniel Harrington and James F. Keenan (eds), *Jesus and Virtue Ethics: Building Bridges between New Testament Studies and Moral Theology*. Lanham, MD: Sheed and Ward.

Lawler, Michael G. (2002). *Marriage and the Catholic Church: Disputed Questions*. Collegeville, MN: Liturgical Press.

Lawler, Michael G. (2007). 'A Marital Catechumenate: A Proposal'. *INTAMS Review* 13(2): 161–177.

Legrain, Michel (2009). *L'Eglise catholique et le marriage en Occident et en Afrique*, 3 vols. Paris: L'Harmattan.

Lonergan, Bernard, J. F. (1957). *Insight: A Study of Human Understanding*. London: Longmans.

Macfarlane, Alan (1987). *Marriage and Love in England: Modes of Reproduction 1300–1840*. Oxford: Blackwell.

MacIntyre, Alasdair (1981). *After Virtue: A Study in Moral Theory*. Notre Dame: University of Notre Dame Press.

Ntakarutimana, Emmanuel (1996). 'Being a Child in Central Africa Today'. In *Concilium* 2: 118–125.

Quaife, G. R. (1979). *Wanton Wives and Wayward Wenches: Peasants and Illicit Sex in Early Seventeenth Century England*. London: Croom Helm.

Rémy, Jean (1979). 'The Family: Contemporary Models and Historical Perspective'. In Andrew Greeley (ed.), *The Family in Crisis or Transition. Concilium* 121: 3–14.

Schoen, Robert (1992). 'First Unions and the Stability of First Marriages'. *Journal of Marriage and the Family* 54, 281–284.

Stanley, Scott M. (2005). *The Power of Commitment: A Guide to Active, Life-long Love*. San Francisco: Jossey-Bass.

Stone, Lawrence (1979). *The Family, Sex, and Marriage in England: 1500–1800*. London: Weidenfeld and Nicolson.

Stratman, Daniel (1997). 'Introduction to Virtue Ethics'. In Daniel Stratman (ed.), *Virtue Ethics: A Critical Reader*. Georgetown: Georgetown University Press.

Teachman, Jay D., and Karen A. Polanko (1990). 'Cohabitation and Marital Stability in the United States'. *Social Forces* 69: 207–220.

Tertullian (1844). *Ad Uxorem*. In J. P. Migne (ed.), *Patrologiae Cursus Completus: Series Latina*, 1. Ann Arbor, MI: University of Michigan Press

Thatcher, Adrian 1999. *Marriage after Modernity: Christian Marriage in Postmodern Times*. Sheffield: Sheffield Academic Press.

Waite, Linda J. (2000). 'Cohabitation: A Communitarian Perspective'. In Martin King Whyte (ed.), *Marriage in America: A Communitarian Perspective*. Lanham, MD: Rowman and Littlefield.

CHAPTER 34

....

WIVES AND HUSBANDS

....

THOMAS KNIEPS-PORT LE ROI

CONTEXT

....

Deinstitutionalization

LEGALLY regulated, ritually solemnized, and publicly recognized, the marital union of wives and husbands was for the longest time and for the majority of people in Western civilization the norm and was the only socially accepted way to have a sexual relationship and raise children. Along with this dominant position, marriage also offered a set of fixed social rules that governed the individual's behaviour within it. Although subject to long-term social, economic, and cultural transformations, the marital institution seemed resilient enough to cope with changing contexts and to adjust the social norms it offered to couples accordingly.

In the 1960s and 1970s, however, an accelerated process of disintegration set in, resulting in a scenario without precedence in previous history: increasing divorce rates, a delayed entry into marriage, a rise of cohabitation as a prelude or alternative to marriage, an increase of children being born outside marriage, and a general decline of people projected to ever marry. While some observers speculated that '[f]or perhaps the first time in human history, marriage as an ideal is under a sustained and surprisingly successful attack' (Waite and Gallagher 2000: 1), others bluntly diagnosed and complained of its 'decline' (Popenoe et al. 1996). What could be said with more certainty was that marriage was undergoing a process of 'deinstitutionalization'. By this, social theorists mean that the social norms that define people's behaviour in an institution such as marriage are not just shifting but, more fundamentally, weakening, even to the point of decomposing. US family sociologist Andrew Cherlin (2004: 848) explains:

> In times of social stability, the taken-for-granted nature of norms allows people to go about their lives without having to question their actions or the actions of others. But when social change produces situations outside the reach of established norms,

individuals can no longer rely on shared understandings of how to act. Rather, they must negotiate new ways of acting, a process that is a potential source of conflict and opportunity.

Cherlin describes what has happened to marriage in the twentieth century as the result of two major transformations. The first one is the transition from 'institutional marriage' to 'companionate marriage'. In the single-earner, breadwinner-homemaker family of the first half of the century, husbands and wives still followed a strict script of social roles regulated by a clear division of labour along gender lines. What bound them together, however, was no longer social obligation alone but a shared feeling of companionship that developed on the inside of the marital relationship. Spouses were supposed to be each other's friends, companions, and lovers and thus bring to their union a sense of self-expression and emotional satisfaction that was unimagined by couples in the institutional marriages of the previous era.

This companionate model proved extremely attractive and successful, reaching its zenith in the 1950s with a sharp increase in marriage and childbearing. For the last time, marriage offered a majority of people the default entry into adult and family life. But the recipe for its short success turned out to be its major shortcoming in the long run. The fact that spouses drew their personal gratification and emotional satisfaction from the fulfilment of predetermined marital roles, became increasingly unacceptable for following generations. The second transition took issue with such remaining institutional features and marked the ascendance of a new model. From the 1960s and 1970s on,

> [w]hen people evaluated how satisfied they were with their marriages, they began to think more in terms of the development of their own sense of self and the expression of their feelings, as opposed to the satisfaction they gained through building a family and playing the roles of spouse and parent. The result was a transition from the companionate marriage to what we might call the *individualized marriage*.

> (Cherlin 2004: 852)

According to Cherlin, this second transition was mainly due to the rise of an 'expressive individualism' in American culture. But also on the other side of the Atlantic the growing individualization of personal life conjured up a 'new sentimental order' (Bawin-Legros 2003) which has put institutional marriage under considerable strain.

New Sentimental Order

The idea of marrying for love originated in the late eighteenth century and was widely taken for granted by the end of the twentieth century. The same values, however, that increased people's satisfaction with marriage as a relationship started to undermine the stability of marriage as an institution. As historian Stephanie Coontz points out, '[m]arriage has become more joyful, more loving, and more satisfying for many couples than ever before in history. At the same time it has become optional and more brittle. These two strands of change cannot be disentangled' (2005: 306).

Social theorists of late modernity have analysed how the quest for satisfying intimate relationships collides with the expanding role of personal choice and puts the marital project of an enduring relationship at risk. Anthony Giddens (1992) observes that the romantic love model, which acclaimed relationship permanence ('till death do us part'), has been replaced by what he calls 'confluent love'. What counts in confluent love is the 'special relationship' that is continuously searched for rather than the quality of a 'special person'. The confluent love model features the ideal of the 'pure relationship', one that 'is entered into for its own sake, for what can be derived by each person from a sustained association with another; and which is continued only in so far as it is thought by both parties to deliver enough satisfactions for each individual to stay within it' (1992: 58). Partners in a pure relationship establish trust through intimacy, mutual respect, and intense communication, but driven by a pattern of reflexive autonomy and self-actualization they also allow for the permanent possibility of break-up.

Such internal ambivalences of an era 'which has fallen in love with love' are also explored by Beck and Beck-Gernsheim (1995). One of the paradoxes they see is that '[i]ndividualization may drive men and women apart, but . . . it also pushes them back into one another's arms. *As traditions become diluted, the attractions of a close relationship grow.* Everything that one has lost, is sought in the other' (1995: 32, emphasis original). As a consequence, love becomes a substitute for religion, a secular religion and private sanctuary which 'we are hardly aware of because we ourselves are its temples and our wishes are our prayers' (1995: 177). '[H]idden behind the hope that we can compensate for our mistakes and shortcomings by lavishing love on the beloved is the belief that love is an act of confession and often a gesture against a heartless society' (1995: 179–180). That supreme belief in love remains intact even in the face of the collateral damage it may cause. Worshipping love does not only produce disproportionate expectations vis-à-vis one's partner or spouse, it also allows or forces one to break with partner or family in order not to betray one's personal search for true love. In that sense (1995: 174),

> [a]bandoning one's own children for someone else is not a breach of love but a proof of it. This illustrates the extraordinary power love already exerts over us as well as the contradictions of trying to live up to this ideal while coping with the mundane routine of daily life.

For Zygmunt Bauman (2003) intimate relationships in today's consumerist society even have something absurd about them as the measure of their success is indeed the possibility of their failure. '[H]uman attention tends nowadays to be focused on the satisfaction that relationships are hoped to bring precisely because somehow they have not been found fully and truly satisfactory; and if they do satisfy, the price of the satisfaction they bring has often been found to be excessive and unacceptable' (2003: p. xi). They constantly 'vacillate between a sweet dream and a nightmare, and there is no telling when one turns into the other' (2003: p. viii).

Symbolic Meaning

If contemporary men and women are 'so desperate to 'relate'; and yet wary of the state of 'being related' and particularly of being related 'for good', not to mention forever' (Bauman 2003: p. viii), marriage has understandably lost its stability—but, as Beck and Beck-Gernsheim already predicted in 1995, 'none of its attractiveness' (1995: 172). The interesting question may therefore no longer be 'why so few people are marrying, but rather, why so *many* people are marrying, or planning to marry, or hoping to marry, when cohabitation and single parenthood are widely acceptable options' (Cherlin 2004: 854). As Cherlin shows for the US context, there can be no doubt that marriage is no longer as dominant as it once was, and it is most unlikely that it will regain its former position. Still, it has a chance of retaining a distinctive value amidst alternative forms of partnership and family life, as people may continue to value its 'symbolic meaning' (2004: 855):

> What has happened is that although the practical importance of being married has declined, its symbolic importance has remained high, and may even have increased…It has evolved from a marker of conformity to a marker of prestige. Marriage is a status one builds up to, often by living with a partner beforehand, by attaining steady employment or starting a career, by putting away some savings, and even by having children. Marriage's place in the life course used to come before those investments were made, but now it often comes afterward. It used to be the foundation of adult personal life; now it is sometimes the capstone. It is something to be achieved through one's own efforts rather than something to which one routinely accedes.

Whatever the future of marriage will be in Western societies, Cherlin's informed guess provides a valuable perspective for researchers who have come to realize that in times of deinstitutionalization close relationships still undergo 'processes of institutionalization', however individualized such trajectories may be and whether or not they are conducive to marriage (Kopp et al. 2010).

CHURCH TEACHING AND THEOLOGY

Denominational Perspectives

The Christian churches in the West have been affected by the deinstitutionalizing and individualizing trends of (late) modernity in equal measure (Thatcher 1999). Variances in their respective theological visions and legal practices of marriage, though, have made them face these developments in different ways. John Witte has shown that all Western denominational traditions 'have recognized multiple perspectives on marriage but gave priority to one perspective in order to achieve an integrated understanding' (1997: 2). Witte refers to four perspectives in particular. The first one is a *naturalistic* perspective which regards marriage as an institution given in creation (Gen. 1:1, 27–28; 2:24), ordered towards procreation, and subject to natural laws. Permanently 'hovering in the background', the naturalistic argument adumbrated for the first time in Augustine is perfected by Thomas Aquinas in the thirteenth century, remains largely uncontested in the theology of the Reformation, and holds, up to the Second Vatican Council, a central position in Roman Catholic teaching. A second, *social* perspective deals with marriage as 'a social estate, subject to the expectations and exactions of the local community and to special state laws of contract, property, and inheritance' (Witte 1997: 2). This perspective is strongly emphasized by the Protestant tradition. With their rejection of the sacramental character of marriage and its subordination to celibacy, Martin Luther and his colleagues taught that, although divinely ordained, marriage was a 'worldly undertaking', part of the earthly kingdom of creation, and therefore subject not to the Church but to the civil authorities.

Still from another perspective, marriage is dealt with as a voluntary association formed by the mutual agreement of the spouses. The Latin Church took this *contractual* understanding over from ancient Roman law and from the twelfth century forward built upon it the canonical marriage law which remained predominant in the West. With the period of the Enlightenment the contractarian model of marriage experienced a new heyday—this time, however, dissociated from any rules preset by God, nature, or Church. The terms of the marital bargain were left to the contracting parties themselves: 'Couples should now be able to make their own marital beds, and lie in them or leave them as they saw fit' (Witte 1997: 10). Much of today's secular understanding of marriage has become grounded on such a private contractual model and the attendant idea of consensual intimate relationships.

A fourth perspective is the *religious* one, which according to Witte is characteristic of the Roman Catholic understanding of marriage 'as a spiritual or sacramental association, subject to the creed, cult, and canons of the church community' (1997: 2). '[R]aised by Christ the Lord to the dignity of a sacrament between the baptized' (*Code of Canon Law* 1983: can. 1055 §1), marriage, when validly contracted and consummated, symbolizes the union between Christ and His Church (Eph. 5:21–33) and confers sanctifying grace to the couple. This sacramental perspective renders marriage a central concern of the Church's doctrine, morality, and discipline and thus accounts for the fact that over the past decades the Roman Catholic Church, more than the Protestant Churches, has made considerable efforts to defend and refine its teaching and practice in the face of a prevailing secular mentality and its decomposing effects on the marital institution as such.

Intimate Partnership of Married Life and Love

The Second Vatican Council (1962–1965) marks a major shift in the Roman Catholic teaching on marriage. In its Pastoral Constitution on the Church in the Modern World,

Gaudium et spes, the council speaks of the marital union in terms unheard of in previous church teaching:

> The biblical Word of God several times urges the betrothed and the married to nour-ish and develop their wedlock by pure conjugal love and undivided affection...This love is an eminently human one since it is directed from one person to another through an affection of the will; it involves the good of the whole person, and there-fore can enrich the expressions of body and mind with a unique dignity, ennobling these expressions as special ingredients and signs of the friendship distinctive of marriage. This love God has judged worthy of special gifts, healing, perfecting and exalting gifts of grace and of charity. Such love, merging the human with the divine, leads the spouses to a free and mutual gift of themselves, a gift providing itself by gen-tle affection and by deed, such love pervades the whole of their lives.
>
> (Second Vatican Council 1965: para. 49)

The idea of conjugal love had been absent from previous teaching. Resuming a long-standing tradition of canonical legislation and theological argument, the 1917 Code of Canon Law had defined marriage as a 'contract' by which spouses exchange the right over one another's bodies in view of acts 'apt for procreation' (*The 1917 or Pio-Benedictine Code of Canon Law* 2001: can. 1012 §1, 1013 §1, 1081 §2). Marriage was seen here as an impersonal estate, instituted by divine creation and endowed by nature with specific ends, which the spouses enter into by mutual consent. Friendship and love or, as scholastic theologians had rendered it at the time, 'mutual help' (*mutuum adiuto-rium*) between wife and husband were regarded as a welcome side effect, of the order of a 'secondary end', but in no way essential to the marital union and its intrinsic obligations.

At Vatican II the council fathers break with this tradition and seek to 'describe mar-riage as it is lived, and urge how it ought to be lived, by men and women in the second half of the twentieth century' (Mackin 1982: 267). They insist that marriage has its greatest value not in some goal outside itself such as the continuation of the human race. Its pri-mary meaning and value is in the sharing of the whole of life, in what they call the 'inti-mate partnership of married life and love' (Second Vatican Council 1965: para. 48). As such, it may have 'various benefits and purposes'—the conciliar text mentions the tradi-tional 'good of offspring' (*bonum prolis*) and the good of society, and juxtaposes to them the 'good of the spouses' (*bonum coniugum*)—but all of them originally spring from the communion of conjugal love and are in no way hierarchically subordinated to each other.

The council thus initiates a shift in the Catholic reflection on marriage from an insti-tutional and legal to a person-centred and relational approach. Post-conciliar theology generally acclaims this move but differs in how it has to be interpreted.

Truly Human Love, Nuptial Imagery, and Alternative Practices

A 'revisionist' majority of theologians and ethicists welcomes as the most important development in the theology of marriage that 'the council declared the mutual love of the spouses and their passionate desire to be best friends for life to be of the very essence of marriage' (Lawler 2002: 36). They maintain that the previous model of marriage as a *procreative institution* has been replaced by the model of *interpersonal union* in which 'the emphasis is no longer exclusively on procreation but squarely on the marital union of the spouses' (2002: p. ix). This is underscored by a significant shift in wording since the council departed from calling marriage a legal contract and chose instead to describe it as 'covenant', a biblical term which is 'saturated with overtones of mutual personal and steadfast love' (2002: 36). If lived as Christian marriage, such loving interpersonal union is 'a grace-full way to God, an opportunity to raise in the contemporary world a model, a light, a veritable sacrament, of the steadfastly loving union between God and God's people and between Christ and Christ's Church' (2002: 39). This position puts the reality of the relationship far before any institutional framework for marriage.

In their sexual ethics approach, these scholars develop the 'criterion of the human person adequately considered' into a foundational principle from which human sexuality and marriage have to be judged (Salzman and Lawler 2008: 124). According to Kevin T. Kelly, '[e]ven such a fundamental human institution as marriage does not have any free-standing independent moral criterion of its own. It can only be properly understood and evaluated with reference to that one all-embracing criterion of the good of the human person, integrally and adequately considered' (Kelly 1998: 140). An adequate and integral understanding, however, has to consider the human person primarily in and according to changing historical and sociocultural contexts. If then, for example, women are experiencing marriage as oppressive, a theological critique of that form of marriage is imperative. These authors do not question the goodness and value of marriage but they claim that the starting point for a reflection on marital and sexual morality must not be marriage, but rather the quality of the relationship lived in it, which ought to be of a truly human and justly loving kind.

A 'traditionalist' position, which draws its inspiration mainly from the writing and teaching of the late Pope John Paul II, insists instead that the human person has to be seen as part of a timeless natural order and that marriage occupies a central place in a design in which all humans are called to participate. When John Paul II refers to 'God's original plan of marriage and the family' (1981), he does not primarily have in mind some outward prescriptions of how marriage ought to be lived but a divine script that is impressed on the human person's body. In his 'theology of the body' the human body bears the mark of the self-giving love which is at the origin of the mystery of creation and which humans recognize in their being created as male and female and have to live in accordance with in their sexuality. The '*spousal meaning of the body*' consists in that

> [t]he body, which expresses femininity 'for' masculinity and, vice versa, masculinity 'for' femininity, manifests the reciprocity and the communion of persons. It expresses it through gift as the fundamental characteristic of personal existence…Masculinity-femininity—namely, sex—is the original sign of a creative donation and at the same time 'the sign of a gift' that man, male-female, becomes aware of as a gift lived so to speak in an original way.

> (John Paul II 2006: 183)

This spousal meaning translates into a specific 'language of the body', the grammar of which humans ought not to distort in their sexual behaviour. Essentially, it includes—next to the claim that intimate relations can legitimately be maintained only between heterosexual partners—that sexual intercourse can only take place within an exclusive, faithful, and lifelong marital relationship because the 'total physical self-giving would be a lie if it were not the sign and fruit of a total personal self-giving, in which the whole person, including the temporal dimension, is present' (1981: para. 11); and that each marital act must be open to procreation and may not be 'overlaid, through contraception, by an objectively contradictory language, namely, that of not giving oneself totally to the other' (1981: para. 32). Marriage comes into the frame here not just as a moral requirement or institutional safeguard for sexual relationships but rather as a theologico-anthropological key concept from which sexual difference, love, and fertility have to be understood in their interconnectedness. Proponents of that vision have even further developed the idea that the concrete experience of the spousal relationship between husband and wife is the constitutive core of the 'nuptial mystery' which is 'the key for understanding ... the salient aspects, the dogma, of our faith' as it lies at the basis of the mysteries of the relationship between Christ and the Church, of the event of Christ, and finally of the Trinity itself (Scola 2005: 97–98).

More recently, a new generation of scholars has taken issue with the two strands prevalent in post-conciliar discussion about marriage. Classifying them both as variants of the standard Catholic personalist framework, they accuse the traditionalists of an abstract and idealistic description of the spousal relationship and criticize the revisionists for their narrow focus on private interiority. What they claim instead is an approach that pays attention to the experiences and practices of today's couples and is thus more sensitive to the complexities of contemporary contexts; places marriage within larger accounts of the Christian life as a whole; and brings the counter-cultural potential of the Christian tradition to bear on destructive practices in the current culture (Cloutier 2010).

Florence C. Bourg, for instance, finds much of the theological parlance about conjugal love modelling the reciprocal love between Christ and the Church highly unrealistic. It 'sounds more like the perfect communion within the triune Godhead' while the usual love relationship 'is decidedly less reciprocal' and mirrors the 'earthly, painful, dying-and-rising, hopeful love celebrated at Easter' (Bourg 2004: 79–80). But her advocacy of 'ordinary and imperfect' (spousal and family) relationships also includes a critique of the prevailing romantic model of marriage and family life. In a cultural context 'where privacy and choice are celebrated almost as ends in themselves', the romantic model 'can be interpreted to permit opting out of obligations toward persons with unforeseen special needs, or who change in ways that we do not choose— especially in ways that affect their ability to provide us affirmation and emotional companionship'. Only here is the theological imagery of God's covenantal love in its place, since 'covenant love doesn't disappear simply because one party "isn't having fun anymore" ' (2004: 91).

In a similar vein, Julie H. Rubio insists that the Catholic vision of marriage is in sharp contrast to the popular model of lifelong romance and of the marital dyad. Marriage is not simply or even primarily a personal relationship. 'Speaking of marriage as a relationship says too little about the kind of marriages to which Christians are called' (Rubio 2003: 83). Instead, marriage

> crystallizes the love of the larger church community. The couple is not just two-in-one, but two together within the whole, with specific responsibilities for the whole. They must be strong, because the community needs their strength. They must persevere in love, because the community needs to see God's love actualized among God's people, and this is precisely what people see when they know an outward-focused loving couple. (2003: 38)

David Matzko McCarthy blames modern theologians' interpersonal account of conjugal love for its 'theological romanticism about marriage' (2004: 64). Dyadic love and the commitment to pure relationship, however, fall prey to the market ethos of modern life, as they 'are defined by their ability to regenerate desire, so that the enemy of love is considered to be the practical matters of life that bring a domestication or settling of desire' (2004: 244). The grammar of romantic love conflicts with the 'grammar of belonging' and that is why '[g]reat lovers do not necessarily make for good housekeeping' and '[l]ove and passion die once partners settle in at home' (2004: 64). McCarthy challenges the standard theological view that the conjugal union establishes and sustains the household. '[M]arriage does not set a couple apart in order to begin a family, but puts a husband and wife in the middle of a larger network of preferential loves' (2004: 246). By placing marriage within this larger context of family, friends, and neighbourhood, McCarthy returns to an essentially pre-modern understanding in which kin and social relationships are the foundation of marriage and not the other way around. Forty years after Vatican II marriage is proposed here as an institutional practice—of received roles and duties, of lifelong fidelity and generativity—that defies mainstream cultural trends and much of modern theological thinking.

PERSPECTIVES

Why Marry at All?

Is there any substantial reason to commend marriage over the other forms of living together that have widely been accepted as alternatives in late modern society? Previous generations of theologians could afford to speculate in rather abstract terms about the goods and benefits of marriage since there was little need to persuade people of its advantages. When Augustine set off to counter the Manichaeans' condemnation of procreation he found in marriage a welcome excuse and a way to minimize the risk of succumbing to the almost inevitable sinfulness of sexual intercourse. Over time, the Church pushed aside the idea of the 'relative' goodness of marriage that undergirded Augustine's conception, coming to regard the threefold goods of offspring, fidelity, and indissolubility as simple blessings. Thomas Aquinas did not have to be convinced that marriage was a natural institution and therefore good in itself. Elaborating on the Augustinian *bona*, he laid the groundwork for the idea of the ends or purposes (*fines*) of marriage, thus showing how well and intelligently nature and its heavenly creator had provided for a union in which man and woman assist each other and make use of their sexuality for the overarching purpose of perpetuating the human race through procreation.

Today some still believe that marriage with 'its orientation to the bearing and rearing of children' and 'its distinctive structure, including norms of monogamy and fidelity' (Girgis et al. 2010: 246) does not need any positive endorsement, since it is the natural and thus only legitimate framework for human pair bonds which 'make little sense, and uniquely answer to no human need, apart from reproductive-type union' (2010: 287). Whether grounded on 'common human reason' (2010: 247) or additionally undergirded by theological arguments (Grisez 1993: 633–680), this normative discourse is more intended to convince same-sex couples why they are not entitled to marry than to persuade heterosexual partners why they ought to. The latter, however, is what social scientists have in mind when they conclude, on the basis of empirical evidence, that '[m]arriage is an important social good, associated with an impressively broad array of positive outcomes for children and adults alike' (*Why Marriage Matters* 2002: 6).

Theologians like Don Browning have quickly realized that, notwithstanding its overall plausibility, this discourse is tributary both to a utilitarian perspective and to the use of therapeutic language, making it prone to the late-modern individualistic search for personal gratification that it needs to combat. They have therefore urged that, for a successful promotion of marriage, a moral and religious underpinning is also needed (Browning 2003). Browning is certainly right to claim that Christianity (along with other religious traditions) 'must retrieve their marriage and family traditions' and 'must do so critically' (Browning et al. 1997: 307), but one may wonder whether his own vision of marriage relies more on what sociologists and politicians suppose to be good and egalitarian spousal relationships, than on what the Christian tradition really has to offer.

Many contemporary theologians are in any case more reluctant when it comes to promoting marriage. Margaret A. Farley acknowledges that '[f]or the sake of love and the ones we love, we commit ourselves to institutional frameworks that will hold us faithful to our love', but such frameworks, of which marriage is the most common one, 'ought to be subject to norms of justice. If they are not, we challenge them or forsake them, or we shrivel up within them' (2006: 260). Jana M. Bennett even thinks that 'there is a cultural frenzy regarding marriage' and that many theologians' 'focus on marriage is misplaced and problematic' (2008: 3 and 4). While developing a theology of God's household which is both reflected and realized in a variety of local households, she agrees with Bourg that baptism is the 'root of every Christian's vocation to holiness' (Bourg 2004: 78). She allows thus for a more inclusive approach to a broad variety of types of Christian community than the narrow focus on paradigmatic models of discipleship such as virginity in the past or the spousal union in present theology.

Marriage as Norm?

Joseph Monti has shown a viable path between a normative discourse which imposes marriage as an obligatory requirement for any and all kinds of sexual relations and a moral rhetoric which too easily puts alternative forms of sexual expression on an equal footing with it. At the basis of his argument is the distinction between 'ethical norms' and 'moral rules'. Norms disclose values and provide orientation for moral action but 'are never categorically regulative', i.e. they do not prescribe what has to be done in specific situations and particular circumstances (Monti 1995: 116). Rules on the other hand 'regulate particular circumstances and situations so that the values disclosed by ethical norms might be accomplished as goods' (1995: 119). If ethical norms and moral rules are confused and the distance between them collapses, moral instruction becomes dysfunctional in that '[n]orms fail to disclose and orient our lives around values' and '[r]ules fail to regulate the particular circumstances and behavior of our lives toward the promotion of the good as achievements of these values' (1995: 117). This is what has happened to the Christian discourse on sexual and marital morality:

> In upholding the norm of heterosexual marriage as a rule of behaviour in any and all situations and circumstances, many denominations are making the same analytic mistake of confusing ethical norms and moral rules. A similar confusion exists when it is argued that the particular needs and interests of individuals are enough for the creation of new or parallel norms in Christian sexual morality. And when all such teaching fails to persuade a significant number of Christians, the problem, no matter how sensitively portrayed, is interpreted either as a defect in character—a modernist turning away from the traditional values of love and commitment—or the authoritarian dictates of an archaic and anachronistic Church. Being unpersuaded by either side of the debate, many are left without theological and moral guidance at all, and the Church's teaching voice gives way to the even greater confusions of popular cultures. (1995: 121)

Monti abides by the 'singularity' and 'universality' of the marital norm 'as an identifying character mark of the Church' (1995: 209). As 'ethical norms manifest and model the ideal character-identity of a culture and community—what the community claims to be and wants to become, and how its members are obliged' (1995: 197), marriage became normative in the Christian community because it came to disclose a specific set of values that identified the Christian ideal in the field of sexual experience. And just like all ethical norms, the marital norm can only be appropriated and kept alive by 'critical and hermeneutical acts of remembrance'. On the one hand, it cannot be invented in private nor created from scratch but needs communal acts of historical retrieval. On the other hand, the Christian community cannot refer to any mythic couple or archetypical marriage that would provide moral guidance by simply being re-enacted in the present. 'Values and norms emerge from prior assumptions and interpretations of meaning and truth contained in the conversations and narrations of history, but to remain vital, must always be submitted again to verification and legitimation in every generation of the life of a tradition and community' (1995: 199).

It is in such a critical-hermeneutical conversation and action that the dynamic interaction between norms and rules comes into play. According to Monti, heterosexual marriage must remain the *single* orienting norm for sexual activity in the Christian community because a divergence of norms and values connected to it (e.g. for married and unmarried, for heterosexuals and homosexuals) would be a source of division and fracture. The specific rules for life, however, must be *plural* in view of the heterogeneity and diversity of situations and circumstances that they are supposed to regulate. That is why 'responsible nonmarital heterosexual and homosexual sexual expression—expression guided by the requisite Christian values—are never threats to marriage or to the Church itself; whereas pervasive irresponsible sexual expression of any kind among Christians can be a diagnosis of the failure of the Church's norm to be working effectively' (1995: 211).

Likewise, claiming some 'universal' character of the marital norm does not imply that marriage is 'ahistorically normative' (Monti 1995: 208). Its rise to a normative status has neither been continuous within the Christian tradition itself nor is it certain that whatever happens to the material history of heterosexuality and marriage it will remain the central focus of its remembrance. Moreover, the marital norm may not even be 'applicable to all members of a tradition-informed community' (1995: 199). Not only are those who are not married not 'abnormal' in any social-psychological or even moral sense; also the married 'are themselves always 'off the norm' because 'no single couple or the entire range of married couples embody the norm itself'. 'Particular marriages bring only a familiarity of necessary values and goods to the life of the Church rather than a literal and identifying embodiment' (1995: 239). While husbands and wives have thus a profound social and ecclesiastical obligation and responsibility to actively uphold and support the marital norm, they give the community only 'a glimpse of the ideal values necessary for the guidance of responsible sexual life' (1995: 239).

Monti offers a balanced and compelling account of how Christian communities could hold fast to and commend marriage while acknowledging and supporting 'analogous marital practices' in deviant forms of sexual expression. Love, fidelity, and creativity should thereby be the central patterns of a responsible sexual life modelled by the norm of marriage (1995: cf. 229–239). To propose the marital norm as a 'universal claim' in a context in which the Christian tradition has come to realize its particularity implies what Philippe Bordeyne has called 'moral labour' (*travail moral*) (2010: 230). The witness which Christian faith bears to this universal moral claim can only 'be grounded in marital practices (*pratiques conjugales*) the singularness of which becomes more and more obvious' (2010: 229). Paradoxically, marriage may reveal its value precisely when it is no longer the 'rule' but the exception in today's context.

Marriage as Personal Achievement or Institutional Practice?

According to David McCarthy 'the *institution* of marriage is the dividing line on how newer generations are going to think about and choose marriage' (McCarthy 2008: 61, emphasis added). In times of deinstitutionalization and expressive individualism the popular vision is that a relationship starts with romantic love and emotional intimacy, includes togetherness and cohabitation at some point, and then may, or may not, find its achievement, or 'capstone' in Cherlin's phrasing, in marriage. In this perspective, marriage is just an 'elevated form of living together', a 'value-added cohabitation' (McCarthy 2010: 136). Yet, McCarthy doubts whether this sequence still holds true.

Some people (by their late twenties) are tired of having 'relationships' and are looking to be married. The process might be: identify those with characteristics of a future husband or wife and subsequently hope to develop a relationship. Whether a couple begins with the 'relationship' or the virtues of a good spouse, the institutional features of marriage make the relationship distinctive. It is not a value-added friendship. It is a marriage, not reducible to a general idea of an 'intimate relationship' that endures (McCarthy 2010: 136).

The tension between 'positional-institutional and personal-elaborative claims and codes' (McCarthy 2008: 67) is a major challenge for any contemporary theology of marriage. Roman Catholic teaching and theology again provide a good illustration here. Being a point of disagreement between some theologians and the magisterium in the first half of the twentieth century, the issue surfaced again in the discussions during the Second Vatican Council, was 'settled' by way of compromise in the council's document on marriage, but became acute again in post-conciliar theology. As already mentioned, the council text connected with the twentieth-century experiential reality of marriage, describing it as an interpersonal loving relationship, but grafted the new parlance upon the older, institutional framework, which remained largely intact underneath. At one place the two perspectives are even neatly juxtaposed when the document refers to the procreative function of marriage, a major pillar of the institutional approach: 'By their very nature, the institution of matrimony itself and conjugal love are ordained for the procreation and education of children' (Second Vatican Council 1965: para. 48). The conservative opponents of the new perspective at the council had cautioned that including love in the definition of marriage would provide ammunition for the advocates of divorce. In the aftermath of the council, Pope Paul VI obviously had a similar concern and clarified in an allocution to the Tribunal of the Roman Rota in 1976 how the council text was (not) to be understood:

> Hence we firmly deny that with the failure of some subjective element such as marital love the marriage itself no longer exists as a 'juridical reality'. For this reality has its

origin in a consent once for all juridically efficacious. So far as the law is concerned this 'reality' continues to exist, since it in no way depends on love for its existence. For when they give their free consent the spouses do nothing other than to enter and be fixed in an objective order or institution, which is something greater than themselves and in no way depends on them for either its nature or the laws proper to it. Marriage did not take its origin in the free will of men, but was instituted by God, who willed it to be reinforced and enlightened by his laws.

(Quoted in Mackin 1982: 321)

As divorce and remarriage became a highly debated issue in post-conciliar Catholic theology, theologians of the 'revisionist' strand came to disagree with the institutional claim contained in the pope's understanding of 'indissoluble' marriage, which remains unchanged in the official teaching even today (Congregation for the Doctrine of the Faith 1998). In their understanding, marriage is in essence an interpersonal loving relationship, which develops from initial friendship and love into lifelong commitment as its inherent, yet optional, culmination. If it does, one can only wish and hope that love remains and the relationship endures because—and here they depart from the pope's rectification—there is no exterior instance that could make any claim on its endurance.

Moreover, on the basis of the very same personalist approach that praises the potential of loving commitment on the one side, its proponents are quick to admit love's fragility on the other. According to Margaret Farley, a simple 'appeal to our understanding of the concrete reality of human persons and a theology of human possibilities and limitations' reveals that '[l]ove is notoriously fickle, waxing and waning in ways we cannot always control' (2008: 299). If it does disappear then there is not much that can hold marriage as a relationship: 'Not presently a strong and unquestioned institution, not the love itself, not the sanctioned "laws" of marriage, not even the children born in marriage' (2008: 299). As realistic as this position may appear with regard to the working and ending of present-day relationships, its critics perceive too much optimism, and ultimately also a fatalistic undertone, in the underlying theological rationale which basically 'implies that the relationship is always good; it must be in order to carry the marriage' (McCarthy 2010: 141). But what would an alternative vision then look like, one that sees marriage as an institutional practice in its distinctiveness from intimate relations?

McCarthy suggests reversing the revisionist assumption that the relationship is the beginning and foundation and marriage an additional 'superstructure'. To start with marriage then means to start with public vows that 'are not defined by the married couple' and with spousal roles that are configured to 'lifelong fidelity and generativity' (2010: 138–139). Such an 'institutional and communal foundation of marriage—the vows, the expectations, and social relationships structured on the basis of family, the social tasks of sustaining productive households, and the common calling of raising children—give marriage purposes that an interpersonal relationship cannot sustain' (2010: 139). In this way, a free space could be opened for couples 'to develop relationships that work through a lifetime and . . . to have relationships that are not satisfying'. Spouses would be 'freed from the straight-jacket of total satisfaction and romantic ideas about sharing the "total self" ' and 'from the myth of the soul mate'. Marriage would be the 'beginning of something entirely new' (2010: 138)—not the crowning of a love that has survived against all odds, but the initiation into an ascetic practice that will teach couples to love along the way.

McCarthy lays bare the obvious shortcomings of any theological approach that focuses solely on the interpersonal and subjective elements of the marital union while neglecting its need for external, objective, or institutional structure. His own alternative model, however, falls into the other extreme and remains insensitive to the way most couples today experience and live their intimate relationships. His suggestion to give priority to marital 'roles and duties' comes close to a pre-conciliar and in fact pre-modern understanding of institutional marriage, and one wonders how it could be transferred into effective pastoral care. The merit of his approach lies much more in that he has called attention to the polarity of personal versus institutional viewpoints that tend to exclude each other but in fact need to be kept in balance. Just as pre-modern theologies of marriage had difficulties including subjective and interpersonal elements, late modern theologies tend to abandon too easily institutional supports that the marital union urgently needs to face the current threats to its stability.

It seems that contemporary theologies of marriage have not sufficiently explored the capacity of committed love to transcend the realm of (inter)subjectivity by 'de-privatizing' and 'externalizing' the subjective will in such a way that it appeals to the partners from a quasi-objective position (Lehmann 1972: 62). Phenomenological studies on the concept of 'conjugality' with its attendant characteristics of intimacy, faithfulness, permanence, and openness to children (Jonckheere 2000), and on the 'natural indissolubility' of committed relationships (Lacroix 2001) offer similar perspectives, which deserve further inquiry. Recent research on the role of the wedding ritual (Fopp 2007; Merzyn 2010) and on marital spirituality (Knieps-Port le Roi and Sandor 2008) indicates that on a practical level couples have a desire to disclose the marital union as a locus of a transcendence or divine grace in which they may put their hope for a fulfilling relationship beyond what they are able to realize by their own human competences and capabilities.

REFERENCES

Bauman, Zygmunt (2003). *Liquid Love: On the Frailty of Human Bonds*. Cambridge: Polity Press.

Bawin-Legros, Bernadette (2003). *Le Nouvel Ordre sentimental. A quoi sert la famille aujourd'hui?* Paris: Payot.

Beck, Ulrich, and Elisabeth Beck-Gernsheim (1995). *The Normal Chaos of Love*. Cambridge: Polity Press.

Bennett, Jana M. (2008). *Water is Thicker Than Blood: An Augustinian Theology of Marriage and Singleness*. New York: Oxford University Press.

Bordeyne, Philippe (2010). *L'Ethique du mariage. La Vocation sociale de l'amour*. Paris: Desclée de Brouwer.

Bourg, Florence C. (2004). *Where Two or Three Are Gathered: Christian Families as Domestic Churches*. Notre Dame, IN: University of Notre Dame Press.

Browning, Don S. (2003). *Marriage and Modernization: How Globalization Threatens Marriage and What to Do about It*. Grand Rapids, MI, and Cambridge, UK: William B. Eerdmans.

Browning, Don S., Bonnie J. Miller-McLemore, Pamela D. Couture, K. Brynolf Lyon, and Robert M. Franklyn (1997). *From Culture Wars to Common Ground: Religion and the American Family Debate*. Louisville, Kentucky: Westminster John Knox Press.

Cherlin, Andrew J. (2004). 'The Deinstitutionalization of American Marriage'. *Journal of Marriage and Family*, 66(4): 848–861.

Cloutier, David (2010) (ed.). *Leaving and Coming Home: New Wineskins for Catholic Sexual Ethics*. Eugene, OR: Wipf & Stock.

Code of Canon Law (1983). <http://www.vatican.va/archive/ENG1104/_INDEX.HTM>.

Congregation for the Doctrine of the Faith (1998) (ed.). *Sulla pastorale dei divorziati risposati: Documenti, commenti e studi*. Vatican City: Libreria Editrice Vaticana.

Coontz, Stephanie (2005). *Marriage, a History: How Love Conquered Marriage*. New York: Viking.

Farley, Margaret A. (2006). *Just Love: A Framework for Christian Sexual Ethics*. New York and London: Continuum.

Fopp, Sabine (2007). *Trauung—Spannungsfelder und Segensräume: Empirisch-theologischer Entwurf eines Rituals im Übergang*. Stuttgart: Kohlhammer.

Giddens, Anthony (1992). *The Transformation of Intimacy: Sexuality, Love and Eroticism in Modern Societies*. Stanford, CA: Stanford University Press.

Girgis, Sherif, Robert P. George, and Ryan T. Anderson (2010). 'What is Marriage?' *Harvard Journal of Law & Public Policy*, 34(1): 245–287.

Grisez, Germain (1993). *The Way of the Lord Jesus, ii. Living a Christian Life*. Quincy, IL: Franciscan Press.

John Paul II (1981). *Familiaris consortio*. <http://www.vatican.va/holy_father/john_paul_ii/apost_exhortations/documents/hf_jp-ii_exh_19811122_familiaris-consortio_en.html>.

John Paul II (2006). *Man and Woman He Created Them: A Theology of the Body*. Trans. intro., and indexed Michael Waldstein. Boston: Pauline Books & Media.

Jonckheere, Paul (2000). *La Conjugalité. Le nouveau défi amoureux*. Paris: L'Harmattan.

Kelly, Kevin T. (1998). *New Directions in Sexual Ethics: Moral Theology and the Challenge of AIDS*. London and Washington, DC: Geoffrey Chapman.

Knieps-Port le Roi, Thomas, and Monica Sandor (2008). *Companion to Marital Spirituality*. Leuven: Peeters.

Kopp, Johannes, Daniel Lois, Christian Kunz, and Oliver Arranz Becker (2010). *Verliebt, verlobt, verheiratet: Institutionalisierungsprozesse in Partnerschaften*. Wiesbaden: VS Verlag für Sozialwissenschaften.

Lacroix, Xavier (2001) (ed.). *Oser dire le mariage indissoluble*. Paris: Cerf.

Lawler, Michael G. (2002). *Marriage and the Catholic Church: Disputed Questions*. Collegeville, MN: Liturgical Press.

Lehmann, Karl (1972). 'Zur Sakramentalität der Ehe' (1972). In Franz Henrich and Volker Eid (eds), *Ehe und Ehescheidung: Diskussion unter Christen*. Munich: Kösel Verlag, 57–71.

McCarthy, David Matzko (2004). *Sex and Love in the Home*, 2nd edn. London: SCM Press.

McCarthy, David Matzko (2008). *Theologies of Marriage and Family in a New Generation: An Overwhelming Desire for Home*. CTSA (Catholic Theological Society of America) Proceedings 63: 57–70. <http://ejournals.bc.edu/ojs/index.php/ctsa/article/view/4914/4389>.

McCarthy, David Matzko (2010). *Cohabitation and Marriage*. In Cloutier (2010): 119–143.

Mackin, Theodore (1982). *What is Marriage?* Ramsey, NJ: Paulist Press.

Merzyn, Konrad (2010). *Die Rezeption der kirchlichen Trauung: Eine empirisch-theologische Untersuchung*. Leipzig: Evangelische Verlagsanstalt.

Monti, Joseph (1995). *Arguing about Sex: The Rhetoric of Christian Sexual Morality*. Albany, NY: State University of New York Press.

Popenoe, David, Jean B. Elshtain, and David Blankenhorn (1996) (eds). *Promises to Keep: Decline and Renewal of Marriage in America*. Lanham, MD: Rowman & Littlefield.

Rubio, Julie H. (2003). *A Christian Theology of Marriage and the Family*. New York and Mahwah, NJ: Paulist Press.

Salzman, Todd A., and Michael G. Lawler (2008). *The Sexual Person: Toward a Renewed Catholic Anthropology*. Washington, DC: Georgetown University Press.

Scola, Angelo (2005). *The Nuptial Mystery*. Grand Rapids, MI, and Cambridge, UK: William B. Eerdmans.

Second Vatican Council (1965). *Pastoral Constitution on the Church in the Modern World: Gaudium et spes*. <http://www.vatican.va/archive/hist_councils/ii_vatican_council/documents/vat-ii_const_19651207_gaudium-et-spes_en.html>.

Thatcher, Adrian (1999). *Marriage After Modernity: Christian Marriage in Postmodern Times*. Sheffield: Sheffield Academic Press.

The 1917 or Pio-Benedictine Code of Canon Law (2001). Ed. Edward N. Peeters. San Francisco: Ignatius Press.

Waite, Linda J., and Maggie Gallagher (2000). *The Case for Marriage: Why Married People are Happier, Healthier, and Better off Financially*. New York: Doubleday.

Witte, John Jr. (1997, 2012). *From Sacrament to Contract: Marriage, Religion, and Law in the Western Tradition*. Louisville, KY: Westminster John Knox Press.

Why Marriage Matters: Twenty-One Conclusions from the Social Sciences (2002). New York: Institute for American Values.

CHAPTER 35

....

FAMILIES

....

ADRIAN THATCHER

SOURCES

....

Official Roman Catholic Teaching

(No discussion of families can be had without referring to marriage, so this chapter should be read in conjunction with chapter 34.)

The Vatican II document *Gaudium et spes* uses the term 'family' to mean the family of the entire human race (Paul VI 1965: 2–3, 24, 26, 29, 32–33, 37–9), the family of people who constitute the church (1965: 40), and the individual family which, rightly ordered, contributes to the common good. 'The Gospel's message' is 'that the human race was to become the Family of God' (1965: 32). The Church stands between the family of the human race and the human family unit, 'which is the first and vital cell of society' (John Paul II 1981: 42). 'She' has

> a call to form the family of God's children during the present history of the human race, and to keep increasing it until the Lord returns.... She serves as a leaven and as a kind of soul for human society as it is to be renewed in Christ and transformed into God's family.
>
> (Paul VI 1965: 40)

At the micro-level marriage is said to be fundamental to the flourishing of persons, and therefore to societies and to the broader human race: 'The well-being of the individual person and of human and Christian society is intimately linked with the healthy condition of that community produced by marriage and family' (1965: 47). Why? Because

> ...God Himself is the author of matrimony, endowed as it is with various benefits and purposes. All of these have a very decisive bearing on the continuation of the

human race, on the personal development and eternal destiny of the individual members of a family, and on the dignity, stability, peace and prosperity of the family itself and of human society as a whole.

(Paul VI 1965: 48)

In the 1983 *Charter of the Rights of the Family*, addressed to a more secular audience, the theological tone of the language is understandably more muted. The family is 'a community of love and solidarity'; it is 'the place where different generations come together and help one another to grow in human wisdom and to harmonize the rights of individuals with other demands of social life'; and it is organically related to the broader society in which it exists (Holy See 1983: Preamble, E, F, G). Catholic teaching insists on protecting 'the rights, the fundamental needs, the well-being and the values of the family', while deploring that these 'are often ignored and not rarely undermined by laws, institutions and socio-economic programs', with the result that 'many families are forced to live in situations of poverty which prevent them from carrying out their role with dignity' (1983: Preamble, J, K). John Paul II (d.2005) notes with sadness 'the fact that, in the countries of the so-called Third World, families often lack both the means necessary for survival, such as food, work, housing and medicine, and the most elementary freedoms' (1981: 6).

Communion of Persons

In the Apostolic Exhortation *Familiaris Consortio* Pope John Paul II develops his teaching that the family unit is a 'communion of persons'. Meditating on Genesis 1:27 he observes

> God created man in His own image and likeness: calling him to existence through love, He called him at the same time for love.
>
> God is love and in Himself He lives a mystery of personal loving communion. Creating the human race in His own image and continually keeping it in being, God inscribed in the humanity of man and woman the vocation, and thus the capacity and responsibility, of love and communion. Love is therefore the fundamental and innate vocation of every human being.

(John Paul II 1981: 11)

A relational understanding of the idea of humankind being made in the image of God is clearly brought to the text of Genesis 1: 27. The *imago dei* is given a Trinitarian interpretation. The love that God is, is the 'mystery of personal loving communion', and human persons are created so that they can share in both. The family is explicitly called 'a communion of persons' (John Paul II 1981: 16, 18, 22). In 1994 John Paul II asserted with more confidence the idea that families share in the 'tri-une' life of God. Observing that only 'man' among all beings was created 'in the image and likeness of God', the Pope taught that human fatherhood and motherhood, while remaining *biologically similar* to that of other living beings in nature, contain in an essential and unique way a *'likeness' to God* which is the basis of the family as a community of human life, as a community of persons united in love (*communio personarum*).

(John Paul II 1994: 6 emphasis original)

He was even able to discern how

In the light of the New Testament... *the primordial model of the family is to be sought in God himself*, in the Trinitarian mystery of his life. The divine 'We' is the eternal pattern of the human 'we', especially of that 'we' formed by the man and the woman created in the divine image and likeness.

(John Paul II 1994: 6, emphasis original)

With the term 'primordial model', an ontology of family is reached. The human 'we' of the individual family unit, and the divine 'We' of the three Persons whose unity is their communion of life and love, are allowed to mingle together by means of a two-way analogy which flows both 'downwards' from God and 'upwards' back to God. Both sets of persons are able to be designated *communio personarum*:

The family is in fact a community of persons whose proper way of existing and living together is communion: *communio personarum*. Here too, while always acknowledging the absolute transcendence of the Creator with regard to his creatures, we can see the family's ultimate relationship to the divine 'We'. *Only persons are capable of living 'in communion'*.

(John Paul II 1994: 7, emphasis original)

The Domestic Church

The family unit and the ecclesial 'family of God' intermingle by means of the idea of 'domestic church'. The family unit extends outwards, from 'family communion' to the wider 'community'. There is a distinction between 'the family' and 'the Christian family'. The latter is 'called to experience a new and original communion which confirms and perfects natural and human communion'. This it finds in 'the grace of Jesus Christ' and in the Holy Spirit

who is poured forth in the celebration of the sacraments, [and] is the living source and inexhaustible sustenance of the supernatural communion that gathers believers and links them with Christ and with each other in the unity of the Church of God. The Christian family constitutes a specific revelation and realization of ecclesial communion, and for this reason too it can and should be called 'the domestic church'.

(John Paul II 1981: 21)

Within the family and society, 'it is important to underline the equal dignity and responsibility of women with men' (1981: 22). The Church should 'tirelessly' insist 'that the work of women in the home be recognized and respected by all in its irreplaceable value' (1981: 23). But men and women have 'different vocations', and 'the Church must in her own life promote as far as possible their equality of rights and dignity' (1981: 23). This does not mean, the Pope explains, 'for women a renunciation of their femininity or an imitation of the male role, but the fullness of true feminine humanity which should be expressed in their activity, whether in the family or outside of it, without disregarding the differences of customs and cultures in this sphere' (1981: 23). In the *Letter to Families*, the domestic church is elevated to share the status as the Church of God, considered (in Ephesians 5: 21–32) both as 'a great mystery' and as the 'bride of Christ':

> The family itself is the great mystery of God. As the 'domestic church', it is the bride of Christ. The universal Church, and every particular Church in her, is most immediately revealed as the bride of Christ in the 'domestic church' and in its experience of love: conjugal love, paternal and maternal love, fraternal love, the love of a community of persons and of generations.
>
> (John Paul II 1994: 19)

Critical Familism

The most promising Protestant theological analysis of families in the last twenty years has undoubtedly been the Family, Religion, and Culture project, founded and led by the late Don Browning (*d.*2010) at the University of Chicago. The project defined and advocated 'critical familism'. Browning distinguished critical familism both from the familism 'that blesses and supports cohesive families at any cost', and from 'the divided spheres and soft patriarchy of the so-called traditional family of the industrial era' (Browning 2007: 255). Rather, critical familism 'promotes the ideal of the equal-regard, mother-father partnership where both husband and wife have, in principle, equal access to the responsibilities and privileges of both the public world of citizenship and employment and the domestic sphere of household maintenance and child care' (2007: 255). It is inclusive, advocating 'social support for and connection with already existing families of single parents, stepparents, adults called to a vocation of singleness, and gays and lesbians raising children' (Browning et al. 1997: 3).

Practical Theology

Browning had already written an influential textbook on *practical* theology (Browning 1991), and the project, which produced over twenty major books, followed the methods and approaches of that branch of theology. Practical theology, he stated,

> begins with practical questions, describes the situations from which the questions come, and searches the classic expressions of the Christian faith for guidance. It

moves from a description of practice to theory and then back to a renewed and more critical practice. In the end, it is interested in appropriate transformation of our practices to meet changed circumstances.

(Browning et al. 1997: 8; Browning 2003: 3–4)

The practical questions driving the project were set by 'the massive social and cultural trends' that were producing 'stunning transformations in American families' (Browning et al. 1997: 21). Similar trends are recognizable in probably all Western societies and were summarized as '(1) the drift...toward heightened forms of individualism; (2) the spread of market economics and government bureaucracy into the intimacies of families and private life; (3) the powerful psychological shifts that these forces have produced; and (4) the influences of a declining, yet still active patriarchy' (1997: 21). In turn, the effects of these trends included over 50 per cent of marriages ending in divorce; a great increase in 'out-of-wedlock births'; a rise in single parent-hood and consequent poverty; and the lack of influence on children of absent fathers (1997: 52–58).

Being a practical project driven by a practical theologian, the social action required by critical familism is constantly stressed. The final chapter of the flagship volume was a list of priorities for action on behalf both of churches and of society. *'More than anything else, churches must retrieve their marriage and family traditions, even though they must do so critically'* (Browning et al. 1997: 307, emphasis original). But the critical retrieval of these traditions was to be sharply distinguished from the activity of evangelical lobby groups and American party political posturing: 'Churches should not just promote getting married and staying married; *'they should themselves be sensitive to the power distortions, inequalities, convoluted communications, and failures in intersubjectivity characteristic of families since the beginning of human history'* (1997: 307, emphasis original) They should join with each other, with synagogues and mosques, with 'civil society' and the state in promoting critical familism. They should, among many other practical tasks, advocate 'the idea of the sixty-hour workweek as a goal for dual-income families' (1997: 328) and provide or support marriage education as a matter of public policy. The project acknowledged 'that other religious traditions can contribute to this great cultural work' (1997: 255), and it provided an important resource book to help bring it about (Browning et al. 2006). Convinced that marriage, critically retrieved and understood, made a strong contribution to the common good of children and parents, and to communities and the wider society, a volume was produced which sought to enlist the cooperation of professionals in law, medicine, ministry, therapy, and business (Wall et al. 2002).

Equal-Regard

The 'equal-regard marriage' is based on a rejection of a patriarchal understanding of marriage and of the still popular idea of male 'headship' (Blankenhorn et al. 2004). It is the product of an extensive analysis of love as mutuality; applied to marriage it describes 'a relationship between husband and wife characterized by mutual respect, affection, practical assistance, and justice—a relationship that values and aids the self and other with equal seriousness' (Browning et al. 1997: 2, 287–289). Love as equal-regard was never intended to deny the need for sacrificial or 'agapic' love when it became required, only that self-giving should take place 'in the service of mutuality and not an end in itself. Both husband and wife should equally play the sacrificial role...' (1997: 24).

Kin Altruism

Browning gave theological impetus to the theory of kin altruism developed by the evolutionary psychologist W. D. Hamilton (Browning 2007: 121). The idea of 'kin altruism, the preferential treatment people tend to give to their biologically related family members' (Browning et al. 1997: 71), is a reason why

> the family with intact, biologically related parents should be given a prima facie priority in our cultural, ethical and educational scale of values. *The fundamental issue of our time may be how to retain and honor the intact family without turning it into an object of idolatry and without retaining the inequalities of power, status, and privilege ensconced in its earlier forms.*
>
> (Browning et al. 1997: 71, emphasis original)

Browning thought evolutionary psychology made a 'limited' contribution to family studies by describing the early conditions which 'helped integrate human males into families'. These are '(1) "paternal recognition," or a father's certainty that a particular child was his; (2) the long period of human infant dependency, which required mothers to look for assistance from male consorts; (3) ongoing sexual exchange between mates; and (4) reciprocal altruism (mutual helpfulness) between father and mother'. Browning thought the theory

> gives a partial account as to why the children of intact biological parents seem, on average, to do better in school, jobs, and their own later marital relations. Biological parents are more inclined to identify with and become invested in their offspring. They sense that in caring for the 'other' that is their child they are caring partially for themselves.
>
> (Browning 2007: 121)

Browning often noted similarities between this theory and Aquinas' thoughts about parents loving their offspring more than other children. One's biological children are made in the image of God but also 'in the image of their parents'. Browning claimed that Aquinas' view both emphasized 'the obligation to show a general benevolence toward them' while 'it does not obscure the importance of inclinations in parents to exert special energy on behalf of their own offspring' (2007: 122). The loosening of bonds between fathers and children is a modern curse, and called 'the male problem-atic'—'the increasing tendency of men, partially due to the pressures of modernity and partially because of archaic evolutionary tendencies, to mate and procreate but live separately from their children and often relinquish their parental responsibilities' (Browning 2003: 77; Green 2007: 76–79). But they only *tend* to give it. Christianity is praised for strengthening the bonds between fathers and their children 'through the ideal of male servanthood and the subversion of the honor-shame codes of the Greco-Roman world' (Browning 2003: 79). Christian teaching helped to inculcate parental responsibility and to keep families together, while the loosening of such bonds in the modern period constitutes a grave problem for families. 'The task for our time', argues Browning, 'is to combine a love ethic of equal regard between hus-band and wife with a powerful ethic of parental care and responsibility' (Browning 2003: 82).

Evangelical and Feminist Approaches to Families

Rodney Clapp is an American evangelical Protestant who takes Jesus' relativization of families in the Gospels with unusual seriousness, and asserts that the Church is 'first family' (Clapp 1993, 2012), taking precedence over obligations to biological family mem-bers. Mark 3: 31–35 and similar passages indicate that 'Jesus declared that his disciples were his first or primary family'. The words of Christ, as he hung on the cross, to Mary and to the beloved disciple (John 19: 26–27) constitute 'a new family...on the spot'. Clapp comments

> With such words and deeds, Jesus desacralizes and decenters the family, subordinat-ing it and its good to the pursuit of the kingdom of God. The apostle Paul concurs, teaching that the followers of Jesus are brother and sister to one another. In his view, the old self dies in baptism and enters into the new and now primary sociality of the church, Christ's body. Allegiance to the family is not eliminated but is rendered secondary. In baptism, water is thicker than blood. For these reasons, I taught my daughter that she is first of all my sister in Christ and second (though importantly) my daughter.
>
> (Clapp 2012: 53)

This approach differs considerably from the crass attempt to see the modern nuclear family vindicated by the teachings of Scripture. There is even agreement with Rosemary Radford Ruether regarding the subversive character of Jesus' teaching about fami-lies. Ruether speaks not of 'first family' but of the church's sense of being a 'new fam-ily' (Ruether 2000: 28), both in the 'Palestinian Jesus movement' and in the Pauline churches where Paul's characteristic theological mix of freedom from the law and adop-tion as 'sons of God' now applies to Christians 'who are Abraham's true sons and heirs' (2000: 29). But there the similarity ends. An aim of Ruether is 'to show that shifting ideologies involving the family and "family values" are generally coded messages about women and how they should behave in relation to men' (2000: 28). She advocates 'an acceptance of a postmodern or pluralist understanding of family forms' (2000: 12, 212). Her 'ecofeminist family ethic' sounds remarkably like that of critical familism for it too is 'based on the equality and partnership of men and women in family, work, and society, and on the reconfiguring of work-family relations and economic and political hierarchies to foster a more equitable sharing of wealth within sustainable communities' (2000: 207).

Whereas critical familism advocates marriage, Ruether advocates support for 'a variety of family and household patterns' (2000: 212). Her list is a long one:

> ... the single householder; the gay or lesbian couple, including partners raising children by adoption, former marriages, or artificial insemination; the single parent, male or female; the two-earner heterosexual couple; the three- or four-generation family; families blended through divorce and remarriage; and cohabiting partnerships of two, three, or more people that may or may not include a sexual pair. This diversity is already the reality of American life.
>
> (Ruether 2000: 212)

The 'values of mutuality and commitment' which may be found in egalitarian marriages 'are not lessened but rather expanded when they are affirmed in many forms, and not in one form only that marginalizes and denigrates all the other forms by which people are sustaining their lives in community' (Ruether 2000: 213).

Neo-Augustinian Approaches

The two main approaches to families described earlier have provided stimuli for further work. Clapp's comparison between baptism and birth, between the family of Church and the natural family, is echoed by the title of Jana Bennett's recent monograph *Water is Thicker Than Blood* (2008). Bennett detects a 'cultural frenzy' about marriage (2008: 3) which theologians have replicated, 'participating in a frenzy of their own' (2008: 4). Both the Protestant Family, Religion, and Culture project and the Catholic theology of the domestic church are said to damage ecclesiology. The former sets out on a 'falsely eschatological' path (2008: 8). Marriage and family displace God as the ultimate ground of our hopes: proximate concerns are raised to ultimacy, and marriage and family are overidealized (2008: 10). Browning 'has made these concerns ultimate by suggesting that the savior of the world, or at least of our broken American society, must be a good, functioning, family' (2008: 10).

The troubles of the latter, the 'domestic church', begin with its very name, which is 'grammatically and theologically inconsistent' (Bennett 2008: 10). Bennett thinks supporters of the notion are more concerned with social justice than with 'Christian moral formation'. No strong connection exists between the Church and the 'domestic church', and since marriage in Catholic thought 'belongs exclusively to this age' (2008: 14) it lacks any eschatological future (unlike virginity). The alternative is an

Augustinian theology of redemption. All baptized persons, whether single or married, and therefore representing a diversity of households, belong first of all to the Body of Christ, and it is this that gives them primary identities. Water is thicker than blood. Whereas for the evangelical Clapp the primary bonds which make family relations secondary are constituted by the faith of Christians, for Bennett the primary bonds belong to the fellowship of the Church, sacramentally constituted. Because Christians primarily belong there, they will be nourished there, and provide spiritual nourishment in the various diverse households to which, secondarily, they also belong.

Brent Waters also turns to Augustine and to the eschatological dimension of the family and its purpose. An adequate representation of Christian thought about marriage and family must return to Augustine's 'three goods', not least because these 'serve to embed marriage and family within a nexus of social, political, and ecclesial relationships, providing a useful point of departure for formulating a counter-form of moral discourse to that of late liberalism' (Waters 2007: 136). 'Late liberalism' seems to infect most theological accounts of family. 'The family is the locus of authority established by God for organizing the cooperative tasks of procreation and childrearing' (2007: 174). There is a 'timely ordering of affinity' (2007: 192–206) that flows directly from 'the teleological ordering of the family'. There *is* such an entity as a 'normative Christian family' (Waters 2012: 53). 'In summary, as a witness to God's providential ordering of creation, the family is a human association comprised of biological and social affinities.... The family is characterized by a married couple with children, who are in turn related by blood, marriage, and lineage to an extended range of kin.' There is a 'providential movement and witness of the family' (Waters 2007: 206–229) based on the doctrine of creation and the orientation of the Christian family to the divine destiny of all things through Christ. Against the domestic church Waters asserts 'the church is not a family' (2007: 239–244) and 'the family is not a church' (2007: 244–251). 'Social ordering' is a divine gift: 'late liberalism' (2007: 265–269) and the misguided theologians who are influenced by it disastrously treat it as a human project destined for chaos.

Themes

Personalism

Roman Catholic teaching about families is unrivalled among the churches, in breadth and depth. The personalist analogy of the *communio personarum* between the family unit and the unity of the triune God is novel, and has rightly been called 'a Trinitarian anthropology of the family', the theological legitimacy of which is still apparently becoming established (Ouellet 2006). However, some theologians regard the very personalism by which the Pope articulates his 'primordial model' of the family to be counter-productive and flawed. Earlier Catholic teaching about family as a 'mediating institution', or as 'an organic body that mediates social life', is compromised by 'the modern subjective turn' or 'the interpersonal turn' which 'makes the outward disposition of marriage ambiguous and its social character less distinct' (McCarthy 2001: 112). The emphasis on the family as a 'communion of love' 'opens the way to make conjugal love prior to (as the basis for) the duties and functions of parenthood and family' (2001: 112), so that 'When marriage is defined by inward relations rather than outward roles and duties, connections between interpersonal harmony and the social function of family become loose' (2001: 113).

Domestic Church

Some criticisms of the idea of 'domestic church' have just been noted. Other critics, many of them Roman Catholics, are concerned about the stern and unrelenting tone of papal teaching against abortion in any circumstance, against divorce and further marriage, against sterilization and contraception. The requests of the 1980 Synod of Bishops to the Pope to reintroduce a betrothal ceremony or to allow local variation with regard to different customs for the entry into marriage, were ignored (Grootaers and Selling 1983: 292–293), while the possibility that couples of the same sex might form a union or a family was a possibility far beyond the horizon of the 1980s and 1990s.

Adrian Thatcher (2007: 235–240) identifies three further types of problem caused by identifying families with domestic churches—those of hierarchy, constitution and ministry, and membership. The hierarchical ordering of Churches can appear to authorize authoritarian fathers in the domestic church to require obedience and submission to their paternal rule. Are both the parents priests (or just the father)? Is the ministry of parents sacramental (every bathing of children potentially a baptism, every meal a sacrament)? Does a family have to assume the approved papal form to qualify as a domestic church? Cahill probes the gendered roles of parents in domestic churches. While finding much to applaud in the papal advocacy of women and their equality with men, she observes how the Pope does not practise what he advocates elsewhere: 'women's equality in principle is partly but not fully supported by the kinds of institutional practices he envisions as serving the common good at the concrete level (in marriage, family, church, and civil society in general)' (Cahill 2000: 92). The 'papal eulogization' of mothers, she observes, sounds regressive to many North Americans, and to many others,

> his notion that women are by nature maternal; that, even when not literally mothers, their 'special genius' consists in nurturing, maternal behavior in all other relationships; and that the 'special' feminine vocation to love provides a rationale for exclusion from the church's most respected leadership roles, are simply incredible.
>
> (Cahill 2000: 92)

Respect for 'Non-traditional' Families

Gloria Albrecht argues that critical familism and the marriage movement generally, 'assume race, gender, and economic privileges that are not available to all' (2005: 169). Her reluctant accusation is that by

> ignoring socioeconomic realities for many people, these ideals may mask and reinforce unjust inequalities. In fact, the themes and policies of the defense-of-marriage movement fit nicely with the neoliberal political economy that developed in the second half of the twentieth century.
>
> (Albrecht 2005: 169)

Albrecht argues that 'church and social policies that value families must connect the well-being of all families with a commitment to gender equality and economic justice', and critical familism does not do this sufficiently. That criticism is similar to Cahill's worry that heavy papal insistence on the assumed normative structure of the Christian family inevitably contrasts 'non-normative' family structures in an unfavourable light. While many African American families in the United States are often regarded in this way, Albrecht insists their achievements should instead be justly *celebrated* when the full social and economic context is taken into account (Cahill 2000: 111–129). The project is able to retort that it was careful to avoid tracing simplistic causal connections, and so culpability, between wrong moral choices and family breakdown, and that the evidence on which its analyses were based took such factors as poverty into account. (One important source, The Center for Marriage and Family (2013), continues to update its findings annually.) Its commitment to gender equality is obvious enough. While its economic analysis may have been insufficiently critical of the capitalist economy of the United States, the project sought change within civil society where it was most achievable.

Biblical Interpretation

Critical familism quarried the New Testament for guidance, aided by the best critical scholarship. That endeavour, however, proved difficult. Thatcher has suggested that some of the preferred theology of families has been brought to the New Testament rather than derived from it. The problems are obvious. First, Jesus in the synoptic Gospels is highly critical of families (Mk. 3: 31–35, 10: 28–31; Mt. 12: 46–50, 19: 27–30; Lk. 8: 19–21, 11: 27–28; 18: 29–30) regularly valuing 'Kingdom' above 'kin'. Second, the New Testament speaks of 'households' not families, and these can include many members who are 'fictive-kin' or 'non-kin' (Osiek and Balch 1997: 43). Third, these households are hierarchically ordered, and the Household Codes (Eph. 5: 22–6: 9; Col. 3: 18–4: 1; 1 Pet. 2:18–3:7; 1 Tim. 2: 8–15, 6: 1–2; Tit. 2: 1–10) require the submission of all members to the

paterfamilias. One might also add that the New Testament itself is lukewarm about marriage (Thatcher 2007: 31).

Fourth, the ideals of equal-regard love, equal-regard marriage (indeed equality
between men and women) are not found as straightforwardly in the New Testament
as Browning hoped. Rather, readers of the New Testament quickly discover that
Kingdom is valued over kin; that gender hierarchies are affirmed; that women submit
to men and are silenced in the churches; that heads of households may not have been
self-consciously practising 'servanthood'; and that hints of equality between women
and men may be something different—a unity which nonetheless leaves gender bias
assumed and unchallenged (Thatcher 2007: 25–41).

Browning and his team contend that a contextual reading of these problems mitigates
our difficulties with them. Set in the surrounding world, the young faith 'inspired heightened degrees of female equality, a chastened patriarchy, higher levels of male responsibility and servanthood, less of a double standard in sexual ethics, and deeper respect for
children' (Browning et al. 1997: 131). The family, relativized in the teaching of Jesus, 'was a
patriarchal clan and kinship structure that functioned as a religiopolitical unit . . . and was
generally in tension with other clans, the state, and the national cult' (1997: 134). Elisabeth
Schüssler-Fiorenza's depiction of early Christianity as 'a discipleship of equals' is invoked
(Browning et al. 1997: 135): husbands' love for their wives is characterised by sacrifice and
servanthood. The Gospel engages with the Honour-Shame Codes that regulated ancient
families, and partially transforms them. A favoured metaphor is that of a 'trajectory', discerned in the New Testament as an alleged movement towards the equality of the sexes
and equal-regard marriages. It loses momentum among second and third generation
Christians whose survival under persecution required its temporary suspension.

These readings are plausible ones, no more. If more is built on the biblical texts than
the texts can bear, perhaps that is inevitable, given the place of the Bible in the Protestant
churches of the United States which are principally addressed. But little is ever settled by
an appeal to scripture. As Tertullian taught, 'controversy over the Scriptures can, clearly,
produce no other effect than help to upset either the stomach or the brain' (1885: 16).
Perhaps the claim that a trajectory towards equal-regard may have begun early in the
New Testament, even if it was badly interrupted, can be sustained. More importantly,
the method of practical theology (described in the first part of this chapter) is followed
consistently, and brings together the theological sources of Scripture, Tradition, Reason,
and Experience in a most creative way.

First Church?

A common issue to arise in several of these theological narratives is the status to be
given to Christians either as members of the kingdom of God or as baptized members
of churches. Daughters and sons are primarily the sisters and brothers of their parents
in the 'first family' of church. The bonds of the kingdom are more primary than the
bonds of kin, and the water of baptism is thicker than the bonds of blood. What kind

of assertions are these? While deep interpersonal bonds of *koinònia*, of solidarity or friendship, are undoubtedly achievable within communities of faith, how often are they in practice achieved?

The question is similar to that posed by Philip Lyndon Reynolds (1994) about the sacrament of marriage: is the 'bond' of marriage *existential* or *ontological*? Opting for the former alternative Reynolds argues that there was no mysterious ontological/sacramental quality of marriage apart from the existential *quality* of the marital relationship (1994: 307). What may be happening in the prioritization of the bonds of the kingdom is the borrowing of the language of family relations to express the shared values, experiences and goals of people of faith in order to accentuate their importance. This borrowing of familial language has the hallmarks of metaphor all over it. For example, it makes good sense, but metaphorical good sense, to say with St Paul that Gentile Christians are the *adopted* children of God. But the literalization of the adoption metaphor is likely to cancel the adoptive meaning. If Clapp's daughter is first of all his sister (in Christ), then his responsibility for her as a father cannot be prior to his responsibility for all his sisters and brothers in the household of God. Will he not prioritize the payment of his daughter's university tuition fees or health care costs over those of the daughter or son of anyone else?

Some Christian ethicists have indeed argued valiantly for this extreme position (Hallett 1998), but it is hard to see how real fathers and mothers can consistently hold to an ideal that does not allow them to give priority to their own children. The standard reply, that the children do not *belong* to their parents because they first belong to God and are best thought of as divine gifts, merely leaves unsaid and unspecified the special responsibilities parents have for the children they have brought into the world. Water, then, is *not* thicker than blood. Kin altruism is a better way of underscoring parental responsibility. In the real (and often broken) world of families, the prioritization and idealization of the ecclesial family of God is likely to produce an unacknowledged 'ecclesiolatry' (Scott 2009: 404).

Forms and Norms

Is there a route beyond the polarization between the liberal embrace of all family forms and the more conservative insistence on a particular family form—based on marriage? Four preliminary steps may be necessary if this route is to be followed. First a distinction must be made between support and advocacy. Ruether's list of 'family and household patterns' comes with the exhortation that, without exception, they are all to be supported (whatever 'support' might mean in a practical sense). But some family 'patterns' are actually much better than others in terms of achieving positive outcomes for their members, especially for children, and for the wider society and for the common good. So while all families, in the eyes of Christians, are neighbours to be loved as Christians love themselves, and so are deserving of 'support', Christian ethics cannot be neutral regarding either the tradition about marriage which is peculiarly its own, or about the strong comparative evidence that it works.

The second step just *is* this respect for evidence. John Witte writes

> for most adult parties most of the time, married life is better than single life, marital cohabitation is better than nonmarital cohabitation, married parents do better than single parents in raising their children. According to several recent studies…married folks on average live longer, happier, and safer lives. They are more satisfied, prosperous, and efficient. They receive better hygiene, health care, and coinsurance. Their children develop better emotional, social, and moral skills. These data on the health benefits of marriage are now emerging with increasing alacrity within a variety of modern professions. They have enormous implications for our professional responsibilities to couples and children, and to the institution of marriage itself.
>
> (Witte 2002: 86)

The third step must be the avoidance in liberal thought of equivocation regarding family form. A secular British report, *Rethinking Families*, advocates the abandonment of talk of family forms in favour of 'the notion of *family practices*: what we do rather than what we are' (Williams et al. 2004: 16, original emphasis). But the shift from being to *doing*, or from theory to *practice*, cannot conceal the possibility that people may do badly, and practise poorly, just because a particular form of family is no longer valued. This shift is common enough in theology too; Ruether is not the only example. Herbert Anderson and Susan Johnson (1995) advocate the priority of family *function* or *purpose*, arguing that 'structures of the family have changed over centuries and will continue to change while its purposes have remained more constant' (1995: 49). Purpose and structure can apparently be neatly disconnected. John and Olive Drane (2004) rise to an unwarranted peak of liberal optimism in speaking of 'redesigned families', observing that 'the shape of the new design is not yet clear, nor is it likely to be for some time to come. As a culture we are still at the drawing board stage' (2004: 40). The possibility that late modern culture might be mistaken about, or looking in the wrong place for, its design templates, is not considered. The advantages of marriage should not be dissipated by the refusal to name them in the desire to embrace all families whatever their 'design' (or lack of it). These theologies are equivocal about marriage.

But fourth, it would be necessary to commend marriage as the nucleus of a household in an inclusive way which conservative thought will struggle to accommodate. There should be no stigma attached to unmarried couples. Around half of the children in the United Kingdom are born *outside* of marriage. Registering disapproval of such 'irregularities' is counter-productive and pointless. The inclusion of same-sex couples within marriage should be welcomed by the churches instead of their general pedantic malevolence towards homosexual people. There have been many changes to marriage itself since New Testament times, not least the arrival in the last third of the twentieth century of egalitarian, companionate marriage (Thatcher 2011, 2012). And the churches will do well to recognize that the values that it associates with marriage—fidelity, commitment, unconditionality, fruitfulness, hospitality, and so on—are often found in families where formal marriage vows have never been made. Such recognition, as Ruether has suggested, does not 'lessen' the value of marriage but 'expands' it. There is an irony too in this expansion. Jesus' teaching about the priority of kingdom over kin relativizes all attempts to *insist* on marriage as the sole form by which families calling themselves Christian must manifest themselves.

Future Families

Future theological work on families may still draw principally from the resources of the two main theological providers in this chapter, the Roman Catholic Church and the project of critical familism. But any mix is likely to be both partial and eclectic.

Communio personarum

A way forward may be to confirm the centre-piece of theological thinking about families to be the doctrine of the social Trinity. God, and human families, are in their different ways, each a *communio personarum*. But the image of the triune God is to be found in the loving interplay, in the enabling and restoring, in the forgiving and the disciplining, in the different forms of love and devotion which, thankfully, are to be found (to different degrees) in families, irrespective of whether the core of each is an officially recognized sacramental marriage or a legal union. This extension of the *communio personarum*, cannot and may never be approved by the Roman Magisterium. But it remains a fruitful possibility.

The Persons of God within the Holy Trinity are co-equal. This is a strong element of the analogy between the divine 'Family' and human families, of which Protestant thought still has much to learn. There can be no domination and submission in God's life. That would amount to the heresy of subordinationism. Each divine Person makes the others what they are. Their union allows for real difference between them, and their difference enhances their love. Families are able to ground themselves by their faith and their practice in the flow of the divine love that embraces them. *Ubi caritas et amor, Deus ibi est*. At least two official Roman Catholic documents say this (United States Conference of Catholic Bishops 1994; Benedict XVI 2005), but they say it within the troubling restrictions of marital sacramentality, compulsory heterosexuality, and male gender bias.

Analogia amoris

Perhaps this *analogia amoris* needs extension beyond the limits of Catholic, and indeed all Christian doctrinal and sacramental thought, to embrace people of all faiths and of none, and people of different sexual orientations as well? There can be no love without the presence of the God who is Love. McCarthy's (2001) worry that 'the interpersonal turn' of such thought turns the family inward and minimizes its social character cannot be decisive. Trinitarian love always extends beyond itself, creating what is not itself and embracing it. Richard of St Victor saw this clearly (Thatcher 2007: 84–85). The immanence of divine love *within* families may also be a better way of linking families and Church than by calling families domestic churches.

The Christian Gospel is good news for families. Beginning with God's love and grace, it explains families to themselves. It unveils the possibility of participation in the life of God, in a unique form of intimacy and responsibility. Wherever the divine life is manifest there will be a movement towards 'equal-regard', for that life is a communion of co-equal Persons. Christians commend marriage as the basis of a household partly because of its remarkable powers of re-invention, and because of the fruitfulness of doctrinal development which enables it to be joyfully appropriated from one generation to the next. Marriage is revered as the enduring basis of families because of the enduring values and hopes which are expressed through it. These still render it an aspiration for a large majority of young women and men.

Parenting acquires its deep religious significance not by allowing God the Father and the Virgin Mary to serve as respective role models for fathers and mothers but by fathers and mothers together taking on joint responsibility for the care of their children in the name of the divine Father who loves all creatures that are brought into the world. The dynamic of equal-regard requires a re-appraisal of all aspects of household management—earning, caring, cooking, shopping, cleaning, and so on—not so that partners interchangeably do all of it in a display of pseudo-equality, but because a genuine power-sharing between them results in tasks and responsibilities being mutually assigned and discharged for the good of the whole family. The Love that God is, is distributed in the cooperation of partners, and is well modelled by the idea of divine *perichòrèsis*—the mutual interaction of the Persons of the Trinity within the unity of divine communion. Children, who cannot love their parents reciprocally, will require their 'agapic' love, as they move from complete dependence on their parents to progressive independence.

Parenting and Hospitality

McCarthy (2001) may overstate the danger of families becoming introverted. The boundaries of family are porous. The addition of ageing relatives, the fostering and adoption of children, the temporary accommodation of strangers (and friends), the offering of the home as a place for voluntary activity, these and many more possible additions and activities, may ensure families do not become self-absorbed. The divine Love has never been self-contained. It always flows beyond itself, creating what is not itself, and reconciling what is not itself to itself. Human love is of course less spectacular, needing divine grace in order to begin to approximate to its divine source. Families cannot exist as islands in an alien sea of sociality. Family members interact through school, work, the countless voluntary formal and informal organizations of civil society, and the opportunities provided by local neighbourhoods. For Christian families the local church may be not only a means of integration into the wider community, but the place where family life is hallowed, explained, nurtured and empowered in the way of Christ. From Catholics to Quakers, families are able to draw on the deep resources of faith, differently understood, appropriated and expressed, as they become 'communities of love and solidarity'.

REFERENCES

Albrecht, Gloria H. (2005). 'Ideals and Injuries: The Denial of Difference in the Construction of Christian Family Ideals'. *Journal of the Society of Christian Ethics*, 25(1): 169–195.

Anderson, Herbert and Susan B. W. Johnson (1995). *Regarding Children: A New Respect for Childhood and Families*. Louisville, KY: Westminster John Knox Press.

Benedict XVI (2005). *Deus Caritas Est*. <http://www.vatican.va/holy_father/benedict_xvi/encyclicals/documents/hf_ben-xvi_enc_20051225_deus-caritas-est_en.html>.

Bennett, Jana (2008). *Water Is Thicker than Blood: An Augustinian Theology of Marriage and Singleness*. New York: Oxford University Press.

Blankenhorn David, Don Browning, and Mary Stewart Van Leeuwen (2004) (eds). *Does Christianity Teach Male Headship? The Equal-Regard Marriage and its Critics*. Grand Rapids, MI, and Cambridge: Eerdmans.

Browning, Don S. (1991). *A Fundamental Practical Theology*. Minneapolis: Fortress Press.

Browning, Don S. (2003). *Marriage and Modernization: How Globalization Threatens Marriage and What to Do about It*. Grand Rapids, MI, and Cambridge: Eerdmans.

Browning, Don S. (2007). *Equality and the Family: A Fundamental, Practical Theology of Children, Mothers, and Fathers in Modern Societies*. Grand Rapids, MI , and Cambridge: Eerdmans.

Browning, Don S., Bonnie J. Miller-McLemore, Pamela D. Couture, Brynolf Lyon, K., and Robert M. Franklin (1997). *From Culture Wars to Common Ground: Religion and the American Family Debate*. Louisville, KY: Westminster John Knox Press.

Browning, Don S., M. Christian Green, and John Witte, Jr. (eds) (2006). *Sex, Marriage, & Family in World Religions*. New York: Columbia University Press.

Cahill, Lisa Sowle (2000). *Family: A Christian Social Perspective*. Minneapolis, MN: Fortress Press.

Center for Marriage and Families (2013). <http://www.centerformarriageandfamilies.org/>.

Clapp, Rodney (1993). *Families at the Crossroads: Beyond Traditional and Modern Options*. Leicester: Inter-Varsity Press.

Clapp, Rodney (2012). 'Our first family'. *Christian Century*, 129(9), 2 May: 53.

Drane, John and Olive M. Fleming Drane (2004). *Family Fortunes: Faith-full Caring for Today's Families*. London: Darton, Longman & Todd.

Green, M. Christian (2007). 'Fatherhood, Feminism, and Family Altruism'. In John Witte, Jr., M. Christian Green, and Amy Wheeler (eds), *The Equal-Regard Family and Its Friendly Critics: Don Browning and the Practical Theological Ethics of the Family*. Grand Rapids, MI, and Cambridge: Eerdmans, 69–94.

Grootaers Jan and Joseph A. Selling (1983). *The 1980 Synod of Bishops 'On the Role of the Family'*. Leuven: Leuven University Press.

Hallett, Garth (1998). *Priorities and Christian Ethics*. Cambridge: Cambridge University Press.

Holy See (1983) *Charter of the Rights of the Family*. <http://www.vatican.va/roman_curia/ pontifical_councils/family/documents/rc_pc_family_doc_19831022_family-rights_en.html>.

John Paul II (1981). *Familiaris consortio*. <http://www.vatican.va/holy_father/john_paul_ii/ apost_exhortations/documents/hf_jp-ii_exh_19811122_familiaris-consortio_en.html>.

John Paul II (1994). *Letter to Families*. <http://www.vatican.va/holy_father/john_paul_ii/ letters/documents/hf_jp-ii_let_02021994_families_en.html>.

McCarthy, David Matzko (2001). *Sex and Love in the Home*. London: SCM Press.

Osiek, Carolyn and David L. Balch (1997). *Families in the New Testament World: Households and House Churches*. Louisville, KY: Westminster John Knox Press.

Ouellet, Marc (2006), *Divine Likeness: Toward a Trinitarian Anthropology of the Family*. Grand Rapids, MI, and Cambridge: Eerdmans.

Paul VI (1965). *Gaudium et spes: Pastoral Constitution on the Church in the Modern World*. <http://www.vatican.va/archive/hist_councils/ii_vatican_council/documents/vat-ii_ cons_19651207_gaudium-et-spes_en.html>.

Reynolds, Philip Lyndon (1994). *Marriage in the Western Church: The Christianization of Marriage During the Patristic and Early Medieval Periods*. Leiden: M.J. Brill.

Ruether, Rosemary Radford (2000). *Christianity and the Making of the Modern Family*. Boston: Beacon Press.

Scott, Kieran (2009). Review of Bennett. *Theology Today*, 66(3): 403–5.

Tertullian (1885). *Prescription against Heretics*. From *Ante-Nicene Fathers*: Vol. 3. Buffalo, NY: Christian Literature Publishing Co. <http://www.newadvent.org/fathers/0311.htm>.

Thatcher, Adrian (2007). *Theology and Families*. Malden, MA: Oxford: Blackwell Publishing.

Thatcher, Adrian (2011). *God, Sex and Gender: An Introduction*. Chichester, UK: Wiley-Blackwell.

Thatcher, Adrian (2012). *Making Sense of Sex*. London: SPCK.

United States Conference of Catholic Bishops (1994). *Follow the Way of Love*. <http://old.usccb. org/laity/follow.shtml>.

Wall, John, Don Browning, William J. Docherty, Stephen Post, eds (2002). *Marriage, Health and the Professions: If Marriage is Good for You, What Does This Mean for Law, Medicine, Ministry, Therapy, and Business?* Grand Rapids, MI, and Cambridge: Eerdmans.

Waters, Brent (2007). *The Family in Christian Social and Political Thought*. Oxford: Oxford University Press.

Waters, Brent (2012). 'Is There a Normative Christian Family?' *INTAMS Review: Journal for the Study of Marriage and Spirituality*, 18(1), Summer: 53–63.

Williams, Fiona, ESRC CAVA Research Group (2004). *Rethinking Families*. London: Calouste Gulbenkian Foundation.

Witte, John (2002). 'The Goods and Goals of Marriage: The Health Paradigm in Historical Perspective'. In John Wall et al. (eds), *Marriage, Health and the Professions: If Marriage is Good for You, What Does This Mean for Law, Medicine, Ministry, Therapy, and Business?* Grand Rapids, MI, and Cambridge: Eerdmans, 49–89.

CHAPTER 36

....

GAY AFFECTIONS

....

GERARD LOUGHLIN

ONCE upon a time there were no gay people, and the same may be true in the future, when they will have become historical, passing personages of the twentieth and twenty-first centuries. But this thought offers little solace to those who wish that there were no such people, the dykes, fairies, faggots, homos, poofs, queers, etc. It offers no solace because it is about an identity and not the people identified, who always have been and will be, even if their present naming should cease. This chapter is concerned with how the character of the gay person was constructed in the twentieth century, and what that identity made and makes possible. But it cannot be doubted that there were and always will be people whose erotic affections are for members of their own sex. There is no reason to think that such interests are not stable across cultures and throughout history. And this is what we would expect if such affections are indeed a modality of human nature, like the differences of sex: male, female, and intersex.

We are concerned with people who find their own sex attractive. Brought up to believe that boy meets girl and the rest is history—romance, marriage, family—they find that meeting other boys or other girls is where history begins, but does not end. For while society provides scripts for heterosexual lovers, in which they are tutored from before puberty, it is less ready to guide girls who like girls and boys who like boys into the pleasures and joys of conjugal bliss. Such people have been equally tutored in wanting the other sex, but they find their bodies acting otherwise, with contrary movements of desire and longing. They find themselves differently possessed and dispossessed. They are surprised and taken out of themselves by the flesh of others, overtaken by unforeseen proximity and passion. 'One may want to, or manage to for a while, but despite one's best efforts, one is undone, in the face of the other, by the touch, by the scent, by the feel, by the prospect of the touch, by the memory of the feel' (Butler 2004: 23–24). Judith Butler reminds us that desire is an ecstatic movement, that in wanting to possess—to feel, to touch—we are also undone. The homosexual is doubly undone, drawn out not only from herself, but also from the expectations of family and community, from the lie that it is always the other sex that calls you to yourself.

Society, until relatively recently, offered little to such people, other than to condemn their yearnings and punish their yearnings' fulfilment. Such people had indeed to learn a script and play a part, and sometimes learned it so well that they may never have known that their interests really lay elsewhere than where society prescribed. They may have met the boy to their girl, or girl to their boy, that while not of their dreams was sufficiently companionable for them to find some comfort in their arms, some joy in producing offspring. Or they might have entered religious life; a life dedicated to love beyond the body, where the body's desires were both chastised and chastened to signal a more intimate if also more spiritual companionship. Some, however, found their way to places—nearly always city places—that offered alternate scripts for living: marginal and sometimes criminal ways of life. These were permitted but punishable forms of association, and dangerous because the permission could be withdrawn on a whim and replaced with incarceration and worse.

THE LOVE THAT DARE NOT SPEAK ITS NAME

Lady Windermere's Fan by Oscar Wilde (1854–1900) was first performed in 1892, and it was in that year that Wilde met the Marquess of Queensbury, the father of Wilde's lover, Lord Alfred Douglas (Hyde 1976: 192). The joviality of their initial meeting did not last. In 1895, four days after the opening of Wilde's most famous play, *The Importance of Being Earnest*, the Marquess called at Wilde's Club, the Albermale, and left his card for 'Oscar Wilde posing as a somdomite [*sic*]' (Hyde 1976: 196). Wilde rose to the bait, and sued for libel. By the end of the year it was he and not Queensbury who was in the dock. Wilde was found guilty of 'gross indecency' and imprisoned for two years. Despite Queensbury's card, Wilde escaped the graver charge of sodomy, which carried a penalty of up to ten years in prison.

In 1894, Douglas had written of 'the love that dare not speak its name'. He had done so in the poem 'Two Loves', in which that Love which was 'full sad and sweet', sighing with many sighs, is denounced as Shame by the 'true Love' that fills 'the hearts of boy and girl with mutual flame'. But even if this false Love, which arrived 'unasked by night', had dared to say his name, he could hardly have called himself 'homosexual' love, for the term was but newly minted, and not yet abroad in the world. When it was put to Wilde at his trial that the unspoken name was 'unnatural love', he replied that it was the affection of 'an elder for a younger man', such as there was between 'David and Jonathan, such as Plato made the very basis of his philosophy, and such as you find in the sonnets of Michelangelo and Shakespeare'.

> It is that deep spiritual affection that is as pure as it is perfect … It is in this century misunderstood, so much misunderstood that it may be described as the 'Love that dare not speak its name', and on account of it I am placed where I am today. It is beautiful, it is fine, it is the noblest form of affection. There is nothing unnatural about it.

It is intellectual, and it repeatedly exists between an elder and a younger man, where the elder has intellect and the younger man has all the joy, hope, and glamour of life before him. That it should be so, the world does not understand. The world mocks at it and sometimes puts one in the pillory for it.

(Wilde, quoted in Hyde 1976: 257–258)

The speech won Wilde both applause and derision, and of course he was right that the love he described was as natural as any other. But it was also constructed upon a classical model of pederastic affections, seemingly shorn of physicality and elevated to a purely intellectual, spiritual state. It is a model that was made possible through the teaching of the Classics in public schools and ancient universities (Harding 2013).

Douglas and Wilde may never have thought of themselves as homosexuals, but a hundred years on, and 'homosexual' has become the default term for a person who is attracted to, and falls in love with, people of his or her own sex, and homosexuality is the term for such attraction and love. And of course there are other names, such as gay and queer. One might think that all these names refer to the same kind of person, but if so they evaluate that kind differently. They are said in some contexts and not others, and those contexts—from the academy and hospital to the bar and back alley—evoke different feelings and reactions, different cultural regimes.

A name like 'gay' provides a fascinating example of how cultural context determines meaning and resonance. Many used it happily as an adjective for anything that was light-hearted and cheerful. But it was also a slang term for a homosexual—though with limited use beyond certain circles—and in the nineteenth century it named women prostitutes (Weeks 1977: 3). It was only as homosexuals became more prominent in society that the term became more generally known and used, first abusively and then affirmatively by the abused, as in the Gay Liberation Front, Gay Pride, and the British Gay Christian Movement, founded in 1976 (Gill 1998). While 'homosexual' might be considered a merely descriptive, neutral term, 'gay' was used evaluatively, whether pejoratively or proudly. More recently gay has returned to a more adjectival usage, but now meaning sad or weak or uncool, and so once more demeaning those identified as gay.

Gay and homosexual might seem synonymous, but if so they are inexact equivalents. For they not only carry different evaluations, they have different referents. For while homosexual refers to both men and women, gay was increasingly used of men only, and lesbian became the preferred name for homosexual women. Thus the Gay Christian Movement revised its name in 1987 to become the Lesbian and Gay Christian Movement (Gill 1998: 17 n. 2).

It is because the names for persons who love their own sex are not constant, and carry different ranges of resonance and expectation, that it is necessary to interrogate their formation and history, and to trace them back through history, including the history of the Church. For otherwise we will be in danger of supposing that what someone meant by a 'homosexual' in the late nineteenth century is the same as what was meant by a 'gay' person in the twentieth, let alone a 'sodomite' in the seventeenth or twelfth centuries, or a *molle* or *tribade* in the first.

The issue is whether there is a constant character to which all these terms refer and from which they take their import, or whether the terms are social constructs—concretions of beliefs, fears, and hopes—that form the people to which they are applied, directing and limiting their lives. The first possibility is often called an essentialist viewpoint, while the second is known, not surprisingly, as a constructionist one. The first supposes that gay people today—and straight or heterosexual people as well—are much the same as they ever were. What it means to be a man or a woman, heterosexual or homosexual, doesn't change. The second argues that these things do indeed change, that how people thought and felt in the past may be very different from how they do now. A rose by any other name does not smell as sweet, for by another name the flower is perfumed with different associations. There may be similarities, but these cannot be assumed, and must be established. We are social animals, whose culture mediates everything we otherwise experience as natural, so that the natural always comes to us through the cultural, saturated with contingent meanings and feelings.

Becoming Homosexual

It is often said that the nineteenth century extended into the twentieth, coming to an end only in 1914. But the long nineteenth century may be even longer, for in many ways we still live within its ambit. And we still live with its discovery—or invention—of sexuality, of homosexuality and heterosexuality. For it was only in the nineteenth century—as Michel Foucault must still teach us—that the 'homosexual became a personage, a past, a case history, and a childhood, in addition to being a type of life, a life form, and a morphology, with an indiscreet anatomy and possibly a mysterious physiology'. This newly found 'personage' was completely conditioned and consumed by his sexuality.

> It was everywhere present in him: at the root of all his actions because it was their insidious and indefinitely active principle; written immodestly on his face and body because it was a secret that always gave itself away. It was consubstantial with him, less as a habitual sin than as a singular nature…. Homosexuality appeared as one of the forms of sexuality when it was transposed from the practice of sodomy onto a kind of interior androgyny, a hermaphroditism of the soul. The sodomite had been a temporary aberration; the homosexual was now a species.
>
> (Foucault 1984: 43)

The import of Foucault's claim has often been debated, for a certain carelessness—in either Foucault or his readers—has led to differing interpretations of his always beguiling but elusive text. A common reading is to suppose that here Foucault marks a transition from a concern with same-sex practices to an interest in their practitioners, from sodomitical *acts* to homosexual *persons*. Before, there had been the 'practice of sodomy', a lamentable habit into which anyone might fall, but now there is a 'species', the homo-sexual, the kind of person who would so succumb.

Certainly Foucault wants to note the arrival of the homosexual species as a distinct kind of human, one that is marked by a sexuality that determines all aspects of its char-acter. Moreover, this personage is understood in terms of 'nature' rather than of 'sin'; it is a natural occurrence rather than a moral failing. And this species emerged in the nineteenth century, for it was then, as we have seen, that the terms 'homosexual' and 'homosexuality' were coined, first in German and then in English.

Foucault dates the arrival of these terms to 1870 and to an article on 'contrary sex-ual sensations' by Carl Friedrich Otto Westphal (1833–1890), professor of psychiatry at the University of Berlin. Foucault is not concerned with finding a precise date for the arrival of homosexuality; Westphal's article 'can stand as its date of birth'. He is more concerned to note that homosexuality is not a moral but a 'psychological, psychiatric, medical category', and that it 'constitutes' those it names in terms of a 'sensibility, a cer-tain way of inverting the masculine and the feminine in oneself' (Foucault 1984: 43). This is why it is 'an interior androgyny, a hermaphroditism of the soul'. It is an inward, psychological matter. One can be homosexual without engaging in sexual relations. It is undoubtedly this last point which suggests that Foucault is drawing a distinction between sodomitical acts and homosexual persons. And indeed he has already declared that 'sodomy was a category of forbidden acts; their perpetrator was nothing more than the juridical subject of them' (Foucault 1984: 43). But he has also spoken of the 'sodo-mite' as a character prone to such perpetrations. Thus there are acts and actors, prac-tices and practitioners, whether we are talking about sodomy or homosexuality, pre- or post-1870. But under the earlier regime it is the acts that give rise to the actor, whereas in the later regime it is the other way around, homosexuality being a sensibility before it is an action. But even more importantly for Foucault, these actors are called to the stage by different regimes of discourse. The sodomite is a juridical subject, called by law, civil or ecclesial, to confess his (or her) misdeeds. The homosexual, on the other hand, is named through psychological inspection, a patient of pathology. It is the transition of the homosexual from one regime of discourse to another that interests Foucault. Thus he can name the homosexual prior to the name, the 'nineteenth-century homosexual' who became a 'personage' through his naming (Foucault 1984: 43). The term picks out people who were always present, but changes them in doing so, producing a new con-cept for them to inhabit.

Foucault suggests the like power of Church and clinic to call out their respective subjects, to constitute them as sinners or deviants. Thus the 'nineteenth-century psy-chiatrists' give 'strange baptismal names' to their perverts, viewing their pathologies as 'heresies' against orthodox nature (Foucault 1984: 43). But Foucault also finds a discon-tinuity. For while the ecclesiastics sought the sodomite in order to be rid of an infection, the doctors policed their patients in order to give them and their ailments an 'analytical, visible, and permanent reality'. They sought the specification, not the exclusion, of such 'aberrant sexualities', and found them throughout the social body and in the body of the patient (Foucault 1984: 44).

Foucault credits Westphal (1870) with the invention of homosexuality, but Westphal never used the term, and Karl Maria Kertbeny (1824–1882) is a much better candidate for this, being the first to use the term 'homosexual' in print (1869). But it was Richard von Krafft-Ebing (1840–1902) who established its more general usage through his *Psychopathia sexualis* (1886). It was this work that introduced the character of the homosexual to the English-speaking world when Charles Gilbert Chaddock (1861–1936) published his translation in 1892. It is important to note the late date for the invention of the 'homosexual'—though not as late as the invention of the German 'heterosexual' in 1887 and the English in 1892—for it reminds us that the term was barely available when the nineteenth century's most acclaimed homosexual achieved his greatest fame and notoriety.

Sexuality is now ubiquitous in Western culture. It is understood as an essential erotic interest that can be variously orientated, and which is given—made known—by its *object*, by the *sex* of those who arouse desire. This way of thinking is now so dominant in the West that it appears entirely natural, as just the way things are. But as a way of categorizing and evaluating people it is relatively new, a late child of modernity. Thus, as David Halperin notes, 'although there have been, in many different times and places (including classical Greece), persons who sought sexual contact with other persons of the same sex as themselves, it is only within the last hundred years or so that such persons (or some portion of them, at any rate) have been homosexuals' (1990: 29). It is also only in the last hundred years or so that other people have been heterosexuals, and only more recently that a portion of homosexuals have been gay, lesbian, or queer. Halperin's century is itself becoming long, stretching out beyond 1986, when he first published his essay.

The historicist, Halperian argument—that the past is another country—is not easily grasped. The Church of England report, *Some Issues in Human Sexuality* (2003), for example, fails at the outset, and this despite rehearsing the historicist argument in some detail. Its authors fail to learn from their own learning, and conclude that while such terms 'as "homosexual" and "heterosexual" may be modern', people were always aware 'that there were certain individuals who had an innate attraction to members of their own sex and therefore, although the term "homosexual" may be recent, the idea that lies behind it may be an ancient one' (Church of England 2003: 182). But the 'idea' is precisely not ancient, and no ancient individuals thought that they or others were homosexual, that they could be characterized as having an 'innate attraction to members of their own sex', let alone a 'sexual orientation'. There is no evidence that they thought like this, their texts do not speak like this, and they did not have to. They had other categories for thinking the identities and practices of those who sought companionship and pleasure in the bodies of their own sex. St Paul gives no indication of thinking as we do—but merely refers to men having (some kind of) sex with men, and to women having either (some kind of) sex with women or the wrong kind of sex with men, and, moreover, sex in the context of idolatry (Rom. 1:26; see further Martin 2006: 51–64).

SODOMIA

Foucault, as we have seen, is suspected of having drawn a distinction between the nineteenth century's homosexual and the earlier, temporary figure of the sodomite, which distinction he characterized as one between a 'nature' and an 'act', a disposition and a practice. Sodomy became homosexuality when the act became the man, and for the most part we are talking of men. But the medieval and early modern sodomite may have been less temporary and more of a species than Foucault either knew or acknowledged; a precursor of the homosexual, though conceptually more inchoate and subject to a more 'hysterical' response. Sodomy and the sodomite were no less a matter of invention than homosexuality and the homosexual, but one developed by Christian theology rather than medical science.

Oscar Wilde was accused of being—'posing as'—a sodomite, an entirely biblical character, but one whose named practice, sodomy, is of more recent origin. Mark Jordan (1997) dates the invention of sodomy (*sodomia*) to Peter Damian in the eleventh century. Peter coined the term on the basis of blasphemy (*blasphemia*) in his *Liber Gomorrhianus* (*Book of Gomorrah*).

> And we add this: if blasphemy is the worst, I do not know in what way sodomy is better. Blasphemy makes a man to err; sodomy, to perish. The former divides the soul from God; the latter joins it to the devil. The former casts out of paradise; the latter drowns in Tartarus. The former binds the eyes of the mind; the latter casts into the turmoil of ruin. If we are careful to search into which of these crimes weighs more heavily on the scales of divine scrutiny, sacred scripture fully instructs us in what we seek. Indeed, while the sons of Israel were led into captivity for blaspheming God and worshipping idols, the Sodomites perished in heavenly fire and sulphur, devoured in the holocaust.
>
> (Peter Damian 1982: 89)

Before, there had only been sodomites and their practices, but from now on there would be a new essence and identity, a possibly contagious disposition, which did not have to be acted out in order to be present. The *Book of Gomorrah* was addressed to Pope Leo IX, urging him to take action against those clerics who practised the 'sodomitic vice' or 'sodomy'—which newly coined term was the fateful 'abstraction of an essential sin'. This abstraction was drawn from an already existing character, the 'sodomite', who was thus further constituted as the exemplar of a 'range of human acts, activities, or dispositions' (Jordan 1997: 49, 161). While Peter is repeatedly concerned with the acts that constitute sodomy, these are the acts of a particular character, a particular condition, which, while it might change—Peter is concerned that the sodomite should desist from his actions—will not readily or really do so, since the sodomite is likened to a demoniac and deserving of death, as also those who harbour them (Peter Damian 1982: 39–40). If the sodomite is to be cured it will be in the next life (Jordan 1997: 57–58).

Burdened with the weight of the crime, he cannot arise nor conceal his evil for long in the hiding-place of ignorance. He cannot rejoice here while he lives nor can he hope there when he dies, since he is compelled to bear the disgrace of human derision now and afterwards the torment of eternal damnation. The lamentation of the prophet clearly applies to this soul. 'Look O Lord, upon my distress: my stomach is in ferment, my heart recoils within me because I am full of bitterness: the sword kills without, and at home death is similar.'

(Peter Damian 1982: 65; quoting Lam. 1:20)

Jordan is adamant that medieval sodomy was in no sense modern homosexuality. Like the Bible, 'medieval moral theology' has 'absolutely nothing' to say about homosexuality. 'Homosexuality' is no more discussed by medieval theology than are phlogiston, Newton's inertia, quarks, or any of the other entities hypothesized by one or another modern science. '"Sodomy" is not "homosexuality"' (Jordan 1997: 161). However, in the medieval sodomite Jordan does find a precursor for the modern homosexual in the sense that, like the homosexual, the sodomite is a personage with a definable identity, an 'anatomy and physiology, personal history, and secret community'. The possibility of categorizing people according to their sexual desires was made possible by the medieval invention of the sodomite. When we think of others or ourselves as homosexuals it is because the medievals had first thought of sodomites, people who are defined by a set of sexual practices and desires.

This does not mean, of course, that the Sodomite *is* the nineteenth century's homosexual. The identities are different, as are the notions about identity itself. It does mean that the invention of the homosexual may well have relied on the already familiar category of the Sodomite. The idea that same-sex pleasure constitutes an identity of some kind is clearly the work of medieval theology, not nineteenth-century forensic medicine. So too any rejection of the Christian account of Sodomy may well carry with it the rejection of identity as a necessary category for thinking about same-sex pleasure.

(Jordan 1997: 163–164, author's emphasis)

And Jordan's last point is crucial, for both the notion of the sodomite and of the homosexual make same-sex pleasure the mark of an identity, in the way that a society might imagine left-handedness as the marker of a certain character, a certain type of sinister personage, who gives herself away by writing, or wanting to write, with her left hand. As with the homosexual, the act—writing with the left hand—is the sign of a preceding disposition, a prior and sinister desire. Today most people would think it absurd that left-handedness was a marker of a particular kind of personage, who might be opposed to the dexterous, the right-handed, in the manner that we take sexual orientation to be the marker of a specific, stable, and culturally transcendent identity. But the comparison is not innocent, because the left-handed have been viewed as deviant, portending deeper threats, and requiring correction, enforced normalization.

Soft Men and Hard Women

However, we must further complicate Foucault and Jordan's story. For just as the sodomite might be considered analogous to the homosexual, so the ancient world had a similar personage, at least one similar personage, who was alike constructed in terms of his sexual proclivities. But being analogous this person is also interestingly different from either the sodomite or the homosexual. Bernadette Brooten, in her study of *Love Between Women*, discusses the example of Soranus of Antioch (as translated by Caelius Aurelianus), who, in his two-part treatise *On Acute and On Chronic Diseases* (*Peri oxeōn kai chroniōn pathōn*), details the case of soft men (*molles*), who become effeminate and adopt a passive role with other men, being penetrated rather than penetrating. For Soranus this is a disease of the soul, consequent upon the failure to moderate sexual desires. Since such men can have periods of remission, when they again become penetrators of both boys and women, Soranus' distinction between healthy and unhealthy men is not the modern one between heterosexual and homosexual persons (which categories include both men and women), but an ancient one between active and passive men; between proper men and those who are not, who suffer from desiring to become as if women (Brooten 1996: 148–150; see also Halperin 1990: 22–24).

At one point in his discussion, Soranus likens these soft men to those women—*tribades*—who suffer the reverse disease of pursuing other women, of aspiring to an active, masculine role in sexual congress (Brooten 1996: 150–156). As with the men, the unbridled lust of these women leads them to adopt the contrary of their natural sexual role, and censure falls on their wish to be active rather than passive, as it falls on those men who wish to be passive rather than active. But their partners are blameless, at least with regard to male–male encounters, which further points up that we are not dealing with anything like the modern concept of the homosexual, but with one of its precursors. Except that in some ways the earlier ideas live on in Western culture, as when it is supposed that (active) homosexual men are invariably the corruptors of otherwise (passive) heterosexual boys, and all sexual encounters are imagined as taking place between dominants and submissives. Most importantly, Soranus understood homoerotic desires to be pathological, and debated both their cause and possible cure. He debated whether the condition might be hereditary or congenital, and by way of cure he advocated mind control and, for some women, clitoridectomy (Brooten 1996: 156–159, 162–171).

Soranus studied in Alexandria and practised medicine in Rome at the beginning of the second century AD, so while not contemporaneous with Paul, he demonstrates the possibility that Paul might have known of those among the Gentiles who were deemed to be something like Soranus' *tribades* and *molles* (soft men). So perhaps it was such people of whom Paul was thinking in Romans 1. But whether or not we make this supposition, we cannot say that Paul had any idea of modern homosexuality or of homosexual persons, and we must remember that Paul associated 'unnatural' sexual inclinations and practices with idolatry, with a fundamental misperception of the world. He was not thinking of bishops and priests, of holy men and women.

The ancient world is curiously both different from our own and all too familiar. Its asymmetric view of the sexes still shadows more recent symmetries, its inequality still present in the avowed egalitarianism of the modern world, and nowhere more effectively than in the cultures of the Christian churches. There it is still possible to think that women are but a 'complement' to men, and so unfit for those offices sequestered to the male sex.

Affective Relationships

We have tracked back from the late nineteenth-century homosexual to the first-century *molles* and *tribades* by way of the medieval sodomite, and we have seen that it is not only the nineteenth-century homosexual who might be thought a certain type of character or personage. What these people had in common was a desire for their own sex, an affection for similar flesh. But we have not found a constant character, the continuity of a single identity, stable across the centuries. Each of the persons—the types of person—is different from one another. And yet there are also similarities, though not necessarily the same similarities in all cases.

But now we can track forward from the nineteenth century to the present day, to the homosexuals of the twentieth and twenty-first centuries, to such characters as the lesbian woman and gay man. These latter are as much constructs of the social imaginary as anything that has gone before, and as such they too are unstable, changing over time. We can track their arrival and development, their permutations and perturbations, even their fracturing and dissolution. Above all we can see that the modern homosexual is not one thing.

This story proceeds by way of homosexuality as pathology in modern psychiatry. This is how it was first conceived at the end of the nineteenth century, and the degree to which it should be considered pathological would become a matter for debate in both psychiatry and psychoanalysis. Sigmund Freud understood it as a failure in development, and yet as such natural in everyone, with most, but not all, turning heterosexual as they matured. Homosexuality is thus the universal condition. By 1935 Freud could write to a troubled mother that homosexuality 'is assuredly no advantage, but it is nothing to be ashamed of, no vice, no degradation, it cannot be classified as an illness, we consider it to be a variation of the sexual function produced by a certain arrest of sexual development' (quoted in Abelove 2003: 1).

As the twentieth century wore on, the case for naturalizing homosexuality grew. In 1952 it was still classified as a psychopathic personality disturbance by the highly influential America Psychiatric Association. But by 1968 it had become a mere mental disturbance, and in 1973 it was removed from even this category. It was now what Freud had suggested, a minority variant of human sexuality.

Margaret Farley notes that many of those who opposed the depathologizing of homo-sexuality credited the change to political pressures rather than medical facts, and that they were not wrong to do so (2006: 281 n. 65). For medicine does not escape the cultural. The construction of a pathological homosexuality was itself a political act. Psychiatry, still in its infancy when homosexuality was invented, responded to social valuations of same-sex practices, and continued to do so throughout the twentieth century.

People pathologize that which they think undesirable and find incomprehensible. Doing so provides the comfort of an understandable causal mechanism, and so the promise of intervention and possible elimination: a cure. When psychiatry, for the most part, gave up on doing this, other sciences arose to take its place. Thus genetics offered a different causal mechanism, a different means of manipulation and possible elimina-tion. As Farley notes, homosexuality has been constructed in any number of ways, and nearly always with a political intent: to expunge or extol. 'Depending on the favoured construction, responses have ranged from recommendations for repentance, genetic therapy, psychoanalysis, or political advocacy for the rights and general welfare of gays and lesbians' (Farley 2006: 283).

The naturalization of homosexuality resulted from political agitation, from an array of movements and discourses that argued for the decriminalization of homosexual behaviour, and for homosexuals as but one more minority in any human society, part of humankind's rich tapestry. And while 'homosexuality' was loosed from its psychiatric moorings, losing the sense of pathology, it nevertheless seemed too indebted to those origins, so that many homosexuals turned to naming themselves as 'gay'. As such they were self-named, and positively named, and the meaning of the name was being formed in and through its adoption, in the discovery of what it would be to live as an avowed gay person; free to love whom one would, and free from persecution in doing so. Gay life was a new thing; is a new thing.

More recently the idea of gay men and lesbian women has given way to that of queer folk, of people who refuse to conform to either heterosexual or homosexual expecta-tions, who want to imagine a culture in which affections rather than bodies determine the legitimacy of relationships; in which it matters how you love rather than (the sex of) who you love. This is why for many the arrival of same-sex marriage does not seem like the redefinition of marriage but its further recognition, since recognized as the relation-ship, the mutual commitment, of people, rather than the people committed. Their sex does not affect the relationship, but the relationship affects the nature of their sex (with one another). This stress on relationship rather than prior identity is not so very new. It is not so far from the 'situation ethics' of the 1960s (Fletcher 1966), nor from the teaching of the Jesuit Martin D'Arcy, who in 1945 could write that the 'perfection of love … is to be found in personal friendship, whether between a man and a woman, between man and man or between man and God' (1945: 32–33). It is there in the command to love the neighbour, when the neighbour is not some people but all, when the identity of 'neigh-bour' undoes all other identities, including that of 'enemy'.

And we might think that something similar is being said by those who play down bodily identities in favour of the Christian's relationship to Christ. 'Our sexual affections can no more define who we are than can our class, race or nationality', as the *St Andrew's Day Statement* claims (1997: 7). Sexual identities—gay or straight—are as ephemeral as those of race or class. They will all disappear, 'placed under eschatological erasure', as Elizabeth Stuart puts it.

> They are not matters of ultimate concern. At my death all that has been written on my body will be once again overwritten by my baptism as it was a few weeks after my birth when I was immersed in the waters of death and rebirth and a new character was given to me which nothing can ever destroy ... Gender, race, sexual orientation, family, nationality, and all other culturally constructed identities will not survive the grave. They will pass away, the 'I' that is left, the I am that I am is not, as the popular song would have it, 'my own special creation' nor the creation of human communities, the I am that I am is God's own special creation and that is my only grounds for hope.
>
> (Stuart 2007: 74)

It would thus seem that Stuart and the *St Andrew's Day Statement* are oddly at one; oddly, because the *Statement* is the product of Evangelical Christianity, while Stuart comes from a more Catholic background and writes as a lesbian. Stuart's list of identities is more extensive than those in the *Statement*, especially if we take 'gender' to include 'sex', remembering that sex is always a gendered category (see Butler 1999). Sex is one category that does not pass away in the *Statement*, being somehow more ontological, more eschatological. But both *Statement* and Stuart seem to think gay identity a passing phase. But passing when? To the extent that the *Statement* agrees with Stuart—that the identities we and our cultures construct are eschatologically erased—we have to recognize that both might be advocating a realized eschatology; identities—or some of them—are being erased now.

Gay Silence

Homosexuals, gays, queers, have been asked to speak the nature of their lives, the joys and sorrows of their affections, and in the churches to do so as the Christians they claim to be. And other Christians are asked to listen, to attend to what Oliver O'Donovan has called the 'experience of the human' borne by the 'gay Christian movement' (2009: 17). O'Donovan has wondered if this movement is now of an age that it can speak for itself. The *St Andrew's Day Statement*, to which O'Donovan was a signatory, was intended to elicit just such an account of the gay Christian experience. But the gays failed to deliver, the 'strategy' falling victim to what O'Donovan saw as a 'prevailing hermeneutic of suspicion' (2009: 110).

O'Donovan lamented the failure to start a conversation. 'What the gay experience really is, is a question of huge importance both to gays and non-gays.' Do gays really want marriage, or does the 'roaming character of some gay relations' get closer to the heart of the matter? O'Donovan wanted gays to debate this in public, as doing so would help people like himself to understand 'the dynamic of the [gay] experience'. 'They will need to ask themselves about likenesses of experience and about unlikenesses, about ways in which known patterns illuminate unknown, about the extending of paradigms to encompass new types' (O'Donovan 2009: 111).

It is the likeness and unlikeness of gay experience to non-gay experience that homosexuals have to explain to heterosexuals; that 'elusive and mysterious experience' of which O'Donovan (2009: 112) writes. This calling to account—or invitation to conversation—is remarkable for thinking there is something that can be called the gay experience, an experience we must suppose different from an equally single straight one. O'Donovan is reticent about this experience, for he is calling upon gay people to deliver it in appropriately analogical fashion, but one notes the nice coding of 'roaming' relations. One might suppose that some heterosexuals are also promiscuous, but it is unclear whether this would fall as a likeness or an unlikeness between gay and non-gay experience.

O'Donovan is coy about the gay experience he wants to construct, but that he needs to construct it is clear enough. For if there is one thing we know in this regard, it is that there is no one experience that characterizes being gay. Perhaps there are enough commonalities between people to think that their experiences are not so discrete that we cannot venture some generalizations. Yet at the same time we have to recognize that there are enough varieties of, and vagaries in, the human condition, both within and along the timeline of any society, that we must talk about a plurality of conditions.

Not even the common experience of death—the experience of others' death—is the same for all, since for some it arrives suddenly, unexpectedly, while for others it is seen far off and watched as it approaches. Then it is foreseen and sometimes even longed-for. The death of the young is different from that of the old, and both different in different times and places, in different social classes and cultures of mortality. We may suppose a common core, and that medical or similar discourses will give us purchase on this generality, but the different contexts in which lives are lived affect their ending, as those contexts affect all other common attributes of body and desire.

If this variety of circumstance and emotion can attend something as truly common and similar for all as death, how much more is this the case for personal relationships in all their variety, from fleeting encounters to more permanent accords, which even in marriage change and develop over time? Is this not one reason why we attend to the stories of others, in novels, films, and songs, so that we might know the manifold nature of our human condition, and hope to find there some common ground for our own hurts and joys—unique as these seem to us? And while our own lives—our own 'special creations'—will be less unique than we like to think, is there not a need to keep reading, watching, listening, in order to comprehend, however weakly, the complexity of human affection? And hasn't this been taking place for many years? Haven't gay people been writing, showing, and yes, even singing of their lives and loves?

Rather than supposing a heterosexual or gay experience, we would do better in recognizing a multitude of such, and in recognizing their birth out of a multitude of

differing contexts. So rather than think modern homosexuality or homosexual experience a 'coherent definitional field', we should follow Eve Kosofsky Sedgwick and think
it 'a space of overlapping, contradictory, and conflictual definitional forces' (1994: 45).
And with Sedgwick we would also do better in recognizing that one sexual identity does
not simply give way to another, in a neatly sequential or supersessionist manner, but that
there are also temporal overlaps between such identities or characters. Sedgwick makes
this point against the histories offered by Foucault and Halperin, and it is one that this
chapter has risked also, having suggested a history in which 'one model of same-sex relations is superseded by another, which may again be superseded by another' (1994: 47).
But we have also noted the persistence of earlier forms, and so suppose a more imbri-
cated story. Different models can exist together, and we should not think earlier identities mere remnants or vestiges, soon to pass away, but recognize them as something
more obdurate, troubling any attempt to define a single modern identity or experience.
As a consequence, any such experience is formed by 'unexpectedly plural, varied, and
contradictory historical understandings', the force of which is as palpable today as it ever
was (Sedgwick 1994: 48).

By drawing attention to the continuing life of past understandings, Sedgwick sought
to denaturalize the present, and to 'render less destructively presumable "homosexuality as we know it today"' (1994: 48). O'Donovan does not presume to know such a
homosexuality, but he does assume that there is such a homosexuality to be known, and
that the subjects of this identity or experience can be called upon to debate it for the benefit of others in the churches, who seem to think it so very different from their own experience, and who need to know it in order to know that it is not an 'intrinsic moral evil' as
the Catholic Church has taught (Congregation for the Doctrine of the Faith 1986: 250).

Gay Christians have been telling their stories for years, for as long as it was possible for them to think themselves gay Christians (for example Babuscio 1976). If their
talking, writing, and publishing has seemed like silence, it is not for want of speaking.
And this speaking heard as silence brings us back to the idea that identities are changed
in Christ. Stuart's idea of eschatological erasure is one that seeks to relativize, but not
do away with the identities that allow us to be, happily or unhappily. They remain, but
are overwritten, written differently, and they include the identities of male and female,
which are also rewritable. But this does not seem to be the case for the St Andrew's Day
Statement, where sexed identity is steadfast.

The Statement seems to think that there are only two types of body, and the suspicion must be that they are equally steadfast in their heterosexuality, notwithstanding the claim that at the 'deepest level' there is no such thing as a heterosexual (St
Andrew's Day Statement 1997: 7). For immediately, we are reminded that Christians
are called to 'various forms of self-denial' in their 'struggle against disordered
desires' or the 'misdirection' of 'innocent' ones (St Andrew's Day Statement 1997: 7).
We are reminded that the Bible places the 'phenomena of homosexual behaviour'
in the 'context of human idolatry', a context which seems more certain than modernity's 'theoretical confusion' regarding such phenomena (St Andrew's Day Statement
1997: 8). And finally, we are reminded that the Church still proffers the 'forgiveness of

sins' to 'those who understand themselves as homosexual', calling everyone to either marriage or singleness (*St Andrew's Day Statement* 1997: 8–9). It is thus clear that homosexuality and heterosexuality are not on the same footing. There may be no heterosexuals at the deepest level, but there is heterosexuality, and it is not a problem in the manner of 'homosexual behaviour'. This of course is not surprising. The *Statement* is the product of Evangelical Christianity. But it serves to remind us that talk of rewriting or erasing identities is not without danger.

The story of gay affections as told here is about the emergence of an identity or set of identities; identities that arose from the late nineteenth-century invention of the homosexual, a personage who—as Foucault argued—was the product of medical rather than moral discourse. As such, the homosexual was naturalized, and in the course of the twentieth century re-entered moral discourse, but on his or her own terms, speaking for themselves as gay men and lesbian women. These identities have in turn been questioned, queered, by those who, attending to how discourse builds bodies, have wanted to show the instability of all identities, including, and in particular, the heterosexual—itself the child of the (not-so) far-off nineteenth century.

The destabilizing of sexual identities—the work of queer theory—finds an analogue in the relativizing of identities in Christ, and both share the same danger: that the loosening of identity might be the loss—the destruction—of the persons identified. This is why both theology and theory must attend to the obduracies of the body—those affections of the flesh that trouble some discourses—and those discourses that enable the affectionate relation of bodies. Such discourses include the stories of gay affection that some have heard as silence, but in which silence we might also hear the discourse of the gospel, the story of a relationship that makes possible all other affections. 'When God revealed himself as love, the last fear was removed from man's heart. Neither God nor nature nor other human beings were enemies and a menace. They could all be looked at with interest and love, and in the case of persons love could be mutual' (D'Arcy 1945: 33).

REFERENCES

Abelove, Henry (2003). *Deep Gossip*. Minneapolis: University of Minnesota Press.

Babuscio, Jack (1976). *We Speak for Ourselves: Experiences in Homosexual Counselling*. London: SPCK.

Brooten, Bernadette (1996). *Love Between Women: Early Christian Responses to Female Homoeroticism*. Chicago: University of Chicago Press.

Butler, Judith (1999). *Gender Trouble: Feminism and the Subversion of Identity*, 2nd edn. London: Routledge.

Butler, Judith (2004). *Precarious Life: The Powers of Mourning and Violence*. London: Verso.

Church of England (2003). *Some Issues in Human Sexuality*. London: Church House Publishing.

Congregation for the Doctrine of the Faith (1986). *On the Pastoral Care of Homosexual Persons*. London: Catholic Truth Society.

D'Arcy SJ, M. C. (1945). *The Mind and Heart of Love: Lion and Unicorn in Eros and Agape*. London: Faber & Faber.

Farley, Margaret A. (2006). *Just Love: A Framework for Christian Sexual Ethics*. London: Continuum.

Fletcher, Joseph (1966). *Situation Ethics: The New Morality*. London: SCM Press.

Foucault, Michel (1984). *The History of Sexuality: An Introduction*. Harmondsworth: Peregrine Books.

Gill, Sean (1998). *The Lesbian and Gay Christian Movement: Campaigning for Justice, Truth and Love*. London: Cassell.

Halperin, David M. (1990). 'One Hundred Years of Homosexuality'. In Halperin (ed.), *One Hundred Years of Homosexuality and Other Essays on Greek Love*. New York: Routledge, 15–40.

Harding, James E. (2013). *The Love of David and Jonathan: Ideology, Text, Reception*. London: Equinox.

Hyde, Montgomery H. (1976). *Oscar Wilde*. London: Methuen.

Jordan, Mark D. (1997). *The Invention of Sodomy in Christian Theology*. Chicago: University of Chicago Press.

Kertbeny, Karl Maria (1869). *Paragraph 143 des preussischen Strafgesetzbuches...* Leipzig: Serbe.

von Krafft-Ebing, Richard (1886). *Psychopathia sexualis*. Stuttgart: Ferdinand Enke.

von Krafft-Ebing, Richard (1892). *Psychopathia sexualis*. Trans. C. G. Chaddock. London: F. A. Davis Co.

Martin, Dale B. (2006). *Sex and the Single Savior: Gender and Sexuality in Biblical Interpretation*. Louisville, KY: Westminster John Knox Press.

O'Donovan, Oliver (2009). *A Conversation Waiting to Begin: The Churches and the Gay Controversy*. London: SCM Press.

Peter Damian (1982). *Book of Gomorrah: An Eleventh-Century Treatise against Clerical Homosexual Practices*. Trans. and intro. Pierre J. Payer. Waterloo, ON: Wilfrid Laurier University Press.

St Andrew's Day Statement (1997). In Timothy Bradshaw (ed.), *The Way Forward? Christian Voices on Homosexuality and the Church*. London: Hodder & Stoughton, 5–11.

Sedgwick, Eve Kosofsky (1994). *Epistemology of the Closet*. Harmondsworth: Penguin Books.

Stuart, Elizabeth (2007). 'Sacramental Flesh'. In Gerard Loughlin (ed.), *Queer Theology: Rethinking the Western Body*. Oxford: Blackwell, 65–75.

Weeks, Jeffrey (1977). *Coming Out: Homosexual Politics in Britain, from the Nineteenth Century to the Present*. London: Quartet Books.

Westphal, Carl (1870). 'Die conträre Sexualempfindung, Symptom eines neuropathischen (psychopathischen) Zeustandes'. *Archiv für Psychiatrie und Nervenkrankheiten*, 2: 73–108.

CHAPTER 37

....

LESBIANS

....

LISA ISHERWOOD

It was from the late 1970s to the early 1990s that lesbian theologies found a voice and proliferated. Before the 1970s lesbian theology was understood as part of gay theology and it still remains the case that when Church documents deal with same-sex issues the word 'homosexual' is used, thus making no distinction between men and women. Since the 1990s queer theologies have come to the fore (Loughlin 2007) and have even questioned the notion of lesbian as a category, threatening to make the short-lived visibility of lesbian theology extinct. This is not to say that many lesbians do not still hold on to the identity, despite identity politics being challenged from many sides. It *is* to say that political correctness has in some cases expanded the discourse at the expense of certain lives, but at the same time it has brought others into the discourse. Many of the issues that affect lesbians affect all women and so it is not surprising that feminist theological method underpins much lesbian theology, that is, creating theology from lived experience as well as looking at scripture and history with a hermeneutic of suspicion.

Creating theology from lived experience has, in this case of sexuality, allowed for the development of what has become known as 'sexual theology'. This is a theology based in the lived experience of women and men, one that takes seriously this experience as part of God's self-disclosure. Sexual theology (Nelson 1992) is to be distinguished from the theology of sexuality. The latter takes a far more hierarchical approach to theology. It assumes that all matters of sexuality have been dealt with in the Bible and tradition and therefore that personal and lived experience simply has to conform to some pre-revealed set of principles. Lesbian theologians reject this approach because they understand the destructive effect of biblical so-called 'clobber texts' on lesbian and gay people. These texts condemn and do not lead to a wholeness of being for gay and lesbian people and so are rejected from the powerful belief that the God revealed in Jesus is one of love who looks for life in abundance and wholeness. Such a God could not condemn love wherever it was made manifest.

This assertion is made from experiences of mutuality and growth experienced in mutual relation between lesbian and gay people. It is this experience and a steadfast belief in the love of God that enables lesbian theologians to reject the clobber texts as of another time and within a different understanding of human sexuality. What the lived experience of lesbian people brings to the table is a new consciousness when examining texts that oppress and destroy, even if they are biblical. This does not mean that lesbian theologians do not look into biblical texts, as we shall see in the following section.

BIBLE AND CHURCH HISTORY

Feminist theology has been interested to remember the women in biblical and Christian narratives who have been largely ignored except as putty in the patriarchal plot. That has meant that we can get some insight into how those around Jesus and within the history of Christianity may have been conducting their sexual arrangements. Feminist scholarship has thrown up some amazing results which all add to the creation of a very different reality from that which we have grown to expect. In addition Deryn Guest (2005) has developed what she terms a hermeneutic of hetero-suspicion which she hopes leads away from what at times can be an essentialist feminist form of reading scripture (2005: 108) and opens the way for more creative engagement with texts. While acknowledging the difficulties of identifying a category that may be understood as lesbian she suggests that her strategy consisting of four elements may help us read differently. Her principles are *resistance*, which is commitment to a hermeneutic of hetero-suspicion; *rupture*, which is a commitment to disruption of sex-gender binaries; *re-clamation*, which is commitment to a strategy of appropriation, and *re-engagement*, which is a commitment to making a difference (2005: 110). While there are some commentaries (see West 2000) that take a queer stance or even a gay and lesbian stance, Guest is the only theologian to have actually developed a hermeneutical circle that may be called lesbian. Her approach allows for reading with lesbian eyes and looking at the gaps in the text to let one's own experience speak in them.

Women as Missionary Partners

Mary Rose D'Angelo uses a similar method when she examines the suggestion that there were women missionary partnerships in the early Church and she is curious to understand what that might mean. This is a very queer reading indeed of a world that had restrictions on women. Her interest was aroused by a funerary relief depicting two women with right hands clasped in a common gesture of commitment (D'Angelo 1990: 65–86). It is plain that others have seen it in this light also since it has been defaced in order to make one partner look male. For D'Angelo the existence of such a relief opened the possibility of women as committed partners during the early Church period and made her wonder about the role and relationship of biblical women that we have to date only read through a patriarchal haze.

The very existence of women in pairs, regardless of the physical relationship between them, is of huge significance. In a world, not unlike our own, where the energies of women were supposed to be directed towards men and any valid action of women was supposed to focus on men, to see women taking space and proclaiming a new reality is amazingly inspirational. It is also interesting to consider what kind of role and relationship the women in Jesus' immediate circle may have had since it further illuminates questions regarding his own approach to sexuality. Will we see by an examination of the relationship between Mary and Martha that Jesus was in fact a 'swinger' as Ruether (1974) playfully suggested? D'Angelo reminds us that we think of Mary and Martha as a pair who signal two paths for women, housewife or contemplative, and of course she wishes to challenge this view. Mary is described as the 'sister' of Martha who is usually seen as the dominant figure. We are also told she 'ministers'. It is of significance that they welcomed Jesus to their home since this suggests that they owned it and had some authority within it. In John 12:2 we are told that Martha was present at dinner and 'serving' (*diekonei*) which we should understand in the light of her ministry (*diakonia*) rather than as a female domestic task (D'Angelo 1990: 70). Mary, who is described as the sister of Martha, is also shown to act as a disciple by sitting at the feet of Jesus. So we appear to have a minister and a disciple under the same roof, one taking the dominant role which would possibly sit her within a definition of lesbian as understood in earlier times.

Schüssler-Fiorenza (1983: 30–34) suggests that both 'sister' and 'minister' function as titles of early Christian missionaries and therefore reveal the true role of these women. D'Angelo wishes to take the argument further and see them as a missionary couple. This interpretation is based on their ownership of a house, suggesting that they were heads of a house church just like Prisca and Aquila, and the fact that they are described as sisters in the way that other missionary pairs are described as brother/sister. Paul often uses the word 'brother' to introduce his missionary partner at the same time as describing himself as an apostle. The term is a very fluid one and does not always imply subordination (D'Angelo 1990: 80) but rather a vibrant and equal relationship. It is then possible to re-image Mary and Martha as minister and disciple but also at the very least sitting somewhere along what Adrienne Rich calls the lesbian continuum (Rich 1987: 62). This is a continuum of women friends who by their relationship, be it sexual or otherwise, give their emotional energy to women and thus challenge heteropatriarchy which expects women to dedicate all their energies to men.

What this shows is that the early Jesus movement was very flexible compared to the strictly gendered relationships that were expected at the time. It was then a great place to dislocate the power of patriarchy as exerted through the family. It should also be kept in mind that it was a time when the family was being used to strengthen the Roman Empire through the Augustan reforms relating to childbearing and the dominance of the husband in the family. While it may not be the case that Mary and Martha ventured further into the Empire than their own backyards, there were others who did. It is within this context that the 'queer' nature of their activities should be understood. Their choice of a woman as a partner in Christian mission should be seen as a sexual as well as a social choice in terms of the arrangement of sexuality. It was a blatant rejection of the power inherent in the cultural norm. In the world in which they functioned, one would no doubt have been seen as taking the dominant role, thus being viewed as a man. Like female leadership in the early Christian mission, the practice raised the spectre of the unnatural woman who plays the role of the man (D'Angelo 1990: 84).

D'Angelo concludes by suggesting that these women must have been living along the lesbian continuum to which Rich alerts us. In choosing the company of women, they were making a statement about the value of women that would be both difficult to hear and hugely subversive in a patriarchal context. Whether they had sex together is of course an interesting question beyond the merely curious. The evidence from that period is that many women were in same-sex relationships and that this was a deeply subversive way to live (Brooten: 1996). That they were deeply affectionate towards, and supportive of, one another seems to be beyond question and provides us with a resource denied by a patriarchal reading.

The example of Mary and Martha also provides us with a backdoor glimpse at what may have been happening around Jesus. He lived in a wider world that, while generally disapproving of lesbian relationships, also acknowledged marriage between women (D'Angelo 1990). Marriage was only allowed for a very narrow band of people at that time and so we have to be careful about how we understand the word. There were some high-born women who may have had the privilege of a publicly acknowledged union while others would have declared themselves married simply by living together. There are sources from the second century that show that women did consider themselves married; for example, Megilla is married to Demoriassa who is her wife (*eme gyne*) (D'Angelo 1990: 85).

Lesbian Identity in Antiquity

It still remains the case that there were difficulties in that world even in defining women, let alone those who related to other women. 'Woman' depended very much on social location and 'lesbian', although the word was not used, was understood in terms of those who would be seen to exhibit 'masculine desire' or male cultural power. So it was against this background that Romans 1:26, 'their women exchanged natural relations for unnatural ...', was penned. The 'unnatural' here signals rejection of the passive and submissive women they were expected to be (Brooten 1996). Brooten (1996) in her extensive work does not give us a lesbian theology but demonstrates how women in relation with other women were viewed and treated in early Christianity. Her main point is that 'lesbian' was not a term used, and the main issue for men in those days was the behaviour of women whom they believed wished to take the power of men in relation. This is of course not the kind of definition we use today or the way in which we understand lesbianism to include what one does with other women in terms of sexual acts. Rather, the power question was of utmost importance in early Christian history, an aspect inherited from antiquity (Brooten 1996: 25). Clitoridectomy was often carried out on women who were seen as assuming male power but it is often difficult to know if this was because they were seen as sexually active with other women or simply because they were seen as too powerful.

Brooten's contribution is extremely important because it enables lesbian theologians to show that there was a way to claim a lesbian identity in antiquity and early Christianity, a claim that has until recently been disputed. She also uncovers the power question at the heart of the identity and moves away from understanding lesbianism as a set of sex acts and more as a way of being in the world which is not under male control. Mary Daly (1988) would fully endorse this understanding with her definition of a dyke as a woman who holds back the forces of heteropatriarchy through the use of her body. Both Brooten and D'Angelo open doors to a lesbian heritage in Christianity, indeed a radical one in that we see women resisting dominant heteropatriarchy through their relationships. Perhaps then this is a lesson for contemporary Christian lesbians who argue for acceptance and equality in the patriarchal order?

Moving on from the early Church we also find traces of women loving women throughout Christian history. We can begin to piece together the impact their embodied, woman-desiring selves had on the theology and spirituality of their day. Amongst those who have done some groundbreaking work on queer devotion is Richard Rambuss (1998: 54) who, like Bataille, takes the stance that 'sacred eroticism' and 'eroticism' are the same thing and have to be taken with equal seriousness; that is, the former does not need to be explained away, but rather taken seriously on its own terms and as a fundamental and important aspect of our erotic natures. Rambuss also uncovers the way in which the sacred erotic transgresses the boundaries of vanilla heterosexuality, that form of sexuality that is paradoxically upheld with such vigour by Christian morality. Once again there are similarities with Bataille who signalled the transgressive at the heart of the erotic in its full and religious state. This is summed up neatly by Michael Warner who says 'religion makes available a language of ecstasy, a horizon of significance within which transgressions against the normal order of the world and the boundaries of self can be seen as good things' (Warner in Rambuss 1998: 58).

Rambuss gives many examples of how men erotically desire the male Christ: they penetrate and are penetrated by him. He also shows that women were not just erotically drawn to a male Christ. For example, the body of Christ crosses genders for Catherine of Siena and she is eventually engaged passionately with, sinking into the flesh of, a female Christ, a Christ whom she desires. Margery Kempe is another example of a sexually explicit relationship with the body of Christ in many forms. Margery is a good example of how the fullness of eroticism triggered by an object of desire can lead to transgressive fullness within the sacred. Margery has sexual intimacy with God and with Jesus both of whom become son, lover, and husband in the encounters. She also has sex with God as female (Windeatt 1985: 88). Of course none of the examples given here say anything explicit about lesbian theology but they raise questions about the very fixed nature of gender that much contemporary theology assumes and suggest that lesbian eroticism does have a part to play in Christian spirituality. The desiring of a woman, albeit a female Christ, can end in mystical union and transformation both within the spiritual life but also within lived experience, as perhaps the life of Margery Kempe illustrates best.

CHRISTOLOGIES

Much feminist work had been done in the area of Christology before Heyward actually situated her work in a lesbian body, a move that shocked many people. Her emphasis is on experiencing God as a living reality, not as a plausible abstract concept. This was a huge step in relocating women's agency in their bodies. Heyward makes it abundantly clear how important relating is to the creation of theology, in the introduction to *Touching Our Strength: The Erotic as Power and the Love of God* (1989). Here she tells us that in order to come to the point of being able to write theology she had to ground herself, to situate herself, in her embodiedness through touch, smell, taste, and memory of those she had cared for and of the battles that had been fought and were being fought, both personally and internationally. She had to spend both painstaking and playful time with friends and she had to make love to her lovers. It was the plural of lover that made many people take a breath. Feminist theologies have always understood Christology as an ethical investigation, so that whoever Christ may be, the result cannot be abstract but has to make a difference in the lives of women and men in the everyday process of living. What then might Heyward be implying by use of the plural? She says in that same introduction that all the actions she mentioned grounded her, embodied her, and placed her in relation; this in turn stretched beyond that of the people involved into an ethical relation with the cosmos and all that is in it. Only when she was challenged and expanded in this way could she reflect theologically.

Heyward's starting point for seeking to understand God is taking human experience seriously. She says, 'We are left alone untouched, until we choose to take ourselves—our humanity—more seriously than we have taken our God' (Heyward 1982: p. xix). For Heyward God's creative power is the power to love and to be loved. This love is erotic, not some nicely sanitized and other-worldly love. If God loves us then we are needed, because, as Heyward tells us, a lover needs relation—if for no other reason, in order to love. This also implies that we ought to be passionate lovers in order to learn the open vulnerable mutuality which she understands to be the divine.

Heyward suggests that Jesus saw no difference between our love for our God and our love for our neighbour (Mark 12:28–31). Therefore we are labouring to create a new life based on mutual love, one in which 'We are dealing with a real love for man for his own sake and not for the love of God' (Heyward 1982: 16). There can be no passive observance if we are to be in mutual relation, and this places us very differently in relation to ideas of incarnation. Heyward is not denying the possibility of incarnation; indeed if God is a God of relation then incarnation is bound to be not only a possibility but a desirable necessity. Neither is she devaluing the reality of incarnation but rather exposing the limits of exclusivity. Once we really value Jesus' humanity the dualistic gulf between humanity and God is breached. It becomes possible to assert that our own humanity can touch, heal, and comfort the world and in so doing strengthen God. At the same time it becomes apparent that a God of love is as dependent on us as we are on her. Heyward therefore re-images divinity as something we grow towards by choice and activity. We are drawn by the power of the erotic that is our birthright and lies in us as the power of *dunamis*, a biblical concept that Heyward claims Jesus wished to share. This of course implies the crucial ability to make choices which has been limited for women. Restoring choice as part of the Christological process rather than passive victimhood is contributing to a greater understanding. Heyward believes women loving women have an easier time of reclaiming power and overcoming passivity than their heterosexual sisters.

Re-Imaging Jesus

Heyward embarks on a task she calls 'imaging Jesus'. This is a process of expressing something about reality, of expressing a relation that we know already between ourselves and that which we image. Re-imaging may mean letting go of tradition. One such letting-go is realizing that Jesus only really matters if he was human and if we view his incarnation as a 'relational experience' (Heyward 1982: 31). Heyward believes it is a crippling mistake to see Jesus as a divine person 'rather than as a human being who knew and loved God'. It is crippling because it prevents people claiming their own divinity. By re-imaging Jesus she also re-images human beings by realizing the amazing power and relation that lie dormant in human nature. Although the Gospels tend to imply Jesus' innate divinity, Luke hints at its growth when he says 'and Jesus increased in wisdom, in stature and in favour with God and men' (Luke 2:52). Heyward does not wish to deny God's parenthood of Jesus but wishes to re-image it beyond genetic terms and therefore as the source of power in which Jesus was grounded. Once we really value Jesus' humanity, the dualistic gulf between humanity and God is breached. It becomes possible to assert that our own humanity can touch, heal, and comfort the world, and in so doing strengthen God. At the same time it becomes apparent that a God of love is as dependent on us as we are on her. Heyward is clear that her experiences in the lesbian community demonstrated to her the divine/human ability of touch, comfort, and healing so needed in marginalized communities. Many women have testified that the acceptance and love they receive within such communities and the intimacy they experience help to heal years of pain and distress inflicted by society and Church.

Heyward re-images divinity as something we grow towards by choice and activity. This shift requires her to look critically at the notions of authority and power. She is anxious to move away from the idea that authority is something that is exercised over us by God or state and to come to an understanding of it as self-possessed. She notes that two words are used in the Gospels. One is *exousia* which denotes power that has been granted, whereas *dunamis* which is raw power—innate, spontaneous, and often fearful—is not granted: it is inborn, and this is the authority that Jesus claims (Heyward 1982: 45). This is why Jesus could not answer his interrogators. They were not speaking the same language because they were interested in authority while he was concerned with power. Nor could he be understood by those who wished to equate authority with religious and civil government.

What was new about Jesus' teaching about power was his realization that our *dunamis* is rooted in God and is the force by which we claim our divinity. By acting with *dunamis* we, just like Jesus, act from both our human and divine elements. We can overcome the suspicion of human power and initiative placed in our religious understanding by the story of Eve and her actions in Eden. Of course we have to re-image the kingdom as a place where the lion lies down with the lamb and the tools of destruction are changed into instruments of creativity. When humans dare to acknowledge their divine nature through *dunamis*, this is the kind of kingdom that is imaginable and must be made incarnate through radical love. It is perhaps not surprising to find a Christian lesbian priest theologian examining issues of power and authority. Declaring one's love as legitimate in the face of the power of Church and State requires a great deal of self-belief, a belief possibly based in *dunamis*.

Radical love incarnates the kingdom because intimacy is the deepest quality of relation. Heyward says that to be intimate is to be assured that we are known in such a way that the mutuality of our relation is real, creative, and cooperative. There is no hint here of losing oneself in another even if that other is God. Once again we see Heyward's lived experience coming through in her theology. She claims it is possible to see Jesus' ministry as based on intimacy, since he knew people intuitively, insightfully, and spontaneously. Heyward's re-imaging makes it clear that Jesus does not have exclusive rights to *dunamis*. Indeed he facilitates our knowing and claiming of God as *dunamis* through relation. He reveals to us 'the possibility of our own godding' (Heyward 1982: 47). Of course, time and again people reject this and cling to conformity and Jesus points out, 'You put aside the commandment of God to cling to human traditions' (Mark 7:8). In his own lifetime this rejection led to Jesus' crucifixion and led to the death of God, not because Jesus was exclusively God but because humanity rejected the possibility of its own *dunamis*. Heyward says the crucifixion signals 'the extent to which human beings will go to avoid our own relational possibilities' (1982: 48). There is a further denial of Jesus today by Christians who insist on his other-worldly sonship and divinity and in the name of this exclusivity condemn and marginalize people.

Heyward's Christ is one who meets us where we are between the 'yet' and the 'not yet', and impresses upon us not so much his divine nature but the erotic, relational meaning of who we are (1982: 163). In this way, 'God's incarnations are as many and varied as the persons who are driven by the power in relation to touch and be touched by sisters and brothers' (1982: 164). This is Christology fully embodied, sensuous and erotic, seeking vulnerable commitment, alive with expectancy and power. Heyward is well aware that traditional Christianity will have difficulty accepting such an experientially based Christology, based as it is in lesbian embodiment. It is however her lesbianism that plays a large part in her Christological explorations as it is the ground of her experience of mutuality and her most embodied reality. Indeed, she has since argued that the kind of mutuality she is expounding is most easily found between women. The power dynamics

of gender do not make it an easy matter for men and women to find mutual empowerment in their most intimate acts.

By suggesting that the embodied reality of *eros* is as central to the life of Christ as it is
to our own becoming and relating, Heyward opened the gates for sexual lives to be part
of the basis for the unfolding of the divine and the reflection that becomes doctrinal.
Of course it could be argued that the 'theologians of the erotic' expect too much from it
in terms of morality and do not acknowledge that there is also tragedy involved in the
erotic. They could be accused of ignoring that erotic yearnings can also conflict with
justice-seeking outcomes (Sands 1992: 12). However, for Heyward the erotic leads to a
way of living which is open, mutual, vulnerable, and life-enhancing. This is to be practised in the boardroom just as much as in the bedroom.

FRIENDSHIP

There has been a considerable amount of work done by lesbians on friendship as a
Christian model of relationship. This suggests that it is a good model for overcoming
patriarchal ownership patterns of sexual relations. What we do know is that marriage
as the Christian Church has presented it, is not working. This is evident not only by
the number of divorces but also by the high rate of spousal murder and abuse. There
is something wrong in the basic fabric of the institution when dissatisfaction and even
death can be the result of attempting it. There is a key to be found in the words of those
who wish to blame feminism for the demise of marriage. They say that women have too
much power and freedom and expect too much fulfilment.

Friendship was a theme taken up in lesbian theologies in the 1990s as part of a critique of heterosexual marriage and an apologetic for same-sex relationships (Hunt 1991;
Donoghue 1993). Foremost in this literature was *Just Good Friends: Toward a Lesbian
and Gay Theology of Relationships* written by Elizabeth Stuart (1995). When Stuart wrote
about friendship as a way for lesbians to relate, with its implicit critique of heterosexual
marriage, such an institution was not available for lesbians and gay men. As this is written, gay and lesbian marriage has been accepted in several countries. It is interesting to
ponder whether the new rights and ceremonies will actually override the new models
suggested by Stuart and others. Will the desire for entry into 'normal' marriage arrangements actually blunt the critique of the institution of marriage?

Stuart is in favour of the friendship model as she declares it is a scriptural model of
relationship (Thatcher and Stuart 1996: 306). She claims that God's formal covenants
with people in the Hebrew scriptures make friends of them, while Jesus befriended
the friendless and declared that his disciples were his friends not his servants (John
17:15). In addition to God befriending people we see that friendships such as David and
Jonathan and Ruth and Naomi have over time been held up as models of covenanted
love. Friendship is an inclusive relationship which is based in mutual vulnerability and
freedom. Stuart therefore suggests that this experience of lesbians can form a solid basis

for rethinking a theology of marriage which she believes will transform gender relationality (Thatcher and Stuart 1996: 309).

Stuart was not without her critics, some lesbian theologians believing that this model presented lesbian couples as celibate, loving maiden aunts, a picture that many wished to deny. Stuart is herself clear that friendship is based in sexuality as she sees all relationality as having an embodied drive for intimacy at its heart, and this, she believes, is sexual in nature if not in practice. Equally there were those who wished to defend marriage as much more than friendship, indeed as a hierarchy, but that misses the point of mutual vulnerability in relation entirely. There were some such as Carter Heyward who also understood lesbian relationship as friendship and included within this definition a critique of monogamy (Heyward 1989: 136). She argued that fidelity does not demand monogamy but rather openness, honesty, and a high degree of caring for the relationships. Like many lesbian feminists Heyward is aware of the way in which monogamy has been used against women throughout history and she, like many others in the wider lesbian community (Easton and Hardy 1997), was attempting to find other ways to relate based in mutuality and vulnerability.

For Heyward 'nonmonogamy' called for people to deepen their sense of self and their ability to relate, to be open to 'godding' in various situations, and to be more of the divine they are called to be through that deep yearning for relation which she understands as the central aspect of God. Others such as Stuart believe that monogamy is required in order to be completely oneself in the assurance that the person one opens to will be there tomorrow because the level of vulnerability we are striving for as Christians also carries with it a real risk of destruction if betrayed (Thatcher and Stuart 1996: 310).

THE LESBIAN *IMAGO DEI*

It has to be said that even when lesbian theology can be identified there is within it a certain assumption of sameness. This has led Lee Chiaramonte to lament the absence of the stone butch in theological discourse. She claims that the stone butch is an apt image for the *imago dei* and one that challenges the androcentric imaging of the concept which has limited who may be seen as God's proxy in the world. The stone butch reimagining this concept allows for women to be included in all their embodied and gendered particularity since the stone butch is one who lures to herself subjects called *femmes* (women) (Chiaramonte 1999: 75). Further, the stone butch manifests women as powerful which has always as we have seen been troubling for the Christian tradition. She assumes power that has hitherto been granted to men but she takes it in a new way, defining 'masculine' in an entirely new light, moving away from hierarchical and patriarchal understandings of it.

This redefinition is not simply a matter of identity politics but also of sexuality. The stone butch worships women. She only has interest in her lovers' pleasure. She refuses stereotypes and certain kinds of embodiment and understands receiving by way of giving as a way of being and becoming. Chiaramonte understands this to be 'a process relational paradigm of God's own action in the world' (1999: 89), a God she understands as permeable and open to the exchange of feeling between Godself and the world. Further, the stone butch's marginalization even within lesbian communities makes her willingness to keep 'showing up' and loving, a deep demonstration of self-respect, emancipatory practice, and commitment to a diverse lesbian community. She presents herself as a 'yearning metaphor for all those different, discredited and yet deserving of valuation' (1999: 90), and in this way, Chiaramonte claims she is an apt *imago dei*.

Marie Cartier (2013) also sees the butch, stone or not, as a figure who gives us theological insight. For her the courage and steadfastness that butches showed in the face of fierce and violent reaction to their existence, coupled with their ability to empower women through the female masculinity they inhabit, makes them in many cases saviours of others but certainly the backbone of creative communities of solidarity. Further, the way in which they love women challenges the whole heteropatriarchal structure, requiring a rethink not just of masculinity but also of femininity (2013: 40). In so doing, Cartier argues, a new spirituality is brought to light, one in which the embodied lover is also the embodied divine and the source of religious engagement. The butch is the most visible face of the lesbian community and the most challenging, since she is certainly a woman in charge of herself who redefines in a visible and lived way what we think we know of gender.

Queering the Old Terrain

No essay on lesbian theologies can avoid the question of gender and an investigation of the category of lesbian itself. The assumed categories of butch/*femme* have been questioned and we have seen the emergence of lesbian men, SM dykes, trans-dykes, and straight and queer lesbians. The term 'lesbian' then is not without need of investigation as is an enquiry into the richness offered to theology by this rainbow of human experience. For some, lesbian theology has come to be equated with straight theology. Since the winning of various rights within the State and some churches being more open, queer theologians tend to view lesbian theology as rather tame, modelling (as they claim) traditional forms of partnership and with that, traditional forms of economic life. I think this seems a little harsh as it seems to remain true that while the rhetoric is more inclusive, the reality is not. Thus lesbians still have some kind of border existence within a patriarchal society. However the point is taken that normalization in the light of our lesbian foresisters should perhaps not be the goal for justice-seeking Christian lesbians.

Gender and Subjectivity

In terms of the investigation of gender, feminist theologians took up where de Beauvoir finished and insisted that women have been without subjective power, being viewed, as they have been through history, as the 'Other'. That is to say they have had no access to the symbolic or even linguistic realms in which culture and theology are created by those who are central to these areas: men. It seems fair to say that if heterosexual women were viewed as the 'Other' then those who did not fit that model were doubly or even triply 'othered', considered way outside the realms of real humanness.

The feminist arguments for the subjectivity of women opened up a whole world and perhaps we were not fully aware that subjectivity will never allow the comfort of the old unified certainties to re-emerge, not even those around who women are, or what women want and how it is for women. What had been done was to actually shatter the unified convenience of 'woman' and opened up a kaleidoscope of potential and a rainbow of glorious harmony and disharmony in the unfolding of the 'reality' of woman. Once we moved from concepts like woman, female, feminine, there would be no end to what was laid before us through the lived reality of women's lives.

Critics of this approach often cite this open space, this embrace of endless possibility, as the weakness of the discipline. Surely we need to fix something in order to have a discipline related to anything at all – surely we need women, lesbian or not, to have feminist theology and one may add heteropatriarchy! But has it not been the simple definitions that have led over the centuries to the exclusions? Butler (2004: 12) provocatively declares that multiplicity is not the thing that makes agency impossible but is rather the very nature of agency, precisely the condition in which agency flourishes. Further she (2004: 180) suggests that it is in the fear of the questions posed by multiplicity that we find the creation of the rhetoric of morals as a defence of politics. She illustrates her point through considering how the Catholic Church deals with issues of gender and sexual difference.

The Curia has called for the United Nations to eliminate the language of gender from its platforms to do with the status of women, declaring that the word is simply a cover for homosexuality which it condemns and does not see as having a place in a rights agenda. It insisted on a return to the word 'sex'. Its rhetoric attempted to indisputably link 'sex' with 'maternal' and 'feminine', reflecting, as they saw it, the divinely ordained 'natural goodness' of things. To those observing the agenda, it was a clear attempt to reverse many of the gains that women had made in relation to human rights, and it was a narrow defining that could be once again placed at the service of containment and control. Butler puts it as follows: 'The Vatican fears the separation of sexuality from sex, for that introduces a notion of sexual practice that is not constrained by putatively natural reproductive ends' (2004: 184). It is then no surprise that the Vatican considers the inclusion of lesbian rights in United Nations legislation as 'anti-human'. Given its understanding of the relation between sex and the human person, such a statement is correct, since the inclusion of 'lesbian' into the realm of the universal would be to expand the boundaries of what is so far defined as human within the conventional limits. In order then that all humans may be recognized it seems that 'the human must become strange to itself' (Butler 2004: 194).

Butler goes on to say that this new human 'will have no ultimate form but it will be one that is constantly negotiating sexual difference in a way that has no natural or necessary consequences for the social organisation of sexuality' (2004: 191). Is it in this enactment of the beyond, the becoming strange to oneself, that all the possibilities of incarnate life find root? Butler reminds us that the body is the site on which language falters (2004: 198) and the signifiers of the body remain for the most part largely unconscious. These signifiers are themselves a language, but one ever unfolding and of many tongues. Performativity is a 'whole body' engagement, just as incarnation is, and both resist the deadening claws of narrow and controlling definitions of personhood: both expand the edges of where we think we inhabit. The examples already given from Christian history demonstrate how women have attempted to perform embodied empowerment along-side other women within rigidly patriarchal structures.

Given Butler's position we perhaps have to look at women in our Christian history such as Thecla in a new light. There is a very strong body of scholarship (see MacDonald 1983), which suggests that the stories in the Apocryphal Acts are folk tales and as such they claim to present history. Folk tales serve two opposing purposes: they stabilize society and at the same time they destabilize society. They can define the identity of those who are dissatisfied with society and become a source of strength for that group. What we find in many of the Christian stories are women who defy physical boundaries and so question social gender and sexual roles by their actions and appearance.

Thecla Reconsidered

Thecla is an interesting character as a woman empowered to spread the gospel. In the early days of lesbian, gay, bisexual, transgender, and intersex (LGBTI) theology she was hailed as a transvestite, transgendered, lesbian, or transsexual. A queer eye asks if this motif of a cross-dressing woman was used to tell us something of significance about the relationship of people who become Christian with their gendered environment, rather than simply about the manifestation in Christian history of other fixed categories of sex and gender. Contemporary scholarship is no longer content to leave the argument that she and others cross-dressed for the sake of safety. In Thecla's story she does not cross-dress from the beginning even though she is travelling and at some risk; she only cross-dresses after baptism (Anson 1974: 1–32). And of course, this is in strict contravention of scriptural command (Deut. 22:5). John Anson suggests that the clue to Thecla may be found when she is thrown to the beasts but not killed. The tale relays that she found herself clothed by God. Anson says that this is a literal fulfilment of the putting on of Christ that Paul speaks about in baptism and so for him the donning of men's clothes is simply another step in this process that started in the arena with the beasts (Anson 1974).

He continues that a faith based in Galatians 3:27–8 would mean followers would embody a state of primal perfection that overcame all distinctions including that of sex. In putting on Christ, followers would attempt to appropriate his male form. There is another way of reading (Althaus-Reid and Isherwood 2009: 3) which is that she embraced the wholeness of God, clothed in the full gender richness of that divine reality. Perhaps her actions were rooted in Montanism where the women prophets Prisca and Maximilla had prominent roles. They had many visions and understood themselves as female Christs. This understanding was based in their reading of Galatians 3:27–8 whereby once the distinctions and divisions were overcome they were free to embrace their divine natures, free of notions of oppositional gender which, as Butler (2004) tells us, impose on us a little death and leave us mourning the loss all our lives.

It can be argued that women like Thecla understood their male attire as connected to overcoming the binary opposites of gender that set in place unequal lived reality. Cross-dressing implies a starting point and a place towards which one is aiming and so serves to highlight gender polarity, since clothes allow us to play with identity and they aid that becoming; they enable a physical embodied performance. Cross-dressing creates an illusion for the user and the observer. It is a luminal space allowing movement across boundaries and transversing margins which confine.

Cross-dressing is an ingenious tool, as it does not fit categories of sex or gender alone. As such it exposes both and so in this way is a form of 'gender iconography' making visible the spaces of possibility which are closed off by dichotomous conceptualization. Ritual cross-dressing which pre-dated Christian cross-dressing (Suthrell 2004) has at its heart the notion of returning to wholeness, because it allows a very deep experience of gender, both one's own and the other. In some societies cross-dressing represents magical qualities which are signalled by the ambiguity. So Christian cross-dressing has a cultural heritage, and in taking seriously the message of equality of the Christian gospel those who did it 'queered' gender in order to find a way of living out that radical equality, rather than remaining primordial males.

Once we engage in confusing categories it leads to their breakdown as oppositional points of reference. We need to ensure that we do not replace them with points along an old axis. So are these women simply categories such as 'lesbian' or 'trans' or are they erasing categories through a challenge based in the baptismal formula and exercised along a lesbian continuum? We may never know but what we see is that they allow for a hermeneutic of hetero-suspicion which is a very welcome space in a once apparently solidly heterosexual and patriarchal Christian heritage.

The Achievement of Lesbian Theology

The queer move in terms of understanding gender offers huge possibilities to Christian theology to understand the nature of incarnation anew. For much of its history Christianity has understood incarnation as a once and for all almost static event, that is to say it happened and all else is laid out in the light of it. Feminist Christologies which have introduced the possibility of an inclusive understanding of incarnation have also paved the way for queer understandings to offer themselves. Lesbian theology as we have seen offers the lesbian body as a site of redemptive praxis and as an *imago dei*, and in so doing questions many of the rigid assumptions that have underpinned our traditional notions of incarnation and salvation. Questioning the rigid nature of gender also questions the rigid nature of incarnation, and a glorious array of possibility opens up in which embodied justice-seeking becomes the bedrock of incarnational ethics, rather than laws and precepts written in a book. Even the most marginalized within any community may claim her divine/human nature. It can be seen that lesbian sexual theology offers challenges to traditional theology but many new insights have emerged from this embodied marginal theology.

REFERENCES

Althaus-Reid, Marcella, and Lisa Isherwood (2004). *The Sexual Theologian: Essays on Sex, God and Politics*. London: T&T Clark.

Althaus-Reid, Marcella, and Lisa Isherwood (2009). *Trans/Formations*. London: SCM Press.

Anson, John (1974). 'The Female Transvestite in Early Monasticism: The Origin and Development of a Motif'. *Viator: Medieval and Renaissance Studies*, 5: 1–32.

Brooten, Bernadette (1996). *Love Between Women: Early Christian Responses to Female Homoeroticism*. Chicago: Chicago University Press.

Butler, Judith (2004). *Undoing Gender*. London: Routledge.

Cartier, Marie (2013). *Baby You're My Religion: Butch Femme Bar Culture*. Durham: Acumen.

Chiaramonte, Lee (1999). 'A Harrisonian Ontology of the Stone Butch as Process Relational Imago Dei'. *Theology & Sexuality*, 11 (Sept.), 75–90.

Daly, Mary (1988). *Websters' First New Intergalactic Wickedary of the English Language Conjured by Mary Daly in Cahoots with Jane Caputi*. London: Women's Press.

D'Angelo, Mary Rose (1990). 'Women Partners in the New Testament'. *Journal of Feminist Studies in Religion*, 6: 65–86.

Donoghue, Emma (1993). *Passion Between Women*. London: Scarlet Press.

Easton, Dossie, and Janet W. Hardy (1997). *The Ethical Slut: A Practical Guide to Polyamory, Open Relationships and Other Adventures*. Berkeley: Celestial Arts.

Guest, Deryn (2005). *When Deborah Met Jael: Lesbian Biblical Hermeneutics*. London: SCM Press.

Heyward, Carter (1982). *The Redemption of God: A Theology of Mutual Relation*. Lanham, MD: University of America Press.

Heyward, Carter (1989). *Touching Our Strength: The Erotic as Power and the Love of God*. New York: Harper Collins.

Hunt, Mary (1991). *Fierce Tenderness: A Theology of Friendship*. New York: Crossroad.

Isherwood, Lisa (2006). *The Power of Erotic Celibacy: Queering Heteropatriarchy*. London: T&T Clark.

Loughlin, Gerard (2007). *Queer Theology: Rethinking the Western Body*. Oxford: Blackwell.

Macdonald, Dennis (1983). *The Legend and the Apostles: The Battle for Paul in Story and Canon*. Philadelphia: Westminster Press.

Mollenkott, Virginia (1993). *Sensuous Spirituality: Out From Fundamentalism*. New York: Crossroad.

Nelson, James (1978). *Embodiment: An Approach to Sexuality and Christian Theology*. Minneapolis: Augsburg.

Nelson, James (1992). *Body Theology*. Louisville, KY: Westminster John Knox.

Rambuss, Richard (1998). *Closet Devotions*. Durham, NC: Duke University Press.

Rich Adrienne (1987). *Of Woman Born: Motherhood As Experience and Institution, 10th Anniversary Edition*. New York: W. W. Norton & Company.

Ruether, Rosemary Radford (1974). *Religion and Sexism: Images of Women in Jewish and Christian Traditions*. New York: Simon & Schuster.

Sands, Kathleen (1992). 'Uses of the Thea[o]logian: Sex and Theodicy in Religious Feminism'. *Journal of Feminist Studies in Religion*, 8: 7–33.

Schüssler-Fiorenza, Elisabeth (1983). *In Memory of Her*. London: SCM Press.

Stuart, Elizabeth (1995). *Just Good Friends: Towards a Lesbian and Gay Theology of Relationships*. London: Mowbray.

Stuart, Elizabeth (2002). *Gay and Lesbian Theologies*. Aldershot: Ashgate.

Suthrell, Charlotte (2004). *Unzipping Gender, Sex, Cross Dressing and Culture*. Oxford: Berg.

Thatcher, Adrian, and Elizabeth Stuart (1996) (eds). *Christian Perspectives on Sexuality and Gender*. Leominster: Gracewing.

West, Mona (2000). *Take Back the Word: A Queer Reading of the Bible*. Cleveland: Pilgrim Press.

Windeatt, B. A. (1985) (trans.). *The Book of Margery Kempe*. London: Penguin.

CHAPTER 38

···

BISEXUAL PEOPLE

···

MARGARET ROBINSON

WHAT IS BISEXUALITY?

BISEXUALITY, as a sexual orientation, emerged into the public consciousness through the work of Dr Alfred Kinsey, whose seven-point scale measured sexual behaviour on a continuum, with exclusive heterosexuality (represented by 0) on one end, exclusive homosexuality (represented by 6) on the other end, and degrees of bisexuality at points 1 through 5. 'Males,' Kinsey wrote, 'do not represent two discrete populations, heterosexual and homosexual. The world is not to be divided into sheep and goats.... The living world is a continuum in each and every one of its aspects' (Kinsey et al. 1948: 639).

Due in large part to Kinsey's scale, bisexuality came to be viewed as a third sexual orientation, defined by 'attraction to both sexes', and conceptualized as in-between heterosexuality and homosexuality. The creation of bisexuality as a distinct orientation made identifying as *a bisexual* possible, and ultimately helped shape the lesbian, gay, bisexual, transexual, and queer (LGBTQ) communities we have today. Since the 1990s, definitions of bisexuality as 'attraction to both sexes' have been criticized for reinforcing a binary system of gender and sex that excludes those who do not fit easily into male or female categories. In response to such critiques, many now define bisexuality as the capacity for attraction to both same-sex and other-sex partners, and that is the definition I will use throughout this chapter.

Researchers typically assess sexual orientation, including bisexuality, by measuring attraction, behaviour, or personal identity. Measures of *sexual attraction* classify as bisexual those who report attractions to both same-sex and other-sex partners, or whose attractions are based on criteria other than a partner's sex (sometimes called 'gender blindness'). Measures of attraction are often used to survey adolescents, who may have limited sexual experience and sexual identities that are not yet fully formed.

Table 38.1 Percentage of population indicating same-sex attractions

Study reference	Men		Women	
	Same-sex attraction only	Bisexual attraction	Same-sex attraction only	Bisexual attraction
Savin-Williams & Ream 2007	1.0	**4.3**	0.6	**12.3**
Mosher et al. 2005	1.5	**5.6**	0.7	**12.9**
Dickson et al. 2003	0.6	**10.0**	0.0	**24.5**
Laumann et al. 1994	2.4	**3.8**	0.3	**4.1**

Bold indicates largest percentage, by sex

Studies suggest that approximately 4–10 per cent of men and 4–24 per cent of women report bisexual attractions (see Table 38.1). Many people who have bisexual attractions never act upon these feelings or develop a bisexual identity. Laumann and colleagues (1994), for example, found that majority of women who report same-sex attractions or behaviour self-identify as heterosexual.

A second measure, *sexual behaviour*, classifies people as bisexual if their sexual history includes same-sex and other-sex partners. Within the United States, approximately 1 per cent of men and 2.9 per cent of women fit this definition (Bauer and Brennan 2013: 154), although Kinsey put this figure as high as 46 per cent (Kinsey et al. 1948: 656). Sometimes called *behaviourally bisexual*, this group includes people who self-identify as heterosexual, gay, or lesbian. Behavioural measures generally do not examine the motives behind sexual activity; paid sex work, for example, is not distinguished from sex motivated by attraction. Behavioural definitions of sexuality are often used in studies of disease transmission, since it is what we do with a partner, rather than our attractions or identities, which determines our health risks.

Measures of *sexual identity* classify as bisexual only those who identify ourselves in this way (see Table 38.2). This measure generates the lowest number of bisexuals, since for many reasons—not least of which is biphobia—those of us with bisexual attractions or histories may identify as straight, gay, or lesbian. Some people who meet the definition of bisexual may describe ourselves as *pan*sexual (attracted to people of *all* sexes or genders), *poly*sexual (attracted to *many* sexes or genders), fluid (having attractions that shift or change over time), or as queer (a slur, reclaimed as an identity). Bisexual people often use more than one label, identifying, for example, as bisexual *and* queer.

Who Identifies as Bisexual?

Bisexuals tend to be younger than gays, lesbians, or heterosexuals (Tjepkma 2008), and are more likely to live in poverty (Tjepkma 2008; Badgett et al. 2013). While 30 per

Table 38.2 Percentage of population self-identifying as gay or bisexual

Study reference	Men		Women	
	Gay	Bisexual	Lesbian	Bisexual
Office for National Statistics 2012	**1.5**	0.3	**0.7**	0.5
Chandra et al. 2011	**1.7**	1.1	1.1	**3.5**
Chandra et al. 2011	**2.3**	1.8	1.3	**2.8**
Tjepkema 2008	**1.4**	0.7	0.7	**0.9**
Rissel et al. 2003	**1.6**	0.9	0.8	**1.4**
Laumann et al. 1994	**2.0**	0.8	**0.9**	0.5
Janus & Janus 1993	4.0	**5.0**	2.0	**3.0**

Bold indicates largest percentage, by sex

cent of gays, lesbians, and heterosexuals are racial minorities, this is true for 50 per cent of bisexuals (Gates 2010: ii). Numerous theorists have made connections between the experience of being bisexual and that of being biracial, noting how those of us who do not fit neatly into pre-determined categories of sexuality or race are often portrayed as conflicted, confused, or traitorous. As Table 38.2 shows, the majority of sexual minority women identify as bisexual, while the majority of sexual minority men identify as gay. As a result, bisexual politics has been heavily shaped by feminism. Bisexual feminism is, in part, a counter-discourse to lesbian separatism, which has portrayed bisexual women as lesbians seeking heterosexual privilege, or as heterosexuals invading lesbian space, and therefore as politically and personally untrustworthy.

Some gays and lesbians initially come out as bisexual, and this has led many to view bisexuality as a transitional identity. The inaccuracy of this model is demonstrated by Lisa Diamond's (2008) ten-year longitudinal study, which found that over time more women adopted a bisexual identity than relinquished it. Many bisexuals first come out as gay or lesbian, describing this experience as being 'in the gay closet', or as 'coming out twice'. However, biphobic discourse sometimes portrays those who transition to a bisexual identity as abandoning authenticity in an effort to be socially acceptable. Women who shift from lesbian to bisexual are derogatorily referred to as 'hasbians', and many report being ostracized by their friends and communities. Bisexual theorists have used the term 'compulsory monosexuality' to describe the refusal to accord to bisexuality the same legitimacy that is given to heterosexual, gay, and lesbian identities.

Bisexuals are less likely to be out than gays and lesbians (Gates 2010). Coming out as bisexual is complicated by bisexual invisibility—many bisexuals report not hearing about bisexuality until late adolescence or early adulthood. Those of us who do come out are often met with disbelief, or hostility. Bisexuals have named this tendency to deny, ignore, or reclassify us as 'bisexual erasure'. Unlike monosexuals, bisexuals cannot clearly signal our identity by our gender presentation or the sex of our partner—those of us in same-sex relationships, for example, are assumed to be gay or lesbian. Coming out is further complicated by biphobia from heterosexual, gay, and lesbian people. Gregory Herek (2002) found that heterosexuals viewed bisexuals less favourably than any other social group (save for intravenous drug users). Possibly due to the combination of stigma (both external and internalized) and lack of social support, bisexual women have a heightened risk of depression, substance use, eating disorders, and suicide when compared with heterosexual women and lesbians (Koh and Ross 2006; Tjepkma 2008).

Bisexual people report a broad range of attractions and partners, with only a small minority reporting attraction or sexual activity evenly split between men and women. A recent study of US data found that 41.3 per cent of bisexual women and 51.2 per cent of bisexual men were in relationships with other-sex partners, while 12.6 per cent of bisexual women and 16.5 per cent of bisexual men had same-sex partners. An additional 5.9 per cent of women and 14.2 per cent of men reported no partners at all (Bauer and Brennan 2013: 155).

While bisexuals are stereotyped as promiscuous, most of us form long-term monogamous relationships. Greta Bauer and David Brennan (2013: 156) found that among bisexuals, 59.8 per cent of women and 81.9 per cent of men had had only one sexual partner within the past year. Lisa Diamond (2008: 12) found that 89 per cent of the bisexual women in her study were in long-term monogamous relationships, compared with 70 per cent of lesbians, and 67 per cent of heterosexual women. Despite monogamy's prevalence, between 30–54 per cent of bisexuals describe open (i.e. non-monogamous) relationships as our ideal (Rust 1996: 136; Page 2004: 143). The percentage of bisexuals who report actually being in open relationships varies: one US study put the figure at 33 per cent (Page 2004: 143), while a UK study put the figure at 13 per cent for women (George 1993: 230). Some relationships may be open in theory but monogamous in practice. In my own research, I found 78 per cent of the bisexual women in open relationships were not dating multiple partners at the time of their interview (Robinson 2013: 28).

BISEXUAL THEOLOGY ARISES

The first documented case of theology by self-identified bisexuals emerged among the Quakers in North America, whose newly formed Committee of Friends on Bisexuality issued the 'Ithaca Statement on Bisexuality' in New York in June 1972. Bisexual activist Stephen Donaldson (née Bob Martin), recalled events leading up to the statement: 'I organized an impromptu workshop on bisexuality and was astonished to find 130 Quakers, one of every ten General Conference attendees, overflowing into five meeting rooms and an auditorium for two days of lively discussion based more on experience than on abstract theories' (Donaldson 1995: 34).

Although it emerged from a Christian denomination, the Ithaca Statement was primarily political, asking if fellow Quakers were aware of the 'massive and inescapable bigotry' that non-heterosexuals encountered in employment, housing, media, and other institutions (Martin 1972: 456). Reports on the meeting were published in both *The Advocate*, a magazine with a primarily gay and lesbian audience, and the Quaker newsletter *Friends Journal*. Donaldson described the Ithaca Statement as 'the first public declaration of the bisexual movement' and 'the first statement on bisexuality issued by an American religious assembly, at a time when the term "bisexuality" itself was still unknown to large numbers of people' (1995: 34).

Bisexual theology appeared regularly in a number of bisexual anthologies published between 1991 and 2006, in some cases occupying up to a quarter of each book. Two features distinguished this theology from that done by gays and lesbians. First, it included a range of religious traditions, rather than focusing primarily on Christianity. *Bi Any Other Name*, for example, included essays from Wiccan, Jewish, Pagan, and Buddhist perspectives, as well as the text of the closing ritual from the First National Bisexual Conference in San Francisco (Hutchins and Kaahumanu 1991). Second, whereas early work by gay and lesbian theologians such as John J. McNeill and Virginia Ramey Mollenkott had focused on apologetics directed at the heterosexual Christian mainstream, bisexual theology spoke to a primarily bisexual audience, eschewed apologetics, and focused on personal experience. Far from offering a bisexual orthodoxy, these anthologies emphasized a multiplicity of options for spiritual and religious fulfilment.

The most significant milestone in the development of bisexual theology was the release of *Blessed Bi Spirit* (Kolodny 2000), the first collection to focus exclusively upon the spiritual experiences of bisexual people. In the Introduction, lesbian theologian Mary Hunt proposes that 'symbolically and epistemologically', bisexual theology 'is a giant step forward', bringing insights that may help theologians to move past hierarchical dualisms such as 'God/world, human/animal, male/female, white/black, heterosexual/homosexual' (Kolodny 2000: p. xv). A good starting point, Hunt suggests, might be a reflection upon the bisexual experience of the divine. In her own contribution to the book, Amanda Udis-Kessler does exactly that. She writes: 'God does not invite us by demanding that we abandon our deepest selves.... I must ask what Jesus has to say to me as a bisexual person, capable of emotionally and sexually loving both women and men, often mistrusted and sometimes rejected by both heterosexuals and lesbian/gay people' (2000: 11).

As Udis-Kessler suggests, bisexual theology has been shaped by our experiences of rejection and marginalization as well as by our experiences of love and intimate connection. As I will show in the section below, this call to develop bisexual theology emerges, for the most part, in a vacuum where bisexuality has rarely been addressed.

Bisexuality in Mainstream Theology

Traditionally, Christian theology has ignored bisexuality, instead defining homosexuality as encompassing all same-sex attraction and expression. Gianfrancesco Zuanazzi, of the John Paul II Institute for Studies on Marriage and Family, asserts that bisexuality is actually 'ambivalent or mixed homosexuality', and he dismisses bisexual identity claims as an attempt to avoid 'being regarded as homosexual' (1997: 9). John F. Harvey, the founder of Courage International, a conservative ministry for Catholics with same-sex attraction, writes that 'apparently bisexual persons are either homosexual or hetero-sexual' (1987: 29). From the perspective of Harvey or Zuanazzi, whether an individual identifies as gay, lesbian, or bisexual is irrelevant, for they all share the 'problem' of homosexual attraction to varying degrees.

The Catholic magisterium defines human sexuality as two-fold in purpose (procrea-tion and union), and sees this purpose expressed in the Genesis story and reflected in the physical and psychological structures of human beings themselves (Congregation for the Doctrine of the Faith 1986: 6; Catholic Church 2000: 2332). Such theology ele-vates heterosexuality as an ideal to which all who are able (including bisexuals) should strive—a position that LGBTQ scholars have named as heterosexism. Anglican state-ments have also taken a heteronormative position on human sexuality. The Church of England House of Bishops Report (1991) rejects the suggestion that same-sex rela-tionships are 'parallel' or 'alternative' to heterosexuality, which they characterized as 'complete'. This approach defines same-sex attraction as a kind of defect—possibly con-genital—that prevents one from achieving heterosexual functioning.

The same Report stands out as the first time a religious body significantly addressed bisexuality. The bishops wrote:

> We recognize that there are those whose sexual orientation is ambiguous, and who can find themselves attracted to partners of either sex. Nevertheless it is clear that bisexual activity must always be wrong for this reason, if no other, that it inevitably involves being unfaithful. The Church's guidance to bisexual Christians is that if they are capable of heterophile relationships and of satisfaction within them, they should follow the way of holiness in either celibacy or abstinence or heterosexual marriage. In the situation of the bisexual, it can also be that counselling will help the person concerned to discover the truth of their personality and to achieve a degree of inner healing.
>
> (Church of England House of Bishops 1991: 42)

Describing bisexuality as 'ambiguous', effectively defines it as the failure to have a clear orientation at all. That the bishops see bisexual identity as illegitimate is further sup-ported by their suggestion that through therapy we may discover a truth more funda-mental than our claim to bisexuality. As Adrian Thatcher notes, the suggestion that bisexuals need healing implies that we are sick (1993: 156). The bishops respond to Thatcher directly in their follow-up document, *Some Issues in Human Sexuality*, noting that the question of whether or not bisexuals are sick 'is precisely the issue under dis-pute' (Church of England House of Bishops 2003: 216).

The House of Bishops recommends abstinence for gays and lesbians but permit those who cannot live abstinently to choose a 'loving and faithful homophile partnership, in intention lifelong, where mutual self-giving includes the physical expression of their attachment' (Church of England House of Bishops 1991: 41). Some Catholic scholars

have also called for a special exception for 'irreversible' homosexuals, wherein monogamous, permanent same-sex relationships would be permitted as the closest approximation to the heterosexual ideal (Curran and McCormick 1984; Cahill 1992). When it
comes to bisexuals, however, The House of Bishops contend that a faithful and loving
same-sex relationship is not an option:

> If God's overall intention for human activity is that it should take place in the con-
> text of marriage with someone of the opposite sex, then clearly the Church needs to
> encourage bisexual people who are capable of entering into such a relationship to do
> so, and to discourage them from entering into a homosexual one.
>
> (Church of England House of Bishops 2003: 283)

While the Anglican bishops dismiss the possibility of same-sex relationships for bisexual
Christians, others dismiss the possibility of marriage to an other-sex partner. Thatcher
suggests that marriage to an other-sex partner 'may lead to serious complications later'
(1993: 156), and Harvey recommends that bisexuals not marry unless we '*definitively*'
give up our 'homosexual friends and milieu' (1987: 185).

The opposition to bisexuals marrying an other-sex partner lies in mainstream theology's portrayal of us as conflicted, compulsive, or hypersexual. In *The seven big myths
about the Catholic Church*, Christopher Kaczor argues facetiously that 'if there is a right to
marry in accordance with sexual orientation, then a bisexual should be allowed to marry
both a man and a woman at the same time' (2012: 128). The Church of England House of
Bishops (1991) uses the term 'bisexual activity' to describe having concurrent male and
female partners, and then denounce this as promiscuity. While this certainly describes
a minority of bisexuals, it overlooks those in monogamous relationships as well as those
who are single or celibate. The bishops are aware of the opposition to monogamy by some
theologians, but argue that such a view 'flies in the face of all that has been said earlier
about the sacramentality of the body and the importance of proportion between physical intimacy and personal commitment' (1991: 42). This creeping behaviourism rejects
bisexuality as a false identity. Due to the perception that bisexuals have a choice between
same-sex and other-sex partners, heteronormative theology demands that we prioritize
relationships with other-sex partners, and eschew LGBTQ community involvement.

Bisexuality in Gay, Lesbian, and Queer Theology

Like the mainstream theology to which it responds, gay, lesbian, and queer theologies
have failed to be knowledgably inclusive of bisexuals. Beyond reproducing binary categories of sexuality that erase bisexuality, gays and lesbians have also produced some of
the most blatant examples of theological biphobia.

In *The Church and The Homosexual*, gay theologian John J. McNeill distinguishes
between the 'genuine homosexual condition', which he describes as permanent, and
'the behavior of perversion' (1976: 41), which is situational, chosen, and indulgent.

'The pervert,' he argues, 'is not a genuine homosexual; rather, he is a heterosexual who engages in homosexual practices, or a homosexual who engages in heterosexual practices' (1976: 39). McNeill's pervert is thus anyone whose behaviour (and perhaps attraction) spills out of the binary categories of straight and gay/lesbian—which is to say, bisexuals. Using this framework, McNeill argues that the people Paul denounces in Romans 1:26 are perverts (i.e. bisexuals) rather than inverts (gays/lesbians), since Paul describes them as 'abandoning their natural customs'.

While McNeill takes pains to establish that inverts are not responsible for their condition, he argues that perverts freely choose their actions. Pansexual theologian Phillip Bernhardt-House examines McNeill's exegesis and concludes: 'If the heterosexist notion of total sexual dualism is necessary to uphold the possibility of homosexual inclusion and acceptance despite (or even due to) Paul's words, then this leaves bisexuals ... entirely out in the cold as far as visibility and acceptance are concerned' (2010: 59). McNeill (1976: 39) goes on to argue that same-sex relationships are permissible for 'genuine' homosexuals, provided they mirror marriage in their depth of love and commitment. McNeill's exegesis secures freedom for gays and lesbians at the cost of applying Romans 1:26 directly and exclusively to bisexuals.

Lesbian theologians have paid slightly more attention to bisexuality than their male counterparts. This attention, however, has often been a preamble to erasure, with bisexuality being introduced, then quickly dismissed as ineffective. Carter Heyward paved the way for women's ordination in the Episcopal Church. Her portrayal of lesbianism as a strategy for coping with sexism is an important challenge to constructions of sexuality as private and personal, and the norms of mutuality and justice, which she endorses for all sexual relationships, are an improvement over theologies that judge bisexuality against a monosexual norm. When it comes to bisexuality, however, Heyward's theology is a mixed blessing. Her epistemology assumes a fundamental human bisexuality shaped by gender roles and compulsory heterosexuality. 'As boxes go,' Heyward suggests, 'bisexuality isn't bad. It may be (if unknowable truths were known) the most nearly adequate box for *all* persons' (1979: 155). Such universalizing undercuts bisexuality's political content by making it pre-conscious rather than strategic, reinforcing portrayals of bisexuality as immature and underdeveloped.

While Heyward describes herself as attracted to women as well as to men, she resists adopting a bisexual identity:

> The problem with bisexuality in my life (and I can speak only for myself) is that it has been grounded too much in my utopian fantasy of the way things ought to be and too little in the more modest recognition of myself as a participant in this society at this time in this world, in which I have both a concrete desire for personal intimacy with someone else and a responsibility to participate in, and witness to, the destruction of unjust social structures—specifically, the heterosexual box.
>
> (Heyward 1979: 155)

Heyward identifies lesbian identity as best able to provide 'prophetic witness' to the importance of feminism and sexual justice in late 1970s. By contrast, she describes bisexuality as living 'in anticipation of a future that has not arrived'. How this might differ from the eschatological hope for justice common to all Christians is unclear. What is clear is that Heyward sees lesbian identity as able to promote mutuality and justice, and challenge heterosexuality, in a way that bisexual identity cannot. If Heyward is speaking only for herself in rejecting bisexuality as 'utopian' (literally, a 'nowhere' identity), it is difficult to explain why the bulk of her work refers to 'lesbians and straight women' or 'gays and lesbians' as if these are the only identities that are theologically or politically significant. This erasure leaves bisexuality as the only identity unable to be actualized in oppressive environments, and ignores the motives behind bisexual women's identity choices, which may be no less political and strategic than Heyward's own choice to identify as lesbian.

Queer theology emerged in the work of gay theologian Robert Goss. His book, *Jesus acted up: A gay and lesbian manifesto* (1993), abandoned apologia and exegesis in favour of a hermeneutic modelled on liberation theology. Building on the work of theorists such as Michel Foucault, Judith Butler, and Jeffrey Weeks, queer theology analyses how categories of sexuality reinforce power and privilege, and how this connection might be subverted. Rather than joining the mainstream theological conversation, queer theology asks: How is God speaking directly to queer people, and what is being said? Queer theology has produced extensive biblical exegesis, as well as turning its lens on the transcendent within daily life, revealing the work of God within LGBTQ communities. Yet with few exceptions, bisexuality has been referenced only in passing, present only as part of a litany of sexual identities. Perusing the index of queer theology texts, for example, I found more references to bestiality than to bisexuality.

A few queer theologians, such as Robert Goss and Patrick Cheng, stand out in their attempt to grapple with bisexuality on its own terms. Goss notes that bisexuality's epistemology may be incomprehensible or threatening to some:

> Bisexual theologies will certainly undermine gay/lesbian and heterosexual theological discourse. Both gay/lesbian and heterosexual theologies subscribe to the politics of otherness with an either/or paradigm, while bisexual theologies represent a subversive alternative to either/or thinking. They stress a 'both/and' method that undermines either straight or gay methods of theological reflection and promote mediating methods to bridge hetero and gay theological discourses.

(Goss 1999: 52)

In *Radical Love: An Introduction to Queer Theology*, Patrick Cheng takes up the Christology of Marcella Althaus-Reid, and Laurel Dykestra, revealing how Jesus embodies a bisexual epistemology in his approach to hierarchical dualism. Cheng even goes so far as to propose that 'sin can be understood by queer theology to be sexual and gender essentialism' (2011: 74), framing social constructionism as a form of grace.

What is missing from even the relatively bi-friendly queer theologies of Goss and Cheng, however, is the focus on experience that has characterized queer theology's treatment of gay and lesbian identity. The bisexuality that Goss and Cheng address is primarily an epistemology rather than a lived identity. If, as queer theology has argued, God is present in our queer lives, then the erasure of bisexuality is, in effect, a rejection of the complexity of God. Although the move to an inclusive theology is an important one, until the theological implications of bisexuality are fully explored and integrated, queer theologians will insufficiently comprehend the categories they aim to destabilize.

KEY ISSUES IN BISEXUAL THEOLOGY

Bisexuals have a complex relationship with our faith traditions. Darren Sherkat (2002) found that we showed the lowest rates of church attendance, and bisexual women had the lowest frequency of prayer among women. Compared with lesbians and gay men, more bisexuals identify with the faith tradition in which we were raised. Biblical faith was high, with 69.4 per cent of bisexual women and 60.7 per cent of bisexual men believing that the Bible was the actual or inspired word of God (Sherkat 2002: 318). Andrew Yip (2003) found that the vast majority of bisexuals in his study agreed that God is love, immanent, genderless, and concerned with social justice. Compared with gays and lesbians, however, fewer bisexuals felt that God was approachable or responsive to our prayers. Bisexuals in Yip's study tended to hold a low Christology, seeing Jesus as a prophet and moral leader, but were less likely than gays or lesbians to see Jesus as our personal saviour, as the exclusive path to salvation, or as the incarnation of God. More recently, Alex Toft (2012) found that 70 per cent of the bisexuals in his study saw 'personal spiritual exploration' rather than communal worship as central to their religious life. While 66.3 per cent did not read the Bible, 84 per cent made time for prayer (Toft 2012: 195–196). Perhaps most telling, half of Toft's participants felt they could compartmentalize their Christianity from their bisexuality, while the other half felt they must integrate these identities (2012: 196). If bisexual theology emerges only when sexuality and theology are in conversation, then compartmentalization may undermine bisexual theology's very development.

For the most part, bisexual theology emerges from the experience of being doubly marginalized—from mainstream Christianity's rigid gender roles and compulsory heterosexuality, as well as from the triumphalism and biphobia of gay and lesbian theology. With this realization comes a new sense of empowerment, as bisexuals speak about our own experiences of transcendence, redemption, and love. Within bisexual theology to date, a number of common themes emerge, and I will discuss three: (1) a holistic view of sexuality as foundational to the human experience; (2) a tendency toward synthesis, unifying what are often seen as opposite categories; and (3) using an intersectional lens to examine how sexuality is shaped and constructed by categories such as class, race, or gender.

A Holistic View of Sexuality

Christian theology has tended to distinguish between the spiritual and the sexual, associating the latter with the fallen flesh. Sexual approaches to the divine have been seen as a hallmark of pagan religions, and declared illegitimate. Following in the steps of lesbians Carter Heyward and Audre Lorde, bisexual theologians assert that the erotic is sacred, and reject religious frameworks that separate the spiritual from the sexual. Instead, bisexual theologians have argued that sexuality is the ground in which all human relations, including our relation with God, are rooted.

For bisexual theologian Marcella Althaus-Reid, there is no theology that is not *already* a sexual theology (Robinson 2010: 112). What Althaus-Reid views as new, and as essential, is theology done outside of compulsory heterosexuality, compulsory monogamy, misogyny, and phallocentrism. For Althaus-Reid, a theology must be sexual if it is to be authentic and useful. 'If people cannot honestly incorporate the sexual aspect of their lives into their experiences of the divine,' she asks, 'then how can they possibly hope to live with integrity and in right-relation with others?' (Simpson 2005: 99–100). This sense that the sexual and the sacred are not discrete is also present in the groundbreaking anthology, *Bi Any Other Name*. Anthology editors Loraine Hutchins and Lani Ka'ahumanu state that they 'dare to question the dichotomy between sacred and profane' and argue that 'there is a renewed sense that sex is spiritual without contradiction' (1991: 92). Bernhardt-House argues that 'overcoming the compartmentalization of both spirituality/religion and sexuality is key to nondualistic, and therefore bisexual, theological praxis' (2000: 59). Bernhardt-House's own work includes an examination of how Jesus's choice to wash his disciples' feet confounds the expectations around active and passive, upon which Biblical objections to non-heterosexuality are based (2000: 37).

From a holistic perspective, spirituality is not simply an option for bisexuals (equivalent, perhaps, to secularity), but is the basic value upon which bisexuality itself is based. For bisexual theologians, to be bisexual is to be an embodied spirit, embracing our connection with other embodied spirits across boundaries such as sex, race, and class. Theological essays in the bi anthologies of the 1990s integrate spirituality into politics, personal relationship development, and bisexual community building rather than treating bisexual theology as a discourse in conversation with mainstream churches.

A Tendency Toward Synthesis

Bisexual theology seeks to undermine or transcend categories that would split us into halves. This synthesis, and the search for it, is named as redemptive. In their introduction to the 'Spiritualities' edition of the *Journal of Bisexuality*, editors Loraine Hutchins and H. Sharif Williams note that 'one theme for bisexual people in their spiritual lives is being able to heal the painful splits many named—between public and private, female and male, gay and straight, closeted and being out, body and soul, sacred and profane' (2010: 7). This approach is reflected in the titles used for the spirituality sections of our anthologies: Lani Ka'ahumanu and Loraine Hutchins (1991) called their section 'Healing the Splits', and Ron Jackson Suresha and Pete Chvany (2005) called theirs 'Bridge Building in Bisexual Spirit'.

Within a bisexual theological framework, spirituality is the force that draws people together and makes loving across socially constructed and politically policed boundaries possible. In *Blessed Bi Spirit*, Debra Kolodny argues:

> Blessed with the capacity for our intimate relationships to transcend the socially constructed boundaries of gender identity (masculine/feminine) as well as the biologically constructed boundaries (male/female), bisexual people embody and can therefore integrate and constructively deploy powerful theological insights that take others years to cultivate through practice.
>
> (Kolodny 2000: 62)

Bisexual theologians view hierarchical binaries as separating us from one another, and ultimately, from God. Salvation comes from recognizing that categories do not reflect how things are in and of themselves, but only how we choose to organize them. A theology that subverts hierarchical binaries such as man/woman, or heterosexual/homosexual is not easily folded into either mainstream, or gay/lesbian theologies. Indeed, for many, these categories are ontological and symbolic, created by God and reflective of God's likeness. Such categories have been treated as prescriptive rather than as descriptive, and been elevated, whether consciously or not, to sacred status. Bisexual theologians challenge what they perceive as the idolatry of hierarchical binaries, naming such structures as sinful rather than redemptive.

Liberation theologian Marcella Althaus-Reid (2003) frames bisexuality as an epistemological stance that embraces subversive readings, instability, and fluidity of meaning over fixity. For her, this resistance is achieved by bisexuality's association with threes, which she identifies with the trinity as well as with less conventional metaphors such as sexual threesomes. In her book, *The Queer God*, Althaus-Reid portrays the divine as reflected in multiplicity, and she challenges theologies that reduce, control, or eliminate the essential mystery of God by portraying the divine as essentially male, straight, or singular. As I have argued elsewhere, a bisexual epistemology such as that which Althaus-Reid advocates may radically distance us from other Christians: 'To discover the Divine apart from patriarchy, apart from the violent dominance and submission of colonialism, and apart from the sexualized violence of heteronormativity is in effect to discover a different God than the one most Christians would recognize' (Robinson 2010: 117). The fault for this distance, however, lies primarily with mainstream Christianity, whose theologies are so reliant upon heteronormativity, that a theology built upon any other basis seems unrecognizable as Christian.

In her essay 'The Holy Leper and The Bisexual Christian' (2000), Amanda Udis-Kessler argues that the way Jesus challenged distinctions between clean and unclean can serve as a template for challenging the dualistic thinking that undergirds current-day inequality and oppression. Udis-Kessler argues that within the purity system of his day, Jesus' practice of touching and healing the ritually unclean, such as lepers, rendered himself ritually unclean. In touching a leper, Jesus effectively becomes classed as a leper himself, occupying a mysterious position (both holy and unclean) that challenges the politics of purity. It is Jesus' boundary-breaking practice Udis-Kessler writes, that 'offers me hope that my bisexuality, far from being a sin, disease, or case of confusion, might be God's way of working gracefully in me against exclusivism and categorization, on behalf of God's joyful and inclusive kingdom' (2000: 15).

An Intersectional Lens

Since bisexuals are disproportionately poor, female, and racialized, it is not surprising that our theology has been shaped by experiences of poverty, sexism, and racism. Marcella Althaus-Reid, for example, describes herself as a 'Latin American woman brought up in the poverty of Buenos Aires' (2000: 9), and uses a postcolonial, feminist, and post-Marxist theological lens. Citing the role of Christianity in colonialism, and the oppression of women and LGBTQ people, she names the Church as a sinful social structure to which decolonized queers 'do not give authority or recognition' (2003: 165). Traditional theology, she argues, has based its view of sexuality on an androcentric and misogynistic anthropology. Queer theology must begin from a feminist anthropology 'where women are in control of their desires and pleasures, and in complete freedom to express themselves sexually with their own bodies, with other women, with men, or both' (Althaus-Reid 2004: 88–89).

This anthropological project begins, as the hermeneutical circle of liberation theology does, with a reflection on women's lived experience. Althaus-Reid's conceptualization of 'women' is highly particularized, 'at the crossroads of multiple ideological discourses such as those of race, class, sexuality, and religion' (2012: 442). Althaus-Reid (2003) draws upon Marxist analysis, arguing that the Church has claimed a monopoly on the holy, making God's love a commodity to be exchanged for political and social submission. Althaus-Reid challenges us to imagine what sexuality might look like if it were separated from capitalism's individualized and hierarchical profit structure. What if the body were no longer treated as property to be possessed, leased, or sold? What if love and sex were no longer portrayed as being in limited supply, but were instead recognized as present in abundance among the people?

Bisexual theologian Ibrahim Abdurrahman Farajajé (née Elias Farajajé-Jones), argues that heteropatriarchy has colonized our minds and bodies, and focused our energy on assimilating into the heterosexual mainstream. Characterizing bisexual people as 'victims of forced relocations from the very core of our being', Farajajé asserts that psychological decolonization will free us from hierarchical binaries such as male/female, white/black, and enable each of us to express our full gender, sexual, and racial complexity (Farajajé-Jones 2000: 16). Farajajé criticizes black liberation theology, and the Black Church, for being a source of hostility instead of a sanctuary from homophobia and heterosexism:

> Religion, especially African-American Judeo-Christian religion, is still being used to persecute and oppress people who are in-the-life [an identity term Farajajé proposes,

see below]. It forces people to remain closeted. Perhaps one of the worst things about it is that it is used to destroy people's self-esteem and to augment their self-hatred. Religiously-inspired homophobia and biphobia are actually killing people.

(Farajajé-Jones 1993: 143)

Farajajé's contention is supported by recent research. William Jeffries and colleagues (2008) found that while most Black Christian bisexual men were heavily involved in their Church communities, the majority were not out as bisexual, or were out only selectively, for fear of rejection, expulsion, or violence. Farajajé attributes homophobia and biphobia in the Black church to the influence of the white religious right, and suggests that theologians 'need to articulate theologies for the Black Church that teach that we are inclusive, not exclusive; that we are about life and not about death' (Farajajé-Jones 1993: 143). To counter the violence and oppression that racialized people have suffered, he proposes an 'in the life' theology. As I have noted elsewhere (Robinson 2012), identities such as lesbian, gay, and bisexual are heavily shaped by white supremacy, and their claims to universality are made possible only by overwriting racialized sexual identities. Farajajé proposes 'in the life' as a traditional African-American sexual identity that is inclusive of 'a broad spectrum of identities and behaviors' (1993: 140).

FUTURE DIRECTIONS

Despite the relative prevalence of bisexuality, few theologians have come out as bisexual. Even Marcella Althaus-Reid, the most recognized bisexual theologian to date, identified as queer in her written work. Bernhardt-House suggests that the lack of qualified theologians willing to risk identifying themselves as bisexual is responsible for the underdevelopment of bisexual theology (2000: 10). While many bisexuals are undoubtedly living closeted lives in their faith communities, I suspect that those bisexuals who leave the heterosexual or gay/lesbian closets may find themselves also leaving their churches. The theology we inherit from our communities has, as Althaus-Reid (2003) points out, resulted in a God that is a stranger to many of us. If bisexual people see religious reform as unlikely, that explains why we may be reluctant to participate in reform movements.

The religious plurality of bisexual anthologies, coupled with the relative absence of bisexual Christian voices, suggests that bisexual theology will continue to be, as it has been, an inter-religious dialogue, made possible in part, as a result of similar identities and experiences. Bisexual theology's greatest contribution may be manifested not in developing our own theological discourse—another box labelled 'bisexual theology'—but in having our theological insights taken up by all theologians. The identification of compulsory monosexuality and hierarchical binaries as forms of structural sin, for example, are insights from which many theologians could benefit. Mainstream theology may be less receptive to suggestions that the sex (and perhaps number) of our partner(s) is less morally relevant than the quality of our relationship(s).

References

Althaus-Reid, M. (2000). *Indecent Theology: Theological Perversions in Sex, Gender and Politics.* London: Routledge.

Althaus-Reid, M. (2003). *The Queer God.* London: Routledge.

Althaus-Reid, M. (2004). *From Feminist Theology to Indecent Theology: Readings on Poverty, Sexual Identity and God.* London: SCM Press.

Althaus-Reid, M. (2012). 'Doing a Theology from Disappeared Bodies: Theology, Sexuality, and the Excluded Bodies of the Discourses of Latin American Liberation Theology'. In M. McClintock Fulkerson, and S. Briggs (eds), *Oxford Handbook of Feminist Theology.* Oxford: Oxford University Press, 411–455.

Badgett, M. V. L., Durso, L. E., and Schneebaum, S. (2013). *New Patterns of Poverty in the Lesbian, Gay, and Bisexual Community.* The Williams Institute. <http://williamsinstitute. law.ucla.edu/wp-content/uploads/LGB-Poverty-Update-Jun-2013.pdf> (accessed 30 June 2013).

Bauer, G. R. and Brennan, D. J. (2013). 'The Problem with "Behavioral Bisexuality": Assessing Sexual Orientation in Survey Research'. *Journal of Bisexuality,* 13(2): 148–165.

Bernhardt-House, P. A. (2000). Serving Two Masters: Bisexual Theological Foundations. MA Thesis, Gonzaga University.

Bernhardt-House, P. A. (2010). 'Reenforcing Binaries, Downgrading Passions: Bisexual Invisibility in Mainstream Queer Christian Theology'. *Journal of Bisexuality,* 10(2): 54–63.

Cahill, L. S. (1992). *Women and Sexuality.* Madeleva Lecture in Spirituality. New York: Paulist Press.

Catholic Church. (2000). *Catechism of the Catholic Church,* 2nd edn. Vatican: Libreria Editrice Vaticana.

Chandra, A., Mosher, W. D., Copen, C., and Sionean, C. (2011). 'Sexual Behavior, Sexual Attraction, and Sexual Identity in The United States: Data from the 2006–2008 National Survey of Family Growth'. *National Health Statistics Report 36.* Hyattsville, MD: National Center for Health Statistics. <http://www.cdc.gov/nchs/data/nhsr/nhsr036.pdf> (accessed 30 June 2013).

Cheng, P. S. (2011). *Radical Love: An Introduction to Queer Theology.* New York: Church Publishing.

Congregation for the Doctrine of the Faith (1986). *Letter to the Bishops of the Catholic Church on the Pastoral Care of Homosexual Persons.* London: Catholic Truth Society.

Church of England House of Bishops (1991). *Issues in Human Sexuality.* London: Church House Publishing.

Church of England House of Bishops (2003). *Some Issues in Human Sexuality: A Guide to the Debate.* London: Church House Publishing.

Curran, C. E. and McCormick, R. A. (1984). *The Use of Scripture in Moral Theology.* Readings in Moral Theology, vol. 4. New York: Paulist Press.

Diamond, L. M. (2008). 'Female Bisexuality from Adolescence to Adulthood: Results from a 10-Year Longitudinal Study'. *Developmental Psychology,* 44(1): 5–14.

Dickson, N., Paul, C., and Herbison, P. (2003). 'Same-sex Attraction in a Birth Cohort: Prevalence and Persistence in Early Adulthood'. *Social Science & Medicine,* 56(8): 1607–1615.

Donaldson, S. (1995). 'The Bisexual Movement's Beginnings in the 70s: A Personal Retrospective'. In N. Tucker (ed.), *Bisexual Politics: Theories, Queries, & Visions.* New York: Harrington Park Press, 31–45.

Farajaje-Jones, E. (1993). 'Breaking Silence: Toward an In-The-Life Theology'. In J. H. Cone and G. S. Wilmore (eds), *Black Theology: A Documentary History*, vol. II. Maryknoll, NY: Orbis Books, 139–159.

Farajajé-Jones, E. (2000). 'Loving Queer'. *The Family: A Magazine for Lesbians, Gays, Bisexuals, & Their RelationsI*, 6(1): 14–21.

Gates, G. J. (2010). *Sexual Minorities in the 2008 General Social Survey: Coming Out And Demographic Characteristics*. Los Angeles: The Williams Institute, UCLA.

George, S. (1993). *Women and Bisexuality*. London: Scarlet Press.

Goss, R. (1993). *Jesus Acted Up: A Gay And Lesbian Manifesto*. San Francisco: Harper.

Goss, R. (1999). 'Queer Theologies as Transgressive Metaphors: New Paradigms for Hybrid Sexual Theologies'. *Theology and Sexuality*, 5(10): 43–53.

Harvey, J. F. (1987). *The Homosexual Person: New Thinking in Pastoral Care*. San Francisco: Ignatius Press.

Herek, Gregory M. (2002). 'Heterosexuals' Attitudes Toward Bisexual Men and Women in the United States'. *Journal of Sex Research*, 39(4): 264–274.

Heyward, C. (1979). 'Coming Out: Journey Without Maps'. *Christianity and Crisis*, 39(10): 153–156.

Hutchins, L. and Ka'ahumanu, L. (1991). *Bi Any Other Name: Bisexual People Speak Out*. Boston: Alyson Publications.

Hutchins, L. and Williams, H. S. (2010). 'Our Hearts Still Hold These Intimate Connections: An Introduction to The Spiritualities Special Issue of the Journal of Bisexuality'. *Journal of Bisexuality*, 10(1–2): 4–17.

Janus, S. and Janus, C. (1993). *The Janus Report on Sexual Behavior*. New York: John Wiley & Sons.

Jeffries, W. L., Dodge, B., and Sandfort, T. G. M. (2008). 'Religion and Spirituality among Bisexual Black Men in the USA'. *Culture, Health & Sexuality*, 10(5): 463–477.

Kaczor, C. (2012). *The Seven Big Myths about the Catholic Church: Distinguishing Fact from Fiction about Catholicism*. San Francisco: Ignatius Press.

Kinsey, A., Pomeroy, W. B., and Martin, C. E. (1948). *Sexual Behavior in the Human Male*. Bloomington: Indiana University Press.

Koh, A. S., and Ross, L. K. (2006). 'Mental Health Issues: A Comparison of Lesbian, Bisexual And Heterosexual Women'. *Journal of Homosexuality*, 1(1): 33–57.

Kolodny, D. R. (2000). *Blessed Bi Spirit: Bisexual People of Faith*. New York: Continuum Press.

Laumann, E., Gagnon, J. H., Michael, R. T., and Michaels, S. (1994). *The Social Organization Of Sexuality: Sexual Practices in the United States*. Chicago: University of Chicago Press, reprinted 1993.

McNeill, J. J. (1976). *The Church and the Homosexual*. Boston: Beacon Press.

Martin, R. (1972). 'Concern Raised about Bisexuality'. *Friends Journal*, 1 September: 455–456.

Mosher, W. D., Chandra, A., and Jones, J. (2005). 'Sexual Behavior and Selected Health Measures: Men and Women 15–44 Years of Age, United States, 2002'. *Advance Data*, 362: 1–55.

Office for National Statistics. (2012). 'Statistical Bulletin: Integrated Household Survey April 2011 to March 2012: Experimental Statistics'. Available at: <<http://www.ons.gov.uk/ons/dcp171778_280451.pdf> (accessed 30 June 2013).

Page, E. (2004). 'Mental Health Services Experiences of Bisexual Women and Bisexual Men: an Empirical Study'. *Journal of Bisexuality*, 3(3–4): 137–160.

Rissel, C. E., Richters, J., Grulich, A. E., de Visser, R. O., and Smith, A. M. (2003). 'Sex in Australia: Selected Characteristics of Regular Sexual Relationships'. *Australian & New Zealand Journal of Public Health*, 27(2): 124–130.

Robinson, M. (2010). 'Reading Althaus-Reid as a Bi Feminist Theo/Methodological Resource'. *Journal of Bisexuality*, 10(1–2): 108–120.

Robinson, M. (2012). 'Two-Spirited Sexuality and White Universality'. *Plural Space: Postcolonial Networks: Pursuing Global Justice Together*. <http://postcolonialnetworks.com/2012/06/02/two-spirited/> (accessed 30 June 2013).

Robinson, M. (2013). 'Polyamory and Monogamy as Strategic Identities'. *Journal of Bisexuality*, 13(1): 21–38.

Rust, P. (1996). 'Monogamy and Polyamory: Relationship Issues for Bisexuals'. In B. Firestein (ed.), *Bisexuality: The Psychology and Politics of an Invisible Minority*. Thousand Oaks: Sage Publications, 127–148.

Savin-Williams, R. C. and Ream, G. L. (2007). 'Prevalence and Stability of Sexual Orientation Components During Adolescence and Young Adulthood'. *Archives of Sexual Behavior*, 36(3): 385–394.

Sherkat, D. E. (2002). 'Sexuality and Religious Commitment in the United States: An Empirical Examination'. *Journal for the Scientific Study of Religion*, 41(2): 313–323.

Simpson, R. (2005). 'How to be Fashionably Queer: Reminding the Church of the Importance of Sexual Stories'. *Theology and Sexuality*, 11(2): 97–108.

Suresha R., and Chvany, P. (2005). *Bi Men: Coming Out Every Which Way*. Binghampton, NY: Harrington Park Press.

Thatcher, A. (1993). *Liberating Sex: A Christian Sexual Theology*. London: SPCK.

Tjepkema, M. (2008). 'Health Care Use Among Gay, Lesbian and Bisexual Canadians'. *Health Reports*, 19(1): 53–64.

Toft, A. (2012). 'Bisexuality and Christianity: Negotiating Disparate Identities in Church Life'. In S. J. Hunt, and A. K. T. Yip (eds), *Ashgate Research Companion to Contemporary Religion and Sexuality*. Farnham: Ashgate Publishing, 189–203.

Udis-Kessler, A. (2000). 'The Holy Leper and the Bisexual Christian'. In D. R. Kolodny (ed.), *Blessed Bi Spirit: Bisexual People of Faith*. New York: Continuum Press, 11–16. Original article published in 1997.

Yip, A. K. T. (2003). 'Spirituality and Sexuality: An Exploration of the Religious Beliefs of Non-Heterosexual Christians in Great Britain'. *Theology and Sexuality*, 9(1): 137–154.

Zuanazzi, G. (1997). 'The Homosexual Condition I., Definition and Casual Factors'. *L'Osservatore Romano*, 17 (23 April): 9.

CHAPTER 39

....

INTERSEX AND TRANSGENDER PEOPLE

....

SUSANNAH CORNWALL

> It is easy for most Christian churches...to see transgender and intersex
> people as having a *disease* that has to be *cured* or *corrected*, but the idea
> of giving transgender and intersex persons a unique identity and dignity
> within the human community does not make sense to them.
>
> (Quero 2008: 96, emphasis original)

INTERSEX, TRANSGENDER, AND THEOLOGY

....

CHRISTIAN theologians often assume everyone has a clear and stable physical sex, male or female. Some argue that gender identity must match this physical sex only in certain ways in physically, psychologically, and spiritually healthy people. However, the existence of intersex conditions and of transgender identities makes clear, first, that not everyone does have a clear male or female physical sex, and second, that gender identity does not 'match' physical sex typically for everyone.

Many intersex people and transgender people consider themselves unremarkable men or women with no particular need for special treatment or accommodations in the area of sexuality. However, the specificities of their body-histories may, for some, mean that theologies of sexuality which assume 'good' and 'healthy' bodies are always sexed and gendered only in typical ways, exclude them from signification, or pathologize their unusual bodies or gender identities. Intersex and transgender are discrete issues and should not be conflated. However, both phenomena, and the experiences of both groups, demonstrate the limitations of theologies which assume always stable, binary models of maleness and femaleness. Sexual theologies for all people must therefore acknowledge that intersex and transgender people may face particular challenges surrounding sexuality, and that intersex and transgender themselves pose questions for sexual theologies assuming stable, binary sex, gender, and sexuality. For some scholars, intersex and transgender help to make clear that this model does not tell the whole story. They note that a binary model of sex has not existed in all times and cultures:

> Conservatives believe that humans naturally come in two opposite sexes, and they read that 'truth' into Genesis 1 and Romans 1 as proof that homosexuality is unnatural and heterosexual complementarity, God's creative purpose for the sexes.... However objective it may seem, even the scientific framework for defining the 'two sexes' is a cultural construction.

> (Swancutt 2006: 70–1)

What is Intersex?

All human foetuses' genital regions initially appear identical, and typically, beginning around seven weeks' gestation, most develop along clear male or female lines (Preves 2003: 24–6): XY foetuses usually develop testes, a penis, and scrotum, and are brought up as boys from birth; XX foetuses usually develop ovaries, a clitoris, and vulva, and are brought up as girls. However, people with intersex conditions—about one in every 2,500 people (Preves 2003: 2–3)—have bodies different from typical male or female ones.

Formerly, the term 'hermaphrodite' was used for people with intersex conditions, but this is misleading and is now considered archaic. 'Hermaphrodite' implies someone with a full set of both male and female genitalia. However, intersex conditions mostly fall into two categories:

- those where the external genitalia look 'in between' male and female genitalia (with, for example, a genital tubercle which looks bigger than a clitoris but smaller than a penis);
- those where the external genitalia look unremarkably male or female, but there are unusual combinations of internal and external characteristics (for example, testes and XY chromosomes, and a clitoris, vulva, and vaginal opening).

Until fairly recently, parents of intersex children were encouraged to keep their conditions secret. Many children with unusual genitalia had corrective genital surgery soon after birth (and, sometimes, follow-up surgery through childhood and adolescence). This sometimes involved reducing or entirely removing large clitorises and small penises, with more emphasis placed on appearance than sensation (Preves 2003: 55–6). Most doctors argued early surgery was best for intersex children, so they would grow up as 'normal' boys or girls. This was based in the thought of John Money, an influential psychologist and sexologist, who believed gender identity in young children was flexible (Money

1980: 33), and that children could grow up happily in either gender provided their genitals were altered to reinforce the 'correct' identity (Money and Ehrhardt 1972: 15).

However, from the mid-1990s, many intersex people who had had surgery as children argued that this intervention, coupled with the secrecy surrounding their conditions, had caused them more problems than having unusual genitals would have done. Some said they could not enjoy sex as adults because of physical and psychological scarring caused by early surgery (Kessler 1998: 56). More recently, treatments for intersex are likely to include delayed or less invasive surgery, along with support for children and families as they consider the implications of early, delayed, or no surgery.

Medical approaches to intersex are clearly influenced by cultural understandings of sex, gender, sexuality, health, disease, disability, and embodiment. It is therefore appropriate to ask in what ways these cultural understandings have themselves been influenced by Christian theological accounts, and what standards of goodness and normality in bodies Christian theologians use. The Roman Catholic ethicist Margaret Farley says,

> The question for all of us is not only what treatment should be given for a condition considered to be pathological, but whether the condition is pathological or not. In other words, if a culture were less preoccupied with male/female sexual division and with boy/girl, man/woman gender differentiation, would the medical imperative regarding intersexed persons remain as it is? Or more fundamentally, is gender assignment as a 'pure' male or female, man or woman, essential to human flourishing?
>
> (Farley 2006: 151)

WHAT IS TRANSGENDER?

Transgender people feel their gender identity does not 'fit' their biological sex. Whilst most biological females identify as women and most biological males as men, transgender men are biologically female but identify as men, and transgender women are biologically male but identify as women. 'Transgender' refers to people with a disjunction between their physical sex and gender identity; 'transsexualism' refers more specifically to people who have undertaken surgery or hormone therapy to make their bodies 'fit' their gender identities.

It is unclear what causes transgender. Unlike intersex, where there is a clear variation from typical male or female anatomy, there is not uncontested evidence of a physical difference in transgender people. Some scientists argue that there is a disparity between the brains of transgender and non-transgender people, with some 'female' physical brain characteristics in transgender women (Zhou et al. 1995; Gooren 2006), but this is contested. Some believe transgender people have variant genes (Bentz et al. 2008; Hare et al. 2009). Others believe transgender is caused by foetal exposure to unusual levels of hormones during pregnancy (Schneider et al. 2006). Still others, following the early work of

Harry Benjamin, a pioneer in transgender research, believe there is no clear biological basis for transgender and that it arises for other reasons, such as psychological trauma or particular dynamics within families.

There may be many people with feelings of gender dysphoria who never actually transition gender. Up until 2010, about 12,500 people in the UK had sought medical treatment for gender dysphoria (GIRES 2011). In Britain, about 80 per cent of people seeking treatment are male-to-female, and 20 per cent female-to-male (Reed et al. 2009: 4), but elsewhere in Europe, the ratio is nearer 50–50 (Reed et al. 2009: 17). The average age for starting transition is 42 (GIRES 2011). According to GIRES (Gender Identity Research and Education Society), about 7,500 people in the UK have legally changed their documents since the Gender Recognition Act 2004 (GRA) was passed.[1]

Like intersex, transgender is under-acknowledged within Christian theology. Some of the theological work done in the area, such as the Church of England's 2003 document *Some Issues in Human Sexuality* (Archbishop's Council 2003) did not, suggest critics, take sufficient account of the experiences of transgender people (Beardsley 2005). However, transgender theologians have interpreted the experience of gender transition as a good site of God's revelation (Tanis 2003).

INTERSEX, TRANSGENDER AND SAME-SEX RELATIONSHIPS

Some Christian theologians believe all sexual relationships between same-sex partners are illegitimate. Many point to the Bible, which they argue condemns homosexual activity; others point to concepts such as Natural Law or the 'orders of creation' and claim that, since a major function of sexual activity is procreation, non-procreative sex (including sex between same-sex partners) is illegitimate. Robert Gagnon explicitly links gender transition with homosexuality, saying, 'Transsexuality is...an even more extreme version of the problem of homosexuality: an explicit denial of the integrity of one's own sex and an overt attempt at marring the sacred image of maleness and femaleness formed by God.... It is a decisive complaint or rebellion against God for having created oneself as male or female' (Gagnon 2007: 3–4).

---

[1] The Gender Recognition Act 2004 in British law allows transgender people to have the gender in which they now live (their 'acquired gender') legally recognized. This means a transgender person can obtain a new birth certificate listing the acquired gender rather than the gender originally assigned at birth, and their new name if this differs from the name given at birth. The Act also affords transgender people the right to marry someone of the opposite gender (i.e. the same biological sex), although clergy in the Church of England and Church in Wales are not obliged to marry someone they believe to be living in an acquired gender. The Act does not change someone's legal status as parent to an existing child. The full text of the Act is available at <http://www.legislation.gov.uk/ukpga/2004/7/contents>.

Alice Domurat Dreger, a historian of medical understandings of unusual bodies, notes that, in nineteenth-century France, doctors were concerned to 'enunciate a science of "inverted" sexuality' (Dreger 1998: 128). Many medics and scientists explored how and why some people's sexuality was 'inverted', causing attraction to the same sex rather than 'natural' attraction to the opposite sex, and analysed the causes and outworkings of so-called hermaphroditism. Some believed that homosexual inclination was itself a kind of hermaphroditism (Dreger 1998: 135). Transgender has also been understood, at times, as a logical outworking of same-sex desire: if it is 'natural' to desire people of the opposite sex, runs this logic, then if one is a man attracted to another man, one must 'really' be a woman.

However, even when they are not characterized as maximized versions of homosexuality, transgender and intersex pose particular challenges to the assertion that same-sex activity is wrong. Both phenomena demonstrate that it is not always clear *which* definitions of sex and gender are being used by theologians who oppose same-sex relationships. John Hare notes that Church of England teaching on sexuality and marriage 'depends... on the ability to define and recognize two sexes, male and female; to assign appropriate roles to each; and to define their appropriate behaviour' (Hare 2007: 99). He believes that intersex, in particular, has profound implications for Church of England debates on gender, sexuality, and same-sex relationships.

The existence of intersex may raise problems for theologians who assert that marriage may only occur between men and women, since some intersex people will, for example, be legally classified as women despite having XY ('male') chromosomes. If an intersex woman with Androgen Insensitivity Syndrome[2] married a non-intersex XY man, this would be two XY people marrying, which some Christians might class as a same-sex marriage. If the significant factor is not chromosomes but gender identity, this implies that marriages where one partner is transgender should also be legitimate, since, again, they might both have XY chromosomes, but one has a masculine and one a feminine gender identity.

This is, in fact, however, not what most theologians claim. Many theologians oppose marriage where one partner is transgender precisely because this would constitute a 'same-sex' marriage. In this instance, biology at birth is deemed to be the irreducible fact about someone. A man who lost his genitals in an accident would still be male, argues Oliver O'Donovan, so someone who has 'lost' his genitals by design, via sex reassignment surgery, is still male too (O'Donovan 1983: 145). God intended male bodies to be oriented toward female bodies; humans must accept this 'givenness' gladly (O'Donovan 1983: 152) and not transcend the boundaries of what it is appropriate to do in, through, and to our bodies (O'Donovan 1983: 150–1). A marriage where one partner is transsexual, says O'Donovan, 'will not be the union of a man and a

---

[2] Androgen Insensitivity Syndrome is a condition where an XY foetus, which would usually develop into a male, cannot respond to androgens ('male' hormones), so although there are internal male features such as testes, the external genitalia are female, with a vaginal opening, clitoris, and labia. Almost all people with AIS are brought up as girls and continue to live as women in adulthood.

woman, and so will not be a marriage at all' (O'Donovan 1983: 156). This is echoed in the United Kingdom Evangelical Alliance's document, *Transsexuality*, which states, 'A transsexual relationship...cannot be regarded as truly being contracted between a man and a woman but between two partners of the same sex, one of whom has adopted a gender identity which is at variance with their biological sex' (Evangelical Alliance 2000: 30). The Evangelical Alliance's guide for churches to the UK Gender Recognition Act 2004 says, 'Under the GRA it is now legally possible for a transgendered person to "marry" someone of the same biological sex' (Evangelical Alliance 2006: 4). The use of inverted commas makes it clear that this is not a *real* marriage as far as the Evangelical Alliance is concerned, despite being legally recognized. The Evangelical Alliance believes marriages involving transgender people 'pass on to others experience of gender confusion and distort common-sense understanding of what constitutes family' (Evangelical Alliance 2006: 9). It also holds that 'by definition transsexual relationships involve a lifestyle that excludes authentic sexual relations' (Evangelical Alliance 2006: 26).

Many Christian theologians who oppose same-sex relationships, and believe same-sex marriage is impossible, do not define exactly what they believe constitutes sex. If pressed, many would probably—in common with contemporary social norms—appeal to chromosomes or gonads as 'irreducibly' defining sex. However, this will not be a good arbiter in the case of intersex people, who have some combination of chromosomes, gonads, genitals, sex cells, and gender identity different from that typical for males or females. All these should be considered in any analysis of what constitutes sex—and thus 'same-sex' relationships—for intersex people.

TYPES OF SEXUAL ACTIVITY AND CHALLENGES OF UNUSUAL ANATOMY

What logic underlies the Evangelical Alliance's assertion that transsexual relationships exclude 'authentic sexual relations'? In some Christian denominations, marriages are deemed to have been consummated only once full sexual intercourse has occurred. This is usually defined, as by the Roman Catholic Church, as intercourse in which the erect male penis penetrates the female vagina followed by male ejaculation within the vagina. Rodney Holder, an Anglican, argues that transsexualism might pose a problem for marriage: it may be impossible for people who have had genital surgery to consummate their marriages (Holder 1998a: 90, 1998b: 130). Nonetheless, Holder does not believe that transgender marriages are illegitimate, since the *intention* of the transgender partner is to enter into what they understand as a heterosexual marriage (Holder 1998b: 131, 134), and the genitals have been altered 'to remedy a severe disfunction' (Holder 1998b: 132).

It is true that penetrative vaginal sexual intercourse may be impossible for some transgender and intersex people. Intersex people with 'ambiguous' genitalia may not have a vaginal opening capable of being penetrated, or a penis capable of penetrating a vagina and/or ejaculating. Intersex people's ability to have this kind of sexual intercourse may have been compromised by genital surgery, designed to make the genitals appear more typical, which has left scarring. For some transgender people, penetrative sexual intercourse will be impossible either because they have not had genital surgery and so their genital anatomy still resembles that of their partner, or because the surgically-altered anatomy they do have still does not allow for penetrative sexual intercourse.

The question, then, is whether penetrative vaginal sex followed by male ejaculation inside the vagina must *always* be deemed to have a different cosmic and/or theological significance from other kinds of sexual activity. One reason why it should is that this is how children are most commonly conceived. Potentially procreative sex is often understood, theologically, as different in kind from deliberately non-procreative sex—variously held to include sex between same-sex partners, heterosexual sex using contraception, and heterosexual sexual activity avoiding male ejaculation in the vagina, such as oral, anal, and intercrural (between the thighs) sex. For some Roman Catholic theologians in particular, sex where contraception is used prevents sex signifying all it is designed to signify, namely openness and hospitality to one's partner and any children who may be conceived.

However, for many transgender and intersex people, the question of procreative sex is moot: they are unlikely to be able to conceive in any case. For transgender people in heterosexual relationships (with people of the same biological sex but the opposite gender as themselves), conception via penetrative sex will not be possible because their partner makes the same gametes (eggs or sperm) as they do. For some intersex people, penetrative sex is impossible because of the specific nature of their genital anatomy. For some other intersex people, penetration may be possible but conception may not: women with Androgen Insensitivity Syndrome usually have vaginas, but have no uterus or ovaries, so cannot conceive children. For these groups of people, if a type of sexual activity of which they are physically incapable is given cosmic significance over and above other kinds of sexual activity of which they are capable, their own sexual activity may be written out of signification. There are overlaps here with the experiences of some people with disabilities, who may similarly be unable to take part in penetrative vaginal intercourse followed by male ejaculation inside the vagina because of specific physical limitations.

Many Christian denominations do legitimize the use of contraception for married couples, which means that the procreative meaning of sexual activity has already been separated out from its other meanings, namely union and sexual fulfilment for the partners. Theologies which legitimize contraception may find it harder to justify the continued insistence that penetrative vaginal sex is cosmically different from other sexual activity (Williams 2002).

THE PRIVILEGING OF PENETRATION?

Some theologians appeal to the biblical notion that sexual intercourse mystically joins the partners so that—per Genesis 2:24 and 1 Corinthians 6:17—their spirits are united and they become 'one flesh' (see discussion in Woodhead 1997: 115–118; see also e.g. Hollinger 2009: 98). However, the Bible never makes explicit exactly *what kind* of physical activity carries this mystical power. We cannot assume on the grounds of the Bible alone that only penetrative vaginal sex followed by male ejaculation inside the vagina is spiritually significant in this way.

The theological privileging of penetrative vaginal sex may also represent a bias toward male sexual experience: Shere Hite famously argued, on the grounds of research with hundreds of women, that most do not find penetration sexually stimulating in its own right and are unlikely to experience orgasm through penetration alone (Hite 1976). Theologies which insist that only penetrative vaginal sex is 'real' risk excluding some transgender and some intersex people. They risk failing to engage as fully as they could with the ethical and moral significance of a range of sexual activity. This leaves other kinds of sexual activity in a strange limbo where they are either not acknowledged as significant at all, or are deemed perverse in some way.

In an essay setting out his opposition to sex reassignment surgery for transgender people, O'Donovan argues that respecting living forms means recognizing the limits of how it is legitimate to alter them. He says, 'To known [*sic*] oneself as body is to know that there are only certain things that one can do and be, because one's freedom must be responsible to a given form, which is the form of one's own experience in the material world' (O'Donovan 1983: 151). Furthermore, O'Donovan believes that genitals constructed artificially for a transsexual person are not really part of the person's body. He says,

> Whatever the surgeon may be able to do, and whatever he may yet learn to do, he cannot make self out of not-self. He cannot turn an artifact into a human being's body. The transsexual can never say with justice: 'These organs are my bodily being, and their sex is my sex'.

(O'Donovan 1983: 152)

As a result, for O'Donovan, whatever these genitals may communicate during sexual activity with a partner, it is less than the whole truth.

A similar argument occurs in Roman Catholic theology. In Roman Catholic Canon Law, consummation of a marriage is rendered impossible if either spouse is deemed permanently organically impotent. Circumstances constituting permanent organic impotence in a woman include having a vagina constructed from artificial materials (Dacanáy 2000: 37–38, 40). The argument is that a vagina which has not been created from human materials is not entirely a human organ. It therefore cannot be legitimately used for sexual acts performed 'in a human fashion', one of the criteria which must be satisfied in order for consummation to have occurred. The case for vaginas made artificially but from human materials is less certain, though Dacanáy states explicitly that the affirmation of the constructed vagina as a human organ 'could not be made for transsexual surgeries' (Dacanáy 2000: 40).

PATHOLOGY OR BENIGN VARIATION?

Physical differences such as those caused by intersex have sometimes been understood as pathological. Cultural representations of 'hermaphrodites' sometimes figure them as monsters, freaks, or degenerates. In contemporary Christian theology, intersex people are more likely to be treated compassionately, but their bodies may nonetheless be understood as problematic, not innocuous variations but pathological deviations from legitimate maleness or femaleness. For example, Dennis P. Hollinger, a conservative evangelical theologian, understands intersex conditions as 'results of the fallen condition of our world, including the natural world.... All distortions in the world are to be judged against the divine creational givens. In a fallen world there will be chaos and confusion that extends even to human sexuality' (Hollinger 2009: 84). Charles Colson describes intersex people as 'afflicted with [a] deformity', saying, 'The Bible teaches that the Fall into sin affected biology itself—that nature is now marred and distorted from its original perfection. This truth gives us a basis for fighting evil, for working to alleviate disease and deformity—including helping those unfortunate children born with genital deformities' (Colson 1996). Hollinger and Colson are not saying intersex people are unusually sinful, or have done something wrong to cause their conditions. Nonetheless, they understand intersex as evidence of something amiss in the world. Hollinger and Colson appeal to what they understand as God's creational norms, which mean that humans are male and female by design, any deviation from this representing a mistake or a problem.

A SPECTRUM OF EMBODIMENT?

However, other theologians maintain that human sex is more complicated than that. For Virginia Ramey Mollenkott, the binary male and female system represents a distortion of the reality of a *spectrum* of sexed embodiment. Christians, suggests Mollenkott, should celebrate more different kinds of identity and embodiment. In what she calls an 'omnigender' world, intersex bodies are not problems, but 'reminders of Original Perfection' (Mollenkott 2007: 99), from a time before narrow human social norms were concretized. An intersex woman, Angela Moreno, uses similar imagery herself when she describes her large clitoris, surgically removed when she was 12:

> I loved it...I had this wonderful relationship with it...I think of that time that I had,...maybe six months before surgery from the time that I noticed it and started

to love it 'til the time that it was taken from me,... [as] this time in the pleasure garden before the fall.

(Moreno, speaking in Chase 1996)

Justin Tanis, too, appeals to Genesis, claiming, 'The act of creation, even while differentiating between elements of creation, still leaves space for "in between" things: dusk,
dawn, intersexed persons. God blesses all those parts of creation, calling them good'
(Tanis 2003: 59). Mollenkott's notion of omnigender has its own problems: for example,
she seems to advocate glossing over differences between sexes and genders (Mollenkott
2007: 186), a tactic which might ironically end up erasing rather than endorsing variation. However, her acknowledgement that binary sex as a system stems, at least partly,
from social constructions about what bodies signify, means her theology is more open
to intersex and transgender variations than many theologies grounded in a strongly
binary-sexed model.

Intersex and transgender people have often worked hard to convince others
that they are not 'mistakes', but good creations of God. Some scholars suggest there
are overlaps between non-pathologizing discourses of *intersex* embodiment and
non-pathologizing discourses of *variant* embodiment for people with disabilities
(Koyama 2006; Cornwall 2009). Intersex bodies and disabled bodies might both be
figured as differing from the statistical norm in some way, and posing particular challenges in their own right, but also, at least in part, made more problematic because of
social reactions to them.

Some theologians note that, often, impaired people are told by well-meaning
Christians that they will inevitably be healed in the afterlife (Lewis 2007: 65–75). This
shifts the problems faced by disabled people back onto disabled bodies, not social
failure to accommodate them. It may also reinforce links between disability and sin,
whether personal or the general effects of sin on creation (Yong 2011: 60–61). The idea
of healing might be empowering for some disabled people, but others find the notion
that their impairment might be removed difficult, fearing this could compromise
their identity. Consequently, J. David Hester suggests that Christians should be cir-
cumspect about discussing 'healing' in terms of the *removal* of a physical difference.
In the case of intersex, he argues, ' "Healing" is not "healing from", but living comfortably and healthily with oneself as intersex' (Hester 2006: 48). Furthermore, 'healing'
might be for *whole* societies as they learn to navigate and celebrate living in relation
to God and other humans in a variety of bodies. Hester says, 'Unquestioning acceptance of intersexed bodies as normal and natural seems to be a powerful means of 'healing'.... Intersex people whose bodies diverge from the gender ideal nevertheless find
"health" through integration into the community and acceptance of their own bodies'
(Hester 2006: 52).

Hester notes that many intersex people who have 'found healing' have joined support groups where they can talk and share experiences with intersex people like
themselves (Hester 2006: 54–55, 65). But Christian communities might, similarly, be
understood as places where love and a shared identity in Christ provide healing from

the rejection some intersex and transgender people experience in society. What Hester finds in the intersex people's testimonies he analyses is 'a rhetoric of truth-telling that seeks to undo the implicit pathology of the condition, a pathology that has been orchestrated by silence and paternalism' (Hester 2006: 55). Truth-telling in Christian communities might therefore mean exposing how Christian narratives have been complicit in reinforcing narrowly-sexed social norms, and appealing to a greater legitimacy for bodies grounded in their status as creations of God. In this way, intersex people might be liberated from the burden of being forced into a box their bodies were never intended to fit.

Ethical Issues Surrounding Surgery

Whilst many issues facing intersex people and transgender people theologically and socially are similar, there are also important differences between them, some of which have led to tensions between the groups. For example, whilst many transgender people choose to pursue surgery and/or hormone therapy to make their bodies 'match' their gender identities, many intersex people have experienced 'corrective' genital surgery against their will. Some intersex people understand these surgeries as invasive, abusive, and damaging to the integrity of the people they originally were.

An important difference between transgender and intersex experiences of surgery is that, in most cases, sex reassignment surgery for transgender people does not take place until they are over 18 and have lived publicly for a year in their acquired gender. Some transgender people report difficulty in accessing surgical intervention, especially where such surgery is very expensive and transgender people must pay for it themselves or convince 'gatekeeper' doctors or insurance companies that it is medically necessary. By contrast, most initial surgery for intersex takes place on babies and young children, and many need repeat operations throughout their lives. Whilst surgery and other medical intervention for transgender people might endorse their agency and capacity to make decisions about their bodies, surgery for intersex people is likely—especially if it occurred when they were very young, or without their consent—to be understood as invading or compromising their agency.

How can theologies for intersex and transgender people simultaneously endorse the goodness of 'bodies as they are' in the case of intersex, and acknowledge that pre-surgery bodies are sometimes sources of frustration, anxiety, and even disgust for some transgender people? One significant theological consideration here is 'givenness'. As we saw above, some Christian opponents to sex reassignment surgery for transgender people believe it is wrong for humans to alter their bodies in this way, because bodies are given by God as they are. However, intersex Christians have also argued that their bodies are how God made them and intended them to be, and that God does not make mistakes. Interestingly, some transgender people also appeal to 'givenness' as a good, but for them it is *gender* that is 'given' and therefore should not be changed, rather than bodily sex. Rachel Mann, a transgender Christian, says of her sex reassignment surgery,

> It was an act of violence against the normal course of things. And yet without it I would not have achieved the degree and depth of self-reconciliation that I have.... There is part of me that can see that life would have been easier and simpler if... I could have accepted my maleness and male body; but the fact is that, as painful as the surgery was, I would choose it again and again rather than be a man.

> (Mann 2012: 94)

Surgery may have implications for intersex and transgender people's capacity to enjoy sexual activity, and this raises its own ethical questions. Some critics of corrective surgery on intersex babies and children argue that, in the past, surgeons were more concerned about the finished genitals' cosmetic appearance than their capacity to feel sexual pleasure. Appearance is not unimportant, especially if the child will be getting changed in front of other people during sports or swimming lessons, or at the beach. But to what extent is it ethically legitimate to privilege appearance over capacity for sensation? In particular, some critics have accused surgeons of sexism, constructing vaginas understood mainly as passive holes or penis-receptacles, rather than body-parts which can feel sexual pleasure in their own right (Dreger 1998: 184; Kessler 1998: 55–56; Preves 2003: 56). As a result, more recently, some intersex activists have argued that no aesthetic surgery for intersex should take place before the child is old enough to understand the implications of conducting or not conducting surgery, and to be involved in the decision-making process.

Despite the differences between intersex and transgender concerns about surgery, then, some similar sets of ethical questions arise. Should surgery take place at all? If so, when and how? Who should decide? Issues of autonomy and self-determination apply to both intersex and transgender people. Sexual theologies for intersex and transgender people should acknowledge that their bodily integrity is as important as anyone else's, and that their experiences of undergoing unwanted surgery, or being unable to access surgery they consider necessary, may negatively affect their body-image, sense of self, and capacity to find sexual activity pleasurable and enjoyable. Sexual theologies for transgender and intersex people should celebrate them as they are, stand with those whose bodies discomfit or disturb them, and support them in decisions about their bodies, whether this involves surgical intervention or not.

Vulnerability in Sexual Encounter

Sexual relationships always involve vulnerability. Physically, being wholly or partially naked, and exposing one's genitals in someone else's presence, puts one in a position where one cannot easily defend oneself from attack. Emotionally, sexual intercourse as an expression of intimacy means opening one's private inner self up to another person and trusting that they will not abuse the privilege. Any sexual relationship, whether with a long-term partner or a relative stranger, has an element of risk attached.

Intersex and transgender people may find themselves at particular risk in sexual relationships. For some, their unusual genital appearance (whether because they have been born with ambiguous genitalia, or because they have had surgery to alter their genitalia) is a source of fear and disquiet which makes them wary of getting into sexual relationships because they do not know how others will react. They may also lack confidence because of their genital appearance. For some transgender people, especially those who have transitioned gender but not had genital surgery, there may be a 'mismatch' between the gender in which they 'pass' and their genital appearance. This puts them at risk of violence or attack when sexual partners first learn (before, during, or after sex) that they are transgender. Sadly, there are numerous cases of transpeople having been assaulted, wounded, and even killed by sexual partners who felt they had been 'deceived'.

For intersex and transgender people even more than others, then, trust and confidence in sexual partners' goodwill and acceptance will be important in order to ensure, as far as possible, physical and emotional safety. What Christian ethical resources are there for promoting just and life-affirming sexualities? Farley suggests seven principles for just sexual behaviour which Christians should take into account. These are:

- *Do no unjust harm.* Since sexual activity makes people vulnerable to one another, we should not abuse this vulnerability by deliberately betraying or deceiving our sexual partners (Farley 2006: 217).
- *Free consent.* We should not be violent or coercive in our sexual relationships, but should be truthful, keep our promises, and be transparent with our partners (Farley 2006: 219).
- *Mutuality.* Sex should be a reciprocal aspect of relationships in which both partners give and receive freely, not something to be forced or endured (Farley 2006: 222).
- *Equality.* Unequal amounts of power in a relationship will lead to coercion and exploitation (Farley 2006: 223).
- *Commitment.* This entails both a commitment of time, giving sexual relationships a chance to deepen and mature, and a commitment to equality, mutuality, and justice (Farley 2006: 226).
- *Fruitfulness.* Sexual interactions have consequences for other people beyond the partners themselves. Just, loving sexual relationships should free the participants to look outwards and promote love and inclusion for others in their community, not to be entirely absorbed in each other (Farley 2006: 228).
- *Social justice.* This entails always treating other people as ends in themselves, and taking responsibility for our sexual choices and their consequences (Farley 2006: 229).

Conclusion: the Goodness of Different Types of Embodiment

When considering sexual theologies for intersex and transgender people, it is important to note that both groups have, at times, suffered from stereotypes and projections from others about their sexual selves. Both intersex and transgender people have sometimes been figured as excessively or peculiarly sexual, with prurient media fascination about genital anatomy and sexual behaviour surrounding the coverage of early high-profile transpeople such as Christine Jorgensen, and with intersex people sometimes having been characterized as insatiable, super-sexual 'hermaphrodites'. Conversely, intersex people in particular have also suffered a sometime characterization as *a*sexual, unable to participate in 'normal' sex at all and therefore somehow lacking in sexuality (Colligan 2004: 50). Ironically, intersex people's asexualization may have been exacerbated by the desire of some activists and allies to distance intersex conditions from the queer and the lesbian, gay, bisexual, and trangender (LGBT) identity politics with which they were sometimes associated in the 1990s—but intersex activist Emi Koyama says that 'for intersex people to truly achieve acceptance, it makes no sense to retreat from the conversations about gender and sexuality' (Koyama 2006). It almost goes without saying that, in actual fact, transgender people and intersex people are *sexed* and *sexual*, but no more or less so by virtue of their conditions than non-transgender and non-intersex people. Abby L. Wilkerson (2012: 185) argues that, since oppressed people often also find themselves oppressed or marginalized sexually—or made to play out their sexuality only in particular stereotypical ways—for some groups, eroticization on their own terms may be an important way of resisting stereotyped characterization. Wilkerson adds that intersex people's 'public reflections on sexuality' are valuable, making clear that healthy sexualities might 'encompass a range of pleasures and identities, rather than evaluating the eroticism of bodily configurations and practices on the basis of their proximity to a predetermined norm' (Wilkerson 2012: 202).

This kind of logic underlies efforts by intersex and transgender people to identify proto-intersex and proto-transgender figures in the Bible, to endorse the goodness, naturalness and non-pathology of such body-identities. In this way, they aim to show that Christian theological assertions about only non-transgender maleness and femaleness being desirable, good, 'real' identities are inadequate. For some intersex and transgender people, the scriptural eunuchs are important, representing people who stood outside conventional sex-gender categories and, sometimes, had atypical genital anatomy. One intersex Christian, David, notes of Jesus' teaching about eunuchs in Matthew 19,

> I scoured the Bible to find out anything to do with intersex and I was thrilled when I discovered that Jesus spoke about it. My interpretation of what Jesus said about eunuchs...I thought that was wonderful, yes. And that was the springboard for my faith. I thought, Jesus knows I exist! I'm not on my own. Because I thought I was the only one in the world, you see.

(David 2012)

LIBERATION

Liberating theologies for transgender and intersex people will endorse the good-ness of different kinds of embodiment, and critique interventions more concerned with upholding conservative social norms than respecting the agency and integrity of the bodies in question. This does not mean all gender should be eradicated or ren-dered obsolete: for people who have fought long and hard for the specificities of their body-identities to be recognized as legitimate, good sites of God's grace, declaring an end to gender difference may risk disappearance of their specificity or a new silencing of their voices. Indeed, remarks Farley,

> Once we see other possibilities for gendering, gender is itself rendered at once more important and less. It is more important for those who must struggle to discover their gender identity and come to be at home in it. It is less important as a way to exclude some identities from the circle of our common humanity.
>
> (Farley 2006: 155)

Liberation means being supported to live safely in a particular body, even if it is unusual and troubling, even if it is 'ambiguous', and even if it is not the body that others believe one 'should' have. Liberation also means emancipation from tired stereotypes about sex and gender in social and cultural terms, and from theological anthropologies grounded in outmoded medical and scientific paradigms. This entails being critical of how theolo-gians and the Christian Churches have discussed sex and gender in the past: in an essay on intersex, Roman Catholic ethicist Patricia Beattie Jung comments, 'It is reasonable to expect magisterial interpretations of biblical texts to be readily corroborated not only by the best of biblical scholarship but also to cohere with cogent interpretations of relevant human experiences and with the best scientific data and philosophical arguments avail-able' (Jung 2006: 305).

The assumption that transgender always stems from psychological disturbance seems to go hand in hand, in some theological accounts, with the assumption that reproduc-tive sexual activity is *the* divinely-ordained ideal and that anyone who deliberately chooses to render reproduction impossible via sex reassignment surgery cannot be psy-chologically healthy (Central Board of Finance 1991: 26–27). Appeals to gender com-plementarity also recur in this literature (Central Board of Finance 1991: 37–38). I have noted elsewhere that 'holding as pre-existent "known fact" that all transgender people are mentally ill or delusional profoundly undermines their legitimacy as authors and actors of their own identities, and fails to disturb the genital-centric model of human sex' (Cornwall 2010: 125). Liberating theologies for transgender and intersex people allow them to make decisions about their own bodies and bodily expressions without an automatic assumption that they are incapable of responsibly and reflectively doing so.

Indeed, argues transgender theologian Vanessa Sheridan, 'Seeking personal spir-itual liberation through the good news of Jesus Christ will help us to accept our responsibilities and benefits as gender variant individuals, allowing us to more fully celebrate our transgendered orientation and identity as the true blessings from God that they are' (Sheridan 2001: 99). This, she suggests, means refusing the definitions of themselves as peculiarly damaged or pathological which many transgender people encounter: 'Liberation always begins when someone makes a decision to refuse the imposed definitions of others' (Sheridan 2001: 100). Sheridan suggests that the biblical Exodus narrative, which she interprets as narrating an 'alternative social vision for God's people', can 'speak directly to the hearts and spirits of contemporary transgendered Christians' (Sheridan 2001: 105).

Gender as a 'Calling'

Tanis suggests transgender people might be liberated by figuring gender as a *calling*: a discovery of who God intends them to be, recognizing that callings can emerge gradually, are ongoing, and can be permanent or for a season (Tanis 2003: 156). Through coming into their calling, suggests Tanis, transgender people might experience 'truth, realness, and integrity in which we come to know ourselves better than we did before.... We experience the affirmation that we are fully revealed and known to God' (Tanis 2003: 168). Mann notes that this does not necessarily entail denying one's own former history, but that transpeople's relationships with their histories in another gender may nonetheless be difficult or painful for themselves and others: 'One of the costs of my emergent identity has been to make it difficult for my family to speak confidently about my early life as a boy and young man. There is a sense in which, for my family as a whole, my early life has been lost' (Mann 2012: 22).

Finally, liberating sexual theologies for intersex and transgender people must be grounded in a conviction that, like other people, they are created in the image of God and that their embodiment is good. As Tanis remarks, 'The nature of God is to embody all genders, and thus it is natural for those of us who do as well. Rather than being outside of the divine order, intersexed and transgendered individuals are an integral part of creation, a creation that God declared was good' (Tanis 2003: 138). In fact, the Christian tradition already contains resources for understanding difference and otherness as occurring along more than sexed and gendered lines; Christianity's association with the dynamics of clear and unambiguous gender and sex can be, at most, only an ambivalent one.

References

Archbishops' Council (2003). *Some Issues in Human Sexuality, A Guide to the Debate: A Discussion Document from the House of Bishops' Group on Issues in Human Sexuality.* London: Church House Publishing.

Beardsley, Christina (2005). 'Taking Issue: The Transsexual Hiatus in Some Issues in Human Sexuality'. *Theology*, 58(845): 338–346.

Bentz, E., Hefler, L. A., Kaufmann, U., Huber, J. C., Kolbus, A., and Tempfer, C. B. (2008). 'A Polymorphism of the CYP17 Gene Related to Sex Steroid Metabolism is Associated with Female-to-Male but not Male-to-Female Transsexualism'. *Fertility and Sterility*, 90(1): 56–59.

Central Board of Finance of the Church of England (1991). *Issues in Human Sexuality: A Statement by the House of Bishops*. London: Church House Publishing.

Chase, Cheryl (1996) (director). *Hermaphrodites Speak!* Video. Rohnert Park, CA: Intersex Society of North America.

Colligan, Sumi (2004). 'Why the Intersexed Shouldn't be Fixed: Insights from Queer Theory and Disability Studies'. In Bonnie G. Smith and Beth Hutchison (eds), *Gendering Disability*. New Brunswick, NJ: Rutgers University Press, 45–60.

Colson, Charles (1996). 'Blurred Biology: How Many Sexes Are There?' <http://www.breakpoint.org/commentaries/5213-blurred-biology>.

Cornwall, Susannah (2009). 'Theologies of Resistance: Intersex, Disability and Queering the "Real World"'. In Morgan Holmes (ed.), *Critical Intersex (Queer Interventions)*. Aldershot: Ashgate, 215–243.

Cornwall, Susannah (2010). *Sex and Uncertainty in the Body of Christ: Intersex Conditions and Christian Theology*. London: Equinox.

Dacanáy, Adolfo N. (2000). *Canon Law on Marriage: Introductory Notes and Comments*. Quezon City: Ateneo de Manila University Press.

David (pseudonym) (2012). Interview with Susannah Cornwall as part of Intersex, Identity and Disability: Issues for Public Policy, Healthcare and the Church project.

Dreger, Alice Domurat (1998). *Hermaphrodites and the Medical Invention of Sex*. Cambridge, MA: Harvard University Press.

Evangelical Alliance Policy Commission (2000). *Transsexuality*. London: Evangelical Alliance.

Evangelical Alliance (2006). *Gender Recognition: A Guide for Churches to the Gender Recognition Act (UK)*. London: Evangelical Alliance and Parakaleo Ministry.

Farley, Margaret A. (2006). *Just Love: A Framework for Christian Sexual Ethics*. New York, NY: Continuum.

Gagnon, Robert A. J. (2007). 'Transsexuality and Ordination'. <http://robgagnon.net/Articles/transsexualityordination.pdf>.

Gender Identity Research and Education Society (GIRES) (2011). 'The Number of Gender Variant People in the UK—Update 2011'. <http://www.gires.org.uk/Prevalence2011.pdf>.

Gooren, Louis (2006). 'The Biology of Human Psychosexual Differentiation'. *Hormones and Behavior*, 50(4): 589–601.

Hare, John (2007). '"Neither Male nor Female": The Case of Intersexuality'. In Duncan Dormor and Jeremy Morris (eds), *An Acceptable Sacrifice? Homosexuality and the Church*. London: SPCK, 98–111.

Hare, L., P. Bernard, F. Sanchez, P. Baird, E. Vilain, T. Kennedy, and V. Harley (2009). 'Androgen Receptor Repeat Length Polymorphism Associated with Male-to-Female Transsexualism'. *Biological Psychiatry*, 65(1): 93–96.

Hester, J. David (2006). 'Intersex and the Rhetorics of Healing'. In Sharon E. Sytsma (ed.), *Ethics and Intersex*. Dordrecht: Springer, 47–71.

Hite, Shere (1976). *The Hite Report: A Nationwide Study of Female Sexuality*. New York, NY: Macmillan.

Holder, Rodney (1998a). 'The Ethics of Transsexualism, Part 1: The Transsexual Condition and the Biblical Background to an Ethical Response.' *Crucible*, 37(2): 89–99.

Holder, Rodney (1998b). 'The Ethics of Transsexualism, Part 2: A Christian Response to the Issues Raised.' *Crucible*, 37(3): 125–136.

Hollinger, Dennis P. (2009). *The Meaning of Sex: Christian Ethics and the Moral Life*. Grand Rapids, MI: Baker Academic.

Jung, Patricia Beattie (2006). 'Christianity and Human Sexual Polymorphism: Are They Compatible?' In Sharon E. Sytsma (ed.), *Ethics and Intersex*. Dordrecht: Springer, 293–309.

Kessler, Suzanne J. (1998). *Lessons from the Intersexed*. New Brunswick, NJ: Rutgers University Press.

Koyama, Emi (2006). 'From "Intersex" to "DSD": Toward a Queer Disability Politics of Gender'. Keynote speech presented at Translating Identity conference. University of Vermont, February 2006. <http://www.ipdx.org/articles/intersextodsd.html>.

Lewis, Hannah (2007). *Deaf Liberation Theology*. Aldershot: Ashgate.

Mann, Rachel (2012). *Dazzling Darkness: Gender, Sexuality, Illness and God*. Glasgow: Wild Goose Publications.

Mollenkott, Virginia Ramey (2007). *Omnigender: A Trans-Religious Approach*, revised and expanded edn. Cleveland, OH: Pilgrim Press.

Money, John (1980). *Love and Love Sickness: The Science of Sex, Gender Difference, and Pair-Bonding*. Baltimor, MD: The Johns Hopkins University Press.

Money, John and Anke A. Ehrhardt (1972). *Man and Woman, Boy and Girl: The Differentiation and Dimorphism of Gender Identity from Conception to Maturity*. Baltimore, MD: The Johns Hopkins University Press.

O'Donovan, Oliver (1983). 'Transsexualism and Christian Marriage'. *Journal of Religious Ethics*, 11(1): 135–162.

Preves, Sharon E. (2003). *Intersex and Identity: The Contested Self*. New Brunswick, NJ: Rutgers University Press.

Quero, Martín Hugo Córdova (2008). 'This Body Trans/Forming Me: Indecencies in Transgender/Intersex Bodies, Body Fascism and the Doctrine of the Incarnation'. In Marcella Althaus-Reid and Lisa Isherwood (eds), *Controversies in Body Theology*. London: SCM Press, 80–128.

Reed, Bernard, Stephenne Rhodes, Pietà Schofield, and Kevan Wylie (2009). *Gender Variance in the UK: Prevalence, Incidence, Growth and Geographic Distribution*. Ashtead: Gender Identity Research and Education Society.

Schneider, H, J. Pickel, and G. Stalla (2006). 'Typical Female 2nd–4th Finger Length (2D:4D) Ratios in Male-to-Female Transsexuals—Possible Implications for Prenatal Androgen Exposure'. *Psychoneuroendocrinology*, 31(2): 265–269.

Sheridan, Vanessa (2001). *Crossing Over: Liberating the Transgender Christian*. Cleveland, OH: Pilgrim Press.

Swancutt, Diana M. (2006). 'Sexing the Pauline Body of Christ: Scriptural Sex in the Context of the American Christian Culture War'. In Virginia Burrus and Catherine Keller (eds), *Toward a Theology of Eros: Transfiguring Passion at the Limits of Discipline*. New York: Fordham University Press, 65–98.

Tanis, Justin (2003). *Trans-Gendered: Theology, Ministry, and Communities of Faith*. Cleveland, OH: Pilgrim Press.

Wilkerson, Abby L. (2012). 'Normate Sex and its Discontents'. In Robert McRuer and Anna Mollow (eds), *Sex and Disability*. Durham, NC: Duke University Press, 183–207.

Williams, Rowan (2002). 'The Body's Grace'. In Eugene F. Rogers (ed.), *Theology and Sexuality: Classic and Contemporary Readings*. Oxford: Blackwell, 309–321.

Woodhead, Linda (1997). 'Sex in a Wider Context.' In Jon Davies and Gerard Loughlin (eds), *Sex These Days: Essays on Theology, Sexuality and Society*. Sheffield: Sheffield Academic Press, 98–120.

Yong, Amos (2011). *The Bible, Disability, and the Church: A New Vision of the People of God*. Grand Rapids, MI: Eerdmans.

Zhou, Jiang-Ning, Michel A. Hofman, Louis J. Gooren, and Dick F. Swaab (1995). 'A Sex Difference in the Human Brain and its Relation to Transsexuality'. *Nature*, 378: 68–70.

CHAPTER 40

....

DISABLED PEOPLE

....

DEBORAH BETH CREAMER

INTRODUCTION

....

ISSUES of sexuality inform disabled people in much the same way as they inform people who do not have disabilities—for example, there are single disabled people, coupled disabled people, straight disabled people, queer disabled people, celibate disabled people, and so on—and a great portion of what has been written elsewhere in this volume will be relevant regardless of one's ability status. Yet people with disabilities also face unique challenges and possibilities in relation to sexuality. Significant barriers to full sexual expression by people with disabilities still exist, and sexual theologies that are inclusive of people with disabilities—let alone ones that are based on the experiences and insights of people with disabilities—have received scant attention in academic or professional settings.

This chapter will begin with a brief description of various models and definitions of disability, as an attempt to complicate and nuance our understandings of disability and of what we might mean when we reference the experiences of people with disabilities. It will then explore how disability relates both to sexuality and to theology separately, and will close with some tentative proposals for what sexual theologies of disability might encompass. This chapter will not attempt to suggest a single or segregated sexual theology for disabled people, but rather will seek both to argue that every sexual theology ought to be accessible to people with disabilities (among other reasons, because all of us are likely to experience disability at some point in our lives) and to make the case that reflection on disability can enhance and improve all sexual theologies, even for those people who understand themselves presently as non-disabled.

DEFINING DISABILITY

....

Defining disability may seem unnecessary. Each of us already holds tacit and embedded understandings of what is (and is not) disability, and who is (and is not) disabled.

If asked to define disability, many of us will first list impairments (blindness, deafness, paralysis) or diagnoses (spinal cord injury, multiple sclerosis, Down's syndrome), and will likely focus primarily on a person's functional limitations or what it seems she or he cannot do. These interpretations draw on a *medical* understanding of disability, beginning with an ideal of a 'normal' and 'healthy' body and then applying the label of 'disabled' to any part of the body or mind that is perceived as deviating from this ideal (Altman 2001). The medical model encourages us to respond to disability by 'fixing' the impairment if possible and by 'normalizing' the situation (as much as possible) if the impairment cannot be completely fixed. In other words, disability is perceived as a problem that is located within an individual body, and is to be avoided whenever possible. For many of us, this medical understanding seems like nothing but common sense. We think, 'of course a person who is blind or cannot walk is disabled, and of course they would want to "get better" if they could'. Yet the medical model does not tell the full story of disability, nor does it capture the diversity and breadth of experiences of people who live with disabilities.

Most significantly, the medical model has fallen under great suspicion due to the work of disability advocates who argue that the 'problem' of disability is not so much located in individual bodies as it is in society's response (or lack of response) to the full range of human embodied experiences (Pelka 1997). From this perspective, disability is an issue of architecture and attitudes, of designing physical and social spaces based on an arbitrary and impossible ideal. Thus if we imagine a wheelchair user at the base of a flight of stairs, while the medical model would suggest that the problem of disability is a body that cannot walk or climb stairs, one might instead suggest that the problem is in the building that does not offer a ramp or lift, or in people who did not imagine that wheelchair users might wish to enter it.

This approach is often referred to as the *social* model of disability, as it sees disability as a social problem rather than one that is intrinsic to an individual body (Shakespeare 2013). This model also suggests both that disability is somewhat arbitrary (socially constructed) and that our engagement with disability can change (socially fluid). We can observe this when we reflect on the ways that the label of disability itself has been applied differently across time (think of leprosy or autism) as well as the dramatic ways that the daily lives of people with disabilities have changed (for example, as laws have been enacted to require barrier-free public spaces or as technology has increased access to communication and employment). Closely related to the social model is the *minority* model of disability, which recognizes people with disabilities as an oppressed or excluded group who face prejudice and discrimination, and where ableism needs to be considered in the same sorts of ways as racism or sexism (Pelka 1997; Charlton 1998). The social and minority models highlight, for example, the ways in which conditions such as under- or unemployment or lack of access to health care and public transport are at least as significant as impairments for people with disabilities as are any embodied limitations or architectural barriers, and that prejudice and bias ought to be our real loci of concern.

Another understanding of disability comes in the *moral* model (Eiesland 1998). This perspective is perhaps most apparent in ancient literature, where disability was often conflated with demon possession or with some sort of special or saintly status. Disability or other physical difference here is seen as a curse or a blessing, a punishment or a reward. It carries moral weight and value. While this sort of interpretation might be most clearly observed in older times—when one might have talked openly about disability as being the result of sin or as a test of faith, for example—this model still persists today. People with disabilities are often described as being inspirational even before we know anything about their journeys, or, at the other extreme, we express pity or regret for them without knowing any details about their lives or how they experience their own disability. Thus, moral value is assigned to experiences of disability, simply because of the presence of disability. Attention to this lens reminds us that disability is rarely engaged or perceived as a neutral category, and thus our reflection on disability cannot be reduced to seemingly impartial biomedical or social determinations either.

A final lens, the *limits* model, offers another important reminder: none of us experience life without impairments and limits (Creamer 2009). Disability, when we stop to think about it, is a 'normal' part of human existence. The World Health Organization estimates that a billion people, or 15 per cent of the world population, have some sort of disability (World Health Organization 2013). And many of us will experience disability at some point in our lives, particularly as we grow older. Beyond this, most people experience impairments that are not socially considered to be disabling, and use adaptive technologies in response to these impairments: eyeglasses to read or to drive, medication for headaches or strained muscles, a stepstool to reach high shelves. The limits model also highlights the ways in which we are all interdependent: we may think of people with disabilities as the ones who are 'dependent', but independence itself is a sort of illusion: we rely on each other for food, clothing, and shelter; we depend on technology for transportation, communication, and employment. None of us is truly independent. From this perspective, the category of 'disability' emerges as a somewhat artificial designation that distorts humanity into categories of 'us' and 'them' when really things are far more blurry and messy.

These lenses, and others not named here, remind us that when we are exploring issues of disability, we must attend to multiple layers of meaning and interpretation. Beyond this, it is also important to remember that disability is as diverse a category as any other identity grouping, engaging a vast range of embodied experiences and other sociocultural expressions. There is no intrinsic reason to group together a wheelchair user, a person with a learning difference, and a person who experiences chronic pain. Even within one single category—say, those who use wheelchairs—we will find a wide range of embodied experiences (temporary v. permanent, different levels of function, etc.), divergent attitudes towards those experiences, and a vast array of other identity characteristics and situational factors (including gender, race, economic status, political leanings, taste in music, and so on). Disability is an artificial category, sometimes useful—especially insofar as it allows for access to services, support, advocacy, research, community, and so on—but artificial nonetheless. As we consider sexual theologies for people with disabilities, it is important to keep these layers, and their complexities and contestations, in mind.

DISABILITY AND SEXUALITY

Sexuality has been a difficult and complicated issue for many people with disabilities, at both practical and symbolic levels. A first significant issue is that the dominant culture often imagines people with disabilities to be either asexual (particularly for people with noticeable disfiguration or mobility impairment) or hypersexual (as for people with Down's syndrome or other cognitive differences). As Mollow and McRuer (2012: 1) observe, 'when sex and disability are linked in contemporary American cultures, the conjunction is most often the occasion for marginalization or marveling; the sexuality of disabled people is typically depicted in terms of either tragic deficiency or freakish excess'. At one level, this follows from a common cultural impression that 'the sexiest people are healthy, fit, and active ... rarely are disabled people regarded as either desiring subjects or objects of desire' (Mollow and McRuer 2012: 1). Social assumptions about disability and sexuality often follow from the interplay of moral notions of disability with moral notions of sexuality. When sex is seen as focused on desire and disability is seen as undesirable, we imagine people with disabilities as antithetical to sexuality. When sex is seen as bad or impure and people with disabilities are seen as inspirational or heroic, we imagine people with disabilities as asexual. If we imagine sex as deviant and people with disabilities as deviant, we might overly conflate the two to the point of hypersexuality. Even apart from moral interpretations, if we simply think of sexuality as a normal physical expression, and people with disabilities as physically abnormal, we might not consider sexuality to even be relevant for people with disabilities. On the other hand, 'fetish' stories emphasizing particular impairments or disabilities abound. Teasing apart and reconstructing such caricatured images around sex and disability is essential before we can even begin to articulate a sexual theology for people with disabilities.

Disabled people often face significant barriers that limit their ability for sexual self-expression and for partnership. People who live with disability throughout their lives might lack access to sexuality education, or have limited opportunities for social interactions with age-group peers, or have minimal privacy in their living situations. When people experience disability later in life, information about sexuality (including discussion of adaptive sexual practices) is often missing from rehabilitation protocols and practices; when sexuality is discussed, it is often presented in narrow (heterosexual, procreative) ways. This is not the case in all situations, of course, and often tends to vary depending on the type of impairment as well as other social and identity factors (including gender, sexual orientation, partnership status, and age). But sexuality is consistently an area of struggle for people with disabilities. As Finger (1992: 9) writes, 'It's easier for us [people with disabilities] to talk about—and formulate strategies for changing—discrimination in employment, education, and housing than to talk about our exclusion from sexuality and reproduction'. Only recently have resources emerged that highlight holistic notions of health and embodiment which are more open to creativity around understandings of sexual expression, call more boldly for sexual rights for people with disabilities (Kaufman et al. 2007), and begin to imagine 'what if disability were sexy?' (Mollow and McRuer 2012: 1).

Of course, there is more to sexuality than access to information or opportunities for sexual activity, and it is important to look at systemic as well as individual issues. The intersection of disability and sexuality is entangled with a long and disturbing record of legal, political, and relational violations of people with disabilities. People with disabilities have been denied access to marriage and parenting and have been the victims of forced sterilization and of termination of parental rights (Longmore and Umansky 2001; Longmore 2003; Watson et al. 2012; Davis 2013). Conversations about prenatal testing and whether or not a disabled child is 'desirable' or avoidable, and even concerns about eugenics, are at stake here as well (Ladd 2003; Shakespeare 2008; Creamer 2013; Hubbard 2013). People with disabilities experience domestic and sexual abuse at rates far higher than the general population, perhaps because they are perceived as less able to defend themselves and less likely to be believed if they report the abuse (Kaufman et al. 2007; Walker-Hirsch 2007). People with developmental or cognitive disabilities are at particular risk of being targets of sexual predators, for example entering into unequal sexual relationships in the hopes of gaining acceptance or avoiding rejection (Walker-Hirsch 2007). Others may stay in abusive relationships due to a variety of personal and systemic barriers, including finances, transportation, daily care, or limited social support (Kaufman et al. 2007; Fitzsimons 2009). If we are to talk about sexuality and disability, we cannot ignore these substantial issues.

Yet, with this said, we also must be careful that our discussion of sexuality and disability does not only emphasize the pathological or the problematic. Echoing Mollow and McRuer, disability can be sexy! Artists with disabilities highlight the ways in which differences in human form can be beautiful and desirable (Bartlett et al. 2011; Beale et al. 2013). Narrative works describe the fullness of life of people with disabilities, with sexuality as an intrinsic and unsurprising element (Fries 1997; Driedger 2010). Guidebooks highlight not just disability-possible sex, but disability-positive sex (Kaufman et al. 2007; Maxwell et al. 2007). Critical scholarly works attempt to reframe our theoretical and discursive notions of disability and sex (McRuer 2006; Hall 2011; McRuer and Mollow 2012). Woven throughout all of these projects is an attitude not just that sexuality can be modified for people with disabilities, but also that the creative and imaginative ways in which people with disabilities engage with sexuality might serve as a positive example for those who are currently non-disabled, for example by vividly challenging the 'impairment' of the able-bodied tendency to think that sex only refers to particular practices and outcomes or that is relevant only to specific body parts, or that only certain formulations of the human body can be experienced as beautiful, sexy, or desirable. Taking these examples alongside our earlier discussion of disability models, it is undeniable that disability and sexuality are already well engaged with each other, and so our task becomes that of working to reduce individual and systemic impediments while simultaneously being open to the possibility that 'disabled sex' might have something to offer all of us.

DISABILITY AND THEOLOGY

The engagement of theology with disability is by no means new, although it has taken a very different tone since the late 1990s. Most major religious traditions include some sort of significant attention to issues of physical and/or spiritual healing, and offer moral as well as practical teachings about embodiment more generally. This has been particularly apparent within Christianity, which, as Margaret Miles reminds us, can be described as 'the religion of the incarnation' (Miles 2005: 1). Disability emerges as a major theme in both Hebrew Bible and New Testament texts (Avalos et al. 2007; Moss and Schipper 2011). Some of Christianity's earliest institutional history (and, likely, a significant factor in its initial growth) was as a site of physical, as well as spiritual, healing (Stark 1996; Avalos 1999; Pilch 2000). The body was a contested site in early Christian doctrinal formulations, as leaders debated questions around Jesus' nature (as human and/or divine) and questioned whether the body was a necessary evil or part of the goodness of creation (Brown 1988). Early Church leaders and theologians engaged questions of disability, directly or indirectly (Brock and Swinton 2012). And, of course, some of these theologians were people with disabilities themselves and reflected on their own embodied experiences as part of their work (Creamer 2009). Similar intersections of religion and disability can be traced within other faith traditions as well (Abrams 1998; Gahly 2010; Schumm and Stoltzfus 2011a, 2011b; Richardson 2012).

While Christian theologies have not been silent about issues of disability, they also often have not been particularly helpful. Much of this stems from moral interpretations of disability: as mentioned earlier, disability was seen as a punishment for sin, a test of faith, an opportunity to inspire others, a demonstration of God's healing power, or simply a mysterious act of God (Creamer 2012). Religious communities have demonstrated resistance to social and minority interpretations of disability, for example arguing for exemption from the US Americans with Disabilities Act of 1990 and being slow to embrace architectural modifications or inclusive hiring practices (Eiesland and Saliers 1998). Until recently, written work on disability has focused primarily on providing pastoral care for people or families with disabilities (Colston 1978), adapting religious education programmes for children with intellectual disabilities (Bogardus 1963), or providing inspirational or devotional reflections (Tada 1976). While a few works highlighted issues of inclusion or attended to diversity within disability experiences (Hauerwas 1973; Wilke 1980), disability was primarily seen as problematic, and people with disabilities rarely encountered full welcome in congregations or other sites of religious life (Webb-Mitchell 1994).

A major shift occurred with the publication of Nancy Eiesland's *The Disabled God* in 1994. Rather than beginning with moral or even medical understandings of disability, Eiesland started with minority and social interpretations. As a person with a disability herself, she described what she experienced as a significant rift between her faith and her activism, insofar as her religious communities seemed unaware of or uninterested in the disability rights movement and disability groups seemed apathetic or angry towards religious perspectives. As she looked for answers, she began to play with an image of the disabled God, specifically 'God in a sip-puff wheelchair ...Not an omnipotent, self-sufficient God, but neither a pitiable, suffering servant' (Eiesland 2002: 13). For her, this connected with the resurrection stories of Jesus (Luke 24:36–39), where Jesus is depicted as having scars that are not caused by sin, do not make him the subject of pity, and do not keep him from connecting with or providing significant leadership to other people. Grounded in this image, Eiesland began to explore a theology that is radically inclusive of people with disabilities—not in spite of their disabilities, but in the midst of them—and even suggesting that people with disabilities have an epistemological privilege (reminiscent of other works in liberation theology). Rather than beginning with the belief that physical impairment is the problem to be addressed or solved, this approach names intolerance, injustice, and exclusion—and, importantly, the people and structures that perpetuate these injustices—as the 'problem' of disability. And, Eiesland persuasively argues, God is not one of the perpetuators of this injustice, but rather sides with the oppressed and their allies (Eiesland 1994).

Eiesland's work opened the floodgates for new creative work at the intersection of religion and disability. Other scholars began to propose images of God that not only were not antithetical to disability but also highlighted positive characteristics of God or divinity that might be aligned with disability, such as authenticity (Creamer 1995), interdependence (Black 1996), and inclusivity (Block 2002)—each attempting to challenge the idea that God is wholly other than what it means to be disabled. Others built on these liberatory images and carried them forward into particular contexts and practices of ministry, such as preaching (Black 1996), religious education (Webb-Mitchell 1996), biblical interpretation (Bishop 1995), and other elements of religious practice (Eiesland and Saliers 1998).

Over time, scholarship around disability and theology has grown more nuanced and diverse. The original evocative image of a disabled God has been pushed to its less comfortable edges. What if we propose a Deaf God (Lewis 2007)? Or, perhaps more provocatively, what if we imagine God with a cognitive disability or mental illness (Swinton 2003; Creamer 2009)? Theological engagement with experiences of autism (Reynolds 2008), dementia (Swinton 2012), Down's syndrome (Yong 2007) or profound intellectual disability (Reinders 2008; Haslam 2011) has led to interesting questions around how we attribute value to individuals and interpersonal relationships within religious frameworks. Theological anthropology has become a significant area of concern, and the process of exploring the nature of the human person has led to the naming of inadequacies of the social model and of the instability of disability identity itself (Davis 2002; Creamer 2009). Drawing on insights from post-colonial and queer theories, this stream of work rejects the binary division of able and disabled, and proposes that 'normal' is nothing but an illusion—and one that is dangerous, deceitful, and needs significant theological deconstruction (Creamer 2009). This leads to opportunities for a critical analysis of theological structures, conventions, and world views that carry far beyond the narrow field of disability studies (Betcher 2007). For example, within biblical studies, attention to disability is becoming understood not as a speciality concern but rather as part of responsible interpretation, perhaps like feminist interpretation before it (Avalos et al. 2007; Moss and Schipper 2011). More and more, it is recognized that the insights from disability are widely relevant within theology and religious studies, both because disability is a common experience and because insights about embodiment, inclusion, labelling, liminality, fluidity, and so on have deep and widespread significance.

Towards a Sexual Theology for People with Disabilities

As is hopefully clear from the preceding discussion, it is no easy task to tease out a sexual theology for people with disabilities. Much work remains to be done, both by scholars and by advocates, and the stories and insights of people with disabilities themselves (with a variety of experiences and expressions of disability) need to be foregrounded. Rather than predicting or restricting what such projects might look like, I would instead suggest four features that are likely to appear within any successful sexual theology for people with disabilities.

First, taking a cue from the campaign for people-first language (Creamer 2013: 226), I would suggest that sexual theologies must recall that people with disabilities are, first and foremost, people. This campaign highlighted the ways in which phrases such as 'disabled person' or 'blind man' or 'retarded child' put the diagnosis or impairment first, rather than describing a *person* who has unique characteristics and experiences (person with a disability, person who experiences blindness, person with a cognitive difference). As we have learned, word-order alone does not correct narrow perceptions, and there is ongoing debate within the disability community over whether it is actually better to say 'person with a disability' or 'disabled person' as each construction simultaneously highlights and minimizes significant factors, leads people into an unhelpful concern with political correctness, and fails to take into account regional and contextual variations. But the overall point is still well taken: if we are to consider theologies (including sexual theologies) that will be inclusive of disability, we perhaps need to begin by remembering that disability is not the only factor that defines a person, and that they are, always, a person first, with all the limits and foibles and messiness and possibilities that humanness brings. This part of the Handbook, part 8, 'Sexual Theologies for all People', and all the essays in it (Chapters 30–41), have been designed to fulfil the principle: 'people first'.

The second, and necessarily related, feature is that we cannot forget that disability is, many times, still a significant factor in people's lives. It is a false and easy liberalism that suggests that 'we are all disabled' or that disability is something we can tune in and out of as we choose or that is superficially laid on top of a person's identity, even when we talk about something like sexuality. As the previous discussion has noted, people with disabilities face significant individual as well as structural barriers, and we cannot simply wish these away. Disability still remains a significant issue of civil rights. People with disabilities experience some of the highest levels of poverty and unemployment and are disproportionately the victims of crime and abuse. Political challenges to health care funding, government programmes, and rights-based legislation make this population even more vulnerable.

Disability is also a significant issue of identity, such that a person with a disability may experience their disability as central to their lives and fundamental to how they understand themselves. It is also an embodied experience, and issues such as pain deserve attention as well; even as we notice structural issues, we must ask about and attend to bodily experiences and not just social ones. All of these complex issues require consideration by theologians and other religious leaders (including theologians and religious leaders with disabilities), both to address ways in which worship and faith communities can be models of inclusion and access (Carter 2007; Webb-Mitchell 2010) and to provide leadership around these questions of such significant concern.

Third, and somewhat in tension with the previous point, is the reminder that disability is a common, unsurprising, and ordinary part of the human experience. Most of us will experience some degree of disability at some point in our lives; we are, at most, temporarily able-bodied. Disability cannot be perceived only as a special interest issue based on categories of 'us' and 'them'; it is a fluid and unstable category, and we are all in it together. Thus, one might argue that every sexual theology ought to be attentive to disability, or that sexual theologies of disability might be relevant to us all. And in the midst of this commonality we must also recognize immense diversity. It is absurd to think that sexuality for an amputee would automatically be the same as sexuality for a person with a cognitive difference or for a person who experiences obsessive compulsive tendencies. Just as sexual theologies more generally might need to be simultaneously broad and narrow (talking about commonalities of partnered experiences alongside a sense that each relationship is different, for example), one would also expect a sexual theology of disability to encounter both the commonality of the human person (as part of the goodness of creation, from Genesis 1, for example) and simultaneously the particularity of each instantiation of human difference (each with different gifts, as in 1 Corinthians 12).

And last, a final commitment here is that sexual theologies of disability must draw on insights that come from experiences of disability themselves, and must approach disability as a source of insight and wisdom, not only as an experience of loss or a deficiency. Disability reminds us to attend to embodiment more authentically, not as an idealized and imposed norm, but rather in the messiness and imperfection and goodness of real life. This also highlights valuable characteristics that are often embedded in experiences of disability, such as creativity, perseverance, and interdependence (Creamer 2009). Attention to disability as such offers new possibilities for sexual theology, not just for disabled people but for the (temporarily) non-disabled as well.

References

Abrams, Judith (1998). *Judaism and Disability: Portrayals in Ancient Texts from the Tanach through the Bavli*. Washington, DC: Gallaudet University Press.

Altman, Barbara M. (2001). 'Disability Definitions, Models, Classification Schemes, and Applications'. In Gary L. Albrecht, Katherine D. Seelman, and Michael Bury (eds), *The Handbook of Disability Studies*. Thousand Oaks, CA: Sage, 97–122.

Avalos, Hector (1999). *Health Care and the Rise of Christianity*. Peabody, MA: Hendrickson.

Avalos, Hector, Sarah Melcher, and Jeremy Schipper (2007) (eds). *This Abled Body: Rethinking Disabilities in Biblical Studies*. Atlanta: Society of Biblical Literature.

Bartlett, Jennifer, Sheila Black, and Michael Northen (2011) (eds). *Beauty is a Verb: The New Poetry of Disability*. El Paso, TX: Cinco Puntos Press.

Beale, Elaine, Patty Berne, Vanessa Huang, Nomy Lamm, Leroy Franklin Moore Jr., and Todd Herman (2013). *Sins Invalid: An Unashamed Claim to Beauty in the Face of Invisibility*. <http://www.sinsinvalid.org>.

Betcher, Sharon (2007). *Spirit and the Politics of Disablement*. Minneapolis: Fortress Press.

Bishop, Marilyn E. (1995). *Religion and Disability: Essays in Scripture, Theology, and Ethics*. Kansas City, MO: Sheed and Ward.

Black, Kathy (1996). *A Healing Homiletic: Preaching and Disability*. Nashville: Abingdon.

Black, Sheila, Jennifer Bartlett, and Michael Northen (2011). *Beauty is a Verb: The New Poetry of Disability*. El Paso, TX: Cinco Puntos Press.

Block, Jennie Weiss (2002). *Copious Hosting: A Theology of Access for People with Disabilities*. New York: Continuum.

Bogardus, LaDonna (1963). *Christian Education for Retarded Children and Youth*. New York: Abingdon Press.

Brock, Brian, and John Swinton (2012) (eds). *Disability in the Christian Tradition: A Reader*. Grand Rapids, MI: Eerdmans.

Brown, Peter (1988). *The Body and Society: Men, Women, and Sexual Renunciation in Early Christianity*. New York: Columbia University Press.

Carter, Eric (2007). *Including People with Disabilities in Faith Communities: A Guide for Service Providers, Families, and Congregations*. Baltimore: Paul H. Brookes.

Charlton, James I. (1998). *Nothing About Us Without Us: Disability, Oppression and Empowerment*. Berkeley and Los Angeles: University of California Press.

Colston, Lowell (1978). *Pastoral Care with Handicapped Persons*. Philadelphia: Fortress.

Creamer, Deborah B. (1995). 'Finding God in Our Bodies: Theology from the Perspective of People with Disabilities'. *Journal of Religion in Disability and Rehabilitation*, 2: 27–42, 67–87.

Creamer, Deborah B. (2009). *Disability and Christian Theology: Embodied Limits and Constructive Possibilities*. Oxford: Oxford University Press.

Creamer, Deborah B. (2010). 'Embracing Limits, Queering Embodiment: Creating/Creative Possibilities for Disability Theology'. *Journal of Feminist Studies in Religion*, 26(2): 123–127.

Creamer, Deborah B. (2012). 'Disability Theology'. *Religion Compass*, 6/7: 339–346.

Creamer, Deborah B. (2013). 'Disability Liberative Ethics'. In Miguel De La Torre (ed.), *Ethics: A Liberative Approach*. Minneapolis: Fortress Press, 223–238.

Davis, Lennard J. (2002). *Bending Over Backwards: Disability, Dismodernism, and Other Difficult Positions*. New York: New York University Press.

Davis, Lennard J. (2013) (ed.). *The Disability Studies Reader*, 4th edn. New York: Routledge.

Driedger, Diane (2010) (ed.). *Living the Edges: A Disabled Women's Reader*. Toronto: Inanna.

Eiesland, Nancy (1994). *The Disabled God: Toward a Liberatory Theology of Disability*. Nashville: Abingdon Press.

Eiesland, Nancy (1998). 'Barriers and Bridges: Relating the Disability Rights Movement and Religious Organizations'. In Eiesland and Saliers (1998), 200–229.

Eiesland, Nancy (2002). 'Encountering the Disabled God'. *The Other Side*, 38(5): 10–15.

Eiesland, Nancy, and Don Saliers (1998) (eds). *Human Disability and the Service of God: Reassessing Religious Practice*. Nashville: Abingdon.

Finger, Anne (1992). 'Forbidden Fruit'. *New Internationalist*, 233: 8–10.

Fitzsimons, Nancy M. (2009). *Combating Violence and Abuse of People with Disabilities: A Call to Action*. Baltimore: Paul H. Brookes.

Fries, Kenny (1997) (ed.). *Staring Back: The Disability Experience from the Inside Out*. New York: Plume.

Gahly, Mohammed (2010). *Islam and Disability: Perspectives in Theology and Jurisprudence*. New York: Routledge.

Hall, Kim Q. (2011) (ed.). *Feminist Disability Studies*. Bloomington, IN: Indiana University Press.

Haslam, Molly (2011). *A Constructive Theology of Intellectual Disability: Human Being as Mutuality and Response*. New York: Fordham University Press.

Hauerwas, Stanley (1973). 'Christian Care of the Retarded'. *Theology Today*, 30: 130–137.

Hubbard, Ruth (2013). 'Abortion and Disability: Who Should and Should Not Inhabit the World?' In Davis (2013), 74–86.

Kaufman, Miriam, Cory Silverberg, and Fran Odette (2007). *The Ultimate Guide to Sex and Disability: For All of Us Who Live with Disabilities, Chronic Pain, and Illness*, 2nd edn. San Francisco: Cleis Press.

Ladd, Paddy (2003). *Understanding Deaf Culture: In Search of Deafhood*. Clevedon, England: Multilingual Matters.

Lewis, Hannah (2007). *Deaf Liberation Theology*. Burlington, VT: Ashgate.

Longmore, Paul K. (2003). *Why I Burned My Book and Other Essays on Disability*. Philadelphia: Temple University Press.

Longmore, Paul K., and Lauri Umansky (2001). *The New Disability History: American Perspectives*. New York: New York University Press.

McRuer, Robert (2006). *Crip Theory: Cultural Signs of Queerness and Disability*. New York: New York University Press.

McRuer, Robert, and Anna Mollow (2012) (eds). *Sex and Disability*. Durham, NC: Duke University Press.

Maxwell, Jane, Julia Watts Belser, and Darlena David (2007). *A Health Handbook for Women with Disabilities*. Berkeley, CA: Hesperian.

Miles, Margaret (2005). *The Word Made Flesh: A History of Christian Thought*. Malden, MA: Blackwell.

Mollow, Anna, and Robert McRuer (2012). 'Introduction'. In McRuer and Mollow (2012), 1–34.

Moss, Candida, and Jeremy Schipper (2011) (eds). *Disability Studies and Biblical Literature*. New York: Palgrave Macmillan.

Pelka, Fred (1997). *The ABC-CLIO Companion to the Disability Rights Movement*. Santa Barbara, CA: ABC-CLIO.

Pilch, John (2000). *Healing in the New Testament: Insights from Medical and Mediterranean Anthropology*. Minneapolis: Fortress Press.

Reinders, Hans (2008). *Receiving the Gift of Friendship: Profound Disability, Theological Anthropology, and Ethics.* Grand Rapids, MI: Eerdmans.

Reynolds, Thomas (2008). *Vulnerable Communion: A Theology of Disability and Hospitality.* Grand Rapids, MI: Brazos.

Richardson, Kristina (2012). *Disability and Difference in the Medieval Islamic World: Blighted Bodies.* Edinburgh: Edinburgh University Press.

Schumm, Darla and Michael Stoltzfus (2011a) (eds). *Disability and Religious Diversity: Cross-Cultural and Interreligious Perspectives.* New York: Palgrave Macmillan.

Schumm, Darla and Michael Stoltzfus (2011b) (eds). *Disability in Judaism, Christianity, and Islam: Sacred Texts, Historical Traditions, and Social Analysis.* New York: Palgrave Macmillan.

Shakespeare, Tom (2008). 'Disability, Genetics, and Eugenics'. In John Swain and Sally French (eds), *Disability on Equal Terms.* Los Angeles: Sage, 21–30.

Shakespeare, Tom (2013). 'The Social Model of Disability'. In Davis (2013), 214–221.

Stark, Rodney (1996). *The Rise of Christianity: A Sociologist Reconsiders History.* Princeton: Princeton University Press.

Swinton, John (2003). 'The Body of Christ has Down's Syndrome: Theological Reflections on Disability, Vulnerability and Graceful Communities'. *Journal of Pastoral Theology*, 13: 66–78.

Swinton, John (2012). *Dementia: Living in the Memories of God.* Grand Rapids, MI: Eerdmans.

Tada, Joni Eareckson (1976). *Joni.* Minneapolis: World Wide Publications.

Walker-Hirsch, Leslie (2007). *The Facts of Life … And More: Sexuality and Intimacy for People with Intellectual Disabilities.* Baltimore: Paul H. Brookes.

Watson, Nick, Alan Roulstone, and Carol Thomas (2012) (eds). *Routledge Handbook of Disability Studies.* New York: Routledge.

Webb-Mitchell, Brett (1994). *Unexpected Guests at God's Banquet: Welcoming People with Disabilities into the Church.* New York: Crossroad.

Webb-Mitchell, Brett (1996). *Dancing with Disabilities: Opening the Church to All God's Children.* Cleveland: United Church Press.

Webb-Mitchell, Brett (2010). *Beyond Accessibility: Toward Full Inclusion of People with Disabilities in Faith Communities.* New York: Church Publishing.

Wilke, Harold H. (1980). *Creating the Caring Congregation: Guidelines for Ministering with the Handicapped.* Nashville: Abingdon.

World Health Organization (2013). *Fact Sheet 352: Disability and Health.* <http://www.who.int/mediacentre/factsheets/fs352/en/index.html.

Yong, Amos (2007). *Theology and Down Syndrome: Reimagining Disability in Late Modernity.* Waco, TX: Baylor University Press.

CHAPTER 41

FRIENDS AND FRIENDSHIP

INTRODUCTION

> I don't want to fake you out
> Take or shake or forsake you out
> I ain't lookin' for you to feel like me
> See like me or be like me
> All I really want to do
> Is, baby, be friends with you.

ON 9 June 1964 Bob Dylan recorded 'All I Really Wanna Do': amongst myriads of pop songs that extolled erotic love and sexual desire, this one addressed friendship. Throughout the song Dylan's apophatic description outlines features of opposite-sex friendship—it is not about hurting, constraining, dissecting, bringing down, or defining. Here, in the last verse he notes a vital point; similitude is not necessary for friendship—one does not have to feel, see, or be like a friend, for difference is no impediment to the relationship. So, was Dylan describing a 1960's ideal that has no enduring relevance, or was he onto something? In what follows I will seek to outline something of friendship's pedigree, and the way in which we encounter it in twenty-first century.

Like the erotic love so celebrated in popular music, friendship is love too: but why is it even necessary to make this point explicit? In contemporary Western culture there is significant ambiguity around the word 'friendship', so exploring its characteristics is important, not least because of its social and ecclesial implications. Currently, friends might be entries in 'Facebook', colleagues from work, those we meet at the gym, those we encounter in an online forum, a life-long companion and so on. In our cultural context, friendship is not understood uniformly. Compounding this, friendship is a complex relationship, not least due to gender dynamics and social conventions. Being a friend in a twenty-first-century Western setting is both similar to, and significantly different from, being a friend at other points in history, or in another cultural setting.

FRIENDSHIP—AN OVERVIEW

Let us consider some of friendship's characteristics, and some influential contributors to its understanding. There are benefits and opportunities afforded by being a friend, and challenges too, due to the constant flux in understanding the human person and relationality. As a relationship, friendship has experiential complexity, yet at its most basic it might be described as simply 'being liked'. For others, it might be expressed more deeply as being known and loved by another. Even seeking to define what friendship is, one realizes that cultural propriety and social norms dictate how we express (in word and action) our loving relationships. Would a British heterosexual male openly say to his friend (of whatever gender) that he loved them? Would this cross an unspoken cultural boundary that in another context would not even exist?

Here is one root of the complexity—understanding friendship's nature has as much to do with the context of social *mores* and definitions of love, as it has with the specificity of what being a friend actually means. Defining a relationship cannot be universally applicable; there must always be room for the exception, the recognition that it is not this way for everyone. Nonetheless it *is* possible to explore friendship's nature at a general level, through observation and philosophical insight, for universality is not the only criterion of value. So it is possible to say, for example, that for some teenagers considerable focused thought is given to relationships that begin in sexual attraction. Perhaps not so much effort is expended reflecting on the familial bonds that may exist by default, or indeed to bonds of friendship that one often falls into by chance, and that may seldom be maintained with any level of purposed reflection as they grow older: for some, friendship just happens.

Robert Paine, in his 1969 study of friendship in the USA, wrote that 'The basic meaning of friendship is the sense of worth one may get from it. Friendship says to you that someone is enjoying you and understands you. A friend can also explain you to yourself' (Paine 1969: 514). A more penetrating analysis is offered by the French philosopher Simone Weil: 'From the fact that the desire to please and the desire to command are not found in pure friendship, it has in it, at the same time as affection, something not unlike complete indifference' (Weil 1977: 128). On the surface this seems a cold definition, but within it is the notion of friendship as a love that seeks to allow 'the other' to be fully who they are, rather than moulding them to our own preferences. Here it is already apparent that friendship has a level of relational profundity and differing qualities of expression— in the notion of 'pure' friendship—that may seldom be considered.

Reflecting on our own friends, we may recognize something of a spectrum in the nature of their relationship to us. We have occasional friends, friends who are on the fringe of our lives, and some who are at the centre, those who are good for us, perhaps those who are not. We may know the experience of meeting old friends only very occasionally, and yet picking up after many years as if we had never been apart. There are those in whose company we feel relaxed, and others to whom we feel like lifestyle accessories, rather than an integral part of their social network. Is there a common thread within such variety?

Initially we can identify some key components in friendship's character. It contains affection, the promotion of self-worth and, most obviously, the companionship and pleasure that one gets through human relationship. Depending on the social context in which the friendship is located, there may be an expectation of practical support should it be required. This is noted by Glenn Adams and Victoria C. Plaut, in an interview-based survey of North American and Ghanaian participants to determine how they viewed friendship. In the USA, having a large number of friends was taken to be a good thing, and was primarily about affirming the individual's likeability and social value. In Ghana it was different: friendship was rooted in a collectivist understanding of personhood, and the prevalence of poverty meant that its primary benefit was in a commitment to receiving (and providing) material assistance. Having many friends was therefore considered with caution. It led the researchers to state that 'friendship is not a universal form; instead, it takes different forms in different cultural worlds' (Adams and Plaut 2003: 334).

Unlike familial bonds, friendship is usually elective; whereas blood relations or those inherited through marriage are given, one normally selects one's friends. There is another dimension, hinted at by Paine and Weil, to consider: the capacity for self-understanding and self-betterment. This might be considered to be the 'virtuous capacity' of friendship, or the moral or ethical development achieved when one gains understanding of one's motivations, and seeks to improve through that insight. This is what Paine alludes to: the friend who can 'explain you to yourself' need not do so in formal communication. The friendship is the conversation.

Then there is the activity of seeking the good of another, for no other gain than *their* happiness or betterment. For this to be more than philanthropy the relationship must incorporate the element of reciprocity or mutuality; thus there must be some sense of equality for this to take place. However, even if this is so, 'equality' need not be understood solely in terms of material wealth or social status. The capacity to reciprocate love and nourish a friend is not financially dependent. However, if there is no mutually agreed understanding of that friendship's nature—if the friends are seeking different things from the relationship, and have personal gain as the motivation—then one might well question the moral nature of that friendship. Similarly, if there is an unequal balance of power, affection, or support—over a sustained period of time—it would be reasonable to ask what the nature of that relationship was, and perhaps whether it could be considered a friendship at all.

A Philosophical Insight

Moving towards a clearer definition, the writings of ancient Greece reveal an investment in exploring friendship's nature. Homer[1] around the eighth century BCE underpins

---

[1] I assume for these purposes that he exists as an actual writer, rather than invest time discussing the possible 'Homeric School'.

his poetry with observation of the human condition, not least in his elevation of male friendship in combat as described in the *Iliad*, in which we see an example of the depth of feeling that exists between Achilles and Patroclus. When Menelaus brings the news that Patroclus has been killed in battle, Achilles responds, 'What pleasure is this to me since my dear companion is dead, Patroclus, whom I loved beyond all other companions, as well as I love my own life' (*Iliad* 18.80–82). The intense bond of mutual love and commitment to one's friend is evident here, for Achilles realizes that in returning to avenge his friend's death he too will be killed. This deep bond had developed as the two grew up and fought together, leading to a friendship in which the value of one life was linked to that of the other; even into self-sacrifice.

Beyond poetry, both Plato and Aristotle offer differently nuanced understandings of friendship. In the *Lysis*, Plato outlines, through the device of a conversation between young men, a discussion of friendship's nature and value. It is a relationship that elevates the friends to enjoying the higher values of life. Whilst friends *may* be similar to each other (the principle of 'like attracting like'), this is by no means essential, as Plato's interlocutors recognize the problem of competition or rivalry between friends who may be very similar. Conversely, the notion of opposites attracting is also rejected, for patently good is not attracted to bad, nor the just to the unjust. Plato sees the attraction of 'the good' to 'the good' as the basis of friendship, rather than 'personality type' (in twenty-first century terminology) being the crucial factor. The pursuit of the good is the key to a happy life, and the delight of enjoying the good in 'the other' becomes the basis of friendship's attraction.

Developing Plato's stance, it is Aristotle who provides perhaps the most expansive exposition of friendship. For him, friendship is at the heart of the social order of free citizens in the *polis*, contributing positively to participative society and to a good (which includes a morally responsible) and happy life. Aristotle is not concerned with friendships between a slave and a free man—they are different creatures and could not hope to engage in the highest form of friendship: such is his starting prejudice. For Aristotle, a friend seeks the good of the other; they want the other to flourish and live well. Friendship is robust and enduring, it includes the affirmation and delight found in the company of the friend, but it also has room for challenge and rebuke. He outlines three types of friendship in *The Nicomachean Ethics*:

- Friendships of utility are based on friends who share common connections and circumstances, often through a common workplace. They are bound together by circumstance and are useful to each other. The skills and character of the friends are beneficial to each other and there is a common understanding of this benefit— friends can help us out in times of need.
- Friendships of pleasure are based on a mutual enjoyment of each other in some shared activity. These are friends one might have a great time with, through some shared experience. In this category might be shared sexual pleasure, which featured significantly in Aristotle's social context. Of these first two categories, Aristotle says 'Such friendships, then, are easily dissolved, if the parties do not remain like

themselves; for if the one party is no longer pleasant or useful the other ceases to love him' (Aristotle 2009: VIII.3.19–20).

- The third category he identifies is 'perfect' or virtuous friendship rooted in the nature of the friends themselves. Such friends love 'the good' in each other. This friendship is not based on external factors such as shared interests or mutually shared pleasures which, when they have passed, leave the friends with little connection. This friendship (being rooted in the lasting virtue of pursuit of the good) is morally superior and mutually beneficial. Such friends are as 'another self' to each other; each mirroring who they are to the other, so that something of their own goodness is visible in that other. Each is of such value as to live on in the other's heart, were one friend to die.

There are some fundamental assumptions in these Greek accounts that seem alien in contemporary Western society: the centrality of the *polis* structure to living well, the social inequality that depended upon slavery, the relegation of women to secondary social status. We also note an understanding of the person as being vitally connected to others—being dyadic rather than individuated as in contemporary Western culture— and a commitment to the pursuit of that which is good and virtuous. Do such social and cultural mismatches render the insights of Plato and Aristotle irrelevant to a contemporary setting? Are there so few points of contact that we cannot recognize ourselves in their description of the human person and what allows them to flourish? Is the notion of seeking 'the good' in 'the other' a quaint and outdated naiveté in a society dedicated to the pursuit of individual fulfilment? The answer to these questions must be 'no'. Whilst ancient Greek societal structures offered friendship a place in the public sphere, that has now largely shifted to the private, the capacity for nourishing and morally beneficial friendships can still be seen as attractive, alongside friendships that are more functional or transitory.

Moving beyond Antiquity, further insight into friendship's nature may be found by considering some areas where friendship faces complexity and pressure, through insights from the study of theology, sexuality, and gender.

Friendship's Complexity—Aelred and Kierkegaard

In conversation with Abbot Notker Wolf (at the time Abbot Primate of the Benedictine Confederation of the Order of St Benedict) I asked his view of the place of friendship in a monastic community. His answer was frank, and acknowledged deep ambivalence. He recognized its importance but, based on experience, was also aware that friendship held the potential to be destructive to the community: specifically he felt its danger lay in exclusivity. He countered this by stating that a friendship should always be open to another joining it; 'friendship should not be me and the other, but me and you, and the other'. He recalled his own experience as an abbot dealing with the aftermath of friendships that had become 'corrupting', resulting in exclusion and deceit through attempts to hide those friendships from others in the community. The outcome, he stated, was always destructive and led to a tension between recognizing friendship's value in the community, and being wary of its potential to harm.[2] So, in the context of a monastery, characterized by a commitment to the common life, friendship's particularity (if understood as exclusivity) could indeed corrode community: but does it have to?

This concern also appears in the preface to Aelred of Rievaulx's *Spiritual Friendship*. As Douglass Roby writes;

> The very earliest Fathers of the Desert had alternately treasured their friends as guides and helpers on the path to virtue, and rejected any personal entanglements which could keep them from the purity of heart which they prized above all. As the cenobitic tradition developed after Pachomius, monastic legislators became more suspicious of the divisive effects of 'particular friendships' which could lead to favouritism and grumbling in the community.
>
> (Roby preface to Aelred 1977: 16)

Aelred (1109–1166 CE) became abbot of the Cistercian Rievaulx Abbey. His *Spiritual Friendship*, heavily influenced by Cicero's *de Amicitia*, is reworked into a specifically Christian discussion of monastic friendship in three 'books' or sections. Contrary to the concerns above, Aelred believes the absolute commitment of friends to each other is exemplified in the sharing of common property. He acknowledges, however, that corruption of true friendship can occur by the incursion of sin that debases its virtue into acquisitive love. It is evident that he sees friendship as having an ethical and spiritual dimension that lifts it above merely enjoying the company of the other; in particular, friendship can provide a window into the love of God.[3] Aelred is dialogical, seeking to raise and then resolve honest questions about the propriety and challenges of being a Christian friend in a monastic community.

In the first section of *Spiritual Friendship*, Aelred describes all 'friendship love' as being rooted in the God who loves all; retaining an Augustinian understanding of God as 'lover', 'loved', and the 'love between them'. Aelred then expands on the consequences of this understanding as he outlines a conversation between himself and fellow monk, Ivo:

IVO: What does all this add up to? Shall I say of friendship what John, the friend of Jesus, says of charity: 'God is friendship'?

AELRED: That would be unusual, to be sure, nor does it have the sanction of the Scriptures. But still what is true of charity, I surely do not hesitate to grant to friendship, since 'he that abides in friendship, abides in God, and God in him'.

(Aelred 1977: I.69–70).

---

[2]   Extracts of a conversation held 4 September 2007 at Chichester Cathedral cloisters, based on notes taken afterwards.

[3]   A slight reworking of Augustine's belief that one loves God through loving one's friend, and that the earthly apogee of friendship is Christian friendship, enabled by the Holy Spirit. See *Confessions* 4.4.7; *City of God* 15.22.

This conciliatory tone and the ability to develop a theology by extrapolating from what is known to what might be experienced, so that his community will be drawn into knowledge of God, is typical of Aelred's approach.

In the second section, he discusses the issue of the physical expression of love, and admits that physicality is necessary: the spiritual kiss between friends can be physical, yet denote the 'mingling of spirits' (Aelred 1977: II.26). Here, to the surprise of Gratian (Aelred's conversation partner in this section), who clearly expects a prohibition on physical contact, he describes the kiss as given almost by proxy, from Christ *via* the Christian brother. The relaxed discussion of friendship in Aelred's writing challenged his contemporary monastic environment in which physicality was treated with some suspicion, for fear of inflaming sexual passion. Aelred's approach is typically controlled, advocating reasoned permission over prohibition. For Aelred, a friendship that has passed through a period of discernment and been subjected to his four stages of 'clearing', has no fear; it will be mutually beneficial to the friends' spiritual well-being. His clearing process is described thus; 'one climbs to the perfection of friendship: the first is selection, the second probation, the third admission, and the fourth perfect harmony in matters human and divine with charity and benevolence' (Aelred 1977: III.8).

Crucially, Aelred (1977: III.82, 83) locates the particularity of friendship within the matrix of a loving community, as he states in the third section.

> ... as I was walking the round of the cloister of the monastery, the brethren were sitting around forming as it were a most loving crown.... In that multitude of brethren I found no one whom I did not love, and no one by whom, I felt sure, I was not loved.
>
> We embrace very many with every affection, but in such a way that we do not admit them to the secrets of friendship, which consists especially in the revelation of all our confidences and plans'.

Aelred sees no conflict with the love of many and the particular love of friends, and in this regard challenges a concern in Christian theology. Does the love of particular individuals as friends undermine the universality of loving all?[4] To love a friend, Aelred argues, one must discipline oneself, 'allowing nothing which is unbecoming and refusing nothing which is profitable' (1977: III.129). This rule not only applies to those who are friends but is expanded to those who are neighbours. Having started with this larger group (Aelred 1977: III.129, 130):

> ... then let him choose from among them one whom he can admit in familiar fashion to the mysteries of friendship, and upon whom he can bestow his affection in abundance, laying bare his mind and heart, even to their sinews and marrow.... Let such a friend be chosen, moreover, not according to the caprice of affection but rather

---

[4] For a detailed analysis of this issue, see Summers (2009: ch. 6).

according to the foresight of reason, because of similarity of character and the contemplation of virtue.

Aelred's reasoning exhibits an openness to 'the other' that is not evident in, for example, Søren Kierkegaard's contribution to the conversation on friendship. Kierkegaard (1813–1855 CE) is deeply suspicious of friendship's particularity and states in *Works of Love*, 'If anyone thinks that a man by falling in love, or by having found a friend, has learned to know the Christian love, then he is seriously mistaken' (Kierkegaard 1946: 47). He argues that there is no element of choice to friendship; it happens when a spark ignites between two people, who then are bonded to the exclusion of others. Friendship then is selfish and inward-looking with a propensity to feed the ego. Ultimately the only proper expression of Christian love is in the choice of loving one's neighbour—love of one's neighbour being the only appropriate, open relationship that can be selfless. In this regard he sees 'love of neighbour' as being opposed to 'love of friend'. One's neighbour is 'whoever one meets' and so neighbour-love is truly open, inclusive and, crucially, a matter of conscience. This is vital for Kierkegaard, for 'love. . . is not a matter of impulse and inclination; nor is it a matter of emotion, nor a matter for intellectual calculation' (Kierkegaard 1946: 116). His desire is for unconditionality—love uncontaminated by selfish desire; open to any and all. In this, Kierkegaard sees the expression of true faith—loving that which is already given, not that which one would choose (Kierkegaard 1946: 129). Here, Kierkegaard's emotional asceticism emerges, thriving on self-denial and the renunciation of desire. Yet he maintains that this love is not cold or clinical—it has passion, and is exercised in the dutiful loving response to a command of God.

As we have seen, Aelred knows nothing of Kierkegaard's fearful limitation, but offers a context of supportive love in which human relationality can flourish; but was Aelred offering an unrealistic model that practicality could never allow? Certainly his writings did not endure as a major force in monasticism; yet Aelred's work has persisted, doggedly resurfacing to offer his profoundly human treatment of the subject matter through practical example. Liz Carmichael suggests that in his day Aelred was treated with suspicion by the Cistercian General Chapter and that 'His interest in friendship and his provision of opportunities for it, were probably seen as laxity' (Carmichael 2004: 97). Perhaps only an abbot with Aelred's interpersonal skills would be capable of leading such a community, by holding in tension the advantages and risks of such open friendship. So, expanding Aelred's principles, is there a place for friendship in the life of the Church? We will return to this question, but first must explore some further areas of complexity facing friendship in contemporary culture.

FRIENDSHIP UNDER PRESSURE

There are several areas in which friendship is being stretched or re-shaped by social change. These are worth considering, as they help to further clarify what friendship is (and what it is not). As an example, current suspicion and fear of 'cronyism' in politics and business can make friendship in the world of work problematic, requiring careful thought about boundaries: this reflects a marked change throughout the twentieth century and into the twenty-first.

Sexuality and Friendship

We begin by considering friendships between those of the opposite sex. By way of clarifying any ambiguity: in English the word 'love' is used for many relational permutations, however there is a variety in Greek that allows more nuanced expression. Although not consistently applied, as with many languages, in general the differing terms for 'love' are; *eros*—sexual attraction, the overwhelming experience of 'being in love' and characterized by desire for the other; *storge*—the loving bond of affection between parent and child; *philia*—the bond between brothers, friendship love; *agape*—charity or love that parallels divine love: it is the constituent of 'love for God' and is generally thought of as being of a different order to love for fellow humanity. The most influential proponent of this differentiation is C. S. Lewis in his book *The Four Loves* (1960). At the very least, this variety allows insight into what may be going on in the spectrum of our relationships.

Aristotle treats opposite sex friendship in passing: it does not merit serious treatment in his androcentric world, mainly due to perceptions of inequality that would hamper genuine reciprocity. However, relating to husband and wife, he states; 'both utility and pleasure seem to be found in this kind of friendship. But this friendship may be based also on virtue, if the parties are good; for each has its own virtue, and they will delight in the fact' (Aristotle 2009: 8.12.1162a.25). The heterosexual male–female friendship question emerges in literature and memorably in the 1989 comedy film 'When Harry Met Sally' directed by Rob Reiner, which asks the question; is it possible for a male and female to be friends, that is experiencing *philia* friendship love, without the component of *eros* erotic love? For Harry the answer is no: the complication of *eros* will always intrude into the friendship, somehow 'corrupting' the purity of friendship with sexual desire. Harry's opinion is not shared by all, however.

Some anthropological research into the nature of opposite-sex friendship has been carried out, for example, the USA-based survey by Joel D. Block with 2,063 respondents and 500 interviews ran from 1975 to 1978, and catalogued the variety of friendship types. Of opposite-sex friends he claims, 'In sexual matters our culture remains divided and confused. In truth, most of us are ambivalent about our sexuality with opposite-sex friends and do not know how to resolve the dilemma comfortably' (Block 1980: 92). Such surveys confirm that the significant majority of friendships are between people of the same sex, with opposite-sex friendships being in the minority, but not unusual. Block's study is already dated, and there has been a shift in perception into the twenty-first century, in part due to the equality movement which, although not definitive, has affected the manner in which men and women perceive each other. We can observe significant progress when compared to the prejudice evident in the philosopher and writer George Santayana, who in his 1920 publication *Little Essays* wrote,

> Friendship with a woman is therefore apt to be more or less than friendship: less, because there is no intellectual parity; more, because (even when the relationship remains wholly dispassionate, as in respect to old ladies) there is something mysterious and oracular about a woman's mind which inspires a certain instinctive deference and puts it out of the question to judge what she says by masculine standards.

> (Santayana 1920: 38)

Regardless of the disturbing insight this provides into Santayana's mind, it may be that despite obvious social progress, there persists a deeply rooted sexual inequality, with its foundations in a basic misunderstanding of human identity. This emerges in an apparent suspicion of intimacy outside the traditional role of male and female in a sexual relationship. Such a traditional relationship can quite easily mask a power/gender imbalance, and indeed in certain marriages it is quite overt. When the relationship is a friendship, this imbalance is challenged from the outset, for friendship is based on the recognition of, and a commitment to, equality and reciprocity. So, paralleling any concerns around sexual innuendo, there may be a more profound justice issue, focused on the affirmation of equality, which may be a contributory factor in Western culture's apparent dis-ease with opposite-sex friendships.

What then of same-sex friendships? If we return to the *eros* issue and sexual attraction, the situation is clarified in the scenario of two same-sex friends, when one is of a homosexual orientation. Is this then the equivalent of heterosexual opposite-sex friendship? Is this relationship damaged by the 'intrusion' of *eros*? Should it be treated with suspicion? The inconsistency is evident—of course not every relationship is determined by sexual attraction and governed by 'desire for the other' as an object of sexual fulfilment. Furthermore, since gender is a component of human identity, in the same way that ethnicity, intellect and personality type are, is it reasonable to identify only gender as being the determinative factor in relationality? The answer may emerge that on some occasions sexual attraction is a factor, but not all human encounter is reducible to a formula into which the component parts of an individual are plugged and a friendship emerges.

This is merely acknowledging the mystery of human relationship; the attraction that allows friendship (like any loving relationship) to blossom is not formulaic. Who knows why we have a connection with one person and not another? Sometimes we are friends with the most unlikely people: sometimes people like ourselves but sometimes those who are polar opposites. This brings the discussion back to Aristotle's (and Plato's) dilemma—why are friends attracted to each other? In their terms, the 'pursuit of the good' may be a vocabulary alien to our culture, but is the principle recognizable? In Antiquity, the pursuit of *eudaimonia* was a prime goal; translated as 'happiness' or 'well-being', or even better 'living the best possible life'[5] because it is more than an

---

[5] See for example P. J. Wadell's (1989: 31) interpretation.

emotional state. It is activity that has a pleasurable result associated with it. If *eudaimonia* is the goal and arena of friendship, it is achieved in community for 'virtue cannot be attained in solitude' (Wadell 1989: 64). This concept, if extracted from its ancient vocabulary, may yet be identifiable as a twenty-first-century goal. The striking difference is that, with our monadic understanding of the self, we might pursue the best possible life as a solitary project. Aristotle recognizes that one needs friends to provide the means by which to execute the good habits and deeds which are the evidence, and expression of, living that 'best possible life'. Whatever the gender or sexual orientation of our friends, this mutuality is surely the most important focus.

Marriage and Life-partnership

Husband and wife are partners whose relationship is recognized as having *eros* as a primary component; marriage vows make explicit that sexual fidelity is characteristic of that relationship, and that monogamy is a defining social marker. In UK civil partnerships, the set vows acknowledge free consent and companionship, but fidelity and monogamy are not cited. With friendship, we are in a different realm from either.

First, there is no declaration of friendship that is marked by a public ceremony—it has no official public form that describes its nature. Beyond the school playground 'blood-brothers' ritual, friendship tends not to be ritually noted. This has not always been so, and there have been times in Western society that such rituals were evident. Alan Bray has traced the phenomenon of 'sworn friendship' between friends of the same sex, resulting in shared graves, with examples on tombstones dating from Istanbul in 1391, up to the grave of Cardinal John Henry Newman in Warwick in 1890, where he is buried with his friend Fr. Ambrose St John, who had died some fifteen years previously. In his survey, Bray discovers a socially recognized ceremony of friendship that could sit alongside marriage vows.[6] One significant aspect of Bray's book is his refusal to simplify human relationality to the polarities of either friendship *or* homosexual love. He recognizes the complexity of human relationships, and particularly friendship, which (due to its depth and life-giving nature) elicits a desire to mark it out publically. The potential marbling of *eros* and *philia* is not the interesting point for Bray; he focuses on the love of friends, and seeks to explore what that means for embodied people. It may or may not involve a sexual component, for this is not where friendship love is defined.

Secondly, there is an expectation that friendship is not monogamous, but is deliberately 'polygamous' or we might even say 'flirtatious', in that it seeks to encourage and forge other friendship bonds. It would be considered oppressive in our cultural context to have only one friend who would feel 'cheated on' if we struck up another friendship with someone else (the existence of so called 'best friends' accepted). In fact, as noted in

---

[6] This does not directly equate to *adelphopoiesis*—the Greek Orthodox liturgy of 'brother making', apparently known in medieval times, and explored by Boswell (1994).

the Adams and Plaut study, Western culture values having multiple friends—it indicates social status through being evidently popular and 'likeable'. Perhaps this is most evident in the desire to gather proof of multiple friends on one's social networking page: but are 'Facebook Friends' real friends? We generally recognize a variety of intensities in our friendships, and seem to accept that friendship's 'polygamous' nature does not detract from its essential nature, in fact it may even enhance it. Someone with many friends may have the problem of not having enough time to spend with them all, but the essential nature of the friendships (their ontology) is not called into question, such that all their friendships are seen as being somehow diluted, untrustworthy, or betrayed because of multiple 'partners'.

Longevity

By the beginning of the twenty-first century, the increase in average lifespan has brought sharp pressure to bear on social services and pension funds. However, material resources are not the only ones being stretched. As people live and function socially for significantly longer, and have significant periods of leisure time, relationships spanning many decades are not unusual. Life partners and spouses live longer, placing pressure on loving relationships and life-long friendships. If life expectancy continues to increase, and the anticipated quality of that life keeps pace, then a sense of vigour and animation in these relationships must also be expected. Can friendships retain their virtuous and sustaining nature for such a period? Evidence of this pressure is emerging, and it is not unusual for a marriage that has lasted over thirty years to come to an end, the 'spark' having died out. Perhaps we are seeing a relationship where the companionship is much like Aristotle's 'pleasure' or 'utility' friendship; and when circumstances change, the relationship founders. Perhaps the friendship has run its course, and with it, the marriage?

Aligned with this issue is the increasingly commonplace situation of a wife or husband dying, for example aged 70, and the surviving spouse living for another 20 or more years. There may be no particular desire to embark on a second (or third, or fourth) marriage when in one's 70s or 80s: because of complications with inheritance provision for children, or there is no emotional desire to 'replace' the deceased partner, or for other reasons. However, the desire for companionship, friendship, or a sexual relationship may still be present. Here emerges a pressure; in part exacerbated by the liberality of the contemporary Western moral climate, in which cohabitation is an accepted status. This social permission can sit in tension with deep-seated Christian (or generational) antipathy to such a lifestyle. The option to share a lifestyle based on companionship or friendship may be simultaneously accessible, tempting, and distressing for a certain social or ecclesial demographic. It requires us to reflect on what marriage relationships mean, with awareness that the contemporary Western understandings are not universally accepted, and that social pragmatism and friendship feature more prominently in those of other cultures.

Virtual Friendship

This is an area of specific relevance for contemporary culture, where friendship is under a new pressure. The rise of social media, enabled by swift technological advances, has brought communication to a place never before seen in human history, and such developments have particular relevance for relationality. In living memory, relationships once reliant on the medium of handwriting have become instantaneous and global. Through broadband technology and high-definition image, they have developed to the extent that a virtual face-to-face encounter is possible with a degree of reality that goes beyond an 'approximation' of the person. Facial expressions and emotions are recognizable so that a 'true conversation' is possible. This is a significant step-change from the previously limited medium of typed online chat.

Is there a qualitative difference in this medium, or does this virtual encounter equate to the real thing? The challenges fall into two areas: how virtual friendship is impacted by the nature of physically dispersed community, and how this relates to human embodiment. First then; the challenge of dispersed community. The online encounter is a highly selective one—opening up only a narrow slice of a whole life, at a mutually convenient time. Due to the (usually) distant nature of the communication, there is little possibility that any aspect of the participant's 'off-screen' existence will be accessible. I can only know of my online friend what they choose to reveal to me, and the friendship will be predicated on this limitation—we are unlikely to meet up at the corner shop by chance.

However, there are at least two responses to this initial challenge. First, through the networked nature of virtual relationships in social media websites such as Facebook, a multidimensional view of a person, though the shared viewpoints of a variety of friends, emerges. It is difficult for the friendship to remain as one dimensional as one maintained by phone call or letter. Secondly, many 'real world' friendships are also selective in their knowledge of the participants. Friends made at work, at a weekly football match or at college, may see and know only that facet of each other's lives. Although the capacity for an accidental encounter outside of the normal arena of the friendship is possible, it is in practice unlikely; yet the *possibility* of such real world relationships to develop and grow into spheres other than their initiating arenas, seems enough to avoid the criticism levelled at virtual friendships. Of course, even if there is a continental divide between online friends, the possibility of meeting may be remote, but not impossible.

This leads into the second challenge of 'virtual friendship'. As embodied beings we recognize the importance of the other's face and of human contact. Despite the quality of digital image and the authentic rendering of voice, as yet, one cannot shake hands with, hug or kiss a virtual friend. This absence is in part a negation of who one is as an embodied being, a significant hiatus in how one communicates, knows, and is known. Yet countering this is the reality that many friends who do meet regularly may touch only occasionally, if at all. Does this negate or even impair their friendship?[7]

[7] The behavioural study by Jourard (1966), observed friends talking in a café in various countries. During the hour, in England they did not touch at all, in the USA they touched twice, in France 110 times, and in Puerto Rico 180 times!

There is, according to Emmanuel Levinas, a profound challenge in the corporeality of another person for how we understand 'otherness'. Their bodily existence asserts their distinctiveness and their visage questions me, reminding me that they are 'other' and will always remain unknown and unassimilable to me (Levinas 1969: 45). But is Levinas' desire to assert the absolute otherness of the other sustainable? It asserts a profoundly Cartesian view of the human self that overlooks fundamental human connectedness. It is evident that what I see in the face of another human being reveals, at a fundamental level, not just otherness, but a commonality that must surely soften his claim of their radical unknowability. Nonetheless, their corporeality challenges my anthropological arrogance, lest I assume that I have full control of my world. Since they cannot be reduced to a concept or idea when they face me; their very presence questions and relocates me.

Thus we can question whether the digital image, central to the most lifelike virtual friendship, can truly substitute for the *presence* of the other? Do embodied beings have to be 'in the presence' of the other in order to 'be present' to them? There is a caution here for advocates of Virtual Church (VC). Travis Pickell states (citing Bazin and Cottin), 'In advocating for standalone virtual congregations, VC enthusiasts unwittingly (and sometimes wittingly) send a message that relativizes the human body. The Church should engage the virtual world in the name of the gospel but 'making a place for Christianity in the virtual world does not mean that Christianity should itself become virtual or disembodied' (Pickell 2010: 78).

Returning then to friendship through social media—if it does not describe ourselves, we co-exist with a generation of 'digital natives' whose familiarity with social networking render it the primary and instinctive method of interaction and communication. This demographic faces a challenge, for a casualty of relational fluidity and freedom is friendship's value. Does the world of 'Facebook Friends' commodify friendship; making it a means of enhancing status without allowing the nature of such friendship to be the primary driver? Such virtual friendship is condemned by Fröding and Peterson as a 'second rate' form of the relationship, because it has lost its potential for virtue. Their concern is primarily ethical, in that, under an Aristotelian understanding, friendship has a moral component that is fundamental and emerges in 'substantial real life interaction'. Virtual friendship may have mutual admiration, equality of status, and even the spending of time together, in common with the highest form of friendship but, they argue, its selectivity means that virtual friends; 'miss out on important, potentially problematic and complex, aspects of the friends' personality. Therefore the agent ends up admiring and loving parts of the friend rather than the whole of her' (Fröding and Peterson 2012: 205).

Self-sacrifice and Constructed Friendships

In Jesus' short treatise on friendship, as presented in John's gospel (John 15:12–14), he states; 'This is my commandment, that you love one another as I have loved you. No one has greater love than this, to lay down one's life for one's friends. You are my friends if you do what I command you' (NRSV). The command in question was to love one another, and here, friendship is described in contrast with servanthood. Servants have no insight into their master's will, but friends have equal status; they understand and share confidence and purpose. Whilst this text is central to friendship's importance for the Church in general, I highlight it here in relation to the depth of commitment that friendship love allows, and indeed requires. Contemporary culture, with its commitment to individuation and self-satisfaction, might ignore the possibilities of the self-sacrificial love proposed by Homer in the *Iliad*. It is tempting to see friendship as purely elective; we do choose our friends and can break those friendships: we can have an ex-friend as surely as an ex-husband. However, in the cited biblical text there is no self-selection; the disciples are told, 'you did not choose me but I chose you' (John 15:16). Yet the expectation is that deep bonds will be formed, and this proves to be the case in John's account of their behaviour following the crucifixion and resurrection.

The notion of constructed friendships is nothing new. It is essential to military life, which, for example, trains soldiers to live and fight together with the expectation of self-sacrifice. In conversation with a group of UK Army Chaplains, they described how the process of binding new recruits together into workable units is carefully controlled to achieve a desired result.[8] In basic training, new recruits are brought together in small groups of four; they experience the stripping away of the familiarity and freedom of civilian life with its decision making and self-sufficiency. In this new regime, the Army becomes provider and decider. Through physical hardship, competition, and the learning of new skills, the team learns to suffer and rejoice together. They are dependent upon each other for success in team tasks and activities; the victory or failure of the group becomes a corporate responsibility. They live in close proximity to each other, getting to know the best and worst of each other's characters—there is no respite or opt-out in this formation process. The result, in the overwhelming majority of cases, is a fighting unit that trusts each other, and is capable of going into combat under extreme peril. They have *forged* the bond of friendship.

It is notable that in the tragic reports of deaths in combat, comrades of those who have died in battle describe their willingness to lay down their lives, not so much for the regiment (although loyalty here can be significant), but for their 'mates' or friends. Similarly those who have left life in the armed forces will regularly turn to military friends for support before civilian agencies, due to this deep connectedness and loyalty. So, it would appear that friendship, whilst usually associated with self-selection, is not exclusively so. It is possible, in the right circumstances, to create the deepest of friendships that are not transitory. In a final connection back to the *Iliad*, Homer's most prized form of friendship is that between two males, and is forged in combat; violence providing both opportunity and fuel for this most passionate and self-sacrificial of loves. Like any good author, his material reflects his readers' interests.[9]

---

[8] Seminar with UK Army Chaplains at Amport House, 2 December 2009, based on notes taken after the conversations.
[9] In contemporary UK culture, note the extraordinary appetite for fact-based fiction around the bravery and self-sacrifice of military Special Forces.

CONCLUSION

The implications of loving one another to such an extent that one is willing to lay down one's life for a friend need not remain consigned to the world of film or literature. Inspired by Jesus' command that his disciples were to love one another, and reinforced by his statement 'You are my friends', the Church has an opportunity to discover this in practice. The equality and reciprocity inherent in that relationship, offers a model of Christian relationality that begins in hospitable welcome and continues to the mutuality of shared discipleship. The self-understanding of the Church and its mission as being primarily relational rather than structural, has the capacity to transform Christian community. It can challenge a process-oriented, metrics-driven notion of mission, and offer an appreciation of human connectedness in embracing the otherness of 'the other' without requiring that they become like us. In this hospitable approach—treating those who are not yet friends as if they were friends—it may be possible to take the risk of forging relationality that is not commodity based; that does not consume the other as a product. Thus, the uncertainty around friendship's social and even personal value, that appears evident in contemporary Western culture, provides opportunity for the Church to reveal a friendship that is robust, life-giving, and virtuous: gifted by Christ and resourced by the Holy Spirit.

REFERENCES

Adams G. and V. C. Plaut (2003). 'The Cultural Grounding of Personal Relationship: Friendship in North American and West African Worlds'. *Personal Relationships*, 10(3): 333–347.

Aelred of Rievaulx (1977). *Spiritual Friendship*, trans. M. E. Laker. Kalamazoo, MI: Cistercian Publications.

Aristotle (2009). *The Nicomachean Ethics*. Trans. D. Ross. Oxford: Oxford University Press.

Block, J. D. (1980). *Friendship*. New York: Macmillan.

Boswell, J. (1994). *Same-Sex Unions in Pre-Modern Europe*. New York: Random House.

Bray, A. (2003). *The Friend*. Chicago & London: University of Chicago Press.

Carmichael, L., (2004) *Friendship: Interpreting Christian Love*. London: T&T Clark.

Fröding, B. and M. Peterson (2012). 'Why Virtual Friendship Is No Genuine Friendship'. *Ethics and Information Technology*, 14: 201–207.

Jourard, Sidney (1966). 'An Exploratory Study of Body-Accessibility'. *British Journal of Social & Clinical Psychology*, 5(3): 221–231.

Kierkegaard, S. (1946). *Works of Love*. Trans. D. F. and L. M. Swenson. Princeton: Princeton University Press.

Levinas, E. (1969). *Totality and Infinity: An Essay on Exteriority*. Trans. A. Lingis. Pittsburgh: Duquesne University Press.

Lewis, C. S. (1960). *The Four Loves*. London: Geoffrey Bles.

Paine, R. (1969). 'In Search of Friendship: An Exploratory Analysis in Middle-class Culture'. *Man*, New Series, 4(4): 505–524.

Pickell, T. (2010). ' "Thou Hast Given Me a Body": Theological Anthropology and the Virtual Church'. *Princeton Theological Review*, Fall: 67–79.

Santayana, G. (1920). *Little Essays Drawn from the Writings of George Santayana*. Ed. Logan Pearsall Smith. New York: Charles Scribner's Sons,

Summers, S. (2009). *Friendship: Exploring its Implications for the Church in Postmodernity*. London: T&T Clark.

Wadell, P. J. (1989). *Friendship and the Moral Life*. Notre Dame, ID: University of Notre Dame Press.

Weil, S. (1977). *Waiting on God: Letters and Essays*. Trans. E. Crawford. London: Fount.

Index